REASON

AND

RESPONSIBILITY

REASON
AND
RESPONSIBILITY

READINGS
IN SOME BASIC PROBLEMS
OF PHILOSOPHY

Fifth Edition

edited by
Joel Feinberg
University of Arizona

WADSWORTH PUBLISHING COMPANY
BELMONT, CALIFORNIA
A DIVISION OF WADSWORTH, INC.

Philosophy Editor: Kenneth King
Production Editor: Diane Sipes
Copy Editor: Anne Draus

Printed in the United States of America

4   5   6   7   8   9   10—85   84   83

Library of Congress Cataloging in Publication Data

Feinberg, Joel, 1926–   ed.
   Reason and responsibility.

   Bibliography: p.
   1.   Philosophy—Addresses, essays, lectures.
I.   Title.
B21.F4 1981   100   80-21179
ISBN 0-534-00924-7

ISBN 0-534-00924-7

CONTENTS

PART 6   SELF-LOVE AND THE CLAIMS OF MORALITY   474

PREFACE

The conviction underlying this volume is that for the purpose of introducing the modern college student to philosophy it is far preferable to have a small number of representative problems examined in great detail than to have a "little bit of everything," with each "branch" of philosophy, each major "ism," and each major historical period represented with scrupulous impartiality even though the articles may have little relevance to one another. I have selected articles from both classical and contemporary sources on such topics as religion, knowledge, mind, personal identity, death, freedom, responsibility, duty, and selfishness. The problems that concern philosophers under these headings are not mere idle riddles, but rather questions of vital interest to any reflective person. Each set of problems is plumbed in considerable depth in essays expressing different, and often opposing, views. My hope is that exposure to this argumentative give-and-take will encourage students to take part in the process themselves and develop, through practice, their powers of philosophical reasoning.

This fifth edition of *Reason and Responsibility* represents a very substantial revision of the earlier editions. It opens with a new introductory essay by the editor entitled "What Is Philosophy?" which attempts to provide for the beginner a clear, though somewhat rough, map to the philosophical subject matter. A short glossary of philosophical terms has also been included. In response to the suggestions of various reviewers, I have added new materials to all sections of the book except Part Five, and I have substantially overhauled Parts Three and Six. Part One now contains the eighteenth-century formulation of the cosmological argument that Hume criticized in his *Dialogues,* namely that of Samuel Clarke, as well as William Rowe's careful discussion of that argument. The section on philosophy of religion now also includes Walter T. Stace's sympathetic discussion of mysticism and Stephen Stich's unsympathetic analysis of Pascal's "Wager." Part Two now contains Godfrey Vesey's analysis of Berkeley's famous "heat-pain argument." The compatible position on determinism and free will in Part Four is now presented by Walter T. Stace, an unusually clear writer, whose works are readily understandable by the beginner.

There are seven new articles in Part Three. Godfrey Vesey's fictitious dialogue between Descartes and Princess Elizabeth of Bohemia is based on the actual correspondence between those historical figures, and marks the transition between Part Two (which is dominated by Descartes' *Meditations*) and Part Three on the philosophy of mind. John Locke's discussion of material and spiritual substances provides background for critical treatment of the central doctrine of Descartes' philosophy of mind—that mind is itself a substance. Jerome Shaffer provides the clearest sophisticated account available of current theories of the "subject of consciousness" and the mind-body problem. The most innovative change in Part Three in this edition is the inclusion of a whole subsection on the concept of a self (personal identity).

The most thoroughly restructured section of the book, however, is Part Six on moral philosophy. To the subsection on ethical skepticism I have added Walter T. Stace's essay on ethical relativism—a subject of keen interest to many undergraduates. The following subsection on psychological egoism now includes not only my own essay but also two new essays that draw philosophical lessons from the teachings of modern biology. The first, by the distinguished biological theorist Stephen Gould, attempts to explain how altruism could survive and flourish in a Darwinian world. The second, by the philosopher Howard Kahane, gives the account of moral motivation that he thinks is supported by the theories of sociobiology. The largest addition to Part Six is the nearly complete classic by John Stuart Mill, *Utilitarianism*. Paul Taylor's treatment of "Ethical Egoism" rounds out the subsection on normative principles. The concluding subsection, "Why Be Moral?" has been enriched by Immanuel Kant's moral catechism and Paul Taylor's discerning "The Ultimate Question."

One important change made in the fourth edition has been preserved in the fifth edition. In Part Two, "Human Knowledge: Its Grounds and Limits," I have given up the effort to carry over from the other parts of the book the general principle of organization by specific separate problems. That part now contains no subsections. By means of this change from the earlier edition, I have avoided the proliferation of inappropriately technical essays on riddles concerning the various types of knowledge—our knowledge of the past, of the future, of ourselves, of other minds, of mathematical truths, and so on—and I have also avoided, I hope, offensive splintering of classic texts into little bits and snippets. Instead, I have included in their unabridged entirety both Descartes' *Meditations* and Berkeley's *Three Dialogues,* as well as a very substantial part of Hume's *Inquiry concerning Human Understanding*. These systematic works develop answers to the smaller questions in a natural manner and sequence and give the student the opportunity to study fully elaborated systems of thought in their original sources.

This volume now contains two complete classics (Descartes' *Meditations* and Berkeley's *Dialogues*), two other classics virtually or nearly complete (Hume's *Dialogues* and Mill's *Utilitarianism*), and very substantial sections of still two others (Hume's *Inquiry* and Plato's *Republic*). It is now quite feasible to use this text to teach an introductory course based solidly on a reading of these classics, with more recent articles thrown in as a kind of dividend. The book contains many articles by contemporary philosophers, including nine addressed specifically to beginning students and written expressly for this book (those by William Rowe, Wesley Salmon who wrote two, James Cornman, John Perry, Phillip Montague, Howard Kahane, and two from the editor).

I do not presume to dictate one necessary and natural order of sequence through these materials. The book begins with the philosophy of religion since its problems are likely to be already familiar to many beginners. But it is just as "natural" to begin with Part Two, since the question of our knowledge of God presupposes the question of the "grounds and limits of human knowledge" generally. Similarly, there is no reason why one could not begin with the mind-body problem (Part Three) or the problem of determinism and free will (Part Four). Indeed, many professors have told me that they prefer to begin with ethics (Part Six) and work their way from there toward the front of the book.

In selecting materials for this fifth edition I have been helped by the advice, positive and negative, of the following critics: Joan C. Callahan, of the University of Maryland; Richard M. Gale, of the University of Pittsburgh; Jeffrey Gold, of East Tennessee State University; Kenneth C. Kennard, of Illinois State University; Richard Kraut, of the University of Illinois, Chicago Circle; Daniel Rochowiak, of Merrimack College; and G. A. Spangler, of California State University, Long Beach. I am grateful for their help, and also for the skillful typing and assistance in assembling the manuscript of Kay Clark, Amanda Cisco, and Ann Hickman.

Joel Feinberg

REASON

AND

RESPONSIBILITY

Introduction: What Is Philosophy?

With few exceptions, the beginning college student will not have encountered any course labeled "philosophy" in a high school curriculum. The student may well realize that philosophy is not a branch of one of the more familiar academic disciplines like history, mathematics, or one of the experimental sciences. It is usually classified as one of the humanities, along with art and literature, although it is not simply a form of literature like poetry or the novel. Philosophy has a subject matter of its own, but exactly what does one study in philosophy? To begin an answer to this question, one studies in philosophy a certain set of intellectual problems, the solutions proposed to those problems by thinkers who have grappled with them, and the arguments for and against those solutions offered by their proponents and their critics.

The distinctive problems of academic philosophy are usually classified under headings called branches or fields of philosophy. These headings also provide the names of the various courses in philosophy that one finds in college catalogues. There are various ways of dividing the philosophical subject matter, however, and some of them overlap one another. Perhaps the most common scheme is to divide the subject into the following basic subjects.

1. *Epistemology* (also called the "Theory of Knowledge"). This is the branch of philosophy concerned with questions about knowledge: What are the theoretical limits, if any, to what human beings can know? What are the grounds and sources of knowledge? How is genuine knowledge distinguished from its counterfeits? How is knowledge related to belief? to understanding? to probability? What is the ultimate evidence for our ordinary beliefs? What are the ultimate grounds for our knowledge in mathematics and in science? How do we know that there are laws of nature to be discovered (as opposed to mere coincidental regularities) and that what has held true in the past will continue to hold true in the future? Do we really *know* anything at all? These and similar questions, and the more technical problems they presuppose (for example, questions about reason and experience, reasonableness, rationality, and faith, meaning and truth) are called epistemological questions.

2. *Metaphysics* (sometimes called "Ontology"). In its grandest definition, this basic branch of philosophy is characterized as the study of "the nature of reality." Metaphysics presses the everyday distinction between appearance and reality to its ultimate sources and limits. Some things truly exist, whereas other things seem to exist but in reality are only illusions. How do we distinguish between them? And of those things that do exist, which are the ultimately real things? Flowers and trees are the appearances that collections of cells present to our senses; the cells in turn are composed of complex molecules, themselves divisible into atoms made of still more material constituents. What then is the most

basic "stuff" that everything real is "made" of? What is that of which everything else is an appearance, but which is not in turn the appearance of anything else? Is this ultimate reality *material* stuff, as our examples suggest? Is there just one such kind of ultimate thing or many kinds? Perhaps minds and their experiences are ultimately real too, even though they do not seem to be "made" of anything material. What does it mean anyway to say that something exists in its own right or has reality?

Metaphysical questions also arise when we are tempted to posit the existence of various kinds of "queer entities" in our catalogue of types of ultimately real things. Suppose someone were to argue, for example, that in addition to all the ordinary human beings, there also exist some utterly extraordinary entities called "the average man" and "the average woman." The average man has 1.99 arms and 1.8 children and during some periods of history he becomes younger every year! We are, of course, too sophisticated to be fooled by this metaphysical claim. We know that statements about "the average man" are merely useful ways of speaking, expressions we use to avoid more cumbersome, but less paradoxical, language. To say that the average man has 1.99 arms, for example, is to say only that the total number of arms on men divided by the total number of men is 1.99. (It is not surprising that the number is less than two because we know that some men have lost arms through accidents and genetic defects whereas no man has more than two arms.) Therefore, statements about the average man can be analyzed into statements about real men, and the average man himself can be "reduced" to, or is a mere "construction" of, more basic elements.

Typical metaphysical questions ask whether other allegedly ultimate categories can be similarly reduced or analyzed. Can all our statements about minds and experiences be reduced in principle to statements about physical processes? If so, then matter is closer to the ultimate than mind. On the other hand, perhaps it can be shown that such reductive analyses cannot work or that the reduction goes in the other direction instead, reducing material objects to mental experiences. In the end, a complete metaphysical theory will be a kind of conceptual picture of reality as consisting ultimately, for example, of atoms in the void, or of material objects in orderly motion, laws of nature, and minds, or of persons and God, or of particular things (like this man and this chair) and classes or universals (like humanity and chairness). Questions about the reducible or irreducible status of a certain kind of entity are also called metaphysical questions.

3. *Ethics* (also called "Moral Philosophy"). This is the branch of philosophy concerned with standards of right conduct and with the nature of good and evil. Just as epistemology attempts to characterize the general kinds of knowledge rather than try to make an exhaustive list of all the specific items of knowledge, and just as metaphysics attempts to describe the ultimate category or categories of being rather than try to list all the specific things that have existence, so ethics is concerned to make and defend only very general ethical and evaluative judgments. The moral philosopher does not pass judgment on the character of each and every person and the rightness of each and every act. Rather, the moral philosopher tries to formulate correct *standards* of estimable character and right conduct. The concern of ethics is not so much with the questions of which acts are right and which are wrong, but rather with what *makes* right acts right and what *makes* wrong acts wrong. Similarly, when the moral philosopher is concerned with questions of value (goodness) and disvalue (badness), he or she wishes to discover what *kinds* of things are good as ends in themselves, not simply as means to other ends.

The focus of the philosopher's interest—whether in epistemology, metaphysics, or ethics—is on "where the buck stops," that is on what is *ultimate* evidence, what is *ultimately* real, and what is *ultimately* good.

4. *Logic* (sometimes taught in courses called "Critical Thinking"). Logic is concerned with formulating the standards of correct reasoning that enable us to criticize reasons as cogent or weak, relevant or irrelevant, valid or invalid. The subject matter of logic can be expressed in one word: *arguments*. In logic, an argument is a set of statements of which one is a conclusion and the others constitute the reason or evidence for the conclusion. The latter are said to be the *premises* from which the conclusion follows. When the conclusion does not actually follow from the premises the argument is defective or *invalid*. When the conclusion does follow from the premises in accordance with the canons of correct reasoning, the argument is *valid*.

Strictly speaking, the terms "valid" and "invalid" are applied only to *deductive arguments*. A valid deductive argument is such that if the premises are true then the conclusion *must* be true (it cannot possibly be false). The classic textbook example is: (1) All men are mortal; (2) Socrates is a man; therefore (3) Socrates is mortal. If the premises of a deductive argument are true and the conclusion false, it follows that the argument is invalid. All other combinations of truth values, however, are possible in valid deductive arguments. A valid argument may proceed from true premises to true conclusion (in which case it is called *sound*), from false premises to false conclusion (for example: "The earth is flat; therefore at least one planet is flat"), or from false premises to true conclusion (for example: "All Americans are dogs; all dogs are human beings; therefore all Americans are human beings"). No matter what the actual truth value of the premises and the conclusion may be, to characterize the deductive argument as valid is to say that its *form* is such that if the premises are true then the conclusion must be true.

An *inductive argument,* however, may be a very good argument of its kind, but it does not even purport to establish its conclusion with necessity. Hence it is not usually called "valid," even when its premises lend support to its conclusion. Rather, its form is such that if its premises are true then *probably* its conclusion is true. (Consider: "Nine of the ten balls in this urn are red; therefore if I reach in and pull out one at random, it will be red.")

Any question that asks whether one proposition is a good (or poor) or valid (or invalid) reason for another proposition is a logical question, and logic is the branch of philosophy that attempts to answer logical questions, not case by case, but in a general way. Logic is concerned with the general characteristics of all good or valid reasons by which they are good or valid reasons.

The distinctions between the types of questions and the branches of philosophy listed previously are not clear-cut. A course in epistemology is likely to get involved with metaphysical as well as epistemological questions, and vice versa. Similarly, one can raise epistemological, metaphysical, and logical questions about ethics. Indeed the branch of moral philosophy that raises such questions has its own name: *ethical theory* (or "metaethics"). Among the epistemological problems addressed by ethical theory are such questions as: Is there such a thing as moral knowledge? If so, how is it related to scientific knowledge, and what are its grounds and limits? The chief metaphysical question addressed by ethical theory is: Must one include moral properties (for example, goodness and badness) among the ultimate constituents of reality, or can they be reduced to, or analysed into, characteristics of some other kind?

The distinctions between basic kinds of philosophical questions also enable us to define branches of philosophy that provide the names for further particular academic courses. Epistemology, metaphysics, ethics, and logic can be regarded as the core areas of philosophy, but other branches of philosophy raise epistemological, metaphysical, logical, and ethical questions in special contexts. These derivative branches and courses often have titles with the form "Philosophy of X" where X stands for some other discipline or practice. The following is a partial but representative list.

1. *Philosophy of Religion,* which the first section of this text is devoted to, raises metaphysical questions about the existence of God; epistemological questions about the limits of knowledge and the roles of reason, experience, and faith in the acquisition of knowledge; ethical questions about the necessity or dispensability of religious doctrines for the support of moral principles; and logical questions about the cogency of various traditional arguments for the existence of God.

2. *Philosophy of Mind,* which the third section of this text is largely devoted to, includes epistemological problems about the grounds and limits of our knowledge of minds, both our own and those of others. It involves metaphysical questions about the distinguishing characteristics of the mind, the dispensable or indispensable status of mind in a catalogue of kinds of ultimately real entities, and the relationship between minds and "their" bodies or brains. The philosophy of mind also provides some data for a problem of vital interest to those moral philosophers interested in moral responsibility, namely the famous problem of determinism and free will (see Part Four of this text).

3. *Philosophy of Science* addresses epistemological questions about the grounds and limits of scientific knowledge, in particular the status of knowledge derived from inductive arguments and the distinctive characteristics of scientific explanation. It deals with metaphysical questions about the ultimate presuppositions of science, the ultimate or derivative status of the individual sciences (for example, can psychology in principle be reduced to physics?), the status of unobservable entities in scientific theories, and the scientific use of such metaphysical categories as substance, causation, space, and time. The philosophy of science involves ethical questions about the uses of science and technology, and logical questions about the distinctive methods of science and the evaluation of scientific hypotheses, inferences, and experiments.

4. *Philosophy of Politics* (more commonly called "political" or "social" philosophy) raises such metaphysical questions as whether propositions about the state can be analysed into more complicated statements about individual persons. But mostly, it deals with ethical questions about the legitimacy or authority of governments, the grounds and limits of the obligation of obedience to law and government, and the comparative evaluation of various basic types of government.

5. *Philosophy of Art* ("philosophical aesthetics") raises metaphysical questions that concern the status of the art object. (Is the poem one and the same as the black marks—printed words—on the paper? Is the painting the same as the chemical pigments on the canvas? If not, then what is the contribution of the perceiving mind?) Philosophy of art

deals with epistemological questions such as whether art has meaning and truth, and ethical questions about the appropriate standards for criticizing art and the social value of art.

Not only is the above list of derivative branches of philosophy not exhaustive; it is in principle indefinitely expansible. Philosophical questions can be asked about any basic form of human experience and activity, including philosophy itself. Indeed this introduction can be interpreted as a sketchy essay in the "philosophy of philosophy." A more thorough investigation would try to state what epistemological, metaphysical, ethical, and logical questions have in common (for which they have a common description— "philosophical") and how these philosophical questions are contrasted with the subject matter of the sciences, mathematics, art, history, and theology.

Some writers say that all philosophical questions are either *conceptual* or *normative*. Conceptual questions call for the clarification or analysis of general concepts, and the answers take the form of definitions of the words that express those concepts. Philosophers undertake conceptual inquiries when they attempt to define "God," "knowledge," "substance," "cause," "mind," "freedom," "justice," "science," or "philosophy," or when they try to clarify such conceptual distinctions as between appearance and reality, knowledge and belief, means and end. Normative questions are those posed in such terms as "good," "bad," "right," "wrong," "valid," "invalid," "justified" and "unjustified," which call for critical judgments and evaluations. Sometimes philosophers try to justify basic beliefs such as that material objects exist, or institutions such as political democracy. In doing so they are attacking questions that are irreducibly normative—the questions cannot be answered entirely by the methods of science and the other nonphilosophical disciplines.

If the questions of philosophy are defined as (1) well-formed, legitimate questions, as opposed to pseudo questions so muddled in their formulation that they pose no real question at all (for example, "How much does justice weigh?"), and (2) questions that are not of mathematics, science, history, or any other well-defined discipline—then it is debatable whether there are any philosophical questions at all. Skeptics might maintain that all legitimate intellectual questions are scientific, mathematical, historical, and so on, and any leftover questions belonging to none of these disciplines are pseudo questions incapable even in principle of being answered. But such a belief would itself be taking a stand on a meaningful philosophical question in the philosophy of philosophy. The question of whether all legitimate intellectual questions are scientific (and so on) is itself a *real question* that is not a scientific question. The independence of philosophy is thus vindicated by its capacity to transcend itself by including itself within the scope of its own subject matter.

The questions of the philosophy of philosophy include epistemological issues (for example, "Can we *know* the answers to philosophical questions?"); metaphysical issues (for example, "If there can be uniquely philosophical knowledge, is there a distinctive realm of being that it is knowledge about?"); ethical issues (for example, "What social value might there be in the study of philosophy?" "What claim does it have on our resources?"); and logical issues about the standards of proper reasoning in philosophy itself. These questions are as difficult and fascinating as those of any other branch of philosophy, but they are, in a way, parasitical. They can be seriously and systematically studied only by a person who has already studied the other branches of philosophy that this highly derivative branch is about. The philosophy of philosophy, in short, should be a final destination, not an initial launching position.

The point, after all, of this brief essay has been merely to introduce the student to philosophy, not to raise and settle philosophical questions about philosophy. The best introduction to philosophy, however, (as to anything else) is to become quickly and directly acquainted with the subject itself. And if you are a normally curious, reflective, and intellectually sensitive person, you will find your new acquaintance frustrating at times but endlessly intriguing and engrossing.

Glossary of Technical Terms

Argument: A set of statements of which one is a conclusion and others constitute the reason or evidence for the conclusion.

Conceptual question: A question that calls for the definition of some general term that will clarify its meaning or render it more explicit.

Deductive argument: An argument whose conclusion is said to follow necessarily from its premises.

Epistemological question: A question that inquires about the ultimate grounds, sources, or limits of knowledge.

Epistemology: That basic branch or core area of philosophy which studies the nature of knowledge and tries to map its limits.

Ethical theory (Metaethics): That branch of philosophy which tries to answer epistemological, metaphysical, and logical questions about ethics, that is, about moral concepts, rules, judgments, and principles.

Ethics: That basic branch or core area of philosophy which tries to state the ultimate standards of right and wrong conduct, and the criteria for intrinsically good and evil states of affairs.

Inductive argument: An argument that purports to establish its conclusion with probability.

Logic: That basic branch or core area of philosophy which tries to state the standards of correct reasoning and the rules for assessing arguments.

Logical question: A question that inquires generally about the cogency of reasons for given conclusions or the criteria for correct reasoning.

Metaphysical question: A question that inquires about the ultimate reality of some given class of things or seeks to determine more generally which entities are the ultimate constituents of reality.

Metaphysics (Ontology): That basic branch or core area of philosophy which seeks to determine generally the basic constituents of reality and the nature of existence.

Normative question: A question that applies to some class of things a norm or standard of rightness or wrongness, goodness or badness, or some other term of critical appraisal.

Premise: A statement in an argument that provides the reason or evidence for the conclusion.

Pseudo question: A "question" which may be well-formed grammatically, but which is so muddled conceptually it can have no correct answer, only an explanation of why and how it is ill-formed and unanswerable.

Reductive analysis: A proposed translation of all statements containing a given term or phrase into equivalent statements not containing that term or phrase in order to rebut the argument that the term or phrase in question refers to an ultimate existent.

Sound deductive argument: An argument that (1) is valid and (2) contains only true premises.

Valid deductive argument: An argument whose form is such that if its premises are true then its conclusion must be true (whatever the actual truth values of the premises and conclusion happen to be).

PART 1 REASON AND

What can reason tell us about such vast topics as the origin of the universe and the existence and nature of God? Most of us have beliefs about these matters—beliefs derived from religious authorities or based on faith; but is there any way to demonstrate that these beliefs are reasonable or unreasonable? This question provides the unifying theme for the readings in Part One.

Traditional arguments for the existence of God are often divided into two groups: those whose premises are justified *a posteriori* (based on experience) and those whose premises are known *a priori* (independently of experience). In fact, however, only one mode of argument has ever purported to be wholly independent of experience, namely, the *ontological argument,* invented by St. Anselm in the eleventh century and defended in one form or another by Descartes, Spinoza, and Leibniz in the seventeenth century. (For Descartes' version of the argument, see his fifth Meditation, p. 131.) According to this argument, the very concept of God (or definition of the word *God*) entails that God must exist. If the argument is correct, any rational being who has an idea of God—even if that being has no knowledge whatever of the kind derived from sense experience—has conclusive rational grounds for believing that God exists. The ontological argument still has defenders among philosophers of religion today, but among those who agree to reject it, perhaps a majority of the philosophers, there is little agreement over precisely what is wrong with the argument. One recent discussion of the argument is included here. William L. Rowe's essay sets forth Anselm's argument clearly, step by step (including steps that are only implicit in Anselm's own formulation), summarizes the three most important objections to the argument, and then presents his own criticism. Rowe concludes that the ontological argument is defective, but that it is nevertheless a ''work of genius'' which, despite its apparent simplicity, raises philosophical questions about the nature of existence that are subtle and fascinating in their own right.

Other arguments for God's existence are often called a priori, but these always contain at least one premise that asserts some simple experiential fact. Factual premises summariz-

RELIGIOUS BELIEF

ing some facet of our experience are found in the various versions of the *cosmological argument*—illustrated in this section by the selections from St. Thomas Aquinas and Samuel Clarke. For the first three of his "Five Ways," Aquinas begins each argument by citing a familiar fact of experience: Some things are in motion; there are causes and effects; things are generated and corrupted. He then tries to show that this fact can be explained only by the existence of God, since alternative explanations lead to logical absurdities. In his second article in this section, William L. Rowe examines the cosmological argument in the form given it by Samuel Clarke and other seventeenth- and eighteenth-century philosophers. Put simply, the argument goes as follows:

1. Every being (that exists or ever did exist) is either a dependent being or self-existent being.
2. Not every being can be a dependent being.
3. Therefore, there exists a self-existent being.

The argument clearly is valid; that is, *if* its premises are true, then its conclusion is true. But the premises, especially the second, are highly controversial. Rowe reviews the dialectic of the debate, pro and con, over the truth of the second premise, before cautiously concluding that the premise has not yet been conclusively shown to be true.

Both the ontological and the cosmological arguments are *deductive* in form; that is, they purport to demonstrate that if their premises are true, then their conclusions must necessarily be true. It is logically impossible for a valid deductive argument to have both true premises and false conclusion. The *teleological argument* (more commonly called "the argument from design") for God is more modest. It argues not that its conclusion follows necessarily from its premises, but only that its premises establish a probability that the conclusion is true. It is therefore what logicians call an *inductive* argument. The famous argument from design, which is given classic formulations in William Paley's *Natural Theology* (1802) and by Cleanthes, a character in David Hume's *Dialogues*

(1779), has the inductive form. More precisely, it is an argument by analogy, with the form:

1. *a, b, c,* and *d* all have properties *P* and *Q*.
2. *a, b,* and *c* all have property *R* as well.
3. Therefore, *d* has property *R* too (probably).

The closer the similarity between *d* and *a, b,* and *c,* the more probable is the conclusion. Cleanthes' argument can be rendered as follows:

1. Boats, houses, watches, and the whole experienced world have such properties as "mutual adjustment of parts to whole" and "curious adapting of means to ends."
2. Boats, houses, and watches have the further property of having been produced by design.
3. Therefore, it is probable that the universe also has this further property, that it too was produced by design.

The conclusion of this argument, that a designer of the world exists, has the same logical role as a scientific hypothesis designed to explain the facts of experience, and must be accepted or rejected according to whether it meets the criteria of adequacy by which hypotheses are appraised in science and in everyday life.

The case against the argument from design is stated with great force and ingenuity by Philo, probably speaking for David Hume himself. The analogies cited by the argument, he claims, are weak, partly because we know only one small part of the universe and cannot with confidence infer from it the nature of the whole. Moreover, he argues, there are other equally plausible ways of accounting for the observed order in the world. One of these alternative explanations, called by Philo in Part VII the "Epicurean Hypothesis," bears striking resemblance to the Darwinian theory that biological adaptations are the result of chance variations and the survival of the fittest.

In Parts X and XI occurs one of the most famous discussions of "the problem of evil," so central to religious belief. Here Philo concedes that if the existence of God has already been established by some a priori argument, then perhaps one can account for the appearance of evil in the world. But, he goes on to argue, one cannot infer the existence of an all-good and all-powerful being from the appearance of evil; that is, the former can hardly be an *explanation* of the latter. The twentieth-century philosopher J. L. Mackie uses the traditional problem of evil to launch a much stronger attack against belief in a God with the attributes normally ascribed to Him by the Western monotheistic religions. Mackie argues that those attributes, specifically omnipotence and benevolence, are inconsistent with the existence of evil in the world. The reader is then challenged either to modify his or her conception of the deity, to fault Mackie's logic, or to locate the premise or premises in Mackie's arguments that the reader thinks are false.

Many contemporary philosophers reject all attempts to interpret theological doctrines in the manner suggested by the argument from design as "larger scientific hypotheses" whose primary function is to explain the world we experience. According to these writers, there is at least one crucial difference between the two: Scientific hypotheses are in principle falsifiable. We can at least conceive of an experience that we would count as evidence against Newton's laws, but the true believer's faith in God is compatible with anything that might happen. And, it has been urged, a doctrine that is consistent with everything possible can explain nothing actual. In the selection from a symposium on theology and falsification, the contemporary British philosopher Antony Flew challenges his fellow symposiasts to describe any conceivable occurrence that they would accept as evidence against the existence of a loving God. If nothing can ever be allowed to count against the assertion of his existence, Flew argues, then that assertion is not in principle falsifiable and therefore explains nothing. His challenge is met in quite different ways. R. M. Hare rejects the view that religious doctrines are explanatory assertions, yet argues that they are no worse for that. His Oxford colleague Basil Mitchell, on the other hand, would allow the fact of pain to count against—but not decisively against—Christian doctrine.

What if it should turn out (as many philosophers now believe) that all traditional arguments for the existence of God, a priori and a posteriori, are defective, or at least inconclusive? Would it follow that religious belief is unreasonable? Walter T. Stace, in his essay "What Is Mysticism?" discusses various accounts of mystic experiences that are literally indescribable, in which there is allegedly a direct experience of an infinite undifferentiated unity—"naturally but not necessarily" thought to be God. To those in all religious traditions who have reported such phenomena, the experience is so vivid and intense that while under its influence, one cannot doubt its authenticity. To a person subject to such experiences it must seem that all talk of proofs and hypotheses are totally irrelevant. Stace sympathizes with the view that it is entirely reasonable for mystics to believe they are in touch with an independent reality that is not otherwise knowable. Bertrand Russell, however, in his critique of mysticism, is more skeptical. "From a scientific point of view," he writes, "we can make no distinction between the man who eats little and sees heaven and the man who drinks much and sees snakes." Perhaps the key issue is whether an abnormal physical condition might be a necessary condition for some kinds of experiences of external reality, or whether physiological abnormality is itself always a strong reason to discount what is experienced.

Mystical experiences, while having nothing to do with argument, might nevertheless be considered a kind of "evidence" for their attendant beliefs. The question posed by William James in the final selection in this section, however, is whether beliefs based on no evidence whatever can nevertheless be, in some circumstances, reasonable. His ingenious essay answers this question in a cautious affirmative. (The careful reader might well ask himself, however, whether James's strict conditions for the proper exercise of "the will to believe" are in fact ever satisfied.) If there is one thing that William James, the nineteenth-century Protestant, has in common with Blaise Pascal, the seventeenth-century Catholic (whose famous "wager argument" for faith is sharply criticized here by Stephen Stitch), it is the conviction that the primary function of religious belief is not simply to allay philosophical curiosity about things. Both writers are aware that, to many, religious belief is a vital practical need; and each in his own way urges that this be taken into account when the reasonableness of belief is assessed.

The Existence and Nature of God

SAINT ANSELM

The Ontological Argument, from *Proslogium**

Saint Anselm (1033–1109) was Archbishop of Canterbury.

CHAPTER II

Truly there is a God, although the fool hath said in his heart, There is no God.

And so, Lord, do thou, who dost give understanding to faith, give me, so far as thou knowest it to be profitable, to understand that thou art as we believe; and that thou art that which we believe. And, indeed, we believe that thou art a being than which nothing greater can be conceived. Or is there no such nature, since the fool hath said in his heart, there is no God? (Psalms xiv. 1). But, at any rate, this very fool, when he hears of this being of which I speak—a being than which nothing greater can be conceived—understands what he hears, and what he understands is in his understanding; although he does not understand it to exist.

For, it is one thing for an object to be in the understanding, and another to understand that the object exists. When a painter first conceives of what he will afterwards perform, he has it in his understanding, but he does not yet understand it to be, because he has not yet performed it. But after he has made the painting, he both has it in his understanding, and he understands that it exists, because he has made it.

Hence, even the fool is convinced that something

*From *St. Anselm: Basic Writings,* trans. S. N. Deane, with an Introduction by Charles Hartshorne (La Salle, Ill.: Open Court, 1961). Reprinted by permission of the publisher.

exists in the understanding, at least, than which nothing greater can be conceived. For, when he hears of this, he understands it. And whatever is understood, exists in the understanding. And assuredly that, than which nothing greater can be conceived, cannot exist in the understanding alone. For, suppose it exists in the understanding alone: then it can be conceived to exist in reality; which is greater.

Therefore, if that, than which nothing greater can be conceived, exists in the understanding alone, the very being, than which nothing greater can be conceived, is one, than which a greater can be conceived. But obviously this is impossible. Hence, there is no doubt that there exists a being, than which nothing greater can be conceived, and it exists both in the understanding and in reality.

CHAPTER III

God cannot be conceived not to exist.—God is that, than which nothing greater can be conceived.—That which can be conceived not to exist is not God.

And it assuredly exists so truly, that it cannot be conceived not to exist. For, it is possible to conceive of a being which cannot be conceived not to exist; and this is greater than one which can be conceived not to exist. Hence, if that, than which nothing greater can be conceived, can be conceived not to exist, it is not that than which nothing greater can be conceived. But this is an irreconcilable contradiction. There is, then, so truly a being than which nothing greater can be conceived to exist, that it cannot even be conceived not to exist; and this being thou art, O Lord, our God.

So truly, therefore, dost thou exist, O Lord, my God, that thou canst not be conceived not to exist; and rightly. For, if a mind could conceive of a being better than thee, the creature would rise above the Creator; and this is most absurd. And, indeed, whatever else there is, except thee alone, can be conceived not to exist. To thee alone, therefore, it belongs to exist more truly than all other beings, and hence in a higher degree than all others. For, whatever else exists does not exist so truly, and hence in a higher degree than all others. For, whatever else exists does not exist so truly, and hence in a less degree it belongs to it to exist. Why, then, has the fool said in his heart, there is no God (Psalms xiv. I), since it is so evident, to a rational mind, that thou dost exist in the highest degree of all? Why, except that he is dull and a fool?

CHAPTER IV

How the fool has said in his heart what cannot be conceived.—A thing may be conceived in two ways: (1) when the word signifying it is conceived; (2) when the thing itself is understood. As far as the word goes God can be conceived not to exist; in reality he cannot.

But how has the fool said in his heart what he could not conceive; or how is it that he could not conceive what he said in his heart? since it is the same to say in the heart, and to conceive.

But, if really, nay, since really, he both conceived, because he said in his heart; and did not say in his heart, because he could not conceive; there is more than one way in which a thing is said in the heart or conceived. For, in one sense, an object is conceived, when the word signifying it is conceived; and in another, when the very entity, which the object is, is understood.

In the former sense, then, God can be conceived not to exist; but in the latter, not at all. For no one who understands what fire and water are can conceive fire to be water, in accordance with the nature of the facts themselves, although that is possible according to the words. So, then, no one who understands what God is can conceive that God does not exist; although he says these words in his heart, either without any, or with some foreign signification. For, God is that than which a greater cannot be conceived. And he who thoroughly understands this, assuredly understands that this being so truly exists, that not even in concept can it be non-existent. Therefore, he who understands that God so exists, cannot conceive that he does not exist.

I thank thee, gracious Lord, I thank thee; because what I formerly believed by thy bounty, I now so understand by thine illumination, that if I were unwilling to believe that thou dost exist, I should not be able to understand this to be true.

CHAPTER V

God is whatever it is better to be than not to be; and he, as the only self-existent being, creates all things from nothing.

What art thou, then, Lord God, than whom nothing greater can be conceived? But what art thou, except that which, as the highest of all beings, alone exists through itself, and creates all other things from nothing? For, whatever is not this is less than a thing which can be conceived of. But this cannot be conceived of thee. What good, therefore, does the supreme Good lack, through which every good is? Therefore, thou art just, truthful, blessed, and whatever it is better to be than not to be. For it is better to be just than not just; better to be blessed than not blessed.

WILLIAM L. ROWE

The Ontological Argument*

William L. Rowe (1931–   ) teaches philosophy at Purdue University.

Arguments for the existence of God are commonly divided into a posteriori and a priori arguments. An a posteriori argument depends on a principle or premise that can be known only by means of our experience of the world. An a priori argument, on the other hand, purports to rest on principles which can be known independently of our experience of the world, just by reflecting on and understanding them. Of the three major arguments for the existence of God—the Cosmological, Teleological, and Ontological—only the last is entirely a priori. In the Cosmological argument one starts from some simple fact about the world, such as the fact that it contains things which are caused to exist by other things. In the Teleological argument a somewhat more complicated fact about the world serves as a starting point: the fact that the world exhibits order and design. In the Ontological argument, however, one begins simply with a concept of God.

I

It is perhaps best to think of the Ontological argument as a family of arguments, each member of which begins with a concept of God, and by appealing only to a priori principles, endeavors to establish that God actually exists. Within this family of arguments the most important historically is the argument set forth by Anselm in the second chapter of his *Proslogium* (A Discourse).[1] Indeed, the Ontological argument begins with chapter II of Anselm's *Proslogium*. In

an earlier work, *Monologium* (A Soliloquy), Anselm had endeavored to establish the existence and nature of God by weaving together several versions of the Cosmological argument. In the Preface to *Proslogium* Anselm remarks that after the publication of *Monologium* he began to search for a single argument which alone would establish the existence and nature of God. After much strenuous but unsuccessful effort, he reports that he sought to put the project out of his mind in order to turn to more fruitful tasks. The idea, however, continued to haunt him until one day the proof he had so strenuously sought became clear to his mind. Anselm sets forth this proof in the second chapter of *Proslogium*.

Before discussing Anselm's argument in step-by-step fashion, there are certain concepts that will help us understand some of the central ideas of the argument. Suppose we draw a vertical line in our imagination and agree that on the left side of our line are all the things which exist, while on the right side of the line are all the things which don't exist. We might then begin to make a list of some of the things on both sides of our imaginary line, as follows:

THINGS WHICH EXIST	THINGS WHICH DON'T EXIST
The Empire State Building	The Fountain of Youth
Dogs	Unicorns
The planet Mars	The Abominable Snowman

Now each of the things (or sorts of things) listed thus far has (have) the following feature: it (they) logically might have been on the other side of the line. The Fountain of Youth, for example, is on the right side of the line, but *logically* there is no absurdity in the idea that it might have been on the left side of the line. Similarly, although dogs do exist, we surely can imagine without logical absurdity that they might not have existed, that they might have been on the right side of the line. Let us then record this feature of the things thus far listed by introducing the idea of a *contingent thing* as a thing that logically might have been on the other side of the line from the side it actually is on. The planet Mars and the Abominable Snowman are contingent things, even though the former happens to exist and the latter does not.

Suppose we add to our list the phrase "the object which is completely round and completely square at the same time" on the right side of our line. The round square, however, unlike the other things thus far listed on the right side of our line, is something that *logically could not* have been on the left side of the line. Noting this, let us introduce the idea of an *impossible thing* as a thing that is on the right side of the line and logically could not have been on the left side of the line.

Looking again at our list, we wonder if there is anything on the left side of our imaginary line which, unlike the things thus far listed on the left side, *logically could not* have been on the right side of the line. At this point we don't have to answer this question, but it is useful to have a concept to apply to any such things, should there be any. Accordingly, let us say that a *necessary thing* is a thing on the left side of our imaginary line and logically could not have been on the right side of the line.

Finally, a *possible thing* is any thing that is either on the left side of our imaginary line or logically might have been on the left side of the line. Possible things, then, will be all those things that are not impossible things—that is, all those things that are either contingent or necessary. If there are no necessary things, then all possible things will be contingent and all contingent things will be possible. If there is a necessary thing, however, then there will be a possible thing which is not contingent.

Armed with these concepts, we can clarify certain important distinctions and ideas in Anselm's thought. The first of these is his distinction between *existence in the understanding* and *existence in reality*. Anselm's notion of existence in reality is the same as our notion of existence; that is, being on the left side of our imaginary line. Since the Fountain of Youth is on the right side of the line, it does not exist in reality. The things which exist are, to use Anselm's phrase, the things which exist in reality. Anselm's notion of existence in the understanding, however, is not the same as any idea we normally employ. When we

think of a certain thing, say the Fountain of Youth, then that thing, on Anselm's view, exists in the understanding. Also, when we think of an existing thing like the Empire State Building, it, too, exists in the understanding. So some of the things on both sides of our imaginary line exist in the understanding, but only those on the left side of our line exist in reality. Are there any things that don't exist in the understanding? Undoubtedly there are, for there are things, both existing and non-existing, of which we have not really thought. Now suppose I assert that the Fountain of Youth does not exist. Since to meaningfully deny the existence of something I have to have that thing in mind, I have to think of it, it follows on Anselm's view that whenever someone asserts that some thing does not exist, that thing *does* exist in the understanding.[2] So in asserting that the Fountain of Youth does not exist, I imply that the Fountain of Youth does exist in the understanding. And in asserting that it does not exist I have asserted (on Anselm's view) that it does not exist in reality. This means that my simple assertion amounts to the somewhat more complex claim that the Fountain of Youth exists in the understanding but does not exist in reality—in short, that the Fountain of Youth exists *only* in the understanding.

We can now understand why Anselm insists that anyone who hears of God, thinks about God, or even denies the existence of God is, nevertheless, committed to the view that God exists in the understanding. Also, we can understand why Anselm treats what he calls "the fool's claim" that God does not exist as the claim that God exists *only* in the understanding—that is, that God exists in the understanding but does not exist in reality.

In *Monologium* Anselm sought to prove that among those beings which do exist there is one which is the greatest, highest, and the best. But in *Proslogium* he undertakes to prove that among those beings which exist there is one which is not just the greatest among existing beings, but is such that no conceivable being is greater. We need to distinguish these two ideas: (1) a being than which *no existing being* is greater, and (2) a being than which *no conceivable being* is greater. If the only things in existence were a stone, a frog, and a man, the last of these would satisfy our first idea but not our second—for we can conceive of a being (an angel or God) greater than a man. Anselm's idea of God, as he expresses it in *Proslogium* II, is the same as (2) above; it is the idea of "a being than which nothing greater can be conceived.'' It will facilitate our understanding of Anselm's argument if we make two slight changes in the way he has expressed his idea of God. For his phrase I shall substitute the following: '*the being than which none greater is possible.*'[3] This idea says that if a certain being is God then no *possible being* can be greater than it, or conversely, if a certain being is such that it is even *possible* for there to be a being greater than it, then that being is not God. What Anselm proposes to prove, then, is that the being than which none greater is possible exists in reality. If he proves this he will have proved that God, as he conceives of Him, exists in reality.

But what does Anselm mean by ''greatness''? Is a building, for example, greater than a man? In *Monologium,* chapter II, Anselm remarks: ''But I do not mean physically great, as a material object is great, but that which, the greater it is, is the better or the more worthy—wisdom, for instance.'' Contrast wisdom with size. Anselm is saying that wisdom is something that contributes to the greatness of a thing. If a thing comes to have more wisdom than it did before then (given that its other characteristics remain the same), that thing has become a greater, better, more worthy thing than it was. Wisdom, Anselm is saying, is a great-making quality. However, the mere fact that something increases in size (physical greatness) does not make that thing a better thing than it was before, so size is not a great-making quality. By ''greater than'' Anselm means ''better than,'' ''superior to,'' or ''more worthy than,'' and he believes that some characteristics, like wisdom and moral goodness, are great-making characteristics in that anything which has them is a *better thing* than it would be (other characteristics of it remaining the same) were it to lack them.

We come now to what we may call the *key idea* in Anselm's Ontological argument. Anselm believes that *existence in reality is a great-making quality.* Does Anselm mean that anything that exists is a greater thing than anything that doesn't? Although he does not ask or answer the question, it is perhaps reasonable to believe that Anselm did not mean this. When he discusses wisdom as a great-making quality he is careful not to say that any wise thing is better than any unwise thing—for he recognizes that a just but unwise man might be a better being than a wise but unjust man.[4] I suggest that what Anselm means is

that anything that doesn't exist but might have existed (is on the right side of our line but might have been on the left) would have been a greater thing if it had existed (if it had been on the left side of our line). He is not comparing two different things (one existing and one not existing) and saying that the first is therefore greater than the second. Rather, he is talking about *one* thing and pointing out that if it does not exist but might have existed, then *it* would have been a greater thing if it had existed. Using Anselm's distinction between existence in the understanding and existence in reality, we may express the key idea in Anselm's reasoning as follows: If something exists only in the understanding but might have existed in reality, then it might have been greater than it is. Since the Fountain of Youth, for example, exists only in the understanding but (unlike the round square) might have existed in reality, it follows by Anselm's principle that the Fountain of Youth might have been a greater thing than it is.

II

We can now consider the step-by-step development of Anselm's Ontological argument. I shall use the term ''God'' in place of the longer phrase ''the being than which none greater is possible''—wherever the term ''God'' appears we are to think of it as simply an abbreviation of the longer phrase.

1. God exists in the understanding.

As we have noted, anyone who hears of the being than which none greater is possible is, on Anselm's view, committed to premise (1).

2. God might have existed in reality (God is a possible being).

Anselm, I think, assumes the truth of (2) without making it explicit in his reasoning. By asserting (2) I do not mean to imply that God does not exist in reality, but that, unlike the round square, God is a possible being.

3. If something exists only in the understanding and might have existed in reality, then it might have been greater than it is.

As we noted, this is the key idea in Anselm's Ontological argument. It is intended as a general principle, true of anything whatever.

Steps (1)–(3) constitute the basic premises of Anselm's Ontological argument. From these three items, Anselm believes, it follows that God exists in reality. But how does Anselm propose to convince us that if we accept (1)–(3) we are committed by the rules of logic to accept his conclusion that God exists in reality? Anselm's procedure is to offer what is called a *reductio ad absurdum* proof of his conclusion. Instead of showing directly that the existence of God follows from steps (1)–(3), Anselm invites us to *suppose* that God does not exist (i.e., that the conclusion he wants to establish is false) and then shows how this supposition, when conjoined with steps (1)–(3), leads to an absurd result, a result that couldn't possibly be true because it is contradictory. Since the supposition that God does not exist leads to an absurdity, that supposition must be rejected in favor of the conclusion that God does exist.

Does Anselm succeed in reducing the "fool's belief" that God does not exist to an absurdity? The best way to answer this question is to follow the steps of his argument.

4. Suppose God exists only in the understanding.

This supposition, as we saw earlier, is Anselm's way of expressing the belief that God does not exist.

5. God might have been greater than He is. (2, 4, and 3)[5]

Step (5) follows from steps (2), (4), and (3). Since (3), if true, is true of anything whatever, it will be true of God. Therefore, (3) implies that if God exists only in the understanding and might have existed in reality, then God might have been greater than He is. If so, then given (2) and (4), (5) must be true. For what (3) says when applied to God is that given (2) and (4), it follows that (5).

6. God is a being than which a greater is possible. (5)

Surely if God is such that He logically might have been greater, then He is such than which a greater is possible.

We can now appreciate Anselm's *reductio* argument. He has shown that if we accept steps (1)–(4), we must accept step (6). But (6) is unacceptable; it is the absurdity Anselm was after. By replacing "God" in (6) with the longer phrase it abbreviates, we see that (6) amounts to the absurd assertion:

7. The being than which none greater is possible is a being than which a greater is possible.

Now since steps (1)–(4) have led us to an obviously false conclusion, and if we accept Anselm's basic

premises (1)–(3) as true, then (4), the supposition that God exists only in the understanding, must be rejected as false. Thus we have shown that:

8. It is false that God exists only in the understanding.

But since premise (1) tells us that God does exist in the understanding and (8) tells us that God does not exist only there, we may infer that

9. God exists in reality as well as in the understanding. (1, 8)

III

Most of the philosophers who have considered this argument have rejected it because of a basic conviction that from the logical analysis of a certain idea or concept we can never determine that there exists in reality anything answering to that idea or concept. We may examine and analyse, for example, the idea of an elephant or the idea of a unicorn, but it is only by our experience of the world that we can determine that there exist things answering to our first idea and not to the second. Anselm, however, believes that the concept of God is utterly unique—from an analysis of this concept he believes that it can be determined that there exists in reality a being which answers to it. Moreover, he presents us with an argument to show that it can be done in the case of the idea of God. We can, of course, simply reject Anselm's argument on the grounds that it violates the basic conviction noted above. Many critics, however, have sought to prove more directly that it is a bad argument and to point out the particular step that is mistaken. Next we shall examine the three major objections that have been advanced by the argument's critics.

The first criticism was advanced by a contemporary of Anselm's, a monk named "Gaunilo," who wrote a response to Anselm entitled, "On Behalf of the Fool."[6] Gaunilo sought to prove that Anselm's reasoning is mistaken by applying it to things other than God, things which we know don't exist. He took as his example the island than which none greater is possible. No such island really exists. But, argues Gaunilo, if Anselm's reasoning were correct we could show that such an island really does exist. For since it is greater to exist than not to exist, if the island than which none greater is possible doesn't exist then it is an island than which a greater is possible. But it is impossible for the island than which none greater is possible to be an island than which a greater is possible. Therefore, the island than which none greater is possible must exist. About this argument Gaunilo remarks:

If a man should try to prove to me by such reasoning that this island truly exists, and that its existence should no longer be doubted, either I should believe that he was jesting, or I know not which I ought to regard as the greater fool: myself, supposing I should allow this proof; or him, if he should suppose that he had established with any certainty the existence of this island.[7]

Gaunilo's strategy is clear: by using the very same reasoning Anselm employs in his argument, we can prove the existence of things we know don't exist. Therefore, Anselm's reasoning in his proof of the existence of God must be mistaken. In reply to Gaunilo, Anselm insisted that his reasoning applies only to God and cannot be used to establish the existence of things other than God. Unfortunately, Anselm did not explain just why his reasoning cannot be applied to things like Gaunilo's island.

In defense of Anselm against Gaunilo's objection, there are two difficulties in applying Anselm's reasoning to things like Gaunilo's island. The first derives from the fact that Anselm's principle that existence is a great-making quality was taken to mean that if something does not exist then it is not as great *a thing* (being) as it would have been had it existed. Now if we use precisely this principle in Gaunilo's argument, all we will prove is that if Gaunilo's island does not exist then the island than which none greater is possible is an island than which *a greater thing* is possible. But this statement is not an absurdity. For the island than which no greater *island* is possible can be something than which *a greater thing* is possible—an unsurpassable island may be a surpassable thing. (A perfect man might be a greater thing than a perfect island.) Consequently, if we follow Anselm's reasoning exactly, it does not appear that we can derive an absurdity from the supposition that the island than which none greater is possible does not exist.

A second difficulty in applying Anselm's reasoning to Gaunilo's island is that we must accept the premise that Gaunilo's island is a possible thing. But this seems to require us to believe that some finite, limited thing (an island) might have unlimited perfections. It is not at all clear that this is possible. Try to think, for example, of a hockey player than which none

greater is possible. How fast would he have to skate? How many goals would he have to score in a game? How fast would he have to shoot the puck? Could he ever fall down, be checked, or receive a penalty? Although the phrase, "the hockey player than which none greater is possible," seems meaningful, as soon as we try to get a clear idea of what such a being would be like we discover that we can't form a coherent idea of it all. For we are being invited to think of some limited, finite thing—a hockey player or an island—and then to think of it as exhibiting unlimited, infinite perfections. Perhaps, then, since Anselm's reasoning applies only to possible things, Anselm can reject its application to Gaunilo's island on the grounds that the island than which none greater is possible is, like the round square, an impossible thing.

By far the most famous objection to the Ontological argument was set forth by Immanuel Kant in the eighteenth century. According to this objection the mistake in the argument is its claim, implicit in premise (3), that existence is a quality or predicate that adds to the greatness of a thing. There are two parts to this claim: (1) existence is a quality or predicate, and (2) existence, like wisdom and unlike physical size, is a great-making quality or predicate. Someone might accept (1) but object to (2); the objection made famous by Kant, however, is directed at (1). According to this objection, existence is not a predicate at all. Therefore, since in its second premise Anselm's argument implies that existence *is* a predicate, the argument must be rejected.

The central point in the philosophical doctrine that existence is not a predicate concerns what we do when we ascribe a certain quality or predicate to something: for example, when we say of a man next door that he is intelligent, six feet tall, or fat. In each case we seem to assert or presuppose that there *exists* a man next door and then go on to ascribe to him a certain predicate—"intelligent," "six feet tall," or "fat." And many proponents of the doctrine that existence is not a predicate claim that this is a *general feature* of predication. They hold that when we ascribe a quality or predicate to anything we assert or presuppose that the thing exists and then ascribe the predicate to it. Now if this is so, then it is clear that existence cannot be a predicate which we may ascribe to or deny of something. For if it were a predicate, then when we assert of some thing (things) that it (they) exists (exist) we would be asserting or presupposing that it (they) exists (exist) and then going on to predicate existence of it (them). For example, if existence were a predicate, then in asserting "tigers exist" we would be asserting or presupposing that tigers exist and then going on to predicate existence of them. Furthermore, in asserting "dragons do not exist" we would be asserting or presupposing, if existence were a predicate, that dragons do exist and then going on to deny that existence attaches to them. In short, if existence were a predicate, the affirmative existential statement "tigers exist" would be a redundancy and the negative existential statement "dragons do not exist" would be contradictory. But clearly "tigers exist" is not a redundancy; and "dragons do not exist" is true and, therefore, not contradictory. What this shows, according to the proponents of Kant's objection, is that existence is not a genuine predicate.

According to the proponents of the above objection, when we assert that tigers exist and that dragons do not we are not saying that certain things (tigers) have and certain other things (dragons) do not have a peculiar predicate, *existence;* rather, we are saying something about the *concept* of a tiger and the *concept* of a dragon. We are saying that the concept of a tiger applies to something in the world and that the concept of a dragon does not apply to anything in the world.

Although this objection to the Ontological argument has been widely accepted, it is doubtful that it provides us with a conclusive refutation of the argument. It may be true that existence is not a predicate, that in asserting the existence of something we are not ascribing a certain predicate or attribute to that thing. But the arguments presented for this view seem to rest on mistaken or incomplete claims about the nature of predication. For example, the argument which we stated earlier rests on the claim that when we ascribe a predicate to anything we assert or presuppose that that thing exists. But this claim appears to be mistaken. In asserting that Dr. Doolittle is an animal lover I seem to be ascribing the predicate "animal lover" to Dr. Doolittle, but in doing so I certainly am not asserting or presupposing that Dr. Doolittle actually exists. Dr. Doolittle doesn't exist, but it is nevertheless true that he is an animal lover. The plain fact is that we can talk about and ascribe predicates to many things which do not exist and never did. Merlin, for example, no less than Houdini, was a magician, although Houdini existed but Merlin did not. If, as these examples suggest, the claim that whenever we ascribe a predicate to something we assert or presuppose that the thing exists is a false claim, then we will need a better argument for the doctrine that existence is not

a predicate. There is some question, however, whether anyone has succeeded in giving a really conclusive argument for this doctrine.[8]

A third objection against the Ontological argument calls into question the premise that God might have existed in reality (God is a possible being). As we saw, this premise claims that the being than which none greater is possible is not an impossible object. But is this true? Consider the series of positive integers: 1, 2, 3, 4, etc. We know that any integer in this series, no matter how large, is such that a larger integer than it is possible. Therefore, the positive integer than which none larger is possible is an impossible object. Perhaps this is also true of the being than which none greater is possible. That is, perhaps no matter how great a being may be, it is possible for there to be a being greater than it. If this were so, then, like the integer than which none larger is possible, Anselm's God would not be a possible object. The mere fact that there are degrees of greatness, however, does not entitle us to conclude that Anselm's God is like the integer than which none larger is possible. There are, for example, degrees of size in angles—one angle is larger than another—but it is not true that no matter how large an angle is it is possible for there to be an angle larger than it. It is logically impossible for an angle to exceed four right angles. The notion of an angle, unlike the notion of a positive integer, implies a degree of size beyond which it is impossible to go. Is Anselm's God like a largest integer, and therefore impossible, or like a largest angle, and therefore possible? Some philosophers have argued that Anselm's God is impossible,[9] but the arguments for this conclusion are not very compelling. Perhaps, then, this objection is best construed not as proving that Anselm's God is impossible, but as raising the question whether any of us is in a position to know that the being than which none greater is possible is a possible object. For Anselm's argument cannot be a successful proof of the existence of God unless its premises are not just true but are really *known* to be true. Therefore, if we do not know that Anselm's God is a possible object, then his argument cannot prove the existence of God to us, cannot enable us to know that God exists.

IV

Finally, I want to present a somewhat different critique of Anselm's argument, a critique suggested by the basic conviction noted earlier; namely that from the mere logical analysis of a certain idea or concept we can never determine that there exists in reality anything answering to that idea or concept.

Suppose someone comes to us and says:

I propose to define the term ''God'' as *an existing, wholly perfect being*. Now since it can't be true that an existing, wholly perfect being does not exist, it can't be true that God, as I've defined Him, does not exist. Therefore, God must exist.

His argument appears to be a very simple Ontological argument. It begins with a particular idea or concept of God and ends by concluding that God, so conceived, must exist. What can we say in response? We might start by objecting to his definition, claiming: (1) that only predicates can be used to define a term, and (2) that existence is not a predicate. But suppose he is not impressed by this response—either because he thinks that no one has fully explained what a predicate is or proved that existence isn't one, or because he thinks that anyone can define a word in whatever way he pleases. Can we allow him to define the word ''God'' in any way he pleases and still hope to convince him that it will not follow from that definition that there actually exists something to which his concept of God applies? I think we can. Let us first invite him, however, to consider some concepts other than his peculiar concept of God.

Earlier we noted that the term ''magician'' may be applied both to Houdini and Merlin, even though the former existed and the latter did not. Noting that our friend has used ''existing'' as part of his definition of ''God,'' suppose we agree with him that we can define a word in any way we please, and, accordingly, introduce the following definitions:

A ''magican'' is defined as *an existing magician*.
A ''magico'' is defined as *a non-existing magician*.

Here we have introduced two words and used ''existing'' or ''non-existing'' in their definitions. Now something of interest follows from the fact that ''existing'' is part of our definition of a ''magican.'' For while it is true that Merlin was a *magician,* it is not true that Merlin was a *magican*. And something of interest follows from our including ''non-existing'' in the definition of a ''magico''—it is true that Houdini was a *magician,* but it is not true that Houdini was a *magico*. Houdini was a *magician*

and a *magican,* but not a *magico;* Merlin was a *magician* and a *magico,* but not a *magican*.

We have just seen that introducing ''existing'' or ''non-existing'' into the definition of a concept has a very important implication. If we introduce ''existing'' into the definition of a concept, it follows that no non-existing thing can exemplify that concept. And if we introduce ''non-existing'' into the definition of a concept, it follows that no existing thing can exemplify that concept. No non-existing thing can be a *magican,* and no existing thing can be a *magico*.

But must some existing thing exemplify the concept ''magican''? No! From the fact that ''existing'' is included in the definition of ''magican'' it does not follow that some existing thing is a magican— all that follows is that no non-existing thing is a magican. If there were no magicans in existence there would be nothing to which the term ''magican'' would apply. This being so, it clearly does not follow merely from our definition of ''magican'' that some existing thing is a magican. Only if magicians exist will it be true that some existing thing is a magican.

We are now in a position to help our friend see that the mere fact that ''God'' is defined as an existing, wholly perfect being it will not follow that some existing being is God. Something of interest does follow from his definition; namely that no non-existing being can be God. But whether some existing thing is God will depend entirely on whether some existing thing is a wholly perfect being. If no wholly perfect being exists there will be nothing to which his concept of God can apply. This being so, it clearly does not follow merely from his definition of ''God'' that some existing thing is God. Only if a wholly perfect being exists will it be true that God, as he conceives of Him, exists.

The implications of these considerations for Anselm's ingenious argument can now be traced. Anselm conceives of God as a being than which none greater is possible. He then claims that existence is a great-making quality and something that has it is greater than it would have been had it lacked existence. Clearly then, no non-existing thing can exemplify Anselm's concept of God. For if we suppose that some non-existing thing exemplifies Anselm's concept of God and also suppose that that non-existing thing might have existed in reality (is a possible thing) then we are supposing that that non-existing thing (1) might have been a greater thing, and (2) is, nevertheless, a thing than which a greater is not possible. Thus far Anselm's reasoning is, I believe, impeccable. But what follows from it? All that follows from it is that no non-existing thing can be God (as Anselm conceives of God). All that follows is that given Anselm's concept of God, the proposition, "Some non-existing thing is God," cannot be true. But, as we saw earlier, this is also the case with the proposition, "Some non-existing thing is a magican." What remains to be shown is that some existing thing exemplifies Anselm's concept of God. What really does follow from his reasoning is that the only thing that logically could exemplify his concept of God is something which actually exists. And this conclusion is not without interest. But from the mere fact that nothing but an existing thing could exemplify Anselm's concept of God, it does not follow that some existing thing actually does exemplify his concept of God—no more than it follows from the mere fact that no non-existing thing can be a magican that some existing thing is a magican.[10]

There is, however, one major difficulty in this critique of Anselm's argument. This difficulty arises when we take into account Anselm's implicit claim that God is a possible thing. To see just what this difficulty is, let us return to the idea of a possible thing, which is any thing that either is on the left side of our imaginary line or logically might have been on the left side of the line. Possible things, then, will be all those things that, unlike the round square, are not impossible things. Suppose we concede to Anselm that God, as he conceives of Him, is a possible thing. Now, of course, the mere knowledge that something is a possible thing does not enable us to conclude that that thing is an existing thing. Many possible things, like the Fountain of Youth, do not exist. But if something is a possible thing then it is either an existing thing or a non-existing thing. The set of possible things can be exhaustively divided into those possible things which actually exist and those possible things which do not exist. Therefore, if Anselm's God is a possible thing it is either an existing thing or a non-existing thing. We have concluded, however, that no non-existing thing can be Anselm's God; therefore, it seems we must conclude with Anselm that some actually existing thing does exemplify his concept of God.

To see the solution to this major difficulty we need to return to an earlier example. Let us consider again the idea of a "magican," an existing magician. It so happens that some magicians have

existed—Houdini, the Great Blackstone, etc. But, of course, it might have been otherwise. Suppose, for the moment that no magicians have ever existed. The concept "magician" would still have application, for it would still be true that Merlin was a magician. But would any possible object be picked out by the concept of a "magican"? No, for no non-existing thing could exemplify the concept "magican." And on the supposition that no magicians ever existed, no existing thing would exemplify the concept "magican."[11] We then would have a coherent concept "magican" which would not be exemplified by any possible object at all. For if all the possible objects which are magicians are non-existing things, none of them would be a magican and, since no possible objects which exist are magicians, none of them would be a magican. Put in this way, our result seems paradoxical. We are inclined to think that only contradictory concepts like "the round square" are not exemplified by any possible things. The truth is, however, that when "existing" is included in or implied by a certain concept, it may be the case that no possible object does in fact exemplify that concept. For no possible object that doesn't exist will exemplify a concept like "magican" in which "existing" is included; and if there are no existing things which exemplify the other features included in the concept—for example, "being a magician" in the case of the concept "magican"—then no possible object that exists will exemplify the concept. Put in its simplest terms, if we ask whether any possible thing is a magican the answer will depend entirely on whether any existing thing is a magician. If no existing things are magicians then no possible things are magicans. Some possible object is a magican just in the case some actually existing thing is a magician.

Applying these considerations to Anselm's argument, we can find the solution to our major difficulty. Given Anselm's concept of God and his principle that existence is a great-making quality, it really does follow that the only thing that logically could exemplify his concept of God is something which actually exists. But, we argued, it doesn't follow from these considerations alone that God actually exists, that some existing thing exemplifies Anselm's concept of God. The difficulty we fell into, however, is that when we add the premise that God is a possible thing, that some possible object exemplifies his concept of God, it really does follow that God actually exists, that some actually existing thing exemplifies Anselm's concept of God. For if some possible object exemplifies his concept of God, that object is either an existing thing or a non-existing thing. But since no non-existing thing could exemplify Anselm's concept of God, it follows that the possible object which exemplifies his concept of God must be a possible object that actually exists. Therefore, given (1) Anselm's concept of God, (2) his principle that existence is a great-making quality, and (3) the premise that God, as conceived by Anselm, is a possible thing, it really does follow that Anselm's God actually exists. But we now can see that in granting Anselm the premise that God is a possible thing we have granted far more than we intended. All we thought we were conceding is that Anselm's concept of God, unlike the concept of a round square, is not contradictory or incoherent. But without realizing it we were in fact granting much more than this, as became apparent when we considered the idea of a magican. There is nothing contradictory in the idea of a magican, an existing magician. But in asserting that a magican is a possible thing we are, as we saw, directly implying that some existing thing is a magician. For if no existing thing is a magician, the concept of a magican will apply to no possible object whatever. The same point holds with respect to Anselm's God. Since Anselm's concept of God logically cannot apply to some non-existing thing, the only possible objects to which it could apply are possible objects which actually exist. Therefore, in granting that Anselm's God is a possible thing we are conceding far more than that his idea of God isn't incoherent or contradictory. Suppose, for example, that every existing being has some defect which it might not have had. Without realizing it we were denying this when we granted that Anselm's God is a possible being. If every existing being has a defect it might not have had, then every existing being might have been greater. But if every existing being might have been greater, then Anselm's concept of God will apply to no possible object whatever. Therefore, if we allow Anselm his concept of God and his principle that existence is a great-making quality, then in granting that God, as Anselm conceives of Him, is a possible being we will be granting much more than that his concept of God is not contradictory. We will be

conceding, for example, that some existing thing is as perfect as it can be. The fact is that Anselm's God is a possible thing only if some *existing* thing is as perfect as it can be.

Our final critique of Anselm's argument is simply this. In granting that Anselm's God is a possible thing we are in fact granting that Anselm's God actually exists. But since the purpose of the argument is to prove to us that Anselm's God exists, we cannot be asked to grant as a premise a statement which is virtually equivalent to the conclusion that is to be proved. Anselm's concept of God may be coherent and his principle that existence is a great-making quality may be true. But all that follows from this is that no non-existing thing can be Anselm's God. If we add to all of this the premise that God is a possible thing it will follow that God actually exists. But the additional premise claims more than that Anselm's concept of God isn't incoherent or contradictory. It amounts to the assertion that some existing being is supremely great. And since this is, in part, the point the argument endeavors to prove, the argument begs the question: it assumes the point it is supposed to prove.

If the above critique is correct, Anselm's argument fails as a proof of the existence of God. This is not to say, however, that the argument is not a work of genius. Perhaps no other argument in the history of thought has raised so many basic philosophical questions and stimulated so much hard thought. Even if it fails as a proof of the existence of God, it will remain as one of the high achievements of the human intellect.

NOTES

1. Some philosophers believe that Anselm sets forth a different and more cogent argument in chapter III of his *Proslogium*. For this viewpoint see Charles Hartshorne, *Anselm's Discovery* (LaSalle, Ill.: Open Court Publishing Co., 1965); and Norman Malcolm, "Anselm's Ontological Arguments," *The Philosophical Review* LXIX, No. 1 (January 1960): 41–62. For an illuminating account both of Anselm's intentions in *Proslogium II* and *III* and of recent interpretations of Anselm see Arthur C. McGill's essay "Recent Discussions of Anselm's Argument" in *The Many-faced Argument,* ed. John Hick and Arthur C. McGill (New York: The Macmillan Co., 1967), pp. 33–110.

2. Anselm does allow that someone may assert the sentence "God does not exist" without having in his understanding the object or idea for which the word 'God' stands (see *Proslogium,* chapter IV). But when a person does understand the object for which a word stands, then when he uses that word in a sentence denying the existence of that object he must have that object in his understanding. It is doubtful, however, that Anselm thought that incoherent or contradictory expressions like 'the round square' stand for objects which may exist in the understanding.

3. Anselm speaks of "a being" rather than "the being" than which none greater can be conceived. His argument is easier to present if we express his idea of God in terms of "the being." Secondly, to avoid the psychological connotations of "can be conceived" I have substituted "possible."

4. See *Monologium*, chapter XV.

5. The numbers in parentheses refer to the earlier steps in the argument from which the present step is derived.

6. Gaunilo's brief essay, Anselm's reply, and several of Anselm's major works, as translated by S. N. Deane, are collected in *Saint Anselm: Basic Writings* (LaSalle, Ill.: Open Court Publishing Co., 1962).

7. *Saint Anselm: Basic Writings*, p. 151.

8. Perhaps the most sophisticated presentation of the objection that existence is not a predicate is William P. Alston's "The Ontological Argument Revisited" in *The Philosophical Review* 69 (1960): 452–74.

9. See, for example, C. D. Broad's discussion of the Ontological Argument in *Religion, Philosophy, and Psychical Research* (New York: Harcourt, Brace & World, 1953).

10. An argument along the lines just presented may be found in J. Shaffer's illuminating essay "Existence, Predication and the Ontological Argument," *Mind* 71 (1962): 307–325.

11. I am indebted to Professor William Wainwright for bringing this point to my attention.

SAINT THOMAS AQUINAS

The Five Ways, from *Summa Theologica**

Saint Thomas Aquinas (1225–1274) is the philosopher and theologian whose teachings are most favored by the Roman Catholic Church.

[Part I, Question 2, Article 3]

The existence of God can be proved in five ways.

The first and more manifest way is the argument from motion. It is certain, and evident to our senses, that in the world some things are in motion. Now whatever is moved is moved by another, for nothing can be moved except it is in potentiality to that towards which it is moved; whereas a thing moves inasmuch as it is in act. For motion is nothing else than the reduction of something from potentiality to actuality. But nothing can be reduced from potentiality to actuality, except by something in a state of actuality. Thus that which is actually hot, as fire, makes wood, which is potentially hot, to be actually hot, and thereby moves and changes it. Now it is not possible that the same thing should be at once in actuality and potentiality in the same respect, but only in different respects. For what is actually hot cannot simultaneously be potentially hot; but it is simultaneously potentially cold. It is therefore impossible that in the same respect and in the same way a thing should be both mover and moved, *i.e.*, that it should move itself. Therefore, whatever is moved must be moved by another. If that by which it is moved be itself moved, then this also must needs be moved by another, and that by another again. But this cannot go on to infinity, because then there would be no first mover, and consequently no other mover, seeing that subsequent movers move only inasmuch as they are moved by the first mover; as the staff moves only because it is moved by the hand. Therefore it is necessary to arrive at a first mover, moved by no other; and this everyone understands to be God.

The second way is from the nature of efficient cause. In the world of sensible things we find there is an order of efficient causes. There is no case known (neither is it, indeed, possible) in which a thing is found to be the efficient cause of itself; for so it would be prior to itself, which is impossible. Now in efficient causes it is not possible to go on to infinity, because in all efficient causes following in order, the first is the cause of the intermediate cause, and the intermediate is the cause of the ultimate cause,

*From *The Basic Writings of Saint Thomas Aquinas,* ed. Anton C. Pegis (New York: Random House; London: Burns & Oates, 1945), pp. 22–23. Copyright © 1945 Random House, Inc. Reprinted by permission of the publishers.

whether the intermediate cause be several, or one only. Now to take away the cause is to take away the effect. Therefore, if there be no first cause among efficient causes, there will be no ultimate, nor any intermediate, cause. But if in efficient causes it is possible to go on to infinity, there will be no first efficient cause, neither will there be an ultimate effect, nor any intermediate efficient causes; all of which is plainly false. Therefore it is necessary to admit a first efficient cause, to which everyone gives the name of God.

The third way is taken from possibility and necessity, and runs thus. We find in nature things that are possible to be and not to be, since they are found to be generated, and to be corrupted, and consequently, it is possible for them to be and not to be. But it is impossible for these always to exist, for that which can not-be at some time is not. Therefore, if everything can not-be, then at one time there was nothing in existence. Now if this were true, even now there would be nothing in existence, because that which does not exist begins to exist only through something already existing. Therefore, if at one time nothing was in existence, it would have been impossible for anything to have begun to exist; and thus even now nothing would be in existence—which is absurd. Therefore, not all beings are merely possible, but there must exist something the existence of which is necessary. But every necessary thing either has its necessity caused by another, or not. Now it is impossible to go on to infinity in necessary things which have their necessity caused by another, as has been already proved in regard to efficient causes. Therefore we cannot but admit the existence of some being having of itself its own necessity, and not

receiving it from another, but rather causing in others their necessity. This all men speak of as God.

The fourth way is taken from the gradation to be found in things. Among beings there are some more and some less good, true, noble, and the like. But *more* and *less* are predicated of different things according as they resemble in their different ways something which is the maximum, as a thing is said to be hotter according as it more nearly resembles that which is hottest; so that there is something which is truest, something best, something noblest, and, consequently, something which is most being, for those things that are greatest in truth are greatest in being, as it is written in *Metaph.* ii.[1] Now the maximum in any genus is the cause of all in that genus, as fire, which is the maximum of heat, is the cause of all hot things, as is said in the same book.[2] Therefore there must also be something which is to all beings the cause of their being, goodness, and every other perfection; and this we call God.

The fifth way is taken from the governance of the world. We see that things which lack knowledge, such as natural bodies, act for an end, and this is evident from their acting always, or nearly always, in the same way, so as to obtain the best result. Hence it is plain that they achieve their end, not fortuitously, but designedly. Now whatever lacks knowledge cannot move towards an end, unless it be directed by some being endowed with knowledge and intelligence; as the arrow is directed by the archer. Therefore some intelligent being exists by whom all natural things are directed to their end; and this being we call God.

NOTES
1. [Aquinas refers here to Aristotle's *Metaphysics*, Ia 1 (993b30).]

2. [*Metaphysics*, Ia 1 (993b25).]

SAMUEL CLARKE

A Modern Formulation of the Cosmological Argument*

Samuel Clarke (1675–1729), English theologian and philosopher, was one of the first to be greatly influenced by Isaac Newton's physics.

There has existed from eternity some one unchangeable and independent being. For since something must needs have been from eternity; as hath been already proved, and is granted on all hands: either there has always existed one unchangeable and *independent* Being, from which all other beings that are or ever were in the universe, have received their original; or else there has been an infinite succession of changeable and *dependent* beings, produced one from another in an endless progression, without any original cause at all: which latter supposition is so very absurd, that tho' all atheism must in its account of most things (as shall be shown hereafter) terminate in it, yet I think very few atheists ever were so weak as openly and directly to defend it. For it is plainly impossible and contradictory to itself. I shall not argue against it from the supposed impossibility of infinite succession, *barely and absolutely considered in itself*; for a reason which shall be mentioned hereafter: but, if we consider such an infinite progression, as *one* entire endless *series* of *dependent* beings; 'tis plain this whole *series* of beings can have no cause

from without, of its existence; because in it are supposed to be included *all things* that are or ever were in the universe: and 'tis plain it can have no reason *within itself,* of its existence; because no one being in this infinite succession is supposed to be self-existent or *necessary* (which is the only ground or reason of existence of any thing, that can be imagined *within the thing itself,* as will presently more fully appear), but every one *dependent* on the foregoing: and where *no part* is necessary, 'tis manifest *the whole* cannot be necessary; absolute necessity of existence, not being an outward, relative, and accidental determination; but an inward and essential property of the nature of the thing which so exists. An infinite succession therefore of merely *dependent* beings, without any original independent cause; is a *series* of beings, that has neither necessity nor cause, nor any reason *at all* of its existence, neither *within itself* nor *from without:* that is, 'tis an express contradiction and impossibility; 'tis a supposing *something* to be *caused,* (because it's granted in every one of its stages of succession, not to be necessary and from itself); and yet that in the whole it is caused *absolutely by nothing*: Which every man knows is a contradiction to be done *in time*; and because duration in this case makes no diference, 'tis equally a contradiction to suppose it done from eternity: And consequently there must *on the contrary,* of necessity have existed from eternity, *some one* immutable and *independent* Being: Which, what it is, remains in the next place to be inquired.

*From Samuel Clarke, *A Demonstration of the Being and Attributes of God* (1705), Part II.

WILLIAM L. ROWE

The Cosmological Argument*

Since ancient times thoughtful people have sought to justify their religious beliefs. Perhaps the most basic belief for which justification has been sought is the belief that there is a God. The effort to justify belief in the existence of God has generally started either from facts available to believers and nonbelievers alike or from facts, such as the experience of God, normally available only to believers. In this and the next two chapters, we shall consider some major attempts to justify belief in God by appealing to facts supposedly available to any rational person, whether religious or not. By starting from such facts theologians and philosophers have developed arguments for the existence of God, arguments which, they have claimed, prove beyond reasonable doubt that there is a God.

STATING THE ARGUMENT

Arguments for the existence of God are commonly divided into *a posteriori* arguments and *a priori* arguments. An *a posteriori* argument depends on a principle or premise that can be known only by means of our experience of the world. An *a priori* argument, on the other hand, purports to rest on principles all of which can be known independently of our experience of the world, by just reflecting on and understanding them. Of the three major arguments for the existence of God—the Cosmological, the Teleological, and the Ontological—only the last of these is entirely *a priori*. In the Cosmological Argument one starts from some simple fact about the world, such as that it contains things which are caused to exist by other things. In the Teleological Argument a somewhat more complicated fact about the world serves as a starting point,

the fact that the world exhibits order and design. In the Ontological Argument, however, one begins simply with a concept of God. In this chapter we shall consider the Cosmological Argument. . . .

Before we state the Cosmological Argument itself, we shall consider some rather general points about the argument. Historically, it can be traced to the writings of the Greek philosophers, Plato and Aristotle, but the major developments in the argument took place in the thirteenth and in the eighteenth centuries. In the thirteenth century, Aquinas put forth five distinct arguments for the existence of God, and of these, the first three are versions of the Cosmological Argument.[1] In the first of these he started from the fact that there are things in the world undergoing change and reasoned to the conclusion that there must be some ultimate cause of change that is itself unchanging. In the second he started from the fact that there are things in the world that clearly are caused to exist by other things and reasoned to the conclusion that there must be some ultimate cause of existence whose own existence is itself uncaused. And in the third argument he started from the fact that there are things in the world which need not have existed at all, things which do exist but which we can easily imagine might not, and reasoned to the conclusion that there must be some being that had to be, that exists and could not have failed to exist. Now it might be objected that even if Aquinas' arguments do prove beyond doubt the existence of an unchanging changer, an uncaused cause, and a being that could not have failed to exist, the arguments fail to prove the existence of the theistic God. For the theistic God, as we saw, is supremely good, omnipotent, omniscient, and creator of but separate from and independent of the world. How do we know, for example, that the unchanging changer isn't evil or slightly ignorant? The answer to this ob-

*From William L. Rowe, *Philosophy of Religion* (Belmont, Calif.: Wadsworth Publishing Co., 1978), pp. 16–30. Reprinted by permission of the publisher and the author.

jection is that the Cosmological Argument has two parts. In the first part the effort is to prove the existence of a special sort of being, for example, a being that could not have failed to exist, or a being that causes change in other things but is itself unchanging. In the second part of the argument the effort is to prove that the special sort of being whose existence has been established in the first part has, and must have, the features—perfect goodness, omnipotence, omniscience, and so on—which go together to make up the theistic idea of God. What this means, then, is that Aquinas' three arguments are different versions of only the first part of the Cosmological Argument. Indeed, in later sections of his *Summa Theologica* Aquinas undertakes to show that the unchanging changer, the uncaused cause of existence, and the being which had to exist are one and the same being and that this single being has all of the attributes of the theistic God.

We noted above that a second major development in the Cosmological Argument took place in the eighteenth century, a development reflected in the writings of the German philosopher, Gottfried Leibniz (1646–1716), and especially in the writings of the English theologian and philosopher, Samuel Clarke (1675–1729). In 1704 Clarke gave a series of lectures, later published under the title *A Demonstration of the Being and Attributes of God.* These lectures constitute, perhaps, the most complete, forceful, and cogent presentation of the Cosmological Argument we possess. The lectures were read by the major skeptical philosopher of the century, David Hume (1711–1776), and in his brilliant attack on the attempt to justify religion in the court of reason, his *Dialogues Concerning Natural Religion,* Hume advanced several penetrating criticisms of Clarke's arguments, criticisms which have persuaded many philosophers in the modern period to reject the Cosmological Argument. In our study of the argument we shall concentrate our attention largely on its eighteenth-century form and try to assess its strengths and weaknesses in the light of the criticisms which Hume and others have advanced against it.

The first part of the eighteenth-century form of the Cosmological Argument seeks to establish the existence of a self-existent being. The second part of the argument attempts to prove that the self-existent being is the theistic God, that is, has the features which we have noted to be basic elements in the theistic idea of God. We shall consider mainly the first part of the argument, for it is against the first part that philoso-

phers from Hume to Russell have advanced very important objections.

In stating the first part of the Cosmological Argument we shall make use of two important concepts, the concept of a *dependent being* and the concept of a *self-existent being*. By "a dependent being" we mean a *being whose existence is accounted for by the causal activity of other things.* Recalling Anselm's division into the three cases: "explained by another," "explained by nothing," and "explained by itself," it's clear that a dependent being is a being whose existence is explained by another. By "a self-existent being" we mean a *being whose existence is accounted for by its own nature.* This idea, as we saw in the preceding chapter, is an essential element in the theistic concept of God. Again, in terms of Anselm's three cases, a self-existent being is a being whose existence is explained by itself. Armed with these two concepts, the concept of a dependent being and the concept of a self-existent being, we can now state the first part of the Cosmological Argument.

1. Every being (that exists or ever did exist) is either a dependent being or a self-existent being.
2. Not every being can be a dependent being.

Therefore,

3. There exists a self-existent being.

DEDUCTIVE VALIDITY

Before we look critically at each of the premises of this argument, we should note that this argument is, to use an expression from the logician's vocabulary, *deductively valid.* To find out whether an argument is deductively valid we need only ask the question: If its premises were true would its conclusion have to be true? If the answer is yes, the argument is deductively valid. If the answer is no, the argument is deductively invalid. Notice that the question of the validity of an argument is entirely different from the question of whether its premises are in fact true. The following argument is made up entirely of false statements, but it is deductively valid.

1. Babe Ruth is the President of the U.S.
2. The President of the U.S. is from Indiana.

Therefore,

3. Babe Ruth is from Indiana.

The argument is deductively valid because even though its premises are false, if they were true its conclusion would have to be true. Even God, Aquinas would say, cannot bring it about that the premises of this argument are true and yet its conclusion is false, for God's power extends only to what is possible, and it is an absolute impossibility that Babe Ruth be the President, the President be from Indiana, and yet Babe Ruth not be from Indiana.

The Cosmological Argument (that is, its first part) is a deductively valid argument. If its premises are or were true its conclusion would have to be true. It's clear from our example about Babe Ruth, however, that the fact that an argument is deductively valid is insufficient to establish the truth of its conclusion. What else is required? Clearly that we know or have rational grounds for believing that the premises are true. If we know that the Cosmological Argument is deductively valid and can establish that its premises are true, we shall thereby have proved that its conclusion is true. Are, then, the premises of the Cosmological Argument true? To this more difficult question we must now turn.

PSR AND THE FIRST PREMISE

At first glance the first premise might appear to be an obvious or even trivial truth. But it is neither obvious nor trivial. And if it appears to be obvious or trivial, we must be confusing the idea of a self-existent being with the idea of a being that is not a dependent being. Clearly, it is obviously true that any being is either a dependent being (explained by other things) or it is not a dependent being (not explained by other things). But what our premise says is that any being is either a dependent being (explained by other things) or it is a self-existent being (explained by itself). Consider again Anselm's three cases.

a. explained by another
b. explained by nothing
c. explained by itself

What our first premise asserts is that each being that exists (or ever did exist) is either of sort *a* or of sort *c*. It denies that any being is of sort *b*. And it is this denial that makes the first premise both significant and controversial. The obvious truth we must not confuse it with is the truth that any being is either of sort *a* or not of sort *a*. While this is true it is neither very significant nor controversial.

Earlier we saw that Anselm accepted as a basic principle that whatever exists has an explanation of its existence. Since this basic principle denies that any thing of sort *b* exists or ever did exist, it's clear that Anselm would believe the first premise of our Cosmological Argument. The eighteenth-century proponents of the argument also were convinced of the truth of the basic principle we attributed to Anselm. And because they were convinced of its truth, they readily accepted the first premise of the Cosmological Argument. But by the eighteenth century, Anselm's basic principle had been more fully elaborated and had received a name, ''the Principle of Sufficient Reason.'' Since this principle (PSR, as we shall call it) plays such an important role in justifying the premises of the Cosmological Argument, it will help us to consider it for a moment before we continue our enquiry into the truth or falsity of the premises of the Cosmological Argument.

The Principle of Sufficient Reason (PSR), as it was expressed by both Leibniz and Samuel Clarke, is a very general principle and is best understood as having two parts. In its first part it is simply a restatement of Anselm's principle that there must be an explanation of the *existence* of any being whatever. Thus if we come upon a man in a room, PSR implies that there must be an explanation of the fact that that particular man exists. A moment's reflection, however, reveals that there are many facts about the man other than the mere fact that he exists. There is the fact that the man in question is in the room he's in, rather than somewhere else, the fact that he is in good health, and the fact that he is at the moment thinking of Paris, rather than, say, London. Now the purpose of the second part of PSR is to require an explanation of these facts as well. We may state PSR, therefore, as the principle that *there must be an explanation (a) of the existence of any being, and (b) of any positive fact whatever*. We are now in a position to study the role this very important principle plays in the Cosmological Argument.

Since the proponent of the Cosmological Argument accepts PSR in both its parts, it is clear that he will appeal to its first part, PSRa, as justification for the first premise of the Cosmological Argument. Of course, we can and should enquire into the deeper question of whether the proponent of the argument is rationally justified in accepting PSR itself. But we shall put this question aside for the moment. What we need to see first is whether he is correct in thinking that *if* PSR is true then both of the premises of the Cosmological Argument are true. And what we have just seen is that if only the first part of PSR, that is,

Argument will be true. But what of the second premise of the Argument? For what reasons does the proponent think that it must be true?

THE SECOND PREMISE

According to the second premise, not every being that exists can be a dependent being, that is, can have the explanation of its existence in some other being or beings. Presumably, the proponent of the argument thinks there is something fundamentally wrong with the idea that every being that exists is dependent, that each existing being was caused by some other being which in turn was caused by some other being, and so on. But just what does he think is wrong with it? To help us in understanding his thinking, let's simplify things by supposing that there exists only one thing now, A_1, a living thing perhaps, that was brought into existence by something else A_2, which perished shortly after it brought A_1 into existence. Suppose further that A_2 was brought into existence in similar fashion some time ago by A_3, and A_3 by A_4, and so forth back into the past. Each of these beings is a *dependent* being, it owes its existence to the preceding thing in the series. Now if nothing else ever existed but these beings, then what the second premise says would not be true. For if every being that exists or ever did exist is an A and was produced by a preceding A, then every being that exists or ever did exist would be dependent and, accordingly, premise two of the Cosmological Argument would be false. If the proponent of the Cosmological Argument is correct there must, then, be something wrong with the idea that every being that exists or did exist is an A and that they form a causal series, A_1 caused by A_2, A_2 caused by A_3, A_3 caused by A_4, . . . A_n caused by A_{n+1}. How does the proponent of the Cosmological Argument propose to show us that there is something wrong with this view?

A popular but mistaken idea of how the proponent tries to show that something is wrong with the view that every being might be dependent is that he uses the following argument to reject it.

1. There must be a *first being* to start any causal series.
2. If every being were dependent there would be no *first being* to start the causal series.
Therefore,
3. Not every being can be a dependent being.

Although this argument is deductively valid and its second premise is true, its first premise overlooks the distinct possibility that a causal series might be *infinite,* with no first member at all. Thus if we go back to our series of A beings, where each A is dependent, having been produced by the preceding A in the causal series, it's clear that if the series existed it would have no first member, for every A in the series there would be a preceding A which produced it, *ad infinitum.* The first premise of the argument just given assumes that a causal series must stop with a first member somewhere in the distant past. But there seems to be no good reason for making that assumption.

The eighteenth-century proponents of the Cosmological Argument recognized that the causal series of dependent beings could be infinite, without a first member to start the series. They rejected the idea that every being that is or ever was is dependent not because there would then be no first member to the series of dependent beings, but because there would then be no explanation for the fact that there are and have always been dependent beings. To see their reasoning let's return to our simplification of the supposition that the only things that exist or ever did exist are dependent beings. In our simplification of that supposition only one of the dependent beings exists at a time, each one perishing as it produces the next in the series. Perhaps the first thing to note about this supposition is that there is no individual A in the causal series of dependent beings whose existence is unexplained—A_1 is explained by A_2, A_2 by A_3, and A_n by A_{n+1}. So the first part of PSR, PSRa, appears to be satisfied. There is no particular being whose existence lacks an explanation. What, then, is it that lacks an explanation, if every particular A in the causal series of dependent beings has an explanation? It is the *series itself* that lacks an explanation. Or, as I've chosen to express it, *the fact that there are and have always been dependent beings.* For suppose we ask why it is that there are and have always been As in existence. It won't do to say that As have always been producing other As—we can't explain why there have always been As by saying there always have been As. Nor, on the supposition that only As have ever existed, can we explain the fact that there have always been As by appealing to something other than an A—for no such thing would have existed. Thus the supposition that the only things that exist or ever existed are dependent things leaves us with a fact for which there can be no explanation; namely, the fact that there are and have always been dependent beings.

QUESTIONING THE JUSTIFICATION OF
THE SECOND PREMISE

Critics of the Cosmological Argument have raised several important objections against the claim that if every being is dependent the series or collection of those beings would have no explanation. Our understanding of the Cosmological Argument, as well as of its strengths and weaknesses, will be deepened by a careful consideration of these criticisms.

The first criticism is that the proponent of the Cosmological Argument makes the mistake of treating the collection or series of dependent beings as though it were itself a dependent being, and, therefore, requires an explanation of its existence. But, so the objection goes, the collection of dependent beings is not itself a dependent being any more than a collection of stamps is itself a stamp.

A second criticism is that the proponent makes the mistake of inferring that because each member of the collection of dependent beings has a cause the collection itself must have a cause. But, as Bertrand Russell noted, such reasoning is as fallacious as to infer that the human race (that is, the collection of human beings) must have a mother because each member of the collection (each human being) has a mother.

A third criticism is that the proponent of the argument fails to realize that for there to be an explanation of a collection of things is nothing more than for there to be an explanation of each of the things making up the collection. Since in the infinite collection (or series) of dependent beings, each being in the collection does have an explanation—by virtue of having been caused by some preceding member of the collection—the explanation of the collection, so the criticism goes, has already been given. As David Hume remarked, "Did I show you the particular causes of each individual in a collection of twenty particles of matter, I should think it very unreasonable, should you afterwards ask me, what was the cause of the whole twenty. This is sufficiently explained in explaining the cause of the parts."[2]

Finally, even if the proponent of the Cosmological Argument can satisfactorily answer these objections, he must face one last objection to his ingenious attempt to justify premise two of the Cosmological Argument. For someone may agree that if nothing exists but an infinite collection of dependent beings, the infinite collection will have no explanation of its existence, and still refuse to conclude from this that there is something wrong with the idea that every being is a dependent being. Why, he might ask, should we think that everything has to have an explanation? What's wrong with admitting that the fact that there are and have always been dependent beings is a *brute fact,* a fact having no explanation whatever? Why does everything have to have an explanation anyway? We must now see what can be said in response to these several objections.

RESPONSES TO CRITICISM

It is certainly a mistake to think that a collection of stamps is itself a stamp, and very likely a mistake to think that the collection of dependent beings is itself a dependent being. But the mere fact that the proponent of the argument thinks that there must be an explanation not only for each member of the collection of dependent beings but for the collection itself is not sufficient grounds for concluding that he must view the collection as itself a dependent being. The collection of human beings, for example, is certainly not itself a human being. Admitting this, however, we might still seek an explanation of why there is a collection of human beings, of why there are such things as human beings at all. So the mere fact that an explanation is demanded for the collection of dependent beings is no proof that the person who demands the explanation must be supposing that the collection itself is just another dependent being.

The second criticism attributes to the proponent of the Cosmological Argument the following bit of reasoning:

1. Every member of the collection of dependent beings has a cause or explanation.
Therefore,
2. The collection of dependent beings has a cause or explanation.

As we noted in setting forth this criticism, arguments of this sort are often unreliable. It would be a mistake to conclude that a collection of objects is light in weight simply because each object in the collection is light in weight, for if there were many objects in the collection it might be quite heavy. On the other hand, if we know that each marble weighs more than one ounce we could infer validly that the collection of marbles weighs more than an ounce. Fortunately, however, we don't need to decide whether the inference from (1.) to (2.) is valid or invalid. We need not decide this question because the proponent of the

Cosmological Argument need not use this inference to establish that there must be an explanation of the collection of dependent beings. He need not use this inference because he has in PSR a principle from which it follows immediately that the collection of dependent beings has a cause or explanation. For according to PSR every positive fact must have an explanation. If it is a fact that there exists a collection of dependent beings then, according to PSR, that fact too must have an explanation. So it is PSR that the proponent of the Cosmological Argument appeals to in concluding that there must be an explanation of the collection of dependent beings, and not some dubious inference from the premise that each member of the collection has an explanation. It seems, then, that neither of the first two criticisms is strong enough to do any serious damage to the reasoning used to support the second premise of the Cosmological Argument.

The third objection contends that to explain the existence of a collection of things is the same thing as to explain the existence of each of its members. If we consider a collection of dependent beings where each being in the collection is explained by the preceding member which caused it, it's clear that no member of the collection will lack an explanation of its existence. But, so the criticism goes, if we've explained the existence of every member of a collection we've explained the existence of the collection—there's nothing left over to be explained. This forceful criticism, originally advanced by David Hume, has gained considerable support in the modern period. But the criticism rests on an assumption that the proponent of the Cosmological Argument would not accept. The assumption is that to explain the existence of a collection of things it is *sufficient* to explain the existence of every member in the collection. To see what is wrong with this assumption is to understand the basic issue in the reasoning by which the proponent of the Cosmological Argument seeks to establish that not every being can be a dependent being.

In order for there to be an explanation of the existence of the collection of dependent beings, it's clear that the eighteenth-century proponents would require that the following two conditions be satisfied:

C1. There is an explanation of the existence of each of the members of the collection of dependent beings.
C2. There is an explanation of why there are *any* dependent beings.

According to the proponents of the Cosmological Ar-

gument if every being that exists or ever did exist is a dependent being—that is, if the whole of reality consists of nothing more than a collection of dependent beings—C1 will be satisfied, but C2 will not be satisfied. And since C2 won't be satisfied there will be no explanation of the collection of dependent beings. The third criticism, therefore, says in effect that if C1 is satisfied C2 will be satisfied, and, since in a collection of dependent beings each member will have an explanation in whatever it was that produced it, C1 will be satisfied. So, therefore, C2 will be satisfied and the collection of dependent beings will have an explanation.

Although the issue is a complicated one, I think it is possible to see that the third criticism rests on a mistake: the mistake of thinking that if C1 is satisfied C2 must also be satisfied. The mistake is a natural one to make for it is easy to imagine circumstances in which if C1 is satisfied C2 also will be satisfied. Suppose, for example, that the whole of reality includes not just a collection of dependent beings but also a self-existent being. Suppose further that instead of each dependent being having been produced by some other dependent being every dependent being was produced by the self-existent being. Finally, let us consider both the possibility that the collection of dependent beings is finite in time and has a first member and the possibility that the collection of dependent beings is infinite in past time, having no first member. Using "G" for the self-existent being, the first possibility may be diagrammed as follows:

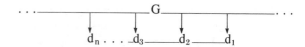

G, we shall say, has always existed and always will. We can think of d_1 as some presently existing dependent being, d_2, d_3, and so forth as dependent beings that existed at some time in the past, and d_n as the first dependent being to exist. The second possibility may be portrayed as follows:

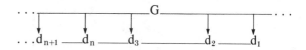

On this diagram there is no first member of the collection of dependent beings. Each member of the infinite collection, however, is explained by reference to the self-existent being G which produced it. Now the interesting point about both these cases is that the explanation that has been provided for the members of the collection of dependent beings carries with it, at least in part, an answer to the question of why there are any dependent beings at all. In both cases we may explain why there are dependent beings by pointing out that there exists a self-existent being that has been engaged in producing them. So one we have learned that the existence of each member of the collection of dependent beings has its existence explained by the fact that G produced it, we have already learned why there are dependent beings.

Someone might object that we haven't really learned why there are dependent beings until we also learn *why* G has been producing them. But, of course, we could also say that we haven't really explained the existence of a particular dependent being, say d$_3$, until we also learn not just that G produced it but *why* G produced it. The point we need to grasp, however, is that once we admit that every dependent being's existence is explained by G, we must admit that the fact that there are dependent beings has also been explained. So it is not unnatural that someone should think that to explain the existence of the collection of dependent beings is nothing more than to explain the existence of its members. For, as we've seen, to explain the collection's existence is to explain each member's existence and to explain why there are any dependent beings at all. And in the examples we've considered, in doing the one (explaining why each dependent being exists) we've already done the other (explained why there are any dependent beings at all). We must now see, however, that on the supposition that the whole of reality consists *only* of a collection of dependent beings, to give an explanation of each member's existence is not to provide an explanation of why there are dependent beings.

In the examples we've considered we have gone *outside* of the collection of dependent beings in order to explain the members' existence. But if the only beings that exist or ever existed are dependent beings then each dependent being will be explained by some other dependent being, ad infinitum. This does not mean that there will be some particular dependent being whose existence is unaccounted for. Each dependent being has an explanation of its existence; namely, in the dependent being which preceded it and

produced it. So C1 is satisfied: there is an explanation of the existence of each member of the collection of dependent beings. Turning to C2, however, we can see that it will not be satisfied. We cannot explain why there are (or have ever been) dependent beings by appealing to all the members of the infinite collection of dependent beings. For if the question to be answered is why there are (or have ever been) any dependent beings at all, we cannot answer that question by noting that there always have been dependent beings, each one accounting for the existence of some other dependent being. Thus on the supposition that every being is dependent it seems there will be no explanation of why there are dependent beings. C2 will not be satisfied. Therefore, on the supposition that every being is dependent there will be no explanation of the existence of the collection of dependent beings.

THE TRUTH OF PSR

We come now to the final criticism of the reasoning supporting the second premise of the Cosmological Argument. According to this criticism, it is admitted that the supposition that every being is dependent implies that there will be a *brute fact* in the universe, a fact, that is, for which there can be no explanation whatever. For there will be no explanation of the fact that dependent beings exist and have always been in existence. It is this brute fact that the proponents of the argument were describing when they pointed out that if every being is dependent the series or collection of dependent beings would lack an explanation of *its* existence. The final criticism asks what is wrong with admitting that the universe contains such a brute, unintelligible fact. In asking this question the critic challenges the fundamental principle, PSR, on which the Cosmological Argument rests. For, as we've seen, the first premise of the argument denies that there exists a being whose existence has no explanation. In support of this premise the proponent appeals to the first part of PSR. The second premise of the argument claims that not every being can be dependent. In support of this premise the proponent appeals to the second part of PSR, the part which states that there must be an explanation of any positive fact whatever.

The proponent reasons that if every being were a dependent being then although the first part of PSR would be satisfied—every being would have an explanation—the second part would be violated, there would be no explanation for the positive fact that there are and have always been dependent beings. For first, since every being is supposed to be dependent, there would be nothing outside of the collection of dependent beings to explain the collection's existence. Second, the fact that each member of the collection has an explanation in some other dependent being is insufficient to explain why there are and have always been dependent beings. And, finally, there is nothing about the collection of dependent beings that would suggest that it is a self-existent collection. Consequently, if every being were dependent, the fact that there are and have always been dependent beings would have no explanation. But this violates the second part of PSR. So the second premise of the Cosmological Argument must be true, not every being can be a dependent being. This conclusion, however, is no better than the principle, PSR, on which it rests. And it is the point of the final criticism to question the truth of PSR. Why, after all, should we accept the idea that every being and every positive fact must have an explanation? Why, in short, should we believe PSR? These are important questions, and any final judgment of the Cosmological Argument depends on how they are answered.

Most of the theologians and philosophers who accept PSR have tried to defend it in either of two ways. Some have held that PSR is (or can be) known *intuitively* to be true. By this they mean that if we fully understand and reflect on what is said by PSR we can see that it must be true. Now, undoubtedly, there are statements which are known intuitively to be true. "Every triangle has exactly three angles" or "No physical object can be in two different places in space at one and the same time" are examples of statements whose truth we can apprehend just by understanding and reflecting on them. The difficulty with the claim that PSR is intuitively true, however, is that a number of very able philosophers fail to apprehend its truth, and some even claim that the principle is false. It is doubtful, therefore, that many of us, if any, know intuitively that PSR is true.

The second way philosophers and theologians who accept PSR have sought to defend it is by claiming that although it is not known to be true, it is, nevertheless, a presupposition of reason, a basic assumption that rational people make, whether or not they reflect sufficiently to become aware of the assumption. It's probably true that there are some assumptions we all make about our world, assumptions which are so basic that most of us are unaware of them. And, I suppose, it might be true that PSR is such an assumption. What bearing would this view of PSR have on the Cosmological Argument? Perhaps the main point to note is that even if PSR is a presupposition we all

share, the premises of the Cosmological Argument could still be false. For PSR itself could still be false. The fact, if it is a fact, that all of us *presuppose* that every existing being and every positive fact has an explanation does not imply that no being exists, and no positive fact obtains, without an explanation. Nature is not bound to satisfy our presuppositions. As the American philosopher, William James, once remarked in another connection, "In the great boarding house of nature, the cakes and the butter and the syrup seldom come out so even and leave the plates so clear."

Our study of the first part of the Cosmological Argument has led us to the fundamental principle on which its premises rest, the Principle of Sufficient Reason. Since we do not seem to know that PSR is true we cannot reasonably claim to know that the premises of the Cosmological Argument are true. They might be true. But unless we do know them to be true they cannot *establish* for us the conclusion that there exists a being that has the explanation of its existence within its own nature. If it were shown, however, that even though we do not *know* that PSR is true we all, nevertheless, *presuppose* PSR to be true, then, whether PSR is true or not, to be consistent we should accept the Cosmological Argument. For, as we've seen, its premises imply its conclusion and its premises do seem to follow from PSR. But no one has succeeded in *showing* that PSR is an assumption that most or all of us share. So our final conclusion must be that although the Cosmological Argument might be a *sound* argument (valid with true premises), it does not provide us with good rational grounds for believing that among those beings that exist there is one whose existence is accounted for by its own nature. Having come to this conclusion we may safely put aside the second part of the argument. For even if it succeeded in showing that a self-existent being would have the other attributes of the theistic God, the Cosmological Argument would still not provide us with good rational grounds for belief in God, having failed in its first part to provide us with good rational grounds for believing that there is a self-existent being.

NOTES

1. See St. Thomas Aquinas, *Summa Theologica*, 1a. 2, 3.

2. David Hume, *Dialogues Concerning Natural Religion*, Part IX, ed. H. D. Aiken (New York: Hafner Publishing Company, 1948), pp. 59–60.

WILLIAM PALEY

The Argument from Design*

William Paley (1743–1805) was an English philosopher of religion and ethics.

CHAPTER ONE: STATE OF THE ARGUMENT

In crossing a heath, suppose I pitched my foot against a *stone* and were asked how the stone came to be there, I might possibly answer that for anything I knew to the contrary it had lain there forever; nor would it, perhaps, be very easy to show the absurdity of this answer. But suppose I had found a *watch* upon the ground, and it should be inquired how the watch happened to be in that place, I should hardly think of the answer which I had before given, that for anything I knew the watch might have always been there. Yet why should not this answer serve for the watch as well as for the stone; why is it not as admissible in the second case as in the first? For this reason, and for no other, namely, that when we come to inspect the watch, we perceive—what we could not discover in the stone—that its several parts are framed and put together for a purpose, e.g., that they are so formed and adjusted as to produce motion, and that motion so regulated as to point out the hour of the day; that if the different parts had been differently shaped from what they are, or placed after any other manner or in any other order than that in which they are placed, either no motion at all would have been carried on in the machine, or none which would have answered the use that is now served by it. To reckon up a few of the plainest of these parts and of their offices, all tending to one result: we see a cylindrical box containing a coiled elastic spring, which, by its endeavor to relax itself, turns round the box. We next observe a flexible chain—artificially wrought for the sake of flexure—communicating the action of the spring from the box to the fusee. We then find a series of wheels, the teeth of which catch in and apply to each other, conducting the motion from the fusee to the balance and from the balance to the pointer, and at the same time, by the size and shape of those wheels, so regulating that motion as to terminate in causing an index, by an equable and measured progression, to pass over a given space in a given time. We take notice that the wheels are made of brass, in order to keep them from rust; the springs of steel, no other metal being so elastic; that over the face of the watch there is placed a glass, a material employed in no other part of the work, but in the room of which, if there had been any other than a transparent substance, the hour could not be seen without opening the case. This mechanism being observed—it requires indeed an examination of the instrument, and perhaps some previous knowledge of the subject, to perceive and understand it; but being once, as we have said, observed and understood—the inference we think is inevitable, that the watch must have had a maker—that there must have existed, at some time and at some place or other, an artificer or artificers who formed it for the purpose which we find it actually to answer, who completely comprehended its construction and designed its use.

I. Nor would it, I apprehend, weaken the conclusion, that we had never seen a watch made—that we had never known an artist capable of making one—that we were altogether incapable of executing such a piece of workmanship ourselves, or of understanding in what manner it was performed; all this being no more than what is true of some exquisite remains of ancient art, of some lost arts, and, to the generality of mankind, of the more curious productions of modern manufacture. Does one man in a million know how oval frames are turned? Ignorance of this kind exalts our opinion of the unseen and

*From *Natural Theology* (1802).

unknown artist's skill, if he be unseen and unknown, but raises no doubt in our minds of the existence and agency of such an artist, at some former time and in some place or other. Nor can I perceive that it varies at all the inference, whether the question arise concerning a human agent or concerning an agent of a different species, or an agent possessing in some respects a different nature.

II. Neither, secondly, would it invalidate our conclusion, that the watch sometimes went wrong or that it seldom went exactly right. The purpose of the machinery, the design, and the designer might be evident, and in the case supposed, would be evident, in whatever way we accounted for the irregularity of the movement, or whether we could account for it or not. It is not necessary that a machine be perfect in order to show with what design it was made: still less necessary, where the only question is whether it were made with any design at all.

III. Nor, thirdly, would it bring any uncertainty into the argument, if there were a few parts of the watch, concerning which we could not discover or had not yet discovered in what manner they conduced to the general effect; or even some parts, concerning which we could not ascertain whether they conduced to that effect in any manner whatever. For, as to the first branch of the case, if by the loss, or disorder, or decay of the parts in question, the movement of the watch were found in fact to be stopped, or disturbed, or retarded, no doubt would remain in our minds as to the utility or intention of these parts, although we should be unable to investigate the manner according to which, or the connection by which, the ultimate effect depended upon their action or assistance; and the more complex the machine, the more likely is this obscurity to arise. Then, as to the second thing supposed, namely, that there were parts which might be spared without prejudice to the movement of the watch, and that we had proved this by experiment, these superfluous parts, even if we were completely assured that they were such, would not vacate the reasoning which we had instituted concerning other parts. The indication of contrivance remained, with respect to them, nearly as it was before.

IV. Nor, fourthly, would any man in his senses think the existence of the watch with its various machinery accounted for, by being told that it was one out of possible combinations of material forms; that whatever he had found in the place where he found the watch, must have contained some internal configuration or other; and that this configuration might be the structure now exhibited, namely, of the works of a watch, as well as a different structure.

V. Nor, fifthly, would it yield his inquiry more satisfaction, to be answered that there existed in things a principle of order, which had disposed the parts of the watch into their present form and situation. He never knew a watch made by the principle of order; nor can he even form to himself an idea of what is meant by a principle of order distinct from the intelligence of the watchmaker.

VI. Sixthly, he would be surprised to hear that the mechanism of the watch was no proof of contrivance, only a motive to induce the mind to think so:

VII. And not less surprised to be informed that the watch in his hand was nothing more than the result of the laws of *metallic* nature. It is a perversion of language to assign any law as the efficient, operative cause of any thing. A law presupposes an agent, for it is only the mode according to which an agent proceeds: it implies a power, for it is the order according to which that power acts. Without this agent, without this power, which are both distinct from itself, the *law* does nothing, is nothing. The expression, "the law of metallic nature," may sound strange and harsh to a philosophic ear; but it seems quite as justifiable as some others which are more familiar to him, such as "the law of vegetable nature," "the law of animal nature," or, indeed, as "the law of nature" in general, when assigned as the cause of phenomena, in exclusion of agency and power, or when it is substituted into the place of these.

VIII. Neither, lastly, would our observer be driven out of his conclusion or from his confidence in its truth by being told that he knew nothing at all about the matter. He knows enough for his argument; he knows the utility of the end; he knows the subserviency and adaptation of the means to the end. These points being known, his ignorance of other points, his doubts concerning other points affect not the certainty of his reasoning. The consciousness of knowing little need not beget a distrust of that which he does know.

CHAPTER TWO: STATE OF THE ARGUMENT CONTINUED

Suppose, in the next place, that the person who found the watch should after some time discover that, in addition to all the properties which he had hitherto observed in it, it possessed the unexpected property of producing in the course of its movement another watch like itself—the thing is conceivable; that it contained within it a mechanism, a system of parts—a mold, for instance, or a complex adjustment of lathes, files, and other tools—evidently and separately calculated for this purpose; let us inquire what effect ought such a discovery to have upon his former conclusion.

I. The first effect would be to increase his admiration of the contrivance, and his conviction of the consummate skill of the contriver. Whether he regarded the object of the contrivance, the distinct apparatus, the intricate, yet in many parts intelligible mechanism by which it was carried on, he would perceive in this new observation nothing but an additional reason for doing what he had already done—for referring the construction of the watch to design and to supreme art. If that construction *without* this property, or, which is the same thing, before this property had been noticed, proved intention and art to have been employed about it, still more strong would the proof appear when he came to the knowledge of this further property, the crown and perfection of all the rest.

II. He would reflect that, though the watch before him were *in some sense* the maker of the watch which was fabricated in the course of its movements, yet it was in a very different sense from that in which a carpenter, for instance, is the maker of a chair—the author of its contrivance, the cause of the relation of its parts to their use. With respect to these, the first watch was no cause at all to the second; in no such sense as this was it the author of the constitution and order, either of the parts which the new watch contained, or of the parts by the aid and instrumentality of which it was produced. We might possibly say, but with great latitude of expression, that a stream of water ground corn; but no latitude of expression would allow us to say, no stretch of conjecture could lead us to think that the stream of water built the mill, though it were too ancient for us to know who the builder was. What the stream of water does in the affair is neither more nor less than this: by the application of an unintelligent impulse to a mechanism previously arranged, arranged independently of it and arranged by intelligence, an effect is produced, namely, the corn is ground. But the effect results from the arrangement. The force of the stream cannot be said to be the cause or the author of the effect, still less of the arrangement. Understanding and plan in the formation of the mill were not the less necessary for any share which the water has in grinding the corn; yet is this share the same as that which the watch would have contributed to the production of the new watch, upon the supposition assumed in the last section. Therefore,

III. Though it be now no longer probable that the individual watch which our observer had found was made immediately by the hand of an artificer, yet this alteration does not in anywise affect the inference that an artificer had been originally employed and concerned in the production. The argument from design remains as it was. Marks of design and contrivance are no more accounted for now than they were before. In the same thing, we may ask for the cause of different properties. We may ask for the cause of the color of a body, of its hardness, of its heat; and these causes may be all different. We are now asking for the cause of that subserviency to a use, that relation to an end, which we have remarked in the watch before us. No answer is given to this question by telling us that a preceding watch produced it. There cannot be design without a designer; contrivance without a contriver; order without choice; arrangement without anything capable of arranging; subserviency and relation to a purpose without that which could intend a purpose; means suitable to an end, and executing their office in accomplishing that end, without the end ever having been contemplated or the means accommodated to it. Arrangement, disposition of parts, subserviency of means to an end, relation of instruments to a use imply the presence of intelligence and mind. No one, therefore, can rationally believe that the insensible, inanimate watch, from which the watch before us issued, was the proper cause of the mechanism we so much admire in it—could be truly said to have constructed the instrument, disposed its parts, assigned their office, determined their order, action, and mutual dependency, combined their several motions into one result, and that also a result connected with the utilities of other beings. All these properties, therefore, are as much unaccounted for as they were before.

IV. Nor is anything gained by running the difficulty farther back, that is, by supposing the watch before us to have been produced from another watch, that from a former, and so on indefinitely. Our going back ever so far brings us no nearer to the least degree of satisfaction upon the subject. Contrivance is still unaccounted for. We still want a contriver. A designing mind is neither supplied by this supposition nor dispensed with. If the difficulty were diminished the farther we went back, by going back indefinitely we might exhaust it. And this is the only case to which this sort of reasoning applies. Where there is a tendency, or, as we increase the number of terms, a continual approach toward a limit, *there,* by supposing the number of terms to be what is called infinite, we may conceive the limit to be attained; but where there is no such tendency or approach, nothing is effected by lengthening the series. There is no difference as to the point in question, whatever there may be as to many points, between one series and another—between a series which is finite and a series which is infinite. A chain composed of an infinite number of links can no more support itself than a chain composed of a finite number of links. And of this we are assured, though we never *can* have tried the experiment; because, by increasing the number of links, from ten, for instance, to a hundred, from a hundred to a thousand, etc., we make not the smallest approach, we observe not the smallest tendency toward self-support. There is no difference in this respect—yet there may be a great difference in several respects—between a chain of a greater or less length, between one chain and another, between one that is finite and one that is infinite. This very much resembles the case before us. The machine which we are inspecting demonstrates, by its construction, contrivance and design. Contrivance must have had a contriver, design a designer, whether the machine immediately proceeded from another machine or not. That circumstance alters not the case. That other machine may, in like manner, have proceeded from a former machine: nor does that alter the case; the contrivance must have had a contriver. That former one from one preceding it: no alteration still; a contriver is still necessary. No tendency is perceived, no approach toward a diminution of this necessity. It is the same with any and every succession of these machines—a succession of ten, of a hundred, of a thousand; with one series, as with another—a series which is finite, as with a series which is infinite. In whatever other respects they may differ, in this they do not. In all equally, contrivance and design are unaccounted for.

The question is not simply, how came the first watch into existence?—which question, it may be pretended, is done away by supposing the series of watches thus produced from one another to have been infinite, and consequently to have had no such *first* for which it was necessary to provide a cause. This, perhaps, would have been nearly the state of the question, if nothing had been before us but an unorganized, unmechanized substance, without mark or indication of contrivance. It might be difficult to show that such substance could not have existed from eternity, either in succession—if it were possible, which I think it is not, for unorganized bodies to spring from one another—or by individual perpetuity. But that is not the question now. To suppose it to be so is to suppose that it made no differennce whether he had found a watch or a stone. As it is, the metaphysics of that question have no place; for, in the watch which we are examining are seen contrivance, design, an end, a purpose, means for the end, adaptation to the purpose. And the question which irresistably presses upon our thoughts is, whence this contrivance and design? The thing required is the intending mind, the adapted hand, the intelligence by which that hand was directed. This question, this demand is not shaken off by increasing a number or succession of substances destitute of these properties; nor the more, by increasing that number to infinity. If it be said that, upon the supposition of one watch being produced from another in the course of that other's movements and by means of the mechanism within it, we have a cause for the watch in my hand, namely, the watch from which it proceeded; I deny that for the design, the contrivance, the suitableness of means to an end, the adaptation of instruments to a use, all of which we discover in the watch, we have any cause whatever. It is in vain, therefore, to assign a series of such causes or to allege that a series may be carried back to infinity; for I do not admit that we have yet any cause at all for the phenomena, still less any series of causes either finite or infinite. Here is contrivance but no contriver; proofs of design, but no designer.

V. Our observer would further also reflect that the maker of the watch before him was in truth and reality the maker of every watch produced from it: there being no difference, except that the latter manifests a more exquisite skill, between the making of another watch with his own hands, by the mediation of files, lathes, chisels, etc., and the disposing, fixing, and inserting of these instruments, or of others equivalent to them, in the body of the watch already made, in such a manner as to form a new watch in the course of the movements which he had given to the old one. It is only working by one set of tools instead of another.

The conclusion which the *first* examination of the watch, of its works, construction, and movement, suggested, was that it must have had, for cause and author of that construction, an artificer who understood its mechanism and designed its use. This conclusion is invincible. A *second* examination presents us with a new discovery. The watch is found, in the course of its movement, to produce another watch similar to itself; and not only so, but we perceive in it a system or organization separately calculated for that purpose. What effect would this discovery have or ought it to have upon our former inference? What, as has already been said, but to increase beyond measure our admiration of the skill which had been employed in the formation of such a machine? Or shall it, instead of this, all at once turn us round to an opposite conclusion, namely, that no art or skill whatever has been concerned in the business, although all other evidences of art and skill remain as they were, and this last and supreme piece of art be now added to the rest? Can this be maintained without absurdity? Yet this is atheism . . .

CHAPTER FIVE: APPLICATION OF THE ARGUMENT CONTINUED

Every observation which was made in our first chapter concerning the watch may be repeated with strict propriety concerning the eye, concerning animals, concerning plants, concerning, indeed, all the organized parts of the works of nature. As,

I. When we are inquiring simply after the *existence* of an intelligent Creator, imperfection, inaccuracy, liability to disorder, occasional irregularities may subsist in a considerable degree without inducing any doubt into the question; just as a watch may frequently go wrong, seldom perhaps exactly right, may be faulty in some parts, defective in some,

without the smallest ground of suspicion from thence arising that it was not a watch, not made, or not made for the purpose ascribed to it. When faults are pointed out, and when a question is started concerning the skill of the artist or the dexterity with which the work is executed, then, indeed, in order to defend these qualities from accusation, we must be able either to expose some intractableness and imperfection in the materials or point out some invincible difficulty in the execution, into which imperfection and difficulty the matter of complaint may be resolved; or, if we cannot do this, we must adduce such specimens of consummate art and contrivance. proceeding from the same hand as may convince the inquirer of the existence, in the case before him, of impediments like those which we have mentioned, although, what from the nature of the case is very likely to happen, they be unknown and unperceived by him. This we must do in order to vindicate the artist's skill, or at least the perfection of it; as we must also judge of his intention and of the provisions employed in fulfilling that intention, not from an instance in which they fail but from the great plurality of instances in which they succeed. But, after all, these are different questions from the question of the artist's existence; or, which is the same, whether the thing before us be a work of art or not; and the questions ought always to be kept separate in the mind. So likewise it is in the works of nature. Irregularities and imperfections are of little or no weight in the consideration when that consideration relates simply to the existence of a Creator. When the argument respects his attributes, they are of weight; but are then to be taken in conjunction—the attention is not to rest upon them, but they are to be taken in conjunction with the unexceptional evidences which we possess of skill, power, and benevolence displayed in other instances; which evidences may, in strength, number, and variety, be such and may so overpower apparent blemishes as to induce us, upon the most reasonable ground, to believe that these last ought to be referred to some cause, though we be ignorant of it, other than defect of knowledge or of benevolence in the author . . .

DAVID HUME

Dialogues concerning Natural Religion*

David Hume (1711–1776) was a leading philosopher of the Enlightenment, the author of a famous history of England, and the tutor of Adam Smith in political economy. He spent most of his life in Edinburgh.

PART II

I must own, Cleanthes, said Demea, that nothing can more surprise me than the light in which you have all along put this argument. By the whole tenor of your discourse, one would imagine that you were maintaining the Being of a God against the cavils of atheists and infidels, and were necessitated to become a champion for that fundamental principle of all religion. But this, I hope, is not by any means a question among us. No man, no man at least of common sense, I am persuaded, ever entertained a serious doubt with regard to a truth so certain and self-evident. The question is not concerning the *being* but the *nature* of God. This I affirm, from the infirmities of human understanding, to be altogether incomprehensible and unknown to us. The essence of that supreme Mind, his attributes, the manner of his existence, the very nature of his duration—these and every particular which regards so divine a Being are mysterious to men. Finite, weak, and blind creatures, we ought to humble ourselves in his august presence, and, conscious of our frailties, adore in silence his infinite perfections which eye hath not seen, ear hath not heard, neither hath it entered into the heart of man to conceive. They are covered in a deep cloud from human curiosity; it is profaneness to attempt penetrating through these sacred obscurities, and, next to the impiety of denying his existence, is the temerity of prying into his nature and essence, decrees and attributes.

But lest you should think that my *piety* has here

*First published in 1779.

got the better of my *philosophy,* I shall support my opinion, if it needs any support, by a very great authority. I might cite all the divines, almost from the foundation of Christianity, who have ever treated of this or any other theological subject; but I shall confine myself, at present, to one equally celebrated for piety and philosophy. It is Father Malebranche who, I remember, thus expresses himself.[1] "One ought not so much," says he, "to call God a spirit in order to express positively what he is, as in order to signify that he is not matter. He is a Being infinitely perfect—of this we cannot doubt. But in the same manner as we ought not to imagine, even supposing him corporeal, that he is clothed with a human body, as the anthropomorphites asserted, under colour that that figure was the most perfect of any, so neither ought we to imagine that the spirit of God has human ideas or bears any resemblance to our spirit, under colour that we know nothing more perfect than a human mind. We ought rather to believe that as he comprehends the perfections of matter without being material . . . he comprehends also the perfections of created spirits without being spirit, in the manner we conceive spirit: that his true name is *He that is,* or, in other words, Being without restriction, All Being, the Being infinite and universal."

After so great an authority, Demea, replied Philo, as that which you have produced, and a thousand more which you might produce, it would appear ridiculous in me to add my sentiment or express my approbation of your doctrine. But surely, where reasonable men treat these subjects, the question can never be concerning the *being* but only the *nature* of the Deity. The former truth, as you well observe, is unquestionable and self-evident. Nothing exists without a cause; and the original cause of this universe (whatever it be) we call God, and piously ascribe to him every species of perfection. Whoever scruples this fundamental truth deserves every punishment which can be inflicted among philosophers, to wit, the greatest ridicule, contempt, and disapprobation. But as all perfection is entirely relative, we ought never to imagine that we comprehend the attributes of this divine Being, or to suppose that his perfections have any analogy or likeness to the perfections of a human creature. Wisdom, thought, design, knowledge—these we justly ascribe to him because these words are honourable among men, and we have no other language or other conceptions by which we can express our adoration of him. But let us beware lest we think that our ideas anywise correspond to his perfections, or that his attributes have any resemblance to these qualities among men. He is infinitely superior to our limited view and comprehension, and is more the object of worship in the temple than of disputation in the schools.

In reality, Cleanthes, continued he, there is no need of having recourse to that affected scepticism so displeasing to you in order to come at this determination. Our ideas reach no further than our experience. We have no experience of divine attributes and operations. I need not conclude my syllogism, you can draw the inference yourself. And it is a pleasure to me (and I hope to you, too) that just reasoning and sound piety here concur in the same conclusion, and both of them establish the adorably mysterious and incomprehensible nature of the Supreme Being.

Not to lose any time in circumlocutions, said Cleanthes, addressing himself to Demea, much less in replying to the pious declamations of Philo, I shall briefly explain how I conceive this matter. Look round the world, contemplate the whole and every part of it: you will find it to be nothing but one great machine, subdivided into an infinite number of lesser machines, which again admit of subdivisions to a degree beyond what human senses and faculties can trace and explain. All these various machines, and even their most minute parts, are adjusted to each other with an accuracy which ravishes into admiration all men who have ever contemplated them. The curious adapting of means to ends, throughout all nature, resembles exactly, though it much exceeds, the productions of human contrivance—of human design, thought, wisdom, and intelligence. Since therefore the effects resemble each other, we are led to infer, by all the rules of analogy, that the causes also resemble, and that the Author of nature is somewhat similar to the mind of man, though possessed of much larger faculties, proportioned to the grandeur of the work which he has executed. By this argument *a posteriori,* and by this argument alone, do we prove at once the existence of a Deity and his similarity to human mind and intelligence.

I shall be so free, Cleanthes, said Demea, as to tell you that from the beginning I could not approve of your conclusion concerning the similarity of the Deity to men, still less can I approve of the mediums by which you endeavour to establish it. What! No demonstration of the Being of God! No abstract arguments! No proofs *a priori!* Are these which have hitherto been so much insisted on by philosophers all fallacy, all sophism? Can we reach no farther in this subject than experience and probability? I will not say that this is betraying the cause of a Deity; but surely, by this affected candour, you give advantages to atheists which they never could obtain by the mere dint of argument and reasoning.

What I chiefly scruple in this subject, said Philo, is not so much that all religious arguments are by Cleanthes reduced to experience, as that they appear not to be even the most certain and irrefragable of that inferior kind. That a stone will fall, that fire will burn, that the earth has solidity, we have observed a thousand and a thousand times; and when any new instance of this nature is presented, we draw without hesitation the accustomed inference. The exact similarity of the cases gives us a perfect assurance of a similar event, and a stronger evidence is never desired nor sought after. But wherever you depart, in the least, from the similarity of the cases, you diminish proportionably the evidence, and may at last bring it to a very weak *analogy,* which is confessedly liable to error and uncertainty. After having experienced the circulation of the blood in human creatures, we make no doubt that it takes place in Titius and Maevius; but from its circulation in frogs and fishes it is only a presumption, though a strong one, from analogy that it takes place in men and other animals. The analogical reasoning is much weaker when we infer the circulation of the sap in vegetables from our experience that the blood circulates in animals; and those who hastily followed that imperfect analogy are found, by more accurate experiments, to have been mistaken.

If we see a house, Cleanthes, we conclude, with the greatest certainty, that it had an architect or builder because this is precisely that species of effect which we have experienced to proceed from that species of cause. But surely you will not affirm that the universe bears such a resemblance to a house that we can with the same certainty infer a similar cause, or that the analogy is here entire and perfect. The dissimilitude is so striking that the utmost you can here pretend to is a guess, conjecture, a presumption concerning a similar cause; and how that pretension will be received in the world, I leave you to consider.

It would surely be very ill received, replied Cleanthes; and I should be deservedly blamed and detested did I allow that the proofs of Deity amounted to no more than a guess or conjecture. But is the whole adjustment of means to ends in a house and in the universe so slight a resemblance? the economy of final causes? the order, proportion, and arrangement of every part? Steps of a stair are plainly contrived that human legs may use them in mounting; and this inference is certain and infallible. Human legs are also contrived for walking and mounting; and this inference, I allow, is not altogether so certain because of the dissimilarity which you remark; but does it, therefore, deserve the name only of presumption or conjecture?

Good God! cried Demea, interrupting him, where are we? Zealous defenders of religion allow that the proofs of a Deity fall short of perfect evidence! And you, Philo, on whose assistance I depended in proving the adorable mysteriousness of the Divine Nature, do you assent to all these extravagant opinions of Cleanthes? For what other name can I give them? or, why spare my censure when such principles are advanced, supported by such an authority, before so young a man as Pamphilus?

You seem not to apprehend, replied Philo, that I argue with Cleanthes in his own way, and, by showing him the dangerous consequences of his tenets, hope at last to reduce him to our opinion. But what sticks most with you, I observe, is the representation which Cleanthes has made of the argument *a posteriori;* and, finding that the argument is likely to escape your hold and vanish into air, you think it so disguised that you can scarcely believe it to be set in its true light. Now, however much I may dissent, in other respects, from the dangerous principle of Cleanthes, I must allow that he has fairly represented that argument, and I shall endeavour so to state the matter to you that you will entertain no further scruples with regard to it.

Were a man to abstract from everything which he knows or has seen, he would be altogether incapable, merely from his own ideas, to determine what kind of scene the universe must be, or to give the preference to one state or situation of things above another. For as nothing which he clearly conceives could be esteemed impossible or implying a contradiction, every chimera of his fancy would be upon an equal footing; nor could he assign any just reason why he adheres to one idea or system, and rejects the others which are equally possible.

Again, after he opens his eyes and contemplates the world as it really is, it would be impossible for him at first to assign the cause of any one event, much less of the whole of things, or of the universe. He might set his fancy a rambling, and she might bring him in an infinite variety of reports and representations. These would all be possible, but, being all equally possible, he would never of himself give a satisfactory account for his preferring one of them to the rest. Experience alone can point out to him the true cause of any phenomenon.

Now, according to this method of reasoning, Demea, it follows (and is, indeed, tacitly allowed by Cleanthes himself) that order, arrangement, or the adjustment of final causes, is not of itself any proof of design, but only so far as it has been experienced to proceed from that principle. For aught we can know *a priori,* matter may contain the source or spring of order originally within itself, as well as mind does; and there is no more difficulty in conceiving that the several elements, from an internal unknown cause, may fall into the most exquisite arrangement, than to conceive that their ideas, in the great universal mind, from a like internal unknown cause, fall into that arrangement. The equal possibility of both these suppositions is allowed. But, by experience, we find (according to Cleanthes) that there is a difference between them. Throw several pieces of steel together, without shape or form, they will never arrange themselves so as to compose a watch. Stone and mortar and wood, without an architect, never erect a house. But the ideas in a human mind, we see, by an unknown, inexplicable economy, arrange themselves so as to form the plan of a watch or house. Experience, therefore, proves that there is an original principle of order in mind, not in matter. From similar effects we infer similar causes. The adjustment of means to ends is alike in the universe, as in a machine of human contrivance. The causes, therefore, must be resembling.

I was from the beginning scandalized, I must own, with this resemblance which is asserted between the Deity and human creatures, and must conceive it to imply such a degradation of the Supreme Being as no sound theist could endure. With your assistance, therefore, Demea, I shall endeavour to defend what you justly call the adorable mysteriousness of the Divine Nature, and shall refute this reasoning of Cleanthes, provided he allows that I have made a fair representation of it.

When Cleanthes had assented, Philo, after a short pause, proceeded in the following manner.

That all inferences, Cleanthes, concerning fact are founded on experience, and that all experimental reasonings are founded on the supposition that similar causes prove similar effects, and similar effects similar causes, I shall not at present much dispute with you. But observe, I entreat you, with what extreme caution all just reasoners proceed in the transferring of experiments to similar cases. Unless the cases be exactly similar, they repose no perfect confidence in applying their past observation to any particular phenomenon. Every alteration of circumstances occasions a doubt concerning the event; and it requires new experiments to prove certainly that the new circumstances are of no moment or importance. A change in bulk, situation, arrangement, age, disposition of the air, or surrounding bodies—any of these particulars may be attended with the most unexpected consequences. And unless the objects be quite familiar to us, it is the highest temerity to expect with assurance, after any of these changes, an event similar to that which before fell under our observation. The slow and deliberate steps of philosophers here, if anywhere, are distinguished from the precipitate march of the vulgar, who, hurried on by the smallest similitude, are incapable of all discernment or consideration.

But you can think, Cleanthes, that your usual phlegm and philosophy have been preserved in so wide a step as you have taken when you compared to the universe houses, ships, furniture, machines, and, from their similarity in some circumstances, inferred a similarity in their causes? Thought, design, intelligence, such as we discover in men and other animals, is no more than one of the springs and principles of the universe, as well as heat or cold, attraction or repulsion, and a hundred others which fall under daily observation. It is an active cause by which some particular parts of nature, we find, produce alterations on other parts. But can a conclusion, with any propriety, be transferred from parts to the whole? Does not the great disproportion bar all comparison and inference? From observing the growth of a hair, can we learn anything concerning the generation of a man? Would the manner of a leaf's blowing, even though perfectly known, afford us any instruction concerning the vegetation of a tree?

But allowing that we were to take the *operations* of one part of nature upon another for the foundation of our judgment concerning the *origin* of the whole (which never can be admitted), yet why select so minute, so weak, so bounded a principle as the reason and design of animals is found to be upon this planet? What peculiar privilege has this little agitation of the brain which we call *thought,* that we must thus make it the model of the whole universe? Our partiality in our own favour does indeed present it on all occasions, but sound philosophy ought carefully to guard against so natural an illusion.

So far from admitting, continued Philo, that the operations of a part can afford us any just conclusion concerning the origin of the whole, I will not allow any one part to form a rule for another part if the latter be very remote from the former. Is there any reasonable ground to conclude that the inhabitants of other planets possess thought, intelligence, reason, or anything similar to these faculties in men? When nature has so extremely diversified her manner of operation in this small globe, can we imagine that she incessantly copies herself throughout so immense a universe? And if thought, as we may well suppose, be confined merely to this narrow corner and has even there so limited a sphere of action, with what propriety can we assign it for the original cause of all things? The narrow views of a peasant who makes his domestic economy the rule for the government of kingdoms is in comparison a pardonable sophism.

But were we ever so much assured that a thought and reason resembling the human were to be found throughout the whole universe, and were its activity elsewhere vastly greater and more commanding than it appears in this globe, yet I cannot see why the operations of a world constituted, arranged, adjusted, can with any propriety be extended to a world which is in its embryo state, and is advancing towards that constitution and arrangement. By observation we know somewhat of the economy, action, and nourishment of a finished animal, but we must transfer with great caution that observation to the growth of a foetus in the womb, and still more to the formation of an animalcule in the loins of its male parent. Nature, we find, even from our limited experience, possesses an infinite number of springs and principles which incessantly discover themselves on every change of her position and situation. And what new and unknown principles would actuate her in so new and unknown a situation as that of the formation of a universe, we cannot, without the utmost temerity, pretend to determine.

A very small part of this great system, during a very short time, is very imperfectly discovered to us; and do we thence pronounce decisively concerning the origin of the whole?

Admirable conclusion! Stone, wood, brick, iron, brass, have not, at this time, in this minute globe of earth, an order or arrangement without human art and contrivance; therefore, the universe could not originally attain its order and arrangement without something similar to human art. But is a part of nature a rule for another part very wide of the former? Is it a rule for the whole? Is a very small part a rule for the universe? Is nature in one situation a certain rule for nature in another situation vastly different from the former?

And can you blame me, Cleanthes, if I here imitate the prudent reserve of Simonides, who, according to the noted story, being asked by Hiero, *What God was?* desired a day to think of it, and then two days more; and after that manner continually prolonged the term, without ever bringing in his definition or description? Could you even blame me if I had answered, at first, *that I did not know,* and was sensible that this subject lay vastly beyond the reach of my faculties? You might cry out sceptic and rallier, as much as you pleased; but, having found in so many other subjects much more familiar the imperfections and even contradictions of human reason, I never should expect any success from its feeble conjectures in a subject so sublime and so remote from the sphere of our observation. When two *species* of objects have always been observed to be conjoined together, I can *infer,* by custom, the existence of one wherever I *see* the existence of the other; and this I call an argument from experience. But how this argument can have place where the objects, as in the present case, are single, individual, without parallel or specific resemblance, may be difficult to explain. And will any man tell me with a serious countenance

that an orderly universe must arise from some thought and art like the human because we have experience of it? To ascertain this reasoning it were requisite that we had experience of the origin of worlds; and it is not sufficient, surely, that we have seen ships and cities arise from human art and contrivance.

Philo was proceeding in this vehement manner, somewhat between jest and earnest, as it appeared to me, when he observed some signs of impatience in Cleanthes, and then immediately stopped short. What I had to suggest, said Cleanthes, is only that you would not abuse terms, or make use of popular expressions to subvert philosophical reasonings. You know that the vulgar often distinguish reason from experience, even where the question relates only to matter of fact and existence, though it is found, where that *reason* is properly analyzed, that it is nothing but a species of experience. To prove by experience the origin of the universe from mind is not more contrary to common speech than to prove the motion of the earth from the same principle. And a caviller might raise all the same objections to the Copernican system which you have urged against my reasonings. Have you other earths, might he say, which you have seen to move? Have . . .

Yes! cried Philo, interrupting him, we have other earths. Is not the moon another earth, which we see to turn around its centre? Is not Venus another earth, where we observe the same phenomenon? Are not the revolutions of the sun also a confirmation, from analogy, of the same theory? All the planets, are they not earths which revolve about the sun? Are not the satellites moons which move round Jupiter and Saturn, and along with these primary planets round the sun? These analogies and resemblances, with others which I have not mentioned, are the sole proofs of the Copernican system; and to you it belongs to consider whether you have any analogies of the same kind to support your theory.

In reality, Cleanthes, continued he, the modern system of astronomy is now so much received by all inquirers, and has become so essential a part even of our earliest education, that we are not commonly very scrupulous in examining the reasons upon which it is founded. It is now become a matter of mere curiosity to study the first writers of that subject who had the full force of prejudice to encounter, and were obliged to turn their arguments on every side in order to render them popular and convincing. But if we peruse Galileo's famous *Dialogues* concerning the system of the world, we shall find that the great genius, one of the sublimest that ever existed, first bent all his endeavours to prove that there was no foundation for the distinction commonly made between elementary and celestial substances. The schools, proceeding from the illusions of sense, had carried this distinction very far; and had established the latter substances to be ingenerable, incorruptible, unalterable, impassible; and had assigned all the opposite qualities to the former. But Galileo, beginning with the moon, proved its similarity in every particular to the earth: its convex figure, its natural darkness when not illuminated, its density, its distinction into solid and liquid, the variations of its phases, the mutual illuminations of the earth and moon, their mutual eclipses, the inequalities of the lunar surface, etc. After many instances of this kind, with regard to all the planets, men plainly saw that these bodies became proper objects of experience, and that the similarity of their nature enabled us to extend the same arguments and phenomena from one to the other.

In this cautious proceeding of the astronomers you may read your own condemnation, Cleanthes, or rather may see that the subject in which you are engaged exceeds all human reason and inquiry. Can you pretend to show any such similarity between the fabric of a house and the generation of a universe? Have you ever seen nature in any such situation as resembles the first arrangement of the elements? Have worlds ever been formed under your eye, and have you had leisure to observe the whole progress of the phenomenon, from the first appearance of order to its final consummation? If you have, then cite your experience and deliver your theory.

PART III

How the most absurd argument, replied Cleanthes, in the hands of a man of ingenuity and invention, may acquire an air of probability! Are you not aware, Philo, that it became necessary for Copernicus and his first disciples to prove the similarity of the terrestrial and celestial matter because several philosophers, blinded by old systems and supported by some sensible appearances, had denied this similarity? But that it is by no means necessary that theists should prove the similarity of the works of *nature* to those of *art* because this similarity is self-evident

and undeniable? The same matter, a like form; what more is requisite to show an analogy between their causes, and to ascertain the origin of all things from a divine purpose and intention? Your objections, I must freely tell you, are no better than the abstruse cavils of those philosophers who denied motion, and ought to be refuted in the same manner—by illustrations, examples, and instances rather than by serious argument and philosophy.

Suppose, therefore, that an articulate voice were heard in the clouds, much louder and more melodious than any which human art could ever reach; suppose that this voice were extended in the same instant over all nations and spoke to each nation in its own language and dialect; suppose that the words delivered not only contain a just sense and meaning, but convey some instruction altogether worthy of a benevolent Being superior to mankind—could you possibly hesitate a moment concerning the cause of this voice, and must you not instantly ascribe it to some design or purpose? Yet I cannot see but all the same objections (if they merit that appellation) which lie against the system of theism may also be produced against this inference.

Might you not say that all conclusions concerning fact were founded on experience; that, when we hear an articulate voice in the dark and thence infer a man, it is only the resemblance of the effects which leads us to conclude that there is a like resemblance in the cause; but that this extraordinary voice, by its loudness, extent, and flexibility to all languages, bears so little analogy to any human voice that we have no reason to suppose any analogy in their causes; and, consequently, that a rational, wise, coherent speech proceeded, you know not whence, from some accidental whistling of the winds, not from any divine reason or intelligence? You see clearly your own objections in these cavils, and I hope too you see clearly that they cannot possibly have more force in the one case than in the other.

But to bring the case still nearer the present one of the universe, I shall make two suppositions which imply not any absurdity or impossibility. Suppose that there is a natural, universal, invariable language, common to every individual of human race, and that books are natural productions which perpetuate themselves in the same manner with animals and vegetables, by descent and propagation. Several expressions of our passions contain a universal language: all brute animals have a natural speech, which, however limited, is very intelligible to their own species. And as there are infinitely fewer parts and less contrivance in the finest composition of eloquence than in the coarsest organized body, the propagation of an *Iliad* or *Aeneid* is an easier supposition than that of any plant or animal.

Suppose, therefore, that you enter into your library thus peopled by natural volumes containing the most refined reason and most exquisite beauty; could you possibly open one of them and doubt that its original cause bore the strongest analogy to mind and intelligence? When it reasons and discourses; when it expostulates, argues, and enforces its views and topics; when it applies sometimes to the pure intellect, sometimes to the affections; when it collects, disposes, and adorns every consideration suited to the subject; could you persist in asserting that all this, at the bottom, had really no meaning, and that the first formation of this volume in the loins of its original parent proceeded not from thought and design? Your obstinacy, I know, reaches not that degree of firmness; even your sceptical play and wantonness would be abashed at so glaring an absurdity.

But if there be any difference, Philo, between this supposed case and the real one of the universe, it is all to the advantage of the latter. The anatomy of an animal affords many stronger instances of design than the perusal of Livy or Tacitus; and any objection which you start in the former case, by carrying me back to so unusual and extraordinary a scene as the first formation of worlds, the same objection has place on the supposition of our vegetating library. Choose, then, your party, Philo, without ambiguity or evasion; assert either that a rational volume is no proof of a rational cause or admit of a similar cause to all the works of nature.

Let me here observe, too, continued Cleanthes, that this religious argument, instead of being weakened by that scepticism so much affected by you, rather acquires force from it and becomes more firm and undisputed. To exclude all argument or reasoning of every kind is either affectation or madness. The declared profession of every reasonable sceptic is only to reject abstruse, remote, and refined arguments; to adhere to common sense and the plain instincts of nature; and to assent, wherever any reasons strike him with so full a force that he cannot, without the greatest violence, prevent it. Now the arguments for natural religion are plainly of this kind; and nothing but the most perverse, obstinate metaphysics can reject them. Consider, anatomize

the eye, survey its structure and contrivance, and tell me, from your own feeling, if the idea of a contriver does not immediately flow in upon you with a force like that of sensation. The most obvious conclusion, surely, is in favour of design; and it requires time, reflection, and study, to summon up those frivolous though abstruse objections which can support infidelity. Who can behold the male and female of each species, the correspondence of their parts and instincts, their passions and whole course of life before and after generation, but must be sensible that the propagation of the species is intended by nature? Millions and millions of such instances present themselves through every part of the universe, and no language can convey a more intelligible irresistible meaning than the curious adjustment of final causes. To what degree, therefore, of blind dogmatism must one have attained to reject such natural and such convincing arguments?

Some beauties in writing we may meet with which seem contrary to rules, and which gain the affections and animate the imagination in opposition to all the precepts of criticism and to the authority of the established masters of art. And if the argument for theism be, as you pretend, contradictory to the principles of logic, its universal, its irresistible influence proves clearly that there may be arguments of a like irregular nature. Whatever cavils may be urged, an orderly world, as well as a coherent, articulate speech, will still be received as an incontestable proof of design and intention.

It sometimes happens, I own, that the religious arguments have not their due influence on an ignorant savage and barbarian, not because they are obscure and difficult, but because he never asks himself any question with regard to them. Whence arises the curious structure of an animal? From the copulation of its parents. And these whence? From *their* parents? A few removes set the objects at such a distance that to him they are lost in darkness and confusion; nor is he actuated by any curiosity to trace them farther. But this is neither dogmatism nor scepticism, but stupidity: a state of mind very different from your sifting, inquisitive disposition, my ingenious friend. You can trace causes from effects; you can compare the most distant and remote objects; and your greatest errors proceed not from barrenness of thought and invention, but from too luxuriant a fertility which suppresses your natural good sense by a profusion of unnecessary scruples and objections.

Here I could observe, Hermippus, that Philo was a little embarrassed and confounded; but, while he hesitated in delivering an answer, luckily for him, Demea broke in upon the discourse and saved his countenance.

Your instance, Cleanthes, said he, drawn from books and language, being familiar, has, I confess, so much more force on that account; but is there not some danger, too, in this very circumstance, and may it not render us presumptuous, by making us imagine we comprehend the Deity and have some adequate idea of his nature and attributes? When I read a volume, I enter into the mind and intention of the author; I become him, in a manner, for the instant, and have an immediate feeling and conception of those ideas which revolved in his imagination while employed in that composition. But so near an approach we never surely can make to the Deity. His ways are not our ways, his attributes are perfect but incomprehensible. And this volume of nature contains a great and inexplicable riddle, more than any intelligible discourse or reasoning.

The ancient Platonists, you know, were the most religious and devout of all the pagan philosophers, yet many of them, particularly Plotinus, expressly declare that intellect or understanding is not to be ascribed to the Deity, and that our most perfect worship of him consists, not in acts of veneration, reverence, gratitude, or love, but in a certain mysterious self-annihilation or total extinction of all our faculties. These ideas are, perhaps, too far stretched, but still it must be acknowledged that, by representing the Deity as so intelligible and comprehensible, and so similar to a human mind, we are guilty of the grossest and most narrow partiality, and make ourselves the model of the whole universe.

All the *sentiments* of the human mind, gratitude, resentment, love, friendship, approbation, blame, pity, emulation, envy, have a plain reference to the state and situation of man, and are calculated for preserving the existence and promoting the activity of such a being in such circumstances. It seems, therefore, unreasonable to transfer such sentiments to a supreme existence or to suppose him actuated by them; and the phenomena, besides, of the universe will not support us in such a theory. All our *ideas* derived from the senses are confessedly false and illusive, and cannot therefore be supposed to have place in a supreme intelligence. And as the ideas of internal sentiment, added to those of the external senses, composed the whole furniture of human understanding, we may conclude that none of the *materials* of thought are in any respect similar in the human and in the divine intelligence. Now, as to the *manner* of thinking, how can we make any comparison between them or suppose them anywise resembling? Our thought is fluctuating, uncertain, fleeting, successive, and compounded; and were we to remove these circumstances, we absolutely annihilate its essence, and it would in such a case be an abuse of terms to apply to it the name of thought or reason. At least, if it appear more pious and respectful (as it really is) still to retain these terms when we mention the Supreme Being, we ought to acknowledge that their meaning, in that case, is totally incomprehensible, and that the infirmities of our nature do not permit us to reach any ideas which in the least correspond to the ineffable sublimity of the Divine attributes.

PART IV

It seems strange to me, said Cleanthes, that you, Demea, who are so sincere in the cause of religion, should still maintain the mysterious, incomprehensible nature of the Deity, and should insist so strenuously that he has no manner of likeness or resemblance to human creatures. The Deity, I can readily allow, possesses many powers and attributes of which we can have no comprehension; but, if our ideas, so far as they go, be not just and adequate and correspondent to his real nature, I know not what there is in this subject worth insisting on. Is the name, without any meaning, of such mighty importance? Or how do you mystics, who maintain the absolute incomprehensibility of the Deity, differ from sceptics or atheists, who assert that the first cause of all is unknown and unintelligible? Their temerity must be very great if, after rejecting the production by a mind—I mean a mind resembling the human (for I know of no other)—they pretend to assign, with certainty, any other specific intelligible cause; and their conscience must be very scrupulous, indeed, if they refuse to call the universal unknown cause a God or Deity, and to bestow on him as many sublime eulogies and unmeaning epithets as you shall please to require of them.

Who could imagine, replied Demea, that Cleanthes, the calm philosophical Cleanthes, would attempt to refute his antagonists by affixing a nickname to them, and, like the common bigots and inquisitors of the age, have recourse to invective and declamation instead of reasoning? Or does he not perceive that these topics are easily retorted, and that *anthropomorphite* is an appellation as invidious, and implies as dangerous consequences, as the epithet of *mystic* with which he has honoured us? In reality, Cleanthes, consider what it is you assert when you represent the Deity as similar to the human mind and understanding. What is the soul of man? A composition of various faculties, passions, sentiments, ideas—united, indeed, into one self or person, but still distinct from each other. When it reasons, the ideas which are the parts of its discourse arrange themselves in a certain form or order which is not preserved entire for a moment, immediately gives place to another arrangement. New opinions, new passions, new affections, new feelings arise which continually diversify the mental scene and produce in it the greatest variety and most rapid succession imaginable. How is this compatible with that perfect immutability and simplicity which all true theists ascribe to the Deity? By the same act, say they, he sees past, present, and future; his love and hatred, his mercy and justice, are one individual operation; he is entire in every point of space, and complete in every instant of duration. No succession, no change, no acquisition, no diminution. What he is implies not in it any shadow of distinction or diversity. And what he is this moment he ever has been and ever will be, without any new judgment, sentiment, or operation. He stands fixed in one simple, perfect state; nor can you ever say, with any propriety, that this act of his is different from that other, or that this judgment or idea has been lately formed and will give place, by succession, to any different judgment or idea.

I can readily allow, said Cleanthes, that those who maintain the perfect simplicity of the Supreme Being, to the extent in which you have explained it, are complete mystics, and chargeable with all the consequences which I have drawn from their opinion. They are, in a word, atheists, without knowing it. For though it be allowed that the Deity possesses attributes of which we have no comprehension, yet ought we never to ascribe to him any attributes which are absolutely incompatible with that intelligent nature essential to him. A mind whose acts and sentiments and ideas are not distinct and successive, one that is wholly simple and totally immutable, is a mind which has no thought, no reason, no will,

no sentiment, no love, no hatred; or, in a word, is no mind at all. It is an abuse of terms to give it that appellation, and we may as well speak of limited extension without figure, or of number without composition.

Pray consider, said Philo, whom you are at present inveighing against. You are honouring with the appellation of *atheist* all the sound, orthodox divines, almost, who have treated of this subject; and you will at last be, yourself, found, according to your reckoning, the only sound theist in the world. But if idolaters be atheists, as, I think, may justly be asserted, and Christian theologians the same, what becomes of the argument, so much celebrated, derived from the universal consent of mankind?

But, because I know you are not much swayed by names and authorities, I shall endeavor to show you, a little more distinctly, the inconveniences of that anthropomorphism which you have embraced, and shall prove that there is no ground to suppose a plan of the world to be formed in the Divine mind, consisting of distinct ideas, differently arranged, in the same manner as an architect forms in his head the plan of a house which he intends to execute.

It is not easy, I own, to see what is gained by this supposition, whether we judge of the matter by *reason* or by *experience*. We are still obliged to mount higher in order to find the cause of this cause which you had assigned as satisfactory and conclusive.

If *reason* (I mean abstract reason derived from inquiries *a priori*) be not alike mute with regard to all questions concerning cause and effect, this sentence at least it will venture to pronounce: that a mental world or universe of ideas requires a cause as much as does a material world or universe of objects, and, if similar in its arrangement, must require a similar cause. For what is there in this subject which should occasion a different conclusion or inference? In an abstract view, they are entirely alike; and no difficulty attends the one supposition which is not common to both of them.

Again, when we will needs force *experience* to pronounce some sentence, even on these subjects which lie beyond her sphere, neither can she perceive any material difference in this particular between those two kinds of worlds, but finds them to be governed by similar principles, and to depend upon an equal variety of causes in their operations. We have specimens in miniature of both of them. Our own mind resembles the one; a vegetable or animal body the other. Let experience, therefore, judge from these samples. Nothing seems more delicate, with regard to its causes, than thought; and as these causes never operate in two persons after the same manner, so we never find two persons who think exactly alike. Nor indeed does the same person think exactly alike at any two different periods of time. A difference of age, of the disposition of his body, of weather, of food, of company, of books, of passions—any of these particulars, or others more minute, are sufficient to alter the curious machinery of thought and communicate to it very different movements and operations. As far as we can judge, vegetables and animal bodies are not more delicate in their motions, nor depend upon a greater variety or more curious adjustment of springs and principles.

How, therefore, shall we satisfy ourselves concerning the cause of that Being whom you suppose the Author of nature, or, according to your system of anthropomorphism, the ideal world into which you trace the material? Have we not the same reason to trace that ideal world into another ideal world or new intelligent principle? But if we stop and go no farther, why go so far? Why not stop at the material world? How can we satisfy ourselves without going on *in infinitum?* And, after all, what satisfaction is there in that infinite progression? Let us remember the story of the Indian philosopher and his elephant. It was never more applicable than to the present subject. If the material world rests upon a similar ideal world, this ideal world must rest upon some other, and so on without end. It were better, therefore, never to look beyond the present material world. By supposing it to contain the principle of its order within itself, we really assert it to be God: and the sooner we arrive at that Divine Being, so much the better. When you go one step beyond the mundane system, you only excite an inquisitive humour which it is impossible ever to satisfy.

To say that the different ideas which compose the reason of the Supreme Being fall into order of themselves and by their own nature is really to talk without any precise meaning. If it has a meaning, I would fain know why it is not as good sense to say that the parts of the material world fall into order of themselves and by their own nature. Can the one opinion be intelligible, while the other is not so?

We have, indeed, experience of ideas which fall into order of themselves and without any *known* cause. But, I am sure, we have a much larger experience of matter which does the same, as in all instances of generation and vegetation where the accurate analysis of the cause exceeds all human comprehension. We have also experience of particular systems of thought and of matter which have no order; of the first in madness, of the second in corruption. Why, then, should we think that order is more essential to one than the other? And if it requires a cause in both, what do we gain by your system, in tracing the universe of objects into a similar universe of ideas? The first step which we make leads us on for ever. It were, therefore, wise in us to limit all our inquiries to the present world, without looking farther. No satisfaction can ever be attained by these speculations which so far exceed the narrow bounds of human understanding.

It was usual with the Peripatetics, you know, Cleanthes, when the cause of any phenomenon was demanded, to have recourse to their *faculties* or *occult qualities,* and to say, for instance, that bread nourished by its nutritive faculty, and senna purged by its purgative. But it has been discovered that this subterfuge was nothing but the disguise of ignorance, and that these philosophers, though less ingenuous, really said the same thing with the sceptics or the vulgar who fairly confessed that they knew not the cause of these phenomena. In like manner, when it is asked, what cause produced order in the ideas of the Supreme Being, can any other reason be assigned by you, anthropomorphites, than that it is a *rational* faculty, and that such is the nature of the Deity? But why a similar answer will not be equally satisfactory in accounting for the order of the world, without having recourse to any such intelligent creator as you insist on, may be difficult to determine. It is only to say that *such* is the nature of material objects, and that they are all originally possessed of a *faculty* of order and proportion. These are only more learned and elaborate ways of confessing our ignorance; nor has the one hypothesis any real advantage above the other, except in its greater conformity to vulgar prejudices.

You have displayed this argument with great emphasis, replied Cleanthes: You seem not sensible how easy it is to answer it. Even in common life, if I assign a cause for any event, is it any objection, Philo, that I cannot assign the cause of that cause, and answer every new question which may incessantly be started? And what philosophers could possibly submit to so rigid a rule?—philosophers who confess ultimate causes to be totally unknown, and are sensible that the most refined principles into which they trace the phenomena are still to them as inexplicable as these phenomena themselves are to the vulgar. The order and arrangement of nature, the curious adjustment of final causes, the plain use and intention of every part and organ—all these bespeak in the clearest language an intelligent cause or author. The heavens and the earth join in the same testimony: The whole chorus of nature raises one hymn to the praises of its Creator. You alone, or almost alone, disturb this general harmony. You start abstruse doubts, cavils, and objections; you ask me what is the cause of this cause? I know not; I care not; that concerns not me. I have found a Deity; and here I stop my inquiry. Let those go farther who are wiser or more enterprising.

I pretend to be neither, replied Philo; and for that very reason I should never, perhaps, have attempted to go so far, especially when I am sensible that I must at last be contented to sit down with the same answer which, without further trouble, might have satisfied me from the beginning. If I am still to remain in utter ignorance of causes and can absolutely give an explication of nothing, I shall never esteem it any advantage to shove off for a moment a difficulty which you acknowledge must immediately, in its full force, recur upon me. Naturalists indeed very justly explain particular effects by more general causes, though these general causes themselves should remain in the totally inexplicable, but they never surely thought it satisfactory to explain a particular effect by a particular cause which was no more to be accounted for than the effect itself. An ideal system, arranged of itself, without a precedent design, is not a whit more explicable than a material one which attains its order in a like manner; nor is there any more difficulty in the latter supposition than in the former.

PART V

But to show you still more inconveniences, continued Philo, in your anthropomorphism, please to take a new survey of your principles. *Like effects prove like causes.* This is the experimental argument; and this, you say too, is the sole theological argument. Now it is certain that the liker the effects which are seen and the liker the causes which are inferred, the stronger is the argument. Every departure on either side diminishes the probability and

renders the experiment less conclusive. You cannot doubt of the principle; neither ought you to reject its consequences.

All the new discoveries in astronomy which prove the immense grandeur and magnificence of the works of nature are so many additional arguments for a Deity, according to the true system of theism; but, according to your hypothesis of experimental theism, they become so many objections, by removing the effect still farther from all resemblance to the effects of human art and contrivance. For if Lucretius, even following the old system of the world, could exclaim:

Quis regere immensi summam, quis habere profundi
Indu manu validas potis est moderanter habenas?
Quis pariter coelos omnes convertere? et omnes
Ignibus aetheriis terras suffire feraces?
Omnibus inque locis esse omni tempore praesto?[2]

If Tully [Cicero] esteemed this reasoning so natural as to put it into the mouth of his Epicurean:

Quibus enim oculis animi intueri potuit vester Plato fabricam illam tanti operis, qua construi a Deo atque aedificari mundum facit? quae molitio? quae ferramenta? qui vectes? quae machinae? qui ministri tanti muneris fuerunt? quemadmodum autem obedire et parere voluntati architecti aer, ignis, aqua, terra potuerunt?[3]

If this argument, I say, had any force in former ages, how much greater must it have at present when the bounds of Nature are so infinitely enlarged and such a magnificent scene is opened to us? It is still more unreasonable to form our idea of so unlimited a cause from our experience of the narrow productions of human design and invention.

The discoveries by microscopes, as they open a new universe in miniature, are still objections, according to you, arguments, according to me. The further we push our researches of this kind, we are still led to infer the universal cause of all to be vastly different from mankind, or from any object of human experience and observation.

And what say you to the discoveries in anatomy, chemistry, botany? . . . These surely are no objections, replied Cleanthes; they only discover new instances of art and contrivance, it is still the image of mind reflected on us from innumerable objects.

Add a mind *like the human,* said Philo. I know of no other, replied Cleanthes. And the liker, the better, insisted Philo. To be sure, said Cleanthes.

Now, Cleanthes, said Philo, with an air of alacrity and triumph, mark the consequences. *First,* by this method of reasoning you renounce all claim to infinity in any of the attributes of the Deity. For, as the cause ought only to be proportioned to the effect, and the effect, so far as it falls under our cognizance, is not infinite, what pretensions have we, upon your suppositions, to ascribe that attribute to the Divine Being? You will still insist that, by removing him so much from similarity to human creatures, we give in to the most arbitrary hypothesis, and at the same time weaken all proofs of his existence.

Secondly, you have no reason, on your theory, for ascribing perfection to the Deity, even in his finite capacity, or for supposing him free from every error, mistake, or incoherence, in his undertakings. There are many inexplicable difficulties in the works of nature which, if we allow a perfect author to be proved *a priori,* are easily solved, and become only seeming difficulties from the narrow capacity of man, who cannot trace infinite relations. But according to your method of reasoning, these difficulties become all real, and, perhaps, will be insisted on as new instances of likeness to human art and contrivance. At least, you must acknowledge that it is impossible for us to tell, from our limited views, whether this system contains any great faults or deserves any considerable praise if compared to other possible and even real systems. Could a peasant, if the *Aeneid* were read to him, pronounce that poem to be absolutely faultless, or even assign to it its proper rank among the productions of human wit, he who had never seen any other production?

But were this world ever so perfect a production, it must still remain uncertain whether all the excellences of the work can justly be ascribed to the workman. If we survey a ship, what an exalted idea must we form of the ingenuity of the carpenter who framed so complicated, useful, and beautiful a machine? And what surprise must we feel when we find him a stupid mechanic who imitated others, and copied an art which, through a long succession of ages, after multiplied trials, mistakes, corrections, deliberations, and controversies, had been gradually improving? Many worlds might have been botched and bungled, throughout an eternity, ere this system was struck out; much labour lost, many fruitless trials made, and a slow but continued improvement carried on during infinite ages in the art of world-making. In such subjects, who can determine where the truth, nay, who can conjecture where the probability lies, amidst a great number of hypotheses which may be proposed, and a still greater which may be imagined?

And what shadow of an argument, continued Philo, can you produce from your hypothesis to prove the unity of the Deity? A great number of men join in building a house or ship, in rearing a city, in framing a commonwealth; why may not several deities combine in contriving and framing a world? This is only so much greater similarity to human affairs. By sharing the work among several, we may so much further limit the attributes of each, and get rid of that extensive power and knowledge which must be supposed in one deity, and which, according to you, can only serve to weaken the proof of his existence. And if such foolish, such vicious creatures as man can yet often unite in framing and executing one plan, how much more those deities or demons, whom we may suppose several degrees more perfect!

To multiply causes without necessity is indeed contrary to true philosophy, but this principle applies not to the present case. Were one deity antecedently proved by your theory who were possessed of every attribute requisite to the production of the universe, it would be needless, I own (though not absurd) to suppose any other deity existent. But while it is still a question whether all these attributes are united in one subject or dispersed among several independent beings, by what phenomena in nature can we pretend to decide the controversy? Where we see a body raised in a scale, we are sure that there is in the opposite scale, however concealed from sight, some counterposing weight equal to it; but it is still allowed to doubt whether that weight be an aggregate of several distinct bodies or one uniform united mass. And if the weight requisite very much exceeds anything which we have ever seen conjoined in any single body, the former supposition becomes still more probable and natural. An intelligent being of such vast power and capacity as is necessary to produce the universe, or, to speak in the language of ancient philosophy, so prodigious an animal exceeds all analogy and even comprehension.

But further, Cleanthes: Men are mortal, and renew their species by generation; and this is common to all living creatures. The two great sexes of male and female, says Milton, animate the world. Why must this circumstance, so universal, so essential, be excluded from those numerous and limited deities? Behold, then, the theogeny of ancient times brought back upon us.

And why not become a perfect anthropomorphite? Why not assert the deity or deities to be corporeal, and to have eyes, a nose, mouth, ears, etc.? Epicurus maintained that no man had ever seen reason but in a human figure; therefore, the gods must have a human figure. And this argument, which is deservedly so much ridiculed by Cicero, becomes, according to you, solid and philosophical.

In a word, Cleanthes, a man who follows your hypothesis is able, perhaps, to assert or conjecture that the universe sometime arose from something like design; but beyond that position he cannot ascertain one single circumstance, and is left afterwards to fix every point of his theology by the utmost license of fancy and hypothesis. This world, for aught he knows, is very faulty and imperfect, compared to a superior standard, and was only the first rude essay of some infant deity who afterwards abandoned it, ashamed of his lame performance; it is the work only of some dependent, inferior deity, and is the object of derision to his superiors; it is the production of old age and dotage in some superannuated deity, and ever since his death has run on at adventures, from the first impulse and active force which it received from him. You justly give signs of horror, Demea, at these strange suppositions; but these, and a thousand more of the same kind, are Cleanthes' suppositions, not mine. From the moment the attributes of the Deity are supposed finite, all these have place. And I cannot, for my part, think that so wild and unsettled a system of theology is, in any respect, preferable to none at all.

These suppositions I absolutely disown, cried Cleanthes: they strike me, however, with no horror, especially when proposed in that rambling way in which they drop from you. On the contrary, they give me pleasure when I see that, by the utmost indulgence of your imagination, you never get rid of the hypothesis of design in the universe, but are obliged at every turn to have recourse to it. To this concession I adhere steadily; and this I regard as a sufficient foundation for religion.

PART VI

It must be a slight fabric, indeed, said Demea, which can be erected on so tottering a foundation.

While we are uncertain whether there is one deity or many, whether the deity or deities, to whom we owe our existence, be perfect or imperfect, subordinate or supreme, dead or alive, what trust or confidence can we repose in them? What devotion or worship address to them? What veneration or obedience pay them? To all the purposes of life the theory of religion becomes altogether useless; and even with regard to speculative consequences its uncertainty, according to you, must render it totally precarious and unsatisfactory.

To render it still more unsatisfactory, said Philo, there occurs to me another hypothesis which must acquire an air of probability from the method of reasoning so much insisted on by Cleanthes. That like effects arise from like causes—this principle he supposes the foundation of all religion. But there is another principle of the same kind, no less certain and derived from the same source of experience, that, where several known circumstances are observed to be similar, the unknown will also be found similar. Thus, if we see the limbs of a human body, we conclude that it is also attended with a human head, though hid from us. Thus, if we see, through a chink in a wall, a small part of the sun, we conclude that were the wall removed we should see the whole body. In short, this method of reasoning is so obvious and familiar that no scruple can ever be made with regard to its solidity.

Now, if we survey the universe, so far as it falls under our knowledge, it bears a great resemblance to an animal or organized body, and seems actuated with a like principle of life and motion. A continual circulation of matter in it produces no disorder; a continual waste in every part is incessantly repaired; the closest sympathy is perceived throughout the entire system; and each part or member, in performing its proper offices, operates both to its own preservation and to that of the whole. The world, therefore, I infer, is an animal; and the Deity is the *soul* of the world, actuating it, and actuated by it.

You have too much learning, Cleanthes, to be at all surprised at this opinion which, you know, was maintained by almost all the theists of antiquity, and chiefly prevails in their discourses and reasonings. For though, sometimes, the ancient philosophers reason from final causes, as if they thought the world the workmanship of God, yet it appears rather their favourite notion to consider it as his body whose organization renders it subservient to him. And it must be confessed that, as the universe resembles more a human body than it does the works of human art and contrivance, if our limited analogy could ever, with any propriety, be extended to the whole of nature, the inference seems juster in favour of the ancient than the modern theory.

There are many other advantages, too, in the former theory which recommended it to the ancient theologians. Nothing more repugnant to all their notions because nothing more repugnant to common experience than mind without body, a mere spiritual substance which fell not under their senses nor comprehension, and of which they had not observed one single instance throughout all nature. Mind and body they knew because they felt both; an order, arrangement, organization, or internal machinery, in both they likewise knew, after the same manner; and it could not but seem reasonable to transfer this experience to the universe, and to suppose the divine mind and body to be also coeval and to have, both of them, order and arrangement naturally inherent in them and inseparable from them.

Here, therefore, is a new species of *anthropomorphism,* Cleanthes, on which you may deliberate, and a theory which seems not liable to any considerable difficulties. You are too much superior, surely, to *systematical prejudices* to find any more difficulty in supposing an animal body to be, originally, of itself or from unknown causes, possessed of order and organization, than in supposing a similar order to belong to mind. But the *vulgar prejudice* that body and mind ought always to accompany each other ought not, one should think, to be entirely neglected; since it is founded on *vulgar experience,* the only guide which you profess to follow in all these theological inquiries. And if you assert that our limited experience is an unequal standard by which to judge of the unlimited extent of nature, you entirely abandon your own hypothesis, and must thenceforward adopt our mysticism, as you call it, and admit of the absolute incomprehensibility of the Divine Nature.

This theory, I own, replied Cleanthes, has never before occurred to me, though a pretty natural one; and I cannot readily, upon so short an examination and reflection, deliver any opinion with regard to it. You are very scrupulous, indeed, said Philo. Were I to examine any system of yours, I should not have acted with half that caution and reserve in stating objections and difficulties to it. However, if anything occur to you, you will oblige us by proposing it.

Why then, replied Cleanthes, it seems to me that, though the world does, in many circumstances, resemble an animal body, yet is the analogy also defective in many circumstances the most material: no organs of sense; no seat of thought or reason; no one precise origin of motion and action. In short, it seems to bear a stronger resemblance to a vegetable than to an animal, and your inference would be so far inconclusive in favour of the soul of the world.

But, in the next place, your theory seems to imply the eternity of the world; and that is a principle which, I think, can be refuted by the strongest reasons and probabilities. I shall suggest an argument to this purpose which, I believe, has not been insisted on by any writer. Those who reason from the late origin of arts and sciences, though their inference wants not force, may perhaps be refuted by considerations derived from the nature of human society, which is in continual revolution between ignorance and knowledge, liberty and slavery, riches and poverty; so that it is impossible for us, from our limited experience, to foretell with assurance what events may or may not be expected. Ancient learning and history seem to have been in great danger of entirely perishing after the inundation of the barbarous nations; and had these convulsions continued a little longer or been a little more violent, we should not probably have now known what passed in the world a few centuries before us. Nay, were it not for the superstition of the popes, who preserved a little jargon of Latin in order to support the appearance of an ancient and universal church, that tongue must have been utterly lost; in which case the Western world, being totally barbarous, would not have been in a fit disposition for receiving the Greek language and learning, which was conveyed to them after the sacking of Constantinople. When learning and books had been extinguished, even the mechanical arts would have fallen considerably to decay; and it is easily imagined that fable or tradition might ascribe to them a much later origin than the true one. This vulgar argument, therefore, against the eternity of the world seems a little precarious.

But here appears to be the foundation of a better argument. Lucullus was the first that brought cherry-trees from Asia to Europe, though that tree thrives so well in many European climates that it grows in the woods without any culture. Is it possible that, throughout a whole eternity, no European had ever passed into Asia and thought of transplanting so delicious a fruit into his own country? Or if the tree was once transplanted and propagated, how could it ever afterwards perish? Empires may rise and fall, liberty and slavery succeed alternately, ignorance and knowledge give place to each other; but the cherry-tree will still remain in the woods of Greece, Spain, and Italy, and will never be affected by the revolutions of human society.

It is not two thousand years since vines were transplanted into France, though there is no climate in the world more favourable to them. It is not three centuries since horses, cows, sheep, swine, dogs, corn, were known in America. Is it possible that during the revolutions of a whole eternity there never arose a Columbus who might open the communication between Europe and that continent? We may as well imagine that all men would wear stockings for ten thousand years, and never have the sense to think of garters to tie them. All these seem convincing proofs of the youth or rather infancy of the world, as being founded on the operation of principles more constant and steady than those by which human society is governed and directed. Nothing less than a total convulsion of the elements will ever destroy all the European animals and vegetables which are now to be found in the Western world.

And what argument have you against such convulsions? replied Philo. Strong and almost incontestable proofs may be traced over the whole earth that every part of this globe has continued for many ages entirely covered with water. And though order were supposed inseparable from matter, and inherent in it, yet may matter be susceptible of many and great revolutions, through the endless periods of eternal duration. The incessant changes to which every part of it is subject seem to intimate some such general transformations; though, at the same time, it is observable that all the changes and corruptions of which we have ever had experience are but passages from one state of order to another; nor can matter ever rest in total deformity and confusion. What we see in the parts, we may infer in the whole; at least, that is the method of reasoning on which you rest your whole theory. And were I obliged to defend any particular system of this nature, which I never willingly should do, I esteem none more plausible than that which ascribes an eternal inherent principle of order to the world, though attended with great and continual revolutions and alterations. This at once solves all difficulties; and

if the solution, by being so general, is not entirely complete and satisfactory, it is at least a theory that we must sooner or later have recourse to, whatever system we embrace. How could things have been as they are, were there not an original inherent principle of order somewhere, in thought or in matter? And it is very indifferent to which of these we give the preference. Chance has no place, on any hypothesis, sceptical or religious. Everything is surely governed by steady, inviolable laws. And were the inmost essence of things laid open to us, we should then discover a scene of which, at present, we can have no idea. Instead of admiring the order of natural beings, we should clearly see that it was absolutely impossible for them, in the smallest article, ever to admit of any other disposition.

Were anyone inclined to revive the ancient pagan theology which maintained, as we learned from Hesiod, that this globe was governed by 30,000 deities, who arose from the unknown powers of nature, you would naturally object, Cleanthes, that nothing is gained by this hypothesis; and that it is as easy to suppose all men animals, beings more numerous but less perfect, to have sprung immediately from a like origin. Push the same inference a step further, and you will find a numerous society of deities as explicable as one universal deity who possesses within himself the powers and perfections of the whole society. All these systems, then, of Scepticism, Polytheism, and Theism, you must allow, on your principles, to be on a like footing, and that no one of them has any advantage over the others. You may thence learn the fallacy of your principles.

PART VII

But here, continued Philo, in examining the ancient system of the soul of the world there strikes me, all of a sudden, a new idea which, if just, must go near to subvert all your reasoning, and destroy even your first inferences on which you repose such confidence. If the universe bears a greater likeness to animal bodies and to vegetables than to the works of human art, it is more probable that its cause resembles the cause of the former than that of the latter, and its origin ought rather to be ascribed to generation or vegetation than to reason or design. Your conclusion, even according to your own principles, is therefore lame and defective.

Pray open up this argument a little further, said Demea, for I do not rightly apprehend it in that concise manner in which you have expressed it.

Our friend Cleanthes, replied Philo, as you have heard, asserts that, since no question of fact can be proved otherwise than by experience, the existence of a Deity admits not of proof from any other medium. The world, says he, resembles the works of human contrivance; therefore its cause must also resemble that of the other. Here we may remark that the operation of one very small part of nature, to wit, man, upon another very small part, to wit, that inanimate matter lying within his reach, is the rule by which Cleanthes judges of the origin of the whole; and he measures objects, so widely disproportioned, by the same individual standard. But to waive all objections drawn from this topic, I affirm that there are other parts of the universe (besides the machines of human invention) which bear still a greater resemblance to the fabric of the world, and which, therefore, afford a better conjecture concerning the universal origin of this system. These parts are animals and vegetables. The world plainly resembles more an animal or a vegetable than it does a watch or a knitting-loom. Its cause, therefore, it is more probable, resembles the cause of the former. The cause of the former is generation or vegetation. The cause, therefore, of the world we may infer to be something similar or analogous to generation or vegetation.

But how is it conceivable, said Demea, that the world can arise from anything similar to vegetation or generation?

Very easily, replied Philo. In like manner as a tree sheds its seed into the neighboring fields and produces other trees, so the great vegetable, the world, or this planetary system, produces within itself certain seeds which, being scattered into the surrounding chaos, vegetate into new worlds. A comet, for instance, is the seed of a world; and after it has been fully ripened, by passing from sun to sun, and star to star, it is, at last, tossed into the unformed elements which everywhere surround this universe, and immediately sprouts up into a new system.

Or if, for the sake of variety (for I see no other advantage), we should suppose this world to be an animal: a comet is the egg of this animal; and in like manner as an ostrich lays its egg in the sand, which, without any further care, hatches the egg and pro-

duces a new animal, so . . . I understand you, says Demea. But what wild, arbitrary suppositions are these! What *data* have you for such extraordinary conclusions? And is the slight, imaginary resemblance of the world to a vegetable or an animal sufficient to establish the same inference with regard to both? Objects which are in general so widely different, ought they to be a standard for each other?

Right, cries Philo: This is the topic on which I have all along insisted. I have still asserted that we have no *data* to establish any system of cosmogony. Our experience, so imperfect in itself and so limited both in extent and duration, can afford us no probable conjecture concerning the whole of things. But if we must needs fix on some hypothesis, by what rule, pray, ought we to determine our choice? Is there any other rule than the greater similarity of the objects compared? And does not a plant or an animal, which springs from vegetation or generation, bear a stronger resemblance to the world than does any artificial machine, which arises from reason and design?

But what is this vegetation and generation of which you talk? said Demea. Can you explain their operations, and anatomize that fine internal structure on which they depend?

As much, at least, replied Philo, as Cleanthes can explain the operations of reason, or anatomize that internal structure on which it depends. But without any such elaborate disquisitions, when I see an animal, I infer that it sprang from generation; and that with as great certainty as you conclude a house to have been reared by design. These words *generation, reason* mark only certain powers and energies in nature whose effects are known, but whose essence is incomprehensible; and one of these principles, more than the other, has no privilege for being made a standard to the whole of nature.

In reality, Demea, it may reasonably be expected that the larger the views are which we take of things, the better will they conduct us in our conclusions concerning such extraordinary and such magnificent subjects. In this little corner of the world alone, there are four principles, *reason, instinct, generation, vegetation,* which are similar to each other, and are the causes of similar effects. What a number of other principles may we naturally suppose in the immense extent and variety of the universe could we travel from planet to planet, and from system to system, in order to examine each part of this mighty fabric? Any one of these four principles above mentioned (and a hundred others which lie open to our conjecture) may afford us a theory by which to judge of the origin of the world; and it is a palpable and egregious partiality to confine our view entirely to that principle by which our own minds operate. Were this principle more intelligible on that account, such a partiality might be somewhat excusable; but reason, in its internal fabric and structure, is really as little known to us as instinct or vegetation; and, perhaps, even that vague, undeterminate word *nature,* to which the vulgar refer everything is not at the bottom more inexplicable. The effects of these principles are all known to us from experience; but the principles themselves and their manner of operation are totally unknown; nor is it less intelligible or less conformable to experience to say that the world arose by vegetation, from seed shed by another world, than to say that it arose from a divine reason or contrivance, according to the sense in which Cleanthes understands it.

But methinks, said Demea, if the world had a vegetative quality and could sow the seeds of new worlds into the infinite chaos, this power would be still an additional argument for design in its author. For whence could arise so wonderful a faculty but from design? Or how can order spring from anything which perceives not that order which it bestows?

You need only look around you, replied Philo, to satisfy yourself with regard to this question. A tree bestows order and organization on that tree which springs from it, without knowing the order; an animal in the same manner on its offspring; a bird on its nest; and instances of this kind are even more frequent in the world than those of order which arise from reason and contrivance. To say that all this order in animals and vegetables proceeds ultimately from design is begging the question; nor can that great point be ascertained otherwise than by proving, *a priori,* both that order is, from its nature, inseparably attached to thought and that it can never of itself or from original unknown principles belong to matter.

But further, Demea, this objection which you urge can never be made use of by Cleanthes, without renouncing a defense which he has already made against one of my objections. When I inquired concerning the cause of that supreme reason and intelligence into which he resolves everything, he told me that the impossibility of satisfying such inquiries could never be admitted as an objection in any species of philosophy. *We must stop somewhere,* says he; *nor is it ever within the reach of human capacity to explain ultimate causes or show the last connections of any objects. It is sufficient if any steps, as far as we go, are supported by experience and observation.* Now that vegetation and generation, as well as reason, are experienced to be principles of order in nature is undeniable. If I rest my system of cosmogony on the former, preferably to the latter, it is at my choice. The matter seems entirely arbitrary. And when Cleanthes asks me what is the cause of my great vegetative or generative faculty, I am equally entitled to ask him the cause of his great reasoning principle. These questions we have agreed to forbear on both sides; and it is chiefly his interest on the present occasion to stick to this agreement. Judging by our limited and imperfect experience, generation has some privileges above reason; for we see every day the latter arise from the former, never the former from the latter.

Compare, I beseech you, the consequences on both sides. The world, say I, resembles an animal; therefore it is an animal, therefore it arose from generation. The steps, I confess, are wide, yet there is some small appearance of analogy in each step. The world, says Cleanthes, resembles a machine; therefore it is a machine, therefore it arose from design. The steps are here equally wide, and the analogy less striking. And if he pretends to carry on *my* hypothesis a step further, and to infer design or reason from the great principle of generation on which I insist, I may, with better authority, use the same freedom to push further *his* hypothesis, and infer a divine generation or theogony from his principle of reason. I have at least some faint shadow of experience, which is the utmost that can ever be attained in the present subject. Reason, in innumerable instances, is observed to arise from the principle of generation, and never to arise from any other principle.

Hesiod and all the ancient mythologists were so struck with this analogy that they universally explained the origin of nature from an animal birth, and copulation. Plato, too, so far as he is intelligible, seems to have adopted some such notion in his *Timaeus.*

The Brahmins assert that the world arose from an infinite spider, who spun this whole complicated mass from his bowels, and annihilates afterwards the whole or any part of it, by absorbing it again and resolving it into his own essence. Here is a species of cosmogony which appears to us ridiculous because a spider is a little contemptible animal whose operations we are never likely to take for a model of the whole universe. But still here is a new species of analogy, even in our globe. And were there a planet wholly inhabited by spiders (which is very possible), this inference would there appear as natural and irrefragable as that which in our planet ascribes the origin of all things to design and intelligence, as explained by Cleanthes. Why an orderly system may not be spun from the belly as well as from the brain, it will be difficult for him to give a satisfactory reason.

I must confess, Philo, replied Cleanthes, that, of all men living, the task which you have undertaken, of raising doubts and objections, suits you best and seems, in a manner, natural and unavoidable to you. So great is your fertility of invention than I am not ashamed to acknowledge myself unable, on a sudden, to solve regularly such out-of-the-way difficulties as you incessantly start upon me, though I clearly see, in general, their fallacy and error. And I question not, but you are yourself, at present, in the same case, and have not the solution so ready as the objection, while you must be sensible that common sense and reason are entirely against you, and that such whimsies as you have delivered may puzzle but never can convince us.

PART VIII

What you ascribe to the fertility of my invention, replied Philo, is entirely owing to the nature of the subject. In subjects adapted to the narrow compass of human reason there is commonly but one determination which carries probability or conviction with it; and to a man of sound judgment all other suppositions but that one appear entirely absurd and chimerical. But in such questions as the present, a hundred contradictory views may preserve a kind of imperfect analogy, and invention has here full scope to exert itself. Without any great effort of thought, I believe that I could, in an instant, propose other systems of cosmogony which would have some faint appearance of truth, though it is a thousand, a million to one if either yours or any one of mine be the true system.

For instance, what if I should revive the old Epicurean hypothesis? This is commonly, and I believe justly, esteemed the most absurd system that has yet been proposed; yet I know not whether, with a few alterations, it might not be brought to bear a

faint appearance of probability. Instead of supposing matter infinite, as Epicurus did, let us suppose it finite. A finite number of particles is only susceptible of finite transpositions; and it must happen, in an eternal duration, that every possible order or position must be tried an infinite number of times. This world, therefore, with all its events, even the most minute, has before been produced and destroyed, and will again be produced and destroyed, without any bounds and limitations. No one who has a conception of the powers of infinite, in comparison of finite, will ever scruple this determination.

But this supposes, said Demea, that matter can acquire motion without any voluntary agent or first mover.

And where is the difficulty, replied Philo, of that supposition? Every event, before experience, is equally difficult and incomprehensible; and every event, after experience, is equally easy and intelligible. Motion, in many instances, from gravity, from elasticity, from electricity, begins in matter, without any known voluntary agent; and to suppose always, in these cases, an unknown voluntary agent is mere hypothesis and hypothesis attended with no advantages. The beginning of motion in matter itself is as conceivable a priori as its communication from mind and intelligence.

Besides, why may not motion have been propagated by impulse through all eternity, and the same stock of it, or nearly the same, be still upheld in the universe? As much is lost by the composition of motion, as much is gained by its resolution. And whatever the causes are, the fact is certain that matter is and always has been in continual agitation, as far as human experience or tradition reaches. There is not probably, at present, in the whole universe, one particle of matter at absolute rest.

And this very consideration, too, continued Philo, which we have stumbled on in the course of the argument, suggests a new hypothesis of cosmogony that is not absolutely absurd and improbable. Is there a system, an order, an economy of things, by which matter can preserve that perpetual agitation which seems essential to it, and yet maintain a constancy in the forms which it produces? There certainly is such an economy, for this is actually the case with the present world. The continual motion of matter, therefore, in less than infinite transpositions, must produce this economy or order, and by its very nature, that order, when once established, supports itself for many ages if not to eternity. But wherever matter is so poised, arranged, and adjusted, as to continue in perpetual motion, and yet preserve a constancy in the forms, its situation must, of necessity, have all the same appearance of art and contrivance which we observe at present. All the parts of each form must have a relation to each other and to the whole; and the whole itself must have a relation to the other parts of the universe, to the element in which the form subsists, to the materials with which it repairs its waste and decay, and to every other form which is hostile or friendly. A defect in any of these particulars destroys the form, and the matter of which it is composed is again set loose, and is thrown into irregular motions and fermentations till it unite itself to some other regular form. If no such form be prepared to receive it, and if there be a great quantity of this corrupted matter in the universe, the universe itself is entirely disordered, whether it be the feeble embryo of a world in its first beginnings that is thus destroyed or the rotten carcase of one languishing in old age and infirmity. In either case, a chaos ensues till finite though innumerable revolutions produce, at last, some forms whose parts and organs are so adjusted as to support the forms amidst a continued succession of matter.

Suppose (for we shall endeavour to vary the expression) that matter were thrown into any position by a blind, unguided force; it is evident that this first position must, in all probability, be the most confused and most disorderly imaginable, without any resemblance to those works of human contrivance which, along with a symmetry of parts, discover an adjustment of means to ends and a tendency to self-preservation. If the actuating force cease after this operation, matter must remain for ever in disorder and continue an immense chaos, without any proportion or activity. But suppose that the actuating force, whatever it be, still continues in matter, this first position will immediately give place to a second which will likewise, in all probability, be as disorderly as the first, and so on through many successions of changes and revolutions. No particular order or position ever continues a moment unaltered. The original force, still remaining in activity, gives a perpetual restlessness to matter. Every possible situation is produced and instantly destroyed. If a glimpse or dawn of order appears for a moment, it is instantly hurried away and confounded by that never-ceasing force which actuates every part of matter.

Thus the universe goes on for many ages in a continued succession of chaos and disorder. But is it not possible that it may settle at last, so as not to lose its motion and active force (for that we have supposed inherent in it), yet so as to preserve an uniformity of appearance, amidst the continual motion and fluctuation of its parts? This we find to be the case with the universe at present. Every individual is perpetually changing, and every part of every individual; and yet the whole remains, in appearance, the same. May we not hope for such a position or rather be assured of it from the eternal revolutions of unguided matter; and may not this account for all the appearing wisdom and contrivance which is in the universe? Let us contemplate the subject a little, and we shall find that this adjustment if attained by matter of a seeming stability in the forms, with a real and perpetual revolution or motion of parts, affords a plausible, if not a true, solution of the difficulty.

It is in vain, therefore, to insist upon the uses of the parts in animals or vegetables, and their curious adjustment to each other. I would fain know how an animal could subsist unless its parts were so adjusted? Do we not find that it immediately perishes whenever this adjustment ceases, and that its matter, corrupting, tries some new form? It happens indeed that the parts of the world are so well adjusted that some regular form immediately lays claim to this corrupted matter; and if it were not so, could the world subsist? Must it not dissolve, as well as the animal, and pass through new positions and situations till in great but finite succession it fall, at last, into the present or some such order?

It is well, replied Cleanthes, you told us that this hypothesis was suggested on a sudden, in the course of the argument. Had you had leisure to examine it, you would soon have perceived the insuperable objections to which it is exposed. No form, you say, can subsist unless it possess those powers and organs requisite for its subsistence; some new order or economy must be tried, and so on, without intermission, till at last some order which can support and maintain itself is fallen upon. But according to this hypothesis, whence arise the many conveniences and advantages which men and all animals possess? Two eyes, two ears are not absolutely necessary for the subsistence of the species. The human race might have been propagated and preserved without horses, dogs, cows, sheep, and those innumerable fruits and products which serve to our satisfaction and enjoyment. If no camels had been created for the use of man in the sandy deserts of Africa and Arabia, would the world have been dissolved? If no loadstone had been framed to give that wonderful and useful direction to the needle, would human society and the human kind have been immediately extinguished? Though the maxims of nature be in general very frugal, yet instances of this kind are far from being rare; and any one of them is a sufficient proof of design—and of a benevolent design—which gave rise to the order and arrangement of the universe.

At least, you may safely infer, said Philo, that the foregoing hypothesis is so far incomplete and imperfect, which I shall not scruple to allow. But can we ever reasonably expect greater success in any attempts of this nature? Or can we ever hope to erect a system of cosmogony that will be liable to no exceptions, and will contain no circumstance repugnant to our limited and imperfect experience of the analogy of nature? Your theory itself cannot surely pretend to any such advantage, even though you have run into *anthropomorphism,* the better to preserve a conformity to common experience. Let us once more put it to trial. In all instances which we have ever seen, ideas are copied from real objects, and are ectypal, not archetypal, to express myself in learned terms. You reverse this order and give thought the precedence. In all instances which we have ever seen, thought has no influence upon matter except where that matter is so conjoined with it as to have an equal reciprocal influence upon it. No animal can move immediately anything but the members of its own body; and, indeed, the equality of action and reaction seems to be an universal law of nature; but your theory implies a contradiction to this experience. These instances, with many more which it were easy to collect (particularly the supposition of a mind or system of thought that is eternal or, in other words, an animal ingenerable and immortal)—these instances, I say, may teach all of us sobriety in condemning each other, and let us see that as no system of this kind ought ever to be received from a slight analogy, so neither ought any to be rejected on account of a small incongruity. For that is an inconvenience from which we can justly pronounce no one to be exempted.

All religious systems, it is confessed, are subject to great and insuperable difficulties. Each disputant triumphs in his turn, while he carries on an offensive war, and exposes the absurdities, barbarities, and pernicious tenets of his antagonist. But all of them, on the whole, prepare a complete triumph for the *sceptic,* who tells them that no system ought ever to be embraced with regard to such subjects: for this plain reason that no absurdity ought ever to be assented to with regard to any subject. A total suspense of judgment is here our only reasonable resource. And if every attack, as is commonly observed, and no defence among theologians is successful, how complete must be *his* victory who remains always, with all mankind, on the offensive, and has himself no fixed station or abiding city which he is ever, on any occasion, obliged to defend?

PART IX

But if so many difficulties attend the argument *a posteriori,* said Demea, had we not better adhere to that simple and sublime argument *a priori* which, by offering to us infallible demonstration, cuts off at once all doubt and difficulty? By this argument, too, we may prove the *infinity* of the Divine attributes, which, I am afraid, can never be ascertained with certainty from any other topic. For how can an effect which either is finite or, for aught we know, may be so—how can such an effect, I say, prove an infinite cause? The unity, too, of the Divine Nature it is very difficult, if not absolutely impossible, to deduce merely from contemplating the works of nature; nor will the uniformity alone of the plan, even were it allowed, give us any assurance of that attribute. Whereas the argument *a priori* . . .

You seem to reason, Demea, interposed Cleanthes, as if those advantages and conveniences in the abstract argument were full proofs of its solidity. But it is first proper, in my opinion, to determine what argument of this nature you choose to insist on; and we shall afterwards, from itself, better than from its *useful* consequences, endeavour to determine what value we ought to put upon it.

The argument, replied Demea, which I would insist on is the common one. Whatever exists must have a cause or reason of its existence, it being absolutely impossible for anything to produce itself or be the cause of its own existence. In mounting up, therefore, from effect to causes, we must either go on in tracing an infinite succession, without any ultimate cause at all, or must at least have recourse to some ultimate cause that is *necessarily* existent. Now that the first supposition is absurd may be thus proved. In the infinite chain or succession of causes and effects, each single effect is determined to exist by the power and efficacy of that cause which immediately preceded; but the whole eternal chain or succession, taken together, is not determined or caused by anything, and yet it is evident that it requires a cause or reason, as much as any particular object which begins to exist in time. The question is still reasonable why this particular succession of causes existed from eternity, and not any other succession or no succession at all. If there be no necessarily existent being, any supposition which can be formed is equally possible; nor is there any more absurdity in *nothing's* having existed from eternity than there is in that succession of causes which constitutes the universe. What was it, then, which determined *something* to exist rather than *nothing,* and bestowed being on a particular possibility, exclusive of the rest? *External causes,* there are supposed to be none. *Chance* is a word without a meaning. Was it *nothing?* But that can never produce anything. We must, therefore, have recourse to a necessarily existent Being who carries the *reason* of his existence in himself, and who cannot be supposed not to exist, without an express contradiction. There is, consequently, such a Being—that is, there is a Deity.

I shall not leave it to Philo, said Cleanthes, though I know that starting objections is his chief delight, to point out the weakness of this metaphysical reasoning. It seems to me so obviously ill-grounded, and at the same time of so little consequence to the cause of true piety and religion, that I shall myself venture to show the fallacy of it.

I shall begin with observing that there is an evident absurdity in pretending to demonstrate a matter of fact, or to prove it by arguments *a priori.* Nothing is demonstrable unless the contrary implies a contradiction. Nothing that is distinctly conceivable implies a contradiction. Whatever we conceive as existent, we can also conceive as non-existent. There is no being, therefore, whose non-existence implies a contradiction. Consequently there is no being whose existence is demonstrable. I propose this argument as entirely decisive, and am willing to rest the whole controversy upon it.

It is pretended that the Deity is a necessarily existent being; and this necessity of his existence is attempted to be explained by asserting that, if we knew his whole essence or nature, we should perceive it to be as impossible for him not to exist, as for twice two not to be four. But it is evident that

this can never happen, while our faculties remain the same as at present. It will still be possible for us, at any time, to conceive the nonexistence of what we formerly conceived to exist; nor can the mind ever lie under a necessity of supposing any object to remain always in being; in the same manner as we lie under a necessity of always conceiving twice two to be four. The words, therefore, *necessary existence* have no meaning or, which is the same thing, none that is consistent.

But further, why may not the material universe be the necessarily existent Being, according to this pretended explication of necessity? We dare not affirm that we know all the qualities of matter; and, for aught we can determine, it may contain some qualities which, were they known, would make its non-existence appear as great a contradiction as that twice two is five. I find only one argument employed to prove that the material world is not the necessarily existent Being; and this argument is derived from the contingency both of the matter and the form of the world. "Any particle of matter," it is said, "may be *conceived* to be annihilated, and any form may be *conceived* to be altered. Such an annihilation or alteration, therefore, is not impossible."[4] But it seems a great partiality not to perceive that the same argument extends equally to the Deity, so far as we have any conception of him, and that the mind can at least imagine him to be nonexistent or his attributes to be altered. It must be some unknown, inconceivable qualities which can make his non-existence appear impossible or his attributes unalterable; and no reason can be assigned why these qualities may not belong to matter. As they are altogether unknown and inconceivable, they can never be proved incompatible with it.

Add to this that in tracing an eternal succession of objects it seems absurd to inquire for a general cause or first author. How can anything that exists from eternity have a cause, since that relation implies a priority in time and a beginning of existence?

In such a chain, too, or succession of objects, each part is caused by that which preceded it, and causes that which succeeds it. Where then is the difficulty? But the *whole,* you say, wants a cause. I answer that the uniting of several distinct countries into one kingdom, or several distinct members into one body is performed merely by an arbitrary act of the mind, and has no influence on the nature of things. Did I show you the particular causes of each individual in a collection of twenty particles of matter, I should think it very unreasonable should you afterwards ask me what was the cause of the whole twenty. This is sufficiently explained in explaining the cause of the parts.

Though the reasonings which you have urged, Cleanthes, may well excuse me, said Philo, from starting any further difficulties, yet I cannot forbear insisting still upon another topic. It is observed by arithmeticians that the products of 9 compose always either 9 or some lesser product of 9 if you add together all the characters of which any of the former products is composed. Thus, of 18, 27, 36, which are products of 9, you make 9 by adding 1 to 8, 2 to 7, 3 to 6. Thus 369 is a product also of 9; and if you add 3, 6, and 9, you make 18, a lesser product of 9.[5] To a superficial observer so wonderful a regularity may be admired as the effect either of chance or design; but a skillful algebraist immediately concludes it to be the work of necessity, and demonstrates that it must for ever result from the nature of these numbers. Is it not probable, I ask, that the whole economy of the universe is conducted by a like necessity, though no human algebra can furnish a key which solves the difficulty? And instead of admiring the order of natural beings, may it not happen that, could we penetrate into the intimate nature of bodies, we should clearly see why it was absolutely impossible they could ever admit of any other disposition? So dangerous is it to introduce this idea of necessity into the present question! and so naturally does it afford an inference directly opposite to the religious hypothesis!

But dropping all these abstractions, continued Philo, and confining ourselves to more familiar topics, I shall venture to add an observation that the argument *a priori* has seldom been found very convincing, except to people of a metaphysical head who have accustomed themselves to abstract reasoning, and who, finding from mathematics that the understanding frequently leads to truth through obscurity, and contrary to first appearances, have transferred the same habit of thinking to subjects where it ought not to have place. Other people, even of good sense and the best inclined to religion, feel always some deficiency in such arguments, though they are not perhaps able to explain distinctly where it lies—a certain proof that men ever did and ever

will derive their religion from other sources than from this species of reasoning.

PART X

It is my opinion, I own, replied Demea, that each man feels, in a manner, the truth of religion within his own breast, and, from a consciousness of his imbecility and misery rather than from any reasoning, is led to seek protection from that Being on whom he and all nature is dependent. So anxious or so tedious are even the best scenes of life that futurity is still the object of all our hopes and fears. We incessantly look forward and endeavour, by prayers, adoration, and sacrifice, to appease those unknown powers whom we find, by experience, so able to afflict and oppress us. Wretched creatures that we are! What resource for us amidst the innumerable ills of life did not religion suggest some methods of atonement, and appease those terrors with which we are incessantly agitated and tormented?

I am indeed persuaded, said Philo, that the best and indeed the only method of bringing everyone to a due sense of religion is by just representations of the misery and wickedness of men. And for that purpose a talent of eloquence and strong imagery is more requisite than that of reasoning and argument. For is it necessary to prove what everyone feels within himself? It is only necessary to make us feel it, if possible, more intimately and sensibly.

The people, indeed, replied Demea, are sufficiently convinced of this great and melancholy truth. The miseries of life, the unhappiness of man, the general corruptions of our nature, the unsatisfactory enjoyment of pleasures, riches, honours—these phrases have become almost proverbial in all languages. And who can doubt of what all men declare from their own immediate feeling and experience?

In this point, said Philo, the learned are perfectly agreed with the vulgar; and in all letters, *sacred* and *profane,* the topic of human misery has been insisted on with the most pathetic eloquence that sorrow and melancholy could inspire. The poets, who speak from sentiment, without a system, and whose testimony has therefore the more authority, abound in images of this nature. From Homer down to Dr. Young, the whole inspired tribe have ever been sensible that no other representation of things would suit the feeling and observation of each individual.

As to authorities, replied Demea, you need not seek them. Look round this library of Cleanthes. I shall venture to affirm that, except authors of particular sciences, such as chemistry or botany, who have no occasion to treat of human life, there is scarce one of those innumerable writers from whom the sense of human misery has not, in some passage or other, extorted a complaint and confession of it. At least, the chance is entirely on that side; and no one author has ever, so far as I can recollect, been so extravagant as to deny it.

There you must excuse me, said Philo: Leibniz has denied it, and is perhaps the first[6] who ventured upon so bold and paradoxical an opinion; at least, the first who made it essential to his philosophical system.

And by being the first, replied Demea, might he not have been sensible of his error? For is this a subject in which philosophers can propose to make discoveries especially in so late an age? And can any man hope by a simple denial (for the subject scarcely admits of reasoning) to bear down the united testimony of mankind, founded on sense and consciousness?

And why should man, added he, pretend to an exemption from the lot of all other animals? The whole earth, believe me, Philo, is cursed and polluted. A perpetual war is kindled amongst all living creatures. Necessity, hunger, want stimulate the strong and courageous; fear, anxiety, terror agitate the weak and infirm. The first entrance into life gives anguish to the new-born infant and to its wretched parent; weakness, impotence, distress attend each stage of that life, and it is, at last finished in agony and horror.

Observe, too, says Philo, the curious artifices of nature in order to embitter the life of every living being. The stronger prey upon the weaker and keep them in perpetual terror and anxiety. The weaker, too, in their turn, often prey upon the stronger, and vex and molest them without relaxation. Consider that innumerable race of insects, which either are bred on the body of each animal or, flying about, infix their stings in him. These insects have others still less than themselves which torment them. And thus on each hand, before and behind, above and below, every animal is surrounded with enemies which incessantly seek his misery and destruction.

Man alone, said Demea, seems to be, in part, an exception to this rule. For by combination in society he can easily master lions, tigers, and bears, whose greater strength and agility naturally enable them to prey upon him.

On the contrary, it is here chiefly, cried Philo, that the uniform and equal maxims of nature are most apparent. Man, it is true, can, by combination, surmount all his *real* enemies and become master of the whole animal creation; but does he not immediately raise up to himself *imaginary* enemies, the demons of his fancy, who haunt him with superstitious terrors and blast every enjoyment of life? His pleasure, as he imagines, becomes in their eyes a crime; his food and repose give them umbrage and offence; his very sleep and dreams furnish new materials to anxious fear; and even death, his refuge from every other ill, presents only the dread of endless and innumerable woes. Nor does the wolf molest more the timid flock than superstition does the anxious breast of wretched mortals.

Besides, consider, Demea: This very society by which we surmount those wild beasts, our natural enemies, what new enemies does it not raise to us? What woe and misery does it not occasion? Man is the greatest enemy of man. Oppression, injustice, contempt, contumely, violence, sedition, war, calumny, treachery, fraud—by these they mutually torment each other, and they would soon dissolve that society which they had formed were it not for the dread of still greater ills which must attend their separation.

But though these external insults, said Demea, from animals, from men, from all the elements, which assault us from a frightful catalogue of woes, they are nothing in comparison of those which arise within ourselves, from the distempered condition of our mind and body. How many lie under the lingering torment of disease? Hear the pathetic enumeration of the great poet.

> Intestine stone and ulcer, colic-pangs,
> Demoniac frenzy, moping melancholy,
> And moon-struck madness, pining atrophy
> Marasmus, and wide-wasting pestilence.
> Dire was the tossing, deep the groans: *Despair*
> Tended the sick, busiest from couch to couch
> And over them triumphant *Death* his dart
> Shook: but delay'd to strike, though oft invok'd
> With vows, as their chief good and final hope.[7]

The disorders of the mind, continued Demea, though more secret, are not perhaps less dismal and vexatious. Remorse, shame, anguish, rage, disappointment, anxiety, fear, dejection, despair—who has ever passed through life without cruel inroads from these tormentors? How many have scarcely ever felt any better sensations? Labour and poverty, so abhorred by everyone, are the certain lot of the far greater number; and those few privileged persons who enjoy ease and opulence never reach contentment or true felicity. All the goods of life united would not make a very happy man, but all the ills united would make a wretch indeed; and any one of them almost (and who can be free from every one?), nay, often the absence of one good (and who can possess all?) is sufficient to render life ineligible.

Were a stranger to drop on a sudden into this world, I would show him, as a specimen of its ills, an hospital full of diseases, a prison crowded with malefactors and debtors, a field of battle strewed with carcases, a fleet floundering in the ocean, a nation languishing under tyranny, famine, or pestilence. To turn the gay side of life to him and give him a notion of its pleasures—whither should I conduct him? To a ball, to an opera, to court? He might justly think that I was only showing him a diversity of distress and sorrow.

There is no evading such striking instances, said Philo, but by apologies which still further aggravate the charge. Why have all men, I ask, in all ages, complained incessantly of the miseries of life? . . . They have no just reason, says one: these complaints proceed only from their discontented, repining, anxious disposition. . . . And can there possibly, I reply, be a more certain foundation of misery than such a wretched temper?

But if they were really as unhappy as they pretend, says my antagonist, why do they remain in life? . . .

Not satisfied with life, afraid of death—

This is the secret chain, say I, that holds us. We are terrified, not bribed to the continuance of our existence.

It is only a false delicacy, he may insist, which a few refined spirits indulge, and which has spread these complaints among the whole race of mankind. . . . And what is this delicacy, I ask, which you blame? Is it anything but a greater sensibility to all the pleasures and pains of life? And if the man of a delicate, refined temper, by being so much more alive than the rest of the world, is only so much more unhappy, what judgment must we form in general of human life?

Let me remain at rest, says our adversary, and they will be easy. They are willing artificers of their own misery. . . . No! reply I: an anxious languor follows their repose; disappointment, vexation, trouble, their activity and ambition.

I can observe something like what you mention in some others, replied Cleanthes, but I confess I feel little or nothing of it in myself, and hope that it is not so common as you represent it.

If you feel not human misery yourself, cried Demea, I congratulate you on so happy a singularity. Others, seemingly the most prosperous, have not been ashamed to vent their complaints in the most melancholy strains. Let us attend to the great, the fortunate emperor, Charles V, when tired with human grandeur, he resigned all his extensive dominions into the hands of his son. In the last harangue which he made on that memorable occasion, he publicly avowed *that the greatest prosperities which he had ever enjoyed had been mixed with so many adversities that he might truly say he had never enjoyed any satisfaction or contentment.* But did the retired life in which he sought for shelter afford him any greater happiness? If we may credit his son's account, his repentance commenced the very day of his resignation.

Cicero's fortune, from small beginnings, rose to the greatest lustre and renown; yet what pathetic complaints of the ills of life do his familiar letters, as well as philosophical discourses, contain? And suitably to his own experience, he introduces Cato, the great, the fortunate Cato protesting in his old age that had he a new life in his offer he would reject the present.

Ask yourself, ask any of your acquaintance, whether they would live over again the last ten or twenty years of their life. No! but the next twenty, they say, will be better:

And from the dregs of life, hope to receive
What the first sprightly running could not give. [8]

Thus, at last, they find (such is the greatness of human misery, it reconciles even contradictions) that they complain at once of the shortness of life and of its vanity and sorrow.

And it is possible, Cleanthes, said Philo, that after all these reflections, and infinitely more which might be suggested, you can still persevere in your anthropomorphism, and assert the moral attributes of the Deity, his justice, benevolence, mercy, and rectitude, to be of the same nature with these virtues in human creatures? His power, we allow, is infinite; whatever he wills is executed; but neither man nor any other animal is happy; therefore, he does not will their happiness. His wisdom is infinite; he is never mistaken in choosing the means to any end; but the course of nature tends not to human or animal felicity; therefore, it is not established for that purpose. Through the whole compass of human knowledge there are no inferences more certain and infallible than these. In what respect, then, do his benevolence and mercy resemble the benevolence and mercy of men?

Epicurus' old questions are yet unanswered.

"Is he willing to prevent evil, but not able? then is he impotent. Is he able, but not willing? then is he malevolent. Is he both able and willing? whence then is evil?"

You ascribe, Cleanthes (and I believe justly), a purpose and intention to nature. But what, I beseech you, is the object of that curious artifice and machinery which she has displayed in all animals—the preservation alone of individuals, and propagation of the species? It seems enough for her purpose, if such a rank be barely upheld in the universe, without any care or concern for the happiness of the members that compose it. No resource for this purpose: no machinery in order merely to give pleasure or ease; no fund of pure joy and contentment; no indulgence without some want or necessity accompanying it. At least, the few phenomena of this nature are over-balanced by opposite phenomena of still greater importance.

Our sense of music, harmony, and indeed beauty of all kinds, gives satisfaction, without being absolutely necessary to the preservation and propagation of the species. But what racking pains, on the other hand, arise from gouts, gravels, megrims, toothaches, rheumatisms, where the injury to the animal machinery is either small or incurable? Mirth, laughter, play, frolic seem gratuitous satisfactions which have no further tendency; spleen, melancholy, discontent, superstition are pains of the same nature. How then does the Divine benevolence display itself, in the sense of you anthropomorphites? None but we mystics, as you were pleased to call us, can account for this strange mixture of phenomena, by deriving it from attributes infinitely perfect but incomprehensible.

And have you, at last, said Cleanthes smiling, betrayed your intentions, Philo? Your long agreement with Demea did indeed a little surprise me, but I find you were all the while erecting a concealed battery against me. And I must confess that you have now fallen upon a subject worthy of your noble spirit

of opposition and controversy. If you can make out the present point, and prove mankind to be unhappy or corrupted, there is an end at once of all religion. For to what purpose establish the natural attributes of the Deity, while the moral are still doubtful and uncertain?

You take umbrage very easily, replied Demea, at opinions the most innocent and the most generally received, even amongst the religious and devout themselves; and nothing can be more surprising than to find a topic like this—concerning the wickedness and misery of man—charged with no less than atheism and profaneness. Have not all pious divines and preachers who have indulged their rhetoric on so fertile a subject, have they not easily, I say, given a solution of any difficulties which may attend it? This world is but a point in comparison of the universe; this life but a moment in comparison of eternity. The present evil phenomena, therefore, are rectified in other regions, and in some future period of existence. And the eyes of men, being then opened to larger views of things, see the whole connection of general laws, and trace, with adoration, and benevolence and rectitude of the Deity through all the mazes and intricacies of his providence.

No! replied Cleanthes, no! These arbitrary suppositions can never be admitted, contrary to matter of fact, visible and uncontroverted. Whence can any cause be known but from its known effects? Whence can any hypothesis be proved but from the apparent phenomena? To establish one hypothesis upon another is building entirely in the air; and the utmost we ever attain by these conjectures and fictions is to ascertain the bare possibility of our opinion, but never can we, upon such terms, establish its reality.

The only method of supporting Divine benevolence—and it is what I willingly embrace—is to deny absolutely the misery and wickedness of man. Your representations are exaggerated; your melancholy views mostly fictitious; your inferences contrary to fact and experience. Health is more common than sickness; pleasure than pain; happiness than misery. And for one vexation which we meet with, we attain, upon computation, a hundred enjoyments.

Admitting your position, replied Philo, which yet is extremely doubtful, you must at the same time allow that, if pain be less frequent than pleasure, it is infinitely more violent and durable. One hour of it is often able to outweigh a day, a week, a month of our common insipid enjoyments; and how many days, weeks, and months are passed by several in the most acute torments? Pleasure, scarcely in one instance, is ever able to reach ecstasy and rapture; and in no one instance can it continue for any time at its highest pitch and altitude. The spirits evaporate, the nerves relax, the fabric is disordered, and the enjoyment quickly degenerates into fatigue and uneasiness. But pain often, good God, how often! rises to torture and agony; and the longer it continues, it becomes still more genuine agony and torture. Patience is exhausted, courage languishes, melancholy seizes us, and nothing terminates our misery but the removal of its cause or another event which is the sole cure of all evil, but which, from our natural folly, we regard with still greater horror and consternation.

But not to insist upon these topics, continued Philo, though most obvious, certain, and important, I must use the freedom to admonish you, Cleanthes, that you have put the controversy upon a most dangerous issue, and are unawares introducing a total scepticism into the most essential articles of natural and revealed theology. What! no method of fixing a just foundation for religion unless we allow the happiness of human life, and maintain a continued existence even in this world, with all our present pains, infirmities, vexations, and follies, to be eligible and desirable! But this is contrary to everyone's feeling and experience; it is contrary to an authority so established as nothing can subvert. No decisive proofs can ever be produced against this authority; nor is it possible for you to compute, estimate, and compare all the pains and all the pleasures in the lives of all men and of all animals; and thus, by your resting the whole system of religion on a point which, from its very nature, must for ever be uncertain, you tacitly confess that that system is equally uncertain.

But allowing you what never will be believed, at least, what you never possibly can prove, that animal or, at least, human happiness in this life exceeds its misery, you have yet done nothing; for this is not, by any means, what we expect from infinite power, infinite wisdom, and infinite goodness. Why is there any misery at all in the world? Not by chance, surely. From some cause then. Is it from the intention of the Deity? But he is perfectly benevolent. Is it contrary to his intention? But he is

almighty. Nothing can shake the solidity of this reasoning, so short, so clear, so decisive, except we assert that these subjects exceed all human capacity, and that our common measures of truth and falsehood are not applicable to them—a topic which I have all along insisted on, but which you have, from the beginning, rejected with scorn and indignation.

But I will be contented to retire still from this intrenchment, for I deny that you can ever force me in it. I will allow that pain or misery in man is *compatible* with infinite power and goodness in the Deity, even in your sense of these attributes: what are you advanced by all these concessions? A mere possible compatibility is not sufficient. You must *prove* these pure, unmixt, and uncontrollable attributes from the present mixt and confused phenomena, and from these alone. A hopeful undertaking! Were the phenomena ever so pure and unmixt, yet, being finite, they would be insufficient for that purpose. How much more, where they are also so jarring and discordant!

Here, Cleanthes, I find myself at ease in my argument. Here I triumph. Formerly, when we argued concerning the natural attributes of intelligence and design, I needed all my sceptical and metaphysical subtilty to elude your grasp. In many views of the universe and of its parts, particularly the matter, the beauty and fitness of final causes strike us with such irresistible force that all objections appear (what I believe they really are) mere cavils and sophisms; nor can we then imagine how it was ever possible for us to repose any weight on them. But there is no view of human life or the condition of mankind from which, without the greatest violence, we can infer the moral attributes or learn that infinite benevolence, conjoined with infinite power and infinite wisdom, which we must discover by the eyes of faith alone. It is your turn now to tug the labouring oar, and to support your philosophical subtilties against the dictates of plain reason and experience.

PART XI

I scruple not to allow, said Cleanthes, that I have been apt to suspect the frequent repetition of the word *infinite,* which we meet with in all theological writers, to savour more of panegyric than of philosophy, and that any purposes of reasoning, and even of religion, would be better served were we to rest contented with more accurate and more moderate expressions. The terms *admirable, excellent, superla-*

tively great, wise, and *holy*—these sufficiently fill the imaginations of men, and anything beyond, besides that it leads into absurdities, has no influence on the affections or sentiments. Thus, in thy present subject, if we abandon all human analogy, as seems your intention, Demea, I am afraid we abandon all religion and retain no conception of the great object of our adoration. If we preserve human analogy, we must forever find it impossible to reconcile any mixture of evil in the universe with infinite attributes; much less can we ever prove the latter from the former. But supposing the Author of nature to be finitely perfect, though far exceeding mankind, a satisfactory account may then be given of natural and moral evil, and every untoward phenomenon be explained and adjusted. A less evil may then be chosen in order to avoid a greater; inconveniences be submitted to in order to reach a desirable end; and, in a word, benevolence, regulated by wisdom and limited by necessity, may produce just such a world as the present. You, Philo, who are so prompt at starting views and reflections and analogies, I would gladly hear, at length, without interruption, your opinion of this new theory; and if it deserve our attention, we may afterwards, at more leisure, reduce it into form.

My sentiments, replied Philo, are not worth being made a mystery of; and, therefore, without any ceremony, I shall deliver what occurs to me with regard to the present subject. I must, I think, be allowed that, if a very limited intelligence whom we shall suppose utterly unacquainted with the universe were assured that it were the production of a very good, wise, and powerful Being, however finite, he would, from his conjectures, form *beforehand* a different notion of it from what we find it to be by experience; nor would he ever imagine, merely from these attributes of the cause of which he is informed, that the effect could be so full of vice and misery and disorder, as it appears in this life. Supposing now that this person were brought into the world, still assured that it was the workmanship of such a sublime and benevolent Being, he might, perhaps, be surprised at the disappointment, but would never retract his former belief if founded on any very solid argument, since such a limited intelligence must be sensible of his own blindness and ignorance, and must allow that there may be many solutions of those phenomena which will for ever escape his comprehension. But supposing, which is the real case with regard to man, that this creature is not antecedently convinced of a supreme intelligence, benevolent, and powerful, but is left to gather such a belief from the appearances of things—this entirely alters the case, nor will he ever find any reason for such a conclusion. He may be fully convinced of the narrow limits of his understanding, but this will not help him in forming an inference concerning the goodness of superior powers, since he must form that inference from what he knows, not from what he is ignorant of. The more you exaggerate his weakness and ignorance, the more diffident you render him, and give him the greater suspicion that such subjects are beyond the reach of his faculties. You are obliged, therefore, to reason with him merely from the known phenomena, and to drop every arbitrary supposition or conjecture.

Did I show you a house or palace where there was not one apartment convenient or agreeable, where the windows, doors, fires, passsages, stairs, and the whole economy of the building were the source of noise, confusion, fatigue, darkness, and the extremes of heat and cold, you would certainly blame the contrivance, without any further examination. The architect would in vain display his subtilty, and prove to you that, if this door or that window were altered, greater ills would ensue. What he says may be strictly true: the alteration of one particular, while the other parts of the building remain, may only augment the inconveniences. But still you would assert in general that, if the architect had had skill and good intentions, he might have formed such a plan of the whole, and might have adjusted the parts in such a manner as would have remedied all or most of these inconveniences. His ignorance, or even your own ignorance of such a plan, will never convince you of the impossibility of it. If you find any inconveniences and deformities in the building, you will always, without entering into any detail, condemn the architect.

In short, I repeat the question: Is the world, considered in general and as it appears to us in this life, different from what a man or such a limited being would, *beforehand,* expect from a very powerful, wise, and benevolent Deity? It must be strange prejudice to assert the contrary. And from thence I conclude that, however consistent the world may be, allowing certain suppositions and conjectures with the idea of such a Deity, it can never afford us an inference concerning his existence. The consistency is not absolutely denied, only the inference. Conjectures, especially where infinity is excluded from the Divine attributes, may perhaps be sufficient to prove a consistency, but can never be foundations from any inference.

There seem to be *four* circumstances on which depend all or the greatest part of the ills that molest sensible creatures; and it is not impossible but all these circumstances may be necessary and unavoidable. We know so little beyond common life, or even of common life, that, with regard to the economy of a universe, there is no conjecture, however wild, which may not be just, nor any one, however plausible, which may not be erroneous. All that belongs to human understanding, in this deep ignorance and obscurity, is to be sceptical or at least cautious, and not to admit of any hypothesis whatever, much less of any which is supported by no appearance of probability. Now this I assert to be the case with regard to all the causes of evil and the circumstances on which it depends. None of them appear to human reason in the least degree necessary or unavoidable, nor can we suppose them such, without the utmost licence of imagination.

The *first* circumstance which introduces evil is that contrivance or economy of the animal creation by which pains, as well as pleasures, are employed to excite all creatures to action, and make them vigilant in the great work of self-preservation. Now pleasure alone, in its various degrees, seems to human understanding sufficient for this purpose. All animals might be constantly in a state of enjoyment; but when urged by any of the necessities of nature, such as thirst, hunger, weariness, instead of pain, they might feel a diminution of pleasure by which they might be prompted to seek that object which is necessary to their subsistence. Men pursue pleasure as eagerly as they avoid pain; at least, they might have been so constituted. It seems, therefore, plainly possible to carry on the business of life without any pain. Why then is any animal ever rendered susceptible of such a sensation? If animals can be free from it an hour, they might enjoy a perpetual exemption from it, and it required as particular a contrivance of their organs to produce that feeling as to endow them with sight, hearing, or any of the senses. Shall we conjecture that such a contrivance was necessary, without any appearance of reason, and shall we build on that conjecture as on the most certain truth?

But a capacity of pain would not alone produce pain were it not for the *second* circumstance, viz., the conducting of the world by general laws; and this seems nowise necessary to a very perfect Being. It is true, if everything were conducted by particular volitions, the course of nature would be perpetually broken, and no man could employ his reason in the conduct of life. But might not other particular volitions remedy this inconvenience? In short, might not the Deity exterminate all ill, wherever it were to be found, and produce all good, without any preparation or long progress of causes and effects?

Besides, we must consider that, according to the present economy of the world, the course of nature, though supposed exactly regular, yet to us appears not so, and many events are uncertain, and many disappoint our expectations. Health and sickness, calm and tempest, with an infinite number of other accidents whose causes are unknown and variable, have a great influence both on the fortunes of particular persons and on the prosperity of public societies; and indeed all human life, in a manner, depends on such accidents. A being, therefore, who knows the secret springs of the universe might easily, by particular volitions, turn all these accidents to the good of mankind and render the whole world happy, without discovering himself in any operation. A fleet whose purposes were salutary to society might always meet with a fair wind. Good princes enjoy sound health and long life. Persons born to power and authority be framed with good tempers and virtuous dispositions. A few such events as these, regularly and wisely conducted, would change the face of the world, and yet would no more seem to disturb the course of nature or confound human conduct than the present economy of things where the causes are secret and variable and compounded. Some small touches given to Caligula's brain in his infancy might have converted him into a Trajan. One wave, a little higher than the rest, by burying Caesar and his fortune in the bottom of the ocean, might have restored liberty to a considerable part of mankind. There may, for aught we know, be good reasons why Providence interposes not in this manner, but they are unknown to us; and, though the mere supposition that such reasons exist may be sufficient to *save* the conclusion concerning the Divine attributes, yet surely it can never be sufficient to *establish* that conclusion.

If everything in the universe be conducted by general laws, and if animals be rendered susceptible of pain, it scarcely seems possible but some ill must arise in the various shocks of matter and the various concurrence and opposition of general laws; but this ill would be very rare were it not for the *third* circumstance which I proposed to mention, viz., the great frugality with which all powers and faculties are distributed to every particular being. So well adjusted are the organs and capacities of all animals, and so well fitted to their preservation, that, as far as history or tradition reaches, there appears not to be any single species which has yet been extinguished in the universe. Every animal has the requisite endowments, but these endowments are bestowed with so scrupulous an economy that any considerable diminution must entirely destroy the creature. Wherever one power is increased, there is a proportional abatement in the others. Animals which excel in swiftness are commonly defective in force. Those which possess both are either imperfect in some of their senses or are oppressed with the most craving wants. The human species, whose chief excellence is reason and sagacity, is of all others the most necessitous, and the most deficient in bodily advantages, without clothes, without arms, without food, without lodging, without any convenience of life, except what they owe to their own skill and industry. In short, nature seems to have formed an exact calculation of the necessities of her creatures, and, like a *rigid master,* has afforded them little more powers or endowments than what are strictly sufficient to supply those necessities. An *indulgent parent* would have bestowed a large stock in order to guard against accidents, and secure the happiness and welfare of the creature in the most unfortunate concurrence of circumstances. Every course of life would not have been so surrounded with precipices that the least departure from the true path, by mistake or necessity, must involve us in misery and ruin. Some reserve, some fund, would have been provided to ensure happiness, nor would the powers and the necessities have been adjusted with so rigid an economy. The Author of nature is inconceivably powerful; his force is supposed great, if not altogether inexhaustible, nor is there any reason, as far as we can judge, to make him observe this strict frugality in his dealings with his creatures. It would have been better, were his power extremely limited, to have created fewer animals, and to have endowed these with more faculties for their happiness and preservation. A builder is never esteemed prudent who undertakes a plan beyond what his stock will enable him to finish.

In order to cure most of the ills of human life, I require not that man should have the wings of the eagle, the swiftness of the stag, the force of the ox, the arms of the lion, the scales of the crocodile or rhinoceros; much less do I demand the sagacity of an angel or cherubim. I am contented to take an increase in one single power or faculty of his soul. Let him be endowed with a greater propensity to industry and labour, a more vigorous spring and activity of mind, a more constant bent to business and application. Let the whole species possess naturally an equal diligence with that which many individuals are able to attain by habit and reflection, and the most beneficial consequences, without any allay of ill, is the immediate and necessary result of this endowment. Almost all the moral as well as natural evils of human life arise from idleness; and were our species, by the original constitution of their frame, exempt from this vice or infirmity, the perfect cultivation of land, the improvement of arts and manufactures, the exact execution of every office and duty, immediately follow; and men at once may fully reach that state of society which is so imperfectly attained by the best regulated government. But as industry is a power, and the most valuable of any, nature seems determined, suitably to her usual maxims, to bestow it on man with a very sparing hand, and rather to punish him severely for his deficiency in it than to reward him for his attainments. She has so contrived his frame that nothing but the most violent necessity can oblige him to labour; and she employs all his other wants to overcome, at least in part, the want of diligence, and to endow him with some share of a faculty of which she has thought fit naturally to bereave him. Here our demands may be allowed very humble, and therefore the more reasonable. If we required the endowments of superior penetration and judgment, of a more delicate taste of beauty, of a nicer sensibility to benevolence and friendship, we might be told that we impiously pretend to break the order of nature, that we want to exalt ourselves into a higher rank of being, that the presents which we require, not being suitable to our state and condition, would only be pernicious to us. But it is hard, I dare to repeat it, it is hard that, being placed in a world so full of wants and necessities, where almost every being and element is either our foe or refuses its assistance . . . we should also have our own temper to struggle with, and should be deprived of that faculty which can alone fence against these multiplied evils.

The *fourth* circumstance whence arises the misery and ill of the universe is the inaccurate workmanship of all the springs and principles of the great machine of nature. It must be acknowledged that there are few parts of the universe which seem not to serve some purpose, and whose removal would not produce a visible defect and disorder in the whole. The parts hang all together, nor can one be touched without affecting the rest, in a greater or less degree. But at the same time, it must be observed that none of these parts or principles, however useful, are so accurately adjusted as to keep precisely within those bounds in which their utility consists; but they are, all of them, apt, on every occasion, to run into the one extreme or the other. One would imagine that this grand production had not received the last hand of the maker—so little finished is every part, and so coarse are the strokes with which it is executed. Thus the winds are requisite to convey the vapours along the surface of the globe, and to assist men in navigation; but how often, rising up to tempests and hurricanes, do they become pernicious? Rains are necessary to nourish all the plants and animals of the earth; but how often are they defective? how often excessive? Heat is requisite to all life and vegetation, but is not always found in the due proportion. On the mixture and secretion of the humours and juices of the body depend the health and prosperity of the animal; but the parts perform not regularly their proper function. What more useful than all the passions of the mind, ambition, vanity, love, anger? But how often do they break their bounds and cause the greatest convulsions in society? There is nothing so advantageous in the universe but what frequently becomes pernicious, by its excess or defect; nor has nature guarded, with the requisite accuracy, against all disorder or confusion. The irregularity is never perhaps so great as to destroy any species, but is often sufficient to involve the individuals in ruin and misery.

On the concurrence, then, of these *four* circumstances does all or the greatest part of natural evil depend. Were all living creatures incapable of pain, or were the world administered by particular volitions, evil never could have found access into the universe; and were animals endowed with a large stock of powers and faculties, beyond what strict necessity requires, or were the several springs and principles of the universe so accurately framed as to preserve always the just temperament and medium, there must have been very little ill in comparison of what we feel at present. What then shall we pronounce on this occasion? Shall we say that these circumstances are not necessary, and that they might easily have been altered in the contrivance of the universe? This decision seems too presumptuous for creatures so blind and ignorant. Let us be more modest in our conclusions. Let us allow that, if the goodness of the Deity (I mean a goodness like the human) could be established on any tolerable reasons *a priori,* these phenomena, however untoward, would not be sufficient to subvert that principle, but might easily, in some unknown manner, be reconcilable to it. But let us still assert that, as this goodness is not antecedently established but must be inferred from the phenomena, there can be no grounds for such an inference while there are so many ills in the universe, and while these ills might so easily have been remedied, as far as human understanding can be allowed to judge on such a subject. I am sceptic enough to allow that the bad appearances, notwithstanding all my reasonings, may be compatible with such attributes as you suppose, but surely they can never prove these attributes. Such a conclusion cannot result from scepticism, but must arise from the phenomena, and from our confidence in the reasonings which we deduce from these phenomena.

Look round this universe. What an immense profusion of beings, animated and organized, sensible and active! You admire this prodigious variety and fecundity. But inspect a little more narrowly these living existences, the only beings worth regarding. How hostile and destructive to each other! How insufficient all of them for their own happiness! How contemptible or odious to the spectator! The whole presents nothing but the idea of a blind nature, impregnated by a great vivifying principle, and pouring forth from her lap, without discernment or parental care, her maimed and abortive children!

Here the Manichaean system occurs as a proper hypothesis to solve the difficulty; and, no doubt, in some respects it is very specious and has more probability than the common hypothesis, by giving a plausible account of the strange mixture of good and ill which appears in life. But if we consider, on the other hand, the perfect uniformity and agreement of the parts of the universe, we shall not discover in it any marks of the combat of a malevolent with a benevolent being. There is indeed an opposition of pains and pleasures in the feelings of sensible creatures; but are not all the operations of nature carried on by an opposition of principles, of hot and cold, moist and dry, light and heavy? The true conclusion is that the original Source of all things is entirely indifferent to all these principles, and has no more regard to good above ill than to heat above cold, or to drought above moisture, or to light above heavy.

There may *four* hypotheses be framed concerning the first causes of the universe: that they are endowed with perfect goodness; that they have perfect malice; that they are opposite and have both goodness and malice; that they have neither goodness nor malice. Mixed phenomena can never prove the two former unmixed principles; and the uniformity and steadiness of general laws seem to oppose the third. The fourth, therefore, seems by far the most probable.

What I have said concerning natural evil will apply to moral with little or no variation; and we have no more reason to infer that the rectitude of the Supreme Being resembles human rectitude than that his benevolence resembles the human. Nay, it will be thought that we have still greater cause to exclude from him moral sentiments, such as we feel them, since moral evil, in the opinion of many, is much more predominant above moral good than natural evil above natural good.

But even though this should not be allowed, and though the virtue which is in mankind should be acknowledged much superior to the vice, yet, so long as there is any vice at all in the universe, it will very much puzzle you anthropomorphites how to account for it. You must assign a cause for it, without having recourse to the first cause. But as every effect must have a cause, and that cause another, you must either carry on the progression *in infinitum* or rest on that original principle, who is the ultimate cause of all things . . .

Hold! hold! cried Demea: Whither does your imagination hurry you? I joined in alliance with you in order to prove the incomprehensible nature of the Divine Being, and refute the principles of Cleanthes, who would measure everything by human rule and standard. But I now find you running into all the topics of the greatest libertines and infidels, and betraying that holy cause which you seemingly espoused. Are you secretly, then, a more dangerous enemy than Cleanthes himself?

And are you so late in perceiving it? replied Cleanthes. Believe me, Demea, your friend Philo, from the beginning, has been amusing himself at both our expense; and it must be confessed that the injudicious reasoning of our vulgar theology has given him but too just a handle of ridicule. The total infirmity of human reason, the absolute incomprehensibility of the Divine Nature, the great and universal misery, and still greater wickedness of men—these are strange topics, surely, to be so fondly cherished by orthodox divines and doctors. In ages of stupidity and ignorance, indeed, these principles may safely be espoused; and perhaps no views of things are more proper to promote superstition than such as encourage the blind amazement, the diffidence, and melacholy of mankind. But at present . . .

Blame not so much, interposed Philo, the ignorance of these reverend gentlemen. They know how to change their style with the times. Formerly, it was a most popular theological topic to maintain that human life was vanity and misery, and to exaggerate all the ills and pains which are incident to men. But of late years, divines, we find, begin to retract this position and maintain, though still with some hesitation, that there are more goods than evils, more pleasures than pains, even in this life. When religion stood entirely upon temper and education, it was thought proper to encourage melancholy, as, indeed, mankind never have recourse to superior powers so readily as in that disposition. But as men have now learned to form principles and to draw consequences, it is necessary to change the batteries, and to make use of such arguments as will endure at least some scrutiny and examination. This variation is the same (and from the same causes) with that which I formerly remarked with regard to scepticism.

Thus Philo continued to the last his spirit of opposition, and his censure of established opinions. But I could observe that Demea did not at all relish the latter part of the discourse; and he took occasion soon after, on some pretence or other, to leave the company.

NOTES

1. *Recherche de la Verité,* liv. 3, cap. 9.

2. *De Rerum Natura,* lib. XI [II], 1094. (Who can rule the sum, who hold in his hand with controlling force the strong reins, of the immeasurable deep? Who can at once make all the different heavens to roll and warm with ethereal fires all the fruitful earths, or be present in all places at all times?)—(Translation by H. A. J. Munro, G. Bell & Sons, 1920.)

3. *De Natura Deorum,* lib. I [cap. VIII]. (For with what eyes could your Plato see the construction of so vast a work which, according to him, God was putting together and building? What materials, what tools, what bars, what machines, what servants were employed in such gigantic work? How could the air, fire, water, and earth pay obedience and submit to the will of the architect?)

4. Dr. Clarke [Samuel Clarke, the rationalist theologian (1675–1729)].

5. *Republique des Lettres,* Aut 1685.

6. That sentiment had been maintained by Dr. King and some few others before Leibniz, though by none of so great fame as that German philosopher.

7. Milton: *Paradise Lost,* Bk. XI.

8. John Dryden, *Aureng-Zebe,* Act IV, sc. 1.

J. L. M A C K I E

Evil and Omnipotence*

J. L. Mackie (1917–   ) teaches philosophy at University College, Oxford.

The traditional arguments for the existence of God have been fairly thoroughly criticized by philosophers. But the theologian can, if he wishes, accept this criticism. He can admit that no rational proof of God's existence is possible. And he can still retain all that is essential to his position, by holding that God's existence is known in some other, nonrational way. I think, however, that a more telling criticism can be made by way of the traditional problem of evil. Here it can be shown, not that religious beliefs lack rational support, but that they are positively irrational, that the several parts of the essential theological doctrine are inconsistent with one another, so that the theologian can maintain his position as a whole only by a much more extreme rejection of reason than in the former case. He must now be prepared to believe, not merely what cannot be proved, but what can be *disproved* from other beliefs that he also holds.

The problem of evil, in the sense in which I shall be using the phrase, is a problem only for someone who believes that there is a God who is both omnipotent and wholly good. And it is a logical problem, the problem of clarifying and reconciling a number of

beliefs: it is not a scientific problem that might be solved by further observations, or a practical problem that might be solved by a decision or an action. These points are obvious; I mention them only because they are sometimes ignored by theologians, who sometimes parry a statement of the problem with such remarks as "Well, can you solve the problem yourself?" or "This is a mystery which may be revealed to us later" or "Evil is something to be faced and overcome, not to be merely discussed."

In its simplest form the problem is this: God is omnipotent; God is wholly good; and yet evil exists. There seems to be some contradiction between these three propositions, so that if any two of them were true the third would be false. But at the same time all three are essential parts of most theological positions: the theologian, it seems, at once *must* adhere and *cannot consistently* adhere to all three. (The problem does not arise only for theists, but I shall discuss it in the form in which it presents itself for ordinary theism.)

However, the contradiction does not arise immediately; to show it we need some additional premises, or perhaps some quasi-logical rules connecting the terms "good," "evil," and "omnipotent." These additional principles are that good is opposed to evil, in such a way that a good thing always eliminates evil as far as it can, and that there are no limits to what an omnipotent thing can do. From these it follows that a good omnipotent thing eliminates evil com-

*From *Mind,* Vol. LXIV, No. 254 (1955). Reprinted by permission of the author and Basil Blackwell, Publisher.

pletely, and then the propositions that a good omnipotent thing exists, and that evil exists, are incompatible.

ADEQUATE SOLUTIONS

Now once the problem is fully stated it is clear that it can be solved, in the sense that the problem will not arise if one gives up at least one of the propositions that constitute it. If you are prepared to say that God is not wholly good, or not quite omnipotent, or that evil does not exist, or that good is not opposed to the kind of evil that exists, or that there are limits to what an omnipotent thing can do, then the problem of evil will not arise for you.

There are, then, quite a number of adequate solutions of the problem of evil, and some of these have been adopted, or almost adopted, by various thinkers. For example, a few have been prepared to deny God's omnipotence, and rather more have been prepared to keep the term ''omnipotence'' but severely to restrict its meaning, recording quite a number of things that an omnipotent being cannot do. Some have said that evil is an illusion, perhaps because they held that the whole world of temporal, changing things is an illusion, and that what we call evil belongs only to this world, or perhaps because they held that although temporal things *are* much as we see them, those that we call evil are not really evil. Some have said that what we call evil is merely the privation of good, that evil in a positive sense, evil that would really be opposed to good, does not exist. Many have agreed with Pope that disorder is harmony not understood, and that partial evil is universal good. Whether any of these views is *true* is, of course, another question. But each of them gives an adequate solution of the problems of evil in the sense that if you accept it this problem does not arise for you, though you may, of course, have *other* problems to face.

But often enough these adequate solutions are only *almost* adopted. The thinkers who restrict God's power, but keep the term ''omnipotence,'' may reasonably be suspected of thinking, in other contexts, that his power is really unlimited. Those who say that evil is an illusion may also be thinking, inconsistently, that this illusion is itself an evil. Those who say that ''evil'' is merely privation of good may also be thinking, inconsistently, that privation of good is an evil . . . If Pope meant what he said in the first line of his couplet, that ''disorder'' is only harmony not understood, the ''partial evil'' of the second line must, for consistency, mean ''that

which, taken in isolation, falsely appears to be evil,'' but it would more naturally mean ''that which, in isolation, really is evil.'' The second line, in fact, hesitates between two views, that ''partial evil'' isn't really evil, since only the universal quality is real, and that ''partial evil'' is really an evil, but only a little one.

In addition, therefore, to adequate solutions, we must recognize unsatisfactory inconsistent solutions, in which there is only a half-hearted or temporary rejection of one of the propositions which together constitute the problem. In these, one of the constituent propositions is explicitly rejected, but it is covertly reasserted or assumed elsewhere in the system.

FALLACIOUS SOLUTIONS

Besides these half-hearted solutions, which explicitly reject but implicitly assert one of the constituent propositions, there are definitely fallacious solutions which explicitly maintain all the constituent propositions, but implicitly reject at least one of them in the course of the argument that explains away the problem of evil.

There are, in fact, many so-called solutions which purport to remove the contradiction without abandoning any of its constituent propositions. These must be fallacious, as we can see from the very statement of the problem, but it is not so easy to see in each case precisely where the fallacy lies. I suggest that in all cases the fallacy has the general form suggested above: in order to solve the problem one (or perhaps more) of its constituent propositions is given up, but in such a way that it appears to have been retained, and can therefore be asserted without qualification in other contexts. Sometimes there is a further complication: the supposed solution moves to and fro between, say, two of the constituent propositions, at one point asserting the first of these but covertly abandoning the second, at another point asserting the second but covertly abandoning the first. These fallacious solutions often turn upon some equivocation with the words ''good'' and ''evil,'' or upon some vagueness about the way in which good and evil are opposed to one another, or about how much is meant by ''omnipotence.'' I propose to examine some of these so-called solutions, and to exhibit their fallacies in detail. Incidentally, I shall also be considering whether an adequate solution could be reached by a minor modification of one or more of the constituent propositions, which would, however, still satisfy all the essential requirements of ordinary theism.

1. "Good cannot exist without evil" or "Evil is necessary as a counterpart to good."

It is sometimes suggested that evil is necessary as a counterpart to good, that if there were no evil there could be no good either, and that this solves the problem of evil. It is true that it points to an answer to the question "Why should there be evil?" But it does so only by qualifying some of the propositions that constitute the problem.

First, it sets a limit to what God can do, saying that God *cannot* create good without simultaneously creating evil, and this means either that God is not omnipotent or that there are *some* limits to what an omnipotent thing can do. It may be replied that these limits are always presupposed, that omnipotence has never meant the power to do what is logically impossible, and on the present view the existence of good without evil would be a logical impossibility. This interpretation of omnipotence may, indeed, be accepted as a modification of our original account which does not reject anything that is essential to theism, and I shall in general assume it in the subsequent discussion. It is, perhaps, the most common theistic view, but I think that some theists at least have maintained that God can do what is logically impossible. Many theists, at any rate, have held that logic itself is created or laid down by God, that logic is the way in which God arbitrarily chooses to think. (This is, of course, parallel to the ethical view that morally right actions are those which God arbitrarily chooses to command, and the two views encounter similar difficulties.) And *this* account of logic is clearly inconsistent with the view that God is bound by logical necessities—unless it is possible for an omnipotent being to bind himself, an issue which we shall consider later, when we come to the Paradox of Omnipotence. This solution of the problem of evil cannot, therefore, be consistently adopted along with the view that logic is itself created by God.

But, secondly, this solution denies that evil is opposed to good in our original sense. If good and evil are counterparts, a good thing will not "eliminate evil as far as it can." Indeed, this view suggests that good and evil are not strictly qualities of things at all. Perhaps the suggestion is that good and evil are related in much the same way as great and small. Certainly, when the term "great" is used relatively as a condensation of "greater than so-and-so," and "small" is used correspondingly, greatness and smallness are counterparts and cannot exist without each other. But in this sense greatness is not a quality, not an intrinsic feature of anything; and it would be absurd to think of a movement in favor of greatness and against smallness in this sense. Such a movement would be self-defeating, since relative greatness can be promoted only by a simultaneous promotion of relative smallness. I feel sure that no theists would be content to regard God's goodness as analogous to this—as if what he supports were not the *good* but the *better,* and as if he had the paradoxical aim that all things should be better than other things.

This point is obscured by the fact that "great" and "small" seem to have an absolute as well as a relative sense. I cannot discuss here whether there is absolute magnitude or not, but if there is, there could be an absolute sense for "great," it could mean of at least a certain size, and it would make sense to speak of all things getting bigger, of a universe that was expanding all over, and therefore it would make sense to speak of promoting greatness. But in *this* sense great and small are not logically necessary counterparts: either quality could exist without the other. There would be no logical impossibility in everything's being small or in everything's being great.

Neither in the absolute nor in the relative sense, then, of "great" and "small" do these terms provide an analogy of the sort that would be needed to support this solution of the problem of evil. In neither case are greatness and smallness *both* necessary counterparts *and* mutually opposed forces or possible objects for support and attack.

It may be replied that good and evil are necessary counterparts in the same way as any quality and its logical opposite: redness can occur, it is suggested, only if nonredness also occurs. But unless evil is merely the privation of good, they are not logical opposites, and some further argument would be needed to show that they are counterparts in the same way as genuine logical opposites. Let us assume that this could be given. There is still doubt of the correctness of the metaphysical principle that a quality must have a real opposite: I suggest that it is not really impossible that everything should be, say, red, that the truth is merely that if everything were red we should not notice redness, and so we should have no word "red"; we observe and give names to qualities only if they have real opposites. If so, the principle that a term must have an opposite would belong only to our language or to our thought, and would not be an ontological principle, and, correspondingly, the rule that good cannot exist without evil would not state a logical necessity of a sort that God would just have to put up with. God might have made everything good, though *we* should not have noticed it if he had.

But, finally, even if we concede that this *is* an ontological principle, it will provide a solution for the problem of evil only if one is prepared to say, "Evil exists, but only just enough evil to serve as the counterpart of good." I doubt whether any theist will accept this. After all, the *ontological* requirement that nonredness should occur would be satisfied even if all the universe, except for a minute speck, were red, and, if there were a corresponding requirement for evil as a counterpart to good, a minute dose of evil would presumably do. But theists are not usually willing to say, in all contexts, that all the evil that occurs is a minute and necessary dose.

2. "Evil is necessary as a means to good."

It is sometimes suggested that evil is necessary for good not as a counterpart but as a means. In its simple form this has little plausibility as a solution of the problem of evil, since it obviously implies a severe restriction of God's power. It would be a *causal* law that you cannot have a certain end without a certain means, so that if God has to introduce evil as a means to good, he must be subject to at least some causal laws. This certainly conflicts with what a theist normally means by omnipotence. This view of God as limited by causal laws also conflicts with the view that causal laws are themselves made by God, which is more widely held than the corresponding view about the laws of logic. This conflict would, indeed, be resolved if it were possible for an omnipotent being to bind himself, and this possibility has still to be considered. Unless a favorable answer can be given to this question, the suggestion that evil is necessary as a means to good solves the problem of evil only by denying one of its constituent propositions, either that God is omnipotent or that "omnipotent" means what it says.

3. "The universe is better with some evil in it than it could be if there were no evil."

Much more important is a solution which at first seems to be a mere variant of the previous one, that evil may contribute to the goodness of a whole in which it is found, so that the universe as a whole is better as it is, with some evil in it, than it would be if there were no evil. This solution may be developed in either of two ways. It may be supported by an aesthetic analogy, by the fact that contrasts heighten beauty, that in a musical work, for example, there may occur discords which somehow add to the beauty of the work as a whole. Alternatively, it may be worked out in connection with the notion of progress, that the best possible organization of the universe will not be static, but progressive, that the gradual overcoming of evil by good is really a finer thing than would be the eternal unchallenged supremacy of good.

In either case, this solution usually starts from the assumption that the evil whose existence gives rise to the problem of evil is primarily what is called physical evil, that is to say, pain. In Hume's rather half-hearted presentation of the problem of evil, the evils that he stresses are pain and disease, and those who reply to him argue that the existence of pain and disease makes possible the existence of sympathy, benevolence, heroism, and the gradually successful struggle of doctors and reformers to overcome these evils. In fact, theists often seize the opportunity to accuse those who stress the problem of evil of taking a low, materialistic view of good and evil, equating these with pleasure and pain, and of ignoring the more spiritual goods which can arise in the struggle against evils.

But let us see exactly what is being done here. Let us call pain and misery "first order evil" or "evil (1)." What contrasts with this, namely, pleasure and happiness, will be called "first order good" or "good (1)." Distinct from this is "second order good" or "good (2)" which somehow emerges in a complex situation in which evil (1) is a necessary component—logically, not merely causally, necessary. (Exactly *how* it emerges does not matter: in the crudest version of this solution good [2] is simply the heightening of happiness by the contrast with misery, in other versions it includes sympathy with suffering, heroism in facing danger, and the gradual decrease of first order evil and increase of first order good.) It is also being assumed that second order good is more important than first order good or evil, in particular that it more than outweighs the first order evil it involves.

Now this is a particularly subtle attempt to solve the problem of evil. It defends God's goodness and omnipotence on the ground that (on a sufficiently long view) this is the best of all logically possible worlds because it includes the important second order goods, and yet it admits that real evils, namely first order evils, exist. But does it still hold that good and evil are opposed? Not, clearly, in the sense that we set out originally: good does not tend to eliminate evil in general. Instead, we have a modified, a more complex pattern. First order good (e.g., happiness) *contrasts with* first order evil (e.g., misery): these two are opposed in a fairly mechanical way; some second order goods (e.g., benevolence) try to maximize first order good and minimize first order evil; but God's goodness is not this, it is rather the will to maximize *second* order good. We might, therefore, call God's goodness an example of a third order goodness, or good (3). While this account is different from our original one, it might well be held to be an improvement on it, to give a more accurate description of the way in which good is opposed to evil, and to be consistent with the essential theist position.

There might, however, be several objections to this solution.

First, some might argue that such qualities as benevolence—and a fortiori the third order goodness which promotes benevolence—have a merely derivative value, that they are not higher sorts of good, but merely means to good (1), that is, to happiness, so that it would be absurd for God to keep misery in existence in order to make possible the virtues of benevolence, heroism, etc. The theist who adopts the present solution must, of course, deny this, but he can do so with some plausibility, so I should not press this objection.

Secondly, it follows from this solution that God is not in our sense benevolent or sympathetic: he is not concerned to minimize evil (1), but only to promote good (2); and this might be a disturbing conclusion for some theists.

But, thirdly, the fatal objection is this. Our analysis shows clearly the possibility of the existence of a *second* order evil, an evil (2) contrasting with good (2) as evil (1) contrasts with good (1). This would include malevolence, cruelty, callousness, coward-ice, and states in which good (1) is decreasing and

evil (1) increasing. And just as good (2) is held to be the important kind of good, the kind that God is concerned to promote, so evil (2) will, by analogy, be the important kind of evil, the kind which God, if he were wholly good and omnipotent, would eliminate. And yet evil (2) plainly exists, and indeed most theists (in other contexts) stress its existence more than that of evil (1). We should, therefore, state the problem of evil in terms of second order evil, and against this form of the problem the present solution is useless.

An attempt might be made to use this solution again, at a higher level, to explain the occurrence of evil (2): indeed the next main solution that we shall examine does just this, with the help of some new notions. Without any fresh notions, such a solution would have little plausibility: for example, we could hardly say that the really important good was a good (3), such as the increase of benevolence in proportion to cruelty, which logically required for its occurrence the occurrence of some second order evil. But even if evil (2) could be explained in this way, it is fairly clear that there would be third order evils contrasting with this third order good: and we should be well on the way to an infinite regress, where the solution of a problem of evil, stated in terms of evil (n), indicated the existence of an evil (n + 1), and a further problem to be solved.

4. "Evil is due to human free will."

Perhaps the most important proposed solution of the problem of evil is that evil is not to be ascribed to God at all, but to the independent actions of human beings, supposed to have been endowed by God with freedom of the will. This solution may be combined with the preceding one: first order evil (e.g., pain) may be justified as a logically necessary component in second order good (e.g., sympathy) while second order evil (e.g., cruelty) is not *justified*, but is so ascribed to human beings that God cannot be held responsible for it. This combination evades my third criticism of the preceding solution.

The free-will solution also involves the preceding solution at a higher level. To explain why a wholly good God gave men free will although it would lead to some important evils, it must be argued that it is better on the whole that men should act freely, and sometimes err, than that they should be innocent automata, acting rightly in a wholly determined way. Freedom, that is to say, is now treated as a third order good, and as being more valuable than second order goods (such as sympathy and heroism) would be if they were deterministically produced, and it is being assumed that second order evils, such as cruelty, are logically necessary accompaniments of freedom, just as pain is a logically necessary precondition of sympathy.

I think that this solution is unsatisfactory primarily because of the incoherence of the notion of freedom of the will: but I cannot discuss this topic adequately here, although some of my criticisms will touch upon it.

First I should query the assumption that second order evils are logically necessary accompaniments of freedom. I should ask this: if God has made men such that in their free choices they sometimes prefer what is good and sometimes what is evil, why could he not have made men such that they always freely choose the good? If there is no logical impossibility in a man's freely choosing the good on one, or on several occasions, there cannot be a logical impossibility in his freely choosing the good on every occasion. God was not, then, faced with a choice between making innocent automata and making beings who, in acting freely, would sometimes go wrong: there was open to him the obviously better possibility of making beings who would act freely but always go right. Clearly, his failure to avail himself of this possibility is inconsistent with his being both omnipotent and wholly good.

If it is replied that this objection is absurd, that the making of some wrong choices is logically necessary for freedom, it would seem that "freedom" must here mean complete randomness or indeterminacy, including randomness with regard to the alternatives good and evil, in other words that men's choices and consequent actions can be "free" only if they are not determined by their characters. Only on this assumption can God escape the responsibility for men's actions; for if he made them as they are, but did not determine their wrong choices, this can only be because the wrong choices are not determined by men as they are. But then if freedom is randomness, how can it be a characteristic of *will*? And, still more, how can it be the most important good? What value or merit would there be in free choices if these were random actions which were not determined by the nature of the agent?

I conclude that to make this solution plausible two different senses of "freedom" must be confused, one sense which will justify the view that freedom is a third order good, more valuable than other goods would be without it, and another sense, sheer randomness, to prevent us from ascribing to God a deci-

sion to make men such that they sometimes go wrong when he might have made them such that they would always freely go right.

This criticism is sufficient to dispose of this solution. But besides this there is a fundamental difficulty in the notion of an omnipotent God creating men with free will, for if men's wills are really free this must mean that even God cannot control them, that is, that God is no longer omnipotent. It may be objected that God's gift of freedom to men does not mean that he *cannot* control their wills, but that he always *refrains* from controlling their wills. But why, we may ask, should God refrain from controlling evil wills? Why should he not leave men free to will rightly, but intervene when he sees them beginning to will wrongly? If God could do this, but does not, and if he is wholly good, the only explanation could be that even a wrong free act of will is not really evil, that its freedom is a value which outweighs its wrongness, so that there would be a loss of value if God took away the wrongness and the freedom together. But this is utterly opposed to what theists say about sin in other contexts. The present solution of the problem of evil, then, can be maintained only in the form that God has made men so free that he *cannot* control their wills.

This leads us to what I call the "Paradox of Omnipotence": can an omnipotent being make things which he cannot subsequently control? Or, what is practically equivalent to this, can an omnipotent being make rules which then bind himself? (These are practically equivalent because any such rules could be regarded as setting certain things beyond his control, and vice versa.) The second of these formulations is relevant to the suggestions that we have already met, that an omnipotent God creates the rules of logic or causal laws, and is then bound by them.

It is clear that this is a paradox: the questions cannot be answered satisfactorily either in the affirmative or in the negative. If we answer "Yes," it follows that if God actually makes things which he cannot control, or makes rules which bind himself, he is not omnipotent once he had made them: there are *then* things which he cannot do. But if we answer "No," we are immediately asserting that there are things which he cannot do, that is to say that he is already not omnipotent.

It cannot be replied that the question which sets this paradox is not a proper question. It would make perfectly good sense to say that a human mechanic has made a machine which he cannot control: if there is any difficulty about the question it lies in the notion of omnipotence itself.

This, incidentally, shows that although we have approached this paradox from the free-will theory, it is equally a problem for a theological determinist. No one thinks that machines have free will, yet they may well be beyond the control of their makers. The determinist might reply that anyone who makes anything determines its ways of acting, and so determines its subsequent behavior: even the human mechanic does this by his *choice* of materials and structure for his machine, though he does not know all about either of these: the mechanic thus determines, though he may not foresee, his machine's actions. And since God is omniscient, and since his creation of things is total, he both determines and foresees the ways in which his creatures will act. We may grant this, but it is beside the point. The question is not whether God *originally* determined the future actions of his creatures, but whether he can *subsequently* control their actions, or whether he was able in his original creation to put things beyond his subsequent control. Even on determinist principles the answers "Yes" and "No" are equally irreconcilable with God's omnipotence.

Before suggesting a solution of this paradox, I would point out that there is a parallel Paradox of Sovereignty. Can a legal sovereign make a law restricting its own future legislative power? For example, could the British parliament make a law forbidding any future parliament to socialize banking, and also forbidding the future repeal of this law itself? Or could the British parliament, which was legally sovereign in Australia in, say, 1899, pass a valid law, or series of laws, which made it no longer sovereign in 1933? Again, neither the affirmative nor the negative answer is really satisfactory. If we were to answer "Yes," we should be admitting the validity of a law which, if it were actually made, would mean that parliament was no longer sovereign. If we were to answer "No," we should be admitting that there is a law, not logically absurd, which parliament cannot validly make, that is, that parliament is not now a legal sovereign. This paradox can be solved in the following way. We should distinguish between first order laws, that is, laws governing the actions of individuals and bodies other than the legislature,

and second order laws, that is, laws about laws, laws governing the actions of the legislature itself. Correspondingly, we should distinguish two orders of sovereignty, first order sovereignty (sovereignty [1]) which is unlimited authority to make first order laws, and second order sovereignty (sovereignty [2]) which is unlimited authority to make second order laws. If we say that parliament is sovereign we might mean that any parliament at any time has sovereignty (1), or we might mean that parliament has both sovereignty (1) and sovereignty (2) at present, but we cannot without contradiction mean both that the present parliament has sovereignty (2) and that every parliament at every time has sovereignty (1), for if the present parliament has sovereignty (2) it may use it to take away the sovereignty (1) of later parliaments. What the paradox shows is that we cannot ascribe to any continuing institution legal sovereignty in an inclusive sense.

The analogy between omnipotence and sovereignty shows that the paradox of omnipotence can be solved in a similar way. We must distinguish between first order omnipotence (omnipotence [1]), that is, unlimited power to act, and second order omnipotence (omnipotence [2]), that is, unlimited power to determine what powers to act things shall have. Then we could consistently say that God all the time has omnipotence (1), but if so no beings at any time have powers to act independently of God. Or we could say that God at one time had omnipotence (2), and used it to assign independent powers to act to certain things, so that God thereafter did not have omnipotence (1). But what the paradox shows is that we cannot consistently ascribe to any continuing being omnipotence in an inclusive sense.

An alternative solution of this paradox would be simply to deny that God is a continuing being, that any times can be assigned to his actions at all. But on this assumption (which also has difficulties of its own) no meaning can be given to the assertion that God made men with wills so free that he could not control them. The paradox of omnipotence can be avoided by putting God outside time, but the free-will solution of the problem of evil cannot be saved in this way, and equally it remains impossible to hold that an omnipotent God *binds himself* by causal or logical laws.

CONCLUSION

Of the proposed solutions of the problem of evil which we have examined, none has stood up to criticism. There may be other solutions which require examination, but this study strongly suggests that there is no valid solution of the problem which does not modify at least one of the constituent propositions in a way which would seriously affect the essential core of the theistic position.

Quite apart from the problem of evil, the paradox of omnipotence has shown that God's omnipotence must in any case be restricted in one way or another, that unqualified omnipotence cannot be ascribed to any being that continues through time. And if God and his actions are not in time, can omnipotence, or power of any sort, be meaningfully ascribed to him?

ANTONY FLEW, R. M. HARE, BASIL MITCHELL

Symposium on Theology and Falsification*

Antony Flew (1923–   ) teaches philosophy at University of Reading in England. R. M. Hare (1919–   ) is perhaps the leading British moral philosopher. He teaches at Corpus Christi College, Oxford. Basil Mitchell (1917–   ) teaches at Oriel College, Oxford.

ANTONY FLEW

Let us begin with a parable. It is a parable developed from a tale told by John Wisdom in his haunting and revelatory article 'Gods.'[1] Once upon a time two explorers came upon a clearing in the jungle. In the clearing were growing many flowers and many weeds. One explorer says, 'Some gardener must tend this plot.' The other disagrees, 'There is no gardener.' So they pitch their tents and set a watch. No gardener is ever seen. 'But perhaps he is an invisible gardener.' So they set up a barbed-wire fence. They electrify it. They patrol with bloodhounds. (For they remember how H. G. Wells's *The Invisible Man* could be both smelt and touched though he could not be seen.) But no shrieks ever suggest that some intruder has received a shock. No movements of the wire ever betray an invisible climber. The bloodhounds never give cry. Yet still the Believer is not convinced. 'But there is a gardener, invisible, intangible, insensible to electric shock, a gardener who has no scent and makes no sound, a gardener who comes secretly to look after the garden which he loves.' At last the Sceptic despairs, 'But what remains of your original assertion? Just how does what you call an invisible, intangible, eternally elusive gardener differ from an imaginary gardener or even from no gardener at all?'

In this parable we can see how what starts as an assertion, that something exists or that there is some analogy between certain complexes of phenomena, may be reduced step by step to an altogether different status, to an expression perhaps of a 'picture preference.'[2] The Sceptic says there is no gardener. The Believer says there is a gardener (but invisible, etc.). One man talks about sexual behaviour. Another man prefers to talk of Aphrodite (but knows that there is not really a superhuman person additional to, and somehow responsible for, all sexual phenomena).[3] The process of qualification may be checked at any point before the original assertion is completely withdrawn and something of that first assertion will remain (Tautology). Mr. Wells's invisible man could not, admittedly, be seen, but in all other respects he

*Antony Flew, R. M. Hare, and Basil Mitchell, "Theology and Falsification," *University*, 1950–51. Reprinted in A. Flew and A. MacIntyre, eds., *New Essays in Philosophical Theology* (New York: Macmillan, 1955), pp. 96–108. The discussion is reprinted here by permission of the Macmillan Company. First published 1955 by SCM Press Ltd. First American paperback edition published 1964.

was a man like the rest of us. But though the process of qualification may be, and of course usually is, checked in time, it is not always judiciously so halted. Someone may dissipate his assertion completely without noticing that he has done so. A fine brash hypothesis may thus be killed by inches, the death by a thousand qualifications.

And in this, it seems to me, lies the peculiar danger, the endemic evil, of theological utterance. Take such utterances as 'God has a plan,' 'God created the world,' 'God loves us as a father loves his children.' They look at first sight very much like assertions, vast cosmological assertions. Of course, this is no sure sign that they either are, or are intended to be, assertions. But let us confine ourselves to the cases where those who utter such sentences intend them to express assertions. (Merely remarking parenthetically that those who intend or interpret such utterances as crypto-commands, expressions of wishes, disguised ejaculations, concealed ethics, or as anything else but assertions, are unlikely to succeed in making them either properly orthodox or practically effective.)

Now to assert that such and such is the case is necessarily equivalent to denying that such and such is not the case.[4] Suppose then that we are in doubt as to what someone who gives vent to an utterance is asserting, or suppose that, more radically, we are sceptical as to whether he is really asserting anything at all, one way of trying to understand (or perhaps it will be to expose) his utterance is to attempt to find what he would regard as counting against, or as being incompatible with, its truth. For if the utterance is indeed an assertion, it will necessarily be equivalent to a denial of the negation of that assertion. And anything which would count against the assertion, or which would induce the speaker to withdraw it and to admit that it had been mistaken, must be part of (or the whole of) the meaning of the negation of that assertion. And to know the meaning of the negation of an assertion, is as near as makes no matter, to know the meaning of that assertion.[5] And if there is nothing which a putative assertion denies then there is nothing which it asserts either: and so it is not really an assertion. When the Sceptic in the parable asked the Believer, 'Just how does what you call an invisible, intangible, eternally elusive gardener differ from an imaginary gardener or even from no gardener at all?' he was suggesting that the Believer's earlier statement had been so eroded by qualification that it was no longer an assertion at all.

Now it often seems to people who are not religious as if there was no conceivable event or series of events the occurrence of which would be admitted by sophisticated religious people to be a sufficient reason for conceding 'there wasn't a God after all' or 'God does not really love us then.' Someone tells us that God loves us as a father loves his children. We are reassured. But then we see a child dying of inoperable cancer of the throat. His earthly father is driven frantic in his efforts to help, but his Heavenly Father reveals no obvious sign of concern. Some qualification is made—God's love is 'not a merely human love' or it is 'an inscrutable love,' perhaps—and we realize that such sufferings are quite compatible with the truth of the assertion that 'God loves us as a father (but, of course, . . .).' We are reassured again. But then perhaps we ask: what is this assurance of God's (appropriately qualified) love worth, what is this apparent guarantee really a guarantee against? Just what would have to happen not merely (morally and wrongly) to tempt but also (logically and rightly) to entitle us to say 'God does not love us' or even 'God does not exist'? I therefore put to the succeeding symposiasts the simple central question, 'What would have to occur or to have occurred to constitute for you a disproof of the love of, or of the existence of, God?'

R. M. HARE[6]

I wish to make it clear that I shall not try to defend Christianity in particular, but religion in general— not because I do not believe in Christianity, but because you cannot understand what Christianity is, until you have understood what religion is.

I must begin by confessing that, on the ground marked out by Flew, he seems to me to be completely victorious. I therefore shift my ground by relating another parable. A certain lunatic is convinced that all dons want to murder him. His friends introduce him to all the mildest and most respectable dons that they can find, and after each of them has retired, they say, 'You see, he doesn't really want to murder you; he spoke to you in the most cordial manner; surely you are convinced now?' But the lunatic replies, 'Yes, but that was only his diabolical cunning; he's really plotting against me the whole time, like the rest of them; I know it I tell you.' However many kindly dons are produced, the reaction is still the same.

Now we say that such a person is deluded. But what is he deluded about? About the truth or falsity of an assertion? Let us apply Flew's test to him. There is no behaviour of dons that can be enacted which he will accept as counting against his theory; and therefore his theory, on this test, asserts nothing. But it does not follow that there is no difference between what he thinks about dons and what most of us think about them—otherwise we should not call him a lunatic and ourselves sane, and dons would have no reason to feel uneasy about his presence in Oxford.

Let us call that in which we differ from this lunatic, our respective *bliks*. He has an insane *blik* about dons; we have a sane one. It is important to realize that we have a sane one, not no *blik* at all; for there must be two sides to any argument—if he has a wrong *blik*, then those who are right about dons must have a right one. Flew has shown that a *blik* does not consist in an assertion or system of them; but nevertheless it is very important to have the right *blik*.

Let us try to imagine what it would be like to have different *bliks* about other things than dons. When I am driving my car, it sometimes occurs to me to wonder whether my movements of the steering-wheel will always continue to be followed by corresponding alterations in the direction of the car. I have never had a steering failure, though I have had skids, which must be similar. Moreover, I know enough about how the steering of my car is made, to know the sort of thing that would have to go wrong for the steering to fail—steel joints would have to part, or steel rods break, or something—but how do I know that this won't happen? The truth is, I don't know; I just have a *blik* about steel and its properties, so that normally I trust the steering of my car; but I find it not at all difficult to imagine what it would be like to lose this *blik* and acquire the opposite one. People would say I was silly about steel; but there would be no mistaking the reality of the difference between our respective *bliks*—for example, I should never go in a motorcar. Yet I should hesitate to say that the difference between us was the difference between contradictory assertions. No amount of safe arrivals or bench-tests will remove my *blik* and restore the normal one; for my *blik* is compatible with any finite number of such tests.

It was Hume who taught us that our whole commerce with the world depends upon our *blik* about the world; and that difference between *bliks* about the world cannot be settled by observation of what

happens in the world. That was why, having performed the interesting experiment of doubting the ordinary man's *blik* about the world, and showing that no proof could be given to make us adopt one *blik* rather than another, he turned to backgammon to take his mind off the problem. It seems, indeed, to be impossible even to formulate as an assertion the normal *blik* about the world which makes me put my confidence in the future reliability of steel joints, in the continued ability of the road to support my car, and not gape beneath it revealing nothing below; in the general non-homicidal tendencies of dons; in my own continued well-being (in some sense of that word that I may not now fully understand) if I continue to do what is right according to my lights; in the general likelihood of people like Hitler coming to a bad end. But perhaps a formulation less inadequate than most is to be found in the Psalms: 'The earth is weak and all the inhabiters thereof: I bear up the pillars of it.'

The mistake of the position which Flew selects for attack is to regard this kind of talk as some sort of *explanation,* as scientists are accustomed to use the word. As such, it would obviously be ludicrous. We no longer believe in God as an Atlas—*nous n'avons pas besoin de cette hypothèse.*[7] But it is nevertheless true to say that, as Hume saw, without a *blik* there can be no explanation; for it is by our *bliks* that we decide what is and what is not an explanation. Suppose we believe that everything that happened, happened by pure chance. This would not of course be an assertion; for it is compatible with anything happening or not happening, and so, incidentally, is its contradictory. But if we had this belief, we should not be able to explain or predict or plan anything. Thus, although we should not be *asserting* anything different from those of a more normal belief, there would be a great difference between us; and this is the sort of difference that there is between those who really believe in God and those who really disbelieve in him.

The word 'really' is important, and may excite suspicion. I put it in, because when people have had a good Christian upbringing, as have most of those who now profess not to believe in any sort of religion, it is very hard to discover what they really believe. The reason why they find it so easy to think that they are not religious, is that they have never got into the frame of mind of one who suffers from the doubts to which religion is the answer. Not for them the terrors of the primitive jungle. Having abandoned some of the more picturesque fringes of religion, they think that they have abandoned the whole thing—whereas in fact they still have got, and could not live without, a religion of a comfortably substantial, albeit highly sophisticated, kind, which differs from that of many 'religious people' in little more than this, that 'religious people' like to sing Psalms about theirs—a very natural and proper thing to do. But nevertheless there may be a big difference lying behind—the difference between two people who, though side by side, are walking in different directions. I do not know in what direction Flew is walking; perhaps he does not know either. But we have had some examples recently of various ways in which one can walk away from Christianity, and there are any number of possibilities. After all, man has not changed biologically since primitive times; it is his religion that has changed, and it can easily change again. And if you do not think that such changes make a difference, get acquainted with some Sikhs and some Mussulmans of the same Punjabi stock; you will find them quite different sorts of people.

There is an important difference between Flew's parable and my own which we have not yet noticed. The explorers do not *mind* about their garden; they discuss it with interest, but not with concern. But my lunatic, poor fellow, minds about dons; and I mind about the steering of my car; it often has people in it that I care for. It is because I mind very much about what goes on in the garden in which I find myself, that I am unable to share the explorers' detachment.

BASIL MITCHELL

Flew's article is searching and perceptive, but there is, I think, something odd about his conduct of the theologian's case. The theologian surely would not deny that the fact of pain counts against the assertion that God loves men. This very incompatibility generates the most intractable of theological problems—the problem of evil. So the theologian *does* recognize the fact of pain as counting against Christian doctrine. But it is true that he will not allow it—or anything—to count decisively against it; for he is committed by his faith to trust in God. His attitude is not that of the detached observer, but of the believer.

Perhaps this can be brought out by yet another parable. In time of war in an occupied country, a member of the resistance meets one night a stranger who deeply impresses him. They spend that night together in conversation. The Stranger tells the partisan that he himself is on the side of the resistance—indeed that he is in command of it, and urges the partisan to have faith in him no matter what happens. The partisan is utterly convinced at that meeting of the Stranger's sincerity and constancy and undertakes to trust him.

They never meet in conditions of intimacy again. But sometimes the Stranger is seen helping members of the resistance, and the partisan is grateful and says to his friends, 'He is on our side.'

Sometimes he is seen in the uniform of the police handing over patriots to the occupying power. On these occasions his friends murmur against him: but the partisan still says, 'He is on our side.' He still believes that, in spite of appearances, the Stranger did not deceive him. Sometimes he asks the Stranger for help and receives it. He is then thankful. Sometimes he asks and does not receive it. Then he says, 'The Stranger knows best.' Sometimes his friends, in exasperation, say 'Well, what *would* he have to do for you to admit that you were wrong and that he is not on our side?' But the partisan refuses to answer. He will not consent to put the Stranger to the test. And sometimes his friends complain, 'Well, if *that's* what you mean by his being on our side, the sooner he goes over to the other side the better.'

The partisan of the parable does not allow anything to count decisively against the proposition 'The Stranger is on our side.' This is because he has committed himself to trust the Stranger. But he of course recognizes that the Stranger's ambiguous behavior *does* count against what he believes about him. It is precisely this situation which constitutes the trial of his faith.

When the partisan asks for help and doesn't get it, what can he do? He can (a) conclude that the Stranger is not on our side or; (b) maintain that he is on our side, but that he has reasons for withholding help.

The first he will refuse to do. How long can he uphold the second position without its becoming just silly?

I don't think one can say in advance. It will depend on the nature of the impression created by the Stranger in the first place. It will depend, too, on the manner in which he takes the Stranger's behavior. If he blandly dismisses it as of no consequence, as having no bearing upon his belief, it will be assumed that he is thoughtless or insane. And it quite obviously won't do for him to say easily, 'Oh, when used of the Stranger the phrase "is on our side" *means* ambiguous behavior of this sort.' In that case he would be like the religious man who says blandly of a terrible disaster 'It is God's will.' No, he will only be regarded as sane and reasonable in his belief, if he experiences in himself the full force of the conflict.

It is here that my parable differs from Hare's. The partisan admits that many things may and do count against his belief: whereas Hare's lunatic who has a *blik* about dons doesn't admit that anything counts against his *blik*. Nothing *can* count against *bliks*. Also the partisan has a reason for having in the first instance committed himself, viz, the character of the Stranger; whereas the lunatic has no reason for his *blik* about dons—because, of course, you can't have reasons for *bliks*.

This means that I agree with Flew that theological utterances must be assertions. The partisan is making an assertion when he says, 'The Stranger is on our side.'

Do I want to say that the partisan's belief about the Stranger is, in any sense, an explanation? I think I do. It explains and makes sense of the Stranger's behaviour: it helps to explain also the resistance movement in the context of which he appears. In each case it differs from the interpretation which the others put upon the same facts.

'God loves men' resembles 'the Stranger is on our side' (and many other significant statements, e.g. historical ones) in not being conclusively falsifiable. They can both be treated in at least three different ways: (1) As provisional hypotheses to be discarded if experience tells against them; (2) As significant articles of faith; (3) As vacuous formulae (expressing, perhaps, a desire for reassurance) to which experience makes no difference and which make no difference to life.

The Christian, once he has committed himself, is precluded by his faith from taking up the first attitude: 'Thou shalt not tempt the Lord thy God.' He is in constant danger, as Flew has observed, of slipping into the third. But he need not; and, if he does, it is a failure in faith as well as in logic.

ANTONY FLEW

It has been a good discussion: and I am glad to have helped to provoke it. But now—at least in *University*—it must come to an end: and the Editors of *University* have asked me to make some concluding remarks. Since it is impossible to deal with all the issues raised or to comment separately upon each contribution, I will concentrate on Mitchell and Hare, as representative of two very different kinds of response to the challenge made in 'Theology and Falsification.'

The challenge, it will be remembered, ran like this. Some theological utterances seem to, and are intended to, provide explanations or express assertions. Now an assertion, to be an assertion at all, must claim that things stand thus and thus; *and not otherwise*. Similarly an explanation, to be an explanation at all, must explain why this particular thing occurs; *and not something else*. Those last clauses are crucial. And yet sophisticated religious people—or so it seemed to me—are apt to overlook this, and tend to refuse to allow, not merely that anything actually does occur, but that anything conceivably could occur, which would count against their theological assertions and explanations. But in so far as they do this their supposed explanations are actually bogus, and their seeming assertions are really vacuous.

Mitchell's response to this challenge is admirably direct, straightforward, and understanding. He agrees 'that theological utterances must be assertions.' He agrees that if they are to be assertions, there must be something that would count against their truth. He agrees, too, that believers are in constant danger of transforming their would-be assertions into 'vacuous formulae.' But he takes me to task for an oddity in my 'conduct of the theologian's case. The theologian surely would not deny that the fact of pain counts against the assertion that God loves men. This very incompatibility generates the most intractable of theological problems, the problem of evil.' I think he is right. I should have made a distinction between two very different ways of dealing with what looks like evidence against the love of God: the way I stressed was the expedient of qualifying the original assertion; the way the theologian usually takes, at first, is to admit that it looks bad but to insist that there is—there must be—some explanation which will show that, in spite of appearances, there really is a God who loves us. His difficulty, it seems to me, is that he has given God attributes which rule out all possible saving explanations. In Mitchell's parable of the Stranger it is easy for the believer to find plausible excuses for ambiguous behavior: for the Stranger is a man. But suppose the Stranger is God. We cannot say that he would like to help but cannot: God is omnipotent. We cannot say that he would help if he only knew: God is omniscient. We cannot say that he is not responsible for the wickedness of others: God creates those others. Indeed an omnipotent, omniscient God must be an accessory before (and during) the fact to every human misdeed; as well as being responsible for every non-moral defect in the universe. So, though I entirely concede that Mitchell was absolutely right to insist against me that the theologian's first move is to look for an *explanation,* I still think that in the end, if relentlessly pursued, he will have to resort to the avoiding action of *qualification.* And there lies the danger of that death by a thousand qualifications, which would, I agree, constitute 'a failure in faith as well as in logic.'

Hare's approach is fresh and bold. He confesses that 'on the ground marked out by Flew, he seems to me to be completely victorious.' He therefore introduces the concept of *blik.* But while I think that there is room for some such concept in philosophy, and that philosophers should be grateful to Hare for his invention, I nevertheless want to insist that any attempt to analyse Christian religious utterances as expressions or affirmations of a *blik* rather than as (at least would-be) assertions about the cosmos is fundamentally misguided. *First,* because thus interpreted they would be entirely unorthodox. If Hare's religion really is a *blik,* involving no cosmological assertions about the nature and activities of a supposed personal creator, then surely he is not a Christian at all? *Second,* because thus interpreted, they could scarcely do the job they do. If they were not even intended as assertions then many religious activities would become fraudulent, or merely silly. If 'You ought *because* it is God's will' asserts no more than 'You ought,' then the person who prefers the former

phraseology is not really giving a reason, but a fraudulent substitute for one, a dialectical dud cheque. If 'My soul must be immortal *because* God loves his children, etc.' asserts no more than 'My soul must be immortal,' then the man who reassures himself with theological arguments for immortality is being as silly as the man who tries to clear his overdraft by writing his bank a cheque on the same account. (Of course neither of these utterances would be distinctively Christian: but this discussion never pretended to be so confined.) Religious utterances may indeed express false or even bogus assertions: but I simply do not believe that they are not both intended and interpreted to be or at any rate to presuppose assertions, at least in the context of religious practice; whatever shifts may be demanded, in another context, by the exigencies of theological apologetic.

One final suggestion. The philosophers of religion might well draw upon George Orwell's last appalling nightmare *1984* for the concept of *doublethink.* '*Doublethink* means the power of holding two contradictory beliefs simultaneously, and accepting both of them. The party intellectual knows that he is playing tricks with reality, but by the exercise of *doublethink* he also satisfies himself that reality is not violated' (*1984,* p. 220). Perhaps religious intellectuals too are sometimes driven to doublethink in order to retain their faith in a loving God in face of the reality of a heartless and indifferent world. But of this more another time, perhaps.

NOTES

1. *P.A.S.,* 1944–5, reprinted as Ch. X of *Logic and Language,* Vol. I (Blackwell, 1951), and in his *Philosophy and Psychoanalysis* (Blackwell, 1953).

2. Cf. J. Wisdom, 'Other Minds,' *Mind,* 1940; reprinted in his *Other Minds* (Blackwell, 1952).

3. Cf. Lucretius, *De Rerum Natura, II,* 655–60.

4. For those who prefer symbolism: $p \equiv \sim\sim p$.

5. For by simply negating $\sim p$ we get $p: \sim\sim p \equiv p$.

6. Some references to intervening discussion have been excised by the editors of *New Essays in Philosophical Theology.*

7. We have no need of this hypothesis.

W A L T E R   T.   S T A C E

What Is Mysticism?*

Walter T. Stace (1886–1967) served in the British Civil Service in Ceylon before moving to the United States where he taught at Princeton University from 1932 to 1955.

(1) *A New Kind of Consciousness.* In his book *The Varieties of Religious Experience* William James suggests, as a result of his psychological researches, that "our normal consciousness, rational consciousness as we call it, is but one special type of consciousness, whilst all about it, parted from it by the filmiest of screens, there lie potential forms of consciousness entirely different." This statement exactly fits mystical consciousness. It is entirely unlike our everyday consciousness and is wholly incommensurable with it. What are the fundamental characteristics or elements of our ordinary consciousness? We may think of it as being like a building with three floors. The ground floor consists of physical sensations— sights, sounds, smells, tastes, touch sensations, and organic sensations. The second floor consists of images, which we tend to think of as mental copies of sensations. The third floor is the level of the intellect, which is the faculty of concepts. On this floor we find abstract thinking and reasoning processes. This account of the mind may be open to cavil. Some philosophers think that colors, sounds, and so on, are not properly called "sensations"; others that images

are not "copies" of sensations. These fine points, however, need not seriously concern us. Our account is sufficiently clear to indicate what we are referring to when we speak of sensations, images, and concepts as being the fundamental elements of the cognitive aspects of our ordinary consciousness. Arising out of these basic cognitive elements and dependent upon them are emotions, desires, and volitions. In order to have a name for it we may call this whole structure—including sensations, images, concepts, and their attendant desires, emotions, and volitions —our *sensory-intellectual consciousness.*

Now the mystical consciousness is quite different from this. It is not merely that it involves different kinds of sensation, thought, or feeling. We are told that some insects or animals can perceive ultraviolet color and infrared color; and that some animals can hear sounds which are inaudible to us; even that some creatures may have a sixth sense quite different from any of our five senses. These are all, no doubt, kinds of sensations different from any we have. But they are still sensations. And the mystical consciousness is destitute of any sensations at all. Nor does it contain any concepts or thoughts. It is not a sensory-intellectual consciousness at all. Accordingly, it cannot be described or analyzed in terms of any of the elements of the sensory-intellectual consciousness, with which it is wholly incommensurable.

This is the reason why mystics always say that their experiences are "ineffable." All words in all languages are the products of our sensory-intellectual consciousness and express or describe its elements or

*From W. T. Stace, ed., *The Teachings of the Mystics* (New York: New American Library of World Literature, 1960), pp. 12–28. Reprinted by permission of Mrs. Blanche Stace. Section headings renumbered.

some combination of them. But as these elements (with the doubtful exception of emotions) are not found in the mystical consciousness, it is felt to be impossible to describe it in any words whatever. In spite of this the mystics do describe their experiences in roundabout ways, at the same time telling us that the words they use are inadequate. This raises a serious problem for the philosophy of mysticism, but it is not possible for us to dwell on it here.

The incommensurability of the mystical with the sensory-intellectual consciousness is also the ultimate reason why we have to exclude visions and voices, telepathy, precognition, and clairvoyance from the category of the mystical. Suppose someone sees a vision of the Virgin Mary. What he sees has shape, the shape of a woman, and color—white skin, blue raiment, a golden halo, and so on. But these are all images or sensations. They are therefore composed of elements of our sensory-intellectual consciousness. The same is true of voices. Or suppose one has a precognition of a neighbor's death. The components one is aware of—a dead man, a coffin, etc.—are composed of elements of our sensory-intellectual consciousness. The only difference is that these ordinary elements are arranged in unfamiliar patterns which we have come to think cannot occur, so that if they do occur they seem supernormal. Or the fact that such elements are combined in an unusual way so as to constitute the figure of a woman up in the clouds, perhaps surrounded by other humanlike figures with wings added to them—all this does not constitute a different *kind* of consciousness at all. And just as sensory elements of any sort are excluded from the mystical consciousness, so are conceptual elements. It is not that the thoughts in the mystical consciousness are different from those we are accustomed to. It does not include any thoughts at all. The mystic, of course, expresses thoughts about his experience after that experience is over, and he remembers it when he is back again in his sensory-intellectual consciousness. But there are no thoughts *in* the experience itself.

If anyone thinks that a kind of consciousness without either sensations, images, or thoughts, because it is totally unimaginable and inconceivable to most of us, cannot exist, he is surely being very stupid. He supposes that the possibilities of this vast universe are confined to what can be imagined and understood by the brains of average human insects who crawl on a minute speck of dust floating in illimitable space.

On the other hand, there is not the least reason to suppose that the mystical consciousness is miraculous or supernatural. No doubt it has, like our ordinary consciousness, been produced by the natural process of evolution. Its existence in a few rare men is a psychological fact of which there is abundant evidence. To deny or doubt that it exists as a psychological fact is not a reputable opinion. It is ignorance. Whether it has any value or significance beyond itself, and if so what—these, of course, are matters regarding which there can be legitimate differences of opinion. Owing to the comparative rarity of this kind of consciousness, it should no doubt be assigned to the sphere of abnormal psychology.

(2) *The Core of Mysticism.* I shall, for the present, treat it as an hypothesis that although mystical experiences may in certain respects have different characteristics in different parts of the world, in different ages, and in different cultures, there are nevertheless a number of fundamental common characteristics. I shall also assume that the agreements are more basic and important, the differences more superficial and relatively less important. This hypothesis can only be fully justified by an elaborate empirical survey of the descriptions of their experiences given by mystics and collected from all over the world. But I believe that enough of the evidence for it will appear in the following pages[1] to convince any reasonable person.

The most important, the central characteristics in which all *fully developed* mystical experiences agree, and which in the last analysis is definitive of them and serves to mark them off from other kinds of experiences, is that they involve the apprehension of *an ultimate nonsensuous unity in all things,* a oneness or a One to which neither the senses nor the reason can penetrate. In other words, it entirely transcends our sensory-intellectual consciousness.

It should be carefully noted that only fully developed mystical experiences are necessarily apprehensive of the One. Many experiences have been recorded which lack this central feature but yet possess other mystical characteristics. These are borderline cases, which may be said to shade off from the central core of cases. They have to the central core the relation which some philosophers like to call "family resemblance."

We should also note that although at this stage of our exposition we speak of mystical experience as an apprehension *of* the Unity, the mystics of the Hindu and Buddhist cultures, as well as Plotinus and many others, generally insist that this is incorrect since it supposes a division between subject and object. We should rather say that the experience *is* the One. Thus Plotinus writes: "We should not speak of seeing, but instead of seen and seer, speak boldly of a simple Unity for in this seeing we neither distinguish nor are there two." But we will leave the development of this point till later. And often for convenience' sake we shall speak of the experience *of* the unity.

(3) *Extrovertive Mysticism.* There appear to be two main distinguishable types of mystical experience, both of which may be found in all the higher cultures. One may be called extrovertive mystical experience, the other introvertive mystical experience. Both are apprehensions of the One, but they reach it in different ways. The extrovertive way looks outward and through the physical senses into the external world and finds the One there. The introvertive way turns inward, introspectively, and finds the One at the bottom of the self, at the bottom of the human personality. The latter far outweighs the former in importance both in the history of mysticism and in the history of human thought generally. The introvertive way is the major strand in the history of mysticism, the extrovertive way a minor strand. I shall only briefly refer to extrovertive mysticism and then pass on, and shall take introvertive mysticism as the main subject of this book.

The extrovertive mystic with his physical senses continues to perceive the same world of trees and hills and tables and chairs as the rest of us. But he sees these objects transfigured in such manner that the Unity shines through them. Because it includes ordinary sense perceptions, it only partially realizes the description given in section (1). For the full realization of this we have to wait for the introvertive experience. I will give two brief historical instances of extrovertive experience. The great Catholic mystic Meister Eckhart (circa 1260–1329) wrote as follows: "Here [i.e., in this experience] all blades of grass, wood, and stone, all things are One. . . . When is a man in mere understanding? When he sees one thing separated from another. And when is he above mere understanding? When he sees all in all, then a man stands above mere understanding."

In this quotation we note that according to Eckhart seeing a number of things as separate and distinct, seeing the grass and the wood and the stone as three different things, is the mark of the sensory-intellectual consciousness. For Eckhart's word "understanding" means the conceptual intellect. But if one passes beyond the sensory-intellectual consciousness into the

mystical consciousness, then one sees these three things as being "all one." However, it is evident that in this extrovertive experience the distinctions between things have not wholly disappeared. There is no doubt that what Eckhart means is that he sees the three things as distinct and separate and yet at the same time as not distinct but identical. The grass is identical with the stone, and the stone with the wood, although they are all different. Rudolph Otto, commenting on this, observes that it is as if one said that black is the same as white, white the same as black, although at the same time white remains white and black remains black. Of course this is a complete paradox. It is in fact contradictory. But we shall find that paradoxicality is one of the common characteristics of all mysticism. And it is no use saying that this is all logically impossible, and that no consciousness of this kind can exist, unless we wish, on these a priori grounds, to refuse to study the evidence—which is overwhelming.

What some mystics simply call the One other mystics often identify with God. Hence we find Jakob Böhme (1575–1624) saying much the same thing about the grass and the trees and the stones as Eckhart does, but saying that they are all God instead of just all One. The following is a statement of one of his experiences: "In this light my spirit saw through all things and into all creatures and I recognized God in grass and plants."

It is suggested that the extrovertive type of experience is a kind of halfway house to the introvertive. For the introvertive experience is wholly nonsensuous and nonintellectual. But the extrovertive experience is sensory-intellectual in so far as it still perceives physical objects but is nonsensuous and nonintellectual in so far as it perceives them as "all one."

We may sum up this short account of the extrovertive consciousness by saying that it is a perception of the world as transfigured and unified in one ultimate being. In some cultures the one being is identified with God; and since God is then perceived as the inner essence of all objects, this type of experience tends toward pantheism. But in some cultures—for example, Buddhism—the unity is not interpreted as God at all.

(4) *Introvertive Mysticism.* Suppose that one could shut all physical sensations out of one's consciousness. It may be thought that this would be easy as regards some of the senses, namely sight, hearing,

taste, and smell. One can shut one's eyes, stop up one's ears, and hold one's nose. One can avoid taste sensations by keeping one's mouth empty. But one cannot shut off tactual sensations in any simple way of this kind. And it would be even more difficult to get rid of organic sensations. However, one can perhaps suppose it possible somehow to thrust tactual and organic sensations out of conscious awareness—perhaps into the unconscious. Mystics do not, as far as I know, descend to the ignominious level of holding their noses and stopping their ears. My only point is that it is possible to conceive of getting rid of all sensations, and in one way or other mystics claim that they do this.

Suppose now, after this has been done, we next try to get rid of all sensuous *images* from our minds. This is very difficult. Most people, try as they will not to picture anything at all, will find vague images floating about in consciousness. Suppose, however, that it is possible to suppress all images. And suppose finally that we manage to stop all thinking and reasoning. Having got rid of the whole empirical content of sensations, images, and thoughts, presumably all emotions and desires and volitions would also disappear, since they normally exist only as attachments to the cognitive content. What, then, would be left of consciousness? What would happen? It is natural to suppose that with all the elements of consciousness gone consciousness itself would lapse and the subject would fall asleep or become *un*conscious.

Now it happens to be the case that this total suppression of the whole empirical content of consciousness is precisely what the introvertive mystic claims to achieve. And he claims that what happens is not that all consciousness disappears but that only the ordinary sensory-intellectual consciousness disappears and is replaced by an entirely new kind of consciousness, the mystical consciousness. Naturally we now ask whether any description of this new consciousness can be given. But before trying to answer that difficult question, I propose to turn aside for a brief space to speak about the methods which mystics use to suppress sensuous images, and thinking, so as to get rid of their sensory-intellectual consciousness. There are the Yoga techniques of India; and Christian mystics in Catholic monasteries also evolved their own methods. The latter usually call their techniques ''prayers,'' but they are not prayers in the vulgar sense of asking God for things; they are much more like the ''meditation'' and ''concentration'' of Yogis than may be commonly supposed. This is too vast a subject to be discussed in detail here. But I will give two elementary illustrations.

Everyone has heard of the breathing exercises undertaken by the Yogis of India seeking samadhi—samadhi being the Indian name for mystical consciousness. What is this special method of breathing, and what is it supposed to accomplish? The theory of the matter is, I understand, something like this: It is practically impossible, or at least very difficult, to stop all sensing, imaging, and thinking by a forcible act of the will. What comes very near to it, however, is to concentrate one's attention on some single point or object so that all other mental content falls away and there is left nothing but the single point of consciousness. If this can be done, then ultimately that single point will itself disappear because contrast is necessary for our ordinary consciousness, and if there is only one point of consciousness left, there is nothing to form a contrast to it.

The question then is: On what single thing should one concentrate? A simple way is to concentrate on the stream of one's own breath. Simple instructions which I have heard given are these. One first adopts a suitable physical position with spine and neck perfectly erect. Then breathe in and out slowly, evenly, and smoothly. Concentrate your attention on this and nothing else. Some aspirants, I believe, count their breaths, 1, 2, 3, . . . up to 10, and then begin the count again. Continue this procedure till you attain the desired results.

A second method is to keep repeating in one's mind some short formula of words over and over again till the words lose all meaning. So long as they carry meaning, of course, the mind is still occupied with the thought of this meaning. But when the words become meaningless there is nothing left of consciousness except the monotonous sound image, and that too, like the consciousness of one's breath, will in the end disappear. There is an interesting connection between this method and a remark made by the poet Tennyson. From childhood up Tennyson had frequent mystical experiences. They came to him spontaneously, without effort, and unsought. But he mentions the curious fact that he could induce them at will by the odd procedure of repeating his own name over and over again to himself. I know of no evidence that he studied mysticism enough to understand the theory of his own procedure, which would presumably be that the constantly repeated sound image served as the focus of the required one-pointed attention.

This leads to another curious reflection. Mystics who follow the procedure of constantly repeating a verbal formula often, I believe, tend to choose some religious set of words, for instance a part of the Lord's Prayer or a psalm. They probably imagine that these uplifting and inspirational words will carry them upwards toward the divine. But Tennyson's procedure suggests that any nonsense words would probably do as well. And this seems to agree with the general theory of concentration. It doesn't seem to matter what is chosen as the single point of concentration, whether it be one's breathing, or the sound of one's own name, or one's navel, or anything else, provided only it serves to shut off all other mental content.

Another point on which mystics usually insist in regard to spiritual training is what they call "detachment." Emphasis on this is found just as much in Hinduism and Buddhism as in Christianity. What is sought is detachment from desire, the uprooting of desire, or at any rate of all self-centered desires. The exact psychology of the matter presents great difficulties. In Christian mysticism the idea of detachment is usually given a religious and moral twist by insisting that it means the destruction of self-will or any kind of self-assertiveness, especially the rooting out of pride and the attainment of absolute humility. In non-Christian mysticism detachment does not usually get this special slant. But in the mysticism of all cultures detachment from desires for sensations and sensory images is emphasized.

We will now return to the main question. Supposing that the sensory-intellectual consciousness has been successfully supplanted by the mystical consciousness, can we find in the literatures of the subject any descriptions of this consciousness that will give us any idea of what it is like? The answer is that although mystics frequently say that their experiences are ineffable and indescribable, they nevertheless do often in fact describe them, and one can find plenty of such descriptive statements in the literature. They are usually extremely short—perhaps only three or four lines. And frequently they are indirect and not in the first person singular. Mystics more often than not avoid direct references to themselves.

I will give here a famous description which occurs in the Mandukya Upanishad. The Upanishads are supposed to have been the work of anonymous forest seers in India who lived between three thousand and twenty-five hundred years ago. They are among the oldest records of mysticism in the world. But they are of an unsurpassable depth of spirituality. For long ages and for countless millions of men in the East they have been, and they remain, the supreme source of the spiritual life. Of the introvertive mystical consciousness the Mandukya says that it is "beyond the senses, beyond the understanding, beyond all expression. . . . It is the pure unitary consciousness, wherein awareness of the world and of multiplicity is completely obliterated. It is ineffable peace. It is the Supreme Good. It is One without a second. It is the Self."

It will repay us, not to just slur over this passage, but to examine it carefully clause by clause. The first sentence is negative, telling us only what the experience is *not*. It is "beyond the senses, beyond the understanding." That is to say, it is beyond the sensory-intellectual consciousness; and there are in it no elements of sensation or sensuous imagery and no elements of conceptual thought. After these negatives there comes the statement that "it is the unitary consciousness, wherein all awareness of multiplicity has been obliterated." The core of the experience is thus described as an undifferentiated unity—a oneness or unity in which there is no internal division, no multiplicity.

I happen to have quoted a Hindu source. But one can find exactly the same thing in Christian mysticism. For instance the great Flemish mystic Jan van Ruysbroeck (1293–1381) says of what he calls "the God-seeing man" that "his spirit is undifferentiated and without distinction, and therefore it feels nothing but the unity." We see that the very words of the faithful Catholic are almost identical with those of the ancient Hindu, and I do not see how it can be doubted that they are describing the same experience. Not only in Christianity and Hinduism but everywhere else we find that the essence of the experience is that it is an *undifferentiated unity,* though each culture and each religion interprets this undifferentiated unity in terms of its own creeds or dogmas.

It may be objected that "undifferentiated unity" is a conceptual thought, and this is inconsistent with our statement that the experience is wholly nonintellectual. The answer is that concepts such as "one," "unity," "undifferentiated," "God," "Nirvana," etc., are only applied to the experience *after* it has passed and when it is being *remembered*. None can be applied during the experience itself.

The passage of the Upanishad goes on to say that the undifferentiated unity "is the Self." Why is this? Why is the unity now identified with the Self? The answer is plain. We started with the full self or mind of our ordinary everyday consciousness. What was it full of? It was full of the multiplicity of sensations, thoughts, desires, and the rest. But the mind was not merely this multiplicity. These disparate elements were held together in a unity, the unity of the single mind or self. A multiplicity without a unity in which the multiple elements are together is inconceivable —e.g., many objects in one space. Now when we emptied all the multiple contents out of this unity of the self what is left, according to the Upanishad, is the unity of the self, the original unity minus its contents. And this is the self. The Upanishads go further than this. They always identify this individual self with the Universal Self, the soul of the world. [. . . But] for the moment we may continue to think in terms of the individual self, the pure ego of you or me. The undifferentiated unity is thought to be the pure ego.

I must draw the reader's attention to several facts about this situation. In the first place it flatly contradicts what David Hume said in a famous passage about the self.[2] He said that when he looked introspectively into himself and searched for the I, the self, the ego, all he could ever introspect was the multiplicity of the sensations, images, thoughts, and feelings. He could never observe any I, any pure self apart from its contents, and he inferred that the I is a fiction and does not really exist. But now a vast body of empirical evidence, that of the mystics from all over the world, affirms that Hume was simply mistaken on a question of psychological fact, and that it is possible to get rid of all the mental contents and find the pure self left over and to experience this. This evidence need not mean that the self is a thing or a "substance," but can be taken as implying that it is a pure unity, the sort of being which Kant called the "transcendental unity" of the self.

The next thing to note is that the assertion of this new kind of consciousness is completely paradoxical. One way of bringing out the paradox is to point out that what we are left with here, when the contents of consciousness are gone, is a kind of consciousness which has no objects. It is not a consciousness *of* anything, but yet it is still consciousness. For the contents of our ordinary daily consciousness, the colors, sounds, wishes, thoughts are the same as the objects of consciousness, so that when the contents are gone the objects are gone. This consciousness of the mystics is not even a consciousness of consciousness, for then there would be a duality which is incompatible with the idea of an undifferentiated unity. In India it is called *pure* consciousness. The word "pure" is used in somewhat the same sense as Kant used it— meaning "without any empirical contents."

Another aspect of the paradox is that this pure consciousness is simultaneously both positive and negative, something and nothing, a fullness and an emptiness. The positive side is that it is an actual and positive consciousness. Moreover, all mystics affirm that it is pure peace, beatitude, joy, bliss, so that it has a positive affective tone. The Christians call it "the peace of God which passeth all understanding." The Buddhists call it Nirvana. But although it has this positive character, it is quite correct to say also that when we empty out all objects and contents of the mind *there is nothing whatever left*. That is the negative side of the paradox. What is left is sheer Emptiness. This is fully recognized in all mystical literature. In Mahayan Buddhism this total emptiness of the mystical consciousness is called the Void. In Christian mysticism the experience is identified with God. And this causes Eckhart and others to say that God, or the Godhead, is pure Nothingness, is a "desert," or "wilderness," and so on. Usually the two sides of the paradox are expressed in metaphors. The commonest metaphor for the positive side is light and for the negative side darkness. This is the darkness of God. It is called darkness because all distinctions disappear in it just as all distinctions disappear in a physical darkness.

We must not say that what we have here is a light *in* the darkness. For that would be no paradox. The paradox is that the light *is* the darkness, and the darkness *is* the light. This statement can be well documented from the literature of different cultures. I will give two examples, one from Christianity, one from Buddhism—and from the Buddhism of Tibet of all places in the world. Dionysius the Areopagite, a Christian, speaks of God as "the dazzling obscurity which outshines all brilliance with the intensity of its darkness." And the Tibetan book of the Dead puts the same paradox in the words, "the clear light of the Void." In Dionysius we see that the obscurity, or the darkness, *is* the brilliance, and in the Tibetan book we see that the Void itself *is* a clear light.

(5) *Mysticism and Religion*. Most writers on mysticism seem to take it for granted that mystical experience is a religious experience, and that mysticism is necessarily a religious phenomenon. They seem to think that mysticism and religious mysticism are one and the same thing. But this is far from being correct. It is true that there is an important connection between mysticism and religion, but it is not nearly so direct and immediate as most writers have seemed to think, nor can it be simply taken for granted as an obvious fact.

There are several grounds for insisting that intrinsically and in itself mystical experience is not a religious phenomenon at all and that its connection with religions is subsequent and even adventitious. In the first place, it seems to be clear that if we strip the mystical experience of all intellectual interpretation such as that which identifies it with God, or with the Absolute, or with the soul of the world, what is left is simply the undifferentiated unity. Now what is there that is religious about an undifferentiated unity? The answer seems to be, in the first instance, "Nothing at all." There seems to be nothing religious about an undifferentiated unity as such.

In the theistic religions of the West, in Christianity, Judaism, and Islam, the experience of the undifferentiated unity is interpreted as "union with God." But this is an interpretation and is not the experience itself. It is true that some Christian mystics, such as St. Teresa of Avila, invariably speak simply of having experienced "union with God," and do not talk about an undifferentiated unity. St. Teresa did not have a sufficiently analytical mind to distinguish between the experience and its interpretation. But other Christian mystics who are more analytically minded, such as Eckhart and Ruysbroeck, do speak of the undifferentiated unity.

These considerations are further underlined by the fact that quite different interpretations of the same experience are given in different cultures. The undifferentiated unity is interpreted by Eckhart and Ruysbroeck in terms of the Trinitarian conception of God, but by Islamic mystics as the unitarian God of Islam, and by the leading school of the Vedantists as a more impersonal Absolute. And when we come to Buddhism we find that the experience is not interpreted as any kind of God at all. For the Buddhist it becomes the Void or Nirvana. Buddha denied the existence of a Supreme Being altogether. It is often said that Buddhism is atheistic. And whether this description of Buddhism is true or not, it is certainly the case that there can

exist an atheistic mysticism, a mystical experience naked and not clothed in any religious garb.

In view of these facts, we have a problem on our hands. Why is it that, in spite of exceptions, mysticism *usually* takes on some religious form and is usually found in connection with a definitely religious culture and as being a part of some definite religion? The following are, I think, the main reasons.

First, there is a very important feature of the introvertive mystical experience which I have not mentioned yet. I refer to the experience of the "melting away" into the Infinite of one's own individuality. Such phrases as "melting away," "fading away," "passing away" are found in the mystical literature of Christianity, Islam, Hinduism, and Buddhism. Among the Sufis of Islam there is a special technical term for it. It is called fanā. It must be insisted that this is not an inference or an interpretation or a theory or a speculation. It is an actual experience. The individual, as it were, directly experiences the disappearance of his own individuality, its fading away into the Infinite. To document this, one could quote from Eckhart, or from the Upanishads or the Sufis. But I believe I can bring home the point to a modern reader better by quoting a modern author. I referred earlier to the fact that Tennyson had frequent mystical experiences. His account of them is quoted by William James in his *The Varieties of Religious Experience*. Tennyson wrote, "All at once, as it were out of the intensity of the consciousness of individuality, individuality itself seemed to dissove and fade away into boundless being. . . . the loss of personality, if such it were, seeming no extinction but the only true life." "Boundless being" seems to have the same meaning as "the Infinite." The Infinite is in most minds identified with the idea of God. We are finite beings, God is the only Infinite Being. One can see at once, therefore, how this experience of the dissolution of one's own individuality, its being merged into the Infinite, takes on a religious meaning. In theistic cultures the experience of melting away into boundless being is interpreted as union with God.

A second reason for the connection between mysticism and religion is that the undifferentiated unity is necessarily thought of by the mystics as being *beyond space and beyond time*. For it is without any internal division or multiplicity of parts, whereas the essence of time is its division into an endless multitude of successive parts, and the essence of space is its division into a multitude of parts lying side by side. Therefore the undifferentiated unity, being without any multiplicity of parts, is necessarily spaceless and timeless. Being timeless is the same as being eternal. Hence Eckhart is constantly telling us that the mystical experience transcends time and is an experience of "the Eternal Now." But in religious minds the Eternal, like the Infinite, is another name for God. Hence the mystical experience is thought of as an experience of God.

A third reason for this identification of the undifferentiated unity with God lies in the emotional side of the experience. It is the universal testimony of the mystics that their kind of consciousness brings feelings of an exalted peace, blessedness, and joy. It becomes identified with the peace of God, the gateway of the Divine, the gateway of salvation. This is also why in Buddhism, though the experience is not personified or called God, it nevertheless becomes Nirvana which is the supreme goal of the Buddhist religious life.

Thus we see that mysticism naturally, though not necessarily, becomes intimately associated with whatever is the religion of the culture in which it appears. It is, however, important to realize that it does not favor any particular religion. Mystical experience in iself does not have any tendency to make a man a Christian or a Buddhist. Into the framework of what creed he will fit his experience will tend to depend mostly on the culture in which he lives. In a Buddhist country the mystic interprets his experience as a glimpse of Nirvana, in a Christian country he may interpret it as union with God or even (as in Eckhart) as penetrating into the Godhead which is beyond God. Or if he is a highly sophisticated modern individual, who has been turned by his education into a religious skeptic, he may remain a skeptic as regards the dogmas of the different religions; he may allow his mystical experience to remain naked without any clothing of creeds or dogmas; but he is likely at the same time to feel that in that experience he has found something *sacred*. And this feeling of the sacred may quite properly be called "religious" feeling though it does not clothe itself in any dogmas. And this alone may be enough to uplift his ideals and to revolutionize his life and to give it meaning and purpose.

(6) *The Ethical Aspects of Mysticism*. It is sometimes asserted that mysticism is merely an escape from life and from its duties and responsibilities. The mystic, it is said, retreats into a private ecstasy of bliss, turns his back on the world, and forgets not only his own sorrows but the needs and sorrows of his fellow men. In short, his life is essentially selfish.

It is possible that there have been mystics who deserved this kind of condemnation. To treat the bliss of the mystical consciousness as an end in itself is certainly a psychological possibility. And no doubt there have been men who have succumbed to this temptation. But this attitude is not the mystic ideal, and it is severely condemned by those who are most representative of the mystics themselves. For instance, St. John of the Cross condemns it as "spiritual gluttony." Eckhart tells us that if a man were in mystical ecstasy and knew of a poor man who needed his help, he should leave his ecstasy in order to go and serve the poor man. The Christian mystics especially have always emphasized that mystical union with God brings with it an intense and burning love of God which must needs overflow into the world in the form of love for our fellow men; and that this must show itself in deeds of charity, mercy, and self-sacrifice, and not merely in words.

Some mystics have gone beyond this and have insisted that the mystical consciousness is the secret fountain of all love, human as well as divine; and that since love in the end is the only source of true moral activity, therefore mysticism is the source from which ethical values ultimately flow. For all selfishness and cruelty and evil result from the separateness of one human being from another. This separateness of individuals breeds egoism and the war of all against all. But in the mystical consciousness all distinctions disappear and therefore the distinction between "I" and "you" and "he" and "she." This is the mystical and metaphysical basis of love, namely the realization that my brother and I are one, and that therefore his sufferings are my sufferings and his happiness is my happiness. This reveals itself dimly in the psychological phenomena of sympathy and more positively in actual love. For one who had no touch of the mystical vision all men would be islands. And in the end it is because of mysticism that it is possible to say that "no man is an island" and that on the contrary every man is "a part of the main."

(7) *Alternative Interpretations of Mysticism*. We have seen that the same experience may be interpreted in terms of different religious creeds. There is also another set of alternative interpretations which we ought to mention. We may believe that the mystic really is in touch, as he usually claims, with some being

greater than himself, some spiritual Infinite which transcends the temporal flux of things. Or we may, on the other hand, adopt the alternative solution of the skeptic who will think that the mystical consciousness is entirely subjective and imports nothing outside itself. My own vote would be cast for the former solution. I would agree with the words of Arthur Koestler [. . . when] he speaks of a higher order of reality which for us is like a text written in invisible ink. "I also liked to think," he says, "that the founders of religions, prophets, saints and seers had at moments been able to read a fragment of the invisible text; after which they had so much padded, dramatised and ornamented it, that they themselves could no longer tell what parts of it were authentic."

But I wish to point out that even if one should choose the skeptical alternative and suppose that the mystical consciousness reveals no reality outside its owner's brain, one is far from having disposed of mysticism as some worthless delusion which ought to be got rid of. Even if it is wholly subjective, it still reveals something which is supremely great in human life. It is still the peace which passeth all understanding. It is still the gateway to salvation—not, I mean, in a future life, but as the highest beatitude that a man can reach in this life, and out of which the greatest deeds of love can flow. But it must be added, of course, that it belongs among those things of which Spinoza wrote in those famous words: "If the road which I have shown is very difficult, it yet can be discovered. And clearly it must be very hard if it is so rarely found. For how could it be that it is neglected by practically all, if salvation . . . could be found without difficulty. But all excellent things are as difficult as they are rare."

NOTES

1. [Stace refers here to the anthology for which this essay was an introduction.—Ed.]

2. [In this volume, see p. 299.—Ed.]

B E R T R A N D   R U S S E L L

Critique of Mysticism*

Bertrand Russell (1872–1970) wrote over thirty important books in logic, mathematics, social theory, and philosophy.

Ought we to admit that there is available, in support of religion, a source of knowledge which lies outside science and may properly be described as "revelation"? This is a difficult question to argue, because those who believe that truths have been revealed to them profess the same kind of certainty in regard to them that we have in regard to objects of sense. We believe the man who has seen things through the telescope that we have never seen; why, then, they ask, should we not believe them when they report things that are to them equally unquestionable?

It is, perhaps, useless to attempt an argument such as will appeal to the man who has himself enjoyed mystic illumination. But something can be said as to whether we others should accept this testimony. In the first place, it is not subject to the ordinary tests. When a man of science tells us the result of an experiment, he also tells us how the experiment was performed; others can repeat it, and if the result is not confirmed it is not accepted as true; but many men might put themselves into the situation in which the mystic's vision occurred without obtaining the same revelation. To this it may be answered that a man must use the appropriate sense: a telescope is useless to a man who keeps his eyes shut. The argument as to the credibility of the mystic's testimony may be prolonged almost indefinitely. Science should

*From Bertrand Russell, *Religion and Science,* Home University Library 178 (New York: Oxford University Press, 1961), pp. 177–189. First published in 1935. Reprinted by permission of the publisher.

be neutral, since the argument is a scientific one, to be conducted exactly as an argument would be conducted about an uncertain experiment. Science depends upon perception and inference; its credibility is due to the fact that the perceptions are such as any observer can test. The mystic himself may be certain that he *knows,* and has no need of scientific tests; but those who are asked to accept his testimony will subject it to the same kind of scientific tests as those applied to men who say they have been to the North Pole. Science, as such, should have no expectation, positive or negative, as to the result.

The chief argument in favour of the mystics is their agreement with each other. "I know nothing more remarkable," says Dean Inge, "than the unanimity of the mystics, ancient, mediaeval, and modern, Protestant, Catholic, and even Buddhist or Mohammedan, though the Christian mystics are the most trustworthy." I do not wish to underrate the force of this argument, which I acknowledged long ago in a book called *Mysticism and Logic.* The mystics vary greatly in their capacity of giving verbal expression to their experiences, but I think we may take it that those who succeeded best all maintain: (1) that all division and separateness is unreal, and that the universe is a single indivisible unity; (2) that evil is illusory, and that the illusion arises through falsely regarding a part as self-subsistent; (3) that time is unreal, and that reality is eternal, not in the sense of being everlasting, but in the sense of being wholly outside time. I do not pretend that this is a complete account of the matters on which all mystics concur, but the three propositions that I have mentioned may serve as representatives of the whole. Let us now imagine ourselves a jury in a law-court, whose business it is to decide on the credibility of the witnesses who make these three somewhat surprising assertions.

We shall find, in the first place, that, while the witnesses agree up to a point, they disagree totally when that point is passed, although they are just as certain as when they agree. Catholics, but not Protestants, may have visions in which the Virgin appears; Christians and Mohammedans, but not Buddhists, may have great truths revealed to them by the Archangel Gabriel; the Chinese mystics of the Tao tell us, as a direct result of their central doctrine, that all government is bad, whereas most European and Mohammedan mystics, with equal

confidence, urge submission to constituted authority. As regards the points where they differ, each group will argue that the other groups are untrustworthy; we might, therefore, if we were content with a mere forensic triumph, point out that most mystics think most other mystics mistaken on most points. They might, however, make this only half a triumph by agreeing on the greater importance of the matters about which they are at one, as compared with those as to which their opinions differ. We will, in any case, assume that they have composed their differences, and concentrated the defence at these three points—namely, the unity of the world, the illusory nature of evil, and the unreality of time. What test can we, as impartial outsiders, apply to their unanimous evidence?

As men of scientific temper, we shall naturally first ask whether there is any way by which we can ourselves obtain the same evidence at first hand. To this we shall receive various answers. We may be told that we are obviously not in a receptive frame of mind, and that we lack the requisite humility; or that fasting and religious meditation are necessary; or (if our witness is Indian or Chinese) that the essential prerequisite is a course of breathing exercises. I think we shall find that the weight of experimental evidence is in favour of this last view, though fasting also has been frequently found effective. As a matter of fact, there is a definite physical discipline, called yoga, which is practised in order to produce the mystic's certainty, and which is recommended with much confidence by those who have tried it.[1] Breathing exercises are its most essential feature, and for our purposes we may ignore the rest.

In order to see how we could test the assertion that yoga gives insight, let us artificially simplify this assertion. Let us suppose that a number of people assure us that if, *for a certain time,* we breathe in a certain way, we shall become convinced that time is unreal. Let us go further, and suppose that, having tried their recipe, we have ourselves experienced a state of mind such as they describe. But now, having returned to our normal mode of respiration, we are not quite sure whether the vision was to be believed. How shall we investigate this question?

First of all, what can be meant by saying that time is unreal? If we really mean what we say, we must mean that such statements as "this is before that" are mere empty noise, like "twas brillig." If we suppose anything less than this—as, for example, that there is a relation between events which puts them in the same order as the relation of earlier and later, but that it is a different relation—we shall not have made any assertion that makes any real change in our outlook. It will be merely like supposing that the Iliad was not written by Homer, but by another man of the same name. We have to suppose that there are no "events" at all; there must be only the one vast whole of the universe, embracing whatever is real in the misleading appearance of a temporal procession. There must be nothing in reality corresponding to the apparent distinction between earlier and later events. To say that we are born, and then grow, and then die, must be just as false as to say that we die, then grow small, and finally are born. The truth of what seems an individual life is merely the illusory isolation of one element in the timeless and indivisible being of the universe. There is no distinction between improvement and deterioration, no difference between sorrows that end in happiness and happiness that ends in sorrow. If you find a corpse with a dagger in it, it makes no difference whether the man died of the wound or the dagger was plunged in after death. Such a view, if true, puts an end, not only to science, but to prudence, hope, and effort; it is incompatible with worldly wisdom, and— what is more important to religion—with morality.

Most mystics, of course, do not accept these conclusions in their entirety, but they urge doctrines from which these conclusions inevitably follow. Thus Dean Inge rejects the kind of religion that appeals to evolution, because it lays too much stress upon a temporal process. "There is no law of progress, and there is no universal progress," he says. And again: "The doctrine of automatic and universal progress, the lay religion of many Victorians, labours under the disadvantage of being almost the only philosophical theory which can be definitely disproved." On this matter, which I shall discuss at a later stage, I find myself in agreement with the Dean, for whom, on many grounds, I have a very high respect. But he naturally does not draw from his premises all the inferences which seem to me to be warranted.

It is important not to caricature the doctrine of mysticism, in which there is, I think, a core of wisdom. Let us see how it seeks to avoid the extreme consequences which seem to follow from the denial of time.

The philosophy based upon mysticism has a great tradition, from Parmenides to Hegel. Parmenides says: "What is, is uncreated and indestructible; for it is complete, immovable, and without end. Nor was it ever, nor will it be; for now *it is,* all at once, a continuous one."[2] He introduced into metaphysics the distinction between reality and appearance, or the way of truth and the way of opinion, as he calls them. It is clear that whoever denies the reality of time must introduce some such distinction, since obviously the world *appears* to be in time. It is also clear that, if everyday experience is not to be *wholly* illusory, there must be some relation between appearance and the reality behind it. It is at this point, however, that the greatest difficulties arise: if the relation between appearance and reality is made too intimate, all the unpleasant features of appearance will have their unpleasant counterparts in reality, while if the relation is made too remote, we shall be unable to make inferences from the character of appearance to that of reality, and reality will be left a vague Unknowable, as with Herbert Spencer. For Christians, there is the related difficulty of avoiding pantheism: if the world is *only* apparent, God created nothing, and the reality corresponding to the world is a part of God; but if the world is in any degree real and distinct from God, we abandon the wholeness of everything, which is an essential doctrine of mysticism, and we are compelled to suppose that, in so far as the world is real, the evil which it contains is also real. Such difficulties make thoroughgoing mysticism very difficult for an orthodox Christian. As the Bishop of Birmingham says: "All forms of pantheism . . . as it seems to me, must be rejected because, if man is actually a part of God, the evil in man is also in God."

All this time I have been supposing that we are a jury, listening to the testimony of the mystics, and trying to decide whether to accept or reject it. If, when they deny the reality of the world of sense, we took them to mean "reality" in the ordinary sense of the law-courts, we should have no hesitation in rejecting what they say, since we should find that it runs counter to all other testimony, and even to their own in their mundane moments. We must therefore look for some other sense. I believe that, when the mystics contrast "reality" with "appearance," the word "reality" has not a logical, but an emotional, significance: it means what is, in some sense, important. When it is said that time is "unreal," what should be said is that, in some sense and on some occasions, it is important to conceive the universe as a whole, as the Creator, if He existed, must have conceived it in deciding to create it. When so conceived, all process is within one completed whole; past, present, and future, all exist, in some sense, together, and the present does not have that pre-eminent reality which it has to our usual ways of apprehending the world. If this interpretation is accepted, mysticism expresses an emotion, not a fact; it does not assert anything, and therefore can be neither confirmed nor contradicted by science. The fact that mystics do make assertions is owing to their inability to separate emotional importance from scientific validity. It is, of course, not to be expected that they will accept this view, but it is the only one, so far as I can see, which, while admitting something of their claim, is not repugnant to the scientific intelligence.

The certainty and partial unanimity of mystics is no conclusive reason for accepting their testimony on a matter of fact. The man of science, when he wishes others to see what he has seen, arranges his microscope or telescope; that is to say, he makes changes in the external world, but demands of the observer only normal eyesight. The mystic, on the other hand, demands changes in the observer, by fasting, by breathing exercises, and by a careful abstention from external observation. (Some object to such discipline, and think that the mystic illumination cannot be artificially achieved; from a scientific point of view, this makes their case more difficult to test than that of those who rely on yoga. But nearly all agree that fasting and an ascetic life are helpful.) We all know that opium, hashish, and alcohol produce certain effects on the observer, but as we do not think these effects admirable we take no account of them in our theory of the universe. They may even, sometimes, reveal fragments of truth; but we do not regard them as sources of general wisdom. The drunkard who sees snakes does not imagine, afterwards, that he has had a revelation of a reality hidden from others, though

some not wholly dissimilar belief must have given rise to the worship of Bacchus. In our own day, as William James related,[3] there have been people who considered that the intoxication produced by laughing-gas revealed truths which are hidden at normal times. From a scientific point of view, we can make no distinction between the man who eats little and sees heaven and the man who drinks much and sees snakes. Each is in an abnormal physical condition, and therefore has abnormal perceptions. Normal perceptions, since they have to be useful in the struggle for life, must have some correspondence with fact; but in abnormal perceptions there is no reason to expect such correspondence, and their testimony, therefore, cannot outweigh that of normal perception.

The mystic emotion, if it is freed from unwarranted beliefs, and not so overwhelming as to remove a man wholly from the ordinary business of life, may give something of very great value—the same kind of thing, though in a heightened form, that is given by contemplation. Breadth and calm and profundity may all have their source in this emotion, in which, for the moment, all self-centred desire is dead, and the mind becomes a mirror for the vastness of the universe. Those who have had this experience, and believe it to be bound up unavoidably with assertions about the nature of the universe, naturally cling to these assertions. I believe myself that the assertions are inessential, and that there is no reason to believe them true. I cannot admit any method of arriving at truth except that of science, but in the realm of the emotions I do not deny the value of the experiences which have given rise to religion. Through association with false beliefs, they have led to much evil as well as good; freed from this association, it may be hoped that the good alone will remain.

NOTES

1. As regards yoga in China, see Waley, *The Way and Its Power*, pp. 117–18.

2. Quoted from Burnet's *Early Greek Philosophy*, p. 199.

3. See his *Varieties of Religious Experience*.

Reason and Faith

BLAISE PASCAL

The Wager*

Blaise Pascal (1623–1662) was a French mathematician and philosopher.

Infinite—nothing.—Our soul is cast into a body, where it finds number, time, dimension. Thereupon it reasons, and calls this nature, necessity, and can believe nothing else.

Unity joined to infinity adds nothing to it, no more than one foot to an infinite measure. The finite is annihilated in the presence of the infinite, and becomes a pure nothing. So our spirit before God, so our justice before divine justice. There is not so great disproportion between our justice and that of God, as between unity and infinity.

The justice of God must be vast like His compassion. Now, justice to the outcast is less vast, and ought less to offend our feelings than mercy towards the elect.

We know that there is an infinite, and are ignorant of its nature. As we know it to be false that numbers are finite, it is therefore true that there is an infinity in number. But we do not know what it is. It is false that it is even, it is false that it is odd; for the addition of a unit can make no change in its nature. Yet it is a number, and every number is odd or even (this is certainly true of every finite number). So we may well know that there is a God without knowing what He is. Is there not one substantial truth, seeing there are so many things which are not the truth itself?

We know then the existence and nature of the finite, because we also are finite and have extension. We know the existence of the infinite, and are ignorant of its nature, because it has extension like us, but not limits like us. But we know neither the existence nor the nature of God, because He has neither extension nor limits.

But by faith we know His existence; in glory we shall know His nature. Now, I have already shown that we may well know the existence of a thing, without knowing its nature.

Let us now speak according to natural lights.

If there is a God, He is infinitely incomprehensible, since, having neither parts nor limits, He has no affinity to us. We are then incapable of knowing either what He is or if He is. This being so, who will dare to undertake the decision of the question? Not we, who have no affinity to Him.

Who then will blame Christians for not being able to give a reason for their belief, since they profess a religion for which they cannot give a reason? They declare, in expounding it to the world, that it is a foolishness, *stultitiam;* and then you complain that they do not prove it! If they proved it, they would not keep their words; it is in lacking proofs, that they are not lacking in sense. "Yes, but although this excuses those who offer it as such, and take away from them the blame of putting it forward without reason, it does not excuse those who receive it." Let us then examine this point, and say, "God is, or He is not." But to which side shall we incline? Reason can decide nothing here. There is an infinite chaos which separates us. A game is being played at the extremity of

*From Blaise Pascal, *Thoughts,* trans. W. F. Trotter (New York: P. F. Collier & Son, 1910), p. 233. This material reprinted with the kind permission of Crowell Collier and Macmillan, Inc.

this infinite distance where heads or tails will turn up. What will you wager? According to reason, you can do neither the one thing nor the other; according to reason, you can defend neither of the propositions.

Do not then reprove for error those who have made a choice; for you know nothing about it. "No, but I blame them for having made, not this choice, but a choice; for again both he who chooses heads and he who chooses tails are equally at fault, they are both in the wrong. The true course is not to wager at all."

—Yes; but you must wager. It is not optional. You are embarked. Which will you choose then; Let us see. Since you must choose, let us see which interests you least. You have two things to lose, the true and the good; and two things to stake, your reason and your will, your knowledge and your happiness; and your nature has two things to shun, error and misery. Your reason is no more shocked in choosing one rather than the other, since you must of necessity choose. This is one point settled. But your happiness? Let us weigh the gain and the loss in wagering that God is. Let us estimate these two chances. If you gain, you gain all; if you lose, you lose nothing. Wager them without hesitation that He is.—"That is very fine. Yes, I must wager; but I may perhaps wager too much."—Let us see. Since there is an equal risk of gain and of loss, if you had only to gain two lives, instead of one, you might still wager. But if there were three lives to gain, you would have to play (since you are under the necessity of playing), and you would be imprudent, when you are forced to play, not to chance your life to gain three at a game where there is an equal risk of loss and gain. But there is an eternity of life and happiness. And this being so, if there were an infinity of chances, of which one only would be for you, you would still be right in wagering one to win two, and you would act stupidly, being obliged to play, by refusing to stake one life against three at a game in which out of an infinity of an infinitely happy life to gain. But there is here an infinity of an infinitely happy life to gain, a chance of gain against a finite number of chances of loss, and what you stake is finite. It is all divided; wherever the infinite is and there is not an infinity of chances of loss against that of gain, there is no time to hesitate, you must give all. And thus, when one is forced to play, he must renounce reason to preserve his life, rather than

risk it for infinite gain, as likely to happen as the loss of nothingness.

For it is no use to say it is uncertain if we will gain, and it is certain that we risk, and that the infinite distance between the *certainty* of what is staked and the *uncertainty* of what will be gained, equals the finite good which is certainly staked against the uncertain infinite. It is not so, as every player stakes a certainty to gain an uncertainty, and yet he stakes a finite certainty to gain a finite uncertainty, without transgressing against reason. There is not an infinite distance between the certainty staked and the uncertainty of the gain; that is untrue. In truth, there is an infinity between the certainty of gain and the certainty of loss. But the uncertainty of the gain is proportioned to the certainty of the stake according to the proportion of the chances of gain and loss. Hence it comes that, if there are as many risks on one side as on the other, the course is to play even; and then the certainty of the stake is equal to the uncertainty of the gain, so far is it from the fact that there is an infinte distance between them. And so our proposition is of infinite force, when there is the finite to stake in a game where there are equal risks of gain and of loss, and the infinite to gain. This is demonstrable; and if men are capable of any truths, this is one.

"I confess it, I admit it. But still is there no means of seeing the faces of the cards?"—Yes, Scripture and the rest, &c.—"Yes, but I have my hands tied and my mouth closed; I am forced to wager, and am not free. I am not released, and am so made that I cannot believe. What then would you have me do?"

"True. But at least learn your inability to believe, since reason brings you to this, and yet you cannot believe. Endeavour then to convince yourself, not by increase of proofs of God, but by the abatement of your passions. You would like to attain faith, and do not know the way; you would like to cure yourself of unbelief, and ask the remedy for it. Learn of those who have been bound like you, and who now stake all their possessions. These are people who know the way which you would follow, and who are cured of an ill of which you would be cured. Follow the way by which they began; by acting as if they believe, taking the holy water, having masses said, &c. Even this will naturally make you believe, and deaden your acuteness.—"But this is what I am afraid of."—And why? What have you to lose?

But to show you that this leads you there, it is this which will lessen the passions, which are your stumbling-blocks.

The end of this discourse. —Now what harm will befall you in taking this side? You will be faithful, honest, humble, grateful, generous, a sincere friend, truthful. Certainly you will not have those poisonous pleasures, glory and luxury; but will you not have others? I will tell you that you will thereby gain in this life, and that, at each step you take on this road, you will see so great certainty of gain, so much nothingness in what you risk, that you will at last recognize that you have wagered for something certain and infinite, for which you have given nothing.

''Ah! This discourse transports me, charms me,'' &c.

If this discourse pleases you and seems impressive, know that it is made by a man who has knelt, both before and after it, in prayer to that Being, infinite and without parts, before whom he lays all he has, for you also to lay before Him all you have for your own good and for His glory, so that strength may be given to lowliness.

S T E P H E N   P.   S T I C H

Pascal's Wager and Doomsday Scenario Arguments*

Stephen P. Stich (1943–) teaches philosophy at the University of Maryland. His specialty is the philo - sophy of language.

In the argument I want to examine . . . the particular moral judgment being defended is that there should be a total ban on recombinant DNA research. The argument begins with the observation that even in so-called low-risk recombinant DNA experiments there is at least a possibility of catastrophic consequences. We are, after all, dealing with a relatively new and unexplored technology. Thus it is at least possible that a bacterial culture whose genetic makeup has been altered in the course of a recombinant DNA experiment may exhibit completely unexpected pathogenic characteristics. Indeed, it is not impossible that we could find ourselves confronted with a killer strain of, say, *E. coli* and, worse, a strain against which humans can marshal no natural defense. Now if this is possible—if we cannot say with assurance that the probability of it happening is zero—then, the argument continues, all recombinant

DNA research should be halted. For the negative utility of the imagined catastrophe is so enormous, resulting as it would in the destruction of our society and perhaps even of our species, that no work which could possibly lead to this result would be worth the risk.

The argument just sketched, which might be called the ''doomsday scenario'' argument, begins with a premise which no informed person would be inclined to deny. It is indeed *possible* that even a low-risk recombinant DNA experiment might lead to totally catastrophic results. No ironclad guarantee can be offered that this will not happen. And while the probability of such an unanticipated catastrophe is surely not large, there is no serious argument that the probability is zero. Still, I think the argument is a sophistry. To go from the undeniable premise that recombinant DNA research might possibly result in unthinkable catastrophe to the conclusion that such research should be banned requires a moral principle stating that *all* endeavors that might possibly result in such a catastrophe should be prohibited. Once the principle has been stated, it is hard to believe that anyone would take it at all seriously. For the principle entails that, along with recombinant DNA research, almost all scientific research and many other commonplace activities having little to do with science should be prohibited. It is, after all, at least logically possible

*A short excerpt from Stephen P. Stich, ''The Recombinant DNA Debate,'' *Philosophy and Public Affairs,* Vol. 7 (1978). Copyright © 1978 by Princeton University Press. Reprinted by permission of the author and the publisher.

that the next new compound synthesized in an ongoing chemical research program will turn out to be an uncontainable carcinogen many orders of magnitude more dangerous than aerosol plutonium. And, to vary the example, there is a non-zero probability that experiments in artificial pollination will produce a weed that will, a decade from now, ruin the world's food grain harvest.[1]

I cannot resist noting that the principle invoked in the doomsday scenario argument is not new. Pascal used an entirely parallel argument to show that it is in our own best interests to believe in God. For though the probability of God's existence may be very low, if He nonetheless should happen to exist, the disutility that would accrue to the disbeliever would be catastrophic—an eternity in hell. But, as introductory philosophy students should all know, Pascal's argument only looks persuasive if we take our options to be just two: Christianity or atheism. A third possibility is belief in a jealous non-Christian God who will see to our damnation if and only if we *are* Christians. The probability of such a deity existing is again very small, but non-zero. So Pascal's argument is of no help in deciding whether or not to accept Christianity.

For we may be damned if we do and damned if we don't.

I mention Pascal's difficulty because there is a direct parallel in the doomsday scenario argument against recombinant DNA research. Just as there is a non-zero probability that unforeseen consequences of recombinant DNA research will lead to disaster, so there is a non-zero probability that unforeseen consequences of *failing* to pursue the research will lead to disaster. There may, for example, come a time when, because of natural or man-induced climatic change, the capacity to alter quickly the genetic constitution of agricultural plants will be necessary to forestall catastrophic famine. And if we fail to pursue recombinant DNA research now, our lack of knowledge in the future may have consequences as dire as any foreseen in the doomsday scenario argument. . . .

NOTE

1. Unfortunately, the doomsday scenario argument is *not* a straw man conjured only by those who would refute it. Consider, for example, the remarks of Anthony Mazzocchi, spokesman for the Oil, Chemical and Atomic Workers International Union, reported in *Science News,* 19 March 1977, p. 181: "When scientists argue over safe or unsafe, we ought to be very prudent. . . . If critics are correct and the Andromeda scenario has *even the smallest possibility* of occurring, we must assume it will occur on the basis of our experience" (emphasis added).

WILLIAM   JAMES

The Will to Believe*

I

Let us give the name of hypothesis to anything that may be proposed to our belief; and just as the electricians speak of live and dead wires, let us speak of any hypothesis as either *live* or *dead*. A live hypothesis is one which appeals as a real possibility to him to whom it is proposed. If I ask you to believe in the Mahdi, the notion makes no electric connection with your nature—it refuses to scintillate with any credibility at all. As an hypothesis it is completely

dead. To an Arab, however (even if he be not one of the Mahdi's followers), the hypothesis is among the mind's possibilities: It is alive. This shows that deadness and liveness in an hypothesis are not intrinsic properties, but relations to the individual thinker. They are measured by his willingness to act. The maximum of liveness in an hypothesis means willingness to act irrevocably. Practically, that means belief; but there is some believing tendency wherever there is willingness to act at all.

Next, let us call the decision between two hypotheses an *option*. Options may be of several kinds. They may be first, *living* or *dead;* secondly, *forced* or

*Extracts from William James, "The Will to Believe," an Address to the Philosophical Clubs of Yale and Brown Universities. First published in the *New World,* 1896.

avoidable; thirdly, *momentous* or *trivial;* and for our purposes we may call an option a *genuine* option when it is of the forced, living, and momentous kind.

1. A living option is one in which both hypotheses are live ones. If I say to you: "Be a theosophist or be a Mohammedan," it is probably a dead option, because for you neither hypothesis is likely to be alive. But if I say: "Be an agnostic or be a Christian," it is otherwise: trained as you are, each hypothesis makes some appeal, however small, to your belief.

2. Next, if I say to you: "Choose between going out with your umbrella or without it," I do not offer you a genuine option, for it is not forced. You can easily avoid it by not going out at all. Similarly, if I say, "Either love me or hate me," "Either call my theory true or call it false," your option is avoidable. You may remain indifferent to me, neither loving nor hating, and you may decline to offer any judgment as to my theory. But if I say, "Either accept this truth or go without it," I put on you a forced option, for there is no standing place outside of the alternative. Every dilemma based on a complete logical disjunction, with no possibility of not choosing, is an option of this forced kind.

3. Finally, if I were Dr. Nansen and proposed to you to join my North Pole expedition, your option would be momentous; for this would probably be your similar opportunity, and your choice now would either exclude you from the North Pole sort of immortality altogether or put at least the chance of it into your hands. He who refuses to embrace a unique opportunity loses the prize as surely as if he tried and failed. *Per contra,* the option is trivial when the opportunity is not unique, when the stake is insignificant, or when the decision is reversible if it later prove unwise. Such trivial options abound in the scientific life. A chemist finds an hypothesis live enough to spend a year in its verification: he believes in it to that extent. But if his experiments prove inconclusive either way, he is quit for his loss of time, no vital harm being done.

It will facilitate our discussion if we keep all these distinctions well in mind.

II

The next matter to consider is the actual psychology of human opinion. When we look at certain facts, it seems as if our passional and volitional nature lay at the root of all our convictions. When we look at

others, it seems as if they could do nothing when the intellect had once said its say. Let us take the latter facts up first.

Does it not seem preposterous on the very face of it to talk of our opinions being modifiable at will? Can our will either help or hinder our intellect in its perceptions of truth? Can we, by just willing it, believe that Abraham Lincoln's existence is a myth, and that the portraits of him in *McClure's Magazine* are all of some one else? Can we, by any effort of our will, or by any strength of wish that it were true, believe ourselves well and about when we are roaring with rheumatism in bed, or feel certain that the sum of the two one-dollar bills in our pocket must be a hundred dollars? We can *say* any of these things, but we are absolutely impotent to believe them; and of just such things is the whole fabric of the truths that we do believe in made up—matters of fact, immediate or remote, as Hume said, and relations between ideas, which are either there or not there for us if we see them so, and which if not there cannot be put there by any action of our own.

In Pascal's *Thoughts* there is a celebrated passage known in literature as Pascal's wager. In it he tries to force us into Christianity by reasoning as if our concern with truth resembled our concern with the stakes in a game of chance. Translated freely his words are these: You must either believe or not believe that God is—which will you do? Your human reason cannot say. A game is going on between you and the nature of things which at the day of judgment will bring out either heads or tails. Weigh what your gains and your losses would be if you should stake all you have on heads, or God's existence: if you win in such case, you gain eternal beatitude; if you lose, you lose nothing at all. If there were an infinity of chances, and only one for God in this wager, still you ought to stake your all on God; for though you surely risk a finite loss by this procedure, any finite loss is reasonable, even a certain one is reasonable, if there is but the possibility of infinite gain. Go, then, and take holy water, and have masses said; belief will come and stupefy your scruples. . . . Why should you not? At bottom, what have you to lose?

You probably feel that when religious faith expresses itself thus, in the language of the gaming-table, it is put to its last trumps. Surely Pascal's own personal belief in masses and holy water had far other springs; and this celebrated page of his is but an argument for others, a last desperate snatch at a weapon against the hardness of the unbelieving heart. We feel that a faith in masses and holy water adopted wilfully after such a mechanical calculation would lack the inner soul of faith's reality; and if we were ourselves in the place of the Deity, we should probably take particular pleasure in cutting off believers of this pattern from their infinite reward. It is evident that unless there be some preexisting tendency to believe in masses and holy water, the option offered to the will by Pascal is not a living option. Certainly no Turk ever took to masses and holy water on its account; and even to us Protestants these means of salvation seem such foregone impossibilities that Pascal's logic, invoked for them specifically, leaves us unmoved. As well might the Mahdi write to us, saying, "I am the Expected One whom God has created in his effulgence. You shall be infinitely happy if you confess me; otherwise you shall be cut off from the light of the sun. Weigh, then, your infinite gain if I am genuine against your finite sacrifice if I am not!" His logic would be that of Pascal; but he would vainly use it on us, for the hypothesis he offers us is dead. No tendency to act on it exists in us to any degree.

The talk of believing by our volition seems, then, from one point of view, simply silly. From another point of view it is worse than silly, it is vile. When one turns to the magnificent edifice of the physical sciences, and sees how it was reared; what thousands of disinterested moral lives of men lie buried in its mere foundations; what patience and postponement, what choking down of preference, what submission to the icy laws of outer fact are wrought into its very stones and mortar; how absolutely impersonal it stands in its vast augustness—then how besotted and contemptible seems every little sentimentalist who comes blowing his voluntary smoke-wreaths, and pretending to decide things from out of his private dream! Can we wonder if those bred in the rugged and manly school of science should feel like spewing such subjectivism out of their mouths? The whole system of loyalties which grow up in the schools of science go dead against its toleration; so that it is only natural that those who have caught the scientific fever should pass over to the opposite extreme, and write sometimes as if the incorruptibly truthful intellect ought positively to prefer bitterness and unacceptableness to the heart in its cup.

It fortifies my soul to know
That though I perish, Truth is so

sings Clough, while Huxley exclaims: "My only consolation lies in the reflection that, however bad our posterity may become, so far as they hold by the plain rule of not pretending to believe what they have no reason to believe, because it may be to their advantage so to pretend [the word 'pretend' is surely here redundant], they will not have reached the lowest depth of immorality." And that delicious *enfant terrible* Clifford writes: "Belief is desecrated when given to unproved and unquestioned statements for the solace and private pleasure of the believer. . . . Whoso would deserve well of his fellows in this matter will guard the purity of his belief with a very fanaticism of jealous care, lest at any time it should rest on an unworthy object, and catch a stain which can never be wiped away. . . . If [a] belief has been accepted on insufficient evidence [even though the belief be true, as Clifford on the same page explains] the pleasure is a stolen one. . . . It is sinful because it is stolen in defiance of our duty to mankind. That duty is to guard ourselves from such beliefs as from a pestilence which may shortly master our own body and then spread to the rest of the town. . . . It is wrong always, everywhere, and for every one, to believe anything upon insufficient evidence."

III

All this strikes one as healthy, even when expressed, as by Clifford, with somewhat too much of robustious pathos in the voice. Free will and simple wishing do seem, in the matter of our credences, to be only fifth wheels to the coach. Yet if any one should thereupon assume that intellectual insight is what remains after wish and will and sentimental preference have taken wing, or that pure reason is what then settles our opinions, he would fly quite as directly in the teeth of the facts.

It is only our already dead hypotheses that our willing nature is unable to bring to life again. But what has made them dead for us is for the most part a previous action of our willing nature of an antagonistic kind. When I say "willing nature," I do not mean only such deliberate volitions as may have set up habits of belief that we cannot now escape from— I mean all such factors of belief as fear and hope, prejudice and passion, imitation and partisanship, the circumpressure of our caste and set. As a matter of fact we find ourselves believing, we hardly know how or why. Mr. Balfour gives the name of "authority" to all those influences, born of the intellectual climate, that make hypotheses possible or impossible for us, alive or dead. Here in this room, we all of us believe in molecules and the conservation of energy, in democracy and necessary progress, in Protestant Christianity and the duty of fighting for "the doctrine of the immortal Monroe," all for no reasons worthy of the name. We see into these matters with no more inner clearness, and probably with much less, than any disbeliever in them might possess. His unconventionality would probably have some grounds to show for its conclusions; but for us, not insight, but the *prestige* of the opinions, is what makes the spark shoot from them and light up our sleeping magazines of faith. Our reason is quite satisfied, in nine hundred and ninety-nine cases out of every thousand of us, if it can find a few arguments that will do to recite in case our credulity is criticized by some one else. Our faith is faith in some one else's faith, and in the greatest matters this is the most the case. . . .

Evidently, then, our non-intellectual nature does influence our convictions. There are passional tendencies and volitions which run before and others which come after belief, and it is only the latter that are too late for the fair; and they are not too late when the previous passional work has been already in their own direction. Pascal's argument, instead of being powerless, then seems a regular clincher, and is the last stroke needed to make our faith in masses and holy water complete. The state of things is evidently far from simple; and pure insight and logic, whatever they might do ideally, are not the only things that really do produce our creeds.

IV

Our next duty, having recognized this mixedup state of affairs, is to ask whether it be simply reprehensible and pathological, or whether, on the contrary, we must treat it as a normal element in making up our minds. The thesis I defend is, briefly stated, this: *Our passional nature not only lawfully may, but must, decide an option between propositions, whenever it is a genuine option that cannot by its nature be decided on intellectual grounds; for to say, under such circumstances, "Do not decide, but leave the question open," is itself a passional decision—just like deciding yes or no—and is attended with the same risk of losing the truth.* . . .

VII

One more point, small but important, and our preliminaries are done. There are two ways of looking at our duty in the matter of opinion—ways entirely different, and yet ways about whose difference the theory of knowledge seems hitherto to have shown very little concern. *We must know the truth;* and *we must avoid error*—these are our first and great commandments as would-be knowers; but they are not two ways of stating an identical commandment, they are two separable laws. Although it may indeed happen that when we believe the truth A, we escape as an incidental consequence from believing the falsehood B, it hardly ever happens that by merely disbelieving B we necessarily believe A. We may in escaping B fall into believing other falsehoods, C or D, just as bad as B; or we may escape B by not believing anything at all, not even A.

Believe truth! Shun error!—these, we see, are two materially different laws; and by choosing between them we may end by coloring differently our whole intellectual life. We may regard the chase for truth as paramount, and the avoidance of error as secondary; or we may, on the other hand, treat the avoidance of error as more imperative, and let truth take its chance. Clifford, in the instructive passage which I have quoted, exhorts us to the latter course. Believe nothing, he tells us, keep your mind in suspense forever, rather than by closing it on insufficient evidence incur the awful risk of believing lies. You, on the other hand, may think that the risk of being in error is a very small matter when compared with the blessings of real knowledge, and be ready to be duped many times in your investigation rather than postpone indefinitely the chance of guessing true. I myself find it impossible to go with Clifford. We must remember that these feelings of our duty about either truth or error are in any case only expressions of our passional life. Biologically considered, our minds are as ready to grind out falsehood as veracity, and he who says, "Better go without belief forever than believe a lie!" merely shows his own preponderant private horror of becoming a dupe. He may be critical of many of his desires and fears, but this fear he slavishly obeys. He cannot imagine any one questioning its binding force. For my own part, I have also a horror of being duped; but I can believe that worse things than being duped may happen to a man in this world: so Clifford's exhortation has to my ears a thoroughly fantastic sound. It is like a general informing his soldiers that it is better to keep out of battle forever than to risk a single wound. Not so are victories either over enemies or over nature gained. Our errors are surely not such awfully solemn things. In a world where we are so certain to incur them in spite of all our caution, a certain lightness of heart seems healthier than this excessive nervousness on their behalf. At any rate, it seems the fittest thing for the empiricist philosopher.

VIII

And now, after all this introduction, let us go straight at our question. I have said, and now repeat it, that not only as a matter of fact do we find our passional nature influencing us in our opinions, but that there are some options between opinions in which this influence must be regarded both as an inevitable and as a lawful determinant of our choice.

I fear here that some of you my hearers will begin to scent danger, and lend an inhospitable ear. Two first steps of passion you have indeed had to admit as necessary—we must think so as to avoid dupery, and we must think so as to gain truth; but the surest path to those ideal consummations, you will probably consider, is from now onwards to take no further passional step.

Well, of course, I agree as far as the facts will allow. Wherever the option between losing truth and gaining it is not momentous, we can throw the chance of *gaining truth* away, and at any rate save ourselves from any chance of *believing falsehood,* by not making up our minds at all till objective evidence has come. In scientific questions, this is almost always the case; and even in human affairs in general, the need of acting is seldom so urgent that a false belief to act on is better than no belief at all. Law courts, indeed, have to decide on the best evidence attainable for the moment, because a judge's duty is to make law as well as to ascertain it, and (as a learned judge once said to me) few cases are worth spending much time over: the great thing is to have them decided on *any* acceptable principle, and got out of the way. But in our dealings with objective nature we obviously are recorders, not makers, of the truth; and decisions for the mere sake of deciding promptly and getting on to the next business would be wholly out of place. Throughout the breadth of physical nature facts are what they are quite independently of us, and seldom is there any such hurry about them that the risks of being duped by believing a premature theory need be faced. The questions here are always trivial options, the hypotheses are hardly living (at any rate not living for us spectators), the choice between believing truth or falsehood is seldom forced. The attitude of sceptical balance is therefore the absolutely wise one if we would escape mistakes. What difference, indeed, does it make to most of us whether we have or have not a theory of the Röntgen rays, whether we believe or not in mind-stuff, or have a conviction about the causality of conscious states? It makes no difference. Such options are not forced on us. On every account it is better not to make them, but still keep weighing reasons *pro et contra* with an indifferent hand.

I speak, of course, here of the purely judging mind. For purposes of discovery such indifference is to be less highly recommended, and science would be far less advanced than she is if the passionate desires of individuals to get their own faiths confirmed had been kept out of the game. See for example the sagacity which Spencer and Weismann now display. On the other hand, if you want an absolute duffer in an investigation, you must, after all, take the man who has no interest whatever in its results: he is the warranted incapable, the positive fool. The most useful investigator, because the most sensitive observer, is always he whose eager interest in one side of the question is balanced by an equally keen nervousness lest he become deceived.[1] Science has organized this nervousness into a regular *technique,* her so-called method of verification; and she has fallen so deeply in love with the method that one may even say she has ceased to care for truth by itself at all. It is only truth as technically verified that interests her. The truth of truths might come in merely affirmative form, and she would decline to touch it. Such truth as that, she might repeat with Clifford, would be stolen in defiance of her duty to mankind. Human passions, however, are stronger than technical rules. "*Le coeur a ses raisons,*" as Pascal says, "*que la raison ne connait pas*";[2] and however indifferent to all but the bare rules of the game the umpire, the abstract intellect, may be, the concrete players who furnish him the materials to judge of are usually, each one of them, in love with some pet "live hypothesis" of his own. Let us agree, however, that wherever there is no forced option, the dispassionately judicial intellect with no pet hypothesis, saving us, as it does, from dupery at any rate, ought to be our ideal.

The question next arises: Are there not somewhere forced options in our speculative questions, and can we (as men who may be interested at least as much in positively gaining truth as in merely escaping dupery) always wait with impunity till the coercive evidence shall have arrived? It seems *a priori* improbable that the truth should be so nicely adjusted to our needs and powers as that. In the great boarding-house of nature, the cakes and the butter and the syrup seldom come out so even and leave the plates so clean. Indeed, we should view them with scientific suspicion if they did.

IX

Moral questions immediately present themselves as questions whose solution cannot wait for sensible proof. A moral question is a question not of what sensibly exists, but of what is good, or would be good if it did exist. Science can tell us what exists; but to compare the *worths,* both of what exists and of what does not exist, we must consult not science, but what Pascal calls our heart. . . .

Turn now from these wide questions of good to a certain class of questions of fact, questions concerning personal relations, states of mind between one man and another. *Do you like me or not?*—for example. Whether you do or not depends, in countless instances, on whether I meet you halfway, am willing to assume that you must like me, and show you trust and expectation. The previous faith on my part in your liking's existence is in such cases what makes your liking come. But if I stand aloof, and refuse to budge an inch until I have objective evidence, until you shall have done something apt, as the absolutists say, *ad extorquendum assensum meum,* ten to one your liking never comes. How many women's hearts are vanquished by the mere sanguine insistence of some man that they *must* love him! He will not consent to the hypothesis that they cannot. The desire for a certain kind of truth here brings about that special truth's existence; and so it is in innumerable cases of other sorts. . . . *And where faith in a fact can help create the fact,* that would be an insane logic which should say that faith running ahead of scientific evidence is the "lowest kind of immorality" into which a thinking being can fall. Yet such is the logic by which our scientific absolutists pretend to regulate our lives!

X

In truths dependent on our personal action, then, faith based on desire is certainly a lawful and possibly an indispensable thing.

But now, it will be said, these are all childish human cases, and have nothing to do with great cosmical matters, like the question of religious faith. Let us then pass on to that. Religions differ so much in their accidents that in discussing the religious question we must make it very generic and broad. What then do we now mean by the religious hypothesis? Science says things are; morality says some things are better than other things; and religion says essentially two things.

First, she says that the best things are the more eternal things, the overlapping things, the things in the universe that throw the last stone, so to speak, and say the final word. "Perfection is eternal"—this phrase of Charles Secrétan seems a good way of putting this first affirmation of religion, an affirmation which obviously cannot yet be verified scientifically at all.

The second affirmation of religion is that we are better off even now if we believe her first affirmation to be true.

Now, let us consider what the logical elements of this situation are *in case the religious hypothesis in both its branches be really true.* (Of course, we must admit that possibility at the outset. If we are to discuss the question at all, it must involve a living option. If for any of you religion be a hypothesis that cannot, by any living possibility, be true, then you need go no farther. I speak to the "saving remnant" alone.) So proceeding, we see, first, that religion offers itself as a *momentous* option. We are supposed to gain, even now, by our belief, and to lose by our non-belief, a certain vital good. Secondly, religion is a *forced* option, so far as that good goes. We cannot escape the issue by remaining sceptical and waiting for more light, because, although we do avoid error in that way *if religion be untrue,* we lose the good, *if it be true,* just as certainly as if we positively chose to disbelieve. It is as if a man should hesitate indefinitely to ask a certain woman to marry him because he was not perfectly sure that she would prove an angel after he brought her home. Would he not cut himself off from that particular angel-possibility as decisively as if he went and married some one else? Scepticism, then, is not avoidance of option; it is option of a certain particular kind of risk. *Better risk loss of truth than chance of error*—that is your faith-vetoer's exact position. He is actively playing his stake as much as the believer is; he is backing the field against the religious hypothesis, just as the believer is backing the religious hypothesis against the field. To preach scepticism to us as a duty until "sufficient evidence" for religion be found, is tantamount therefore to telling us, when in presence of the religious hypothesis, that to yield to our fear of its being error is wiser and better than to yield to our hope that it may be true. It is not intellect against all passions, then; it is only intellect with one passion laying down its law. And by what, forsooth, is the supreme wisdom of this passion warranted? Dupery for dupery, what proof is there that dupery through hope is so much worse than dupery through fear? I, for one, can see no proof; and I simply refuse obedience to the scientist's command to imitate his kind of option, in a case where my own stake is important enough to give me the right to choose my own form of risk. If religion be true and the evidence for it be still insufficient, I do not wish, by putting your extinguisher upon my nature (which feels to me as if it had after all some business in this matter), to forfeit my sole chance in life of getting upon the winning side—that chance depending, of course, on my willingness to run the risk of acting as if my passional need of taking the world religiously might be prophetic and right.

All this is on the supposition that it really may be prophetic and right, and that, even to us who are discussing the matter, religion is a live hypothesis which may be true. Now, to most of us religion comes in a still further way that makes a veto on our active faith even more illogical. The more perfect and more eternal aspect of the universe is represented in our religions as having personal form. The universe is no longer a mere *It* to us, but a *Thou*, if we are religious; and any relation that may be possible from person to person might be possible here. For instance, although in one sense we are passive portions of the universe, in another we show a curious autonomy, as if we were small active centers on our own account. We feel, too, as if the appeal of religion to us were made to our own active goodwill, as if evidence might be forever withheld from us unless we met the hypothesis halfway to take a trivial illustration: just as a man who in a company of gentle-

men made no advances, asked a warrant for every concession, and believed no one's word without proof, would cut himself off by such churlishness from all the social rewards that a more trusting spirit would earn—so here, one who should shut himself up in snarling logicality and try to make the gods extort his recognition willy-nilly, or not get it at all, might cut himself off forever from his only opportunity of making the gods' acquaintance. This feeling, forced on us we know not whence that by obstinately believing that there are gods (although not to do so would be so easy both for our logic and our life) we are doing the universe the deepest service we can, seems part of the living essence of the religious hypothesis. If the hypothesis *were* true in all its parts, including this one, then pure intellectualism, with its veto on our making willing advances, would be an absurdity; and some participation of our sympathetic nature would be logically required. I therefore, for one, cannot see my way to accepting the agnostic rules for truth-seeking, or wilfully agree to keep my willing nature out of the game. I cannot do so for this plain reason, that *a rule of thinking which would absolutely prevent me from acknowledging certain kinds of truth if those kinds of truth were really there, would be an irrational rule*. That for me is the long and short of the formal logic of the situation, no matter what the kinds of truth might materially be.

I confess I do not see how this logic can be escaped. But sad experience makes me fear that some of you may still shrink from radically saying with me, *in abstracto,* that we have the right to believe at our own risk any hypothesis that is live enough to tempt our will. I suspect, however, that if this is so, it is because you have got away from the abstract logical point of view altogether, and are thinking (perhaps without realizing it) of some particular religious hypothesis which for you is dead. The freedom to "believe what we will" you apply to the case of some patent superstition; and the faith you think of is the faith defined by the schoolboy when he said, "Faith is when you believe something that you know ain't true." I can only repeat that this is misapprehension. *In concreto,* the freedom to believe can only cover living options which the intellect of the individual cannot by itself resolve; and living options never seem absurdities to him who has them to consider. When I look at the religious question as it really puts itself to concrete men, and when I think of all the possibilities which both practically and theoretically it involves, then this command that we shall put a stopper on our heart, instincts, and courage, and *wait*—acting of course meanwhile more or less as if religion were not true[3]—till doomsday, or till such time as our intellect and senses working together may have raked in evidence enough—this command, I say, seems to me the queerest idol ever manufactured in the philosophic cave. Were we scholastic absolutists, there might be more excuse. If we had an infallible intellect with its objective certitudes, we might feel ourselves disloyal to such a perfect organ of knowledge in not trusting to it exclusively, in not waiting for its releasing word. But if we are empiricists, if we believe that no bell in us tolls to let us know for certain when truth is in our grasp, then it seems a piece of idle fantasticality to preach so solemnly our duty of waiting for the bell. Indeed we *may* wait if we will—I hope you do not think that I am denying that—but if we do so, we do so at our peril as much as if we believed. In either case we *act,* taking our life in our hands. No one of us ought to issue vetoes to the other, nor should we bandy words of abuse. We ought, on the contrary, delicately and profoundly to respect one another's mental freedom: then only shall we bring about the intellectual republic; then only shall we have that spirit of inner tolerance without which all our outer tolerance is soulless, and which is empiricism's glory; then only shall we live and let live, in speculative as well as in practical things.

I began by a reference to Fitz-James Stephen; let me end by a quotation from him. "What do you think of yourself? What do you think of the world? . . . These are questions with which all must deal as it seems good to them. They are riddles of the Sphinx, and in some way or other we must deal with them. . . . In all important transactions of life we have to take a leap in the dark. . . . If we decide to leave the riddles unanswered, that is a choice; if we waver in our answer, that, too, is a choice: but whatever choice we make, we make it at our peril. If a man chooses to turn his back altogether on God and the future, no one can prevent him; no one can show beyond reasonable doubt that he is mistaken. If a man thinks otherwise and acts as he thinks, I do not see that any one can prove that he is mistaken. Each must act as he thinks best; and if he is wrong, so much the worse for him. We stand on a mountain pass in the midst of whirling snow and blinding mist, through which we get glimpses now and then of paths which may be deceptive. If we stand still we shall be frozen to death. If we take the wrong road we shall be dashed to pieces. We do not certainly know whether there is any right one. What must we do? 'Be strong and of a good courage.' Act for the best, hope for the best, and take what comes.

. . . If death ends all, we cannot meet death better."

NOTES

1. Compare Wilfrid Ward's Essay "The Wish to Believe," in his *Witnesses to the Unseen* (Macmillan & Co., 1893).

2. "The heart has its reasons which reason does not know."

3. Since belief is measured by action, he who forbids us to believe religion to be true, necessarily also forbids us to act as we should if we did believe it to be true. The whole defence of religious faith hinges upon action. If the action required or inspired by the religious hypothesis is in no way different from that dictated by the naturalistic hypothesis, then religious faith is a pure superfluity, better pruned away, and controversy about its legitimacy is a piece of idle trifling, unworthy of serious minds. I myself believe, of course, that the religious hypothesis gives to the world an expression which specifically determines our reactions, and makes them in a large part unlike what they might be on a purely naturalistic scheme of belief.

4. *Liberty, Equality, Fraternity,* p. 353, 2d edition (London, 1874).

PART 2 HUMAN KNOWLEDGE:

During the great golden age of philosophy, in the seventeenth and eighteenth centuries, problems about the nature of human knowledge divided philosophers into two schools; and despite changing idioms and increased understanding of the methods of science, the division to a large degree persists. On the one hand, the *empiricists*, whose leading thinkers were John Locke (1632–1704), George Berkeley (1685–1753), and David Hume (1711–1776), held that all our ideas come from experience and that no proposition about any matter of fact can be known to be true independently of experience. On the other hand, the *rationalists*, whose most important representatives were René Descartes (1596–1650), Baruch Spinoza (1632–1677), and Gottfried Leibniz (1646–1716), maintained that there are "innate ideas," and that certain general propositions (usually called "necessary" or "a priori" propositions) can be known to be true in advance of, or in the absence of, empirical verification.[1]

Advocates of the theory of innate ideas did not, of course, hold that we are born literally thinking certain thoughts, but rather that we are born with inherited dispositions to have thoughts of a certain form and structure. Just as dehydrated milk has the disposition to become milk when water is added to it, so the mind, on this theory, has from birth the disposition to acquire the concepts of being, substance, duration—even infinitude and God—once a certain amount of experience is "added to it." Thus, rationalism holds that there can be in the mind ideas and truths that were not first present in experience but only later activated by experience. For the empiricist, on the other hand, the mind is (as Locke put it) like a tablet on which nothing has been written (a *tabula rasa*) until experience writes its message on it.

The writings of René Descartes, a leading mathematician and man of science as well as a philosopher, are a clear example not only of the rationalistic doctrine and method but also of the rationalistic temper of mind. In the autobiographical *Discourse on Method,*

---

[1]It should be noted that both the rationalist and the empiricist are "rationalists" in the wider sense of the term—that is, as opposed to fideism, romanticism, or irrationalism. Both can support rational inquiry as the sole road to truth, but they differ in their conceptions of what rational inquiry is, particularly regarding the role that sense experience plays in it.

ITS GROUNDS AND LIMITS

Descartes compares the state of the sciences and philosophy to an ancient European town, grown helter-skelter from an older village, with crooked streets, random walls, and poor sanitation. Of course, we are not accustomed to rip down whole cities in order to start from scratch the task of rational redesign; but individuals can without arrogance or absurdity think of ripping down and rebuilding their own homes:

> . . . and the same I thought was true of any similar project for reforming the body of the Sciences, or the order of teaching them established in the Schools: but as for the opinions which up to that time I had embraced, I thought that I could not do better than resolve at once to sweep them wholly away, that I might afterwards be in a position to admit either others more correct, or even perhaps the same ones when they had undergone the scrutiny of reason. I firmly believed that in this way I should much better succeed in the conduct of my life, than if I built only upon old foundations, and leaned upon principles which, in my youth, I had taken upon trust.

Thus Descartes begins his dramatic quest for new "foundations," doubting everything that can be doubted until he finds a solid basis for reconstruction in the indubitable fact of his own existence as a "thinking substance." What makes the argument for his own existence so convincing, Descartes decides, is its "clearness and distinctness." Hence, he has a working criterion of truth to use in the voyage away from his skeptical starting point: Whatever he conceives clearly and distinctly is true.

In his third Meditation, Descartes finds in himself the idea of an infinite God. The idea, he argues, could not be his own invention, nor could it be derived from merely finite experience. Its only possible cause must be the actually existing deity. He then goes on to prove that this deity is no deceiver. Therefore, (a) since God has given us a powerful disposition to believe in the existence of material objects (such as human bodies), and (b) since God would be a deceiver if no such objects existed, and (c) since God is not a deceiver—it follows that such objects do exist and that human knowledge is reliable. Intellectual error, then, when it occurs, springs from a kind of hasty willfulness in ourselves and not from God.

Though many philosophers today would quarrel with particular steps in Descartes' arguments, there is no denying that his general method has left its mark on most of his successors. For three centuries philosophers have tried to give a rational reconstruction of our knowledge, beginning with the relatively indubitable and building on it, and taking very seriously as they work the nagging claims of imaginary skeptics that what we think we know with certainty we may not really know at all.

Skeptical doubts are especially likely to torment the empiricist philosopher. Since empiricism holds that the sole source ultimately of our knowledge of things external to us is sense experience, it is a matter of importance to empiricists to explain just how that knowledge is derived from the "impressions" made upon our various sense organs. John Locke rested a great part of his theory upon a crucial distinction first used in antiquity and then revived by Galileo—namely, the distinction between *primary and secondary qualities* of physical objects. Primary qualities are intrinsic characteristics of the object itself—characteristics such as solidity, extension in space (size), figure (shape), motion or rest, and number. These are qualities that the objects would continue to possess even if there were no perceiving beings in the world. Secondary qualities, on the other hand (such qualities as color, taste, smell, sound, warmth, and cold), exist only when actually sensed, and then only "in the mind" of the one who senses them. The primary quality itself is inseparable from the material object and is found in every part of it, no matter how small. Every conceivable unit of matter, from a celestial body to an atom, must have some size and shape. (On the other hand, no mere atom could have color.)

Locke also contributed to the terminology of subsequent empiricists the technical term "idea" to stand for "whatever is the object of the understanding when a man thinks" or, more generally, for any direct object of awareness or consciousness.[2] And, again, the "ideas" that result from our perception of primary qualities are different from our "ideas" of secondary qualities. When we perceive a primary quality, according to Locke, our "idea" of this quality exactly resembles the corresponding primary quality in the material object itself. In contrast, when we perceive a secondary quality, our "idea" of this quality has no resemblance to a corresponding property of the thing itself. That is, our "idea" of, for instance, color or odor in an object is produced in us by virtue of the object's "power" to reflect and absorb light waves of certain frequencies, or to emit molecules in certain degrees of vibration. Because of these capacities or "powers" of material objects, color and odor can come into existence. Yet without eyes, there could be no color; without noses, no odor; and without minds, no "secondary qualities" at all.

Locke's theory of perception, then, does seem to have strong support from scientifically sophisticated common sense. It often contrasted with another possible theory of perception (a theory held by no reputable philosopher), which is sometimes ascribed (quite unfairly) to the scientifically unsophisticated common sense of "the ordinary man." According to the latter theory, called *naive realism,* the qualities that Locke called "primary" and those he called "secondary" are both strictly part of physical objects, and both can exist quite independently of perceiving minds.[3] It follows from naive realism

---

[2]David Hume's usage was somewhat narrower. In the *Treatise of Human Nature,* his earlier more formal exposition of the views included here, Hume explains that he will use the word "impression" to mean "all our sensations, passions, and emotions, as they make their first appearance in the soul." By "ideas" he means "the faint images of these in thinking and reasoning."

[3]The Spanish-American philosopher George Santayana (*Winds of Doctrine* [London: J. M. Dent and Sons, New York: Charles Scribner's Sons, 1940], p. 146) once lampooned a similar view about the ethical characteristic "goodness" by likening it to the claim that whiskey is "intoxicating in itself, without reference to any animal; that it is pervaded, as it were, by an inherent intoxication, and stands dead drunk in its bottle!"

that a world without perceiving minds might yet be a colorful, clamorous, and smelly place. Locke's view, in contrast, is that physical substances and their primary qualities can exist independently of sentient minds, and only the secondary qualities are mind-dependent. This theory can be called *sophisticated realism:* "sophisticated" because it seems to accord with what science tells us about secondary qualities; "realism" because it allows that material objects have a real existence independent of minds. Locke's view is often called *representative realism,* because of the tenet that ideas ("in the mind") faithfully mirror or "represent" material objects to us in perception, even though the material objects and the "ideas" by which we come to know them are quite distinct entities. The textbooks also call Locke's view the *causal theory of perception* because of the tenet that material objects are the causes of the ideas, or appearances, or sense data we have of them. The material substance itself is distinct from its own qualities, even from its own primary qualities, and, not being directly perceivable, must simply be posited as an unknowable "substratum" for its powers and properties. (Locke's conception of substance was rejected by most later empiricists, who preferred to think of a material thing as a mere "bundle of attributes," not as a mysterious entity "underlying" or "possessing" its own attributes.)

The realism of John Locke, roughly sketched in the preceding paragraphs, must be understood as the primary target of the arguments of George Berkeley, Bishop of Cloyne.[4] Locke would have approved of Berkeley's systematic demonstration that secondary qualities are mental. Berkeley argues for the conclusion in two ways. First of all, he maintains that extreme degrees of each secondary quality are inseparable in our consciousness from pain. Hence, if it is absurd to imagine that pain is, for example, *in* or *part of* the stove, then it is equally absurd to imagine that the heat is literally in the stove. This famous argument by Berkeley is subjected to critical scrutiny by twentieth-century philosopher Godfrey Vesey in his article in this section. Berkeley's second argument is the famous "argument from the relativity of perception." If I put one ice-chilled hand and one warm hand into a tub of tepid water, the water will feel hot to my cold hand and cold to my hot hand; but the water itself cannot be both hot and cold. Hence, both heat and cold must be "in the mind" only.

But Berkeley then turns the tables on Locke by arguing in quite similar ways for the necessarily mental status of *primary qualities* too. If the supporter of Locke accepts these latter arguments, there is nothing left of his conception of an external object beyond that of an unknowable "substratum." Berkeley easily disposes of the concept of a substratum as theoretically superfluous and unintelligible. He is left then with a world in which only perceiving minds ("subjects") and their "ideas" (the appearances of primary and secondary qualities) exist. Hence, the universe is through and through mental. This theory of reality bears the name *subjective idealism.* (Perhaps "ideaism" would be less misleading, since the theory has nothing whatever to do with ideals.)

Berkeley was as concerned as Descartes or Locke to find a solid alternative to skepticism. As an empiricist, he was resolved to show that all of our ideas, insofar as they are genuine (not merely confused), are derived from experience. What, then, of our idea of corporeal objects such as trees, tables, bodies? Berkeley was driven by his logic and his empiricist startings to conclude that physical objects, insofar as we have any clear

[4]There is no selection from Locke in this section, but the summary of his relevant views included here provides a useful background for the study of Berkeley's writings. See Part 3, pp. 251–254, for Locke's account of material and spiritual substances.

idea of them at all, are simply collections of sense impressions. Those corporeal substances, of which Descartes was at last able to form a "clear and distinct idea," turn out on analysis to be the figments of muddled thought.

Has empiricism then truly reconstructed our knowledge of the world, if this is its conclusion? Doesn't Berkeley's conception of a world "through and through mental" give a violent jolt to common sense? Not so, replies Berkeley's spokesman Philonous. Berkeley's idealism implies that tables and trees and bodies are just exactly what they seem—colored, shaped, hard, and so on. There is indeed nothing to these things except the qualities they seem to have. Moreover, it is not true that tables "vanish" or "pop out of existence" the moment we turn our backs on them (that *would* be repugnant to common sense); for God is always perceiving them, and therefore they continue to exist as ideas in His mind. To many later empiricists this use of God seemed a desperate expedient to save Berkeley's theory from embarrassment. John Stuart Mill (1806–1873) was typical of later empiricists (often called *phenomenalists*) who found ways to make the rejection of "corporeal substance" more palatable to common sense without invoking a *deus ex machina*. According to Mill, if we say that the table continues to exist when unperceived, all we can mean by this is that *if* someone were to look in a certain place, then he would have sense impressions of a certain (table-like) kind; for material objects are not simply bundles of actual sense impressions but are rather to be understood as "permanent possibilities of sensation," and this conception exhausts whatever clear idea we have of them. Some writers have suggested that phenomenalism (the view of David Hume as well as of Mill) can be thought of as "Berkeley's view without Berkeley's God."

A famous philosopher who argued (against Berkeley and Hume) in support of the independent existence of physical objects[5] was Bertrand Russell (1872–1970). In the two chapters of his elementary text *The Problems of Philosophy* (1912) included here, Russell is willing to concede to Berkeley and Hume that a table, for example, is "not *immediately* known to us at all." But unlike the idealists and phenomenalists, Russell maintains that the existence of a table, or any other material object of any size or construction, can be inferred from what *is* directly perceived, namely our "sense-data" (what Berkeley called "ideas"). This natural inference, Russell insists, is to a hypothesis (the existence of material things) that "simplifies and systemizes" the account we give of our experiences better than any alternative.

David Hume in the eighteenth century applied the empiricist philosophy not only to the concept of a material substance but to other basic concepts as well, with results that even he called skeptical. Unlike Berkeley, who regarded skepticism as a charge to be rebutted, Hume thought of it as a position to be reluctantly adopted. In the selections included here, he examines the concept of causation and finds no more sense in the idea of a "necessary connection" between cause and effect (when we drop a stone, it *must* fall—so we think) than Berkeley did in the idea of "corporeal substance." We may continue to talk, as Hume himself does, of one thing's causing another, but all we can *mean* is that events of the first kind are in fact constantly conjoined with events of the second kind; and the so-called necessity that the second follow the first is simply the reflection of our habitual expectation. Hume would not have us deny the plain reports of our senses or the fruits or our mathematical deductions; he merely points out that there is no logically infallible method of achieving truth about matters of fact, and indeed no method at all for reasoning

---

[5]One of many different philosophical theories that bear the name "realism."

about matters that lie beyond all experience. But this kind of skepticism need not force us into a permanent suspension of judgment about all things, even in the practical affairs of life; for we will (as Hume elsewhere puts it) continue to leave buildings by the first-floor door rather than the upstairs window, and "Nature will always maintain her rights and prevail in the end over any abstract reasoning whatever."

The article "An Encounter with David Hume" was written specifically for the third edition of this volume by Wesley C. Salmon of the University of Arizona. It is meant to show the beginning student of philosophy and science ("Physics 1a") how natural Hume's doubts can seem to one who ponders the methods and results of the exact sciences, and how important it is to our conception of scientific knowledge to come to terms with those doubts. In particular, Salmon discusses such scientific notions as causation, inductive inference, probability, laws of nature, the regularity of nature, necessity, and predictability, in the light of Hume's empiricism. Salmon's essay views these matters through the eyes of a sensitive undergraduate student of physics who comes to wonder whether all science rests ultimately on a kind of "faith" in the uniformity of nature that cannot be rationally demonstrated to be correct. If that is so, he asks (with a certain amount of anguish), how can physics be shown to be a more reliable guide to knowledge of the future than, say, astrology or crystal gazing? These questions pose in a very rough way what has come to be called "the problem of induction" or "Hume's riddle of induction." Salmon concludes by sketching the main strategies that have been proposed by philosophers for coming to terms with Hume's skeptical doubts about scientific method.

RENÉ DESCARTES

Meditations on First Philosophy*

René Descartes (1596–1650) is commonly said to be the founder of modern philosophy. Among his other achievements was the invention of analytical geometry.

SYNOPSIS OF THE SIX
FOLLOWING MEDITATIONS

In the first Meditation I set forth the reasons for which we may, generally speaking, doubt about all things and especially about material things, at least so long as we have no other foundations for the sciences than those which we have hitherto possessed. But although the utility of a Doubt which is so general does not at first appear, it is at the same time very great, inasmuch as it delivers us from every kind of prejudice, and sets out for us a very simple way by which the mind may detach itself from the senses; and finally it makes it impossible for us ever to doubt those things which we have once discovered to be true.

In the second Meditation, mind, which making use of the liberty which pertains to it, takes for granted that all those things of whose existence it has the least doubt, are non-existent, recognises that it is however absolutely impossible that it does not itself exist. This point is likewise of the greatest moment, inasmuch as by this means a distinction is easily drawn between the things which pertain to mind—that is to say to the intellectual nature—and those which pertain to body.

But because it may be that some expect from me in this place a statement of the reasons establishing the immortality of the soul, I feel that I should here make known to them that having aimed at writing nothing in all this Treatise of which I do not possess

very exact demonstrations, I am obliged to follow a similar order to that made use of by the geometers, which is to begin by putting forward as premises all those things upon which the proposition that we seek depends, before coming to any conclusion regarding it. Now the first and principal matter which is requisite for thoroughly understanding the immortality of the soul is to form the clearest possible conception of it, and one which will be entirely distinct from all the conceptions which we may have of body; and in this Meditation this has been done. In addition to this it is requisite that we may be assured that all the things which we conceive clearly and distinctly are true in the very way in which we think them; and this could not be proved previously to the Fourth Meditation. Further we must have a distinct conception of corporeal nature, which is given partly in this Second, and partly in the Fifth and Sixth Meditations. And finally we should conclude from all this, that those things which we conceive clearly and distinctly as being diverse substances, as we regard mind and body to be, are really substances essentially distinct one from the other; and this is the conclusion of the Sixth Meditation. This is further confirmed in this same Meditation by the fact that we cannot conceive of body excepting in so far as it is divisible, while the mind cannot be conceived of excepting as indivisible. For we are not able to conceive of the half of a mind as we can do of the smallest of all bodies; so that we see that not only are their natures different but even in some respects contrary to one another. I have not however dealt further with this matter in this Treatise, both because what I have said is sufficient to show clearly enough that the extinction of the mind does not follow from the corruption of the body, and also to give men the hope of another life after death, as also because the premises from which the immortality of the soul may be deduced depend on an elucidation of a complete system of Physics. This would mean

*René Descartes, *Meditations on First Philosophy*, trans. Elizabeth Haldane and G. R. T. Ross (London: Cambridge University Press, 1931). Reprinted by permission of the publisher. First published in Latin in 1641.

to establish in the first place that all substances generally—that is to say all things which cannot exist without being created by God—are in their nature incorruptible, and that they can never cease to exist unless God, in denying to them his concurrence, reduce them to nought; and secondly that body, regarded generally, is a substance, which is the reason why it also cannot perish, but that the human body, inasmuch as it differs from other bodies, is composed only of a certain configuration of members and of other similar accidents, while the human mind is not similarly composed of any accidents, but is a pure substance. For although all the accidents of mind be changed, although, for instance, it think certain things, will others, perceive others, etc., despite all this it does not emerge from these changes another mind: the human body on the other hand becomes a different thing from the sole fact that the figure or form of any of its portions is found to be changed. From this it follows that the human body may indeed easily enough perish, but the mind [or soul of man (I make no distinction between them)] is owing to its nature immortal.

In the Third Meditation it seems to me that I have explained at sufficient length the principal argument of which I make use in order to prove the existence of God. But none the less, because I did not wish in that place to make use of any comparisons derived from corporeal things, so as to withdraw as much as I could the minds of readers from the senses, there may perhaps have remained many obscurities which, however, will, I hope, be entirely removed by the Replies which I have made to the Objections which have been set before me. Amongst others there is, for example, this one, 'How the idea in us of a being supremely perfect possesses so much objective reality (that is to say participates by representation in so many degrees of being and perfection) that it necessarily proceeds from a cause which is absolutely perfect.' This is illustrated in these Replies by the comparison of a very perfect machine, the idea of which is found in the mind of some workman. For as the objective contrivance of this idea must have some cause, i.e. either the science of the workman or that of some other from whom he has received the idea, it is similarly impossible that the idea of God which is in us should not have God himself as its cause.

In the Fourth Meditation it is shown that all these things which we very clearly and distinctly perceive are true, and at the same time it is explained in what the nature of error or falsity consists. This must of necessity be known both for the confirmation of the preceding truths and for the better comprehension of those that follow. (But it must meanwhile be remarked that I do not in any way there treat of sin— that is to say of the error which is committed in the pursuit of good and evil, but only of that which arises in the deciding between the true and the false. And I do not intend to speak of matters pertaining to the Faith or the conduct of life, but only of those which concern speculative truths, and which may be known by the sole aid of the light of nature.)

In the Fifth Meditation corporeal nature generally is explained, and in addition to this the existence of God is demonstrated by a new proof in which there may possibly be certain difficulties also, but the solution of these will be seen in the Replies to the Objections. And further I show in what sense it is true to say that the certainty of geometrical demonstrations is itself dependent on the knowledge of God.

Finally in the Sixth I distinguish the action of the understanding [intellectio] from that of the imagination [imaginatio]; the marks by which this distinction is made are described. I here show that the mind of man is really distinct from the body, and at the same time that the two are so closely joined together that they form, so to speak, a single thing. All the errors which proceed from the senses are then surveyed, while the means of avoiding them are demonstrated, and finally all the reasons from which we may deduce the existence of material things are set forth. Not that I judge them to be very useful in establishing that which they prove, to wit, that there is in truth a world, that men possess bodies, and other such things which never have been doubted by anyone of sense; but because in considering these closely we come to see that they are neither so strong nor so evident as those arguments which lead us to the knowledge of our mind and of God; so that these last must be the most certain and most evident facts which can fall within the cognizance of the human mind. And this is the whole matter that I have tried to prove in these Meditations, for which reason I here omit to speak of many other questions with which I dealt incidentally in this discussion.

MEDITATION I

Of the things which may be brought within the sphere of the doubtful.

It is now some years since I detected how many were the false beliefs that I had from my earliest youth admitted as true, and how doubtful was everything I had since constructed on this basis; and from that time I was convinced that I must once for all seriously undertake to rid myself of all the opinions which I had formerly accepted, and commence to build anew from the foundation, if I wanted to establish any firm and permanent structure in the sciences. But as this enterprise appeared to be a very great one, I waited until I had attained an age so mature that I could not hope that at any later date I should be better fitted to execute my design. This reason caused me to delay so long that I should feel that I was doing wrong were I to occupy in deliberation the time that yet remains to me for action. To-day, then, since very opportunely for the plan I have in view I have delivered my mind from every care [and am happily agitated by no passions] and since I have procured for myself an assured leisure in a peaceable retirement, I shall at last seriously and freely address myself to the general upheaval of all my former opinions.

Now for this object it is not necessary that I should show that all of these are false—I shall perhaps never arrive at this end. But inasmuch as reason already persuades me that I ought no less carefully to withhold my assent from matters which are not entirely certain and indubitable than from those which appear to me manifestly to be false, if I am able to find in each one some reason to doubt, this will suffice to justify my rejecting the whole. And for that end it will not be requisite that I should examine each in particular, which would be an endless undertaking; for owing to the fact that the destruction of the foundations of necessity brings with it the downfall of the rest of the edifice, I shall only in the first place attack those principles upon which all my former opinions rested.

All that up to the present time I have accepted as most true and certain I have learned either from the senses or through the senses; but it is sometimes proved to me that these senses are deceptive, and it is wiser not to trust entirely to any thing by which we have once been deceived.

But it may be that although the senses sometimes deceive us concerning things which are hardly perceptible, or very far away, there are yet many others to be met with as to which we cannot reasonably have any doubt, although we recognize them by their means. For example, there is the fact that I am here, seated by the fire, attired in a dressing gown, having this paper in my hands and other similar matters. And how could I deny that these hands and this body are mine, were it not perhaps that I compare myself to certain persons, devoid of sense, whose cerebella are so troubled and clouded by the violent vapours of black bile, that they constantly assure us that they think they are kings when they are really quite poor, or that they are clothed in purple when they are really without covering, or who imagine that they have an earthenware head or are nothing but pumpkins or are made of glass. But they are mad, and I should not be any the less insane were I to follow examples so extravagant.

At the same time I must remember that I am a man, and that consequently I am in the habit of sleeping, and in my dreams representing to myself the same things or sometimes even less probable things, than do those who are insane in their waking moments. How often has it happened to me that in the night I dreamt that I found myself in this particular place, that I was dressed and seated near the fire, whilst in reality I was lying undressed in bed! At this moment it does indeed seem to me that it is with eyes awake that I am looking at this paper; that this head which I move is not asleep, that it is deliberately and of set purpose that I extend my hand and perceive it; what happens in sleep does not appear so clear nor so distinct as does all this. But in thinking over this I remind myself that on many occasions I have in sleep been deceived by similar illusions, and in dwelling carefully on this reflection I see so manifestly that there are no certain indications by which we may clearly distinguish wakefulness from sleep that I am lost in astonishment. And my astonishment is such that it is almost capable of persuading me that I now dream.

Now let us assume that we are asleep and that all these particulars, e.g. that we open our eyes, shake our head, extend our hands, and so on, are but false delusions; and let us reflect that possibly neither our hands nor our whole body are such as they appear to us to be. At the same time we must at least confess that the things which are represented to us in sleep are like painted representations which can only have been formed as the counterparts of something real and true, and that in this way those general things at least, i.e. eyes, a head, hands, and a whole body, are not imaginary things, but things really existent. For, as a matter of fact, painters, even when they study with the greatest skill to represent sirens and satyrs by forms the most strange and extraordinary, cannot give them natures which are entirely new, but merely make a certain medley of the members of different animals; or if their imagination is extravagant enough to invent something so novel that nothing similar has ever before been seen, and that then their work represents a thing purely fictitious and absolutely false, it is certain all the same that the colours of which this is composed are necessarily real. And for the same reason, although these general things, to wit, [a body], eyes, a head, hands, and such like, may be imaginary, we are bound at the same time to confess that there are at least some other objects yet more simple and more universal, which are real and true; and of these just in the same way as with certain real colours, all these images of things which dwell in our thoughts, whether true and real or false and fantastic, are formed.

To such a class of things pertains corporeal nature in general, and its extension, the figure of extended things, their quantity or magnitude and number, as also the place in which they are, the time which measures their duration, and so on.

That is possibly why our reasoning is not unjust when we conclude from this that Physics, Astronomy, Medicine and all other sciences which have as their end the consideration of composite things, are very dubious and uncertain; but that Arithmetic, Geometry and other sciences of that kind which only treat of things that are very simple and very general, without taking great trouble to ascertain whether they are actually existent or not, contain some measure of certainty and an element of the indubitable. For whether I am awake or asleep, two and three together always form five, and the square can never have more than four sides, and it does not seem possible that truths so clear and apparent can be suspected of any falsity [or uncertainty].

Nevertheless I have long had fixed in my mind the belief that an all-powerful God existed by whom I have been created such as I am. But how do I know that He has not brought it to pass that there is no earth, no heaven, no extended body, no magnitude, no place, and that nevertheless [I possess the perceptions of all these things and that] they seem to me to exist just exactly as I now see them? And, besides, as I sometimes imagine that others deceive themselves in the things which they think they know best, how do I know that I am not deceived every time that I add two and three, or count the sides of a square, or judge of things yet simpler, if anything simpler

can be imagined? But possibly God has not desired that I should be thus deceived, for He is said to be supremely good. If, however, it is contrary to His goodness to have made me such that I constantly deceive myself, it would also appear to be contrary to His goodness to permit me to be sometimes deceived, and nevertheless I cannot doubt that He does permit this.

There may indeed be those who would prefer to deny the existence of a God so powerful, rather than believe that all other things are uncertain. But let us not oppose them for the present, and grant that all that is here said of a God is a fable; nevertheless in whatever way they suppose that I have arrived at the state of being that I have reached—whether they attribute it to fate or to accident, or make out that it is by a continual succession of antecedents, or by some other method—since to err and deceive oneself is a defect, it is clear that the greater will be the probability of my being so imperfect as to deceive myself ever, as is the Author to whom they assign my origin the less powerful. To these reasons I have certainly nothing to reply, but at the end I feel constrained to confess that there is nothing in all that I formerly believed to be true, of which I cannot in some measure doubt, and that not merely through want of thought or through levity, but for reasons which are very powerful and maturely considered; so that henceforth I ought not the less carefully refrain from giving credence to these opinions than to that which is manifestly false, if I desire to arrive at any certainty [in the sciences].

But it is not sufficient to have made these remarks, we must also be careful to keep them in mind. For these ancient and commonly held opinions still revert frequently to my mind, long and familiar custom having given them the right to occupy my mind against my inclination and rendered them almost masters of my belief; nor will I ever lose the habit of deferring to them or of placing my confidence in them, so long as I consider them as they really are, i.e. opinions in some measure, doubtful, as I have just shown, and at the same time highly probable, so that there is much more reason to believe in than to deny them. That is why I consider that I shall not be acting amiss, if, taking of set purpose a contrary belief, I allow myself to be deceived, and for a certain time pretend that all these opinions are entirely false and imaginary, until at last, having thus balanced my former prejudices with my latter [so that they cannot divert my opinions more to one side than to the other], my judgment will no longer be dominated by bad usage or turned away from the right knowledge of the truth. For I am assured that there can be neither peril nor error in this course, and that I cannot at present yield too much to distrust, since I am not considering the question of action, but only of knowledge.

I shall then suppose, not that God who is supremely good and the fountain of truth, but some evil genius not less powerful than deceitful, has employed his whole energies in deceiving me; I shall consider that the heavens, the earth, colours, figures, sound, and all other external things are nought but the illusions and dreams of which this genius has availed himself in order to lay traps for my credulity; I shall consider myself as having no hands, no eyes, no flesh, no blood, nor any senses, yet falsely believing myself to possess all these things; I shall remain obstinately attached to this idea, and if by this means it is not in my power to arrive at the knowledge of any truth, I may at least do what is in my power [i.e. suspend my judgment], and with firm purpose avoid giving credence to any false thing, or being imposed upon by this arch deceiver, however powerful and deceptive he may be. But this task is a laborious one, and insensibly a certain lassitude leads me into the course of my ordinary life. And just as a captive who in sleep enjoys an imaginary liberty, when he begins to suspect that his liberty is but a dream, fears to awaken, and conspires with these agreeable illusions that the deception may be prolonged, so insensibly of my own accord I fall back into my former opinions, and I dread awakening from this slumber, lest the laborious wakefulness which would follow the tranquility of this repose should have to be spent not in daylight, but in the excessive darkness of the difficulties which have just been discussed.

MEDITATION II

Of the Nature of the Human Mind; and that it is more easily known than the Body.

The Meditation of yesterday filled my mind with so many doubts that it is no longer in my power to forget them. And yet I do not see in what manner I can resolve them; and, just as if I had all of a sudden fallen into very deep water, I am so disconcerted that I can neither make certain of setting my feet on the bottom, nor can I swim and so support myself on the surface. I shall nevertheless make an effort and follow anew the same path as that on which I yesterday entered, i.e. I shall proceed by setting aside all that in which the least doubt could be supposed to exist, just as if I had discovered that it was absolutely false; and I shall ever follow in this road until I have met with something which is certain, or at least, if I can do nothing else, until I have learned for certain that there is nothing in the world that is certain. Archimedes, in order that he might draw the terrestrial globe out of its place, and transport it elsewhere, demanded only that one point should be fixed and immovable; in the same way I shall have the right to conceive high hopes if I am happy enough to discover one thing only which is certain and indubitable.

I suppose, then, that all the things that I see are false; I persuade myself that nothing has ever existed of all that my fallacious memory represents to me. I consider that I possess no senses; I imagine that body, figure, extension, movement and place are but the fictions of my mind. What, then, can be esteemed as true? Perhaps nothing at all, unless that there is nothing in the world that is certain.

But how can I know there is not something different from those things that I have just considered, of which one cannot have the slightest doubt? Is there not some God, or some other being by whatever name we call it, who puts these reflections into my mind? That is not necessary, for is it not possible that I am capable of producing them myself? I myself, am I not at least something? But I have already denied that I had senses and body. Yet I hesitate, for what follows from that? Am I so dependent on body and senses that I cannot exist without these? But I was persuaded that there was nothing in all the world, that there was no heaven, no earth, that there were no minds, nor any bodies: was I not then likewise persuaded that I did not exist? Not at all; of a surety I myself did exist since I persuaded myself of something [or merely because I thought of something]. But there is some deceiver or other, very powerful and very cunning, who ever employs his ingenuity in deceiving me. Then without doubt I exist also if he deceives me, and let him deceive me as much as he will, he can never cause me to be nothing so long as I think that I am something. So that after having reflected well and carefully examined all things, we must come to the definite conclusion that this proposition: I am, I exist, is necessary true each time that I pronounce it, or that I mentally conceive it.

But I do not yet know clearly enough what I am, I who am certain that I am; and hence I must be careful to see that I do not imprudently take some other object in place of myself, and thus that I do not go astray in respect of this knowledge that I hold to be the most certain and most evident of all that I have formerly learned. That is why I shall now consider anew what I believed myself to be before I embarked upon these last reflections; and of my former opinions I shall withdraw all that might even in a small degree be invalidated by the reasons which I have just brought forward, in order that there may be nothing at all left beyond what is absolutely certain and indubitable.

What then did I formerly believe myself to be? Undoubtedly I believed myself to be a man. But what is a man? Shall I say a reasonable animal? Certainly not; for then I should have to inquire what an animal is, and what is reasonable; and thus from a single question I should insensibly fall into an infinitude of others more difficult; and I should not wish to waste the little time and leisure remaining to me in trying to unravel subtleties like these. But I shall rather stop here to consider the thoughts which of themselves spring up in my mind, and which were not inspired by anything beyond my own nature alone when I applied myself to the consideration of my being. In the first place, then, I considered myself as having a face, hands, arms, and all that system of members composed of bones and flesh as seen in a corpse which I designated by the name of body. In addition to this I considered that I was nourished, that I walked, that I felt, and that I thought, and I referred all these actions to the soul: but I did not stop to consider what the soul was, or if I did stop. I imagined that it was something extremely rare and subtle like a wind, a flame, or an ether, which was spread throughout my grosser parts. As to body I had no manner of doubt about its nature, but thought I had a very clear knowledge of it; and if I had desired to explain it according to the notions that I had then formed of it, I should have described it thus: By the body I understand all that which can be defined by a certain figure: something which can be confined in a certain place, and which can fill a given space in such a way that every other body will be excluded from it; which can be perceived either by touch, or by sight, or by hearing, or by taste, or by smell: which can be moved in many ways not, in truth,

by itself, but by something which is foreign to it, by which it is touched [and from which it receives impressions]: for to have the power of self-movement, as also of feeling or of thinking, I did not consider to appertain to the nature of body: on the contrary, I was rather astonished to find that faculties similar to them existed in some bodies.

But what am I, now that I suppose that there is a certain genius which is extremely powerful, and, if I may say so, malicious, who employs all his powers in deceiving me? Can I affirm that I possess the least of all those things which I have just said pertain to the nature of body? I pause to consider, I revolve all these things in my mind, and I find none of which I can say that it pertains to me. It would be tedious to stop to enumerate them. Let us pass to the attributes of soul and see if there is any one which is in me? What of nutrition or walking [the first mentioned]? But if it is so that I have no body it is also true that I can neither walk nor take nourishment. Another attribute is sensation. But one cannot feel without body, and besides I have thought I perceived many things during sleep that I recognised in my waking moments as not having been experienced at all. What of thinking? I find here that thought is an attribute that belongs to me; it alone cannot be separated from me. I am, I exist, that is certain. But how often? Just when I think; for it might possibly be the case if I ceased entirely to think, that I should likewise cease altogether to exist. I do not now admit anything which is not necessarily true: to speak accurately I am not more than a thing which thinks, that is to say a mind or a soul, or an understanding, or a reason, which are terms whose significance was formerly unknown to me. I am, however, a real thing and really exist; but what thing? I have answered: a thing which thinks.

And what more? I shall exercise my imagination [in order to see if I am not something more]. I am not a collection of members which we call the human body: I am not a subtle air distributed through these members, I am not a wind, a fire, a vapour, a breath, or anything at all which I can imagine or conceive; because I have assumed that all these were nothing. Without changing that supposition I find that I only leave myself certain of the fact that I am somewhat. But perhaps it is true that these same things which I supposed were non-existent because they are unknown to me, are really not different from the self which I know. I am not sure about this, I shall not dispute about it now; I can only give judgment on things that are known to me. I know that I exist, and I inquire what I am, I whom I know to exist. But it is very certain that the knowledge of my existence taken in its precise significance does not depend on things whose existence is not yet known to me; consequently it does not depend on those which I can feign in imagination. And indeed the very term *feign* in imagination proves to me my error, for I really do this if I image myself a something, since to imagine is nothing else than to contemplate the figure or image of a corporeal thing. But I already know for certain that I am, and that it may be that all these images, and, speaking generally, all things that relate to the nature of body are nothing but dreams [and chimeras]. For this reason I see clearly that I have as little reason to say, 'I shall stimulate my imagination in order to know more distinctly what I am,' than if I were to say, 'I am now awake, and I perceive somewhat that is real and true: but because I do not yet perceive it distinctly enough, I shall go to sleep of express purpose, so that my dreams may represent the perception with greatest truth and evidence.' And, thus, I know for certain that nothing of all that I can understand by means of my imagination belongs to this knowledge which I have of myself, and that it is necessary to recall the mind from this mode of thought with the utmost diligence in order that it may be able to know its own nature with perfect distinctness.

But what then am I? A thing which thinks. What is a thing which thinks? It is a thing which doubts, understands, [conceives], affirms, denies, wills, refuses, which also imagines and feels.

Certainly it is no small matter if all these things pertain to my nature. But why should they not so pertain? Am I not that being who now doubts nearly everything, who nevertheless understands certain things, who affirms that one only is true, who denies all the others, who desires to know more, is averse from being deceived, who imagines many things, sometimes indeed despite his will, and who perceives many likewise, as by the intervention of the bodily organs? Is there nothing in all this which is as true as it is certain that I exist, even though I should always sleep and though he who has given me being employed all his ingenuity in deceiving me? Is there likewise any one of these attributes which can be distinguished from my thought, or which might be said to be separated from myself? For it is so evident of itself that it is I who doubt, who understand, and who desire, that there is no reason here to add anything to explain it. And I have certainly the power of imagining likewise; for although it may happen (as I formerly supposed) that none of the things which I imagine are true, nevertheless this power of imagining does not cease to be really in use, and it forms part of my thought. Finally, I am the same who feels, that is to say, who perceives certain things, as by the organs of sense, since in truth I see light, I hear noise, I feel heat. But it will be said that these phenomena are false and that I am dreaming. Let it be so; still it is at least quite certain that it seems to me that I see light, that I hear noise and that I feel heat. That cannot be false; properly speaking it is what is in me called feeling; and used in this precise sense that is no other thing than thinking.

From this time I begin to know what I am with a little more clearness and distinction than before; but nevertheless it still seems to me, and I cannot prevent myself from thinking, that corporeal things, whose images are framed by thought, which are tested by the senses, are much more distinctly known than that obscure part of me which does not come under the imagination. Although really it is very strange to say that I know and understand more distinctly these things whose existence seems to me dubious, which are unknown to me, and which do not belong to me, than others of the truth of which I am convinced, which are known to me and which pertain to my real nature, in a word, than myself. But I see clearly how the case stands: my mind loves to wander, and cannot yet suffer itself to be retained within the just limits of truth. Very good, let us once more give it the freest rein, so that, when afterwards we seize the proper occasion for pulling up, it may the more easily be regulated and controlled.

Let us begin by considering the commonest matters, those which we believe to be the most distinctly comprehended, to wit, the bodies which we touch and see; not indeed bodies in general, for these general ideas are usually a little more confused, but let us consider one body in particular. Let us take, for example, this piece of wax: it has been taken quite freshly from the hive, and it has not yet lost the sweetness of the honey which it contains; it still retains somewhat of the odour of the flowers from which it has been culled; its colour, its figure, its size are apparent; it is hard, cold, easily handled, and if you strike it with the finger, it will emit a sound. Finally all the things which are requisite to cause us distinctly to recognise a body, are met with in it. But notice that while I speak and approach the fire what remained of the taste is exhaled, the smell evaporates, the colour alters, the figure is destroyed, the size increases, it becomes liquid, it heats, scarcely can one handle it, and when one strikes it, no sound is emitted. Does the same wax remain after this change? We must confess that it remains; none would judge otherwise. What then did I know so distinctly in this piece of wax? It could certainly be nothing of all that the senses brought to my notice, since all these things which fall under taste, smell, sight, touch, and hearing, are found to be changed, and yet the same wax remains.

Perhaps it was what I now think, viz, that this wax was not that sweetness of honey, nor that agreeable scent of flowers, nor that particular whiteness, nor that figure, nor that sound, but simply a body which a little while before appeared to me as perceptible under these forms, and which is now perceptible under others. But what, precisely, is it that I imagine when I form such conceptions? Let us attentively consider this, and, abstracting from all that does not belong to the wax, let us see what remains. Certainly nothing remains excepting a certain extended thing which is flexible and movable. But what is the meaning of flexible and movable? Is it not that I imagine that this piece of wax being round is capable of becoming square and of passing from a square to a triangular figure? No, certainly it is not that, since I imagine it admits of an infinitude of similar changes, and I nevertheless do not know how to compass the infinitude by my imagination, and consequently this conception which I have of the wax is not brought about by the faculty of imagination. What now is this extension? Is it not also unknown? For it becomes greater when the wax is melted, greater when it is boiled, and greater still when the heat increases; and I should not conceive [clearly] according to truth what wax is, if I did not think that even this piece that we are considering is capable of receiving more variations in extension than I have ever imagined. We must then grant that I could not even understand through the imagination what this piece of wax is, and that it is my mind alone which perceives it. I say this piece of wax in particular, for as to wax in general it is yet clearer. But what is this piece of wax which cannot be understood excepting by the [understanding or] mind? It is certainly the same that I see, touch,

imagine, and finally it is the same which I have always believed it to be from the beginning. But what must particularly be observed is that its perception is neither an act of vision, nor of touch, nor of imagination, and has never been such although it may have appeared formerly to be so, but only an intuition of the mind, which may be imperfect and confused as it was formerly, or clear and distinct as it is at present, according as my attention is more or less directed to the elements which are found in it, and of which it is composed.

Yet in the meantime I am greatly astonished when I consider [the great feebleness of mind] and its proneness to fall [insensibly] into error; for although without giving expression to my thoughts I consider all this in my own mind, words often impede me and I am almost deceived by the terms of ordinary language. For we say that we see the same wax, if it is present, and not that we simply judge that it is the same from its having the same colour and figure. From this I should conclude that I knew the wax by means of vision and not simply by the intuition of the mind; unless by chance I remember that, when looking from a window and saying I see men who pass in the street, I really do not see them, but infer that what I see is men, just as I say that I see wax. And yet what do I see from the window but hats and coats which may cover automatic machines? Yet I judge these to be men. And similarly solely by the faculty of judgment which rests in my mind, I comprehend that which I believed I saw with my eyes.

A man who makes it his aim to raise his knowledge above the common should be ashamed to derive the occasion for doubting from the forms of speech invented by the vulgar; I prefer to pass on and consider whether I had a more evident and perfect conception of what the wax was when I first perceived it, and when I believed I knew it by means of the external senses or at least by the common sense as it is called, that is to say by the imaginative faculty, or whether my present conception is clearer now that I have most carefully examined what it is, and in what way it can be known. It would certainly be absurd to doubt as to this. For what was there in this first perception which was distinct? What was there which might not as well have been perceived by any of the animals? But when I distinguish the wax from its external forms, and when, just as if I had taken from it its vestments, I consider it quite naked, it is certain that although some error may still be found in my judgment, I can nevertheless not perceive it thus without a human mind.

But finally what shall I say of this mind, that is, of myself, for up to this point I do not admit in myself anything but mind? What then, I who seem to perceive this piece of wax so distinctly, do I not know myself, not only with much more truth and certainty, but also with much more distinctness and clearness? For if I judge that the wax is or exists from the fact that I see it, it certainly follows much more clearly that I am or that I exist myself from the fact that I see it. For it may be that what I see is not really wax, it may also be that I do not possess eyes with which to see anything; but it cannot be that when I see, or (for I no longer take account of the distinction) when I think I see, that I myself who think am nought. So if I judge that the wax exists from the fact that I touch it, the same thing will follow, to wit, that I am; and if I judge that my imagination, or some other cause, whatever it is, persuades me that wax exists, I shall still conclude the same. And what I have here remarked of wax may be applied to all other things which are external to me [and which are met with outside of me]. And further, if the [notion or] perception of wax has seemed to me clearer and more distinct, not only after the sight or the touch, but also after many other causes have rendered it quite manifest to me, with how much more [evidence] and distinctness must it be said that I now know myself, since all the reasons which contribute to the knowledge of wax, or any other body whatever, are yet better proofs of the nature of my mind! And there are so many other things in the mind itself which may contribute to the elucidation of its nature, that those which depend on body such as these just mentioned, hardly merit being taken into account.

But finally here I am, having insensibly reverted to the point I desired, for, since it is now manifest to me that even bodies are not properly speaking known by the senses or by the faculty of imagination, but by the understanding only, and since they are not known from the fact that they are seen or touched, but only because they are understood, I see clearly that there is nothing which is easier for me to know than my mind. But because it is difficult to rid oneself so promptly of an opinion to which one was accustomed for so long, it will be well that I should halt a little at this point, so that by the length of my medi-

tation I may more deeply imprint on my memory this new knowledge.

MEDITATION III

Of God: That He exists.

I shall now close my eyes, I shall stop my ears, I shall call away all my senses, I shall efface even from my thoughts all the images of corporeal things, or at least (for that is hardly possible) I shall esteem them as vain and false; and thus holding converse only with myself and considering my own nature, I shall try little by little to reach a better knowledge of and a more familiar acquaintanceship with myself. I am a thing that thinks, that is to say, that doubts, affirms, denies, that knows a few things, that is ignorant of many [that loves, that hates], that wills, that desires, that also imagines and perceives; for as I remarked before, although the things which I perceive and imagine are perhaps nothing at all apart from me and in themselves, I am nevertheless assured that these modes of thought that I call perceptions and imaginations, inasmuch only as they are modes of thought, certainly reside [and are met with] in me.

And in the little that I have just said, I think I have summed up all that I really know, or at least all that hitherto I was aware that I knew. In order to try to extend my knowledge further, I shall now look around more carefully and see whether I cannot still discover in myself some other things which I have not hitherto perceived. I am certain that I am a thing which thinks; but do I not then likewise know what is requisite to render me certain of a truth? Certainly in this first knowledge there is nothing that assures me of its truth, excepting the clear and distinct perception of that which I state, which would not indeed suffice to assure me that what I say is true, if it could ever happen that a thing which I conceived so clearly and distinctly could be false; and accordingly it seems to me that already I can establish as a general rule that all things which I perceive very clearly and very distinctly are true.

At the same time I have before received and admitted many things to be very certain and manifest, which yet I afterwards recognised as being dubious. What then were these things? They were the earth, sky, stars and all other objects which I apprehended by means of the senses. But what did I clearly [and distinctly] perceive in them? Nothing more than that the ideas or thoughts of these things were presented to my mind. And not even now do I deny that these ideas are met with in me. But there was yet another thing which I affirmed, and which, owing to the habit which I had formed of believing it, I thought I perceived very clearly, although in truth I did not perceive it at all, to wit, that there were objects outside of me from which these ideas proceeded, and to which they were entirely similar. And it was in this that I erred, or, if perchance my judgement was correct, this was not due to any knowledge arising from my perception.

But when I took anything very simple and easy in the sphere of arithmetic or geometry into consideration, e.g. that two and three together made five, and other things of the sort, were not these present to my mind so clearly as to enable me to affirm that they were true? Certainly if I judged that since such matters could be doubted, this would not have been so for any other reason than that it came into my mind that perhaps a God might have endowed me with such a nature that I may have been deceived even concerning things which seemed to me most manifest. But every time that this preconceived opinion of the sovereign power of a God presents itself to my thought, I am constrained to confess that it is easy to Him, if He wishes it, to cause me to err, even in matters in which I believe myself to have the best evidence. And, on the other hand, always when I direct my attention to things which I believe myself to perceive very clearly, I am so persuaded of their truth that I let myself break out into words such as these: Let who will deceive me, He can never cause me to be nothing while I think that I am, or some day cause it to be true to say that I have never been, it being true now to say that I am, or that two and three make more or less than five, or any such thing in which I see a manifest contradiction. And, certainly, since I have no reason to believe that there is a God who is a deceiver, and as I have not yet satisfied myself that there is a God at all, the reason for doubt which depends on this opinion alone is very slight, and so to speak metaphysical. But in order to be able altogether to remove it, I must inquire whether there is a God as soon as the occasion presents itself; and if I find that there is a God, I must also inquire whether He may be a deceiver; for without a knowledge of these two truths I do not see that I can ever be certain of anything.

And in order that I may have an opportunity of inquiring into this in an orderly way [without interrupting the order of meditation which I have proposed to myself, and which is little by little to pass from the notions which I find first of all in my mind to those which I shall later on discover in it] it is requisite that I should here divide my thoughts into certain kinds, and that I should consider in which of these kinds there is, properly speaking, truth or error to be found. Of my thoughts some are, so to speak, images of the things, and to these alone is the title 'idea' properly applied; examples are my thought of a man or of a chimera, of heaven, of an angel, or [even] of God. But other thoughts possess other forms as well. For example in willing, fearing, approving, denying, though I always perceive something as the subject of the action of my mind; yet by this action I always add something else to the idea which I have of that thing; and of the thoughts of this kind some are called volitions or affections, and others judgments.

Now as to what concerns ideas, if we consider them only in themselves and do not relate them to anything else beyond themselves, they cannot properly speaking be false; for whether I imagine a goat or a chimera, it is not less true that I imagine the one than the other. We must not fear likewise that falsity can enter into will and into affections, for although I may desire evil things, or even things that never existed, it is not the less true that I desire them. Thus there remains no more than the judgments which we make, in which I must take the greatest care not to deceive myself. But the principal error and the commonest which we may meet with in them, consists in my judging that the ideas which are in me are similar or conformable to the things which are outside me; for without doubt if I considered the ideas only as certain modes of my thoughts, without trying to relate them to anything beyond, they could scarcely give me material for error.

But among these ideas, some appear to me to be innate, some adventitious, and others to be formed [or invented] by myself; for, as I have the power of understanding what is called a thing, or a truth, or a thought, it appears to me that I hold this power from no other source than my own nature. But if now I hear some sound, if I see the sun, or feel heat, I have hitherto judged that these sensations proceeded from certain things that exist outside of me; and finally it appears to me that sirens, hippogryphs, and the like, are formed out of my own mind. But again I may possibly persuade myself that all these ideas are of the nature of those which I term adventitious, or else that they are all innate, or all fictitious: for I have not yet clearly discovered their true origin.

And my principal task in this place is to consider, in respect to those ideas which appear to me to proceed from certain objects that are outside me, what are the reasons which cause me to think them similar to these objects. It seems indeed in the first place that I am taught this lesson by nature; and, secondly, I experience in myself that these ideas do not depend on my will nor therefore on myself—for they often present themselves to my mind in spite of my will. Just now, for instance, whether I will or whether I do not will, I feel heat, and thus I persuade myself that this feeling, or at least this idea of heat, is produced in me by something which is different from me, i.e. by the heat of the fire near which I sit. And nothing seems to me more obvious than to judge that this object imprints its likeness rather than anything else upon me.

Now I must discover whether these proofs are sufficiently strong and convincing. When I say that I am so instructed by nature, I merely mean a certain spontaneous inclination which impels me to believe in this connection, and not a natural light which makes me recognise that it is true. But these two things are very different; for I cannot doubt that which the natural light causes me to believe to be true, as, for example, it has shown me that I am from the fact that I doubt, or other facts of the same kind. And I possess no other faculty whereby to distinguish truth from falsehood, which can teach me that what this light shows me to be true is not really true, and no other faculty that is equally truthworthy. But as far as [apparently] natural impulses are concerned, I have frequently remarked, when I had to make active choice between virtue and vice, that they often enough led me to the part that was worse; and this is why I do not see any reason for following them in what regards truth and error.

And as to the other reason, which is that these ideas must proceed from objects outside me, since they do not depend on my will, I do not find it any the more convincing. For just as these impulses of which I have spoken are found in me, notwithstanding that they do not always concur with my will, so perhaps there is in me some faculty fitted to produce these ideas without the assistance of any external things, even though it is not yet known by me; just as, apparently, they have hitherto always been found in me during sleep without the aid of any external objects.

And finally, though they did proceed from objects different from myself, it is not a necessary consequence that they should resemble these. On the contrary, I have noticed that in many cases there was a difference between the object and its idea. I find, for example, two completely diverse ideas of the sun in my mind; the one derives its origin from the senses, and should be placed in the category of adventitious ideas; according to this idea the sun seems to be extremely small; but the other is derived from astronomical reasonings, i.e. is elicited from certain notions that are innate in me, or else it is formed by me in some other manner; in accordance with it the sun appears to be several times greater than the earth. These two ideas cannot, indeed, both resemble the same sun, and reason makes me believe that the one which seems to have originated directly from the sun itself, is the one which is most dissimilar to it.

All this causes me to believe that until the present time it has not been by a judgment that was certain [or premeditated], but only by a sort of blind impulse that I believed that things existed outside of, and different from me, which, by the organs of my senses, or by some other method whatever it might be, conveyed these ideas or images to me [and imprinted on me their similitudes].

But there is yet another method of inquiring whether any of the objects of which I have ideas within me exist outside of me. If ideas are only taken as certain modes of thought, I recognize amongst them no difference or inequality, and all appear to proceed from me in the same manner; but when we consider them as images, one representing one thing and the other another, it is clear that they are very different one from the other. There is no doubt that those which represent to me substances are something more, and contain so to speak more objective reality within them [that is to say, by representation participate in a higher degree of being or perfection] than those that simply represent modes or accidents; and that idea again by which I understand a supreme God, eternal, infinite, [immutable], omniscient, omnipotent, and Creator of all things which are outside of Himself, has certainly more objective reality in itself than those ideas by which finite substances are represented.

Now it is manifest by the natural light that there must at least be as much reality in the efficient and total cause as in its effect. For, pray, whence can the effect derive its reality, if not from its cause? And in what way can this cause communicate this reality to it, unless it possessed it in itself? And from this it follows, not only that something cannot proceed from nothing, but likewise that what is more perfect—that is to say, which has more reality within itself—cannot proceed from the less perfect. And this is not only evidently true of those effects which possess actual or formal reality, but also of the ideas in which we consider merely what is termed objective reality. To take an example, the stone which has not yet existed not only cannot now commence to be unless it has been produced by something which possesses within itself, either formally or eminently, all that enters into the composition of the stone [i.e. it must possess the same things or other more excellent things than those which exist in the stone] and heat can only be produced in a subject in which it did not previously exist by a cause that is of an order [degree or kind] at least as perfect as heat, and so in all other cases. But further, the idea of heat, or of a stone, cannot exist in me unless it has been placed within me by some cause which possesses within it at least as much reality as that which I conceive to exist in the heat or the stone. For although this cause does not transmit anything of its actual or formal reality to my idea, we must not for that reason imagine that it is necessarily a less real cause; we must remember that [since every idea is a work of the mind] its nature is such that it demands of itself no other formal reality than that which it borrows from my thought, of which it is only a mode [i.e. a manner or way of thinking]. But in order that an idea should contain some one certain objective reality rather than another, it must without doubt derive it from some cause in which there is at least as much formal reality as this idea contains of objective reality. For if we imagine that something is found in an idea which is not found in the cause, it must then have been derived from nought; but however imperfect may be this mode of being by which a thing is objectively [or by representation] in the understanding by its idea, we cannot certainly say that this mode of being is nothing, nor, consequently, that the idea derives its origin from nothing.

Nor must I imagine that, since the reality that I consider in these ideas is only objective, it is not essential that this reality should be formally in the causes of my ideas, but that it is sufficient that it should be found objectively. For just as this mode of objective existence pertains to ideas by their proper nature, so does the mode of formal existence pertain to the causes of those ideas (this is at least true of the first and principal) by the nature peculiar to them. And although it may be the case that one idea gives birth to another idea, that cannot continue to be so indefinitely; for in the end we must reach an idea whose cause shall be so to speak an archetype, in which the whole reality [or perfection] which is so to speak objectively [or by representation] in these ideas is contained formally [and really]. Thus the light of nature causes me to know clearly that the ideas in me are like [pictures or] images which can, in truth, easily fall short of the perfection of the objects from which they have been derived, but which can never contain anything greater or more perfect.

And the longer and the more carefully that I investigate these matters, the more clearly and distinctly do I recognise their truth. But what am I to conclude from it all in the end? It is this, that if the objective reality of any one of my ideas is of such a nature as clearly to make me recognise that it is not in me either formally or eminently, and that consequently I cannot myself be the cause of it, it follows of necessity that I am not alone in the world, but that there is another being which exists, or which is the cause of this idea. On the other hand, had no such an idea existed in me, I should have had no sufficient argument to convince me of the existence of any being beyond myself; for I have made very careful investigation everywhere and up to the present time have been able to find no other ground.

But of my ideas, beyond that which represents me to myself, as to which there can here be no difficulty, there is another which represents a God, and there are others representing corporeal and inanimate things, others angels, others animals, and others again which represent to me men similar to myself.

As regards the ideas which represent to me other men or animals, or angels, I can however easily conceive that they might be formed by an admixture of the other ideas which I have of myself, of corporeal things, and of God, even although there were apart from me neither men nor animals, nor angels, in all the world.

And in regard to the ideas of corporeal objects, I do not recognise in them anything so great or so excellent that they might not have possibly proceeded from myself; for if I consider them more closely, and examine them individually, as I yesterday examined the idea of wax, I find that there is very little in them which I perceive clearly and distinctly. Magnitude or extension in length, breadth, or depth, I do so perceive; also figure which results from a termination of this extension, the situation which bodies of different figure preserve in relation to one another, and movement or change of situation; to which we may also add substance, duration and number. As to other things such as light, colours, sounds, scents, tastes, heat, cold and the other tactile qualities, they are thought by me with so much obscurity and confusion that I do not even know if they are true or false, i.e. whether the ideas which I form of these qualities are actually the ideas of real objects or not [or whether they only represent chimeras which cannot exist in fact]. For although I have before remarked that it is only in judgments that falsity, properly speaking, or formal falsity, can be met with, a certain material falsity may nevertheless be found in ideas, i.e. when these ideas represent what is nothing as though it were something. For example, the ideas which I have of cold and heat are so far from clear and distinct that by their means I cannot tell whether cold is merely a privation of heat, or heat a privation of cold, or whether both are real qualities, or are not such. And inasmuch as [since ideas resemble images] there cannot be any ideas which do not appear to represent some things, if it is correct to say that cold is merely a privation of heat, the idea which represents it to me as something real and positive will not be improperly termed false, and the same holds good of other similar ideas.

To these it is certainly not necessary that I should attribute any author other than myself. For if they are false, i.e. if they represent things which do not exist, the light of nature shows me that they issue from nought, that is to say, that they are only in me in so far as something is lacking to the perfection of my nature. But if they are true, nevertheless because they exhibit so little reality to me that I cannot even clearly distinguish the thing represented from non-being, I do not see any reason why they should not be produced by myself.

As to the clear and distinct idea which I have of corporeal things, some of them seem as though I might have derived them from the idea which I possess of myself, as those which I have of substance, duration, number, and such like. For [even] when I think that a stone is a substance, or at least a thing capable of existing of itself, and that I am a substance also, although I conceive that I am a thing that thinks and not one that is extended, and that the stone on the other hand is an extended thing which does not think, and that thus there is a notable difference between the two conceptions—they seem, nevertheless, to agree in this, that both represent substances. In the same way, when I perceive that I now exist and further recollect that I have in former times existed, and when I remember that I have various thoughts of which I can recognize the number, I acquire ideas of duration and number which I can afterwards transfer to any object that I please. But as to all the other qualities of which the ideas of corporeal things are composed, to wit, extension, figure, situation and motion, it is true that they are not formally in me, since I am only a thing that thinks; but because they are merely certain modes of substance [and so to speak the vestments under which corporeal substance appears to us] and because I myself am also a substance, it would seem that they might be constrained in me eminently.

Hence there remains only the idea of God, concerning which we must consider whether it is something which cannot have proceeded from me myself. By the name God I understand a substance that is infinite [eternal, immutable], independent, all-knowing, all-powerful, and by which I myself and everything else, if anything else does exist, have been created. Now all these characteristics are such that the more diligently I attend to them, the less do they appear capable of proceeding from me alone; hence, from what has been already said, we must conclude that God necessarily exists.

For although the idea of substance is within me owing to the fact that I am substance, nevertheless I should not have the idea of an infinite substance—since I am finite—if it had not proceeded from some substance which was veritably infinite.

Nor should I imagine that I do not perceive the infinite by a true idea, but only by the negation of the finite, just as I perceive repose and darkness by the negation of movement and of light; for, on the contrary, I see that there is manifestly more reality in infinite substance than in finite, and therefore that in some way I have in me the notion of the infinite earlier than the finite—to wit, the notion of God before that of myself. For how would it be possible that I should know that I doubt and desire, that is to say, that something is lacking to me, and that I am not quite perfect, unless I had within me some idea of a Being more perfect than myself, in comparison with which I should recognize the deficiencies of my nature?

And we cannot say that this idea of God is perhaps materially false and that consequently I can derive it from nought [i.e. that possibly it exists in me because I am imperfect], as I have just said is the case with ideas of heat, cold and other such things; for, on the contrary, as this idea is very clear and distinct and contains within it more objective reality than any other, there can be none which is of itself more true, nor any in which there can be less suspicion of falsehood. The idea, I say, of this Being who is absolutely perfect and infinite, is entirely true; for although, perhaps, we can imagine that such a Being does not exist, we cannot nevertheless imagine that His idea represents nothing real to me, as I have said of the idea of cold. This idea is also very clear and distinct; since all that I conceive clearly and distinctly of the real and the true, and of what conveys some perfection, is in its entirety contained in this idea. And this does not cease to be true although I do not comprehend the infinite, or though in God there is an infinitude of things which I cannot comprehend, nor possibly even reach in any way by thought; for it is of the nature of the infinite that my nature, which is finite and limited, should not comprehend it; and it is sufficient that I should understand this, and that I should judge that all things which I clearly perceive and in which I know that there is some perfection, and possibly likewise an infinitude of properties of which I am ignorant, are in God formally or eminently, so that the idea which I have of Him may become the most true, most clear, and most distinct of all the ideas that are in my mind.

But possibly I am something more than I suppose myself to be, and perhaps all those perfections which I attribute to God are in some way potentially in me, although they do not yet disclose themselves, or issue in action. As a matter of fact I am already sensible that my knowledge increases [and perfects itself] little by little, and I see nothing which can prevent it from increasing more and more into infinitude; nor do I see, after it has thus been increased [or perfected], anything to prevent my being able to acquire by its means all the other perfections of the Divine nature; nor finally why the power I have of acquiring these perfections, if it really exist in me, shall not suffice to produce the ideas of them.

At the same time I recognize that this cannot be. For, in the first place, although it were true that

every day my knowledge acquired new degrees of perfection, and that there were in my nature many things potentially which are not yet there actually, nevertheless these excellences do not pertain to [or make the smallest approach to] the idea which I have of God in whom there is nothing merely potential [but in whom all is present really and actually]; for it is an infallible token of imperfection in my knowledge that it increases little by little. And further, although my knowledge grows more and more, nevertheless I do not for that reason believe that it can ever be actually infinite, since it can never reach a point so high that it will be unable to attain to any greater increase. But I understand God to be actually infinite, so that He can add nothing to His supreme perfection. And finally I perceive that the objective being of an idea cannot be produced by a being that exists potentially only, which properly speaking is nothing, but only a being which is formal or actual.

To speak the truth, I see nothing in all that I have just said which by the light of nature is not manifest to anyone who desires to think attentively on the subject; but when I slightly relax my attention, my mind, finding its vision somewhat obscured and so to speak blinded by the images of sensible objects, I do not easily recollect the reason why the idea that I possess of a being more perfect than I, must necessarily have been placed in me by a being which is really more perfect; and this is why I wish here to go on to inquire whether I, who have this idea, can exist if no such being exists.

And I ask, from whom do I then derive my existence? Perhaps from myself or from my parents, or from some other source less perfect than God; for we can imagine nothing more perfect than God, or even as perfect as He is.

But [were I independent of every other and] were I myself the author of my being, I should doubt nothing and I should desire nothing, and finally no perfection would be lacking to me; for I should have bestowed on myself every perfection of which I possessed any idea and should thus be God. And it must not be imagined that those things that are lacking to me are perhaps more difficult of attainment than those which I already possess; for, on the contrary, it is quite evident that it was a matter of much greater difficulty to bring to pass that I, that is to say, a thing or substance that thinks, should emerge out of nothing, than it would be to attain to the knowledge of many things of which I am ignorant, and which are only the accidents of this thinking substance. But it is clear that if I had of myself possessed this greater perfection of which I have just spoken [that is to say, if I had been the author of my own existence], I should not at least have denied myself the things which are the more easy to acquire [to wit, many branches of knowledge of which my nature is destitute]; nor should I have deprived myself of any of the things contained in the idea which I form of God, because there are none of them which seem to me specially difficult to acquire: and if there were any that were more difficult to acquire, they would certainly appear to me to be such (supposing I myself were the origin of the other things which I possess) since I should discover in them that my powers were limited.

But though I assumed that perhaps I have always existed just as I am at present, neither can I escape the force of this reasoning, and imagine that the conclusion to be drawn from this is, that I need not seek for any author of my existence. For all the course of my life may be divided into an infinite number of parts, none of which is in any way dependent on the other; and thus from the fact that I was in existence a short time ago it does not follow that I must be in existence now, unless some cause at this instant, so to speak, produces me anew, that is to say, conserves me. It is as a matter of fact perfectly clear and evident to all those who consider with attention the nature of time, that, in order to be conserved in each moment in which it endures, a substance has need of the same power and action as would be necessary to produce and create it anew, supposing it did not yet exist, so that the light of nature shows us clearly that the distinction between creation and conservation is solely a distinction of the reason.

All that I thus require here is that I should interrogate myself, if I wish to know whether I possess a power which is capable of bringing it to pass that I who now am shall still be in the future; for since I am nothing but a thinking thing, or at least since thus far it is only this portion of myself which is precisely in question at present, if such a power did reside in me, I should certainly be conscious of it. But I am conscious of nothing of the kind, and by this I know clearly that I depend on some being different from myself.

Possibly, however, this being on which I depend is not that which I call God, and I am created either by my parents or by some other cause less perfect than God. This cannot be, because, as I have just said, it is perfectly evident that there must be at least as much reality in the cause as in the effect; and thus since I am a thinking thing, and possess an idea of God within me, whatever in the end be the cause assigned to my existence, it must be allowed that it is likewise a thinking thing and that it possesses in itself the idea of all the perfections which I attribute to God. We may again inquire whether this cause derives its origin from itself or from some other thing. For if from itself, it follows by the reasons before brought forward, that this cause must itself be God; for since it possesses the virtue of self-existence, it must also without doubt have the power of actually possessing all the perfections of which it has the idea, that is, all those which I conceive as existing in God. But if it derives its existence from some other cause than itself, we shall again ask, for the same reason, whether this second cause exists by itself or through another, until from one step to another, we finally arrive at an ultimate cause, which will be God.

And it is perfectly manifest that in this there can be no regression into infinity, since what is in question is not so much the cause which formerly created me, as that which conserves me at the present time.

Nor can we suppose that several causes may have concurred in my production, and that from one I have received the idea of one of the perfections which I attribute to God, and from another the idea of some other, so that all these perfections indeed exist somewhere in the universe, but not as complete in one unity which is God. On the contrary, the unity, the simplicity or the inseparability of all things which are in God is one of the principal perfections which I conceive to be in Him. And certainly the idea of this unity of all Divine perfections cannot have been placed in me by any cause from which I have not likewise received the ideas of all the other perfections; for this cause could not make me able to comprehend them as joined together in an inseparable unity without having at the same time caused me in some measure to know what they are [and in some way to recognise each one of them].

Finally, so far as my parents [from whom it appears I have sprung] are concerned, although all that I have ever been able to believe of them were true, that does not make it follow that it is they who conserve me, nor are they even the authors of my being in any sense, in so far as I am a thinking being; since what they did was merely to implant certain dispositions in that matter in which the self—i.e. the mind, which alone I at present identify with myself—is by me deemed to exist. And thus there can be no difficulty in their regard, but we must of necessity conclude from the fact alone that I exist, or that the idea of a Being supremely perfect—that is of God—is in me, that the proof of God's existence is grounded on the highest evidence.

It only remains to me to examine into the manner in which I have acquired this idea from God; for I have not received it through the senses, and it is never presented to me unexpectedly, as is usual with the ideas of sensible things when these things present themselves, or seem to present themselves, to the external organs of my senses; nor is it likewise a fiction of my mind, for it is not in my power to take from or to add anything to it; and consequently the only alternative is that it is innate in me, just as the idea of myself is innate in me.

And one certainly ought not to find it strange that God, in creating me, placed this idea within me to be like the mark of the workman imprinted on his work; and it is likewise not essential that the mark shall be something different from the work itself. For from the sole fact that God created me it is most probable that in some way he has placed his image and similitude upon me, and that I perceive this similitude (in which the idea of God is contained) by means of the same faculty by which I perceive myself—that is to say, when I reflect on myself I not only know that I am something [imperfect], incomplete and dependent on another, which incessantly aspires after something which is better and greater than myself, but I also know that He on whom I depend possesses in Himself all the great things towards which I aspire [and the ideas of which I find within myself], and that not indefinitely or potentially alone, but really, actually and infinitely; and that thus He is God. And the whole strength of the argument which I have here made use of to prove the existence of God consists in this, that I recognise that it is not possible that my nature should be what it is, and indeed that I should have in myself the idea of a God, if God did not veritably exist—a God, I say, whose idea is in me, i.e. who possesses all those supreme perfections of which our mind may indeed have some idea but without understanding them all, who is liable to no errors or defect [and who has none of all those marks which denote imper-

fection]. From this it is manifest that He cannot be a deceiver, since the light of nature teaches us that fraud and deception necessarily proceed from some defect.

But before I examine this matter with more care, and pass on to the consideration of other truths which may be derived from it, it seems to me right to pause for a while in order to contemplate God Himself, to ponder at leisure His marvellous attributes, to consider, and admire, and adore, the beauty of this light so resplendent, at least as far as the strength of my mind, which is in some measure dazzled by the sight, will allow me to do so. For just as faith teaches us that the supreme felicity of the other life consists only in this contemplation of the Divine Majesty, so we continue to learn by experience that a similar meditation, though incomparably less perfect, causes us to enjoy the greatest satisfaction of which we are capable in this life.

MEDITATION IV
Of the True and the False.

I have been well accustomed these past days to detach my mind from my senses, and I have accurately observed that there are very few things that one knows with certainty respecting corporeal objects, that there are many more which are known to us respecting the human mind, and yet more still regarding God Himself; so that I shall now without any difficulty abstract my thoughts from the consideration of [sensible or] imaginable objects, and carry them to those which, being withdrawn from all contact with matter, are purely intelligible. And certainly the idea which I possess of the human mind inasmuch as it is a thinking thing, and not extended in length, width and depth, nor participating in anything pertaining to body, is incomparably more distinct than is the idea of any corporeal thing. And when I consider that I doubt, that is to say, that I am an incomplete and dependent being, the idea of a being that is complete and independent, that is of God, presents itself to my mind with so much distinctness and clearness—and from the fact alone that this idea is found in me, or that I who possess this idea exist, I conclude so certainly that God exists, and that my existence depends entirely on Him in every moment of my life—that I do not think that the human mind is capable of knowing anything with more evidence and certitude. And it seems to me that I now have before me a road which will lead us from the contemplation of the true God (in whom all the treasures of science and wisdom are contained) to the knowledge of the other objects of the universe.

For, first of all, I recognise it to be impossible that He should ever deceive me; for in all fraud and deception some imperfection is to be found, and although it may appear that the power of deception is a mark of subtilty or power, yet the desire to deceive without doubt testifies to malice or feebleness, and accordingly cannot be found in God.

In the next place I experienced in myself a certain capacity for judging which I have doubtless received from God, like all the other things that I possess; and as He could not desire to deceive me, it is clear that He has not given me a faculty that will lead me to err if I use it aright.

And no doubt respecting this matter could remain, if it were not that the consequence would seem to follow that I can thus never be deceived; for if I hold all that I possess from God, and if He has not placed me in the capacity for error, it seems as though I could never fall into error. And it is true that when I think only of God [and direct my mind wholly to Him], I discover [in myself] no cause of error, or falsity; yet directly afterwards, when recurring to myself, experience shows me that I am nevertheless subject to an infinitude of errors, as to which, when we come to investigate them more closely, I notice that not only is there a real and positive idea of God or of a Being of supreme perfection present to my mind, but also, so to speak, a certain negative idea of nothing, that is, of that which is infinitely removed from any kind of perfection; and that I am in a sense something intermediate between God and nought, i.e. placed in such a manner between the supreme Being and non-being, that there is in truth nothing in me that can lead to error in so far as a sovereign Being has formed me; but that, as I in some degree participate likewise in nought or in non-being, i.e. in so far as I am not myself the supreme Being, and as I find myself subject to an infinitude of imperfections, I ought not to be astonished if I should fall into error. Thus do I recognise that error, in so far as it is such, is not a real thing depending on God, but simply a defect; and therefore, in order to fall into it, that I have no need to possess a special faculty given me by God for this very purpose, but that I fall into error from the fact that the power given me by God for the purpose of distinguishing truth from error is not infinite.

Nevertheless this does not quite satisfy me; for error is not a pure negation [i.e. is not the simple defect or want of some perfection which ought not to be mine], but it is a lack of some knowledge which it seems that I ought to possess. And on considering the nature of God it does not appear to me possible that He should have given me a faculty which is not perfect of its kind, that is, which is wanting in some perfection due to it. For if it is true that the more skillful the artisan, the more perfect is the work of his hands, what can have been produced by this supreme Creator of all things that is not in all its parts perfect? And certainly there is no doubt that God could have created me so that I could never have been subject to error; it is also certain that He ever wills what is best; is it then better that I should be subject to err than that I should not?

In considering this more attentively, it occurs to me in the first place that I should not be astonished if my intelligence is not capable of comprehending why God acts as He does; and that there is thus no reason to doubt of His existence from the fact that I may perhaps find many other things besides this as to which I am able to understand neither for what reason nor how God has produced them. For, in the first place, knowing that my nature is extremely feeble and limited, and that the nature of God is on the contrary immense, incomprehensible, and infinite, I have no further difficulty in recognising that there is an infinitude of matters in His power, the causes of which transcend my knowledge; and this reason suffices to convince me that the species of cause termed final, finds no useful employment in physical [or natural] things; for it does not appear to me that I can without temerity seek to investigate the [inscrutable] ends of God.

It further occurs to me that we should not consider one single creature separately, when we inquire as to whether the works of God are perfect, but should regard all his creations together. For the same thing which might possibly seem very imperfect with some semblance of reason if regarded by itself, is found to be very perfect if regarded as part of the whole universe; and although, since I resolved to doubt all things, I as yet have only known certainly my own existence and that of God, nevertheless since I have recognised the infinite power of God, I cannot deny that He may have produced many other things, or at least that He has the power of producing them, so that I may obtain a place as a part of a great universe.

Whereupon, regarding myself more closely, and considering what are my errors (for they alone testify to there being any imperfection in me), I answer that they depend on a combination of two causes, to wit, on the faculty of knowledge that rests in me, and on the power of choice or of free will— that is to say, of the understanding at the same time of the will. For by the understanding alone I [neither assert nor deny anything, but] apprehend the ideas of things as to which I can form a judgment. But no error is properly speaking found in it, provided the word error is taken in its proper signification; and though there is possibly an infinitude of things in the world of which I have no idea in my understanding, we cannot for all that say that it is deprived of these ideas [as we might say of something which is required by its nature], but simply it does not possess these; because in truth there is no reason to prove that God should have given me a greater faculty of knowledge than He has given me; and however skillful a workman I represent Him to be, I should not for all that consider that He was bound to have placed in each of His works all the perfections which He may have been able to place in some. I likewise cannot complain that God has not given me a free choice or a will which is sufficient, ample and perfect, since as a matter of fact I am conscious of a will so extended as to be subject to no limits. And what seems to me very remarkable in this regard is that of all the qualities which I possess there is no one so perfect and so comprehensive that I do not very clearly recognise that it might be yet greater and more perfect. For, to take an example, if I consider the faculty of comprehension which I possess, I find that it is of very small extent and extremely limited, and at the same time I find the idea of another faculty much more ample and even infinite, and seeing that I can form the idea of it, I recognise from this very fact that it pertains to the nature of God. If in the same way I examine the memory, the imagination, or some other faculty, I do not find any which is not small and circumscribed, while in God it is immense [or infinite]. It is free will alone or liberty of choice which I find to be so great in me that I can conceive no other idea to be more great; it is indeed the case that it is for the most part this will that causes me to know that in some manner I bear the image and similitude of God. For although the power of will is incomparably greater in God than in me, both by reason of the knowledge and the power which, conjoined with it, render it stronger and more efficacious, and by reason of its object, inasmuch as in God it extends to a great many things; it nevertheless does not seem to me greater if I consider it formally and precisely in itself: for the faculty of will consists alone in our having the power of choosing to do a thing or choosing not to do it (that is, to affirm or deny, to pursue or to shun it), or rather it consists alone in the fact that in order to affirm or deny, pursue or shun those things placed before us by the understanding, we act so that we are unconscious that any outside force constrains us in doing so. For in order that I should be free it is not necessary that I should be indifferent as to the choice of one or the other of two contraries; but contrariwise the more I lean to the one—whether I recognise clearly that the reasons of the good and true are to be found in it, or whether God so disposes my inward thought—the more freely do I choose and embrace it. And undoubtedly both divine grace and natural knowledge, far from diminishing my liberty, rather increase it and strengthen it. Hence this indifference which I feel, when I am not swayed to one side rather than to the other by lack of reason, is the lowest grade of liberty, and rather evinces a lack or negation in knowledge than a perfection of will: for if I always recognised clearly what was true and good, I should never have trouble in deliberating as to what judgment or choice I should make, and then I should be entirely free without ever being indifferent.

From all this I recognise that the power of will which I have received from God is not of itself the source of my errors—for it is very ample and very perfect of its kind—any more than is the power of understanding; for since I understand nothing but by the power which God has given me for understanding, there is no doubt that all that I understand, I understand as I ought, and it is not possible that I err in this. Whence then come my errors? They come from the sole fact that since the will is much wider in its range and compass than the understanding, I do not restrain it within the same bounds, but extend it also to things which I do not understand: and as the will is of itself indifferent to these, it easily falls into error and sin, and chooses the evil for the good, or the false for the true.

For example, when I lately examined whether anything existed in the world, and found that from the very fact that I considered this question it followed very clearly that I myself existed, I could not prevent myself from believing that a thing I so clearly conceived was true: not that I found myself compelled to do so by some external cause, but simply because from great clearness in my mind there followed a great inclination of my will; and I believed this with so much the greater freedom or spontaneity as I possessed the less indifference towards it. Now, on the contrary, I not only know that I exist, inasmuch as I am a thinking thing, but a certain representation of corporeal nature is also presented to my mind; and it comes to pass that I doubt whether this thinking nature which is in me, or rather by which I am what I am, differs from this corporeal nature, or whether both are not simply the same thing; and I here suppose that I do not yet know any reason to persuade me to adopt the one belief rather than the other. From this it follows that I am entirely indifferent as to which of the two I affirm or deny, or even whether I abstain from forming any judgment in the matter.

And this indifference does not only extend to matters as to which the understanding has no knowledge, but also in general to all those which are not apprehended with perfect clearness at the moment when the will is deliberating upon them: for, however probable are the conjectures which render me disposed to form a judgment respecting anything, the simple knowledge that I have that those are conjectures alone and not certain and indubitable reasons, suffices to occasion me to judge the contrary. Of this I have had great experience of late when I set aside as false all that I had formerly held to be absolutely true, for the sole reason that I remarked that it might in some measure be doubted.

But if I abstain from giving my judgment on anything when I do not perceive it with sufficient clearness and distinctness, it is plain that I act rightly and am not deceived. But if I determine to deny or affirm, I no longer make use as I should of my free will, and if I affirm what is not true, it is evident that I deceive myself; even though I judge according to truth, this comes about only by chance, and I do not escape the blame of misusing my freedom; for the light of nature teaches us that the knowledge of the understanding should always precede the determination of the will. And it is in the misuse of the free will that the privation which constitutes the characteristic nature of error is met with. Privation, I say, is found in the act, in so far as it proceeds from me, but it is not found in the faculty which I have received from God, nor even in the act in so far as it depends on Him.

For I have certainly no cause to complain that God has not given me an intelligence which is more powerful, or a natural light which is stronger than that which I have received from Him, since it is proper to the finite understanding not to comprehend a multitude of things, and it is proper to a created understanding to be finite; on the contrary, I have every reason to render thanks to God who owes me nothing and who has given me all the perfections I possess, and I should be far from charging Him with injustice, and with having deprived me of, or wrongfully withheld from me, these perfections which He has not bestowed upon me.

I have further no reason to complain that He has given me a will more ample than my understanding, for since the will consists only of one single element, and is so to speak indivisible, it appears that its nature is such that nothing can be abstracted from it [without destroying it]; and certainly the more comprehensive it is found to be, the more reason I have to render gratitude to the giver.

And, finally, I must also not complain that God concurs with me in forming the acts of the will, that is, the judgment in which I go astray, because these acts are entirely true and good, inasmuch as they depend on God; and in a certain sense more perfection accrues to my nature from the fact that I can form them, than if I could not do so. As to the privation in which alone the formal reason of error or sin consists, it has no need of any concurrence from God, since it is not a thing [or an existence], and since it is not related to God as to a cause, but should be termed merely a negation [according to the significance given to these words in the Schools]. For in fact it is not an imperfection in God that He has given me the liberty to give or withhold my assent from certain things as to which He has not placed a clear and distinct knowledge in my understanding; but it is without doubt an imperfection in me not to make a good use of my freedom, and to give my judgment readily on matters which I only understand obscurely. I nevertheless perceive that God could easily have created me so that I never should err, although I still remained free, and endowed with a limited knowledge, viz, by giving to my understanding a clear and distinct intelligence of all things as to which I should ever have to deliberate; or simply by His engraving deeply in my memory the resolution never to form a judgment on anything without having a clear and distinct understanding of it, so that I could never forget it. And it is easy for me to understand that, in so far as I consider myself alone, and as if there were only myself in the world, I should have been much more perfect than I am, if God had created me so that I could never err. Nevertheless I cannot deny that in some sense it is a greater perfection in the whole universe that certain parts should not be exempt from error as others are than that all parts should be exactly similar. And I have no right to complain if God, having placed me in the world, has not called upon me to play a part that excels all others in distinction and perfection.

And further I have reason to be glad on the ground that if He has not given me the power of never going astray by the first means pointed out above, which depends on a clear and evident knowledge of all the things regarding which I can deliberate, He has at least left within my power the other means, which is firmly to adhere to the resolution never to give judgment on matters whose truth is not clearly known to me; for although I notice a certain weakness in my nature in that I cannot continually concentrate my mind on one single thought, I can yet, by attentive and frequently repeated meditation, impress it so forcibly on my memory that I shall never fail to recollect it whenever I have need of it, and thus acquire the habit of never going astray.

And inasmuch as it is in this that the greatest and principal perfection of man consists, it seems to me that I have not gained little by this day's Meditation, since I have discovered the source of falsity and error. And certainly there can be no other source than that which I have explained; for as often as I so restrain my will within the limits of my knowledge that it forms no judgment except on matters which are clearly and distinctly represented to it by the understanding, I can never be deceived; for every clear and distinct conception is without doubt something, and hence cannot derive its origin from what is nought, but must of necessity have God as its author—God, I say, who being supremely perfect, cannot be the cause of any error; and consequently we must conclude that such a conception [or such a judgment] is true. Nor have I only learned to-day what I should avoid in order that I may not err, but also how I should act in order to arrive at a knowledge of the truth; for without doubt I shall arrive at this end if I devote my attention sufficiently to those things which I perfectly understand; and if I separate

from these that which I only understand confusedly and with obscurity. To these I shall henceforth diligently give heed.

MEDITATION V

Of the essence of material things, and, again, of God that He exists.

Many other matters respecting the attributes of God and my own nature or mind remain for consideration; but I shall possibly on another occasion resume the investigation of these. Now (after first noting what must be done or avoided, in order to arrive at a knowledge of the truth) my principal task is to endeavour to emerge from the state of doubt into which I have these last days fallen, and to see whether nothing certain can be known regarding material things.

But before examining whether any such objects as I conceive exist outside of me, I must consider the ideas of them in so far as they are in my thought, and see which of them are distinct and which confused.

In the first place, I am able distinctly to imagine that quantity which philosophers commonly call continuous, or the extension in length, breadth, or depth, that is in this quantity, or rather in the object to which it is attributed. Further, I can number in it many different parts, and attribute to each of its parts many sorts of size, figure, situation and local movements, and, finally, I can assign to each of these movements all degrees of duration.

And not only do I know these things with distinctness when I consider them in general, but, likewise [however little I apply my attention to the matter], I discover an infinitude of particulars respecting numbers, figures, movements, and other such things, whose truth is so manifest, and so well accords with my nature, that when I begin to discover them, it seems to me that I learn nothing new, or recollect what I formerly knew—that is to say, that I for the first time perceive things which were already present to my mind, although I had not as yet applied my mind to them.

And what I here find to be most important is that I discover in myself an infinitude of ideas of certain things which cannot be esteemed as pure negations, although they may possibly have no existence outside of my thought, and which are not framed by me, although it is within my power either to think or not to think them, but which possess natures which are true and immutable. For example, when I imagine a triangle, although there may nowhere in the world be such a figure outside my thought, or ever have been, there is nevertheless in this figure a certain determinate nature, form, or essence, which is immutable and eternal, which I have not invented, and which in no wise depends on my mind, as appears from the fact that diverse properties of that triangle can be demonstrated, viz, that its three angles are equal to two right angles, that the greatest side is subtended by the greatest angle, and the like, which now, whether I wish it or do not wish it, I recognise very clearly as pertaining to it, although I never thought of the matter at all when I imagined a triangle for the first time, and which therefore cannot be said to have been invented by me.

Nor does the objection hold good that possibly this idea of a triangle has reached my mind through the medium of my senses, since I have sometimes seen bodies triangular in shape; because I can form in my mind an infinitude of other figures regarding which we cannot have the least conception of their ever having been objects of sense, and I can nevertheless demonstrate various properties pertaining to their nature as well as to that of the triangle, and these must certainly all be true since I conceive them clearly. Hence they are something, and not pure negation; for it is perfectly clear that all that is true is something, and I have already fully demonstrated that all that I know clearly is true. And even although I had not demonstrated this, the nature of my mind is such that I could not prevent myself from holding them to be true so long as I conceive them clearly; and I recollect that even when I was still strongly attached to the objects of sense, I counted as the most certain those truths which I conceived clearly as regards figures, numbers, and the other matters which pertain to arithmetic and geometry, and, in general, to pure and abstract mathematics.

But now, if just because I can draw the idea of something from my thought, it follows that all which I know clearly and distinctly as pertaining to this object does really belong to it, may I not derive from this an argument demonstrating the existence of God? It is certain that I no less find the idea of God, that is to say, the idea of a supremely perfect Being, in me, than that of any figure or number whatever it is; and I do not know any less clearly and distinctly

that an [actual and] eternal existence pertains to this nature than I know that all that which I am able to demonstrate of some figure or number truly pertains to the nature of this figure or number, and therefore, although all that I concluded in the preceding Meditations were found to be false, the existence of God would pass with me as at least as certain as I have ever held the truths of mathematics (which concern only numbers and figures) to be.

This indeed is not at first manifest, since it would seem to present some appearance of being a sophism. For being accustomed in all other things to make a distinction between existence and essence, I easily persuade myself that the existence can be separated from the essence of God, and that we can thus conceive God as not actually existing. But, nevertheless, when I think of it with more attention, I clearly see that existence can no more be separated from the essence of God than can its having its three angles equal to two right angles be separated from the essence of a [rectilinear] triangle, or the idea of a mountain from the idea of a valley; and so there is not any less repugnance to our conceiving a God (that is, a Being supremely perfect) to whom existence is lacking (that is to say, to whom a certain perfection is lacking), than to conceive of a mountain which has no valley.

But although I cannot really conceive of a God without existence any more than a mountain without a valley, still from the fact that I conceive of a mountain with a valley, it does not follow that there is such a mountain in the world; similarly although I conceive of God as possessing existence, it would seem that it does not follow that there is a God which exists; for my thought does not impose any necessity upon things, and just as I may imagine a winged horse, although no horse with wings exists, so I could perhaps attribute existence to God, although no God existed.

But a sophism is concealed in this objection; for from the fact that I cannot conceive a mountain without a valley, it does not follow that there is any mountain or any valley in existence, but only that the mountain and the valley, whether they exist or do not exist, cannot in any way be separated one from the other. While from the fact that I cannot conceive God without existence, it follows that existence is inseparable from Him, and hence that He really exists; not that my thought can bring this to pass, or impose any necessity on things, but, on the contrary, because the necessity which lies in the thing itself, i.e. the necessity of the existence of God determines me to think in this way. For it is not within my power to think of God without existence (that is of a supremely perfect Being devoid of a supreme perfection) though it is in my power to imagine a horse either with wings or without wings.

And we must not here object that it is in truth necessary for me to assert that God exists after having presupposed that He possesses every sort of perfection, since existence is one of these, but that as a matter of fact my original supposition was not necessary, just as it is not necessary to consider that all quadrilateral figures can be inscribed in the circle; for supposing I thought this, I should be constrained to admit that the rhombus might be inscribed in the circle since it is a quadrilateral figure, which, however, is manifestly false. [We must not, I say, make any such allegations because] although it is not necessary that I should at any time entertain the notion of God, nevertheless whenever it happens that I think of a first and a sovereign Being, and, so to speak, derive the idea of Him from the storehouse of my mind, it is necessary that I should attribute to Him every sort of perfection, although I do not get so far as to enumerate them all, or to apply my mind to each one in particular. And this necessity suffices to make me conclude (after having recognised that existence is a perfection) that this first and sovereign Being really exists; just as though it is not necessary for me ever to imagine any triangle, yet, whenever I wish to consider a rectilinear figure composed only of three angles, it is absolutely essential that I should attribute to it all those properties which serve to bring about the conclusion that its three angles are not greater than two right angles, even although I may not then be considering this point in particular. But when I consider which figures are capable of being inscribed in the circle, it is in no wise necessary that I should think that all quadrilateral figures are of this number; on the contrary, I cannot even pretend that this is the case, so long as I do not desire to accept anything which I cannot conceive clearly and distinctly. And in consequence there is a great difference between the false suppositions such as this, and the true ideas born within me, the first and principal of which is that of God. For really I discern in many ways that this idea is not something factitious, and depending solely on my thought, but that it is the image of a true and immutable nature; first of all, because I cannot conceive anything but God himself to whose essence existence [necessarily]

pertains; in the second place because it is not possible for me to conceive two or more Gods in this same position; and, granted that there is one such God who now exists, I see clearly that it is necessary that He should have existed from all eternity, and that He must exist eternally; and finally, because I know an infinitude of other properties in God, none of which I can either diminish or change.

For the rest, whatever proof or argument I avail myself of, we must always return to the point that it is only those things which we conceive clearly and distinctly that have the power of persuading me entirely. And although amongst the matters which I conceive of in this way, some indeed are manifestly obvious to all, while others only manifest themselves to those who consider them closely and examine them attentively; still, after they have once been discovered, the latter are not esteemed as any less certain than the former. For example, in the case of every right-angled triangle, although it does not so manifestly appear that the square of the base is equal to the squares of the two other sides as that this base is opposite to the greatest angle; still, when this has once been apprehended, we are just as certain of its truth as of the truth of the other. And as regards God, if my mind were not pre-occupied with prejudices, and if my thought did not find itself on all hands diverted by the continual pressure of sensible things, there would be nothing which I could know more immediately and more easily than Him. For is there anything more manifest than that there is a God, that is to say, a Supreme Being, to whose essence alone existence pertains?

And although for a firm grasp of this truth I have need of a strenuous application of mind, at present I not only feel myself to be as assured of it as of all that I hold as most certain, but I also remark that the certainty of all other things depends on it so absolutely, that without this knowledge it is impossible ever to know anything perfectly.

For although I am of such a nature that as long as I understand anything very clearly and distinctly, I am naturally impelled to believe it to be true, yet because I am also of such a nature that I cannot have my mind constantly fixed on the same object in order to perceive it clearly, and as I often recollect having formed a past judgment without at the same time properly recollecting the reasons that led me to make it, it may happen meanwhile that other reasons present themselves to me, which would easily cause me to change my opinion, if I were ignorant of the facts of the existence of God, and thus I should have no true and certain knowledge, but only vague and vacillating opinions. Thus, for example, when I consider the nature of a [rectilinear] triangle, I who have some little knowledge of the principles of geometry recognise quite clearly that the three angles are equal to two right angles, and it is not possible for me not to believe this so long as I apply my mind to its demonstration; but so soon as I abstain from attending to the proof, although I still recollect having clearly comprehended it, it may easily occur that I come to doubt its truth, if I am ignorant of there being a God. For I can persuade myself of having been so constituted by nature that I can easily deceive myself even in those matters which I believe myself to apprehend with the greatest evidence and certainty, especially when I recollect that I have frequently judged matters to be true and certain which other reasons have afterwards impelled me to judge to be altogether false.

But after I have recognised that there is a God—because at the same time I have also recognised that all things depend upon Him, and that He is not a deceiver, and from that have inferred that what I perceive clearly and distinctly cannot fail to be true—although I no longer pay attention to the reasons for which I have judged this to be true, provided that I recollect having clearly and distinctly perceived it, no contrary reason can be brought forward which could ever cause me to doubt of its truth; and thus I have a true and certain knowledge of it. And this same knowledge extends likewise to all other things which I recollect having formerly demonstrated, such as the truths of geometry and the like; for what can be alleged against them to cause me to place them in doubt? Will it be said that my nature is such as to cause me to be frequently deceived? But I already know that I cannot be deceived in the judgment whose grounds I know clearly. Will it be said that I formerly held many things to be true and certain which I have afterwards recognised to be false? But I had not had any clear and distinct knowledge of these things, and not as yet knowing the rule whereby I assure myself of the truth, I had been impelled to give my assent from reasons which I have since recognised to be less strong than I had at the time imagined them to be. What further objection can then be raised? That

possibly I am dreaming (an objection I myself made a little while ago), or that all the thoughts which I now have are no more true than the phantasies of my dreams? But even though I slept the case would be the same, for all that is clearly present to my mind is absolutely true.

And so I very clearly recognise that the certainty and truth of all knowledge depends alone on the knowledge of the true God, in so much that, before I knew Him, I could not have a perfect knowledge of any other thing. And now that I know Him I have the means of acquiring a perfect knowledge of an infinitude of things, not only of those which relate to God Himself and other intellectual matters, but also of those which pertain to corporeal nature in so far as it is the object of pure mathematics [which have no concern with whether it exists or not].

MEDITATION VI

Of the Existence of Material Things, and of the real distinction between the Soul and Body of Man.

Nothing further now remains but to inquire whether material things exist. And certainly I at least know that these may exist in so far as they are considered as the objects of pure mathematics, since in this aspect I perceive them clearly and distinctly. For there is no doubt that God possesses the power to produce everything that I am capable of perceiving with distinctness, and I have never deemed that anything was impossible for Him, unless I found a contradiction in attempting to conceive it clearly. Further, the faculty of imagination which I possess, and of which, experience tells me, I make use when I apply myself to the consideration of material things, is capable of persuading me of their existence; for when I attentively consider what imagination is, I find that it is nothing but a certain application of the faculty of knowledge to the body which is immediately present to it, and which therefore exists.

And to render this quite clear, I remark in the first place the difference that exists between the imagination and pure intellection [or conception]. For example, when I imagine a triangle, I do not conceive it only as a figure comprehended by three lines, but I also apprehend these three lines as present by the power and inward vision of my mind, and this is what I call imagining. But if I desire to think of a chiliagon, I certainly conceive truly that it is a figure composed of a thousand sides, just as easily as I conceive of a triangle that it is a figure of three sides;

but I cannot in any way imagine the thousand sides of a chiliagon [as I do the three sides of a triangle], nor do I, so to speak, regard them as present [with the eyes of my mind]. And although in accordance with the habit I have formed of always employing the aid of my imagination when I think of corporeal things, it may happen that in imagining a chiliagon I confusedly represent to myself some figure, yet it is very evident that this figure is not a chiliagon, since it in no way differs from that which I represent to myself when I think of a myriagon or any other many-sided figure; nor does it serve my purpose in discovering the properties which go to form the distinction between a chiliagon and other polygons. But if the question turns upon a pentagon, it is quite true that I can conceive its figure as well as that of a chiliagon without the help of my imagination; but I can also imagine it by applying the attention of my mind to each of its five sides, and at the same time to the space which they enclose. And thus I clearly recognise that I have need of a particular effort of mind in order to effect the act of imagination, such as I do not require in order to understand, and this particular effort of mind clearly manifests the difference which exists between imagination and pure intellection.

I remark besides that this power of imagination which is in one, inasmuch as it differs from the power of understanding, is in no wise a necessary element in my nature, or in [my essence, that is to say, in] the essence of my mind; for although I did not possess it I should doubtless ever remain the same as I now am, from which it appears that we might conclude that it depends on something which differs from me. And I easily conceive that if some body exists with which my mind is conjoined and united in such a way that it can apply itself to consider it when it pleases, it may be that by this means it can imagine corporeal objects; so that this mode of thinking differs from pure intellection only inasmuch as mind in its intellectual activity in some manner turns on itself, and considers some of the ideas which it possesses in itself; while in imagining it turns towards the body, and there beholds in it something conformable to the idea which it has either conceived of itself or perceived by the senses. I easily understand, I say, that the imagination could be thus constituted if it is true that body exists; and because I can discover no other convenient mode of explaining it, I conjecture with probability that body does exist; but this is only with probability, and although I examine all things with

care, I nevertheless do not find that from this distinct idea of corporeal nature, which I have in my imagination, I can derive any argument from which there will necessarily be deduced the existence of body.

But I am in the habit of imagining many other things besides this corporeal nature which is the object of pure mathematics, to wit, the colours, sounds, scents, pain, and other such things, although less distinctly. And inasmuch as I perceive these things much better through the senses, by the medium of which, and by the memory, they seem to have reached my imagination, I believe that, in order to examine them more conveniently, it is right that I should at the same time investigate the nature of sense perception, and that I should see if from the ideas which I apprehend by this mode of thought, which I call feeling, I cannot derive some certain proof of the existence of corporeal objects.

And first of all I shall recall to my memory those matters which I hitherto held to be true, as having perceived them through the senses, and the foundations on which my belief has rested; in the next place I shall examine the reasons which have since obliged me to place them in doubt; in the last place I shall consider which of them I must now believe.

First of all, then, I perceived that I had a head, hands, feet, and all other members of which this body—which I considered as a part, or possibly even as the whole, of myself—is composed. Further I was sensible that this body was placed amidst many others, from which it was capable of being affected in many different ways, beneficial and hurtful, and I remarked that a certain feeling of pleasure accompanied those that were beneficial, and pain those which were harmful. And in addition to this pleasure and pain, I also experienced hunger, thirst, and other similar appetites, as also certain corporeal inclinations towards joy, sadness, anger, and other similar passions. And outside myself, in addition to extension, figure, and motions of bodies, I remarked in them hardness, heat, and all other tactile qualities, and, further, light and colour, and scents and sounds, the variety of which gave me the means of distinguishing the sky, the earth, the sea, and generally all the other bodies, one from the other. And certainly, considering the ideas of all these qualities which presented themselves to my mind, and which alone I perceived properly or immediately, it was not without reason that I believed myself to perceive objects quite different from my thought, to wit, bodies from which those ideas proceeded; for I found by experience that these ideas presented themselves to me without my consent being requisite, so that I could not perceive any object, however desirous I might be, unless it were present to the organs of sense; and it was not in my power not to perceive it, when it was present. And because the ideas which I receive through the senses were much more lively, more clear, and even, in their own way, more distinct than any of those which I could of myself frame in meditation, or than those I found impressed on my memory, it appeared as though they could not have proceeded from my mind, so that they must necessarily have been produced in me by some other things. And having no knowledge of those objects excepting the knowledge which the ideas themselves gave me, nothing was more likely to occur to my mind than that the objects were similar to the ideas which were caused. And because I likewise remembered that I had formerly made use of my senses rather than my reason, and recognised that the ideas which I formed of myself were not so distinct as those which I perceived through the senses, and that they were most frequently even composed of portions of these last, I persuaded myself easily that I had no idea in my mind which had not formerly come to me through the senses. Nor was it without some reason that I believed that this body (which by a certain special right I call my own) belonged to me more properly and more strictly than any other; for in fact I could never be separated from it as from other bodies; I experienced in it and on account of it all my appetites and affections, and finally I was touched by the feeling of pain and titillation of pleasure in its parts, and not in the parts of other bodies which were separated from it. But when I inquired, why, from some, I know not what, painful sensation, there follows sadness of mind, and from the pleasurable sensation there arises joy, or why this mysterious pinching of the stomach which I call hunger causes me to desire to eat, and dryness of throat causes a desire to drink, and so on, I could give no reason excepting that nature taught me so; for there is certainly no affinity (that I at least can understand) between the craving of the stomach and the desire to eat, any more than between the perception of whatever causes pain and the thought of sadness which arises from this perception. And in the same

way it appeared to me that I had learned from nature all the other judgments which I formed regarding the objects of my senses, since I remarked that these judgments were found in me before I had the leisure to weigh and consider any reasons which might oblige me to make them.

But afterwards many experiences little by little destroyed all the faith which I had rested in my senses; for I from time to time observed that those towers which from afar appeared to me to be round, more closely observed seemed square, and that colossal statues raised on the summit of these towers, appeared as quite tiny statues when viewed from the bottom; and so in an infinitude of other cases I found error in judgments founded on the external senses. And not only in those founded on the external senses, but even in those founded on the internal as well; for is there anything more intimate or more internal than pain? And yet I have learned from some persons whose arms or legs have been cut off, that they sometimes seemed to feel pain in the part which had been amputated, which made me think that I could not be quite certain that it was a certain member which pained me, even although I felt pain in it. And to those grounds of doubt I have lately added two others, which are very general; the first is that I never have believed myself to feel anything in waking moments which I cannot also sometimes believe myself to feel when I sleep, and as I do not think that these things which I seem to feel in sleep, proceed from objects outside of me, I do not see any reason why I should have this belief regarding objects which I seem to perceive while awake. The other was that being still ignorant, or rather supposing my self to be ignorant, of the author of my being, I saw nothing to prevent me from having been so constituted by nature that I might be deceived even in matters which seemed to me to be most certain. And as to the grounds on which I was formerly persuaded of the truth of sensible objects, I had not much trouble in replying to them. For since nature seemed to cause me to lean towards many things from which reason repelled me, I did not believe that I should trust much to the teachings of nature. And although the ideas which I receive by the senses do not depend on my will, I did not think that one should for that reason conclude that they proceeded from things different from myself, since possibly some faculty might be discovered in me—though hitherto unknown to me—which produced them.

But now that I begin to know myself better, and

to discover more clearly the author of my being, I do not in truth think that I should rashly admit all the matters which the senses seem to teach us, but, on the other hand, I do not think that I should doubt them all universally.

And first of all, because I know that all things which I apprehend clearly and distinctly can be created by God as I apprehend them, it suffices that I am able to apprehend one thing apart from another clearly and distinctly in order to be certain that the one is different from the other, since they may be made to exist in separation at least by the omnipotence of God; and it does not signify by what power this separation is made in order to compel me to judge them to be different: and, therefore, just because I know certainly that I exist, and that meanwhile I do not remark that any other thing necessarily pertains to my nature or essence, excepting that I am a thinking thing, I rightly conclude that my essence consists solely in the fact that I am a thinking thing [or a substance whose whole essence or nature is to think]. And although possibly (or rather certainly, as I shall say in a moment) I possess a body with which I am very intimately conjoined, yet because, on the one side, I have a clear and distinct idea of myself inasmuch as I am only a thinking and unextended thing, and as, on the other, I possess a distinct idea of body, inasmuch as it is only an extended and unthinking thing, it is certain that this I [that is to say, my soul by which I am what I am], is entirely and absolutely distinct from my body, and can exist without it.

I further find in myself faculties employing modes of thinking peculiar to themselves, to wit, the faculties of imagination and feeling, without which I can easily conceive myself clearly and distinctly as a complete being; while, on the other hand, they cannot be so conceived apart from me, that is, without an intelligent substance in which they reside, for [in the notion we have of these faculties, or, to use the language of the Schools] in their formal concept, some kind of intellection is comprised, from which I infer that they are distinct from me as its modes are from a thing. I observe also in me some other faculties such as that of change of position, the assumption of different figures and such like, which cannot be conceived, any more than can the preceding, apart from some substance to which they are attached, and consequently cannot exist without it; but it is very clear that these faculties, if it be true that they exist, must be attached to some corporeal or extended and not to an intelligent substance, since in the clear and

distinct conception of these there is some sort of extension found to be present, but no intellection at all. There is certainly further in me a certain passive faculty of perception, that is, of receiving and recognising the ideas of sensible things, but this would be useless to me [and I could in no way avail myself of it], if there were not either in me or in some other thing another active faculty capable of forming and producing these ideas. But this active faculty cannot exist in me [inasmuch as I am a thing that thinks] seeing that it does not presuppose thought, and also that those ideas are often produced in me without my contributing in any way to the same, and often even against my will; it is thus necessarily the case that the faculty resides in some substance different from me in which all the reality which is objectively in the ideas that are produced by this faculty is formally or eminently contained, as I remarked before. And this substance is either a body, that is, a corporeal nature in which there is contained formally [and really] all that which is objectively [and by representation] in those ideas, or it is God Himself, or some other creature more noble than body in which that same is contained eminently. But since God is no deceiver, it is very manifest that He does not communicate to me these ideas immediately and by Himself, nor yet by the intervention of some creature in which their reality is not formally, but only eminently, contained. For since He has given me no faculty to recognise that this is the case, but, on the other hand, a very great inclination to believe [that they are sent to me or] that they are conveyed to me by corporeal objects, I do not see how He could be defended from the accusation of deceit if these ideas were produced by causes other than corporeal objects. Hence we must allow that corporeal things exist. However, they are perhaps not exactly what we perceive by the senses, since this comprehension by the senses is in many instances very obscure and confused; but we must at least admit that all things which I conceive in them clearly and distinctly, that is to say, all things which, speaking generally, are comprehended in the object of pure mathematics, are truly to be recognised as external objects.

As to other things, however, which are either particular only, as, for example, that the sun is of such and such a figure, etc., or which are less clearly and distinctly conceived, such as light, sound, pain and the like, it is certain that although they are very dubious and uncertain, yet on the sole ground that God is not a deceiver, and that consequently He has not permitted any falsity to exist in my opinion which He has not likewise given me the faculty of correcting, I may assuredly hope to conclude that I have within me the means of arriving at the truth even here. And first of all there is no doubt that in all things which nature teaches me there is some truth contained; for by nature, considered in general, I now understand no other thing than either God Himself or else the order and disposition which God has established in created things; and by my nature in particular I understand no other thing than the complexus of all the things which God has given me.

But there is nothing which this nature teaches me more expressly [nor more sensibly] than that I have a body which is adversely affected when I feel pain, which has need of food or drink when I experience the feelings of hunger and thirst, and so on; nor can I doubt there being some truth in all this.

Nature also teaches me by the sensations of pain, hunger, thirst, etc., that I am not only lodged in my body as a pilot in a vessel, but that I am very closely united to it, and so to speak so intermingled with it that I seem to compose with it one whole. For if that were not the case, when my body is hurt, I, who am merely a thinking thing, should not feel pain, for I should perceive this wound by the understanding only, just as the sailor perceives by sight when something is damaged in his vessel; and when my body has need of drink or food, I should clearly understand the fact without being warned of it by confused feelings of hunger and thirst. For all these sensations of hunger, thirst, pain, etc. are in truth none other than certain confused modes of thought which are produced by the union and apparent intermingling of mind and body.

Moreover, nature teaches me that many other bodies exist around mine, of which some are to be avoided, and others sought after. And certainly from the fact that I am sensible of different sorts of colours, sounds, scents, tastes, heat, hardness, etc., I very easily conclude that there are in the bodies from which all these diverse sense-perceptions proceed certain variations which answer to them, although possibly these are not really at all similar to them. And also from the fact that amongst these different sense-perceptions some are very agreeable to me

and others disagreeable, it is quite certain that my body (or rather myself in my entirety, inasmuch as I am formed of body and soul) may receive different impressions agreeable and disagreeable from the other bodies which surround it.

But there are many other things which nature seems to have taught me, but which at the same time I have never really received from her, but which have been brought about in my mind by a certain habit which I have of forming inconsiderate judgments on things; and thus it may easily happen that these judgments contain some error. Take, for example, the opinion which I hold that all space in which there is nothing that affects [or makes an impression on] my senses is void; that in a body which is warm there is something entirely similar to the idea of heat which is in me; that in a white or green body there is the same whiteness or greenness that I perceive; that in a bitter or sweet body there is the same taste, and so on in other instances; that the stars, the towers, and all other distant bodies are of the same figure and size as they appear from far off to our eyes, etc. But in order that in this there should be nothing which I do not conceive distinctly, I should define exactly what I really understand when I say that I am taught somewhat by nature. For here I take nature in a more limited signification than when I term it the sum of all the things given me by God, since in this sum many things are comprehended which only pertain to mind (and to these I do not refer in speaking of nature) such as the notion which I have of the fact that what has once been done cannot ever be undone and an infinitude of such things which I know by the light of nature [without the help of the body]; and seeing that it comprehends many other matters besides which only pertain to body, and are no longer here contained under the name of nature, such as the quality of weight which it possesses and the like, with which I also do not deal; for in talking of nature I only treat of those things given by God to me as a being composed of mind and body. But the nature here described truly teaches me to flee from things which cause the sensation of pain, and seek after the things which communicate to me the sentiment of pleasure and so forth; but I do not see that beyond this it teaches me that from those diverse sense-perceptions we should ever form any conclusion regarding things outside of us, without having [carefully and maturely] mentally examined them beforehand. For it seems to me that it is mind alone, and not mind and body in conjunction, that is requisite to a knowledge of the truth in regard to such things. Thus, although a star makes no larger an impression on my eye than the flame of a little candle there is yet in me no real or positive propensity impelling me to believe that it is not greater than that flame; but I have judged it to be so from my earliest years, without any rational foundation. And although in approaching fire I feel heat, and in approaching it a little too near I even feel pain, there is at the same time no reason in this which could persuade me that there is in the fire something resembling this heat any more than there is in it something resembling the pain; all that I have any reason to believe from this is, that there is something in it, whatever it may be, which excites in me these sensations of heat or of pain. So also, although there are spaces in which I find nothing which excites my senses, I must not from that conclude that these spaces contain no body; for I see in this, as in other similar things, that I have been in the habit of perverting the order of nature, because these perceptions of sense having been placed within me by nature merely for the purpose of signifying to my mind what things are beneficial or hurtful to the composite whole of which it forms a part, and being up to that point sufficiently clear and distinct, I yet avail myself of them as though they were absolute rules by which I immediately determine the essence of the bodies which are outside me, as to which, in fact, they can teach me nothing but what is most obscure and confused.

But I have already sufficiently considered how, notwithstanding the supreme goodness of God, falsity enters into the judgments I make. Only here a new difficulty is presented—one respecting those things the pursuit or avoidance of which is taught me by nature, and also respecting the internal sensations which I possess, and in which I seem to have sometimes detected error [and thus to be directly deceived by my own nature]. To take an example, the agreeable taste of some food in which poison has been intermingled may induce me to partake of the poison, and thus deceive me. It is true, at the same time, that in this case nature may be excused, for it only induces me to desire food in which I find a pleasant taste, and not to desire poison which is unknown to it; and thus I can infer nothing from this fact, except that my nature is not omniscient, at which there is certainly no reason to be astonished, since man, being finite in nature, can only have knowledge the perfectness of which is limited.

But we not unfrequently deceive ourselves even in those things to which we are directly impelled by nature, as happens with those who when they are sick desire to drink or eat things hurtful to them. It will perhaps be said here that the cause of their deceptiveness is that their nature is corrupt, but that does not remove the difficulty, because a sick man is none the less truly God's creature than he who is in health; and it is therefore as repugnant to God's goodness for the one to have a deceitful nature as it is for the other. And as a clock composed of wheels and counterweights no less exactly observes the laws of nature when it is badly made, and does not show the time properly, than when it entirely satisfies the wishes of its maker, and as, if I consider the body of a man as being a sort of machine so built up and composed of nerves, muscles, veins, blood and skin, that though there were no mind in it at all, it would not cease to have the same motions as at present, exception being made of those movements which are due to the direction of the will, and in consequence depend upon the mind [as opposed to those which operate by the disposition of its organs], I easily recognise that it would be as natural to this body, supposing it to be, for example, dropsical, to suffer the parchedness of the throat which usually signifies to the mind the feeling of thirst, and to be disposed by this parched feeling to move the nerves and other parts in the way requisite for drinking, and thus to augment its malady and do harm to itself, as it is natural to it, when it has no indisposition, to be impelled to drink for its good by a similar cause. And although, considering the use to which the clock has been destined by its maker, I may say that it deflects from the order of its nature when it does not indicate the hours correctly; and as, in the same way, considering the machine of the human body as having been formed by God in order to have in itself all the movements usually manifested there, I have reason for thinking that it does not follow the order of nature when, if the throat is dry, drinking does harm to the conservation of health, nevertheless I recognise at the same time that this last mode of explaining nature is very different from the other. For this is but a purely verbal characterisation depending entirely on my thought, which compares a sick man and a badly constructed clock with the idea which I have of a healthy man and a well made clock, and it is hence extrinsic to the things to which it is applied; but according to the other interpretation of the term nature I understand something which is truly found in things and which is therefore not without some truth.

But certainly although in regard to the dropsical body it is only so to speak to apply an extrinsic term when we say that its nature is corrupted, inasmuch as apart from the need to drink, the throat is parched; yet in regard to the composite whole, that is to say, to the mind or soul united to this body, it is not a purely verbal predicate, but a real error of nature, for it to have thirst when drinking would be hurtful to it. And thus it still remains to inquire how the goodness of God does not prevent the nature of man so regarded from being fallacious.

In order to begin this examination, then, I here say, in the first place, that there is a great difference between mind and body, inasmuch as body is by nature always divisible, and the mind is entirely indivisible. For, as a matter of fact, when I consider the mind, that is to say, myself inasmuch as I am only a thinking thing, I cannot distinguish in myself any parts, but apprehend myself to be clearly one and entire; and although the whole mind seems to be united to the whole body, yet if a foot, or an arm, or some other part, is separated from my body, I am aware that nothing has been taken away from my mind. And the faculties of willing, feeling, conceiving, etc. cannot be properly speaking said to be its parts, for it is one and the same mind which employs itself in willing and in feeling and understanding. But it is quite otherwise with corporeal or extended objects, for there is not one of these imaginable by me which my mind cannot easily divide into parts, and which consequently I do not recognise as being divisible; this would be sufficient to teach me that the mind or soul of man is entirely different from the body, if I had not already learned it from other sources.

I further notice that the mind does not receive the impressions from all parts of the body immediately, but only from the brain, or perhaps even from one of its smallest parts, to wit, from that in which the common sense is said to reside, which, whenever it is disposed in the same particular way, conveys the same thing to the mind, although meanwhile the other portions of the body may be differently disposed, as is testified by innumerable experiments which it is unnecessary here to recount.

I notice, also, that the nature of body is such that none of its parts can be moved by another part a little way off which cannot also be moved in the same way by each one of the parts which are between the two, although this more remote part does not act at all. As, for example, in the cord ABCD [which is in tension] if we pull the last part D, the first part A will not be moved in any way differently from what would be the case if one of the intervening parts B or C were pulled, and the last part D were to remain unmoved. And in the same way, when I feel pain in my foot, my knowledge of physics teaches me that this sensation is communicated by means of nerves dispersed through the foot, which, being extended like cords from there to the brain, when they are contracted in the foot, at the same time contract the inmost portions of the brain which is their extremity and place of origin, and then excite a certain movement which nature has established in order to cause the mind to be affected by a sensation of pain represented as existing in the foot. But because these nerves must pass through the tibia, the thigh, the loins, the back and the neck, in order to reach from the leg to the brain, it may happen that although their extremities which are in the foot are not affected, but only certain ones of their intervening parts [which pass by the loins or the neck], this action will excite the same movement in the brain that might have been excited there by a hurt received in the foot, in consequence of which the mind will necessarily feel in the foot the same pain as if it had received a hurt. And the same holds good of all the other perceptions of our senses.

I notice finally that since each of the movements which are in the portion of the brain by which the mind is immediately affected brings about one particular sensation only, we cannot under the circumstances imagine anything more likely than that this movement, amongst all the sensations which it is capable of impressing on it, causes mind to be affected by that one which is best fitted and most generally useful for the conservation of the human body when it is in health. But experience makes us aware that all the feelings with which nature inspires us are such as I have just spoken of; and there is therefore nothing in them which does not give testimony to the power and goodness of the God [who has produced them]. Thus, for example, when the nerves which are in the feet are violently or more than usually moved, their movement, passing through the medulla of the spine to the inmost parts of the brain, gives a sign to the mind which makes it feel somewhat, to wit, pain, as though in the foot, by which the mind is excited to do its utmost to remove the cause of the evil as dangerous and hurtful to the foot. It is true that God could have constituted the nature of man in such a way that this same movement in the brain would have conveyed something quite different to the mind; for example, it might have produced consciousness of itself either in so far as it is in the brain, or as it is in the foot, or as it is in some other place between the foot and the brain, or it might finally have produced consciousness of anything else whatsoever; but none of all this would have contributed so well to the conservation of the body. Similarly, when we desire to drink, a certain dryness of the throat is produced which moves its nerves, and by their means the internal portions of the brain; and this movement causes in the mind the sensation of thirst, because in this case there is nothing more useful to us than to become aware that we have need to drink for the conservation of our health; and the same holds good in other instances.

From this it is quite clear that, notwithstanding the supreme goodness of God, the nature of man, inasmuch as it is composed of mind and body, cannot be otherwise than sometimes a source of deception. For if there is any cause which excites, not in the foot but in some part of the nerves which are extended between the foot and the brain, or even in the brain itself, the same movement which usually is produced when the foot is detrimentally affected, pain will be experienced as though it were in the foot, and the sense will thus naturally be deceived; for since the same movement in the brain is capable of causing but one sensation in the mind, and this sensation is much more frequently excited by a cause which hurts the foot than by another existing in some other quarter, it is reasonable that it should convey to the mind pain in the foot rather than in any other part of the body. And although the parchedness of the throat does not always proceed, as it usually does, from the fact that drinking is necessary for the health of the body, but sometimes comes from quite a different cause, as is the case with dropsical patients, it is yet much better that it should mislead on this occasion than if, on the other hand, it were always to deceive us when the body is in good health; and so on in similar cases.

And certainly this consideration is of great service to me, not only in enabling me to recognise all the errors to which my nature is subject, but also in enabling me to avoid them or to correct them more easily. For knowing that all my senses more frequently indicate to me truth than falsehood respecting the things which concern that which is beneficial to the body, and being able almost always to avail myself of many of them in order to examine one particular thing, and, besides that, being able to make use of my memory in order to connect the present with the past, and of my understanding which already has discovered all the causes of my errors, I ought no longer to fear that falsity may be found in matters every day presented to me by my senses. And I ought to set aside all the doubts of these past days as hyperbolical and ridiculous, particularly that very common uncertainty respecting sleep, which I could not distinguish from the waking state; for at present I find a very notable difference between the two, inasmuch as our memory can never connect our dreams one with the other, or with the whole course of our lives, as it unites events which happen to us while we are awake. And, as a matter of fact, if someone, while I was awake, quite suddenly appeared to me and disappeared as fast as do the images which I see in sleep, so that I could not know from whence the form came nor whither it went, it would not be without reason that I should deem it a spectre or a phantom formed by my brain [and similar to those which I form in sleep], rather than a real man. But when I perceive things as to which I know distinctly both the place from which they proceed, and that in which they are, and the time at which they appeared to me; and when, without any interruption, I can connect the perceptions which I have of them with the whole course of my life, I am perfectly assured that these perceptions occur while I am waking and not during sleep. And I ought in no wise to doubt the truth of such matters, if, after having called up all my senses, my memory, and my understanding, to examine them, nothing is brought to evidence by any one of them which is repugnant to what is set forth by the others. For because God is in no wise a deceiver, it follows that I am not deceived in this. But because the exigencies of action often oblige us to make up our minds before having leisure to examine matters carefully, we must confess that the life of man is very frequently subject to error in respect to individual objects, and we must in the end acknowledge the infirmity of our nature.

GEORGE BERKELEY

Three Dialogues between Hylas and Philonous*

George Berkeley (1685–1753), the Anglican Bishop of Cloyne, was born in Ireland.

THE FIRST DIALOGUE

Philonous. Good morrow, Hylas. I did not expect to find you abroad so early.

Hylas. It is indeed something unusual; but my thoughts were so taken up with a subject I was discoursing of last night that, finding I could not sleep, I resolved to rise and take a turn in the garden.

Phil. It happened well, to let you see what innocent and agreeable pleasures you lose every morning. Can there be a pleasanter time of the day or a more delightful season of the year? That purple sky, these wild but sweet notes of birds, the fragrant bloom upon the trees and flowers, the gentle influence of the rising sun—these and a thousand nameless beauties of nature inspire the soul with secret transports; its faculties, too, being at this time fresh and lively, are fit for those meditations which the solitude of a garden and tranquility of the morning naturally dispose us to. But I am afraid I interrupt your thoughts, for you seemed very intent on something.

Hyl. It is true, I was, and shall be obliged to you if you will permit me to go on in the same vein; not that I would by any means deprive myself of your company, for my thoughts always flow more easily in conversation with a friend than when I am alone; but my request is that you would suffer me to impart my reflections to you.

Phil. With all my heart, it is what I should have requested myself if you had not prevented me.

Hyl. I was considering the odd fate of those men who have in all ages, through an affectation of being distinguished from the vulgar, or some unaccountable turn of thought, pretended either to believe nothing at all or to believe the most extravagant things in the world. This, however, might be borne if their paradoxes and skepticism did not draw after them some consequences of general disadvantage to mankind. But the mischief lies here: that when men of less leisure see them who are supposed to have spent their whole time in the pursuits of knowledge professing an entire ignorance of all things or advancing such notions as are repugnant to plain and commonly received principles, they will be tempted to entertain suspicions concerning the most important truths, which they had hitherto held sacred and unquestionable.

Phil. I entirely agree with you as to the ill tendency of the affected doubts of some philosophers and fantastical conceits of others. I am even so far gone of late in this way of thinking that I have quitted several of the sublime notions I had got in their schools for vulgar opinions. And I give it you on my word, since this revolt from metaphysical notions to the plain dictates of nature and common sense, I find my understanding strangely enlightened, so that I can now easily comprehend a great many things which before were all mystery and riddle.

Hyl. I am glad to find there was nothing in the accounts I heard of you.

Phil. Pray, what were those?

Hyl. You were represented in last night's conversation as one who maintained the most extravagant opinion that ever entered into the mind of man, to wit, that there is no such thing as "material substance" in the world.

Phil. That there is no such thing as what philosophers call "material substance," I am seriously persuaded; but if I were made to see anything absurd or skeptical in this, I should then have the same reason to renounce this that I imagine I have now to reject the contrary opinion.

*First published in 1713.

Hyl. What! Can anything be more fantastical, more repugnant to common sense or a more manifest piece of skepticism than to believe there is no such thing as matter?

Phil. Softly, good Hylas. What if it should prove that you, who hold there is, are, by virtue of that opinion, a greater skeptic and maintain more paradoxes and repugnances to common sense than I who believe no such thing?

Hyl. You may as soon persuade me the part is greater than the whole, as that, in order to avoid absurdity and skepticism, I should ever be obliged to give up my opinion in this point.

Phil. Well then, are you content to admit that opinion for true which, upon examination, shall appear most agreeable to common sense and remote from skepticism?

Hyl. With all my heart. Since you are for raising disputes about the plainest things in nature, I am content for once to hear what you have to say.

Phil. Pray, Hylas, what do you mean by a "skeptic"?

Hyl. I mean what all men mean, one that doubts of everything.

Phil. He then who entertains no doubt concerning some particular point, with regard to that point cannot be thought a skeptic.

Hyl. I agree with you.

Phil. Whether does doubting consist in embracing the affirmative or negative side of a question?

Hyl. In neither; for whoever understands English cannot but know that *doubting* signifies a suspense between both.

Phil. He then that denies any point can no more be said to doubt of it than he who affirms it with the same degree of assurance.

Hyl. True.

Phil. And, consequently, for such his denial is no more to be esteemed a skeptic than the other.

Hyl. I acknowledge it.

Phil. How comes it to pass then, Hylas, that you pronounce me a skeptic because I deny what you affirm, to wit, the existence of matter? Since, for aught you can tell, I am as peremptory in my denial as you in your affirmation

Hyl. Hold, Philonous, I have been a little out in my definition; but every false step a man makes in discourse is not to be insisted on. I said indeed that a "skeptic" was one who doubted of everything, but I should have added: or who denies the reality and truth of things.

Phil. What things? Do you mean the principles and theorems of sciences? But these you know are universal intellectual notions, and consequently independent of matter; the denial therefore of this does not imply the denying them.

Hyl. I grant it. But are there no other things? What think you of distrusting the senses, of denying the real existence of sensible things, or pretending to know nothing of them. Is not this sufficient to denominate a man a skeptic?

Phil. Shall we therefore examine which of us it is that denies the reality of sensible things or professes the greatest ignorance of them, since, if I take you rightly, he is to be esteemed the greatest skeptic?

Hyl. That is what I desire.

Phil. What mean you by "sensible things"?

Hyl. Those things which are perceived by the senses. Can you imagine that I mean anything else?

Phil. Pardon me, Hylas, if I am desirous clearly to apprehend your notions, since this may much shorten our inquiry. Suffer me then to ask you this further question. Are those things only perceived by the senses which are perceived immediately? Or may those things properly be said to be "sensible" which are perceived immediately, or not without the intervention of others?

Hyl. I do not sufficiently understand you.

Phil. In reading a book, what I immediately perceive are the letters, but mediately, or by means of these, are suggested to my mind the notions of God, virtue, truth, etc. Now, that the letters are truly sensible things, or perceived by sense, there is no doubt; but I would know whether you take the things suggested by them to be so too.

Hyl. No, certainly; it were absurd to think God or virtue sensible things, though they may be signified and suggested to the mind by sensible marks with which they have an arbitrary connection.

Phil. It seems, then, that by "sensible things" you mean those only which can be perceived immediately by sense.

Hyl. Right.

Phil. Does it not follow from this that, though I see one part of the sky red, and another blue, and that my reason does thence evidently conclude there must be some cause of that diversity of colors, yet that cause cannot be said to be a sensible thing or perceived by the sense of seeing?

Hyl. It does.

Phil. In like manner, though I hear variety of sounds, yet I cannot be said to hear the causes of those sounds.

Hyl. You cannot.

Phil. And when by my touch I perceive a thing to be hot and heavy, I cannot say, with any truth or propriety, that I feel the cause of its heat or weight.

Hyl. To prevent any more questions of this kind, I tell you once for all that by "sensible things" I mean those only which are perceived by sense, and that in truth the senses perceive nothing which they do not perceive immediately, for they make no inferences. The deducing therefore of causes or occasions from effects and appearances, which alone are perceived by sense, entirely relates to reason.

Phil. This point then is agreed between us—that *sensible things are those only which are immediately perceived by sense.* You will further inform me whether we immediately perceive by sight anything besides light and colors and figures; or by hearing, anything but sounds; by the palate, anything besides tastes; by the smell, besides odors; or by the touch, more than tangible qualities.

Hyl. We do not.

Phil. It seems, therefore, that if you take away all sensible qualities, there remains nothing sensible?

Hyl. I grant it.

Phil. Sensible things therefore are nothing else but so many sensible qualities or combinations of sensible qualities?

Hyl. Nothing else.

Phil. Heat is then a sensible thing?

Hyl. Certainly.

Phil. Does the reality of sensible things consist in being perceived, or is it something distinct from their being perceived, and that bears no relation to the mind?

Hyl. To *exist* is one thing, and to be *perceived* is another.

Phil. I speak with regard to sensible things only; and of these I ask, whether by their real existence you mean a subsistence exterior to the mind and distinct from their being perceived?

Hyl. I mean a real absolute being, distinct from and without any relation to their being perceived.

Phil. Heat therefore, if it be allowed a real being, must exist without the mind?

Hyl. It must.

Phil. Tell me, Hylas, is this real existence equally compatible to all degrees of heat, which we perceive, or is there any reason why we should attribute it to some and deny it to others? And if there be, pray, let me know that reason.

Hyl. Whatever degree of heat we perceive by sense, we may be sure the same exists in the object that occasions it.

Phil. What! the greatest as well as the least?

Hyl. I tell you, the reason is plainly the same in respect of both: they are both perceived by sense; nay, the greater degree of heat is more sensibly perceived; and consequently, if there is any difference, we are more certain of its real existence than we can be of the reality of a lesser degree.

Phil. But is not the most vehement and intense degree of heat a very great pain?

Hyl. No one can deny it.

Phil. And is any unperceiving thing capable of pain or pleasure?

Hyl. No, certainly.

Phil. Is your material substance a senseless being or a being endowed with sense and perception?

Hyl. It is senseless, without doubt.

Phil. It cannot, therefore, be the subject of pain?

Hyl. By no means.

Phil. Nor, consequently, of the greatest heat perceived by sense, since you acknowledge this to be no small pain?

Hyl. I grant it.

Phil. What shall we say then of your external object: is it a material substance, or no?

Hyl. It is a material substance with the sensible qualities inhering in it.

Phil. How then can a great heat exist in it, since you own it cannot in a material substance? I desire you would clear this point.

Hyl. Hold, Philonous, I fear I was out in yielding intense heat to be a pain. It should seem rather that pain is something distinct from heat, and the consequence or effect of it.

Phil. Upon putting your hand near the fire, do you perceive one simple uniform sensation or two distinct sensations?

Hyl. But one simple sensation.

Phil. Is not the heat immediately perceived?

Hyl. It is.

Phil. And the pain?

Hyl. True.

Phil. Seeing therefore they are both immediately perceived at the same time, and the fire affects you only with one simple or uncompounded idea, it follows that this same simple idea is both the intense heat immediately perceived and the pain; and, consequently, that the intense heat immediately perceived is nothing distinct from a particular sort of pain.

Hyl. It seems so.

Phil. Again, try in your thoughts, Hylas, if you can conceive a vehement sensation to be without pain or pleasure.

Hyl. I cannot.

Phil. Or can you frame to yourself an idea of sensible pain or pleasure, in general, abstracted from every particular idea of heat, cold, tastes, smells, etc.?

Hyl. I do not find that I can.

Phil. Does it not therefore follow that sensible pain is nothing distinct from those sensations or ideas—in an intense degree?

Hyl. It is undeniable; and, to speak the truth, I begin to suspect a very great heat cannot exist but in a mind perceiving it.

Phil. What! are you then in that *skeptical* state of suspense, between affirming and denying?

Hyl. I think I may be positive in the point. A very violent and painful heat cannot exist without the mind.

Phil. It has not therefore, according to you, any real being?

Hyl. I own it.

Phil. Is it therefore certain that there is no body in nature really hot?

Hyl. I have not denied there is any real heat in bodies. I only say there is no such thing as an intense real heat.

Phil. But did you not say before that all degrees of heat were equally real, or, if there was any difference, that the greater were more undoubtedly real than the lesser?

Hyl. True; but it was because I did not then consider the ground there is for distinguishing between them, which I now plainly see. And it is this: because intense heat is nothing else but a particular kind of painful sensation, and pain cannot exist but in a perceiving being, it follows that no intense heat can really exist in an unperceiving corporeal substance. But this is no reason why we should deny heat in an inferior degree to exist in such a substance.

Phil. But how shall we be able to discern those degrees of heat which exist only in the mind from those which exist without it?

Hyl. That is no difficult matter. You know the least pain cannot exist unperceived; whatever, therefore,

degree of heat is a pain exists only in the mind. But as for all other degrees of heat nothing obliges us to think the same of them.

Phil. I think you granted before that no unperceiving being was capable of pleasure any more than of pain.

Hyl. I did.

Phil. And is not warmth, or a more gentle degree of heat than what causes uneasiness, a pleasure?

Hyl. What then?

Phil. Consequently, it cannot exist without the mind in an unperceiving substance, or body.

Hyl. So it seems.

Phil. Since, therefore, as well those degrees of heat that are not painful, as those that are, can exist only in a thinking substance, may we not conclude that external bodies are absolutely incapable of any degree of heat whatsoever?

Hyl. On second thoughts, I do not think it is so evident that warmth is a pleasure as that a great degree of heat is pain.

Phil. I do not pretend that warmth is as great a pleasure as heat is a pain. But if you grant it to be even a small pleasure, it serves to make good my conclusion.

Hyl. I could rather call it an "indolence." It seems to be nothing more than a privation of both pain and pleasure. And that such a quality or state as this may agree to an unthinkng substance, I hope you will not deny.

Phil. If you are resolved to maintain that warmth, or a gentle degree of heat, is no pleasure, I know not how to convince you otherwise than by appealing to your own sense. But what think you of cold?

Hyl. The same that I do of heat. An intense degree of cold is a pain; for to feel a very great cold is to perceive a great uneasiness; it cannot therefore exist without the mind; but a lesser degree of cold may, as well as a lesser degree of heat.

Phil. Those bodies, therefore, upon whose application to our own we perceive a moderate degree of heat must be concluded to have a moderate degree of heat or warmth in them; and those upon whose application we feel a like degree of cold must be thought to have cold in them.

Hyl. They must.

Phil. Can any doctrine be true that necessarily leads a man into an absurdity?

Hyl. Without doubt it cannot.

Phil. Is it not an absurdity to think that the same thing should be at the same time both cold and warm?

Hyl. It is.

Phil. Suppose now one of your hands is hot, and the other cold, and that they are both at once put into the same vessel of water, in an intermediate state, will not the water seem cold to one hand, and warm to the other?

Hyl. It will.

Phil. Ought we not therefore, by your principles, to conclude it is really both cold and warm at the same time, that is, according to your own concession, to believe an absurdity?

Hyl. I confess it seems so.

Phil. Consequently, the principles themselves are false, since you have granted that no true principle leads to an absurdity.

Hyl. But, after all, can anything be more absurd than to say, *there is no heat in the fire?*

Phil. To make the point still clearer; tell me whether, in two cases exactly alike, we ought not to make the same judgment?

Hyl. We ought.

Phil. When a pin pricks your finger, does it not rend and divide the fibres of your flesh?

Hyl. It does.

Phil. And when a coal burns your finger, does it any more?

Hyl. It does not.

Phil. Since, therefore, you neither judge the sensation itself occasioned by the pin, nor anything like it to be in the pin, you should not, conformably to what you have now granted, judge the sensation occasioned by the fire, or anything like it, to be in the fire.

Hyl. Well, since it must be so, I am content to yield this point and acknowledge that heat and cold are only sensations existing in our minds. But there still remain qualities enough to secure the reality of external things.

Phil. But what will you say, Hylas, if it shall appear that the case is the same with regard to all other sensible qualities, and that they can no more be supposed to exist without the mind than heat and cold?

Hyl. Then, indeed, you will have done something to the purpose; but that is what I despair of seeing proved.

Phil. Let us examine them in order. What think you of tastes—do they exist without the mind, or no?

Hyl. Can any man in his senses doubt whether sugar is sweet or wormwood bitter?

Phil. Inform me, Hylas. Is a sweet taste a particular kind of pleasure or pleasant sensation, or is it not?

Hyl. It is.

Phil. And is not bitterness some kind of uneasiness or pain?

Hyl. I grant it.

Phil. If therefore, sugar and wormwood are unthinking corporeal substances existing without the mind, how can sweetness and bitterness, that is, pleasure and pain, agree to them?

Hyl. Hold, Philonous. I now see what it was [that] deluded me all this time. You asked whether heat and cold, sweetness and bitterness, were not particular sorts of pleasure and pain; to which I answered simply that they were. Whereas I should have thus distinguished: those qualities as perceived by us are pleasures or pains, but not as existing in the external objects. We must not therefore conclude absolutely that there is no heat in the fire or sweetness in the sugar, but only that heat or sweetness, as perceived by us, are not in the fire or sugar. What say you to this?

Phil. I say it is nothing to the purpose. Our discourse proceeded altogether concerning sensible things, which you defined to be "the things we immediately perceive by our senses." Whatever other qualities, therefore, you speak of, as distinct from these, I know nothing of them, neither do they at all belong to the point in dispute. You may, indeed, pretend to have discovered certain qualities which you do not perceive and assert those insensible qualities exist in fire and sugar. But what use can be made of this to your present purpose, I am at a loss to conceive. Tell me then once more, do you acknowledge that heat and cold, sweetness and bitterness (meaning those qualities which are perceived by the senses), do not exist without the mind?

Hyl. I see it is to no purpose to hold out, so I give up the cause as to those mentioned qualities, though I profess it sounds oddly to say that sugar is not sweet.

Phil. But, for your further satisfaction, take this along with you: that which at other times seems sweet shall, to a distempered palate, appear bitter, and nothing can be plainer than that divers persons perceive different tastes in the same food, since that which one man delights in, another abhors. And how could this be if the taste was something really inherent in the food?

Hyl. I acknowledge I know not how.

Phil. In the next place, odors are to be considered. And with regard to these I would fain know whether what has been said of tastes does not exactly agree to them? Are they not so many pleasing or displeasing sensations?

Hyl. They are.

Phil. Can you then conceive it possible that they should exist in an unperceiving thing?

Hyl. I cannot.

Phil. Or can you imagine that filth and ordure affect those brute animals that feed on them out of choice with the same smells which we perceive in them?

Hyl. By no means.

Phil. May we not therefore conclude of smells, as of the other forementioned qualities, that they cannot exist in any but a perceiving substance or mind?

Hyl. I think so.

Phil. Then as to sounds, what must we think of them, are they accidents really inherent in external bodies or not?

Hyl. That they inhere not in the sonorous bodies is plain from hence; because a bell struck in the exhausted receiver of an air-pump sends forth no sound. The air, therefore, must be thought the subject of sound.

Phil. What reason is there for that, Hylas?

Hyl. Because, when any motion is raised in the air, we perceive a sound greater or less, in proportion to the air's motion; but without some motion in the air we never hear any sound at all.

Phil. And granting that we never hear a sound but when some motion is produced in the air, yet I do not see how you can infer from thence that the sound itself is in the air.

Hyl. It is this very motion in the external air that produces in the mind the sensation of sound. For, striking on the drum of the ear, it causes a vibration which by the auditory nerves being communicated to the brain, the soul is thereupon affected with the sensation called ''sound.''

Phil. What! is sound then a sensation?

Hyl. I tell you, as perceived by us it is a particular sensation in the mind.

Phil. And can any sensation exist without the mind?

Hyl. No, certainly.

Phil. How then can sound, being a sensation, exist in the air if by the ''air'' you mean a senseless substance existing without the mind?

Hyl. You must distinguish, Philonous, between sound as it is perceived by us, and as it is in itself; or (which is the same thing) between the sound we immediately perceive and that which exists without us. The former, indeed, is a particular kind of sensation, but the latter is merely a vibrative or undulatory motion in the air.

Phil. I thought I had already obviated that distinction by the answer I gave when you were applying it in a like case before. But, to say no more of that, are you sure then that sound is really nothing but motion?

Hyl. I am.

Phil. Whatever, therefore, agrees to real sound may with truth be attributed to motion?

Hyl. It may.

Phil. It is then good sense to speak of ''motion'' as of a thing that is *loud, sweet, acute,* or *grave.*

Hyl. I see you are resolved not to understand me. Is it not evident those accidents or modes belong only to sensible sound, or sound in the common acceptation of the word, but not to sound in the real and philosophic sense, which, as I just now told you, is nothing but a certain motion of the air?

Phil. It seems then there are two sorts of sound— the one vulgar, or that which is heard, the other philosophical and real?

Hyl. Even so.

Phil. And the latter consists in motion?

Hyl. I told you so before.

Phil. Tell me, Hylas, to which of the senses, think you, the idea of motion belongs? To the hearing?

Hyl. No, certainly; but to the sight and touch.

Phil. It should follow then that, according to you, real sounds may possibly be *seen* or *felt,* but never *heard.*

Hyl. Look you, Philonous, you may, if you please, make a jest of my opinion, but that will not alter the truth of things. I own, indeed, the inferences you draw me into sound something oddly, but common language, you know, is framed by, and for the use of, the vulgar. We must not therefore wonder if expressions adapted to exact philosophic notions seem uncouth and out of the way.

Phil. Is it come to that? I assure you I imagine

myself to have gained no small point since you make so light of departing from common phrases and opinions, it being a main part of our inquiry to examine whose notions are widest of the common road and most repugnant to the general sense of the world. But can you think it no more than a philosophical paradox to say that "real sounds are never heard," and that the idea of them is obtained by some other sense? And is there nothing in this contrary to nature and the truth of things?

Hyl. To deal ingenuously, I do not like it. And, after the concessions already made, I had as well grant that sounds, too, have no real being without the mind.

Phil. And I hope you will make no difficulty to acknowledge the same of colors.

Hyl. Pardon me; the case of colors is very different. Can anything be plainer than that we see them on the objects?

Phil. The objects you speak of are, I suppose, corporeal substances existing without the mind?

Hyl. They are.

Phil. And have true and real colors inhering in them?

Hyl. Each visible object has that color which we see in it.

Phil. How! is there anything visible but what we perceive by sight?

Hyl. There is not.

Phil. And do we perceive anything by sense which we do not perceive immediately?

Hyl. How often must I be obliged to repeat the same thing? I tell you, we do not.

Phil. Have patience, good Hylas, and tell me once more whether there is anything immediately perceived by the senses except sensible qualities. I know you asserted there was not; but I would now be informed whether you still persist in the same opinion.

Hyl. I do.

Phil. Pray, is your corporeal substance either a sensible quality or made up of sensible qualities?

Hyl. What a question that is! Who ever thought it was?

Phil. My reason for asking was, because in saying "each visible object has that color which we see in it," you make visible objects to be corporeal substances, which implies either that corporeal substances are sensible qualities or else that there is something

besides sensible qualities perceived by sight; but as this point was formerly agreed between us, and is still maintained by you, it is a clear consequence that your corporeal substance is nothing distinct from sensible qualities.

Hyl. You may draw as many absurd consequences as you please and endeavor to perplex the plainest things, but you shall never persuade me out of my senses. I clearly understand my own meaning.

Phil. I wish you would make me understand it, too. But, since you are unwilling to have your notion of corporeal substance examined, I shall urge that point no further. Only be pleased to let me know whether the same colors which we see exist in external bodies or some other.

Hyl. The very same.

Phil. What! are then the beautiful red and purple we see on yonder clouds really in them? Or do you imagine they have in themselves any other form than that of a dark mist of vapor?

Hyl. I must own, Philonous, those colors are not really in the clouds as they seem to be at this distance. They are only apparent colors.

Phil. "Apparent" call you them? How shall we distinguish these apparent colors from real?

Hyl. Very easily. Those are to be thought apparent which, appearing only at a distance, vanish upon a nearer approach.

Phil. And those, I suppose, are to be thought real which are discovered by the most near and exact survey.

Hyl. Right.

Phil. Is the nearest and exactest survey made by the help of a microscope or by the naked eye?

Hyl. By a microscope, doubtless.

Phil. But a microscope often discovers colors in an object different from those perceived by the unassisted sight. And, in case we had microscopes magnifying to any assigned degree, it is certain that no object whatsoever, viewed through them, would appear in the same color which it exhibits to the naked eye.

Hyl. And what will you conclude from all this? You cannot argue that there are really and naturally no colors on objects because by artificial managements they may be altered or made to vanish.

Phil. I think it may evidently be concluded from your own concessions that all the colors we see with our naked eyes are only apparent as those on the clouds, since they vanish upon a more close and accurate inspection which is afforded us by a microscope. Then, as to what you say by way of prevention: I ask you whether the real and natural state of an object is better discovered by a very sharp and piercing sight or by one which is less sharp?

Hyl. By the former without doubt.

Phil. Is it not plain from dioptrics that microscopes make the sight more penetrating and represent objects as they would appear to the eye in case it were naturally endowed with a most exquisite sharpness?

Hyl. It is.

Phil. Consequently, the microscopical representation is to be thought that which best sets forth the real nature of the thing, or what it is in itself. The colors, therefore, by it perceived are more genuine and real than those perceived otherwise.

Hyl. I confess there is something in what you say.

Phil. Besides, it is not only possible but manifest that there actually are animals whose eyes are by nature framed to perceive those things which by reason of their minuteness escape our sight. What think you of those inconceivably small animals perceived by glasses? Must we suppose they are all stark blind? Or, in case they see, can it be imagined their sight has not the same use in preserving their bodies from injuries which appears in that of all other animals? And if it has, is it not evident they must see particles less than their own bodies, which will present them with a far different view in each object from that which strikes our senses? Even our own eyes do not always represent objects to us after the same manner. In the jaundice everyone knows that all things seem yellow. Is it not therefore highly probable those animals in whose eyes we discern a very different texture from that of ours, and whose bodies abound with different humors, do not see the same colors in every object that we do? From all which should it not seem to follow that all colors are equally apparent, and that none of those which we perceive are really inherent in any outward object?

Hyl. It should.

Phil. The point will be past all doubt if you consider that, in case colors were real properties or affections inherent in external bodies, they could admit of no alteration without some change wrought in the very bodies themselves; but is it not evident from what has been said that, upon the use of microscopes, upon a change happening in the humors of the eye, or a variation of distance, without any manner of real alteration in the thing itself, the colors of any object are either changed or totally disappear? Nay, all other circumstances remaining the same,

change but the situation of some objects and they shall present different colors to the eye. The same thing happens upon viewing an object in various degrees of light. And what is more known than that the same bodies appear differently colored by candlelight from what they do in the open day? Add to these the experiment of a prism which, separating the heterogeneous rays of light alters the color of any object and will cause the whitest to appear of a deep blue or red to the naked eye. And now tell me whether you are still of opinion that every body has its true real color inhering in it; and if you think it has, I would fain know further from you what certain distance and position of the object, what peculiar texture and formation of the eye, what degree or kind of light is necessary for ascertaining that true color and distinguishing it from apparent ones.

Hyl. I own myself entirely satisfied that they are all equally apparent and that there is no such thing as color really inhering in external bodies, but that it is altogether in the light. And what confirms me in this opinion is that in proportion to the light colors are still more or less vivid; and if there be no light, then are there no colors perceived. Besides, allowing there are colors on external objects, yet, how is it possible for us to perceive them? For no external body affects the mind unless it acts first on our organs of sense. But the only action of bodies is motion, and motion cannot be communicated otherwise than by impulse. A distant object, therefore, cannot act on the eye, nor consequently make itself or its properties perceivable to the soul. Whence it plainly follows that it is immediately some contiguous substance which, operating on the eye, occasions a perception of colors; and such is light.

Phil. How! is light then a substance?

Hyl. I tell you, Philonous, external light is nothing but a thin fluid substance whose minute particles, being agitated with a brisk motion and in various manners reflected from the different surfaces of outward objects to the eyes, communicate different motions to the optic nerves; which, being propagated to the brain, cause therein various impressions, and these are attended with the sensations of red, blue, yellow, etc.

Phil. It seems, then, the light does no more than shake the optic nerves.

Hyl. Nothing else.

Phil. And, consequent to each particular motion

of the nerves, the mind is affected with a sensation which is some particular color.

Hyl. Right.

Phil. And these sensations have no existence without the mind.

Hyl. They have not.

Phil. How then do you affirm that colors are in the light, since by ''light'' you understand a corporeal substance external to the mind?

Hyl. Light and colors, as immediately perceived by us, I grant cannot exist without the mind. But in themselves they are only the motions and configurations of certain insensible particles of matter.

Phil. Colors, then, in the vulgar sense, or taken for the immediate objects of sight, cannot agree to any but a perceiving substance.

Hyl. That is what I say.

Phil. Well then, since you give up the point as to those sensible qualities which are alone thought colors by all mankind besides, you may hold what you please with regard to those invisible ones of the philosophers. It is not my business to dispute them; only I would advise you to bethink yourself whether, considering the inquiry we are upon, it be prudent for you to affirm—*the red and blue which we see are not real colors, but certain unknown motions and figures which no man ever did or can see are truly so.* Are not these shocking notions, and are not they subject to as many ridiculous inferences as those you were obliged to renounce before in the case of sounds?

Hyl. I frankly own, Philonous, that it is in vain to stand out any longer. Colors, sounds, tastes, in a word, all those termed ''secondary qualities,'' have certainly no existence without the mind. But by this acknowledgment I must not be supposed to derogate anything from the reality of matter or external objects; seeing it is no more than several philosophers maintain, who nevertheless are the farthest imaginable from denying matter. For the clearer understanding of this you must know sensible qualities are by philosophers divided into ''primary'' and ''secondary.'' The former are extension, figure, solidity, gravity, motion, and rest. And these they hold exist really in bodies. The latter are those above enumerated, or, briefly, all sensible qualities besides the primary, which they assert are only so many sensations or ideas existing nowhere but in the mind. But all this, I doubt not, you are already apprised of. For my part

I have been a long time sensible there was such an opinion current among philosophers, but was never thoroughly convinced of its truth till now.

Phil. You are still then of opinion that *extension* and *figures* are inherent in external unthinking substances?

Hyl. I am.

Phil. But what if the same arguments which are brought against secondary qualities will hold good against these also?

Hyl. Why then I shall be obliged to think they too exist only in the mind.

Phil. Is it your opinion the very figure and extension which you perceive by sense exist in the outward object or material substance?

Hyl. It is.

Phil. Have all other animals as good grounds to think the same of the figure and extension which they see and feel?

Hyl. Without doubt, if they have any thought at all.

Phil. Answer me, Hylas. Think you the senses were bestowed upon all animals for their preservation and well-being in life? Or were they given to men alone for this end?

Hyl. I make no question but they have the same use in all other animals.

Phil. If so, is it not necessary they should be enabled by them to perceive their own limbs and those bodies which are capable of harming them?

Hyl. Certainly.

Phil. A mite therefore must be supposed to see his own foot, and things equal or even less than it, as bodies of some considerable dimension, though at the same time they appear to you scarce discernible or at best at so many visible points?

Hyl. I cannot deny it.

Phil. And to creatures less than the mite they will seem yet larger?

Hyl. They will.

Phil. Insomuch that what you can hardly discern will to another extremely minute animal appear as some huge mountain?

Hyl. All this I grant.

Phil. Can one and the same thing be at the same time in itself of different dimensions?

Hyl. That were absurd to imagine.

Phil. But from what you have laid down it follows that both the extension by you perceived and that perceived by the mite itself, as likewise all those perceived by lesser animals, are each of them the true extension of the mite's foot; that is to say, by your own principles you are led into an absurdity.

Hyl. There seems to be some difficulty in the point.

Phil. Again, have you not acknowledged that no real inherent property of any object can be changed without some change in the thing itself?

Hyl. I have.

Phil. But, as we approach to or recede from an object, the visible extension varies, being at one distance ten or a hundred times greater than at another. Does it not therefore follow from hence likewise that it is not really inherent in the object?

Hyl. I own I am at a loss what to think.

Phil. Your judgment will soon be determined if you will venture to think as freely concerning this quality as you have done concerning the rest. Was it not admitted as a good argument that neither heat nor cold was in the water because it seemed warm to one hand and cold to the other?

Hyl. It was.

Phil. Is it not the very same reasoning to conclude there is no extension or figure in an object because to one eye it shall seem little, smooth, and round, when at the same time it appears to the other great, uneven, and angular?

Hyl. The very same. But does this latter fact ever happen?

Phil. You may at any time make the experiment by looking with one eye bare and with the other through a microscope.

Hyl. I know not how to maintain it, and yet I am loath to give up *extension;* I see so many odd consequences following upon such a concession.

Phil. Odd, say you? After the concessions already made, I hope you will stick at nothing for its oddness. [But,[1] on the other hand, should it not seem very odd if the general reasoning which includes all other sensible qualities did not also include extension? If it be allowed that no idea nor anything like an idea can exist in an unperceiving substance, then surely it follows that no figure or mode of extension, which we can either perceive or imagine, or have any idea of, can be really inherent in matter, not to mention the peculiar difficulty there must be in conceiving a material substance, prior to and distinct from extension, to be the *substratum* of extension. Be the sensible quality what it will—figure or sound or color—it seems alike impossible it should subsist in that which does not perceive it.]

Hyl. I give up the point for the present, reserving still a right to retract my opinion in case I shall hereafter discover any false step in my progress to it.

Phil. That is a right you cannot be denied. Figures and extension being dispatched, we proceed next to *motion.* Can a real motion in any external body be at the same time both very swift and very slow?

Hyl. It cannot.

Phil. Is not the motion of a body swift in a reciprocal proportion to the time it takes up in describing any given space? Thus a body that describes a mile in an hour moves three times faster than it would in case it described only a mile in three hours.

Hyl. I agree with you.

Phil. And is not time measured by the succession of ideas in our minds?

Hyl. It is.

Phil. And is it not possible ideas should succeed one another twice as fast in your mind as they do in mine, or in that of some spirit of another kind?

Hyl. I own it.

Phil. Consequently, the same body may to another seem to perform its motion over any space in half the time that it does to you. And the same reasoning will hold as to any other proportion; that is to say, according to your principles (since the motions perceived are both really in the object) it is possible one and the same body shall be really moved the same way at once, both very swift and very slow. How is this consistent with common sense or with what you just now granted?

Hyl. I have nothing to say to it.

Phil. Then as for *solidity;* either you do not mean any sensible quality by that word, and so it is beside our inquiry; or if you do, it must be either hardness or resistance. But both the one and the other are plainly relative to our senses: it being evident that what seems hard to one animal may appear soft to another who has greater force and firmness of limbs. Nor is it less plain that the resistance I feel is not in the body.

Hyl. I own the very sensation of resistance, which is all you immediately perceive, is not in the *body,* but the cause of that sensation is.

Phil. But the causes of our sensations are not things immediately perceived, and therefore not sensible. This point I thought had been already determined.

Hyl. I own it was; but you will pardon me if I seem a little embarrassed; I know not how to quit my old notions.

Phil. To help you out, do but consider that if

extension be once acknowledged to have no existence without the mind, the same must necessarily be granted of motion, solidity, and gravity, since they all evidently suppose extension. It is therefore superfluous to inquire particularly concerning each of them. In denying extension, you have denied them all to have any real existence.

Hyl. I wonder, Philonous, if what you say be true, why those philosophers who deny the secondary qualities any real existence should yet attribute it to the primary. If there is no difference between them, how can this be accounted for?

Phil. It is not my business to account for every opinion of the philosophers. But, among other reasons which may be assigned for this, it seems probable that pleasure and pain being rather annexed to the former than the latter may be one. Heat and cold, tastes and smells have something more vividly pleasing or disagreeable than the ideas of extension, figure, and motion affect us with. And, it being too visibly absurd to hold that pain or pleasure can be in an unperceiving substance, men are more easily weaned from believing the external existence of the secondary than the primary qualities. You will be satisfied there is something in this if you recollect the difference you made between an intense and more moderate degree of heat, allowing the one a real existence while you denied it to the other. But, after all, there is no rational ground for that distinction, for surely an indifferent sensation is as truly a *sensation* as one more pleasing or painful, and consequently should not any more than they be supposed to exist in an unthinking subject.

Hyl. It is just come into my head, Philonous, that I have somewhere heard of a distinction between *absolute* and *sensible* extension. Now though it be acknowledged that *great* and *small,* consisting merely in the relation which other extended beings have to the parts of our own bodies, do not really inhere in the substances themselves, yet nothing obliges us to hold the same with regard to *absolute* extension, which is something abstracted from *great* and *small,* from this or that particular magnitude or figure. So likewise as to motion: *swift* and *slow* are altogether relative to the succession of ideas in our own minds. But it does not follow, because those modifications of motion exist not without the mind, that therefore absolute motion abstracted from them does not.

Phil. Pray what is it that distinguishes one motion, or one part of extension, from another? Is it not something sensible, as some degree of swiftness or slowness, some certain magnitude or figure peculiar to each?

Hyl. I think so.

Phil. These qualities, therefore, stripped of all sensible properties, are without all specific and numerical differences, as the schools call them.

Hyl. They are.

Phil. That is to say, they are extension in general, and motion in general.

Hyl. Let it be so.

Phil. But it is a universally received maxim that *everything which exists is particular.* How then can motion in general, or extension in general, exist in any corporeal substance?

Hyl. I will take time to solve your difficulty.

Phil. But I think the point may be speedily decided. Without doubt you can tell whether you are able to frame this or that idea. Now I am content to put our dispute on this issue. If you can frame in your thoughts a distinct abstract idea of motion or extension divested of all those sensible modes as swift and slow, great and small, round and square, and the like, which are acknowledged to exist only in the mind, I will then yield the point you contend for. But if you cannot, it will be unreasonable on your side to insist any longer upon what you have no notion of.

Hyl. To confess ingenuously, I cannot.

Phil. Can you even separate the ideas of extension and motion from the ideas of all those qualities which they who make the distinction term "secondary"?

Hyl. What! is it not an easy matter to consider extension and motion by themselves, abstracted from all other sensible qualities? Pray how do the mathematicians treat of them?

Phil. I acknowledge, Hylas, it is not difficult to form general propositions and reasonings about those qualities without mentioning any other, and, in this sense, to consider or treat of them abstractedly. But how does it follow that, because I can pronounce the word "motion" by itself, I can form the idea of it in my mind exclusive of body? Or because theorems may be made of extension and figures, without any mention of *great* or *small,* or any other sensible mode or quality, that therefore it is possible such an abstract idea of extension, without any particular size or figure or sensible quality, should be distinctly formed and apprehended by the mind? Mathematicians treat of quantity without regarding what other sensible qualities it is attended with, as being altogether indifferent to their demonstrations. But when, laying aside the words, they contemplate the bare ideas, I believe you will find they are not the pure abstracted ideas of extension.

Hyl. But what say you to *pure intellect?* May not abstracted ideas be framed by that faculty?

Phil. Since I cannot frame abstract ideas at all, it is plain I cannot frame them by the help of pure intellect, whatsoever faculty you understand by those words. Besides, not to inquire into the nature of pure intellect and its spiritual objects, as *virtue, reason, God,* or the like, thus much seems manifest that sensible things are only to be perceived by sense or represented by the imagination. Figures, therefore, and extension, being originally perceived by sense, do not belong to pure intellect; but, for your further satisfaction, try if you can frame the idea of any figure abstracted from all particularities of size or even from other sensible qualities.

Hyl. Let me think a little—I do not find that I can.

Phil. And can you think it possible that [an idea] should really exist in nature which implies a repugnancy in its comception?

Hyl. By no means.

Phil. Since therefore it is impossible even for the mind to disunite the ideas of extension and motion from all other sensible qualities, does it not follow that where the one exist there necessarily the other exist likewise?

Hyl. It should seem so.

Phil. Consequently, the very same arguments which you admitted as conclusive against the secondary qualities are, without any further application of force, against the primary, too. Besides, if you will trust your senses, is it not plain all sensible qualities coexist, or to them appear as being in the same place? Do they ever represent a motion or figure as being divested of all other visible and tangible qualities?

Hyl. You need say no more on this head. I am free to own, if there be no secret error or oversight in our proceedings hitherto, that all sensible qualities are alike to be denied existence without the mind. But my fear is that I have been too liberal in my former concessions, or overlooked some fallacy or other. In short, I did not take time to think.

Phil. For that matter, Hylas, you may take what time you please in reviewing the progress of our inquiry. You are at liberty to recover any slips you might have made, or offer whatever you have omitted which makes for your first opinion.

Hyl. One great oversight I take to be this—that I did not sufficiently distinguish the *object* from the *sensation.* Now, though this latter may not exist without the mind, yet it will not thence follow that the former cannot.

Phil. What object do you mean? The object of the senses?

Hyl. The same.

Phil. It is then immediately perceived?

Hyl. Right.

Phil. Make me to understand the difference between what is immediately perceived and a sensation.

Hyl. The sensation I take to be an act of the mind perceiving; besides which there is something perceived, and this I call the "object." For example, there is red and yellow on that tulip. But then the act of perceiving those colors is in me only, and not in the tulip.

Phil. What tulip do you speak of? Is it that which you see?

Hyl. The same.

Phil. And what do you see besides color, figure, and extension?

Hyl. Nothing.

Phil. What you would say then is that the red and yellow are coexistent with the extension; is it not?

Hyl. That is not all; I would say they have a real existence without the mind, in some unthinking substance.

Phil. That the colors are really in the tulip which I see is manifest. Neither can it be denied that this tulip may exist independent of your mind or mine; but that any immediate object of the senses—that is, any idea, or combination of ideas—should exist in an unthinking substance, or exterior to all minds, is in itself an evident contradiction. Nor can I imagine how this follows from what you said just now, to wit, that the red and yellow were on the tulip *you saw,* since you do not pretend to *see* that unthinking substance.

Hyl. You have an artful way, Philonous, of diverting our inquiry from the subject.

Phil. I see you have no mind to be pressed that way. To return then to your distinction between *sensation* and *object;* if I take you right, you distinguish in every perception two things, the one an action of the mind, the other not.

Hyl. True.

Phil. And this action cannot exist in, or belong to, any unthinking thing, but whatever besides is implied in a perception may?

Hyl. That is my meaning.

Phil. So that if there was a perception without any act of the mind, it were possible such a perception should exist in an unthinking substance?

Hyl. I grant it. But it is impossible there should be such a perception.

Phil. When is the mind said to be active?

Hyl. When it produces, puts an end to, or changes anything.

Phil. Can the mind produce, discontinue, or change anything but by an act of the will?

Hyl. It cannot.

Phil. The mind therefore is to be accounted *active* in its perceptions so far forth as *volition* is included in them?

Hyl. It is.

Phil. In plucking this flower I am active, because I do it by the motion of my hand, which was consequent upon my volition; so likewise in applying it to my nose. But is either of these smelling?

Hyl. No.

Phil. I act, too, in drawing the air through my nose, because my breathing so rather than otherwise is the effect of my volition. But neither can this be called "smelling," for if it were I should smell every time I breathed in that manner?

Phil. Smelling then is somewhat consequent to all this?

Hyl. It is.

Phil. But I do not find my will concerned any further. Whatever more there is—as that I perceive such a particular smell, or any smell at all—this is independent of my will, and therein I am altogether passive. Do you find it otherwise with you, Hylas?

Hyl. No, the very same.

Phil. Then, as to seeing, is it not in your power to open your eyes or keep them shut, to turn them this or that way?

Hyl. Without doubt.

Phil. But does it in like manner depend on your will that in looking on this flower you perceive *white* rather than any other color? Or, directing your open eyes toward yonder part of the heaven, can you avoid seeing the sun? Or is light or darkness the effect of your volition?

Hyl. No, certainly.

Phil. You are then in these respects altogether passive?

Hyl. I am.

Phil. Tell me now whether *seeing* consists in perceiving light and colors or in opening and turning the eyes?

Hyl. Without doubt, in the former.

Phil. Since, therefore, you are in the very perception of light and colors altogether passive, what is become of that action you were speaking of as an ingredient in every sensation? And does it not follow from your own concessions that the perception of light and colors, including no action in it, may exist in an unperceiving substance? And is not this a plain contradiction?

Hyl. I know not what to think of it.

Phil. Besides, since you distinguish the *active* and *passive* in every perception, you must do it in that of pain. But how is it possible that pain, be it as little active as you please, should exist in an unperceiving substance? In short, do but consider the point and then confess ingenuously whether light and colors, tastes, sounds, etc., are not all equally passions or sensations in the soul. You may indeed call them "external objects" and give them in words what subsistence you please. But examine your own thoughts and then tell me whether it be not as I say?

Hyl. I acknowledge, Philonous, that, upon a fair observation of what passes in my mind, I can discover nothing else but that I am a thinking being affected with variety of sensations; neither is it possible to conceive how a sensation should exist in an unperceiving substance. But then, on the other hand, when I look on sensible things in a different view, considering them as so many modes and qualities, I find it necessary to suppose a material *substratum,* without which they cannot be conceived to exist.

Phil. "Material substratum" call you it? Pray, by which of your senses came you acquainted with that being?

Hyl. It is not itself sensible; its modes and qualities only being perceived by the senses.

Phil. I presume then it was by reflection and reason you obtained the idea of it?

Hyl. I do not pretend to any proper positive idea of it. However, I conclude it exists because qualities cannot be conceived to exist without a support.

Phil. It seems then you have only a relative notion of it, or that you conceive it not otherwise than by conceiving the relation it bears to sensible qualities?

Hyl. Right.

Phil. Be pleased, therefore, to let me know wherein that relation consists.

Hyl. Is it not sufficiently expressed in the term "substratum" or "substance"?

Phil. If so, the word "substratum" should import that it is spread under the sensible qualities or accidents?

Hyl. True.

Phil. And consequently under extension?

Hyl. I own it.

Phil. It is therefore somewhat in its own nature distinct from extension?

Hyl. I tell you extension is only a mode, and matter is something that supports modes. And is it not evident the thing supported is different from the thing supporting?

Phil. So that something distinct from, and exclusive of, extension is supposed to be the *substratum* of extension?

Hyl. Just so.

Phil. Answer me, Hylas, can a thing be spread without extension, or is not the idea of extension necessarily included in *spreading?*

Hyl. It is.

Phil. Whatsoever therefore you suppose spread under anything must have in itself an extension distinct from the extension of that thing under which it is spread?

Hyl. It must.

Phil. Consequently, every corporeal substance being the *substratum* of extension must have in itself another extension by which it is qualified to be a *substratum,* and so on to infinity? And I ask whether this be not absurd in itself and repugnant to what you granted just now, to wit, that the *substratum* was something distinct from and exclusive of extension?

Hyl. Aye, but, Philonous, you take me wrong. I do not mean that matter is *spread* in a gross literal sense under extension. The word "substratum" is used only to express in general the same thing with "substance."

Phil. Well then, let us examine the relation implied in the term "substance." Is it not that it stands under accidents?

Hyl. The very same.

Phil. But that one thing may stand under or support another, must it not be extended?

Hyl. It must.

Phil. Is not therefore this supposition liable to the same absurdity with the former?

Hyl. You still take things in a strict literal sense; that is not fair, Philonous.

Phil. I am not for imposing any sense on your words; you are at liberty to explain them as you please. Only, I beseech you, make me understand something by them. You tell me matter supports or stands under accidents. How! is it as your legs support your body?

Hyl. No; that is the literal sense.

Phil. Pray let me know any sense, literal or not literal, that you understand it in.—How long must I wait for an answer, Hylas?

Hyl. I declare I know not what to say. I once thought I understood well enough what was meant by matter's supporting accidents. But now, the more I think on it, the less can I comprehend it; in short, I find that I know nothing of it.

Phil. It seems then you have no idea at all, neither relative nor positive, of matter? you know neither what it is in itself nor what relation it bears to accidents?

Hyl. I acknowledge it.

Phil. And yet you asserted that you could not conceive how qualities or accidents should really exist without conceiving at the same time a material support of them?

Hyl. I did.

Phil. That is to say, when you conceive the real existence of qualities, you do withal conceive something which you cannot conceive?

Hyl. It was wrong I own. But still I fear there is some fallacy or other. Pray, what think you of this? It is just come into my head that the ground of all our mistake lies in your treating of each quality by itself. Now I grant that each quality cannot singly subsist without the mind. Color cannot without extension, neither can figure without some other sensible quality. But, as the several qualities united or blended together form entire sensible things, nothing hinders why such things may not be supposed to exist without the mind.

Phil. Either, Hylas, you are jesting or have a very bad memory. Though, indeed, we went through all the qualities by name one after another, yet my arguments, or rather your concessions, nowhere tended to prove that the secondary qualities did not subsist each alone by itself, but that they were not *at all* without the mind. Indeed, in treating of figure and motion we concluded they could not exist without the mind, because it was impossible even in thought to separate them from all secondary qualities, so as to conceive them existing by themselves. But then this was not the only argument made use of upon that occasion. But (to pass by all that has been hitherto said and reckon it for nothing, if you will have it so) I am content to put the whole upon this issue. If you can conceive it possible for any mixture or combination of qualities, or any sensible object whatever, to exist without the mind, then I will grant it actually to be so.

Hyl. If it comes to that the point will soon be decided. What more easy than to conceive a tree or house existing by itself, independent of, and unperceived by, any mind whatsoever? I do at this present time conceive them existing after that manner.

Phil. How say you, Hylas, can you see a thing which is at the same time unseen?

Hyl. No, that were a contradiction.

Phil. Is it not as great a contradiction to talk of *conceiving* a thing which is *unconceived?*

Hyl. It is.

Phil. The tree or house, therefore, which you think of is conceived by you?

Hyl. How should it be otherwise?

Phil. And what is conceived is surely in the mind?

Hyl. Without question, that which is conceived is in the mind.

Phil. How then came you to say you conceived a house or tree existing independent and out of all minds whatsoever?

Hyl. That was I own an oversight, but stay, let me consider what let me into it.—It is a pleasant mistake enough. As I was thinking of a tree in a solitary place where no one was present to see it, methought that was to conceive a tree as existing unperceived or unthought of, not considering that I myself conceived it all the while. But now I plainly see that all I can do is to frame ideas in my own mind. I may indeed conceive in my own thoughts the idea of a tree, or a house, or a mountain, but that is all. And this is far from proving that I can conceive them *existing out of the minds of all spirits*.

Phil. You acknowledge then that you cannot possibly conceive how any one corporeal sensible thing should exist otherwise than in a mind?

Hyl. I do.

Phil. And yet you will earnestly contend for the truth of that which you cannot so much as conceive?

Hyl. I profess I know not what to think; but still there are some scruples remain with me. Is it not certain I see things at a distance? Do we not perceive the stars and moon, for example, to be a great way off? Is not this, I say, manifest to the senses?

Phil. Do you not in a dream, too, perceive those or the like objects?

Hyl. I do.

Phil. And have they not then the same appearance of being distant?

Hyl. They have.

Phil. But you do not thence conclude the apparitions in a dream to be without the mind?

Hyl. By no means.

Phil. You ought not therefore to conclude that sensible objects are without the mind, from their appearance or manner wherein they are perceived.

Hyl. I acknowledge it. But does not my sense deceive me in those cases?

Phil. By no means. The idea or thing which you immediately perceive, neither sense nor reason informs you that it actually exists without the mind. By sense you only know that you are affected with such certain sensations of light and colors, etc. And these you will not say are without the mind.

Hyl. True, but, besides all that, do you not think the sight suggests something of *outness* or *distance?*

Phil. Upon approaching a distant object, do the visible size and figure change perpetually or do they appear the same at all distances?

Hyl. They are in a continual change.

Phil. Sight, therefore, does not suggest or any way inform you that the visible object you immediately perceive exists at a distance,[2] or will be perceived when you advance farther onward, there being a continued series of visible objects succeeding each other during the whole time of your approach.

Hyl. It does not; but still I know, upon seeing an object, what object I shall perceive after having passed over a certain distance? no matter whether it be exactly the same or no, there is still something of distance suggested in the case.

Phil. Good Hylas, do but reflect a little on the point, and then tell me whether there be any more in it than this. From the ideas you actually perceive by sight, you have by experience learned to collect what other ideas you will (according to the standing order of nature) be affected with, after such a certain succession of time and motion.

Hyl. Upon the whole, I take it to be nothing else.

Phil. Now is it not plain that if we suppose a

man born blind was on a sudden made to see, he could at first have no experience of what may be suggested by sight?

Hyl. It is.

Phil. He would not then, according to you, have any notion of distance annexed to the things he saw, but would take them for a new set of sensations existing only in his mind?

Hyl. It is undeniable.

Phil. But to make it more plain: is not *distance* a line turned endwise to the eye?

Hyl. It is.

Phil. And can a line so situated be perceived by sight?

Hyl. It cannot.

Phil. Does it not therefore follow that distance is not properly and immediately perceived by sight?

Hyl. It should seem so.

Phil. Again, is it your opinion that colors are at a distance?

Hyl. It must be acknowledged they are only in the mind.

Phil. But do not colors appear to the eye as coexisting in the same place with extension and figures?

Hyl. They do.

Phil. How can you then conclude from sight that figures exist without, when you acknowledge colors do not; the sensible appearances being the very same with regard to both?

Hyl. I know not what to answer.

Phil. But allowing that distance was truly and immediately perceived by the mind, yet it would not thence follow it existed out of the mind. For whatever is immediately perceived is an idea; and can any *idea* exist out of the mind?

Hyl. To suppose that were absurd; but, inform me, Philonous, can we perceive or know nothing besides our ideas?

Phil. As for the rational deducing of causes from effects, that is beside our inquiry. And by the senses you can best tell whether you perceive anything which is not immediately perceived. And I ask you whether the things immediately perceived are other than your own sensations or ideas? You have indeed more than once, in the course of this conversation, declared yourself on those points, but you seem, by this last question, to have departed from what you then thought.

Hyl. To speak the truth, Philonous, I think there are two kinds of objects: the one perceived immediately, which are likewise called "ideas"; the other

are real things or external objects, perceived by the mediation of ideas which are their images and representations. Now I own ideas do not exist without the mind, but the latter sort of objects do. I am sorry I did not think of this distinction sooner; it would probably have cut short your discourse.

Phil. Are those external objects perceived by sense or by some other faculty?

Hyl. They are perceived by sense.

Phil. How! is there anything perceived by sense which is not immediately perceived?

Hyl. Yes, Philonous, in some sort there is. For example, when I look on a picture or statue of Julius Caesar, I may be said, after a manner, to perceive him (though not immediately) by my senses.

Phil. It seems then you will have our ideas, which alone are immediately perceived, to be pictures of external things: and that these also are perceived by sense inasmuch as they have a conformity or resemblance to our ideas?

Hyl. That is my meaning.

Phil. And in the same way that Julius Caesar, in himself invisible, is nevertheless perceived by sight, real things, in themselves imperceptible, are perceived by sense.

Hyl. In the very same.

Phil. Tell me, Hylas, when you behold the picture of Julius Caesar, do you see with your eyes any more than some colors and figures, with a certain symmetry and composition of the whole?

Hyl. Nothing else.

Phil. And would not a man who had never known anything of Julius Caesar see as much?

Hyl. He would.

Phil. Consequently, he has his sight and the use of it in as perfect a degree as you?

Hyl. I agree with you.

Phil. Whence comes it then that your thoughts are directed to the Roman emperor, and his are not? This cannot proceed from the sensations or ideas of sense by you then perceived, since you acknowledge you have no advantage over him in that respect. It should seem therefore to proceed from reason and memory, should it not?

Hyl. It should.

Phil. Consequently, it will not follow from that instance that anything is perceived by sense which is not immediately perceived. Though I grant we may, in one acceptation, be said to perceive sensible things mediately by sense—that is, when, from a frequently perceived connection, the immediate perception of ideas by one sense suggest to the mind others, perhaps belonging to another sense, which are wont to be connected with them. For instance, when I hear a coach drive along the streets, immediately I perceive only the sound; but from the experience I have had that such a sound is connected with a coach, I am said to hear the coach. It is nevertheless evident that, in truth and strictness, nothing can be *heard* but *sound;* and the coach is not then properly perceived by sense, but suggested from experience. So likewise when we are said to see a red-hot bar of iron; the solidity and heat of the iron are not the objects of sight, but suggested to the imagination by the color and figure which are properly perceived by that sense. In short, those things alone are actually and strictly perceived by any sense which would have been perceived in case that same sense had then been first conferred on us. As for other things, it is plain they are only suggested to the mind by experience grounded on former perceptions. But, to return to your comparison of Caesar's picture, it is plain, if you keep to that, you must hold the real things or archetypes of our ideas are not perceived by sense, but by some internal faculty of the soul, as reason or memory. I would, therefore, fain know what arguments you can draw from reason for the existence of what you call "real things" or "material objects," or whether you remember to have seen them formerly as they are in themselves, or if you have heard or read of anyone that did.

Hyl. Philonous, you are disposed to railery; but that will never convince me.

Phil. My aim is only to learn from you the way to come at the knowledge of "material beings." Whatever we perceive is perceived either immediately or mediately—by sense, or by reason and reflection. But, as you have excluded sense, pray show me what reason you have to believe their existence, or what *medium* you can possibly make use of to prove it, either to mine or your own understanding.

Hyl. To deal ingenuously, Philonous, now [that] I consider the point, I do not find I can give you any good reason for it. But this much seems pretty plain, that it is at least possible such things may really exist. And as long as there is no absurdity in supposing them, I am resolved to believe as I did, till you bring good reasons to the contrary.

Phil. What! is it come to this, that you only believe the existence of material objects, and that your belief is founded barely on the possibility of its being true? Then you will have me bring reasons against it, though another would think it reasonable the proof should lie on him who holds the affirmative. And, after all, this very point which you are now resolved to maintain, without any reason, is in effect what you have more than once during this discourse seen good reason to give up. But to pass over all this—if I understand you rightly, you say our ideas do not exist without the mind, but that they are copies, images, or representations of certain originals that do?

Hyl. You take me right.

Phil. They are then like external things?

Hyl. They are.

Phil. Have those things a stable and permanent nature, independent of our senses, or are they in a perpetual change, upon our producing any motions in our bodies, suspending, exerting, or altering our faculties or organs of sense?

Hyl. Real things, it is plain, have a fixed and real nature, which remains the same notwithstanding any change in our senses or in the posture and motion of our bodies; which indeed may affect the ideas in our minds, but it were absurd to think they had the same effect on things existing without the mind.

Phil. How then is it possible that things perpetually fleeting and variable as our ideas should be copies or images of anything fixed and constant? Or, in other words, since all sensible qualities, as size, figure, color, etc., that is, our ideas, are continually changing upon every alteration in the distance, medium, or instruments of sensation—how can any determinate material objects be properly represented or painted forth by several distinct things each of which is so different from and unlike the rest? Or, if you say it resembles some one only of our ideas, how shall we be able to distinguish the true copy from all the false ones?

Hyl. I profess, Philonous, I am at a loss. I know not what to say to this.

Phil. But neither is this all. Which are material objects in themselves—perceptible or imperceptible?

Hyl. Properly and immediately nothing can be perceived but ideas. All material things, therefore, are in themselves insensible and to be perceived only by their ideas.

Phil. Ideas then are sensible, and their archetypes or originals insensible?

Hyl. Right.

Phil. But how can that which is sensible be like that which is insensible? Can a real thing, in itself *invisible,* be like a *color,* or a real thing which is not *audible* be like a *sound?* In a word, can anything be like a sensation or idea, but another sensation or idea?

Hyl. I must own, I think not.

Phil. Is it possible there should be any doubt on the point? Do you not perfectly know your own ideas?

Hyl. I know them perfectly, since what I do not perceive or know can be no part of my idea.

Phil. Consider, therefore, and examine them, and then tell me if there be anything in them which can exist without the mind, or if you can conceive anything like them existing without the mind?

Hyl. Upon inquiry I find it impossible for me to conceive or understand how anything but an idea can be like an idea. And it is most evident that *no idea can exist without the mind.*

Phil. You are, therefore, by your principles forced to deny the reality of sensible things, since you made it to consist in an absolute existence exterior to the mind. That is to say, you are a downright skeptic. So I have gained my point, which was to show your principles led to skepticism.

Hyl. For the present I am, if not entirely convinced, at least silenced.

Phil. I would fain know what more you would require in order to a perfect conviction. Have you not had the liberty of explaining yourself all manner of ways? Were any little slips in discourse laid hold and insisted on? Or were you not allowed to retract or reinforce anything you had offered, as best served your purpose? Has not everything you could say been heard and examined with all the fairness imaginable? In a word, have you not in every point been convinced out of your own mouth? And, if you can at present discover any flaw in any of your former concessions, or think of any remaining subterfuge, any new distinction, color, or comment whatsoever, why do you not produce it?

Hyl. A little patience, Philonous. I am at present so amazed to see myself ensnared, and as it were imprisoned in the labyrinths you have drawn me into, that on the sudden it cannnot be expected I should find my way out. You must give me time to look about me and recollect myself.

Phil. Hark; is not this the college bell?

Hyl. It rings for prayers.

Phil. We will go in then, if you please, and meet here again tomorrow morning. In the meantime, you may employ your thoughts on this morning's discourse and try if you can find any fallacy in it, or invent any new means to extricate yourself.

Hyl. Agreed.

THE SECOND DIALOGUE

Hylas. I beg your pardon, Philonous, for not meeting you sooner. All this morning my head was so filled with our late conversation that I had not leisure to think of the time of the day, or indeed of anything else.

Philonous. I am glad you were so intent upon it, in hopes if there were any mistakes in your concessions, or fallacies in my reasonings from them, you will now discover them to me.

Hyl. I assure you I have done nothing ever since I saw you but search after mistakes and fallacies, and, with that [in] view, have minutely examined the whole series of yesterday's discourse; but all in vain, for the notions it led me into, upon review, appear still more clear and evident; and the more I consider them, the more irresistibly do they force my assent.

Phil. And is not this, think you, a sign that they are genuine, that they proceed from nature and are conformable to right reason? Truth and beauty are in this alike, that the strictest survey sets them both off to advantage, while the false luster of error and disguise cannot endure being reviewed or too nearly inspected.

Hyl. I own there is a great deal in what you say. Nor can anyone be more entirely satisfied of the truth of those odd consequences so long as I have in view the reasonings that lead to them. But when these are out of my thoughts, there seems, on the other hand, something so satisfactory, so natural and intelligible in the modern way of explaining things that I profess I know not how to reject it.

Phil. I know not what you mean.

Hyl. I mean the way of accounting for our sensations or ideas.

Phil. How is that?

Hyl. It is supposed the soul makes her residence in some part of the brain, from which the nerves take their rise, and are thence extended to all parts of the body; and that outward objects, by the different impressions they make on the organs of sense, communicate certain vibrative motions to the nerves, and these, being filled with spirits, propagate them to the brain or seat of the soul, which, according to the various impressions or traces thereby made in the brain, is variously affected with ideas.

Phil. And call you this an explication of the manner whereby we are affected with ideas?

Hyl. Why not, Philonous; have you anything to object against it?

Phil. I would first know whether I rightly understand your hypothesis. You make certain traces in the brain to be the causes or occasions of our ideas. Pray tell me whether by the "brain" you mean any sensible thing.

Hyl. What else think you I could mean?

Phil. Sensible things are all immediately perceivable; and those things which are immediately perceivable are ideas, and these exist only in the mind. This much you have, if I mistake not, long since agreed to.

Hyl. I do not deny it.

Phil. The brain therefore you speak of, being a sensible thing, exists only in the mind. Now I would fain know whether you think it reasonable to suppose that one idea or thing existing in the mind occasions all other ideas. And if you think so, pray how do you account for the origin of that primary idea or brain itself?

Hyl. I do not explain the origin of our ideas by that brain which is perceivable to sense, this being itself only a combination of sensible ideas, but by another which I imagine.

Phil. But are not things imagined as truly *in the mind* as things perceived?

Hyl. I must confess they are.

Phil. It comes, therefore, to the same thing; and you have been all this while accounting for ideas by certain motions or impressions of the brain, that is, by some alteration in an idea, whether sensible or imaginable it matters not.

Hyl. I begin to suspect my hypothesis.

Phil. Besides spirits, all that we know or conceive are our own ideas. When, therefore, you say all ideas are occasioned by impressions in the brain, do you conceive this brain or no? If you do, then you talk of ideas imprinted in an idea causing that same idea, which is absurd. If you do not conceive it, you talk unintelligibly, instead of forming a reasonable hypothesis.

Hyl. I now clearly see it was a mere dream. There is nothing in it.

Phil. You need not be much concerned at it, for, after all, this way of explaining things, as you called it, could never have satisfied any reasonable man. What connection is there between a motion in the nerves and the sensations of sound or color in the mind? Or how is it possible these should be the effect of that?

Hyl. But I could never think it had so little in it as now it seems to have.

Phil. Well then, are you at length satisfied that no sensible things have a real existence, and that you are in truth an arrant *skeptic?*

Hyl. It is too plain to be denied.

Phil. Look! are not the fields covered with a delightful verdure? Is there not something in the woods and groves, in the rivers and clear springs, that soothes, that delights, that transports the soul? At the prospect of the wide and deep ocean, or some huge mountain whose top is lost in the clouds, or of an old gloomy forest, are not our minds filled with a pleasing horror? Even in rocks and deserts is there not an agreeable wildness? How sincere a pleasure is it to behold the natural beauties of the earth! To preserve and renew our relish for them, is not the veil of night alternately drawn over her face, and does she not change her dress with the seasons? How aptly are the elements disposed! What variety and use in the meanest productions of nature! What delicacy, what beauty, what contrivance in animal and vegetable bodies! How exquisitely are all things suited, as well to their particular ends as to constitute apposite parts of the whole! And while they mutually aid and support, do they not also set off and illustrate each other? Raise now your thoughts from this ball of earth to all those glorious luminaries that adorn the high arch of heaven. The motion and situation of the planets, are they not admirable for use and order? Were those (miscalled "erratic") globes ever known to stray in their repeated journeys through the pathless void? Do they not measure areas round the sun ever proportioned to the times? So fixed, so immutable are the laws by which the unseen Author of nature actuates the universe. How vivid and radiant is the luster of the fixed stars! How magnificent and rich that negligent profusion with which they appear to be scattered throughout the whole azure vault! Yet, if you take the telescope, it brings into your sight a new host of stars that escape the naked eye. Here they seem contiguous and minute, but to a nearer view, immense orbs of light at various distances, far sunk in the abyss of space. Now you must call imagination to your aid. The feeble narrow sense cannot descry innumerable worlds revolving round the central fires, and in those worlds the energy of an all-perfect Mind displayed in endless forms. But neither sense nor imagination are big enough to comprehend the boundless extent with all its glittering furniture. Though the laboring mind exert and strain each power to its utmost reach, there still stands out ungrasped a surplusage immeasurable. Yet all the vast bodies that compose this mighty frame, how distant and remote soever, are by some secret mechanism, some divine art and force, linked in a mutual dependence and intercourse with each other, even with this earth, which was almost slipt from my thoughts and lost in the crowd of worlds. Is not the whole system immense, beautiful, glorious beyond expression and beyond thought! What treatment, then, do those philosophers deserve who would deprive these noble and delightful scenes of all reality? How should those principles be entertained that lead us to think all the visible beauty of the creation a false imaginary glare? To be plain, can you expect this skepticism of yours will not be thought extravagantly absurd by all men of sense?

Hyl. Other men may think as they please, but for your part you have nothing to reproach me with. My comfort is you are as much a skeptic as I am.

Phil. There, Hylas, I must beg leave to differ from you.

Hyl. What! have you all along agreed to the premises, and do you now deny the conclusion and leave me to maintain those paradoxes by myself which you led me into? This surely is not fair.

Phil. I deny that I agreed with you in those notions that led to skepticism. You indeed said the *reality* of sensible things consisted in an *absolute existence* out of the minds of spirits, or distinct from their being perceived. And, pursuant to this notion of reality, you are obliged to deny sensible things any real existence; that is, according to your own definition, you profess yourself a skeptic. But I neither said nor thought the reality of sensible things was to be defined after that manner. To me it is evident, for the reasons you allow of, that sensible things cannot exist otherwise than in a mind or spirit. Whence I conclude, not that they have no real existence, but that, seeing they depend not on my thought and have an existence distinct from being perceived by me, *there must be some other mind wherein they exist.* As sure,

therefore, as the sensible world really exists, so sure is there an infinite omnipresent Spirit, who contains and supports it.

Hyl. What! this is no more than I and all Christians hold; nay, and all others, too, who believe there is a God and that He knows and comprehends all things.

Phil. Aye, but here lies the difference. Men commonly believe that all things are known or perceived by God, because they believe the being of a God; whereas I, on the other side, immediately and necessarily conclude the being of a God, because all sensible things must be perceived by him.

Hyl. But so long as we all believe the same thing, what matter is it how we come by that belief?

Phil. But neither do we agree in the same opinion. For philosophers, though they acknowledge all corporeal beings to be perceived by God, yet they attribute to them an absolute subsistence distinct from their being perceived by any mind whatever, which I do not. Besides, is there no difference between saying, *there is a God, therefore He perceives all things,* and saying, *sensible things do really exist; and if they really exist, they are necessarily perceived by an infinite mind: therefore there is an infinite mind, or God?* This furnishes you with a direct and immediate demonstration, from a most evident principle, of the *being of a God.* Divines and philosophers had proved beyond all controversy, from the beauty and usefulness of the several parts of the creation, that it was the workmanship of God. But that—setting aside all help of astronomy and natural philosophy, all contemplation of the contrivance, order and adjustment of things—an infinite mind should be necessarily inferred from the bare *existence* of the sensible world is an advantage peculiar to them only who have made this easy reflection, that the sensible world is that which we perceive by our several senses; and that nothing is perceived by the senses besides ideas; and that no idea or archetype of an idea can exist otherwise than in a mind. You may now, without any laborious search into the sciences, without any subtlety of reason or tedious length of discourse, oppose and baffle the most strenuous advocate for atheism, those miserable refuges, whether in an eternal succession of unthinking causes and effects or in a fortuitous concourse of atoms; those wild imaginations of Vanini,

Hobbes, and Spinoza: in a word, the whole system of atheism, is it not entirely overthrown by this single reflection on the repugnancy included in supposing the whole or any part, even the most rude and shapeless, of the visible world to exist without a mind? Let any one of those abettors of impiety but look into his own thoughts, and there try if he can conceive how so much as a rock, a desert, a chaos, or confused jumble of atoms, how anything at all, either sensible or imaginable, can exist independent of a mind, and he need go no further to be convinced of his folly. Can anything be fairer than to put a dispute on such an issue and leave it to a man himself to see if he can conceive, even in thought, what he holds to be true in fact, and from a notional to allow it a real existence?

Hyl. It cannot be denied there is something highly serviceable to religion in what you advance. But do you not think it looks very like a notion entertained by some eminent moderns, of *seeing all things in God?*

Phil. I would gladly know that opinion; pray explain it to me.

Hyl. They conceive that the soul, being immaterial, is incapable of being united with material things so as to perceive them in themselves, but that she perceives them by her union with the substance of God, which, being spiritual, is therefore purely intelligible, or capable of being the immediate object of a spirit's thought. Besides, the divine essence contains in it perfections correspondent to each created being, and which are, for that reason, proper to exhibit or represent them to the mind.

Phil. I do not understand how our ideas, which are things altogether passive and inert, can be the essence or any part (or like any part) of the essence or substance of God, who is an impassive, indivisible, purely active being. Many more difficulties and objections there are which occur at first view against this hypothesis; but I shall only add that it is liable to all the absurdities of the common hypothesis, in making a created world exist otherwise than in the mind of a Spirit. Beside all which it has this peculiar to itself that it makes that material world serve to no purpose. And if it pass for a good argument against other hypotheses in the sciences that they suppose nature or the divine wisdom to make something in vain, or do that by tedious roundabout methods which might have been performed in a much more easy and compendious way, what shall we think of that hypothesis which supposes the whole world made in vain?

Hyl. But what say you, are not you too of opinion that we see all things in God? If I mistake not, what you advance comes near it.

Phil. [Few men think, yet all have opinions. Hence men's opinions are superficial and confused. It is nothing strange that tenets which in themselves are ever so different should nevertheless be confounded with each other by those who do not consider them attentively. I shall not therefore be surprised if some men imagine that I run into the enthusiasm of Malebranche, though in truth I am very remote from it. He builds on the most abstract general ideas, which I entirely disclaim. He asserts an absolute external world, which I deny. He maintains that we are deceived by our senses and know not the real natures or the true forms and figures of extended beings; of all which I hold the direct contrary. So that upon the whole there are no principles more fundamentally opposite than his and mine. It must be owned.][3] I entirely agree with what the holy Scripture says, "That in God we live and move and have our being." But that we see things in His essence, after the manner above set forth, I am far from believing. Take here in brief my meaning: It is evident that the things I perceive are my own ideas, and that no idea can exist unless it be in a mind. Nor is it less plain that these ideas or things by me perceived, either themselves or their archetypes, exist independently of my mind; since I know myself not to be their author, it being out of my power to determine at pleasure what particular ideas I shall be affected with upon opening my eyes or ears. They must therefore exist in some other mind, whose will it is they should be exhibited to me. The things, I say, immediately perceived are ideas or sensations, call them which you will. But how can any idea or sensation exist in, or be produced by, anything but a mind or spirit? This indeed is inconceivable; and to assert that which is inconceivable is to talk nonsense, is it not?

Hyl. Without doubt.

Phil. But, on the other hand, it is very conceivable that they should exist in and be produced by a spirit, since this is no more than I daily experience in myself, inasmuch as I perceive numberless ideas, and, by an act of my will, can form a great variety of them and raise them up in my imagination; though, it must be confessed, these creatures of the fancy are not altogether so distinct, so strong, vivid, and permanent as those perceived by my senses, which latter are called "real things." From all which I conclude, *there is a Mind which affects me every moment with all the sensible impressions I perceive.* And from the variety, order, and manner of these I conclude the Author of them to be *wise, powerful, and good beyond comprehension.* Mark it well; I do not say I see things by perceiving that which represents them in the intelligible Substance of God. This I do not understand; but I say the things by me perceived are known by the understanding and produced by the will of an infinite Spirit. And is not all this most plain and evident? Is there any more in it than what a little observation of our own minds, and that which passes in them, not only enables us to conceive but also obliges us to acknowledge?

Hyl. I think I understand you very clearly and own the proof you give of a Deity seems no less evident than it is surprising. But allowing that God is the supreme and universal cause of all things, yet may there not be still a third nature besides spirits and ideas? May we not admit a subordinate and limited cause of our ideas? In a word, may there not for all that be *matter?*

Phil. How often must I inculcate the same thing? You allow the things immediately perceived by sense to exist nowhere without the mind; but there is nothing perceived by sense which is not perceived immediately: therefore there is nothing sensible that exists without the mind. The matter, therefore, which you still insist on is something intelligible, I suppose something that may be discovered by reason, and not by sense.

Hyl. You are in the right.

Phil. Pray let me know what reasoning your belief of matter is grounded on, and what this matter is in your present sense of it.

Hyl. I find myself affected with various ideas whereof I know I am not the cause; neither are they the cause of themselves or of one another, or capable of subsisting by themselves, as being altogether inactive, fleeting, dependent beings. They have therefore some cause distinct from me and them, of which I pretend to know no more than that it is *the cause of my ideas.* And this thing, whatever it be, I call "matter."

Phil. Tell me, Hylas, has everyone a liberty to change the current proper signification annexed to a common name in any language? For example, suppose a traveler should tell you that in a certain country men pass unhurt through the fire; and, upon explain-

ing himself, you found he meant by the word "fire" that which others call "water"; or, if he should assert that there are trees that walk upon two legs, meaning men by the term "trees." Would you think this reasonable?

Hyl. No, I should think it very absurd. Common custom is the standard of propriety in language. And for any man to affect speaking improperly is to pervert the use of speech, and can never serve to a better purpose than to protract and multiply disputes where there is no difference in opinion.

Phil. And does not "matter," in the common current acceptation of the word, signify an extended, solid, movable, unthinking, inactive substance?

Hyl. It does.

Phil. And has it not been made evident that no such substance can possibly exist? And though it should be allowed to exist, yet how can that which is *inactive* be a *cause,* or that which is *unthinking* be a *cause of thought?* You may, indeed, if you please, annex to the word "matter" a contrary meaning to what is vulgarly received, and tell me you understand by it an unextended, thinking, active being which is the cause of our ideas. But what else is this than to play with words and run into that very fault you just now condemned with so much reason? I do by no means find fault with your reasoning, in that you collect a cause from the phenomena; but I deny that the cause deducible by reason can properly be termed "matter."

Hyl. There is indeed something in what you say. But I am afraid you do not thoroughly comprehend my meaning. I would by no means be thought to deny that God, or an infinite Spirit, is the Supreme Cause of all things. All I contend for is that, subordinate to the Supreme Agent, there is a cause of a limited and inferior nature which concurs in the production of our ideas, not by any act of will or spiritual efficiency, but by that kind of action which belongs to matter, *viz.,* motion.

Phil. I find you are at every turn relapsing into your old exploded conceit, of a movable and consequently an extended substance existing without the mind. What! have you already forgotten you were convinced, or are you willing I should repeat what has been said on that head? In truth, this is not fair dealing in you still to suppose the being of that which you have so often acknowledged to have no being. But, not to insist further on what has been so largely handled, I ask whether all your ideas are not perfectly passive and inert, including nothing of action in them.

Hyl. They are.

Phil. And are sensible qualities anything else but ideas?

Hyl. How often have I acknowledged that they are not.

Phil. But is not motion a sensible quality?

Hyl. It is.

Phil. Consequently, it is no action?

Hyl. I agree with you. And indeed it is very plain that when I stir my finger it remains passive, but my will which produced the motion is active.

Phil. Now I desire to know, in the first place, whether, motion being allowed to be no action, you can conceive any action besides volition; and, in the second place, whether to say something and conceive nothing be not to talk nonsense; and, lastly, whether, having considered the premises, you do not perceive that to suppose any efficient or active cause of our ideas other than *spirit* is highly absurd and unreasonable?

Hyl. I give up the point entirely. But, though matter may not be a cause, yet what hinders its being an *instrument* subservient to the Supreme Agent in the production of our ideas?

Phil. An instrument say you; pray what may be the figure, springs, wheels, and motions of that instrument?

Hyl. Those I pretend to determine nothing of, both the substance and its qualities being entirely unknown to me.

Phil. What! You are then of opinion it is made up of unknown parts, that it has unknown motions and an unknown shape?

Hyl. I do not believe that it has any figure or motion at all, being already convinced that no sensible qualities can exist in an unperceiving substance.

Phil. But what notion is it possible to frame of an instrument void of all sensible qualities, even extension itself?

Hyl. I do not pretend to have any notion of it.

Phil. And what reason have you to think this unknown, this inconceivable somewhat does exist? Is it that you imagine God cannot act as well without it, or that you find by experience the use of some such thing when you form ideas in your own mind?

Hyl. You are always teasing me for reasons of my belief. Pray what reasons have you not to believe it?

Phil. It is to me a sufficient reason not to believe the existence of anything if I see no reason for believing it. But, not to insist on reasons for believing, you will not so much as let me know what it is you would have me believe, since you say you have no manner of notion of it. After all, let me entreat you to consider whether it be like a philosopher, or even like a man of common sense, to pretend to believe you know not what, and you know not why.

Hyl. Hold, Philonous. When I tell you matter is an *instrument,* I do not mean altogether nothing. It is true I know not the particular kind of instrument, but, however, I have some notion of *instrument in general,* which I apply to it.

Phil. But what if it should prove that there is something, even in the most general notion of *instrument,* as taken in a distinct sense from *cause,* which makes the use of it inconsistent with the divine attributes?

Hyl. Make that appear and I shall give up the point.

Phil. What mean you by the general nature or notion of instrument?

Hyl. That which is common to all particular instruments composes the general notion.

Phil. Is it not common to all instruments that they are applied to the doing those things only which cannot be performed by the mere act of our wills? Thus, for instance, I never use an instrument to move my finger, because it is done by a volition. But I should use one if I were to remove part of a rock or tear up a tree by the roots. Are you of the same mind? Or can you show any example where an instrument is made use of in producing an effect immediately depending on the will of the agent?

Hyl. I own I cannot.

Phil. How, therefore, can you suppose that an all-perfect Spirit, on whose will all things have an absolute and immediate dependence, should need an instrument in his operations or, not needing it, make use of it? Thus it seems to me that you are obliged to own the use of a lifeless inactive instrument to be incompatible with the infinite perfection of God, that is, by your own confession, to give up the point.

Hyl. It does not readily occur what I can answer you.

Phil. But methinks you should be ready to own the truth when it has been fairly proved to you. We, indeed, who are beings of finite powers, are forced to make use of instruments. And the use of an instrument shows the agent to be limited by rules of another's prescription, and that he cannot obtain his end but in such a way and by such conditions. Whence it seems a clear consequence that the Supreme Unlimited Agent uses no tool or instrument at all. The will of an Omnipotent Spirit is no sooner exerted than executed, without the application of means, which, if they are employed by inferior agents, it is not upon account of any real efficacy that is in them, or necessary aptitude to produce any effect, but merely in compliance with the laws of nature or those conditions prescribed to them by the First Cause, who is Himself above all limitation or prescription whatsoever.

Hyl. I will no longer mantain that matter is an instrument. However, I would not be understood to give up its existence neither, since, notwithstanding what has been said, it may still be an *occasion*.

Phil. How many shapes is your matter to take? Or how often must it be proved not to exist before you are content to part with it? But to say no more of this (though by all the laws of disputation I may justly blame you for so frequently changing the signification of the principal term), I would fain know what you mean by affirming that matter is an "occasion," having already denied it to be a cause. And when you have shown in what sense you understand occasion, pray, in the next place, be pleased to show me what reason induces you to believe there is such an occasion of our ideas?

Hyl. As to the first point: by "occasion" I mean an inactive unthinking being, at the presence whereof God excites ideas in our minds.

Phil. And what may be the nature of that inactive unthinking being?

Hyl. I know nothing of its nature.

Phil. Proceed then to the second point and assign some reason why we should allow an existence to this inactive, unthinking, unknown thing.

Hyl. When we see ideas produced in our minds after an orderly and constant manner, it is natural to think they have some fixed and regular occasions at the presence of which they are excited.

Phil. You acknowledge then God alone to be the cause of our ideas, and that He causes them at the presence of those occasions.

Hyl. That is my opinion.

Phil. Those things which you say are present to God, without doubt He perceives.

Hyl. Certainly; otherwise they could not be to Him an occasion of acting.

Phil. Not to insist now on your making sense of this hypothesis, or answering all the puzzling questions and difficulties it is liable to: I only ask whether the order and regularity observable in the series of our ideas, or the course of nature, be not sufficiently accounted for by the wisdom and power of God; and whether it does not derogate from those attributes to suppose He is influenced, directed, or put in mind, when and what He is to act, by an unthinking substance? And, lastly, whether, in case I granted all you contend for, it would make anything to your purpose, it not being easy to conceive how the external or absolute existence of an unthinking substance, distinct from its being perceived, can be inferred from my allowing that there are certain things perceived by the mind of God which are to Him the occasion of producing ideas in us?

Hyl. I am perfectly at a loss what to think, this notion of occasion seeming now altogether as groundless as the rest.

Phil. Do you not at length perceive that in all these different acceptations of matter you have been only supposing you know not what, for no manner of reason and to no kind of use?

Hyl. I freely own myself less fond of my notions since they have been so accurately examined. But still, methinks, I have some confused perception that there is such a thing as matter.

Phil. Either you perceive the being of matter immediately or mediately. If immediately, pray inform me by which of the senses you perceive it. If mediately, let me know by what reasoning it is inferred from those things which you perceive immediately. So much for the perception. Then for the matter itself, I ask whether it is object, substratum, cause, instrument, or occasion? You have already pleaded for each of these, shifting your notions and making matter to appear sometimes in one shape, then in another. And what you have offered has been disapproved and rejected by yourself. If you have anything new to advance I would gladly hear it.

Hyl. I think I have already offered all I had to say on those heads. I am at a loss what more to urge.

Phil. And yet you are loath to part with your old prejudice. But to make you quit it more easily, I desire that, besides what has been hitherto suggested, you will further consider whether, upon supposition that matter exists, you can possibly conceive how you should be affected by it? Or, supposing it did not exist, whether it be not evident you might for all that be affected with the same ideas you now are, and consequently have the very same reason to believe its existence that you now can have?

Hyl. I acknowledge it is possible we might perceive all things just as we do now, though there was no matter in the world; neither can I conceive, if there be matter, how it should produce any idea in our minds. And I do further grant you have entirely satisfied me that it is impossible there should be such a thing as matter in any of the foregoing acceptations. But still I cannot help supposing that there is *matter* in some sense or other. What that is I do not indeed pretend to determine.

Phil. I do not expect you should define exactly the nature of that unknown being. Only be pleased to tell me whether it is a substance—and if so, whether you can suppose a substance without accidents; or in case you suppose it to have accidents or qualities, I desire you will let me know what those qualities are, at least what is meant by "matter's supporting them"?

Hyl. We have already argued on those points. I have no more to say to them. But, to prevent any further questions, let me tell you I at present understand by "matter" neither substance nor accident, thinking nor extended being, neither cause, instrument, nor occasion, but something entirely unknown, distinct from all these.

Phil. It seems then you include in your present notion of matter nothing but the general abstract idea of *entity*.

Hyl. Nothing else, save only that I superadd to this general idea the negation of all those particular things, qualities, or ideas that I perceive, imagine, or in anywise apprehend.

Phil. Pray where do you suppose this unknown matter to exist?

Hyl. Oh Philonous! now you think you have entangled me; for if I say it exists in place, then you will infer that it exists in the mind, since it is agreed that place or extension exists only in the mind; but I am not ashamed to own my ignorance. I know not where it exists; only I am sure it exists not in place. There is a negative answer for you. And you must expect no other to all the questions you put for the future about matter.

Phil. Since you will not tell me where it exists, be pleased to inform me after what manner you sup-

pose it to exist, or what you mean by its "existence"?

Hyl. It neither thinks nor acts, neither perceives nor is perceived.

Phil. But what is there positive in your abstracted notion of its existence?

Hyl. Upon a nice observation, I do not find I have any positive notion or meaning at all. I tell you again, I am not ashamed to own my ignorance. I know not what is meant by its existence or how it exists.

Phil. Continue, good Hylas, to act the same ingenuous part and tell me sincerely whether you can frame a distinct idea of entity in general, prescinded from and exclusive of all thinking and corporeal beings, all particular things whatsoever.

Hyl. Hold, let me think a little—I profess, Philonous, I do not find that I can. At first glance methought I had some dilute and airy notion of pure entity in abstract, but, upon closer attention, it has quite vanished out of sight. The more I think on it, the more am I confirmed in my prudent resolution of giving none but negative answers and not pretending to the least degree of any positive knowledge or conception of matter, its *where,* its *how,* its *entity,* or anything belonging to it.

Phil. When, therefore, you speak of the existence of matter, you have not any notion in your mind?

Hyl. None at all.

Phil. Pray tell me if the case stands not thus: at first, from a belief of material substance, you would have it that the immediate objects existed without the mind; then, that they are archetypes; then, causes; next, instruments; then, occasions: lastly, *something in general,* which being interpreted proves *nothing.* So matter comes to nothing. What think you, Hylas, is not this a fair summary of your whole proceeding?

Hyl. Be that as it will, yet I still insist upon it, that our not being able to conceive a thing is no argument against its existence.

Phil. That from a cause, effect, operation, sign, or other circumstance there may reasonably be inferred the existence of a thing not immediately perceived; and that it were absurd for any man to argue against the existence of that thing, from his having no direct and positive notion of it, I freely own. But where there is nothing of all this, where neither reason nor revelation induces us to believe the existence of a thing, where we have not even a relative notion of it, where an abstraction is made from perceiving and being perceived, from spirit and idea, lastly, where there is not so much as the most inadequate or faint idea pretended to, I will not, indeed, thence conclude against the reality of any notion or existence of anything; but my inference shall be that you mean nothing at all, that you employ words to no manner of purpose, without any design or signification whatsoever. And I leave it to you to consider how mere jargon should be treated.

Hyl. To deal frankly with you, Philonous, your arguments seem in themselves unanswerable, but they have not so great an effect on me as to produce that entire conviction, that hearty acquiescence, which attends demonstration. I find myself still relapsing into an obscure surmise of I know not what—*matter.*

Phil. But are you not sensible, Hylas, that two things must concur to take away all scruple and work a plenary assent in the mind? Let a visible object be set in never so clear a light, yet, if there is any imperfection in the sight, or if the eye is not directed toward it, it will not be distinctly seen. And though a demonstration be never so well grounded and fairly proposed, yet, if there is withal a stain of prejudice or a wrong bias on the understanding, can it be expected on a sudden to perceive clearly and adhere firmly to the truth? No, there is need of time and pains: the attention must be awakened and detained by a frequent repetition of the same thing placed oft in the same, oft in different lights. I have said it already, and find I must still repeat and inculcate, that it is an unaccountable license you take in pretending to maintain you know not what, for you know not what reason, to you know not what purpose. Can this be paralleled in any art or science, any sect or profession of men? Or is there anything so barefacedly groundless and unreasonable to be met with even in the lowest of common conversation? But, perhaps, you will still say, matter may exist, though at the same time you neither know what is meant by "matter" or by its "existence." This indeed is surprising, and the more so because it is altogether voluntary, you not being led to it by any one reason, for I challenge you to show me that thing in nature which needs matter to explain or account for it.

Hyl. The reality of things cannot be maintained without supposing the existence of matter. And is not this, think you, a good reason why I should be earnest in its defense?

Phil. The reality of things! What things, sensible or intelligible?

Hyl. Sensible things.

Phil. My glove, for example?

Hyl. That or any other thing perceived by the senses.

Phil. But to fix on some particular thing, is it not a sufficient evidence to me of the existence of this *glove* that I see it and feel it and wear it? Or, if this will not do, how is it possible I should be assured of the reality of this thing which I actually see in this place by supposing that some unknown thing, which I never did or can see, exists after an unknown manner, in an unknown place, or in no place at all? How can the supposed reality of that which is intangible be a proof that anything tangible really exists? Or of that which is invisible, that any visible thing or, in general, of anything which is imperceptible, that a perceptible exists? Do but explain this and I shall think nothing too hard for you.

Hyl. Upon the whole, I am content to own the existence of matter is highly improbable; but the direct and absolute impossibility of it does not appear to me.

Phil. But granting matter to be possible, yet, upon that account merely, it can have no more claim to existence than a golden mountain or a centaur.

Hyl. I acknowledge it, but still you do not deny it is possible; and that which is possible, for aught you know, may actually exist.

Phil. I deny it to be possible; and have, if I mistake not, evidently proved, from your own concessions, that it is not. In the common sense of the word "matter," is there any more implied than an extended, solid, figured, movable substance existing without the mind? And have not you acknowledged, over and over, that you have seen evident reason for denying the possibility of such a substance?

Hyl. True, but that is only one sense of the term "matter."

Phil. But is it not the only proper genuine received sense? And if matter in such a sense be proved impossible, may it not be thought with good grounds absolutely impossible? Else how could anything be proved impossible? Or, indeed, how could there be any proof at all one way or other to a man who takes the liberty to unsettle and change the common signification of words?

Hyl. I thought philosophers might be allowed to speak more accurately than the vulgar, and were not always confined to the common acceptation of a term.

Phil. But this now mentioned is the common received sense among philosophers themselves. But, not to insist on that, have you not been allowed to take matter in what sense you pleased? And have you not used this privilege in the utmost extent, sometimes entirely changing, at others leaving out or putting into the definition of it whatever, for the present, best served your design, contrary to all the known rules of reason and logic? And has not this shifting, unfair method of yours spun out our dispute to an unnecessary length, matter having been particularly examined and by your own confession refuted in each of those senses? And can any more be required to prove the absolute impossibility of a thing than the proving it impossible in every particular sense that either you or anyone else understands it in?

Hyl. But I am not so thoroughly satisfied that you have proved the impossibility of matter in the last most obscure abstracted and indefinite sense.

Phil. When is a thing shown to be impossible?

Hyl. When a repugnancy is demonstrated between the ideas comprehended in its definition.

Phil. But where there are no ideas, there no repugnancy can be demonstrated between ideas?

Hyl. I agree with you.

Phil. Now, in that which you call the obscure indefinite sense of the word "matter," it is plain, by your own confession, there was included no idea at all, no sense except an unknown sense, which is the same thing as none. You are not, therefore, to expect I should prove a repugnancy between ideas where there are no ideas, or the impossibility of matter taken in an *unknown* sense, that is, no sense at all. My business was only to show you meant *nothing;* and this you were brought to own. So that, in all your various senses, you have been shown either to mean nothing at all or, if anything, an absurdity. And if this be not sufficient to prove the impossibility of a thing, I desire you will let me know what is.

Hyl. I acknowledge you have proved that matter is impossible, nor do I see what more can be said in defense of it. But, at the same time that I give up this, I suspect all my other notions. For surely none could be more seemingly evident than this once was; and yet it now seems as false and absurd as ever it did true before. But I think we have discussed the point sufficiently for the present. The remaining part of the day I would willingly spend in running over in my thoughts the several heads of this morning's conversation, and tomorrow shall be glad to meet you here again about the same time.

Phil. I will not fail to attend you.

THE THIRD DIALOGUE

Philonous. Tell me, Hylas, what are the fruits of yesterday's meditation? Has it confirmed you in the same mind you were in at parting, or have you since seen cause to change your opinion?

Hylas. Truly my opinion is that all our opinions are alike vain and uncertain. What we approve today, we condemn tomorrow. We keep a stir about knowledge and spend our lives in pursuit of it, when, alas! we know nothing all the while; nor do I think it possible for us ever to know anything in this life. Our faculties are too narrow and too few. Nature certainly never intended us for speculation.

Phil. What! say you we can know nothing, Hylas?

Hyl. There is not that single thing in the world whereof we can know the real nature, or what it is in itself.

Phil. Will you tell me I do not really know what fire or water is?

Hyl. You may indeed know that fire appears hot, and water fluid; but this is no more than knowing what sensations are produced in your own mind upon the application of fire and water to your organs of sense. Their internal constitution, their true and real nature, you are utterly in the dark as to *that*.

Phil. Do I not know this to be a real stone that I stand on, and that which I see before my eyes to be a real tree?

Hyl. Know? No, it is impossible you or any man alive should know it. All you know is that you have such a certain idea or appearance in your own mind. But what is this to the real tree or stone? I tell you that color, figure, and hardness, which you perceive, are not the real natures of those things, or in the least like them. The same may be said of all other real things or corporeal substances which compose the world. They have, none of them, anything in themselves, like those sensible qualities by us perceived. We should not, therefore, pretend to affirm or know anything of them, as they are in their own nature.

Phil. But surely, Hylas, I can distinguish gold, for example, from iron; and how could this be if I knew not what either truly was?

Hyl. Believe me, Philonous, you can only distinguish between your own ideas. That yellowness, that weight, and other sensible qualities, think you they are really in the gold? They are only relative to the senses and have no absolute existence in nature. And in pretending to distinguish the species of real things by the appearances in your mind, you may perhaps act as wisely as he that should conclude two men were of a different species because their clothes were not of the same color.

Phil. It seems, then, we are altogether put off with the appearances of things, and those false ones, too. The very meat I eat, and the cloth I wear, have nothing in them like what I see and feel.

Hyl. Even so.

Phil. But is it not strange the whole world should be thus imposed on and so foolish as to believe their senses? And yet I know not how it is, but men eat, and drink, and sleep, and perform all the offices of life as comfortably and conveniently as if they really knew the things they are conversant about.

Hyl. They do so; but you know ordinary practice does not require a nicety of speculative knowledge. Hence the vulgar retain their mistakes, and for all that make a shift to bustle through the affairs of life. But philosophers know better things.

Phil. You mean they know that they *know nothing.*

Hyl. That is the very top and perfection of human knowledge.

Phil. But are you all this while in earnest, Hylas; and are you seriously persuaded that you know nothing real in the world? Suppose you are going to write, would you not call for pen, ink, and paper, like another man; and do you not know what it is you call for?

Hyl. How often must I tell you that I know not the real nature of any one thing in the universe? I may indeed upon occasion make use of pen, ink, and paper. But what any one of them is in its own true nature, I declare positively I know not. And the same is true with regard to every other corporeal thing. And what is more, we are not only ignorant of the true and real nature of things, but even of their existence. It cannot be denied that we perceive such certain appearances or ideas, but it cannot be concluded from thence that bodies really exist. Nay, now I think on it, I must, agreeably to my former concessions, further declare that it is impossible any real corporeal thing should exist in nature.

Phil. You amaze me. Was ever anything more wild and extravagant than the notions you now maintain? And is it not evident you are led into all these extravagances by the belief of *material substance?* This makes you dream of those unknown natures in everything. It is this occasions your distinguishing

between the reality and sensible appearances of things. It is to this you are indebted for being ignorant of what everybody else knows perfectly well. Nor is this all: you are not only ignorant of the true nature of everything, but you know not whether any thing really exists or whether there are any true natures at all, forasmuch as you attribute to your material beings an absolute or external existence wherein you suppose their reality consists. And as you are forced in the end to acknowledge such an existence means either a direct repugnancy or nothing at all, it follows that you are obliged to pull down your own hypothesis of material substance and positively to deny the real existence of any part of the universe. And so you are plunged into the deepest and most deplorable skepticism that ever man was. Tell me, Hylas, is it not as I say?

Hyl. I agree with you. "Material substance" was no more than a hypothesis, and a false and groundless one, too. I will no longer spend my breath in defense of it. But whatever hypothesis you advance or whatsoever scheme of things you introduce in its stead, I doubt not it will appear every whit as false; let me but be allowed to question you upon it. That is, suffer me to serve you in your own kind, and I warrant it shall conduct you through as many perplexities and contradictions to the very same state of skepticism that I myself am in at present.

Phil. I assure you, Hylas, I do not pretend to frame any hypothesis at all. I am of a vulgar cast, simple enough to believe my senses and leave things as I find them. To be plain, it is my opinion that the real things are those very things I see and feel, and perceive by my senses. These I know and, finding they answer all the necessities and purposes of life, have no reason to be solicitous about any other unknown beings. A piece of sensible bread, for instance, would stay my stomach better than ten thousand times as much of that insensible, unintelligible real bread you speak of. It is likewise my opinion that colors and other sensible qualities are on the objects. I cannot for my life help thinking that snow is white, and fire hot. You, indeed, who by "snow" and "fire" mean certain external, unperceived, unperceiving substances are in the right to deny whiteness or heat to be affections inherent in them. But I who understand by those words the things I see and feel am obliged to think like other folks. And as I am no skeptic with regard to the nature of things, so neither am I as to their existence. That a thing should be really perceived by my senses and at the same time not really exist is to me a plain contradiction, since I cannot prescind or abstract, even in thought, the existence of a sensible thing from its being perceived. Wood, stones, fire, water, flesh, iron, and the like things which I name and discourse of are things that I know. And I should not have known them but that I perceived them by my senses; and things perceived by the senses are immediately perceived; and things immediately perceived are ideas; and ideas cannot exist without the mind; their existence therefore consists in being perceived; when, therefore, they are actually perceived, there can be no doubt of their existence. Away then with all that skepticism, all those ridiculous philosophical doubts. What a jest is it for a philosopher to question the existence of sensible things till he has it proved to him from the veracity of God, or to pretend our knowledge in this point falls short of intuition or demonstration! I might as well doubt of my own being as of the being of those things I actually see and feel.

Hyl. Not so fast, Philonous: You say you cannot conceive how sensible things should exist without the mind. Do you not?

Phil. I do.

Hyl. Supposing you were annihilated, cannot you conceive it possible that things perceivable by sense may still exist?

Phil. I can, but then it must be in another mind. When I deny sensible things an existence out of the mind, I do not mean my mind in particular, but all minds. Now it is plain they have an existence exterior to my mind, since I find them by experience to be independent of it. There is therefore some other mind wherein they exist during the intervals between the times of my perceiving them, as likewise they did before my birth, and would do after my supposed annihilation. And as the same is true with regard to all other finite created spirits, it necessarily follows there is an *omnipresent external Mind* which knows and comprehends all things, and exhibits them to our view in such a manner and according to such rules as He Himself has ordained and are by us termed the "laws of nature."

Hyl. Answer me, Philonous. Are all our ideas perfectly inert beings? Or have they any agency included in them?

Phil. They are altogether passive and inert.

Hyl. And is not God an agent, a being purely active?

Phil. I acknowledge it.

Hyl. No idea, therefore, can be like unto or represent the nature of God.

Phil. It cannot.

Hyl. Since, therefore, you have no idea of the mind of God, how can you conceive it possible that things should exist in His mind? Or, if you can conceive the mind of God without having an idea of it, why may not I be allowed to conceive the existence of matter, notwithstanding I have no idea of it?

Phil. As to your first question: I own I have properly no *idea* either of God or any other spirit; for these, being active, cannot be represented by things perfectly inert as our ideas are. I do nevertheless know that I, who am a spirit or thinking substance, exist as certainly as I know my ideas exist. Further, I know what I mean by the terms "I" and "myself"; and I know this immediately or intuitively, though I do not perceive it as I perceive a triangle, a color, or a sound. The mind, spirit, or soul is that indivisible unextended thing which thinks, acts, and perceives. I say "indivisible," because unextended; and "unextended," because extended, figured, movable things are ideas; and that which perceives ideas, which thinks and wills, is plainly itself no idea, nor like an idea. Ideas are things inactive and perceived. And spirits a sort of beings altogether different from them. I do not therefore say my soul is an idea, or like an idea. However, taking the word "idea" in a large sense, my soul may be said to furnish me with an idea, that is, an image or likeness of God, though indeed extremely inadequate. For all the notion I have of God is obtained by reflecting on my own soul, heightening its powers, and removing its imperfections. I have, therefore, though not an inactive idea, yet in *myself* some sort of an active thinking image of the Deity. And though I perceive Him not by sense, yet I have a notion of Him, or know Him by reflection and reasoning. My own mind and my own ideas I have an immediate knowledge of; and, by the help of these, do mediately apprehend the possibility of the existence of other spirits and ideas. Further, from my own being, and from the dependency I find in myself and my ideas, I do, by an act of reason, necessarily infer the existence of a God and of all created things in the mind of God. So much for your first question. For the second: I suppose by this time you can answer it yourself. For you neither perceive matter objectively, as you do an inactive being or idea, nor know it, as you do yourself by a reflex act; neither do you mediately apprehend it by similitude of the one or the other, nor yet collect it by reasoning from that which you know immediately. All which makes the case of *matter* widely different from that of the *Deity*.

[*Hyl.*[4] You say your own soul supplies you with some sort of an idea or image of God. But, at the same time, you acknowledge you have, properly speaking, no idea of your own soul. You even affirm that spirits are a sort of beings altogether different from ideas. Consequently, that no idea can be like a spirit. We have, therefore, no idea of any spirit. You admit nevertheless that there is spiritual substance, although you have no idea of it, while you deny there can be such a thing as material substance, because you have no notion or idea of it. Is this fair dealing? To act consistently, you must either admit matter or reject spirit. What say you to this?

Phil. I say, in the first place, that I do not deny the existence of material substance merely because I have no notion of it, but because the notion of it is inconsistent, or, in other words, because it is repugnant that there should be a notion of it. Many things, for aught I know, may exist whereof neither I nor any other man has or can have any idea or notion whatsoever. But then those things must be possible, that is, nothing inconsistent must be included in their definition. I say, secondly, that, although we believe things to exist which we do not perceive, yet we may not believe that any particular thing exists without some reason for such belief; but I have no reason for believing the existence of matter. I have no immediate intuition thereof, neither can I immediately from my sensations, ideas, notions, actions, or passions infer an unthinking, unperceiving, inactive substance, either by probable deduction or necessary consequence. Whereas the being of my self, that is, my own soul, mind, or thinking principle, I evidently know by reflection. You will forgive me if I repeat the same things in answer to the same objections. In the very notion or definition of "material substance" there is included a manifest repugnance and inconsistency. But this cannot be said of the notion of spirit. That ideas should exist in what does not perceive, or be produced by what does not act, is repugnant. But it is no repugnancy to say that a perceiving thing should be the subject of ideas, or an active thing the cause of them. It is granted we have neither an immediate evidence nor a demonstrative knowledge of the existence of other finite spirits, but it will not thence follow that such spirits are on a foot with material substances, if to

suppose the one be inconsistent, and it be not inconsistent to suppose the other; if the one can be inferred by no argument, and there is a probability for the other; if we see signs and effects indicating distinct finite agents like ourselves, and see no sign or symptom whatever that leads to a rational belief of matter. I say, lastly, that I have a notion of spirit, though I have not, strictly speaking, an idea of it. I do not perceive it as an idea, or by means of an idea, but know it by reflection.

Hyl. Notwithstanding all you have said, to me it seems that, according to your own way of thinking, and in consequence of your own principles, it should follow that you are only a system of floating ideas without any substance to support them. Words are not to be used without a meaning. And, as there is no more meaning in *spiritual* substance than in *material* substance, the one is to be exploded as well as the other.

Phil. How often must I repeat that I know or am conscious of my own being, and that I *myself* am not my ideas, but somewhat else, a thinking, active principle that perceives, knows, wills, and operates about ideas. I know that I, one and the same self, perceive both colors and sounds, that a color cannot perceive a sound, nor a sound a color, that I am therefore one individual principle distinct from color and sound, and, for the same reason, from all other sensible things and inert ideas. But I am not in like manner conscious either of the existence or essence of matter. On the contrary, I know that nothing inconsistent can exist, and that the existence of matter implies an inconsistency. Further, I know what I mean when I affirm that there is a spiritual substance or support of ideas, that is, that a spirit knows and perceives ideas. But I do not know what is meant when it is said that an unperceiving substance has inherent in it and supports either ideas or the archetypes of ideas. There is, therefore, upon the whole no parity of case between spirit and matter.]

Hyl. I own myself satisfied in this point. But do you in earnest think the real existence of sensible things consists in their being actually perceived? If so, how comes it that all mankind distinguish between them? Ask the first man you meet, and he shall tell you, "to be perceived" is one thing, and "to exist" is another.

Phil. I am content, Hylas, to appeal to the common sense of the world for the truth of my notion. Ask the gardener why he thinks yonder cherry tree exists in the garden, and he shall tell you, because he sees and feels it; in a word, because he perceives it by his senses. Ask him why he thinks an orange tree not to be there, and he shall tell you, because he does not perceive it. What he perceives by sense, that he terms a real being and says it "is" or "exists"; but that which is not perceivable, the same, he says, has no being.

Hyl. Yes, Philonous, I grant the existence of a sensible thing consists in being perceivable, but not in being actually perceived.

Phil. And what is perceivable but an idea? And can an idea exist without being actually perceived? These are points long since agreed between us.

Hyl. But be your opinion never so true, yet surely you will not deny it is shocking and contrary to the common sense of men. Ask the fellow whether yonder tree has an existence out of his mind; what answer think you he would make?

Phil. The same that I should myself, to wit, that it does exist out of his mind. But then to a Christian it cannot surely be shocking to say, the real tree, existing without his mind, is truly known and comprehended by (that is, *exists in*) the infinite mind of God. Probably he may not at first glance be aware of the direct and immediate proof there is of this, inasmuch as the very being of a tree, or any other sensible thing, implies a mind wherein it is. But the point itself he cannot deny. The question between the materialists and me is not whether things have a *real* existence out of the mind of this or that person, but, whether they have an *absolute* existence, distinct from being perceived by God, and exterior to all minds. This, indeed, some heathens and philosophers have affirmed, but whoever entertains notions of the Deity suitable to the Holy Scriptures will be of another opinion.

Hyl. But, according to your notions, what difference is there between real things and chimeras formed by the imagination or the visions of a dream, since they are all equally in the mind?

Phil. The ideas formed by the imagination are faint and indistinct; they have, besides, an entire dependence on the will. But the ideas perceived by sense, that is, real things, are more vivid and clear, and, being imprinted on the mind by a spirit distinct from us, have not the like dependence on our will. There is, therefore, no danger of confounding these

with the foregoing, and there is as little of confounding them with the visions of a dream, which are dim, irregular, and confused. And though they should happen to be never so lively and natural, yet, by their not being connected and of a piece with the preceding and subsequent transaction of our lives, they might easily be distinguished from realities. In short, by whatever method you distinguish *things* from *chimeras* on your own scheme, the same, it is evident, will hold also upon mind. For it must be, I presume, by some perceived difference, and I am not for depriving you of any one thing that you perceive.

Hyl. But still, Philonous, you hold there is nothing in the world but spirits and ideas. And this you must needs acknowledge sounds very oddly.

Phil. I own the word "idea," not being commonly used for "thing," sounds something out of the way. My reason for using it was because a necessary relation to the mind is understood to be implied by the term; and it is now commonly used by philosophers to denote the immediate objects of the understanding. But however oddly the proposition may sound in words, yet it includes nothing so very strange or shocking in its sense, which in effect amounts to no more than this, to wit, that there are only things perceiving and things perceived, or that every unthinking being is necessarily, and from the very nature of its existence, perceived by some mind, if not by any finite created mind, yet certainly by the infinite mind of God, in whom "we live, and move, and have our being." Is this as strange as to say the sensible qualities are not on the object or that we cannot be sure of the existence of things, or know anything of their real natures, though we both see and feel them and perceive them by all our senses?

Hyl. And, in consequence of this, must we not think there are no such things as physical or corporeal causes, but that a spirit is the immediate cause of all the *phenomena* in nature? Can there be anything more extravagant than this?

Phil. Yes, it is infinitely more extravagant to say a thing which is inert operates on the mind, and which is unperceiving is the cause of our perceptions. Besides, that which to you I know not for what reason seems so extravagant is no more than the Holy Scriptures assert in a hundred places. In them God is represented as the sole and immediate Author of all those effects which some heathens and philosophers are wont to ascribe to Nature, Matter, Fate, or the like unthinking principle. This is so much the constant language of Scripture that it were needless to confirm it by citations.

Hyl. You are not aware, Philonous, that, in making God the immediate Author of all the motions in nature, you make Him the Author of murder, sacrilege, adultery, and the like heinous sins.

Phil. In answer to that I observe, first, that the imputation of guilt is the same whether a person commits an action with or without an instrument. In case, therefore, you suppose God to act by the mediation of an instrument or occasion called "matter," you as truly make Him the Author of sin as I, who think Him the immediate agent in all those operations vulgarly ascribed to Nature. I further observe that sin or moral turpitude does not consist in the outward physical action or motion, but in the internal deviation of the will from the laws of reason and religion. This is plain, in that the killing an enemy in a battle or putting a criminal legally to death is not thought sinful, though the outward act be the very same with that in the case of murder. Since, therefore, sin does not consist in the physical action, the making God an immediate cause of all such actions is not making Him the Author of sin. Lastly, I have nowhere said that God is the only agent who produces all the motions in bodies. It is true I have denied there are any other agents besides spirits, but this is very consistent with allowing to thinking rational beings, in the production of motions, the use of limited powers, ultimately, indeed, derived from God but immediately under the direction of their own wills, which is sufficient to entitle them to all the guilt of their actions.

Hyl. But the denying matter, Philonous, or corporeal substance, there is the point. You can never persuade me that this is not repugnant to the universal sense of mankind. Were our dispute to be determined by most voices, I am confident you would give up the point without gathering the votes.

Phil. I wish both our opinions were fairly stated and submitted to the judgment of men who had plain common sense, without the prejudices of a learned education. Let me be represented as one who trusts his senses, who thinks he knows the things he sees and feels, and entertains no doubts of their existence; and you fairly set forth with all your doubts, your paradoxes, and your skepticism about you, and I shall willingly acquiesce in the determination of any indifferent person. That there is no substance wherein ideas can exist besides spirit is to me evident, and that the objects immediately perceived are ideas is on

all hands agreed. And that sensible qualities are objects immediately perceived no one can deny. It is therefore evident there can be no *substratum* of those qualities but spirit, in which they exist, not by way of mode or property, but as a thing perceived in that which perceives it. I deny, therefore, that there is any unthinking *substratum* of the objects of sense, and in that acceptation that there is any material substance. But if by "material substance" is meant only sensible body, that which is seen and felt (and the unphilosophical part of the world, I dare say, mean no more), then I am more certain of matter's existence than you or any other philosopher pretend to be. If there be anything which makes the generality of mankind averse from the notions I espouse, it is a misapprehension that I deny the reality of sensible things; but as it is you who are guilty of that and not I, it follows that in truth their aversion is against your notions and not mine. I do therefore assert that I am as certain as of my own being that there are bodies or corporeal substances (meaning the things I perceive by my senses), and that, granting this, the bulk of mankind will take no thought about, nor think themselves at all concerned in the fate of, those unknown natures and philosophical quiddities which some men are so fond of.

Hyl. What say you to this? Since, according to you, men judge of the reality of things by their senses, how can a man be mistaken in thinking the moon a plain lucid surface, about a foot in diameter, or a square tower, seen at a distance, round, or an oar, with one end in the water, crooked?

Phil. He is not mistaken with regard to the ideas he actually perceives, but in the inferences he makes from his present perceptions. Thus, in the case of the oar, what he immediately perceives by sight is certainly crooked, and so far he is in the right. But if he thence conclude that upon taking the oar out of the water he shall perceive the same crookedness, or that it would affect his touch as crooked things are wont to do, in that he is mistaken. In like manner, if he shall conclude, from what he perceives in one station, that, in case he advances toward the moon or tower, he should still be affected with the like ideas, he is mistaken. But his mistake lies not in what he perceives immediately and at present (it being a manifest contradiction to suppose he should err in respect of that), but in the wrong judgment he makes concerning the ideas he apprehends to be connected with those immediately perceived, or, concerning the ideas, that from what he perceives at present he imagines would be perceived in other circumstances. The case is the same with regard to the Copernican system. We do not here perceive any motion of the earth, but it were erroneous thence to conclude that, in case we were placed at as great a distance from that as we are now from the other planets, we should not then perceive its motion.

Hyl. I understand you and must needs own you say things plausible enough, but give me leave to put you in mind of one thing. Pray, Philonous, were you not formerly as positive that matter existed as you are now that it does not?

Phil. I was. But here lies the difference. Before, my positiveness was founded, without examination, upon prejudice, but now, after inquiry, upon evidence.

Hyl. After all, it seems our dispute is rather about words than things. We agree in the thing, but differ in the name. That we are affected with ideas from without is evident; and it is no less evident that there must be (I will not say archetypes, but) powers without the mind corresponding to those ideas. And as these powers cannot subsist by themselves, there is some subject of them necessarily to be admitted, which I call "matter," and you call "spirit." This is all the difference.

Phil. Pray, Hylas, is that powerful being, or subject of powers, extended?

Hyl. It has not extension, but it has the power to raise in you the idea of extension.

Phil. It is therefore itself unextended?

Hyl. I grant it.

Phil. Is it not also active?

Hyl. Without doubt; otherwise, how could we attribute powers to it?

Phil. Now let me ask you two questions: *First,* whether it be agreeable to the usage either of philosophers or others to give the name "matter" to an unextended active being? And, secondly, whether it be not ridiculously absurd to misapply names contrary to the common use of language?

Hyl. Well then, let it not be called "matter," since you will have it so, but some "third nature," distinct from matter and spirit. For what reason is there why you should call it spirit? Does not the notion of spirit imply that it is thinking as well as active and unextended?

Phil. My reason is this: because I have a mind to have some notion or meaning in what I say, but I have no notion of any action distinct from volition, neither can I conceive volition to be anywhere but in a spirit; therefore, when I speak of an active being I am obliged to mean a spirit. Besides, what can be plainer than that a thing which has no ideas in itself cannot impart them to me; and, if it has ideas, surely it must be a spirit. To make you comprehend the point still more clearly, if it be possible: I assert as well as you that, since we are affected from without, we must allow powers to be without, in a being distinct from ourselves. So far we are agreed. But then we differ as to the kind of this powerful being. I will have it to be spirit, you matter or I know not what (I may add, too, you know not what) third nature. Thus I prove it to be spirit. From the effects I see produced I conclude there are actions; and because actions, volitions; and because there are volitions, there must be a will. Again, the things I perceive must have an existence, they or their archetypes, out of my mind; but, being ideas, neither they nor their archetypes can exist otherwise than in an understanding, there is therefore an understanding. But will and understanding constitute in the strictest sense a mind or spirit. The powerful cause, therefore, of my ideas is in strict propriety of speech a *spirit.*

Hyl. And now I warrant you think you have made the point very clear, little suspecting that what you advance leads directly to a contradiction. Is it not an absurdity to imagine any imperfection in God?

Phil. Without a doubt.

Hyl. To suffer pain is an imperfection?

Phil. Are we not sometimes affected with pain and uneasiness by some other being?

Phil. We are.

Hyl. And have you not said that being is a spirit, and is not that spirit God?

Phil. I grant it.

Hyl. But you have asserted that whatever ideas we perceive from without are in the mind which affects us. The ideas, therefore, of pain and uneasiness are in God, or, in other words, God suffers pain; that is to say, there is an imperfection in the divine nature, which, you acknowledge, was absurd. So you are caught in a plain contradiction.

Phil. That God knows or understands all things, and that He knows, among other things, what pain is, even every sort of painful sensation, and what it is for His creatures to suffer pain, I make no question. But that God, though He knows and sometimes causes painful sensations in us, can Himself suffer pain I positively deny. We, who are limited and dependent spirits, are liable to impressions of sense, the effects of an external agent, which, being produced against our wills, are sometimes painful and uneasy. But God, whom no external being can affect, who perceives nothing by sense as we do, whose will is absolute and independent, causing all things, and liable to be thwarted or resisted by nothing, it is evident such a Being as this can suffer nothing, nor be affected with any painful sensation or, indeed, any sensation at all. We are chained to a body; that is to say, our perceptions are connected with corporeal motions. By the law of our nature we are affected upon every alteration in the nervous parts of our sensible body; which sensible body, rightly considered, is nothing but a complexion of such qualities or ideas as have no existence distinct from being perceived by a mind; so that this connection of sensations with corporeal motions means no more than a correspondence in the order of nature between two sets of ideas, or things immediately perceivable. But God is a pure spirit, disengaged from all such sympathy or natural ties. No corporeal motions are attended with the sensations of pain or pleasure in His mind. To know everything knowable is certainly a perfection, but to endure or suffer or feel anything by sense is an imperfection. The former, I say, agrees to God, but not the latter. God knows or has ideas, but His ideas are not conveyed to Him by sense, as ours are. Your not distinguishing where there is so manifest a difference makes you fancy you see an absurdity where there is none.

Hyl. But all this while you have not considered that the quantity of matter has been demonstrated to be proportional to the gravity of bodies. And what can withstand demonstration?

Phil. Let me see how you demonstrate that point.

Hyl. I lay it down for a principle that the moments or quantities of motion in bodies are in a direct compounded reason of the velocities and quantities of matter contained in them. Hence, where the velocities are equal, it follows the moments are directly as the quantity of matter in each. But it is found by experience that all bodies (bating the small inequalities arising from the resistance of the air) descend with an equal velocity; the motion therefore of descending bodies, and consequently their gravity, which is the cause or principle of that motion, is proportional to the quantity of matter, which was to be demonstrated.

Phil. You lay it down as a self-evident principle that the quantity of motion in any body is proportional to the velocity and matter taken together; and this is made use of to prove a proposition from whence the existence of matter is inferred. Pray is not this arguing in a circle?

Hyl. In the premise I only mean that the motion is proportional to the velocity, jointly with the extension and solidity.

Phil. But allowing this to be true, yet it will not thence follow that gravity is proportional to matter in your philosophic sense of the word, except you take it for granted that unknown *substratum,* or whatever else you call it, is proportional to those sensible qualities which to suppose is plainly begging the question. That there is magnitude and solidity or resistance perceived by sense I readily grant, as likewise, that gravity may be proportional to those qualities I will not dispute. But that either these qualities as perceived by us, or the powers producing them, do exist in a *material substratum*—this is what I deny, and you, indeed, affirm but, notwithstanding your demonstration, have not yet proved.

Hyl. I shall insist no longer on that point. Do you think, however, you shall persuade me the natural philosophers have been dreaming all this while? Pray what becomes of all their hypotheses and explications of the phenomena which suppose the existence of matter?

Phil. What mean you, Hylas, by the "phenomena"?

Hyl. I mean the appearances which I perceive by my senses.

Phil. And the appearances perceived by sense, are they not ideas?

Hyl. I have told you so a hundred times.

Phil. Therefore, to explain the phenomena is to show how we come to be affected with ideas in that manner and order wherein they are imprinted on our senses. Is it not?

Hyl. It is.

Phil. Now, if you can prove that any philosopher has explained the production of any one idea in our minds by the help of *matter,* I shall forever acquiesce and look on all that has been said against it as nothing; but if you cannot, it is vain to urge the explication of phenomena. That a being endowed with knowledge and will should produce or exhibit ideas is easily understood. But that a being which is utterly destitute of these faculties should be able to produce ideas, or in any sort to affect an intelligence, this I can never understand. This I say, though we had some positive conception of matter, though we knew its qualities and could comprehend its existence, would yet be so far from explaining things that it is itself the most inexplicable thing in the world. And yet, for all this, it will not follow that philosophers have been doing nothing; for by observing and reasoning upon the connection of ideas, they discover the laws and methods of nature, which is a part of knowledge both useful and entertaining.

Hyl. After all, can it be supposed God would deceive all mankind? Do you imagine He would have induced the whole world to believe the being of matter if there was no such thing?

Phil. That every epidemical opinion arising from prejudice, or passion, or thoughtlessness may be imputed to God, as the Author of it, I believe you will not affirm. Whatsoever opinion we father on Him, it must be either because He has discovered it to us by supernatural revelation or because it is so evident to our natural faculties, which were framed and given us by God, that it is impossible we should withhold our assent from it. But where is the revelation? Or where is the evidence that extorts the belief of matter? Nay, how does it appear that matter, taken for something distinct from what we perceive by our senses is thought to exist by all mankind, or, indeed, by any except a few philosophers who do not know what they would be at? Your question supposes these points are clear; and, when you have cleared them, I shall think myself obliged to give you another answer. In the meantime let it suffice that I tell you I do not suppose God has deceived mankind at all.

Hyl. But the novelty, Philonous, the novelty! There lies the danger. New notions should always be discountenanced; they unsettle men's minds, and nobody knows where they will end.

Phil. Why the rejecting a notion that has no foundation, either in sense or in reason or in Divine authority, should be thought to unsettle the belief of such opinions as are grounded on all or any of these, I cannot imagine. That innovations in government and religion are dangerous and ought to be discountenanced, I freely own. But is there the like reason why they should be discouraged in philosophy? The making anything known which was unknown before is an innovation in knowledge; and if all such inno-

vations had been forbidden, men would [not] have made a notable progress in the arts and sciences. But it is none of my business to plead for novelties and paradoxes. That the qualities we perceive are not on the objects, that we must not believe our senses, that we know nothing of the real nature of things and can never be assured even of their existence, that real colors and sounds are nothing but certain unknown figures and motions, that motions are in themselves neither swift nor slow, that there are in bodies absolute extensions without any particular magnitude or figure, that a thing stupid, thoughtless, and inactive operates on a spirit, that the least particle of a body contains innumerable extended parts—these are the novelties, these are the strange notions which shock the genuine uncorrupted judgment of all mankind, and, being once admitted, embarrass the mind with endless doubts and difficulties. And it is against these and the like innovations I endeavor to vindicate Common Sense. It is true, in doing this I may, perhaps, be obliged to use some ambages and ways of speech not common. But if my notions are once thoroughly understood, that which is most singular in them will, in effect, be found to amount to no more than this—that it is absolutely impossible and a plain contradiction to suppose any unthinking being should exist without being perceived by a mind. And if this notion be singular, it is a shame it should be so at this time of day and in a Christian country.

Hyl. As for the difficulties other opinions may be liable to, those are out of the question. It is your business to defend your own opinion. Can anything be plainer than that you are for changing all things into ideas? You, I say, who are not ashamed to charge me with skepticism. This is so plain, there is no denying it.

Phil. You mistake me. I am not for changing things into ideas but rather ideas into things, since those immediate objects of perception, which, according to you, are only appearances of things, I take to be the real things themselves.

Hyl. Things! you may pretend what you please; but it is certain you leave us nothing but the empty forms of things, the outside only which strikes the senses.

Phil. What you call the empty forms and outside of things seem to me the very things themselves. Nor are they empty or incomplete otherwise than upon your supposition that matter is an essential part of all corporeal things. We both, therefore, agree in this, that we perceive only sensible forms; but herein we differ: you will have them to be empty appearances, I real beings. In short, you do not trust your senses, I do.

Hyl. You say you believe your senses, and seem to applaud yourself that in this you agree with the vulgar. According to you, therefore, the true nature of a thing is discovered by the senses. If so, whence comes that disagreement? Why, is not the same figure, and other sensible qualities, perceived all manner of ways? And why should we use a microscope the better to discover the true nature of a body, if it were discoverable to the naked eye?

Phil. Strictly speaking, Hylas, we do not see the same object that we feel; neither is the same object perceived by the microscope which was by the naked eye. But in case every variation was thought sufficient to constitute a new kind of individual, the endless number or confusion of names would render language impracticable. Therefore, to avoid this as well as other inconveniences which are obvious upon a little thought, men combine together several ideas, apprehended by divers senses, or by the same sense at different times or in different circumstances, but observed, however, to have some connection in nature, either with respect to coexistence or succession; all which they refer to one name and consider as one thing. Hence it follows that when I examine by my other senses a thing I have seen, it is not in order to understand better the same object which I had perceived by sight, the object of one sense not being perceived by the other senses. And when I look through a microscope, it is not that I may perceive more clearly what I perceived already with my bare eyes, the object perceived by the glass being quite different from the former. But in both cases my aim is only to know what ideas are connected together; and the more a man knows of the connection of ideas, the more he is said to know of the nature of things. What, therefore, if our ideas are variable, what if our senses are not in all circumstances affected with the same appearances? It will not thence follow they are not to be trusted or that they are inconsistent either with themselves or anything else, except it be with your preconceived notion of (I know not what) one single, unchanged, unperceivable, real nature, marked by each name; which prejudice seems to have taken its rise from not rightly understanding the common language of men speaking of several distinct ideas as united into one thing by the mind. And, indeed, there is cause to suspect several erroneous conceits of the philosophers are owing to the same original: while they began to build their schemes not so much on notions as words which were framed by the vulgar merely for convenience and dispatch in the common actions of life, without any regard to speculation.

Hyl. Methinks I apprehend your meaning.

Phil. It is your opinion the ideas we perceive by our senses are not real things, but images or copies of them. Our knowledge, therefore, is no further real than as our ideas are the true representations of those originals. But as these supposed originals are in themselves unknown, it is impossible to know how far our ideas resemble them, or whether they resemble them at all. We cannot, therefore, be sure we have any real knowledge. Further, as our ideas are perpetually varied, without any change in the supposed real things, it necessarily follows they cannot all be true copies of them, if some are and others are not, it is impossible to distinguish the former from the latter. And this plunges us yet deeper in uncertainty. Again, when we consider the point, we cannot conceive how any idea, or anything like an idea, should have an absolute existence out of a mind, nor consequently, according to you, how there should be any real thing in nature. The result of all which is that we are thrown into the most hopeless and abandoned skepticism. Now give me leave to ask you, *first,* whether your referring ideas to certain absolutely existing unperceived substances, as their originals, be not the source of all this skepticism? *Secondly,* whether you are informed, either by sense or reason, of the existence of those unknown originals? And in case you are not, whether it be not absurd to suppose them? *Thirdly,* whether, upon inquiry, you find there is anything distinctly conceived or meant by the ''absolute or external existence of unperceiving substances''; *Lastly,* whether, the premises considered, it be not the wisest way to follow nature, trust your senses, and, laying aside all anxious thought about unknown natures or substances, admit with the vulgar those for real things which are perceived by the senses?

Hyl. For the present I have no inclination to the answering part. I would much rather see how you can get over what follows. Pray, are not the objects perceived by the senses of one likewise perceivable to others present? If there were a hundred more here, they would all see the garden, the trees and flowers, as I see them. But they are not in the same manner affected with the ideas I frame in my imagination. Does not this make a difference between the former sort of objects and the latter?

Phil. I grant it does. Nor have I ever denied a difference between the objects of sense and those of imagination. But what would you infer from thence? You cannot say that sensible objects exist unperceived because they are perceived by many.

Hyl. I own I can make nothing of that objection, but it has led me into another. Is it not your opinion that by our senses we perceive only the ideas existing in our minds?

Phil. It is.

Hyl. But the same idea which is in my mind cannot be in yours or in any other mind. Does it not, therefore, follow from your principles that no two can see the same thing? And is not this highly absurd?

Phil. If the term "same" be taken in the vulgar acceptation, it is certain (and not at all repugnant to the principles I maintain) that different persons may perceive the same thing, or the same thing or idea exist in different minds. Words are of arbitrary imposition; and since men are used to apply the word "same" where no distinction or variety is perceived, and I do not pretend to alter their perceptions, it follows that, as men have said before, *several saw the same thing,* so they may, upon like occasions, still continue to use the same phrase without any deviation either from propriety of language or the truth of things. But if the term "same" be used in the acceptation of philosophers who pretend to an abstracted notion of identity, then, according to their sundry definitions of this notion (for it is not yet agreed wherein that philosophic identity consists), it may or may not be possible for divers persons to perceive the same thing. But whether philosophers shall think fit to call a thing the "same" or no is, I conceive, of small importance. Let us suppose several men together, all endued with the same faculties, and consequently affected in like sort by their senses, and who had yet never known the use of language; they would without question agree in their perceptions. Though perhaps, when they came to the use of speech, some regarding the uniformness of what was perceived might call it the "same" thing; others, especially regarding the diversity of persons who perceived, might choose the denomination of "different" things. But who sees not that all the dispute

is about a word, to wit, whether what is perceived by different persons may yet have the term "same" applied to it? Or suppose a house whose walls or outward shell remaining unaltered, the chambers are all pulled down, and new ones built in their place, and that you should call this the "same," and I should say it was not the "same," house—would we not, for all this, perfectly agree in our thoughts of the house considered in itself? And would not all the difference consist in a sound? If you should say we differed in our notions, for that you superadded to your idea of the house the simple abstracted idea of identity, whereas I did not, I would tell you I know not what you mean by that "abstracted idea of identity," and should desire you to look into your own thoughts and be sure you understood yourself.— Why so silent, Hylas? Are you not yet satisfied men may dispute about identity and diversity without any real difference in their thoughts and opinions abstracted from names? Take this further reflection with you—that, whether matter be allowed to exist or no, the case is exactly the same as to the point in hand. For the materialists themselves acknowledge what we immediately perceive by our senses to be our own ideas. Your difficulty, therefore, that no two see the same thing makes equally against the materialists and me.

Hyl. But they suppose an external archetype to which referring their several ideas they may truly be said to perceive the same thing.

Phil. And (not to mention your having discarded those archetypes) so may you suppose an external archetype on my principles; *external,* I mean, to your own mind, though, indeed, it must be supposed to exist in that mind which comprehends all things; but then, this serves all the ends of *identity,* as well as if it existed out of a mind. And I am sure you yourself will not say it is less intelligible.

Hyl. You have indeed clearly satisfied me either that there is no difficulty at bottom in this point or, if there be, that it makes equally against both opinions.

Phil. But that which makes equally against two contradictory opinions can be a proof against neither.

Hyl. I acknowledge it. But, after all, Philonous, when I consider the substance of what you advance against skepticism, it amounts to no more than this: we are sure that we really see, hear, feel, in a word, that we are affected with sensible impressions.

Phil. And how are we concerned any further? I see this cherry, I feel it, I taste it, and I am sure *nothing* cannot be seen or felt or tasted; it is therefore *real*. Take away the sensations of softness, moisture, redness, tartness, and you take away the cherry. Since it is not a being distinct from sensations, a cherry, I say, is nothing but a congeries of sensible impressions, or ideas perceived by various senses, which ideas are united into one thing (or have one name given them) by the mind because they are observed to attend each other. Thus, when the palate is affected with such a particular taste, the sight is affected with a red color, the touch with roundness, softness, etc. Hence, when I see and feel and taste in sundry certain manners, I am sure the cherry exists or is real, its reality being in my opinion nothing abstracted from those sensations. But if by the word "cherry" you mean an unknown nature distinct from all those sensible qualities, and by its "existence" something distinct from its being perceived, then, indeed, I own neither you nor I, nor anyone else, can be sure it exists.

Hyl. But what would you say, Philonous, if I should bring the very same reasons against the existence of sensible things in a mind which you have offered against their existing in a material *substratum?*

Phil. When I see your reasons, you shall hear what I have to say to them.

Hyl. Is the mind extended or unextended?

Phil. Unextended, without doubt.

Hyl. Do you say the things you perceive are in your mind?

Phil. They are.

Hyl. Again, have I not heard you speak of sensible impressions?

Phil. I believe you may.

Hyl. Explain to me now, O Philonous! how is it possible there should be room for all those trees and houses to exist in your mind. Can extended things be contained in that which is unextended? Or are we to imagine impressions made on a thing void of all solidity? You cannot say objects are in your mind, as books in your study, or that things are imprinted on it, as the figure of a seal upon wax. In what sense, therefore, are we to understand those expressions? Explain me this if you can, and I shall then be able to answer all those queries you formerly put to me about my *substratum.*

Phil. Look you, Hylas, when I speak of objects as existing in the mind or imprinted on the senses, I would not be understood in the gross literal sense— as when bodies are said to exist in a place or a seal to make an impression upon wax. My meaning is only that the mind comprehends or perceives them, and that it is affected from without or by some being distinct from itself. This is my explication of your difficulty; and how it can serve to make your tenet of an unperceiving material *substratum* intelligible, I would fain know.

Hyl. Nay, if that be all, I confess I do not see what use can be made of it. But are you not guilty of some abuse of language in this?

Phil. None at all. It is no more than common custom, which you know is the rule of language, has authorized, nothing being more usual than for philosophers to speak of the immediate objects of the understanding as things existing in the mind. Nor is there anything in this but what is conformable to the general analogy of language; most part of the mental operations being signified by words borrowed from sensible things, as is plain in the terms "comprehend," "reflect," "discourse," etc., which, being applied to the mind, must not be taken in their gross original sense.

Hyl. You have, I own, satisfied me in this point. But there still remains one great difficulty which I know not how you will get over. And, indeed, it is of such importance that if you could solve all others without being able to find a solution for this, you must never expect to make me a proselyte to your principles.

Phil. Let me know this mighty difficulty.

Hyl. The Scripture account of the creation is what appears to me utterly irreconcilable with your notions. Moses tells us of a creation—a creation of what? of ideas? No, certainly, but of things, of real things, solid corporeal substances. Bring your principles to agree with this and I shall perhaps agree with you.

Phil. Moses mentions the sun, moon, and stars, earth and sea, plants and animals. That all these do really exist and were in the beginning created by God, I make no question. If by "ideas" you mean fictions and fancies of the mind, then these are no ideas. If by "ideas" you mean immediate objects of the understanding, or sensible things which cannot exist unperceived, or out of a mind, then these things are ideas. But whether you do or do not call them "ideas," it matters little. The difference is only about a name. And whether that name be retained or rejected, the sense, the truth, and reality of things continues the same. In common talk, the objects of our senses are not termed "ideas" but "things."

Call them so still, provided you do not attribute to them any absolute external existence, and I shall never quarrel with you for a word. The creation, therefore, I allow to have been a creation of things, of *real* things. Neither is this in the least inconsistent with my principles, as is evident from what I have now said; and would have been evident to you without this if you had not forgotten what had been so often said before. But as for solid corporeal substances, I desire you to show where Moses makes any mention of them; and if they should be mentioned by him or any other inspired writer, it would still be incumbent on you to show those words were not taken in the vulgar acceptation for things falling under our senses, but in the philosophic acceptation for matter or an unknown quiddity with an absolute existence. When you have proved these points, then (and not till then) may you bring the authority of Moses into our dispute.

Hyl. It is in vain to dispute about a point so clear. I am content to refer it to your own conscience. Are you not satisfied there is some peculiar repugnancy between the Mosaic account of the creation and your notions?

Phil. If all possible sense which can be put on the first chapter of Genesis may be conceived as consistently with my principles as any other, then it has no peculiar repugnancy with them. But there is no sense you may not as well conceive, believing as I do. Since, besides spirits, all you conceive are ideas, and the existence of these I do not deny. Neither do you pretend they exist without the mind.

Hyl. Pray let me see any sense you can understand it in.

Phil. Why, I imagine that if I had been present at the creation, I should have seen things produced into being—that is become perceptible—in the order prescribed by the sacred historian. I ever before believed the Mosaic account of the creation, and now find no alteration in my manner of believing it. When things are said to begin or end their existence, we do not mean this with regard to God, but His creatures. All objects are eternally known by God, or, which is the same thing, have an eternal existence in His mind; but when things, before imperceptible to creatures, are, by a decree of God, made perceptible to them, then are they said to begin a relative existence with respect to created minds. Upon reading therefore the Mosaic account of the creation, I understand that the several parts of the world became gradually perceivable to finite spirits endowed with proper faculties, so that, whoever such were present, they were in truth perceived by them. This is the literal obvious sense suggested to me by the words of the Holy Scripture, in which is included no mention or thought either of *substratum,* instrument, occasion, or absolute existence. And, upon inquiry, I doubt not it will be found that most plain honest men who believe the creation never think of those things any more than I. What metaphysical sense you may understand it in, you only can tell.

Hyl. But, Philonous, you do not seem to be aware that you allow created things in the beginning only a relative and consequently hypothetical being; that is to say, upon supposition there were men to perceive them, without which they have no actuality of absolute existence wherein creation might terminate. Is it not, therefore, according to you, plainly impossible the creation of any inanimate creatures should precede that of man? And is not this directly contrary to the Mosaic account?

Phil. In answer to that, I say, *first,* created beings might begin to exist in the mind of other created intelligences besides men. You will not, therefore, be able to prove any contradiction between Moses and my notions unless you first show there was no other order of finite created spirits in being before man. I say further, in case we conceive the creation as we should at this time a parcel of plants or vegetables of all sorts produced by an invisible power in a desert where nobody was present—that this way of explaining or conceiving it is consistent with my principles, since they deprive you of nothing, either sensible or imaginable; that it exactly suits with the common, natural, and undebauched notions of mankind; that it manifests the dependence of all things on God, and consequently has all the good effect or influence, which it is possible that important article of our faith should have in making men humble, thankful, and resigned to their Creator. I say, moreover, that, in this naked conception of things, divested of words, there will not be found any notion of what you call the "actuality of absolute existence." You may indeed raise a dust with those terms and so lengthen our dispute to no purpose. But I entreat you calmly to look into your own thoughts and then tell me if they are not a useless and unintelligible jargon.

Hyl. I own I have no very clear notion annexed to them. But what say you to this? Do you not make the existence of sensible things consist in their being in a mind? And were not all things externally in the mind of God? Did they not therefore exist from all eternity, according to you? And how could that which was eternal be created in time? Can anything be clearer or better connected than this?

Phil. And are not you too of opinion that God knew all things from eternity?

Hyl. I am.

Phil. Consequently, they always had a being in the Divine intellect.

Hyl. This I acknowledge.

Phil. By your own confession, therefore, nothing is new, or begins to be, in respect of the mind of God. So we are agreed in that point.

Hyl. What shall we make then of the creation?

Phil. May we not understand it to have been entirely in respect of finite spirits, so that things, with regard to us, may properly be said to begin their existence, or be created, when God decreed they should become perceptible to intelligent creatures in that order and manner which He then established and we now call the laws of nature? You may call this a "relative," or "hypothetical existence," if you please. But so long as it supplies us with the most natural, obvious, and literal sense of the Mosaic history of the creation, so long as it answers all the religious ends of that great article, in a word, so long as you can assign no other sense or meaning in its stead, why should we reject this? Is it to comply with a ridiculous skeptical humor of making everything nonsense and unintelligible? I am sure you cannot say it is for the glory of God. For allowing it to be a thing possible and conceivable that the corporeal world should have an absolute existence extrinsical to the mind of God, as well as to the minds of all created spirits, yet how could this set forth either the immensity or omniscience of the Deity or the necessary and immediate dependence of all things on Him? Nay, would it not rather seem to derogate from those attributes?

Hyl. Well, but as to this decree of God's for making things perceptible, what say you, Philonous, is it not plain God did either execute that decree from all eternity or at some certain time began to will what He had not actually willed before, but only designed to will? If the former, then there could be no creation or beginning of existence in finite things. If the latter, then we must acknowledge something new to befall the Deity, which implies a sort of change; and all change argues imperfection.

Phil. Pray consider what you are doing. Is it not evident this objection concludes equally against a creation in any sense, nay, against every other act of the Deity discoverable by the light of nature? None of which can we conceive otherwise than as performed in time and having a beginning. God is a Being of transcendent and unlimited perfections; His Nature, therefore, is incomprehensible to finite spirits. It is not, therefore, to be expected that any man, whether *materialist* or *immaterialist,* should have exactly just notions of the Deity, His attributes, and ways of operation. If then you would infer anything against me, your difficulty must not be drawn from the inadequateness of our conceptions of the Divine nature, which is unavoidable on any scheme, but from the denial of matter, of which there is not one word, directly or indirectly, in what you have now objected.

Hyl. I must acknowledge the difficulties you are concerned to clear are such only as arise from the nonexistence of matter and are peculiar to that notion. So far you are in the right. But I cannot by any means bring myself to think there is no such peculiar repugnancy between the creation and your opinion, though, indeed, where to fix it I do not distinctly know.

Phil. What would you have? Do I not acknowledge a two-fold state of things, the one ectypal or nature, the other archetypal and eternal? The former was created in time, the latter existed from everlasting in the mind of God. Is not this agreeable to the common notions of divines? Or is any more than this necessary in order to conceive the creation? But you suspect some peculiar repugnancy, though you know not where it lies. To take away all possibility of scruple in the case, do but consider this one point: either you are not able to conceive the creation on any hypothesis whatsoever, and if so, there is no ground for dislike or complaint against my particular opinion on that score; or you are able to conceive it, and if so, why not on my principles, since thereby nothing conceivable is taken away? You have all along been allowed the full scope of sense, imagination, and reason. Whatever, therefore, you could before apprehend, either immediately or mediately by your senses, or by ratiocination from your senses, whatever you could perceive, imagine, or understand, remains still with you. If, therefore, the notion you have of the creation by other principles be intelligible, you have it still upon mine; if it be not intelligible, I conceive it to be no notion at all, and so there is no loss of it. And, indeed, it seems to me very plain that the supposition of matter, that is, a thing perfectly unknown and inconceivable, cannot serve to make us conceive anything. And I hope it need not be proved to you that if the existence of matter does not make the creation conceivable, the creation's being without it inconceivable can be no objection against its non-existence.

Hyl. I confess, Philonous, you have almost satisfied me in this point of the creation.

Phil. I would fain know why you are not quite satisfied. You tell me indeed of a repugnancy between the Mosaic history and immaterialism, but you know not where it lies. Is this reasonable, Hylas? Can you expect I should solve a difficulty without knowing what it is? But, to pass by all that, would not a man think you were assured there is no repugnancy between the received notions of materialists and the inspired writings?

Hyl. And so I am.

Phil. Ought the historical part of Scripture to be understood in a plain obvious sense or in a sense which is metaphysical and out of the way?

Hyl. In the plain sense, doubtless.

Phil. When Moses speaks of herbs, earth, water, etc., as having been created by God, think you not the sensible things commonly signified by those words are suggested to every unphilosophical reader?

Hyl. I cannot help thinking so.

Phil. And are not all ideas, or things perceived by sense, to be denied a real existence by the doctrine of the materialists?

Hyl. This I have already acknowledged.

Phil. The creation, therefore, according to them, was not the creation of things sensible, which have only a relative being, but of certain unknown natures which have an absolute being wherein creation might terminate?

Hyl. True.

Phil. Is it not, therefore, evident the assertors of matter destroy the plain obvious sense of Moses, with which their notions are utterly inconsistent, and instead of it obtrude on us I know not what, something equally unintelligible to themselves and me?

Hyl. I cannot contradict you.

Phil. Moses tells us of a creation. A creation of what? of unknown quiddities, of occasions, or *substratum?* No, certainly, but of things obvious to the

senses. You must first reconcile this with your notions if you expect I should be reconciled to them.

Hyl. I see you can assault me with my own weapons.

Phil. Then as to *absolute existence,* was there ever known a more jejune notion than that? Something it is so abstracted and unintelligible that you have frankly owned you could not conceive it, much less explain anything by it. But allowing matter to exist and the notion of absolute existence to be as clear as light, yet, was this ever known to make the creation more credible? Nay, has it not furnished the atheists and infidels of all ages with the most plausible arguments against a creation? That a corporeal substance which has an absolute existence without the minds of spirits should be produced out of nothing, by the mere will of a spirit, has been looked upon as a thing so contrary to all reason, so impossible and absurd, that not only the most celebrated among the ancients, but even divers modern and Christian philosophers have thought matter coeternal with the Deity. Lay these things together and then judge you whether materialism disposes men to believe the creation of things.

Hyl. I own, Philonous, I think it does not. This of the creation is the last objection I can think of; and I must needs own it has been sufficiently answered as well as the rest. Nothing now remains to be overcome but a sort of unaccountable backwardness that I find in myself toward your notions.

Phil. When a man is swayed, he knows not why, to one side of a question, can this, think you, be anything else but the effect of prejudice, which never fails to attend old and rooted notions? And, indeed, in this respect I cannot deny the belief of matter to have very much the advantage over the contrary opinion with men of a learned education.

Hyl. I confess it seems to be as you say.

Phil. As a balance, therefore, to this weight of prejudice, let us throw into the scale the great advantages that arise from the belief of immaterialism, both in regard to religion and human learning. The being of a God and incorruptibility of the soul, those great articles of religion, are they not proved with the clearest and most immediate evidence? When I say the being of a *God,* I do not mean an obscure general cause of things whereof we have no conception, but *God* in the strict and proper sense of the word, a Being whose spirituality, omnipresence, providence, omniscience, infinite power, and goodness are as conspicuous as the existence of sensible things, of which (notwithstanding the fallacious pretenses and affected scruples of skeptics) there is no more reason to doubt than of our own being. Then, with relation to human sciences: in Natural Philosophy, what intricacies, what obscurities, what contradictions has the belief of matter led men into! To say nothing of the numberless disputes about its extent, continuity, homogeneity, gravity, divisibility, etc.—do they not pretend to explain all things by bodies operating on bodies, according to the laws of motion? And yet, are they able to comprehend how any one body should move another? Nay, admitting there was no difficulty in reconciling the notion of an inert being with a cause, or in conceiving how an accident might pass from one body to another, yet, by all their strained thoughts and extravagant suppositions, have they been able to reach the mechanical production of any one animal or vegetable body? Can they account, by the laws of motion, for sounds, tastes, smells, or colors, or for the regular course of things? Have they accounted, by physical principles, for the aptitude and contrivance even of the most inconsiderable parts of the universe? But laying aside matter and corporeal causes and admitting only the efficiency of an All-perfect Mind, are not all the effects of nature easy and intelligible? If the *phenomena* are nothing else but *ideas,* God is a *spirit,* but matter an unintelligent, unperceiving being. If they demonstrate an unlimited power in their cause, God is active and omnipotent, but matter an inert mass. If the order, regularity, and usefulness of them can never be sufficiently admired, God is infinitely wise and provident, but matter destitute of all contrivance and design. These surely are great advantages in physics. Not to mention that the apprehension of a distant Deity naturally disposes men to a negligence of their moral actions, which they would be more cautious of, in case they thought him immediately present and acting on their minds without the interposition of matter or unthinking second causes. Then in metaphysics: what difficulties concerning entity in abstract, substantial forms, hylarchic principles, plastic natures, substance and accident, principle of individuation, possibility of matter's thinking, origin of ideas, the manner how two independent substances so widely different as *spirit* and *matter* should mutually operate on each other? What difficulties, I say, and endless disquisitions concerning these and innumerable other the like points do we escape by supposing only spirits and ideas? Even the mathematics themselves, if we take away the absolute existence of extended things,

become much more clear and easy, the most shocking paradoxes and intricate speculations in those sciences depending on the infinite divisibility of finite extension, which depends on that supposition. But what need is there to insist on the particular sciences? Is not that opposition to all science whatsoever, that frenzy of the ancient and modern skeptics, built on the same foundation? Or can you produce so much as one argument against the reality of corporeal things or in behalf of that avowed utter ignorance of their natures which does not suppose their reality to consist in an external absolute existence? Upon this supposition, indeed, the objections from the change of colors in a pigeon's neck, or the appearance of the broken oar in the water, must be allowed to have weight. But these and the like objections vanish if we do not maintain the being of absolute external originals, but place the reality of things in ideas, fleeting, indeed, and changeable; however, not changed at random, but according to the fixed order of nature. For herein consists that constancy and truth of things which secures all the concerns of life, and distinguishes that which is real from the irregular visions of the fancy.

Hyl. I agree to all you have now said and must own that nothing can incline me to embrace your opinion more than the advantages I see it is attended with. I am by nature lazy, and this would be a mighty abridgment in knowledge. What doubts, what hypotheses, what labyrinths of amusement, what fields of disputation, what an ocean of false learning may be avoided by that single notion of *immaterialism!*

Phil. After all, is there anything further remaining to be done? You may remember you promised to embrace that opinion which upon examination should appear most agreeable to common sense and remote from skepticism. This, by your own confession, is that which denies matter or the absolute existence of corporeal things. Nor is this all; the same notion has been proved several ways, viewed in different lights, pursued in its consequences, and all objections against it cleared. Can there be a greater evidence of its truth? Or is it possible it should have all the marks of a true opinion and yet be false?

Hyl. I own myself entirely satisfied for the present in all respects. But what security can I have that I shall still continue the same full assent to your opinion and that no unthought-of objection or difficulty will occur hereafter?

Phil. Pray, Hylas, do you in other cases, when a point is once evidently proved, withhold your assent on account of objections or difficulties it may be liable to? Are the difficulties that attend the doctrine of incommensurable quantities, of the angle of contact, of the asymptotes to curves, or the like, sufficient to make you hold out against mathematical demonstration? Or will you disbelieve the Providence of God because there may be some particular things which you know not how to reconcile with it? If there are difficulties attending immaterialism, there are at the same time direct and evident proofs of it. But for the existence of matter there is not one proof, and far more numerous and insurmountable objections lie against it. But where are those mighty difficulties you insist on? Alas! you know not where or what they are; something which may possibly occur hereafter. If this be a sufficient pretense for withholding your full assent, you should never yield it to any proposition, how free soever from exceptions, how clearly and solidly soever demonstrated.

Hyl. You have satisfied me, Philonous.

Phil. But to arm you against all future objections, do but consider that which bears equally hard on two contradictory opinions can be proof against neither. Whenever, therefore, any difficulty occurs, try if you can find a solution for it on the hypothesis of the materialists. Be not deceived by words, but sound your own thoughts. And in case you cannot conceive it easier by the help of materialism, it is plain it can be no objection against immaterialism. Had you proceeded all along by this rule, you would probably have spared yourself abundance of trouble in objecting, since of all your difficulties I challenge you to show one that is explained by matter, nay, which is not more unintelligible with than without that supposition, and consequently makes rather *against* than *for* it. You should consider, in each particular, whether the difficulty arises from the *nonexistence of matter.* If it does not, you might as well argue from the infinite divisibility of extension against the Divine prescience as from such a difficulty against immaterialism. And yet, upon recollection, I believe you will find this to have been often if not always the case. You should likewise take heed not to argue on a *petitio principii.* One is apt to say the unknown substances ought to be esteemed real things rather than the ideas in our minds; and who can tell but the unthinking external substance may concur as a cause or instrument in the productions of our ideas? But is not this proceeding on a supposition that there are such external substances? And to suppose this, is it not begging the question? But above all things, you should beware of imposing on yourself by that vulgar sophism which is called *ignoratio elenchi.* You talked often as if you thought I maintained the nonexistence of sensible things, whereas in truth no one can be more thoroughly assured of their existence than I am; and it is you who doubt, I should have said, positively deny it. Everything that is seen, felt, heard, or any way perceived by the senses is, on the principles I embrace, a real being, but not on yours. Remember, the matter you contend for is an unknown somewhat (if indeed it may be termed "somewhat"), which is quite stripped of all sensible qualities, and can neither be perceived by sense, nor apprehended by the mind. Remember, I say that it is not any object which is hard or soft, hot or cold, blue or white, round or square, etc.— for all these things I affirm do exist. Though, indeed, I deny they have an existence distinct from being perceived, or that they exist out of all minds whatsoever. Think on these points; let them be attentively considered and still kept in view. Otherwise you will not comprehend the state of the question, without which your objections will always be wide of the mark and, instead of mine, may possibly be directed (as more than once they have been) against your own notions.

Hyl. I must needs own, Philonous, nothing seems to have kept me from agreeing with you more than this same *mistaking the question.* In denying matter, at first glimpse I am tempted to imagine you deny the things we see and feel, but, upon reflection, find there is no ground for it. What think you, therefore, of retaining the name "matter" and applying it to *sensible things?* This may be done without any change in your sentiments; and, believe me, it would be a means of reconciling them to some persons who may be more shocked at an innovation in words than in opinion.

Phil. With all my heart; retain the word "matter" and apply it to the objects of sense, if you please, provided you do not attribute to them any subsistence distinct from their being perceived. I shall never quarrel with you for an expression. "Matter" or "material substance" are terms introduced by philosophers, and, as used by them, imply a sort of independence, or a subsistence distinct from being perceived by a mind; but are never used by common people, or, if ever, it is to signify the immediate objects of sense. One would think, therefore, so long as the names of all particular things with the terms "sensible," "substance," "body," "stuff," and the like, are retained, the word "matter" should be never missed in common talk. And in philosophical discourses it seems the best way to leave it quite out, since there is not, perhaps, any one thing that has more favored and strengthened the depraved bent of the mind toward atheism than the use of that general confused term.

Hyl. Well, but, Philonous, since I am content to give up the notion of an unthinking substance exterior to the mind, I think you ought not to deny me the privilege of using the word "matter" as I please, and annexing it to a collection of sensible qualities subsisting only in the mind. I freely own there is no other substance, in a strict sense, than spirit. But I have been so long accustomed to the term "matter" that I know not how to part with it. To say there is no matter in the world is still shocking to me. Whereas to say there is no matter if by that term be meant an unthinking substance existing without the mind, but if by matter is meant some sensible thing whose existence consists in being perceived, then there is matter—this distinction gives it quite another turn; and men will come into your notions with small difficulty when they are proposed in that manner. For, after all, the controversy about matter in the strict acceptation of it lies altogether between you and the philosophers, whose principles, I acknowledge, are not near so natural or so agreeable to the common sense of mankind and Holy Scripture as yours. There is nothing we either desire or shun but as it makes, or is apprehended to make, some part of our happiness or misery. But what has happiness or misery, joy or grief, pleasure or pain to do with absolute existence or with unknown entities abstracted from all relation to us? It is evident things regard us only as they are pleasing or displeasing; and they can please or displease only so far forth as they are perceived. Further, therefore, we are not concerned; and thus far you leave things as you found them. Yet still there is something new in this doctrine. It is plain, I do not now think with the philosophers, nor yet altogether with the vulgar. I would

know how the case stands in that respect, precisely what you have added to or altered in my former notions.

Phil. I do not pretend to be a setter-up of new notions. My endeavors tend only to unite and place in a clearer light that truth which was before shared between the vulgar and the philosophers, the former being of opinion that *those things they immediately perceive are the real things,* and the latter, that *the things immediately perceived are ideas which exist only in the mind.* Which two notions put together do, in effect, constitute the substance of what I advance.

Hyl. I have been a long time distrusting my senses; methought I saw things by a dim light and through false glasses. Now the glasses are removed and a new light breaks in upon my understanding. I am clearly convinced that I see things in their native forms and am no longer in pain about their *unknown natures* or *absolute existence.* This is the state I find myself in at present, though, indeed, the course that brought me to it I do not yet thoroughly comprehend. You set out upon the same principles that Academics, Cartesians, and the like sects usually do, and for a long time it looked as if you were advancing their philosophical skepticism; but, in the end, your conclusions are directly opposite to theirs.

Phil. You see, Hylas, the water of yonder fountain, how it is forced upwards, in a round column, to a certain height, at which it breaks and falls back into the basin from whence it rose, its ascent as well as descent proceeding from the same uniform law or principle of gravitation. Just so, the same principles which, at first view, lead to skepticism, pursued to a certain point, bring men back to common sense.

NOTES

1. [The remainder of the present paragraph did not appear in the first and second editions.]

2. [See Berkeley's *An Essay towards a New Theory of Vision* (1709) and *The Theory of Vision Vindicated and Explained* (1733).]

3. [The bracketed portion of this paragraph did not appear in the first and second editions.]

4. [The four paragraphs following did not appear in the first and second editions.]

GODFREY VESEY

The Heat-Pain Argument*

Godfrey Vesey is a contemporary British philosopher who has taught at the University of London and the Open University. He has published numerous important works on the philosophy of mind.

All that I ever learned at college of philosophy had been a conception of the external world as a colorless and sound-less wilderness whose true nature one could never know, which one could not even imagine—but which I did, none the less, imagine as a vast landscape of polar spaces in whose eternal twilight one wandered, preoccupied and de-luded by a flicker of magic-lantern pictures which danced inside one's mind and for ever remained private to oneself.

Edmund Wilson, *I Thought of Daisy*

I have the impression that the man in Edmund Wilson's novel, *I Thought of Daisy,* did not like what he had learned at college of philosophy. He preferred another conception of the world, the conception of it as a familiar, warm, colorful, sound-filled place to be shared with others—and perhaps especially with Daisy. I sympathize.

The logical thing to do, however, is not to turn one's back on philosophy in general, but to look for mistakes in the particular philosophy of which the conception of the world as "external," colorless, and so on, is a part.

What emerges when we do this is that the philosophy in question was originally fashioned to suit scientists. Scientists found themselves able to explain how one event causes another in the physical world without supposing objects in that world to have all the qualities we perceive them as having. Sometimes the

scientist and the philosopher were one and the same person. As scientist he adopted a certain method of explaining things; as philosopher he tried to go one step further, he tried to justify his scientific methodology with arguments intended to prove that the things he did not need in his explanations—objective colors, sounds, and so on—did not exist. He tried to prove that colors, sounds, etc., existed only in the perceiver's mind.

The argument that is to be found most frequently in the writings of the philosophers who held this conception does not in fact relate to colors and sounds, though colors and sounds certainly received a good deal of attention. It relates to heat. Perhaps this was because Galileo had claimed of heat that its "generally accepted notion comes very far from the truth . . . inasmuch as it is supposed to be a true accident, affection, and quality really residing in the thing which we perceive to be heated."[1]

The problem for the philosophers was: how to *prove* the generally accepted notion to be false.

I think it was the French philosopher René Descartes (1596–1650) who first formulated what I have called "the heat-pain argument." He wrote:

I have a sensation of heat as I approach the fire; but when I approach the same fire too closely, I have a sensation of pain; so there is nothing to convince me that something in the fire resembles heat, any more than the pain; it is just that there must be something in it (whatever this may turn out to be) that produces the sensations of heat or pain.[2]

The British philosopher, John Locke (1632–1704) put the argument like this:

He that will consider that the same fire that at one distance produces in us the sensation of warmth, does at a nearer approach produce in us the far different sensation of pain,

*Godfrey Vesey, "The World Without," from *Philosophy in the Open,* ed. Godfrey Vesey (Milton Keynes, England: Open University Press, 1974), pp. 9–19. Reprinted by permission of the publisher and author.

ought to bethink himself what reason he has to say, that his idea of warmth which was produced in him by the fire, is actually in the fire, and his idea of pain which the same fire produced in him the same way is not in the fire.[3]

Another British philosopher, George Berkeley (1685–1753), expounded the argument in a dialogue between two imaginary characters, Hylas and Philonous. Hylas is persuaded to admit that when he puts his hand uncomfortably near the fire he cannot distinguish between the heat he feels, and the pain. It is, he admits, "one simple uniform sensation." And being *one* sensation, what is true of the pain must be true of the heat. Like the pain, it "cannot exist but in a mind perceiving it."[4]

Hylas, in Berkeley's dialogue, is a born loser. I have written another dialogue, in which I have allowed Hylas to fight back. Philonous, in my dialogue, is much the same as he was in Berkeley's dialogue. But Hylas is a changed character.

I think the man in Edmund Wilson's novel would have liked the new Hylas. They are on the same side.

HYLAS FIGHTS BACK

Phil. Good morning, Hylas. I expected you an hour ago, but tell me now, what are the fruits of your further thought? Are you of the same mind as yesterday? Or have you had cause to change your opinion in the meantime?

Hyl. I'm sorry, Philonous, for not meeting you sooner. All this morning my head was so filled with our conversation that I hadn't leisure to think of the time of day, or indeed of anything else.

Phil. In that case I freely forgive you. I am glad you were so intent upon our conversation. Now, if you have found any mistakes in your concessions, or fallacies in my reasonings from them, please let me hear them.

Hyl. To see mistakes and fallacies, Philonous, I would need to have a clearer and more certain grasp of the arguments than I confess I have. Would you bear with me if I rehearse the steps, and you can put me right if I go wrong?

Phil. It shall be my pleasure, though I must admit to some surprise, for yesterday I thought you had achieved a clear vision of the truth that heat cannot exist but in a mind perceiving it.

Hyl. If you would rather that we . . .

Phil. No, no, no. Rehearse the steps, I beg you, do.

Hyl. The argument turned—correct me if I'm wrong—the argument turned on whether or not intense heat is a pain.

Phil. Yes. *You* had said that pain is something distinct from heat, the consequence or effect of it. And *I* . . .

Hyl. And *you* asked me to consider whether, when I put my hand near the fire, I perceive both heat and pain, or but one simple sensation.

Phil. To which you replied . . .

Hyl. To which I replied "But one simple sensation."

Phil. Yes.

Hyl. Yes. "But one simple sensation." In other words—now this is it, isn't it, Philonous?—my hand feels hot when I hold it near the fire, so very hot that it is painful. And the heat and the pain are one—one simple uniform sensation in my hand.

Phil. Yes [*Pause*] But, of course, not literally in your hand. Not in your hand, Hylas, as are the bones and sinews.

Hyl. The sensation? No. No, of course not. Though we do *talk* of having sensations in parts of our bodies.

Phil. Indeed, but it is in your hand as part of a being endowed with sense and perception that the pain exists. Were you a senseless being you could not be the subject of pain.

Hyl. That is true. So the pain is in my hand, but only in so far as my hand is part of me, a being endowed with sense and perception. Literally, we might say, the pain is in my mind.

Phil. Exactly. And pain cannot exist in what has no mind. A fire, for example, cannot feel pain, because it is a senseless being.

Hyl. Yes, I quite see that.

Phil. Well then, since you have conceded that when you hold your hand near the fire, the heat and the pain are one and the same sensation, and that the pain cannot exist in a senseless being, you must, to be consistent, grant that the heat cannot exist in a senseless being.

Hyl. Such as the fire?

Phil. Such as the fire. Heat cannot exist but in a mind perceiving it.

Hyl. In other words, the fire itself is not hot. And yet, I tell you Philonous, it is. It is evident to my senses that it is. Can anything be more absurd than to deny it? I reach out my hand to the fire and . . . it's . . . hot.

Phil.   [*Stating, not asking*] Your hand.

Hyl.   No, the fire.

Phil.   But, Hylas, there is only the one simple sensation, and you have conceded that it is one with the pain in your hand. You may, because of it, *infer* there to be something in the fire that *causes* it . . .

Hyl.   The heat of the fire I feel by putting my hand near it?

Phil.   . . . but, if I may remind you of what you yourself said yesterday, the only things perceived by the senses are those perceived *immediately*. Causes are inferred, and the senses make no inferences. You cannot know, by the senses, anything of the cause you infer to be in the fire; and moreover, it cannot even be *like* the sensation in your hand, for the sensation requires a being endowed with senses and perception for its existence, and the fire is not such a being.

Hyl.   So by my own concessions I must be wrong in thinking I feel the heat of the fire.

Phil.   Yes.

Hyl.   Either I'm wrong or there was a mistake in my concessions?

Phil.   Yes.

Hyl.   [*After pause*] Hmm. We supposed the heat of the fire to be intense, did we not?

Phil.   We did.

Hyl.   So intense that my hand feels painfully hot?

Phil.   Yes.

Hyl.   But suppose the fire to have died down, to be but warm ashes. I touch them, and their temperature is not such as to make me feel hot.

Phil.   Is it a pleasurable sensation?

Hyl.   Suppose I say it is?

Phil.   Well then, since pleasure cannot exist in a senseless being, neither can the warmth you feel.

Hyl.   [*After pause*] But when I say it is a pleasurable sensation I mean that I take pleasure in it, just as I do in your conversation. Surely it does not follow from your conversation being pleasurable that it exists only in my mind! And anyway I might feel the warmth of the ashes with complete indifference. [*Pause*] But my point is this. I don't have to feel warm to feel the warmth of the ashes. Rather the opposite. I am more likely to feel warmth if I feel cold.

Phl.   Oh, come Hylas!

Hyl.   No, I mean it. If my hands feel cold when I put them on the ashes I shall be more, not less, sensible of the warmth. [*Pause*] And you admitted as much, yourself, Philonous, yesterday. Don't you remember? You said that if one of your hands is hot and the other cold, and you put them both in a bowl of tepid water it will seem cold to the hot hand and warm to the cold one.

Phil.   I said: if one of my hands *is* hot and the other cold, not if one of my hands *feels* hot and the other cold.

Hyl.   All right. But you will admit, won't you, that there is such a thing as one's hands feeling cold? For instance, in the winter, when one has come out without gloves?

Phil.   Of course I admit it. If I come out in the winter without gloves, and you shake hands with me, certainly my hands will feel cold to you. But it doesn't follow that the coldness is anywhere else but in our minds.

Hyl.   [*Sighs*] No, you haven't seen what I'm getting at.

Phil.   [*Slightly irritated*] Well, you said "There is such a thing as one's hands feeling cold" and I agreed.

Hyl.   Yes, but I didn't mean their feeling cold to someone else's touch, or even to your own touch. They . . . simply . . . feel . . . cold.

Phil.   Hylas.

Hyl.   What, Philonous?

Phil.   [*Deliberately*] How is one aware of their coldness if not by touch?

Hyl.   That's the whole point. Don't you see? There's a coldness, a bodily sensation, of which one is aware, but not by touch, or by any other means. It's not an objective quality like the coldness of snow, it's simply a feeling.

Phil.   But the coldness of snow is simply a feeling. So what is the difference?

Hyl.   No, you can't say that.

Phil.   What?

Hyl.   That the coldness of snow is simply a feeling.

Phil.   Why not?

Hyl.   Because that is what you, Philonous, are supposed to be arguing for. It'd be begging the question to introduce it as an objection to what I'm saying.

Phil.   I'm afraid, Hylas, I'm not at all clear what it is you are saying.

Hyl.   I'm saying this. We use words like "hot" and "cold" and "warm" and "chilly" sometimes to say how *we* feel, and sometimes to say how things feel to us. Sometimes for our "bodily sensations" and sometimes for the qualities of fire and snow, and so on. [*Pause*] Suppose I say "My feet feel cold." I may say this, having touched them. They feel cold to my hand. They would feel cold to your hand. Or I may say it without having touched them. I have a sensation of coldness in my feet. But it—the sensation—isn't something which you, or I for that matter, could feel by touching them.

Phil. Of course not; the sensation is in your mind. It's not literally in your feet. But we've been into all that.

Hyl. Yes, but what I want you to see is that we don't use words like "cold" and "hot" *only* to describe how we feel, that is, our bodily sensations. We use them to describe things like snow and fire, and that use is not reducible to the other. When I say snow is cold I don't mean it has feelings of coldness. I don't expect it to start shivering or asking for warm clothing. Its coldness is a *quality* it has, not an *experience* it has. When I say that snow is cold and you say that material substances are senseless and therefore cannot be the subject of sensations, we're not disagreeing.

Phil. All right, but it doesn't follow that you're justified in using "hot" and "cold" of fire and snow.

Hyl. Why not?

Phil. Well, if I've understood you aright, you hold that there's a sort of dual use of words like "hot" and "cold"?

Hyl. [*Agreeing noise*]

Phil. That is, you would say, sometimes we use them to say how we feel, and at other times to describe things like fire and snow.

Hyl. Yes, all right, that's what I'm saying.

Phil. Right. Now, my question to you is this. Given that "hot" and "cold" are names of feelings, what justifies us in using them to describe things like fire and snow? Surely if two things are properly called by the same name it must be because they have something in common. They must be like one another in some respect; else why should we call them by the same name? Yet how can anything in a senseless object, like a fire, be like something, a feeling, that can exist only in a being endowed with senses? In the absence of an explanation of that, it seems to me that we have no reason to call a fire hot, or snow cold.

Hyl. We have a reason, namely that the fire feels hot, the snow cold.

Phil. What I meant was that we have no reason to use the *same* words of fire and snow as we use for what you call our bodily sensations.

Hyl. Ah, well now, Philonous, there are two things I want to say about that.

Phil. Go on.

Hyl. First of all, it seems to me that you've put the cart before the horse, if you'll pardon the expression.

Phil. What do you mean?

Hyl. You said: "Given that 'hot' and 'cold' are names of feelings, what justifies us in using them to describe things like fire and snow?" But it seems to me that it is our use of them to describe fire and snow that is primary. What is problematic is our use of them to express our feelings. Now this comes out in how a child is taught the words. I can point at snow, and say "That's cold." But I can't point at the child's feelings. How a child comes to use words like "pain" and "fear" and "pleasure" as the rest of us do, is the problem, not how it comes to use words like "white" and "round" and "furry." It's a problem precisely because sensations and feelings are not objective in the way colors and shapes and so on, are. And secondly, I think the explanation of our using a word like "cold" for a bodily sensation as well as for a property of snow need not be of the kind you describe.

Phil. What do you mean, Hylas?

Hyl. I mean it need not be in terms of our having noticed some resemblance between a bodily sensation and the coldness the snow has.

Phil. But if it comes to us naturally to use the word "cold" for how we feel, surely . . .

Hyl. Surely there's an explanation? Yes. But the explanation doesn't have to be some supposed resemblance. You said it comes naturally to us to use the word "cold" for how we feel. Well, the explanation may be equally natural.

Phil. What do you mean?

Hyl. Consider how we use words like "giddy" and "dizzy." They are used to describe someone's state of balance: "He's unsteady, swaying about." But they're also used to describe how the person feels. Now, we don't use them in these two ways because we notice a resemblance between a certain feeling and the state of being unbalanced. We call the feeling one of dizziness because it's the feeling that usually goes with being dizzy, that is, being unbalanced. And why should we call it anything else?

Phil. And what about coldness?

Hyl. The same. We call the feeling in our feet one of coldness because it's the feeling that usually goes with their being cold, in the sense in which their being cold is something to be found out by touching them or using a thermometer on them. It's as simple as that.

There's no reason why we should use any other word than the one that's ready to hand, that is, the one for the related state of the body. So we use it—naturally.

Phil. All right, but that doesn't show that heat and cold really are *in* things like fire and snow.

Hyl. No, Philonous. But it demolishes one argument for saying they're not, and as far as I can see it's the only argument you've advanced that even seemed like getting anywhere. I know you've got other arguments and I'll be happy to discuss them with you, but perhaps when the sun has gone down. It is so hot.

Phil. You mean it makes you feel hot.

Hyl. No, Philonous, that's not what I mean. The sun *is* hot. Goodbye!

PROOF IN PHILOSOPHY

In Berkeley's own dialogue, Hylas concedes. In mine it is Philonous who finally says "All right" (though note that it is followed by "but"). Philosophers in dialogues may be persuaded by their opponents in twenty minutes of fast talk. Philosophers in real life are more resistant to persuasion. Let me illustrate this by relating some of the history of my "Hylas Fights Back" dialogue.

I had for a long time been trying to find a way of showing the heat-pain argument to be invalid, because I could not accept the conclusion, that heat exists only as a sensation in the mind. I had reached the point of distinguishing between the use of words like "hot" and "cold" to say how we feel, and their use to describe things like fire and snow. And I was trying to grasp, in terms of this distinction, the significance of Philonous' insistence, in Berkeley's dialogue, that material things are "senseless beings." It struck me that Berkeley's argument must really be as follows:

We use the same word for a quality of material things as we use for a bodily sensation. We are justified in using it for a quality of material things only if the quality is like the bodily sensation. But they cannot be alike, since one of them requires a sentient being for its existence while the other does not. Therefore we are not justified in using it for a quality of material things.

If I was right in supposing this to be the nub of his argument then a prior question to be considered was: "Do people in fact suppose themselves to be justified in using the word 'hot' of material things, like fires, because they think there is something in the fire like

what is in them when they feel hot?" To this the answer seemed to me to be "No." And there, for the time being, I stuck, without being able to see how to make any headway. What could explain the dual use of words like "hot" and "cold" if not a resemblance in the things of which they were used?

I returned to Berkeley's argument some time later, having in the meantime read Ludwig Wittgenstein's *Blue and Brown Books,* and in particular, his treatment of the question "What is it that bodily and mental strain have in common?"[5] I tried to apply what Wittgenstein says about the dual use of the word "strain" to the dual use of the word "hot," and wrote up my conclusions in a paper entitled "Berkeley and Sensations of Heat."[6] In the course of the paper I addressed myself to the question "Why is it that people unhesitatingly talk of feeling hot as well as of feeling the heat of things?" I wrote:

There is nothing impossible about a person's forehead feeling cold to him, although, when he touches it, it feels hot to his hand. But this is an exception to the rule. It is the sort of thing which would happen only if the person was in some unusual condition, such as a fever. Usually if a part of the body *is* hot, or *is* cold, it *feels* hot or cold, to the person whose body it is.

Suppose, however, that there were not this degree of regularity. Suppose, first, that what is true to a limited extent of pain were true to a much greater extent of feelings of hot and cold. What is true of pain is that a bodily feeling which is usually painful may, under certain conditions, be enjoyed. Suppose that, similarly, the effect of a hot bath depended on, say, our emotional state, rather as whether we feel an icicle down our backs as an icicle or as a red-hot dagger depends on what we have been led to expect.

Usually we would feel warm but sometimes we would feel cold. The closer the number of times we felt cold came to equalling the number of times we felt warm, the more inclined we would be to think of the words "warm" and "cold" as applying to the sensation only indirectly. That is, the sensation itself we would apprehend as, perhaps, a mild, diffused prickling, and the warmth and coldness would be our classification of it as "the sort of sensation which is usually caused by being in hot water" and "the sort of sensation which is usually caused by being in cold water."

If there were no regularity at all, if the sort of sensation which is caused by being in hot water were equally often caused by being in cold water, and vice versa, then we would be denied even the possibility of this notional classification. But, as things stand, cases of a person feeling cold when conditions are such as would ordinarily make him feel warm are the exception to the rule.

Now, is it not possible that it is this rule which is the explanation of our referring to the feelings produced in our bodies by prolonged contact with hot or cold objects, as "hot" and "cold"? Is it not possible that we apprehend them as feelings of hotness and coldness because the feelings are usually of one sort when our bodies *are* hot, and of another sort when our bodies *are* cold? If this were so, then any inclination we may have to think that the heat we attribute to external objects and the bodily sensation of being hot must be alike derives from our using the same word for a quality of external objects and for a sensation, and not vice versa. That is, we refer to our sensations as "hot" and "cold" because they are the sensations which usually go with our bodies being hot or cold; and it is not the case that we call external things hot and cold because we think there is something in common between them and our bodily sensations. So the fact that material things are "senseless beings," and hence that the heat which is perceived and the bodily sensation cannot be alike, cannot constitute a proof that we are not justified in attributing heat and cold to material things. What justifies us in attributing heat and cold to material things is our perceiving them to be hot and cold; and they could still feel hot and cold to us even if we never felt hot or cold ourselves.

The persuasiveness of Berkeley's argument about heat and pain depends on two things: (i) our readiness to distinguish between feeling heat and feeling hot, and (ii) our hav-

ing the idea that if two things are called by the same name it must be because we suppose them to be like one another. Only if both these things are accepted can the further point that material things are "senseless beings" be used to promote the conclusion that we are not justified in attributing heat to material things. . . .

NOTES

1. E. A. Burtt, *The Metaphysical Foundations of Modern Science,* rev. ed. (London: Kegan Paul, Trench, Trubner & Co., 1932), p. 75.

2. René Descartes, *Philosophical Writings,* trans. E. Anscombe and P. T. Geach (London: Nelson, 1954), pp. 118–19.

3. John Locke, *An Essay Concerning Human Understanding* ed. A. S. Pringle-Pattison (Oxford: Oxford University Press, 1924), p. 69.

4. George Berkeley, *The Principles of Human Knowledge* (London: Collins, 1962), pp. 152–56.

5. Ludwig Wittgenstein, *The Blue and Brown Books* (Oxford: Basil Blackwell, 1958), p. 132.

6. G. N. A. Vesey, "Berkeley and Sensations of Heat," *The Philosophical Review,* Vol. 69 (1960), pp. 201–210. Reprinted by permission.

B E R T R A N D   R U S S E L L

from *The Problems of Philosophy**

CHAPTER I: APPEARANCE AND REALITY

Is there any knowledge in the world which is so certain that no reasonable man could doubt it? This question, which at first sight might not seem difficult, is really one of the most difficult that can be asked. When we have realised the obstacles in the way of a straightforward and confident answer, we shall be well launched on the study of philosophy—for philosophy is merely the attempt to answer such ultimate questions, not carelessly and dogmatically, as we do in ordinary life and even in the sciences, but critically, after exploring all that makes such questions

puzzling, and after realizing all the vagueness and confusion that underlie our ordinary ideas.

In daily life, we assume as certain many things which, on a closer scrutiny, are found to be so full of apparent contradictions that only a great amount of thought enables us to know what it is that we really may believe. In the search for certainty, it is natural to begin with our present experiences, and in some sense, no doubt, knowledge is to be derived from them. But any statement as to what it is that our immediate experiences make us know is very likely to be wrong. It seems to me that I am now sitting in a chair, at a table of a certain shape, on which I see sheets of paper with writing or print. By turning my head I see out of the window buildings and clouds and the sun. I believe that the sun is about ninety-

*From Bertrand Russell, *The Problems of Philosophy* (New York and London: Oxford University Press, 1952), Chapter I (pp. 9–25) and Chapter II (pp. 26–41). Reprinted by permission of Oxford University Press.

three million miles from the earth; that it is a hot globe many times bigger than the earth; that, owing to the earth's rotation, it rises every morning, and will continue to do so for an indefinite time in the future. I believe that, if any other normal person comes into my room, he will see the same chairs and tables and books and papers as I see, and that the table which I see is the same as the table which I feel pressing against my arm. All this seems to be so evident as to be hardly worth stating, except in answer to a man who doubts whether I know anything. Yet all this may be reasonably doubted, and all of it requires much careful discussion before we can be sure that we have stated it in a form that is wholly true.

To make our difficulties plain, let us concentrate attention on the table. To the eye it is oblong, brown and shiny, to the touch it is smooth and cool and hard; when I tap it, it gives out a wooden sound. Any one else who sees and feels and hears the table will agree with this description, so that it might seem as if no difficulty would arise; but as soon as we try to be more precise our troubles begin. Although I believe that the table is "really" of the same colour all over, the parts that reflect the light look much brighter than the other parts, and some parts look white because of reflected light. I know that, if I move, the parts that reflect the light will be different, so that the apparent distribution of colours on the table will change. It follows that if several people are looking at the table at the same moment, no two of them will see exactly the same distribution of colours, because no two can see it from exactly the same point of view, and any change in the point of view makes some change in the way the light is reflected.

For most practical purposes these differences are unimportant, but to the painter they are all-important: the painter has to unlearn the habit of thinking that things seem to have the colour which common sense says they "really" have, and to learn the habit of seeing things as they appear. Here we have already the beginning of one of the distinctions that cause most trouble in philosophy—the distinction between "appearance" and "reality," between what things seem to be and what they are. The painter wants to know what things seem to be, the practical man and the philosopher want to know what they are; but the philosopher's wish to know this is stronger than the practical man's, and is more troubled by knowledge as to the difficulties of answering the question.

To return to the table. It is evident from what we have found, that there is no colour which preeminently appears to be *the* colour of the table, or even of any one particular part of the table—it appears to be of different colours from different points of view, and there is no reason for regarding some of these as more really its colour than others. And we know that even from a given point of view the colour will seem different by artificial light, or to a colour-blind man, or to a man wearing blue spectacles, while in the dark there will be no colour at all, though to touch and hearing the table will be unchanged. Thus colour is not something which is inherent in the table, but something depending upon the table and the spectator and the way the light falls on the table. When, in ordinary life, we speak of *the* colour of the table, we only mean the sort of colour which it will seem to have to a normal spectator from an ordinary point of view under usual conditions of light. But the other colours which appear under other conditions have just as good a right to be considered real; and therefore, to avoid favouritism, we are compelled to deny that, in itself, the table has any one particular colour.

The same thing applies to the texture. With the naked eye one can see the grain, but otherwise the table looks smooth and even. If we look at it through a microscope, we should see roughnesses and hills and valleys, and all sorts of differences that are imperceptible to the naked eye. Which of these is the "real" table? We are naturally tempted to say that what we see through the microscope is more real, but that in turn would be changed by a still more powerful microscope. If, then, we cannot trust what we see with the naked eye, why should we trust what we see through a microscope? Thus, again, the confidence in our senses with which we began deserts us.

The *shape* of the table is no better. We are all in the habit of judging as to the "real" shapes of things, and we do this so unreflectingly that we come to think we actually see the real shapes. But, in fact, as we all have to learn if we try to draw, a given thing looks different in shape from every different point of view. If our table is "really" rectangular, it will look, from almost all points of view, as if it had two acute angles and two obtuse angles. If opposite sides are parallel, they will look as if they converged to a point away from the spectator; if they are of equal length, they will look as if the nearer side were longer. All these things are not commonly noticed in looking at a table, because experience has taught us to construct the "real" shape from the apparent shape, and the "real" shape is what interests us as practical men. But the "real" shape is not what we see; it is something inferred from what we see. And what we see is constantly changing in shape as we move about the room; so that here again the senses seem not to give us the truth about the table itself, but only about the appearance of the table.

Similar difficulties arise when we consider the sense of touch. It is true that the table always gives us a sensation of hardness, and we feel that it resists pressure. But the sensation we obtain depends upon how hard we press the table and also upon what part of the body we press with; thus the various sensations due to various pressures or various parts of the body cannot be supposed to reveal *directly* any definite property of the table, but at most to be *signs* of some property which perhaps *causes* all the sensations, but is not actually apparent in any of them. And the same applies still more obviously to the sounds which can be elicited by rapping the table.

Thus it becomes evident that the real table, if there is one, is not the same as what we immediately experience by sight or touch or hearing. The real table, if there is one, is not *immediately* known to us at all, but must be an inference from what is immediately known. Hence, two very difficult questions at once arise; namely, (1) Is there a real table at all? (2) If so, what sort of object can it be?

It will help us in considering these questions to have a few simple terms of which the meaning is definite and clear. Let us give the name of "sense-data" to the things that are immediately known in sensation: such things as colours, sounds, smells, hardnesses, roughnesses, and so on. We shall give the name "sensation" to the experience of being immediately aware of these things. Thus, whenever we see a colour, we have a sensation *of* the colour, but the colour itself is a sense-datum, not a sensation. The color is that *of* which we are immediately aware, and the awareness itself is the sensation. It is plain that if we are to know anything about the table, it must be by means of the sense-data—brown colour, oblong shape, smoothness, etc.—which we associate with the table; but for the reasons which have been given, we cannot say that the table *is* the sense-data, or even that the sense-data are directly properties of the table. Thus a problem arises as to the relation of the sense-data to the real table, supposing there is such a thing.

The real table, if it exists, we will call a "physical object." Thus we have to consider the relation of sense-data to physical objects. The collection of all physical objects is called "matter." Thus our two questions may be re-stated as follows: (1) Is there any such thing as matter? (2) If so, what is its nature?

The philosopher who first brought prominently forward the reasons for regarding the immediate objects of our senses as not existing independently of us was Bishop Berkeley (1685–1753). His *Three Dialogues between Hylas and Philonous, in Opposition to Sceptics and Atheists,* undertake to prove that there is no such thing as matter at all, and that the world consists of nothing but minds and their ideas. Hylas has hitherto believed in matter, but he is no match for Philonous, who mercilessly drives him into contradictions and paradoxes, and makes his own denial of matter seem, in the end, as if it were almost common sense. The arguments employed are of very different value: some are important and sound, others are confused or quibbling. But Berkeley retains the merit of having shown that the existence of matter is capable of being denied without absurdity, and that if there are any things that exist independently of us they cannot be the immediate objects of our sensations.

There are two different questions involved when we ask whether matter exists, and it is important to keep them clear. We commonly mean by "matter" something which is opposed to "mind," something which we think of as occupying space and as radically incapable of any sort of thought or consciousness. It is chiefly in this sense that Berkeley denies matter; that is to say, he does not deny that the sense-data which we commonly take as signs of the existence of the table are really signs of the existence of *something* independent of us, but he does deny that this something is non-mental, that it is neither mind nor ideas entertained by some mind. He admits that there must be something which continues to exist when we go out of the room or shut our eyes, and that what we call seeing the table does really give us reason for believing in something which persists even when we are not seeing it. But he thinks that this something cannot be radically different in nature from what we see, and cannot be independent of seeing altogether, though it must be independent of *our* seeing. He is thus led to regard the "real" table as an idea in the mind of God. Such an idea has the required permanence and independence of ourselves, without being—as matter would otherwise be—something quite unknowable, in the sense that we can only infer it, and can never be directly and immediately aware of it.

Other philosophers since Berkeley have also held that, although the table does not depend for its existence upon being seen by me, it does depend upon being seen (or otherwise apprehended in sensation) by *some* mind—not necessarily the mind of God, but more often the whole collective mind of the universe. This they hold, as Berkeley does, chiefly because they think there can be nothing real—or at any rate nothing known to be real—except minds and their thoughts and feelings. We might state the argument by which they support their view in some such way as this: "Whatever can be thought of is an idea in the mind of the person thinking of it; therefore nothing can be thought of except ideas in minds; therefore anything else is inconceivable, and what is inconceivable cannot exist."

Such an argument, in my opinion, is fallacious; and of course those who advance it do not put it so shortly or so crudely. But whether valid or not, the argument has been very widely advanced in one form or another; and very many philosophers, perhaps a majority, have held that there is nothing real except minds and their ideas. Such philosophers are called "idealists." When they come to explaining matter, they either say, like Berkeley, that matter is really nothing but a collection of ideas, or they say, like Leibniz (1646–1716), that what appears as matter is really a collection of more or less rudimentary minds.

But these philosophers, though they deny matter as opposed to mind, nevertheless, in another sense, admit matter. It will be remembered that we asked two questions; namely, (1) Is there a real table at all? (2) If so, what sort of object can it be? Now both Berkeley and Leibniz admit that there is a real table, but Berkeley says it is certain ideas in the mind of God, and Leibniz says it is a colony of souls. Thus both of them answer our first question in the affirmative, and only diverge from the views of ordinary mortals in their answer to our second question. In fact, almost all philosophers seem to be agreed that there is a real table: they almost all agree that, however much our sense-data—colour, shape, smoothness, etc.—may depend upon us, yet their occurrence is a sign of something existing independently of us, something differing, perhaps, completely from our sense-data, and yet to be regarded as causing those sense-data whenever we are in a suitable relation to the real table.

Now obviously this point in which the philosophers are agreed—the view that there *is* a real table, whatever its nature may be—is vitally important, and it will be worth while to consider what reasons there are for accepting this view before we go on to the further question as to the nature of the real table. Our next chapter, therefore, will be concerned with the reasons for supposing that there is a real table at all.

Before we go farther it will be well to consider for a moment what it is that we have discovered so far. It has appeared that, if we take any common object of the sort that is supposed to be known by the senses, what the senses *immediately* tell us is not the truth about the object as it is apart from us, but only the truth about certain sense-data which, so far as we can see, depend upon the relations between us and the object. Thus what we directly see and feel is merely "appearance," which we believe to be a sign of some "reality" behind. But if the reality is not what appears, have we any means of knowing whether there is any reality at all? And if so, have we any means of finding out what it is like?

Such questions are bewildering, and it is difficult to know that even the strangest hypotheses may not be true. Thus our familiar table, which has roused but the slightest thoughts in us hitherto, has become a problem full of surprising possibilities. The one thing we know about it is that it is not what it seems. Beyond this modest result, so far, we have the most complete liberty of conjecture. Leibniz tells us it is a community of souls; Berkeley tells us it is an idea in the mind of God; sober science, scarcely less wonderful, tells us it is a vast collection of electric charges in violent motion.

Among these surprising possibilities, doubt suggests that perhaps there is no table at all. Philosophy, if it cannot *answer* so many questions as we could wish, has at least the power of *asking* questions which increase the interest of the world, and show the strangeness and wonder lying just below the surface even in the commonest things of daily life.

CHAPTER II: THE EXISTENCE OF MATTER

In this chapter we have to ask ourselves whether, in any sense at all, there is such a thing as matter. Is there a table which has a certain intrinsic nature, and continues to exist when I am not looking, or is the table merely a product of my imagination, a dream-table in a very prolonged dream? This question is of the greatest importance. For if we cannot be sure of the independent existence of objects, we cannot be sure of the independent existence of other people's bodies, and therefore still less of other people's minds, since we have no grounds for believing in their minds except such as are derived from observing their bodies. Thus if we cannot be sure of the independent existence of objects, we shall be left alone in a desert—it may be that the whole outer world is nothing but a dream, and that we alone exist. This is an uncomfortable possibility; but although it cannot be strictly *proved* to be false, there is not the slightest reason to suppose that it is true. In this chapter we have to see why this is the case.

Before we embark upon doubtful matters, let us try to find some more or less fixed point from which to start. Although we are doubting the physical existence of the table, we are not doubting the existence of the sense-data which made us think there was a table; we are not doubting that, while we look, a certain colour and shape appear to us, and while we press, a certain sensation of hardness is experienced by us. All this, which is psychological, we are not calling in question. In fact, whatever else may be doubtful, some at least of our immediate experiences seem absolutely certain.

Descartes (1596–1650), the founder of modern philosophy, invented a method which may still be used with profit—the method of systematic doubt. He determined that he would believe nothing which he did not see quite clearly and distinctly to be true. Whatever he could bring himself to doubt, he would doubt, until he saw reason for not doubting it. By applying this method he gradually became convinced that the only existence of which he could be *quite* certain was his own. He imagined a deceitful demon, who presented unreal things to his senses in a perpetual phantasmagoria; it might be very improbable that such a demon existed, but still it was possible, and therefore doubt concerning things perceived by the senses was possible.

But doubt concerning his own existence was not possible, for if he did not exist, no demon could deceive him. If he doubted, he must exist; if he had any experiences whatever, he must exist. Thus his own existence was an absolute certainty to him. "I think, therefore I am," he said (*Cogito, ergo sum*); and on the basis of this certainty he set to work to build up again the world of knowledge which his doubt had laid in ruins. By inventing the method of doubt, and by showing that subjective things are the most certain, Descartes performed a great service

to philosophy, and one which makes him still useful to all students of the subject.

But some care is needed in using Descartes' argument. "*I* think, therefore *I* am" says rather more than is strictly certain. It might seem as though we were quite sure of being the same person to-day as we were yesterday, and this is no doubt true in some sense. But the real Self is as hard to arrive at as the real table, and does not seem to have that absolute, convincing certainty that belongs to particular experiences. When I look at my table and see a certain brown colour, what is quite certain at once is not "*I* am seeing a brown colour," but rather, "a brown colour is being seen." This of course involves something (or somebody) which (or who) sees the brown colour; but it does not of itself involve that more or less permanent person whom we call "I." So far as immediate certainty goes, it might be that the something which sees the brown colour is quite momentary, and not the same as the something which has some different experience the next moment.

Thus it is our particular thoughts and feelings that have primitive certainty. And this applies to dreams and hallucinations as well as to normal perceptions: when we dream or see a ghost, we certainly do have the sensations we think we have, but for various reasons it is held that no physical object corresponds to these sensations. Thus the certainty of our knowledge of our own experiences does not have to be limited in any way to allow for exceptional cases. Here, therefore, we have, for what it is worth, a solid basis from which to begin our pursuit of knowledge.

The problem we have to consider is this: Granted that we are certain of our own sense-data, have we any reason for regarding them as signs of the existence of something else, which we can call the physical object? When we have enumerated all the sensations which we should naturally regard as connected with the table, have we said all there is to say about the table, or is there still something else—something not a sensation, something which persists when we go out of the room? Common sense unhesitatingly answers that there is. What can be bought and sold and pushed about and have a cloth laid on it, and so on, cannot be a *mere* collection of sense-data. If the cloth completely hides the table, we shall derive no sense-data from the table, and therefore, if the table were merely sense-data, it would have ceased to exist, and the cloth would be suspended in empty air, resting, by a miracle, in the place where the table formerly was. This seems plainly absurd; but whoever wishes to become a philosopher must learn not to be frightened by absurdities.

One great reason why it is felt that we must secure a physical object in addition to the sense-data, is that we want the *same* object for different people. When ten people are sitting round a dinner-table, it seems preposterous to maintain that they are not seeing the same tablecloth, the same knives and forks and spoons and glasses. But the sense-data are private to each separate person; what is immediately present to the sight of one is not immediately present to the sight of another: they all see things from slightly different points of view, and therefore see them slightly differently. Thus, if there are to be public neutral objects, which can be in some sense known to many different people, there must be something over and above the private and particular sense-data which appear to various people. What reason, then, have we for believing that there are such public neutral objects?

The first answer that naturally occurs to one is that, although different people may see the table slightly differently, still they all see more or less similar things when they look at the table, and the variations in what they see follow the laws of perspective and reflection of light, so that it is easy to arrive at a permanent object underlying all the different people's sense-data. I bought my table from the former occupant of my room; I could not buy *his* sense-data, which died when he went away, but I could and did buy the confident expectation of more or less similar sense-data. Thus it is the fact that different people have similar sense-data, and that one person in a given place at different times has similar sense-data, which makes us suppose that over and above the sense-data there is a permanent public object which underlies or causes the sense-data of various people and various times.

Now in so far as the above considerations depend upon supposing that there are other people besides ourselves, they beg the very question at issue. Other people are represented to me by certain sense-data, such as the sight of them or the sound of their voices, and if I had no reason to believe that there were physical objects independent of my sense-data, I should have no reason to believe that other people exist except as part of my dream. Thus, when we are trying to show that there must be objects independent of our own sense-data, we cannot appeal to the testimony of other people, since this testimony itself consists of sense-data, and does not reveal other people's experiences unless our own sense-data are signs of things existing independently of us. We must therefore, if possible, find, in our own purely private experiences, characteristics which show, or tend to show, that there are in the world things other than ourselves and our private experiences.

In one sense it must be admitted that we can never *prove* the existence of things other than ourselves and our experiences. No logical absurdity results from the hypothesis that the world consists of myself and my thoughts and feelings and sensations, and that everything else is mere fancy. In dreams a very complicated world may seem to be present, and yet on waking we find it was a delusion; that is to say, we find that the sense-data in the dream do not appear to have corresponded with such physical objects as we should naturally infer from our sense-data. (It is true that, when the physical world is assumed, it is possible to find physical causes for the sense-data in dreams: a door banging, for instance, may cause us to dream of a naval engagement. But although, in this case, there is a physical *cause* for the sense-data, there is not a physical object *corresponding* to the sense-data in the way in which an actual naval battle would correspond.) There is no logical impossibility in the supposition that the whole of life is a dream, in which we ourselves create all the objects that come before us. But although this is not logically impossible, there is no reason whatever to suppose that it is true; and it is, in fact, a less simple hypothesis, viewed as a means of accounting for the facts of our own life, than the common-sense hypothesis that there really are objects independent of us, whose action on us causes our sensations.

The way in which simplicity comes in from supposing that there really are physical objects is easily seen. If the cat appears at one moment in one part of the room, and at another in another part, it is natural to suppose that it has moved from the one to the other, passing over a series of intermediate positions. But if it is merely a set of sense-data, it cannot have ever been in any place where I did not see it; thus we shall have to suppose that it did not exist at all while I was not looking, but suddenly sprang into being in a new place. If the cat exists whether I see it or not, we can understand from our own experience how it gets hungry between one meal and the next;

but if it does not exist when I am not seeing it, it seems odd that appetite should grow during non-existence as fast as during existence. And if the cat consists only of sense-data, it cannot be *hungry,* since no hunger but my own can be a sense-datum to me. Thus the behaviour of the sense-data which represent the cat to me, though it seems quite natural when regarded as an expression of hunger, becomes utterly inexplicable when regarded as mere movements and changes of patches of colour, which are as incapable of hunger as a triangle is of playing football.

But the difficulty in the case of the cat is nothing compared to the difficulty in the case of human beings. When human beings speak—that is, when we hear certain noises which we associate with ideas, and simultaneously see certain motions of lips and expressions of face—it is very difficult to suppose that what we hear is not the expression of a thought, as we know it would be if we emitted the same sounds. Of course similar things happen in dreams, where we are mistaken as to the existence of other people. But dreams are more or less suggested by what we call waking life, and are capable of being more or less accounted for on scientific principles if we assume that there really is a physical world. Thus every principle of simplicity urges us to adopt the natural view, that there really are objects other than our selves and our sense-data which have an existence not dependent upon our perceiving them.

Of course it is not by argument that we originally come by our belief in an independent external world. We find this belief ready in ourselves as soon as we begin to reflect: it is what may be called an *instinctive* belief. We should never have been led to question this belief but for the fact that, at any rate in the case of sight, it seems as if the sense-datum itself were instinctively believed to be the independent object, whereas argument shows that the object cannot be identical with the sense-datum. This discovery, however—which is not at all paradoxical in the case of taste and smell and sound, and only slightly so in the case of touch—leaves undiminished our instinctive belief that there *are* objects *corresponding* to our sense-data. Since this belief does not lead to any difficulties, but on the contrary tends to simplify and systematise our account of our experiences, there seems no good reason for rejecting it. We may therefore admit—though with a slight doubt derived from dreams—that the external world does really exist, and is not wholly dependent for its existence upon our continuing to perceive it.

The argument which has led us to this conclusion is doubtless less strong than we could wish, but it is typical of many philosophical arguments, and it is therefore worth while to consider briefly its general character and validity. All knowledge, we find, must be built up upon our instinctive beliefs, and if these are rejected, nothing is left. But among our instinctive beliefs some are much stronger than others, while many have, by habit and association, become entangled with other beliefs, not really instinctive, but falsely supposed to be part of what is believed instinctively.

Philosophy should show us the hierarchy of our instinctive beliefs, beginning with those we hold most strongly, and presenting each as much isolated and as free from irrelevant additions as possible. It should take care to show that, in the form in which they are finally set forth, our instinctive beliefs do not clash, but form a harmonious system. There can never be any reason for rejecting one instinctive belief except that it clashes with others; thus, if they are found to harmonise, the whole system becomes worthy of acceptance.

It is of course *possible* that all or any of our beliefs may be mistaken, and therefore all ought to be held with at least some slight element of doubt. But we cannot have *reason* to reject a belief except on the ground of some other belief. Hence, by organising our instinctive beliefs and their consequences, by considering which among them it is most possible, if necessary, to modify or abandon, we can arrive, on the basis of accepting as our sole data what we instinctively believe, at an orderly systematic organisation of our knowledge, in which, though the *possibility* of error remains, its likelihood is diminished by the interrelation of the parts and by the critical scrutiny which has preceded acquiescence.

This function, at least, philosophy can perform. Most philosophers, rightly or wrongly, believe that philosophy can do much more than this—that it can give us knowledge, not otherwise attainable, concerning the universe as a whole, and concerning the nature of ultimate reality. Whether this be the case or not, the more modest function we have spoken of can certainly be performed by philosophy, and certainly suffices, for those who have once begun to doubt the adequacy of common sense, to justify the arduous and difficult labours that philosophical problems involve.

DAVID HUME

An Inquiry concerning Human Understanding*

SECTION II. OF THE ORIGIN OF IDEAS

Everyone will readily allow that there is a considerable difference between the perceptions of the mind when a man feels the pain of excessive heat or the pleasure of moderate warmth, and when he afterwards recalls to his memory this sensation or anticipates it by his imagination. These faculties may mimic or copy the perceptions of the senses, but they never can entirely reach the force and vivacity of the original sentiment. The utmost we say of them, even when they operate with greatest vigor, is that they represent their object in so lively a manner that we could *almost* say we feel or see it. But, except the mind be disordered by disease or madness, they never can arrive at such a pitch of vivacity as to render these perceptions altogether undistinguishable. All the colors of poetry, however splendid, can never paint natural objects in such a manner as to make the description be taken for a real landscape. The most lively thought is still inferior to the dullest sensation.

We may observe a like distinction to run through all the other perceptions of the mind. A man in a fit of anger is actuated in a very different manner from one who only thinks of that emotion. If you tell me that any person is in love, I easily understand your meaning and form a just conception of his situation, but never can mistake that conception for the real disorders and agitations of the passion. When we reflect on our past sentiments and affections, our thought is a faithful mirror and copies its objects truly, but the colors which it employs are faint and dull in comparison of those in which our original perceptions were clothed. It requires no nice discern-

*David Hume, *An Inquiry Concerning Human Understanding*, Sections II, IV–VII. First published in 1748.

ment or metaphysical head to mark the distinction between them.

Here, therefore, we may divide all the perceptions of the mind into two classes or species, which are distinguished by their different degrees of force and vivacity. The less forcible and lively are commonly denominated "thoughts" or "ideas." The other species want a name in our language, and in most others; I suppose, because it was not requisite for any but philosophical purposes to rank them under a general term or appellation. Let us, therefore, use a little freedom and call them "impressions," employing that word in a sense somewhat different from the usual. By the term "impression," then, I mean all our more lively perceptions, when we hear, or see, or feel, or love, or hate, or desire, or will. And impressions are distinguished from ideas, which are the less lively perceptions of which we are conscious when we reflect on any of those sensations or movements above mentioned.

Nothing, at first view, may seem more unbounded than the thought of man, which not only escapes all human power and authority, but is not even restrained within the limits of nature and reality. To form monsters and join incongruous shapes and appearances costs the imagination no more trouble than to conceive the most natural and familiar objects. And while the body is confined to one planet, along which it creeps with pain and difficulty, the thought can in an instant transport us into the most distant regions of the universe, or even beyond the universe into the unbounded chaos where nature is supposed to lie in total confusion. What never was seen or heard of, may yet be conceived, nor is anything beyond the power of thought except what implies an absolute contradiction.

But though our thought seems to possess this

unbounded liberty, we shall find upon a nearer examination that it is really confined within very narrow limits, and that all this creative power of the mind amounts to no more than the faculty of compounding, transposing, augmenting, or diminishing the materials afforded us by the senses and experience. When we think of a golden mountain, we only join two consistent ideas, "gold" and "mountain," with which we were formerly acquainted. A virtuous horse we can conceive, because, from our own feeling, we can conceive virtue; and this we may unite to the figure and shape of a horse, which is an animal familiar to us. In short, all the materials of thinking are derived either from our outward or inward sentiment; the mixture and composition of these belongs alone to the mind and will, or, to express myself in philosophical language, all our ideas or more feeble perceptions are copies of our impressions or more lively ones.

To prove this, the two following arguments will, I hope, be sufficient. *First,* when we analyze our thoughts or ideas, however compounded or sublime, we always find that they resolve themselves into such simple ideas as were copied from a precedent feeling or sentiment. Even those ideas which at first view seem the most wide of this origin are found, upon a nearer scrutiny, to be derived from it. The idea of God, as meaning an infinitely intelligent, wise, and good Being, arises from reflecting on the operations of our own mind and augmenting, without limit, those qualities of goodness and wisdom. We may prosecute this inquiry to what length we please; where we shall always find that every idea which we examine is copied from a similar impression. Those who would assert that this position is not universally true, nor without exception, have only one, and that an easy, method of refuting it by producing that idea which, in their opinion, is not derived from this source. It will then be incumbent on us, if we would maintain our doctrine, to produce the impression or lively perception which corresponds to it.

Secondly, if it happen, from a defect of the organ, that a man is not susceptible of any species of sensation, we always find that he is as little susceptible of the correspondent idea. A blind man can form no notion of colors, a deaf man of sounds. Restore either of them that sense in which he is deficient by opening this new inlet for his sensations, you also open an inlet for the ideas, and he finds no difficulty in conceiving these objects. The case is the same if the object proper for exciting any sensation has never

been applied to the organ. A Laplander . . . has no notion of the relish of wine. And though there are few or no instances of a like deficiency in the mind where a person has never felt or is wholly incapable of a sentiment or passion that belongs to his species, yet we find the same observation to take place in a less degree. A man of mild manners can form no idea of inveterate revenge or cruelty, nor can a selfish heart easily conceive the heights of friendship and generosity. It is readily allowed that other beings may possess many senses of which we can have no conception, because the ideas of them have never been introduced to us in the only manner by which an idea can have access to the mind, to wit, by the actual feeling and sensation.

There is, however, one contradictory phenomenon which may prove that it is not absolutely impossible for ideas to arise independent of their correspondent impressions. I believe it will readily be allowed that the several distinct ideas of color, which enter by the eye, or those of sound, which are conveyed by the ear, are really different from each other, though at the same time resembling. Now, if this be true of different colors, it must be no less so of the different shades of the same color; and each shade produces a distinct idea, independent of the rest. For if this should be denied, it is possible, by the continual gradation of shades, to run a color insensibly into what is most remote from it; and if you will not allow any of the means to be different, you cannot, without absurdity, deny the extremes to be the same. Suppose, therefore, a person to have enjoyed his sight for thirty years and to have become perfectly acquainted with colors of all kinds, except one particular shade of blue, for instance, which it never has been his fortune to meet with; let all the different shades of that color, except that single one, be placed before him, descending gradually from the deepest to the lightest, it is plain that he will perceive a blank where that shade is wanting, and will be sensible that there is a greater distance in that place between the contiguous colors than in any other. Now I ask whether it be possible for him, from his own imagination, to supply this deficiency and raise up to himself the idea of that particular shade, though it had never been conveyed to him by his senses? I believe there are few but will be of opinion that he can; and this may serve as a proof that the simple ideas are not always, in every instance, derived from the correspondent impressions, though this instance is so singular that it is scarcely worth our observing, and does not merit that for it alone we should alter our general maxim.

Here, therefore, is a proposition which not only seems in itself simple and intelligible, but, if a proper use were made of it, might render every dispute equally intelligible, and banish all that jargon which has so long taken possession of metaphysical reasonings and drawn disgrace upon them. All ideas, especially abstract ones, are naturally faint and obscure. The mind has but a slender hold of them. They are apt to be confounded with other resembling ideas; and when we have often employed any term, though without a distinct meaning, we are apt to imagine it has a determinate idea annexed to it. On the contrary, all impressions, that is, all sensations either outward or inward, are strong and vivid. The limits between them are more exactly determined, nor is it easy to fall into any error or mistake with regard to them. When we entertain, therefore, any suspicion that a philosophical term is employed without any meaning or idea (as is but too frequent), we need but inquire, *from what impression is that supposed idea derived?* And if it be impossible to assign any, this will serve to confirm our suspicion. By bringing ideas in so clear a light, we may reasonably hope to remove all dispute which may arise concerning their nature and reality.[1]

SECTION IV. SKEPTICAL DOUBTS CONCERNING THE OPERATIONS OF THE UNDERSTANDING

PART I

All the objects of human reason or inquiry may naturally be divided into two kinds, to wit, "Relations of Ideas," and "Matters of Fact." Of the first kind are the sciences of Geometry, Algebra, and Arithmetic, and, in short, every affirmation which is either intuitively or demonstratively certain. *That the square of the hypotenuse is equal to the square of the two sides* is a proposition which expresses a relation between these figures. *That three times five is equal to the half of thirty* expresses a relation between these numbers. Propositions of this kind are discoverable by the mere operation of thought, without dependence on what is anywhere existent in the universe. Though there never were a circle or triangle

in nature, the truths demonstrated by Euclid would forever retain their certainty and evidence.

Matters of fact, which are the second objects of human reason, are not ascertained in the same manner, nor is our evidence of their truth, however great, of a like nature with the foregoing. The contrary of every matter of fact is still possible, because it can never imply a contradiction and is conceived by the mind with the same facility and distinctness as if ever so conformable to reality. *That the sun will not rise tomorrow* is no less intelligible a proposition and implies no more contradiction than the affirmation *that it will rise.* We should in vain, therefore, attempt to demonstrate its falsehood. Were it demonstratively false, it would imply a contradiction and could never be distinctly conceived by the mind.

It may, therefore, be a subject worthy of curiosity to inquire what is the nature of that evidence which assures us of any real existence and matter of fact beyond the present testimony of our senses or the records of our memory. This part of philosophy, it is observable, had been little cultivated either by the ancients or moderns; and, therefore, our doubts and errors in the prosecution of so important an inquiry may be the more excusable while we march through such difficult paths without any guide or direction. They may even prove useful by exciting curiosity and destroying that implicit faith and security which is the bane of all reasoning and free inquiry. The discovery of defects in the common philosophy, if any such there be, will not, I presume, be a discouragement, but rather an incitement, as is usual, to attempt something more full and satisfactory than has yet been proposed to the public.

All reasonings concerning matter of fact seem to be founded on the relation of *cause* and *effect.* By means of that relation alone we can go beyond the evidence of our memory and senses. If you were to ask a man why he believes any matter of fact which is absent, for instance, that his friend is in the country or in France, he would give you a reason, and this reason would be some other fact: as a letter received from him or the knowledge of his former resolutions and promises. A man finding a watch or any other machine in a desert island would conclude that there had once been men in that island. All our reasonings concerning fact are of the same nature. And here it is constantly supposed that there is a connection between the present fact and that which is inferred from it. Were there nothing to bind them together, the inference would be entirely precarious. The hearing of an articulate voice and rational discourse in the dark assures us of the presence of some person. Why? Because these are the effects of the human make and fabric, and closely connected with it. If we anatomize all the other reasonings of this nature, we shall find that they are founded on the relation of cause and effect, and that this relation is either near or remote, direct or collateral. Heat and light are collateral effects of fire, and the one effect may justly be inferred from the other.

If we would satisfy ourselves, therefore, concerning the nature of that evidence which assures us of matters of fact, we must inquire how we arrive at the knowledge of cause and effect.

I shall venture to affirm, as a general proposition which admits of no exception, that the knowledge of this relation is not, in any instance, attained by reasonings *a priori,* but arises entirely from experience, when we find that any particular objects are constantly conjoined with each other. Let an object be presented to a man of ever so strong natural reason and abilities—if that object be entirely new to him, he will not be able, by the most accurate examination of its sensible qualities, to discover any of its causes or effects. Adam, though his rational faculties be supposed, at the very first, entirely perfect, could not have inferred from the fluidity and transparency of water that it would suffocate him, or from the light and warmth of fire that it would consume him. No object ever discovers, by the qualities which appear to the senses, either the causes which produced it or the effects which will arise from it; nor can our reason, unassisted by experience, ever draw any inference concerning real existence and matter of fact.

This proposition, *that causes and effects are discoverable, not by reason, but by experience,* will readily be admitted with regard to such objects as we remember to have once been altogether unknown to us, since we must be conscious of the utter inability which we then lay under of foretelling what would arise from them. Present two smooth pieces of marble to a man who has no tincture of natural philosophy; he will never discover that they will adhere together in such a manner as to require great force to separate them in a direct line, while they make so small a resistance to a lateral pressure. Such events as bear little analogy to the common course of nature are also readily confessed to be known only by experience, nor does any man imagine that the explosion of gunpowder or the attraction of a loadstone could

ever be discovered by arguments *a priori.* In like manner, when an effect is supposed to depend upon an intricate machinery or secret structure of parts, we make no difficulty in attributing all our knowledge of it to experience. Who will assert that he can give the ultimate reason why milk or bread is proper nourishment for a man, not for a lion or tiger?

But the same truth may not appear at first sight to have the same evidence with regard to events which have become familiar to us from our first appearance in the world, which bear a close analogy to the whole course of nature, and which are supposed to depend on the simple qualities of objects without any secret structure of parts. We are apt to imagine that we could discover these effects by the mere operation of our reason without experience. We fancy that, were we brought on a sudden into this world, we could at first have inferred that one billiard ball would communicate motion to another upon impulse, and that we needed not to have waited for the event in order to pronounce with certainty concerning it. Such is the influence of custom that where it is strongest it not only covers our natural ignorance but even conceals itself, and seems not to take place, merely because it is found in the highest degree.

But to convince us that all the laws of nature and all the operations of bodies without exception are known only by experience, the following reflections may perhaps suffice. Were any object presented to us, and were we required to pronounce concerning the effect which will result from it without consulting past observation, after what manner, I beseech you, must the mind proceed in this operation? It must invent or imagine some event which it ascribes to the object as its effect; and it is plain that this invention must be entirely arbitrary. The mind can never possibly find the effect in the supposed cause by the most accurate scrutiny and examination. For the effect is totally different from the cause, and consequently can never be discovered in it. Motion in the second billiard ball is a distinct event from motion in the first, nor is there anything in the one to suggest the smallest hint of the other. A stone or piece of metal raised into the air and left without any support immediately falls. But to consider the matter *a priori,* is there anything we discover in this situation which can beget the idea of a downward rather than an upward or any other motion in the stone or metal?

And as the first imagination or invention of a

particular effect in all natural operations is arbitrary where we consult not experience, so must we also esteem the supposed tie or connection between the cause and effect which binds them together and renders it impossible that any other effect could result from the operation of that cause. When I see, for instance, a billiard ball moving in a straight line toward another, even suppose motion in the second ball should by accident be suggested to me as the result of their contact or impulse, may I not conceive that a hundred different events might as well follow from that cause? May not both these balls remain at absolute rest? May not the first ball return in a straight line or leap off the second in any line or direction? All these suppositions are consistent and conceivable. Why, then, should we give the preference to one which is no more consistent or conceivable than the rest? All our reasonings *a priori* will never be able to show us any foundation for this preference.

In a word, then, every effect is a distinct event from its cause. It could not, therefore, be discovered in the cause, and the first invention or conception of it *a priori,* must be entirely arbitrary. And even after it is suggested, the conjunction of it with the cause must appear equally arbitrary, since there are always many other effects which, to reason, must seem fully as consistent and natural. In vain, therefore, should we pretend to determine any single event or infer any cause or effect without the assistance of observation and experience.

Hence we may discover the reason why no philosopher who is rational and modest has ever pretended to assign the ultimate cause of any natural operation, or to show distinctly the action of that power which produces any single effect in the universe. It is confessed that the utmost effort of human reason is to reduce the principles productive of natural phenomena to a greater simplicity, and to resolve the many particular effects into a few general causes, by means of reasonings from analogy, experience, and observation. But as to the causes of these general causes, we should in vain attempt their discovery, nor shall we ever be able to satisfy ourselves by any particular explication of them. These ultimate springs and principles are totally shut up from human curiosity and inquiry. Elasticity, gravity, cohesion of parts, communication of motion by impulse— these are probably the ultimate causes and principles which we shall ever discover in nature; and we may

esteem ourselves sufficiently happy if, by accurate inquiry and reasoning, we can trace up the particular phenomena to, or near to, these general principles. The most perfect philosophy of the natural kind only staves off our ignorance a little longer, as perhaps the most perfect philosophy of the moral or metaphysical kind serves only to discover larger portions of it. Thus the observation of human blindness and weakness is the result of all philosophy, and meets us, at every turn, in spite of our endeavors to elude or avoid it.

Nor is geometry, when taken into the assistance of natural philosophy, ever able to remedy this defect or lead us into the knowledge of ultimate causes by all that accuracy of reasoning for which it is so justly celebrated. Every part of mixed mathematics proceeds upon the supposition that certain laws are established by nature in her operations, and abstract reasonings are employed either to assist experience in the discovery of these laws or to determine their influence in particular instances where it depends upon any precise degree of distance and quantity. Thus it is a law of motion, discovered by experience, that the moment or force of any body in motion is in the compound ratio or proportion of its solid contents and its velocity, and, consequently, that a small force may remove the greatest obstacle or raise the greatest weight if by any contrivance or machinery we can increase the velocity of that force so as to make it an overmatch for its antagonist. Geometry assists us in the application of this law by giving us the just dimensions of all the parts and figures which can enter into any species of machine, but still the discovery of the law itself is owing merely to experience; and all the abstract reasonings in the world could never lead us one step toward the knowledge of it. When we reason *a priori* and consider merely any object or cause as it appears to the mind, independent of all observation, it never could suggest to us the notion of any distinct object, such as its effect, much less show us the inseparable and inviolable connection between them. A man must be very sagacious who could discover by reasoning that crystal is the effect of heat, and ice of cold, without being previously acquainted with the operation of these qualities.

PART II

But we have not yet attained any tolerable satisfaction with regard to the question first proposed. Each solution still gives rise to a new question as difficult as the foregoing and leads us on to further inquiries. When it is asked, *What is the nature of all our reasonings concerning matter of fact?* the proper answer seems to be, That they are founded on the relation of cause and effect. When again it is asked, *What is the foundation of all our reasonings and conclusions concerning that relation?* it may be replied in one word, *experience*. But if we still carry on our sifting humor and ask, *What is the foundation of all conclusions from experience?* this implies a new question which may be of more difficult solution and explication. Philosophers that give themselves airs of superior wisdom and sufficiency have a hard task when they encounter persons of inquisitive dispositions, who push them from every corner to which they retreat, and who are sure at last to bring them to some dangerous dilemma. The best expedient to prevent this confusion is to be modest in our pretensions and even to discover the difficulty ourselves before it is objected to us. By this means we may make a kind of merit of our very ignorance.

I shall content myself in this section with an easy task and shall pretend only to give a negative answer to the question here proposed. I say, then, that even after we have experience of the operations of cause and effect, our conclusions from that experience are *not* founded on reasoning or any process of understanding. This answer we must endeavor both to explain and to defend.

It must certainly be allowed that nature has kept us at a great distance from all her secrets and has afforded us only the knowledge of a few superficial qualities of objects, while she conceals from us those powers and principles on which the influence of these objects entirely depends. Our senses inform us of the color, weight, and consistency of bread, but neither sense nor reason can ever inform us of those qualities which fit it for the nourishment and support of the human body. Sight or feeling conveys an idea of the actual motion of bodies, but as to what wonderful force or power which would carry on a moving body forever in a continued change of place, and which bodies never lose but by communicating it to others, of this we cannot form the most distant conception. But notwithstanding this ignorance of natural powers[2] and principles, we always presume when we see like sensible qualities that they have like secret powers, and expect that effects similar to those which we have experienced will follow from them. If a body of like color and consistency with that bread which we have formerly eaten be presented to us, we make no scruple of repeating the experiment and foresee with certainty like nourishment and support. Now this is a process of the mind or thought of which I would willingly know the foundation. It is allowed on hands that there is no known connection between the sensible qualities and the secret powers, and, consequently, that the mind is not led to form such a conclusion concerning their constant and regular conjunction by anything which it knows of their nature. As to past *experience,* it can be allowed to give *direct* and *certain* information of those precise objects only, and that precise period of time which fell under its cognizance: But why this experience should be extended to future times and to other objects which, for aught we know, may be only in appearance similar, this is the main question on which I would insist. The bread which I formerly ate nourished me; that is, a body of such sensible qualities was, at that time, endued with such secret powers. But does it follow that other bread must also nourish me at another time, and that like sensible qualities must always be attended with like secret powers? the consequence seems nowise necessary. At least, it must be acknowledged that there is here a consequence drawn by the mind, a certain step taken, a process of thought, and an inference which wants to be explained. These two propositions are far from being the same: *I have found that such an object has always been attended with such an effect,* and *I foresee that other objects which are in appearance similar will be attended with similar effects*. I shall allow, if you please, that the one proposition may justly be inferred from the other: I know, in fact, that it always is inferred. But if you insist that the inference is made by a chain of reasoning, I desire you to produce that reasoning. The connection between these propositions is not intuitive. There is required a medium which may enable the mind to draw such an inference, if indeed it be drawn by reasoning and argument. What that medium is I must confess passes my comprehension; and it is incumbent on those to produce it who assert that it really exists and is the original of all our conclusions concerning matter of fact.

This negative argument must certainly, in process of time, become altogether convincing if many penetrating and able philosophers shall turn their inquiries this way, and no one be ever able to discover any connecting proposition or intermediate step which supports the understanding in this conclusion. But as the question is yet new, every reader may not trust so far to his own penetration as to conclude, because an argument escapes his inquiry, that therefore it does not really exist. For this reason it may be requisite to venture upon a more difficult task, and, enumerating all the branches of human knowledge, endeavor to show that none of them can afford such an argument.

All reasonings may be divided into two kinds, namely, demonstrative reasoning, or that concerning relations of ideas, and moral reasoning, or that concerning matter of fact and existence. That there are no demonstrative arguments in the case seems evident, since it implies no contradiction that the course of nature may change and that an object, seemingly like those which we have experienced, may be attended with different or contrary effects. May I not clearly and distinctly conceive that a body, falling from the clouds and which in all other respects resembles snow, has yet the taste of salt or feeling of fire? Is there any more intelligible proposition than to affirm that all the trees will flourish in December and January, and will decay in May and June? Now, whatever is intelligible and can be distinctly conceived implies no contradiction and can never be proved false by any demonstrative argument or abstract reasoning *a priori*.

If we be, therefore, engaged by arguments to put trust in past experience and make it the standard of our future judgment, these arguments must be probable only, or such as regard matter of fact and real existence, according to the division above mentioned. But that there is no argument of this kind must appear if our explication of that species of reasoning be admitted as solid and satisfactory. We have said that all arguments concerning existence are founded on the relation of cause and effect, that our knowledge of that relation is derived entirely from experience, and that all our experimental conclusions proceed upon the supposition that the future will be conformable to the past. To endeavor, therefore, the proof of this last supposition by probable arguments, or arguments regarding existence, must be evidently going in a circle and taking that for granted which is the very point in question.

In reality, all arguments from experience are founded on the similarity which we discover among natural objects, and by which we are induced to expect effects similar to those which we have found

to follow from such objects. And though none but a fool or madman will ever pretend to dispute the authority of experience or to reject that great guide of human life, it may surely be allowed a philosopher to have so much curiosity at least as to examine the principle of human nature which gives this mighty authority to experience and makes us draw advantage from that similarity which nature has placed among different objects. From causes which appear similar, we expect similar effects. This is the sum of our experimental conclusions. Now it seems evident that, if this conclusion were formed by reason, it would be as perfect at first, and upon one instance, as after ever so long a course of experience; but the case is far otherwise. Nothing so like as eggs, yet no one, on account of this appearing similarity, expects the same taste and relish in all of them. It is only after a long course of uniform experiments in any kind that we attain a firm reliance and security with regard to a particular event. Now, where is that process of reasoning which, from one instance, draws a conclusion so different from that which it infers from a hundred instances that are nowise different from that single one? This question I propose as much for the sake of information as with an intention of raising difficulties. I cannot find, I cannot imagine any such reasoning. But I keep my mind still open to instruction if anyone will vouchsafe to bestow it on me.

Should it be said that, from a number of uniform experiments, we *infer* a connection between the sensible qualities and the secret powers, this, I must confess, seems the same difficulty, couched in different terms. The question still occurs, On what process of argument is this *inference* founded? Where is the medium, the interposing ideas which join propositions so very wide of each other? It is confessed that the color, consistency, and other sensible qualities of bread appear not of themselves to have any connection with the secret powers of nourishment and support; for otherwise we could infer these secret powers from the first appearance of these sensible qualities without the aid of experience, contrary to the sentiment of all philosophers, and contrary to plain matter of fact. Here, then, is our natural state of ignorance with regard to the powers and influence of all objects. How is this remedied by experience? It only shows us a number of uniform effects resulting from certain objects, and teaches us that those particular objects, at that particular time, were endowed with such powers and forces. When a new object endowed with similar sensible qualities is produced, we expect similar powers and forces, and look for a like effect. From a body of like color and consistency with bread, we expect like nourishment and support. But this surely is a step or progress of the mind which wants to be explained. When a man says, *I have found, in all past instances, such sensible qualities, conjoined with such secret powers,* and when he says, *similar sensible qualities will always be conjoined with similar secret powers,* he is not guilty of a tautology, nor are these propositions in any respect the same. You say that the one proposition is an inference from the other; but you must confess that the inference is not intuitive, neither is it demonstrative. Of what nature is it then? To say it is experimental is begging the question. For all inferences from experience suppose, as their foundation, that the future will resemble the past and that similar powers will be conjoined with similar sensible qualities. If there be any suspicion that the course of nature may change, and that the past may be no rule for the future, all experience becomes useless and can give rise to no inference or conclusion. It is impossible, therefore, that any arguments are founded on the supposition of that resemblance. Let the course of things be allowed hitherto ever so regular, that alone, without some new argument or inference, proves not that for the future it will continue so. In vain do you pretend to have learned the nature of bodies from your past experience. Their secret nature, and consequently all their efforts and influence, may change without any change in their sensible qualities. This happens sometimes, and with regard to some objects. Why may it not happen always, and with regard to all objects? What logic, what process of argument secures you against this supposition? My practice, you say, refutes my doubts. But you mistake the purport of my question. As an agent, I am quite satisfied in the point; but as a philosopher who has some share of curiosity, I will not say skepticism, I want to learn the foundation of this inference. No reading, no inquiry has yet been able to remove my difficulty or give me satisfaction in a matter of such importance. Can I do better than propose the difficulty to the public, even though, perhaps, I have small hopes of obtaining a solution? We shall at least, by this means, be sensible of our ignorance, if we do not augment our knowledge.

I must confess that a man is guilty of unpardonable arrogance who concludes, because an argument has escaped his own investigation, that therefore it does not really exist. I must also confess that, though all the learned, for several ages, should have employed themselves in fruitless search upon any subject, it may still, perhaps, be rash to conclude positively that the subject must therefore pass all human comprehension. Even though we examine all the sources of our knowledge and conclude them unfit for such a subject, there may still remain a suspicion that the enumeration is not complete or the examination not accurate. But with regard to the present subject, there are some considerations which seem to remove all this accusation of arrogance or suspicion of mistake.

It is certain that the most ignorant and stupid peasants, nay infants, nay even brute beasts, improve by experience and learn the qualities of natural objects by observing the effects which result from them. When a child has felt the sensation of pain from touching the flame of a candle, he will be careful not to put his hand near any candle, but will expect a similar effect from a cause which is similar in its sensible qualities and appearance. If you assert, therefore, that the understanding of the child is led into this conclusion by any process of argument or ratiocination, I may justly require you to produce that argument, nor have you any pretense to refuse so equitable a demand. You cannot say that the argument is abstruse and may possibly escape your inquiry, since you confess that it is obvious to the capacity of a mere infant. If you hesitate, therefore, a moment or if, after reflection, you produce an intricate or profound argument, you, in a manner, give up the question and confess that it is not reasoning which engages us to suppose the past resembling the future, and to expect similar effects from causes which are to appearance similar. This is the proposition which I intended to enforce in the present section. If I be right, I pretend not to have made any mighty discovery. And if I be wrong, I must acknowledge myself to be indeed a very backward scholar, since I cannot now discover an argument which, it seems, was perfectly familiar to me long before I was out of my cradle.

SECTION V. SKEPTICAL SOLUTION OF THESE DOUBTS

PART I

The passion for philosophy, like that for religion, seems liable to this inconvenience, that though it aims at the correction of our manners and extirpation of our vices, it may only serve, by imprudent management, to foster a predominant inclination and push the mind with more determined resolution toward that side which already *draws* too much by the bias and propensity of the natural temper. It is certain that, while we aspire to the magnanimous firmness of the philosophic sage and endeavor to confine our pleasures altogether within our own minds, we may, at last, render our philosophy, like that of Epictetus and other Stoics, only a more refined system of selfishness, and reason ourselves out of all virtue as well as social enjoyment. While we study with attention the vanity of human life and turn all our thoughts toward the empty and transitory nature of riches and honors, we are, perhaps, all the while flattering our natural indolence which, hating the bustle of the world and drudgery of business, seeks a pretense of reason to give itself a full and uncontrolled indulgence. There is, however, one species of philosophy which seems little liable to this inconvenience, and that because it strikes in with no disorderly passion of the human mind, nor can mingle itself with any natural affection or propensity; and that is the Academic or Skeptical philosophy. The Academics always talk of doubt and suspense of judgment, of danger in hasty determinations, of confining to very narrow bounds the inquiries of the understanding, and of renouncing all speculations which lie not within the limits of common life and practice. Nothing, therefore, can be more contrary than such a philosophy to the supine indolence of the mind, its rash arrogance, its lofty pretensions, and its superstitious credulity. Every passion is mortified by it, except the love of truth; and that passion never is nor can be carried to too high a degree. It is surprising, therefore, that this philosophy, which in almost every instance must be harmless and innocent, should be the subject of so much groundless reproach and obloquy. But, perhaps, the very circumstance which renders it so innocent is what chiefly exposes it to the public hatred and resentment. By flattering no irregular passion, it gains few partisans. By opposing so many vices and follies, it raises to itself abundance of enemies who stigmatize it as libertine, profane, and irreligious.

Nor need we fear that this philosophy, while it endeavors to limit our inquiries to common life,

should ever undermine the reasonings of common life and carry its doubts so far as to destroy all action as well as speculation. Nature will always maintain her rights and prevail in the end over any abstract reasoning whatsoever. Though we should conclude, for instance, as in the foregoing section, that in all reasonings from experience there is a step taken by the mind which is not supported by any argument or process of the understanding, there is no danger that these reasonings, on which almost all knowledge depends, will ever be affected by such a discovery. If the mind be not engaged by argument to make this step, it must be induced by some other principle of equal weight and authority; and that principle will preserve its influence as long as human nature remains the same. What that principle is may well be worth the pains of inquiry.

Suppose a person, though endowed with the strongest faculties of reason and reflection, to be brought on a sudden into this world; he would, indeed, immediately observe a continual succession of objects and one event following another, but he would not be able to discover anything further. He would not at first, by any reasoning, be able to reach the idea of cause and effect, since the particular powers by which all natural operations are performed never appear to the senses; nor is it reasonable to conclude, merely because one event in one instance precedes another, that therefore the one is the cause, the other the effect. The conjunction may be arbitrary and casual. There may be no reason to infer the existence of one from the appearance of the other: and, in a word, such a person without more experience could never employ his conjecture or reasoning concerning any matter of fact or be assured of anything beyond what was immediately present to his memory or senses.

Suppose again that he has acquired more experience and has lived so long in the world as to have observed similar objects or events to be constantly conjoined together—what is the consequence of this experience? He immediately infers the existence of one object from the appearance of the other, yet he has not, by all his experience, acquired any idea or knowledge of the secret power by which the one object produces the other, nor is it by any process of reasoning he is engaged to draw this inference; but still he finds himself determined to draw it, and though he should be convinced that his understanding has no part in the operation, he would nevertheless continue in the same course of thinking. There is some other principle which determines him to form such a conclusion.

This principle is *custom* or *habit*. For whatever the repetition of any particular act or operation produces a propensity to renew the same act or operation without being impelled by any reasoning or process of the understanding, we always say that this propensity is the effect of *custom*. By employing that word we pretend not to have given the ultimate reason of such a propensity. We only point out a principle of human nature which is universally acknowledged, and which is well known by its effects. Perhaps we can push our inquiries no further or pretend to give the cause of this cause, but must rest contented with it as the ultimate principle which we can assign of all our conclusions from experience. It is sufficient satisfaction that we can go so far without repining at the narrowness of our faculties, because they will carry us no further. And it is certain we here advance a very intelligible proposition at least, if not a true one, when we assert that after the constant conjunction of two objects, heat and flame, for instance, weight and solidity, we are determined by custom alone to expect the one from the appearance of the other. This hypothesis seems even the only one which explains the difficulty why we draw from a thousand instances an inference which we are not able to draw from one instance that is in no respect different from them. Reason is incapable of any such variation. The conclusions which it draws from considering one circle are the same which it would form upon surveying all the circles in the universe. But no man, having seen only one body move after being impelled by another, could infer that every other body will move after a like impulse. All inferences from experience, therefore, are effects of custom, not of reasoning.[3]

Custom, then, is the great guide of human life. It is that principle alone which renders our experience useful to us and makes us expect, for the future, a similar train of events with those which have appeared in the past. Without the influence of custom we should be entirely ignorant of every matter of fact beyond what is immediately present to the memory and senses. We should never know how to adjust means to ends or to employ our natural powers in the production of any effect. There would be an end at once of all action as well as of the chief part of speculation.

But here it may be proper to remark that though our conclusions from experience carry us beyond our memory and senses and assure us of matters of fact which happened in the most distant places and most remote ages, yet some fact must always be present to the senses or memory from which we may first proceed in drawing these conclusions. A man who should find in a desert country the remains of pompous buildings would conclude that the country had, in ancient times, been cultivated by civilized inhabitants; but did nothing of this nature occur to him, he could never form such an inference. We learn the events of former ages from history, but then we must peruse the volume in which this instruction is contained, and thence carry up our inferences from one testimony to another, till we arrive at the eye-witnesses and spectators of these distant events. In a word, if we proceed not upon some fact present to the memory or senses, our reasonings would be merely hypothetical; and however the particular links might be connected with each other, the whole chain of inferences would have nothing to support it, nor could we ever, by its means, arrive at the knowledge of any real existence. If I ask why you believe any particular matter of fact which you relate, you must tell me some reason; and this reason will be some other fact connected with it. But as you cannot proceed after this manner *in infinitum,* you must at last terminate in some fact which is present to your memory or senses or must allow that your belief is entirely without foundation.

What, then, is the conclusion of the whole matter? A simple one, though, it must be confessed, pretty remote from the common theories of philosophy. All belief of matter of fact or real existence is derived merely from some object present to the memory or senses and a customary conjunction between that and some other object; or, in other words, having found, in many instances, that any two kinds of objects, flame and heat, snow and cold, have always been conjoined together: if flame or snow be presented anew to the senses, the mind is carried by custom to expect heat or cold, and to *believe* that such a quality does exist and will discover itself upon a nearer approach. This belief is the necessary result of placing the mind in such circumstances. It is an operation of the soul, when we are so situated, as unavoidable as to feel the passion of love, when we receive benefits; or hatred, when we meet with injuries. All these operations are a species of natural instincts, which no reasoning or process of the thought and understanding is able either to produce or to prevent. At this point it would be very allowable for us to stop our philosophical researches. In most questions we can never make a single step further; and in all questions we must terminate here at last, after our most restless and curious inquiries. But still our curiosity will be pardonable, perhaps commendable, if it carry us on to still further researches and make us examine more accurately the nature of this *belief* and of the *customary conjunction* whence it is derived. By this means we may meet with some explications and analogies that will give satisfaction, at least to such as love the abstract sciences, and can be entertained with speculations which, however accurate, may still retain a degree of doubt and uncertainty. As to readers of a different taste, the remaining part of this Section is not calculated for them; and the following inquiries may well be understood, though it be neglected.

PART II

Nothing is more free than the imagination of man, and though it cannot exceed that original stock of ideas furnished by the internal and external senses, it has unlimited power of mixing, compounding, separating, and dividing these ideas in all the varieties of fiction and vision. It can feign a train of events with all the appearance of reality, ascribe to them a particular time and place, conceive them as existent, and paint them out to itself with every circumstance that belongs to any historical fact which it believes with the greatest certainty. Wherein, therefore, consists the difference between such a fiction and belief? It lies not merely in any peculiar idea which is annexed to such a conception as commands our assent, and which is wanting to every known fiction. For as the mind has authority over all its ideas, it could voluntarily annex this particular idea to any fiction, and consequently be able to believe whatever it pleases, contrary to what we find by daily experience. We can, in our conception, join the head of a man to the body of a horse, but it is not in our power to believe that such an animal has ever really existed.

It follows, therefore, that the difference between *fiction* and *belief* lies in some sentiment or feeling which is annexed to the latter, not to the former, and which depends not on the will, nor can be de-

manded at pleasure. It must be excited by nature like all other sentiments and must rise from the particular situation in which the mind is placed at any particular juncture. Whenever any object is presented to the memory or senses, it immediately, by the force of custom, carries the imagination to conceive that object which is usually conjoined to it; and this conception is attended with a feeling or sentiment different from the loose reveries of the fancy. In this consists the whole nature of belief. For as there is no matter of fact which we believe so firmly that we cannot conceive the contrary, there would be no difference between the conception assented to and that which is rejected were it not for some sentiment which distinguishes the one from the other. If I see a billiard ball moving toward another on a smooth table, I can easily conceive it to stop upon contact. This conception implies no contradiction, but still it feels very differently from that conception by which I represent to myself the impulse and the communication of motion from one ball to another.

Were we to attempt a *definition* of this sentiment, we should, perhaps, find it a very difficult, if not an impossible, task; in the same manner as if we should endeavor to define the feeling of cold, or passion of anger, to a creature who never had any experience of these sentiments. Belief is the true and proper name of this feeling, and no one is ever at a loss to know the meaning of that term, because every man is every moment conscious of the sentiment represented by it. It may not, however, be improper to attempt a *description* of this sentiment, in hopes we may by that means arrive at some analogies which may afford a more perfect explication of it. I say that belief is nothing but a more vivid, lively, forcible, firm, steady conception of an object than what the imagination alone is ever able to attain. This variety of terms, which may seem so unphilosophical, is intended only to express that act of the mind which renders realities, or what is taken for such, more present to us than fictions, causes them to weigh more in the thought, and gives them a superior influence on the passions and imagination. Provided we agree about the thing, it is needless to dispute about the terms. The imagination has the command over all its ideas and can join and mix and vary them in all the ways possible. It may conceive fictitious objects with all the circumstances of place and time. It may set them in a manner before our eyes, in their true colors, just as they might have existed. But as it is impossible that this faculty of imagination can ever, of itself, reach belief, it is evident that belief consists not in the peculiar nature or order of ideas, but in the *manner* of their conception and in their *feeling* to the mind. I confess that it is impossible perfectly to explain this feeling or manner of conception. We may make use of words which express something near it. But its true and proper name, as we observed before, is "belief," which is a term that everyone sufficiently understands in common life. And in philosophy we can go no further than assert that *belief* is something felt by the mind, which distinguishes the ideas of the judgment from the fictions of the imagination. It gives them more weight and influence, makes them appear of greater importance, enforces them in the mind, and renders them the governing principle of our actions. I hear at present, for instance, a person's voice with whom I am acquainted, and the sound comes as from the next room. This impression of my senses immediately conveys my thought to the person, together with all the surrounding objects. I pain them out to myself as existing at present, with the same qualities and relations of which I formerly knew them possessed. These ideas take faster hold of my mind than ideas of an enchanted castle. They are very different from the feeling and have a much greater influence of every kind, either to give pleasure or pain, joy or sorrow.

Let us, then, take in the whole compass of this doctrine and allow that the sentiment of belief is nothing but a conception more intense and steady than what attends the mere fictions of the imagination, and that this *manner* of conception arises from a customary conjunction of the object with something present to the memory or senses. I believe that it will not be difficult, upon these suppositions, to find other operations of the mind analogous to it and to trace up these phenomena to principles still more general.

We have already observed that nature has established connections among particular ideas, and that no sooner one idea occurs to our thoughts than it introduces its correlative and carries our attention toward it by a gentle and insensible movement. These principles of connection or association we have reduced to three, namely, "resemblance," "contiguity," and "causation," which are the only bonds that unite our thoughts together and beget that regular train of reflection or discourse which, in a greater or less degree, takes place among all mankind. Now here arises a question on which the solution of the present difficulty will depend. Does it happen in all these relations that when one of the objects is presented to the senses or memory, the mind is not only carried to the conception of the correlative, but reaches a steadier and stronger conception of it than what otherwise it would have been able to attain? This seems to be the case with that belief which arises from the relation of cause and effect. And if the case be the same with the other relations or principles of association, this may be established as a general law which takes place in all the operations of the mind.

We may, therefore, observe, as the first experiment to our present purpose, that upon the appearance of the picture of an absent friend our idea of him is evidently enlivened by the *resemblance,* and that every passion which that idea occasions, whether of joy or sorrow, acquires new force and vigor. In producing this effect there concur both a relation and a present impression. Where the picture bears him no resemblance, at least was not intended for him, it never so much as conveys our thought to him. And where it is absent, as well as the person, though the mind may pass from the thought of one to that of the other, it feels its idea to be rather weakened than enlivened by that transition. We take a pleasure in viewing the picture of a friend when it is set before us; but when it is removed, rather choose to consider him directly than by reflection on an image which is equally distant and obscure.

The ceremonies of the Roman Catholic religion may be considered as instances of the same nature. The devotees of that superstition usually plead, in excuse for the mummeries with which they are upbraided, that they feel the good effect of those external motions, and postures, and actions in enlivening their devotion and quickening their fervor, which otherwise would decay if directed entirely to distant and immaterial objects. We shadow out the objects of our faith, say they, in sensible types and images, and render them more present to us by the immediate presence of these types than it is possible for us to do merely by an intellectual view and contemplation. Sensible objects have always a greater influence on the fancy than any other, and this influence they readily convey to those ideas to which they are related and which they resemble. I shall only infer from these practices and this reasoning that the effect of resemblance in enlivening the ideas is very common; and as in every case a resemblance and a present impression must concur, we are abundantly supplied with experiments to prove the reality of the foregoing principle.

We may add force to these experiments by others of a different kind, in considering the effects of *contiguity* as well as of *resemblance*. It is certain that distance diminishes the force of every idea and that, upon our approach to any object, though it does not discover itself to our senses, it operates upon the mind with an influence which imitates an immediate impression. The thinking on any object readily transports the mind to what is contiguous; but it is only the actual presence of an object that transports it with a superior vivacity. When I am a few miles from home, whatever relates to it touches me more nearly than when I am two hundred leagues distant, though even at that distance the reflecting on anything in the neighborhood of my friends or family naturally produces an idea of them. But, as in this latter case, both the objects of the mind are ideas, notwithstanding there is an easy transition between them; that transition alone is not able to give a superior vivacity to any of the ideas, for want of some immediate impression.[4]

No one can doubt but *causation* has the same influence as the other two relations of resemblance and contiguity. Superstitious people are fond of the relics of saints and holy men, for the same reason that they seek after types or images in order to enliven their devotion and give them a more intimate and strong conception of those exemplary lives which they desire to imitate. Now it is evident that one of the best relics which a devotee could procure would be the handiwork of a saint; and if his clothes and furniture are ever to be considered in this light, it is because they were once at his disposal and were moved and affected by him; in which respect they are to be considered as imperfect effects, and as connected with him by a shorter chain of consequences than any of those by which we learn the reality of his existence.

Suppose that the son of a friend who had been long dead or absent were presented to us; it is evident that this object would instantly revive its correlative idea and recall to our thoughts all past intimacies and familiarities in more lively color than they would otherwise have appeared to us. This is another phenomenon which seems to prove the principle above mentioned.

We may observe that in these phenomena the belief of the correlative object is always presupposed, without which the relation could have no effect. The influence of the picture supposes that we *believe* our friend to have once existed. Contiguity to home can never excite our ideas of home unless we *believe* that it really exists. Now I assert that this belief, where it reaches beyond the memory or senses, is of a similar nature and arises from similar causes with the transition of thought and vivacity of conception here explained. When I throw a piece of dry wood into a fire, my mind is immediately carried to conceive that it augments, not extinguishes, the flame. This transition of thought from the cause to the effect proceeds not from reason. It derives its origin altogether from custom and experience. And, as it first begins from an object present to the senses, it renders the idea or conception of flame more strong or lively than any loose floating reverie of the imagination. The idea arises immediately. The thought moves instantly toward it and conveys to it all that force of conception which is derived from the impression present to the senses. When a sword is leveled at my breast, does not the idea of wound and pain strike me more strongly than when a glass of wine is presented to me, even though by accident this idea should occur after the appearance of the latter object? But what is there in this whole matter to cause such a strong conception except only a present object and a customary transition to the idea of another object which we have been accustomed to conjoin with the former? This is the whole operation of the mind in all our conclusions concerning matter of fact and existence; and it is a satisfaction to find some analogies by which it may be explained. The transition from a present object does in all cases give strength and solidity to the related idea.

Here, then, is a kind of pre-established harmony between the course of nature and the succession of our ideas; and though the powers and forces by which the former is governed be wholly unknown to us, yet our thoughts and conceptions have still, we find, gone on in the same train with the other works of nature. Custom is that principle by which this correspondence has been effected, so necessary to the subsistence of our species and the regulation of our conduct in every circumstance and occurrence of human life. Had not the presence of an object instantly excited the idea of those objects commonly conjoined with it, all our knowledge must have been limited to the narrow sphere of our memory and senses, and we should never have been able to adjust means to ends or employ our natural powers either to the producing of good or avoiding of evil. Those who delight in the discovery and contemplation of *final causes* have here ample subject to employ their wonder and admiration.

I shall add, for a further confirmation of the foregoing theory, that as this operation of the mind, by which we infer like effects from like causes, and *vice versa,* is so essential to the subsistence of all human creatures, it is not probable that it could be trusted to the fallacious deductions of our reason, which is slow in its operations, appears not, in any degree, during the first years of infancy, and, at best, is in every age and period of human life extremely liable to error and mistake. It is more conformable to the ordinary wisdom of nature to secure so necessary an act of the mind by some instinct or mechanical tendency which may be infallible in its operations, may discover itself at the first appearance of life and thought, and may be independent of all the labored deductions of the understanding. As nature has taught us the use of our limbs without giving us the knowledge of the muscles and nerves by which they are actuated, so has she implanted in us an instinct which carries forward the thought in a correspondent course to that which she has established among external objects, though we are ignorant of those powers and forces on which this regular course and succession of objects totally depends.

SECTION VI. OF PROBABILITY[5]

Though there be no such thing as *chance* in the world, our ignorance of the real cause of any event has the same influence on the understanding and begets a like species of belief or opinion.

There is certainly a probability which arises from a superiority of chances on any side; and, according as this superiority increases and surpasses the opposite chances, the probability receives a proportionable increase and begets still a higher degree of belief of assent to that side in which we discover the superiority. If a die were marked with one figure or number of spots on four sides, and with another figure or number of spots on the two remaining sides, it would be more probable that the former would turn up than the latter, though, if it had a thousand sides marked in the same manner, and only one side different, the probability would be much higher and our belief or expectation of the even more steady and secure. This process of the thought or reasoning may seem trivial and obvious; but to those who consider it more

narrowly it may, perhaps, afford matter for curious speculation.

It seems evident that when the mind looks forward to discover the event which may result from the throw of such a die, it considers the turning up of each particular side as alike probable; and this is the very nature of chance, to render all the particular events comprehended in it entirely equal. But finding a greater number of sides concur in the one event than in the other, the mind is carried more frequently to that event and meets it oftener in revolving the various possibilities or chances on which the ultimate result depends. This concurrence of several views in one particular event begets immediately, by an explicable contrivance of nature, the sentiment of belief and gives that event the advantage over its antagonist which is supported by a smaller number of views and recurs less frequently to the mind. If we allow that belief is nothing but a firmer and stronger conception of an object than what attends the mere fictions of the imagination, this operation may, perhaps, in some measure be accounted for. The concurrence of these several views or glimpses imprints the idea more strongly on the imagination, gives it superior force and vigor, renders its influence on the passions and affections more sensible, and, in a word, begets that reliance or security which constitutes the nature of belief and opinion.

The case is the same with the probability of causes as with that of chance. There are some cases which are entirely uniform and constant in producing a particular effect, and no instance has ever yet been found of any failure or irregularity in their operation. Fire has always burned, and water suffocated, every human creature. The production of motion by impulse and gravity is a universal law which has hitherto admitted of no exception. But there are other causes which have been found more irregular and uncertain, nor has rhubarb always proved a purge, or opium a soporific, to everyone who has taken these medicines. It is true, when any cause fails of producing its usual effect, philosophers ascribe not this to any irregularity in nature, but suppose that some secret causes in the particular structure of parts have prevented the operation. Our reasonings, however, and conclusions concerning the event are the same as if this principle had no place. Being determined by custom to transfer the past to the future in all our inferences, where the past has been entirely regular and uniform we expect the event with the greatest assurance and leave no room for any contrary supposition. But where different effects have been found to follow from causes which are to *appearance* exactly similar, all these various effects must occur to the mind in transferring the past to the future, and enter into our consideration when we determine the probability of the event. Though we give the preference to that which has been found most usual, and believe that this effect will exist, we must not overlook the other effects, but must assign to each of them a particular weight and authority in proportion as we have found it to be more or less frequent. It is more probable, in almost every country of Europe, that there will be frost sometime in January than that the weather will continue open throughout that whole month, though this probability varies according to the different climates, and approaches to a certainty in the more northern kingdoms. Here, then, it seems evident that when we transfer the past to the future in order to determine the effect which will result from any cause, we transfer all the different events in the same proportion as they have appeared in the past, and conceive one to have existed a hundred times, for instance, another ten times, and another once. As a great number of views do here concur in one event, they fortify and confirm it to the imagination, beget that sentiment which we call "belief," and give its object the preference above the contrary event which is not supported by an equal number of experiments and recurs not so frequently to the thought in transferring the past to the future. Let anyone try to account for this operation of the mind upon any of the received systems of philosophy, and he will be sensible of the difficulty. For my part, I shall think it sufficient if the present hints excite the curiosity of philosophers and make them sensible how defective all common theories are in treating of such curious and such sublime subjects.

SECTION VII. OF THE IDEA OF NECESSARY CONNECTION

PART I

The great advantage of the mathematical sciences above the moral consists in this, that the ideas of the former, being sensible, are always clear and determinate, the smallest distinction between them is immediately perceptible, and the same terms are still expressive of the same ideas without ambiguity or variation. An oval is never mistaken for a circle, nor a hyperbola for an ellipse. The isosceles and scalenum are distinguished by boundaries more exact than vice and virtue, right and wrong. If any term be defined in geometry, the mind readily, of itself substitutes on all occasions the definition for the term defined, or, even when no definition is employed, the object itself may be presented to the senses and by that means be steadily and clearly apprehended. But the finer sentiments of the mind, the operations of the understanding, the various agitations of the passions, though really in themselves distinct, easily escape us when surveyed by reflection, nor is it in our power to recall the original object as often as we have occasion to contemplate it. Ambiguity, by this means, is gradually introduced into our reasonings: similar objects are readily taken to be the same, and the conclusion becomes at last very wide of the premises.

One may safely, however, affirm that if we consider these sciences in a proper light, their advantages and disadvantages nearly compensate each other and reduce both of them to a state of equality. If the mind, with greater facility, retains the ideas of geometry clear and determinate, it must carry on a much longer and more intricate chain of reasoning and compare ideas much wider of each other in order to reach the abstruser truths of that science. And if moral ideas are apt, without extreme care, to fall into obscurity and confusion, the inferences are always much shorter in these disquisitions, and the intermediate steps which led to the conclusion much fewer than in the sciences which treat of quantity and number. In reality, there is scarcely a proposition in Euclid so simple as not to consist of more parts than are to be found in any moral reasoning which runs not into chimera and conceit. Where we trace the principles of the human mind through a few steps, we may be very well satisfied with our progress, considering how soon nature throws a bar to all our inquiries concerning causes and reduces us to an acknowledgment of our ignorance. The chief obstacle, therefore, to our improvements in the moral or metaphysical sciences is the obscurity of the ideas and ambiguity of the terms. The principal difficulty in the mathematics is the length of inferences and compass of thought requisite to the forming of any conclusion. And, perhaps, our progress in natural philosophy is chiefly retarded by the want of proper experiments and phenomena, which are often discovered by chance and cannot always be found when requisite, even by the most diligent and prudent inquiry. As moral philosophy seems hitherto to have received less improvement than either geometry or physics, we may conclude that if there be any difference in this respect among these sciences, the difficulties which obstruct the progress of the former require superior care and capacity to be surmounted.

There are no ideas which occur in metaphysics more obscure and uncertain than those of "power," "force," "energy," or "necessary connection," of which it is every moment necessary for us to treat in all our disquisitions. We shall, therefore, endeavor in this Section to fix, if possible, the precise meaning of these terms and thereby remove some part of that obscurity which is so much complained of in this species of philosophy.

It seems a proposition which will not admit of much dispute that all our ideas are nothing but copies of our impressions, or, in other words, that it is impossible for us to *think* of anything which we have not antecedently *felt,* either by our external or internal senses. I have endeavored[6] to explain and prove this proposition, and have expressed my hopes that by a proper application of it men may reach a greater clearness and precision in philosophical reasonings than what they have hitherto been able to attain. Complex ideas may, perhaps, be well known by definition, which is nothing but an enumeration of those parts or simple ideas that compose them. But when we have pushed up definitions to the most simple ideas and find still some ambiguity and obscurity, what resources are we then possessed of? By what invention can we throw light upon these ideas and render them altogether precise and determinate to our intellectual view? Produce the impressions or original sentiments from which the ideas are copied. These impressions are all strong and sensible. They admit not of ambiguity. They are not only placed in a full light themselves, but may throw light on their correspondent ideas, which lie in obscurity. And by this means we may perhaps obtain a new microscope or species of optics by which, in the moral sciences, the most minute and most simple ideas may be so enlarged as to fall readily under our apprehension and be equally known with the grossest and most sensible ideas that can be the object of our inquiry.

To be fully acquainted, therefore, with the idea of power or necessary connection, let us examine its impression and, in order to find the impression with greater certainty, let us search for it in all the sources from which it may possibly be derived.

When we look about us toward external objects and consider the operation of causes, we are never able, in a single instance, to discover any power or necessary connection, any quality which binds the effect to the cause and renders the one an infallible consequence of the other. We only find that the one does actually in fact follow the other. The impulse of one billiard ball is attended with motion in the second. This is the whole that appears to the *outward* senses. The mind feels no sentiment or *inward* impression from this succession of objects; consequently, there is not, in any single particular instance of cause and effect, anything which can suggest the idea of power or necessary connection.

From the first appearance of an object we never can conjecture what effect will result from it. But were the power or energy of any cause discoverable by the mind, we could foresee the effect, even without experience, and might, at first, pronounce with certainty concerning it by the mere dint of thought and reasoning.

In reality, there is no part of matter that does ever, by its sensible qualities, discover any power or energy, or give us ground to imagine that it could produce anything, or be followed by any other object, which we could denominate its effect. Solidity, extension, motion—these qualities are all complete in themselves and never point out any other event which may result from them. The scenes of the universe are continually shifting, and one object follows another in an uninterrupted succession; the power or force which actuates the whole machine is entirely concealed from us and never discovers itself in any of the sensible qualities of body. We know that, in fact, heat is a constant attendant of flame; but what is the connection between them we have no room so much as to conjecture or imagine. It is impossible, therefore, that the idea of power can be derived from the contemplation of bodies in single instances of their operation, because no bodies ever discover any power which can be the original of this idea.[7]

Since, therefore, external objects as they appear to the senses give us no idea of power or necessary connection by their operation in particular instances, let us see whether this idea be derived from reflection on the operations of our own minds and be copies from any internal impression. It may be said that we are every moment conscious of internal power while we feel that, by the simple command of our will, we can move the organs of our body or direct the faculties of our mind. An act of volition produces motion in our limbs or raises a new idea in our imagination. This influence of the will we know by consciousness. Hence we acquire the idea of power or energy, and are certain that we ourselves and all other intelligent beings are possessed of power. This idea, then, is an idea of reflection since it arises from reflecting on the operations of our own mind and on the command which is exercised by will both over the organs of the body and faculties of the soul.

We shall proceed to examine this pretension and, first, with regard to the influence of volition over the organs of the body. This influence, we may observe, is a fact which, like all other natural events, can be known only by experience, and can never be foreseen from any apparent energy or power in the cause which connects it with the effect and renders the one an infallible consequence of the other. The motion of our body follows upon the command of our will. Of this we are every moment conscious. But the means by which this is effected, the energy by which the will performs so extraordinary an operation—of this we are so far from being immediately conscious that it must forever escape our most diligent inquiry.

For, *first,* is there any principle in all nature more mysterious than the union of soul with body, by which a supposed spiritual substance acquires such an influence over a material one that the most refined thought is able to actuate the grossest matter? Were we empowered by a secret wish to remove mountains or control the planets in their orbit, this extensive authority would not be more extraordinary, nor more beyond our comprehension. But if, by consciousness, we perceived any power or energy in the will, we must know this power; we must know its connection with the effect; we must know the secret union of soul and body, and the nature of both these substances by which the one is able to operate in so many instances upon the other.

Secondly, we are not able to move all the organs of the body with a like authority, though we cannot assign any reason, besides experience, for so remarkable a difference between one and the other. Why has the will an influence over the tongue and fingers, not over the heart or liver? This question would never embarrass us were we conscious of a power in the former case, not in the latter. We should then perceive, independent of experience, why the authority of the will over the organs of the body is circumscribed within such particular limits. Being in that case fully acquainted with the power or force by which it operates, we should also know why its influence reaches precisely to such boundaries, and no further.

A man suddenly struck with a palsy in the leg or arm, or who had newly lost those members, frequently endeavors, at first, to move them and employ them in their usual offices. Here he is as much conscious of power to command such limbs as a man in perfect health is conscious of power to actuate any member which remains in its natural state and condition. But consciousness never deceives. Consequently, neither in the one case nor in the other are we ever conscious of any power. We learn the influence of our will from experience alone. And experience only teaches us how one event constantly follows another, without instructing us in the secret connection which binds them together and renders them inseparable.

Thirdly, we learn from anatomy that the immediate object of power in voluntary motion is not the member itself which is moved, but certain muscles and nerves and animal spirits, and, perhaps, something still more minute and more unknown, through which the motion is successively propagated ere it reach the member itself whose motion is the immediate object of volition. Can there be a more certain proof that the power by which this whole operation is performed, so far from being directly and fully known by an inward sentiment or consciousness, is to the last degree mysterious and unintelligible? Here the mind wills a certain event; immediately another event, unknown to ourselves and totally different from the one intended, is produced. This event produces another, equally unknown, till, at last, through a long succession the desired event is produced. But if the original power were felt, it must be known; were it known, its effect must also be known, since all power is relative to its effect. And, *vice versa,* if the effect be not known, the power cannot be known nor felt. How indeed can we be conscious of a power to move our limbs when we have no such power, but only that to move certain animal spirits which, though they produce at last the motion of our limbs, yet operate in such a manner as is wholly beyond our comprehension?

We may therefore conclude from the whole, I hope, without any temerity, though with assurance, that our idea of power is not copied from any sentiment or consciousness of power within ourselves when we give rise to animal motion or apply our limbs to their proper use and office. That their motion follows the command of the will is a matter of common experience, like other natural events; but the power or energy by which this is effected, like that in other natural events, is unknown and inconceivable.[8]

Shall we then assert that we are conscious of a power or energy in our own minds when, by an act or command of our will, we raise up a new idea, fix the mind to the contemplation of it, turn it on all sides, and at last dismiss it for some other idea when we think that we have surveyed it with sufficient accuracy? I believe the same arguments will prove that even this command of the will gives us no real idea of force or energy.

First, it must be allowed that when we know a power, we know that very circumstance in the cause by which it is enabled to produce the effect, for these are supposed to be synonymous. We must, therefore, know both the cause and effect and the relation between them. But do we pretend to be acquainted with the nature of the human soul and the nature of an idea, or the aptitude of the one to produce the other? This is a real creation, a production of something out of nothing, which implies a power so great that it may seem, at first sight, beyond the reach of any being less than infinite. At least it must be owned that such a power is not felt, nor known, nor even conceivable by the mind. We only feel the event, namely, the existence of an idea consequent to a command of the will; but the manner in which this operation is performed, the power by which it is produced, is entirely beyond our comprehension.

Secondly, the command of the mind over itself is limited, as well as its command over the body; and these limits are not known by reason or any acquaintance with the nature of cause and effect, but only by experience and observation, as in all other natural events and in the operation of external objects. Our authority over our sentiments and passions is much weaker than that over our ideas; and even the latter authority is circumscribed within very narrow boundaries. Will any one pretend to assign the ultimate reason of these boundaries, or show why the power is deficient in one case, not in another?

Thirdly, this self-command is very different at different times. A man in health possesses more of it than one languishing with sickness. We are more master of our thoughts in the morning than in the evening; fasting, than after a full meal. Can we give any reason for these variations except experience? Where then is the power of which we pretend to be conscious? Is there not here, either in a spiritual or material substance, or both, some secret mechanism or structure of parts upon which the effect depends, and which, being entirely unknown to us, renders the power or energy of the will equally unknown and incomprehensible?

Volition is surely an act of the mind with which we are sufficiently acquainted. Reflect upon it. Consider it on all sides. Do you find anything in it like this creative power by which it raises from nothing a new idea and, with a kind of *fiat,* imitates the omnipotence of its Maker, if I may be allowed so to speak, who called forth into existence all the various scenes of nature? So far from being conscious of this energy in the will, it requires as certain experience as that of which we are possessed to convince us that such extraordinary effects do ever result from a simple act of volition.

The generality of mankind never find any difficulty in accounting for the more common and familiar operations of nature, such as the descent of heavy bodies, the growth of plants, the generation of animals, or the nourishment of bodies by food; but suppose that in all these cases they perceive the very force or energy of the cause by which it is connected with its effect, and is forever infallible in its operation. They acquire, by long habit, such a turn of mind that upon the appearance of the cause they immediately expect, with assurance, its usual attendant, and hardly conceive it possible that any other event could result from it. It is only on the discovery of extraordinary phenomena, such as earthquakes, pestilence, and prodigies of any kind, that they find themselves at a loss to assign a proper cause and to explain the manner in which the effect is produced by it. It is usual for men, in such difficulties, to have recourse to some invisible intelligent principle as the immediate cause of that event which surprises them, and which they think cannot be accounted for from the common powers of nature. But philosophers, who carry their scrutiny a little further, immediately perceive that, even in the most familiar events, the energy of the cause is as unintelligible as in the most unusual, and that we only learn by experience the frequent conjunction of objects, without being ever able to comprehend anything like connection between them. Here, then, many philosophers think themselves obliged by reason to have recourse, on all occasions, to the same principle which the vulgar never appeal to but in cases that appear miraculous and supernatural. They acknowledge mind and intelligence to be, not only the ultimate and original cause of all things, but the immediate and sole cause of every event which appears in nature. They pretend that those objects which are commonly denominated "causes" are in reality nothing but "occasions," and that the true and direct principle of every effect is not any power or force in nature, but a volition of the Supreme Being, who wills that such particular objects should forever be conjoined with each other. Instead of saying that one billiard ball moves another by a force which it has derived from the author of nature, it is the Deity himself, they say, who, by a particular volition, moves the second ball, being determined to this operation by the impulse of the first ball, in consequence of those general laws which he has laid down to himself in the government of the universe. But philosophers, advancing still in their inquiries, discover that as we are totally ignorant of the power on which depends the mutual operation of bodies, we are no less ignorant of that power on which depends the operation of mind on body, or of body on mind; nor are we able, either from our senses or consciousness, to assign the ultimate principle in the one case more than in the other. The same ignorance, therefore, reduces them to the same conclusion. They assert that the Deity is the immediate cause of the union between soul and body, and that they are not the organs of sense which, being agitated by external objects, produce sensations in the mind; but that it is a particular volition of our omnipotent Maker which excites such a sensation in consequence of such a motion in the organ. In like manner, it is not any energy in the will that produces local motion in our members: It is God himself, who is pleased to second our will, in itself impotent, and to command that motion which we erroneously attribute to our own power and efficacy. Nor do philosophers stop at this conclusion. They sometimes extend the same inference to the mind itself in its internal operations. Our mental vision or conception of ideas is nothing but a revelation made to us by our Maker. When we voluntarily turn our thoughts to any object and raise up its image in the fancy, it is not the will which creates that idea, it is the universal Creator who discovers it to the mind and renders it present to us.

Thus, according to these philosophers, everything is full of God. Not content with the principle that nothing exists but by his will, that nothing possesses any power but by his concession, they rob nature and all created beings of every power in order to render their dependence on the Deity still more sensible and immediate. They consider not that by this theory they diminish, instead of magnifying, the grandeur of those attributes which they affect so much to celebrate. It argues, surely, more power in the Deity to delegate a certain degree of power to inferior creatures than to produce everything by his own immediate volition. It argues more wisdom to contrive at first the fabric of the world with such perfect foresight that of itself, and by its proper operation, it may serve all the purposes of Providence than if the great Creator were obliged every moment to adjust its parts and animate by his breath all the wheels of that stupendous machine.

But if we would have a more philosophical confutation of this theory, perhaps the two following reflections may suffice:

First, it seems to me that this theory of the universal energy and operation of the Supreme Being is too bold ever to carry conviction with it to a man sufficiently apprised of the weakness of human reason and the narrow limits to which it is confined in all its operations. Though the chain of arguments which conduct to it were ever so logical, there must arise a strong suspicion, if not an absolute assurance, that it has carried us quite beyond the reach of our faculties when it leads to conclusions so extraordinary and so remote from common life and experience. We are got into fairyland long ere we have reached the last steps of our theory; and *there* we have no reason to trust our common methods of arguments or to think that our usual analogies and probabilities have any authority. Our line is too short to fathom such immense abysses. And however we may flatter ourselves that we are guided, in every step which we take, by a kind of verisimilitude and experience, we may be assured that this fancied experience has no authority when we thus apply it to subjects that lie entirely out of the sphere of experience. But on this we shall have occasion to touch afterwards.[9]

Secondly, I cannot perceive any force in the arguments on which this theory is founded. We are ignorant, it is true, of the manner in which bodies operate on each other. Their force or energy is entirely incomprehensible. But are we not equally ignorant of the manner or force by which a mind, even the Supreme Mind, operates, either on itself or on body? Whence, I beseech you, do we acquire any idea of it? We have no sentiment or consciousness of this power in ourselves. We have no idea of the Supreme Being but what we learn from reflection on our own faculties. Were our ignorance, therefore, a good reason for rejecting anything, we should be led into that principle of denying all energy in the Supreme Being, as much as in the grossest matter. We surely comprehend as little the operations of the one as of the other. Is it more difficult to conceive that motion may arise from impulse than that it may arise from volition? All we know is our profound ignorance in both cases.[10]

PART II

But to hasten to a conclusion of this argument, which is already drawn out to too great a length: We have sought in vain for an idea of power or necessary connection in all the sources from which we would suppose it to be derived. It appears that in single instances of the operation of bodies we never can, by our utmost scrutiny, discover anything but one event following another, without being able to comprehend any force or power by which the cause operates or any connection between it and its supposed effect. The same difficulty occurs in contemplating the operations of mind on body, where we observe the motion of the latter to follow upon the volition of the former, but are not able to observe or conceive the tie which binds together the motion and volition, or the energy, by which the mind produces this effect. The authority of the will over its own faculties and ideas is not a whit more comprehensible, so that, upon the whole, there appears not, throughout all nature, any one instance of connection which is conceivable by us. All events seem entirely loose and separate. One event follows another, but we never can observe any tie between them. They seem *conjoined,* but never *connected.* But as we can have no idea of anything which never appeared to our outward sense or inward sentiment, the necessary conclusion *seems* to be that we have no idea of connection or power at all, and that these words are absolutely without any meaning when employed either in philosophical reasonings or common life.

But there still remains one method of avoiding this conclusion, and one source which we have not yet examined. When any natural object or event is presented, it is impossible for us, by any sagacity or penetration, to discover, or even conjecture, without experience, what event will result from it, or to carry our foresight beyond that object which is immediately present to the memory and senses. Even after one instance or experiment where we have observed a particular event to follow upon another, we are not entitled to form a general rule or foretell what will happen in like cases, it being justly esteemed an unpardonable temerity to judge the whole course of nature from one single experiment, however accurate or certain. But when one particular species of events has always, in all instances, been conjoined with another, we make no longer any scruple of foretelling one upon the appearance of the other, and of employing that reasoning which can alone assure us of any matter of fact or existence. We then call the one object "cause," the other "effect." We suppose that there is some connection between them, some power in the one by which it infallibly produces the other and operates with the greatest certainty and strongest necessity.

It appears, then, that this idea of a necessary connection among events arises from a number of similar instances which occur, of the constant conjunction of these events; nor can that idea ever be suggested by any one of these instances surveyed in all possible lights and positions. But there is nothing in a number of instances, different from every single instance, which is supposed to be exactly similar, except only that after a repetition of similar instances the mind is carried by habit, upon the appearance of one event, to expect its usual attendant and to believe that it will exist. This connection, therefore, which we *feel* in the mind, this customary transition of the imagination from one object to its usual attendant, is the sentiment or impression from which we form the idea of power or necessary connection. Nothing further is the case. Contemplate the subject on all sides, you will never find any other origin of that idea. This is the sole difference between one instance, from which we can never receive the idea of connection, and a number of similar instances by which it is suggested. The first time a man saw the communication of motion by impulse, as by the shock of two billiard balls, he could not pronounce that the one event was *connected,* but only that it was *conjoined* with the other. After he has observed several instances of this nature, he then pronounces them to be *connected.* What alteration has happened to give rise to this new idea of *connection?* Nothing but that he now *feels* these events to be *connected* in his imagination, and can readily foretell the existence of one from the appearance of the other. When we say, therefore, that one object is connected with another, we mean only that they have acquired a connection in our thought and gave rise to this inference by which they become proofs of each other's existence—a conclusion which is somewhat extraordinary, but which seems founded on sufficient evidence. Nor will its evidence be weakened by any general diffidence of the understanding or skeptical suspicion concerning every conclusion which is new and extraordinary. No conclusions can be more agreeable to skepticism than such as make discoveries concerning the weakness and narrow limits of human reason and capacity.

And what stronger instance can be produced of the surprising ignorance and weakness of the understanding than the present? For surely, if there be any relation among objects which it imports us to know perfectly, it is that of cause and effect. On this are founded all our reasonings concerning matter of fact or existence. By means of it alone we attain any assurance concerning objects which are removed from the present testimony of our memory and senses. The only immediate utility of all sciences is to teach us how to control and regulate future events by their causes. Our thoughts and inquiries are, therefore, every moment employed about this relation; yet so imperfect are the ideas which we form concerning it that it is impossible to give any just definition of cause, except what is drawn from something extraneous and foreign to it. Similar objects are always conjoined with similar. Of this we have experience. Suitably to this experience, therefore, we may define a cause to be *an object followed by another, and where all the objects, similar to the first, are followed by objects similar to the second.* Or, in other words, *where, if the first object had not been, the second never had existed.* The appearance of a cause always conveys the mind, by a customary transition, to the idea of the effect. Of this also we have experience. We may, therefore, suitably to this experience, form another definition of cause and call it *an object fol-*

lowed by another, and whose appearance always conveys the thought to that other. But though both these definitions be drawn from circumstances foreign to the cause, we cannot remedy this inconvenience or attain any more perfect definition which may point out that circumstance in the cause which gives it a connection with its effect. We have no idea of this connection, nor even any distinct notion what it is we desire to know when we endeavor at a conception of it. We say, for instance, that the vibration of this string is the cause of this particular sound. But what do we mean by that affirmation? We either mean *that this vibration is followed by this sound, and that all similar vibrations have been followed by similar sounds;* or, *that this vibration is followed by this sound, and that, upon the appearance of one, the mind anticipates the senses and forms immediately an idea of the other.* We may consider the relation of cause and effect in either of these two lights; but beyond these we have no idea of it.[11]

To recapitulate, therefore, the reasonings of this Section: Every idea is copied from some preceding impression or sentiment; and where we cannot find any impression, we may be certain that there is no idea. In all single instances of the operation of bodies or minds there is nothing that produces any impression, nor consequently can suggest any idea, of power or necessary connection. But when many uniform instances appear, and the same object is always followed by the same event, we then begin to entertain the notion of cause and connection. We then *feel* a new sentiment or impression, to wit, a customary connection in the thought or imagination between one object and its usual attendant; and this sentiment is the original of that idea which we seek for. For as this idea arises from a number of similar instances, and not from any single instance, it must arise from that circumstance in which the number of instances differ from every individual instance. But this customary connection or transition of the imagination is the only circumstance in which they differ. In every other particular they are alike. The first instance which we saw of motion, communicated by the shock of two billiard balls (to return to this obvious illustration), is exactly similar to any instance that may at present occur to us, except only that we could not at first *infer* one event from the other, which we are enabled to do at present, after so long a course of uniform experience. I know not whether the reader will readily apprehend this reasoning. I am afraid that, should I multiply words about it or throw it into a greater variety of lights, it would only become more obscure and intricate. In all abstract reasonings there is one point of view which, if we can happily hit, we shall go further toward illustrating the subject than by all the eloquence and copious expression in the world. This point of view we should endeavor to reach, and reserve the flowers of rhetoric for subjects which are more adapted to them.

NOTES

1. It is probable that no more was meant by those who denied innate ideas than that all ideas were copies of our impressions, though it must be confessed that the terms which they employed were not chosen with such caution, nor so exactly defined, as to prevent all mistakes about their doctrine. For what is meant by "innate"? If "innate" be equivalent to "natural," then all the perceptions and ideas of the mind must be allowed to be innate or natural, in whatever sense we take the latter word, whether in opposition to what is uncommon, artificial, or miraculous. If by innate he meant contemporary to our birth, the dispute seems to be frivolous, nor is it worth while to inquire at what time thinking begins, whether before, at, or after our birth. Again, the word "idea" seems to be commonly taken in a very loose sense by Locke and others, as standing for any of our perceptions, our sensations and passions, as well as thoughts. Now, in this sense, I should desire to know what can be meant by asserting that self-love, or resentment of injuries, or the passion between the sexes is not innate?

But admitting these terms "impressions" and "ideas" in the sense above explained, and understanding by "innate" what is original or copied from no precedent perception, then may we assert that all our impressions are innate, and our ideas not innate.

To be ingenuous, I must own it to be my opinion that Locke was betrayed into this question by the schoolmen, who, making use of undefined terms, draw out their disputes to a tedious length without ever touching the point in question. A like ambiguity and circumlocution seem to run through that philosopher's reasonings, on this as well as most other subjects.

2. The word "power" is here used in a loose and popular sense. The more accurate explication of it would give additional evidence to this argument. See Section VII.

3. Nothing is more usual than for writers, even on *moral, political,* or *physical* subjects, to distinguish between *reason* and *experience,* and to suppose that these species of argumentation are entirely different from each other. The former are taken for the mere result of our intellectual faculties, which, by considering *a priori* the nature of things, and examining the effects that must follow from their operation, establish particular principles of science and philosophy. The latter are supposed to be derived entirely from sense and observation, by which we learn what has actually resulted from the operation of particular objects, and are thence able to infer what will for the future result from them. Thus, for instance, the limitations and restraints of civil government and a legal constitution may be defended, either from *reason,* which, reflecting on the great frailty and corruption of human nature, teaches that no man can safely be trusted with unlimited authority; or from *experience* and history, which inform us of the enormous abuses that ambition in every age and country has been found to make of so imprudent a confidence.

The same distinction between reason and experience is maintained in all our deliberations concerning the conduct of life,

while the experienced statesman, general physician, or merchant, is trusted and followed, and the unpracticed novice, with whatever natural talents endowed, neglected and despised. Though it be allowed that reason may form very plausible conjectures with regard to the consequences of such a particular conduct in such particular circumstances, it is still supposed imperfect without the assistance of experience, which is alone able to give stability and certainty to the maxim derived from study and reflection.

But notwithstanding that this distinction be thus universally received, both in the active and speculative scenes of life, I shall not scruple to pronounce that it is, at bottom, erroneous, or at least superficial.

If we examine those arguments which, in any of the sciences above mentioned, are supposed to be the mere effects of reasoning and reflection, they will be found to terminate at last in some general principle or conclusion for which we can assign no reason but observation and experience. The only difference between them and those maxims which are vulgarly esteemed the result of pure experience is that the former cannot be established without some process of thought, and some reflection on what we have observed, in order to distinguish its circumstances and trace its consequences—whereas, in the latter, the experienced event is exactly and fully similar to that which we infer as the result of any particular situation. The history of a Tiberius or a Nero makes us dread a like tyranny, were our monarchs freed from the restraints of laws and senates: but the observation of any fraud or cruelty in private life is sufficient, with the aid of a little thought, to give us the same apprehension, while it serves as an instance of the general corruption of human nature, and shows us the danger which we must incur by reposing an entire confidence in mankind. In both cases, it is experience which is ultimately the foundation of our inference and conclusion.

There is no man so young and inexperienced as not to have formed from observation many general and just maxims concerning human affairs and the conduct of life; but it must be confessed that when a man comes to put these in practice he will be extremely liable to error, till time and further experience both enlarge these maxims, and teach him their proper use and application. In every situation or incident there are many particular and seemingly minute circumstances which the man of greatest talents is at first apt to overlook, though on them the justness of his conclusions, and consequently the prudence of his conduct, entirely depend. Not to mention that, to a young beginner, the general observations and maxims occur not always on the proper occasions, nor can be immediately applied with due calmness and distinction. The truth is, an inexperienced reasoner could be no reasoner at all were he absolutely inexperienced; and when we assign that character to anyone, we mean it only in a comparative sense, and suppose him possessed of experience in a smaller and more imperfect degree.

4. [A footnote containing a long quotation from Cicero, deleted.]

5. Mr. Locke divides all arguments into "demonstrative" and "probable." In this view, we must say that it is only probable that all men must die, or that the sun will rise tomorrow. But to conform our language more to common use, we ought to divide arguments into *demonstrations, proofs,* and *probabilities;* by proofs, meaning such arguments from experience as leave no room for doubt or opposition.

6. [In Section II.]

7. Mr. Locke, in his chapter of Power, says that, finding from experience that there are several new productions in matter, and concluding that there must somewhere be a power capable of producing them, we arrive at last by this reasoning at the idea

of power. But no reasoning can ever give us a new, original simple idea, as this philosopher himself confesses. This, therefore, can never be the origin of that idea.

8. It may be pretended, that the resistance which we meet with in bodies, obliging us frequently to exert our force and call up all our power, this gives us the idea of force and power. It is this *nisus* or strong endeavor of which we are conscious, that is the original impression from which this idea is copied. But, *first*, we attribute power to a vast number of objects where we never can suppose this resistance or exertion of force to take place: to the Supreme Being, who never meets with any resistance; to the mind in its command over its ideas and limbs, in common thinking and motion, where the effect follows immediately upon the will, without any exertion or summoning up of force; to inanimate matter, which is not capable of this sentiment. *Secondly,* this sentiment of an endeavor to overcome resistance has no known connection with any event: What follows it we know by experience, but could not know it *a priori*. It must, however, be confessed that the animal *nisus* which we experience, though it can afford no accurate precise idea of power, enters very much into that vulgar, inaccurate idea which is formed of it.

9. Section XII. [Not included here.]

10. I need not examine at length the *vis inertiae* which is so much talked of in the new philosophy, and which is ascribed to matter. We find by experience that a body at rest or in motion continues forever in its present state, till put from it by some new cause; and that a body impelled takes as much motion from the impelling body as it acquires itself. These are facts. When we call this a *vis inertiae,* we only mark these facts, without pretending to have any idea of the inert power, in the same manner as, when we talk of gravity, we mean certain effects without comprehending that active power. It was never the meaning of Sir Isaac Newton to rob second causes of all force or energy, though some of his followers have endeavored to establish that theory upon his authority. On the contrary, that great philosopher had recourse to an ethereal active fluid to explain his universal attraction, though he was so cautious and modest as to allow that it was a mere hypothesis not to be insisted on without more

experiments. I must confess that there is something in the fate of opinions a little extraordinary. Descartes insinuated that doctrine of the universal and sole efficacy of the Deity, without insisting on it. Malebranche and other Cartesians made it the foundation of all their philosophy. It had, however, no authority in England. Locke, Clarke, and Cudworth never so much as take notice of it, but suppose all along that matter has a real, though subordinate and derived, power. By what means has it become so prevalent among our modern metaphysicians?

11. According to these explications and definitions, the idea of *power* is relative as much as that of *cause;* and both have a reference to an effect, or some other event constantly conjoined with the former. When we consider the *unknown* circumstance of an object by which the degree or quantity of its effect is fixed and determined, we call that its power. And accordingly, it is allowed by all philosophers that the effect is the measure of the power. But if they had any idea of power as it is in itself, why could they not measure it in itself? The dispute, whether the force of a body in motion be as its velocity, or the square of its velocity; this dispute, I say, needed not be decided by comparing its effects in equal or unequal times, but by direct mensuration and comparison.

As to the frequent use of the words "force," "power," "energy," etc., which everywhere occur in common conversation as well as in philosophy, that is no proof that we are acquainted, in any instance, with the connecting principle between cause and effect, or can account ultimately for the production of one thing by another. These words, as commonly used, have very loose meanings annexed to them, and their ideas are very uncertain and confused. No animal can put external bodies in motion without the sentiment of a *nisus* or endeavor; and every animal has a sentiment or feeling from the stroke or blow of an external object that is in motion. These sensations, which are merely animal, and from which we can *a priori* draw no inference, we are apt to transfer to inanimate objects, and to suppose that they have some such feelings whenever they transfer or receive motion. With regard to energies, which are exerted without our annexing to them any idea of communicated motion, we consider only the constant experienced conjunction of the events; and as we *feel* a customary connection between the ideas, we transfer that feeling to the objects, as nothing is more usual than to apply to external bodies every internal sensation which they occasion.

WESLEY C. SALMON

An Encounter with David Hume*

Wesley C. Salmon (1925–   ) directs the program in the history and philosophy of science at the University of Arizona.

A DAY IN THE LIFE OF A HYPOTHETICAL STUDENT

In the Physics 1a lecture hall, Professor Salvia[1] has had a bowling ball suspended from a high ceiling by a long rope so that it can swing back and forth like a pendulum. Standing well over to one side of the room, he holds the bowling ball at the tip of his nose. He releases it (taking great care not to give it a push). It swings through a wide arc, gaining considerable speed as it passes through the low portion of its swing beneath the point of suspension from the ceiling. It continues to the other side of the room, where it reaches the end of its path, and then returns. The professor stands motionless as the bowling ball moves faster and faster back toward his nose. As it passes through the midpoint of the return arc, it is again traveling very rapidly, but it begins to slow down, and it stops just at the tip of his nose. Some of the students think he is cool. "This demonstration," he says, "illustrates the faith that the physicist has in nature's regularity." (See Figure 1.)

Imagine that you have witnessed this demonstration just after your philosophy class, where the subject of discussion was Hume's *Enquiry Concerning Human Understanding*. You raise your hand. "How did you *know* that the bowling ball would stop where it did, just short of bashing your nose into your face?" you ask.

"This is a standard demonstration," he replies; "I do it every year in this class, and it has often been used by many other physics teachers." In an attempt to inject a little humor, he adds, "If I had had any doubt about its working, I'd have had the teaching assistant do it."

"Are you saying, then, that you trusted the experiment to work this time simply because it has

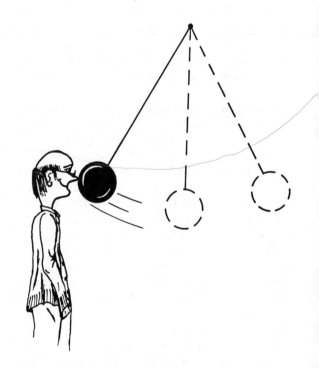

Figure 1.   Prof Salvia's Pendulum. After swinging to the opposite side of the lecture hall, the bowling ball swings right back to the tip of the prof's nose, which remains motionless during the entire procedure.

been tried so many times in the past, and has never failed?'' You recall Hume's discussion of the collisions of billiard balls. In the first instance, according to Hume, before you have any experience with material objects colliding with one another, you would not know what to expect when you see a moving billiard ball approaching a stationary one, but after a good deal of experience you confidently expect some motion to be transferred to the stationary ball as a result of the collision. As your experience accumulates, you learn to predict the exact manner in which the second ball will move after being struck by the first. But you cannot really accept that answer, and neither, you feel sure, will your physics professor. Without waiting for an answer, you follow up your first question with another.

"I have this friend," you continue, "who drives like a maniac. It scares me to ride with him, but he always tells me not to worry—he has never had an accident, or even a traffic ticket. Should I conclude—assuming he is telling the truth (just as I assume you are telling me the truth about this demonstration)—that it is as safe for me to ride with him as it is for you to perform the bowling ball trick?"

"It's not the same thing at all," another student chimes in; "you can prove, mathematically, that the pendulum will not swing back beyond its original starting point, but you certainly can't prove mathematically that your friend won't have a wreck. In a way it's just the opposite; you can prove that he is likely to have an accident if he keeps on driving like that."

"What you say is partly right," says Professor Salvia to the second student, "but it isn't only a matter of mathematics. We have to rely upon the laws of physics as well. With the pendulum we were depending mainly upon the law of conservation of energy, one of the most fundamental laws of nature. As the pendulum goes through its swing, potential energy is transformed into kinetic energy, which is transformed back into potential energy, and so forth. As long as the total amount of energy remains unchanged, my nose is safe."

Since you have not yet studied the concept of energy, you do not worry too much about the details of the explanation. You are satisfied that you will understand why the pendulum behaves as it does when you have learned more about the concepts

and laws that were mentioned. But you do remember something Hume wrote. There are two kinds of reasoning: reasoning concerning relations of ideas, and reasoning concerning matters of fact and existence. Mathematical reasoning falls into the former category (relations of ideas) and consequently, by itself, cannot provide any information about matters of fact. The pendulum and the professor's nose are, however, matters of fact, so we need something in addition to mathematics to get the information we want concerning that situation. Professor Salvia has told us what it is—we need the laws of nature as well.

Since physics is your last class in the morning, you head for the cafeteria when it is over to get a sandwich and coffee. The philosophy class is still bugging you. What was it Hume said about bread? That we do not know the "secret power" by which it nourishes us? Now we do, of course; we understand metabolism, the mechanism by which the body converts food into energy. Hume (living in the eighteenth century) did not understand about power and energy, as he said repeatedly. He did not know why bread is suitable food for humans, but not for tigers and lions. In biology class, you recall, you studied herbiverous, carnivorous, and omniverous species. Biologists must now understand why some species can metabolize vegetables and others cannot. Modern physics, chemistry, and biology can provide a complete explanation of the various forms of energy, the ways they can be converted from one form to another, and the ways in which they can be utilized by a living organism.

Taking a sip of the hot coffee, you recall some other things Hume said—for example, remarks about the "connection" between heat and flame. We now know that heat is really a form of energy; that temperature is a measure of the average kinetic energy of the molecules. Now, it seems, we know a great deal about the "secret powers," "energy," etc., that so perplexed Hume. Modern physics knows that ordinary objects are composed of molecules, which are in turn composed of atoms, which are themselves made up of subatomic particles. Modern science can tell us what holds atoms and molecules together, and why the things that consist of them have the properties they do. What was it that Hume said about a piece of ice and a crystal (e.g., a diamond)? That we do not know why one is caused by cold and the other by heat? I'll just bet, you think, that Salvia could answer that one without a bit of trouble. Why, you wonder, do they make us read these old philosophers who are now so out of date? Hume was, no doubt, a very profound thinker in his day, but why do we have to study him now, when we know the answers to all of those questions? If I were majoring in history that might be one thing, but that doesn't happen to be my field of interest. Oh, I suppose they'd say that getting an education means that you have to learn something about the "great minds of the past," but why doesn't the philosophy professor come right out and tell us the answers to these questions? It's silly to pretend that they are still great mysteries.

After lunch, let's imagine, you go to a class in contemporary social and political problems, a class you particularly like because of the lively discussions. A lot of time is spent talking about such topics as population growth, ecology and the environment, energy demands and uses, food production, and pollution. You discuss population trends, the extrapolation of such trends, and the predication that by the year 2000 A.D., world population will reach 7 billion. You consider the various causes and possible effects of increasing concentrations of carbon dioxide in the atmosphere. You discuss solutions to various of these problems in terms of strict governmental controls, economic sanctions and incentives, and voluntary compliance on the part of enlightened and concerned citizens.

"If people run true to form," you interject, "if they behave as they always have, you can be sure that you won't make much progress relying on the good will and good sense of the populace at large."

"What is needed is more awareness and education," another student remarks, "for people can change if they see the need. During World War II people willingly sacrificed in order to support the war effort. They will do the same again, if they see that the emergency is really serious. That's why we need to provide more education and make stronger appeals to their humanitarian concerns."

"What humanitarian concerns?" asks still another student with evident cynicism.

"People *will* change," says another. "I have been reading that we are entering a new era, the Age of Aquarius, when man's finer, gentler, more considerate nature will be manifest."

"Well, I don't know about all of this astrology," another remarks in earnest tones, "but I do not believe that God will let His world perish if we mend our ways and trust in Him. I have complete faith in His goodness."

You find this statement curiously reminiscent of Professor Salvia's earlier mention of his faith in the regularity of nature.

That night, after dinner, you read an English assignment. By the time you finish it, your throat feels a little scratchy, and you notice that you have a few sniffles. You decide to begin taking large doses of vitamin C; you have read that there is quite some controversy as to whether this helps to ward off colds, but that there is no harm in taking this vitamin in large quantities. Before going to the drug store to buy some vitamin C, you write home to request some additional funds; you mail your letter in the box by the pharmacy. You return with the vitamin C, take a few of the pills, and turn in for the night—confident that the sun will rise tomorrow morning, and hoping that you wont't feel as miserable as you usually do when you catch a cold. David Hume is the farthest thing from your mind.

HUME REVISITED

The next morning, you wake up feeling fine. The sun is shining brightly, and you have no sign of a cold. You are not sure whether the vitamin C cured your cold, or whether it was the good night's sleep, or whether it wasn't going to develop into a real cold regardless. Perhaps, even, it was the placebo effect; in psychology you learned that people can often be cured by totally inert drugs (e.g., sugar pills) if they believe in them. You don't really know what caused your prompt recovery, but frankly, you don't really care. If it was the placebo effect that is fine with you; you just hope it will work as well the next time.

You think about what you will do today. It is Thursday, so you have a philosophy discussion section in the morning and a physics lab in the afternoon. Thursday, you say to yourself, has got to be the lousiest day of the week. The philosophy section is a bore, and the physics lab is a drag. If only it were Saturday, when you have no classes! For a brief moment you consider taking off. Then you remember the letter you wrote last night, think about your budget and your grades, and resign yourself to the prescribed activities for the day.

The leader of the discussion section starts off with

the question, "What was the main problem—I mean the really *basic* problem—bothering Hume in the *Enquiry?*" You feel like saying, "Lack of adequate scientific knowledge" (or words to that effect), but restrain yourself. No use antagonizing the guy who will decide what grade to give you. Someone says that he seemed to worry quite a lot about causes and effects, to which the discussion leader (as usual) responds, "But *why?*" Again, you stifle an impulse to say, "Because he didn't know too much about them."

After much folderal, the leader finally elicits the answer, "Because he wanted to know how we can find out about things we don't actually see (or hear, smell, touch, taste, etc.)."

"In other words," the leader paraphrases, "to examine the basis for making inferences from what we observe to what we cannot (at the moment) observe. Will someone," he continues, "give me an example of something you believe in which you are not now observing?"

You think of the letter you dropped into the box last night, of your home and parents, and of the money you hope to receive. You do not see the letter now, but you are confident it is somewhere in the mails; you do not see your parents now, but you firmly believe they are back home where you left them; you do not yet see the money you hope to get, but you expect to see it before too long. The leader is pleased when you give those examples. "And what do causes and effects have to do with all of this?" he asks, trying to draw you out a little more. Still thinking of your grade you cooperate. "I believe the letter is somewhere in the mails because I wrote it and dropped it in the box. I believe my parents are at home because they are always calling me up to tell me what to do. And I believe that the money will come as an effect of my eloquent appeal." The leader is really happy with that; you can tell you have an A for today's session.

"But," he goes on, "do you see how this leads us immediately into Hume's next question? If cause-effect relations are the whole basis for our knowledge of things and events we do not observe, how do we know whether one event causes another, or whether they just happen together as a matter of coincidence?" Your mind is really clicking now.

"I felt a cold coming on last night, and I took a massive dose of vitamin C," you report. "This

morning I feel great, but I honestly don't know whether the vitamin C actually cured it."

"Well, how could we go about trying to find out," retorts the discussion leader.

"By trying it again when I have the first symptoms of a cold," you answer, "and by trying it on other people as well." At that point the bell rings, and you leave class wondering whether the vitamin C really did cure your incipient cold.

You keep busy until lunch, doing one thing and another, but sitting down and eating, you find yourself thinking again about the common cold and its cure. It seems to be a well-known fact that the cold is caused by one or more viruses, and the human organism seems to have ways of combating virus infections. Perhaps the massive doses of vitamin C trigger the body's defenses, in some way or other, or perhaps it provides some kind of antidote to the toxic effects of the virus. You don't know much about all of this, but you can't help speculating that science has had a good deal of success in finding causes and cures of various diseases. If continued research reveals the physiological and chemical processes in the cold's infection and in the body's response, then surely it would be possible to find out whether the vitamin C really has any effect upon the common cold or not. It seems that we could ascertain whether a causal relation exists in this instance if only we could discover the relevant laws of biology and chemistry.

At this point in your musings, you notice that it is time to get over to the physics lab. You remember that yesterday morning you were convinced that predicting the outcome of an experiment is possible if you know which physical laws apply. That certainly was the outcome of the discussion in the physics class. Now, it seems, the question about the curative power of vitamin C hinges on exactly the same thing—the laws of nature. As you hurry to the lab it occurs to you that predicting the outcome of an experiment, before it is performed, is a first-class example of what you were discussing in philosophy—making inferences from the observed to the unobserved. We observe the set-up for the experiment (or demonstration) before it is performed, and we predict the outcome before we observe it. Salvia certainly was confident about the prediction he made. Also, recalling one of Hume's examples, you were at least as confident, when you went to bed last night, that the sun would rise this morning. But Hume seemed to be saying that the basis for this confidence was the fact that the sun has been observed to rise every morning since the dawn of history. "That's wrong," you say to yourself as you reach the physics lab. "My confidence in the rising of the sun is based upon the laws of astronomy. So here we are back at the laws again."

Inside the lab you notice a familiar gadget; it consists of a frame from which five steel balls are suspended so that they hang in a straight line, each one touching its neighbors. Your little brother got a toy like this, in a somewhat smaller size, for his birthday a couple of years ago. You casually raise one of the end balls, and let it swing back. It strikes the nearest of the four balls left hanging, and the ball at the other end swings out (the three balls in the middle keeping their place). The ball at the far end swings back again, striking its neighbor, and then the ball on the near end swings out, almost to the point from which you let it swing originally. The process goes on for a while, with the two end balls alternately swinging out and back. It has a pleasant rhythm. (See Figure 2.)

While you are enjoying the familiar toy, the lab instructor, Dr. Sagro,[2] comes over to you. "Do you know why just the ball on the far end moves—instead of, say, two on the far end, or all four of the remaining ones—when the ball on this end strikes?"

"Not exactly, but I suppose it has something to do with conservation of energy," you reply, recalling what Salvia said yesterday in answer to the question about the bowling ball.

"That's right," says Dr. Sagro, "but it also depends upon conservation of momentum." Before you have a chance to say anything she continues, "Let me ask you another question. What would happen if you raised two balls at this end, and let them swing together toward the remaining three?"

"I think two balls will swing away at the other end," you reply, remembering the way your brother's toy worked.

"Why don't you test it to find out if you are right?" says the instructor. You do, and you find that the result is as you had predicted. Without saying anything about it, you assume that this, too, can be explained by means of the laws of conservation of energy and momentum.

Dr. Sagro poses another question. "What will happen," she asks, "if you start by swinging three balls from this end?" Since there are only two re-

maining balls you don't know what to say, so you confess ignorance. She suggests you try it, in order to find out what will happen. When you do, you see that three balls swing to the other side, and three swing back again; the middle ball swings back and forth, acting as the third ball in each group. This was a case in which you didn't know what to expect as a result until you tried the experiment.[3] This was like some of Hume's examples; not until you have actually had the experience do you know what result to expect. But there is also something different.

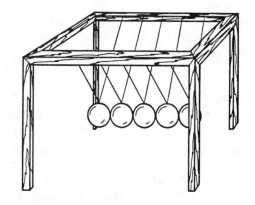

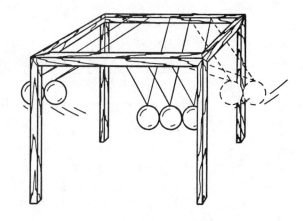

Figure 2. The Energy-Momentum Toy. When two balls at the right collide with the remaining three, two balls swing away from the left side. What happens when three on the right collide with the remaining two?

Hume said that you must try the experiment many times in order to know what to expect; nevertheless, after just one trial you are sure what will happen whenever the experiment is repeated. This makes it rather different from the problem of whether vitamin C cured your cold. In that case, it seemed necessary to try the experiment over and over again, preferably with a number of different people. Reflecting upon this difference, you ask the lab instructor a crucial question, "If you knew the laws of conservation of momentum and energy, but had never seen the experiment with the three balls performed, would you have been able to predict the outcome?"

"Yes," she says simply.

"Well," you murmur inaudibly, "it seems as if the whole answer to Hume's problem regarding inferences about things we do not immediately observe, including predictions of future occurrences, rests squarely upon the laws of nature."

KNOWING THE LAWS

Given that the laws are so fundamental, you decide to find out more about them. The laws of conservation of energy and momentum are close at hand, so to speak, so you decide to start there. "O.K.," you say to the lab instructor, "what are these laws of nature, which enable you to predict so confidently how experiments will turn out before they are performed? I'd like to learn something about them."

"Fine," she says, delighted with your desire to learn; "let's start with conservation of momentum. It's simpler than conservation of energy, and we can demonstrate it quite easily."[4] (See Figure 3.)

Your laboratory contains a standard piece of equipment—an air track—on which little cars move back and forth. The track is made of metal with many tiny holes through which air is blown. The cars thus ride on a thin cushion of air; they move back and forth almost without friction. Some of the cars are equipped with spring bumpers, so that they will bounce off of one another upon impact, while others have coupling devices which lock them together upon contact. Dr. Sagro begins by explaining what is meant by the momentum of a body—namely, its mass multiplied by its velocity.[5] "To speak somewhat quaintly," she says, "the mass is just a measure of the quantity of matter in the body.[6] Since, in all of the experiments we are going to do, it is safe to say that the mass of each body remains unchanged, we need not say more about it. You can see that each car comes with its mass labeled; this one, for instance, has a mass of 200 grams, while this one has a mass of 400 grams. We have a number of different cars with quite a variety of different masses. The velocity," she continues, "is what we ordinarily mean by 'speed' along with the direction of travel. On the air track there are only two possible directions, left to right and right to left. Let us simply agree that motion from left to right has a positive velocity,

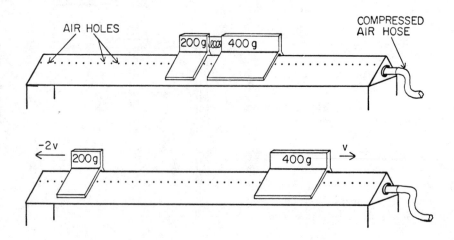

Figure 3. Cars on the Air Track. Top: Cars tied together against spring under tension. Bottom: Cars moving apart after "explosion." $400\,g \times v + 200\,g \times (-2v) = 0$. Momentum is conserved.

while motion from right to left has a negative velocity. Mass, of course, is always a positive quantity. Thus, momentum, which is mass times velocity, may be positive, negative, or zero. When we add the momenta of various bodies together, we must always be careful of the sign (plus or minus)."

With these preliminaries, you begin to perform a variety of experiments. She has various types of fancy equipment for measuring velocities, which she shows you how to use, and she also helps you to make measurements. You find that it is fun pushing cars back and forth on the track, crashing them into one another, and measuring their velocities before and after collisions. You try it with a variety of cars of different masses and with differing velocities. You try it with the ones that bounce apart after impact and with those that stick together. You always find that the *total* momentum (the sum of the momenta for the two cars) before any collision is equal to the *total* momentum after the collision, even though the momenta of the individual cars may change markedly as a result of the collision. This, Dr. Sagro explains, is what the law of conservation of momentum demands: when two bodies (such as the cars) interact with one another (as in a collision), the total momentum of the system consisting of those two bodies is the same before and after the interaction.

You ask her whether this law applies only to collisions; she replies immediately that it applies to all kinds of interactions. "Let's see how it works for a simple type of 'explosion,' " she suggests. She helps you tie together two cars, holding a compressed spring between them. You burn the string which holds them together and they fly apart. You measure the velocities and compute the momenta of each of the cars after the "explosion." It turns out that the momentum of the one car is always equal in amount but opposite in direction to that of the other. This is true whether the cars are of equal or unequal masses and whether the tension on the spring that drives them apart is great or small. "This is just what the law of conservation of momentum tells us to expect," she explains; "the momentum of each car is zero before the 'explosion' because they are not moving (each has velocity equal to zero), and so the two momenta after the 'explosion' (one positive and one negative) must add up to zero. That is what has happened every time.

"There are many other applications of the law of conservation of momentum," she continues. "When a rifle recoils upon being fired, when a jet engine propels an airplane, when a rocket engine lifts an artificial satellite into orbit, or when you step out of an untethered rowboat and are surprised to feel it moving out from under you—these are all cases of conservation of momentum."

"Is this law ever violated?" you ask.

"No," she answers, "there are no known exceptions to it." You leave the lab with the feeling that you know at least one fundamental law, and that you have seen it proved experimentally right before your eyes. You can't wait to tell your philosophy professor about it.

When you go to your philosophy class the next morning, the topic is still Hume's *Enquiry Concerning Human Understanding* and the problem of how we can have knowledge of things we do not observe. As the lecture begins, Professor Philo[7] is saying, "As we saw during the last lecture, Hume maintains that our knowledge of what we do not observe is based entirely upon cause and effect relations, but that raises the question of how we can gain knowledge of these relations. Hume maintained that this knowledge can result only from repeated observation of one type of event (a cause) to see whether it is always followed by an event of another kind (its effect). Hume therefore analyzed the notion of causality in terms of constant conjunction of events. Consider for a moment Hume's favorite example, the colliding billiard balls . . ."

You raise your hand. "It seems to me that Hume was wrong about this," you begin, and then you relate briefly yesterday's experiences in the physics lab. "If you know the relevant laws of nature," you conclude, "you can predict the outcomes of future experiments on the basis of a single trial, or perhaps even without benefit of any trials at all."

"But how," asks Professor Philo, "can we establish knowledge of the laws of nature?"

You had a hunch she might ask some such question, and you are ready with your reply, "We *proved* it experimentally."

"Well," says Professor Philo, "I'm not a physicist, so perhaps you had better explain in a little more detail just what the experimental proof consists of. You mentioned something about an explosion—how did that go?"

You explain carefully how the air track works, how the two cars were joined together with a spring under tension in between, and how they moved apart when the string was burned. "In every case," you conclude, "the momentum of the two cars was equal in amount and opposite in direction, just as the law of conservation of momentum says it should be."

"Now let me see if I understand your line of reasoning," says the professor in a tone that is altogether too calm to suit you. "If the law of conservation of momentum is correct, then the two cars will part in the manner you described. The cars did move apart in just that way. Therefore, the law of conservation of momentum is correct. Is that your argument?"

"I guess so," you reply a bit hesitantly, because it looks as if she is trying to trap you.

"Do you think that kind of argument is valid?" she responds.

"What do you mean?" you ask, beginning to feel a little confused.

"Well," she says, "isn't that rather like the following argument: If this defendant is guilty, he will refuse to testify at his own trial; he does refuse to testify; therefore, he is guilty. Would any judge allow that argument in a court of law?"

"Of course not," you reply, "but it isn't the same thing at all. We tested the law of conservation of momentum many times in many different ways, and in every case we got the expected result (allowing for the usual small inaccuracies in the measurements)."

"If I remember what you said," Ms. Philo goes on, "in one of your experiments you had one car with a mass of 200 grams and another with a mass of 400 grams, and in that case the lighter car recoiled with twice the speed of the more massive one. How many times did you repeat this particular experiment?"

"Once or twice, as nearly as I can recall."

"Yet, you seem to believe that the result would be the same, no matter how many times the experiment was repeated—is that correct?"

"I suppose so," you reply somewhat uncomfortably.

"And with how many different masses and how many different recoil velocities did you try it? Do you believe it would work the same way if the masses were thousands or billions of kilograms instead of a few grams? And do you suppose that it would work the same way if the velocities were very great—somewhere near the speed of light?"

Since you have heard that strange things happen when speeds approach that of light, your hesitancy increases, but you reply tentatively, "Well, the lab instructor told me that there are no exceptions to the law."

"Did she say that," asks Philo, "or did she say no *known* exceptions?"

"I guess that was it," you reply lamely, feeling quite crushed.

Professor Philo endeavors to summarize the discussion. "What is considered experimental 'proof of a law of nature' is actually a process of testing *some* of its logical consequences. That is, you ask what would have to happen *if* your hypothesis is true, and then you perform an experiment to see if it turns out that way *in fact*. Since any law of nature is a generalization,[8] it has an unlimited number of consequences. We can never hope to test them all. In particular, any *useful* law of nature will have consequences that pertain to the future; they enable us to make predictions. We can never test these consequences until it is too late to use them for the purpose of prediction. To suppose that testing *some* of the consequences of a law constitutes a *conclusive proof* of the law would clearly be an outright logical fallacy." The bell rings and you leave the class, convinced that she has merely been quibbling.

During your physics class you brood about the previous discussion in the philosophy class, without paying very close attention to the lecture. Similar thoughts keep nagging at you during lunch. The objections brought up by Professor Philo seem to be well-founded, you conclude, but you wonder how they can be reconciled with the apparent reliability and certainty of scientific knowledge. In desperation, you decide to talk it over with Professor Salvia during his office hour this very afternoon. When you arrive, you don't know exactly where to begin, so you decide to go back to the pendulum demonstration, which was the thing that got you started on this whole mess. "When you performed that demonstration," you ask, "were you *absolutely certain* how it would turn out? Has it ever failed?"

"Well, to be perfectly honest," he says, "it has been known to fail. Once when a friend of mine was doing it in front of a large auditorium, the suspension in the ceiling broke and the ball landed right on his foot. He was in a cast for months!"

"But that's no fault of the law of conservation of energy is it?" you ask. "The breaking of the suspension didn't mean that conservation of energy is false, did it?"

"Of course not," he answers, "we still believe firmly in conservation of energy."

"But are you *certain* of the law of conservation of energy, or any other law of nature?" you ask, and before he has a chance to answer, you tell him about the discussion in the philosophy class this morning.

"So that's what's bothering you," he says, after hearing the whole story. "Professor Philo has an important point. No matter how thoroughly we have tested a scientific law—better, let's say 'hypothesis'—there is always the possibility that new evidence will show up to prove it false. For instance, around the close of the nineteenth century, many physicists seemed virtually certain that Newtonian mechanics was absolutely correct. A wide variety of its consequences had been tested under many different circumstances, and Newton's laws stood up extremely well. But early in the twentieth century it became clear that what we now call 'classical physics' would have to undergo major revisions, and a profound scientific revolution ensued. Modern physics, which includes quantum mechanics and relativity theory, was the result. We can never be sure that any hypothesis we currently accept as correct will not have to be abandoned or modified at some time in the future as a result of new evidence."

"What about the law of conservation of momentum?" you ask, recalling yesterday's experience in the lab. "The lab instructor said it has no known exceptions."

"That is correct," says Salvia, "and it is a rather interesting case. Conservation of momentum is a consequence of Newton's laws of motion; therefore, any consequence of conservation of momentum is a consequence of Newton's laws. But we now regard Newton's laws as not strictly true—they break down, for example, with objects traveling close to the speed of light—but conservation of momentum holds even in these cases. So we have a good example of a case where we believe a lot of consequences, but we do not believe in the laws (Newton's) from which the consequences follow."

It occurs to you that this is a rather important set of supposed laws; perhaps the philosophy professor was not merely quibbling when she said that it was not valid to conclude that a hypothesis is true just because we know many of its consequences to be true.

"Since you cannot be certain of any so-called law of nature," you ask, "why do you believe in them so firmly?"

"Because," answers Salvia, "we consider them very well confirmed. We accept well-confirmed hypotheses, knowing that we may later have to change our minds in the light of new evidence. Science can no longer claim infallible truth."

"Does that mean that scientific results are highly probable, but not absolutely certain?" you ask, trying to be sure you have understood what he has said.

"Yes, you could put it that way," he agrees.

You leave with the feeling that you have a pretty good comprehension of the situation. As a result of your study of physics and philosophy you now understand why science cannot claim infallibility for its findings, but must be content with results that are well confirmed. With that, you take off for the weekend. (And what you do with your weekend is your own business.)

HUME'S BOMBSHELL

A little tired, but basically in a cheerful mood, you arrive at your philosophy class on Monday morning. You meet the professor a few minutes before class outside the room, and you tell her very briefly of your conversation with the physics professor. You explain that you now understand why it is that scientific laws can never be considered completely certain, but only as well-confirmed hypotheses. With her help, and with that of Professor Salvia, you now understand what Hume was driving at—and you see, moreover, that Hume was right. She smiles, and you both go into the classroom, where she begins her lecture.

"Last Friday, as you may recall, we had quite a lively discussion about the status of scientific laws—the law of conservation of momentum, in particular. We saw that such laws cannot be proved conclusively by any amount of experimental evidence. This is a point with which, I am happy to report, many (if not most) contemporary scientists agree. They realize that the most they can reasonably claim for their hypotheses is strong confirmation. Looking at the matter this way, one could conclude that it is wise to believe in scientific predictions, for if they are not certain to be true, they are a good bet. To believe in scientific results is to bet with the best available odds.

"However," she continues, "while this view may be correct as far as it goes, Hume was making a much more fundamental, and I should add, much more devastating point. Hume was challenging not merely our right to claim that scientific predictions will always be right, but also our right to claim that they will usually, or often, or indeed ever, be correct. Take careful note of what he says in Section IV:

Let the course of things be allowed hitherto ever so regular; that alone, without some new argument or inference, proves not that, for the future, it will continue so. In vain do you pretend to have learned the nature of bodies from your past experience. Their secret nature, and consequently all their effects and influence, may change, without any change in their sensible qualities. This happens sometimes, and with regard to some objects: Why may it not happen always and with regard to all objects? What logic, what process of argument secures you against this supposition?

He is saying, as I hope you understood from your reading, that no matter how reliably a law seems to have held in the past, there is no logical reason why it must do so in the future *at all*. It is therefore possible that *every* scientific prediction, based on *any* law or laws whatever, may turn out to be false from this moment on. The stationary billiard ball that is struck by a moving one may remain motionless where it is—while the moving ball may bounce straight back in the direction from whence it came, or it may go straight up in the air, or it might vanish in a puff of smoke. Any of these possibilities can be imagined; none of them involves any logical contradiction. This is the force of Hume's skeptical arguments. The conclusion seems to be that we have no *reason* to believe in scientific predictions—no more reason than to believe on the basis of astrology, crystal gazing, or sheer blind guessing."

You can hardly believe your ears; what is she saying? You raise your hand, and when you are recognized, you can hardly keep your intense irritation from showing as you assert, "But certainly we can say that scientific predictions are more probable than those based, for example, upon astrology." As you speak, you are reminded of the remark in contemporary problems last Wednesday concerning the coming of the Age of Aquarius. Science has got to be better than *that!* As these thoughts cross your mind Professor Philo is saying, ". . . but that depends upon what you mean by 'probable,' doesn't it?"

The physics lecture today is on Newton's law of gravitation, and the professor is explaining that every bit of matter in the universe is attracted to every other by a force proportional to the masses and inversely proportional to the square of the distance between them. He goes on to explain how Kepler's laws of planetary motion and Galileo's law of falling bodies are (when suitably corrected) consequences of Newton's laws. You listen carefully, but you recognize this as another law that enables scientists to make impressive predictions. Indeed, Salvia is now telling how Newton's laws were used to explain the tides on the oceans and to predict the existence of two planets, Neptune and Pluto, that had not been known before. At the same time, you are wondering whether there is anything in what Hume seemed to be saying about such laws. Is it possible that suddenly, at the very next moment, matter would cease to have gravitational attraction, so that the whole solar system would go flying apart? It's a pretty chilling thought.

At lunch you are thinking about this question, and you glance back at some of the readings that were assigned from Hume's *Enquiry*. You notice again Hume's many references to secret powers and forces. Well, gravitation is surely a force, though there has not been any great secret about it since Newton's time. It is the "power" which keeps the solar system together. You remember reading somewhere that, according to Hume, you cannot know that it is safer to leave a building by way of the halls, stairways, and doors than it would be to step out of the third-story window. Well, Newton's law makes it clear why you don't want to step out of the third-story window, but what assurance have you that the building will continue to stand, rather than crashing down around your ears before you can get out? The engineers who design and build towers and bridges have a great deal of knowledge of the "secret powers" of their materials, so they must know a great deal more than Hume did about the hidden properties of things.

At this very moment, a lucky coincidence occurs— you see Dr. Sagro, your physics lab instructor, entering the cafeteria. You wave to her, and she sits down with you, putting her coffee cup on the table. You begin to ask her some questions about structural materials, and she responds by inquiring whether you would be satisfied if she could explain how the table supports the cup of coffee. You recognize it as just the kind of question you have in mind, and urge her to proceed.

"Certain materials, such as the metal in this table," she begins, "have a rather rigid crystalline structure, and for this reason they stick together and maintain their shape unless subjected to large forces. These crystals consist of very regular (and very beautiful) arrays of atoms, and they are held together by forces, essentially electrostatic in origin, among the charged particles that make up the atoms. Have you studied Coulomb's law of electrostatic forces?''

"No," you reply, "we are just doing Newton's law of gravitation. I think Salvia said electricity and magnetism would come up next semester.''

"Well," she says, "these electrostatic forces are a lot like gravitational forces (they vary inversely with the square of the distance), but there are a couple of very important differences. First, as you know, there are two types of charges, positive and negative. The proton in the nucleus of the atom carries a positive charge, and the electrons that circulate about the nuclei have a negative charge. Two particles with opposite signs (such as a proton and an electron) attract one another, while two particles with like signs (e.g., two electrons or two protons) repel each other. This is different from gravity, because all matter attracts all other matter; there is no such thing as gravitational repulsion. The second main difference is that the electrostatic force is fantastically stronger than the gravitational force—roughly a billion billion billion billion times more powerful— but we don't usually notice it because most objects we deal with in everyday life are electrically neutral, containing equal amounts of positive and negative electric charge, or very nearly so. If you could somehow strip all of the electrons away from an apple, and all of the protons away from the earth, the force of attraction between the apple and the earth would be unbelievable.

"It is these *extremely* strong attractive and repulsive forces among the electrons and protons in the metal that maintain a stable and rigid form. That's why the table doesn't collapse. And the reason the coffee cup stays on top of the table, without penetrating its surface or slipping through, is that the electrons in the surface of the cup strongly repel those in the surface of the table. Actually, there is also a quantum mechanical force that prevents the weight of the cup from noticeably compressing the table, but we needn't go into that, because the effect is mostly due to the electrostatic forces.''

Pleased with this very clear explanation, you thank her, but follow it up with another question. "Is there any logical reason why it has to be that way—why opposite charges attract and like charges repel? Can you prove that it is impossible for like charges to attract and unlike charges to repel? What would

happen if *that* were suddenly to become the law?''

"It would certainly result in utter catastrophe," she replies, "with all of the atomic nuclei bunching up together in one place and all of the electrons rushing away from them to congregate elsewhere. But to answer your question, no, there is no logical proof that it couldn't be that way. In our physical world we find that there are, in fact, two types of charges, and they obey the Coulomb law rather than the one you just formulated.''

"Can you prove that the world will not switch from the one law to the other, say, tomorrow?'' you ask.

"No, frankly, I can't," she answers, "but I, and all other physicists assume—call it an article of faith if you like—that it won't happen.''

There's that word "faith" again, you muse as you leave the cafeteria.

The more you think about it, the more clearly you see that the physicists have not shown you how to get around the basic problem Hume raised; rather, they have really reinforced it. Maybe this problem is tougher than I thought, you say to yourself, and you head for Professor Philo's office to talk further about it. "I was thinking about all these 'secret powers' Hume talks about," you begin, "and so I asked my physics instructor about them. She explained, as an example, how a table supports a coffee cup, but she did it on the basis of laws of nature— Coulomb's law of electrostatics was one of them. This law is very well confirmed, I suppose, but she admitted that it is quite possible to imagine that this law would fail tomorrow, and—if you'll pardon the expression—all hell would break loose. Now, my question is, how can we find out about these secret powers that Hume keeps saying we need to know? How can we discover the real underlying causes of what happens?''

"I think you are really beginning to get the point Hume was driving at," she replies, "namely, that there is *no way*, even in principle, of finding any hidden causes or secret powers. You can, of course, find regularities in nature—such as conservation of energy, conservation of momentum, universal gravitation, and electrostatic attraction and repulsion— but these can only be known to have held up to the present. There is no further kind of hidden connection or causal relation that can be discovered by more careful observation, or examination with some kind of super-microscope. Of course, we do discover regularities, and we explain them. For instance, Kepler's laws of planetary motion are regularities that are explained by Newton's laws of motion and gravitation, but these do not reveal any secret powers. They simply provide more general regularities to cover the more restricted ones.

"In his discussion of 'the idea of necessary connection,' Hume tries to bring out precisely this point. We can observe, as you were saying in class the other day, that recoil experiments always yield a particular type of result—namely, momentum is conserved. We have observed this many times. And now we expect, on future trials, that the same thing will happen. But we do not observe, nor can we discover in any way, an *additional* factor which constitutes a necessary connection between the 'explosion' and the subsequent motion of the cars. This seems to be what Hume had in mind when he wrote:

These ultimate springs and principles are totally shut up from human curiosity and enquiry. Elasticity, gravity, cohesion of parts, communication of motion by impulse; these are probably the ultimate causes and principles which we ever discover in nature; and we may esteem ourselves sufficiently happy, if, by accurate inquiry and reasoning, we can trace up the particular phenomena to, or near to, these general principles.[9]

Hume is acknowledging that we can discover general regularities in nature, but he is denying that an additional 'connection' can be found. And Hume was dedicated to the maxim, as are modern scientists, that we have no business talking about things it is impossible in principle for us to know anything about.

"When he asks why we do, in fact, expect so confidently that the future experiments will have outcomes similar to those of the past trials, Hume finds that it is nothing other than a matter of psychological conditioning. When we see one type of cause repeatedly followed by a particular type of effect, we come to expect that the same type of effect will follow the next time we come across that kind of cause. But this is not a matter of logical reasoning. Have you heard of Pavlov's conditioning experiments with dogs?" You nod. "When the bell rings the dog starts to salivate. He is *not* reasoning that, since the sounding of the bell has, in the past, been associated with the bringing of food, therefore, on this occasion the food will (at least probably) appear soon after the bell rings. According to Hume's analysis, what is called 'scientific reasoning' is no more rational or logical than your watering at the mouth when you are hungry and hear the dinner bell. It is something you cannot help doing, Hume says, but that does not mean that it has any logical foundation."

"That brings up a question I've wanted to ask," you say. "Hume seems to think that people necessarily reason in that way—inductive reasoning, I think it is called—but I've noticed that lots of people don't seem to. For instance, many people (including a student in my current problems course) believe in things like astrology; they believe that the configuration of the planets has a bearing on human events, when experience shows that it often doesn't work that way." The professor nods in agreement. You continue, "So if there is no logical justification for believing in scientific predictions, why isn't it just as reasonable to believe in astrological predictions?"

"That," replies the prof, "is a very profound and difficult question. I doubt that any philosopher has a completely satisfactory answer to it."

MODERN ANSWERS[10]

The Wednesday philosophy lecture begins with a sort of rhetorical question, "What reason do we have (Hume is, at bottom, asking) for trusting the scientific method; what grounds do we have for believing that scientific predictions are reliable?" You have been pondering that very question quite a bit in the last couple of days, and—rhetorical or not—your hand shoots up. You have a thing or two to say on the subject.

"Philosophers may have trouble answering such questions," you assert, "but it seems to me there is an obvious reply. As my physics professor has often said, the scientist takes a very practical attitude. He puts forth a hypothesis; if it works he believes in it, and he continues to believe in it as long as it works. If it starts giving him bad predictions, he starts looking for another hypothesis, or for a way of revising his old one. Now the important thing about the scientific method, it seems to me, is that it works. Not only has it led to a vast amount of knowledge about the physical world, but it has been applied in all sorts of practical ways—and although these applications may not have been uniformly beneficial—for better or worse they were successful. Not always, of course, but by and large. Astrology, crystal gazing, and other such superstitious methods simply do not work very well. That's good enough for me."[11]

"That is, indeed, a very tempting answer," Professor Philo replies, "and in one form or another, it has been advanced by several modern philosophers. But Hume actually answered that one himself. You might put it this way. We can all agree that science has, up till now, a very impressive record of success in predicting the future. The question we are asking, however, is this: should we *predict* that science will continue to have the kind of success it has had in the past? It is quite natural to assume that its record will continue, but this is just a case of applying the scientific method to itself. In studying conservation of momentum, you inferred that future experiments would have results similar to those of your past experiments; in appraising the scientific method, you are assuming that its future success will match its past success. But using the scientific method to judge the scientific method is circular reasoning. It is as if a man goes to a bank to cash a check. When the teller refuses, on the grounds that he does not know this man, the man replies, 'That is no problem; permit me to introduce myself—I am John Smith, just as it says on the check.'

"Suppose that I were a believer in crystal gazing. You tell me that your method is better than mine because it has been more successful than mine. You say that this is a good reason for preferring your method to mine. I object. Since you are using your method to judge my method (as well as your method), I demand the right to use my method to evaluate yours. I gaze into my crystal ball and announce the result: from now on crystal gazing will be very successful in predicting the future, while the scientific method is due for a long run of bad luck."

You are about to protest, but she continues.

"The trouble with circular arguments is that they can be used to prove anything; if you assume what you are trying to prove, then there isn't much difficulty in proving it. You find the scientific justification of the scientific method convincing because you already trust the scientific method; if you had equal trust in crystal gazing, I should think you would find the crystal gazer's justification of his method equally convincing. Hume puts it this way:

When a man says, *I have found, in all past instances, such sensible qualities conjoined with such secret powers:* And when he says, *Similar sensible qualities will always be conjoined with similar secret powers,* he is not guilty of a tautology, nor are these propositions in any respect

the same. You can say that the one proposition is an inference from the other. But you must confess that the inference is not intuitive; neither is it demonstrative: Of what nature is it, then? To say it is experimental is begging the question. For all inferences from experience suppose, as their foundation, that the future will resemble the past, and that similar powers will be conjoined with similar sensible qualities.[12]

If the assumption that the future is like the past is the presupposition of the scientific method, we cannot assume that principle in order to justify the scientific method. Once more, we can hardly find a clearer statement than Hume's:

We have said that all arguments concerning existence are founded on the relation of cause and effect; that our knowledge of that relation is derived entirely from experience; and that all our experimental conclusions proceed upon the supposition that the future will be conformable to the past. To endeavour, therefore, the proof of this last supposition by probable arguments, or arguments regarding existence, must evidently be going in a circle, and taking that for granted, which is the very point in question.[13]

"The principle that the future will be like the past, or that regularities which have held up to the present will persist in the future, has traditionally been called *the principle of uniformity of nature.* Some philosophers, most notably Immanuel Kant, have regarded it as an a priori truth.[14] It seems to me, however, that Hume had already provided a convincing refutation of that claim by arguing that irregularities, however startling to common sense, are by no means inconceivable—that is, they cannot be ruled out a priori. Recall what he said:

. . . it implies no contradiction that the course of nature may change, and that an object, seemingly like those which we have experienced, may be attended with different or contrary effects. May I not clearly and distinctly conceive that a body, falling from the clouds, and which, in all other respects, resembles snow, has yet the taste of salt or feeling of fire? . . . Now whatever is intelligible, and can be distinctly conceived, implies no contradiction, and can never be proved false by any demonstrative argument or abstract reasoning a priori.[15]

"Other philosophers have proposed assuming this principle (or something similar) as a postulate; Bertrand Russell, though not the only one to advocate this approach, is by far the most famous.[16] But most philosophers agree that this use of postulation is question-begging. The real question still remains: why should one adopt any such postulate? Russell himself, in another context, summed it up very well: The method of 'postulating' what we want has many advantages; they are the same as the advantages of theft over honest toil."[17]

"Nevertheless," you interject, "can't we still say that scientific predictions are more probable than, say, those of astrology or crystal gazing?"

"It seems to me you raised a similar question once before," Professor Philo replies, "and I seem to recall saying that it depends on what you mean by the term 'probable.' Maybe it would be helpful if I now explain what I meant."[18] You nod encouragement. "The concept of probability—or perhaps I should say 'concepts' of probability—are very tricky. If you were to undertake a systematic study of confirmation and induction, you would have to go into a rather technical treatment of probability, but perhaps I can give a brief hint of what is involved.[19] One thing that has traditionally been meant by this term relates directly to the frequency with which something occurs—as Aristotle put it, the probable is that which happens often. If the weather forecaster says that there is a 90% chance of rain, he presumably means that, given such weather conditions as are now present, rain occurs in nine out of ten cases. If these forecasts are correct, we can predict rain on such occasions and be right nine times out of ten.

"Now, if you mean that scientific predictions are probable in *this* sense, I do not see how you could possibly support your claim. For Hume has argued—cogently, I think—that, for all we know now, *every* future scientific prediction may go wrong. He was not merely saying that science is fallible, that it will sometimes err in its predictions—he was saying that nature might at any moment (for all we can know) become irregular on such a wide scale that any kind of scientific prediction of future occurrences would be utterly impossible. We have not found any reason to believe he was mistaken about this point."

"That must be the concept of probability I had in mind," you remark; "I'm not quite sure how to express it, but it had something to do with what it would be reasonable to believe. I was thinking of the fact that, although we cannot regard scientific

hypotheses as certain, we can consider them well confirmed. It is something like saying that a particular suspect is probably guilty of a crime—that the evidence, taken as a whole, seems to point to him."

"You have put your finger on another important probability concept," the professor replies. "It is sometimes known as the rational credibility concept. The most popular contemporary attempt (I believe) to deal with Hume's problem of inductive reasoning is stated in terms of this concept. The argument can be summarized in the following way. Hume has proved that we cannot *know for sure* that our scientific predictions will be correct, but that would be an unreasonable demand to place upon science. The best we can hope is for scientific conclusions that are probable. But when we ask that they be probable, in this sense, we are only asking that they be based upon the best possible evidence. Now, that is just what scientific predictions are—they are predictions based upon the best possible evidence. The scientist has fashioned his hypotheses in the light of all available information, and he has tested them experimentally on many occasions under a wide variety of circumstances. He has summoned all of the available evidence, and he has brought it to bear on the problem at hand. Such scientific predictions are obviously probable (as we are now construing this term); hence, they are rationally credible.[20] If we say that a belief is irrational, we mean that it runs counter to the evidence, or the person who holds it is ignoring the evidence. And in such contexts, when we speak of evidence, we are referring to inductive or scientific evidence.

"Now, the argument continues, to ask whether it is reasonable to believe in scientific conclusions comes right down to asking whether one ought to fashion his beliefs on the basis of the available evidence. But this is what it means to be rational. Hence, the question amounts to asking whether it is rational to be rational. If the question makes any sense at all, the obvious answer is 'yes.' "

"That answer certainly satisfies me," you say, feeling that Dr. Philo has succeeded admirably in stating the point you were groping for. "I'm glad to know that lots of other philosophers agree with it. Do you think it is a satisfactory answer to Hume's problem of induction?" You are more than a trifle discouraged when she gives a negative response with a shake of her head. "Why not?" you demand.

"This argument seems to me to beg the question," she replies, "for it assumes that the concept of evidence is completely clear. But that is precisely the question at issue. If we could be confident that the kind of experiments you performed in the physics lab to test the law of conservation of momentum do, in fact, provide evidence for that law, then we could say that the law is well supported by evidence. But to suppose that such facts do constitute evidence amounts to saying that what has happened in the past is a sign of what will happen in the future—the fact that momentum was conserved in your 'explosion' experiments is an indication that momentum will be conserved in future experiments of a similar nature. This assumes that the future will be like the past, and that is precisely the point at issue. To say that one fact constitutes evidence for another means, in part, that the one provides some basis for inference to the occurrence of the other. The problem of induction is nothing other than the problem of determining the circumstances under which such inference is justified. Thus, we have to resolve the problem of induction—Hume's problem—before we can ascertain whether one fact constitutes evidence for another. We cannot use the concept of evidence—inductive evidence—to solve the problem of induction.

"There is another way to look at this same argument. If you ask me whether you should use the scientific method, I must find out what you hope to accomplish. If you say that you want to get a job teaching physics, I can tell you right away that you had better use the scientific method, at least in your work, because that is what is expected of a physicist. If you say that you want to enjoy the respect and prestige that accrues to scientists in certain social circles, the answer is essentially the same. If you tell me, however, that you want to have as much success as possible in predicting future events, the answer is by no means as easy. If I tell you to go ahead and make scientific predictions, because that is what is considered reasonable (that is what is meant by fashioning your beliefs on the basis of evidence), then you should ask whether being reasonable in this sense (which is obviously the commonly accepted sense) is a good way to attain your goal. The answer, 'but that's what it means to be reasonable,' is beside the point. You might say, 'I want a method that is reasonable to adopt in order to achieve my goal of successful prediction—that is what I mean by being reasonable. To tell me that the scientific method is what is usually *called* reasonable doesn't help. I want to know whether the method that is *commonly called* reasonable is *actually* a reasonable method

to adopt to attain my goal of successful prediction of the future. The fact that it is usually considered reasonable cuts no ice, because an awareness of Hume's problem of induction has not filtered down into common usage.' That's what I think you should say."

"Couldn't we avoid all of these problems," suggests another student, "if we simply resisted the temptation to generalize? In social science, my area of interest, we find that it is very risky to generalize, say, from one society to another. An opinion survey on students in the far west, for example, will not be valid when applied to students attending eastern schools. Wouldn't we be better off to restrict our claims to the facts we know, instead of trying to extend them inductively to things we really don't know?"

"The opinion you have offered bears a strong resemblance (though it isn't identical) to that of an influential British philosopher.[21] He has presented his ideas persuasively, and has many followers. Hume, he says, has proved conclusively that induction is not a justifiable form of inference; it is, consequently, no part of science. The only kind of logic that has a legitimate place in science is deductive logic. Deductive inferences are demonstrative; their conclusions must be true if their premises are true. These inferences are precisely what Hume called 'reasoning concerning relations of ideas.' The crucial point is that they *do not add to our knowledge* in any way—they enable us to see the content of our premises, but they do not extend that content in the least. Thus, from premises that refer only to events in the past and present, it is impossible to *deduce* any predictions of future facts. Any kind of inference which would enable us to predict the future on the basis of facts already observed would have to be of a different sort; such inference is often called 'ampliative' or 'inductive.' If science contains only deductive inferences, but no inductive inferences, it can never provide us with any knowledge beyond the content of our immediate observations.

"Now this philosopher does not reject scientific knowledge; he simply claims that prediction of the future is no part of the business of science. Accordingly, the function of scientific investigation is to find powerful general hypotheses (he calls them *conjectures*) that adequately explain all known facts that have occurred so far. As long as such a generalization succeeds in explaining the new facts that come along it is retained; if it fails to explain new facts, it must be modified or rejected. The sole purpose of scientific experimentation is to try to find weaknesses in such hypotheses—that is to criticize them or try to refute them. He calls this the 'method of conjectures and refutations,' or sometimes simply, 'the critical approach.'

"The main difficulty with this approach—an insuperable one, in my opinion—is the fact that it completely deprives science of its predictive function. To the question of which method to use for predicting the future, it can give no answer. Astrology, crystal gazing, blind guessing, and scientific prediction are all on a par. To find out what the population of the world will be in 2000 A.D., we might as well employ a psychic seer as a scientific demographer. I find it hard to believe that this can constitute a satisfactory solution to the problem of employing our knowledge to find rational solutions to the problems that face us—problems whose solutions demand that we make predictions of the future course of events. Tempting as it is to try to evade Hume's problem in this way, I do not see how we can be satisfied to admit that there is no rational approach to our problem."

"But perhaps there is no answer to Hume's problem," says still another student; "maybe the only hope for salvation of this world is to give up our blind worship of science and return to religion. We have placed our faith in science, and look where we are as a result. I believe we should adopt a different faith."

There's that word *again,* you note to yourself, as the professor begins her answer: "Though I heartily agree that many of the results of science—*technological* results, I think we should emphasize—have been far from beneficial, I don't think we can properly condemn scientific *knowledge.* Knowledge is one thing; what we choose to do with it is quite another. But that's not the issue we are concerned with. I do not see how anyone could deny that science has had a great deal of success in making predictions; no other approach can possibly present a comparable record of success. And, as time goes on, the capability for predictive success seems only to increase. It would be an utterly astonishing piece of luck, if it were sheer coincidence, that science has been so much luckier than other approaches in making its predictions. If anyone can consistently pick a winner

in every race at every track every day, we are pretty sure he has more than good luck going for him. Science isn't infallible, but it is hard to believe its predictive success is just a matter of chance. I, at least, am not prepared to say that science is just one among many equally acceptable faiths—you pays your money and you takes your choice. I feel rather sure that the scientific approach has a logical justification of some sort." With that, the bell rings, the discussion ends, and everyone leaves—none by way of the window.

It just isn't good enough, you say to yourself, after listening to your physics professor lecturing, with demonstrations, on the law of conservation of angular momentum. You don't know whether you're dizzier from the discussion of Hume's problem in the philosophy class or from watching student volunteers in this class being spun on stools mounted on turntables. In any case, you decide to look up Professor Philo after lunch, and you find her in her office.

"Look," you say a bit brusquely, "I see that Hume was right about our inability to prove that nature is uniform. But suppose that nature does play a trick on us, so to speak. Suppose that after all this time of appearing quite uniform, manifesting all sorts of regularities such as the laws of physics, she turns chaotic. Then there isn't anything we can do anyhow. Someone might make a lucky guess about some future event, but there would be no systematic method for anticipating the chaos successfully. It seems to me I've got a way of predicting the future which will work if nature is uniform—the scientific method, or if you like, the inductive method—and if nature isn't uniform, I'm out of luck whatever I do. It seems to me I've got everything to gain and nothing to lose (except a lot of hard work) if I attempt to adhere to the scientific approach. That seems good enough to me; what do you think?"[22]

"Well," she says quietly, "I tend to agree with that answer, and so do a few others, but we are certainly in the minority. And many difficult problems arise when you try to work it out with precision."

"What sorts of difficulties are these?" you ask.

"There are several kinds," she begins; "for instance, what exactly do you mean by saying that nature is uniform? You cannot mean—to use Hume's quaint language—that like sensible qualities are always conjoined with like secret powers. All of us, including Hume, know this claim is false. Bread which looks and tastes completely harmless may contain a deadly poison. A gas which has exactly the appearance of normal air may suffocate living organisms and pollute the atmosphere. That kind of uniformity principle cannot be the basis of our inferences.''

"That's quite true," you answer, "but perhaps we could say that nature operates according to regular laws. Ever since I began to think about Hume's problem, I have been led back to laws of nature.''

"Your suggestion is a good one," she replies, ''but modern philosophers have found it surprisingly difficult to say precisely what type of statement can qualify as a possible law of nature. It is a law of nature, most physicists would agree, that no material objects travel faster than light; they would refuse to admit, *as a law of nature,* that no golden spheres are more than one mile in diameter. It is not easy to state clearly the basis for this distinction. Both statements are generalizations, and both are true to the best of our knowledge.''[23]

"Isn't the difference simply that you cannot, even in principle, accelerate a material object to the speed of light, while it is possible in principle to fabricate an enormous sphere of gold?''

"That is precisely the question at issue," she replies. "The problem is, what basis do we have for claiming possibility in the one case and impossibility in the other. You seem to be saying that a law of nature prevents the one but not the other, which is obviously circular. And if you bring in the notion of causation—causing something to go faster than light vs. causing a large golden sphere to be created—you only compound the difficulty, for the concept of causation is itself a source of great perplexity.

"Suppose, however, that we had succeeded in overcoming that obstacle—that we could say with reasonable precision which sorts of statements are candidates for the status of laws of nature and which are not. We then face a further difficulty. It is obvious that some tests of scientific laws carry greater weight than others. The discovery of the planet Neptune, for example, confirmed Newton's laws much more dramatically than would a few additional observations of Mars. A test with particles traveling at very high velocities would be much stronger evidence for conservation of momentum than would some more experiments on the air track in the physics lab. It is not easy to see how to measure or compare the weight which different types of evidence lend to different scientific hypotheses.

"Scientific confirmation is a subtle and complex matter to which contemporary philosophers have devoted a great deal of attention; some have tried to construct systems of inductive logic that would capture this kind of scientific reasoning. Such efforts have, at best, met with limited success; inductive logic is in a primitive state compared with deductive logic. Until we have a reasonably clear idea of what such inference consists of, however, it is unlikely that we will be able to go very far in meeting the fundamental challenge Hume issued concerning the justification of scientific reasoning. Unless we can at least say what inductive inference is, and what constitutes uniformity of nature (or natural law), we can hardly argue that inductive reasoning—and only inductive reasoning—will prove successful in predicting the future if nature is uniform. And even if those concepts were clarified, the argument would still be intricate indeed.''

"Do you think there is any chance that answers to such problems can be found?'' you ask.

"I think it's just possible.''

"Thanks," you say as you get up to leave.

"And my thanks to you," she replies. "You cannot possibly know how satisfying it is to talk with someone like you—someone intelligent—who takes such philosophical problems seriously and thinks hard about them. If you keep it up, you might be the very person to find some of the answers. I wish you well.''

NOTES

1. Professor Salvia is a descendant of Salviati, the protagonist in Galileo's dialogues. The name was shortened when the family emigrated to America.

2. Dr. Sagro is married to a descendant of Sagredo, another character in Galileo's dialogues.

3. If you really did know, please accept the author's apologies.

4. Please note that "demonstrate" is ambiguous. In mathematics it means "prove"; in physics it means "exemplify." Hume uses this term only in the mathematical sense.

5. Hume, using the terminology of his day, refers to it as the "moment" of the moving body.

6. This is Newton's definition; it is somewhat out of date, but adequate in the present context.

7. She is a direct descendant of Philo, the protagonist in Hume's "Dialogues Concerning Natural Religion," most of which is reprinted in this anthology.

8. Professor Philo realizes that it would be more accurate to say that a statement or hypothesis expressing a law of nature must be a generalization, but she does not wish to introduce unnecessary terminological distinctions at this point. For further details see W. Salmon, "Determinism and Indeterminism in Modern Science," p. 331 in this anthology.

9. In section IV, part I, anticipating the results of the later discussion.

10. All of the attempts to deal with Hume's problem which are treated in this section are discussed in detail in Wesley C. Salmon, *The Foundations of Scientific Inference* (Pittsburgh: University of Pittsburgh Press, 1967); this book will be cited hereafter as *Foundations*.

11. This is an inductive justification; see *Foundations*, chapter II, section I.

12. David Hume, *An Enquiry Concerning Human Under-standing* (hereafter, *Enquiry*), section IV, part II.

13. Ibid.

14. For discussion of justification by means of synthetic a priori principles, see *Foundations*, chapter II, section 4.

15. *Enquiry*, section IV, part II.

16. For discussion of the postulational approach, see *Foundations*, chapter II, section 6.

17. Bertrand Russell, *Introduction to Mathematical Philosophy* (London: Allen & Unwin, 1919), p. 71.

18. The "probabilistic approach" is discussed in *Foundations*, chapter II, section 7.

19. An elementary survey of philosophical problems of probability is given in *Foundations*, chapters IV–VII. References to additional literature on this subject can be found there.

20. We are assuming, of course, that these predictions are properly made. Scientists are only human, and they do make mistakes. One should not conclude, however, that every false prediction represents a scientific error. Impeccable scientific procedure is fallible, as we have already noted more than once.

21. This refers to the "deductivist" position of Sir Karl Popper. This approach is discussed in *Foundations*, chapter II, section 3.

22. This approach is due mainly to Hans Reichenbach; it is known as a "pragmatic justification" and is discussed in *Foundations*, chapter II, section 8.

23. Further elementary discussion of this issue can be found in Carl G. Hempel, *Philosophy of Natural Science* (Englewood Cliffs, N.J.: Prentice-Hall, Inc., 1966), § 5.3 A more technical and extensive treatment of related issues can be found in Nelson Goodman, *Fact, Fiction, and Forecast*, 2nd ed. (Indianapolis, Ind.: The Bobbs-Merrill Co., 1965).

PART 3 MIND AND

To a large degree, what has come to be known as the "Mind-Body Problem" in philosophy is a product of the philosophy of René Descartes. How can things differing as radically as minds (or souls) and bodies, in Descartes' conception, be so intimately related, as they clearly are, in every human person? Bodies are solid chunks of material stuff, extended in three-dimensional space, publicly observable and measurable, possessed of a certain mass and velocity, and capable of causing things to happen, in accordance with the invariant laws of mechanics, by transmitting their impact in "collisions" with other material things. A mind, on the other hand, is directly "observable" only by the person who owns it; only he can think his thoughts, feel his emotions, suffer his pains. Although, under certain circumstances, someone else can cut open his skull and see and touch his living *brain,* there is no conceivable way for another to see or touch his mind or its beliefs, sensations, and desires. Minds, moreover, have no size or shape or spatial location, no mass, or velocity, or capacity to make impact.

Nevertheless, to common sense, it seems certain that minds and bodies do causally interact. When I will, or wish, or desire (mental events) to raise my arm, up it goes (bodily event); and when a sliver of wood penetrates my flesh (bodily event), I feel pain (mental event). It would surely seem, then, that, in normal volition, mental events *cause* physical ones and that, in sensation and perception, physical events *cause* mental ones. Yet how can this be? How can the mind, a mass-less, weightless, unextended thing, push up against a nerve cell and cause an impulse to be transmitted along a nerve to a muscle? And how can physical stimuli like wood slivers or even light rays penetrate a thing that has no size or location and cause it to have an experience? Isn't this as inconceivable as a collision between a physical object and a ghost? This is the kind of difficulty cited by many of Descartes' own contemporaries in criticism of his philosophy.[1]

---

[1] A number of distinguished philosophers, theologians, and scientists, including Pierre Gassendi, Thomas Hobbes, and Antoine Arnauld, were invited to comment on the manuscript of Descartes' *Meditations* before it was published. Their "Objections" were then forwarded to Descartes, who in turn composed "Replies," and published the whole exchange along with the original work. The entire discussion is strongly recommended to the serious student of Descartes' philosophy.

ITS PLACE IN NATURE

Many important seventeenth-century philosophers, no matter how impressed in other ways by the ''Cartesian philosophy'' (as the philosophy of Descartes came to be called), found Descartes' theory of interaction between mind and body unacceptable. Some, therefore, came to abandon the part of Descartes' philosophy that generated the difficulty: his *dualism,* or theory that mind and matter are distinct and independent kinds of substances, each capable of existing quite independently of the other. *Idealism* of Berkeley's kind of thinking, the theory that the body itself is nothing but a collection of actual or possible sense-data—sights, sounds, touches, smells—was one alternative. According to that theory, there exist only minds and their mental ''contents,'' hence no problem of causal interaction between radically diferent kinds of substances. *Materialism*—the theory that mind is either reducible to, or ultimately dependent upon, matter—was another alternative. Still other philosophers maintained a kind of dualism but abandoned the common-sense view that mind and body really do interact causally. Some held, for example, that the wood sliver's penetration of my flesh does not *cause* me pain; rather, it is the *occasion* for God, whose infinite nature somehow encompasses both mind and matter, to cause me to feel pain, and similarly that my desire to raise my arm is simply the occasion for God's causing my arm to go up. This is the theory called *occasionalism.* Others held the view called *parallelism,* according to which mind and body only appear to interact because of a kind of ''pre-established harmony'' between their life histories. Leibniz likened this parallelism to that between two clocks that strike at the same moment, having been wound up together and each designed to keep accurate time, in causal independence of each other.

This section opens with a fictitious dialogue by the contemporary British philosopher Godfrey Vesey, based on actual correspondence in the seventeenth century between René Descartes and Princess Elizabeth of Bohemia. Vesey provides both an introduction and a commentary. Elizabeth is largely persuaded by Descartes' philosophy but she voices here the doubts and misgivings that assailed many of Descartes' contemporaries about ''the nature of the soul'' and how ''an immaterial thing can move the body.''

John Locke, the great English philosopher who was a much younger contemporary of

Descartes, in the next article examines the concept of *substance,* which does much to generate the mind-body problem. European philosophers had commonly argued that mere properties of things—or "accidents" as they were often called—could not exist by themselves but required a thing, or substance, to inhere in. Thus hardness, redness, and loudness exist only in material substances; thinking, desiring, and fearing only in spiritual substances; omnipotence and omniscience only in infinite substance (God). The main function of substance then is to provide a "substratum" for perceived qualities. But Locke subjects the idea of a substratum to analysis and concludes that it is a confused idea, the idea of an "I know not what." Causal interaction between spiritual substances (minds) and corporeal substances (bodies), he concludes, is no more mysterious than interaction between different material substances.

The twentieth-century philosopher C. D. Broad, in his selection included here, is unwilling to abandon dualism on the alleged ground that it cannot explain how volition and perception are possible. Efforts to solve the mind-body problem by positing such theories as idealism, materialism, occasionalism, or parallelism, he argues, are quite unnecessary. Once we state and consider carefully the reasons that have been urged against two-way causal interaction of mind and body, we can find no basis in them for denying the deliverances of common sense on this matter.

In an extraordinarily useful essay, Jerome Shaffer reviews the arguments for and against not only dualism but also most of the other leading theories about "the subject of consciousness," including the "double-aspect" theory of Baruch Spinoza (1632–1677) and the currently popular "person theory" of Oxford philosopher P. F. Strawson. Spinoza denied that mind and body were distinct and independent substances, each capable of existing entirely on its own. Rather they are two "aspects" of a substance that in itself is neither mental nor physical. Strawson calls this underlying entity the *person*—a being who has both physical attributes such as weight and height, and mental attributes such as beliefs and emotions. It is the person—not the mind or body—who walks, breathes, and digests food, and also who thinks, chooses, and feels anxiety. The person theory has very attractive features, but Shaffer also points out that it has difficulties of its own; most importantly, it does not provide a philosophically adequate account of the human body.

Many twentieth-century philosophers would agree with Broad (and with Shaffer's final tentative suggestion) that some duly modified form of dualism can withstand the traditional attacks against that theory, but the question is still extremely controversial. Probably the leading rivals to dualism in this scientific age are the various forms of materialism.[2] The two leading forms of materialism, each in its own way trying to do justice to the scientific conception of man, are *epiphenomenalism,* which holds that mind is not itself a material thing but rather a distinct but causally impotent by-product (an "epiphenomenon") of the world charted by physics,[3] and *the identity theory,* which holds that mental events (the occurrence of aches and pains, sensations, after-images, desires,

---

[2] "Materialism" as the name of a philosophical theory ought not to be confused with various other senses of the word. A philosophical materialist is *not* (necessarily) "a person who tends to give undue importance to material possessions and comforts." Nor is he (necessarily) "a person who thinks that everybody ought to put his 'material well-being' (as measured in dollars and cents) above all other considerations." A philosophical materialist could, with consistency, denounce materialism in these other senses.

[3] Many philosophers, including Cornman in his essay in this section, prefer to classify epiphenomenalism as a form of dualism in which the interaction is just one way (from body to mind). Epiphenomenalists do, after all, deny that mind is a material thing. But in also denying that mind has causal efficacy, they deny that it is a *substance* at all in the traditional sense.

thoughts) are simply identical with brain processes, "identical" in the same sense as that in which lightning flashes are held to be identical with electrical discharges. The former view—epiphenomenalism—is represented in this volume by the great nineteenth-century biologist Thomas Huxley, who argues from the scientific evidence of his day to the conclusion that states of consciousness in all the higher animals, including human beings, are the effects but not the causes of "molecular changes of the brain-substance." The latter view—the identity theory—is represented here by the essay of James W. Cornman, who argues explicitly against Broad's dualism, Huxley's epiphenomenalism, and a less plausible form (than his own) of the identity thesis itself.

The concluding articles of Part Three relate the discussion back to one of the original concerns of Princess Elizabeth—whether "in death there is an end of me." This question of course presupposes the questions preceding it about the nature of the subject of consciousness. If body and mind are one and the same thing, or if mind is a mere "epiphenomenon" or by-product of body, then it would follow that the disintegration of mind (soul, self) would proceed at the same pace with the disintegration of the body. But if our minds are distinct substances, and causally efficacious in their own right, then it is at least possible that they (we) can survive the death of their (our) bodies. If we are to make philosophical progress in our discussions of the possibility of survival, however, we need to move beyond common understanding of the nature of mind and agreement about the empirical evidence (if any). In addition, we must become clear about a set of prior questions that are not normally treated in works on the mind-body problem; namely, questions about *personal identity*. Who or what am I, this entity whose possible survival of death is under discussion? Am I simply this body and nothing more? What then of my belief that this body "belongs" to me, that the owner is one thing and the body another? Am I simply my mind? Am I a self that somehow encompasses both body and mind? Could I be the *same self* that I am now if I had none of my present memories, or if I suddenly discovered myself with an altogether different body (for example, with four legs and a tail)? How much can I change without ceasing to be the person I am now? These are only some of the riddles associated with the elusive concept of personal identity. Still others are suggested by more recondite possibilities: resurrection of the dead, reincarnation, transmigration of souls, bodily transfers, multiple or alternate possession of a body by various persons, brain transplants, and "brain rejuvenations"—examples drawn from theology, psychic research, abnormal psychology, and science fiction.

The subsection on "the concept of a self" contains three famous philosophical discussions on the nature of personal identity. John Locke argues that it is a person's consciousness, in the form of memories of past experiences, that makes him or her the same person through different times, even as the body completely changes its characteristics and appearance. If the mind of a prince were magically inserted into the body of a cobbler, Locke argues in a famous example, we would all say that the person with the cobbler's appearance is the prince, and that only his body, not his personal identity, had changed. David Hume argues against the view that there is such a thing as an unchanging substantial self as opposed to the relatively fleeting thoughts and feelings revealed in consciousness. All we can mean by a self, Hume concludes, is a "bundle or collection of different perceptions." Thomas Reid (1710–1796) claimed to vindicate common sense in his argument against both Locke and Hume. Against Locke, Reid argues that memory is not the only criterion of personal identity. We may well need to add bodily continuity to the full complex criteria that do justice to our common-sense notions. Against Hume, he argues in various ways, insisting that there cannot be perceptions without a perceiver (something other than the perceptions themselves), just as there cannot be actions without actors.

In the deathbed dialogue that concludes this section, John Perry focuses sharply on the area where the problem of survival and the riddles of personal identity intersect. A dying professor, her old friend a clergyman, and her student, among them bring up quite spontaneously the famous philosophical theories of John Locke, Joseph Butler, and Antony Collins—seminal thinkers of the seventeenth and eighteenth centuries—about personal identity. At issue is the question of what sense, if any, can be made of the very idea of personal survival.

G O D F R E Y   V E S E Y

The Princess and the Philosopher*

1. IS THERE LIFE AFTER DEATH?

In the synopsis of his *Meditations on First Philosophy* (1641) René Descartes (1596–1650) wrote:

What I have said is sufficient to show clearly that the extinction of the mind does not follow from the corruption of the body, and also to give men the hope of another life after death.[1]

In order to "show clearly enough" that there can be life after death Descartes did not have recourse to the alleged discoveries of spiritualists. He did not attend seances, or anything like that. What he did was to shut himself up and *think*. He thought about what he could, and could not, possibly doubt. He could not possibly doubt that he was thinking, and therefore that he existed. Even an all-powerful deceiver could not have deluded him about his own existence. But such a deceiver, he thought, might well have deluded him about everything bodily. There was nothing in the indubitable fact of his thinking to guarantee that he even had a body. He could think of himself as a purely mental being. And surely it could not be beyond God's power to have created him as a purely mental being. But in that case his mind and his body are really distinct, even if they happen to be united in this earthly life. But if they are really distinct then one of them, the mind, can continue to exist when the other, the body, is dead and buried.

*Godfrey Vesey, "The Princess and the Philosopher," from *Philosophy in the Open*, ed. Godfrey Vesey (Milton Keynes, England: Open University Press, 1974), pp. 65–75. Reprinted by permission of the publisher and author. Section numbers added.

The conclusion was attractive, and the argument not an easy one to show to be invalid. But the doctrine that man is two distinct things, a purely spiritual soul on the one hand and a purely physical body on the other, had its difficulties. Chief among them was that of understanding how the two different "substances" can act on one another. How can what does not take up space, the purely spiritual soul, *move* the body, as, in Descartes' view, it must when people make voluntary movements? And how can a "cerebral motion," as Descartes calls it, produce a sensation in the mind, as, in his view, it must when people perceive things?

Descartes welcomed criticisms of his work. Some were from his fellow philosophers, men with established reputations and widely known views, like Thomas Hobbes (1588–1679) and Antoine Arnauld (1612–1694). Their objections to his *Meditations,* and Descartes' replies, were published along with the *Meditations.* But other exchanges were not published in his lifetime. One such was his lengthy correspondence with the Princess Elizabeth of Bohemia, daughter of the Elector Frederick, against whom Descartes had once soldiered. Descartes corresponded with her from 1643 until his death, and the work in which he gave his fullest account of the relationship between soul and body, *The Passions of the Soul* (1649), was originally composed for her.

In a letter to Elizabeth dated 28 June 1643 Descartes made what might seem to be a remarkable concession. Elizabeth had written that she found it hard to understand how the soul, if it is purely spiritual, can bring about a change in the body. She could imagine much more easily that the soul has matter and takes up space—has what philosophers call "extension"—than that, being immaterial, it could move a body, and be affected by changes in it. Descartes replied:

Your Highness makes the remark that it is easier to ascribe matter and extension to the soul than to ascribe to it the power of moving a body and being moved by it without having any matter. Now I would ask your Highness to hold yourself free to ascribe "matter and extension" to the soul; . . .[2]

Could Descartes really have meant this? Could he really have meant to make a concession so damaging to his professed view, which is that the soul is distinct from the body precisely in *not* being a material thing?

The dialogue that follows answers this question. I imagined a meeting between Descartes, the philosopher, and Elizabeth, the princess, and based their discussion on the letters they wrote to one another in the 1640s. Some license has been taken. Not all the arguments attributed to Elizabeth are to be found in her letters to Descartes. The use of a geometrical example towards the end of the dialogue, in particular, comes not from the Descartes-Elizabeth correspondence, but from the objections made to the *Meditations* by Antoine Arnauld.[3] But an effort has been made not to introduce philosophical ideas of later centuries.

2. THE PRINCESS AND THE PHILOSOPHER: A DIALOGUE

[*Conversation and music in a large hall*]

Descartes. . . . Madame, the honor that your Highness does in greeting me is greater than I dared to hope. It is most consoling not only to receive the favor of your commandments in writing, but to encounter you.

Elizabeth. You are welcome, Master. Your letters have given me much pleasure.

Descartes. I am most obliged to your Highness for reading them. Even when you see how badly I explain myself, you still have patience to hear me. [*Slight pause*] But tell me, Madame, how can I help you and what subjects still bemuse your Highness? When I read the traces of your thought on paper, I find a truly amazing comprehension of the abstract matters on which I write. But now, seeing before me a body

such as painters give to angels from which these superhuman sentiments flow, I am ravished like a man come fresh to heaven. Anything you ask, I will answer, if I can.

Elizabeth. Let us move to a quieter room.

[*They move to a quiet room and sit down*]

Elizabeth. I wrote to you, you will remember, about the nature of the soul. I asked you how the soul, if it is an immaterial thing, can move the body. Surely, if one object is to move another, the first must be in physical contact with the second. I cannot play my harpsichord without touching the keys with my fingers. How can the soul, if it is purely spiritual, touch the body to bring about changes in it?

Descartes. Forgive me, Madame, I answered that question, did I not?

Elizabeth. You replied to my letter, but I don't think you answered my question. You wrote that people suppose heaviness to be something that moves objects, and yet moves them without their being touched. Heaviness makes the leaves fall to the ground and this is obviously different from the way that one ball, when it strikes another, makes it move. In other words—and this I took to be your point—we do have a notion of one thing moving another without making contact with it.

Descartes. Ah . . . so you agree with me.

Elizabeth. [*Slight pause—continues puzzled*] But the way in which heaviness moves the leaves is very different from the way the soul moves the body. Heaviness is not immaterial in the way that, according to you, the soul is immaterial. It isn't—how shall I put it?—heaviness isn't a *mental* force. What I can't understand is how a thought can bring about a bodily movement. You aren't saying that it does so by heaviness, are you? In any case, I don't know what that means.

Descartes. No, no, no, no, no. My point is that we do have a notion of things being moved without other things making physical contact with them. [*Slight pause*] As a matter of fact, this notion is misapplied when we use it to understand why things fall to the ground. In my *Physics* I showed that the heaviness of things is not, in fact, something distinct from them. But we do have this notion and I believe we were given it in order to understand how the soul moves the body. If, by using this notion, we can understand how the soul moves the body, we can also see how a man's soul and body are united.

Elizabeth. But all the emphasis, in your *Meditations,* is on their being distinct.

Descartes. Yes, but there are two things to remember about the soul. First, it is a thing which thinks. Second, it is united to the body, and so can act and suffer along with it. I said almost nothing about the second in my *Meditations*. My aim there was to show that the soul is distinct from the body, and it would only have confused matters to have said, at the same time, that they are united.

Elizabeth. [*Interrupting*] Oh yes, but now you must explain. Because if you simply say that the soul and body are united, and leave it at that, I'm really no better off. How can what is spiritual be united with what is corporeal, physical, material, "extended"? Master, I accept that soul and body are united, but if I am to understand how the soul can act on the body, I must understand the principle of their union. How are soul and body, two distinct substances, united?

Descartes. [*Pensively*] Well, it isn't by the intellect, with which we comprehend the soul, that we can also understand the union of soul and body. Nor is it by the intellect aided by the imagination. That leaves only the senses. So it is through the senses that we understand the union of soul and body. When we philosophize on these matters we realize that soul and body are distinct; but so far as our experience is concerned it's as if they were one. When I raise my arm, or have a pain in my back, I don't feel myself to be separate from my arm or my back. But I know, nevertheless, that my soul is distinct from my body.

Elizabeth. You are saying that it *feels* as if body and soul are united?

Descartes. Indeed.

Elizabeth. But that doesn't explain *how* they are united, does it? You said we understand the union of soul and body by the senses. But knowing *that* the soul acts on the body isn't knowing how. [*Pause*] You see, it seems to me that if the soul and body do act on one another, then we ought to be able to understand how they do so. The senses don't seem to provide that sort of knowledge. [*Descartes still does not reply*] It was because I couldn't see how the immaterial soul could act on the physical body that I suggested that the soul, in its substance as distinct from its activity, must be material. If thinking, willing, and so on, are things that the *body* does, instead of things done by a spiritual thing which is distinct from the body, my problem doesn't arise.

Descartes. But what do you mean by "substance"? It's the soul's activities—thinking, willing, and so on—that make it the substance it is. Thought is the essence of the soul, just as "extension"— taking up space—is the essence of matter. No substance can have two essences.

Elizabeth. [*Indignant*] Yet I clearly remember your saying in a letter that I could "ascribe matter and extension to the soul."

Descartes. When was that?

Elizabeth. About three years ago, I think.

Descartes. In what connection?

Elizabeth. I can find the letter for you. [*She rummages*] Yes, here it is. Let me find the place . . . Ah! "Your Highness remarks that it is easier to ascribe matter and extension to the soul than to ascribe to an *im*material thing the ability to move a material thing and be moved by it. Now I would ask your Highness to feel free to ascribe matter and extension to the soul . . ."

Descartes. Ah, but how does it go on?

Elizabeth. Er ". . . matter and extension to the soul; for this is nothing else than to conceive the soul as united to the body."

Descartes. [*Animated*] You see! I was still talking about the soul being united to the body. The soul is, in a sense, extended. For example, when we feel aches and pains in various parts of our bodies. . . . Suppose you prick your finger on a spindle . . .

Elizabeth. Aren't you confusing me with another Princess?

Descartes. I said "suppose." Suppose you prick your finger on a spindle. You feel pain. Where do you feel the pain? In your finger. In a way it's almost as if your soul were extended throughout your body, even into your fingers. But to talk in that way is to talk only of feeling. The pain isn't really in your finger, it's in your soul. You know by your intellect that it isn't in your finger, since you know by your intellect that the soul, which suffers pain, is immaterial. To know the truth of the matter we must trust the intellect.

Elizabeth. The intellect, you say, tells us that the soul is immaterial. But is our intellectual perception of the soul sufficiently clear? Perhaps if we had a clearer perception of its nature we would realize that it is, in fact, material. Isn't there at least this possibility?

Descartes. Not if the argument of my *Meditations* is sound. You remember, I imagined that an extremely powerful, malicious demon does everything he can to deceive us?

Elizabeth. Yes.

Descartes. He may deceive me about everything that has to do with my body, but when it comes to my thinking—well, then he can't deceive me. That I cannot doubt. [*Slowly and emphatically*] Therefore, in so far as I cannot be deceived about my existence I am no more than a thinking thing.

Elizabeth. Agreed. But that is "what you cannot be deceived about." The question I'm raising is a different one. It isn't about what you do or don't know; it's about what is in fact the case. I'm suggesting that although you can suppose yourself not to have bodily attributes it may nevertheless be the case that you do have them.

Descartes. No. They may seem quite different questions—the one about what I know or don't know and the one about what is in fact the case—but they aren't. They're connected.

Elizabeth. How? How are they connected?

Descartes. Well, it's really to do with possibilities. If it is possible for thinking to go on apart from a body then . . .

Elizabeth. [*Interrupting*] But *is* it possible? That's the question.

Descartes. All right, I'm coming to that. I did say "if." If it is possible for thinking, and the body, to exist in separation then . . .

Elizabeth. [*Impatiently*] Yes, yes, then what-does-the-thinking isn't the body. I can quite see that. But what you've got to do is to get rid of the "if." That is, you've got to show it to be possible for thinking to go on apart from a body.

Descartes. Precisely, and that is where what I know and don't know, comes in.

Elizabeth. Go on.

Descartes. Well, I know certainly that I am thinking and at the same time I can doubt that I have bodily attributes. So I can perceive the one thing, the thinking, apart from the other. And since this perception is clear and distinct it must be possible for the one thing to exist apart from the other.

Elizabeth. Just a moment. You said "since this perception is clear and distinct."

Descartes. Yes.

Elizabeth. And you'd say that if you clearly and distinctly perceive yourself as no more than a thinking thing then it would follow that you could exist as no more than a thinking thing?

Descartes. Yes.

Elizabeth. And therefore that you really are no more than a thinking thing?

Descartes. Exactly.

Elizabeth. All right. Well now, isn't it possible that your perception is clear, but only as far as it goes? And that it doesn't go far enough for you to know the truth? In other words, isn't it possible that you really do have bodily properties although your knowledge of yourself doesn't go beyond your mental properties?

Descartes. No. You must distinguish between clearness and completeness. Certainly there may be things about me which I haven't clearly perceived. But that doesn't affect what I have clearly perceived. And, having clearly perceived that I am a thinking thing, I know that I can exist as such. That is, I know that what I am certain of—my intellectual faculty—is enough for me to exist with. And if it is enough for me to exist with, then I really am distinct from anything bodily.

Elizabeth. So, the principle of your argument is: if I can clearly perceive something to be such-and-such while I cannot clearly perceive it to be so-and-so, then it can exist simply as such-and-such.

Descartes. Yes.

Elizabeth. But now, consider this case. A triangle is a plane figure bounded by three straight lines.

Descartes. Mm.

Elizabeth. That is something most people know. But not everyone knows that the angles of a triangle add up to two right angles. That is, someone might know very well that something was a triangle, and yet not know this further fact about its angles. Now, on your reasoning it should be possible for there to be a triangle whose angles did not add up to two right angles. Do you see what I mean?

Descartes. Yes, it's the same point as Father Arnauld made in the fourth set of objections to my *Meditations.* But I do not accept that they are parallel cases. And I say why in my answer to him.

Elizabeth. I'll have to look at that again. [*Pause*] You see, it isn't that I don't want to believe you. Unless you are right about the soul being distinct from the body, I don't see how there can be any hope of life after death. If it is some part of my body that thinks and wills, then when it decays in death there is an end of me. On your view, moreover, God has made man in his likeness. Only if we perceive ourselves to be purely spiritual can we think of God likewise. These thoughts are precious to me, Master Descartes. I accept them as a matter of faith, but I would that faith and reason should go together. [*Sighs*] The soul grows weary of its burdensome shroud of flesh. There are times when I long to be released from it to a happier life above.

Descartes. Madame, I know of the exile that threatens you, and I grieve that there is nothing I can do to help.

Elizabeth. But there is, Master Descartes. There is. Your letters are a great comfort to me and I hope you'll continue to write. Thus shall the months seem weeks, and the weeks days.

Descartes. I wish I could be of more material service to you. I wish . . .

Elizabeth. [*Interrupting*] Go now, good master. Go out and make free of the court which has banished me. Turn their hearts and minds to philosophy as you have turned mine. It is their evil that I must bear. Moderate it if you can . . .

3. EXORCISING THE GHOST IN THE MACHINE

Two questions that Princess Elizabeth asks, in the dialogue, are (i) Is our intellectual perception of the soul sufficiently clear for us to know that it is immaterial? and (ii) If the soul is immaterial, how can it act on the body?

(i) Both these questions received considerable attention from philosophers writing after Descartes. The British empiricist philosopher John Locke (1632–1704) gave a negative answer to the first. Our idea of spiritual substance, he said, is an idea of "a supposed I know not what" that "supports" thinking and willing ("the power of putting body into motion by thought"). Similarly, our idea of material substance is an idea of something about which we know nothing except that it "supports" solidity and "the power of communicating motion by impulse." This being so, we cannot know that the "support" of thinking is not the same thing as the "support" of solidity,

it being impossible for us, by the contemplation of our own ideas without revelation, to discover whether Omnipotency has not given to some systems of matter, fitly disposed, a power to perceive and think, . . . it being, in respect of our notions, not much more remote from our comprehension to conceive that God can, if He pleases, superadd to matter a faculty of thinking, than that he should superadd to it another substance with a faculty of thinking; since we know not wherein thinking consists, nor to what sort of substances the Almighty has been pleased to give that power . . .[4]

Descartes, of course, thought he had proved that it is an immaterial substance that thinks, and not, as we

would ordinarily say, a person; still less, the "system of matter" which is a person's brain. Princess Elizabeth's doubts about his argument have been succinctly expressed by A. M. MacIver:

Descartes tried to prove demonstratively that what thinks in us must be unextended, starting from the *Cogito*.[5] I know that I exist, because I think, and I know this with certainty; but, in knowing myself to exist, I do not know myself to be extended, because, while sure of my own existence, I can still be doubtful of the existence of all bodies; it is therefore concluded that the "I" which is certainly known to exist is a thinking thing but not an extended thing—or in other words, an immaterial mind. This argument, with its professed conclusion, depends on the simple fallacy of supposing that, if we do not know with certainty that something is the case, we certainly know that it is not the case: if I know that I exist but do not know whether or not I am extended, I know that I am not extended.[6]

MacIver points out that Descartes' conclusion is at odds with our everyday way of talking:

If we accept the Platonic and Cartesian account of human nature, we ought strictly to say "*I* think" but "*My body* sits" and "*My body* walks," and if this account came naturally to men, this (or something which made the same distinction) would be normal colloquial usage; but in fact, ordinary language says equally "*I* think," "I sit," "I walk"—implying that *prima facie* the subject is in each case the same.[7]

The view that there is one subject, namely a *person*, such that *both* predicates like "think" *and* predicates like "walk" are equally applicable to it is one for which P. F. Strawson has argued in his book *Individuals*.[8] A crucial step in the argument is "that a necessary condition of states of consciousness being ascribed at all is that they should be ascribed to the *very same things* as certain corporeal characteristics, a certain physical situation.[9]

MacIver holds that Descartes' real reason for believing that the subject that thinks is not extended was not the one he gave in the *Cogito* argument. He holds that Descartes' real reason was his belief that the behavior of extended things could be explained mechanically, and that since thought is obviously not a mechanical process it could not be an extended thing that thinks.[10]

Gilbert Ryle, in *The Concept of Mind,* endorses

MacIver's explanation of how Descartes really came to believe in an unextended substance:

When Galileo showed that his methods of scientific discovery were competent to provide a mechanical theory which should cover every occupant of space, Descartes found in himself two conflicting motives. As a man of scientific genius he could not but endorse the claims of mechanics, yet as a religious and moral man he could not accept, as Hobbes accepted, the discouraging rider to those claims, namely that human nature differs only in degree of complexity from clockwork. The mental could not be just a variety of the mechanical.

He and subsequent philosophers naturally but erroneously availed themselves of the following escape-route. Since mental-conduct words are not to be construed as signifying the occurrence of mechanical processes, they must be construed as signifying the occurrence of non-mechanical processes; . . . so, while some movements of human tongues and limbs are the effects of mechanical causes, others must be the effects of non-mechanical causes, i.e. some issue from movements of particles of matter, others from workings of the mind.[11]

(ii) One of the major difficulties in accepting this "non-mechanical-causes" view is the one to which Princess Elizabeth gave expression, that of explaining how immaterial minds can bring about changes in material bodies.

There are two ways of responding to a philosophical problem like this. One is to accept the terms in which it is formulated, and try to answer it in those terms. The other is to repudiate the terms; that is, to show that some sort of mistake has been made in the setting-up of the problem. Ryle adopts the second of these courses. He says that a "category mistake" had been made in representing the differences between the physical and the mental as "differences inside the common framework of the categories of 'thing,' 'stuff,' 'attribute,' 'state,' 'process,' 'change,' 'cause,' and 'effect.' "[12]

To accept the terms in which the problem has been posed is to try to answer the question "If the soul *is* immaterial, how can it act on the body?" . . .

If the terms in which the problem has been set are repudiated then there will nevertheless remain a question, of some sort, that requires an answer. In this case it is the question: "If a voluntary action is *not* to be understood as a bodily motion caused by an act of 'will,' how *is* it to be understood?" . . .

NOTES

1. René Descartes, *Philosophical Works,* trans. E. S. Haldane and G. T. R. Ross (New York: Dover, 1934), Vol. I, p. 141.

2. René Descartes, *Philosophical Writings,* ed. and trans. E. Anscombe and P. T. Geach (London: Nelson, 1954), p. 281.

3. Descartes, *op. cit.* (footnote 1), Vol. II, pp. 83–85. Descartes' reply to the argument based on the geometrical example is found on pp. 100–102 of the same volume.

4. John Locke, *An Essay Concerning Human Understanding,* ed. A. S. Pringle-Pattison (Oxford: Oxford University Press, 1924), pp. 268–70.

5. *Cogito* is the Latin word for "I think."

6. A. M. MacIver, "Is There Mind-Body Interaction?," *Proceedings of the Aristotelian Society,* Vol. 36 (1936), p. 101.

7. *Ibid.,* p. 99.

8. P. F. Strawson, *Individuals* (London: Methuen, 1964), Chapter 3.

9. *Ibid.,* p. 102.

10. MacIver, *op. cit.,* p. 102.

11. Gilbert Ryle, *The Concept of Mind* (Hardmondsworth, England: Penguin, 1963), p. 20.

12. *Loc. cit.*

JOHN LOCKE

On Material and Spiritual Substances*

John Locke (1632–1704) was one of the greatest of English philosophers. His empiricist theory of knowledge and natural rights political theory have had lasting influence.

Names made at pleasure neither alter the nature of things, nor make us understand them but as they are signs of and stand for determined ideas. And I desire those who lay so much stress on the sound of these two syllables, *substance,* to consider whether, applying it as they do to the infinite incomprehensible God, to finite spirits, and to body, it be in the same sense; and whether it stands for the same idea, when each of those three so different beings are called substances? If so, whether it will not thence follow, that God, spirits, and body, agreeing in the same common nature of substance, differ not any otherwise than in a bare different modification of that substance; as a tree and a pebble, being in the same sense body, and agreeing in the common nature of body, differ only in a bare modification of that common matter; which will be a very harsh doctrine. If they say that they apply it to God, finite spirits, and matter, in three different significations, and that it stands for one idea when God is said to be a substance, for another when the soul is called substance, and for a third when a body is called so — if the name substance stands for three several distinct ideas, they would do well to make known those distinct ideas, or at least to give three distinct names to them, to prevent, in so important a notion, the confusion and errors that will naturally follow from the promiscuous use of so doubtful a term; which is so far from being suspected to have three distinct, that in ordinary use it has scarce one clear distinct signification; and if they can thus make three distinct ideas of substance, what hinders why another may not make a fourth?

They who first ran into the notion of *accidents,* as a sort of real beings that needed something to inhere in, were forced to find out the word *substance* to support them. Had the poor Indian philosopher (who imagined that the earth also wanted something to bear it up) but thought of this word substance, he needed not to have been at the trouble to find an elephant to support it, and a tortoise to support his elephant: the word substance would have done it effectually. And he that inquired, might have taken it for as good an answer from an Indian philosopher, that substance, without knowing what it is, is that which supports the earth, as we take it for a sufficient answer and good doctrine from our European philosophers, that substance, without knowing what it is, is that which supports accidents. So that of substance we have no idea of what it is, but only a confused obscure one of what it does.

The mind being, as I have declared, furnished with a great number of the simple ideas conveyed in by the senses, as they are found in exterior things, or by reflection on its own operations, takes notice also, that a certain number of these simple ideas go constantly together; which being presumed to belong to one thing, and words being suited to common apprehensions, and made use of for quick dispatch, are called, so united in one subject, by one name; which, by inadvertency, we are apt afterward to talk of and consider as one simple idea, which indeed is a complication of many ideas together: because, as I have said, not imagining how these simple ideas can subsist by themselves, we accustom ourselves to suppose some *substratum* wherein they do subsist, and from which they do result, which therefore we call *substance.*

*Extracts from John Locke, *An Essay concerning Human Understanding* (1690), from Book 2, Chap. 13, Sections 18, 19, Chap. 23, Sections 1–5, 15–20, 29, 30; and Book 4, Chap. 3, Section 6.

So that if any one will examine himself concerning his notion of pure substance in general, he will find he has no other idea of it at all, but only a supposition of he knows not what support of such qualities which are capable of producing simple ideas in us; which qualities are commonly called accidents. If anyone should be asked, what is the subject wherein color or weight inheres, he would have nothing to say, but the solid extended parts: and if he were demanded, what is it that that solidity and extension inhere in, he would not be in a much better case than the Indian before mentioned, who saying that the world was supported by a great elephant, was asked, what the elephant rested on; to which his answer was, a great tortoise: but being again pressed to know what gave support to the broad-backed tortoise, replied, something, he knew not what. And thus here, as in all other cases where we use words without having clear and distinct ideas, we talk like children; who being questioned what such a thing is which they know not, readily give this satisfactory answer, that it is *something;* which in truth signifies no more, when so used, either by children or men, but that they know not what; and that the thing they pretend to know, and talk of, is what they have no distinct idea of at all, and so are perfectly ignorant of it, and in the dark. The idea, then, we have, to which we give the general name substance, being nothing but the supposed, but unknown, support of those qualities we find existing, which we imagine cannot subsist *sine re substante,* without something to support them, we call that support *substantia;* which, according to the true import of the word, is, in plain English, standing under, or upholding.

An obscure and relative idea of substance in general being thus made, we come to have the ideas of *particular sorts of substances,* by collecting such combinations of simple ideas as are, by experience and observation of men's senses, taken notice of to exist together, and are therefore supposed to flow from the particular internal constitution or unknown essence of that substance. Thus we come to have the ideas of a man, horse, gold, water, etc., of which substances, whether any one has any other clear idea, farther than of certain simple ideas coexisting together, I appeal to every one's own experience. It is the ordinary qualities observable in iron or a diamond, put together, that make the true complex idea of those substances, which a smith or a jeweller commonly knows better than a philosopher; who, whatever substantial forms he may talk of, has no other idea of those substances than what is framed by a collection of those simple ideas which are to be found in them. Only we must take notice, that our complex ideas of substances, besides all these simple ideas they are made up of, have always the confused idea of something to which they belong and in which they subsist. And therefore, when we speak of any sort of substance, we say it is a thing having such or such qualities; as body is a thing that is extended, figured, and capable of motion; a spirit, a thing capable of thinking; and so hardness, friability, and power to draw iron, we say, are qualities to be found in a loadstone. These and the like fashions of speaking intimate that the substance is supposed always something besides the extension, figure, solidity, motion, thinking, or other observable ideas, though we know not what it is.

Hence, when we talk or think of any particular sort of corporeal substances, as horse, stone, etc., though the idea we have of either of them be but the complication or collection of those several simple ideas of sensible qualities which we used to find united in the thing called horse or stone; yet because we cannot conceive how they should subsist alone, nor one in another, we suppose them existing in, and supported by, some common subject; which support we denote by the name substance, though it be certain we have no clear or distinct idea of that thing we suppose a support.

The same happens concerning the operations of the mind, viz., thinking, reasoning, fearing, etc., which we concluding not to subsist of themselves, nor apprehending how they can belong to body, or be produced by it, we are apt to think these the actions of some other substance, which we call spirit; whereby yet it is evident, that having no other idea or notion of matter, but something wherein those many sensible qualities which affect our senses do subsist; by supposing a substance wherein thinking, knowing, doubting, and a power of moving, etc., do subsist; we have as clear a notion of the substance of spirit as we have of body; the one being supposed to be (without knowing what it is) the *substratum* to those simple ideas we have from without; and the other supposed (with a like ignorance of what it is) to be the *substratum* to those operations which we experiment in ourselves within.

Besides the complex ideas we have of material sensible substances, by the simple ideas we have taken from those operations of our own minds, which we experiment daily in ourselves, we are able to frame the *complex idea of an immaterial spirit*. For putting together the ideas of thinking and willing, or the power of moving or quieting corporeal motion, joined to substance, of which we have no distinct idea, we have the idea of an immaterial spirit; and by putting together the ideas of coherent solid parts, and a power of being moved, joined with substance, of which likewise we have no positive idea, we have the idea of matter. The one is as clear and distinct an idea as the other: the idea of thinking and moving a body being as clear and distinct ideas as the ideas of extension, solidity, and being moved. For our idea of substance is equally obscure, or none at all, in both; it is but a supposed I know not what, to support those ideas we call accidents.

By the complex idea of extended, figured, colored, and all other sensible qualities which is all that we know of it, we are as far from the idea of the substance of body as if we knew nothing at all: nor, after all the acquaintance and familiarity which we imagine we have with matter, and the many qualities men assure themselves they perceive and know in bodies, will it, perhaps, upon examination, be found, that they have any more or clearer primary ideas belonging to body than they have belonging to immaterial spirit.

The primary ideas we have *peculiar to body*, as contra-distinguished to spirit, are *the cohesion of solid,* and consequently separable *parts, and a power of communicating motion by impulse*. These, I think, are the original ideas proper and peculiar to body; for figure is but the consequence of finite extension.

The ideas we have belonging and *peculiar to spirit* are *thinking,* and *will,* or a power of putting body into motion by thought, and, which is consequent to it, liberty. For as body cannot but communicate its motion by impulse to another body, which it meets with at rest; so the mind can put bodies into motion, or forbear to do so, as it pleases. The ideas of existence, duration, and mobility, are common to them both.

There is no reason why it should be thought strange that I make mobility belong to spirit: for having no other idea of motion but change of distance with other beings that are considered as at rest, and finding that spirits as well as bodies cannot operate but where they are, and that spirits do operate at several times in several places, I cannot but attribute change of place to all finite spirits; (for of the infinite Spirit I speak not here). For my soul, being a real being, as well as my body, is certainly as capable of changing distance with

any other body or being as body itself, and so is capable of motion. And if a mathematician can consider a certain distance or a change of that distance between two points, one may certainly conceive a distance and a change of distance between two spirits; and so conceive their motion, their approach or removal, one from another.

Every one finds in himself, that his soul can think, will, and operate on his body, in the place where that is; but cannot operate in a body, or in a place, a hundred miles distant from it. Nobody can imagine, that his soul can think or move a body at Oxford, whilst he is at London; and cannot but know that, being united to his body, it constantly changes place all the whole journey between Oxford and London, as the coach or horse does that carries him; and I think may be said to be truly all that while in motion: or if that will not be allowed to afford us a clear idea enough of its motion, its being separated from the body in death, I think, will: for to consider it as going out of the body, or leaving it, and yet to have no idea of its motion, seems to me impossible.

To conclude: Sensation convinces us, that there are solid, extended substances; and reflection, that there are thinking ones: experience assures us of the existence of such beings; and that one hath a power to move body by impulse, the other by thought; this we cannot doubt of. Experience, I say, every moment furnishes us with the clear ideas both of the one and the other. But beyond these ideas, as received from their proper sources, our faculties will not reach. If we would inquire farther into their nature, causes, and manner, we perceive not the nature of extension clearer than we do of thinking. If we would explain them any farther, one is as easy as the other; and there is no more difficulty to conceive how a substance we know not should by thought set body into motion, than how a substance we know not should by impulse set body into motion. So that we are no more able to discover wherein the ideas belonging to body consist, than those belonging to spirit. From whence it seems probable to me, that the simple ideas we receive from sensation and reflection are the boundaries of our thoughts; beyond which, the mind, whatever efforts it would make, is not able to advance one jot; nor can it make any discoveries when it would pry into the nature and hidden causes of those ideas.

So that, in short, the idea we have of spirit, compared with the idea we have of body, stands thus: The substance of spirit is unknown to us; and so is the substance of body equally unknown to us.

From all which it is evident, that the extent of our knowledge comes not only short of the reality of things, but even of the extent of our own ideas. We have the ideas of a square, a circle, and equality: and yet, perhaps, shall never be able to find a circle equal to a square, and certainly know that it is so. We have the ideas of matter and thinking, but possibly shall never be able to know whether any mere material being thinks or no; it being impossible for us, by the contemplation of our own ideas without revelation, to discover whether Omnipotency has not given to some systems of matter, fitly disposed, a power to perceive and think, or else joined and fixed to matter, so disposed, a thinking immaterial substance: it being, in respect of our notions, not much more remote from our comprehension to conceive that God can, if he pleases, superadd to matter a faculty of thinking, than that he should superadd to it another substance with a faculty of thinking; since we know not wherein thinking consists, nor to what sort of substances the Almighty has been pleased to give that power, which cannot be in any created being, but merely by the good pleasure and bounty of the Creator. What certainty of knowledge can anyone have that some perceptions, such as, e.g., pleasure and pain, should not be in some bodies themselves, after a certain manner modified and moved, as well as that they should be in an immaterial substance upon the motion of the parts of body? Body, as far as we can conceive, being able only to strike and affect body; and motion, according to the utmost reach of our ideas, being able to produce nothing but motion: so that when we allow it to produce pleasure or pain, or the idea of a color or sound, we are fain to quit our reason, go beyond our ideas, and attribute it wholly to the good pleasure of our Maker. For since we must allow He has annexed effects to motion, which we can no way conceive motion able to produce, what reason have we to conclude that He could not order them as well to be produced in a subject we cannot conceive capable of them, as well as in a subject we cannot conceive the notion of matter can any way operate upon? I say not this that I would any way lessen the belief of the soul's immateriality: I am not here speaking of probability, but knowledge; and I think not only that it becomes the modesty of philosophy not to pronounce magisterially, where we want that evidence that can produce knowledge; but also, that it is of use to us to discern how far our knowledge does reach; for the state we are at present in, not being that of vision, we must, in many things, content ourselves with faith and probability: and in the present question about the immateriality of the soul, if our faculties cannot arrive at demonstrative certainty, we need not think it strange. All the great ends of morality and religion are well enough secured, without philosophical proofs of the soul's immateriality; since it is evident that He who made us at first begin to subsist here, sensible intelligent beings, and for several years continued us in such a state, can and will restore us to the like state of sensibility in another world, and make us capable there to receive the retribution He has designed to men according to their doings in this life.

C. D. BROAD

The Traditional Problem of Body and Mind*

Charles Dunbar Broad (1887–1972) taught philosophy for many years at Trinity College, Cambridge.

In the last chapter we considered organisms simply as complicated material systems which behave in certain characteristic ways. We did not consider the fact that some organisms are animated by minds, and that all the minds of whose existence we are certain animate organisms. And we did not deal with those features in the behaviour of certain organisms which are commonly supposed to be due to the mind which animates the organism. It is such facts as these, and certain problems to which they have given rise, which I mean to discuss in the present chapter. There is a question which has been argued about for some centuries now under the name of "Interaction"; this is the question whether minds really do act on the organisms which they animate, and whether organisms really do act on the minds which animate them. (I must point out at once that I imply no particular theory of mind or body by the word "to animate". I use it as a perfectly neutral name to express the fact that a certain mind is connected in some peculiarly intimate way with a certain body, and, under normal conditions with no other body. This is a fact even on a purely behaviouristic theory of mind; on such a view to say that the mind M animates the body B would mean that the body B, in so far as it behaves in certain ways, *is* the mind M. A body which did not act in these ways would be said not to be animated by a mind. And a different Body B′, which acted in the same general way as B, would be said to be animated by a different mind M′.)

The problem of Interaction is generally discussed at the level of enlightened common-sense, where it is

*From C. D. Broad, *The Mind and Its Place in Nature* (London: Routledge & Kegan Paul Ltd; Atlantic Highlands, N.J.: Humanities Press Inc., 1925), pp. 95–97, 103–121. Reprinted by permission of the author and publishers.

assumed that we know pretty well what we mean by "mind", by "matter" and by "causation". Obviously no solution which is reached at that level can claim to be ultimate. If what we call "matter" should turn out to be a collection of spirits of low intelligence, as Leibniz thought, the argument that mind and body are so unlike that their interaction is impossible would become irrelevant. Again, if causation be nothing but regular sequence and concomitance, as some philosophers have held, it is ridiculous to regard psycho-neural parallelism and interaction as mutually exclusive alternatives. For interaction will mean no more than parallelism, and parallelism will mean no less than interaction. Nevertheless I am going to discuss the arguments here at the common-sense level, because they are so incredibly bad and yet have imposed upon so many learned men.

We start then by assuming a developed mind and a developed organism as two distinct things, and by admitting that the two are now intimately connected in some way or other which I express by saying that "this mind *animates* this organism". We assume that bodies are very much as enlightened common-sense believes them to be; and that, even if we cannot define "causation", we have some means of recognising when it is present and when it is absent. The question then is: "Does a mind ever act on the body which it animates, and does a body ever act on the mind which animates it?" The answer which common-sense would give to both questions is: "Yes, certainly". On the face of it, my body acts on my mind whenever a pin is stuck into the former and a painful sensation thereupon arises in the latter. And, on the face of it, my mind acts on the body whenever a desire to move my arm arises in the former and is followed by this movement in the latter. Let us call this common-sense view "Two-sided Interaction". Although it seems so obvious it has been denied by probably a majority of philosophers and a majority of physiologists. So the question is: "Why should so many distinguished men, who have studied the subject, have denied the apparently obvious fact of Two-sided Interaction?"

ARGUMENTS AGAINST INTERACTION

. . . There are, so far as I know, two [scientific arguments against two-sided interaction]. One is supposed to be based on the physical principle of the Conservation of Energy, and on certain experiments which have been made on human bodies. The other is based on the close analogy which is said to exist between the structures of the physiological mechanism of reflex action and that of voluntary action. I will take them in turn.

(1) *The Argument from Energy.* It will first be needful to state clearly what is asserted by the principle of the Conservation of Energy. It is found that, if we take certain material systems, *e.g.,* a gun, a cartridge, and a bullet, there is a certain magnitude which keeps approximately constant throughout all their changes. This is called "Energy". When the gun has not been fired it and the bullet have no motion, but the explosive in the cartridge has great chemical energy. When it has been fired the bullet is moving very fast and has great energy of movement. The gun, though not moving fast in its recoil, has also great energy of movement because it is very massive. The gases produced by the explosion have some energy of movement and some heat-energy, but much less chemical energy than the unexploded charge had. These various kinds of energy can be measured in common units according to certain conventions. To an innocent mind there seems to be a good deal of "cooking" at this stage, *i.e.,* the conventions seem to be chosen and various kinds and amounts of concealed energy seem to be postulated in order to make the principle come out right at the end. I do not propose to go into this in detail, for two reasons. In the first place, I think that the conventions adopted and the postulates made, though somewhat suggestive of the fraudulent company-promoter, can be justified by their coherence with certain experimental facts, and that they are not simply made *ad hoc*. Secondly, I shall show that the Conservation of Energy is absolutely irrelevant to the question at issue, so that it would be a waste of

time to treat it too seriously in the present connexion. Now it is found that the total energy of all kinds in this system, when measured according to these conventions, is approximately the same in amount though very differently distributed after the explosion and before it. If we had confined our attention to a part of this system and *its* energy this would not have been true. The bullet, *e.g.,* had no energy at all before the explosion and a great deal afterwards. A system like the bullet, the gun, and the charge, is called a "Conservative System"; the bullet alone, or the gun and the charge, would be called "Non-conservative Systems". A conservative system might therefore be defined as one whose total energy is redistributed, but not altered in amount, by changes that happen within it. Of course, a given system might be conservative for some kinds of change and not for others.

So far we have merely defined a "Conservative System", and admitted that there are systems which, for some kinds of change at any rate, answer approximately to our definition. We can now state the Principle of the Conservation of Energy in terms of the conceptions just defined. The principle asserts that every material system is either itself conservative, or, if not, is part of a larger material system which is conservative. We may take it that there is good inductive evidence for this proposition.

The next thing to consider is the experiments on the human body. These tend to prove that a living body, with the air that it breathes and the food that it eats, forms a conservative system to a high degree of approximation. We can measure the chemical energy of the food given to a man, and that which enters his body in the form of Oxygen breathed in. We can also, with suitable apparatus, collect, measure and analyse the air breathed out, and thus find its chemical energy. Similarly, we can find the energy given out in bodily movement, in heat, and in excretion. It is alleged that, on the average, whatever the man may do, the energy of his bodily movements is exactly accounted for by the energy given to him in the form of food and of Oxygen. If you take the energy put in in food and Oxygen, and subtract the energy given out in waste-products, the balance is almost exactly equal to the energy put out in bodily movements. Such slight differences as are found are as often on one side as on the other, and are therefore probably due to unavoidable experimental errors. I do not propose to criticise the interpretation of these experiments in detail, because, as I shall show soon, they are completely irrelevant to the problem of whether mind and body interact. But there is just one point that I will make before passing on. It is perfectly clear that such experiments can tell us only what happens on the average over a long time. To know whether the balance was accurately kept at every moment we should have to kill the patient at each moment and analyse his body so as to find out the energy present then in the form of stored-up products. Obviously we cannot keep on killing the patient in order to analyse him, and then reviving him in order to go on with the experiment. Thus it would seem that the results of the experiment are perfectly compatible with the presence of quite large excesses or defects in the total bodily energy at certain moments, provided that these average out over longer periods. However, I do not want to press this criticism; I am quite ready to accept for our present purpose the traditional interpretation which has been put on the experiments.

We now understand the physical principle and the experimental facts. The two together are generally supposed to prove that mind and body cannot interact. What precisely is the argument, when fully stated, would run somewhat as follows: "I will to move my arm, and it moves. If the volition has anything to do with causing the movement we might expect energy to flow from my mind to my body. Thus the energy of my body ought to receive a measurable increase, not accounted for by the food that I eat and the Oxygen that I breathe. But no such physically unaccountable increases of bodily energy are found. Again, I tread on a tin-tack, and a painful sensation arises in my mind. If treading on the tack has anything to do with causing the sensation we might expect energy to flow from my body to my mind. Such energy would cease to be measurable. Thus there ought to be a noticeable decrease in my bodily energy, not balanced by increases anywhere in the physical system. But such unbalanced decreases of bodily energy are not found." So it is concluded that the volition has nothing to do with causing my arm to move, and that treading on the tack has nothing to do with causing the painful sensation.

Is this argument valid? In the first place it is important to notice that the conclusion does not follow from the Conservation of Energy and the experimental facts alone. The real premise is a tacitly assumed proposition about causation; viz., that, if a change in A has anything to do with causing a change in B, energy must leave A and flow into B. This is neither asserted nor entailed by the Conservation of Energy. What *it* says is that, *if* energy leaves A, it must appear in something else, say B; so that A and B together form a conservative system. Since the Conservation of Energy is not itself the premise for the argument against Interaction, and since it does not entail that premise, the evidence for the Conservation of Energy is not evidence against Interaction. Is there any independent evidence for the premise? We may admit that it *is* true of many, though not of all, transactions within the physical realm. But there are cases where it is not true even of purely physical transactions; and, even if it were always true in the physical realm, it would not follow that it must also be true of transphysical causation. Take the case of a weight swinging at the end of a string hung from a fixed point. The total energy of the weight is the same at all positions in its course. It is thus a conservative system. But at every moment the direction and velocity of the weight's motion are different, and the proportion between its kinetic and its potential energy is constantly changing. These changes are caused by the pull of the string, which acts in a different direction at each different moment. The string makes no difference to the total energy of the weight; but it makes all the difference in the world to the particular way in which the energy is distributed between the potential and the kinetic forms. This is evident when we remember that the weight would begin to move in an utterly different course if at any moment the string were cut.

Here, then, we have a clear case even in the physical realm where a system is conservative but is continually acted on by something which affects its movement and the distribution of its total energy. Why should not the mind act on the body in this way? If you say that you can see how a string can affect the movement of a weight, but cannot see how a volition could affect the movement of a material particle, you have deserted the scientific argument and have gone back to one of the philosophical arguments. Your real difficulty is either that volitions are so very unlike movements, or that the volition is in your mind whilst the movement belongs to the physical realm. And we have seen how little weight can be attached to these objections.

The fact is that, even in purely physical systems, the Conservation of Energy does not explain what changes will happen or when they will happen. It merely imposes a very general limited condition on the changes that are possible. The fact that the system composed of bullet, charge, and gun, in our earlier example, is conservative does not tell us that the gun ever will be fired, or when it will be fired if at all, or what will cause it to go off, or what forms of energy will appear if and when it does go off. This change in this case is determined by pulling the trigger. Likewise the mere fact that the human body and its neighbourhood form a conservative system does not explain any particular bodily movement; it does not explain why I ever move at all, or why I sometimes write, sometimes walk, and sometimes swim. To explain the happening of these particular movements at certain times it seems to be essential to take into account the volitions which happen from time to time in my mind; just as it is essential to take the string into account to explain the particular behaviour of the weight, and to take the trigger into account to explain the going off of the gun at a certain moment. The difference between the gun-system and the body-system is that a little energy does flow into the former when the trigger is pulled, whilst it is alleged that none does so when a volition starts a bodily movement. But there is not even this amount of difference between the body-system and the swinging weight.

Thus the argument from energy has no tendency to disprove Two-sided Interaction. It has gained a spurious authority from the august name of the Conservation of Energy. But this impressive principle proves to have nothing to do with the case. And the real premise of the argument is not self-evident, and is not universally true even in purely intra-physical transactions. In the end this scientific argument has to lean on the old philosophic arguments; and we have seen that these are but bruised reeds. Nevertheless, the facts brought forward by the argument from energy do throw some light on the *nature* of the interaction between mind and body, assuming this to happen. They do suggest that all the energy of our bodily actions comes out of and goes back into the physical world, and that minds neither add energy to nor abstract it from the latter. What they do, if they do anything, is to determine that at a given moment so much energy shall change from the chemical form to the form of bodily movement; and they determine this, so far as we can see, without altering the total amount of energy in the physical world.

(2) The Argument from the Structure of the Nervous System. There are purely reflex actions, like sneezing and blinking, in which there is no reason to suppose that the mind plays any essential part. Now we know the nervous structure which is used in such acts as these. A stimulus is given to the outer end of an effect nerve; some change or other runs up this nerve, crosses a synapsis between this and an afferent nerve, travels down the latter to a muscle, causes the muscle to contract, and so produces a bodily movement. There seems no reason to believe that the mind plays any essential part in this process. The process may be irreducibly vital, and not merely physico-chemical; but there seems no need to assume anything more than this. Now it is said that the whole nervous system is simply an immense complication of interconnected nervous arcs. The result is that a change which travels inwards has an immense number of alternative paths by which it may travel outwards. Thus the reaction to a given stimulus is no longer one definite movement, as in the simple reflex. Almost any movement may follow any stimulus according to the part which the afferent disturbance happens to take. This path will depend on the relative resistance of the various synapses at the time. Now a variable response to the same stimulus is characteristic of deliberate as opposed to reflex action.

These are the facts. The argument based on them runs as follows. It is admitted that the mind has nothing to do with the causation of purely reflex actions. But the nervous structure and the nervous processes involved in deliberate action do not differ in kind from those involved in reflex action; they differ only in degree of complexity. The variability which characterises deliberate action is fully explained by the variety of alternative paths and the variable resistances of the synapses. So it is unreasonable to suppose that the mind has any more to do with causing deliberate actions than it has to do with causing reflex actions.

I think that this argument is invalid. In the first place I am pretty sure that the persons who use it have before their imagination a kind of picture of how mind and body must interact if they interact at all. They find that the facts do not answer to this picture, and so they conclude that there is no interaction. The picture is of the following kind. They think of the mind as sitting somewhere in a hole in the brain, surrounded by telephones. And they think of the afferent disturbance as coming to an end at one of these telephones and there affecting the mind. The mind is then supposed to respond by sending an efferent impulse down another of these telephones. As no such hole, with afferent nerves stopping at its walls and efferent nerves starting from them, can be found, they conclude that the mind can play no part in the transaction. But another alternative is that this picture of how the mind must act if it acts at all is wrong. To put it shortly, the mistake is to confuse a gap in an explanation with a spatio-temporal gap, and to argue from the absence of the latter to the absence of the former.

The interactionist's contention is simply that there is a gap in any purely physiological explanation of deliberate action; *i.e.,* that all such explanations fail to account completely for the facts because they leave out one necessary condition. It does not follow in the least that there must be a spatio-temporal breach of continuity in the physiological conditions, and that the missing condition must fill this gap in the way in which the movement of a wire fills the spatio-temporal interval between the pulling of a bell-handle and the ringing of a distant bell. To assume this is to make the mind a kind of physical object, and to make its action a kind of mechanical action. Really, the mind and its actions are not literally in Space at all, and the time which is occupied by the mental event is no doubt *also* occupied by some part of the physiological process. Thus I am inclined to think that much of the force which this argument actually exercises on many people is simply due to the presupposition about the *modus operandi* of interaction, and that it is greatly weakened when this presupposition is shown to be a mere prejudice due to our limited power of envisaging unfamiliar alternative possibilities.

We can, however, make more detailed objections to the argument than this. There is a clear introspective difference between the mental accompaniment of voluntary action and that of reflex action. What goes on in our minds when we decide with difficulty to get out of a hot bath on a cold morning is obviously extremely different from what goes on in our minds when we sniff pepper and sneeze. And the difference is qualitative; it is not a mere difference of complexity. This difference has to be explained somehow; and the theory under discussion gives no plausible explanation of it. The ordinary view that, in the latter case, the mind is not acting on the body at all; whilst, in the former, it is acting on the body in a specific way, does at least make the introspective difference between the two intelligible.

Again, whilst it is true that deliberate action differs from reflex action in its greater variability of response to the same stimulus, this is certainly not the whole or the most important part of the difference between them. The really important difference is that, in deliberate action, the response is varied *appropriately* to meet the special circumstances which are supposed to exist at the time or are expected to arise later; whilst reflex action is not varied in this way, but is blind and almost mechanical. The complexity of the nervous system explains the *possibility* of variation; it does not in the least explain why the alternative which actually takes place should as a rule be appropriate and not merely haphazard. And so again it seems as if some factor were in operation in deliberate action which is not present in reflex action; and it is reasonable to suppose that this factor is the volition in the mind.

It seems to me that this second scientific argument has no tendency to disprove interaction; but that the facts which it brings forward do tend to suggest the particular form which interaction probably takes if it happens at all. They suggest that what the mind does to the body in voluntary action, if it does anything, is to lower the resistance of certain synapses and to raise that of others. The result is that the nervous current follows such a course as to produce the particular movement which the mind judges to be appropriate at the time. On such a view the difference between reflex, habitual, and deliberate actions for the present purpose become fairly plain. In pure reflexes the mind cannot voluntarily affect the resistance of the synapses concerned, and so the action takes place in spite of it. In habitual action it deliberately refrains from interfering with the resistance of the synapses, and so the action goes on like a complicated reflex. But it *can* affect these resistances if it wishes, though often only with difficulty; and it is ready to do so if it judges this to be expedient. Finally, it may lose the power altogether. This would be what happens when a person becomes a slave to some habit, such as drug-taking.

I conclude that, at the level of enlightened common-sense at which the ordinary discussion of Interaction moves, no good reason has been produced for doubting that the mind acts on the body in volition, and that the body acts on the mind in sensation. The philosophic arguments are quite inconclusive; and the scientific arguments, when properly understood, are quite compatible with Two-sided Interaction. At most they suggest certain conclusions as to the form which interaction probably takes it if happens at all.

DIFFICULTIES IN THE DENIAL OF INTERACTION

I propose now to consider some of thè difficulties which would attend the denial of Interaction, still keeping the discussion at the same common-sense level. If a man denies the action of body on mind he is at once in trouble over the causation of new sensations. Suppose that I suddenly tread on an unsuspected tin-tack. A new sensation suddenly comes into my mind. This is an event, and it presumably has some cause. Now, however carefully I introspect and retrospect, I can find no other mental event which is adequate to account for the fact that just that sensation has arisen at just that moment. If I reject the common-sense view that treading on the tack is an essential part of the cause of the sensation, I must suppose either that it is uncaused, or that it is caused by other events in my mind which I cannot discover by introspection or retrospection, or that it is caused telepathically by other finite minds or by God. Now enquiry of my neighbours would show that it is not caused telepathically by any event in their minds which they can introspect or remember. Thus anyone who denies the action of body on mind, and admits that sensations have causes, must postulate either (a) immense numbers of unobservable states in his own mind; or (b) as many unobservable states in his neighbours' minds, together with telepathic action; or (c) some nonhuman spirit together with telepathic action. I must confess that the difficulties which have been alleged against the action of body on mind seem to be mild compared with those of the alternative hypotheses which are involved in the denial of such action.

The difficulties which are involved in the denial of the action of mind on body are at first sight equally great; but I do not think that they turn out to be so serious as those which are involved in denying the action of body on mind. The *prima facie* difficulty is this. The world contains many obviously artificial objects, such as books, bridges, clothes, etc. We know that, if we go far enough back in the history of their production, we always do in fact come on the actions of some human body. And the minds connected with these bodies did design the objects in question, did will to produce them, and did believe that they were initiating and guiding the physical process by means of these designs and volitions. If it be true that the mind does not act on the body, it follows that the designs and volitions in the agents' minds did not in fact play any part in the production of books, bridges, clothes, etc. This appears highly paradoxical. And it is an easy step from it to say that anyone who denies the action of mind on body must admit that books, bridges, and other such objects *could* have been produced even though there had been no minds, no thought of these objects and no desire for them. This consequence seems manifestly absurd to common-sense, and it might be argued that it reflects its absurdity back on the theory which entails it.

The man who denies that mind can act on body might deal with this difficulty in two ways: (1) He might deny that the conclusion *is* intrinsically absurd. He might say that human bodies are extraordinarily complex physical objects, which probably obey irreducible laws of their own, and that we really do not know enough about them to set limits to what their unaided powers could accomplish. This is the line which Spinoza took. The conclusion, it would be argued, *seems* absurd only because the state of affairs which it contemplates is so very unfamiliar. We find it difficult to imagine a body like ours without a mind like ours; but, if we could get over this defect in our powers of imagination, we might have no difficulty in admitting that such a body could do all the things which our bodies do. I think it must be admitted that the difficulty is not so great as that which is involved in denying the action of body on mind. There we had to postulate *ad hoc* utterly unfamiliar entities and modes of action; here it is not certain that we should have to do this.

(2) The other line of argument would be to say that the alleged consequence does not necessarily follow from denying the action of mind on body. I assume that both parties admit that causation is something more than mere *de facto* regularity of sequence and concomitance. If they do not, of course the whole controversy between them becomes futile; for there will certainly be causation between mind and body and between body and mind, in the only sense in which there is causation anywhere. This being presupposed, the following kind of answer is logically possible. When I say that B could not have happened unless A had happened, there are two alternative possibilities. (a) A may itself be an indispensable link in any chain of causes which ends up with B. (b) A may not itself be a link in any chain

of causation which ends up with B. But there may be an indispensable link α in any such chain of causation, and A may be a necessary accompaniment or sequent of α. These two possibilities may be illustrated by diagrams. (a) is represented by the figure below:—

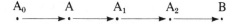

The two forms of (b) are represented by the two figures below:—

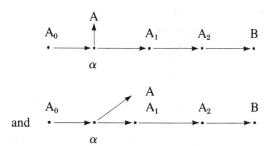

Evidently, if B cannot happen unless α precedes, and if α cannot happen without A accompanying or immediately following it, B will not be able to happen unless A precedes it. And yet A will have had no part in causing B. It will be noticed that, on this view α has a complex effect AA_1 of which a certain part, viz., A_1 is sufficient by itself to produce A_2 and ultimately B. Let us apply this abstract possibility to our present problem. Suppose that B is some artificial object, like a book or a bridge. If we admit that this could not have come into existence unless a certain design and volition had existed in a certain mind, we could interpret the facts in two ways. (a) We could hold that the design and volition are themselves an indispensable link in the chain of causation which ends in the production of a bridge or a book. This is the common view, and it requires us to admit the action of mind on body. (b) We might hold that the design and the volition are not themselves a link in the chain of causation which ends in the production of the artificial object; but that they are a necessary accompaniment or sequent of something which is an indispensable link in this chain of causation. On this view the chain consists wholly of physical events; but one of these physical events (viz., some event in the brain) has a complex consequent. One part of this consequent is purely physical, and leads by purely physical causation to the ultimate production of a bridge or a book. The other is purely mental, and consists of a certain design and volition in the mind

which animates the human body concerned. If this has any consequences they are purely mental. Each part of this complex consequent follows with equal necessity; this particular brain-state could no more have existed without such and such a mental state accompanying or following it than it could have existed without such and such a bodily movement following it. If we are willing to take some such view as this, we can admit that certain objects could not have existed unless there had been designs of them and desires for them; and yet we could consistently deny that these desires and designs have any effect on the movements of our bodies.

It seems to me then that the doctrine which I will call "One-sided Action of Body on Mind" is logically possible; *i.e.,* a theory which accepts the action of body on mind but denies the action of mind on body. But I do not see the least reason to accept it, since I see no reason to deny that mind acts on body in volition. One-sided Action has, I think, generally been held in the special form called "Epiphenomenalism." I take this doctrine to consist of the following four propositions: (1) Certain bodily events cause certain mental events. (2) No mental event plays any part in the causation of any bodily event. (3) No mental event plays any part in the causation of any other mental event. Consequently (4) all mental events are caused by bodily events and by them only. Thus Epiphenomenalism is just One-sided Action of Body on Mind, together with a special theory about the nature and structure of mind. This special theory does not call for discussion here, where I am dealing only with the relations between minds and bodies, and am not concerned with a detailed analysis of mind. . . .

ARGUMENTS IN FAVOUR OF INTERACTION

The only arguments *for* One-sided Action of Body on Mind or for Parallelism are the arguments *against* Two-sided Interaction; and these, as we have seen, are worthless. Are there any arguments in favour of Two-sided Interaction? I have incidentally given two which seem to me to have considerable weight. In favour of the action of mind on body is the fact that we seem to be immediately aware of a causal relation when we voluntarily try to produce a bodily movement, and that the arguments to show that this cannot be true are invalid. In favour of the action of body on mind are the insuperable difficulties which I have pointed out in accounting for the happening of new sensations on any other hypothesis. There are, however, two other arguments which have often been thought to prove the action of mind on body. These are (1) an evolutionary argument, first used, I believe, by William James; and (2) the famous "telegram argument." They both seem to be quite obviously invalid.

(1) The evolutionary argument runs as follows: It is a fact, which is admitted by persons who deny Two-sided Interaction, that minds increase in complexity and power with the growth in complexity of the brain and nervous system. Now, if the mind makes no difference to the actions of the body, this development on the mental side is quite unintelligible from the point of view of natural selection. Let us imagine two animals whose brains and nervous systems were of the same degree of complexity; and suppose, if possible, that one had a mind and the other had none. If the mind makes no difference to the behaviour of the body the chance of survival and of leaving descendants will clearly be the same for the two animals. Therefore natural selection will have no tendency to favour the evolution of mind which has actually taken place. I do not think that there is anything in this argument. Natural selection is a purely negative process; it simply tends to eliminate individuals and species which have variations unfavourable to survival. Now, by hypothesis, the possession of a mind is not *unfavourable* to survival; it simply makes no difference. Now it may be that the existence of a mind of such and such a kind is an inevitable consequence of the existence of a brain and nervous system of such and such a degree of complexity. Indeed we have seen that some such view is essential if the opponent of Two-sided Interaction is to answer the common-sense objection that artificial objects could not have existed unless there had been a mind which designed and desired them. On this hypothesis there is no need to invoke natural selection twice over, once to explain the evolution of the brain and nervous system, and once to explain the evolution of the mind. If natural selection will account for the evolution of the brain and nervous system, the evolution of the mind will follow inevitably, even though it adds nothing to the survival-value of the organism. The plain fact is that natural selection does not account for the origin or for the growth in complexity of anything whatever; and therefore it is no objection to any particular theory of

the relations of mind and body that, if it were true, natural selection would not explain the origin and development of mind.

(2) The "telegram argument" is as follows: Suppose there were two telegrams, one saying "Our son has been killed", and the other saying: "Your son has been killed". And suppose that one or other of them was delivered to a parent whose son was away from home. As physical stimuli they are obviously extremely alike, since they differ only in the fact that the letter "Y" is present in one and absent in the other. Yet we know that the reaction of the person who received the telegram might be very different according to which one he received. This is supposed to show that the reactions of the body cannot be wholly accounted for by bodily causes, and that the mind must intervene causally in some cases. Now I have very little doubt that the mind does play a part in determining the action of the recipient of the telegram; but I do not see why this argument should prove it to a person who doubted or denied it. If two very similar stimuli are followed by two very different results, we are no doubt justified in concluding that these stimuli are not the complete causes of the reactions which follow them. But of course it would be admitted by every one that the receipt of the telegram is not the complete cause of the recipient's reaction. We all know that his brain and nervous system play an essential part in any reaction that he may make to the stimulus. The question then is whether the minute structure of his brain and nervous system, including in this the supposed traces left by past stimuli and past reactions, is not enough to account for the great difference in his behaviour on receiving two very similar stimuli. Two keys may be very much alike, but one may fit a certain lock and the other may not. And, if the lock be connected with the trigger of a loaded gun, the results of "stimulating" the system with one or other of the two keys will be extremely different. We know that the brain and nervous system are very complex, and we commonly suppose that they contain more or less permanent traces and linkages due to past stimuli and reactions. If this be granted, it is obvious that two very similar stimuli may produce very different results, simply because one fits in with the internal structure of the brain and nervous system whilst the other does not. And I do not see how we can be sure that anything more is needed to account for the mere difference of reaction adduced by the "telegram argument."

JEROME A. SHAFFER

The Subject of Consciousness*

Jerome A. Shaffer (1929–   ) teaches philosophy at the University of Connecticut. He is a leading figure in the philosophy of mind.

It would seem to be an undeniable fact that consciousness does exist and that any account of the world will have to give some place to it. But what place? What is the relation of consciousness to whatever else does exist? In particular, what is the relation of consciousness to the organic and inorganic matter that makes up so great a part of the world? And, more particularly, what is the relation of consciousness to those organic systems we know as human bodies? . . .

We can begin our inquiry by asking what is the subject of consciousness, in other words, *what* is conscious when consciousness exists? Well, what sorts of things have consciousness? One pretty indisputable case is that of . . . human beings. But what is a . . . human being? Is he just a particular kind of matter formed in a particular way? Or is there more to the story, and if so what more? If a man is *more* than a particularly formed kind of matter, then is it some part of that *more* which is the subject of consciousness?

To make the discussion manageable, let us confine ourselves to that form of consciousness which consists in having what I shall call mental events: those particular occasions which consist in the having of some thought, the feeling of some sensation, the imaging of some mental picture, the entertaining of some wish, etc. Our problem, then, will be to determine *what* it is that has the thought, feels the sensation, images the mental picture, entertains the wish, etc.

The various theories concerning *what* has the mental events fall into three basic categories. (1) There is

the view that they happen to purely *nonmaterial* things. Proponents of such a view usually admit the existence of purely *material* things in addition to these purely nonmaterial things; hence they are called dualists. (2) There is the view that they happen to purely *material* things; we shall call this materialism. And (3) there is the view that they happen to things which are neither purely material nor purely nonmaterial; we shall call this the person theory. Each shall be considered and evaluated in turn.

DUALISM

The most systematic dualistic theory is that which was presented by the French philosopher Descartes. He held that the subject of consciousness is the *mind* and that the mind is a thing or entity separate and distinct from the body. The body is a thing or entity whose essence (defining characteristic) is occupying space, i.e., having shape, size, and location in space; and it is in no sense conscious. The mind, on the other hand, is completely different in its nature. It is utterly nonspatial, having neither shape, size, nor location. Its essence (defining characteristic) is simply having consciousness, that is, thoughts, feelings, memories, perceptions, desires, emotions, etc.

Descartes held that since the mind and the body are separate entities, each can exist without the other. It is obvious and undeniable that Descartes is at least correct in holding that *some* bodies—e.g., stones and lakes—do indeed exist without minds. Descartes himself believed that animals (other than man) were also examples of bodies without minds. Some people might disagree with him there, and there would be even more disagreement with his thesis that minds could exist without bodies. Descartes believed that minds were immortal, that they continue to exist as disembodied minds after the body has perished in death.

*Jerome A. Shaffer, *Philosophy of Mind*, © 1968, pp. 34–59. Reprinted by permission of the author and Prentice-Hall, Inc., Englewood Cliffs, New Jersey.

There is an important gap in Descartes' account, a gap which can be noted in the summary just given. From the fact that the essence of the mind is one thing, having consciousness, and the essence of the body is another, occupying space, it does not follow that the mind and the body are *two separate entities*. What is to rule out the possibility that one and the same thing can have *both* these properties, be *both* a thinking thing and at the very same time an extended thing? The essence, that is, the defining characteristic, of being a husband is being a married man and the essence of being a parent is having offspring, but one and the same person can be both a husband *and* a parent (and, obviously, can be one without being the other). This gap in Descartes' reasoning was first pointed out by Spinoza, who had been a follower of Descartes. Spinoza realized that "although two attributes may be conceived as really distinct," and here he has in mind thinking and extension, "we cannot nevertheless thence conclude that they constitute two beings or two different substances."[1] Then, breaking decisively with Descartes, Spinoza went on to maintain that in the case of human beings (and, as a matter of fact, for Spinoza, in everything else as well), both thinking *and* space-occupancy were characteristics of one and the same thing. This view shall be discussed later under the heading of double aspect theory.

Nevertheless, Descartes held that one and the same thing could not be both a space-occupier and a thinking thing. He seems to have thought that these characteristics were simply so different in their natures that one and the same thing *could* not have both. Thus he cites the fact that extended things are divisible, whereas thinking things are not divisible (see his sixth *Meditation*). But this is a very weak line of argument. Since thinking and occupying space are different characteristics, there will naturally be differences between them. Extended things will necessarily be divisible (I take it Descartes is here thinking of *spatially* dividing something), and things which are nonextended, say disembodied minds, will not be so divisible. But this is just to say that we have different characteristics here. A thing which thinks would be divisible if it were at the same time an extended thing. So pointing out differences between extension and thinking does not show us that things which have the one characteristic cannot have the other. Perhaps Descartes had in mind the point that extension and thinking are *so very* different, so basically different.

Of course one object could be both red and round, he might say, but could one object be both red and thinking? Here again, however, the line of argument is weak. Being red and being valuable and being holy are *very* different sorts of properties, yet one and the same object, say a particular jewel, might be all three. So we still do not have a very good reason for thinking that thinking things could not be extended and vice versa.

Even if the dualist fails to give us a reason for holding that thinking things and extended things are *different* entities, still such a view might be correct. And we have not yet seen any reason for thinking it is *not* correct. So let us, for the moment, grant the dualist his claim that they are different entities. If we do so, the question arises how these two different entities are related to each other, if at all. Here we find ourselves faced with what is traditionally known in philosophy as the mind-body problem.

THE TRADITIONAL MIND-BODY PROBLEM

. . . In order to get a better grasp of dualism we will here take a brief look at the various theories [of the mind-body problem] that have been proposed. Descartes himself believed that sometimes the mind could causally affect the body and sometimes the body could causally affect the mind; this view is called interactionism. An example of the former would be a case in which, after deliberation, I decide (a mental event) to press the button and then my hand reaches out to press it (a bodily event); an example of the latter would be a case in which the moving hand (a bodily event) comes in contact with the button, causing in me a feeling of fear (a mental event) at what will happen if I do press the button.

Interactionism is not the only dualistic theory of the relation between mind and body. Some philosophers have held that there is only *one-way* causality, from body to mind; this view is known as epiphenomenalism. The epiphenomenalist accepts one half of the interactionist contention, that part which holds that bodily events can cause mental events. But he denies the other half; he denies that mental events can ever cause bodily events. Whatever happens in the mind is merely a by-product of bodily activity (most plausibly, brain activity). No important philosopher has ever held what we might call reverse epiphenomenalism, namely that bodily events are *always* merely effects of mental activity. The religion of Christian Science comes somewhat close to this view, holding that bodily events, particularly those concerning health and disease, are results of mental activity. Many Christian Scientists would go so far as to maintain that *all* bodily events, for example the activity in our sense organs during perception, are caused solely by mental activity. This is the view of the eighteenth-century Irish philosopher George Berkeley, that anything that ever happens at all happens only in the mind. Berkeley's view is no longer dualism; he holds that only minds exist and that matter and in particular bodies do not exist at all, except in the mind.

Finally, there is the dualist theory known as parallelism. The parallelist admits the close connection of events in the mind and events in the body, but does not wish to say that the connection is a causal one, for he holds that the mind and the body are too utterly different to be able to interact causally with each other. So the parallelist holds that the mind and the body are like two clocks, each with its own mechanism and with no causal connection between them, yet always in phase keeping the same time.

OBJECTIONS TO DUALISM

Dualist theories are not very much in favor these days. There are two main sources of discontent with them. (1) Many philosophers have grave doubts that the notion of the mind as a thing or entity can be rendered intelligible. (2) Even if it could be made intelligible, the view of the world which results seems to many unnecessarily complex. We will discuss these two sources of discontent in order.

(1) Dualists tell us that in addition to the familiar objects of everyday life, tables, rocks, hair, trees, clouds, air, in short material things, there also exist things of a quite different kind—minds. These minds are real things, real objects, real entities, but they are fundamentally different sorts of things from material things. Well then, what is a mind? Is it a peculiar kind of stuff, immaterial matter, insubstantial substance, bodiless body? It is supposed to have no extension, that is, no shape, size, or capacity to occupy space; it is not visible to the eye, tangible to the touch, nor is it visible under any microscope however powerful, [or] tangible to the most delicate of probing instruments. Perhaps the mind is like a gravitational, magnetic, or electrical field? But it cannot be, for on the dualist's hypothesis the mind is in no way physical; if it were like them, or like physical energy of some sort, then it would be a *physical* phenomenon and we would no longer be dualists. Yet if it is in no way like such things, in what sense is the mind a thing at all? What

meaning can we give to the notion of the mind as an existent thing?

The problem comes out in two particular ways, in the problem of identification and the problem of individuation. The former problem concerns how we can tell when we are in the presence of some other mind A rather than B or even in the presence of any other mind at all. Since, on the dualist account, another mind is not detectible by any observations we could make, it is impossible that we should have any reason to think we could ever identify another mind as mind A or B. So we could never justifiably believe we were, for example, talking to someone. And a concept of a mind which made it impossible justifiably to apply that concept to any other thing would be utterly useless, even if intelligible.

The problem of individuation concerns what makes two minds distinct, assuming there could be two distinct minds. One answer might be that they have different mental histories, each having had different mental events at certain times. But it seems perfectly intelligible to suppose that at some time we might have two distinct minds with exactly the same history of mental events (each might have grown up in exactly the same way). And, if this supposition of two exactly similar minds is intelligible, then what would make them two distinct minds rather than one and the same mind? The dualist does not seem to have an answer. He must say they are distinct, and yet he cannot say how or in what respect they differ. Does that make any sense?

(2) Even if we were able to give some *meaning* to the claim that minds exist, many contemporary philosophers would reject the claim that in fact minds do exist. They would make the remark attributed to the French astronomer Laplace in reply to Napoleon's question about the role of God in the system: said Laplace, "Sire, I have no need of that hypothesis." Thus many philosophers would argue that everything that happens in the world can be explained without using the notion of minds, strictly on the basis of physical phenomena and physical laws.

The view that minds do not exist at all and that only the physical exists is called materialism. We shall now turn to this view.

MATERIALISM

Materialism is one of the very oldest theories. It was a familiar doctrine to the ancient Greeks of the fourth and fifth centuries B.C. The spokesman for this view, Democritus, held that nothing exists but material atoms and the void and that everything in the world is nothing but the interactions of these atoms as they move through the void. Even the most complex behavior of human beings can be resolved into interactions between the atoms. A modern materialist would allow a more complicated picture than "atoms and the void." He would bring in subatomic particles and antiparticles, electromagnetic waves, a relativized view of "the void," various kinds of forces and energies, and the rest of the conceptual apparatus of contemporary physics. But he would still hold that nothing exists but such physical phenomena; if such terms as "thought," "feeling," "wish," etc., have any meaning at all, they must refer in the last analysis to physical phenomena. So-called mental events are really nothing but physical events occurring to physical objects.

We should, at the outset, distinguish materialism as characterized here from another doctrine which has already been mentioned, epiphenomenalism. . . . The latter is a dualistic theory which allows that the mind is separate and distinct from the body but also insists that the mind is utterly dependent causally upon the body, that everything which happens in the mind is a result of events in the body, and that the mind is utterly powerless to affect the body in any way. Such a view is often called materialistic, since it places the highest *importance* on the material side of things. It is in this sense that Karl Marx was materialistic, for he held that "conceiving, thinking, the mental intercourse of men, appear at [the earliest] stage as the direct efflux of their material behavior."[2] Notice that Marx is not saying men's conceiving, thinking, and mental intercourse *are nothing but* their material behavior. That would be materialism as here characterized. He is saying that they are the "efflux," i.e., a *separate, nonmaterial* outflow which originates and derives from material behavior. Such a view is not materialistic in our sense.

The materialist holds that nothing but the physical exists—matter, energy, and the void. But then what *are* thoughts, feelings, wishes, and the other so-called mental phenomena? Here four different answers have been seriously proposed. The most radical view, supported by very few, is that such terms have *no real meaning at all* and should be dropped from the language. They represent an accretion to our language which was conceived in ignorance and superstition, nurtured by the vested interests of religion and the black arts, and condoned by human lethargy. On this view, mentalistic terms should be allowed to suffer the fate of the language of witchcraft and demonic possession. Let us call this the unintelligibility thesis.

The unintelligibility thesis has not gained much support among contemporary philosophers. In the first place, it is clear why notions of witchcraft and demonic possession died out—it has been shown pretty conclusively by science that no such phenomena in fact exist. There might have been witches, and, in that case, there could have been a science which studied them and the ways in which they achieved their effects; but the evidence indicates that there are no such things. But this is hardly the case with mentalistic terms. What kind of discoveries could show that in fact there are no thoughts, feelings, wishes, and the like? On the contrary, is it not as plain as anything can be that there are such things? And, secondly, we could not dispense with mentalistic terms, even if our theories told us it was most desirable to do so, nor does it seem likely we will be able to do for the foreseeable future. This is because we often want to tell our thoughts, describe our feelings, express our wishes, and there is no other way available of doing so than saying I just had the thought . . . , I feel . . . , I wish. . . . To abandon such expressions would be to impoverish our language to the point of bankruptcy.

Another materialistic reply to the question "What are thoughts, feelings, wishes, and the like?" is called the avowal theory. This theory allows that sentences like "I feel bored" have meaning all right, but are not used to make *statements,* are not used to describe or report or assert anything. They are simply bits of behavior, the effects of certain inner (physical) conditions. If I yawn, twiddle my thumbs, or say "Ho hum," I am not describing, reporting, or asserting anything; I am not making a statement which is either true or false. The avowal theory takes "I feel bored" to be a (learned) bit of behavior, like "Ho hum," which results from certain inner (physical) conditions, and not a statement, description, report, or assertion at all. And the same would go for utterances of the form "I just had the thought that . . . ," "I wish that . . . ," and the like.

It cannot be denied that there is some truth in the avowal theory. Certainly such utterances are sometimes used in this way, as expressions of inner states—"I feel bored" is sometimes uttered in the way that "God, I'm bored!" or even "Oh God, what boredom!" is uttered, and it is clear at least in the latter case that no statement, description, report, or assertion is being made. Yet the avowal theory falls down in two important respects. First, it is utterly implausible when applied to third-person statements, e.g., "He is bored." In no way can such a remark be taken as the expression of an inner state. Second, even in their first-person use, such utterances are often used merely to report or describe. If someone asks me why I keep looking at my watch, I may say "Because I am bored," making a report which explains my behavior. Furthermore, I can use such utterances to make *false* statements, as when I am lying. "Ho hum" cannot be used to explain anything or to lie about anything. So the avowal theory will not do.

Another materialistic account is to allow that expressions referring to thoughts, feelings, wishes, and the like have meaning, but to insist that their meanings can be expressed in purely physicalistic terms. What physicalistic terms? The most plausible candidate is the set of terms which refer to physical *behavior*. This account [is] known as behaviorism. . . .

This behavioristic version of materialism has had a strong appeal for philosophers over the years. In contrast with the unintelligibility thesis, it allows sentences containing mentalistic terms to have meaning, and, in contrast, with the avowal theory, it allows them to be either true or false in the situations in which they are used. And by using the concept of *disposition to behave,* it allows such sentences to be true even where the person is not at that moment behaving in any particular fashion. Yet by tying the meaning to *behavior* the theory allows sentences with mentalistic terms to be testable by observation in an open and public way. To determine whether someone has a headache we only have to see if, under suitable conditions, he behaves in the appropriate ways.

This view, however, is open to a fundamental objection. . . . No matter what sort of behavior or behavioral dispositions we imagine as allegedly constituting a particular mental event, we can always imagine just that behavior or those dispositions *without* that mental event. We can imagine that behavior as coming from some *other* cause, or even as inexplicably *spontaneous*. Therefore behavior and behavioral dispositions do not furnish an exhaustive analysis of these mentalistic terms. There is something left out by such accounts.

The last version of materialism we shall consider, and currently the most seriously discussed, is known

as the identity theory. It is the theory that thoughts, feelings, wishes, and the rest of so-called mental phenomena are identical with, one and the same thing as, states and processes of the *body* (and, perhaps, more specifically, states and processes of the nervous system, or even of the brain alone). Thus the having of a thought is identical with having such and such bodily cells in such and such states, other cells in other states.

In one respect the identity theory and behaviorism are very much alike. This comes out when we ask ourselves what the "dispositions" of the behavorist are. If an object has a "disposition," then *it is in a particular state* such that when certain things happen to it, other things will happen to it. Thus if an object is brittle, it is in a particular state such that when subject to a sudden force it will shatter. And similarly dispositions of a body to behave in particular ways are *states of that body*. So it is fair to say that both identity theorists and behaviorists identify the mental with *bodily states*. But one important way in which they differ concerns how those states are to be defined or characterized. As we have seen, behaviorists wish to define those states in terms of what changes they result in when certain specifiable conditions obtain. Identity theorists wish to define them in terms of identifiable structures of the body, ongoing processes and states of the bodily organs, and, in the last analysis, the very cells which go to make up those organs.

There is another important respect in which the identity theory differs from behaviorism. The behaviorist offered his notion of dispositions to behave in certain ways as an analysis of the very meaning of mentalistic terms. But the identity theorist grants that it is wildly implausible to claim that what I *mean* when I say, for example, that I just had a particular thought is that certain events were going on in my nervous system. For I have no idea what those events are, nor does even the most advanced neurophysiologist at the present time, and yet I know what I mean when I say I just had a particular thought. So, since I know what I mean by those words, I cannot mean by them something I know nothing about (viz., unknown events in my nervous system). Hence the identity theory is not intended to be an analysis of the *meanings* of mentalistic terms as behaviorism purports to be. What, then, is the theory that mental phenomena are "identical" with the body intended to be?

The sense of "identity" relevant here is that in which we say, for example, that the morning star is "identical" with the evening star. It is not that the expression "morning star" means the same as the expression "evening star"; on the contrary, these expressions mean something different. But the object referred to by the two expressions is one and the same; there is just one heavenly body, namely, Venus, which when seen in the morning is called the morning star and when seen in the evening is called the evening star. The morning star is identical with the evening star; they are one and the same object.

Of course, the identity of the mental with the physical is not exactly of this sort, since it is held to be simultaneous identity rather than the identity of a thing at one time with the same thing at a later time. To take a closer example, one can say that lightning is a particularly massive electrical discharge from one cloud to another or to the earth. Not that the word "lightning" *means* "a particularly massive electrical discharge . . ."; when Benjamin Franklin discovered that lightning was electrical, he did not make a discovery about the meaning of words. Nor when it was discovered that water was H_2O was a discovery made about the meanings of words; yet water is identical with H_2O.

In a similar fashion, the identity theorist can hold that thoughts, feelings, wishes, and the like are identical with physical states. Not "identical" in the sense that mentalistic terms are synonymous in meaning with physicalistic terms but "identical" in the sense that the actual events picked out by mentalistic terms are one and the same events as those picked out by physicalistic terms.

It is important to note that the identity theory does not have a chance of being true unless a particular sort of correspondence obtains between mental events and physical events, namely, that whenever a mental event occurs, a physical event of a particular sort (or at least one of a number of particular sorts) occurs, and vice versa. If it turned out to be the case that when a particular mental event occurred it seemed a matter of chance what physical events occurred or even whether any physical event at all occurred, or vice versa, then the identity theory would not be true. So far as our state of knowledge at the present time is concerned, it is still too early to say what the empirical facts are, although it must be said that many scientists do believe that there exists the kind of correspondences

needed by identity theorists. But even if these correspondences turn out to exist, that does not mean that the identity theory will be true. For identity theorists do not hold merely that mental and physical events are correlated in a particular way but that they are one and the same events, i.e., not like lightning and thunder (which are correlated in lawful ways but not identical) but like lightning and electrical discharges (which always go together because they are one and the same).

What are the advantages of the identity theory? As a form of materialism, it does not have to cope with a world which has in it both mental phenomena and physical phenomena, and it does not have to ponder how they might be related. There exist only the physical phenomena, although there do exist two different ways of talking about such phenomena: physicalistic terminology and, in at least some situations, mentalistic terminology. We have here a dualism of language, but not a dualism of entities, events, or properties.

SOME DIFFICULTIES IN THE IDENTITY THEORY

But do we have merely a dualism of languages and no other sort of dualism? In the case of Venus, we do indeed have only one object, but the expression "morning star" picks out one phase of that object's history, where it is in the mornings, and the expression "evening star" picks out another phase of that object's history, where it is in the evenings. If that object did not have these two distinct aspects, it would not have been a *discovery* that the morning star and the evening star were indeed one and the same body, and, further, there would be no point to the different ways of referring to it.

Now it would be admitted by identity theorists that physicalistic and mentalistic terms do not refer to different phases in the history of one and the same object. What sort of identity is intended? Let us turn to an allegedly closer analogy, that of the identity of lightning and a particular sort of electrical phenomenon. Yet here again we have two distinguishable aspects, the appearance to the naked eye on the one hand and the physical composition on the other. And this is also not the kind of identity which is plausible for mental and physical events. The appearance *to the naked eye* of a neurological event is utterly different from the experience of having a thought or a pain.

It is sometimes suggested that the physical aspect results from looking at a particular event "from the outside," whereas the mental results from looking at the same event "from the inside." When the brain surgeon observes my brain he is looking at it from the outside, whereas when I experience a mental event I am "looking" at my brain "from the inside."

Such an account gives us only a misleading analogy, rather than an accurate characterization of the relationship between the mental and the physical. The analogy suggests the difference between a man who knows his own house from the inside, in that he is free to move about within, seeing objects from different perspectives, touching them, etc., but can never get outside to see how it looks from there, and a man who cannot get inside and therefore knows only the outside appearance of the house, and perhaps what he can glimpse through the windows. But what does this have to do with the brain? Am I free to roam about inside my brain, observing what the brain surgeon may never see? Is not the "inner" aspect of my brain far more accessible to the brain surgeon than to me? He has the X rays, probes, electrodes, scalpels, and scissors for getting at the inside of my brain. If it is replied that this is only an analogy, not to be taken literally, then the question still remains how the mental and the physical are related.

Usually identity theorists at this point flee to even vaguer accounts of the relationship. They talk of different "levels of analysis," or of different "perspectives," or of different "conceptual schemes," or of different "language games." The point of such suggestions is that the difference between the mental and the physical is not a basic, fundamental, or intrinsic one, but rather a difference which is merely relative to different human purposes or standpoints. The difference is supposed to exist not in the thing itself but in the eye of the beholder.

But these are only hints. They do not tell us in precise and literal terms how the mental and the physical differ and are related. They only try to assure us that the difference does not matter to the real nature of things. But until we are given a theory to consider, we cannot accept the identity theorists' assurance that some theory will do only he does not know what it is.

One of the leading identity theorists, J. J. C. Smart, holds that mentalistic discourse is simply a vaguer, more indefinite way of talking about what could be talked about more precisely by using physiological terms. If I report a red afterimage, I mean (roughly) that something is going on which is like what goes on when I really see a red patch. I do not actually *mean* that a particular sort of brain process is occurring, but when I say something is going on I refer (very vaguely, to be sure) to just that brain

process. Thus the thing referred to in my report of an afterimage is a brain process. Hence there is no need to bring in any nonphysical features. Thus even the taint of dualism is avoided.

Does this ingenious attempt to evade dualistic implications stand up under philosophical scrutiny? I am inclined to think it will not. Let us return to the man reporting the red afterimage. He was aware of the occurrence of something or other, of some feature or other. Now it seems to me obvious that he was not necessarily aware of the state of his brain at that time (I doubt that most of us are ever aware of the sate of our brain) nor, in general, necessarily aware of any physical features of his body at that time. He might, of course, have been incidentally aware of some physical feature but not insofar as he was aware of the red afterimage as such. Yet he was definitely aware of something, or else how could he have made that report? So he must have been aware of some nonphysical feature. That is the only way of explaining how he was aware of anything at all.

Of course, the thing that our reporter of the afterimage was aware of might well have had further features which he was *not* aware of, particularly, in this connection, physical features. I may be aware of certain features of an object without being aware of others. So it is not ruled out that the event our reporter is aware of might be an event with predominantly physical features—he just does not notice those. But he must be aware of some of its features, or else it would not be proper to say he was aware of *that* event. And if he is not aware of any physical features, he must be aware of something else. And that shows that we cannot get rid of those nonphysical features in the way that Smart suggests.

One would not wish to be dogmatic in saying that identity theorists will never work out this part of their theory. Much work is being done on this problem at the present time, for it arises in other areas of philosophy as well as in the philosophy of mind. In particular philosophers of science are concerned with the problem. We saw that the identity theory used such analogies as the identity of lightning with electrical phenomena and the identity of water with molecules consisting of hydrogen and oxygen. But the question to be raised is what kind of identity we are dealing with in such cases. Do we have mere duality of terms in these cases, duality of features, properties, or aspects, or even duality of substances? Very similar issues arise. So it is quite possible that further work on this problem of identity will be useful in clarifying the identity theory of the mental and the physical. But at the present the matter is by no means as clear as it should be.

Even if the identity theorist could clarify the sense of "identity" to be used in his theory, he would still face two other problems. These concern coexistence in time and space. Coexistence in time and space are conditions that must be met if there is to be identity. That is to say, for two apparently different things to turn out to be one and the same, they must exist at the same time and in the same location. If we could show that Mr. A existed at a time when Mr. B did not, or that Mr. A existed in a place where Mr. B did not, then this would show that Mr. A and Mr. B were different men. It is by virtue of these facts about identity that an alibi can exonerate a suspect: if Mr. A was not in Chicago at the time, then he could not be one and the same with the man who stole the diamonds in Chicago.

So if mental events are to be identical with physical events, then they must fulfill the conditions of coexistence in time and space. The question is, Do they?

So far as coexistence in time is concerned, very little is known. The most relevant work consists in direct stimulation of an exposed part of the brain during surgery. Since only a local anesthetic is necessary in many such cases the patient may well be fully conscious. Then, as the surgeon stimulates different parts of his brain, the patient may report the occurrence of mental events—memories, thoughts, sensations. Do the physical events in the brain and the mental events occur at precisely the same time? It is impossible to say. All that would be required is a very small time gap to prove that the physical events were not identical with the mental events. But it is very difficult to see how the existence of so small a time gap could be established. And even if it were, what would it prove? Only that the mental event was not identical with just that physical event; it would not prove it was nonidentical with any physical event. So it could well be that coexistence in time is present or is not. I do not think that we shall get much decisive information from empirical work of the sort here described. The identity theorist, then, does not have to fear refutation from this quarter, at least not for a long time.

How about coexistence in space? Do mental events occur in the same place the corresponding physical events occur? This is also a very difficult question to answer, for two reasons. First our present ignorance of neurophysiology, especially concerning the brain and how it functions, allows us to say very little about the location of the relevant physical events. This much does seem likely: they are located in the brain. Much more than that we do not at present know, although as the time passes, we should learn much more. The second reason for our difficulty in telling if there is coexistence in space has to do with the location of mental events. Where do thoughts, feelings, and wishes occur? Do they occur in the brain? Suppose you suddenly have the thought that it is almost suppertime; where does that occur? The most sensible answer would be that it occurs wherever you are when you have that thought. If you are in the library when you have that thought, then the thought occurs in the library. But it would be utterly unnatural to ask where inside your body the thought occurred; in your foot, or your liver, or your heart, or your head? It is not that any one of these places is more likely than another. They are all wrong. Not because thoughts occur somewhere *else* within your body than your foot, liver, heart, or head—but because it *makes no sense at all* to locate the occurrence of a thought at some place within your body. We would not understand someone who pointed to a place in his body and claimed that it was *there* that his entertaining of a thought was located. Certainly, if one *looked* at that place, one would not *see* anything resembling a thought. If it were replied to this that pains can be located in the body without being seen there, then it should be pointed out that one *feels* the pain there but one hardly feels a thought in the body.

The fact that it makes no sense at all to speak of mental events as occurring at some point within the body has the result that the identity theory cannot be true. This is because the corresponding physical events do occur at some point within the body, and if those physical events are identical with mental events, then those mental events must occur at the same point within the body. But those mental events do not occur at any point within the body, because any statement to the effect that they occurred here, or there, would be senseless. Hence the mental events cannot meet the condition of coexistence in space, and therefore cannot be identical with physical events.

Our inability to give the location within the body of mental events is different from our inability to give the location of the corresponding physical events within the body. In the latter case, it is that we do not know enough about the body, particularly the brain. Some day, presumably, we will know enough to pin down pretty exactly the location of the relevant physical events. But in the case of mental events it is not simply that at present we are ignorant but that someday we may well know. What would it be like to discover the location of a thought in the brain? What kind of information would we need to be able to say that the thought occurred exactly *here*? If by X rays or some other means we were able to see every event which occurred in the brain, we would never get a glimpse of a thought. If, to resort to fantasy, we could so enlarge a brain or so shrink ourselves that we could wander freely through the brain, we would still never observe a thought. All we could ever observe in the brain would be the *physical* events which occur in it. If mental events had location in the brain, there should be some means of detecting them there. But of course there is none. The very idea of it is senseless.

Some identity theorists believe this objection can be met. One approach is to reply that this objection begs the question: if the identity theory is true, and mental events are identical with brain events, then, paradoxical as it may sound, mental events do indeed have location, and are located precisely where the physical events are located. Another approach is to reply that the relevant physical events should be construed as events which happen to the body as a whole, and therefore occur where the body as a whole is located; then it is not so paradoxical to give location to the mental events, for they would be located where the body is located but would not be located in any particular part of the body.

We have carried our discussion of the identity theory to the very frontier of present philosophical thinking. We can only leave it to the reader to decide how well it can meet the objections which are raised to it.

There is a mixed theory which is relevant at this point. A person might hold that, although mental and physical events are different sorts of events and in no sense identical, nevertheless the subjects to which they both occur are *material* objects. Thus we have a theory which preserves materialism so far as the *subject* of these events is concerned, but represents an important departure from materialism in accepting a dualism of *events,* the existence of nonmaterial events which happen to material objects in addition to the material events which happen to them.

It would be a mere verbal evasion at this point to argue that so-called mental events are really physical, in this mixed theory, since they occur to physical objects. What would have to be faced is the fact that thoughts, feelings, wishes, and the like are happenings of a quite different sort from the changes in size, shape, location, charge, spin, energy level, etc., which are countenanced in present physical theory. And if we did find even more occult and unfamiliar sorts of physical events, we would still have to face the question whether these events are identical with thoughts, feelings, etc. And any attempt to argue for identity would face all the problems we have already observed to arise for the identity theory.

If we were to accept a dualism of events, then to that extent we would be abandoning materialism. We would be admitting that what exists is not merely or purely or wholly material. Objects would have a nonmaterial dimension; they would be subject to nonmaterial happenings and nonmaterial states. To that extent, objects would not be merely material in nature. On the other hand, there would be no merely or purely or wholly nonmaterial objects which were subjects of mental events either. So we would not be back in a full-fledged dualism either. The kind of theory we would have is a neutralist theory: what at the beginning of this chapter we called the person theory. It is time we turned to a full examination of that theory.

A DOUBLE ASPECT ACCOUNT

We have considered the view that mental events happen to purely immaterial substances and the view that so-called mental events are physical events which happen to purely material substances. We have seen both advantages and disadvantages in each of these main lines of approach. Dualism does justice to what we take to be the wide gulf between the conscious, on the one hand, and matter on the other, but at the expense of introducing the very mysterious notion of the purely thinking substance. Materialism dispenses with such a notion, but at the expense of obliterating what we take to be an ineradicable gulf between the conscious and matter. We will shortly look at a recent attempt to find a compromise between these two theories. We will call it the person theory. It is the view that mental events happen neither to purely immaterial substances nor to purely material substances, but to some thing which is *neither immaterial nor material;* let us call them persons. Mental events happen to *persons,* and persons are subject to *both* mental *and* material happenings.

The historical ancestor of the person theorist is Spinoza, the Dutch philosopher of the seventeenth century. Confronted on the one side by the English materialist Hobbes and on the other side by the French dualist Descartes, Spinoza said, in effect, a plague on both your houses. The mental and the physical are both of them simply aspects of something which in itself is neither mental nor physical. A man can equally well be considered as an extended, physical thing or as a thinking thing, although each of these characterizations only brings out one aspect of the man. The analogy has been proposed of an undulating line which at a given moment may be concave from one point of view and convex from the other. The line itself is not completely described by either term, but only by the use of both terms. Yet it is not that there are two different things, one concave and the other convex. There is only one thing which is, from one point of view, concave and, from another point of view, convex. So with man. He is both a thinking thing and an extended, physical thing—not that he is two things but rather that he is one thing with these two aspects. Such a view is traditionally known as a double aspect view. It is like some versions of the identity theory, but, at least in Spinoza's case, differs with respect to the conception of the thing that has the two aspects. For Spinoza what has the two aspects is not material (nor is it mental either), whereas for the identity theory as we have discussed it what has the two aspects is material.

Although we cannot examine the details of Spinoza's theory, we might note that Spinoza believed *everything* which existed had these two aspects. This view is called panpsychism. It is the view that consciousness occurs wherever anything exists and thus that every tree, rock, cloud, and even every atom is conscious to some degree. To be sure, Spinoza did not believe that all things had so fully developed a consciousness as man has; presumably a rock's mind is so crude and inferior that it is only barely conscious at all. Still, for Spinoza, it is conscious to some degree.

For a double aspect theory, there are two issues of crucial importance—what is the nature of the underlying stuff which has the aspects, and what exactly are "aspects"? Unfortunately in Spinoza's theory both of these are left in deep obscurity. Each man, and, in fact, everything else that exists, is just a particular instance or specimen of what Spinoza calls "Substance" and also calls "God" or "Nature." But it is very difficult to understand what this stuff is. An indication of the difficulty is that since Spinoza's time there has been an unending controversy whether Spinoza was an atheist or what one commentator called "a God-intoxicated man." If an issue so general as that cannot be settled, then it is unlikely that we can hope for much clarification about the nature of this underlying stuff. The second question, What is an "aspect"?, is equally important to answer, for we do not know what it means to say that the mental and the physical are "aspects" of the same thing until we know what an "aspect" is. Again, Spinoza is not of much help. In his theory, the mental and the physical are both basic attributes of the underlying stuff but he never says how they are related or, indeed, how one and the same thing could have such *different* attributes. As we saw in our discussion of the identity theory. . . , it is very difficult to explain with any precision in what sense the mental and the physical are "aspects." The suggestion, by analogy with perception, is that they are different appearances of the thing, the thing as seen from different points of view, but when we try to replace the analogy with a literal characterization, we find ourselves unable to say very much.

THE PERSON THEORY

In recent philosophy, a modified version of the double aspect theory which we will call the person theory has been presented by P. F. Strawson.[3] It is the view that the mental and the physical are both of them attributes of *persons*; the person is the underlying entity which has both mental and physical attributes. Thus we could say of the *person* that he is six feet tall, weighs one hundred and seventy-five pounds, is moving at the rate of three miles an hour (all physical attributes), and we could also say of the very same entity, that person, that he is now thinking about a paper he is writing, feels a pang of anxiety about that paper, and then wishes it were already over and done with (all mental attributes). We have here neither attributions to two different subjects, a mind and a body (dualism), nor attributions to a body (materialism), but attributions to a person. We may say that the person has a mind and a body, but all that means is that both mental and physical attributes are applicable to him.

Why does Strawson reject materialism and hold that mental states must be attributed to a *person* rather than to a body? His argument is very difficult to grasp but it appears to be as follows.[4] Unless we are to accept the unintelligibility thesis or the avowal theory . . .—theories which Strawson rejects as too paradoxical to consider—we must admit that we often do ascribe states of consciousness to things; e.g., we say of some particular subject that the subject had a headache. Now Strawson wishes to argue that the notion of attributing a state of consciousness to a subject cannot be analyzed as the notion of attributing a state of consciousness to a body. Consider the epiphenomenalist, who claims that to say "Subject A has a headache" is synonymous with saying "Body *a* is producing a headache." Now the epiphenomenalist would grant that this contention—that all of subject A's headaches are produced by body *a*—is *controversial,* and that some argumentation is needed. But what exactly is the contention? It is not that *all* headaches are produced by body *a*. That is obviously false. Only subject A's headaches are produced by body *a*. But if "Subject A has a headache" is synonymous with "Body *a* is producing a headache," then to say "All subject A's headaches are produced by body *a*" is simply to say "All the headaches produced by body *a* are produced by body *a*." And that is a claim about which controversy would be impossible, since it is an utter tautology. Exactly the same reasoning would be directed by Strawson against the kind of materialsim which holds that "Subject A has a headache" means "Body *a* has a headache."

Strawson's point, if we are interpreting him properly, is that in order for materialists and epiphenomenalists even to formulate their claim, they must have a concept of a subject of mental states which is different from the concept of a material body. For they wish to single out sets of mental states and go on to make the nontrivial claim about each of those sets that it is dependent upon some particular body. So they cannot use the body to single out the sets. Hence, their notion of a subject of states of consciousness must be different from their notion of a material body. Otherwise their claim degenerates into the triviality that all those states of consciousness dependent upon a body are dependent upon that body, a claim too empty to be worth asserting.

I believe that this argument is sound. But it is important to note what it does and does not establish. It establishes the *logical* distinctness of subjects of consciousness and bodies. That is to say, it establishes that expressions referring to the one cannot *mean* the same as expressions referring to the other; they cannot

be synonymous; the one cannot be analyzed in terms of the other. But the argument does not rule out some form of the identity theory, i.e., the claim that the *entities* which exemplify the one set of expressions are one and the same as the entities which exemplify the other.[5] Even if the expression "subject of consciousness" does not *mean* a body of a certain sort, it still might turn out that whatever is a subject of consciousness is identical with a body of a certain sort. We shall return to this issue shortly.

In rejecting the logical identity of persons (i.e., subjects of consciousness) and bodies, Strawson might be suspected of accepting dualism. But this would be a mistake. Strawson also rejects dualism, at least in the Cartesian form we have discussed it above; he rejects the view that the subject of states of consciousness is a wholly immaterial, nonphysical thing, a thing to which nothing but states of consciousness can be ascribed. His argument is as follows.[6] If someone has the concept of a subject of consciousness, then he must be willing to allow that there could be other subjects than himself, i.e., that he might be only one self among many. To have the concept of other subjects of consciousness is to be able to distinguish one from another, pick out or identify different subjects, be able to say on some occasions at least that here is one subject rather than another. (If one had no idea how to distinguish one subject from another, then one would not have the concept of *different* subjects.) Now if other subjects of consciousness were wholly immaterial, then there would be no way of distinguishing one subject from another—how could we possibly tell how many such subjects were around us right now or which subject was which? And if there was no way of distinguishing one subject from another, then, as was just pointed out, one would not have the concept of other subjects. And therefore, as was pointed out at the beginning of this argument, one would not have the concept of a subject of consciousness at all. So the Cartesian concept of the subject as wholly immaterial is without meaning.

Therefore, if we do have a concept of a subject of consciousness, as we surely do, then it can be neither merely the concept of a body (as materialism holds) nor merely the concept of an immaterial thing (as the dualist holds). It must be the concept of an entity to which both physical and mental attributions can be made. That is to say, this subject must be not only conscious but physical as well. Strawson calls entities which admit of both mental and physical attributes *persons*.

The person theory has very attractive features. It gives full weight to the distinction between mental and physical attributes, allowing them to be attributes of basically different natures. Yet it also does justice to the fact that they seem to be attributes of one and the same subject; we say, "As he fell through space, he wondered if the parachute would ever open," not "As his body fell through space, his mind wondered if the parachute would ever open." Nor do we seem committed to that curious entity, the immaterial, extensionless thinking substance of Descartes' dualism.

WHAT IS A PERSON?

And yet, alas, there are difficulties with the person theory. These begin to emerge when we begin probing deeper into the concept of the *person* which is involved here. Strawson defines "person" very simply, as "a type of entity such that *both* predicates ascribing states of consciousness *and* predicates ascribing corporeal characteristics, a physical situation, etc. are equally applicable to a single individual of that single type."[7] But such a definition does not help us very much. That it does not comes out when we ask how the person theory differs from the identity theory.

Identity theorists wish to say that mental attributes are attributes of bodies. Furthermore, most of them wish to say that in some sense the mental attributes are reducible to physical attributes. Not all hold to the latter thesis, however. Herbert Feigl holds that where mentalistic terms are appropriate the basic and underlying reality is *mental* and physicalistic terms refer to this mental reality.[8] Thus Feigl seems to admit a dualism of attributes, mental and physical. Yet his is an identity theory both in the sense that the basic subjects of consciousness are bodies and in the sense that certain mentalistic and physicalistic terms have one and the same referent (although some of these terms will have a *mental* referent). Now Strawson would certainly reject the contention that mental attributes are reducible in any sense to physical attributes. But would he reject the claim that they are attributes of bodies? Does he wish to say that persons are bodies of a certain sort, namely bodies which have mental attributes as well?

It is clear that Strawson holds persons to be things which have bodily attributes. But that does not make them bodies any more than the fact that something has red in it makes it red. For, unlike ordinary bodies, persons are things which have mental attributes as well. Furthermore, for Strawson it is not the case that persons are things which just happen to have bodily attributes (but might not have had them), nor is it the case that they are things which just happen to have mental attributes (but might not have had them). It is essential to persons, on Strawson's conception of them, that they be entities which necessarily have *both* mental and bodily attributes. And that means that they are things which differ essentially from bodies (which have only bodily attributes necessarily). They are different types of stuffs or substances or entities. And therefore the person theory is fundamentally different from materialism of any sort. It is dualistic in holding that there are two different types of subjects in the natural world, physical bodies and persons. Physical bodies necessarily have solely the physical dimension; persons necessarily have two dimensions, a physical and a mental dimension. It is the latter contention which distinguishes it from Spinoza's double aspect theory; for Spinoza, everything which exists in the world is, in Strawson's sense, a person, i.e., a thing which necessarily has both a mental and a physical dimension.

If we cannot say, on the person theory, that a person *is* a body, perhaps we can say that a person is, *in part*, a body (in the way that a thing which has red in it may be in part red). But this will not do either, for it inevitably raises the question what the rest of it is. That is, it suggests that a person is some sort of an amalgam, a compound of a body and something else (perhaps a soul?). Such suggestions are precisely what the person theory attempts to combat.

Can we even say that a person *has* a body? I suppose that Strawson would want to be able to say that. But what would it mean on the person theory? Doubtless it means that persons have bodily attributes. But does it mean any more? Is it to say anything about a relation between a person and a *body?* Not on the person theory. For a *body* is something which necessarily has solely bodily attributes and such a thing has nothing to do with persons, which, as we saw, are things which necessarily have both bodily and mental attributes.

Does very much hang on this question of the relation (on the person theory) between persons and bodies? A good deal. For example, consider the laws of nature which hold for bodies, the laws of physics, chemistry, biology. Surely we would want to be able to say that these laws are true for human bodies as well as other bodies.   it is true, in its Newtonian formulation, that "a *body* continues its state of rest or steady motion unless . . . ," we would want this to hold for the bodies of persons as well as for all other bodies. Yet if we cannot even say that a person's "body" is a *body* in the same sense that rocks and trees are bodies, then these laws of nature, which apply to *bodies,* cannot be applied to the "bodies" of persons. And that would be so great an inconvenience, to say nothing of its absurdity, as to count against the person theory.

To be sure, the term "body" is used in many ways besides the Newtonian one cited above, some of which tie better with the person theory. For example, consider the old song "Gin a body meet a body comin' thro the rye." Here of course we are not envisioning a collision of solids but an encounter between persons. In this context, the term "body" is simply used to mean a person. (Sometimes the reverse is the case. When we say "They searched his person," we are using "person" to mean a body.)

There is another use which comes even closer to the Strawsonian conception of a body. If someone said "They found a body in the lake today," we would be very surprised if he meant a rock, or a tree trunk, or an old, sunken boat, or a fish, although all of these are, in the Newtonian sense, bodies. Here "body" means "corpse," i.e., a dead human being (a dead *animal* is called a carcass rather than a corpse). A corpse or "body" in this sense is what is left when a person dies, although it is not a *part* of a living person or something which he *has* while he is alive (he does have the right to say what is to be done with it after he dies). This concept of the body becomes gruesomely explicit when we refer to it as "the remains."

It is this conception of the body which comes closest to that found in the person theory. For, in that theory, as we have seen, a body is not a person, nor is it a part of a person, nor is it something a person has. At most it is the person insofar as he is thought of as the subject of bodily attributes. It is then an abstraction, an intellectual construction, rather than a reality. But it becomes a reality at death. It materializes into that thing we call a corpse. On the person theory, a human body is what would be the person's corpse if he died; the only way we can talk about a person's body is if we consider him as if he were dead.

It, is, then, one of the paradoxical implications of the person theory that the body which a person has cannot be conceived of as a physical object subject to the laws of the physical world. In its attempt to establish the unity of the person (against dualism) without sacrificing the thesis that persons are conscious (against materialism), the person theory seems to end with the absurdity that a person's body is not a *physical* thing.

A RECONSIDERATION OF DUALISM

In view of the grave difficulties in materialism and the person theory, it might be useful to review the objections to dualism and see if they can be met in some way. After all, dualism does have the advantage over materialism of accounting for the inability to reduce mental phenomena to material phenomena and the advantage over the person theory of allowing for the treatment of the human body as a material body in principle no different from other material bodies. It would be desirable to preserve these advantages, if we could overcome the disadvantages which seem to rule dualism out.

We noted that one source of discontent with dualism was that it seemed to commit us to the existence of a very peculiar kind of entity, a something which persists in time, has states, undergoes changes, and engages in processes, and yet is invisible, intangible, without size or shape or mass. What a curious something it is; it does not even seem *intelligible* that there should be such a thing. Nothing can be said about it except that it is a subject of consciousness! And that hardly makes clear what it is.

I do not think that this difficulty can be met directly. If the dualist is correct, then the notion of a nonmaterial subject of consciousness is perplexing and obscure, and nothing can be done about that. But we can weaken the force of the difficulty. It depends upon an implicit comparison of the immaterial subject of consciousness with the material subject of material states, material events, and material processes. It is suggested by this implicit comparison that the notion of the latter is clear and intelligible whereas the notion of the former is not. But it is not true that the notion of a material thing is clear and intelligible. We can raise parallel objections to it. We may ask of a material thing which has states, undergoes changes, and engages in processes: *What is it* which has these states, undergoes changes, and engages in processes? What *is* a material thing? On reflection we will see that the only thing which can be said is that it is a something which is the subject of certain sorts of states, events, and processes, namely material ones. Nothing more can be said than that. But precisely that sort of thing, no more and no less, can be said of an immaterial thing, namely that it is a something which is the subject of certain sorts of states, events, and processes, namely ones involving consciousness. So in this respect, immaterial things are no worse off than material things.

However, we are still left with two particular problems here, which we referred to earlier as the problem of identification and the problem of individuation. . . .

So far as identification is concerned, it does seem to be the case that we can only tell we are in the presence of another consciousness and can only tell whose consciousness it is by observing *physical* phenomena. We have no way of getting at the other mind directly. Of course, the problem of identification would be easier if mental telepathy were a common phenomenon. Then one could communicate with another mind without resort to ordinary sense observation and one might tell, by the content of the communication, whom one was communicating with. Thus if it communicated information which only your uncle could know, that would be good reason to think it was your uncle you were in communication with. There is some question even here how much such inferences are based upon what we know about the world through sense observation; for example, you would think it was something only your uncle could know because you know, perhaps, that only he was in the room at the time (as established by observing, through the window, his body and the otherwise empty room). So if in the end sense observation must be depended upon, telepathy will not help. But even if it did help it is not available to us for determining the identity of other consciousnesses. So we must depend upon sense observations of material bodies, especially human bodies. And that leaves mental things in a weaker position, at least epistemologically, than material things.

So far as individuation is concerned, too, mental entities seem to have a weaker status than material entities. For it does seem to be possible for there to be two different persons who have exactly the same mental history, exactly the same set of mental states and events throughout their life. The only thing that could distinguish the two would be the existence of different bodies in different places (although having exactly similar mental histories would necessitate their having exactly similar bodies and environments). This indicates that mental entities depend in part on material entities for their individuation.

We must conclude that any theory of the nature of the subject of consciousness must include some reference to the material bodies, although it may not be necessary to *identify* the subject of consciousness with the material body. Indeed, we have seen that there are grave difficulties in attempts to defend such an identification. Yet a dualism which includes the concept of an immaterial subject of consciousness utterly independent of material bodies is unable to deal with the problems of identification and individuation. So we must turn to a closer look at the relation of consciousness and the body. . . .

NOTES

1. *Ethics,* Part I, Prop. x, note.

2. Karl Marx and Friedrich Engels, *The German Ideology* (New York: International Publishers, 1947), p. 14.

3. P. F. Strawson, *Individuals* (London: Methuen & Co., 1959), Chapter 3.

4. *Ibid.,* pp. 95–98.

5. See James W. Cornman, ''Strawson's 'Person','' *Theoria,* XXX (1964), pp. 146–47.

6. *Individuals,* pp. 99–104.

7. *Ibid.* p. 102.

8. Herbert Feigl, ''The 'Mental' and the 'Physical','' *Minnesota Studies* in the Philosophy of Science, Vol. II (Minneapolis: University of Minnesota Press, 1958), pp. 474–75. The essay has been reprinted as a separate monograph (Minneapolis: University of Minnesota Press, 1967); a postscript contains Feigl's most recent thoughts on this matter. See also Feigl's contribution to Sidney Hook, ed., *Dimensions of Mind* (New York: New York University Press, 1961): ''Mind-Body, Not a Pseudo-problem,'' pp. 33–34.

T. H. HUXLEY

Animals and Human Beings as Conscious Automata*

Thomas Henry Huxley (1825–1895) was the leading contemporary interpreter and defender of the theories of his friend, Charles Darwin.

. . . There remains a doctrine to which Descartes attached great weight, so that full acceptance of it became a sort of note of a thorough-going Cartesian, but which, nevertheless, is so opposed to ordinary prepossessions that it attained more general notoriety, and gave rise to more discussion, than almost any other Cartesian hypothesis. It is the doctrine that brute animals are mere machines or automata, devoid not only of reason, but of any kind of consciousness, which is stated briefly in the *Discourse on Method,* and more fully in the "Replies to the Fourth Objection," and in the correspondence with Henry More.

The process of reasoning by which Descartes arrived at this startling conclusion is well shown in the following passage of the "Réponses":

But as regards the souls of beasts, although this is not the place for considering them, and though, without a general exposition of physics, I can say no more on this subject than I have already said in the fifth part of my Treatise on Method; yet, I will further state, here, that it appears to me to be a very remarkable circumstance that no movement can take place, either in the bodies of beasts, or even in our own, if these bodies have not in themselves all the organs and instruments by means of which the very same move-

ments would be accomplished in a machine. So that, even in us, the spirit, or the soul, does not directly move the limbs, but only determines the course of that very subtle liquid which is called the animal spirits, which, running continually from the heart by the brain into the muscles, is the cause of all the movements of our limbs, and often may cause many different motions, one as easily as the other.

And it does not even always exert this determination; for among the movements which take place in us, there are many which do not depend on the mind at all, such as the beating of the heart, the digestion of food, the nutrition, the respiration of those who sleep; and even in those who are awake, walking, singing, and other similar actions, when they are performed without the mind thinking about them. And, when one who falls from a height throws his hands forward to save his head, it is in virtue of no ratiocination that he performs this action; it does not depend upon his mind, but takes place merely because his senses being affected by the present danger, some change arises in his brain which determines the animal spirits to pass thence into the nerves, in such a manner as is required to produce this motion, in the same way as in a machine, and without the mind being able to hinder it. Now since we observe this in ourselves, why should we be so much astonished if the light reflected from the body of a wolf into the eye of a sheep has the same force to excite in it the motion of flight?

After having observed this, if we wish to learn by reasoning, whether certain movements of beasts are comparable to those which are effected in us by the operation of the mind, or, on the contrary, to those which depend only on the animal spirits and the disposition of the organs, it is necessary to consider the difference between the two, which I have explained in the fifth part of the *Discourse on*

---

*From T. H. Huxley, "On the Hypothesis that Animals are Automata and Its History" in *Methods and Results* (New York and London: D. Appleton and Co., 1874).

Method (for I do not think that any others are discoverable), and then it will easily be seen, that all the actions of beasts are similar only to those which we perform without the help of our minds. For which reason we shall be forced to conclude, that we know of the existence in them of no other principle of motion than the disposition of their organs and the continual affluence of animal spirits produced by the heat of the heart, which attenuates and subtilises the blood; and, at the same time, we shall acknowledge that we have had no reason for assuming any other principle, except that, not having distinguished these two principles of motion, and seeing that the one, which depends only on the animal spirits and the organs, exists in beasts as well as in us, we have hastily concluded that the other, which depends on mind and on thought, was also possessed by them.

REFLEX ACTION AND CONSCIOUSLY MOTIVATED BEHAVIOR

Descartes' line of argument is perfectly clear. He starts from reflex action in man, from the unquestionable fact that, in ourselves, co-ordinate, purposive, actions may take place, without intervention of consciousness or volition, or even contrary to the latter. As actions of a certain degree of complexity are brought about by mere mechanism, why may not actions of still greater complexity be the result of a more refined mechanism? What proof is there that brutes are other than a superior race of marionettes, which eat without pleasure, cry without pain, desire nothing, know nothing, and only simulate intelligence as a bee simulates a mathematician?

The Port Royalists adopted the hypothesis that brutes are machines, and are said to have carried its practical applications so far as to treat domestic animals with neglect, if not with actual cruelty. . . . Modern research has brought to light a great multitude of facts, which not only show that Descartes' view is defensible, but render it far more defensible than it was in his day.

It must be premised, that it is wholly impossible absolutely to prove the presence or absence of consciousness in anything but one's own brain, though, by analogy, we are justified in assuming its existence in other men. Now if, by some accident, a man's spinal cord is divided, his limbs are paralysed, so far as his volition is concerned, below the point of injury; and he is incapable of experiencing all those states of consciousness which, in his uninjured state, would be excited by irritation of those nerves which

come off below the injury. If the spinal cord is divided in the middle of the back, for example, the skin of the feet may be cut, or pinched, or burned, or wetted with vitriol, without any sensation of touch, or of pain, arising, in consciousness. So far as the man is concerned, therefore, the part of the central nervous system which lies beyond the injury is cut off from consciousness. It must indeed be admitted, that, if any one think fit to maintain that the spinal cord below the injury is conscious, but that it is cut off from any means of making its consciousness known to the other consciousness in the brain, there is no means of driving him from his position by logic. But assuredly there is no way of proving it, and in the matter of consciousness, if in anything, we may hold by the rule, *De non apparentibus et de non existentibus eadem est ratio.** However near the brain the spinal cord is injured, consciousness remains intact, except that the irritation of parts below the injury is no longer represented by sensation. On the other hand, pressure upon the anterior division of the brain, or extensive injuries to it, abolish consciousness. Hence, it is a highly probable conclusion, that consciousness in man depends upon the integrity of the anterior division of the brain, while the middle and hinder divisions of the brain, and the rest of the nervous centres, have nothing to do with it. And it is further highly probable, that what is true for man is true for other vertebrated animals.

We may assume, then, that in a living vertebrated animal, any segment of the cerebro-spinal axis (or spinal cord and brain) separated from that anterior division of the brain which is the organ of consciousness, is as completely incapable of giving rise to consciousness as we know it to be incapable of carrying out volitions. Nevertheless, this separated segment of the spinal cord is not passive and inert. On the contrary, it is the seat of extremely remarkable powers. In our imaginary case of injury, the man would, as we have seen, be devoid of sensation in his legs, and would have not the least power of moving them. But, if the soles of his feet were tickled, the legs would be drawn up just as vigorously as they would have been before the injury. We know exactly what happens when the soles of the feet are tickled; a molecular change takes place in the sensory nerves of the skin, and is propagated along them and through the posterior roots of the spinal nerves,

*That what is not given in experience may be treated as nonexistent.'' [Ed.]

which are constituted by them, to the grey matter of the spinal cord. Through that grey matter the molecular motion is reflected into the anterior roots of the same nerves, constituted by the filaments which supply the muscles of the legs, and, travelling along these motor filaments, reaches the muscles, which at once contract, and cause the limbs to be drawn up.

In order to move the legs in this way, a definite co-ordination of muscular contractions is necessary; the muscles must contract in a certain order and with duly proportioned force; and moreover, as the feet are drawn away from the source of irritation, it may be said that the action has a final cause, or is purposive.

Thus it follows, that the grey matter of the segment of the man's spinal cord, though it is devoid of consciousness, nevertheless responds to a simple stimulus by giving rise to a complex set of muscular contractions, co-ordinated towards a definite end, and serving an obvious purpose.

EFFECT OF BRAIN DAMAGE IN A LOWER ANIMAL

If the spinal cord of a frog is cut across, so as to provide us with a segment separated from the brain, we shall have a subject parallel to the injured man, on which experiments can be made without remorse; as we have a right to conclude that a frog's spinal cord is not likely to be conscious, when a man's is not.

Now the frog behaves just as the man did. The legs are utterly paralysed, so far as voluntary movement is concerned; but they are vigorously drawn up to the body when any irritant is applied to the foot. But let us study our frog a little farther. Touch the skin of the side of the body with a little acetic acid, which gives rise to all the signs of great pain in an uninjured frog. In this case, there can be no pain, because the application is made to a part of the skin supplied with nerves which come off from the cord below the point of section; nevertheless, the frog lifts up the limb of the same side, and applies the foot to rub off the acetic acid; and, what is still more remarkable, if the limb be held so that the frog cannot use it, it will, by and by, move the limb of the other side, turn it across the body, and use it for the same rubbing process. It is impossible that the frog, if it were in its entirety and could reason, should perform actions more purposive than these: and yet we have most complete assurance that, in this case, the frog is not acting from purpose, has no consciousness, and is a mere insensible machine.

But now suppose that, instead of making a section of the cord in the middle of the body, it had been made in such a manner as to separate the hindermost division of the brain from the rest of the organ, and suppose the foremost two-thirds of the brain entirely taken away. The frog is then absolutely devoid of any spontaneity; it sits upright in the attitude which a frog habitually assumes; and it will not stir unless it is touched; but it differs from the frog which I have just described in this, that, if it be thrown into the water, it begins to swim, and swims just as well as the perfect frog does. But swimming requires the combination and successive co-ordination of a great number of muscular actions. And we are forced to conclude, that the impression made upon the sensory nerves of the skin of the frog by the contact with the water into which it is thrown, causes the transmission to the central nervous apparatus of an impulse which sets going a certain machinery by which all the muscles of swimming are brought into play in due co-ordination. If the frog be stimulated by some irritating body, it jumps or walks as well as the complete frog can do. The simple sensory impression, acting through the machinery of the cord, gives rise to these complex combined movements.

It is possible to go a step farther. Suppose that only the anterior division of the brain—so much of it as lies in front of the "optic lobes"—is removed. If that operation is performed quickly and skillfully, the frog may be kept in a state of full bodily vigour for months, or it may be for years; but it will sit unmoved. It sees nothing: it hears nothing. It will starve sooner than feed itself, although food put into its mouth is swallowed. On irritation, it jumps or walks; if thrown into the water it swims. If it be put on the hand, it sits there, crouched, perfectly quiet, and would sit there forever. If the hand be inclined very gently and slowly, so that the frog would naturally tend to slip off, the creature's fore paws are shifted on to the edge of the hand, until he can just prevent himself from falling. If the turning of the hand be slowly continued, he mounts up with great care and deliberation, putting first one leg forward and then another, until he balances himself with perfect precision upon the edge; and if the turning of the hand is continued, he goes through the needful set of muscular operations, until he comes to be seated in security, upon the back of the hand. The doing of all this requires a delicacy of co-ordination, and a precision of adjustment of the muscular apparatus of the body, which are only comparable to those of a rope-dancer. To the ordinary influences of light, the frog, deprived of its cerebral hemispheres, appears to be blind. Nevertheless, if the animal be put upon a table, with a book at some little distance between it and the light, and the skin of the hinder part of its body is then irritated, it will jump forward, avoiding the book by passing to the right or left of it. Therefore, although the frog appears to have no sensation of light, visible objects act through its brain upon the motor mechanism of its body.

It is obvious, that had Descartes been acquainted with these remarkable results of modern research, they would have furnished him with far more power-ful arguments than he possessed in favour of his view of the automatism of brutes. The habits of a frog, leading its natural life, involve such simple adapta-tions to surrounding conditions, that the machinery which is competent to do so much without the inter-vention of consciousness, might well do all. And this argument is vastly strengthened by what has been learned in recent times of the marvellously complex operations which are performed mechani-cally, and to all appearance without consciousness, by men, when, in consequence of injury or disease, they are reduced to a condition more or less compara-ble to that of a frog, in which the anterior part of the brain has been removed. A case has recently been published by an eminent French physician, Dr. Mesnet, which illustrates this condition so remark-ably, that I make no apology for dwelling upon it at considerable length.

THE CASE OF SERGEANT F.

A sergeant of the French army, F____, twenty-seven years of age, was wounded during the battle of Bazeilles, by a ball which fractured his left parietal bone. He ran his bayonet through the Prussian soldier who wounded him, but almost immediately his right arm became paralysed; after walking about two hun-dred yards, his right leg became similarly affected, and he lost his senses. When he recovered them, three weeks afterwards, in a hospital at Mayence, the right half of the body was completely paralysed, and remained in this condition for a year. At present, the only trace of the paralysis which remains is a slight weakness of the right half of the body. Three or four months after the wound was inflicted, periodi-cal disturbances of the functions of the brain made their appearance, and have continued ever since. The disturbances last from fifteen to thirty hours; the intervals at which they occur being from fifteen to thirty days.

For four years, therefore, the life of this man has been divided into alternating phases—short abnormal states intervening between long normal states.

In the periods of normal life, the ex-sergeant's health is perfect; he is intelligent and kindly, and performs, satisfactorily, the duties of a hospital attendant. The commencement of the abnormal state is ushered in by an uneasiness and a sense of weight about the forehead, which the patient compares to the constriction of a circle of iron; and, after its termination, he complains, for some hours, of dull-ness and heaviness of the head. But the transition from the normal to the abnormal state takes place in a few minutes, without convulsions or cries, and without anything to indicate the change to a by-stander. His movements remain free and his expres-sion calm, except for a contraction of the brow, an incessant movement of the eyeballs, and a chewing motion of the jaws. The eyes are wide open, and their pupils dilated. If the man happens to be in a place to which he is accustomed, he walks about as usual; but, if he is in a new place, or if obstacles are intentionally placed in his way, he stumbles gently against them, stops, and then, feeling over the objects with his hands, passes on one side of them. He offers no resistance to any change of direc-tion which may be impressed upon him, or to the forcible acceleration or retardation of his movements. He eats, drinks, smokes, walks about, dresses and undresses himself, rises and goes to bed at the accus-tomed hours. Nevertheless, pins may be run into his body, or strong electric shocks may be sent through it, without causing the least indication of pain; no odorous substance, pleasant or unpleasant, makes the least impression; he eats and drinks with avidity whatever is offered, and takes asafoetida, or vinegar, or quinine, as readily as water; no noise affects him; and light influences him only under certain condi-tions. Dr. Mesnet remarks, that the sense of touch alone seems to persist, and indeed to be more acute and delicate than in the normal state: and it is by means of the nerves of touch, almost exclusively, that his organism is brought into relation with the external world. Here a difficulty arises. It is clear from the facts detailed, that the nervous apparatus by which, in the normal state, sensations of touch are excited, is that by which external influences determine the movements of the body, in the abnormal state. But does the state of consciousness, which we term a tactile sensation, accompany the operation of this nervous apparatus in the abnormal state? Or is consciousness utterly absent, the man being reduced to an insensible mechanism?

It is impossible to obtain direct evidence in favour of the one conclusion or the other; all that can be said is, that the case of the frog shows that the man may be devoid of any kind of consciousness.

A further difficult problem is this. The man is insensible to sensory impressions made through the ear, the nose, the tongue, and, to a great extent, the eye; nor is he susceptible of pain from causes operating during his abnormal state. Nevertheless, it is possible so to act upon his tactile apparatus, as to give rise to those molecular changes in his sensorium, which are ordinarily the causes of associated trains of ideas. I give a striking example of this process in Dr. Mesnet's words:

He was taking a walk in the garden under a bunch of trees. We placed in his hand his walking stick which he had let fall a few minutes before. He feels it, passes his hand over the bent handle a few times, becomes attentive, seems to extend his ear, and suddenly calls out, "Henry," then, "Here they are. There are about twenty to our two! We have reached our end." And then, with his hand behind his back, as if about to leap, he prepares to attack with his weapon. He crouches in the level, green grass, his head concealed by a tree, in the position of a hunter, and follows all the short-distance movements of the enemy which he believes he sees, with accompanying movements of his hands and shoulders.

In a subsequent abnormal period, Dr. Mesnet caused the patient to repeat this scene by placing him in the same conditions. Now, in this case, the question arises whether the series of actions constituting this singular pantomime was accompanied by the ordinary states of consciousness, the appropriate train of ideas, or not? Did the man dream that he was skirmishing? Or was he in the condition of one of Vaucauson's automata—a senseless mechanism worked by molecular changes in his nervous system? The analogy of the frog shows that the latter assumption is perfectly justifiable.

The ex-sergeant has a good voice, and had, at one time, been employed as a singer at a café. In one of his abnormal states he was observed to begin humming a tune. He then went to his room, dressed himself carefully, and took up some parts of a periodical novel, which lay on his bed, as if he were trying to find something. Dr. Mesnet, suspecting that he was seeking his music, made up one of these into a roll and put it into his hand. He appeared satisfied, took his cane and went downstairs to the door. Here Dr. Mesnet turned him round, and he walked quite contentedly, in the opposite direction, towards the room of the concierge. The light of the sun shining through a window now happened to fall upon him, and seemed to suggest the foot-lights of the stage on which he was accustomed to make his appearance. He stopped, opened his roll of imaginary music, put himself into the attitude of a singer, and sang, with perfect execution, three songs, one after the other. After which he wiped his face with his handkerchief and drank, without a grimace, a tumbler of strong vinegar and water which was put into his hand.

INNATE AND AUTOMATIC BEHAVIOR PATTERNS

An experiment which may be performed upon the frog deprived of the fore part of its brain, well known as Goltz's "Quak-versuch," affords a parallel to this performance. If the skin of a certain part of the back of such a frog is gently stroked with the finger, it immediately croaks. It never croaks unless it is so stroked, and the croak always follows the stroke, just as the sound of a repeater follows the touching of the spring. In the frog, this "song" is innate—so to speak *a priori*—and depends upon a mechanism in the brain governing the vocal apparatus, which is set at work by the molecular change set up in the sensory nerves of the skin of the back by the contact of a foreign body.

In man there is also a vocal mechanism, and the cry of an infant is in the same sense innate and *a priori*, inasmuch as it depends on an organic relation between its sensory nerves and the nervous mechanism which governs the vocal apparatus. Learning to speak, and learning to sing, are processes by which the vocal mechanism is set to new tunes. A song which has been learned has its molecular equivalent, which potentially represents it in the brain, just as a musical box, wound up, potentially represents an overture. Touch the stop and the overture begins;

send a molecular impulse along the proper afferent nerve and the singer begins his song.

Again, the manner in which the frog, though apparently insensible to light, is yet, under some circumstances, influenced by visual images, finds a singular parallel in the case of the ex-sergeant.

Sitting at a table, in one of his abnormal states, he took up a pen, felt for paper and ink, and began to write a letter to his general, in which he recommended himself for a medal, on account of his good conduct and courage. It occurred to Dr. Mesnet to ascertain experimentally how far vision was concerned in this act of writing. He therefore interposed a screen between the man's eyes and his hands; under these circumstances he went on writing for a short time, but the words became illegible, and he finally stopped, without manifesting any discontent. On the withdrawal of the screen he began to write again where he had left off. The substitution of water for ink in the inkstand had a similar result. He stopped, looked at his pen, wiped it on his coat, dipped it in the water, and began again with the same effect.

On one occasion, he began to write upon the topmost of ten superimposed sheets of paper. After he had written a line or two, this sheet was suddenly drawn away. There was a slight expression of surprise, but he continued his letter on the second sheet exactly as if it had been the first. This operation was repeated five times, so that the fifth sheet contained nothing but the writer's signature at the bottom of the page. Nevertheless, when the signature was finished, his eyes turned to the top of the blank sheet, and he went through the form of reading over what he had written, a movement of the lips accompanying each word; moreover, with his pen, he put in such corrections as were needed, in that part of the blank page which corresponded with the position of the words which required correction, in the sheets which had been taken away. If the five sheets had been transparent, therefore, they would, when superimposed, have formed a properly written and corrected letter.

Immediately after he had written his letter, F____ got up, walked down to the garden, made himself a cigarette, lighted and smoked it. He was about to prepare another, but sought in vain for his tobacco-pouch, which had been purposely taken away. The pouch was now thrust before his eyes and put under his nose, but he neither saw nor smelt it; yet, when it was placed in his hand, he at once seized it, made a fresh cigarette, and ignited a match to light the latter. The match was blown out, and another lighted match placed close before his eyes, but he made no attempt to take it and if his cigarette was lighted for him, he made no attempt to smoke. All this time the eyes were vacant, and neither winked, nor exhibited any contraction of the pupils. From these and other experiments, Dr. Mesnet draws the conclusion that his patient sees some things and not others; that the sense of sight is accessible to all things which are brought into relation with him by the sense of touch, and, on the contrary, insensible to things which lie outside this relation. He sees the match he holds and does not see any other.

Just so the frog "sees" the book which is in the way of his jump, at the same time that isolated visual impressions take no effect upon him.

As I have pointed out, it is impossible to prove that F____ is absolutely unconscious in his abnormal state, but it is no less impossible to prove the contrary; and the case of the frog goes a long way to justify the assumption that, in the abnormal state, the man is a mere insensible machine.

If such facts as these had come under the knowledge of Descartes, would they not have formed an apt commentary upon that remarkable passage in the *Traité de l'Homme*, which I have quoted elsewhere, but which is worth repetition:

All the functions which I have attributed to this machine (the body), as the digestion of food, the pulsation of the heart and of the arteries; the nutrition and the growth of the limbs; respiration, wakefulness, and sleep; the reception of light, sounds, odours, flavours, heat, and such like qualities, in the organs of the external senses; the impression of the idea of these in the organ of common sensation and in the imagination; the retention or the impression of these ideas on the memory; the internal movements of the appetites and the passions; and lastly the external movements of all the limbs, which follow so aptly, as well the action of the objects which are presented to the senses, as the impressions which meet in the memory, that they imitate as nearly as possible those of a real man; I desire, I say, that you should consider that these functions in the machine naturally proceed from the mere arrangement of its organs, neither more nor less than do the movements of a clock, or other automaton, from that of its weights and its wheels; so that, so far as these are concerned, it is not necessary to conceive any other vegetative or sensitive soul, nor any other principle of motion or of life, than the blood and the spirits agitated by the fire which burns continually in the heart, and which is no wise essentially different from all the fires which exist in inanimate bodies. And would Descartes not have been justified in asking why we need deny that animals are machines, when men, in a state of unconsciousness, perform, mechanically, actions as complicated and as seemingly rational as those of any animals?

ANIMALS ARE CONSCIOUS AUTOMATA

But though I do not think that Descartes' hypothesis can be positively refuted, I am not disposed to accept it. The doctrine of continuity is too well established for it to be permissible to me to suppose that any complex natural phenomenon comes into existence suddenly, and without being preceded by simpler modifications; and very strong arguments would be needed to prove that such complex phenomena as those of consciousness, first make their appearance in man. We know, that, in the individual man, consciousness grows from a dim glimmer to its full light, whether we consider the infant advancing in years or the adult emerging from slumber and swoon. We know, further, that the lower animals possess, though less developed, that part of the brain which we have every reason to believe to be the organ of consciousness in man; and as, in other cases, function and organ are proportional, so we have a right to conclude it is with the brain; and that the brutes, though they may not possess our intensity of consciousness, and though from the absence of language, they can have no trains of thoughts, but only trains of feelings, yet have a consciousness which, more or less distinctly, foreshadows our own.

I confess that, in view of the struggle for existence which goes on in the animal world, and of the frightful quantity of pain with which it must be accompanied, I should be glad if the probabilities were in favour of Descartes' hypothesis; but, on the other hand, considering the terrible practical consequences to domestic animals which might ensue from any error on our part, it is as well to err on the right side, if we err at all, and deal with them as weaker brethren, who are bound, like the rest of us, to pay their toll for living, and suffer what is needful for the general good. As Hartley finely says, "We seem to be in the place of God to them"; and we may justly follow the precedents He sets in nature in our dealings with them.

But though we may see reason to disagree with Descartes' hypothesis that brutes are unconscious machines, it does not follow that he was wrong in regarding them as automata. They may be more or less conscious, sensitive, automata; and the view that they are such conscious machines is that which is implicitly, or explicitly, adopted by most persons. When we speak of the actions of the lower animals being guided by instinct and not by reason, what we really mean is that, though they feel as we do, yet their actions are the results of their physical organisation. We believe, in short, that they are machines, one part of which (the nervous system) not only sets the rest in motion, and co-ordinates its movements in relation with changes in surrounding bodies, but is provided with special apparatus, the function of which is the calling into existence of those states of consciousness which are termed sensations, emotions, and ideas. I believe that this generally accepted view is the best expression of the facts at present known.

It is experimentally demonstrable—any one who cares to run a pin into himself may perform a sufficient demonstration of the fact—that a mode of motion of the nervous system is the immediate antecedent of a state of consciousness. All but the adherents of "Occasionalism," or of the doctrine of "Pre-established Harmony" (if any such now exist), must admit that we have as much reason for regarding the mode of motion of the nervous system as the cause of the state of consciousness, as we have for regarding any event as the cause of another. How the one phenomenon causes the other we know, as much or as little, as in any other case of causation; but we have as much right to believe that the sensation is an effect of the molecular change, as we have to believe that motion is an effect of impact; and there is as much propriety in saying that the brain evolves sensation, as there is in saying that an iron rod, when hammered, evolves heat.

As I have endeavoured to show, we are justified in supposing that something analogous to what happens in ourselves takes place in the brutes, and that the affections of their sensory nerves give rise to molecular changes in the brain, which again give rise to, or evolve, the corresponding states of consciousness. Nor can there be any reasonable doubt that the emotion of brutes, and such ideas as they possess, are similarly dependent upon molecular brain changes. Each sensory impression leaves behind a record in the structure of the brain—an "ideagenous" molecule, so to speak, which is competent, under certain conditions, to reproduce, in a fainter condition, the state of consciousness which corresponds with that sensory impression; and it is these "ideagenous molecules" which are the physical basis of memory.

It may be assumed, then, that molecular changes in the brain are the causes of all the states of consciousness of brutes. Is there any evidence that these states of consciousness may, conversely, cause those molecular changes which give rise to muscular motion? I see no such evidence. The frog walks, hops, swims, and goes through his gymnastic performances quite as well without consciousness, and consequently without volition, as with it; and, if a frog, in his natural state, possesses anything corresponding with what we call volition, there is no reason to think that it is anything but a concomitant of the molecular changes in the brain which form part of the series involved in the production of motion.

The consciousness of brutes would appear to be related to the mechanism of their body simply as a collateral product of its working, and to be as completely without any power of modifying that working as the steam-whistle which accompanies the work of a locomotive engine is without influence upon its machinery. Their volition, if they have any, is an emotion indicative of physical changes, not a cause of such changes.

This conception of the relations of states of consciousness with molecular changes in the brain—of *psychoses* with *neuroses*—does not prevent us from ascribing free will to brutes. For an agent is free when there is nothing to prevent him from doing that which he desires to do. If a greyhound chases a hare, he is a free agent, because his action is in entire accordance with his strong desire to catch the hare; while so long as he is held back by the leash he is not free, being prevented by external force from following his inclination. And the ascription of freedom to the greyhound under the former circumstances is by no means inconsistent with the other aspect of the facts of the case—that he is a machine impelled to the chase, and caused, at the same time, to have the desire to catch the game by the impression which the rays of light proceeding from the hare make upon his eyes, and through them upon his brain.

Much ingenious argument has at various times been bestowed upon the question: How is it possible to imagine that volition, which is a state of consciousness, and, as such, has not the slightest community of nature with matter in motion, can act upon the moving matter of which the body is composed, as it is

assumed to do in voluntary acts? But if, as is here suggested, the voluntary acts of brutes—or, in other words, the acts which they desire to perform—are as purely mechanical as the rest of their actions, and are simply accompanied by the state of consciousness called volition, the inquiry, so far as they are concerned, becomes superfluous. Their volitions do not enter into the chain of causation of their actions at all. . . .

THE SAME CONCLUSION APPLIES TO HUMAN BEINGS

It will be said, that I mean that the conclusions deduced from the study of the brutes are applicable to man, and that the logical consequences of such application are fatalism, materialism, and atheism—whereupon the drums will beat the *pas de charge*.

One does not do battle with drummers; but I venture to offer a few remarks for the calm consideration of thoughtful persons, untrammelled by foregone conclusions, unpledged to shore-up tottering dogmas, and anxious only to know the true bearings of the case.

It is quite true that, to the best of my judgment, the argumentation which applies to brutes holds equally good of men; and, therefore, that all states of consciousness in us, as in them, are immediately caused by molecular changes of the brain-substance. It seems to me that in men, as in brutes, there is no proof that any state of consciousness is the cause of change in the motion of the matter of the organism. If these positions are well based, it follows that our mental conditions are simply the symbols in consciousness of the changes which take place automatically in the organism; and that, to take an extreme illustration, the feeling we call volition is not the cause of a voluntary act, but the symbol of that state of the brain which is the immediate cause of that act. We are conscious automata, endowed with free will in the only intelligible sense of that much-abused term—inasmuch as in many respects we are able to do as we like—but nonetheless parts of the great series of causes and effects which, in unbroken continuity, composes that which is, and has been, and shall be—the sum of existence.

As to the logical consequences of this conviction of mine, I may be permitted to remark that logical consequences are the scarecrows of fools and the beacons of wise men. The only question which any wise man can ask himself, and which any honest man will ask himself, is whether a doctrine is true or false. Consequences will take care of themselves; at most their importance can only justify us in testing with extra care the reasoning process from which they result.

So that if the view I have taken did really and logically lead to fatalism, materialism, and atheism, I should profess myself a fatalist, materialist, and atheist; and I should look upon those who, while they believed in my honesty of purpose and intellectual competency, should raise a hue and cry against me, as people who by their own admission preferred lying to truth, and whose opinions therefore were unworthy of the smallest attention.

But, as I have endeavored to explain on other occasions, I really have no claim to rank myself among fatalistic, materialistic, or atheistic philoso- phers. Not among the fatalists, for I take the concep- tion of necessity to have a logical, and not a physical foundation; not among materialists, for I am utterly incapable of conceiving the existence of matter if there is no mind in which to picture that existence; not among atheists, for the problem of the ultimate cause of existence is one which seems to me to be hopelessly out of reach of my poor powers. Of all the senseless babble I have ever had occasion to read, the demonstrations of these philosophers who under- take to tell us all about the nature of God would be the worst, if they were not surpassed by the still greater absurdities of the philosophers who try to prove that there is no God. . . .

JAMES W. CORNMAN

A Nonreductive Identity Thesis about Mind and Body*

James W. Cornman (1929–1978) taught philosophy at the University of Pennsylvania.

In his paper, "The Traditional Problem of Mind and Body," C. D. Broad discusses and defends the dualistic thesis derived from René Descartes that is known as dualistic interactionism, or as Broad calls it, "two-sided interactionism."[1] It consists of two theses. First, there are mental phenomena (such as sensations of pain, feelings of pleasure, thoughts, desires, and hopes) over and above the physical parts and processes of the human body (such as the brain, brain processes, nerve fibers, nerve impulses, molecules, and molecular motion). Thus the view is dualistic because it proposes two distinct kinds of entities—mental and physical. Second, these two sorts of entities causally interact in the sense that some physical events (for example, a pin pricking a finger) cause mental events (for example, a feeling of pain), and some mental events (a feeling of pain) cause physical events (a scream). Thus the theory proposes "two-sided" causation. And it is because of this that many people have rejected the theory. One of Broad's central concerns in his paper is to show that this rejection is not justified. My present aim is to show that Broad fails in his attempt and to argue that a quite different mind-body thesis should be accepted instead.

DUALISTIC INTERACTIONISM

Broad clearly and carefully delineates the main strengths and weaknesses of dualistic interactionism. He examines several arguments for and several others against the thesis, including two against the thesis that are derived from facts of science. Al- though he successfully rebuts many of these argu- ments, my claim is that his reply to what he calls "the argument from energy" is inadequate, and that a version of that argument casts serious doubt on dualistic interactionism.[2]

MENTAL CAUSATION AND THE CONSERVATION OF ENERGY AND MOMENTUM

If a mental event, such as a feeling of pain, or what Broad calls a volition or an act of will, causally affects something that is physical, it is generally accepted that it would directly affect the brain in some way. The main problem facing dualistic interactionism is that the two most plausible sorts of ways this might occur violate either the principle of the conservation of mass-energy or the principle of the conservation of linear-momentum. Thus, because these principles are well justified, the interaction theory becomes implausible and should be rejected.

One way that brain processes are causally affected is by stimulation of neurons or nerve fibers in the brain so that the neurons fire and cause series of nerve impulses to move through the brain. Might a feeling of pain or a volition affect the brain in this way? If either one did this, then the total energy of the affected neurons would be increased without any corresponding decrease in energy of the cause, which, because it is mental, has no mass and therefore no energy. But it seems quite reasonable, as Broad notes, that each human body is a conservative system. In other words, it is a physical system, as Broad says, "whose total energy is redistributed, but not altered in amount, by changes that happen within it," that is, by changes within it that are not the result of external physical causes.[3] But, it seems, no human body would be a conservative system if affected by this first sort of mental cause.

It might be replied, however, that we need not accept this conclusion. Perhaps bodies affected by these mental causes remain conservative, because each of the many times that neurons in a human brain are stimulated to fire by mental phenomena, each of the corresponding human bodies loses a compensating amount of energy to its physical environment. However, not only does it seem implausible that all these many equalizing losses of energy occur, but such a thesis would also seem to violate the principle of mass-energy conservation. As Broad puts it, the principle states that "every material system is either itself conservative, or, if not, is part of a larger material system which is conservative."[4] So, given this principle, the total physical universe is conservative. But if the preceding reply were correct, then the physical universe would not be conservative, because its total energy would be increased without a corresponding loss to some other physical system. The same problem would be created by another reply which denies that each human body is a conservative system so that its total energy can increase without corresponding loss by any other physical system. Since each of these bodies is part of the physical universe, the total energy of the universe would also increase from within, contrary to the conservation of mass-energy.

So far, nothing said would disturb Broad's reply to this objection of dualistic interactionism. This is because he suggests that the mind affects the brain in a different way, a way that involves no change of energy and thus avoids any conflict with the conservation of mass-energy. We can begin to understand his suggestion by considering his example:

Take the case of a weight swinging at the end of a string hung from a fixed point. The total energy of the weight is the same at all positions in its course. It is thus a conservative system. But at every moment the direction and velocity of the weight's motion are different, and the proportion between its kinetic and its potential energy is constantly changing. These changes are caused by the pull of the string, which acts in a different direction at each different moment. The string makes no difference to the total energy of the weight; but it makes all the difference in the world to the particular way in which the energy is distributed between the potential and the kinetic forms. . . .

Here, then, we have a clear case even in the physical realm where a system is conservative but is continually acted on by something which affects its movement and the distribution of its total energy. Why should not the mind act on the body in this way?[5]

Broad's example is helpful in two ways. First, it shows how a system can be causally affected by something without the total energy of the system being affected. Second, it helps us see how a system can have different effects itself, without its own cause affecting its total energy. Just imagine that a swinging weight activates different machines by hitting different buttons at the top of its arc. Also imagine that at certain times the length of the string is changed. Then the radius and position of the arc are changed, so the weight hits a different button and starts a different machine. Yet the total energy of the weight remains unchanged.

Is it reasonable that mental phenomena affect brains in some way like the way the string affects the weight? Again we can turn to Broad for what I believe to be the most plausible suggestion. He says that certain facts

JAMES W. CORNMAN   287

suggest that what the mind does to the body in voluntary action, if it does anything, is to lower the resistance of certain synapses and to raise that of others. The result is that the nervous current follows such a course as to produce the particular movement which the mind judges to be appropriate at the time.[6]

The point is that the route that a nerve current takes through a brain depends on which neurons are "excited," that is, which are caused by other neurons to be stimulated to have electrical impulses. And whether a neuron is excited by another depends on what Broad calls the "resistance" at the synapse or junction connecting the two neurons. As Broad puts it, if the resistance is high at the synapse joining two neurons, n_1 and n_2, then, even when there is a nerve impulse in n_1, the other neuron, n_2, is not excited because of the high resistance. As a result, one series of nerve impulses is stopped, and so one route of nerve current through the brain is blocked. But if the resistance at this synapse is low, then when neuron n_1 is excited, it causes n_2 to become excited and that particular series of nerve impulses continues through the brain. But because different nerve currents, or series of brain impulses, in a brain cause different bodily behavior, changes in the amounts of resistance at certain synapses result in different bodily behavior. Broad's suggestion is that mental phenomena, such as volitions, affect a brain, and thereby bodily behavior, by changing the distribution of resistance among a certain group of synapses without affecting the total resistance of this group of synapses. As a result, mental phenomena affect bodily behavior without changing the total energy of the brain.

Broad's proposal shows how mental phenomena might affect bodily behavior without violating the conservation of energy principle. But this does not solve all problems for his thesis, because if it is correct, mental phenomena would seem to change the total linear-momentum within the brain by changing the resistances of synapses. The linear-momentum of something equals its mass times its velocity, where velocity is a vector quantity. That is, it is specified not only by a magnitude but also by a direction. Thus momentum is also a vector quantity. Now, each nerve impulse traveling through a neuron is caused by movements of charged particles, or ions, across a membrane in the neuron. Consequently, because each series of nerve impulses involves different neurons,

it seems clear that the linear-momentum of the ions involved in each series differs from that for every other one, even if, implausibly, the total mass of the ions moving into and out of the neurons, and the magnitude of their velocities should be identical for each series. Given this, then if, by changing the resistance at certain synapses, a volition stopped one series of nerve impulses but allowed another one to continue instead, the resultant total linear-momentum of the brain would be different from what it would have been if this volition had not affected the synapses. But, by the principle of the conservation of linear-momentum, any change of a system's total linear-momentum requires that some net external physical force affect the system. The only appropriate physical forces are gravitational, which require mass, and electromagnetic, which require electrical charge. But, for a dualist, no mental phenomenon has either one. So it surely seems that no brain is subject to any force from a volition. We can conclude, then, that this conservation principle requires that no volition affects any brain in the way that Broad has proposed.

The preceding discussion shows it is reasonable that two of the most plausible ways a mental phenomenon might affect a brain violate either the principle of mass-energy conservation or the principle of linear-momentum conservation. Consequently, although Broad was correct to claim that mental causation of physical events does not require the violation of the mass-energy conservation principle, he overlooked another conservation principle which his suggested hypothesis seems to violate. It is reasonable, therefore, to conclude that dualistic interactionism violates one or the other of these well-established conservation principles and should be rejected for some other mind-body theory that avoids such a violation.

EPIPHENOMENALISM

Broad briefly mentions a dualistic theory that avoids the preceding crucial objection to two-sided interactionism. This is epiphenomenalism, which is one species of the theory of "one-sided action of body on mind."[7] Thomas Huxley, who championed this theory, stated it as follows:

All states of consciousness, in us, as in [brutes], are immediately caused by molecular changes of the brain-substance. It seems to me that in men, as in brutes, there is no proof that any state of consciousness is the cause of change in the motion of the matter of the organism. If these positions are well based, it follows that our mental conditions are simply the symbols in consciousness of the changes which take place automatically in the organism; and that, to take an extreme illustration, the feeling we call volition is not the cause of a voluntary act, but the symbol of that state of the brain which is the immediate cause of that act. We are conscious automata . . .[8]

Huxley's claim is that we human beings, and also some brute animals, are conscious automata in the sense that, although we have mental phenomena, such as volitions and pains, that are distinct from anything physical, all these mental entities are merely epiphenomena, that is, by-products, of ongoing physical processes. In other words, mental events are effects of physical processes, such as nerve impulses in the brain, but no mental event causally affects anything else at all—whether mental or physical. Thus, contrary to the two-sided interaction theory, none of my desires, hopes, fears, or feelings of pain or pleasure ever affect my bodily behavior. Instead, it is always some brain event that produces each mental phenomenon, such as a pain, and also causes the eventual bodily behavior, such as a scream.

Epiphenomenalism has appealed to scientists for several reasons. These include one that attracted Huxley, namely, that it is well-suited to the Darwinian theory of evolution. As more and more complex physical systems evolved, it seems quite natural that certain by-products would also result. Why should not one of these be a conscious mental life? Another attractive feature for scientists is that if epiphenomenalism is correct, then it seems that the physical sciences would be able to explain the behavior of human beings in the same ways they explain the behavior of nonliving physical objects. A third advantage, which is most important for our purposes, is that a one-sided action theory avoids the preceding objection to interaction theories. There is no mental causation of physical events to violate conservation laws for physical systems.

Should we, then, adopt epiphenomenalism? It seems appealing and it does avoid a serious objection. But we must first pause to do two things. We should consider whether this theory faces any objections uniquely its own, and then attempt to discover whether any of its rivals prove to be more reasonable than it is. Regarding the first task, it is important to see that the way in which epiphenomenalism avoids the crucial objection to interactionism results in two undesirable features which detract from the appeal and reasonableness of the theory.

TWO OBJECTIONS TO EPIPHENOMENALISM: THE MENTAL AS A MERE BY-PRODUCT

Broad points out the first undesirable feature when he says, "In favour of the action of mind on body is the fact that we seem to be immediately aware of a causal relation when we voluntarily try to produce a bodily movement."[9] That is, it seems intuitively obvious to us that often, for example, when we will or choose to raise our arm, it goes up *because of* our choosing. And it seems clear to us that, all too often, a feeling of pain will cause us to scream and writhe and squirm. Consequently, any theory like epiphenomenalism that denies such effects of the mental is quite counterintuitive and its reasonableness is decreased accordingly. Nevertheless, an epiphenomenalist could counter this objection and lessen its force somewhat by postulating that the almost constant correlation of mental choosings to do something (for example, my choosing to raise my arm) with the ensuing bodily movement (my arm going up) misleads us into the mistaken belief that the choosing causes the movement. Instead, both these choosings and these bodily movements have the same physical causes in the brain. That is why they regularly accompany each other and why we mistake one effect of the common cause for the cause of the other effect.

Nevertheless, as Broad stresses, we do seem to be aware of the effect of our choices on our own bodily movements. Surely, if all else should prove equal, a theory that accommodates what is so hard for us to deny is preferable to epiphenomenalism, which denies it.

The second weakness that the denial of mental causation creates for epiphenomenalism is less telling than the first, but it is well worth noting. It is stated by the contemporary philosopher, Herbert Feigl:

[Epiphenomenalism] accepts two fundamentally different sorts of laws—the usual causal laws and laws of psycho-physiological correspondence. The physical (causal) laws connect the events in the physical world in the manner of a complex network, while the correspondence laws involve relations of physical events with purely mental "danglers." These correspondence laws are peculiar in that they may be said to postulate "effects" (mental states as dependent variables) which by themselves do not function, or at least do not seem to be needed, as "causes" (independent variables) for any observable behavior.[10]

Feigl's point is that, unlike its main rivals, epiphenomenalism is forced to assume that there are two distinct sorts of causal laws, and this is scientifically unsatisfactory. According to Feigl, mental entities would be "nomological danglers" if epiphenomenalism were true. These entities are mentioned in psychophysical laws (that is, scientific laws linking mental and physical phenomena), but neither they nor these laws would have any function in the scientific explanation and prediction of human behavior. In this sense, mental phenomena would "dangle" uselessly. But physical phenomena and physical laws are quite different. Both are crucial to the explanation and prediction of the behavior of both animate and inanimate objects, as, ideally, all scientifically respectable entities and laws should be.

As before, I believe we can agree that if all else should prove equal, a theory that avoids this consequence would be more reasonable than epiphenomenalism. Yet if this were the only objection to epiphenomenalism, it is not at all clear that it would be unreasonable to adopt the theory. After all, although it may violate an ideal of scientific theory, it requires no change whatsoever in the procedures of observation, experimentation, and theory development that scientists actually use.

REDUCTIVE MATERIALISM

Epiphenomenalism is flawed, but not overwhelmingly so. Nevertheless, we should consider whether there is a preferable alternative to it. For many people, reductive materialism is just such a theory. Consider the version attributed to Thomas Hobbes. He held that sense experience is the source of all man's thoughts, dreams, imaginings, and rememberings, "for there is no conception in a man's mind, which hath not at first, totally or by parts, been begotten upon the organs of sense. The rest are derived from that original."[11] Given this, we can see why Hobbes has been interpreted as a materialist because of his claim that sense experience is "some internal motion in the sentient, generated by some internal motion, of the parts of the object, and propagated through all the media to the innermost part of the organ."[12] It seems, then, that Hobbes might well hold the view that everything, whether living or not, is a purely physical object which is itself, and whose

internal parts are, either in motion or at rest. It is true that some of these physical bodies that have sense organs also have sense experience, thoughts, dreams, and the like. But all of these mental phenomena are nothing but physical motion within these bodies, caused there originally by the effects of physical stimuli on the physical sense organs of the body. This is surely reductive materialism, because all mental phenomena are claimed to be reduced to—that is, nothing but—certain motions (perhaps, certain nerve currents) within the human body.

But it is worth noting that Hobbes may not be a reductive materialist, as another passage indicates. He says that "sense, in all cases, is nothing else but original fancy, caused, as I have said, by the pressure, that is by the motion, of external things upon our eyes, ears, and other organs there unto ordained."[13] Here Hobbes seems to be saying that sense experience is "fancy" which is caused by motion, rather than being identical with motion. Indeed, he holds that fancy is merely the appearance of motion.[14] But appearances—seemingly, mental images such as dream images—are quite different from physical bodies or motion. It may be we should consider Hobbes to be a mind-body dualist who is an epiphenomenalist.

Our main task here, however, is not to uncover the best construal of Hobbes' views. It is likely he was confused and did not hold one clear, consistent thesis. Nevertheless, his confusion is a clue to us. We should clearly delineate the principal mind-body theories before we critically compare them and adopt one as the most reasonable. We can do this for reductive materialism by first stating and then explaining its central thesis:

RM Each mental phenomenon is nothing but (that is, reduced to) some physical phenomenon (presumably, a brain part or process).

That is, a human being is nothing but a physical body. In this respect, the theory is monistic rather than dualistic. For dualistic theories, each volition, thought, or feeling is something distinct from everything physical, including the brain and its processes. For reductive materialism, each mental phenomenon is identical with something physical, such as some part of the brain. So, although we may be conscious automata as Huxley claimed, consciousness is reduced to brain activity rather than being its nonphysical by-product. This is one central difference between epiphenomenalism and reductive materialism. An important similarity, which distinguishes both from dualistic interactionism, is their thesis that all causes are physical.

CONCERNING THE MENTAL BEING "NOTHING BUT" THE PHYSICAL

The crucial phrase in thesis *RM* is 'nothing but.' What is it for *A* to be nothing but *B*? For one thing, if *A* is nothing but *B*, then *A* is identical with *B*. Thus reductive materialism implies that each mental phenomenon (for example, a pain I feel) is identical with a physical phenomenon (for example, stimulated nerve fibers in my brain). But this raises the question of what is required for *A* to be identical with *B*. Following what is known as Leibniz's Principle of the Identity of Indiscernibles, we can say, somewhat roughly, that *A* is identical with *B* if *A* and *B* have exactly the same properties; and *A* is *not* identical with *B* if one of them has a property the other one lacks. For example, the president of the United States who resigned is identical with Richard M. Nixon, because that president and Nixon have exactly the same properties. But Nixon is not identical with the president who was impeached because, among other things, Nixon has the property of living in the 20th century, but the impeached president lacked that property.

If *A* is nothing but *B*, then *A* is identical with *B*. But the converse is false. *A* can be identical with *B*, yet not be nothing but *B*. Identity is a symmetrical relationship. Thus, if *A* is identical with *B*, then *B* is identical with *A*. But it is false that if *A* is nothing but *B*, then *B* is nothing but *A*. The latter relationship is nonsymmetrical. Consequently, mere identity is not sufficient for the reduction that 'nothing but' implies. It is, however, very hard to uncover just what more is needed. Perhaps some examples will help clarify the difference between the two. Consider the following sentences:

(1) The object that frightened you in the cemetery last night *is identical with* the gnarled tree behind Jones' grave.
(2) The gnarled tree behind Jones' grave *is identical with* the object that frightened you in the cemetery last night.

(3) The object that frightened you last night *is nothing but* the gnarled tree behind Jones' grave.
(4) The gnarled tree behind Jones' grave *is nothing but* the object that frightened you last night.

We can easily conceive of situations in which (1), (2), and (3) are true, but (4) sounds quite odd, indeed, false even when (1), (2), and (3) are true. How can a tree be nothing more than something that frightens someone? It has properties, such as having bark, branches, and leaves, that are over and above the properties something has in virtue of it being something that frightens you. That is, a tree is not reducible to a frightening object. But, as (3) states, a frightening object which last night seemed to you to have ghostly properties, turns out to be nothing but an ordinary tree. That is, it is reduced to a tree, which is an object that, aside from its effect on you, has only those properties it has because it is a tree. Thus because (4) is false when (3) is true, 'nothing but' is a nonsymmetrical relationship.

How does this help clarify reductive materialism? Considering pains again, we can now understand better the claim of a reductive materialist that all pains are nothing but stimulated nerve fibers in brains. No pains have properties that are different from those they have because they are stimulated nerve fibers, and so they have no psychological properties.[15] In this sense, then, pains and other mental phenomena are, according to reductive materialism, reduced to something physical. In other words, each mental entity is identical with something physical, contrary to all dualistic theories; each has physical properties; but none has psychological or mental properties that are distinct from physical properties.

Reductive materialism has much appeal. It has all those features that attract many scientists to epiphenomenalism, including its avoidance of the central objection to dualistic interactionism. But, helpfully, materialism avoids this objection in a way that also allows it to bypass the two objections to epiphenomenalism. If each mental phenomenon, such as a volition or a choosing, is identical with something in the brain, as a reductive materialist would claim, then no causal activity by something mental violates any physical conservation law because that same causal activity is activity by something physical. Thus even if volitions cause brain activity either by initiating nerve impulses within the brain or by redistributing the resistance at synapses in the brain, this would violate no conservation principles. All volitions would be physical brain occurrences, and so they would be capable of changes in energy or momentum that counterbalance any changes they bring about in other brain activity.

Notice also how neatly reductive materialism avoids the two objections to epiphenomenalism. Being a monistic rather than a dualistic theory, materialism requires no nomological danglers and allows all mental events to be causes as well as effects, as we can easily see. If each mental event is identical with a brain event, and each brain event is a link in an ongoing causal process in which each link is caused by a preceding one and then causes a subsequent one, then each mental event is both an effect and a cause. And, also, psychophysical laws, which relate mental to physical phenomena, would relate entities that are identical with brain phenomena to certain physical entities, all of which would function in some way or other to explain and predict human behavior.

AN OBJECTION TO REDUCTIVE MATERIALISM: THE ACHINESS OF PAINS

So far, reductive materialism seems clearly superior to the two dualistic theories previously discussed. Unfortunately, however, it faces one fatal objection, uniquely its own. Recall some of the pains you have had, and consider those properties you were sure that they had. Probably you have often been convinced that many pains you felt were intense, stabbing, throbbing, and ached unbearably. Such properties with which pains all too often seem to confront us are not the same as those physical properties that physiologists or physicists discover or ascribe to physical phenomena such as nerve impulses and molecular activity. They are mental or psychological properties which are quite distinct from the physical properties of brain parts and processes. Consequently, if, as surely is undeniable to someone when he experiences pain, pains have these properties, then it is false that all mental phenomena are nothing but physical phenomena. That is, it is false that they have only those properties they have because they are physical entities, such as stimulated nerve fibers in human brains. And this is also true of other mental phenomena, such as itching, tickling, or tingling sensations, and feelings of pleasure, fear, or anxiety. Thus, each person's own experiences of his own bodily sensations, feelings, and emotions

provide him with compelling reason to reject reductive materialism, in spite of its many attractive features.

INTERIM CONCLUSION: ALL THE PRECEDING THEORIES ARE DEFICIENT

Where has our investigation led us? Must we reject all mind-body theories? Perhaps not, because, although defective, epiphenomenalism seems not to be severely damaged. Yet I would hope we can do better. Indeed, I think we can. Recall which feature of reductive materialism allows it to retain the strengths of epiphenomenalism while avoiding its weaknesses. It is its monistic claim that each mental phenomenon is identical with something physical, presumably a brain entity. This identity claim is all that is required to avoid the objection to dualistic interactionism that it violates some conservation principle, and the objections to epiphenomenalism about its nomological danglers and its denial of the causal efficacy of anything mental. Again, no more than the identity of the mental with something physical is needed to maintain what many scientists find appealing about epiphenomenalism, namely, its being well suited to the theory of evolution and its allowing for the explanation of all human bodily behavior by the physical sciences. Might we then devise a mind-body identity theory which has all these advantages yet avoids what devastates reductive materialism?

We have seen that identity is a symmetrical relationship, but reduction is not. Furthermore, identity of A and B requires only that A and B have exactly the same properties. That is, unlike the claim that A is nothing but (reduced to) B, the claim that A is identical with B puts no restrictions on the sorts of properties that A has. Consequently, a pain can be identical with certain stimulated nerve fibers, and still have its psychological properties of being intense, throbbing, stabbing, aching, and the like. And, of course, mere identity would also allow such a pain to have the physical and physiological properties of that brain entity with which it is identical. That is, one and the same entity might have both psychological properties and physical properties.

THE NEUTRAL IDENTITY THEORY

A view that proposes such nonreductive, monistic identities was adumbrated in the writings of Benedict

Spinoza, who said, "the mind and the body are one and the same thing conceived at one time under the attribute of thought [that is, when understood as something with mental properties], and at another under the attribute of extension [that is, when understood as something with physical properties]."[16] Because this one entity has both of these aspects according to Spinoza, his theory is often called, "the double aspect theory." I believe, however, that a more accurate title for the theory we shall discuss is "the neutral identity theory." The entities proposed by such a theory are neither purely physical nor purely mental. They are some third sort of neutral entity, because they have psychological properties which nothing purely physical has, and they have physical properties which nothing purely mental has.

We can state this nonreductive, neutral, monistic theory more precisely in terms of the following thesis:

NI For each existing mental phenomenon, *m:* (a) *m* is identical with some physical phenomenon (presumably, a brain entity), and (b) *m* has both certain psychological properties and the physical properties of the physical phenomenon with which it is identical.

It is, as previously mentioned, clause (a) of *NI* that affords the neutral identity theory the advantages and appeal of epiphenomenalism and reductive materialism without the deficiencies of epiphenomenalism. It is clause (b) that provides the means for this neutral theory to avoid the fatal objection to reductive materialism, because it allows mental phenomena, such as our pains, to have whatever psychological properties we find so hard to deny them when we experience them. The neutral identity theory, then, seems clearly superior to the other theories we have examined. But, of course, once again we must search for its flaws before drawing any conclusion about its reasonableness.

FOUR OBJECTIONS TO THE NEUTRAL IDENTITY THEORY

What objections might there be to the neutral identity theory? I confess I find it hard to uncover any that have much force at all. Nevertheless, let me suggest four that seem to be either the most plausible or the most appealing of those I have considered.

First Objection: The Neutral Theory Implies Something Meaningless. The first objection is one type of argument that is quite popular among contemporary linguistic philosophers. It is an attempt to argue from statements about language to conclusions about nonlinguistic facts, such as claims about identity. In this particular case, the objection argues from the oddity of certain sentences that the neutral theory seems to imply to their meaninglessness and the rejection of the theory. If the neutral theory is true, and, for example, each pain is identical with a group of stimulated nerve fibers, then the sentences 'Some of my nerve fibers are aching and throbbing' and 'My present pain is constituted of a group of molecules' are both true. But according to this first objection, neither is true. Indeed, both seem to be linguistically odd and even meaningless, much like 'Next Saturday is in bed.' And nothing meaningless is true. So the neutral theory is not true.

I find it clearly debatable whether the oddity of 'My present pain is constituted of molecules' and 'Some of my nerve fibers are aching and throbbing' should be classified with the seemingly clear meaninglessness of 'Next Saturday is in bed.' After all, it seems absurd to assign some spatial location, such as being in bed, to a duration of time. But it is not clear it is equally absurd to attribute these properties to pains and nerve fibers. It may sound odd and most unusual, but that is not always a sign of meaninglessness. Consider, for example, how odd and unusual it must have sounded when someone first proposed that each motionless, clear, liquid pool of water is identical with a swarm of discrete particles each of which is constantly in motion. Nevertheless, by now we have become used to such statements and would never claim they are meaningless.

Let us, however, assume for present purposes that the two preceding sentences about pains and nerve fibers are meaningless. Would that refute the neutral identity theory? It would if the following deductively valid argument is successful:

(1) If clause (a) of *NI* is true, then my present pain is identical with (let us assume) stimulated nerve fibers.
(2) If clause (b) of *NI* is true and each pain is identical with stimulated nerve fibers, then it is true that each pain has the physical properties of stimulated nerve fibers.
(3) All nerve fibers are constituted of molecules
(4) The property of being constituted of molecules is a physical property.

(5) If *NI* is true, then it is true that my present pain is constituted of molecules.

(6) But it is meaningless (and so not true) that my present pain is constituted of molecules.

Therefore

(7) *NI* is not true (and so should be rejected).

The only way that a neutral identity theorist who accepts (6) can rebut this objection is by attacking premises (1) and (2). All the other premises are clearly true. One way to launch an attack is by arguing that anyone who accepts *NI* and also (6) should replace the word 'pain' in premises (1) and (2) to avoid committing his theory to the meaningless consequences that (1) and (2) require of it. I suggest that he might devise new technical terms, such as 'fibain' which can be defined as follows:

x is a fibain = df. *x* is an entity that has the properties all pains have, and the properties all stimulated nerve fibers have.

Then a neutral theorist could replace premise (1) by:

(1') If clause (a) of *NI* is true, then the aching entity that I am now experiencing is not a pain but rather a fibain.

And he could replace (2) by:

(2') If clause (b) of *NI* is true and each aching entity is not a pain but rather a fibain, then it is true that each aching entity has the physical properties of fibains.

Now the four premises no longer yield conclusion (5), but rather:

(5') If *NI* is true, then it is true that the fibain I am now experiencing is constituted of molecules.

And, now, not only is (6) irrelevant to the argument, but its replacement that would yield (7) is false:

(6') It is meaningless that the fibain I am now experiencing is constituted of molecules.

The main point emphasized by this reply is that an objection that is aimed at a nonlinguistic ontological thesis but which is based on claims solely about language is often easy to circumvent by avoiding the language that seems to raise the problem. In the present case we assumed a debatable claim about certain sentences being meaningless. The crucial question then becomes whether this claim about language established anything about a mind-body identity thesis. The answer seems clearly to be that it merely required an identity theorist to avoid certain language in stating the consequences of his theory. Thus this first objection fails, even granting the claim about meaninglessness. Of course, the objection does not even arise if, as is not unreasonable, we should reject that claim rather than grant it.

Second Objection: The Implausibility of Only Brains with Psychological Properties. The second objection I wish to consider is, like the first, based on the view that the neutral theory has odd consequences. But the oddity ascribed to the theory by the second objection is not a linguistic one implying meaninglessness; it is rather a nonlinguistic one implying implausibility. The objection is based on two premises. First, if the neutral identity theory is true, then only certain groups of molecules in only certain brains of only certain animals have psychological properties. All other groups have only their usual physical properties. But, second, this consequence of the theory is odd or unusual enough to be implausible. Therefore, the theory itself is implausible.

The problem with this objection is that neither of its premises is reasonable. Indeed, the first one is clearly false. The neutral identity theory does not require that only certain groups of molecules have psychological properties. The theory is mute about any properties of all other groups of molecules. Indeed, it is clearly consistent with the panpsychism with which Spinoza combines his double aspect theory. That is, it is consistent with the thesis that every object with physical properties also has psychological properties, whether or not we can discover them. Panpsychism, however, is quite implausible in its ascription of some undiscoverable low-level mental life even to inanimate objects such as rocks. I would propose, then, that a neutral identity theorist should adopt the view, in addition to his basic theory, that only certain very special groups of molecules have psychological properties. This does make these groups of molecules unique and unusual, but I disagree with the second premise of the present objection which states that any theory that requires there to be such unique and unusual groups of molecules is implausible.

Regardless of whether groups of molecules in the human brain have psychological properties, it must be admitted that this brain is unique and unusual in the complexity of its structure and constituents. Consequently, it is not implausible to think that it would have some very unusual properties. Indeed, I find it plausible to consider psychological properties to be what are called "emergent" properties that emerge in the development of the universe only when a group of molecules is of a certain complex sort—perhaps only when it constitutes a certain complex system of interconnected nerve fibers. There are other sorts of emergent properties, that is, properties that certain groups of atomic and subatomic particles have which none of the individual constituents of the groups have.[17] Why should we not construe psychological properties this way also?

Consider, for example, that certain systems of *NaCl* molecules have the properties of salt—they are white, crystalline, and soluble in water. But neither sodium and chlorine ions, nor their constituents—protons, neutrons, and electrons—have any of these properties individually. Or take *DNA* molecules. Only when their many constituents form together the required double helix is there something that has the unique, unusual, but not implausible biological properties of a living cell. When these constituents are not united in this way none of these emergent properties of a cell result. Likewise, I suggest, when and only when certain sorts of molecules form certain very complex systems, as in the brains of humans and some other living things, do the unique, unusual, but not implausible emergent psychological properties arise. Furthermore, this view of the emergence of psychological properties fits quite nicely with the Darwinian theory of evolution. We can, then, I find, reject this second objection to the neutral theory on the grounds that it has failed to show that what would be unique and unusual about certain brains would also be implausible.

Third Objection: Extrasensory Perception and Minds Distinct from Bodies. The third objection is quite different from the first two. I find it considerably even less plausible than they are, but it may be quite appealing to some. It is based on the claim that no acceptable theory about the relationship between mind and body should require the rejection of any thesis, no matter how odd or unusual, for which there is at least some scientific evidence. And, according to this objection, more and more evidence is accumulating in favor of the hypothesis that some human beings have extrasensory perception. In particular, the evidence is mounting that there is mental telepathy and communication among human beings without reliance on any sense organs. But any means of communication which involves no sense organs requires some sort of mental contact between people, and that is impossible unless there are mental phenomena quite distinct from what is merely physical. So we should reject identity theories for some sort of dualism.

There are two claims made in this objection which we can accept. First, what little evidence there is favors the view that some sort of communication among people occurs without the use of sense organs. The evidence, however, is far from conclusive. Nevertheless, there is enough to justify considerably more research and investigation. Second, any philosophical thesis that presupposes an answer to justified scientific research whose results are far from determined, faces a significant objection. However, whether it is serious enough to require the rejection of the thesis depends on how damaging the problems are that face the competing theories which avoid this particular objection. For example, although dualistic interactionism seems particularly well suited to accommodate extrasensory perception, the objection that it violates some conservation law seems too serious to resurrect it because of this one advantage.

Fortunately, however, we are not forced to choose between a theory that violates some conservation law and a theory that precludes extrasensory perception. This is because, in addition to the two preceding claims which are plausible, the objection rests on two others which are quite dubious. The first is that communication between human beings that does not involve sense organs requires there to be some sort of nonphysical, mental means of communication. But it has not been established that there are no purely physical processes by which one person's brain can affect another person's brain without affecting any of his sense organs. Until, if ever, there comes a time when extrasensory communication is shown to be plausible, and such nonsensory *physical* communication between brains is shown to be implausible, extrasensory perception is not even an objection to a theory which rejects causation by entities with psychological properties. Thus, at present, it is not even an objection to epiphenomenalism and reductive materialism. And it is even less of a threat to the neutral identity theory which allows causation by entities with both physical and psychological properties.

The second claim is more dubious than the first. It is the claim that mental communication and telepathy require mental causes that are distinct from anything physical. That is, it requires dualistic interactionism. It is true that if there should be *mental* telepathy, then epiphenomenalism and reductive materialism would be false. But the neutral theory would be quite compatible with it. It may be that one nonphysical, mental, emergent property of certain very complex physical systems is an ability to send and receive nonphysical signals that require no physical medium whatsoever. Admittedly, such communication seems very mysterious, given our present level of knowledge. And, insofar as it affects the brain of the person who receives it, it seems to violate some conservation law. But it is no more mysterious or less plausible than communication between minds which are distinct from bodies, although causally related to them. Thus, for two reasons, this third objection to the neutral theory fails.

Fourth Objection: Communication with the Dead and Disembodied Minds. It may be protested at this point that the preceding refutation of the third objection depends on the dubious thesis that all extrasensory communication consists in some living human being receiving extrasensory information from another living human being. But surely communication with the dead requires the existence of mental activity after death, and this is incompatible with the neutral theory, as well as with epiphenomenalism and reductive materialism. So, according to this fourth objection, we should reject all three of these theories for dualistic interactionism which is compatible with messages from the dead, and with disembodied life in the hereafter.

For many people, this may be the most appealing and persuasive objection of the four. It is indeed true that if the neutral theory is correct, then, when that brain activity with which a mental phenomenon is identical ceases, the mental phenomenon also ceases to exist. And when death occurs, all such brain activity ceases. Thus, if the neutral theory is true, there is no life after death and also no communication from anyone who is dead. Of course, this is also a consequence of reductive materialism with its reduction of the mental to brain activity, and of epiphenomenalism for which the mental is merely a by-product of that brain activity. But does this provide reason to reject these three theories? It does, only if it is reasonable to think there is such communication.

I believe that a neutral theorist should admit that psychical research has uncovered many reports of experiences that provide some evidence for the thesis of communication from the dead. For example, C. J. Ducasse mentions a case "of a father whose apparition some time after death revealed to one of his sons the existence and location of an unsuspected second will, benefiting him, which was then found as indicated."[18] Ducasse also notes phenomena of a different sort: "Sometimes the same mark of identity of a dead person, or the same message from him, or complementary parts of one message, are obtained independently from two mediums in different parts of the world."[19] These many reports cannot be ignored, and even if the great majority are fraudulent, it is still true, as Ducasse says, that "they cannot all just be laughed off; for to accept the hypothesis of fraud or malobservation would often require more credulity than to accept the facts reported."[20]

It seems reasonable, then, that some of these strange experiences occur. That is, sometimes people are caused to have these apparitions, and sometimes mediums are caused to believe they are receiving messages. But, as Ducasse points out, the crucial question is how these phenomena are to be explained. If we follow Ducasse here, then we would agree that only two explanatory hypotheses are even remotely plausible, namely, communication from the dead, and, where a medium is involved, unconscious, extrasensory communication from living persons, often far away from the medium and unknown by him. I think, however, that, in spite of what Ducasse says, we should also consider the hypothesis that each of these experiences is a case of "malobservation" or hallucination—especially when "apparitions" are experienced. At present, none of these three hypotheses is clearly more reasonable than the other two. And no fourth explanation seems to be any more reasonable than these three. This fact provides a neutral theorist with what he needs to justify the rejection of this objection. Both extrasensory communication and hallucination are compatible with the neutral theory and also with the conservation laws of physics. But communication from the dead would seem to violate some conservation law, because it would seem to require that nonphysical causes affect the brains and bodily behavior of the mediums and the persons having apparitions. Therefore, because, at the present time, communication from the dead is not clearly a better explanation of these phenomena than its two chief rivals, and, of the three, only it seems to violate a conservation law, we should, at least for now, reject the explanation that the phenomena result from communication from the dead.

CONCLUSION: THE NEUTRAL IDENTITY THEORY SHOULD BE ACCEPTED

We have examined the four objections to the neutral identity theory that I have found most plausible or most appealing. I have argued that we have reason to reject all of these objections. If I am right, then, the neutral theory not only avoids all the unrefuted objections to its chief rivals, namely, dualistic interactionism, epiphenomenalism, and reductive materalism, but it also faces none of its own. On that basis, I conclude, the neutral identity theory is not only more reasonable than the other theories about the relationship between mind and body, but is also reasonable enough to be clearly acceptable. It is, consequently, the hypothesis we should adopt—at least until, if ever, new evidence arises that forces its reevaluation.

NOTES

1. C. D. Broad, "The Traditional Problem of Body and Mind," in this anthology, p. 255.

2. *Ibid.*, pp. 255–257.

3. *Ibid.*, p. 256.

4. *Ibid.*

5. *Ibid.*, p. 257.

6. *Ibid.*, p. 259.

7. *ibid.*, p. 261.

8. T. H. Huxley, "Animals and Human Beings as Conscious Automata," in this anthology, p. 271.

9. Broad, p. 261.

10. H. Feigl, "Mind-Body, *Not* a Pseudoproblem," in S. Hook, ed., *Dimensions of Mind* (New York: Collier Books, 1961), p. 37.

11. T. Hobbes, *Hobbes Selections,* edited by F. J. E. Woodbridge (New York: Scribner's, 1930), p. 139.

12. *Ibid.*, p. 107

13. *Ibid.*, p. 140.

14. *Ibid.*, pp. 139–40.

15. For a more detailed discussion and definition of materialism, see my *Materialism and Sensations* (New Haven: Yale University Press, 1971), pp. 1–19. In this book I claim that, strictly speaking, materialism requires no more than that each "instance" of a psychological property (e.g., the particular aching of my present pain) be identical with some "instance" of a physical property. This allows each psychological property (e.g., achiness) to be distinct from all physical properties. Nevertheless, I argue in *Perception, Common Sense, and Science* (New Haven: Yale University Press, 1975), Appendix, that, contrary to materialism, some instances of psychological properties are not identical with any instance of a physical property.

16. B. Spinoza, *Spinoza Selections,* edited by J. Wild (New York: Scribner's, 1930), p. 209.

17. For a more detailed discussion of emergent properties, see my *Materialism and Sensations,* pp. 249–51.

18. C. J. Ducasse, "Is Life after Death Possible?" U. Cal. Press, 1947.

19. *Ibid.*

20. *Ibid.*

The Concept of a Self

JOHN LOCKE

The Prince and the Cobbler*

. . . If the identity of *soul alone* makes the same *man,* and there be nothing in the nature of matter why the same individual spirit may not be united to different bodies, it will be possible that those men, living in distant ages, and of different tempers, may have been the same man: which way of speaking must be from a very strange use of the word man, applied to an idea out of which body and shape are excluded. . . .

An animal is a living organized body; and consequently the same animal, as we have observed, is the same continued *life* communicated to different particles of matter, as they happen successively to be united to that organized living body. And whatever is talked of other definitions, ingenious observation puts it past doubt, that the idea in our minds, of which the sound "man" in our mouths is the sign, is nothing else but of an animal of such a certain form. . . .

I presume it is not the idea of a thinking or rational being alone that makes the *idea of a man* in most people's sense: but of a body, so and so shaped, joined to it; and if that be the idea of a man, the same successive body not shifted all at once, must, as well as the same immaterial spirit, go to the making of the same man.

This being premised, to find wherein personal identity consists, we must consider what *person* stands for;—which, I think, is a thinking intelligent being, that has reason and reflection, and can consider itself as itself, the same thinking thing, in different times and places; which it does only by that consciousness which is inseparable from thinking, and, as it seems to me, essential to it: it being impossible for any one to perceive without *perceiving* that he does perceive. When we see, hear, smell, taste, feel, meditate, or will anything, we know that we do so. Thus it is always as to our present sensations and perceptions: and by this every one is to himself that which he calls self:—it not being considered, in this case, whether the same self be continued in the same or divers substances. For, since consciousness always accompanies thinking, and it is that which makes every one to be what he calls self, and thereby distinguishes himself from all other thinking things, in this alone consists personal identity, i.e. the sameness of a rational being: and as far as this consciousness can be extended backwards to any past action or thought, so far reaches the identity of that person; it is the same self now it was then; and it is by the same self with this present one that now reflects on it, that that action was done.

But it is further inquired, whether it be the same identical substance. This few would think they had reason to doubt of, if these perceptions, with their consciousness, always remained present in the mind, whereby the same thinking thing would be always consciously present, and, as would be thought, evidently the same to itself. But that which seems to make the difficulty is this, that this consciousness being interrupted always by forgetfulness, there being no moment of our lives wherein we have the whole train of all our past actions before our eyes in one

*From John Locke, *An Essay concerning Human Understanding,* Book II, Chapter 27, "Of Ideas of Identity and Diversity." First published in 1690.

view, but even the best memories losing the sight of one part whilst they are viewing another; and we sometimes, and that the greatest part of our lives, not reflecting on our past selves, being intent on our present thoughts, and in sound sleep having no thoughts at all, or at least none with that consciousness which remarks our waking thoughts,—I say, in all these cases, our consciousness being interrupted, and we losing the sight of our past selves, doubts are raised whether we are the same thinking thing, i.e. the same *substance* or no. Which, however reasonable or unreasonable, concerns not *personal* identity at all. The question being what makes the same person; and not whether it be the same identical substance, which always thinks in the same person, which, in this case, matters not at all: different substances, by the same consciousness (where they do partake in it) being united into one person, as well as different bodies by the same life are united into one animal, whose identity is preserved in that change of substances by the unity of one continued life. For, it being the same consciousness that makes a man be himself to himself, personal identity depends on that only, whether it be annexed solely to one individual substance, or can be continued in a succession of several substances. For as far as any intelligent being *can* repeat the idea of any past action with the same consciousness it had of it at first, and with the same consciousness it has of any present action; so far it is the same personal self. For it is by the consciousness it has of its present thoughts and actions, that it is *self to itself* now, and so will be the same self, as far as the same consciousness can extend to actions past or to come; and would be by distance of time, or change of substance, no more two persons, than a man be two men by wearing other clothes today than he did yesterday, with a long or a short sleep between: the same consciousness uniting those distant actions in the same person, whatever substances contributed to their production.

That this is so, we have some kind of evidence in our very bodies, all whose particles, whilst vitally united to this same thinking conscious self, so that *we feel* when they are touched, and are affected by, and conscious of good or harm that happens to them, are a part of ourselves; i.e. of our thinking conscious self. Thus, the limbs of his body are to every one a part of himself; he sympathizes and is concerned for them. Cut off a hand, and thereby separate it from that consciousness he had of its heat, cold, and other affec-

tions, and it is then no longer a part of that which is himself, any more than the remotest part of matter. Thus, we see the *substance* whereof personal self consisted at one time may be varied at another, without the change of personal identity; there being no question about the same person, though the limbs which but now were a part of it, be cut off. . . .

And thus may we be able, without any difficulty, to conceive the same person at the resurrection, though in a body not exactly in make or parts the same which he had here,—the same consciousness going along with the soul that inhabits it. But yet the soul alone, in the change of bodies, would scarce to any one but to him that makes the soul the man, be enough to make the same man. For should the soul of a prince, carrying with it the consciousness of the prince's past life, enter and inform the body of a cobbler, as soon as deserted by his own soul, every one sees he would be the same *person* with the prince, accountable only for the prince's actions: but who would say it was the same *man*? The body too goes to the making the man, and would, I guess, to everybody determine the man in this case, wherein the soul, with all its princely thoughts about it, would not make another man: but he would be the same cobbler to every one besides himself. I know that, in the ordinary way of speaking, the same person, and the same man, stand for one and the same thing. And indeed every one will always have a liberty to speak as he pleases, and to apply what articulate sounds to what ideas he thinks fit, and change them as often as he pleases. But yet, when we will inquire what makes the same *spirit, man,* or *person,* we must fix the ideas of spirit, man, or person in our minds; and having resolved with ourselves what we mean by them, it will not be hard to determine in either of them, or the like, when it is the same, and when not.

But though the immaterial substance or soul does not alone, wherever it be, and in whatsoever state, make the same *man;* yet it is plain, consciousness, as far as ever it can be extended—should it be to ages past—unites existences and actions very remote in time into the same *person,* as well as it does the existences and actions of the immediately preceding moment: so that whatever has the consciousness of present and past actions, is the same person to whom they both belong. Had I the same consciousness that I saw the ark and Noah's flood, as that I saw an overflowing of the Thames last winter, or as that I write now, I could no more doubt that I who write this now, that saw the Thames overflowed last winter, and that viewed the flood at the general deluge, was the same *self,* — place that self in what *substance* you please—than that I who write this am the same *myself* now whilst I write (whether I consist of all the same substance, material or immaterial, or no) that I was yesterday. For as to this point of being the same self, it matters not whether this present self be made up of the same or other substances—I being as much concerned, and as justly accountable for any action that was done a thousand years since, appropriated to me now by this self-consciousness, as I am for what I did the last moment. . . .

But yet possibly it will still be objected, — Suppose I wholly lose the memory of some parts of my life, beyond a possibility of retrieving them, so that perhaps I shall never be conscious of them again; yet am I not the same person that did those actions, had those thoughts that I once was conscious of, though I have now forgot them? To which I answer, that we must here take notice what the word *I* is applied to; which, in this case, is the *man* only. And the same man being presumed to be the same person, I is easily here supposed to stand also for the same person. But if it be possible for the same man to have distinct incommunicable consciousness at different times, it is past doubt the same man would at different times make different persons; which, we see, is the sense of

mankind in the solemnest declaration of their opinions, human laws not punishing the mad man for the sober man's actions, nor the sober man for what the mad man did, —thereby making them two persons: which is somewhat explained by our way of speaking in English when we say such an one is "not himself," or is "beside himself"; in which phrases it is insinuated, as if those who now, or at least first used them, thought that self was changed; the selfsame person was no longer in that man.

But yet it is hard to conceive that Socrates, the same individual man, should be two persons. To help us a little in this, we must consider what is meant by Socrates, or the same individual *man.*

First, it must be either the same individual, immaterial, thinking substance; in short, the same numerical soul, and nothing else.

Secondly, or the same animal, without any regard to an immaterial soul.

Thirdly, or the same immaterial spirit united to the same animal.

Now, take which of these suppositions you please, it is impossible to make personal identity to consist in anything but consciousness; or reach any further than that does.

DAVID HUME

The Self*

There are some philosophers, who imagine we are every moment intimately conscious of what we call our Self; that we feel its existence and its continuance in existence; and are certain, beyond the evidence of a demonstration, both of its perfect identity and simplicity. . . .

Unluckily all these positive assertions are contrary to that very experience, which is pleaded for them,

*From David Hume, *A Treatise of Human Nature.* First published in England in 1738.

nor have we any idea of *self,* after the manner it is here explained. For from what impression could this idea be derived? This question 'tis impossible to answer without a manifest contradiction and absurdity; and yet 'tis a question, which must necessarily be answered, if we would have the idea of self pass for clear and intelligible. It must be some one impression, that gives rise to every real idea. But self or person is not any one impression, but that to which our several impressions and ideas are supposed to have a reference. If any impression gives rise to the idea of self, that impression must continue invariably the same, through the whole course of our lives; since self is supposed to exist after that manner. But there is no impression constant and invariable. Pain and pleasure, grief and joy, passions and sensations succeed each other, and never all exist at the same time. It cannot, therefore, be from any of these impressions, or from any other, that the idea of self is derived; and consequently there is no such idea.

But farther, what must become of all our particular perceptions upon this hypothesis? All these are different, and distinguishable, and separable from each other, and may be separately considered, and may exist separately, and have no need of any thing to support their existence. After what manner, therefore, do they belong to self; and how are they connected with it? For my part, when I enter most intimately into what I call *myself,* I always stumble on some particular perception or other, of heat or cold, light or shade, love or hatred, pain or pleasure. I never can catch *myself* at any time without a perception, and never can observe any thing but the perception. When my perceptions are removed for any time, as by sound sleep; so long am I insensible of *myself,* and may truly be said not to exist. And were all my perceptions removed by death, and could I neither think, nor feel, nor see, nor love, nor hate after the dissolution of my body, I should be entirely annihilated, nor do I conceive what is farther requisite to make me a perfect nonentity. If any one upon serious and unprejudiced reflection, thinks he has a different notion of *himself,* I must confess I can reason no longer with him. All I can allow him is, that he may be in the right as well as I, and that we are essentially different in this particular. He may, perhaps, perceive something simple and continued, which he calls *himself;* though I am certain there is no such principle in me.

But setting aside some metaphysicians of this kind, I may venture to affirm of the rest of mankind, that they are nothing but a bundle or collection of different perceptions, which succeed each other with an inconceivable rapidity, and are in a perpetual flux and movement. Our eyes cannot turn in their sockets without varying our perceptions. Our thought is still more variable than our sight; and all our other senses and faculties contribute to this change; nor is there any single power of the soul, which remains unalterably the same, perhaps for one moment. The mind is a kind of theatre, where several perceptions successively make their appearance; pass, re-pass, glide away, and mingle in an infinite variety of postures and situations. There is properly no *simplicity* in it at one time, nor *identity* in different; whatever natural propension we may have to imagine that simplicity and identity. The comparison of the theatre must not mislead us. They are the successive perceptions only, that constitute the mind; nor have we the most distant notion of the place, where these scenes are represented, or of the materials, of which it is composed.

What then gives us so great a propension to ascribe an identity to these successive perceptions, and to suppose ourselves possessed of an invariable and uninterrupted existence through the whole course of our lives? . . .

We have a distinct idea of an object, that remains invariable and uninterrupted through a supposed variation of time; and this idea we call that of *identity* or *sameness.* We have also a distinct idea of several different objects existing in succession, and connected together by a close relation; and this to an accurate view affords as perfect a notion of *diversity,* as if there was no manner of relation among the objects. But though these two ideas of identity, and a succession of related objects be in themselves perfectly distinct, and even contrary, yet 'tis certain, that in our common way of thinking they are generally confounded with each other. That action of the imagination, by which we consider the uninterrupted and invariable object, and that by which we reflect on the succession of related objects, are almost the same to the feeling, nor is there much more effort of thought required in the latter case than in the former. The relation facilitates the transition of the mind from one object to another, and renders its passage as smooth as if it contemplated one continued object. This resemblance is the cause of the confusion and mistake, and makes us substitute the notion of identity, instead of that of related objects. . . .

Thus we feign the continued existence of the perceptions of our senses, to remove the interruption; and run into the notion of a *soul,* and *self,* and *substance,* to disguise the variation. But we may farther observe, that where we do not give rise to such a fiction, our propension to confound identity with relation is so great, that we are apt to imagine something unknown and mysterious, connecting the parts, beside their relation; and this I take to be the case with regard to the identity we ascribe to plants and vegetables. And even when this does not take place, we still feel a propensity to confound these ideas, though we are not able fully to satisfy ourselves in that particular, nor find any thing invariable and uninterrupted to justify our notion of identity.

Thus the controversy concerning identity is not merely a dispute of words. For when we attribute identity, in an improper sense, to variable or interrupted objects, our mistake is not confined to the expression, but is commonly attended with a fiction, either of something invariable and uninterrupted, or of something mysterious and inexplicable, or at least with a propensity to such fictions. What will suffice to prove this hypothesis to the satisfaction of every fair enquirer, is to show from daily experience and observation, that the objects, which are variable or interrupted, and yet are supposed to continue the same, are such only as consist of a succession of parts, connected together by resemblance, contiguity, or causation. . . .

A ship, of which a considerable part has been changed by frequent reparations, is still considered as the same: nor does the difference of the materials hinder us from ascribing an identity to it. The common end, in which the parts conspire, is the same under all their variations, and affords an easy transition of the imagination from one situation of the body to another. . . .

Though every one must allow, that in a very few years both vegetables and animals endure a *total* change, yet we still attribute identity to them, while their form, size, and substance are entirely altered. An oak, that grows from a small plant to a large tree, is still the same oak; though there be not one particle of matter, or figure of its parts the same. An infant becomes a man, and is sometimes fat, sometimes lean, without any change in his identity. . . . A man, who hears a noise, that is frequently interrupted and renewed, says, it is still the same noise; though 'tis evident the sounds have only a specific identity or resemblance, and there is nothing numerically the same, but the cause, which produced them. In like manner it may be said without breach of the propriety of language, that such a church, which was formerly of brick, fell to ruin, and that the parish rebuilt the same church of free-stone, and according to modern architecture. Here neither the form nor materials are the same, nor is there any thing common to the two objects, but their relation to the inhabitants of the parish; and yet this alone is sufficient to make us denominate them the same. . . .

From thence it evidently follows, that identity is nothing really belonging to these different perceptions, and uniting them together; but is merely a quality, which we attribute to them, because of the union of their ideas in the imagination, when we reflect upon them. . . .

The only question, therefore, which remains, is, by what relations this uninterrupted progress of our thought is produced, when we consider the successive existence of a mind or thinking person. And here 'tis evident we must confine ourselves to resemblance and causation. . . . Also, as memory alone acquaints us with the continuance and extent of this succession of perceptions, 'tis to be considered, upon that account chiefly, as the source of personal identity. Had we no memory, we never should have any notion of causation, nor consequently of that chain of causes and effects, which constitute our self or person.

THOMAS REID

Critique of Locke and Hume on Behalf of Common Sense*

Thomas Reid (1710–1796) was, next to Hume, the most influential Scottish philosopher.

. . . It is proper to consider what is meant by identity in general, what by our own personal identity, and how we are led into that invincible belief and conviction which every man has of his own personal identity, as far as his memory reaches.

Identity in general I take to be a relation between a thing which is known to exist at one time, and a thing which is known to have existed at another time. If you ask whether they are one and the same, or two different things, every man of common sense understands the meaning of your question perfectly. Whence we may infer with certainty, that every man of common sense has a clear and distinct notion of identity.

If you ask a definition of identity, I confess I can give none; it is too simple a notion to admit of logical definition. . . .

I see evidently that identity supposes *an uninterrupted continuance of existence*. That which has ceased to exist cannot be the same with that which afterwards begins to exist; for this would be to suppose a being to exist after it ceased to exist, and to have had existence before it was produced, which are manifest contradictions. Continued uninterrupted existence is therefore necessarily implied in identity. Hence we may infer, that identity cannot, in its proper sense, be applied to our pains, our pleasures, our thoughts, or any operation of our minds. The pain felt this day is not the same individual pain which I felt yesterday, though they may be *similar* in kind and de-

gree, and have the same cause. The same may be said of every feeling, and of every operation of mind. They are all successive in their nature, like time itself, no two moments of which can be the same moment. It is otherwise with the parts of absolute space. They always are, and were, and will be the same. So far, I think, we proceed upon clear ground in fixing the notion of identity in general.

NATURE AND ORIGIN OF OUR IDEA OF PERSONAL IDENTITY

It is perhaps more difficult to ascertain with precision the meaning of *personality;* but it is not necessary in the present subject: it is sufficient for our purpose to observe, that all mankind place their personality in something that *cannot be divided, or consist of parts.* A part of a person is a manifest absurdity. When a man loses his estate, his health, his strength, he is still the same person, and has lost nothing of his personality. If he has a leg or an arm cut off, he is the same person he was before. The amputated member is no part of his person, otherwise it would have a right to a part of his estate, and be liable for a part of his engagements. It would be entitled to a share of his merit and demerit, which is manifestly absurd. A person is something indivisible, and is what Leibniz calls a *monad.*

My personal identity, therefore, implies the continued existence of that indivisible thing which I call *myself.* Whatever this self may be, it is something which thinks, and deliberates, and resolves, and acts, and suffers. I am not thought, I am not action, I am not feeling; I am something that thinks, and acts, and suffers. My thoughts, and actions, and feelings, change every moment; they have no continued, but a successive, existence; but that *self,* or *I,* to which they belong, is permanent, and has the same relation to all

*Edited by Tom L. Beauchamp from two sources: Thomas Reid, *Essays on the Intellectual Powers of Man,* first published in England in 1785, and Thomas Reid, *An Inquiry into the Human Mind on the Principles of Common Sense,* first published in 1764. Reprinted by permission of Professor Beauchamp.

the succeeding thoughts, actions, and feelings which I call mine.

Such are the notions that I have of my personal identity. But perhaps it may be said, this may all be fancy without reality. How do you know,—what evidence have you,—that there is such a permanent self which has a claim to all the thoughts, actions, and feelings which you call yours?

To this I answer, that the proper evidence I have of all this is *remembrance*. I remember that twenty years ago I conversed with such a person; I remember several things that passed in that conversation: my memory testifies, not only that this was done, but that it was done by me who now remember it. If it was done by me, I must have existed at that time, and continued to exist from that time to the present: if the identical person whom I call myself had not a part in that conversation, my memory is fallacious; it gives a distinct and positive testimony of what is not true. Every man in his senses believes what he distinctly remembers, and everything he remembers convinces him that he existed at the same time remembered.

Although memory gives the most irresistible evidence of my being the identical person that did such a thing, at such a time, I may have other good evidence of things which befell me, and which I do not remember: I know who bore me, and suckled me, but I do not remember these events.

It may here be observed, (though the observation would have been unnecessary, if some great philosophers had not contradicted it), that it is not my remembering any action of mine that *makes* me to be the person who did it. This remembrance makes me to *know* assuredly that I did it; *but I might have done it, though I did not remember it.* That relation to me, which is expressed by saying that *I did it,* would be the same, though I had not the least remembrance of it. . . .

When we pass judgment on the identity of other persons than ourselves, we proceed upon other grounds, and determine from a variety of circumstances, which sometimes produce the firmest assurance, and sometimes leave room for doubt. The identity of persons has often furnished matter of serious litigation before tribunals of justice. But no man of a sound mind ever doubted of his own identity, as far as he distinctly remembered. . . .

Thus it appears, that the evidence we have of our own identity, as far back as we remember, is totally of a different kind from the evidence we have of the identity of other persons, or of objects of sense. The first is grounded on *memory,* and gives undoubted certainty. The last is grounded on *similarity,* and on other circumstances, which in many cases are not so decisive as to leave no room for doubt.

It may likewise be observed, that the identity of *objects of sense* is never perfect. All bodies, as they consist of innumerable parts that may be disjoined from them by a great variety of causes, are subject to continual changes of their substance, increasing, diminishing, changing insensibly. When such alterations are gradual, because languages could not afford a different name for every different state of such a changeable being, it retains the same name, and is considered as the same thing. Thus we say of an old regiment, that it did such a thing a century ago, though there now is not a man alive who then belonged to it. We say a tree is the same in the seed-bed and in the forest. A ship of war, which has successively changed her anchors, her tackle, her sails, her masts, her planks, and her timbers, while she keeps the same name, is the same.

The identity, therefore, which we ascribe to bodies, whether natural or artificial, is not perfect identity; it is rather something which, for the conveniency of speech, we call identity. It admits of a great change of the subject, providing the change be *gradual;* sometimes, even of a total change. And the changes which in common language are made consistent with identity differ from those that are thought to destroy it, not in *kind,* but in *number* and *degree.* It has no fixed nature when applied to bodies; and questions about the identity of a body are very often questions about words. But identity, when applied to persons, has no ambiguity, and admits not of degrees, or of more and less. It is the foundation of all rights and obligations, and of all accountableness; and the notion of it is fixed and precise.

STRICTURES ON LOCKE'S ACCOUNT OF PERSONAL IDENTITY

In a long chapter, *Of Identity and Diversity,* Mr. Locke has made many ingenious and just observations, and some which I think cannot be defended. . . .

This doctrine has some strange consequences, which the author was aware of. (1) Such as, that if the same consciousness can be transferred from one intelligent being to another, which he thinks we cannot show to be impossible, *then two or twenty intelligent beings may be the same person.* (2) And if the intelligent being may lose the consciousness of the actions done by him, which surely is possible, then he is not the person that did those actions; so that *one intelligent being may be two or twenty different persons,* if he shall so often lose the consciousness of his former actions.

(3) There is another consequence of this doctrine, which follows no less necessarily, though Mr. Locke probably did not see it. It is, *that a man may be, and at the same time not be, the person that did a particular action.* Suppose a brave officer to have been flogged when a boy at school for robbing an orchard, to have taken a standard from the enemy in his first campaign, and to have been made a general in advanced life; suppose, also, which must be admitted to be possible, that, when he took the standard, he was conscious of his having been flogged at school, and that, when made a general, he was conscious of his taking the standard, but had absolutely lost the consciousness of his flogging. These things being supposed, it follows, from Mr. Locke's doctrine, that he who was flogged at school is the same person who took the standard, and that he who took the standard is the same person who was made a general. Whence it follows, if there be any truth in logic, that the general is the same person with him who was flogged at school. But the general's consciousness does not reach so far back as his flogging; therefore, according to Mr. Locke's doctrine, he is not the person who was flogged. Therefore the general is, and at the same time is not, the same person with him who was flogged at school.

Leaving the consequences of this doctrine to those who have leisure to trace them, we may observe, with regard to the doctrine itself,—

First, that Mr. Locke attributes to consciousness the conviction we have of our past actions, as if a man may now be conscious of what he did twenty years ago. It is impossible to understand the meaning of this, unless by *consciousness* he meant *memory,* the only faculty by which we have an immediate knowledge of our past actions. . . .

When, therefore, Mr. Locke's notion of personal identity is properly expressed, it is, that personal identity *consists in distinct remembrance;* for, even in the popular sense, to say that I am conscious of a past action means nothing else than that I distinctly remember that I did it.

Secondly, it may be observed, that, in this doctrine, not only is consciousness confounded with memory, but, which is still more strange, *personal identity* is confounded with *the evidence which we have of our personal identity.*

It is very true, that my remembrance that I did such a thing is the evidence I have that I am the identical person who did it. And this, I am apt to think, Mr. Locke meant. But to say that my remembrance that I did such a thing, or my consciousness, *makes* me the person who did it, is, in my apprehension, an absurdity too gross to be entertained by any man who attends to the meaning of it; for it is to attribute to memory or consciousness a strange magical power of producing its object, though that object must have existed before the memory or consciousness which produced it. Consciousness is the testimony of one faculty; memory is the testimony of another faculty; and to say that the testimony is the cause of the thing testified, this surely is absurd, if any thing be, and could not have been said by Mr. Locke, if he had not confounded the testimony with the thing testified.

When a horse that was stolen is found and claimed by the owner, the only evidence he can have, or that a judge or witnesses can have, that this is the very identical horse which was his property, is similitude. But would it not be ridiculous from this to infer that the identity of a horse *consists* in similitude only? The only *evidence* I have that I am the identical person who did such actions is, that I remember distinctly I did them; or, as Mr. Locke expresses it, I am conscious I did them. To infer from this, that personal identity consists in consciousness, is an argument which, if it had any force, would prove the identity of a stolen horse to consist solely in similitude.

Thirdly, is it not strange that the sameness or identity of a person should consist in a thing *which is continually changing,* and is not any two minutes the same?

Our consciousness, our memory, and every operation of the mind, are still flowing like the water of a river, or like time itself. The consciousness I have this moment can no more be the same consciousness I had last moment, than this moment can be the last moment. Identity can only be affirmed of things which have a continued existence. Consciousness, and every kind of thought, are transient and momentary, and have no continued existence; and, therefore, if personal identity consisted in consciousness, it would certainly follow, that *no man is the same person any two moments of his life;* and as the right and justice of reward and punishment are founded on personal identity, no man could be responsible for his actions. . . .

Fourthly, there are many expressions used by Mr. Locke, in speaking of personal identity, which to me are altogether unintelligible, unless we suppose that he confounded that sameness or identity which we ascribe to an individual with the identity which, in common discourse, is often ascribed to many individuals of the same species.

When we say that pain and pleasure, consciousness and memory, are the same in all men, this sameness can only mean similarity, or sameness *of kind.* That the pain of one man can be the same individual pain with that of another man is no less impossible, than that one man should be another man: the pain felt by me yesterday can no more be the pain I feel today, than yesterday can be this day; and the same thing may be said of every passion and of every operation of the mind. The same kind or species of operation may be in different men, or in the same man at different times; but it is impossible that the same individual operation should be in different men, or in the same man at different times.

When Mr. Locke, therefore, speaks of "the same consciousness being continued through a succession of different substances"; when he speaks of "repeating the idea of a past action, with the same consciousness we had of it at the first," and of "the same consciousness extending to actions past and to come"; these expressions are to me unintelligible, unless he means not the same individual consciousness, but a consciousness that is similar, or of the same kind. If our personal identity consists in consciousness, as this consciousness cannot be the same individually any two moments, but only of the *same kind,* it would follow, that we are not for any two moments the same individual persons, but the same *kind* of persons. As our consciousness sometimes ceases to exist, as in sound sleep, our personal identity must cease with it. Mr. Locke allows, that the same thing cannot have two beginnings of existence, so that our identity would be irrecoverably gone every time we cease to think, if it was but for a moment. . . .

STRICTURES ON HUME'S ACCOUNT OF PERSONAL IDENTITY

Locke's principle must be, that identity consists in remembrance; and consequently a man must lose his personal identity with regard to every thing he forgets.

Nor are these the only instances whereby our philosophy concerning the mind appears to be very fruitful in creating doubts, but very unhappy in resolving them.

Descartes, Malebranche, and Locke, have all employed their genius and skill, to prove the existence of a material world; and with very bad success. . . .

The present age, I apprehend, has not produced two more acute or more practised in this part of philosophy than [George Berkeley] the Bishop of Cloyne, and the author of the Treatise of Human Nature [David Hume, who] . . . undoes the world of spirits, and leaves nothing in nature but ideas and impressions, without any subject on which they may be impressed.

It seems to be a peculiar strain of humor in this author, to set out in his introduction, by promising with a grave face, no less than a complete system of the sciences, upon a foundation entirely new, to wit, that of human nature; when the intention of the whole work is to show, that there is neither human nature nor science in the world. It may perhaps be unreasonable to complain of this conduct in an author, who neither believes his own existence, nor that of his reader; and therefore could not mean to disappoint him, or to laugh at his credulity. Yet I cannot imagine, that the author of the Treatise of Human Nature is so skeptical as to plead this apology. He believed, against his principles, that he should be read, and that he should retain his personal identity, till he reaped the honor and reputation justly due to his metaphysical *acumen.* Indeed he ingenuously acknowledges, that it was only in solitude and retirement that he could yield any assent to his own philosophy; society, like daylight, dispelled the darkness and fogs of skepticism, and made him yield to the dominion of common sense. Nor did I ever hear him charged with doing any thing, even in solitude, that argued such a degree of skepticism, as his principles maintain. . . .

That the natural issue of this system is skepticism with regard to every thing except the existence of our ideas, and of their necessary relations which appear upon comparing them, is evident: for ideas being the only objects of thought, and having no existence but when we are conscious of them, it necessarily follows, that there is no object of our thought, which can have a continued and permanent existence. Body and spirit, cause and effect, time and space, to which we were wont to ascribe an existence independent of our thought, are all turned out of existence by this short dilemma: Either these things are ideas of sensation or reflection, or they are not: if they are ideas of sensation or reflection, they can have no existence but when we are conscious of them; if they are not ideas of sensation or reflection, they are words without any meaning.

Neither Descartes nor Locke perceived this consequence of their system concerning ideas. Bishop Berkeley was the first who discovered it. . . . But with regard to the existence of spirits or minds, he does not admit the consequence; and if he had admitted it, he must have been an absolute skeptic. . . .

Thus we see, that Descartes and Locke take the road that leads to skepticism, without knowing the end of it; but they stop short for want of light to carry them farther. Berkeley, frighted at the appearance of the dreadful abyss, starts aside, and avoids it. But the author of the Treatise of Human Nature, more daring and intrepid, without turning aside to the right hand or to the left, like Virgil's Alecto, shoots directly into the gulf. . . .

We ought, however, to do this justice both to the bishop of Cloyne and to the author of the Treatise of Human Nature, to acknowledge, that their conclusions are justly drawn from the doctrine of ideas, which has been so universally received. On the other hand, from the character of bishop Berkeley, and of his predecessors Descartes, Locke, and Malebranche, we may venture to say, that if they had seen all the consequences of this doctrine, as clearly as the author before mentioned did, they would have suspected it vehemently, and examined it more carefully than they appear to have done.

The theory of ideas, like the Trojan horse, had a specious appearance both of innocence and beauty; but if those philosophers had known that it carried in its belly death and destruction to all science and common sense, they would not have broken down their walls to give it admittance. . . .

It is certain, no man can conceive or believe smelling to exist of itself, without a mind, or something that has the power of smelling, of which it is called a sensation, an operation or feeling. Yet if any man should demand a proof, that sensation cannot be without a mind or sentient being, I confess that I can give none; and that to pretend to prove it, seems to me almost as absurd as to deny it.

This might have been said without any apology before the Treatise of Human Nature appeared in the world. For till that time, no man, as far as I know, ever thought either of calling in question that principle, or of giving a reason for his belief of it. Whether thinking beings were of an ethereal or igneous nature, whether material or immaterial, was variously disputed; but that thinking is an operation of some kind of being or other, was always taken for granted, as a principle that could not possibly admit of doubt. . . .

If there are certain principles, as I think there are, which the constitution of our nature leads us to believe, and which we are under a necessity to take for granted in the common concerns of life, without being able to give a reason for them; these are what we call the principles of common sense; and what is manifestly contrary to them, is what we call absurd. . . .

It is a fundamental principle of [Hume's] ideal system, that every object of thought must be an impression, or an idea, that is, a faint copy of some preceding impression. This is a principle so commonly received, that the author above mentioned, although his whole system is built upon it, never offers the least proof of it. It is upon this principle, as a fixed point, that he erects his metaphysical engines, to overturn heaven and earth, body and spirit. And indeed, in my apprehension, it is altogether sufficient for the purpose. For if impressions and ideas are the only objects of thought, then heaven and earth, and body and spirit, and every thing you please, must signify only impressions and ideas, or they must be words without any meaning. It seems, therefore, that this notion, however strange, is closely connected with the received doctrine of ideas, and we must either admit the conclusion, or call in question the premises. . . .

The triumph of ideas was completed by the Treatise of Human Nature, which discards spirits also, and leaves ideas and impressions as the sole existences in the universe. What if at last, having nothing else to contend with, they should fall foul of one another, and leave no existence in nature at all? This would surely bring philosophy into danger; for what should we have left to talk or to dispute about? However, hitherto these philosophers acknowledge the existence of impressions and ideas; they acknowledge certain laws of attraction, or rules of precedence, according to which ideas and impressions range themselves in various forms, and succeed one another: but that they should belong to a mind, as its proper goods and chattels, this they have found to be a vulgar error. These ideas are as free and independent as the birds of the air. . . . They make the whole furniture of the universe; starting into existence, or out of it, without any cause; combining into parcels which the vulgar call *minds;* and succeeding one another by fixed laws, without time, place, or author of those laws. . . .

The Treatise of Human Nature . . . seems to have made but a bad return, by bestowing upon them this independent existence; since thereby they are turned out of house and home, and set adrift in the world, without friend or connection, without a rag to cover their nakedness; and who knows but the whole system of ideas may perish by the indiscreet zeal of their friends to exalt them?

However this may be, it is certainly a most amazing discovery that thought and ideas may be without any thinking being: a discovery big with consequences which cannot easily be traced by those deluded mortals who think and reason in the common track. We were always apt to imagine, that thought supposed a thinker, and love a lover, and treason a traitor: but this, it seems, was all a mistake; and it is found out, that there may be treason without a traitor, and love without a lover, laws without a legislator, and punishment without a sufferer, succession without time, and motion without any thing moved, or space in which it may move: or if, in these cases, ideas are the lover, the sufferer, the traitor, it were to be wished that the author of this discovery had farther condescended to acquaint us, whether ideas can converse together, and be under obligations of duty or gratitude to each other; whether they can make promises, and enter into leagues and covenants, and fulfil or break them, and be punished for the breach? If one set of ideas makes a covenant, another breaks it, and a third is punished for it, there is reason to think that justice is no natural virtue in this system.

It seemed very natural to think, that the Treatise of Human Nature required an author, and a very ingenious one too; but now we learn, that it is only a set of ideas which came together, and arranged themselves by certain associations and attractions.

After all, this curious system appears not to be fitted to the present state of human nature. How far it may suit some choice spirits, who are refined from the dregs of common sense, I cannot say. It is acknowledged, I think, that even these can enter into this system only in their most speculative hours, when they soar so high in pursuit of those self-existent ideas, as to lose sight of all other things. But when they condescend to mingle again with the human race, and to converse with a friend, a companion, or a fellow citizen, the ideal system[1] vanishes; common sense, like an irresistible torrent, carries them along; and, in spite of all their reasoning and philosophy, they believe their own existence, and the existence of other things. . . .

This philosophy is like a hobby-horse, which a man in bad health may ride in his closet, without hurting his reputation; but if he should take him abroad with him to church, or to the exchange, or to the play house, his heir would immediately call a jury, and seize his estate.

NOTE
1. [Berkeley's idealism.]

Personal Identity and the Survival of Death

JOHN PERRY

A Dialogue on Personal Identity and Immortality*

John Perry (1943–   ) teaches philosophy at Stanford University.

(This is a record of conversations of Gretchen Weirob, a teacher of philosophy at a small midwestern college, and several of her friends. They took place in her hospital room, the three nights before she died from injuries sustained in a motorcycle accident. Sam Miller is a chaplain and a long-time friend of Weirob's; Dave Cohen is a former student of hers.)

THE FIRST NIGHT

Cohen: I can hardly believe what you say, Gretchen, You are lucid and do not appear to be in great pain. And yet you say things are hopeless?

Weirob: These devices can keep me alive for another day or two at most. Some of my vital organs have been injured beyond anything the doctors know how to repair, apart from certain rather radical measures I have rejected. I am not in much pain. But as I understand it that is not a particularly good sign. My brain was uninjured and I guess that's why I am as lucid as I ever am. The whole situation is a bit depressing, I fear. But here's Sam Miller. Perhaps he will know how to cheer me up.

Miller: Good evening Gretchen. Hello, Dave. I guess there's not much point in beating around the bush, Gretchen; the medics tell me you're a goner. Is there anything I can do to help?

Weirob: Crimenentley, Sam! You deal with the

dying every day. Don't you have anything more comforting to say than "Sorry to hear you're a goner?"

Miller: Well to tell you the truth, I'm a little at a loss for what to say to you. Most people I deal with are believers like I am. We talk of the prospects for survival. I give assurance that God, who is just and merciful, would not permit such a travesty as that our short life on this earth should be the end of things. But you and I have talked about religious and philosophical issues for years. I have never been able to find in you the least inclination to believe in God; indeed, it's a rare day when you are sure that your friends have minds, or that you can see your own hand in front of your face, or that there is any reason to believe that the sun will rise tomorrow. How can I hope to comfort you with the prospect of life after death, when I know you will regard it as having no probability whatsoever?

Weirob: I would not require so much to be comforted, Sam. Even the possibility of something quite improbable can be comforting, in certain situations. When we used to play tennis, I beat you no more than one time in twenty. But this was enough to establish the possibility of beating you on any given occasion, and by focusing merely on the possibility, I remained eager to play. Entombed in a secure prison, having thought our situation quite hopeless, we might find unutterable joy in the information that there was, after all, a possibility of escape, however slim the chances of actually succeeding. Hope provides comfort, and hope does not always require probability. But we must believe that what we hope for is at least possible. So I will set an easier task for you. Simply persuade me that my survival, after the death of this body, is *possible,* and I promise to be comforted. Whether you succeed or not, your attempts will be a diversion, for you know I like to talk philosophy more than anything else.

Miller: But what is possibility, if not reasonable probability?

Weirob: I do not mean possible in the sense of likely, or even in the sense of comforming to the known laws of physics or biology. I mean possible only in the weakest sense, of being conceivable, given the unavoidable facts. Within the next couple of days, this body will die. It will be buried, and it will rot away. I ask that, given these facts, you explain to me how it even makes *sense* to talk of me continuing to exist. Just explain to me what it is I am to *imagine,* when I imagine surviving, that is consistent with these facts, and I shall be comforted.

Miller: But then what is there to do? There are many conceptions of immortality, of survival past the grave, which all seem to make good sense. Surely not the possibility, but only the probability, can be doubted. Take your choice! Christians believe in life, with a body, in some Hereafter—the details vary, of course, from sect to sect. There is the Greek idea of the body as a prison, from which we escape at death—so we have continued life without a body. Then there are conceptions, in which we, so to speak, merge with the flow of being . . .

Weirob: I must cut short your lesson in comparative religion. Survival means surviving, no more, no less. I have no doubts that I shall merge with being; plants will take roots in my remains, and the chemicals that I am will continue to make their contribution to life. I am enough of an ecologist to be comforted. But survival, if it is anything, must offer comforts of a different sort, the comforts of *anticipation.* Survival means that tomorrow, or sometime in the future, there will be someone who will experience, who will see and touch and smell—or at least, at the very least, think and reason and remember. And this person will be *me.* This person will be related to me in such a way that it is correct for me to anticipate, to look forward to, those future experiences. And I am related to her in such a way that it will be right for her to remember what I have thought and done, to feel remorse for what I have done wrong, and pride in what I have done right. And the only relation that supports anticipation and memory in this way,

is simply *identity*. For it is never correct to anticipate, as happening to oneself, what will happen to someone else, is it? Or to remember, as one's own thoughts and deeds, what someone else did? So don't give me merger with being, or some such nonsense. Give me identity, or lets talk about baseball or fishing—but I'm sorry to get so emotional. I just react so strongly when words which mean one thing are used for another—when one talks about survival, but does not mean to say that the same person will continue to exist. It's such a sham!

Miller: I'm sorry. I was just trying to stay in touch with the times, if you want to know the truth, for when I read modern theology or talk to my students who have studied eastern religions, the notion of survival as simply continued existence of the same person seems out of date. Merger with Being! Merger with Being! That's all I hear. My own beliefs are quite simple, if somewhat vague. I think you will live again—with or without a body, I don't know— *I* draw comfort from my belief that you and I will be together again, after I also die. We will communicate, somehow. We will continue to grow spiritually. That's what I believe, as surely as I believe that I am sitting here. For I don't know how God could be excused, if this small sample of life is all that we are allotted; I don't know why he should have created us, if this few years of toil and torment are the end of it . . .

Weirob: Remember our deal, Sam. You don't have to convince me that survival is probable, for we both agree you would not get to first base. You have only to convince me that it is possible. The only condition is that it be real survival we are talking about, not some up-to-date ersatz survival, which simply amounts to what any ordinary person would call ceasing totally to exist.

Miller: I guess I just miss the problem then. Of course it's possible. You just continue to exist, after your body dies. What's to be defended or explained? You want details? OK. Two people meet a thousand years from now, in a place that may or may not be part of this physical universe. I am one and you are the other. So you must have survived. Surely you can imagine that. What else is there to say?

Weirob: But in a few days *I* will quit breathing, *I* will be put into a coffin, *I* will be buried. And in a few months or a few years *I* will be reduced to so much humus. That I take it is obvious, is given.

How then can you say that I am one of these persons a thousand years from now?

Suppose I took this box of kleenex and lit fire to it. It is reduced to ashes and I smash the ashes and flush them down the john. Then I say to you, go home and on the shelf will be *that very box of kleenex*. It has survived! Wouldn't that be absurd? What sense could you make of it? And yet that is just what you say to me. I will rot away. And then, a thousand years later, there I will be. What sense does that make?

Miller: There could be an *identical* box of kleenex at your home, one just like it in every respect. And, in this sense, there is no difficulty in there being someone identical to you in the Hereafter, though your body has rotted away.

Weirob: You are playing with words again. There could be an *exactly similar* box of kleenex on my shelf. We sometimes use "identical" to mean "exactly similar" as when we talk of "identical twins." But I am using "identical," in a way in which *identity* is the condition of memory and correct anticipation. If I am told that tomorrow though I will be dead, someone else that looks and sounds and thinks just like me will be alive, would that be comforting? Could I correctly *anticipate* having her experiences? Would it make sense for me to fear her pains and look forward to her pleasures? Would it be right for her to feel remorse at the harsh way I am treating you? Of course not. Similarity, however exact, is not identity. I use identity to mean there is but one thing. If I am to survive, there must be one person who is here in this bed now, and who is talking to someone in your Hereafter ten or a thousand years from now. After all, what comfort could there be in the notion of a Heavenly imposter, walking around getting credit for the few good things I have done?

Miller: I'm sorry. I see that I was simply confused. Here is what I should have said. If you were merely a live human body—as the kleenex box is merely cardboard and glue in a certain arrangement—then the death of your body would be the end of you. But surely you are more than that, fundamentally more than that. What is fundamentally you is not your body, but your soul or self or mind.

Weirob: Do you mean these words, "soul," "self," or "mind" to come to the same thing?

Miller: I have heard fine distinctions made, but usually cannot follow them. They are the nonphysical, nonmaterial, aspects of you. They are your

consciousness. It is this that I get at with these words, and I am not clever enough to attempt any further distinction.

Weirob: Consciousness? I am conscious, for a while yet. I see, I hear, I think, I remember. But "to be conscious"—that is a verb. What is the subject of the verb, the thing which is conscious? Isn't it just this body, the same object that is overweight, injured, and lying in bed? And which will be buried, and not be conscious in a day or a week at the most?

Miller: As you are a philosopher, I would expect you to be less muddled about these issues. Did Descartes not draw a clear distinction between the body and the mind, between that which is overweight and that which is conscious? Your mind or soul is immaterial, lodged while you are on earth in your body. They are intimately related, but not identical. Now clearly, what concerns us in survival is your mind or soul. It is this which must be identical between the person before me now, and the one I expect to see in a thousand years in heaven.

Weirob: So I am not really this body, but a soul or mind or spirit? And this soul cannot be seen or felt or touched or smelt? That is implied, I take it, by the fact that it is immaterial?

Miller: That's right. Your soul sees and smells, but cannot be seen or smelt.

Weirob: Let me see if I understand you. You would admit that I am the very same person with whom you ate lunch last week at Dorsey's?

Miller: Of course you are.

Weirob: Now when you say I am the same person, if I understand you, that is not a remark about this body you see and could touch and I fear can smell. Rather it is a remark about a soul, which you cannot see or touch or smell. The fact that the same body was across the booth from you at Dorsey's as is now lying in front of you on the bed—that would not mean that the same *person* was present on both occasions, if the same soul were not. And if, through some strange turn of events, the same soul were present on both occasions, but lodged in different bodies, then it *would* be the same person. Is that right?

Miller: You have understood me perfectly. But surely, you understood all of this before!

Weirob: But wait. I can repeat it, but I'm not sure I understand it. If you cannot see or touch or in any way perceive my soul, what makes you think the one you are confronted with now *is* the very same soul you were confronted with at Dorsey's?

Miller: But I just explained. To say it is the same soul and to say it is the same person, are the same. And, of course, you are the same person you were before. Who else would you be if not yourself? You *were* Gretchen Weirob, and you *are* Gretchen Weirob.

Weirob: But how do you know you are talking to Gretchen Weirob at all, and not someone else, say Barbara Walters or even Mark Spitz!

Miller: Well, it's just obvious. I can see who I am talking to.

Weirob: But all you can see is my body. You can see, perhaps, that the same body is before you now that was before you last week at Dorsey's. But you have just said that Gretchen Weirob is not a body but a soul. In judging that the same person is before you now as was before you then, you must be making a judgement about souls—which, you said, cannot be seen or touched or smelled or tasted. And so, I repeat, how do you know?

Miller: Well, I *can* see that it is the same body before me now that was across the table at Dorsey's. And I know that the same soul is connected with the body as was connected with it before. That's how I know it's you. I see no difficulty in the matter.

Weirob: You reason on the principle, "same body, same self."

Miller: Yes.

Weirob: And would you reason conversely also? If there were in this bed Barbara Walter's body—that is, the body you see every night on the news—would you infer that it was not me, Gretchen Weirob, in the bed?

Miller: Of course I would. How would you have come by Barbara Walter's body?

Weirob: But then merely extend this principle to Heaven, and you will see that your conception of survival is without sense. Surely this very body, which will be buried and, as I must so often repeat, *rot away,* will not be in your Hereafter. Different body, different person. Or do you claim that a body can rot away on earth, and then still wind up somewhere else? Must I bring up the kleenex box again?

Miller: No, I do not claim that. But I also do not extend a principle, found reliable on earth, to such a different situation as is represented by the Hereafter. That a correlation between bodies and souls has been found on earth, does not make it inconceivable or impossible that they should separate. Principles found to work in one circumstance may not be assumed to work in vastly altered circumstances.

January and snow go together here, and one would be a fool to expect otherwise. But the principle does not apply in California.

Weirob: So the principle, "same body, same soul," is a well-confirmed regularity, not something you know "a priori."

Miller: By "a priori" you philosophers mean something which can be known without observing what actually goes on in the world, as I can know that two plus two equals four just by thinking about numbers, and that no bachelors are married just by thinking about the meaning of "bachelor?"

Weirob: Yes.

Miller: Then you are right. If it was part of the meaning of "same body" that wherever we have the same body, we have the same soul, it would have to obtain universally, in Heaven as well as on earth. But I just claim it is a generalization we know by observation on earth, and it need not automatically extend to Heaven.

Weirob: But where do you get this principle? It simply amounts to a correlation between being confronted with the same body and being confronted with the same soul. To establish such a correlation in the first place, surely one must have some *other* means of judging sameness of soul. You do not have such a means; your principle is without foundation; either you really do not know the person before you now is Gretchen Weirob, the very same person you lunched with at Dorsey's, or what you do know has nothing to do with sameness of some immaterial soul.

Miller: Hold on, hold on. You know I can't follow you when you start spitting out arguments like that. Now what is this terrible fallacy I'm supposed to have committed?

Weirob: I'm sorry. I get carried away. Here, have one of my chocolates by way of a peace offering.

Miller: Very tasty, thank you.

Weirob: Now why did you choose that one?

Miller: Because it had a certain swirl on the top which shows that it is a caramel.

Weirob: That is, a certain sort of swirl is correlated with a certain type of filling—the swirls with caramel, the rosettes with orange, and so forth.

Miller: Yes. When you put it that way, I see an analogy. Just as I judged that the filling would be the same in this piece as in the last piece that I ate with such a swirl, so I judge that the soul with which I am conversing is the same as the last soul with which I conversed when sitting across from that body. We *see* the outer wrapping and infer to what is inside.

Weirob: But how did you come to realize that swirls of that sort and caramel insides were so associated?

Miller: Why from eating a great many of them over the years. Whenever I bit into a candy with that sort of swirl, it was filled with this sort of caramel.

Weirob: Could you have established the correlation had you never been allowed to bite into a candy and never seen what happened when someone else bit into one? You could have formed the hypothesis, "same swirl, same filling." But could you have ever established it?

Miller: It seems not.

Weirob: So your inference, in a particular case, to the identity of filling from the identity of swirl would be groundless?

Miller: Yes, it would. I think I see what is coming.

Weirob: I'm sure you do. Since you can never, so to speak, bite into my soul, can never see or touch it, you have no way of testing your hypothesis that sameness of body means sameness of self.

Miller: I daresay you are right. But now I'm a bit lost. What is supposed to follow from all of this?

Weirob: If identity of persons consisted in identity of immaterial unobservable souls as you claim, then judgements of personal identity of the sort we make every day whenever we greet a friend or avoid a pest are really judgements about such souls.

Miller: Right.

Weirob: But if such judgements were really about souls, they would all be groundless and without foundation. For we have no direct method of observing sameness of soul, and so—and this is the point made by the candy example—can have no indirect method either.

Miller: That seems fair.

Weirob: But our judgements about persons are not all simply groundless and silly, so we must not be judging of immaterial souls after all.

Miller: Your reasoning has some force. But I suspect the problem lies in my defense of my position, and not the position itself. Look here. There *is* a way to test the hypothesis of a correlation after all. When I entered the room, I expected you to react just as you did. Agrumentatively and skeptically. Had the person with this body reacted completely different perhaps I would have been forced to conclude it was not you. For example, had she complained about not being able to appear on the six o'clock news, and missing Harry Reasoner, and so forth, I might have eventually been persuaded it *was* Barbara Walters and not you. Similarity of psychological characteristics, a person's attitudes, beliefs, memories, prejudices, and the like, is observable. These are correlated with identity of body on the one side, and of course with sameness of soul on the other. So the correlation between body and soul can be established after all by this intermediate link.

Weirob: And how do you know that?

Miller: Know what?

Weirob: That where we have sameness of psychological characteristics, we have sameness of soul.

Miller: Well now you are really being just silly. The soul or mind just is that which is responsible for one's character, memory, belief. These are aspects of or states of mind, just as one's height, weight, and appearance are aspects of the body.

Weirob: Let me grant, for the sake of argument, that belief, character, memory, and so forth are states of mind. That is, I suppose, I grant that what one thinks and feels is due to the state one's mind is in at that time. And I shall even grant that a mind is an immaterial thing—though I harbor the gravest doubts that this is so. I do not see how it follows from that, that similarity of such traits requires, or is evidence to the slightest degree, for identity of the mind or soul.

Let me explain my point with an analogy. If we were to walk out of this room, down past the mill and out toward Wilbur, what would we see?

Miller: We would come to the Blue River, among other things.

Weirob: And how would you recognize the Blue River? I mean, of course if you left from here, you would scarcely expect to hit the Platte or Niobrara. But suppose you were actually lost, and came across the Blue River in your wandering, just at that point where an old dam partly blocks the flow. Couldn't you recognize it?

Miller: Yes, I'm sure as soon as I saw that part of the river I would again know where I was.

Weirob: And how would you recognize it?

Miller: Well, the turgid brownness of the water, the sluggish flow, the filth washed up on the banks, and such.

Weirob: In a word, the state of the water which makes up the river at the time you see it.

Miller: Right.

Weirob: If you saw blue clean water, with bass jumping, you would know it wasn't the Blue River.

Miller: Of course.

Weirob: So you expect, each time you see the Blue, to see the water, which makes it up, in similar states—not always exactly the same, for sometimes it's a little dirtier, but by and large, similar.

Miller: Yes, but what do you intend to make of this?

Weirob: Each time you see the Blue, it consists of *different* water. The water that was in it a month ago may be in Tuttle Creek Reservoir, or in the Mississippi, or in the Gulf of Mexico by now. So the *similarity* of states of water, by which you judge the sameness of river, does not require *identity* of the water which is in those states at these various times.

Miller: And?

Weirob: And so just because you judge as to personal identity by reference to similarity of states of mind, it does not follow that the mind, or soul, is the same in each case. My point is this. For all you know, the immaterial soul which you think is lodged in my body might change from day to day, from hour to hour, from minute to minute, replaced each time by another soul psychologically similar. You cannot see it or touch it, so how would you know?

Miller: Are you saying I don't really know who you are?

Weirob: Not at all. *You* are the one who says personal identity consists in sameness of this immaterial, unobservable, invisible, untouchable soul. I merely point out that *if* it did consist in that, you *would* have no idea who I am. Sameness of body would not necessarily mean sameness of person. Sameness of psychological characteristics would not necessarily mean sameness of person. I am saying that if you do know who I am then you are wrong that personal identity consists in sameness of immaterial soul.

Miller: I see. But wait. I believe my problem is that I simply forgot a main tenet of my theory. The correlation can be established in my own case. I know that *my* soul and my body are intimately and consistently found together. From this one case I can generalize, at least as concerns life in this world, that sameness of body is a reliable sign of sameness of soul. This leaves me free to regard it as intelligible, in the case of death, that the link between the particular soul and the particular body it has been joined with is broken.

Weirob: This would be quite an extrapolation, wouldn't it, from one case directly observed, to a couple of billion in which only the body is observed? For I take it that we are in the habit of assuming, for every man now on earth, as well as those who have already come and gone, that the principle "one body, one soul" is in effect.

Miller: This does not seem an insurmountable obstacle. Since there is nothing special about my case, I assume the arrangement I find in it applies universally, until given some reason to believe otherwise. And I never have been.

Weirob: Let's let that pass. I have another problem that is more serious. How is it that you know in your own case that there is a single soul which has been so consistently connected with your body?

Miller: Now you really cannot be serious, Gretchen. How can I doubt that I am the same person I was? Is there anything more clear and distinct, less susceptible to doubt? How do you expect me to prove anything to you, when you are capable of denying my own continued existence from second to second? Without knowledge of our own identity, everything we think and do would be senseless. How could I think if I did not suppose that the person who begins my thought is the one who completes it? When I act, do I not assume that the person who forms the intention is the very one who performs the action?

Weirob: But I grant you that a single *person* has been associated with your body since you were born. The question is whether one immaterial soul has been, or more precisely, whether you are in a position to know it. You believe that a judgement that one and the same person has had your body all these many years is a judgement that one and the same immaterial soul has been lodged in it. I say that such judgements concerning the soul are totally mysterious, and that if our knowledge of sameness of persons consisted in knowledge of sameness of immaterial soul, it too would be totally mysterious. To point out, as you do, that it is not, but perhaps the most secure knowledge we have, the foundation of all reason and action, is simply to make the point that it cannot consist of knowledge of identity of immaterial self.

Miller: You have simply asserted, and not established, that my judgement that a single soul has been lodged in my body these many years is mysterious.

Weirob: Well, consider these possibilities. One is that a single soul, one and the same, has been with this body I call mine since it was born. The other is that one soul was associated with it until five years ago and then another, psychologically similar, inheriting all the memories and beliefs, took over. A third hypothesis is that every five years a new soul takes over. A fourth is that every five minutes a new soul takes over. The most radical is that there is a constant flow of souls through this body, each psychologically similar to the preceding, as there is a constant flow of water molecules down the Blue. What evidence do I have that the first hypothesis, the "single soul hypothesis," is true, and not one of the others? Because I am the same person I was five minutes or five years ago? But the issue in question is simply whether from sameness of person, which isn't in doubt, we can infer sameness of soul. Sameness of body? But how do I establish a stable relationship between soul and body? Sameness of thoughts and sensations? But they are in constant flux. By the nature of the case, if the soul cannot be observed, it cannot be observed to be the same. Indeed, no sense has ever been assigned to the phrase "same soul." Nor could any sense be attached to it! One would have to say what a single soul looked like or felt like, how an encounter with a single soul at different times differed from encounters with different souls. But this can hardly be done, since a soul on your conception doesn't look or feel like *anything* at all. And so of course "souls" can afford no principle of identity. And so they cannot be used to bridge the gulf between my existence now and my existence in the hereafter.

Miller: Do you doubt the existence of your own soul?

Weirob: I haven't based my argument on there being no immaterial souls of the sort you describe, but merely on their total irrelevance to questions of personal identity, and so to questions of personal survival. I do indeed harbor grave doubts whether there are any immaterial souls of the sort to which you appeal. Can we have a notion of a soul unless we have a notion of the *same* soul? But I hope you do not think that means I doubt my own existence. I think I lie here, overweight and conscious. I think you can see me, not just some outer wrapping, for I think I am just a live human body. But that is not the basis of my argument. I give you these souls. I merely observe they can by their nature provide no principle of personal identity.

Miller: I admit I have no answer.

I'm afraid I do not comfort you, though I have perhaps provided you with some entertainment. Emerson said that a little philosophy turns one away from religion, but that deeper understanding brings one back. I know no one who has thought so long and hard about philosophy as you have. Will it never lead you back to a religious frame of mind?

Weirob: My former husband used to say that a little philosophy turns one away from religion, and more philosophy makes one a pain in the neck. Perhaps he was closer to the truth than Emerson.

Miller: Perhaps he was. But perhaps by tomorrow night I will have come up with some argument that will turn you around.

Weirob: I hope I live to hear it.

THE SECOND NIGHT

Weirob: Well, Sam, have you figured out a way to make sense of the identity of immaterial souls?

Miller: No, I have decided it was a mistake to build my argument on such a dubious notion.

Weirob: Have you then given up on survival? I think such a position would be a hard one for a clergyman to be talked into, and would feel bad about having pushed you so far.

Miller: Don't worry. I'm more convinced than ever. I stayed up late last night thinking and reading, and I'm sure I can convince you now.

Weirob: Get with it, time is running out.

Miller: First, let me explain why, independently of my desire to defend survival after death, I am dissatisfied with your view that personal identity is just bodily identity. My argument will be very similar to the one you used to convince me that personal identity could not be identified with identity of an immaterial soul.

Consider a person waking up tomorrow morning, conscious, but not yet ready to open her eyes and look around and, so to speak, let the new day officially begin.

Weirob: Such a state is familiar enough, I admit.

Miller: Now couldn't such a person tell who she was? That is, even before opening her eyes and looking around, and in particular before looking at her body or making any judgements about it, wouldn't she be able to say who she was? Surely most of us, in the morning, know who we are before opening our eyes and recognizing our own bodies, do we not?

Weirob: You seem to be right about that.

Miller: But such a judgement as this person makes—we shall suppose she judges "I am Gretchen Weirob"—is a judgement of personal identity. Suppose she says to herself, "I am the very person who was arguing with Sam Miller last night." This is clearly a statement about her identity with someone who was alive the night before. And she could make this judgement without examining her body at all. You could have made just this judgement this morning, before opening your eyes.

Weirob: Well, in fact I did so. I remembered our conversation of last night and said to myself, "Could I be the rude person who was so hard on Sam Miller's attempts to comfort me?" And, of course, my answer was that I not only could be but was that very rude person.

Miller: But then by the same principle you used last night, personal identity cannot be bodily identity. For you said that it could not be identity of immaterial soul because we were not judging as to identity of immaterial soul when we judge as to personal identity. But by the same token, as my example shows, we are not judging as to bodily identity when we judge as to personal identity. For we can judge who we are, and that we are the very person who did such and such and so and so, without having to make any judgements at all about the body. So, personal identity, while it may not consist of identity of an immaterial soul, does not consist in identity of material body either.

Weirob: I did argue as you remember. But I also said that the notion of the identity of an immaterial, unobservable, unextended soul seemed to make no sense at all. This is one reason such souls cannot be what we are judging about, when we judge as to personal identity. Bodily identity at least makes sense. Perhaps we are just assuming sameness of body, without looking.

Miller: Granted. But you do admit that we do not in our own cases need to actually make a judgement of bodily identity in order to make a judgement of personal identity.

Weirob: I don't think I will admit it. I will let it pass, so that we may proceed.

Miller: OK. Now it seems to me we are even able to imagine awakening and finding ourselves to have a *different* body than the one we had before. Suppose yourself just as I have described you. And now suppose you finally open your eyes and see, not the body you have grown so familiar with over the years, but one of a fundamentally different shape and size.

Weirob: Well I should suppose I had been asleep for a very long time and lost a lot of weight—perhaps I was in a coma for a year or so.

Miller: But isn't it at least conceivable that it

should not be your old body at all? I seem to be able to imagine awakening with a totally new body.

Weirob: And how would you suppose that this came about?

Miller: That's beside the point. I'm not saying I can imagine a procedure that would bring this about. I'm saying I can imagine it happening to me. In Kafka's *The Metamorphosis,* someone awakens as a cockroach. I can't imagine what would make this happen to me or anyone else, but I can imagine awakening with the body of a cockroach. It is incredible that it should happen—that I do not deny. I simply mean I can imagine experiencing it. It doesn't seem contradictory or incoherent, simply unlikely and inexplicable.

Weirob: So, if I admit this can be imagined, what follows then?

Miller: Well, I think it follows that personal identity does not just amount to bodily identity. For I would not, finding that I had a new body, conclude that I was not the very same person I was before. I would be the same *person,* though I did not have the same *body.* So we would have identity of person but not identity of body. So personal identity cannot just amount to bodily identity.

Weirob: Well, suppose—and I emphasize *suppose*—I grant you all of this. Where does it leave you? What do you claim I have recognized as the same, if not my body and not my immaterial soul?

Miller: I don't claim that you have recognized anything as the same, except the person involved, that is, you yourself.

Weirob: I'm not sure what you mean.

Miller: Let me appeal again to the Blue River. Suppose I take a visitor to the stretch of river by the old Mill, and then drive him toward Manhattan. After an hour or so drive we see another stretch of river, and I say, "That's the same river we saw this morning." As you pointed out yesterday, I don't thereby imply that the very same molecules of water are seen both times. And the places are different, perhaps a hundred miles apart. And the shape and color and level of pollution might all be different. What do I see later in the day that is identical with what I saw earlier in the day?

Weirob: Nothing, except the river itself.

Miller: Exactly. But now notice that what I see, strictly speaking, is not the whole river but only a part of it. I see different parts of the same river at the two different times. So really, if we restrict ourselves to what I literally see, I do not judge identity at all, but something else.

Weirob: And what might that be?

Miller: In saying that the river seen earlier and the river seen later are one and the same river, do I mean any more than that the stretch of water seen later and that stretch of water seen earlier are connected by other stretches of water?

Weirob: That's about right. If the stretches of water are so connected, there is but one river of which they are both parts.

Miller: Yes, that's what I mean. The statement of identity, "This river is the same one we saw this morning," is in a sense about rivers. But in a way it is also about stretches of water or river parts.

Weirob: So, is all of this something special about rivers?

Miller: Not at all. It is a recurring pattern. After all, we constantly deal with objects extended in space and time. But we are seldom aware of the objects as a whole, but only of their parts or stretches of their histories. When a statement of identity is not just something trivial, like "This bed is this bed," it is usually because we are really judging that different parts fit together, in some appropriate pattern, into a certain kind of whole.

Weirob: I'm not sure I see just what you mean yet.

Miller: Let me give you another example. Suppose we are sitting together watching the first game of a doubleheader. You ask me, "Is this game identical with this game?" This is a perfectly stupid question, though, of course, strictly speaking it makes sense and the answer is "yes."

But now suppose you leave in the sixth inning to go for hot dogs. You are delayed, and return after about forty-five minutes or so. You ask, "Is this the same game I was watching?" Now your question is not stupid, but perfectly appropriate.

Weirob: Because the first game might still be going on or it might have ended, and the second game begun, by the time I return.

Miller: Exactly. Which is to say somehow different parts of the game—different innings, or at least different plays—were somehow involved in your question. That's why it wasn't stupid or trivial but significant.

Weirob: So, you think that judgements as to the identity of an object of a certain kind—rivers or base-

ball games or whatever—involve judgements as to the *parts* of those things being connected in a certain way, and are significant only when different parts are involved. Is that your point?

Miller: Yes, and I think it is an important one. How foolish it would be, when we ask a question about the identity of baseball games, to look for something *else*, other than the game as a whole, which had to be the same. It could be the same game, even if different players were involved. It could be the same game, even if it had been moved to a different field. These other things, the innings, the plays, the players, the field, don't have to be the same at the different times for the game to be the same, they just have to be related in certain ways so as to make that complex whole we call a single game.

Weirob: You think we were going off on a kind of wild goose chase when we asked whether it was the identity of soul or body that was involved in the identity of persons?

Miller: Yes. The answer I should now give is neither. We are wondering about the identity of the person. Of course, if by "soul" we just mean "person," there is no problem. But if we mean, as I did yesterday, some other thing whose identity is already understood, which has to be the same when persons are the same, we are just fooling ourselves with words.

Weirob: With rivers and baseball games, I can see that they are made up of parts connected in a certain way. The connection is, of course, different in the two cases, as is the sort of "part" involved. River parts must be connected physically with other river parts to form a continuous whole. Baseball innings must be connected so that the score, batting order, and the like are carried over from the earlier inning to the latter one according to the rules. Is there something analagous we are to say about persons?

Miller: Writers who concern themselves with this speak of "person-stages." That is just a stretch of consciousness, such as you and I are aware of now. I am aware of a flow of thoughts and feelings that are mine, you are aware of yours. A person is just a whole composed of such stretches as parts, not some substance that underlies them, as I thought yesterday, and not the body in which they occur, as you seem to think. That is the conception of a person I wish to defend today.

Weirob: So when I awoke and said to myself, "I am the one who was so rude to Sam Miller last night,'' I was judging that a certain stretch of consciousness I was then aware of, and an earlier one I remembered having been aware of, form a single whole of the appropriate sort—a single stream of consciousness, we might say.

Miller: Yes, that's it exactly. You need not worry about whether the same immaterial soul is involved, or whether that even makes sense. Nor need you worry about whether the same body is involved, as indeed you do not since you don't even have to open your eyes and look. Identity is not, so to speak, something under the person-stages, nor in something they are attached to, but something you build from them.

Now survival, you can plainly see, is no problem at all once we have this conception of personal identity. All you need suppose is that there is, in Heaven, a conscious being, and that the person-stages that make her up are in the appropriate relation to those that now make you up, so that they are parts of the same whole—namely, you. If so, you have survived. So will you admit now that survival is at least possible?

Weirob: Hold on, hold on. Comforting me is not that easy. You will have to show that it is possible that these person-stages or stretches of consciousness be related in the appropriate way. And to do that, won't you have to tell me what that way is?

Miller: Yes, of course, I was getting ahead of myself. It is right at this point that my reading was particularly helpful. In a chapter of his *Essay on Human Understanding* Locke discusses this very question. He suggests that the relation between two person-stages or stretches of consciousness that makes them stages of a single person is just that the later one contains memories of the earlier one. He doesn't say this in so many words—he talks of ''extending our consciousness back in time.'' But he seems to be thinking of memory.

Weirob: So, any past thought or feeling or intention or desire that I can remember having is mine?

Miller: That's right. I can remember only my own past thoughts and feelings, and you only yours. Of course, everyone would readily admit that. Locke's insight is to take this relation as the source of identity and not just its consequence. To remember—or more plausibly, to be able to remember—the thoughts and feelings of a person who was conscious in the past is just what it is to be that person.

Now you can easily see that this solves the problem of the possibility of survival. As I was saying, all you need to do is imagine someone at some future time, not on this earth and not with your present thoughts and feelings, remembering the very conversation we are having now. This does not require sameness of anything else, but it amounts to sameness of person. So, now will you admit it?

Weirob: No, I don't.

Miller: Well, what's the problem now?

Weirob: I admit that if I remember having a certain thought or feeling had by some person in the past, then I must indeed be that person. Though I can remember watching others think, I cannot remember their thinking, any more than I can experience it at the time it occurs if it is theirs and not mine. This is the kernel of Locke's idea, and I don't see that I could deny it.

But we must distinguish—as I'm sure you will agree—between *actually* remembering and merely *seeming* to remember. Many men who think that they are Napoleon claim to remember losing the battle of Waterloo. We may suppose them to be sincere, and to really seem to remember it. But, they do not actually remember, because they were not there and are not Napoleon.

Miller: Of course, I admit that we must distinguish between actually remembering and only seeming to.

Weirob: And you will admit too, I trust, that the thought of some person at some far place and some distant time seeming to remember this conversation I am having with you would not give me the sort of comfort that the prospect of survival is supposed to provide. I would have no reason to anticipate future experiences of this person, simply because she is to *seem* to remember my experiences. The experiences of such a deluded imposter are not ones I can look forward to having.

Miller: I agree.

Weirob: So, the mere possibility of someone in the future seeming to remember this conversation does not show the possibility of my surviving. Only the possibility of someone actually remembering this conversation—or, to be precise, the experiences I am having—would show that.

Miller: Of course. But what are you driving at? Where is the problem? I can imagine someone being deluded, but also someone actually being you and remembering your present thoughts.

Weirob: But, what's the difference? How do you know *which* of the two you are imagining, and *what* you have shown possible?

Miller: Well, I just imagine the one and not the other. I don't see the force of your argument.

Weirob: Let me try to make it clear with another example. Imagine two persons. One is talking to you, saying certain words, having certain thoughts, and so on. The other is not talking to you at all, but is in the next room being hypnotized. The hypnotist gives to this person a posthypnotic suggestion that upon awakening he will remember having had certain thoughts and having uttered certain words to you. The thoughts and words he mentions happen to be just the thoughts and words which the first person actually thinks and says. Do you understand the situation?

Miller: Yes, continue.

Weirob: Now, in a while, both of the people are saying sentences which begin, "I remember saying to Sam Miller . . ." and "I remember thinking as I talked to Sam Miller . . ." And they both report remembering just the same thoughts and utterances. One of these will be remembering and the other only seeming to remember, right?

Miller: Of course.

Weirob: Now, which one is *actually* remembering?

Miller: Why the very one who was in the room talking to me, of course. The other one is just under the influence of the suggestion made by the hypnotist and not remembering talking to me at all.

Weirob: Now you agree that the difference between them does not consist in the content of what they are now thinking or saying.

Miller: Agreed. The difference is in the relation to the past thinking and speaking. In the one case the relation of memory obtains. In the other, it does not.

Weirob: But they both satisfy part of the conditions of remembering, for they both *seem to remember.* So there must be some further condition that the one satisfies and the other does not. I am trying to get you to say what that further condition is.

Miller: Well, I said that the one who had been in this room talking would be remembering.

Weirob: In other words, given two putative rememberers of some past thought or action, the real rememberer is the one who, in addition to seeming to remember the past thought or action, actually thought it or did it.

Miller: Yes.

Weirob: That is to say, the one who is identical with the person who did the past thinking and uttering.

Miller: Yes, I admit it.

Weirob: So, your argument just amounts to this. Survival is possible, because imaginable. It is imaginable, because my identity with some Heavenly person is imaginable. To imagine it, we imagine a person in Heaven who, first, seems to remember my thoughts and actions, and second, is me.

Surely, there could hardly be a tighter circle. If I have doubts that the Heavenly person is me, I will have doubts as to whether she is really remembering or only seeming to. No one could doubt the possibility of some future person who, after his or her death, seemed to remember the things he or she thought and did. But that possibility does not resolve the issue about the possibility of survival. Only the possibility of someone *actually* remembering could do that, for that, as we agree, is sufficient for identity. But doubts about survival and identity simply go over without remainder into doubts about whether the memories would be actual or merely apparent. You guarantee me no more than the possibility of a deluded Heavenly imposter.

Cohen: But wait, Gretchen. I think Sam was less than fair to his own idea just now.

Weirob: You think you can break out of the circle of using real memory to explain identity, and identity to mark the difference between real and apparent memory? Feel free to try.

Cohen: Let us return to your case of the hypnotist. You point out that we have two putative rememberers. You ask what marks the difference, and claim the answer must be the circular one that the real rememberer is the person who actually had the experiences both seem to remember.

But that is not the only possible answer. The experiences themselves cause the later apparent memories in the one case, the hypnotist causes them in the other. We can say that the rememberer is the one of the two whose memories were *caused in the right way* by the earlier experiences. We thus distinguish between the rememberer and the hypnotic subject, without appeal to identity.

The idea that real memory amounts to apparent memory plus identity is misleading anyway. I seem to remember knocking over the menorah so the candles fell into and ruined a tureen of soup when I was a small child. And I did actually perform such a feat. So we have apparent memory and identity. But I do *not* actually remember; I was much too young when I did this to remember it now. I have simply been told the story so often I seem to remember.

Here the suggestion that real memory is apparent memory that was caused in the appropriate way by the past events fares better. Not my experience of pulling over the menorah, but my parents' later recounting of the tragedy, cause my memory-like impressions.

Weirob: You analyze personal identity into memory, and memory into apparent memory which is caused in the right way. A person is a certain sort of causal process.

Cohen: Right.

Weirob: Suppose now for the sake of argument I accept this. How does it help Sam in his defense of the possibility of survival? In ordinary memory, the causal chain from remembered event to memory of it never leads us outside the confines of a single body. Indeed, the normal process of which you speak surely involves storage of information somehow in the brain. How can the states of my brain, when I die, influence in the appropriate way the apparent memories of the Heavenly person Sam takes to be me?

Cohen: Well, I didn't intend to be defending the possibility of survival. That is Sam's problem. I just like the idea that personal identity can be explained in terms of memory, and not just in terms of identity of the body.

Miller: But surely, this does provide me with the basis for further defense. Your challenge, Gretchen, was to explain the difference between two persons in Heaven, one who actually remembers your experience—and so is you—and one who simply seems to remember it. But can I not just say that the one who is you is the one whose states were caused in the appropriate way? I do not mean the way they would be in a normal case of earthly memory. But in the case of the Heavenly being who is you, God would have created her with the brain states (or whatever) she has *because* you had the ones you had at death. Surely it is not the exact form of the dependence of my later memories on my earlier perceptions that makes them really to be memories, but the fact that the process involved has preserved information.

Weirob: So if God creates a Heavenly person, designing her brain to duplicate the brain I have upon death, that person is me. If, on the other hand, a Heavenly being should come to be with those very same memory-like states by accident (if there are accidents in Heaven) it would not be me.

Miller: Exactly. Are you satisfied now that survival makes perfectly good sense?

Weirob: No, I'm still quite unconvinced.

The problem I see is this. If God could create one person in Heaven, and by designing her after me, make her me, why could He not make two such bodies, and cause this transfer of information into both of them? Would both of these Heavenly persons then be me? It seems as clear as anything in philosophy that from

A is B

and

C is B

where by "is" we mean identity, we can infer,

A is C.

So, if each of these Heavenly persons is me, they must be each other. But then they are not two but one. But my assumption was that God creates two, not one. He could create them physically distinct, capable of independent movement, perhaps in widely separated Heavenly locations, each with her own duties to perform, her own circle of Heavenly friends, and the like.

So either God, by creating a Heavenly person with a brain modeled after mine does not really create someone identical with me but merely someone similar to me, or God is somehow limited to making only one such being. I can see no reason why, if there were a God, He should be so limited. So I take the first option. He could create someone similar to me, but not someone who would *be* me. Either your analysis of memory is wrong, and such a being does not, after all, remember what I am doing or saying, or memory is not sufficient for personal identity. Your theory has gone wrong somewhere, for it leads to absurdity.

Cohen: But wait. Why can't Sam simply say that if God makes one such creature, she is you, while if He makes more, none of them are you? It's possible that He makes only one. So it's possible that you survive. Sam always meant to allow that it's *possible* that you won't survive. He had in mind the case in which there is no God to make the appropriate Heavenly persons, or God exists, but just doesn't make even one. You have simply shown that there is another way of not surviving. Instead of making too few Heavenly rememberers, He makes too many.

So what? He might make the right number, and then you would survive.

Weirob: Your remarks really amount to a change in your position. Now you are not claiming that memory alone is enough for personal identity. Now, it is memory *plus* lack of competition, the absence of other rememberers, that is needed for personal identity.

Cohen: It does amount to a change of position. But what of it? Is there anything untenable about the position as changed?

Weirob: Let's look at this from the point of view of the Heavenly person. She says to herself, "Oh, I must be Gretchen Weirob, for I remember doing what she did and saying what she said." But now that's a pretty tenuous conclusion, isn't it? She is really only entitled to say, "Oh, either I'm Gretchen Weirob, or God has created more than one being like me, and none of us are." Identity has become something dependent on things wholly extrinsic to her. Who she is now turns on not just her states of mind and their relation to my states of mind, but on the existence or nonexistence of other people. Is this really what you want to maintain?

Or look at it from my point of view. God creates one of me in Heaven. Surely I should be glad if convinced this was to happen. Now He creates another, and I should despair again, for this means I won't survive after all. How can doubling a good deed make it worthless?

Cohen: Are you saying that there is some contradiction in my suggestion that only a unique Heavenly Gretchen counts as your survival?

Weirob: No, it's not contradictory, as far as I can see. But it seems odd in a way that shows that something somewhere is wrong with your theory. Here is a certain relationship I have with a Heavenly person. There being such a person, to whom I am related in this way, is something that is of great importance to me, a source of comfort. It makes it appropriate for me to anticipate having her experiences, since she is just me. Why should my having that relation to another being destroy my relation to this one? You say because then I will not be identical with either of them. But since you have provided a theory about what that identity consists in, we can look and see what it amounts to for me to be or not to be identical. If she is to remember my experience, I can rightly anticipate hers. But then it seems the doubling makes no difference. And yet it must, for one cannot

be identical with two. So you add, in a purely *ad hoc* manner, that her memory of me isn't enough to make my anticipation of her experiences appropriate, if there are two rather than one so linked. Isn't it more reasonable to conclude, since memory does not secure identity when there are two Heavenly Gretchens, it also doesn't when there is only one?

Cohen: There is something *ad hoc* about it, I admit. But perhaps that's just the way our concept works. You have not elicited a contradiction . . .

Weirob: An infinite pile of absurdities has the same weight as a contradiction. And absurdities can be generated from your account without limit. Suppose God created this Heavenly person before I died. Then He in effect kills me; if He has already created her, then you really are not talking to whom you think, but someone new, created by Gretchen Weirob's strange death moments ago. Or suppose He first creates one being in Heaven, who is me. Then He created another. Does the first cease to be me? If God can create such beings in Heaven, surely He can do so in Albuquerque. And there is nothing on your theory to favor this body before you as Gretchen Weirob's, over the one belonging to the person created in Albuquerque. So I am to suppose that if God were to do this, I would suddenly cease to be. I'm tempted to say I would cease to be Gretchen Weirob. But that would be a confused way of putting it. There would be here, in my place, a new person with false memories of having been Gretchen Weirob, who has just died of competition—a strange death, if ever there was one. She would have no right to my name, my bank account, or the services of my doctor, who is paid from insurance premiums paid for by deductions from Gretchen Weirob's past salary. Surely this is nonsense; however carefully God should choose to duplicate me, in Heaven or in Albuquerque, I would not cease to be, or cease to be who I am. You may reply that God, being benevolent, would never create an extra Gretchen Weirob. But I do not say that He would, but only that if He did this would not, as your theory implies, mean that I cease to exist. Your theory gives the wrong answer in this possible circumstance, so it must be wrong. I think I have been given no motivation to abandon the most obvious and straightforward view on these matters. I am a live body, and when that body dies, my existence will be at an end.

THE THIRD NIGHT

Weirob: Well, Sam, are you here for a third attempt to convince me of the possibility of survival?

Miller: No, I have given up. I suggest we talk about fishing or football or something unrelated to your imminent demise. You will outwit any straightforward attempts to comfort you, but perhaps I can at least divert your mind.

Cohen: But before we start on fishing . . . although I don't have any particular brief for survival, there is one point in our discussion of the last two evenings that still bothers me. Would you mind discussing for a while the notion of personal identity itself, without worrying about the more difficult case of survival after death?

Weirob: I would enjoy it. What point bothers you?

Cohen: Your position seems to be that personal identity amounts to identity of a human body, nothing more, nothing less. A person is just a live human body, or more precisely, I suppose, a human body that is alive and has certain capacities—consciousness and perhaps rationality. Is that right?

Weirob: Yes, it seems that simple to me.

Cohen: But I think there has actually been an episode which disproves that. I am thinking of the strange case of Julia North, which occurred in California a few months ago. Surely you remember it.

Weirob: Yes, only too well. But you had better explain it to Sam, for I'll wager he has not heard of it.

Cohen: Not heard of Julia North? But the case was all over the headlines.

Miller: Well, Gretchen is right. I know nothing of it. She knows that I only read the sports page.

Cohen: You only read the sports page!

Weirob: It's an expression of his unconcern with earthly matters.

Miller: Well, that's not quite fair, Gretchen. It's a matter of preference. I much prefer to spend what time I have for reading in reading about the eighteenth century, rather than the drab and miserable century into which I had the misfortune to be born. It was really a much more civilized century, you know. But let's not dwell on my peculiar habits. Tell me about Julia North.

Cohen: Very well. Julia North was a young woman who was run over by a street car while saving the life of a young child who wandered onto the tracks. The child's mother, one Mary Frances Beaudine, had a stroke while watching the horrible scene. Julia's healthy brain and wasted body, and Mary Frances' healthy body and wasted brain, were transported to a hospital where a brilliant neurosurgeon, Dr. Matthews, was in residence. He had worked out a procedure for what he called a "body transplant." He removed the brain from Julia's head and placed it in Mary Frances', splicing the nerves, etc., using techniques not available until quite recently. The survivor of all this was obviously Julia, as everyone agreed—except, unfortunately, Mary Frances' husband. His shortsightedness and lack of imagination led to great complications and drama and made the case more famous in the history of crime than in the history of medicine. I shall not go into the details of this sorry aspect of the case—they are well reported in a book by Barbara Harris called *Who Is Julia?*, in case you are interested.

Miller: Fascinating!

Cohen: Well, the relevance of this case is obvious. Julia North had one body up until the time of the accident, and another body after the operation. So one person had two bodies. So a person cannot be simply *identified* with a human body. So something must be wrong with your view, Gretchen. What do you say to this?

Weirob: I'll say to you just what I said to Dr. Matthews . . .

Cohen: You have spoken with Dr. Matthews?

Weirob: Yes. He contacted me shortly after my accident. My physician had phoned him up about my case. Matthews said he could perform the same operation for me he did for Julia North. I refused.

Cohen: You refused! But Gretchen, why. . .?

Miller: Gretchen, I *am* shocked. Your decision practically amounts to suicide! You passed up an opportunity to continue living? Why on earth . . .?

Weirob: Hold on, hold on. You are both making an assumption I reject. If the case of Julia North amounts to a counterexample to my view that a person is just a live human body, and if my refusal to submit to this procedure amounts to passing up an option to survive, then the survivor of such an operation must be reckoned as the same person as the brain donor. That is, the survivor of Julia North's operation must have been Julia, and the survivor of the operation on me would have to be me. This is the assumption you both make in criticizing me. But I reject it. I think Jack Beaudine was right. The survivor of the operation involving Julia North's brain was Mary Frances Beaudine, and the survivor of the operation which was to involve my brain would not have been me.

Miller: Gretchen, how on earth can you say that? Will you not give up your view that personal identity is just bodily identity, no matter how clear the counterexample? I really think you simply have an irrational attachment to the lump of material that is your body.

Cohen: Yes, Gretchen, I agree with Sam. You are being preposterous! The survivor of Julia North's operation had no idea who Mary Frances Beaudine was. She remembered being Julia . . .

Weirob: She *seemed* to remember being Julia. Have you forgotten so quickly the importance of this distinction? In my opinion, the effect of the operation was that Mary Frances Beaudine survived deluded, thinking she was someone else.

Cohen: But as you know, the case was litigated. It went to the Supreme Court. They said that the survivor was Julia.

Weirob: That argument is unworthy of you, Dave. Is the Supreme Court infallible?

Cohen: No, they aren't. But I don't think it's such a stupid point.

Look at it this way, Gretchen. This is a case in which two criteria we use to make judgements of identity conflict. Usually we expect personal identity to involve both bodily identity and psychological continuity. That is, we expect that if we have the same body, then the beliefs, memories, character traits and the like also will be enormously similar. In this case, these two criteria which usually coincide do not. If we choose one criterion, we say that the survivor is Mary Frances Beaudine and she has undergone drastic psychological changes. If we choose the other, we say that Julia has survived with a new body. We have to choose which criterion is more important. It's a matter of choice of how to use our language, how to extend the concept "same person" to a new situation. The overwhelming majority of people involved in the case took the survivor to be Julia. That is, society chose to use the concept one way rather than the other. The Supreme Court is *not* beside the point. One of their functions is to settle just how old concepts shall be applied to new circumstances—how "freedom of the press" is to be understood when applied to movies or television, whose existence was not foreseen when the concept was shaped, or to say whether "murder" is to include the abortion of a foetus. They are fallible on points of fact, but they are the final authority on the development of certain important concepts used in law. The notion of *person* is such a concept.

Weirob: You think that *who* the survivor was, was a matter of convention, of how we choose to use language?

Cohen: Yes.

Weirob: I can show the preposterousness of all that with an example.

Let us suppose that I agree to the operation. I lie in bed, expecting my continued existence, anticipating the feelings and thoughts I shall have upon awakening after the operation. Dr. Matthews enters and asks me to take several aspirin, so as not to have a headache when I awake. I protest that aspirins upset my stomach; he asks whether I would have a terrible headache tomorrow or a mild stomachache now, and I agree that it would be reasonable to take them.

Let us suppose you enter at this point with bad news. The Supreme Court has changed its mind! So the survivor will not be me. So, I say, "Oh, then I will not take the aspirin, for it's not me that will have a headache, but someone else. Why should I endure a stomachache, however mild, for the comfort of someone else? After all, I am already donating my brain to that person."

Now this is clearly absurd. If I was correct, in the first place, to anticipate having the sensations and thoughts that the survivor is to have the next day, the decision of nine old men a thousand or so miles away wouldn't make me wrong. And if I was wrong so to anticipate, their decision couldn't make me right. How can the correctness of my anticipation of survival be a matter of the way we use our words? If it is not such a matter, then my identity is not either. My identity with the survivor, my survival, is a question of fact, not of convention.

Cohen: Your example is persuasive. I admit I am befuddled. On the one hand, I cannot see how the matter can be other than I have described. When we know all the facts what can remain to be decided but how we are to describe them, how we are to use our language? And yet I can see that it seems absurd to suppose that the correctness or incorrectness of anticipation of future experience is a matter for convention to decide.

Miller: Well, I didn't think the business about convention was very plausible anyway. But I should like to return you to the main question, Gretchen. Fact or convention, it still remains. Why will you not admit that the survivor of this operation would be you?

Weirob: Well, *you* tell *me,* why do you think she would be me?

Miller: I can appeal to the theory I developed last night. You argued that the idea that personal identity consists in memory would not guarantee the possibility of survival after death. But you said nothing to shake its plausibility as an account of personal identity. It has the enormous advantage, remember, of making sense of our ability to judge our own identity, without examination of our bodies. I should argue that it is the correctness of this theory that explains the *almost* universal willingness to say that the survivor of Julia's operation was Julia. We need not deliberate over how to extend our concept, we need only apply the concept we already have. Memory is sufficient for identity and bodily identity is *not* necessary for it. The survivor remembered Julia's thoughts and actions, and so was Julia. Would you but submit to the operation, the survivor would remember your thoughts and actions, would remember this very conversation we are now having, and would be you.

Cohen: Yes, I now agree completely with Sam. The theory that personal identity is to be analyzed in terms of memory is correct, and according to it you will survive if you submit to the operation.

Let me add another argument against your view and in favor of the memory theory. You have emphasized that identity is the condition of *anticipation.* That means, among other things, that we have a particular concern for that person in the future whom we take to be ourselves. If I were told that any of the three of us were to suffer pain tomorrow, I should be sad. But if it were you or Sam that were to be hurt, my concern would be altruistic or unselfish. That is because I would not anticipate having the painful experience myself. Here I do no more than repeat points you have made earlier in our conversations.

Now what is there about mere sameness of body that makes sense of this asymmetry, between the way we look at our own futures, and the way we look at the futures of others? In other words, why is the identity of your body—that mere lump of matter, as Sam put it—of such great importance? Why care so much about it?

Weirob: You say, and I surely agree, that identity of person is a very special relationship—so special as perhaps not even happily called a relationship at all. And you say that since my theory is that identity of person is identity of body, I should be able to explain the importance of the one in terms of the importance of the other.

I'm not sure I can do that. But does the theory that personal identity consists in memory fare better on this score?

Cohen: Well, I think it does. Those properties of persons which make persons of such great value, and mark their individuality, and make one person so special to his friends and loved ones, are ultimately psychological or mental. One's character, personality, beliefs, attitudes, convictions—they are what make every person so unique and special. A skinny Gretchen would be a shock to us all, but not a Gretchen diminished in any important way. But a Gretchen who was not witty, or not gruff, or not as honest to the path an argument takes as is humanly possible—those would be fundamental changes. Is it any wonder that the survivor of that California fiasco was reckoned as Julia North? Would it make sense to take her to be Mary Jane Beaudine, when she had none of her beliefs or attitudes or memories?

Now if such properties are what is of importance about a person to others, is it not reasonable that they are the basis of one's importance to oneself? And these are just the properties that personal identity preserves when it is taken to consist in links of memory. Do we not have, in this idea, at least the beginning of an explanation of the importance of identity?

Weirob: So on two counts you two favor the memory theory. First, you say it explains how it is possible to judge as to one's own identity, without having to examine one's body. Second, you say it explains the importance of personal identity.

Cohen: Now surely you must agree the memory theory is correct. Do you agree? There may still be time to contact Dr. Matthews . . .

Weirob: Hold on, hold on. I'm still not persuaded. Granted the survivor will *think* she is me, will *seem* to remember thinking my thoughts. But recall the importance of distinguishing between real and merely apparent memory . . .

Cohen: But *you* recall that this distinction is to be made on the basis of whether the apparent memories were or were not caused by the prior experiences in the appropriate way. The survivor will not seem to remember your thoughts because of hypnosis or by coincidence or overweening imagination. She will seem to remember them because the traces those experiences left on your brain now activate her mind in the usual way. She will seem to remember them because she does remember them, and will be you.

Weirob: Let's go over this slowly. We all argue

that the fact that the survivor of this strange operation Dr. Matthews proposes would *seem* to remember doing what I have done. Let us even suppose she would take herself to be me, claim to be Gretchen Weirob—and have no idea who else she might be. (We are then assuming that she differs from me in one aspect—her theory of personal identity. But that does not show her not to be me, for I could change my mind by then.) We all first agree that this much does not make her me. For this could all be true of someone suffering a delusion or a subject of hypnosis.

Cohen: Yes, this is all agreed.

Weirob: But now you think that some *further* condition is satisfied, which makes her apparent memories *real* memories. Now what exactly is this further condition?

Cohen: Well, that the same brain was involved in the perception of the events, and their later *memory.* Thus a causal chain of just the same sort as when only a single body is involved is involved here. That is, perceptions when the event occurs leave a trace in the brain, which is later responsible for the content of the memory. And we agreed, did we not, that apparent memory, caused in the right way, is real memory?

Weirob: Now is it absolutely crucial that the same brain is involved?

Cohen: What do you mean?

Weirob: Let me explain again by reference to Dr. Matthews. In our conversation he explained a new procedure on which he was working called a *brain rejuvenation.* By this process, which is not yet available—only the feasibility of developing it is being studied—a new brain could be made which is an exact duplicate of my brain. That is, an exact duplicate in terms of psychologically relevant states. It might not duplicate all the properties of my brain; for example, the blood vessels in the new brain might be stronger than in the old brain.

Miller: What is the point of developing such a macabre technique?

Weirob: Dr. Matthews' idea is that when weaknesses which might lead to stroke or other brain injury are noted, a healthy duplicate could be made, and replace the original, forestalling the problem.

Now Dave, suppose my problem were not with my liver and kidneys and such, but with my brain. Would you recommend such an operation as to my benefit?

Cohen: You mean, do I think the survivor of such an operation would be you?

Weirob: Exactly. You may assume that Dr. Matthews' technique works perfectly so the causal process involved is no less reliable than that involved in ordinary memory.

Cohen: Then I would say it was you . . . No! Wait! No, it wouldn't be you. Absolutely not!

Miller: But why the sudden reversal? It seems to me it would be her. Indeed, I should try such an operation myself, if it would clear up my dizzy spells and leave me otherwise unaffected.

Cohen: No, don't you see, she is leading us into a false trap. If we say it *is* her, then she will say, "Then what if he makes two duplicates, or three or ten? They can't all be me, they all have an equal claim, so none will be me." It would be the argument of last night, reapplied on earth. So the answer is no, absolutely not, it wouldn't be you. Duplication of self does not preserve identity. Identity of the person requires identity of the brain.

Miller: Quite right.

Weirob: Now let me see if I have your theory straight. Suppose we have two bodies, A and B. My brain is put into A, a duplicate into B. The survivor of this, call them "A-Gretchen" and "B-Gretchen," both seem to remember giving this very speech. Both are in this state of seeming to remember, as the last stage in an information-preserving causal chain, initiated by my giving this speech. Both have my character, personality, beliefs, and the like. But one is *really* remembering, the other is not. A-Gretchen is really me, B-Gretchen is not.

Cohen: Precisely. Is this incoherent?

Weirob: No, I guess there is nothing incoherent about it. But look what has happened to the advantages you claimed for the memory theory.

First, you said, it explains how I can know who I am without opening my eyes and recognizing my body. But in your theory Gretchen-A and Gretchen-B cannot know who they are even if they do open their eyes and examine their bodies. How is Gretchen-A to know whether she has the original brain and is who she seems to be, or has the duplicate and is a new person, only a few minutes old, and with no memories but my delusions? If the hospital kept careless records, or the surgeon thought it was of no great importance to keep track of who got the original and who got the duplicate, she might never know who she was. By making identity of person turn into identity of brain, your theory makes the ease with which I can determine who I am not less, but more mysterious than my theory.

Second, you said, your theory explains why my concern for Gretchen-A, who is me whether she knows it or not, would be selfish, and my anticipation of her experience correct while my concern for Gretchen-B with her duplicated brain would be unselfish, and my anticipation of having her experiences incorrect. And it explains this, you said, because by insisting on the links of memory, we preserve in personal identity more psychological characteristics which are the most important features of a person.

But Gretchen-A and Gretchen-B are psychologically indistinguishable. Though they will go their separate ways, at the moment of awakening they could well be exactly similar in every psychological respect. In terms of character and belief and the contents of their minds, Gretchen-A is no more like me than Gretchen-B. So there is nothing in your theory after all, to explain why anticipation is appropriate when we have identity, and not otherwise.

You said, Sam, that I had an irrational attachment for this unworthy material object, my body. But you too are as irrationally attached to your brain. I have never seen my brain. I should have easily given it up, for a rejuvenated version, had that been the choice with which I was faced. I have never seen it, never felt it, and have no attachment to it. But my body? That seems to me all that I am. I see no point in trying to evade its fate.

Perhaps I miss the merit of your arguments. I am tired, and perhaps my poor brain, feeling slighted, has begun to desert me . . .

Cohen: Oh don't worry Gretchen, you are still clever. Again you have left me befuddled. I don't know what to say. But answer me this. Suppose you are right and we are wrong. But suppose these arguments had not occurred to you, and, sharing in our error, you had agreed to the operation. You anticipate the operation until it happens, thinking you will survive. You are happy. The survivor takes herself to be you, and thinks she made a decision before the operation which has now turned out to be right. She is happy. Your friends are happy. Who would be worse off, either before or after the operation?

Suppose even that you realize identity would not be preserved by such an operation but have it done anyway, and as the time for the operation approaches, you go ahead and anticipate the experiences of the survivor. Where exactly is the mistake? Do you really have any less reason to care for the survivor than for yourself? Can mere identity of body, the lack of which alone keeps you from being her, mean that much? Perhaps we were wrong, after all, in focusing on identity as the necessary condition of anticipation . . .

Miller: It's too late, Dave.

NOTES

The First Night: The arguments against the position that personal identity consists in identity of an immaterial soul are similar to those found in John Locke, "Of Identity and Diversity," Chapter 27 of Book II of *Essay Concerning Human Understanding.* This chapter first appeared in the second edition of 1694.

The Second Night: The arguments against the view that personal identity consists in bodily identity are also suggested by Locke, as is the theory that memory is what is crucial. The argument that the memory theory is circular was made by Joseph Butler in "Of Personal Identity," an Appendix to his *Analogy of Religion,* first published in 1736. Locke's memory theory has been developed by a number of modern authors, including Sydney Shoemaker. The possibility of circumventing Butler's charge of circularity by an appeal to causation is noted by David Wiggins in *Identity and Spatial Temporal Continuity.* The "duplication argument" was apparently first used by the eighteenth-century free thinker, Antony Collins. Collins assumed that something like Locke's theory of personal identity was correct, and used the duplication argument to raise problems for the doctrine of immortality.

The Third Night: Who Is Julia, by Barbara Harris, is an engaging novel published in 1972. (Dr. Matthews had not yet thought of brain rejuvenations.)

Locke considers the possibility of the "consciousness" of a prince being transferred to the body of a cobbler. The idea of using the removal of a brain to suggest how this might happen comes from Sydney Shoemaker's seminal book, *Self-Knowledge and Self-Identity* (1963). Bernard Williams has cleverly and articulately resisted the memory theory and the view that such a brain removal would amount to a body transplant in a number of important articles which are collected in his book *Problems of the Self* (1973). In particular, Williams has stressed the relevance of the duplication argument even in questions of terrestrial personal identity. Weirob's position in this essay is more inspired by Williams than anyone else. I have discussed Williams' arguments and related topics in "Can the Self Divide?" (*Journal of Philosophy,* 1972) and a review of his book (*Journal of Philosophy,* 1976).

An important article on the themes which emerge toward the end of the dialogue is Derek Parfit's "Personal Identity" (*Philosophical Review,* 1971). This article, along with Locke's chapter and a number of other important chapters and articles by Hume, Shoemaker, Williams, and others are collected in my anthology *Personal Identity* (1975). A number of new articles on personal identity appear in Amelie Rorty (ed.), *The Identities of Persons* (1976).

PART 4 DETERMINISM

What are we asking when we ask *why* something happened? Will an adequate explanation show us that in some sense or other the event to be explained *had* to happen in the way it did? Are voluntary human actions in principle subject to the same kinds of explanations as physical events? If everything that happens can in principle be explained by science, is there then no such thing in the universe as random chance, genuine contingency, and uncertainty? The essay by Wesley C. Salmon that begins this section addresses such questions as these. The theory of explanation, of course, has great interest to the philosopher in its own right; but it is also of great strategic importance to the continuing arguments over the ancient riddle of determinism and free will.

Determinism is the theory that all events, including human actions and choices, are, without exception, totally determined. What does it mean to say that an event (a past event, E, for instance) is "totally determined"? To this question various answers have been given which for our present purposes we can take to be roughly equivalent.[1]

1. E was completely caused.
2. There were antecedent sufficient conditions for E; that is, conditions such that given their occurrence E *had* to occur.
3. It was causally necessary that E occur.
4. Given what preceded it, it was inevitable that E take place.
5. E is subsumable under a universal law of nature; that is, the occurrence of E was deducible from a description of the conditions that obtained before its occurrence and certain universal laws.
6. The occurrence of E is subject in principle to scientific explanation.
7. The occurrence of E was in principle predictable.
8. There are circumstances and laws which, if they had been known, would have made it possible for one to predict the occurrence and exact nature of E.

[1] Speaking more strictly, definitions 1–6 are "roughly equivalent" to one another, and definitions 7 and 8 are "roughly equivalent" to one another, although one should beware of subtle differences even within these classes. Basically, there are two types of definitions: those in terms of prior sufficient conditions and those in terms of predictability.

AND FREE WILL

Indeterminism, the logical contradictory of determinism, is the theory that some events are not determined. Most (but by no means all) exponents of indeterminism hold that the events that are not determined are human actions.

There are a number of common-sense considerations that should at least incline a reflective person toward determinism. Whenever we plug in a machine, or plant seeds, or prepare for a storm, we act in the expectation that physical events will occur in accordance with known laws of nature. Hardly anyone would deny, moreover, that physical characteristics of human beings—the color of their eyes, the cellular structure of their brains, glands, and other organs—are determined exactly by their genetic inheritance. And pediatricians and mothers of large broods have often observed that *temperament* is determined, at least to a large degree, right from birth. To a large extent our characters, personalities, and intellects are a consequence of our inherited physical capacities and temperamental proclivities, and our choices in turn reflect our characters. Similarly, our early childhood training, family environment, and education have formative influences on character. We do what we do because we are what we are, and we are what we are, at least to a large extent, because our genes and the influencing conduct of others have made us that way.

At the same time, common sense recognizes that human beings *do* do some things "of their own free will", that is, act in circumstances in which they might very well have done something else instead. This common-sense observation seems hard to reconcile with determinism, which seems to imply that every event that occurs is the only one that could have occurred in the circumstances. This in turn seems to imply that no matter what I did a moment ago, I *could not have done otherwise*—which, in turn, seems to say that I *had* to do what I did, that I was not a free agent. But, most of us would agree, my ability to do otherwise is a necessary condition of praise or blame, reward or punishment—in short, for my *being responsible*. Therefore, if determinism cannot be reconciled with the ability to do otherwise, it cannot be reconciled with moral responsibility either. But we *do* hold people responsible for what they do (indeed, some say we *must* hold people responsible);

therefore (some have argued), so much the worse for determinism. Such is the common-sense case against determinism.

Common sense, however, is no more pleased with indeterminism, which seems to give no satisfactory answer at all to any query of the form "Why did *this* happen rather than some other thing?" The reply "It just happened, that's all" inevitably leaves us unsatisfied. If we drop a stone and, to our astonishment, it rises straight up in the air instead of falling, we won't rest content with the "explanation" that "it was just one of those things—a totally random chance occurrence without rhyme or reason." We are even less likely to accept "chance" as an "explanation" for human actions. Such an explanation, we feel, makes all human actions arbitrary and unintelligible; it also seems to destroy the intimate bond between a person and his actions that is required by judgments of moral responsibility. Yet just insofar as a person's action was uncaused, just so far does it seem to have occurred "without rhyme or reason," as a "matter of pure chance." In the words of one determinist: "in proportion as an act of volition starts of itself without cause it is exactly, so far as the freedom of the individual is concerned, as if it had been thrown into his mind from without—'suggested to him by a freakish demon.'"[2]

Common sense thus is tied up in knots. It looks with little favor either on determinism or indeterminism in respect to human actions. Yet since these two theories are defined as logical contradictories, one of them *must* be true. The plight of common sense thus takes the form of a *dilemma;* that is, an argument of the form

1. If P is true, then Q is true.
2. If not-P is true, then Q is true.
3. Either P is true or not-P is true.
4. Therefore, Q is true (where Q is something repugnant or antecedently unacceptable).

The dilemma of determinism can be stated thus:

1. If determinism is true, we can never do other than we do; hence, we are never responsible for what we do.
2. If indeterminism is true, then some events—namely, all human actions—are random, hence not free; hence, we are never responsible for what we do.
3. Either determinism is true or else indeterminism is true.
4. Therefore, we are never responsible for what we do.

There are several ways we might try to escape being gored by the "horns of the dilemma," but one way is *not* open to us. We may not deny the third premise; for, given our definitions of "determinism" and "indeterminism," it amounts simply to the statement that either determinism is true or else it is not—surely an innocuous claim! We are, in short, not able in this case to get "between the horns of the dilemma" by denying its disjunctive premise.

We are thus left with three possibilities. We can deny the first premise and hold that determinism is, after all, perfectly compatible with free will and responsibility; or we can deny the second premise and hold that an act can be both free and intelligible, and hence responsible, though it was not traceable to determining causes outside the actor himself; or finally we can accept the entire argument just as it stands and argue on independent grounds that its conclusion is not so "repugnant" or so "antecedently unacceptable" as it seems on first appearance.

[2]R. E. Hobart, "Free-Will as Involving Determinism and Inconceivable Without it," *Mind,* 43 (1934).

The first way of attempting to resolve the dilemma is often called "soft determinism." Although that label is now firmly fixed by convention, it is somewhat unfortunate, bringing with it pejorative associations of "tender-mindedness." Perhaps "reconciling determinism" would be a better name, for this theory is, after all, the conjunction of two theses: (1) that determinism is true, and (2) that determinism is compatible with free will and responsibility. Reconciling determinism—the view of Thomas Hobbes, John Locke, David Hume, and John Stuart Mill—is represented here by the selection from Walter T. Stace. Common to all these philosophers is the view that the key phrase "He could have done otherwise" is properly understood as hypothetical, meaning roughly "He would have done otherwise *if* he had so chosen (intended, wished)." In this hypothetical sense, I could have done otherwise than I did, even if determinism is true. I just wrote the word "true," but *if* I had instead chosen to write another word (say, "right"), I should have done so (unless somebody intervened with a gun or knife to prevent me); and this is true even though I was determined to choose to write "true." In short, according to this theory, if I can do what I choose, I am free in the only sense of "free" used in ordinary parlance and in ascriptions of responsibility, and it matters not whether my choice itself was causally determined.

Reconciling determinists often take great pains to distinguish the determinism they espouse from a theory called *fatalism,* which they reject. To say of an event that it was fated to happen is to say more than that it was causally determined. It is to say that it would have happened no matter what the person involved might have done to avoid it. In this sense all of us are fated to die (at some time or other); but only a fatalist would say that a person is fated from birth to die at a definite place and at a definite time. A determinist would admit that it was determined that Abraham Lincoln die in Washington in 1865; but to say that it was *fated* that he so die is to imply, among other things, that even had Lincoln tried to shoot himself in Springfield, Illinois, in 1850, or even had he not gone to the theater on the fatal night, somehow he would have met the same fate he in fact met, in Washington, D.C., in 1865. That *all* events are so fated is a doctrine with strange mystic overtones, and has rarely been defended by philosophers.[3]

The second way of attempting to resolve the dilemma (that is, by denying that an uncaused act is necessarily a random event "without rhyme or reason") is found in the writings of Aristotle, Thomas Reid, and Immanuel Kant, among others, and is represented here by the essays of C. A. Campbell and Richard Taylor. Proponents of the view that human actions are neither determined nor fortuitous—the theory called *libertarianism*—remind us that human actions, unlike other events in nature, are subject to a special kind of explanation: the actor's own *reasons* for acting. An uncaused action, done deliberately for some reason, would therefore be a perfectly intelligible one, and adequately explained by an account of its reasons. The libertarian denies both theses of the reconciling determinist; he denies that determinism and freedom are compatible, and he denies that determinism is true.[4]

The compatibility of free will and determinism is also denied by those who respond to the dilemma in the third way (that is, by embracing the conclusion of the dilemma, instead of trying to avoid it). This is the approach of the "non-reconciling determinists"

[3]One outstanding exception to this generalization is Richard Taylor. See his *Metaphysics* (Englewood Cliffs, N.J.: Prentice-Hall, Inc., 1974), Chapter 6.

[4]All libertarians, therefore, are indeterminists (by definition), but not all indeterminists are libertarians. It is possible for one to hold that all actions are uncaused and *therefore* occur by random chance. That view would be indeterministic but not libertarian.

(usually called "hard determinists"), who, instead of abandoning determinism as the libertarians do, jettison free will and moral responsibility. Non-reconciling determinism was the view of Spinoza and Arthur Schopenhauer, among others, and is represented here by the selection from John Hospers.

In recent years, the debate over determinism has taken a somewhat different turn. Some writers have argued forcefully that, quite apart from any assumption about freedom and responsibility, genuine deliberation and decision cannot possibly be determined, since the very concepts of "deliberating" and "deciding," as we ordinarily understand them, entail an absence of prior causal determination. In his article included here Richard Taylor has taken just such a stand. If determinism is true, according to this kind of argument, then it is at least possible for a person to "discover" in advance what his future decisions will be. But if that is so, then those future "decisions," the argument continues, cannot be genuine decisions at all. Such a startling consequence may yet be true, Taylor concedes, but he points out that if we accept it simply on the grounds that it is implied by a highly speculative philosophical theory (determinism) we will be paying an exorbitantly high price in terms of our ordinary common-sense beliefs. Alvin Goldman, on the other hand, finds less difficulty in the idea that actions and decisions can be predicted well in advance on scientific grounds, even by the person whose actions and decisions they will be. In dealing with this question, Goldman considers the most dramatic crucial case—the possible existence, for each person, of a "book of life" in which is written in advance a description of each voluntary action and each deliberate decision the person will eventually bring about on his own. Goldman attempts to show that it is conceivable that a person might discover such a "book" with his own name on it, read what he will in fact do in the future, and yet, in time, deliberate over whether he shall do what it is written he *will* do. On the success or failure of such efforts as Goldman's the tenability of determinism may very well hinge, for if it fails, Taylor's common-sense case against determinism could carry the day.

Harry Frankfurt offers an analysis of "freedom of the will" that he claims to be neutral in respect to the controversy between the determinists and their opponents. But if his analysis is correct, and if (as he claims) it makes freedom of the will compatible with determinism (as well as with indeterminism) then it takes away the primary motive of the libertarian (to vindicate free will) and the main argument against his determinist rival. The reader should bear in mind that the concept Frankfurt analyzes is not freedom to *act* (as one chooses) but rather freedom to will (as one wants to will)—a kind of "second-order freedom" to which only *persons* can aspire.

The final article in this section, by Elizabeth Beardsley, considers whether or not determinism is consistent with the practice of praising and blaming persons for what they do. She thus touches on a controversy that divides not only (some) determinists from libertarians, but also splits the hard determinists from the soft determinists. Beardsley's ingenious article has the effect of reconciling the two camps of determinists. It also throws light on the very complex concept of blame itself, making a bridge to the topics of Part Five. By distinguishing between the various "perspectives" from which judgments of praise and blame are made, she goes a long way toward settling the question whether praise and blame can be reasonable, if determinism should happen to be true.

Soft Determinism, Hard Determinism, and Libertarianism

WESLEY C. SALMON

Determinism and Indeterminism in Modern Science*

According to a famous legend, the stoic philosopher Epictetus, who was a slave, broke a vase that his master, who was also a philosopher, treasured. When the master began to beat him, Epictetus protested, "By the philosophy to which we both adhere, it was predestined from the beginning of the world that I should break the vase; I am not to blame and I should not be beaten." His master replied, "By that same philosophy, it was determined for all time that I should beat you," and he continued to do so. This anecdote sums up much of the frustration that people down through the ages have felt when confronted with the problem of "free will and determinism." The main purpose of the present essay is to attempt to clarify the notion of determinism, and some other concepts closely related to it. Except for a few incidental remarks, I shall leave the problem of free will to other authors.

Determinism is a doctrine that comes in many forms. In ancient mythology, as well as some later religions, it was a crude sort of fatalism. The fates, with conscious intent, decide at the time of one's birth what is going to happen to him, and nothing anyone can do will make it otherwise. The following passage nicely illustrates the fatalistic view.

DEATH SPEAKS: There was a merchant in Bagdad who sent his servant to market to buy provisions and in a little while the servant came back, white and trembling, and said, Master, just now when I was in the market-place I was jostled by a woman in the crowd and when I turned I saw it was Death that jostled me. She looked at me and made a threatening gesture; now, lend me your horse, and I will ride away from this city and avoid my fate. I will go to Samarra and there Death will not find me. The merchant lent him his horse, and the servant mounted it, and he dug his spurs in its flanks and as fast as the horse would gallop he went. Then the merchant went down to the marketplace and he saw me standing in the crowd and he came to me and said, Why did you make a threatening gesture to my servant when you saw him this morning? That was not a threatening gesture, I said, it was only a start of surprise. I was astonished to see him in Bagdad, for I had an appointment with him tonight in Samarra.[1]

Certain sects of Christianity have maintained that God, who created the world and holds it in his all-powerful control, fore-ordains exactly what is to happen. This view is known as *predestinarianism,* and it is reinforced by the doctrine of God's omniscience. If God knows with complete certainty and in precise detail what will occur in the future—including whether *you* will go to heaven or to hell—the future is determined to be just exactly what God knows it is going to be. The individual has no power over his future and can do nothing to change it. Even his own acts, and his apparently free decisions, are predetermined by something outside of him, over which he has no influence. The feeling of freedom which accompanies many of our decisions and actions is a mere illusion.

Both fatalism and predestinarianism attribute the control of human "fate" or "destiny" to some supernatural agency. Most of us, nowadays, reject fatalism as primitive superstition, and few still believe in predestination. Agnostics and atheists find no basis for believing in God at all, and contemporary theists generally believe that God allows man some measure of freedom. However, it has long been suspected that even a "hard-headed" scientific world-view would lead to a determinism just as inimical to freedom of choice and action as are fatalism and predestinarianism.

1. DETERMINISM IN CLASSICAL PHYSICS

In his famous poem *De Rerum Natura,* Lucretius maintains that everything in the universe consists solely of atoms which move about in otherwise empty space, colliding with one another and forming complex arrangements. The earth and the sun, rocks and trees, human beings and other animals—all are just complicated collections of various kinds of atoms. Everything that happens in the universe, including human thought and action, is simply the result of the movements of atoms. Lucretius realized that free will is problematic if we conceive the motions of atoms to be strictly determined by mechanical laws; he writes, ". . . if all movement is always interconnected, the new arising from the old in a determinate order . . . what is the source of the free will possessed by living things throughout the earth?"[2]

Lucretius tried to resolve the problem by claiming that atoms sometimes swerve spontaneously and without any cause from their otherwise determined courses. Believing that freedom of the will is an established fact, he was led to deny determinism. His argument can be set out as follows:

(1) If determinism is true, man does not have free will. Man has free will.

Determinism is False.

On the basis of this argument, Lucretius accepted indeterminism as the correct world-view.

Lucretius wrote in the first century B.C., hundreds of years before Newton formulated the laws that govern the motions and collisions of those tiny lumps of matter the Greek atomists postulated. Before Newton, one could have speculated as to whether the laws of mechanics completely determine the motions of material particles; after Newton, that question seemed to be closed. From 1686, when the *Principia*[3] was first published, until about 1900, Newton's mechanics was tested and retested, confirmed and reconfirmed. Not only did it explain the approximate correctness of Galileo's law of falling bodies and Kepler's laws of planetary motion, but is also accounted for the behavior of the tides, and the bulging of the Earth at its equator. Moreover, when a delicate laboratory experiment made possible the direct measurement of the gravitational attraction between a large ball of lead and a small one, Newton was found to be right.[4] Newton's laws explained why the orbits of the planets are not perfect ellipses, as Kepler had said, by bringing in the mutual gravitational attractions among the planets themselves, instead of considering only the attraction between each planet and the sun. Indeed, when the planet Uranus appeared not to conform to Newton's laws, Neptune was postulated to account for the deviation. Newton's laws enabled astronomers to predict the location of Neptune, and telescopic observation confirmed its existence. These laws led to the discovery of a theretofore unobserved planet. Later, when Neptune seemed to violate Newton's laws, Pluto was postulated and then observed.[5]

It is almost impossible to overestimate the impressive success of Newtonian mechanics. As more sophisticated experimental and mathematical techniques were developed to extend the application of Newton's laws to new phenomena, confirming evidence continued to mount. One of the greatest mathematical physicists to contribute to the application of Newtonian mechanics to planetary motion was P. S. Laplace, who, early in the nineteenth century, wrote,

All events, even those which on account of their insignificance do not seem to follow the great laws of nature, are a result of it just as necessarily as the revolutions of the sun. In ignorance of the ties which unite such events to the entire system of the universe, they have been made to depend upon final causes or upon hazard, according as they occur and are repeated with regularity, or appear without regard to order; but these imaginary causes have gradually receded with the widening bounds of knowledge and disappear entirely before sound philosophy, which sees in them only the expression of our ignorance of the true causes.[6]

Here is a classic statement of the determinist's position. All events, no matter how large or small, no matter how significant or insignificant, are completely determined by strict laws of mechanics. When people attribute events to final causes (e.g., fate or divine intervention) or hazard (i.e., pure accident or chance) it is only because they are ignorant of the actual facts. The success of Newtonian mechanics offered convincing evidence that all natural phenomena could be explained by the laws of mechanics. As the application of scientific knowledge is pushed further and further, we see that nothing is in principle incapable of explanation on a purely mechanical basis. The argument of Lucretius resulted from the imperfect state of ancient science; if we still accept the first premise, the argument must continue as follows:

(2) If determinism is true, man does not have free will. Determinism is true.

Man does not have free will.

Both of these arguments are logically valid; they differ with respect to their second premises. Newtonian mechanics—so it seemed to Laplace and countless other philosophers and scientists—clearly turned the tide against Lucretius in favor of determinism. Although Lucretius' argument is logically valid, its second premise is not true. What appears to Lucretius to be free will, free choice, or free action is in fact determined, according to Laplace, and any appearance of indeterminacy is only the result of incomplete knowledge of all the causes.

2. DETERMINISM AND THE SCIENCES OF LIFE AND MIND

If one believed, with Lucretius and Laplace, that there is nothing more than atoms and their motions, determinism seemed unavoidable in the Newtonian era. But not everyone found this materialistic outlook entirely compelling. Descartes had argued persuasively that there are two realms, the physical and the psychological, and that they are quite distinct from one another.[7] One could agree with Descartes that the laws of mechanics, which govern the material world, are strictly deterministic, and still maintain that freedom exists in the mental domain. It is essential to remember the difference between the scientific evidence for determinism in physics and the philosophical speculation that everything is entirely reducible to material atoms and their motions.

Descartes held that only man, among all the animals, has a mental life; other animals are mere mechanisms. This doctrine reflects the Christian view that only man has an immortal soul. It suffered a sharp setback when Charles Darwin's epoch-making work on evolution in mid-nineteenth century showed that man and the other animals are not utterly distinct, but closely related.[8] In the face of this result, it might be tempting to suggest that the deepest gulf is not between man and everything else, but rather, between living and non-living things. Darwin's work on the origin of species and the descent of man did not, after all, explain the origin of life itself. But Darwin's work has an aspect that bears upon this distinction as well. Instead of explaining the existence of various species of living things as a result of purposeful "special creation" as recounted in *Genesis,* he explains them in terms of non-purposive mechanisms of natural selection. Add to that the chemical synthesis of the "organic compound" urea from exclusively inorganic substances, and the sharp separation between the biological and the physical realms begins to look less tenable.[9]

In spite of strong indications of continuity between the physical phenomena whose behavior was explained deterministically by Newtonian mechanics and the biological realm of living things, and in spite of man's kinship with the rest of the animal kingdom, there still remained the mysterious phenomena of consciousness that seem the almost exclusive property of the human race. One could speculate that chimpanzees, apes, dogs, and horses may have a very primitive mental life, and even, perhaps, a low degree of free will; nevertheless, in man the conscious aspect is extremely conspicuous (especially to himself), and that might be the locus of his freedom. Man might be so constructed that his physiological aspects are governed by deterministic laws, but his mental life is still governed by psychological laws that are indeterministic. That is what Descartes had maintained from the outset.

At this point, another intellectual giant of the nineteenth century steps into the picture. In an attempt to understand mental illness, Sigmund Freud developed a psychological theory according to which all mental occurrences, even those of the seemingly most trivial sorts, are as strictly caused as are any physical phenomena.[10] Freud postulated unconscious mechanisms that give rise to dreams and neurotic symptoms, and he offered causal explanations of such trivia as slips of the tongue and the pen. Freud's theories were no idle philosophical speculations; they were designed to explain observable phenomena, and they were tested by experience. I do not mean to argue that Freud's theories are still totally acceptable as current theories; neither, for that matter, are Newton's laws. There can be little doubt, however, that he heralded dramatically the possibility that psychological phenomena may be subject to laws just as deterministic as those of Newtonian mechanics. He offers the strong suggestion that our conscious deliberations and "free" choices can be explained as deterministically as the result of the collision of two billiard balls on a table. By the close of the nineteenth century, determinism seemed well on the way to being a scientifically well grounded view of the entire universe in all of its aspects—physical, biological, psychological, and even social.

3. DETERMINISM AND CONTEMPORARY SCIENCE

Twentieth-century science has, in some ways, confirmed and extended the grounds for holding a deterministic world-view, and in others it has seemed to undermine determinism. Spectacular progress in the biological sciences has extended enormously the degree to which processes in living organisms can be understood strictly in terms of chemistry and physics. The most striking achievement has been in the field of molecular biology, where the mechanisms of heredity are explained in exclusively chemical terms. The gene is recognized as a large and complex molecule whose properties are fully determined by its chemical structure, and whose capabilities for self-replication are thereby explained.[11] Protein molecules, the "building blocks of life," are known to be constructed out of amino acids. Amino acids have been synthesized, and so have protein molecules. More recently—just as this article was going to press—H. Gobind Khorana, a Nobel Prize winner at the University of Wisconsin, and associates, synthesized a gene. In the not too distant future, man will very probably succeed in synthesizing a viable living organism from inorganic chemicals. These developments constitute an important extension of Darwin's beginnings, and it no longer seems justifiable to deny that the laws that govern the behavior of atoms have complete dominion in the biological realm.

The science of psychology was in its infancy at the turn of the century, but it too has lived up to its nineteenth-century promise. The scientific study of human and animal behavior—from the psychoanalytic, behavioristic, and physiological standpoints—has borne considerable fruit in showing that human experience, feeling, deliberation, choice, and action can be understood in terms of strict psychological laws. It is perhaps too soon to say whether these laws are ultimately reducible to those of physiology, and thence to those of physics and chemistry, but many indications point in that direction. Even Freud believed that the psychoanalytic mechanisms he postulated would eventually be explained in physiological terms. Subsequent neurological studies suggest that it may soon be feasible to explain learning in terms of specific chemical changes that occur in the brain cells, and psycho-pharmacological developments suggest that chemical understanding of feelings and emotions is not too far away. It is certainly plausible at this point, to suppose that the laws that govern the behavior of atoms also govern our thoughts, feelings, emotions, decisions, and ultimately, all of our actions.[12]

What sort of picture does this give of a person as a thinking, deliberating, considering, choosing agent? His life begins when two cells, a sperm and an egg, unite, and following the laws of physics and chemistry, the genes that are present begin to replicate. The individual's heredity, which determines in large measure what he will become both physically and psychologically, is passed on to him from his parents through the genes that carry "the genetic code." From the beginning, outside influences impinge upon him—even before birth—and these too have a bearing upon what he will become and how he will react to further outside influences. Among prenatal influences are, for example, such disease viruses as that of German measles, which may affect the sense organs of the unborn child and deprive him for life of experiences most of us have. When the infant leaves the womb, social factors begin to operate. Again, external causes—vaguely known as "environmental influences"—become effective. How the person grows depends in part upon such social factors as the personality of the parents and the economic condition of the family, and in part upon what he has already become as a result of the hereditary, physiological, and environmental influences that have already operated upon him. Where, if at all, does the individual's genuine choice—freely made— enter the picture? If he grows up to commit murder, is that not just a part of the inexorable causal process in which he is caught up? Is he not just as much a complete victim of his heredity and environment as Oedipus was of his fate? Is this not the most reasonable inference from the scientific knowledge that is presently available? Before we try to draw a conclusion, it will be best to take another look at the laws of physics that seem to be fundamental to the whole scheme of things.

As the twentieth century dawned, physics, which seemed so secure, was approaching a crisis. Two great revolutions were about to shake it to its very foundations. One of these revolutions, which consisted in the replacement of Newtonian mechanics by Einstein's special (1905) and general (1916) theories of relativity, did nothing to upset the deterministic character of physics. Newton's laws of mechanics turned out to be not quite correct, so they had to be replaced by some revised laws of mechanics, but ones that were no less deterministic.[13]

The other revolution had a profound bearing upon determinism. According to the theories of electromagnetic radiation available at the end of the nineteenth century, a light beam entering a dark box with a small hole will produce inside the box an infinite amount of radiant energy in the ultraviolet region of the spectrum, thus giving rise to a holocaust more terrible than the worst nuclear bomb. This consequence was later aptly called "the ultraviolet catastrophe." Since no such cataclysms occur, something must be drastically wrong with classical physics. In 1900, Max Planck introduced the quantum hypothesis, and showed that it yields a far more satisfactory account of "black body radiation."[14] In 1913, Neils Bohr applied quantization to the orbits of electrons in hydrogen atoms, and showed that he could thereby explain the spectral lines emitted by hydrogen gas when it is excited by passage of an electric current. Bohr's theory, unfortunately, did not work at all well for the spectra of helium and the more complex atoms. By about 1925, Werner Heisenberg, Erwin Schrödinger, Max Born, and others had worked out the details of a more satisfactory quantum mechanics, but the theory they produced was fundamentally statistical. The physics of atoms had become indeterministic. For example, it is a consequence of quantum mechanics that atoms of silver, when shot between the poles of a magnet, will be deflected either up or down, but there is no way, even in principle, of determining beforehand which way a particular atom will go. Each one has a 50-50 chance of going either way, and that is all there is to it.[15] Thus, for reasons

entirely different from those of Lucretius, modern physicists also attribute indeterministic swerves to atoms in motion.

A natural reaction to examples of this kind is to say that there are real causes that determine which atom will be deflected in which direction, but that we have not yet found them. There exists, however, a highly technical proof that such an interpretation is not admissible, for the present theory *cannot* be supplemented in such a way as to make it deterministic. It is intrinsically indeterministic. Any attempt to make it deterministic, by postulating additional causes, will render it logically self-contradictory.[16] At the same time, the present quantum mechanics could be replaced—not merely supplemented—by a thoroughly deterministic theory. Einstein, for one, was never satisfied with the irreducibly statistical character of quantum mechanics—"God does not play dice with the universe" is his oft-quoted remark. Some first-rate physicists are presently working to find a deterministic theory to replace the current quantum mechanics, one by which it will be possible to explain what now seems irreducibly statistical by means of "hidden variables" that cannot occur in the present theory. No one can say for sure whether they will succeed; any new theory, deterministic or indeterministic, has to stand the test of experiment. The current quantum theory does show, however, that the world *may* be fundamentally and irremediably indeterministic, for according to the best currently available knowledge, it is.

4. WHAT IS DETERMINISM?

So far, the discussion has proceeded as if a number of the fundamental concepts we have been using are clear. Since this is a rather dubious supposition, let us focus attention upon some of them in the hope of enhancing our understanding. We will do well to begin with the classic definition of determinism given by Laplace. At this point, our aim is not to argue the truth or falsity of determinism, but only to say what it means. Laplace writes,

Given for one instant an intelligence which could comprehend all the forces by which nature is animated and the respective situation of the beings who compose it—an intelligence sufficiently vast to submit these data to analysis—it would embrace in the same formula the movements of the greatest bodies in the universe and those of the lightest atom; for it, nothing would be uncertain and the future, as the past, would be present to its eyes.[17]

The intelligence mentioned in this statement has sometimes been called "Laplace's demon," but he never intended to imply that such a demon actually exists—or an omniscient God for that matter. According to a famous anecdote, when Napoleon learned of Laplace's great work, *The System of the World,* he asked Laplace where God fit into the system; Laplace replied, "Sir, I have no need of that hypothesis." What he was trying to do was to capture the import of determinism. To affirm determinism is to maintain that the precise condition of the entire universe at any one instant, together with the laws of nature, logically entail the condition of the universe in its totality at any future instant. Newtonian mechanics is deterministic, for if the precise position and momentum of each and every particle at one moment—say 12:00 noon, Greenwich mean time, April 15, 1970—is known, and if the laws of Newtonian mechanics are the true laws of nature, then anyone who could solve sufficiently complicated mathematical equations could deduce with perfect exactitude and rigor the precise state of the universe at any subsequent moment. From these data and these laws, Laplace's demon could calculate any future occurrence. He could ascertain exactly what you will have for breakfast on April 15, 1980, and if you should drop a bit of egg, precisely where it will spot your tie.

No determinist seriously believes that human beings are at present capable of ascertaining the total future of the universe in all detail, or that we will ever be able to do so. He is saying, instead, that it is possible in principle to make such inferences because the laws of nature and the state of the universe at any one time actually do determine the state of the universe at all future times. The fact that we are unable to make perfect predictions in all cases is, to the determinist, the result of human ignorance and other limitations; it is not because nature is lacking in precise determination.

To what, then, is the indeterminist committed? For him, the combination of laws and total state of the universe at one moment do not completely determine the states of the universe at other moments. It is not a failure of our intelligence, a limitation on our knowledge of the laws of nature, or a partial ignorance of the state of the universe at the given

moment. Instead, *given* complete knowledge of the state of the universe at some instant, *given* perfectly accurate formulations of the laws of nature, and *given* unlimited ability to solve mathematical equations, the complete state of the universe at some other moment simply does not follow. This is what it means to deny that determinism, as held by Laplace, is true. For example, Lucretius said that the atoms, all originally falling downward through space at a uniform speed, spontaneously swerved from their courses. In our latter-day wisdom, we know that space does not, by itself, have a downward direction, and that there is no physical way to distinguish uniform motion through space from rest. Lucretius might just as well have said that the atoms were all sitting there motionless, when some of them started dancing around and bumping into one another. Given a precise knowledge of the size, shape, location, and state of motion (rest) of each atom, and given all the laws which govern their motion, there is no way to infer which atom will move, when it will move, in what direction it will move, and what other atoms it will collide with. If you object that there must be *some* reason why one of these atoms moved at the time and in the manner it did, Lucretius will staunchly deny it. It is not just that we do not know the reason— there is no reason!

In this context, I think we can feel the compelling force of the determinist viewpoint. To suppose that atoms start moving about without any cause at all strains our conceptions. It is easy to protest, with the determinist, that there must be some reason; it is tempting to say that the indeterminist is not even offering an intelligible account, let alone a true one. And, indeed, many philosophers have elevated determinism to the status of an a priori truth—one that cannot rationally be denied. It is sometimes called *the principle of sufficient reason,* "a thing cannot occur without a cause that produces it," and sometimes *the law of universal causation,* "everything that happens presupposes something from which it follows according to a rule."[18]

Notice that two very different grounds have been offered in support of determinism. In the first place, it has been regarded as a very general statement that is strongly supported by the success of science in explaining all kinds of phenomena by means of deterministic laws. In the second place, it has been taken as an a priori truth that cannot be rejected without logical absurdity. If it genuinely enjoys the status of an a priori truth, it needs no support from scientific evidence, and science can never conceivably offer any evidence against it.

In view of the results of modern quantum mechanics, it seems inadvisable to regard determinism as an a priori principle. Quantum mechanics, in the form it now has, may not be true, but its truth or falsity is a matter of its correspondence with the facts, not the violation of an a priori principle. Quantum mechanics has shown that science can operate with indeterministic laws without degenerating into unintelligibility or logical absurdity. It seems reasonable to conclude that determinism is not an inviolable a priori principle; rather, its truth or falsity is a very fundamental and general fact about nature that we can hope to establish only more or less certainly on the basis of scientific evidence. If we are tempted to make determinism an a priori principle of reason, it may be because common sense tells us what "stands to reason." Contemporary common sense seems to have assimilated a good deal of the Newtonian world-view, but it has not yet come to terms with the statistical and probabilistic aspects of twentieth-century science.

5. TYPES OF DETERMINISM AND INDETERMINISM

It is traditional to distinguish two kinds of causation, *efficient* causation and *final* causation. Efficient causation has a rather mechanical character, in the sense that effect follows cause without reference to purposes, intentions, or ends. If running water erodes the earth from beneath a rock, and the rock rolls down a hill, the whole process is normally regarded as one in which efficient causes are operating mechanically. If the rock crashes into the home of a mine owner who has been exploiting his employees, and people think it is God's way of punishing him, they are treating it as a case of final causation, inasmuch as this account does involve reference to purposes. The view that God created the separate species of living things in order to realize certain of His purposes takes the origin of species to be an example of final causation. Darwin's view, that the species develop by natural selection, regards the same result as the effect of efficient causes. Biological evolution does not have to be considered an instance of efficient causation, however, for theologians can still maintain that evolution is God's way of bringing about the realization of His purposes.

Whether one believes in efficient causation or final causation or a mixture of the two, it is still possible to be a determinist or an indeterminist. Let us adopt traditional terms and say that a person who believes that nature operates only with efficient causes, but never with final causes, is a *mechanist*. Let us say that anyone who believes that there are final causes is a *teleologist*. To be a mechanist or a teleologist is to make a commitment as to *what kinds* of causes there are, but not as to the pervasiveness of causation of either type. A determinist is one who takes a stand on the question of how extensively causes, of whatever type, operate, but not necessarily a commitment on what type of causes there are. We can, consequently, define four distinct positions:

1. *Mechanistic determinism:* Every event is completely determined by causes, and these causes are efficient, not final, causes. Laplace is the classic representative of this position.
2. *Teleological determinism:* Every event is completely determined by causes, and at least some of these causes are final causes. Calvinistic predestinarianism is the most familiar example.
3. *Mechanistic indeterminism:* Events are not completely determined by causes, but to whatever extent they are determined, it is by efficient causes alone. Lucretius, with his indeterministic atomism, would seem to represent this view, as would most modern physicists who consider quantum mechanics basically indeterministic.
4. *Teleological indeterminism:* Events are not completely determined by causes, but some events are determined to some extent by final causes. An ancient fatalist might represent this view; for instance, the significant events in the life of Oedipus, such as killing his father and marrying his mother, were determined by final causes, but the less important ones, such as the exact positions of the drops of his father's blood, may well have been left to chance.

Scientific progress seems, historically, to be associated with a transition from teleology to mechanism. Artistotle's physics, which dominated the scene for several centuries before Newton, incorporated final causes. Newton's mechanics was entirely non-teleological. Biology before Darwin tended to be teleological, but Darwin, as we noted, introduced a mechanistic conception of biological evolution through natural selection. Subsequently, even the psychological and social sciences have tended to reject teleological conceptions. The question of whether teleological or mechanical conceptions are appropriate is, it seems to me, a matter to be decided by the success or failure of theories and explanations that employ them. On the whole, it appears, experience has strongly suggested that mechanical approaches are more fruitful than teleological ones, but this is an extremely complex issue.[19] The important point is to show how the two types of causation give rise to two types of determinism and two types of indeterminism.

6. LAWS OF NATURE

The laws that are written in law books (also called "statutes") are concocted by humans to *prescribe* how people shall behave. The people who are governed by such laws may conform to them or violate them. The laws of nature, by contrast, *describe* the ways in which various kinds of things in the universe operate, and there is no possibility of violation. If things did not conform to a purported law, it would not be an actual law of nature. Laws of nature, moreover, do not involve a legislator, human or divine, and we should certainly avoid thinking that the existence of laws of nature presupposes a supernatural lawmaker. To fall victim to such an inference would be entrapment by a bad pun.

In science, one often hears of Hooke's law, Kepler's laws, Newton's laws, etc. In each case there are one or more statements, propounded by the individual whose name is attached, which *purport* to describe how things like springs, planets, and bullets behave. If these statements do, in fact, state accurately how such things behave, then they express laws of nature. The law of nature itself is a general uniformity or regularity in nature; the statement that is written in the science text seeks to describe this regularity. There is an elementary, but crucial, distinction between the words used to state a law, and the fact of nature that is being described. The word "table," for instance, is a linguistic entity with five letters, but neither legs nor a flat surface; the word is not to be confused with a piece of furniture. Similarly, the statement of a law is a linguistic entity, which must not be confused with the regularity that nature actually exhibits. If the sentence in the book is true, it expresses a law; when we assert the statement, we do so because we believe it expresses a law, but

we may be quite wrong in thinking so. For example, it was long believed that Newton's so-called laws of motion were true, but we no longer think so; although we still refer to them as "laws," we do not really believe they express genuine laws of nature. We presently believe, however, that the speed of light is the greatest speed at which signals of any kind can be transmitted across empty space, and that law is fundamental to Einstein's special theory of relativity.

The doctrine of determinism, as formulated by Laplace, makes essential reference to the laws of nature. It is of utmost importance to remember that such references do not pertain to statements that are found in textbooks, but rather, to the actual regularities that exist in nature. At any given time, of course, we do not know for certain which statements express actual regularities, and any statement we make purporting to express a law of nature may be incorrect, but that does not imply that we cannot speak meaningfully about the actual laws of nature (as opposed merely to our conceptions of the laws of nature). We do not know for certain that a given bottle actually contains Scotch whiskey, but we quite properly talk about the contents of such bottles even in the absence of certainty. When I take a drink from such a bottle, it is the contents of the bottle I shall be drinking, not merely my conception—I hardly ever drink a conception. If it were never permissible to say anything of which we are not absolutely certain, we could never say anything about the physical world.

7. DETERMINISM AND EXPLANATION

There are many kinds of explanation, such as explaining the meaning of an unfamiliar word, or explaining how to operate a new camera. Some explanations are answers to the question "Why?" and scientific explanations are frequently, if not always, of that type. For example, suppose a small plane crashed upon take-off from an airport near Denver on July 15, 1970, and we ask why the crash occurred. A satisfactory answer might point out that the plane failed to clear an obstacle 100 feet high located a certain distance from the end of the runway, and it might cite such relevant conditions as the length of the runway, the type of aircraft involved and the load it was carrying, the altitude of the airport, the air temperature, the wind velocity and direction, and the relative humidity. These specific factors would be related to the crash by general laws; e.g., that increase of altitude, air temperature, and relative humidity increase the distance needed for take-off. In offering this kind of explanation, two basic kinds of elements are involved, namely, specific conditions obtaining prior to the event to be explained (let us call them *initial conditions*) and *general laws*. The explanation consists in citing the initial conditions and the general laws, and pointing out that the occurrence of the event to be explained follows logically from those premises. An explanation of this type can be schematized as follows:

(3) Statements of initial conditions
Statements of general laws

_____

Statement that the event to be explained occurs

Such an explanation can be regarded as an argument to the effect that the event to be explained was to be expected, in the light of the initial conditions and the general laws, because its occurrence follows from them.[20]

There is a striking similarity between this characterization of explanation and Laplace's formulation of determinism. Recall that his demon requires (i) knowledge of the condition of the universe at some particular moment, i.e., initial conditions, (ii) knowledge of the laws of nature, obviously, general laws, and (iii) ability to carry out mathematical deductions, i.e., the ability to establish the validity of the argument. If determinism, as Laplace conceives it, is true, *every future event* is explainable in terms of the laws of nature and some initial conditions. If you want to explain the entire state of the universe at some future time, you would presumably have to take as initial conditions the entire state of the universe at some antecedent time, as well as all of the laws of nature. But to explain some relatively limited and isolated event, such as the plane crash, only some of the conditions obtaining before the crash would be needed (weather conditions in Hong Kong would not be relevant), and some laws of nature would probably be dispensable. In either case, whether you are trying to explain the condition of the whole universe at some time, or merely some particular event in it, both laws and initial conditions are required.

In view of the close relationship between determinism and one type of scientific explanation, it is tempting to conclude that events that are causally determined can be explained, and those that can be explained are causally determined. From this point, it is easy to take another step and say that when

human actions and decisions can be explained they are determined. One more step leads to the conclusion that to explain human behavior and choices is to show that they cannot be free. To explain human behavior seems to amount to *explaining away* human responsibility! There are, however, a number of dubious steps in this inference.

Whether determinism is true or not, there are many cases in which we do not have enough facts to be able to construct an explanation which demonstrates that the event to be explained must have occurred, given the initial conditions and the laws. For example, we say that John Jones recovered from his streptococcus infection because he was given penicillin, knowing that not all, but only most, streptococcus infections respond to penicillin. We do not have any set of laws and initial conditions from which it follows that the recovery *must* occur; at best, we can show that it is highly probable. It seems there are at least two types of explanation, and they differ from one another in two fundamental ways. The first type, illustrated by the plane crash example, is known as *deductive* explanation; the second type, illustrated by the streptococcus infection example, is known as *inductive* explanation.[21] They differ in the following two ways. First, although both types require the use of general laws, deductive explanations incorporate *universal laws* which hold without exception, while inductive explanations employ *statistical laws*. For instance, the Bernoulli principle, which is fundamental to aerodynamics, states that *in all cases,* the greater the velocity of flow of a fluid (liquid or gas), the smaller is the pressure it exerts perpendicular to the direction of flow. Universal laws have the overall form, "All F are G." Statistical laws are also generalizations, but instead of saying that something happens in every case, they say that it happens in a certain percentage of cases. The percentage may be specified by a precise number, as in "51% of all babies born are male," or it may be given by a vague word, as in "Most cases of streptococcus infection clear up promptly when penicillin is administered." Second, although each type of explanation consists in an argument, the arguments are deductive (i.e., the conclusion follows with necessity from the premises) and inductive (i.e., the premises confer a high probability upon the conclusion) respectively.

If we understand that schema (3) may represent

either an inductive or a deductive argument, both types of explanation conform to it. More explicitly, however, the simplest examples of the two types of explanation can be compared and contrasted via the following two schemas:

(4) All F are G.
   x is F.
   _____
   x is G.

(5) Most F are G.
   x is F.
   _____ [p]
   x is G.

In each case, the first premise is a general law (statistical laws are general in that they refer to a whole class F, but they are not universal in that they do not assert that every member of the class has the property G), the second premise gives the initial conditions, and the conclusion asserts the occurrence of the event to be explained. The single line in (4) signifies a deductive relation between premises and conclusion; the double line in (5) signifies an inductive relation, the number p at the side indicating the degree of probability of the conclusion given the premises. If the probability p attaching to the inductive inference in (5) is near enough to one, we can say that the event to be explained was to be expected in view of the explanatory facts, though it did not necessarily have to happen given these circumstances.

There are still other cases, however, in which we seem to be able to explain occurrences even though the explanatory facts do not make the event very probable—cases, in fact, in which the non-occurrence of the event is more probable than its occurrence, even in the presence of the explanatory conditions. To cite an example that has been widely discussed, if a person contracts syphilis, and it goes through the primary, secondary, and latent stages without treatment with penicillin, he may develop paresis. This is one form of tertiary syphilis, but only a small percentage of those who have untreated latent syphilis become paretic. At the same time, the only people who develop paresis are victims of syphilis. If an individual develops paresis, we offer as an explanation the fact that he had untreated latent syphilis, even though the probability of a latent untreated syphilitic becoming paretic is considerably less than

one half. There are no known characteristics by means of which to predict which cases will develop paresis and which will not.[22]

It is easy to say that explanations of this sort are partial and rudimentary, due to our lack of knowledge of all of the factors surrounding syphilis and its various manifestations. Such an attitude is probably well founded. Scientific experience indicates that further investigation is likely to provide answers to the question of what makes one syphilitic develop paresis and another not. The explanation provides some understanding of what happened and why, but we have good reason to believe that further research will make possible more complete explanations. The same can be said for the streptococcus infection. Even though the explanation of the cure conferred a high probability upon it, there is good reason to suppose that eventually we will find an objective characteristic of certain streptococcus bacilli which makes them resistant to penicillin. When it has been found, we will be able to tell exactly which streptococcus infections can be successfully treated by penicillin and which cannot. When that information is available, it will be possible to give a deductive explanation of the cure of this particular infection by penicillin.

This discussion of types of explanations and how they can be supplemented has a direct bearing upon determinism. If determinism is true, then it is possible in principle to supplement any explanation that is inductive or probabilistic in such a way as to transform it into a deductive explanation. Whenever we use a statistical generalization in an explanation, according to a determinist, it is because our knowledge is incomplete, not because the basic laws of nature are genuinely statistical. On the deterministic view, any reference to chance or probability is, as Laplace remarked above, merely an expression of our ignorance of the true laws of nature.

The indeterminist, by contrast, is committed to saying that there are at least some events for which it is impossible to provide deductive explanations; the best we can hope for is some kind of statistical explanation. While the indeterminist might agree that the statistical character of the laws cited in the medical examples is a reflection of the incompleteness of biological science, he might maintain that in physics there are events that are not amenable to deductive explanation. Lucretius, if he were here and could talk our jargon, might explain the spontaneous movement of an atom by saying that there are various kinds of atoms—large and small, rough and smooth—and that the small smooth ones have a certain probability of jumping even though they are not bumped by other atoms. Such characteristics are the only ones that are relevant to whether the atoms engage in spontaneous movement, so the best explanation we can give is in terms of such probabilities. If we were to tell him that there *must* be *some* reason why this small smooth atom rather than another started to move at that moment, we would merely be expressing a deterministic prejudice.

Leaving this historical fiction, we find a similar situation in modern physics. The atoms of certain elements are unstable, and they suffer radioactive decay. The uranium atom, for example, may decay by emitting an alpha-particle from its nucleus. The nucleus constitutes a strong enclosure, and the alpha-particle races frantically back and forth, bumping into the wall of the nucleus about 10^{21} ($= 1,000,000,000,000,000,000,000$) times per second, and on the average an alpha-particle makes it out in about a billion years. In other words, it has about one chance in 10^{38} of getting out any time it bombards the barrier of its nuclear prison.[23] When we ask why a particular uranium atom decayed in this manner at this particular time, the answer is that an alpha-particle "tunnelled out" of its nucleus. When we ask why the alpha-particle escaped on that particular trial, having failed on countless other occasions, the answer is simply that there is a probability of about 10^{-38} of such an outcome on any given bombardment of the wall. That is all there is to it. Perhaps you want to say that there must be some reason for the success on this trial and the failures on the others, but we do not yet know what it is. According to current quantum mechanics, however, that is not the case. We are, according to that theory, dealing with an irremediably indeterministic process.

The situation in quantum mechanics arises out of what seems to be a pervasive feature of the atomic and sub-atomic world. It has been described by an unfortunate phrase, "the uncertainty principle." When one speaks of uncertainty, it is natural to suppose that there is something to be known, but we do not know it for sure. Thus, it has sometimes been said that there is an inescapable uncertainty if one attempts to ascertain the values of both the position and momentum of a particle, and similarly for energy and time. If we ascertain the position of an electron with great precision, we will be unable to ascertain its momentum very exactly, and conversely. There is

a limit to the joint precision with which two so-called complementary parameters can be known. This way of speaking, as well as many popular attempts to explain the uncertainty principle, strongly suggests that the electron has, at any given moment, an exact position and an exact momentum, but we are not able to find out what both of those values are. This is a serious misinterpretation of the uncertainty principle, as many experts agree.[24] We should say instead that particles such as the electron and our alpha-particle are actually in physical states that are not characterized by exact values of position and momentum, energy and time. We *can* ascertain the state of the particle, but the state, together with all of the pertinent laws of nature, does not provide the basis for deterministic prediction or deductive explanation of such events as the alpha-particle tunnelling out of the uranium nucleus. Even Laplace's demon could not reliably predict the time at which a particular uranium atom would experience radioactive decay.

8. EXPLANATION AND RELEVANCE

If the world is actually indeterministic, in the way modern physics suggests, you might infer that some things cannot be explained. Such a conclusion would, I think, be unjustified.[25] It is true that some events could not be explained deductively, but the supposition that there is no other kind of explanation is simply another aspect of the deterministic view. If we embrace indeterminism, we must adopt a suitable conception of explanation to go along with it. For the indeterminist, some events will have to be explained statistically—I do not say "inductively," because I shall be suggesting a different sort of statistical explanation. Moreover, it looks as if we will have to come to terms with events that are extremely improbable; 10^{-38} is a very small number. Shall we conclude that only events with high probabilities can be explained—that those with low probabilities are inexplicable? This result will be forced upon us if we think that explanations, deductive or statistical, must be *arguments* showing that the event to be explained *was to be expected,* for that requires high probability if deductive certainty is lacking. I am inclined to believe, however, that this way of characterizing statistical explanation is inappropriate. The key to an alternative approach will be the concept of *statistical relevance.*

Suppose a life insurance company is considering

issuing a policy to a certain person, Frank Smith, and suppose that at the premium set, the company will make a profit if he lives for at least ten years. The company must decide whether to sell him life insurance at that rate, and so they would like to know whether he will survive for at least a decade. From mortality tables, they can find the probability that an unspecified American will live that long, but they know in addition that he is male and 37 years old. Again the mortality tables will furnish the probability of a 37-year-old American male living ten years longer. His age and sex are relevant because the probability of survival for a male is different from that for a female, and the probability certainly varies with age. In order to make the decision, the company will secure further evidence about him, e.g., his state of health, his occupation, his personal habits, his marital status, and his hobbies. We know, for example, that the probability of survival is different for heavy cigarette smokers than for non-smokers, different for diabetics than for people in normal health, different for steeplejacks than for clergymen, and different for married men than for bachelors. Any specification of characteristics of Frank Smith that alters the probability of his living to the age of 47 *is statistically relevant* to the case at hand. Characteristics that do not change the probability are irrelevant. Examples of irrelevant characteristics would be the color of his eyes (but not of his skin), whether his social security number is odd or even, and whether his first child is a boy or a girl.

The insurance company would like to know whether Frank Smith will live another ten years, and whether or not Laplace's demon could predict that fact with certainty, the insurance company cannot. Hence, they must be content with probabilities, and indeed, that is the entire basis of their business. In making decisions as to whom to insure, they try to take into consideration the statistically relevant factors, and they try to avoid getting involved with irrelevant ones.

The same considerations, I believe, enter into statistical explanation. When we ask why John Jones' streptococcus infection cleared up quickly, we mention the fact that he was given penicillin, for that is a highly relevant fact. The probability of a streptococcus infection going away promptly is quite different, depending upon whether the patient received penicillin or not. When we ask for an explanation of the fact that John Doe contracted paresis, the fact that he had latent untreated syphilis is cited, for the probability of anyone developing paresis is very different, depending upon whether he ever arrives at the condition of untreated latent syphilis. If we find such explanations incomplete, it is because we reasonably believe that there are additional relevant factors, as yet unknown, that have a bearing upon the probability of recovery from streptococcus infection, or the occurrence of paresis.

Now it might occur to you that an incredible variety of factors could be relevant to, say, the contraction of paresis. Whether John Doe's parents are of Latin or Anglo-Saxon extraction might have some bearing upon his attitudes toward sex, and hence, upon the likelihood of his contracting syphilis, and finally upon the chance of his becoming paretic. His socio-economic status might also be relevant in a number of ways, including the probability of his seeking medical treatment should the symptoms of a venereal disease appear. Nevertheless, although such factors may be indirectly relevant in the absence of more detailed information about his medical condition, they become irrelevant in the light of further information. Once it is known that the victim has contracted syphilis, the probability of his picking up a venereal disease is irrelevant. Once it is known that he has arrived at the stage of latent untreated syphilis, the likelihood of his seeking medical treatment in the early stages of the disease is irrelevant. The more immediate conditions, so to speak, screen off the relevance of the more remote ones.[26]

The determinist and the indeterminist alike, in attempting to explain an event, are trying to assemble a *total set of relevant conditions*. By a total set of relevant conditions, I mean a set of conditions that cannot be supplemented in any way that would change the probability of the given outcome. This aim is achieved more readily than you might offhand suppose. If you have a universal law of the form, "All F are G"—for example, all copper conducts electricity—then the probability of a piece of copper being an electric conductor is one, and nothing can be added to change that. If you add that the piece of copper was formed into a penny, the probability of its conductivity is still one. If you add that it was originally mined in northern Michigan, the probability of conductivity is still one. Unless the general statement was false in the first place (in which case it did not express a genuine law), what is true of all copper is true of any specific type of copper: We have, indeed, found a total set of conditions relevant to conductivity. Similar considerations apply to negative universal generalizations such as "No whales are fish," the probability in such cases being zero instead of one.

The determinist is very happy with the total sets of relevant conditions that are embodied in universal laws, for these are just the kinds of laws he wants for his deductive explanations. When the laws are statistical, he feels, the explanations are incomplete because there are further relevant conditions to be found. He maintains, in other words, that the only way to achieve a total set of relevant conditions is to find universal laws. The indeterminist takes a different view. He maintains that there are other ways of arriving at total sets of relevant conditions. When asked why an atom experienced spontaneous radioactive decay, he might answer that it is an atom of uranium 238, and that it has a half-life of about eight billion years (which is a convenient way of expressing its probability of disintegration). To say merely that it is a uranium atom would not be sufficient, for the different isotopes of uranium have different half-lives, but once the isotope has been specified, nothing further is relevant. It does not matter whether the atom is in a block of pure metallic uranium 238, whether it is alloyed with other uranium isotopes or other metallic elements, whether it is in chemical compound with other elements (e.g., an oxide), whether it is in a magnetic field, or whether it has been blessed by the Pope. In such cases, according to the indeterminist, there is a certain probability of spontaneous decay, and nothing we can add has any bearing upon that probability. If the determinist says that there must be some further relevant factor that has not yet been found, the indeterminist could appropriately reply, "Perhaps it would be nice if there were, but what guarantee have we that nature is so accommodating to our wishes?"

If indeterminism is true, it does not follow that there are events that are incapable of being explained. To offer an explanation, as I have suggested, is to assemble a total set of relevant conditions for the event to be explained, and to cite the probability of that event in the presence of these conditions. This view of explanation, unlike the standard account of deductive and inductive explanation, does not view an explanation as an argument showing that the event was to be expected on the basis of the explanatory facts. The explanation is, rather, a presentation of the conditions relevant to the occurrence of the event,

and a statement of the degree of probability of the event given these conditions. That degree of probability may be high, middling, or low, but whatever its size, it is an index of the degree to which we would have been justified in expecting it.

A point of clarification must be added lest complete misunderstanding arise. The general laws, be they universal or statistical, that provide the relevant conditions, may themselves be explained on a different level, so to speak. If we invoke the general law that all copper conducts electricity, this provides a total set of conditions relevant to the fact that a particular piece of copper, such as a penny placed behind a blown fuse, conducts electricity. However, that does not exclude the possibility of explaining electrical conductivity itself in terms of the behavior of electrons. The fact that such further explanation is possible does not mean that the original explanation of the conductivity of the penny was incomplete; it only means that facts adduced to explain other facts may in turn be explained on a more general or theoretical level.[27]

9. CAUSES VS. STATISTICAL CORRELATIONS

In recent years, evidence of a significant statistical correlation between cigarette smoking and various diseases has been widely publicized. The tobacco industry, in its frequent protest that "no causal connection" has been found, has emphatically reiterated the distinction between causal connection and "mere statistical correlation." While I believe that the statements on behalf of the cigarette manufacturers are wrong, and that extremely strong evidence of a causal connection between cigarette smoking and disease has been presented, that is not the major point here. We are interested in determinism and in explanation, and each of these concepts seems to have a deep causal component. When we think of determinism we think of causal determination, and when we ask "why," the natural answer is "because. . . ." To ask why the airplane crashed is to ask what caused the crash.

A persistent statistical correlation—that is, a genuine statistical relevance relation—is strongly indicative of a causal relation of some sort. Consider some examples. Both fever and characteristic types of spots are symptoms of measles. The fever does not cause the spots and the spots do not cause the fever, yet there is a marked statistical relevance of the one to the other. The reason, of course, is that they are distinct effects of a common cause, and the common cause explains the statistical relation. In similar fashion, there is a high degree of statistical relevance between the drop in barometer reading and the occurrence of a storm, but neither causes the other. Both the storm and the falling barometer are the result of meteorological conditions that barometers are designed to indicate. The main danger in confusing statistical correlation with genuine causation is the danger of confusing symptoms with causes. In medicine, engineering, social work, politics and other practical pursuits, we know the futility of treating the symptoms when we want to correct the conditions giving rise to them.

In discussing the search for total sets of relevant conditions, I mentioned the fact that some relevant conditions can render others irrelevant by what is called "screening off." The screening off phenomenon is basically a matter of causal proximity. The measles infection is more closely related to both the fever and the spots than are the spots and fever to each other. The barometer reading is more remote from the storm than is the set of atmospheric conditions responsible for the storm. Primary syphilis is causally more remote from paresis than is secondary or latent syphilis.

What do these causal relationships amount to? It seems that the world is full of processes that go on in a relatively continuous way. Billiard balls roll around on tables, bouncing off the cushions and colliding with one another, according to the laws of classical mechanics. Light rays are propagated in accordance with the laws of optics. Springs can be extended and contracted as described by Hooke's law. When the temperature of a gas is increased, without changing the size of the container, the pressure increases. These are processes that are governed by universal laws of the kind found in classical physics and used in deductive explanations.[28] If everything that happens in the world follows from antecedent conditions by processes that conform to such laws, we say that the universe is *causally* deterministic. In this case, we could say with Laplace, "We ought then to regard the present state of the universe as the effect of its anterior state and as the cause of the one which is to follow."[29] If, however, the causal processes are governed by laws that have an irreducibly statistical character, such as we find

in contemporary quantum mechanics, then the world is causally indeterministic. It would be a mistake to suppose, however, that there are real connections among events over and above the perfect or imperfect correlations that are embodied in the laws of nature. David Hume's discussion of this point in *An Enquiry Concerning Human Understanding*[30] is a philosophic classic.[31]

10. FREE WILL AND INDETERMINISM

Suppose indeterminism, of the sort suggested by modern quantum mechanics, is true. No one knows for sure whether it is, but it might be, and it is interesting to see what bearing that would have on the problem of human free will.

There is good evidence that radiation of the sort emitted in radioactive decay of unstable nuclei can have profound effects upon genetic structure and can induce mutations. Suppose that the father of a child was in the vicinity of radioactive materials just prior to its conception, and that a chance disintegration of an unstable atom emitted a gamma-ray which altered a gene that was passed on to the child. Suppose, to make the case dramatic, that the genetic damage of the gamma-ray results in the child becoming a congenital criminal, although he would have developed normal character and personality if that atom had not disintegrated just when it did. Would we be inclined to say that this person's criminal acts are done freely, because of the chance occurrence in his heredity, while his non-criminal acts would have been unfree if chance were unable to influence his genetic make-up? Hardly.

But, you might say, the indeterministic event was not part of him. It happened before he was conceived, it came from outside him and his father, and its results were passed onto him (suppose) in a fully deterministic manner. Very well. Suppose a person eats some food which, unknown to him, is contaminated with radioactive material. One of these unstable atoms decays, indeterministically, at a vital place in his body; as a result he contracts cancer. Is there any element of freedom introduced because the chance event took place inside of his body? Hardly.

But, you might continue, the onset of cancer does not involve any element of thought, deliberation, decision, or choice, and these are vitally involved in freedom. That seems to be a sound point. Suppose, therefore, that you are trying to make up your mind about experimenting with marijuana. If determinism were true, your heredity, your environment, and the physiological processes in your nervous system would totally determine the outcome of your deliberation. If you decided to go ahead and try it, the decision would be a causally determined result of the chemistry of your brain at that moment. Under these circumstances, you might seriously doubt that the choice is free. Suppose, however, that determinism is not true. At the crucial point in your brain is an unstable atom. Its relation to the decision process is something like a trigger mechanism. If that atom disintegrates at the proper moment, it will start a process that will lead causally to the decision to smoke pot. If it does not disintegrate, you will decide against it. Does the decision now seem free? Hardly.

These science fiction speculations are designed for one purpose: to raise the question of whether the problem of free will is really connected with determinism in the way it seems to be. Having seen that determinism seems to raise very serious difficulties in connection with freedom of choice and action, we are tempted to jump unreflectively to the conclusion that all will be rosy if we just abandon determinism. When we go on to postulate indeterminism, however, the net result seems to be absolutely no progress at all in the direction of free will. The problem is just as difficult and puzzling—if not more so—under the assumption of indeterminism than it was in the context of determinism. It appears that we can construct the following argument:

(6) If indeterminism is true, man does not have free will. Indeterminism is true.

_____

Man does not have free will.

We do not know for sure whether the second premise of this argument is true, but modern quantum mechanics makes it at least plausible. That, however, is not the crucial point. Argument (6) can be combined with argument (2) as follows:

(7) If determinism is true, man does not have free will. If indeterminism is true, man does not have free will. Either determinism is true or indeterminism is true.

_____

Man does not have free will.

This argument is a dilemma, and it is logically valid.[32] Moreover, its third premise is necessarily true, for indeterminism holds if determinism does not, and conversely. There are two avenues to follow from here. One can accept all three premises and

draw the conclusion that freedom of will, freedom of decision, freedom of choice, and freedom of action are all illusory. The other avenue, and by far the more promising one, I believe, is to reexamine the first premise of arguments (1) and (2), which is the same as the first premise of (7). This premise, which was accepted so facilely at the beginning, has taken us down the long path to argument (7), which might aptly be called "the dilemma of free will." Perhaps the premise is not as self-evident as it appeared at the outset. It may turn out that the question of whether the breaking of the vase by Epictetus was causally determined is far less important than the question of how many vases he, and other slaves, broke after his beating. Legend does not, as far as I know, provide a clear answer to this latter question.[33]

NOTES

1. From the play "Sheppey," by W. Somerset Maugham (copyright, 1933, by W. Somerset Maugham), published in 1933 by William Heinemann, London, and in 1934 by Doubleday and Company, Inc. Reprinted by permission of A. P. Watt & Son, as literary agents to the late Mr. Maugham and on behalf of Messrs. William Heinemann, Ltd.

2. Lucretius, _The Nature of the Universe,_ trans. by R. E. Latham (Baltimore: Penguin Books, 1951).

3. Sir Isaac Newton, _Philosophiae Naturalis Principia Mathematica_ (Mathematical Principles of Natural Philosophy).

4. The so-called "torsion-balance experiment," first performed by Henry Cavendish in 1798. All previous confirmations of Newton's gravitational theory involved either one or two bodies of astronomic proportions: the influence of the earth on falling bodies, the mutual attraction between the sun and the planets, the influence of the moon on the tides. The Cavendish experiment detected the gravitational attraction between two ordinary medium-size terrestrial objects.

5. The explanation of the "perturbations of Uranus" by the planet Neptune was accomplished in 1843 by John C. Adams, and independently about two years later by U. J. J. Leverrier. Neptune was observed and identified as a planet by J. G. Galle in 1846. In similar fashion, Pluto was discovered in 1930. Leverrier also determined that there was a small deviation in the path of Mercury, and he postulated a planet Vulcan to explain it, but Vulcan was never found. The deviation received a more satisfactory explanation in Einstein's general theory of relativity, but even this explanation is challenged by some contemporary physicists, most notably, R. H. Dicke of Princeton University.

6. Pierre Simon, Marquis de Laplace, _A Philosophical Essay on Probabilities,_ trans. by Frederick Wilson Truscott and Frederick Lincoln Emery (New York: Dover Publications, Inc., 1951), p. 3.

7. René Descartes, _Meditations._ In saying that his arguments were persuasive, I do not mean to ignore the severe difficulty of the problem of interaction between mind and matter to which his mind-body dualism led. This problem becomes even more acute if one admits that there is a great deal of interaction between mind and matter, and simultaneously wants to claim determinism

for the physical realm and indeterminism for the psychological realm.

8. Darwin published *The Origin of Species* in 1859 and *The Descent of Man* in 1871.

9. The synthesis of urea was accomplished by Friedrich Wöhler in 1828.

10. See especially Freud's *Psychopathology of Everyday Life* and *The Interpretation of Dreams,* both published in *The Basic Writings of Sigmund Freud,* ed. by A. A. Brill (New York: Random House, 1938). Although Freud lived and worked well into the twentieth century, many of the most significant ideas were developed before the turn of the century.

11. Isaac Asimov, *The Genetic Code* (New York: New American Library, Signet Science Books, 1962), provides an accurate and readable popular account of the most important developments in molecular biology; James Watson, *The Double Helix* (New York: Atheneum Publishers, 1968; reprinted as a Signet paperback by the New American Library), is a fascinating biographical account of the discovery of the structure of the DNA molecule by one of its co-discoverers.

12. For a collection of articles from the *Scientific American* discussing recent developments in this area, see McGaugh, Weinberger, and Whalen, eds., *Psychobiology: The Biological Bases of Behavior* (San Francisco: W. H. Freeman & Co., 1967). See also, Dean Wooldridge, *The Machinery of the Brain* (New York: McGraw-Hill Book Co., 1963).

13. A. d'Abro, *The Evolution of Scientific Thought* (New York: Dover Publications, Inc., 1950), provides an excellent nontechnical account of the development of relativity theory.

14. A. d'Abro, *The Rise of the New Physics* (New York: Dover Publications, Inc., 1951), provides an excellent non-technical account of the development of quantum theory.

15. This is the famous Stern-Gerlach experiment, and it has considerable fundamental importance in quantum theory. See d'Abro, *The Rise of the New Physics,* pp. 599–601.

16. The proof is due to John von Neumann, and is given in his treatise *Mathematical Foundations of Quantum Theory* (Princeton: Princeton University Press, 1955). The significance of this proof is, however, a matter for serious dispute among able physicists.

17. Laplace, *op. cit.,* p. 4.

18. These formulations are due to G. W. Leibniz and Immanuel Kant, respectively.

19. For discussions of some of the complexities involved in the issue of teleology, see *Purpose in Nature,* ed. by John V. Canfield (Englewood Cliffs, N.J.: Prentice-Hall, Inc., 1966).

20. This view of explanation is presented and discussed very clearly by Hospers.

21. Carl G. Hempel in *Aspects of Scientific Explanation* (New York: The Free Press, 1965) has given the clearest and most exhaustive technical discussion of these two types of explanation (which he calls "deductive-nomological" and "inductive-statistical" respectively). He also provided this example of inductive explanation.

22. ". . . 72 out of 100 untreated persons [with latent syphilis] go through life without the symptoms of late [tertiary] syphilis, but 28 out of 100 untreated persons were known to have developed serious outcomes [paresis and others] and there is no way to predict what will happen to an untreated infected person." Edwin Gurney Clark, M.D., and William O. Mortimer Harris, M.D., "Venereal Diseases," *Encyclopaedia Britannica,* 1961, Vol. XXIII, p. 44.

23. See George Gamow, *The Atom and its Nucleus* (Englewood Cliffs, N.J.: Prentice-Hall, Inc., 1961), pp. 111–115. Gamow was responsible for the theoretical explanation of this phenomenon in 1928.

24. See Adolf Grünbaum, "Complementarity in Quantum Physics and its Philosophical Generalization," *Journal of Philosophy,* LIV (1957), pp. 713–727, for an extremely clear discussion of this issue.

25. I have offered a detailed and technical account of explanation in "*Statistical Explanation and Statistical Relevance*" (Pittsburgh: University of Pittsburgh Press, 1971). The present discussion of explanation and relevance is a highly oversimplified version.

26. This concept of *screening off* is of crucial importance in the discussion of explanation and statistical relevance; it is discussed at length in the book cited in the preceding note.

27. See Hospers' article for a clear exposition of this point.

28. There is an exceedingly difficult problem, to which no satisfactory answer has yet been given, as to how causal laws are to be distinguished from other universal or statistical generalizations. The book cited in note 25 goes into some details of this problem.

29. Laplace, *op. cit.,* p. 4.

30. [See pp. 198–220 in this anthology.]

31. See the discussion of Hume's view in my article, "An Encounter with David Hume," p. 227 in this anthology.

32. This type of argument is discussed in my *Logic in Foundations of Philosophy Series* (Englewood Cliffs, N.J.: Prentice-Hall, Inc., 1963; 2nd ed., 1973), §9.

33. To my mind, the best approach to the problem of the relation of free will to determinism is given by Charles Stevenson, "Ethical Judgments and Avoidability," in his *Facts and Values* (New Haven: Yale University Press, 1963), pp. 138–152.

WALTER T. STACE

The Problem of Free Will*

[A] great problem which the rise of scientific naturalism has created for the modern mind concerns the foundations of morality. The old religious foundations have largely crumbled away, and it may well be thought that the edifice built upon them by generations of men is in danger of collapse. A total collapse of moral behavior is, as I pointed out before, very unlikely. For a society in which this occurred could not survive. Nevertheless the danger to moral standards inherent in the virtual disappearance of their old religious foundations is not illusory.

I shall first discuss the problem of free will, for it is certain that if there is no free will there can be no morality. Morality is concerned with what men ought and ought not to do. But if a man has no freedom to choose what he will do, if whatever he does is done under compulsion, then it does not make sense to tell him that he ought not to have done what he did and that he ought to do something different. All moral precepts would in such case be meaningless. Also if he acts always under compulsion, how can he be held morally responsible for his actions? How can he, for example, be punished for what he could not help doing?

It is to be observed that those learned professors of philosophy or psychology who deny the existence of free will do so only in their professional moments and in their studies and lecture rooms. For when it comes to doing anything practical, even of the most trivial kind, they invariably behave as if they and others were free. They inquire from you at dinner whether you will choose this dish or that dish. They will ask a child why he told a lie, and will punish him for not having chosen the way of truthfulness. All of which is inconsistent with a disbelief in free will. This should

cause us to suspect that the problem is not a real one; and this, I believe, is the case. The dispute is merely verbal, and is due to nothing but a confusion about the meanings of words. It is what is now fashionably called a semantic problem.

How does a verbal dispute arise? Let us consider a case which, although it is absurd in the sense that no one would ever make the mistake which is involved in it, yet illustrates the principle which we shall have to use in the solution of the problem. Suppose that someone believed that the word "man" means a certain sort of five-legged animal; in short that "five-legged animal" is the correct *definition* of man. He might then look around the world, and rightly observing that there are no five-legged animals in it, he might proceed to deny the existence of men. This preposterous conclusion would have been reached because he was using an incorrect definition of "man." All you would have to do to show him his mistake would be to give him the correct definition; or at least to show him that his definition was wrong. Both the problem and its solution would, of course, be entirely verbal. The problem of free will, and its solution, I shall maintain, is verbal in exactly the same way. The problem has been created by the fact that learned men, especially philosophers, have assumed an incorrect definition of free will, and then finding that there is nothing in the world which answers to their definition, have denied its existence. As far as logic is concerned, their conclusion is just as absurd as that of the man who denies the existence of men. The only difference is that the mistake in the latter case is obvious and crude, while the mistake which the deniers of free will have made is rather subtle and difficult to detect.

Throughout the modern period, until quite recently, it was assumed, both by the philosophers who denied free will and by those who defended it, that *determinism is inconsistent with free will*. If a man's ac-

*From *Religion and the Modern Mind* by Walter T. Stace (J. B. Lippincott Company). Copyright 1952 by W. T. Stace. Reprinted by permission of Harper & Row, Publishers, Inc.

tions were wholly determined by chains of causes stretching back into the remote past, so that they could be predicted beforehand by a mind which knew all the causes, it was assumed that they could not in that case be free. This implies that a certain definition of actions done from free will was assumed, namely that they are actions *not* wholly determined by causes or predictable beforehand. Let us shorten this by saying that free will was defined as meaning indeterminism. This is the incorrect definition which has led to the denial of free will. As soon as we see what the true definition is we shall find that the question whether the world is deterministic, as Newtonian science implied, or in a measure indeterministic, as current physics teaches, is wholly irrelevant to the problem.

Of course there is a sense in which one can define a word arbitrarily in any way one pleases. But a definition may nevertheless be called correct or incorrect. It is correct if it accords with a *common usage* of the word defined. It is incorrect if it does not. And if you give an incorrect definition, absurd and untrue results are likely to follow. For instance, there is nothing to prevent you from arbitrarily defining a man as a five-legged animal, but this is incorrect in the sense that it does not accord with the ordinary meaning of the word. Also it has the absurd result of leading to a denial of the existence of men. This shows that *common usage is the criterion for deciding whether a definition is correct or not.* And this is the principle which I shall apply to free will. I shall show that indeterminism is not what is meant by the phrase "free will" *as it is commonly used.* And I shall attempt to discover the correct definition by inquiring how the phrase is used in ordinary conversation.

Here are a few samples of how the phrase might be used in ordinary conversation. It will be noticed that they include cases in which the question whether a man acted with free will is asked in order to determine whether he was morally and legally responsible for his acts.

Jones. I once went without food for a week.

Smith. Did you do that of your own free will?

Jones. No. I did it because I was lost in a desert and could find no food.

But suppose that the man who had fasted was Mahatma Gandhi. The conversation might then have gone:

Gandhi. I once fasted for a week.

Smith. Did you do that of your own free will?

Gandhi. Yes. I did it because I wanted to compel the British Government to give India its independence.

Take another case. Suppose that I had stolen some bread, but that I was as truthful as George Washington. Then, if I were charged with the crime in court, some exchange of the following sort might take place:

Judge. Did you steal the bread of your own free will?

Stace. Yes. I stole it because I was hungry.

Or in different circumstances the conversation might run:

Judge. Did you steal of your own free will?

Stace. No. I stole because my employer threatened to beat me if I did not.

At a recent murder trial in Trenton some of the accused had signed confessions, but afterwards asserted that they had done so under police duress. The following exchange might have occurred:

Judge. Did you sign this confession of your own free will?

Prisoner. No. I signed it because the police beat me up.

Now suppose that a philosopher had been a member of the jury. We could imagine this conversation taking place in the jury room.

Foreman of the Jury. The prisoner says he signed the confession because he was beaten, and not of his own free will.

Philosopher. This is quite irrelevant to the case. There is no such thing as free will.

Foreman. Do you mean to say that it makes no difference whether he signed because his conscience made him want to tell the truth or because he was beaten?

Philosopher. None at all. Whether he was caused to sign by a beating or by some desire of his own—the desire to tell the truth, for example—in either case his signing was causally determined, and therefore in neither case did he act of his own free will. Since there is no such thing as free will, the question whether he signed of his own free will ought not to be discussed by us.

The foreman and the rest of the jury would rightly conclude that the philosopher must be making some mistake. What sort of a mistake could it be? There is only one possible answer. The philosopher must be using the phrase "free will" in some peculiar way of his own which is not the way in which men usually use it when they wish to determine a question of moral responsibility. That is, he must be using an incorrect definition of it as implying action not determined by causes.

Suppose a man left his office at noon, and were questioned about it. Then we might hear this:

Jones. Did you go out of your own free will?
Smith. Yes. I went out to get my lunch.

But we might hear:

Jones. Did you leave your office of your own free will?
Smith. No. I was forcibly removed by the police.

We have now collected a number of cases of actions which, in the ordinary usage of the English language, would be called cases in which people have acted of their own free will. We should also say in all these cases that they *chose* to act as they did. We should also say that they could have acted otherwise, if they had chosen. For instance, Mahatma Gandhi was not compelled to fast; he chose to do so. He could have eaten if he had wanted to. When Smith went out to get his lunch, he chose to do so. He could have stayed and done some more work, if he had wanted to. We have also collected a number of cases of the opposite kind. They are cases in which men were not able to exercise their free will. They had no choice. They were compelled to do as they did. The man in the desert did not fast of his own free will. He had no choice in the matter. He was compelled to fast because there was nothing for him to eat. And so with the other cases. It ought to be quite easy, by an inspection of these cases, to tell what we ordinarily mean when we say that a man did or did not exercise free will. We ought therefore to be able to extract from them the proper definition of the term. Let us put the cases in a table:

Free Acts	Unfree Acts
Gandhi fasting because he wanted to free India.	The man fasting in the desert because there was no food.
Stealing bread because one is hungry.	Stealing because one's employer threatened to beat one.

Signing a confession because one wanted to tell the truth.	Signing because the police beat one.
Leaving the office because one wanted one's lunch.	Leaving because forcibly removed.

It is obvious that to find the correct definition of free acts we must discover what characteristic is common to all the acts in the left-hand column, and is, at the same time, absent from all the acts in the right-hand column. This characteristic which all free acts have, and which no unfree acts have, will be the defining characteristic of free will.

Is being uncaused, or not being determined by causes, the characteristic of which we are in search? It cannot be, because although it is true that all the acts in the right-hand column have causes, such as the beating by the police or the absence of food in the desert, so also do the acts in the left-hand column. Mr. Gandhi's fasting was caused by his desire to free India, the man leaving his office by his hunger, and so on. Moreover there is no reason to doubt that these causes of the free acts were in turn caused by prior conditions, and that these were again the results of causes, and so on back indefinitely into the past. Any physiologist can tell us the causes of hunger. What caused Mr. Gandhi's tremendously powerful desire to free India is no doubt more difficult to discover. But it must have had causes. Some of them may have lain in peculiarities of his glands or brain, others in his past experiences, others in his heredity, others in his education. Defenders of free will have usually tended to deny such facts. But to do so is plainly a case of special pleading, which is unsupported by any scrap of evidence. The only reasonable view is that all human actions, both those which are freely done and those which are not, are either wholly determined by causes, or at least as much determined as other events in nature. It may be true, as the physicists tell us, that nature is not as deterministic as was once thought. But whatever degree of determinism prevails in the world, human actions appear to be as much determined as anything else. And if this is so, it cannot be the case that what distinguishes actions freely chosen from those which are not free is that the latter are determined by causes while the former are not. Therefore, being uncaused or being undetermined by causes, must be an incorrect definition of free will.

What, then, is the difference between acts which are freely done and those which are not? What is the characteristic which is present to all the acts in the left-hand column and absent from all those in the right-hand column? Is it not obvious that, although both sets of actions have causes, the causes of those in the left-hand column are *of a different kind* from the causes of those in the right-hand column? The free acts are all caused by desires, or motives, or by some sort of internal psychological states of the agent's mind. The unfree acts, on the other hand, are all caused by physical forces or physical conditions, outside the agent. Police arrest means physical force exerted from the outside; the absence of food in the desert is a physical condition of the outside world. We may therefore frame the following rough definitions. *Acts freely done are those whose immediate causes are psychological states in the agent. Acts not freely done are those whose immediate causes are states of affairs external to the agent.*

It is plain that if we define free will in this way, then free will certainly exists, and the philosopher's denial of its existence is seen to be what it is— nonsense. For it is obvious that all those actions of men which we should ordinarily attribute to the exercise of their free will, or of which we should say that they freely chose to do them, are in fact actions which have been caused by their own desires, wishes, thoughts, emotions, impulses, or other psychological states.

In applying our definition we shall find that it usually works well, but that there are some puzzling cases which it does not seem exactly to fit. These puzzles can always be solved by paying careful attention to the ways in which words are used, and remembering that they are not always used consistently. I have space for only one example. Suppose that a thug threatens to shoot you unless you give him your wallet, and suppose that you do so. Do you, in giving him your wallet, do so of your own free will or not? If we apply our definition, we find that you acted freely, since the immediate cause of the action was not an actual outside force but the fear of death, which is a psychological cause. Most people, however, would say that you did not act of your own free will but under compulsion. Does this show that our definition is wrong? I do not think so. Aristotle, who gave a solution of the problem of free will substantially the same as ours (though he did not use the term "free will")

admitted that there are what he called "mixed" or borderline cases in which it is difficult to know whether we ought to call the acts free or compelled. In the case under discussion, though no actual force was used, the gun at your forehead so nearly approximated to actual force that we tend to say the case was one of compulsion. It is a borderline case.

Here is what may seem like another kind of puzzle. According to our view an action may be free though it could have been predicted beforehand with certainty. But suppose you told a lie, and it was certain beforehand that you would tell it. How could one then say, "You could have told the truth"? The answer is that it is perfectly true that you could have told the truth *if* you had wanted to. In fact you would have done so, for in that case the causes producing your action, namely your desires, would have been different, and would therefore have produced different effects. It is a delusion that predictability and free will are incompatible. This agrees with common sense. For if, knowing your character, I predict that you will act honorably, no one would say when you do act honorably, that this shows you did not do so of your own free will.

Since free will is a condition of moral responsibility, we must be sure that our theory of free will gives a sufficient basis for it. To be held morally responsible for one's actions means that one may be justly punished or rewarded, blamed or praised, for them. But it is not just to punish a man for what he cannot help doing. How can it be just to punish him for an action which it was certain beforehand that he would do? We have not attempted to decide whether, as a matter of fact, all events, including human actions, are completely determined. For that question is irrelevant to the problem of free will. But if we assume for the purposes of argument that complete determinism is true, but that we are nevertheless free, it may then be asked whether such a deterministic free will is compatible with moral responsibility. For it may seem unjust to punish a man for an action which it could have been predicted with certainty beforehand that he would do.

But that determinism is incompatible with moral responsibility is as much a delusion as that it is incompatible with free will. You do not excuse a man for doing a wrong act because, knowing his character, you felt certain beforehand that he would do it. Nor do you deprive a man of a reward or prize because, knowing his goodness or his capabilities, you felt certain beforehand that he would win it.

Volumes have been written on the justification of punishment. But so far as it affects the question of free will, the essential principles involved are quite simple. The punishment of a man for doing a wrong act is justified, either on the ground that it will correct his own character, or that it will deter other people from doing similar acts. The instrument of punishment has been in the past, and no doubt still is, often unwisely used; so that it may often have done more harm than good. But that is not relevant to our present problem. Punishment, if and when it is justified, is justified only on one or both of the grounds just mentioned. The question then is how, if we assume determinism, punishment can correct character or deter people from evil actions.

Suppose that your child develops a habit of telling lies. You give him a mild beating. Why? Because you believe that his personality is such that the usual motives for telling the truth do not cause him to do so. You therefore supply the missing cause, or motive, in the shape of pain and the fear of future pain if he repeats his untruthful behavior. And you hope that a few treatments of this kind will condition him to the habit of truth-telling, so that he will come to tell the truth without the infliction of pain. You assume that his actions are determined by causes, but that the usual causes of truth-telling do not in him produce their usual effects. You therefore supply him with an artificially injected motive, pain and fear, which you think will in the future cause him to speak truthfully.

The principle is exactly the same where you hope, by punishing one man, to deter others from wrong actions. You believe that the fear of punishment will cause those who might otherwise do evil to do well.

We act on the same principle with non-human, and even with inanimate, things, if they do not behave in the way we think they ought to behave. The rose bushes in the garden produce only small and poor blooms, whereas we want large and rich ones. We supply a cause which will produce large blooms, namely fertilizer. Our automobile does not go properly. We supply a cause which will make it go better, namely oil in the works. The punishment for the man, the fertilizer for the plant, and the oil for the car, are all justified by the same principle and in the same way. The only difference is that diferent kinds of things require different kinds of causes to make them do what they should. Pain may be the appropriate remedy to apply, in certain cases, to human beings, and oil to the machine. It is, of course, of no use to inject motor oil into the boy or to beat the machine.

Thus we see that moral responsibility is not only consistent with determinism, but requires it. The assumption on which punishment is based is that human behavior is causally determined. If pain could not be a cause of truth-telling there would be no justification at all for punishing lies. If human actions and volitions were uncaused, it would be useless either to punish or reward, or indeed to do anything else to correct people's bad behavior. For nothing that you could do would in any way influence them. Thus moral responsibility would entirely disappear. If there were no determinism of human beings at all, their actions would be completely unpredictable and capricious, and therefore irresponsible. And this is in itself a strong argument against the common view of philosophers that free will means being undetermined by causes.

JOHN HOSPERS

Free Will and Psychoanalysis*

John Hospers (1918–   ) is the author of numerous books in ethics, politics, and aesthetics. He teaches philosophy at the University of Southern California.

> O Thou who didst with pitfall and with gin
> Beset the Road I was to wander in,
>   Thou wilt not with Predestined Evil round
> Enmesh, and then impute my Fall to Sin!
>   —Edward FitzGerald,
>   *The Rubaiyat of Omar Khayyam*

. . . It is extremely common for nonprofessional philosophers and iconoclasts to deny that human freedom exists, but at the same time to have no clear idea of what it is that they are denying to exist. The first thing that needs to be said about the free-will issue is that any meaningful term must have a meaningful opposite: if it is meaningful to assert that people are not free, it must be equally meaningful to assert that people *are* free, whether this latter assertion is in fact true or not. Whether it is true, of course, will depend on the meaning that is given the weasel-word "free." For example, if freedom is made dependent on indeterminism, it may well be that human freedom is nonexistent. But there seem to be no good grounds for asserting such a dependence, especially since lack of causation is the furthest thing from people's minds when they call an act free. Doubtless there are other senses that can be given to the word "free"—such as "able to do anything we want to do"—in which no human beings are free. But the first essential point about which the denier of freedom must be clear is *what* it is that he is denying. If one knows what it is like for people not to be free, one must know what it *would* be like for them to *be* free.

Philosophers have advanced numerous senses of "free" in which countless acts performed by human beings can truly be called free acts. The most common conception of a free act is that according to which an act is free if and only if it is a *voluntary* act. But the word "voluntary" does not always carry the same meaning. Sometimes to call an act voluntary means that we can do the act *if* we choose to do it: in other words, that it is physically and psychologically possible for us to do it, so that the occurrence of the act follows upon the decision to do it. (One's decision to raise his arm is in fact followed by the actual raising of his arm, unless he is a paralytic; one's decision to pluck the moon from the sky is not followed by the actual event.) Sometimes a voluntary act is conceived (as by G. E. Moore[1]) as an act which would not have occurred if, just beforehand, the agent had chosen not to perform it. But these senses are different from the sense in which a voluntary act is an act resulting from *deliberation,* or perhaps merely from *choice.* For example, there are many acts which we could have avoided, if we had chosen to do so, but which we nevertheless did not *choose* to perform, much less *deliberate* about them. The act of raising one's leg in the process of taking a step while out for a walk, is one which a person could have avoided by choosing to, but which, after one has learned to walk, takes place automatically or semi-automatically through habit, and thus is not the result of choice. (One may have chosen to

*John Hospers, "Meaning and Free Will," *Philosophy and Phenomenological Research,* X (1950), 313–330, reprinted by permission of the author and the editor. The selection appearing here is the abridged version printed as "Free Will and Psychoanalysis" in Wilfred Sellars and John Hospers, eds., *Readings in Ethical Theory* (New York: Appleton-Century-Crofts, 1952), pp. 560–575. For a later discussion of the problem of this paper and one more in accord with the author's present views, see Professor Hospers' *Human Conduct* (New York: Harcourt, Brace & World, 1961), pp. 493–524.

take the walk, but not to take this or that step while walking.) Such acts are free in Moore's sense but are not free in the sense of being deliberate. Moreover, there are classes of acts of the same general character which are not even covered by Moore's sense: sudden outbursts of feeling, in some cases at least, could not have been avoided by an immediately preceding volition, so that if these are to be included under the heading of voluntary acts, the proviso that the act could have been avoided by an immediately preceding volition must be amended to read "could have been avoided by a volition or series of volitions by the agent *at some time in the past*"—such as the adoption of a different set of habits in the agent's earlier and more formative years.

(Sometimes we call *persons,* rather than their acts, free. S. Stebbing, for example, declares that one should never call acts free, but only the doers of the acts.[2] But the two do not seem irreconcilable: can we not speak of a *person* as free *with respect to a certain act* (never just free in general) if that *act* is free—whatever we may then go on to mean by saying that an act is free? Any statement about a free act can then be translated into a statement about the doer of the act.)

Now, no matter in which of the above ways we may come to define "voluntary," there are still acts which are voluntary *but which we would be very unlikely to think of as free.* Thus, when a person submits to the command of an armed bandit, he may do so voluntarily in every one of the above senses: he may do so as a result of choice, even of deliberation, and he could have avoided doing it by willing not to—he could, instead, have refused and been shot. The man who reveals a state secret under torture does the same: he could have refused and endured more torture. Yet such acts, and persons in respect of such acts, are not generally called free. We say that they were performed *under compulsion,* and if an act is performed under compulsion we do not call it free. We say, "He wasn't free because he was forced to do as he did," though of course his act was voluntary.

This much departure from the identification of free acts with voluntary acts almost everyone would admit. Sometimes, however, it would be added that this is all the departure that can be admitted. According to Moritz Schlick, for example,

Freedom means the opposite of compulsion; a man *is free* if he does not act under *compulsion,* and he is com-

pelled or unfree when he is hindered from without in the realization of his natural desires. Hence he is unfree when he is locked up, or chained, or when someone forces him at the point of a gun to do what otherwise he would not do. This is quite clear, and everyone will admit that the everyday or legal notion of the lack of freedom is thus correctly interpreted, and that a man will be considered quite free . . . if no such external compulsion is exerted upon him.[3]

Schlick adds that the entire vexed free-will controversy in philosophy is so much wasted ink and paper, because compulsion has been confused with causality and necessity with uniformity. If the question is asked whether every event is caused, the answer is doubtless yes; but if it is whether every event is compelled, the answer is clearly no. Free acts are uncompelled acts, not uncaused acts. Again, when it is said that some state of affairs (such as water flowing downhill) is necessary, if "necessary" means "compelled," the answer is no; if it means merely that it always happens that way, the answer is yes: universality of application is confused with compulsion. And this, according to Schlick, is the end of the matter.

Schlick's analysis is indeed clarifying and helpful to those who have fallen victim to the confusion he exposes—and this probably includes most persons in their philosophical growing-pains. But *is* this the end of the matter? Is it true that all acts, though caused, are free as long as they are not compelled in the sense which he specifies? May it not be that, while the identification of "free" with "uncompelled" is acceptable, the area of compelled acts is vastly greater than he or most other philosophers have ever suspected? (Moore is more cautious in this respect than Schlick; while for Moore an act is free if it is voluntary in the sense specified above, he thinks there may be another sense in which human beings, and human acts, are not free at all.[4]) We remember statements about human beings being pawns of their early environment, victims of conditions beyond their control, the result of causal influences stemming from their parents, and the like, and we ponder and ask, "Still, are we really free?" Is there not something in what generations of sages have said about man being fettered? Is there not perhaps something too facile, too sleight-of-hand, in Schlick's cutting of the Gordian knot? For example, when a metropolitan newspaper headlines an article with the words "Boy Killer is Doomed Long before He Is Born,"[5] and then goes on to describe how a twelve-year-old boy has been sentenced to prison for the murder of a girl, and how his parental background includes records of drunkenness, divorce, social maladjustment, and paresis, are we still to say that his act, though voluntary and assuredly *not* done at the point of a gun, is free? The boy has early displayed a tendency toward sadistic activity to hide an underlying masochism and "prove that he's a man"; being coddled by his mother only worsens this tendency, until, spurned by a girl in his attempt on her, he kills her—not simply in a fit of anger, but calculatingly, deliberately. Is he free in respect of his criminal act, or for that matter in most of the acts of his life? Surely to ask this question is to answer it in the negative. Perhaps I have taken an extreme case; but it is only to show the superficiality of the Schlick analysis the more clearly. Though not everyone has criminotic tendencies, everyone has been molded by influences which in large measure at least determine his present behavior; he is literally the product of these influences, stemming from periods prior to his "years of discretion," giving him a host of character traits that he cannot change now even if he would. So obviously does what a man is depend upon how a man comes to be, that it is small wonder that philosophers and sages have considered man far indeed from being the master of his fate. It is not as if man's will were standing high and serene above the flux of events that have molded him; it is itself caught up in this flux, itself carried along on the current. An act is free when it is determined by the man's character, say moralists; but what if the most decisive aspects of his character were already irrevocably acquired before he could do anything to mold them? What if even the degree of will power available to him in shaping his habits and disciplining himself now to overcome the influence of his early environment is a factor over which he has no control? What are we to say of this kind of "freedom"? Is it not rather like the freedom of the machine to stamp labels on cans when it has been devised for just that purpose? Some machines can do so more efficiently than others, but only because they have been better constructed.

It is not my purpose here to establish this thesis in general, but only in one specific respect which has received comparatively little attention, namely, the field referred to by psychiatrists as that of unconscious motivation. In what follows I shall restrict my attention to it because it illustrates as clearly as anything the points I wish to make.

Let me try to summarize very briefly the psychoanalytic doctrine on this point.[6] The conscious life of the human being, including the conscious decisions and volitions, is merely a mouthpiece for the unconscious—not directly for the enactment of unconscious drives, but of the compromise between unconscious drives and unconscious reproaches. There is a Big Three behind the scenes which the automaton called the conscious personality carries out: the id, and "eternal gimme," presents its wish and demands its immediate satisfaction; the super-ego says no to the wish immediately upon presentation, and the unconscious ego, the mediator between the two, tries to keep peace by means of compromise.[7]

To go into examples of the functioning of these three "bosses" would be endless; psychoanalytic case books supply hundreds of them. The important point for us to see in the present context is that *it is the unconscious that determines what the conscious impulse and the conscious action shall be.* Hamlet, for example, had a strong Oedipus wish, which was violently counteracted by super-ego reproaches; these early wishes were vividly revived in an unusual adult situation in which his uncle usurped the coveted position from Hamlet's father and won his mother besides. This situation evoked strong strictures on the part of Hamlet's super-ego, and it was this that was responsible for his notorious delay in killing his uncle. A dozen times Hamlet could have killed Claudius easily; but every time Hamlet "decided" not to: a free choice, moralists would say—but no, listen to the super-ego: "What you feel such hatred toward your uncle for, what you are plotting to kill him for, is precisely the crime which you yourself desire to commit: to kill your father and replace him in the affections of your mother. Your fate and your uncle's are bound up together." This paralyzes Hamlet into inaction. Consciously all he knows is that he is unable to act; this conscious inability he rationalizes, giving a different excuse each time.[8] We have always been conscious of the fact that we are not masters of our fate in every respect—that there are many things which we cannot do, that nature is more powerful than we are, that we cannot disobey laws without danger of reprisals, etc. We have become "officially" conscious, too, though in our private lives we must long have been aware of it, that we are not free with respect to the emotions that we feel—whom we love or hate, what types we admire, and the like. More lately still we have been reminded that there are unconscious motivations for our basic attractions and repulsions, our compulsive actions or inabilities to act. But what is not welcome news is that our very acts of volition, and the entire train of deliberations leading up to them, are but façades for the expression of unconscious wishes, or rather, unconscious compromises and defenses.

A man is faced by a choice: shall he kill another person or not? Moralists would say, here is a free choice—the result of deliberation, an action consciously entered into. And yet, though the agent himself does not know it, and has no awareness of the forces that are at work within him, his choice is already determined for him: his conscious will is only an instrument, a slave, in the hands of a deep unconscious motivation which determines his action. If he has a great deal of what the analysts call "free-floating guilt," he will not; but if the guilt is such as to demand immediate absorption in the form of self-damaging behavior, this accumulated guilt will have to be discharged in some criminal action. The man himself does not know what the inner clockwork is; he is like the hands on the clock, thinking they move freely over the face of the clock.

A woman has married and divorced several husbands. Now she is faced with a choice for the next marriage: shall she marry Mr. A, or Mr. B, or nobody at all? She may take considerable time to "decide" this question, and her decision may appear as a final triumph of her free will. Let us assume that A is a normal, well-adjusted, kind, and generous man, while B is a leech, an impostor, one who will become entangled constantly in quarrels with her. If she belongs to a certain classifiable psychological type, she will inevitably choose B, and she will do so even if her previous husbands have resembled B, so that one would think that she "had learned from experience." Consciously, she will of course "give the matter due consideration," etc., etc. To the psychoanalyst all this is irrelevant chaff in the wind—only a camouflage for the inner workings about which she knows nothing consciously. If she is of a certain kind of masochistic strain, as exhibited in her previous set of symptoms, she *must* choose B: her super-ego, always out to maximize the torment in the situation, seeing what dazzling possibilities for self-damaging behavior are promised by the choice of B, compels

her to make the choice she does, and even to conceal the real basis of the choice behind an elaborate façade of rationalizations.

A man is addicted to gambling. In the service of his addiction he loses all his money, spends what belongs to his wife, even sells his property and neglects his children. For a time perhaps he stops; then, inevitably, he takes it up again. The man does not know that he is a victim rather than an agent; or, if he sometimes senses that he is in the throes of something-he-knows-not-what, he will have no inkling of its character and will soon relapse into the illusion that he (his conscious self) is freely deciding the course of his own actions. What he does not know, of course, is that he is still taking out on his mother the original lesion to his infantile narcissism, getting back at her for her fancied refusal of his infantile wishes—and this by rejecting everything identified with her, namely education, discipline, logic, common sense, training. At the roulette wheel, almost alone among adult activities, chance—the opposite of all these things—rules supreme; and his addiction represents his continued and emphatic reiteration of his rejection of Mother and all she represents to his unconscious.

This pseudo-aggression of his is of course masochistic in its effects. In the long run he always loses; he can never quit while he is winning. And far from playing in order to win, rather one can say that his losing is a *sine qua non* of his psychic equilibrium (as it was for example with Dostoyevsky): guilt demands punishment, and in the ego's "deal" with the super-ego the super-ego has granted satisfaction of infantile wishes in return for the self-damaging conditions obtaining. Winning would upset the neurotic equilibrium.[9]

A man has wash-compulsion. He must be constantly washing his hands—he uses up perhaps 400 towels a day. Asked why he does this, he says, "I need to, my hands are dirty"; and if it is pointed out to him that they are not really dirty, he says, "They feel dirty anyway; I feel better when I wash them." So once again he washes them. He "freely decides" every time; he feels that he must wash them, he deliberates for a moment perhaps, but always ends by washing them. What he does not see, of course, are the invisible wires inside him pulling him inevitably to do the things he does: the infantile id-wish concerns preoccupation with dirt, the super-ego charges him with this, and the terrified ego must respond, "No, I don't like dirt, see how clean I like to be, look how I wash my hands!"

Let us see what further "free acts" the same patient engages in (this is an actual case history): he is taken to a concentration camp, and given the worst of treatment by the Nazi guards. In the camp he no longer chooses to be clean; does not even try to be—on the contrary, his choice is now to wallow in filth as much as he can. All he is aware of now is a disinclination to be clean, and every time he must choose he chooses not to be. Behind the scenes, however, another drama is being enacted: the super-ego, perceiving that enough torment is being administered from the outside, can afford to cease pressing its charges in this quarter—the outside world is doing the torturing now, so the super-ego is relieved of the responsibility. Thus the ego is relieved of the agony of constantly making terrified replies in the form of washing to prove that the super-ego is wrong. The defense no longer being needed, the person slides back into what is his natural predilection anyway, for filth. This becomes too much even for the Nazi guards: they take hold of him one day, saying "We'll teach you how to be clean!", drag him into the snow, and pour bucket after bucket of icy water over him until he freezes to death. Such is the end-result of an original id-wish, caught in the machinations of a destroying super-ego.

Let us take, finally, a less colorful, more everyday example. A student at a university, possessing wealth, charm, and all that is usually considered essential to popularity, begins to develop the following personality-pattern: although well taught in the graces of social conversation, he always makes a *faux pas* somewhere, and always in the worst possible situation; to his friends he makes cutting remarks which hurt deeply—and always apparently aimed in such a way as to hurt the most: a remark that would not hurt A but would hurt B he invariably makes to B rather than to A, and so on. None of this is conscious. Ordinarily he is considerate of people, but he contrives always (unconsciously) to impose on just those friends who would resent it most, and at just the times when he should know that he should not impose: at 3 o'clock in the morning, without forewarning, he phones a friend in a near-by city demanding to stay at his apartment for the weekend; naturally the friend is offended, but the person himself is not aware that he has provoked the grievance

("common sense" suffers a temporary eclipse when the neurotic pattern sets in, and one's intelligence, far from being of help in such a situation, is used in the interest of the neurosis), and when the friend is cool to him the next time they meet, he wonders why and feels unjustly treated. Aggressive behavior on his part invites resentment and aggression in turn, but all that he consciously sees is others' behavior towards him—and he considers himself the innocent victim of an unjustified "persecution."

Each of these acts is, from the moralist's point of view, free: he chose to phone his friend at 3 A.M., he chose to make the cutting remark that he did, etc. What he does not know is that an ineradicable masochistic pattern has set in. His unconscious is far more shrewd and clever than is his conscious intellect; it sees with uncanny accuracy just what kind of behavior will damage him most, and unerringly forces him into that behavior. Consciously, the student "doesn't know why he did it"—he gives different "reasons" at different times, but they are all, once again, rationalizations cloaking the unconscious mechanism which propels him willy-nilly into actions that his "common sense" eschews.

The more of this sort of thing one observes, the more he can see what the psychoanalyst means when he talks about *the illusion of freedom*. And the more of a psychiatrist one becomes, the more he is overcome with a sense of what an illusion this free will can be. In some kinds of cases most of us can see it already: it takes no psychiatrist to look at the epileptic and sigh with sadness at the thought that soon this person before you will be as one possessed, not the same thoughtful intelligent person you knew. But people are not aware of this in other contexts, for example when they express surprise at how a person whom they have been so good to could treat them so badly. Let us suppose that you help a person financially or morally or in some other way, so that he is in your debt; suppose further that he is one of the many neurotics who unconsciously identify kindness with weakness and aggression with strength, then he will unconsciously take your kindness to him as weakness and use it as the occasion for enacting some aggression against you. He can't help it, he may regret it himself later; still, he will be driven to do it. If we gain a little knowledge of psychiatry, we can look at him with pity, that a person otherwise so worthy should be so unreliable—but we will exercise realism too, and be aware that there are some types of people that you cannot be good to. In "free" acts of their conscious volition, they will use your own goodness against you.

Sometimes the persons themselves will become dimly aware that "something behind the scenes" is determining their behavior. The divorcee will sometimes view herself with detachment, as if she were some machine (and indeed the psychoanalyst does call her a "repeating-machine"): "I know I'm caught in a net, that I'll fall in love with this guy and marry him and the whole ridiculous merry-go-round will start all over again."

We talk about free will, and we say, for example, the person is free to do so-and-so if he *can* do so *if* he wants to—and we forget that his wanting to is itself caught up in the stream of determinism, that unconscious forces drive him into the wanting or not wanting to do the thing in question. The analogy of the puppet whose motions are manipulated from behind by invisible wires, or better still, by springs inside, is a telling one at almost every point.

And the glaring fact is that it all started so early, before we knew what was happening. The personality-structure is inelastic after the age of five, and comparatively so in most cases after the age of three. Whether one acquires a neurosis or not is determined by that age—and just as involuntarily as if it had been a curse of God. If, for example, a masochistic pattern was set up, under pressure of hyper-narcissism combined with real or fancied infantile deprivation, then the masochistic snowball was on its course downhill long before we or anybody else knew what was happening, and long before anyone could do anything about it. To speak of human beings as "puppets" in such a context is no idle metaphor, but a stark rendering of a literal fact: only the psychiatrist knows what puppets people really are; and it is no wonder that the protestations of philosophers that "the act which is the result of a volition, a deliberation, a conscious decision, is free" leave these persons, to speak mildly, somewhat cold.

But, one may object, all the states thus far described have been abnormal, neurotic ones. The well-adjusted (normal) person at least is free.

Leaving aside the question of how clearly and on what grounds one can distinguish the neurotic from the normal, let me use an illustration of a proclivity that everyone would call normal, namely, the decision of a man to support his wife and possibly a family, and consider briefly its genesis, according to psychoanalytic accounts.[10]

Every baby comes into the world with a full-fledged case of megalomania—interested only in himself, acting as if believing that he is the center of the universe and that others are present only to fulfill his wishes, and furious when his own wants are not satisfied immediately no matter for what reason. Gratitude, even for all the time and worry and care expended on him by the mother, is an emotion entirely foreign to the infant, and as he grows older it is inculcated in him only with the greatest difficulty; his natural tendency is to assume that everything that happens to him is due to himself, except for denials and frustrations, which are due to the "cruel, denying" outer world, in particular the mother; and that he owes nothing to anyone, is dependent on no one. This omnipotence-complex, or illusion of non-dependence, has been called the "autarchic fiction." Such a conception of the world is actually fostered in the child by the conduct of adults, who automatically attempt to fulfill the infant's every wish concerning nourishment, sleep, and attention. The child misconceives causality and sees in these wish-fulfillments not the results of maternal kindness and love, but simply the result of his own omnipotence.

This fiction of omnipotence is gradually destroyed by experience, and its destruction is probably the deepest disappointment of the early years of life. First of all, the infant discovers that he is the victim of organic urges and necessities: hunger, defecation, urination. More important, he discovers that the maternal breast, which he has not previously distinguished from his own body (he has not needed to, since it was available when he wanted it), is not a part of himself after all, but of another creature upon whom he is dependent. He is forced to recognize this, e.g., when he wants nourishment and it is at the moment not present; even a small delay is most damaging to the "autarchic fiction." Most painful of all is the experience of weaning, probably the greatest tragedy in every baby's life, when his dependence is most cruelly emphasized; it is a frustrating experience because what he wants is no longer there at all; and if he has been able to some extent to preserve the illusion of non-dependence heretofore, he is not able to do so now—it is plain that the source of his nourishment is not dependent on him, but he on it. The shattering of the autarchic fiction is a great disillusionment to every child, a tremendous blow to his ego which he will, in one way or another, spend the rest of his life trying to repair. How does he do this?

First of all, his reaction to frustration is anger and fury; and he responds by kicking, biting, etc., the only ways he knows. But he is motorically helpless, and these measures are ineffective, and only serve to emphasize his dependence the more. Moreover, against such responses of the child the parental reaction is one of prohibition, often involving deprivation of attention and affection. Generally the child soon learns that this form of rebellion is profitless, and brings him more harm than good. He wants to respond to frustration with violent aggression, and at the same time learns that he will be punished for such aggression, and that in any case the latter is ineffectual. What face-saving solution does he find? Since he must "face facts," since he must in any case "conform" if he is to have any peace at all, he tries to make it seem as if he himself is the source of the commands and prohibitions: the *external* prohibitive force is *internalized*—and here we have the origin of conscience. By making the prohibitive agency seem to come from within himself, the child can "save face"—as if saying, "The prohibition comes from within me, not from outside, so I'm not subservient to external rule, I'm only obeying rules I've set up myself," thus to some extent saving the autarchic fiction, and at the same time avoiding unpleasant consequences directed against himself by complying with parental commands.

Moreover, the boy[11] has unconsciously never forgiven the mother for his dependence on her in early life, for nourishment and all other things. It has upset his illusion of non-dependence. These feelings have been repressed and are not remembered; but they are acted out in later life in many ways— e.g., in the constant deprecation man has for woman's duties such as cooking and housework of all sorts ("All she does is stay home and get together a few meals, and she calls that work"), and especially in the man's identification with the mother in his sex experiences with women. By identifying with someone one cancels out in effect the person with whom he identifies—replacing that person, unconsciously denying his existence, and the man, identifying with his early mother, playing the active role in "giving" to his wife as his mother has "given" to him, is in effect the denial of his mother's existence, a fact which is narcissistically embarrassing to his ego

because it is chiefly responsible for shattering his autarchic fiction. In supporting his wife, he can unconsciously deny that his mother gave to him, and that he was dependent on her giving. Why is it that the husband plays the provider, and wants his wife to be dependent on no one else, although twenty years before he was nothing but a parasitic baby? This is a face-saving device on his part: he can act out the reasoning, "See, I'm not the parasitic baby; on the contrary I'm the provider, the giver." His playing the provider is a constant face-saving device, to deny his early dependence which is so embarrassing to his ego. It is no wonder that men generally dislike to be reminded of their babyhood, when they were dependent on women.

Thus we have here a perfectly normal adult reaction which is unconsciously motivated. The man "chooses" to support a family—and his choice is as unconsciously motivated as anything could be. (I have described here only the "normal" state of affairs, uncomplicated by the well-nigh infinite number of variations that occur in actual practice.)

Now what of the notion of responsibility? What happens to it on our analysis?

Let us begin with an example, not a fictitious one. A woman and her two-year-old baby are riding on a train to Montreal in mid-winter. The child is ill. The woman wants badly to get to her destination. She is, unknown to herself, the victim of a neurotic conflict whose nature is irrelevant here except for the fact that it forces her to behave aggressively toward the child, partly to spite her husband whom she despises and who loves the child, but chiefly to ward off super-ego charges of masochistic attachment. Consciously she loves the child, and when she says this she says it sincerely, but she must behave aggressively toward it nevertheless, just as many children love their mothers but are nasty to them most of the time in neurotic pseudo-aggression. The child becomes more ill as the train approaches Montreal; the heating system of the train is not working, and the conductor pleads with the woman to get off the train at the next town and get the child to a hospital at once. The woman refuses. Soon after, the child's condition worsens, and the mother does all she can to keep it alive, without, however, leaving the train, for she declares that it is absolutely necessary that she reach her destination. But before she gets there the child is dead. After that, of course, the mother grieves, blames herself, weeps hysterically, and joins the church to gain surcease from the guilt that constantly overwhelms her when she thinks of how her aggressive behavior has killed her child.

Was she responsible for her deed? In ordinary life, after making a mistake, we say, "Chalk it up to experience." Here we should say, "Chalk it up to the neurosis." *She* could not help it if her neurosis forced her to act this way—she didn't even know what was going on behind the scenes, her conscious self merely acted out its assigned part. This is far more true than is generally realized: criminal actions in general are not actions for which their agents are responsible; the agents are passive, not active—they are victims of a neurotic conflict. Their very hyper-activity is unconsciously determined.

To say this is, of course, not to say that we should not punish criminals. Clearly, for our own protection, we must remove them from our midst so that they can no longer molest and endanger organized society. And, of course, if we use the word "responsible" in such a way that justly to hold someone responsible for a deed is by definition identical with being justified in punishing him, then we can and do hold people responsible. But this is like the sense of "free" in which free acts are voluntary ones. It does not go deep enough. In a deeper sense we cannot hold the person responsible: we can hold his neurosis responsible, but *he is not responsible for his neurosis*, particularly since the age at which its onset was inevitable was an age before he could even speak.

The neurosis is responsible—but isn't the neurosis a part of *him*? We have been speaking all the time as if the person and his unconscious were two separate beings; but isn't he one personality, including conscious and unconscious departments together?

I do not wish to deny this. But it hardly helps us here; for what people want when they talk about freedom, and what they hold to when they champion it, is the idea that the *conscious* will is the master of their destiny. "I am the master of my fate, I am the captain of my soul"—and they surely mean their conscious selves, the self that they can recognize and search and introspect. Between an unconscious that willy-nilly determines your actions, and an external force which pushes you, there is little if anything to choose. The unconscious is just *as if* it were an outside force; and indeed, psychiatrists will assert that the inner Hitler (your super-ego) can torment you far more than any external Hitler can. Thus the kind of freedom that people want, the only kind they will settle for, is precisely the kind that psychiatry says they cannot have.

Heretofore it was pretty generally thought that, while we could not rightly blame a person for the color of his eyes or the morality of his parents, or even for what he did at the age of three, or to a large extent what impulses he had and whom he fell in love with, one *could* do so for other of his adult activities, particularly the acts he performed voluntarily and with premeditation. Later this attitude was shaken. Many voluntary acts came to be recognized, at least in some circles, as compelled by the unconscious. Some philosophers recognized this too—Ayer[12] talks about the kleptomaniac being unfree, and about a person being unfree when another person exerts a habitual ascendancy over his personality. But this is as far as he goes. The usual examples, such as the kleptomaniac and the schizophrenic, apparently satisfy most philosophers, and with these exceptions removed, the rest of mankind is permitted to wander in the vast and alluring fields of freedom and responsibility. So far, the inroads upon freedom left the vast majority of humanity untouched; they began to hit home when psychiatrists began to realize, though philosophers did not, that the domination of the conscious by the unconscious extended, not merely to a few exceptional individuals, but to all human beings, that the "big three behind the scenes" are not respecters of persons, and dominate us all, even including that *sanctum sanctorum* of freedom, our conscious will. To be sure, the domination by the unconscious in the case of "normal" individuals is somewhat more benevolent than the tyranny and despotism exercised in neurotic cases, and therefore the former have evoked less comment; but the principle remains in all cases the same: the unconscious is the master of every fate and the captain of every soul.

We speak of a machine turning out good products most of the time but every once in a while it turns out a "lemon." We do not, of course, hold the product responsible for this, but the machine, and via the machine, its maker. Is it silly to extend to inanimate objects the idea of responsibility? Of course. But is it any less so to employ the notion in speaking of human creatures? Are not the two kinds of cases analogous in countless important ways? Occasionally a child turns out badly too, even when his environment and training are the same as that of his brothers and sisters who turn out "all right." He is the "bad penny." His acts of rebellion against parental discipline in adult life (such as the case of the gambler, already cited) are traceable to early experiences of real or fancied denial of infantile wishes. Sometimes the denial has been real, though many denials are absolutely necessary if the child is to grow up to observe the common decencies of civilized life; sometimes, if the child has an unusual quantity of narcissism, every event that occurs is interpreted by him as a denial of his wishes, and nothing a parent could do, even granting every humanly possible wish, would help. In any event, the later neurosis can be attributed to this. Can the person himself be held responsible? Hardly. If he engages in activities which are a menace to society, he must be put into prison, of course, but responsibility is another matter. The time when the events occurred which rendered his neurotic behavior inevitable was a time long before he was capable of thought and decision. As an adult, he is a victim of a world he never made—only this world is inside him.

What about the children who turn out "all right"? All we can say is that "it's just lucky for them" that what happened to their unfortunate brother didn't happen to them; *through no virtue of their own* they are not doomed to the life of unconscious guilt, expiation, conscious depression, terrified ego-gestures for the appeasement of a tyrannical super-ego, that he is. The machine turned them out with a minimum of damage. But if the brother cannot be blamed for his evils, neither can they be praised for their good; unless, of course, we should blame people for what is not their fault, and praise them for lucky accidents.

We all agree that machines turn out "lemons," we all agree that nature turns out misfits in the realm of biology—the blind, the crippled, the diseased; but we hesitate to include the realm of the personality, for here, it seems, is the last retreat of our dignity as human beings. Our ego can endure anything but this; this island at least must remain above the encroaching flood. But may not precisely the same analysis be made here also? Nature turns out psychological "lemons" too, in far greater quantities than any other kind; and indeed all of us are "lemons" in some respect or other, the difference being one of degree. Some of us are lucky enough not to have a gambling-neurosis or criminotic tendencies or masochistic mother-attachment or overdimensional repetition-compulsion to make our lives miserable, but most of our actions, those usually considered

the most important, are unconsciously dominated just the same. And, if a neurosis may be likened to a curse of God, let those of us, the elect, who are enabled to enjoy a measure of life's happiness without the hell-fire of neurotic guilt, take this, not as our own achievement, but simply for what it is—a gift of God.

Let us, however, quit metaphysics and put the situation schematically in the form of a deductive argument.

1. An occurrence over which we had no control is something we cannot be held responsible for.
2. Events E, occurring during our babyhood, were events over which we had no control.
3. Therefore events E were events which we cannot be held responsible for.
4. But if there is something we cannot be held responsible for, neither can we be held responsible for something that inevitably results from it.
5. Events E have as inevitable consequence Neurosis N, which in turn has inevitable consequence Behavior B.
6. Since N is the inevitable consequence of E and B is the inevitable consequence of N, B is the inevitable consequence of E.
7. Hence, not being responsible for E, we cannot be responsible for B.

In Samuel Butler's Utopian satire *Erewhon* there occurs the following passage, in which a judge is passing sentence on a prisoner:

It is all very well for you to say that you came of unhealthy parents, and had a severe accident in your childhood which permanently undermined your constitution; excuses such as these are the ordinary refuge of the criminal; but they cannot for one moment be listened to by the ear of justice. I am not here to enter upon curious metaphysical questions as to the origin of this or that—questions to which there would be no end were their introduction once tolerated, and which would result in throwing the only guilt on the tissues of the primordial cell, or on the elementary gases. There is no question of how you came to be wicked, but only this—namely, are you wicked or not? This has been decided in the affirmative, neither can I hesitate for a single moment to say that it has been decided justly. You are a bad and dangerous person, and stand branded in the eyes of your fellow countrymen with one of the most heinous known offenses.[13]

As moralists read this passage, they may perhaps nod with approval. But the joke is on them. The sting comes when we realize what the crime is for which the prisoner is being sentenced: namely, consumption. The defendant is reminded that during the previous year he was sentenced for aggravated bronchitis, and is warned that he should profit from experience in the future. Butler is employing here his familiar method of presenting some human tendency (in this case, holding people responsible for what isn't their fault) to a ridiculous extreme and thereby reducing it to absurdity.

Assuming the main conclusions of this paper to be true, is there any room left for freedom?

This, of course, all depends on what we mean by "freedom." In the senses suggested at the beginning of this paper, there are countless free acts, and unfree ones as well. When "free" means "uncompelled," and only external compulsion is admitted, again there are countless free acts. But now we have extended the notion of compulsion to include determination by unconscious forces. With this sense in mind, our question is, "With the concept of compulsion thus extended, and in the light of present psychoanalytic knowledge, is there any freedom left in human behavior?"

If practicing psychoanalysts were asked this question, there is little doubt that their answer would be along the following lines: they would say that they were not accustomed to using the term "free" at all, but that if they had to suggest a criterion for distinguishing the free from the unfree, they would say that a person's freedom is present *in inverse proportion to his neuroticism;* in other words, the more his acts are determined by a *malevolent* unconscious, the less free he is. Thus they would speak of *degrees* of freedom. They would say that as a person is cured of his neurosis, he becomes more free—free to realize capabilities that were blocked by the neurotic affliction. The psychologically well-adjusted individual is in this sense comparatively the most free. Indeed, those who are cured of mental disorders are sometimes said to have *regained their freedom:* they are freed from the tyranny of a malevolent unconscious which formerly exerted as much of a domination over them as if they had been abject slaves of a cruel dictator.

But suppose one says that a person is free only to the extent that his acts are *not unconsciously determined at all,* be they unconscious benevolent *or* malevolent? If this is the criterion, psychoanalysts would say, most human behavior cannot be called free at all: our impulses and volitions having to do

with our basic attitudes toward life, whether we are optimists or pessimists, tough-minded or tender-minded, whether our tempers are quick or slow, whether we are "naturally self-seeking" or "naturally benevolent" (and *all the acts consequent upon these things*), what things annoy us, whether we take to blondes or brunettes, old or young, whether we become philosophers or artists or businessmen—all this has its basis in the unconscious. If people generally call most acts free, it is not because they believe that compelled acts should be called free, it is rather through not knowing how large a proportion of our acts actually are compelled. Only the comparatively "vanilla-flavored" aspects of our lives—such as our behavior toward people who don't really matter to us—are exempted from this rule.

These, I think, are the two principal criteria for distinguishing freedom from the lack of it which we might set up on the basis of psychoanalytic knowledge. Conceivably we might set up others. In every case, of course, it remains trivially true that "it all depends on how we choose to use the word." The facts are what they are, regardless of what words we choose for labeling them. But if we choose to label them in a way which is not in accord with what human beings, however vaguely, have long had in mind in applying these labels, as we would be doing if we labeled as "free" many acts which we know as much about as we now do through modern psychoanalytic methods, then we shall only be manipulating words to mislead our fellow creatures.

NOTES

1. *Ethics,* pp. 15–16.
2. *Philosophy and the Physicists,* p. 212.
3. *The Problems of Ethics,* Rynin translation, p. 150.
4. *Ethics,* Chapter 6, pp. 217ff.
5. *New York Post,* Tuesday, May 18, 1948, p. 4.
6. I am aware that the theory presented below is not accepted by all practicing psychoanalysts. Many non-Freudians would disagree with the conclusions presented below. But I do not believe that this fact affects my argument, as long as the concept of unconscious motivation is accepted. I am aware, too, that much of the language employed in the following descriptions is animistic and metaphorical; but as long as I am presenting a view I would prefer to "go the whole hog" and present it in its most dramatic form. The theory can in any case be made clearest by the use of such language, just as atomic theory can often be made clearest to students with the use of models.

7. This view is very clearly developed in Edmund Bergler, *Divorce Won't Help,* especially Chapter 1.

8. See *The Basic Writings of Sigmund Freud,* Modern Library Edition, p. 310. (In *The Interpretation of Dreams.*) Cf. also the essay by Ernest Jones, "A Psycho-analytical Study of Hamlet."

9. See Edmund Bergler's article on the pathological gambler in *Diseases of the Nervous System* (1943). Also "Suppositions about the Mechanism of Criminosis," *Journal of Criminal Psychopathology* (1944) and "Clinical Contributions to the Psycho-genesis of Alcohol Addiction," *Quarterly Journal of Studies on Alcohol,* 5:434 (1944).

10. E.g., Edmund Bergler, *The Battle of the Conscience,* Chapter 1.

11. The girl's development after this point is somewhat different. Society demands more aggressiveness of the adult male, hence there are more super-ego strictures on tendencies toward passivity in the male; accordingly his defenses must be stronger.

12. A. J. Ayer, "Freedom and Necessity," *Polemic* (September-October 1946), pp. 40–43.

13. Samuel Butler, *Erewhon* (Modern Library edition), p. 107.

RICHARD   TAYLOR

Freedom and Determinism*

Richard Taylor (1919–   ) teaches philosophy at the University of Rochester.

SOFT DETERMINISM

. . . All versions of this theory have in common three claims, by means of which, it is naively supposed, a reconciliation is achieved between determinism and freedom. Freedom being, furthermore, a condition of moral responsibility and the only condition that metaphysics seriously questions, it is supposed by the partisans of this view that determinism is perfectly compatible with such responsibility. This, no doubt, accounts for its great appeal and wide acceptance, even by some men of considerable learning.

The three claims of soft determinism are (1) that the thesis of determinism is true, and that accordingly all human behavior, voluntary or other, like the behavior of all other things, arises from antecedent conditions, given which no other behavior is possible—in short, that all human behavior is caused and determined; (2) that voluntary behavior is nonetheless free to the extent that it is not externally constrained or impeded; and (3) that, in the absence of such obstacles and constraints, the causes of voluntary behavior are certain states, events, or conditions withing the agent himself; namely, his own acts of will or volitions, choices, decisions, desires, and so on.

*Richard Taylor, *Metaphysics,* 2nd edition, © 1974, pp. 48–57. Reprinted by permission of Prentice-Hall, Inc., Englewood Cliffs, New Jersey.

Thus, on this view, I am free, and therefore sometimes responsible for what I do, provided nothing prevents me from acting according to my own choice, desire, or volition, or constrains me to act otherwise. There may, to be sure, be other conditions for my responsibility—such as, for example, an understanding of the probable consequences of my behavior, and that sort of thing—but absence of constraint or impediment is, at least, one such condition. And, it is claimed, it is a condition that is compatible with the supposition that my behavior is caused—for it is, by hypothesis, caused by my own inner choices, desires, and volitions.

THE REFUTATION OF THIS

The theory of soft determinism looks good at first—so good that it has for generations been solemnly taught from numberless philosophical chairs and implanted in the minds of students as sound philosophy—but no great acumen is needed to discover that far from solving any problem, it only camouflages it.

My free actions are those unimpeded and unconstrained motions that arise from my own inner desires, choices, and volitions; let us grant this provisionally. But now, whence arise those inner states that determine what my body shall do? Are they within my control or not? Having made my choice or decision and acted upon it, could I have chosen otherwise or not?

Here the determinist, hoping to surrender nothing and yet to avoid the problem implied in that question, bids us not to ask it; the question itself, he announces, is without meaning. For to say that I could have done otherwise, he says, means only that I *would* have done otherwise *if* those inner states that determined my action had been different; if, that is, I had decided or chosen differently. To ask, accordingly, whether I could have chosen or decided differently is only to ask whether, had I decided to decide differently or chosen to choose differently, or willed to will differently, I would have decided or chosen or willed differently. And this, of course, *is* unintelligible nonsense.

But it is not nonsense to ask whether the causes of my actions—my own inner choices, decisions, and desires—are themselves caused. And of course they are, if determinism is true, for on that thesis everything is caused and determined. And if they are, then we cannot avoid concluding that, given the causal conditions of those inner states, I could not have decided, willed, chosen, or desired otherwise than I in fact did, for this is a logical consequence of the very definition of determinism. Of course we can still say that, *if* the causes of those inner states, whatever they were, had been different, then their effects, those inner states themselves, would have been different, and that in this hypothetical sense I could have decided, chosen, willed, or desired differently—but that only pushes our problem back still another step. For we will then want to know whether the causes of those inner states were within my control; and so on, *ad infinitum*. We are, at each step, permitted to say "could have been otherwise" only in a provisional sense—provided, that is, something else had been different—but must then retract it and replace it with "could not have been otherwise" as soon as we discover, as we must at each step, that whatever would have to have been different could not have been different.

EXAMPLES

Such is the dialectic of the problem. The easiest way to see the shadowy quality of soft determinism, however, is by means of examples.

Let us suppose that my body is moving in various ways, that these motions are not externally constrained or impeded, and that they are all exactly in accordance with my own desires, choices, or acts of will and what not. When I will that my arm should move in a certain way, I find it moving in that way, unobstructed and unconstrained. When I will to speak, my lips and tongue move, unobstructed and unconstrained, in a manner suitable to the formation of the words I choose to utter. Now given that this is a correct description of my behavior, namely, that it consists of the unconstrained and unimpeded motions of my body in response to my own volitions, then it follows that my behavior is free, on the soft determinist's definition of "free." It follows further that I am responsible for that behavior; or at least, that if I am not, it is not from any lack of freedom on my part.

But if the fulfillment of these conditions renders my behavior free—that is to say, if my behavior satisfies the conditions of free action set forth in the theory of soft determinism—then my behavior will be no less free if we assume further conditions that are perfectly consistent with those already satisfied.

We suppose further, accordingly, that while my behavior is entirely in accordance with my own volitions, and thus "free" in terms of the conception of freedom we are examining, my volitions themselves are caused. To make this graphic, we can suppose that an ingenious physiologist can induce in me any volition he pleases, simply by pushing various buttons on an instrument to which, let us suppose, I am attached by numerous wires. All the volitions I have in that situation are, accordingly, precisely the ones he gives me. By pushing one button, he evokes in me the volition to raise my hand; and my hand, being unimpeded, rises in response to that volition. By pushing another, he induces the volition in me to kick, and my foot, being unimpeded, kicks in response to that volition. We can even suppose that the physiologist puts a rifle in my hands, aims it at some passer-by, and then, by pushing the proper button, evokes in me the volition to squeeze my finger against the trigger, whereupon the passer-by falls dead of a bullet wound.

This is the description of a man who is acting in accordance with his inner volitions, a man whose body is unimpeded and unconstrained in its motions, these motions being the effects of those inner states. It is hardly the description of a free and responsible agent. It is the perfect description of a puppet. To render a man your puppet, it is not necessary forcibly to constrain the motions of his limbs, after the fashion that real puppets are moved. A subtler but no less effective means of making a man your puppet would be to gain complete control of his inner states, and ensuring, as the theory of soft determinism does ensure, that his body will move in accordance with them.

The example is somewhat unusual, but it is no worse for that. It is perfectly intelligible, and it does appear to refute the soft determinist's conception of freedom. One might think that, in such a case, the agent should not have allowed himself to be so rigged in the first place, but this is irrelevant; we can suppose that he was not aware that he was, and was hence unaware of the source of those inner states that prompted his bodily motions. The example can, moreover, be modified in perfectly realistic ways, so as to coincide with actual and familiar cases. One can, for instance, be given a compulsive desire for certain drugs, simply by having them administered to him over a course of time. Suppose, then, that I do, with neither my knowledge nor consent, thus become a victim of such a desire and act upon it. Do I act freely, merely by virtue of the fact that I am unimpeded in my quest for drugs? In a sense I do, surely, but I am hardly free with respect to whether or not I shall use drugs. I never chose to have the desire for them inflicted upon me.

Nor does it, of course, matter whether the inner states which allegedly prompt all my ''free'' activity are evoked in me by another agent or by perfectly impersonal forces. Whether a desire which causes my body to behave in a certain way is inflicted upon me by another person, for instance, or derived from hereditary factors, or indeed from anything at all, matters not the least. In any case, if it is in fact the cause of my bodily behavior, I cannot but act in accordance with it. Wherever it came from, whether from personal or impersonal origins, it was entirely caused or determined, and not within my control. Indeed, if determinism is true, as the theory of soft determinism holds it to be, all those inner states which cause my body to behave in whatever ways it behaves must arise from circumstances that existed before I was born; for the chain of causes and effects is infinite, and none could have been the least different, given those that preceded.

SIMPLE INDETERMINISM

We might at first now seem warranted in simply denying determinism, and saying that, insofar as they are free, my actions are not caused; or that, if they are caused by my own inner states—my own desires, impulses, choices, volitions, and whatnot—

then these, in any case, are not caused. This is a perfectly clear sense in which a man's action, assuming that it was free, could have been otherwise. If it was uncaused, then, even given the conditions under which it occurred and all that preceded, some other act was nonetheless possible, and he did not have to do what he did. Or if his action was the inevitable consequence of his own inner states, and could not have been otherwise given these, we can nevertheless say that these inner states, being uncaused, could have been otherwise, and could thereby have produced different actions.

Only the slightest consideration will show, however, that this simple denial of determinism has not the slightest plausibility. For let us suppose it is true, and that some of my bodily motions—namely, those that I regard as my free acts—are not caused at all or, if caused by my own inner states, that these are not caused. We shall thereby avoid picturing a puppet, to be sure—but only by substituting something even less like a man; for the conception that now emerges is not that of a free man, but of an erratic and jerking phantom, without any rhyme or reason at all.

Suppose that my right arm is free, according to this conception; that is, that its motions are uncaused. It moves this way and that from time to time, but nothing causes these motions. Sometimes it moves forth vigorously, sometimes up, sometimes down, sometimes it just drifts vaguely about—these motions all being wholly free and uncaused. Manifestly I have nothing to do with them at all; they just happen, and neither I nor anyone can ever tell what this arm will be doing next. It might seize a club and lay it on the head of the nearest bystander, no less to my astonishment than his. There will never be any point in asking why these motions occur, or in seeking any explanation of them, for under the conditions assumed there is no explanation. They just happen, from no causes at all.

This is no description of free, voluntary, or responsible behavior. Indeed, so far as the motions of my body or its parts are entirely uncaused, such motions cannot even be ascribed to me as my behavior in the first place, since I have nothing to do with them. The behavior of my arm is just the random motion of a foreign object. Behavior that is mine must be behavior that is within my control, but motions that occur from no causes are without the control of anyone. I can have no more to do with, and no more control over, the uncaused motions of my limbs than a gambler has over the motions of an honest roulette wheel. I can only, like him, idly wait to see what happens.

Nor does it improve things to suppose that my bodily motions are caused by my own inner states, so long as we suppose these to be wholly uncaused. The result will be the same as before. My arm, for example, will move this way and that, sometimes up and sometimes down, sometimes vigorously and sometimes just drifting about, always in response to certain inner states, to be sure. But since these are supposed to be wholly uncaused, it follows that I have no control over them and hence none over their effects. If my hand lays a club forcefully on the nearest bystander, we can indeed say that this motion resulted from an inner club-wielding desire of mine; but we must add that I had nothing to do with that desire, and that it arose, to be followed by its inevitable effect, no less to my astonishment than to his. Things like this do, alas, sometimes happen. We are all sometimes seized by compulsive impulses that arise we know not whence and we do sometimes act upon these. But because they are far from being examples of free, voluntary, and responsible behavior, we need only to learn that behavior was of this sort to conclude that it was not free, voluntary, or responsible. It was erratic, impulsive, and irresponsible.

DETERMINISM AND SIMPLE INDETERMINISM AS THEORIES

Both determinism and simple indeterminism are loaded with difficulties, and no one who has thought much on them can affirm either of them without some embarrassment. Simple indeterminism has nothing whatever to be said for it, except that it appears to remove the grossest difficulties of determinism, only, however, to imply perfect absurdities of its own. Determinism, on the other hand, is at least initially plausible. Men seem to have a natural inclination to believe in it; it is, indeed, almost required for the very exercise of practical intelligence. And beyond this, our experience appears always to confirm it, so long as we are dealing with everyday facts of common experience, as distinguished from the esoteric researches of theoretical physics. But determinism, as applied to human behavior, has implications which few men can casually accept, and they appear to be implications which no modification of the theory can efface.

Both theories, moreover, appear logically irreconcilable to the two items of data that we set forth at the outset; namely, (1) that my behavior is sometimes the outcome of my deliberation, and (2) that in these and other cases it is sometimes up to me what I do. Because these were our data, it is important to see, as must already be quite clear, that these theories cannot be reconciled to them.

I can deliberate only about my own future actions, and then only if I do not already know what I am going to do. If a certain nasal tickle warns me that I am about to sneeze, for instance, then I cannot deliberate whether to sneeze or not; I can only prepare for the impending convulsion. But if determinism is true, then there are always conditions existing antecedently to everything I do, sufficient for my doing just that, and such as to render it inevitable. If I can know what those conditions are and what behavior they are sufficient to produce, then I can in every such case know what I am going to do and cannot then deliberate about it.

By itself this only shows, of course, that I can deliberate only in ignorance of the causal conditions of my behavior; it does not show that such conditions cannot exist. It is odd, however, to suppose that deliberation should be a mere substitute for clear knowledge. Ignorance is a condition of speculation, inference, and guesswork, which have nothing whatever to do with deliberation. A prisoner awaiting execution may not know when he is going to die, and he may even entertain the hope of reprieve, but he cannot deliberate about this. He can only speculate, guess—and wait.

Worse yet, however, it now becomes clear that I cannot deliberate about what I am going to do, if it is even possible for me to find out in advance, whether I do in fact find out in advance or not. I can deliberate only with the view to deciding what to do, to making up my mind; and this is impossible if I believe that it could be inferred what I am going to do, from conditions already existing, even though I have not made that inference myself. If I believe that what I am going to do has been rendered inevitable by conditions already existing, and could be inferred by anyone having the requisite sagacity, then I cannot try to decide whether to do it or not, for there is simply nothing left to decide. I can at best only guess or try to figure it out myself or, all prognostics failing, I can wait and see; but I cannot deliberate. I deliberate in order to *decide* what *to* do, not to *discover* what it is that I am *going* to do. But if determinism is true, then there are always antecedent conditions sufficient for everything that I do, and this can always be inferred by anyone having the requisite sagacity; that is, by anyone having a knowledge of what those conditions are and what behavior they are sufficient to produce.

This suggests what in fact seems quite clear, that determinism cannot be reconciled with our second datum either, to the effect that it is sometimes up to me what I am going to do. For if it is ever really up to me whether to do this thing or that, then, as we have seen, each alternative course of action must be such that I can do it; not that I can do it in some abstruse or hypothetical sense of "can"; not that I could do it if only something were true that is not true; but in the sense that it is then and there within my power to do it. But this is never so, if determinism is true, for on the very formulation of that theory whatever happens at any time is the only thing that can then happen, given all that precedes it. It is simply a logical consequence of this that whatever I do at any time is the only thing I can then do, given the conditions that precede my doing it. Nor does it help in the least to interpose, among the causal antecedents of my behavior, my own inner states, such as my desires, choices, acts of will, and so on. For even supposing these to be always involved in voluntary behavior—which is highly doubtful in itself—it is a consequence of determinism that these, whatever they are at any time, can never be other than what they then are. Every chain of causes and effects, if determinism is true, is infinite. This is why it is not now up to me whether I shall a moment hence be male or female. The conditions determining my sex have existed through my whole life, and even prior to my life. But if determinism is true, the same holds of anything that I ever am, ever become, or ever do. It matters not whether we are speaking of the most patent facts of my being, such as my sex: or the most subtle, such as my feelings, thoughts, desires, or choices. Nothing could be other than it is, given what was; and while we may indeed say, quite idly, that something—some inner state of mind, for instance—could have been different, had only something else been different, any consolation of this thought evaporates as soon as we add that whatever would have to have been different could not have been different.

It is even more obvious that our data cannot be reconciled to the theory of simple indeterminism. I can deliberate only about my own actions; this is obvious. But the random, uncaused motion of any body whatever, whether it be a part of my body or not, is no action of mine and nothing that is within my power. I might try to guess what these motions will be, just as I might try to guess how a roulette wheel will behave, but I cannot deliberate about them or try to decide what they shall be, simply because these things are not up to me. Whatever is not caused by anything is not caused by me, and nothing could be more plainly inconsistent with saying that it is nevertheless up to me what it shall be.

THE THEORY OF AGENCY

The only conception of action that accords with our data is one according to which men—and perhaps some other things too—are sometimes, but of course not always, self-determining beings; that is, beings which are sometimes the causes of their own behavior. In the case of an action that is free, it must be such that it is caused by the agent who performs it, but such that no antecedent conditions were sufficient for his performing just that action. In the case of an action that is both free and rational, it must be such that the agent who performed it did so for some reason, but this reason cannot have been the cause of it.

Now this conception fits what men take themselves to be; namely, beings who act, or who are agents, rather than things that are merely acted upon, and whose behavior is simply the causal consequence of conditions which they have not wrought. When I believe that I have done something, I do believe that it was I who caused it to be done, I who made something happen, and not merely something within me, such as one of my own subjective states, which is not identical with myself. If I believe that something not identical with myself was the cause of my behavior—some event wholly external to myself, for instance, or even one internal to myself, such as a nerve impulse, volition, or whatnot—then I cannot regard that behavior as being an act of mine, unless I further believe that I was the cause of that external or internal event. My pulse, for example, is caused and regulated by certain conditions existing within me, and not by myself. I do not, accordingly, regard this activity of my body as my action, and would be no more tempted to do so if I became suddenly conscious within myself of those conditions or impulses that produce it. This is behavior with which I have nothing to do, behavior that is not within my immediate control, behavior that is not only not free activity, but not even the activity of an agent to begin with; it is nothing but a mechanical reflex. Had I never learned that my very life depends on this pulse beat, I would regard it with complete indifference, as something foreign to me, like the oscillations of a clock pendulum that I idly contemplate.

Now this conception of activity, and of an agent who is the cause of it, involves two rather strange metaphysical notions that are never applied elsewhere in nature. The first is that of a *self* or *person*—for example, a man—who is not merely a collection of things or events, but a substance and a self-moving being. For on this view it is a man himself, and not merely some part of him or something within him, that is the cause of his own activity. Now we certainly do not know that a man is anything more than an assemblage of physical things and processes, which act in accordance with those laws that describe the behavior of all other physical things and processes. Even though a man is a living being, of enormous complexity, there is nothing, apart from the requirements of this theory, to suggest that his behavior is so radically different in its origin from that of other physical objects, or that an understanding of it must be sought in some metaphysical realm wholly different from that appropriate to the understanding of non-living things.

Second, this conception of activity involves an extraordinary conception of causation, according to which an agent, which is a substance and not an event, can nevertheless be the cause of an event. Indeed, if he is a free agent then he can, on this conception, cause an event to occur—namely, some act of his own—without anything else causing him to do so. This means that an agent is sometimes a cause, without being an antecedent sufficient condition; for if I affirm that I am the cause of some act of mine, then I am plainly not saying that my very existence is sufficient for its occurrence, which would be absurd. If I say that my hand causes my pencil to move, then I am saying that the motion of my hand is, under the other conditions then prevailing, sufficient for the motion of the pencil. But if I then say that I cause my hand to move, I am not saying anything remotely like this, and surely not that the motion of my self is sufficient for the motion of my arm and hand, since these are the only things about me that are moving.

This conception of the causation of events by beings or substances that are not events is, in fact, so different from the usual philosophical conception of a cause that it should not even bear the same name, for "being a cause" ordinarily just means "being an antecedent sufficient condition or set of conditions." Instead, then, of speaking of agents as *causing* their own acts, it would perhaps be better to use another word entirely, and say, for instance, that they *originate* them, *initiate* them, or simply that they *perform* them.

Now this is on the face of it a dubious conception of what a man is. Yet it is consistent with our data, reflecting the presuppositions of deliberation, and appears to be the only conception that is consistent with them, as determinism and simple indeterminism are not. The theory of agency avoids the absurdities of simple indeterminism by conceding that human behavior is caused, while at the same time avoiding the difficulties of determinism by denying that every chain of causes and effects is infinite. Some such causal chains, on this view, have beginnings, and they begin with agents themselves. Moreover, if we are to suppose that it is sometimes up to me what I do, and understand this in a sense which is not consistent with determinism, we must suppose that I am an agent or a being who initiates his own actions, sometimes under conditions which do not determine what action he shall perform. Deliberation becomes, on this view, something that is not only possible but quite rational, for it does make sense to deliberate about activity that is truly my own and that depends in its outcome upon me as its author, and not merely upon something more or less esoteric that is supposed to be intimately associated with me, such as my thoughts, volitions, choices, or whatnot.

One can hardly affirm such a theory of agency with complete comfort, however, and wholly without embarrassment, for the conception of men and their powers which is involved in it is strange indeed, if not positively mysterious. In fact, one can hardly be blamed here for simply denying our data outright, rather than embracing this theory to which they do most certainly point. Our data—to the effect that men do sometimes deliberate before acting, and that when they do, they presuppose among other things that it is up to them what they are going to do—rest upon nothing more than fairly common consent. These data might simply be illusions. It might in fact be that no man ever deliberates, but only imagines that he does, that from pure conceit he supposes himself to be the master of his behavior and the author of his acts. Spinoza has suggested that if a stone, having been thrown into the air, were suddenly to become conscious, it would suppose itself to be the source of its own motion, being then conscious of what it was doing but not aware of the real cause of its behavior. Certainly men are *sometimes* mistaken in believing that they are behaving as a result of choice deliberately arrived at. A man might, for example, easily imagine that his embarking upon matrimony is the result of the most careful and rational deliberation, when in fact the causes, perfectly sufficient for that behavior, might be of an entirely physiological, unconscious origin. If it is sometimes false that we deliberate and then act as the result of a decision deliberately arrived at, even when we suppose it to be true, it might always be false. No one seems able, as we have noted, to describe deliberation without metaphors, and the conception of a thing's being ''within one's power'' or ''up to him'' seems to defy analysis or definition altogether, if taken in a sense which the theory of agency appears to require.

These are, then, dubitable conceptions, despite their being so well implanted in the common sense of mankind. Indeed, when we turn to the theory of fatalism, we shall find formidable metaphysical considerations which appear to rule them out altogether. Perhaps here, as elsewhere in metaphysics, we should be content with discovering difficulties, with seeing what is and what is not consistent with such convictions as we happen to have, and then drawing such satisfaction as we can from the realization that, no matter where we begin, the world is mysterious and the men who try to understand it are even more so. This realization can, with some justification, make one feel wise, even in the full realization of his ignorance.

C. A. CAMPBELL

Has the Self 'Free Will'?*

C. A. Campbell (1897–1974) taught for many years at the University of Glasgow.

. . . It is something of a truism that in philosophic enquiry the exact formulation of a problem often takes one a long way on the road to its solution. In the case of the Free Will problem I think there is a rather special need of careful formulation. For there are many sorts of human freedom; and it can easily happen that one wastes a great deal of labour in proving or disproving a freedom which has almost nothing to do with the freedom which is at issue in the traditional problem of Free Will. The abortiveness of so much of the argument for and against Free Will in contemporary philosophical literature seems to me due in the main to insufficient pains being taken over the preliminary definition of the problem. There is, indeed, one outstanding exception, Professor Broad's brilliant inaugural lecture entitled, 'Determinism, Indeterminism, and Libertarianism',[1] in which forty-three pages are devoted to setting out the problem, as against seven to its solution! I confess that the solution does not seem to myself to follow upon the formulation quite as easily as all that:[2] but Professor Broad's eminent example fortifies me in my decision to give here what may seem at first sight a disproportionate amount of time to the business of determining the essential characteristics of the kind of freedom with which the traditional problem is concerned.

Fortunately we can at least make a beginning with a certain amount of confidence. It is not seriously disputable that the kind of freedom in question is the

*From C. A. Campbell, *On Selfhood And Goodhood* (London: George Allen & Unwin, Ltd. and New Jersey, Humanities Press, Inc., 1957), pp. 158–179. Reprinted by permission of George Allen & Unwin, Ltd.

freedom which is commonly recognised to be in some sense a precondition of moral responsibility. Clearly, it is on account of this integral connection with moral responsibility that such exceptional importance has always been felt to attach to the Free Will problem. But in what precise sense is free will a precondition of moral responsibility, and thus a postulate of the moral life in general? This is an exceedingly troublesome question; but until we have satisfied ourselves about the answer to it, we are not in a position to state, let alone decide, the question whether 'Free Will' in its traditional, ethical, significance is a reality.

Our first business, then, is to ask, exactly what kind of freedom is it which is required for moral responsibility? And as to method of procedure in this inquiry, there seems to me to be no real choice. I know of only one method that carries with it any hope of success; viz. the critical comparison of those acts for which, on due reflection, we deem it proper to attribute moral praise or blame to the agents, with those acts for which, on due reflection, we deem such judgments to be improper. The ultimate touchstone, as I see it, can only be our moral consciousness as it manifests itself in our more critical and considered moral judgments. The 'linguistic' approach by way of the analysis of moral *sentences* seems to me, despite its present popularity, to be an almost infallible method for reaching wrong results in the moral field; but I must reserve what I have to say about this.

The first point to note is that the freedom at issue (as indeed the very name 'Free *Will* Problem' indicates) pertains primarily not to overt acts but to inner acts. The nature of things has decreed that, save in the case of one's self, it is only overt acts which one can directly observe. But a very little reflection serves to show that in our moral judgments upon others their overt acts are regarded as significant only in so far as they are the expression of inner acts. We do not consider the acts of a robot to be morally responsible acts; nor do we consider the acts of a man to be so save in so far as they are distinguishable from those of a robot by reflecting an inner life of choice. Similarly, from the other side, if we are satisfied (as we may on occasion be, at least in the case of ourselves) that a person has definitely elected to follow a course which he believes to be wrong, but has been prevented by external circumstances from translating his inner choice into an overt act, we still regard him

as morally blameworthy. Moral freedom, then, pertains to *inner* acts.

The next point seems at first sight equally obvious and uncontroversial; but, as we shall see, it has awkward implications if we are in real earnest with it (as almost nobody is). It is the simple point that the act must be one of which the person judged can be regarded as the *sole* author. It seems plain enough that if there are any *other* determinants of the act, external to the self, to that extent the act is not an act which the *self* determines, and to that extent not an act for which the self can be held morally responsible. The self is only part-author of the act, and his moral responsibility can logically extend only to those elements within the act (assuming for the moment that these can be isolated) of which he is the *sole* author.

The awkward implications of this apparent truism will be readily appreciated. For, if we are mindful of the influences exerted by heredity and environment, we may well feel some doubt whether there is any act of will at all of which one can truly say that the self is sole author, sole determinant. No man has a voice in determining the raw material of impulses and capacities that constitute his hereditary endowment, and no man has more than a very partial control of the material and social environment in which he is destined to live his life. Yet it would be manifestly absurd to deny that these two factors do constantly and profoundly affect the nature of a man's choices. That this is so we all of us recognise in our moral judgments when we 'make allowances', as we say, for a bad heredity or a vicious environment, and acknowledge in the victim of them a diminished moral responsibility for evil courses. Evidently we do *try,* in our moral judgments, however crudely, to praise or blame a man only in respect of that of which we can regard him as *wholly* the author. And evidently we do recognise that, for a man to be the author of an act in the full sense required for moral responsibility, it is not enough merely that he 'wills' or 'chooses' the act: since even the most unfortunate victim of heredity or environment does, as a rule, 'will' what he does. It is significant, however, that the ordinary man, though well enough aware of the influence upon choices of heredity and environment, does not feel obliged thereby to give up his assumption that moral predicates *are* somehow applicable. Plainly he still believes that there is *something* for which a man is morally responsible, something of which we can fairly say that he is the sole author. *What is this something?* To that question common-sense is not ready with an explicit answer—though an answer is, I think, implicit in the line which its moral judgments take. I shall do what I can to give an explicit answer later in this lecture. Meantime it must suffice to observe that, if we are to be true to the deliverances of our moral consciousness, it is very difficult to deny that *sole* authorship is a necessary condition of the morally responsible act.

Thirdly we come to a point over which much recent controversy has raged. We may approach it by raising the following question. Granted an act of which the agent is sole author, does this 'sole authorship' suffice to make the act a morally free act? We may be inclined to think that it does, until we contemplate the possibility that an act of which the agent is sole author might conceivably occur as a necessary expression of the agent's nature; the way in which, e.g. some philosophers have supposed the Divine act of creation to occur. This consideration excites a legitimate doubt; for it is far from easy to see how a person can be regarded as a proper subject for moral praise or blame in respect of an act which he *cannot help* performing—even if it be his own 'nature' which necessitates it. Must we not recognise it as a condition of the morally free act that the agent 'could have acted otherwise' than he in fact did? It is true, indeed, that we sometimes praise or blame a man for an act about which we are prepared to say, in the light of our knowledge of his established character, that he 'could no other'. But I think that a little reflection shows that in such cases we are not praising or blaming the man strictly for what he does *now* (or at any rate we ought not to be), but rather for those past acts of his which have generated the firm habit of mind from which his *present* act follows 'necessarily'. In other words, our praise and blame, so far as justified, are really retrospective, being directed not to the agent *qua* performing *this* act, but to the agent *qua* performing those past acts which have built up his present character, and in respect to which we presume that he *could* have acted otherwise, that there really *were* open possibilities before him. These cases, therefore, seem to me to constitute no valid exception to what I must take to be the rule, viz. that a man can be morally praised or blamed for an act only if he could have acted otherwise.

Now philosophers today are fairly well agreed that it is a postulate of the morally responsible act that the agent 'could have acted otherwise' in *some* sense of that phrase. But sharp differences of opinion have arisen over the way in which the phrase ought to be interpreted. There is a strong disposition to water down its apparent meaning by insisting that it is not (as a postulate of moral responsibility) to be understood as a straightforward categorical proposition, but rather as a disguised hypothetical proposition. All that we really require to be assured of, in order to justify our holding X morally responsible for an act, is, we are told, that X could have acted otherwise *if* he had *chosen* otherwise (Moore, Stevenson); or perhaps that X could have acted otherwise *if* he had had a different character, or *if* he had been placed in different circumstances.

I think it is easy to understand, and even, in a measure, to sympathise with, the motives which induce philosophers to offer these counter-interpretations. It is not just the fact that 'X could have acted otherwise', as a bald categorical statement, is incompatible with the universal sway of causal law—though this is, to some philosophers, a serious stone of stumbling. The more widespread objection is that it at least looks as though it were incompatible with that causal continuity of an agent's character with his conduct which is implied when we believe (surely with justice) that we can often tell the sort of thing a man will do from our knowledge of the sort of man he is.

We shall have to make our accounts with that particular difficulty later. At this stage I wish merely to show that neither of the hypothetical propositions suggested—and I think the same could be shown for *any* hypothetical alternative—is an acceptable substitute for the categorical proposition 'X could have acted otherwise' as the presupposition of moral responsibility.

Let us look first at the earlier suggestion—'X could have acted otherwise *if* he had chosen otherwise'. Now clearly there are a great many acts with regard to which we are entirely satisfied that the agent is thus situated. We are often perfectly sure that—for this is all it amounts to—if X had chosen otherwise, the circumstances presented no external obstacle to the translation of that choice into action. For example, we often have no doubt at all that X, who in point of fact told a lie, could have told the truth *if* he had so chosen. But does our confidence on this score allay all legitimate doubts about whether X is really blameworthy? Does it entail that X is free in the sense required for moral responsibility? Surely not. The obvious question immediately arises: 'But *could* X have *chosen* otherwise than he did?' It is doubt about the true answer to *that* question which leads most people to doubt the reality of moral responsibility. Yet on this crucial question the hypothetical proposition which is offered as a sufficient statement of the condition justifying the ascription of moral responsibility gives us no information whatsoever.

Indeed this hypothetical substitute for the categorical 'X could have acted otherwise' seems to me to lack all plausibility unless one contrives to forget why it is, after all, that we ever come to feel fundamental doubts about man's moral responsibility. Such doubts are born, surely, when one becomes aware of certain reputable world-views in religion or philosophy, or of certain reputable scientific beliefs, which in their several ways imply that man's actions are necessitated, and thus could not be otherwise than they in fact are. But clearly a doubt so based is not even touched by the recognition that a man could very often act otherwise *if* he so chose. That proposition is entirely compatible with the necessitarian theories which generate our doubt: indeed it is this very compatibility that has recommended it to some philosophers, who are reluctant to give up either moral responsibility or Determinism. The proposition which we *must* be able to affirm if moral praise or blame of X is to be justified is the categorical proposition that X could have acted otherwise because—not if—he could have chosen otherwise; or, since it is essentially the inner side of the act that matters, the proposition simply that X could have chosen otherwise.

For the second of the alternative formulae suggested we cannot spare more than a few moments. But its inability to meet the demands it is required to meet is almost transparent. 'X could have acted otherwise', as a statement of a precondition of X's moral responsibility, really means (we are told) 'X could have acted otherwise *if* he were differently constituted, or *if* he had been placed in different circumstances'. It seems a sufficient reply to this to point out that the person whose moral responsibility is at issue is X; a specific individual, in a specific set of circumstances. It is totally irrelevant to X's moral responsibility that we should be able to say that some person differently constituted from X, or X in a different set of circumstances, could have done something different from what X did.

Let me, then, briefly sum up the answer at which we have arrived to our question about the kind of freedom required to justify moral responsibility. It is that a man can be said to exercise free will in a morally significant sense only in so far as his chosen act is one of which he is the sole cause or author, and only if—in the straightforward, categorical sense of the phrase—he 'could have chosen otherwise'.

I confess that this answer is in some ways a disconcerting one; disconcerting, because most of us, however objective we are in the actual conduct of our thinking, would *like* to be able to believe that moral responsibility is real: whereas the freedom required for moral responsibility, on the analysis we have given, is certainly far more difficult to establish than the freedom required on the analyses we found ourselves obliged to reject. If, e.g. moral freedom entails only that I could have acted otherwise *if* I had chosen otherwise, there is no real 'problem' about it at all. I am 'free' in the normal case where there is no external obstacle to prevent my translating the alternative choice into action, and not free in other cases. Still less is there a problem if all that moral freedom entails is that I could have acted otherwise *if* I had been a differently constituted person, or been in different circumstances. Clearly I am *always* free in *this* sense of freedom. But, as I have argued, these so-called 'freedoms' fail to give us the pre-conditions of moral responsibility, and hence leave the freedom of the traditional free-will problem, the freedom that people are really concerned about, precisely where it was.

Another interpretation of freedom which I am bound to reject on the same general ground, i.e. that it is just not the kind of freedom that is relevant to moral responsibility, is the old idealist view which identifies the *free* will with the *rational* will; the rational will in its turn being identified with the will which wills the moral law in whole-hearted, single-minded obedience to it. This view is still worth at least a passing mention, if only because it has recently been resurrected in an interesting work by Professor A. E. Teale.[3] Moreover, I cannot but feel a certain nostalgic tenderness for a view in which I myself was (so to speak) philosophically cradled. The almost apostolic fervour with which my revered nursing-mother, the late Sir Henry Jones, was wont to impart it to his charges, and, hardly less, his ill-concealed scorn for ignoble natures (like my own) which still hankered after a free will in the old 'vulgar' sense, are vividly recalled for me in Professor Teale's stirring pages.

The true interpretation of free will, according to Professor Teale, the interpretation to which Kant, despite occasional back-slidings, adhered in his better moments, is that 'the will is free in the degree that it is informed and disciplined by the moral principle'.[4]

Now this is a perfectly intelligible sense of the word 'free'—or at any rate it can be made so with a little explanatory comment which Professor Teale well supplies but for which there is here no space. But clearly it is a very different sort of freedom from that which is at issue in the traditional problem of free will. This idealist 'freedom' sponsored by Teale belongs, on his own showing, only to the self in respect of its *good* willing. The freedom with which the traditional problem is concerned, inasmuch as it is the freedom presupposed by moral responsibility, must belong to the self in respect of its *bad*, no less than its *good*, willing. It is, in fact, the freedom to decide between genuinely open alternatives of good and bad willing.

Professor Teale, of course, is not unaware that the freedom he favours differs from freedom as traditionally understood. He recognises the traditional concept under its Kantian title of 'elective' freedom. But he leaves the reader in no kind of doubt about his disbelief in both the reality and the value of this elective freedom to do, or forbear from doing, one's duty.

The question of the reality of elective freedom I shall be dealing with shortly; and it will occupy us to the end of the lecture. At the moment I am concerned only with its value, and with the rival view that all that matters for the moral life is the 'rational' freedom which a man has in the degree that his will is 'informed and disciplined by the moral principle'. I confess that to myself the verdict on the rival view seems plain and inescapable. No amount of verbal ingenuity or argumentative convolutions can obscure the fact that it is in flat contradiction to the implications of moral responsibility. The point at issue is really perfectly straightforward. If, as this idealist theory maintains, my acting in defiance of what I deem to be my duty is not a 'free' act in *any* sense, let alone in the sense that 'I could have acted otherwise', then I cannot be morally blameworthy, and that is all there is to it. Nor, for that matter, is the idealist entitled to say that I am morally praiseworthy if I act dutifully; for although that act *is* a 'free' act in the idealist sense, it is on his own avowal not free in the sense that 'I could have acted otherwise'.

It seems to me idle, therefore, to pretend that if one has to give up freedom in the traditional elective sense one is not giving up anything important. What we are giving up is, quite simply, the reality of the moral life. I recognise that to a certain type of religious nature (as well as, by an odd meeting of extremes, to a certain type of secular nature) that does not appear to matter so very much; but, for myself, I still think it sufficiently important to make it well worthwhile enquiring seriously into the possibility that the elective freedom upon which it rests may be real after all.

Volition = act or faculty of willing.

That brings me to the second, and more constructive, part of this lecture. From now on I shall be considering whether it is reasonable to believe that man does in fact possess a free will of the kind specified in the first part of the lecture. If so, just how and where within the complex fabric of the volitional life are we to locate it?—for although free will must presumably belong (if anywhere) to the volitional side of human experience, it is pretty clear from the way in which we have been forced to define it that it does not pertain simply to volition as such; not even to all volitions that are commonly dignified with the name of 'choices'. It has been, I think, one of the more serious impediments to profitable discussion of the Free Will problem that Libertarians and Determinists alike have so often failed to appreciate the comparatively narrow area within which the free will that is necessary to 'save' morality is required to operate. It goes without saying that this failure has been gravely prejudicial to the case for Libertarianism. I attach a good deal of importance, therefore, to the problem of locating free will correctly within the volitional orbit. Its solution forestalls and annuls, I believe, some of the more tiresome clichés of Determinist criticism.

We saw earlier that Common Sense's practice of 'making allowances' in its moral judgments for the influence of heredity and environment indicates Common Sense's conviction, both that a just moral judgment must discount determinants of choice over which the agent has no control, and also (since it still accepts moral judgments as legitimate) that *something* of moral relevance survives which can be regarded as genuinely self-originated. We are now to try to discover what this 'something' is. And I think we may still usefully take Common Sense as our guide. Suppose one asks the ordinary intelligent citizen *why* he deems it proper to make allowances for X, whose heredity and/or environment are unfortunate. He will tend to reply, I think, in some such terms as these: that X has more and stronger temptations to deviate from what is right than Y or Z, who are normally circumstanced, so that he must put forth a *stronger moral effort* if he is to achieve the same level of external conduct. The intended implication seems to be that X is just as morally praiseworthy as Y or Z *if* he exerts an equivalent moral effort, even though he may not thereby achieve an equal success in conforming his will to the 'concrete' demands of duty. And this implies, again, Common Sense's belief that *in moral effort* we have something for which a man is responsible *without qualification,* something that is *not* affected by heredity and environment but depends *solely* upon the self itself.

Now in my opinion Common Sense has here, in principle, hit upon the one and only defensible answer. Here, and here alone, so far as I can see, in the act of deciding whether to put forth or withhold the moral effort required to resist temptation and rise to duty, is to be found an act which is free in the sense required for moral responsibility; an act of which the self is sole author, and of which it is true to say that 'it could be' (or, after the event, 'could have been') 'otherwise'. Such is the thesis which we shall now try to establish.

The species of argument appropriate to the establishment of a thesis of this sort should fall, I think, into two phases. First, there should be a consideration of the evidence of the moral agent's own inner experience. What *is* the act of moral decision, and what does it imply, from the standpoint of the actual participant? Since there is no way of knowing the act of moral decision—or for that matter any other form of activity—except by actual participation in it, the evidence of the subject, or agent, is on an issue of this kind of palmary importance. It can hardly, however, be taken as in itself conclusive. For even if that evidence should be overwhelmingly to the effect that moral decision does have the characteristics required by moral freedom, the question is bound to be raised—and in view of considerations from other quarters pointing in a contrary direction is *rightly* raised—Can we *trust* the evidence of inner experience? That brings us to what will be the second phase of the argument. We shall have to go on to show, if we are to make good our case, that the extraneous considerations so often supposed to be fatal to the belief in moral freedom are in fact innocuous to it.

In the light of what was said in the last lecture ["Self-Activity and Its Modes"] about the self's experience of moral decision as a *creative* activity, we may perhaps be absolved from developing the first phase of the argument at any great length. The appeal is throughout to one's own experience in the actual taking of the moral decision in the situation of moral temptation. 'Is it possible', we must ask, 'for anyone so circumstanced to *dis*believe that he could be deciding otherwise?' The answer is surely not in doubt. When we decide to exert moral effort to resist a temptation, we feel quite certain that we *could* withhold the effort; just as, if we decide to withhold the effort and yield to our desires, we feel quite certain that we *could* exert it—otherwise we should not blame ourselves afterwards for having succumbed. It may be, indeed, that this conviction is mere self-delusion. But that is not at the moment our concern. It is enough at present to establish that the act of deciding to exert or to withhold moral effort, as we know it from the inside in actual moral living, belongs to the category of acts which 'could have been otherwise'.

Mutatis mutandis, the same reply is forthcoming if we ask, 'Is it possible for the moral agent in the taking of his decision to *dis*believe that he is the *sole* author of that decision?' Clearly he cannot disbelieve that it is *he* who takes the decision. That, however, is not in itself sufficient to enable him, on reflection, to regard himself as *solely* responsible for the act. For his 'character' as so far formed might conceivably be a factor in determining it, and no one can suppose that the constitution of his 'character' is uninfluenced by circumstances of heredity and environment with which *he* has nothing to do. But as we pointed out in the last lecture, the very essence of the moral decision as it is experienced is that it is a decision whether or not to *combat* our strongest desire, and our strongest desire *is* the expression in the situation of our character as so far formed. Now clearly our character cannot be a factor in determining the decision whether or not to *oppose* our character. I think we are entitled to say, therefore, that the act of moral decision is one in which the self is for itself not merely 'author' but 'sole author'.

We may pass on, then, to the second phase of our constructive argument; and this will demand more elaborate treatment. Even if a moral agent *qua* making a moral decision in the situation of 'temptation' cannot help believing that he has free will in the sense at issue—a moral freedom between real alternatives, between genuinely open possibilities—are there, nevertheless, objections to a freedom of this kind so cogent that we are bound to distrust the evidence of 'inner experience'?

I begin by drawing attention to a simple point whose significance tends, I think, to be underestimated. If the phenomenological analysis we have offered is substantially correct, no one while functioning as a moral agent can help believing that he enjoys free will. Theoretically he may be completely convinced by Determinist arguments, but when actually confronted with a personal situation of conflict between duty and desire he is quite certain that it lies with him here and now whether or not he will rise to duty. It follows that if Determinists could produce convincing theoretical arguments against a free will of this kind, the awkward predicament would ensue that man has to deny as a theoretical being what he has to assert as a practical being. Now I think the Determinist ought to be a good deal more worried about this than he usually is. He seems to imagine that a strong case on general theoretical grounds is enough to prove that the 'practical' belief in free will, even if inescapable for us as practical beings, is mere illusion. But in fact it proves nothing of the sort. There is no reason whatever why a belief that we find ourselves obliged to hold *qua* practical beings should be required to give way before a belief which we find ourselves obliged to hold *qua* theoretical beings; or, for that matter, *vice versa*. All that the theoretical arguments of Determinism can prove, unless they are reinforced by a refutation of the phenomenological analysis that supports Libertarianism, is that there is a radical conflict between the theoretical and the practical sides of man's nature, an

antinomy at the very heart of the self. And this is a state of affairs with which no one can easily rest satisfied. I think therefore that the Determinist ought to concern himself a great deal more than he does with phenomenological analysis, in order to show, if he can, that the assurance of free will is not really an inexpugnable element in man's practical consciousness. There is just as much obligation upon him, convinced though he may be of the soundness of his theoretical arguments, to expose the errors of the Libertarian's phenomenological analysis, as there is upon us, convinced though we may be of the soundness of the Libertarian's phenomenological analysis, to expose the errors of the Determinist's theoretical arguments.

However, we must at once begin the discharge of our own obligation. The rest of this lecture will be devoted to trying to show that the arguments which seem to carry the most weight with Determinists are, to say the least of it, very far from compulsive. Fortunately, a good many of the arguments which at an earlier time in the history of philosophy would have been strongly urged against us make almost no appeal to the bulk of philosophers today, and we may here pass them by. That applies to any criticism of 'open possibilities' based on a metaphysical theory about the nature of the universe as a whole. Nobody today *has* a metaphysical theory about the nature of the universe as a whole! It applies also, with almost equal force, to criticisms based upon the universality of causal law as a supposed postulate of science. There have always been, in my opinion, sound philosophic reasons for doubting the validity, as distinct from the convenience, of the causal postulate in its universal form, but at the present time, when scientists themselves are deeply divided about the need for postulating causality even within their own special field, we shall do better to concentrate our attention upon criticisms which are more confidently advanced. I propose to ignore also, on different grounds, the type of criticism of free will that is sometimes advanced from the side of religion, based upon religious postulates of Divine Omnipotence and Omniscience. So far as I can see, a postulate of human freedom is every bit as necessary to meet certain religious demands (e.g. to make sense of the 'conviction of sin'), as postulates of Divine Omniscience and Omnipotence are to meet certain other religious demands. If so, then it can hardly be argued that religious experience as such tells more strongly against than for the position we are defending; and we may be satisfied, in the present context, to leave the matter there. It will be more profitable to discuss certain arguments which contemporary philosophers do think important, and which recur with a somewhat monotonous regularity in the literature of anti-Libertarianism.

These arguments can, I think, be reduced in principle to no more than two: first, the argument from 'predictability'; second, the argument from the alleged meaninglessness of an act supposed to be the self's act and yet not an expression of the self's character. Contemporary criticism of free will seems to me to consist almost exclusively of variations on these two themes. I shall deal with each in turn.

On the first we touched in passing at an earlier stage. Surely it is beyond question (the critic urges) that when we know a person intimately we can foretell with a high degree of accuracy how he will respond to at least a large number of practical situations. One feels safe in predicting that one's dog-loving friend will not use his boot to repel the little mongrel that comes yapping at his heels; or again that one's wife will not pass with incurious eyes (or indeed pass at all) the new hat shop in the city. So to behave would not be (as we say) 'in character'. But, so the criticism runs, you with your doctrine of 'genuinely open possibilities', of a free will by which the self can diverge from its own character, remove all rational basis from such prediction. You require us to make the absurd supposition that the success of countless predictions of the sort in the past has been mere matter of chance. If you *really* believed in your theory, you would not be surprised if tomorrow your friend with the notorious horror of strong drink should suddenly exhibit a passion for whisky and soda, or if your friend whose taste for reading has hitherto been satisfied with the sporting columns of the newspapers should be discovered on a fine Saturday afternoon poring over the works of Hegel. But of course you *would* be surprised. Social life would be sheer chaos if there were not well-grounded social expectations; and social life is not sheer chaos. Your theory is hopelessly wrecked upon obvious facts.

Now whether or not this criticism holds good against some versions of Libertarian theory I need not here discuss. It is sufficient if I can make it clear that against the version advanced in this lecture, according to which free will is localised in a relatively narrow field of operation, the criticism has no relevance whatsoever.

Let us remind ourselves briefly of the setting within which, on our view, free will functions. There is X, the course which we believe we ought to follow, and Y, the course towards which we feel our desire is strongest. The freedom which we ascribe to the agent is the freedom to put forth or refrain from putting forth the moral effort required to resist the pressure of desire and do what he thinks he ought to do.

But then there is surely an immense range of practical situations—covering by far the greater part of life—in which there is no question of a conflict within the self between what he most desires to do and what he thinks he ought to do? Indeed such conflict is a comparatively rare phenomenon for the majority of men. Yet over that whole vast range there is nothing whatever in our version of Libertarianism to prevent our agreeing that character determines conduct. In the absence, real or supposed, of any 'moral' issue, what a man chooses will be simply that course which, after such reflection as seems called for, he deems most likely to bring him what he most strongly desires; and that is the same as to say the course to which his present character inclines him.

Over by far the greater area of human choices, then, our theory offers no more barrier to successful prediction on the basis of character than any other theory. For where there is no clash of strongest desire with duty, the free will we are defending has no business. There is just nothing for it to do.

But what about the situations—rare enough though they may be—in which there *is* this clash and in which free will does therefore operate? Does our theory entail that there, at any rate, as the critic seems to suppose, 'anything may happen'?

Not by any manner of means. In the first place, and by the very nature of the case, the range of the agent's possible choices is bounded by what he thinks he ought to do on the one hand, and what he most strongly desires on the other. The freedom claimed for him is a freedom of decision to make or withhold the effort required to do what he thinks he ought to do. There is no question of a freedom to act in some 'wild' fashion, out of all relation to his characteristic beliefs and desires. This so-called 'freedom of caprice', so often charged against the Libertarian, is, to put it bluntly, a sheer figment of the critic's imagination, with no *habitat* in serious Libertarian theory. Even in situations where free will does come into play it is perfectly possible, on a view like ours, given the appropriate knowledge of a man's character, to predict within certain limits how he will respond.

But 'probable' prediction in such situations can, I think, go further than this. It is obvious that where desire and duty are at odds, the felt 'gap' (as it were) between the two may vary enormously in breadth in different cases. The moderate drinker and the chronic tippler may each want another glass, and each deem it his duty to abstain, but the felt gap between desire and duty in the case of the former is trivial beside the great gulf which is felt to separate them in the case of the latter. Hence it will take a far harder moral effort for the tippler than for the moderate drinker to achieve the same external result of abstention. So much is matter of common agreement. And we are entitled, I think, to take it into account in prediction, on the simple principle that the harder the moral effort required to resist desire the less likely it is to occur. Thus in the example taken, most people would predict that the tippler will very probably succumb to his desires, whereas there is a reasonable likelihood that the moderate drinker will make the comparatively slight effort needed to resist them. So long as the prediction does not pretend to more than a measure of probability, there is nothing in our theory which would disallow it.

I claim, therefore, that the view of free will I have been putting forward is consistent with predictability of conduct on the basis of character over a very wide field indeed. And I make the further claim that that field will cover all the situations in life concerning which there is any empirical evidence that successful prediction is possible.

Let us pass on to consider the second main line of criticism. This is, I think, much the more illuminating of the two, if only because it compels the Libertarian to make explicit certain concepts which are indispensable to him, but which, being desperately hard to state clearly, are apt not to be stated at all. The critic's fundamental point might be stated somewhat as follows:

'Free will as you describe it is completely unintelligible. On your own showing no *reason* can be given, because there just *is* no reason, why a man decides to exert rather than to withhold moral effort, or *vice versa*. But such an act—or more properly, such an "occurrence"—it is nonsense to speak of as an act of a *self*. If there is nothing in the self's character to which it is, even in principle, in any way traceable, the self has nothing to do with it. Your so-called "freedom", therefore, so far from supporting the self's moral responsibility, destroys it as surely as the crudest Determinism could do'.

If we are to discuss this criticism usefully, it is important, I think, to begin by getting clear about two different senses of the word 'intelligible'.

If, in the first place, we mean by an 'intelligible' act one whose occurrence is in principle capable of being inferred, since it follows necessarily from something (though we may not know in fact from what), then it is certainly true that the Libertarian's free will is unintelligible. But that is only saying, is it not, that the Libertarian's 'free' act is not an act which follows necessarily from something! This can hardly rank as a *criticism* of Libertarianism. It is just a description of it. That there can be nothing unintelligible in *this* sense is precisely what the Determinist has got to *prove*.

Yet it is surprising how often the critic of Libertarianism involves himself in this circular mode of argument. Repeatedly it is urged against the Libertarian, with a great air of triumph, that on his view he can't say *why* I now decide to rise to duty, or now decide to follow my strongest desire in defiance of duty. Of course he can't. If he could he wouldn't *be* a Libertarian. To 'account for' a 'free' act is a contradiction in terms. A free will is *ex hypothesi* the sort of thing of which the request for an *explanation* is absurd. The assumption that an explanation must be in principle possible for the act of moral decision deserves to rank as a classic example of the ancient fallacy of 'begging the question'.

But the critic usually has in mind another sense of the word 'unintelligible'. He is apt to take it for granted that an act which is unintelligible in the *above* sense (as the morally free act of the Libertarian undoubtedly is) is unintelligible in the *further* sense that we can attach no meaning to it. And this is an altogether more serious matter. If it could really be shown that the Libertarian's 'free will' were unintelligible in this sense of being meaningless, that, for myself at any rate, would be the end of the affair. Libertarianism would have been conclusively refuted.

But it seems to me manifest that this can *not* be shown. The critic has allowed himself, I submit, to become the victim of a widely accepted but fundamentally vicious assumption. He has assumed that whatever is meaningful must exhibit its meaningfulness to those who view it from the standpoint of external observation. Now if one chooses thus to limit one's self to the rôle of external observer, it is, I think, perfectly true that one can attach no meaning to an act which is the act of something we call a 'self' and yet follows from nothing in that self's character. But then *why should we* so limit ourselves, when what is under consideration is a subjective activity? For the apprehension of subjective acts there is *another* standpoint available, that of *inner experience,* of the practical consciousness in its actual functioning. If our free will should turn out to be something to which we can attach a meaning from *this* standpoint, no more is required. And no more ought to be expected. For I must repeat that only from the inner standpoint of living experience *could* anything of the nature of 'activity' be directly grasped. Observation from without is in the nature of the case impotent to apprehend the active *qua* active. We can from without observe sequences of states. If into these we read activity (as we sometimes do), this can only be on the basis of what we discern in ourselves from the inner standpoint. It follows that if anyone insists upon taking his criterion of the meaningful simply from the standpoint of external observation, he is really deciding in advance of the evidence that the notion of activity, and *a fortiori* the notion of a free will, is 'meaningless'. He looks for the free act through a medium which is in the nature of the case incapable of revealing it, and then, because inevitably he doesn't find it, he declares that it doesn't exist!

But if, as we surely ought in this context, we adopt the inner standpoint, then (I am suggesting) things appear in a totally different light. From the inner standpoint, it seems to me plain, there is no difficulty whatever in attaching meaning to an act which is the self's act and which nevertheless does not follow from the self's character. So much I claim has been established by the phenomenological analysis, in this and the previous lecture, of the act of moral decision in face of moral temptation. It is thrown into particularly clear relief where the moral decision is to make the moral effort required to rise to duty. For the very function of moral effort, as it appears to the agent engaged in the act, is to enable the self to act against the line of least resistance, against the line to which his character as so far formed most strongly inclines him. But if the self is thus conscious here of *combating* his formed character, he surely cannot possibly suppose that the act, although his own act, *issues from* his formed character? I submit,

therefore, that the self knows very well indeed—from the inner standpoint—what is meant by an act which is the *self's* act and which nevertheless does not follow from the self's *character*.

What this implies—and it seems to me to be an implication of cardinal importance for any theory of the self that aims at being more than superficial—is that the nature of the self is for itself something more than just its character as so far formed. The 'nature' of the self and what we commonly call the 'character' of the self are by no means the same thing, and it is utterly vital that they should not be confused. The 'nature' of the self comprehends, but is not without remainder reducible to, its 'character'; it must, if we are to be true to the testimony of our experience of it, be taken as including *also* the authentic creative power of fashioning and re-fashioning 'character'.

The misguided, and as a rule quite uncritical, belittlement, of the evidence offered by inner experience has, I am convinced, been responsible for more bad argument by the opponents of Free Will than has any other single factor. How often, for example, do we find the Determinist critic saying, in effect, '*Either* the act follows necessarily upon precedent states, *or* it is a mere matter of chance and accordingly of no moral significance'. The disjunction is invalid for it does not exhaust the possible alternatives. It seems to the critic to do so only because he *will* limit himself to the standpoint which is proper, and indeed alone possible, in dealing with the physical world, the standpoint of the external observer. If only he would allow himself to assume the standpoint which is not merely proper for, but necessary to, the apprehension of subjective activity, the inner standpoint of the practical consciousness in its actual functioning, he would find himself obliged to recognise the falsity of his disjunction. Reflection upon the act of moral decision as apprehended from the inner standpoint would force him to recognise a *third* possibility, as remote from chance as from necessity, that, namely, of *creative activity,* in which (as I have ventured to express it) nothing determines the act save the agent's doing of it.

There we must leave the matter. But as this lecture has been, I know, somewhat densely packed, it may be helpful if I conclude by reminding you, in bald summary, of the main things I have been trying to say. Let me set them out in so many successive theses.

SUMMARY

1. The freedom which is at issue in the traditional Free Will problem is the freedom which is presupposed in moral responsibility.

2. Critical reflection upon carefully considered attributions of moral responsibility reveals that the only freedom that will do is a freedom which pertains to inner acts of choice, and that these acts must be acts (*a*) of which the self is *sole* author, and (*b*) which the self could have performed otherwise.

3. From phenomenological analysis of the situation of moral temptation we find that the self as engaged in this situation is inescapably convinced that it possesses a freedom of precisely the specified kind, located in the decision to exert or withhold the moral effort needed to rise to duty where the pressure of its desiring nature is felt to urge it in a contrary direction.

Passing to the question of the *reality* of this moral freedom which the moral agent believes himself to possess, we argued:

4. Of the two types of Determinist criticism which seem to have most influence today, that based on the predictability of much human behaviour fails to touch a Libertarianism which confines the area of free will as above indicated. Libertarianism so understood is compatible with all the predictability that the empirical facts warrant. And:

5. The second main type of criticism, which alleges the 'meaninglessness' of an act which is the self's act and which is yet not determined by the self's character, is based on a failure to appreciate that the standpoint of inner experience is not only legitimate but indispensable where what is at issue is the reality and nature of a subjective activity. The creative act of moral decision is inevitably meaningless to the mere external observer; but from the inner standpoint it is as real, and as significant, as anything in human experience.

NOTES

1. Reprinted in *Ethics and the History of Philosophy, Selected Essays*.

2. I have explained the grounds for my dissent from Broad's final conclusion on pp. 27 ff. of *In Defence of Free Will* (Jackson Son & Co., 1938).

3. *Kantian Ethics*.

4. *Op. cit.*, p. 261.

Deliberation, Prediction, and Foreknowledge

ALVIN I. GOLDMAN

Actions, Predictions, and Books of Life*

Alvin I. Goldman (1938–   ) teaches philosophy at the University of Illinois, Chicago Circle.

I

Are actions determined? It is difficult to tell "directly" whether or not actions are governed by universal laws, so some philosophers resort to the following "indirect" argument:

If actions are determined, it is possible to predict them (with certainty).

It is not possible for actions to be predicted (with certainty).
Therefore, actions are not determined.

This position will be called "anti-predictionism," and a defender of it is an "anti-predictionist." The aim of this paper is to rebut anti-predictionism.

Both premises of the anti-predictionist argument will come under attack. The first premise asserts that determinism implies the possibility of prediction, or, in its contrapositive form, that the impossibility of prediction implies indeterminism. But on a reasonable definition of determinism this premise is false. One can specify events which it is logically impossible to predict, but which nonetheless may be determined. Setting such events aside, however, there is a presumptive connection between deter-

*This paper is an abridged and simplified version of a paper with the same title that originally appeared in *American Philosophical Quarterly*, Vol. V, No. 3 (July 1968): 135 –151. A slightly different version appears as Chapter Six. ("Determinism and Predictability") of Alvin I. Goldman, *A Theory of Human Action* (Englewood Cliffs, N.J.: Prentice-Hall, Inc., 1970). For a more rigorous presentation, the reader should consult either of these versions. Reprinted here by permission of the author and the editor of the *American Philosophical Quarterly*.

minism and the possibility of prediction. To support the second premise the anti-predictionist may call attention to a problem concerning the possibility of writing a complete description of someone's life—including his voluntary actions—even before he is born. If actions were determined, it would be possible for such a "book of life" to be written. The anti-predictionist contends, however, that no such book of life could be written, at least not with any assurance that its predictions would come true. For a book of life might be discovered and read by the agent whose actions it predicts; but if the agent reads these predictions, he can choose to falsify them. Hence nobody could write such a book of life with any certainty that his predictions would be fulfilled. Therefore, the anti-predictionist concludes, determinism does not hold. Against this position, I maintain that it may well be possible for books of life to be written, and for the author of such a book to know (with certainty) that its predictions will be fulfilled.

Anti-predictionists generally support their second premise by contrasting the predictability of human behavior with that of physical events. They allege that special difficulties of a purely conceptual sort arise for the prediction of action, difficulties that are unparalleled in the realm of purely physical phenomena. I shall argue that there are no essential differences between actions and physical events with respect to the problem of prediction. More precisely, *conceptual* reflection on the nature of human behavior (as opposed to *empirical* investigation by the special sciences) does not reveal any peculiar immunity of action to prediction.

I am not attempting to prove the thesis that actions are determined; I merely wish to show that the anti-predictionist's arguments fail to prove that actions are not determined. It is, of course, conceivable that actions are undetermined. If so, they are not perfectly predictable. My contention is just that the arguments of philosophers, based on familiar, common-sense features of human action and choice, do not prove that actions are undetermined or immune to prediction. My aim, in other words, is not to establish the *truth,* but merely the *tenability,* of the thesis that actions are determined.

II

Some writers have pointed out that certain actions (under certain descriptions, at least) cannot be predicted: i.e., it is logically impossible for them to be predicted. They have inferred from this that these actions are not determined. I am prepared to concede that it is indeed logically impossible for certain actions (under certain descriptions) to be predicted. But it does not follow from this that they are undetermined.

Before turning to these cases, let us present some relevant definitions. I shall define *determinism* as the view that every event and state of affairs is determined in every detail. An event is *determined* (in a given detail) if and only if it is *deducible from some set of antecedent conditions and laws of nature.* Roughly, a law of nature is any true non-analytic universal statement of unlimited scope which supports counterfactual conditionals. Notice that this definition makes no reference to predictability, and thereby leaves open the connection, if any, between determinism and predictability. When an event is deducible from certain laws and antecedent conditions, I shall say that these antecedent conditions *causally necessitate* this event. I assume that if human actions are determined, then among the events or conditions that causally necessitate them are desires, beliefs, and decisions of the agent.

In our discussion of predictability we need a sense of 'prediction' distinct from mere lucky guesses or precognition. We must be concerned with predictions made on the basis of laws and antecedent conditions. I shall call a prediction a *scientific prediction* if and only if it is made by *deducing* the predicted event from known laws and antecedent conditions. A scientific predictor may learn of the laws and antecedent conditions in any number of ways. (On my definition, most predictions made by actual scientists are not ''scientific predictions,'' since real scientists seldom, if ever, *deduce* subsequent events from laws and prior conditions. But scientific prediction, as defined here, may be regarded as an ideal of prediction to which scientists can aspire.)

With these definitions at hand, let us examine some cases in which actions, or action-related events, are logically impossible to predict. Let the expression 'invent x' mean 'think of x for the very first time.' Now suppose that Sam invents the corkscrew in 1625—in other words, the first thought of the corkscrew occurs in 1625, when Sam thinks of it. It logically follows from this that nobody predicts Sam's invention of the corkscrew. For in order to predict Sam's invention of the corkscrew, the predictor would himself have to think of the corkscrew, and he would have to have such a thought before 1625. But if someone did have such a thought before 1625, then Sam would not *invent* the corkscrew in 1625: Sam's thinking of the corkscrew in 1625 would not count as an inventing of the corkscrew. Thus, it is logically impossible that anyone should (correctly) predict Sam's inventing of the corkscrew.

Does it follow from this that Sam's invention of the corkscrew is undetermined? Certainly not. Although it is logically impossible for anyone to predict Sam's invention of the corkscrew, his invention of the corkscrew may be deducible from laws and antecedent conditions. Consider an analogous case in the realm of purely physical phenomena. Let the expression 'a tornado strikes x *by surprise* at t' mean 'a tornado strikes x at t, and before t nobody thinks of a tornado striking x.' Now suppose that a tornado strikes Timbuktu by surprise at t. It is logically impossible for this event to be predicted, for if someone did predict it, there would be a thought, prior to t, of a tornado striking Timbuktu, and hence there would be no event of a tornado striking Timbuktu *by surprise* at t. But there is no reason to conclude that the event of a tornado striking Timbuktu by surprise is undetermined. We may well suppose that this event is deducible from laws and antecedent conditions. For surely we may suppose that a tornado's striking Timbuktu at t is deducible from prior meteorological conditions and physical laws. But if we simply add to these antecedent conditions the further (antecedent) condition that nobody thinks of a tornado striking Timbuktu before t, we obtain a set of laws and antecedent conditions which jointly entail that a tornado strikes Timbuktu *by surprise* at *t*. We see, then, that the logical impossibility of an event being predicted does not prove that this event is undetermined.

With this point in mind, consider a case involving not actions, but decisions. In his article "Can The Will Be Caused?" Carl Ginet claims that it is impossible ("conceptually impossible") for anyone to predict his own decisions. And he regards this as a reason for concluding that decisions are not caused, i.e., determined. The argument begins by defining 'deciding to do *A*' as 'passing into a state of knowledge (of a certain kind) that one will do, or try to do, *A*.' Now suppose that Sam, at *t*, decides to do *A*. If Sam had predicted that he would make this decision—and if this prediction had involved *knowledge*—then Sam could not, at *t*, decide to do *A*. For if, before *t*, he knew that he would decide to do *A*, then he knew before *t* that he would do, or try to do, *A*. But if he knew, before *t*, that he would do, or try to do, *A*, he could not, at *t*, have *passed into* a state of knowing that he would do, or try to do, *A*. Thus, it is logically impossible for anyone to predict his own decision.

Of course, one might predict one's future decision and then forget about it. Having forgotten about this prediction—i.e., having lost this knowledge—one could later *pass into* a state of (renewed) knowledge that one would do, or try to do, an action. But if one *retains* the foreknowledge, nothing one does later can count as *deciding*.

But does it follow from this that a person's decisions are uncaused, or undetermined? As before, the answer is no. From the fact that it is logically impossible for anyone to predict his own decision (and retain the knowledge contained in this prediction) it does not follow that the decision is not deducible from laws and antecedent conditions. Once we notice that there are certain events, the occurrence of which presupposes that they have not been predicted, we readily see that it is logically impossible for some events to be predicted. But it does not follow that these events are undetermined. Determinism simply does not entail the logical possibility of prediction.

III

Let us set aside the special class of events, including inventions, surprise tornadoes, and decisions, which logically presuppose the absence of prediction or foreknowledge. If we set these aside, it appears that determinism does imply the possibility, in principle, of prediction. For if an event is deducible from laws and antecedent conditions, then if anyone knew these laws and antecedent conditions beforehand, and if he had sufficient reasoning or calculational powers to make the relevant deduction, he could know, beforehand, that the indicated event would occur. In the actual world, of course, there may be no beings with sufficient knowledge of prior conditions and laws, or sufficient deductive powers, to make scientific predictions, especially scientific predictions of (voluntary) human actions. But if we are interested in the possibility, *in principle*, of prediction, we must not confine ourselves to the actual world. We will have to consider certain *non-actual* possible worlds in which a potential predictor is endowed with all relevant information and calculational powers.

The anti-predictionist would contend that there are *no* possible worlds in which scientific predictions are made of an agent's voluntary actions. Or, at any rate, there are no possible worlds in which scientific predictions are made of an agent's voluntary actions and in which the agent learns of these predictions prior to the actions. This is because it is always open to an agent to act contrary to the prediction; in other words, he can always choose to *refute* the prediction, no matter what has been predicted. According to the anti-predictionist, then, there are no possible worlds in which a book of someone's life is written (scientifically) before he is born, a book which he reads during his lifetime, and parts of which he reads prior to the time of the recorded (i.e., predicted) actions. I contend that this claim is mistaken. I think there may well be possible worlds in which books of life are (scientifically) written and yet read at appropriate times by the agent in question. This, then, is an appropriate test of the anti-predictionist's position.

In order to ascertain whether there are possible worlds of the indicated kind, we must try to imagine such worlds. Now we are not interested in possible worlds that are radically different from our own, for the only point of appealing to these possible worlds is to shed light on the actual one. Specifically, we shall want our possible worlds to contain all and only the physical and psychological laws that the actual world contains. Since we do not know all the laws of the actual world, however, we proceed as follows. We see whether we can coherently imagine a world in which scientific predictions of actions are made but which contains no *apparent* difference from our own world with respect to laws of nature. Since this world contains *scientific* predictions, it means that it must be deterministic (at least it must be deterministic with respect to the events being predicted). But this does not beg any questions, for the very fact that such a world does not diverge in any obvious way from the actual world (in terms of laws or regularities) lends credence to the view that the actual world is deterministic. Of course, it does not prove the actual world to be deterministic; but it is not my purpose here to offer such a proof.

My strategy, then, is to sketch a possible world in which a book of life is scientifically written, and in which the agent reads portions of this book. What is problematic and interesting about this is that the book may have a causal effect on the actions it predicts. That is, it may have an effect on the truth or falsity of the statements contained in the book. It is obvious that the prospective author of such a book must take such "reflexivity" into account. Before sketching my possible world, let us examine the structure of prediction-making where the prediction itself has a causal effect on the predicted event.

Consider the problem of an election predictor. He may know what the precise results of the upcoming election will be, if he makes no public prediction of the election. If he publishes a prediction, however, some of the voters, having found out what the results will be, may change their votes and thereby falsify his prediction. How, then, can a pollster make a genuinely scientific and accurate prediction of an election? Can he take into account the effect of the prediction itself? Herbert Simon has shown that, under specifiable conditions, a predictor can do this. Essentially, what the predictor must know is the propensity of the voters in the community to *change* their voting intention in accordance with their expectations of the outcome. If persons are more likely to vote for a candidate when they expect him to win than when they expect him to lose, we have a "bandwagon" effect; if the opposite holds, we have an "underdog" effect.

Let us suppose that a given pollster has ascertained that, two days before the election, 60 percent of the electorate plans to vote for candidate A and 40 percent for B. He also knows that, unless he publishes a prediction, the percentages will be the same on elec-

tion day. Further suppose he knows that there is a certain "bandwagon" effect obtaining in the voting community. (That this bandwagon effect holds in the community could be discovered either by studying previous elections or by deducing it from "higher-level" generalizations found to be true of the community.) When the original intention of the electorate is to vote 60 percent for A, this bandwagon effect can be expressed by the equation $V = 60 + .2(P - 50)$, where P is the percentage vote for A publicly predicted by a pollster, and V is the actual resultant vote for A. Clearly, if the pollster publicly predicts that A will receive 60 percent of the vote, his prediction will be falsified. Putting $P = 60$, the equation tells us that $V = 62$. In other words, the effect of the prediction, combined with the original voting intention of the electorate, would result in a 62 percent vote for A. However, the pollster can easily calculate a value for P which will make $P = V$. He need only solve the two equations, $P = V$ and $V = 60 + .2(P - 50)$. Such a solution yields $P = 62.5$. Thus, the pollster can publish a prediction saying that 62.5 percent of the electorate will vote for A, knowing that his own prediction will bring an additional 2.5 percent of the electorate into the A column, and thereby make his prediction come true.

If someone wishes to predict a single person's behavior and yet let him learn of the prediction, the predictor must employ the same sort of strategy as the pollster. He must take into account the agent's reaction to the prediction. There are several kinds of circumstances in which, having made the appropriate calculations, he will be able to make a correct prediction: (1) The agent learns of the prediction but does not want to falsify it. (2) Upon hearing the prediction, the agent decides to falsify it, but later, when the time of the action approaches, he acquires preponderant reasons for doing what was predicted after all. (3) Having decided to refute the prediction, the agent performs the action conforming with it because he doesn't realize that he is conforming with it. (4) At the time of the action the agent lacks either the ability or the opportunity to do anything but conform with the prediction, though he may have believed that he would be able to falsify it. In any of these four kinds of cases, a predictor would be able to calculate that his prediction, together with numerous other antecedent conditions, would causally necessitate that the agent perform the predicted action. In a case of type (2), for example, the predictor may be able to foresee that the agent will first read his prediction and decide to falsify it. But other factors will crop up—ones which the agent did not originally count on—that will make him change his mind and perform the predicted action after all. And the predictor also foresees this.

In the first three types of cases, (1), (2), and (3), the agent performs the predicted action *voluntarily* (though in (3) he does not realize that what he is doing falls under the description "what was predicted"). In other words, in each of these three kinds of cases, the agent *could have* acted otherwise. Thus, the possibility of a scientific prediction does not require that the agent be *unable* to act in any way different from the prediction. All that is required is that the agent will not *in fact* act in any way different from the prediction. A predictor might know that an agent will in fact act in a certain way, not because he knows the agent will be incapable of doing otherwise, but because he knows that the agent will *choose* or *decide* to act as predicted.

IV

I shall now sketch a possible world in which scientific predictions are made of an agent's life and inscribed in a "book of life," (parts of) which the agent subsequently reads. Obviously I cannot describe the whole of this world, but I shall describe some of its most important and problematic features, namely the interaction between the agent and the book. Unfortunately, I shall have to omit a description of another important part of the world, the part in which the predictor (or predictors) gathers his data and makes his calculations. I am unable to describe this part of the world, first, because I do not know all the laws which the predictor would have at his disposal, and secondly, because I am not able to say just what the structure of this being would be. However, the main features of the predictor's *modus operandi* should be clear from our discussion of the pollster, whose technique is at the heart of such predicting.

While browsing around the library one day, I notice an old dusty tome, quite large, entitled "Alvin I. Goldman." I take it from the shelf and start reading. In great detail, it describes my life as a little boy. It always gibes with my memory and frequently revives my memory of forgotten events. I realize that this purports to be a book of my life and I resolve to test it. Turning to the section with today's date on it, I find the following entry for 2:36 P.M. "He discovers me on the shelf. He takes me down and starts

reading me. . . ." I look at the clock and see that it is 3:03. It is quite plausible, I say to myself, that I found the book about half an hour ago. I turn now to the entry for 3:03. It reads: "He is reading me. He is reading me. He is reading me." I continue looking at the book in this place, meanwhile thinking how remarkable the book is. The entry reads: "He continues to look at me, meanwhile thinking how remarkable I am."

I decide to defeat the book by looking at a future entry. I turn to an entry eighteen minutes hence. It says: "He is reading this sentence." Aha, I say to myself, all I need do is refrain from reading that sentence eighteen minutes from now. I check the clock. To ensure that I won't read that sentence, I close the book. My mind wanders; the book has revived a buried memory and I reminisce about it. I decide to reread the book there and relive the experience. That's safe, I tell myself, because it is an earlier part of the book. I read that passage and become lost in reverie and rekindled emotion. Time passes. Suddenly I start. Oh yes, I intended to refute the book. But what was the time of the listed action?, I ask myself. It was 3:19, wasn't it? But it's 3:21 now, which means I have already refuted the book. Let me check and make sure. I inspect the book at the entry for 3:17. Hmm, that seems to be the wrong place for there it says I'm in a reverie. I skip a couple of pages and suddenly my eyes alight on the sentence: "He is reading this sentence." But it's an entry for 3:21, I notice! So I made a mistake. The action I had intended to refute was to occur at 3:21, not 3:19. I look at the clock, and it is still 3:21. I have not refuted the book after all.

I now turn to the entry for 3:28. It reads, "He is leaving the library, on his way to the President's office." Good heavens, I say to myself, I had completely forgotten about my appointment with the President of the University at 3:30. I suppose I could falsify the book by not going, but it is much more important for me not to be late for that appointment. I'll refute the book some other time! Since I do have a few minutes, however, I turn back to the entry for 3:22. Sure enough, it says that my reading the 3:28 entry has reminded me about the appointment. Before putting the book back on the shelf, and leaving, I turn to an entry for tomorrow at 3:30 P.M. "He's still riding the bus bound for Chicago," it reads. Well, I say to myself, *that* prediction will be easy to refute. I have absolutely no intention of going to Chicago tomorrow.

Despite my decision to refute the book, events later induce me to change my mind and to conform to it, for stronger reasons arise for not refuting it. When I get home that evening I find a note from my wife saying that her father (in Chicago) is ill and that she had to take the car and drive to Chicago. I call her there and she explains what has happened. I tell her about the book. Next morning she calls again with news that her father's condition is deteriorating and that I must come to Chicago immediately. As I hang up I realize that the book may turn out right after all, but the situation nevertheless demands that I go to Chicago. I might still refute it by going by plane or train. However, I call the airlines and am told that the fog is delaying all flights. The railroad says that there are no trains for Chicago till later in the day. So, acquiescing, I take a bus to Chicago, and find myself on it at 3:30.

V

I have given several cases in which the book is not refuted, and the reader should be convinced that I could easily continue this way. But it is important now to reply to several objections which the anti-predictionist is anxious to make against my procedure.

1. *"Your story clearly presupposes determinism. But whether or not determinism is true is the central matter of dispute. Hence, you are begging the question."* Admittedly, my story does presuppose determinism. Unless determinism were true, the imagined predictor could not have figured out what actions the agent would perform and then have written them in the book. However, this does not beg the question. For I am not trying to prove that determinism *is* true. I am merely trying to show that the thesis of determinism is quite compatible with the world as we know it and with human nature as we know it. The world depicted in my story is very much like the real world, except that it contains different antecedent conditions. The fact that this imagined world is determined and contains predictions of actions, and yet resembles the real world so closely, suggests that the real world may also be determined. At any rate, this supposition seems quite tenable, and its tenability is what I seek to establish.

2. *"The story you told was fixed. Events might have been different from the way you described them.*

For example, the fog might not have curtailed all air traffic." No, events could not be different *in the world I am imagining*. That is, in my world all the events I described were causally necessitated by prior antecedent conditions. I did not describe all the antecedent conditions, so perhaps the reader cannot see that each event I did describe was causally necessitated by them. But, since it is a deterministic world, that is so. No one can imagine *my* world and also substitute the negation of one of the events I described. I'm not "fixing" the story by saying that the fog curtailed air traffic; that just is the way my imagined world goes.

3. *"But I can imagine a world in which some putative predictions of actions are refuted."* I have no doubt that you can; that is very easy. You could even imagine a world *somewhat* like the one I have just described, but in which putative predictions are falsified. But this proves nothing at all. I would never deny that one can construct some possible worlds in which putative scientific predictions of actions are not successful. I have only claimed that one can (also) construct *some* possible worlds in which genuine scientific predictions of actions are made (and are successful). The situation with predictions of actions is no different from the one with predictions of physical events. We can construct possible worlds in which predictions of physical phenomena are correct. But we can also construct worlds in which putative scientific predictions of physical phenomena are incorrect. If our ability to construct worlds in which predictions are unsuccessful proves the inherent unpredictableness of the kind of phenomena unsuccessfully predicted, then we can prove the unpredictableness of physical phenomena as easily as the unpredictableness of human action.

4. *"The world you have described, though possible, is a highly improbable world. Worlds in which putative predictions of actions are falsified are much more probable."* The notion of one possible world being "more probable" than another seems to me unintelligible. Surely the statistical sense of probability cannot be intended. There is no way of "sampling" from possible worlds to discover what features most of them have. Perhaps the anti-predictionist means that we can *imagine* more worlds in which putative predictions of actions are falsified. But this too is questionable. I can imagine indefinitely many worlds in which successful predictions of actions are made.

Perhaps the anti-predictionist means that it is

improbable that any such sequence of events as I described would occur in the *real* world. He may well be right on this point. However, to talk about what is probable (in the evidential sense) in the real world is just to talk about what has happened, is happening, and will happen *as a matter of fact.* But the dispute between predictionists and anti-predictionists is, presumably, not about what *will* happen, but about what *could* happen *in principle.* This "in principle" goes beyond the particular facts of the actual world.

5. *"The difference between physical phenomena and action is that predictions of actions can defeat themselves; but predictions of physical events cannot."* This is not so. One can construct worlds in which the causal effect of a putative prediction of a physical event falsifies that prediction. Jones calculates the position of a speck of dust three inches from his nose and the direction and velocity of wind currents in the room. He then announces his prediction that five seconds thence the speck will be in a certain position, neglects to account for the wind expelled from his mouth when he makes the prediction, however, and this factor changes the expected position of the speck of dust. Perhaps one can imagine a wider variety of cases in which predictions affect human action more than physical phenomena. But his is only a difference of *degree,* not of kind.

6. *Predictions of physical events can refute themselves because the predictor may fail to account for the effect of his own prediction. But were he to take this effect into account, he would make a correct prediction. On the other hand, there are conditions connected with the prediction of action in which, no matter what prediction the predictor makes, his prediction will be falsified. Here there is no question of inaccurate calculation or insufficient information. Whatever he predicts will be incorrect. Yet this situation arises only in connection with human action, not physical events."*

This is an important objection and warrants detailed discussion.

VI

Suppose that I wish to predict what action you will perform thirty seconds from now, but that I shall not try to change or affect your behavior except by making my prediction. (Thus, I shall not, for example, predict that you will perform no action at all and then make that prediction come true by killing you.) Further suppose that the following conditions obtain. At this moment you want to falsify any prediction that I shall make of your action. Moreover, you will still have this desire thirty seconds from now, and it will be stronger than any conflicting desire you will have at that time. Right now you intend to do action *A,* but you are prepared to perform *-A* (not *A*) if I predict that you will perform *A.* Thirty seconds hence you will have the ability and opportunity to do *A* and the ability and opportunity to do *-A.* Finally, conditions are such that, if I make a prediction in English in your presence, you will understand it, will remember it for thirty seconds, and will be able to tell whether any of your actions will conform to it or not. Given all these conditions, whatever I predict—at least, if I make the prediction by saying it aloud, in your presence, in English, etc.—will be falsified. If I predict you will do *A,* then you will do *-A,* while if I predict that you will do *-A,* you will proceed to do *A.* In other words, in these conditions any prediction of mine will causally necessitate the non-occurrence of the event I predict.

Notice that this example does not prove that it is impossible "simpliciter" for me to make a scientific prediction of your action. All that it proves is that I cannot make such a prediction *in a certain manner,* viz., by announcing it to you in English. If I predict your action in some other manner, by thinking it to myself or by saying it aloud in Hindustani, for example, the effect on your action would not be the same as if I say it aloud in English. Assume that, if you do not hear me make any prediction or if you hear me say something you fail to understand, you will proceed to perform action *A.* Then it is possible for me to predict your action correctly by announcing the prediction in Hindustani.

In determining whether or not a certain set of events, including (1) a prediction, (2) the event predicted, and (3) certain other assumed conditions, is a "causally compossible" set, it is essential to specify the manner of the prediction. This is true *in general,* not just in the case of predictions of action. A prediction which is "embodied" or expressed in one way will not have the same causal effects as the same prediction expressed in another way. We can see this in the case of the speck of dust. Jones predicted the position of the dust by announcing it orally, and this resulted in the falsification of the prediction. But had he made the same prediction in another fashion—say by moving his toes in a certain conventional pattern—his prediction would not have been falsified, for the position of the dust would not have been affected.

What is the significance of the fact that it is impossible, in some circumstances, for a (correct) prediction of an action to be made in a specified manner? First, this unpredictability does not prove that these actions are undetermined. Indeed, the very construction of the case in which no prediction is possible *presupposed* the existence of laws of nature which, together with a given prediction, would result in a certain action. In short, the case under discussion should, if anything, support rather than defeat the thesis that actions are determined. The only reason one might have for thinking the contrary is the assumption—which should by now appear very dubious—that determinism entails predictability. What our present case shows, I think, is that under some circumstances, even a determined event may not be susceptible of being correctly predicted in a specified manner. This fact can be further supported by adducing a similar case connected with purely physical events. And this brings me to my second point: the case produced above does not reflect a peculiarity of human action, since parallel examples can be found among physical phenomena.

Imagine a certain physical apparatus placed in front of a piano keyboard. A bar extends from the apparatus and is positioned above a certain key. (Only white keys will be considered.) If the apparatus is not disturbed, the bar will strike that key at a certain time. Now let us suppose that the apparatus is sensitive to sound, and, in particular, can discriminate between sounds of varying pitches. If the apparatus picks up a certain sound, the position of the bar will move to the right and proceed to strike the key immediately to the right of the original one (if there is one). Specifically, if the sound has the same pitch as that of the key over which the bar is poised, the bar will move. If the monitored sound has any other pitch, the bar will remain in its position and proceed to strike that key.

Now suppose that someone (or something) wishes to make predictions of the behavior of the apparatus. He wishes to predict what key the bar will strike. But the following restriction is made on the *manner* in which the prediction is to be made. The prediction must be expressed according to a specific set of conventions or symbols. To predict that the bar will strike middle C, for example, the predictor must emit a sound with the pitch of middle C. To predict that the bar will strike D, he must emit a sound with the pitch of that key, etc. All sound emissions are to be made in the neighborhood of the apparatus. Given this restriction on the manner of prediction, it will be causally incompossible for the predictor to make a correct prediction. Suppose that the bar is poised above middle C. If he predicts that it will strike middle C—that is, if he emits a sound of that pitch—the bar will move and proceed to strike D. But if he predicts any other behavior of the bar, for example, that it will strike D, the bar will remain in its original position and strike middle C.

Admittedly, the manner of prediction I have allowed to the predictor of this physical phenomenon is much more narrowly restricted than the manner of prediction allowed to the predictor of human action. But we could imagine physical apparatuses with a greater degree of complexity, able to "refute" predictions made in any of a wider variety of manners. In any case, the principle of the situation is the same for both physical phenomena and human actions, though the manners of prediction which affect one phenomenon may be different from the manners of prediction which affect the other. The latter difference simply reflects the fact that physical objects and human beings do not respond in precisely the same ways to the same causes. But this is equally true of different kinds of physical objects and of different pairs of human beings.

VII

I have shown that there are possible worlds in which voluntary actions are scientifically predicted. Are there possible worlds in which a person predicts one of his *own* actions? I think that there are such worlds, which I shall illustrate by continuing the sketch of the world described earlier.

Having tested my book of life on a very large number of occasions during many months and having failed to refute it, I become convinced that whatever it says is true. I have about as good inductive evidence for this proposition as I do for many another proposition I could be said to know. Finally, I get up enough courage to look at the very end of the book and, as expected, it tells when and how I shall die. Dated five years hence, it describes my committing suicide by jumping off the eighty-sixth floor observation deck of the Empire State Building. From a description of my thoughts which will flash through my mind before jumping, it is clear that the intervening five years will have been terrible. As the result of those experiences, I shall have emotions and desires (and beliefs) which will induce me to jump. Since I trust the book completely, I now conclude that I *shall* commit suicide five years hence. Moreover, I can be said to *know* that I shall commit suicide.

This example shows, contrary to the view of some authors, that we can have knowledge of our own future actions, knowledge which is not based on having already made a decision or formed an intention to perform the future action. In this case, there is a time at which I have certain knowledge of what I shall do (at any rate, about as "certain" as one can be with inductive evidence) and yet I have formed no intention nor made any decision to perform that action. At the time I read the book's prediction, I do not intend to commit suicide. But although I do not intend to commit suicide, I fully believe and know that, five years later, I shall intend to commit suicide. I firmly believe that, at that later time, I shall feel certain emotions and have certain desires which will induce me to jump off the Empire State Building. At the time of my reading the book I do not feel those things, but I commiserate with my future self, much as I commiserate with and understand another person's desires, beliefs, feelings, intentions, etc. Still, my understanding of these states of mind and of the action in which they will issue is the understanding of a spectator; my knowledge of these states and of my future action is purely inductive. Moreover, this knowledge is of a particular *voluntary* act to be performed at a specified time. Though the suicide will be a "desperate" action, it will in no sense be "coerced" or done unknowingly; it will flow from a firm intention, an intention formed very deliberately. But that intention will not be formed until after I have had certain experiences, experiences which, at the time I am reading the book, I have not yet had.

We can imagine two alternative series of events to occur between my reading the book and my suicide. First, I might *forget* what I have learned from the book, and later decide to commit suicide. Secondly, while never forgetting the prediction, the knowledge of my future suicide may gradually change from mere inductive knowledge to knowledge based on intention. In this second alternative, there is never any "moment" of decision. I never pass from a state of complete doubt about committing suicide into a sudden intention of committing suicide. Rather, there

is a gradual change, over the five-year period, from mere inductive knowledge that I shall commit suicide to an intention to commit suicide. When I first read the book I am fully prepared to assent to the proposition that I shall commit suicide. But I am saddened by the thought; my heart isn't in it. Later, as a result of various tragic experiences, my *will* acquiesces in the idea. I begin to welcome the thought of suicide, to entertain the thought of committing suicide with pleasure and relief. When the appointed time comes around, I am *bent* on suicide. This gradual change in attitude constitutes the difference between the kinds of knowledge of my future suicide, the difference between mere inductive knowledge and knowledge based on intention.

Many philosophers are very uncomfortable with the idea of a book of life. They believe that the existence of such books—or of foreknowledge of actions in any form—would deprive us of all the essential characteristics of voluntary behavior: choice, decision, deliberation, etc. I do not think this fear is warranted. I have just shown that even if a person reads what a book of life predicts, and believes this prediction, he can still perform the indicated action voluntarily. Moreover, the existence of predictions which the agent does *not* read leaves ample opportunity for deliberation and decision. An agent may know that a book of his life exists and yet proceed to make decisions and to deliberate as all of us do now. The agent's belief that there is such a book, and his belief that the book's existence implies that his actions are causally necessitated, is compatible with his deliberating whether to do one action or another. Although his future action is causally necessitated, one of the antecedent conditions which necessitate it is his deliberation. Indeed, the prediction in the book of life was made precisely because its writer knew that the agent would deliberate and then decide to do the predicted action. Thus, the book of life can hardly be said to preclude deliberation. Nor does the book of life imply that the agent's deliberation is "for naught," or "irrelevant." On the contrary, his deliberation is a crucial antecedent condition: were he not to deliberate, he probably would not perform the action he eventually does perform. Deliberation and decision are perfectly compatible with the existence of books of life; and they are perfectly compatible with the thesis that they, and the actions in which they issue, are determined.

HARRY G. FRANKFURT

Freedom of the Will and the Concept of a Person*

Harry G. Frankfurt (1929–   ) teaches philosophy at Yale.

What philosophers have lately come to accept as analysis of the concept of a person is not actually analysis of *that* concept at all. Strawson, whose usage represents the current standard, identifies the concept of a person as "the concept of a type of entity such that *both* predicates ascribing states of consciousness *and* predicates ascribing corporeal characteristics . . . are equally applicable to a single individual of that single type."[1] But there are many entities besides persons that have both mental and physical properties. As it happens—though it seems extraordinary that this should be so—there is no common English word for the type of entity Strawson has in mind, a type that includes not only human beings but animals of various lesser species as well. Still, this hardly justifies the misappropriation of a valuable philosophical term.

Whether the members of some animal species are persons is surely not to be settled merely by determining whether it is correct to apply to them, in addition to predicates ascribing corporeal characteristics, predicates that ascribe states of consciousness. It does violence to our language to endorse the application of the term 'person' to those numerous creatures which do have both psychological and material properties but which are manifestly not persons in any normal sense of the word. This misuse

of language is doubtless innocent of any theoretical error. But although the offense is "merely verbal," it does significant harm. For it gratuitously diminishes our philosophical vocabulary, and it increases the likelihood that we will overlook the important area of inquiry with which the term 'person' is most naturally associated. It might have been expected that no problem would be of more central and persistent concern to philosophers than that of understanding what we ourselves essentially are. Yet this problem is so generally neglected that it has been possible to make off with its very name almost without being noticed and, evidently, without evoking any widespread feeling of loss.

There is a sense in which the word 'person' is merely the singular form of 'people' and in which both terms connote no more than membership in a certain biological species. In those senses of the word which are of greater philosophical interest, however, the criteria for being a person do not serve primarily to distinguish the members of our own species from the members of other species. Rather, they are designed to capture those attributes which are the subject of our most humane concern with ourselves and the source of what we regard as most important and most problematical in our lives. Now these attributes would be of equal significance to us even if they were not in fact peculiar and common to the members of our own species. What interests us most in the human condition would not interest us less if it were also a feature of the condition of other creatures as well.

Our concept of ourselves as persons is not to be

*Harry G. Frankfurt, "Freedom of the Will and the Concept of a Person," *The Journal of Philosophy,* Vol. 68 (1971), pp. 5–20. Reprinted by permission of the author and the publisher.

understood, therefore, as a concept of attributes that are necessarily species-specific. It is conceptually possible that members of novel or even of familiar nonhuman species should be persons; and it is also conceptually possible that some members of the human species are not persons. We do in fact assume, on the other hand, that no member of another species is a person. Accordingly, there is a presumption that what is essential to persons is a set of characteristics that we generally suppose—whether rightly or wrongly—to be uniquely human.

It is my view that one essential difference between persons and other creatures is to be found in the structure of a person's will. Human beings are not alone in having desires and motives, or in making choices. They share these things with the members of certain other species, some of whom even appear to engage in deliberation and to make decisions based upon prior thought. It seems to be peculiarly characteristic of humans, however, that they are able to form what I shall call ''second-order desires'' or ''desires of the second order.''

Besides wanting and choosing and being moved *to do* this or that, men may also want to have (or not to have) certain desires and motives. They are capable of wanting to be different, in their preferences and purposes, from what they are. Many animals appear to have the capacity for what I shall call ''first-order desires'' or ''desires of the first order,'' which are simply desires to do or not to do one thing or another. No animal other than man, however, appears to have the capacity for reflective self-evaluation that is manifested in the formation of second-order desires.[2]

I

The concept designated by the verb 'to want' is extraordinarily elusive. A statement of the form ''*A* wants to *X*''—taken by itself, apart from a context that serves to amplify or to specify its meaning—conveys remarkably little information. Such a statement may be consistent, for example, with each of the following statements: (a) the prospect of doing *X* elicits no sensation or introspectible emotional response in *A*; (b) *A* is unaware that he wants to *X*; (c) *A* believes that he does not want to *X*; (d) *A* wants to refrain from *X*-ing; (e) *A* wants to *Y* and believes that it is impossible for him both to *Y* and to *X*; (f) *A* does not ''really'' want to *X*; (g) *A* would rather die than *X*; and so on. It is therefore hardly sufficient to formulate the distinction between first-order and second-order desires, as I have done, by suggesting

merely that someone has a first-order desire when he wants to do or not to do such-and-such, and that he has a second-order desire when he wants to have or not to have a certain desire of the first order.

As I shall understand them, statements of the form ''*A* wants to *X*'' cover a rather broad range of possibilities.[3] They may be true even when statements like (a) through (g) are true: when *A* is unaware of any feelings concerning *X*-ing, when he is unaware that he wants to *X*, when he deceives himself about what he wants and believes falsely that he does not want to *X*, when he also has other desires that conflict with his desire to *X*, or when he is ambivalent. The desires in question may be conscious or unconscious, they need not be univocal, and *A* may be mistaken about them. There is a further source of uncertainty with regard to statements that identify someone's desires, however, and here it is important for my purposes to be less permissive.

Consider first those statements of the form ''*A* wants to *X*'' which identify first-order desires—that is, statements in which the term 'to *X*' refers to an action. A statement of this kind does not, by itself, indicate the relative strength of *A*'s desire to *X*. It does not make it clear whether this desire is at all likely to play a decisive role in what *A* actually does or tries to do. For it may correctly be said that *A* wants to *X* even when his desire to *X* is only one among his desires and when it is far from being paramount among them. Thus, it may be true that *A* wants to *X* when he strongly prefers to do something else instead; and it may be true that he wants to *X* despite the fact that, when he acts, it is not the desire to *X* that motivates him to do what he does. On the other hand, someone who states that *A* wants to *X* may mean to convey that it is this desire that is motivating or moving *A* to do what he is actually doing or that *A* will in fact be moved by this desire (unless he changes his mind) when he acts.

It is only when it is used in the second of these ways that, given the special usage of 'will' that I propose to adopt, the statement identifies *A*'s will. To identify an agent's will is either to identify the desire (or desires) by which he is motivated in some action he performs or to identify the desire (or desires) by which he will or would be motivated when or if he acts. An agent's will, then, is identical with one or more of his first-order desires. But the notion of the will, as I am employing it, is not coextensive with the notion of first-order desires. It is not the notion of something that merely inclines an agent in some degree to act in a certain way. Rather, it is the notion of an *effective* desire—one that moves (or will or would move) a person all the way to action. Thus the notion of the will is not coextensive with the notion of what an agent intends to do. For even though someone may have a settled intention to do X, he may nonetheless do something else instead of doing X because, despite his intention, his desire to do X proves to be weaker or less effective than some conflicting desire.

Now consider those statements of the form "A wants to X" which identify second-order desires— that is, statements in which the term 'to X' refers to a desire of the first order. There are also two kinds of situation in which it may be true that A wants to want to X. In the first place, it might be true of A that he wants to have a desire to X despite the fact that he has a univocal desire, altogether free of conflict and ambivalence, to refrain from X-ing. Someone might want to have a certain desire, in other words, but univocally want that desire to be unsatisfied.

Suppose that a physician engaged in psychotherapy with narcotics addicts believes that his ability to help his patients would be enhanced if he understood better what it is like for them to desire the drug to which they are addicted. Suppose that he is led in this way to want to have a desire for the drug. If it is a genuine desire that he wants, then what he wants is not merely to feel the sensations that addicts characteristically feel when they are gripped by their desires for the drug. What the physician wants, insofar as he wants to have a desire, is to be inclined or moved to some extent to take the drug.

It is entirely possible, however, that, although he wants to be moved by a desire to take the drug, he does not want this desire to be effective. He may not want it to move him all the way to action. He need not be interested in finding out what it is like to take the drug. And insofar as he now wants only to *want* to take it, and not to *take* it, there is nothing in what he now wants that would be satisfied by the drug itself. He may now have, in fact, an altogether univocal desire *not* to take the drug; and he may prudently arrange to make it impossible for him to satisfy the desire he would have if his desire to want the drug should in time be satisfied.

It would thus be incorrect to infer, from the fact that the physician now wants to desire to take the drug, that he already does desire to take it. His second-order desire to be moved to take the drug does not entail that he has a first-order desire to take it. If the drug were now to be administered to him, this might satisfy no desire that is implicit in his desire to want to take it. While he wants to want to take the drug, he may have *no* desire to take it; it may be that *all* he wants is to taste the desire for it. That is, his desire to have a certain desire that he does not have may not be a desire that his will should be at all different than it is.

Someone who wants only in this truncated way to want to X stands at the margin of preciosity, and the fact that he wants to want to X is not pertinent to the identification of his will. There is, however, a second kind of situation that may be described by 'A wants to want to X'; and when the statement is used to describe a situation of this second kind, then it does pertain to what A wants his will to be. In such cases the statement means that A wants the desire to X to be the desire that moves him effectively to act. It is not merely that he wants the desire to X to be among the desires by which, to one degree or another, he is moved or inclined to act. He wants this desire to be effective—that is, to provide the motive in what he actually does. Now when the statement that A wants to want to X is used in this way, it does entail that A already has a desire to X. It could not be true both that A wants the desire to X to move him into action and that he does not want to X. It is only if he does want to X that he can coherently want the desire to X not merely to be one of his desires but, more decisively, to be his will.[4]

Suppose a man wants to be motivated in what he does by the desire to concentrate on his work. It is necessarily true, if this supposition is correct, that he already wants to concentrate on his work. This desire is now among his desires. But the question of whether or not his second-order desire is fulfilled does not turn merely on whether the desire he wants is one of his desires. It turns on whether this desire is, as he wants it to be, his effective desire or will. If, when the chips are down, it is his desire to concentrate on his work that moves him to do what he does, then what he wants at that time is indeed (in the relevant sense) what he wants to want. If it is some other desire that actually moves him when he acts, on the other hand, then what he wants at that time is not (in the relevant sense) what he wants to want. This will be so despite the fact that the desire to concentrate on his work continues to be among his desires.

II

Someone has a desire of the second order either when he wants simply to have a certain desire or when he wants a certain desire to be his will. In situations of the latter kind, I shall call his second-order desires "second-order volitions" or "volitions of the second order." Now it is having second-order volitions, and not having second-order desires generally, that I regard as essential to being a person. It is logically possible, however unlikely, that there should be an agent with second-order desires but with no volitions of the second order. Such a creature, in my view, would not be a person. I shall use the term 'wanton' to refer to agents who have first-order desires but who are not persons because, whether or not they have desires of the second order, they have no second-order volitions.[5]

The essential characteristic of a wanton is that he does not care about his will. His desires move him to do certain things, without its being true of him either that he wants to be moved by those desires or that he prefers to be moved by other desires. The class of wantons includes all nonhuman animals that have desires and all very young children. Perhaps it also includes some adult human beings as well. In any case, adult humans may be more or less wanton; they may act wantonly, in response to first-order desires concerning which they have no volitions of the second order, more or less frequently.

The fact that a wanton has no second-order volitions does not mean that each of his first-order desires is translated heedlessly and at once into action. He may have no opportunity to act in accordance with some of his desires. Moreover, the translation of his desires into action may be delayed or precluded either by conflicting desires of the first order or by the intervention of deliberation. For a wanton may possess and employ rational faculties of a high order. Nothing in the concept of a wanton implies that he cannot reason or that he cannot deliberate concerning how to do what he wants to do. What distinguishes the rational wanton from other rational agents is that he is not concerned with the desirability of his desires themselves. He ignores the question of what his will is to be. Not only does he pursue whatever course of action he is most strongly inclined to pursue, but he does not care which of his inclinations is the strongest.

Thus a rational creature, who reflects upon the suitability to his desires of one course of action or another, may nonetheless be a wanton. In maintaining that the essence of being a person lies not in reason but in will, I am far from suggesting that a creature without reason may be a person. For it is only in virtue of his rational capacities that a person is capable of becoming critically aware of his own will and of forming volitions of the second order. The structure of a person's will presupposes, accordingly, that he is a rational being.

The distinction between a person and a wanton may be illustrated by the difference between two narcotics addicts. Let us suppose that the physiological condition accounting for the addiction is the same in both men, and that both succumb inevitably to their periodic desires for the drug to which they are addicted. One of the addicts hates his addiction and always struggles desperately, although to no avail, against its thrust. He tries everything that he thinks might enable him to overcome his desires for the drug. But these desires are too powerful for him to withstand, and invariably, in the end, they conquer him. He is an unwilling addict, helplessly violated by his own desires.

The unwilling addict has conflicting first-order desires: he wants to take the drug, and he also wants to refrain from taking it. In addition to these first-order desires, however, he has a volition of the second order. He is not a neutral with regard to the conflict between his desire to take the drug and his desire to refrain from taking it. It is the latter desire, and not the former, that he wants to constitute his will; it is the latter desire, rather than the former, that he wants to be effective and to provide the purpose that he will seek to realize in what he actually does.

The other addict is a wanton. His actions reflect the economy of his first-order desires, without his being concerned whether the desires that move him to act are desires by which he wants to be moved to act. If he encounters problems in obtaining the drug or in administering it himself, his responses to his urges to take it may involve deliberation. But it never occurs to him to consider whether he wants the relations among his desires to result in his having the will he has. The wanton addict may be an animal, and thus incapable of being concerned about his will. In any event he is, in respect of his wanton lack of concern, no different from an animal.

The second of these addicts may suffer a first-order conflict similar to the first-order conflict suffered by the first. Whether he is human or not, the wanton may (perhaps due to conditioning) both want to take the drug and want to refrain from taking it. Unlike the unwilling addict, however, he does not prefer that one of his conflicting desires should be paramount over the other; he does not prefer that one first-order desire rather than the other should constitute his will. It would be misleading to say that he is neutral as to the conflict between his desires, since this would suggest that he regards them as equally acceptable. Since he has no identity apart from his first-order desires, it is true neither that he prefers one to the other nor that he prefers not to take sides.

It makes a difference to the unwilling addict, who is a person, which of his conflicting first-order desires wins out. Both desires are his, to be sure; and whether he finally takes the drug or finally succeeds in refraining from taking it, he acts to satisfy what is in a literal sense his own desire. In either case he does something he himself wants to do, and he does it not because of some external influence whose aim happens to coincide with his own but because of his desire to do it. The unwilling addict identifies himself, however, through the formation of a second-order volition, with one rather than with the other of his conflicting first-order desires. He makes one of them more truly his own and, in so doing, he withdraws himself from the other. It is in virtue of this identification and withdrawal, accomplished through the formation of a second-order volition, that the unwilling addict may meaningfully make the analytically puzzling statements that the force moving him to take the drug is a force other than his own, and that it is not of his own free will but rather against his will that this force moves him to take it.

The wanton addict cannot or does not care which of his conflicting first-order desires wins out. His lack of concern is not due to his inability to find a convincing basis for preference. It is due either to his lack of the capacity for reflection or to his mindless indifference to the enterprise of evaluating his own desires and motives.[6] There is only one issue in the struggle to which his first-order conflict may lead: whether the one or the other of his conflicting desires is the stronger. Since he is moved by both desires, he will not be altogether satisfied by what he does no matter which of them is effective. But it makes no difference *to him* whether his craving or his aversion gets the upper hand. He has no stake in the conflict between them and so, unlike the unwilling addict, he can neither win nor lose the struggle in which he is engaged. When a *person* acts, the desire by which he is moved is either the will he wants or a will he wants to be without. When a *wanton* acts, it is neither.

III

There is a very close relationship between the capacity for forming second-order volitions and another capacity that is essential to persons—one that has often been considered a distinguishing mark of the human condition. It is only because a person has volitions of the second order that he is capable both of enjoying and of lacking freedom of the will. The concept of a person is not only, then, the concept of a type of entity that has both first-order desires and volitions of the second order. It can also be construed as the concept of a type of entity for whom the freedom of its will may be a problem. This concept excludes all wantons, both infrahuman and human, since they fail to satisfy an essential condition for the enjoyment of freedom of the will. And it excludes those suprahuman beings, if any, whose wills are necessarily free.

Just what kind of freedom is the freedom of the will? This question calls for an identification of the special area of human experience to which the concept of freedom of the will, as distinct from the concepts of other sorts of freedom, is particularly germane. In dealing with it, my aim will be primarily to locate the problem with which a person is most immediately concerned when he is concerned with the freedom of his will.

According to one familiar philosophical tradition, being free is fundamentally a matter of doing what one wants to do. Now the notion of an agent who does what he wants to do is by no means an altogether clear one: both the doing and the wanting, and the appropriate relation between them as well, require elucidation. But although its focus needs to be sharpened and its formulation refined, I believe that this notion does capture at least part of what is implicit in the idea of an agent who *acts* freely. It misses entirely, however, the peculiar content of the quite different idea of an agent whose *will* is free.

We do not suppose that animals enjoy freedom of the will, although we recognize that an animal may be free to run in whatever direction it wants.

Thus, having the freedom to do what one wants to do is not a sufficient condition of having a free will. It is not a necessary condition either. For to deprive someone of his freedom of action is not necessarily to undermine the freedom of his will. When an agent is aware that there are certain things he is not free to do, this doubtless affects his desires and limits the range of choices he can make. But suppose that someone, without being aware of it, has in fact lost or been deprived of his freedom of action. Even though he is no longer free to do what he wants to do, his will may remain as free as it was before. Despite the fact that he is not free to translate his desires into actions or to act according to the determinations of his will, he may still form those desires and make those determinations as freely as if his freedom of action had not been impaired.

When we ask whether a person's will is free we are not asking whether he is in a position to translate his first-order desires into actions. That is the question of whether he is free to do as he pleases. The question of the freedom of his will does not concern the relation between what he does and what he wants to do. Rather, it concerns his desires themselves. But what question about them is it?

It seems to me both natural and useful to construe the question of whether a person's will is free in close analogy to the question of whether an agent enjoys freedom of action. Now freedom of action is (roughly, at least) the freedom to do what one wants to do. Analogously, then, the statement that a person enjoys freedom of the will means (also roughly) that he is free to want what he wants to want. More precisely, it means that he is free to will what he wants to will, or to have the will he wants. Just as the question about the freedom of an agent's action has to do with whether it is the action he wants to perform, so the question about the freedom of his will has to do with whether it is the will he wants to have.

It is in securing the conformity of his will to his second-order volitions, then, that a person exercises freedom of the will. And it is in the discrepancy between his will and his second-order volitions, or in his awareness that their coincidence is not his own doing but only a happy chance, that a person who does not have this freedom feels its lack. The unwilling addict's will is not free. This is shown by the fact that it is not the will he wants. It is also true, though in a different way, that the will of the wanton addict is not free. The wanton addict neither has the will he wants nor has a will that differs from the will he wants. Since he has no volitions of the second order, the freedom of his will cannot be a problem for him. He lacks it, so to speak, by default.

People are generally far more complicated than my sketchy account of the structure of a person's will may suggest. There is as much opportunity for ambivalence, conflict, and self-deception with regard to desires of the second order, for example, as there is with regard to first-order desires. If there is an unresolved conflict among someone's second-order desires, then he is in danger of having no second-order volition; for unless this conflict is resolved, he has no preference concerning which of his first-order desires is to be his will. This condition, if it is so severe that it prevents him from identifying himself in a sufficiently decisive way with *any* of his conflicting first-order desires, destroys him as a person. For it either tends to paralyze his will and to keep him from acting at all, or it tends to remove him from his will so that his will operates without his participation. In both cases he becomes, like the unwilling addict though in a different way, a helpless bystander to the forces that move him.

Another complexity is that a person may have, especially if his second-order desires are in conflict, desires and volitions of a higher order than the second. There is no theoretical limit to the length of the series of desires of higher and higher orders; nothing except common sense and, perhaps, a saving fatigue prevents an individual from obsessively refusing to identify himself with any of his desires until he forms a desire of the next higher order. The tendency to generate such a series of acts of forming desires, which would be a case of humanization run wild, also leads toward the destruction of a person.

It is possible, however, to terminate such a series of acts without cutting it off arbitrarily. When a person identifies himself *decisively* with one of his first-order desires, this commitment "resounds" throughout the potentially endless array of higher orders. Consider a person who, without reservation or conflict, wants to be motivated by the desire to concentrate on his work. The fact that his second-order volition to be moved by this desire is a decisive one means that there is no room for questions concerning the pertinence of desires or volitions of higher orders. Suppose the person is asked whether he wants to want to want to concentrate on his work. He can properly insist that this question concerning a third-order desire does not arise. It would be a mistake to claim that, because he has not considered whether he wants the second-order volition he has formed, he is indifferent to the question of whether it is with this volition or with some other that he wants his will to accord. The decisiveness of the commitment he has made means that he has decided that no further question about his second-order volition, at any higher order, remains to be asked. It is relatively unimportant whether we explain this by saying that this commitment implicitly generates an endless series of confirming desires of higher orders, or by saying that the commitment is tantamount to a dissolution of the pointedness of all questions concerning higher orders of desire.

Examples such as the one concerning the unwilling addict may suggest that volitions of the second order, or of higher orders, must be formed deliberately and that a person characteristically struggles to ensure that they are satisfied. But the conformity of a person's will to his higher-order volitions may be far more thoughtless and spontaneous than this. Some people are naturally moved by kindness when they want to be kind, and by nastiness when they want to be nasty, without any explicit forethought and without any need for energetic self-control. Others are moved by nastiness when they want to be kind and by kindness when they intend to be nasty, equally without forethought and without active resistance to these violations of their higher-order desires. The enjoyment of freedom comes easily to some. Others must struggle to achieve it.

IV

My theory concerning the freedom of the will accounts easily for our disinclination to allow that this freedom is enjoyed by the members of any species inferior to our own. It also satisfies another condition that must be met by any such theory, by making it apparent why the freedom of the will should be regarded as desirable. The enjoyment of a free will means the satisfaction of certain desires—desires of the second or of higher orders—whereas its absence means their frustration. The satisfactions at stake are those which accrue to a person of whom it may be said that his will is his own. The corresponding frustrations are those suffered by a person of whom it may be said that he is estranged from himself, or

that he finds himself a helpless or a passive bystander to the forces that move him.

A person who is free to do what he wants to do may yet not be in a position to have the will he wants. Suppose, however, that he enjoys both freedom of action and freedom of the will. Then he is not only free to do what he wants to do; he is also free to want what he wants to want. It seems to me that he has, in that case, all the freedom it is possible to desire or to conceive. There are other good things in life, and he may not possess some of them. But there is nothing in the way of freedom that he lacks.

It is far from clear that certain other theories of the freedom of the will meet these elementary but essential conditions: that it be understandable why we desire this freedom and why we refuse to ascribe it to animals. Consider, for example, Roderick Chisholm's quaint version of the doctrine that human freedom entails an absence of causal determination.[7] Whenever a person performs a free action, according to Chisholm, it's a miracle. The motion of a person's hand, when the person moves it, is the outcome of a series of physical causes; but some event in this series, "and presumably one of those that took place within the brain, was caused by the agent and not by any other events". A free agent has, therefore, "a prerogative which some would attribute only to God: each of us, when we act, is a prime mover unmoved".

This account fails to provide any basis for doubting that animals of subhuman species enjoy the freedom it defines. Chisholm says nothing that makes it seem less likely that a rabbit performs a miracle when it moves its leg than that a man does so when he moves his hand. But why, in any case, should anyone *care* whether he can interrupt the natural order of causes in the way Chisholm describes? Chisholm offers no reason for believing that there is a discernible difference between the experience of a man who miraculously initiates a series of causes when he moves his hand and a man who moves his hand without any such breach of the normal causal sequence. There appears to be no concrete basis for preferring to be involved in the one state of affairs rather than in the other.[8]

It is generally supposed that, in addition to satisfying the two conditions I have mentioned, a satisfactory theory of the freedom of the will necessarily provides an analysis of one of the conditions of moral responsibility. The most common recent approach to the problem of understanding the freedom of the will has been, indeed, to inquire what is entailed by the assumption that someone is morally responsible for what he has done. In my view, however, the relation between moral responsibility and the freedom of the will has been very widely misunderstood. It is not true that a person is morally responsible for what he has done only if his will was free when he did it. He may be morally responsible for having done it even though his will was not free at all.

A person's will is free only if he is free to have the will he wants. This means that, with regard to any of his first-order desires, he is free either to make that desire his will or to make some other first-order desire his will instead. Whatever his will, then, the will of the person whose will is free could have been otherwise; he could have done otherwise than to constitute his will as he did. It is a vexed question just how 'he could have done otherwise' is to be understood in contexts such as this one. But although this question is important to the theory of freedom, it has no bearing on the theory of moral responsibility. For the assumption that a person is morally responsible for what he has done does not entail that the person was in a position to have whatever will he wanted.

This assumption *does* entail that the person did what he did freely, or that he did it of his own free will. It is a mistake, however, to believe that someone acts freely only when he is free to do whatever he wants or that he acts of his own free will only if his will is free. Suppose that a person has done what he wanted to do, that he did it because he wanted to do it, and that the will by which he was moved when he did it was his will because it was the will he wanted. Then he did it freely and of his own free will. Even supposing that he could have done otherwise, he would not have done otherwise; and even supposing that he could have had a different will, he would not have wanted his will to differ from what it was. Moreover, since the will that moved him when he acted was his will because he wanted it to be, he cannot claim that his will was forced upon him or that he was a passive bystander to its constitution. Under these conditions, it is quite irrelevant to the evaluation of his moral responsibility to inquire whether the alternatives that he opted against were actually available to him.[9]

In illustration, consider a third kind of addict. Suppose that his addiction has the same physiological basis and the same irresistible thrust as the addictions of the unwilling and wanton addicts, but that he is altogether delighted with his condition. He is a willing addict, who would not have things any other way. If the grip of his addiction should somehow weaken, he would do whatever he could to reinstate it; if his desire for the drug should begin to fade, he would take steps to renew its intensity.

The willing addict's will is not free, for his desire to take the drug will be effective regardless of whether or not he wants this desire to constitute his will. But when he takes the drug, he takes it freely and of his own free will. I am inclined to understand his situation as involving the overdetermination of his first-order desire to take the drug. This desire is his effective desire because he is physiologically addicted. But it is his effective desire also because he wants it to be. His will is outside his control, but, by his second-order desire that his desire for the drug should be effective, he has made this will his own. Given that it is therefore not only because of his addiction that his desire for the drug is effective, he may be morally responsible for taking the drug.

My conception of the freedom of the will appears to be neutral with regard to the problem of determinism. It seems conceivable that it should be causally determined that a person is free to want what he wants to want. If this is conceivable, then it might be causally determined that a person enjoys a free will. There is no more than an innocuous appearance of paradox in the proposition that it is determined, ineluctably and by forces beyond their control, that certain people have free wills and that others do not. There is no incoherence in the proposition that some agency other than a person's own is responsible (even *morally* responsible) for the fact that he enjoys or fails to enjoy freedom of the will. It is possible that a person should be morally responsible for what he does of his own free will and that some other person should also be morally responsible for his having done it.[10]

On the other hand, it seems conceivable that it should come about by chance that a person is free to have the will he wants. If this is conceivable, then it might be a matter of chance that certain people enjoy freedom of the will and that certain others do not. Perhaps it is also conceivable, as a number of philosophers believe, for states of affairs to come about in a way other than by chance or as the outcome of a sequence of natural causes. If it is indeed conceivable for the relevant states of affairs to come about in some third way, then it is also possible that a person should in that third way come to enjoy the freedom of the will.

NOTES

1. P. F. Strawson, *Individuals* (London: Methuen, 1959), pp. 101–102. Ayer's usage of 'person' is similar: "it is characteristic of persons in this sense that besides having various physical properties . . . they are also credited with various forms of consciousness" [A. J. Ayer, *The Concept of a Person* (New York: St. Martin's, 1963), p. 82]. What concerns Strawson and Ayer is the problem of understanding the relation between mind and body, rather than the quite different problem of understanding what it is to be a creature that not only has a mind and a body but is also a person.

2. For the sake of simplicity, I shall deal only with what someone wants or desires, neglecting related phenomena such as choices and decisions. I propose to use the verbs 'to want' and 'to desire' interchangeably, although they are by no means perfect synonyms. My motive in forsaking the established nuances of these words arises from the fact that the verb 'to want', which suits my purposes better so far as its meaning is concerned, does not lend itself so readily to the formation of nouns as does the verb 'to desire'. It is perhaps acceptable, albeit graceless, to speak in the plural of someone's "wants." But to speak in the singular of someone's "want" would be an abomination.

3. What I say in this paragraph applies not only to cases in which 'to *X*' refers to a possible action or inaction. It also applies to cases in which 'to *X*' refers to a first-order desire and in which the statement that '*A* wants to *X*' is therefore a shortened version of a statement—"*A* wants to want to *X*"—that identifies a desire of the second order.

4. It is not so clear that the entailment relation described here holds in certain kinds of cases, which I think may fairly be regarded as nonstandard, where the essential difference between the standard and the nonstandard cases lies in the kind of description by which the first-order desire in question is identified. Thus, suppose that *A* admires *B* so fulsomely that, even though he does not know what *B* wants to do, he wants to be effectively moved by whatever desire effectively moves *B*; without knowing what *B*'s will is, in other words, *A* wants his own will to be the same. It certainly does not follow that *A* already has, among his desires, a desire like the one that constitutes *B*'s will. I shall not pursue here the questions of whether there are genuine counterexamples to the

claim made in the text or of how, if there are, that claim should be altered.

5. Creatures with second-order desires but no second-order volitions differ significantly from brute animals, and, for some purposes, it would be desirable to regard them as persons. My usage, which withholds the designation 'person' from them, is thus somewhat arbitrary. I adopt it largely because it facilitates the formulation of some of the points I wish to make. Hereafter, whenever I consider statements of the form "*A* wants to want to *X*," I shall have in mind statements identifying second-order volitions and not statements identifying second-order desires that are not second-order volitions.

6. In speaking of the evaluation of his own desires and motives as being characteristic of a person, I do not mean to suggest that a person's second-order volitions necessarily manifest a *moral* stance on his part toward his first-order desires. It may not be from the point of view of morality that the person evaluates his first-order desires. Moreover, a person may be capricious and irresponsible in forming his second-order volitions and give no serious consideration to what is at stake. Second-order volitions express evaluations only in the sense that they are preferences. There is no essential restriction on the kind of basis, if any, upon which they are formed.

7. "Freedom and Action," in K. Lehrer, ed., *Freedom and Determinism* (New York: Random House, 1966), pp. 11–44.

8. I am not suggesting that the alleged difference between these two states of affairs is unverifiable. On the contrary, physiologists might well be able to show that Chisholm's conditions for a free action are not satisfied, by establishing that there is no relevant brain event for which a sufficient physical cause cannot be found.

9. For another discussion of the considerations that cast doubt on the principle that a person is morally responsible for what he has done only if he could have done otherwise, see my "Alternate Possibilities and Moral Responsibility," *Journal of Philosophy*, Vol. 66, No. 23 (Dec. 4, 1969): 829–839.

10. There is a difference between being *fully* responsible and being *solely* responsible. Suppose that the willing addict has been made an addict by the deliberate and calculated work of another. Then it may be that both the addict and this other person are fully responsible for the addict's taking the drug, while neither of them is solely responsible for it. That there is a distinction between full moral responsibility and sole moral responsibility is apparent in the following example. A certain light can be turned on or off by flicking either of two switches, and each of these switches is simultaneously flicked to the "on" position by a different person, neither of whom is aware of the other. Neither person is solely responsible for the light's going on, nor do they share the responsibility in the sense that each is partially responsible; rather, each of them is fully responsible.

Determinism and Blame

ELIZABETH L. BEARDSLEY

Determinism and Moral Perspectives*

Elizabeth Beardsley (1914–   ) teaches philosophy at Temple University.

Can determinists find a satisfactory rationale for moral praise and blame? On this question, determinists themselves have long been divided. Although the affirmative answer has enjoyed the status of a majority opinion, the negative answer has at times found very effective support. The force of the negative answer emerges clearly in certain recent writings, in which writers sympathetic to determinism vigorously defend the thesis that determinism removes from the concepts of moral praiseworthiness and blameworthiness all legitimate application whatsoever.[1]

The negative answer to the question posed here is unsatisfactory, I think; but in some ways it is preferable to the affirmative answer as the latter is usually given and supported. In this paper, I shall argue that judgments of moral praise and blame, affirmative as well as negative, can be made within the framework of determinism, provided that we accept a more complex account of these judgments and their foundations than is ordinarily supplied or assumed. I shall maintain that judgments concerning the presence or absence of moral praiseworthiness and blameworthiness are made from several different standpoints, which I shall call "moral perspectives." My primary purpose is to show how an understanding

of these perspectives and their relations can contribute substantially toward relieving the tension widely felt (even by some who are reluctant to admit it) to exist between determinism and certain of our basic ethical concepts.

The terms "praise" and "blame" will be used here with the meaning of "moral praise" and "moral blame." Praise and blame will be treated as correlative concepts such that, for everything that is said about one, a corresponding statement about the other could be made, though it will usually be unnecessary to make it. The term "affirmative judgment of praise" will be used to refer to any explicit attribution of praiseworthiness to a person. A "negative judgment of praise" is an explicit denial that a person is praiseworthy. The general term "judgment of praise" will refer indifferently to either an affirmative or a negative judgment of praise, and similarly for "judgment of blame." Judgments of praise and blame will be treated here as assertions which are true or false, and not as acts which may be useful or useless to perform.

DETERMINIST VIEWS OF PRAISE AND BLAME

Before discussing judgments of praise and blame, it will be helpful to considei briefly certain moral judgments of a different kind. The standpoint from which we affirm or deny that acts are objectively right or wrong I shall call the "perspective of objective rightness or wrongness." A judgment of objective rightness or wrongness is a judgment made about an act, not an agent; and it does not carry with it any implication about the praiseworthiness or blameworthiness of an agent. Statements like "Smith's

*Elizabeth L. Beardsley, "Determinism and Moral Perspectives," *Philosophy and Phenomenological Research,* Vol. XXI (1960), 1–20. Reprinted with permission of the author and the editor of *Philosophy and Phenomenological Research.*

act was objectively right, but he deserves no praise for it'' not only are self-consistent, but are often true; objectively right acts can be committed inadvertently, or from reprehensible motives.

The judgment that an act is objectively right furnishes insufficient evidence for a judgment that its agent is praiseworthy, because certain key facts concerning the causal antecedents of the right act remain to be supplied. The objective rightness or wrongness of an act does not depend in any way on its causal antecedents, but on other considerations, such as its consequences (for teleologists), or its harmony with the will of God, moral rules, or the like (for formalists). It is therefore appropriate to call this perspective a ''noncausal'' one, for it takes no account of whether an act had causal antecedents of one kind rather than another, or indeed had completely determining causal antecedents at all.

Most philosophers, I think, would agree that the use of the moral perspective of objective rightness or wrongness presents no particular problem for the determinist. It is true that certain libertarians have apparently seen something profoundly incongruous in the application of any normative predicates at all to the constituent parts of a determined universe; but this line of thought has persuaded so few that it may be disregarded.

Much less harmony prevails among philosophers who have reflected on the relation between determinism and the concepts of moral praise and blame. Libertarians, of course, maintain that because the truth of determinism would invalidate affirmative judgments of praise and blame, determinism is false, and criteria for praiseworthiness and blameworthiness must include the requirement that an agent should have performed his act ''freely.'' Though determinists are united in rejecting the conclusion of the libertarian argument as false, they differ sharply concerning the acceptability of the conditional premise.

Among leading determinists who believe that valid affirmative judgments of praise and blame can be made, a fairly clear account of the criteria for praiseworthiness and blameworthiness seems to have emerged. I shall call those who subscribe to this account ''Group I determinists.'' Details of the account vary, but a substantial area of agreement remains. It is commonly held that if an agent has acted wrongly, without external constraint (''voluntarily''), without ignorance of relevant facts, and from a mo-

tive or because of a trait that is undesirable, then, and only then, the agent deserves blame for his act.[2] Similar conditions are held to govern praiseworthiness.[3]

Group I determinists deny that there is anything here to conflict with the truth of determinism. They point out that those who make judgments of praise and blame must indeed attend to several key factors among the causal conditions that produced the acts whose agents are judged. But any *other* causal conditions that may have been present, and, in particular, antecedents of antecedents, are to be completely disregarded. Moral praisers and blamers, on this view, are simply not concerned with the nature, or even the existence, of such additional factors. Determinism is thus fully compatible with attributions of praiseworthiness and blameworthiness.[4]

To determinists of a second group—''Group II determinists''—this account seems seriously oversimplified.[5] They contend that the same reasoning which leads us to withhold praise and blame from agents whose acts were committed involuntarily will, when combined with the thesis of determinism, lead on inexorably to the conclusion that no one ever deserves praise or blame for anything. They are haunted by the knowledge that many of the causal antecedents of acts have not been investigated by those who mete out praise and blame on the grounds specified above; and most particularly they are haunted by the knowledge that not all of the causal antecedents of voluntary acts are voluntary acts. Thus they come to believe that no distinction between ''voluntary'' and ''involuntary'' acts that a determinist can consistently make can sustain the moral weight that it must bear if we are to judge men praiseworthy or blameworthy. How, they ask, could we ever be justified in blaming or praising someone for a voluntary act and not an involuntary one, when we know full well that even the voluntary act can be traced back to causes—environmental or hereditary— belonging to a world the agent never made?

I believe that there are elements of truth in each of these brands of determinism, and I shall try to show that this is the case.

THE PERSPECTIVE OF MORAL WORTH

Surely there is no doubt that the conditions for praiseworthiness and blameworthiness set forth in the Group I determinists' account do in fact constitute one important and familiar standard according to which we make judgments of praise and blame. It is highly convenient to introduce a special term for the characteristic of moral value that may be said to belong to an agent who has performed an act that meets the conditions specified. I shall say that an agent has "positive moral worth" if and only if he has acted rightly, voluntarily, with knowledge of relevant facts, and from a desire that is good in its situation.[6] The term "moral worth" will be used to refer to either positive or negative moral worth indifferently, and the standard by which agents are judged to have moral worth (positive or negative) will be called the "standard of moral worth." Elsewhere[7] I have discussed certain features of the concept of moral worth in some detail, and have indicated how conditions for the presence of degrees of moral worth may be set up.

A "judgment of moral worth," which may be affirmative or negative, is a judgment in which moral worth is asserted to be present or absent. We must of course distinguish between a negative judgment of positive moral worth ("Agent A is not morally worthy for act A") and an affirmative judgment of negative moral worth ("Agent Y is morally unworthy for his act B").

I shall call the standpoint from which we make judgments of moral worth the "perspective of moral worth." This is plainly not a wholly noncausal perspective, as is the perspective of objective rightness or wrongness. Because *some* (a strictly limited set) of the circumstances causally relevant to the performance of an act are taken into account when the moral worth of its agent is being judged, this perspective may accurately be called a "causally limited" perspective. The factors taken into account in making judgments from this moral perspective will be termed the "worth-determining" factors.

Group II determinists are likely to feel that the introduction of the term "moral worth" is unobjectionable, and perhaps even useful, provided that judgments of moral worth are not held to imply judgments of praise or blame. Thinkers of this group may be disposed to admit that human beings do indeed have a strong psychological tendency to experience positive feelings when confronted by the gestalt agent-performing-act-under-conditions-for-positive-moral-worth, and to experience negative feelings when confronted by the corresponding negative gestalt. They may contend that, since these feelings cannot be rationally justified, human beings had better try to eliminate them from their psyches as soon as possible. The fact that there is no reason to

believe that this has ever been accomplished is not likely to daunt them. In any case, the important point, for the Group II determinist, is that we should avoid the confusion of believing that persons who happen to form part of the pleasant or unpleasant gestalts just mentioned deserve praise or blame for what they do. Because the crucial distinction between voluntary and involuntary acts is bound to collapse in the end, no one ever deserves praise or blame. Perhaps judgments of praise and blame *are* made from the perspective of moral worth, but they *should* not be.[8]

To this the Group I determinist will reply that, since the conditions for "moral worth" were originally taken directly from an analysis of conditions for praiseworthiness and blameworthiness, it is highly arbitrary, to say the very least, to attempt to purge judgments of moral worth of all association with judgments of praise and blame. Moreover, he will continue, the assertion that human beings have "feelings" which are merely "positive" or "negative," when they encounter persons exhibiting positive or negative moral worth, is decidedly misleading. The "feelings" referred to consists of definite reactions of a specific sort, to which are added, for most moral judges, quite explicit reflective convictions. Human beings feel—and reserve—a very special kind of approval and disapproval for those members of their species who perform acts that have certain salient features. Furthermore, the majority of those who have reflected on the matter seem to have been convinced that approval and disapproval of this special kind are reactions to which the persons in question have a morally justified claim. It is this claim which is put forth in affirmative judgments of praise and blame. In view of these considerations, a heavy burden of proof rests on the Group II determinist, who proposes to eliminate from moral discourse all affirmative judgments of praise and blame. This burden, the Group I determinist charges, has not been effectively sustained.

The Group I determinist will go on to admit readily that, among those features which an act must have if its agent is to merit praise or blame, the requirement that it be voluntary is indeed crucial. But, he will say, to establish voluntariness we need examine only certain of the immediate causal ancestors of an act.[9] Considerations about more remote causal forebears are as irrelevant here as information about a man's grandparents would be if proffered in reply to a query about his parents. Therefore it is the case, not only that we *do* make judgments of praise and blame from the perspective of moral worth, but that this procedure is entirely legitimate, and is not threatened by determinism. Thus, concludes the Group I determinist, the problem of praise and blame has been solved.

The Group I determinist may seem, on the face of it, to have had the better of the argument in the exchange just described. He is right, I think, in maintaining that judgments of praise and blame, affirmative as well as negative, have an extremely strong claim to be retained in moral discourse. He is right, also, in insisting that the distinction between voluntary and involuntary acts which is needed for affirmative judgments of praise and blame can be made by determinists. Finally, he is right in holding that what has been called here the "standard of moral worth" is the standard on which many affirmative and negative judgments of praise and blame are based.

Where the Group I determinist is wrong is in his tacit assumption that *all* judgments of moral praise and blame are made from the perspective of moral worth, and that when a man has been judged praiseworthy or blameworthy from this perspective there is nothing more to say about his moral claim to be praised or blamed for the act under consideration. The truth, as I shall go on to try to show, is much less simple than this. There is indeed a network of causes stretching out in all directions, far beyond the worth-determining factors on which the Group I determinists so resolutely fix their minds. Moreover, these other causal factors are by no means without moral significance. We cannot hope to set up a genuinely effective defense against the Group II determinist's harsh view of what that significance is, unless some other way of doing justice to these additional causal factors can be found.

THE PERSPECTIVE OF MORAL CREDIT

I want now to examine a second moral perspective from which we appraise agents. It is necessary to explain the operation of this perspective somewhat more fully than was the case for moral worth, because it has received little attention from ethical theorists.

When we examine our affirmative and negative judgments of praise and blame, we find that many are made by the standard of moral worth; but we also find, I think, that many are not. A second standard of appraisal often comes into operation after a judgment based on moral worth has been made, when we go on to ask further questions about the individual situation of an agent who has performed an act for which he is judged morally worthy or unworthy. Here individual circumstances which facilitated or hampered the performance of the act are taken into account. What we do, that is, is to investigate factors which made the performance of a certain act by a certain agent particularly "easy" or "difficult" for *him*. On the basis of this information, a further judgment of praise or blame is made.

How do we ascertain that the performance of act A by agent X was "easy" or "difficult?" Not by endeavoring to estimate the intensity of his subjective feelings of effort. What is needed here is an objective correlate;[10] and this, I think, is provided by the concept of circumstances *favorable* or *unfavorable* to the performance of a certain act, i.e., circumstances in whose presence the performance of such an act is either more or less likely to occur than it is in their absence. Given that an act is one for which its agent has positive or negative moral worth, a judgment is made to the effect that the balance of known circumstances causally relevant to the performance of that act was favorable or unfavorable. We try to decide, that is, whether, in view of all the things we know about him, it was antecedently probable that a certain act should have been performed by its agent. If an agent has performed an act for which he has positive moral worth, and if it was antecedently improbable that he should have performed this act, then he is praiseworthy by our new standard as well as by the standard of moral worth. We say that such an act was performed "in spite of obstacles" or "against odds." Similar remarks, of course, could be made regarding blameworthiness as judged by this new standard; and it is convenient at times, though somewhat unidiomatic, to speak of an act for which an agent is morally unworthy and which was antecedently improbable as having also been performed "against odds."

To those who deny that the performance against odds of an act for which the agent is morally worthy or unworthy earns for that agent special praise or blame the only answer can be an invitation to look again, more closely, at the moral appraisals we all make. Evidence confirming the view defended here can be found on all sides. For example, it was maintained not long ago by Auxiliary Bishop Joseph M. Marling of the Roman Catholic Church that the presence of severe neurosis in certain Catholic saints could be admitted, since it not only did not detract from their saintliness, but actually contributed to it, in that a neurosis constitutes a serious obstacle to the achievement of spiritual perfection.[11]

There are strong reasons, I think, for maintaining that the criteria for moral appraisals now being examined constitute a standard separate and distinct from the standard of moral worth. The alternative "single-standard" view (the belief that both sets of criteria can be combined into one complex standard) appears to be widely, though casually, held; but I think it is mistaken. My reasons for this conclusion have been given elsewhere.[12]

By our second standard, then, an agent X is praiseworthy for his act A to some degree if and only if: (1) X has positive moral worth to some degree for A, and (2) X's situation at the time of performing A included among the known circumstances a preponderance or balance of circumstances (other than the amount of "effort" put forth by the agent) which are reasonably judged to be unfavorable to the performance of the act. Similar conditions govern the presence of blameworthiness as judged by this second standard. Agents who perform acts under the conditions for praiseworthiness just specified will be said to have "positive moral credit" for their acts. Like moral worth, moral credit may be present in either a positive or a negative form. A "judgment of moral credit" is an assertion or denial that an agent possesses positive or negative moral credit.[13]

The moral perspective from which judgments of moral credit are made may be called the "perspective of moral credit," and judgments of praise and blame based on the moral credits standard may also be said to be made from this perspective. In order to judge from the perspective of moral credit, we investigate the causal antecedents of an act more extensively than is done for judgments made from the perspective of moral worth. Any instance of any kind of factor which can reasonably be judged to be an unfavorable or favorable circumstance for a given kind of act is potentially a "credit-determining" factor for any agent performing an act of that kind, even though in common practice, to be sure, not all potential credit-determining factors are investigated before judgments are made. The perspective of moral credit, accordingly, may be called a "causally extended" perspective, as compared with our causally limited

perspective of moral worth, and our noncausal perspective of objective rightness or wrongness.

Judgments made from the perspective of moral credit supplement judgments made from the perspective of moral worth. They do not supplant them, any more than judgments about the objective rightness or wrongness of acts are supplanted by judgments about the moral worth of their agents. The latter are self-contained judgments, perfectly satisfactory and significant in their own right. Nevertheless, the perspective of moral credit does set limits to the perspective of moral worth, in that it is important for those who make judgments by the moral worth standard to remember that such judgments do not give us the whole moral truth about an agent. Even when we do not actually go on to ascertain the moral credit-rating of an agent to whom we ascribe positive or negative moral worth, we must bear in mind that further questions along such lines *could* be asked. Judgments of praise and blame made from the perspective of moral worth will be made less dogmatically, with less show of finality, by those who understand that there is another moral perspective from which an individual can be judged. But those who make judgments from the perspective of moral credit must not forget the importance of the perspective of moral worth. Judges who constantly focus their attention on the "ease" or "difficulty" with which something was accomplished need to be reminded at times, to look at the quality of the moral accomplishment itself. Neither of these two moral perspectives can be said to be superior to the other.

It seems clear that the use of the perspective of moral credit is fully compatible with determinism.[14] And the identification of the new standpoint of moral appraisal as a separate moral perspective lends needed strength to the philosophical position of determinism, principally by revealing it to be less dogmatic and impersonal than it is often taken to be. In a more detailed treatment of these matters, the advantages to determinism of recognizing judgments of praise and blame based on moral credit could be explained more fully.

In the end, however, the convinced Group II determinist will always reply that the effort to set up a perspective of moral cred   nnot salvage judgments of praise and blame. He will maintain that judgments of praise and blame based on moral credit are ultimately no more compatible |with determinism than are judgments of praise and blame based on moral worth.[15] As before, he may look tolerantly, or even benevolently, on the procedure of setting up a "perspective of moral credit," just so long as judgments of praise and blame are kept out of the picture. Again his reaction springs from his awareness of additional causal factors, this time of causal factors lying behind those taken into account from the perspective of moral credit. The Group II determinists will say that, although those who make judgments based on moral credit may make extensive inquiries into the factors causally relevant to human acts, sooner or later, because of the limits of time or energy or human knowledge, they must bring their investigations to a close. And when they do, they will not have told the whole causal story; and the part that will remain untold will invalidate judgments of praise and blame made from this moral perspective.

I believe that this charge can be answered, but I want to show first how it might be supported. Let us consider a comparison between two individuals, Jones and Smith. Jones has performed an act having a high degree of positive moral worth in spite of very unfavorable circumstances, whereas Smith, confronted by essentially the same kind of circumstances and placed in a very similar situation, has performed an act having a much lower degree of positive moral worth. It is clear that Jones possesses a higher degree of positive moral credit for his act than does Smith for his,[16] since the circumstances and situation constitute greater obstacles for Jones' act than for Smith's.

Now, no matter how strong our psychological tendency to feel a greater admiration for the achievement of Jones, such an attitude, the Group II determinist would claim, is not justifiable. For moral credit is ascribed on the basis of finding that a preponderance of the *known* circumstances in an agent's situation was unfavorable to the performance of a given act. Judgments of moral credit deal with acts whose performance was improbable; nevertheless, they deal with acts that *were* performed, events that *happened*. If determinism is true, these happenings were caused. Therefore for each act for which an agent possesses moral credit there must exist also a cluster of one or more unknown circumstances causally relevant to the performance of the act, and a preponderance of *these* circumstances must have been favorable, rather than unfavorable. It is all very well, then, to judge that Jones performed under great

odds an act for which he is morally worthy; but such a judgment is superficial and unstable. For, if determinism is true, these vaunted "odds" disappear upon examination; and Jones is seen to have done only what the causal factors in his situation, unknown as well as known, brought forth. So did Smith, and so do we all. How then can praise and blame by the standard of moral credit be justified?

It is evident that this reasoning is too cogent to be set aside. At the close of the preceding section, it was asserted that the causal factors not dealt with in judgments of moral worth were nevertheless morally significant, and would have to be taken care of in some other way. Many of these "left-over" causal factors have now been shown to provide a basis for judgments of praise and blame made from a second moral perspective, the perspective of moral credit. But the Group II determinist now reminds us that behind even the credit-determining factors lie still others, and that these too have a moral significance that cannot be lightly dismissed. His interpretation of the moral significance of this most distant range of causal factors is, as we have seen, simply that they invalidate all affirmative judgments of praise and blame. In the remainder of this paper, I shall try to show that another interpretation is possible, and that it is to be preferred.

THE PERSPECTIVE OF ULTIMATE MORAL EQUALITY

In the course of our discussion, we have now sorted out three groups of factors causally relevant to human behavior: worth-determining factors, credit-determining factors, and what may be called "ultimate" causal factors, which are simply those factors that are left out of account when we make judgments based on moral worth and moral credit. If determinism is true, we may be said to know, for any given act, *that* there are ultimate causal factors. But we do not know *what* they are: if we did know they would take their place among the potential credit-determining factors for the act in question. It is strange that this shadowy group of unknown circumstances should be morally so significant; but I think that there is no doubt that their moral significance is real.

When we are mindful of the existence of the ultimate causal factors, we look at human beings and their acts in a special way. This was brought out by the example of Jones and Smith. When we look at persons in this special way, they are seen to be equals, as far as their claims to moral praise and blame are concerned, or, rather, they are seen to have passed beyond any point at which discriminations of praise-worthiness or blameworthiness are applicable. Seen in this way, all men are members of a moral or spiritual democracy. This is a realm lying behind our distinctions of moral worth and moral credit, a realm in which each is simply the person he is. When we take into account the full range of factors causally relevant to human acts, we must regard human beings as a flock without goats and without sheep.

I propose to say that this special way of looking at persons, in the light of the existence of ultimate causal factors for their behavior, constitutes another moral perspective. This I shall call the "perspective of ultimate moral equality." From this perspective we look at persons and their acts in the widest possible causal contexts, contexts without limits of any kind. Therefore we may call this a "causally un-limited" perspective. As a moral perspective it is, of course, strikingly different in some respects from the others that we have examined. Judgments made from the perspective of moral worth and the perspective of moral credit are judgments of discrimination. This is obvious in the case of comparative judgments, but it is also true of noncomparative ones. Our interest in knowing that X possesses positive moral worth for his honest act, and Y negative moral credit for his cowardly one, stems in large part from the fact that there are honest acts whose agents do not possess positive moral worth, and cowardly acts whose agents earn no negative moral credit. Judgments of praise and blame based on moral worth and moral credit are answers to questions which can in principle be answered either affirmatively or negatively.

This is not true of judgments made from the perspective of ultimate moral equality. Here all are on the same moral footing: none has any ultimate claim to praise or blame, and the judgments made from this perspective are all negative. No matter what acts a person has performed, all that we can say of him from this final moral perspective is that he deserves no praise for what he has done, or that he deserves no blame.

The statement "X is not ultimately praiseworthy for A" is a negative judgment of praise made from the perspective of ultimate moral equality, whereas "Y is not ultimately blameworthy for B" is a negative judgment of blame made from the same perspective. Judgments of praise and blame made from this perspective will here be limited in scope to persons whose acts have earned for them moral worth

or moral credit. That is to say, the statement "X is not ultimately praiseworthy for A" will be permissible if and only if A is an act for which X possesses either positive moral worth or positive moral credit. And the truth-condition for this statement can be stated very briefly: the statement is true if and only if A has ultimate causes. Similarly, "Y is not ultimately blameworthy for B" is permissible if and only if B is an act for which Y possesses negative moral worth or negative moral credit, and true if and only if B has ultimate causes.

But, if determinism is true, we know of any event that it has ultimate causes, and we know this without any specific investigation. The behavior of all men is causally determined, and the nature of what we have called the "ultimate" causes is equally unknown in each case. This eradication of all distinctions in the causal status of acts erases all distinctions in the moral status of their agents. Therefore in one way it can never be news that Brown does not ultimately deserve praise for his kind deed, or that Robinson does not ultimately deserve blame for his unkind one.

In another way, however, these assertions *are* news, and important news. The fact that Brown and Robinson are ultimately moral equals is a vital part of the whole moral truth about them. Compare the situation for a factual account.[17] In factual descriptions of human beings we are interested in the qualities in which they differ, to be sure; but we are also interested in the qualities in which they are alike. For some purposes, and in some contexts, the similarities may be legitimately disregarded; but this does not mean that they can always be left out of account. Sometimes they are more significant than the differences, and they are never more significant than they become when we are in danger of assuming that the differences tell the whole factual story. So it is with moral appraisals of human beings. For the whole moral story, judgments of praise and blame based on moral worth and moral credit need to be supplemented by judgments made from the perspective of ultimate moral equality.

Because this is true, we are justified in regarding the perspective of ultimate moral equality as a genuinely "moral" perspective, even though it eradicates moral discriminations. The knowledge that when persons are viewed in relation to the ultimate causal factors of their behavior moral discriminations no longer apply to them is a piece of moral knowledge, at least in being knowledge about moral matters. It is curious that as we go from a causally limited perspective to a causally extended one we increase our power to make moral discriminations, whereas when we come to a causally unlimited perspective these moral discriminations stop altogether. But the knowledge that this is so is moral knowledge, and it has important bearings on the rest of our moral knowledge.

The relation that holds between the perspective of ultimate moral equality and the other moral perspectives from which judgments of praise and blame are made is analogous in certain ways to the relation between the perspective of moral credit and that of moral worth. Judgments based on moral credit, as we have seen, set limits to judgments based on moral worth. Similarly, the knowledge that human beings can be viewed from a perspective which will show them to be morally equal will remind those who make judgments based on moral worth and moral credit that these judgments of moral inequality do not tell the whole story about the individuals being judged. This knowledge, in turn, will affect the attitudes of those who have it: they will regard themselves and each other with more tolerance than before. Feelings of admiration, contempt, guilt, and pride, will all be experienced more moderately by those who know that no man is ever the *first* cause of good or evil deeds, or *finally* responsible for winning or losing when confronted by moral odds. But this is not to say that such feelings will not be experienced at all, or that they should not be.

For the perspective of ultimate moral equality cannot give us the whole truth about the praiseworthiness and blameworthiness of human beings either. The fact that X has negative moral worth for his act, or that Y has positive moral credit for his, is not cancelled by saying that X does not ultimately deserve blame, or that Y does not ultimately deserve praise. We value in a special way those whose acts meet the standards of moral worth and moral credit, and this is something that we cannot change. As Spinoza saw, it is true—even in a determined universe—that "we desire to form for ourselves an idea of man upon which we may look as a model of human nature."[18] The idea of a man who performs a right act voluntarily, knowingly, and from a good desire, and the idea of a man who, when confronted by odds, can still do these things—these *are* the models we have formed. Conformity to these patterns is what we regard as worthy of praise, and deviation from them in certain ways is what we regard as worthy of blame. We cannot feel about persons who thus conform or deviate as we do about animals or inanimate objects which measure up or fail to measure up to certain other standards. All this being so, judgments of praise and blame based on moral worth and moral credit are not only legitimate but vitally necessary parts of moral discourse. They are answers to questions that we cannot help asking.

The full moral truth about a man and his act, then, might run as follows: that he deserves a low degree of praise for it by the standard of moral worth, a high degree of praise for it by the standard of moral credit, and ultimately no praise for it when he is judged from the perspective of ultimate moral equality. There is no reason why the three statements cannot be true simultaneously. Also, these perspectives seem to be genuinely coordinate, and complementary: we need them all. And, if we distinguish between moral perspectives, we shall be able to avoid the doubling of metaphysical perspectives which Kant found necessary in order to reconcile causality and morality. It is easier to regard a man as blameworthy from one point of view but not from another than to say that his act is both caused and uncaused.

The acquiring of moral wisdom, at least as far as moral appraisals are concerned, does not consist only in learning how to make sound judgments from each moral perspective. It consists also in learning under what circumstances each of the moral perspectives should be used—a large and fundamental problem that cannot be dealt with here.[19] Here let us note only that most of the questions about the praiseworthiness and blameworthiness of human beings that are actually asked are questions to which the appropriate answer is a judgment based on moral worth or one based on moral credit. Writers on ethics[20] have pointed out that we feel something peculiarly objectionable in an attempt by a wrongdoer to exculpate himself on the ground that all his acts were caused and therefore he deserves no blame. Here an inquiry into his blameworthiness is launched from one moral perspective and a reply is made from another. But moral perspectives, however coordinate, are certainly not interchangeable. Questions about praiseworthiness or blameworthiness should be answered from the perspective from which they are asked, whenever it is possible to tell what this is.

Sometimes it will be appropriate, and even very desirable, to add to this answer a judgment made from another moral perspective; but often it will not be. Particular caution must be exercised in advancing judgments made from the perspective of ultimate moral equality. These are illuminating, and even inspiring, when made in the right context, and by those who know how to make accurate discriminations by the standards of moral worth and moral credit. Otherwise they are apt to seem shallow, and somehow sentimental, or cheap.[21]

SOME OBJECTIONS AND REPLIES

The account which has been given of the perspective of ultimate moral equality and its relation to our other perspectives of praise and blame seems likely to arouse objections from all sides. Three of these appear to me to be particularly striking, and in this concluding section I shall try to reply briefly to each one in turn.

(1) The first objection that I shall consider is one that will be raised by Group II determinists. Some of what has been said in the preceding will presumably be acceptable to members of this group; but they will want to know how it can be maintained that the perspective of ultimate moral equality is merely *one* of several perspectives from which agents are appraised. It is rather *the* moral perspective, which, because of its special nature, invalidates all others. It is superior to the others because it is broader in its scope. This is the only perspective that is causally unlimited, the only one from which we view acts in the context of *all* their causes, unknown as well as known. And since we are seeing more broadly, it follows that we are seeing more accurately.

The answer here must be that it is not clear that this does follow. Do we see "better" from a height that takes in a large part of the surrounding territory? The only reply can be "Yes and no." Details which were not seen from a height spring back into view when we climb back down and look at objects in the context of a smaller part of their surroundings; and things which looked alike from above manifest striking differences when seen from a position farther down. In this case, one standpoint does not reveal the "real nature" of the objects better than another one does.

But we must not be lured into pressing our optical metaphor of "perspectives" too far. In any case, the Group II determinist may wish to support his basic contention—that the perspective of ultimate moral equality has a privileged status—in another way. He may claim that it will be impossible, psychologically, for those who have viewed persons from the perspective of ultimate moral equality to go on making the same old judgments of praise and blame from other perspectives. How, he will ask, can we throw ourselves into the task of sorting the worthy from the unworthy, the creditable from the discreditable, when we know that from another standpoint these distinctions will disappear altogether? Will not the view from every perspective but that of ultimate moral equality take on the aspect of something unreal, a mirage without power to deceive for more than a moment?

Part of the answer here is that we cannot, indeed, make moral discriminations in exactly the "same old" way, and that we cannot "throw ourselves" into the sorting and grading processes with quite the zeal of those who have never seen human beings as ultimate moral equals. The difference, however, will be in the quality and intensity of the emotions accompanying judgments of praise and blame based on moral worth and moral credit. The judgments themselves will go on being made; human acts will go on being looked at in causal contexts of varying scope. Our models of human nature, in short, will go on being used. To see whether it is psychologically possible to return from the perspective of ultimate moral perspectives, no determinist needs to look farther than his own experience. It is in truth not possible to do anything else.

(2) A second objection is likely to be raised by certain libertarians. It is the charge that our so-called "perspective of ultimate moral equality" is ignoble and degrading. Such a perspective, it will be said, affords a particularly deplorable example of the levelling tendency which seeks to destroy standards of merit in all areas. Plato's charge against political democracy—that it makes equals of unequals—applies a thousandfold to the "moral democracy" that is claimed to be visible from this distorting perspective. The moral world is hierarchical to the core; to remove the sheep and the goats from the moral landscape is to destroy it. So runs this second charge.

The answer to it divides into two parts. The first point to be made is that moral discriminations have not been permanently eradicated. Viewed from the other moral perspectives (which, as we have seen, are not eliminated by the perspectives of ultimate moral equality), the moral landscape swims back into our ken with sheep and goats intact. Moreover, it is sometimes more appropriate to look at the moral world in this way.

But some will feel that this part of the answer is not enough: that it is wrong *ever* to see all persons as moral equals. Now even though one may be deeply convinced that the perspective of ultimate moral equality, far from being ignoble, is—when appropriately used—exalted and inspiring, it is not altogether easy to know how to argue for this conviction. One may point to the increase in compassion, tolerance, equanimity, that come to those who know how to look at themselves and each other on occasion from the perspective of ultimate moral equality. But it may conceivably be said in reply that these are regarded as benefits only by persons who are antecedently convinced that determinism is, as a matter of fact, true. This reply is not without force. That portion of Spinoza's defense of determinism which shows "what service to our own lives a knowledge of this doctrine is" has not lost its power to move determinists; but what power do his words have over others? If all our acts go back to ultimate causes, then we should indeed look at all human beings with compassion and tolerance; but what if they do not? Libertarians may contend that compassion and tolerance are not spiritual goods if these attitudes are directed toward humans who, because they have misused their freedom, simply do not deserve to be pitied or tolerated. And equanimity in the face of moral iniquity is nothing but extreme moral callousness, particularly unforgivable, it will be said, when the wrongdoer is oneself.

It may prove impossible to disabuse some extreme libertarians of their conviction that human beings should never be regarded as being all morally equal. But it is hard to believe that most people, whatever their metaphysical beliefs, will not find something to which they can respond positively in the attitudes engendered by the perspective of ultimate moral equality. The making of all our judgments of praise and blame with less finality, less assurance that they represent the whole truth, must seem to many an end to be welcomed.[22] Religious teachings which have kept before our eyes the view from something like the perspective of ultimate moral equality ("There but for the grace of God go I") have performed a great service for our moral outlook.[23]

(3) Finally, I want to take note of the contention—in which those of all metaphysical persuasions will doubtless heartily concur—that this account of praise and blame is simply too complicated to be acceptable. How could the average unspeculative mortal ever find his way among such a bewildering variety of moral perspectives? How could he ever make a judgment of praise or blame?

In reply to these questions, two points must be made. First, a single moral judgment arrived at from a single moral perspective is not necessarily made more complicated by the present account than by other accounts.[24] But, secondly, it must be admitted that difficulties do arise when a moral judge is asked to remember that other moral perspectives exist and set limits to the one that he is using at any given time, and when he is asked, as he sometimes must be, to decide on the moral perspective that should be used in a particular situation. We have seen that moral wisdom, on the present view, consists not merely in the ability to make correct moral appraisals from a single perspective, but also in the ability to correlate the perspectives, and, on occasion, to choose among them.

It may well be that few attain this kind of wisdom, yet it is by no means clear that it cannot be attained by unspeculative persons. Perhaps such persons can and do make concrete judgments of moral praise and blame in a balanced and large-minded way, keeping the various relevant considerations in due proportion, and governing their own attitudes accordingly, despite a lack of any grasp of a theoretical basis for what they are doing. But, if it should turn out that we cannot really evade the conclusion that the present account makes moral wisdom harder for an unspeculative person to attain, this conclusion would not necessarily vitiate the account. Why should it not be the case that moral wisdom demands considerable resources of intellect as well as of character?

In this paper, I have been arguing that the question with which we began, "Can determinists find a rationale for moral praise and blame?" can be answered affirmatively. I have tried to show, however, that the unrecognized assumption behind the typical and influential affirmative answers that have been given—the assumption that judgments of praise and blame are made from a single moral perspective—is mistaken. I have maintained that those determinists who give a negative answer to our original question have caught sight of some important truths that the others have missed. In the end, however, with their attempts to set up the perspective of ultimate moral equality as the sole valid perspective for judgments of praise and blame, they have fallen into the same fundamental error as the others. One group eternally confronts the other with the question "How can you deny that human beings can be said to be praiseworthy and blameworthy, in view of the fact that they commit acts that are right or wrong, and at the same time done voluntarily, knowingly, and from good or bad desires?" To which the second group incessantly hurls back a question of its own: "How can you assert that human beings can be said to be praiseworthy or blameworthy, in view of the fact that their acts, like all other events, are wholly subject to causal laws, and must be traced back, in the end, to factors wholly beyond the agents' control?" The account given here, which may be called the "theory of multiple moral perspectives," is designed to help put an end to this durable impasse. I have tried to show that the first group is speaking from the perspective of moral worth, while the second replies from the perspective of ultimate moral equality. Both perspectives are valid; but each perspective is incomplete.

Three moral perspectives are necessary, I have contended, if we are to tell the whole about the praiseworthiness and blameworthiness of human beings. One of these, the perspective of ultimate moral equality, takes form as a consequence of assuming determinism to be true; but its adoption is not without moral and spiritual benefits. The other perspectives can be exhibited in an examination of judgments of praise and blame conducted quite independently of any determinist assumptions; and we can then see that determinism is—at the very least—fully compatible with the use of these moral perspectives. It seems to me that considerable work remains to be done in clarifying and refining these concepts and principles, and in exploring their implications in many directions but if the claims made here are in essentials justified, it follows that determinists need not feel that old familiar uneasiness when confronted by the concepts of moral praise and blame. On the contrary, it may be that we stand here on solid ground.

NOTES

1. See Paul Edwards, "Hard and Soft Determinism," and John Hospers, "What Means This Freedom?" Both in Sidney Hook, *Determinism and Freedom* (New York University Press, 1958); also W. I. Matson, "On the Irrelevance of Freewill to Moral Responsibility," *Mind*, Vol. LXV (1956), pp. 489–497.

Although these writers frame their argument more explicitly in terms of the concept of moral responsibility than in terms of moral praiseworthiness and blameworthiness, the application to the latter concepts is clear. Matson's chief thesis, that libertarianism can validate the concept of moral responsibility no more successfully than determinism can, will not be dealt with in the present paper; the part of his article which bears most directly on what I shall have to say is found in sections 2 and 3.

2. I have found the presentation of this general position by P. H. Nowell-Smith in *Ethics* (London, 1954), particularly helpful here.

3. Note that the terms "blameworthy" and "praiseworthy" have not been defined here and that no definitions of these terms will be offered in this paper.

4. Many would argue, of course, that determinism is much more than merely "compatible" with these judgments, since we cannot speak of an agent's act as "his" act or as arising "from" a motive or trait, unless determinism is assumed to be true. This argument will be deliberately set aside here.

5. My distinction between "Group I" and "Group II" determinism is plainly very similar to Edwards' distinction between "soft" and "hard" determinism. See Edwards, *op. cit.*, and also Edwards and Pap, *A Modern Introduction to Philosophy* (Free Press, 1957), p. 380.

6. I prefer to formulate this last condition in terms of a "desire" rather than of a "trait," because we sometimes make judgments of this kind without having sufficient evidence to ascertain the presence of a trait; but this point is not of central importance here.

7. "Moral Worth and Moral Credit," *The Philosophical Review*, Vol. LXVI (1957), pp. 304–328. In the present treatment I have left the term "moral worth" undefined, and I have also introduced it here to refer to an attribute of agents who are praiseworthy or blameworthy *for* acts rather than to refer to attribute of acts themselves.

8. It is convenient to speak of the point at issue between the Group I and Group II determinists as concerned primarily with the validity of *affirmative* judgments of praise and blame; and I occasionally do this. But it should be understood that the Group II determinist in fact equally denies the validity of any *negative* judgment of praise (or blame) which is made with the assumption that the class of persons who deserve praise (or blame) is not vacuous.

9. If it should be said that so-called "voluntary" acts are not *really* voluntary after all, the Group I determinist would reply in the fashion of Flew, in the latter's discussion of the expression "acting freely." See A. Flew, "Divine Omnipotence and Human Freedom," in Flew and MacIntyre, *New Essays in Philosophical Theology* (Macmillan, 1955), pp. 149–151.

10. There will not, however, be an exact correlation between felt intensity of effort and the criterion proposed.

11. See *Time*, Vol. LXVIII (August 27, 1956), for an account of an address by Auxiliary Bishop Joseph M. Marling of Kansas City, Mo., to the Guild of Catholic Psychiatrists.

12. E. L. Beardsley, *op. cit.*, especially pp. 309–315.

13. See *ibid.* for a detailed discussion of the concept of moral credit and its relation to moral worth. Here I leave "moral credit" undefined, and use it to refer to an attribute of agents rather than of acts.

14. It may be said, I think correctly, that the account of moral credit given here actually presupposes a determinist position, since reliable causal generalizations about human behavior underlie the estimates of probability on which judgments of moral credit, in large part, depend.

15. I disregard here the fact that the Group II determinist would also say that the perspective of moral credit inherits what he takes to be the deficiencies of the perspective of moral worth, since judgments of moral worth are presupposed by judgments of moral credit.

16. On degrees of praiseworthiness by the standard of moral credit, see E. L. Beardsley, *op. cit.,* p. 319.

17. By this manner of speaking I do not mean to rule out the possibility that a naturalistic account of the meaning of basic ethical terms can be given.

18. B. Spinoza, *Ethics* (Oxford Press, 4th ed., 1930), p. 179.

19. One important question to consider in this connection is whether it is ever justifiable to employ the perspective of ultimate moral equality when thinking of one's own future acts and their moral status. Some reflections which bear on this question (though they are not expressed in the language of the present paper) are offered by H. Fingarette in his interesting article "Psychoanalytic Perspectives on Moral Guilt and Responsibility: A Re-Evaluation," *Philosophy and Phenomenological Research,* Vol. XVI (1955–1956), pp. 18–29.

20. See, for example, Nowell-Smith, *op. cit.,* pp. 297–300.

21. Judgments made from the perspective of ultimate moral equality are most effective when directed to individuals whose moral credit has been ascertained, as well as their moral worth. If we go directly from the perspective of moral worth to the perspective of ultimate moral equality without passing through the perspective of moral credit, it appears that something important has been left out.

22. This end is particularly desirable for those more sweeping judgments in which persons are praised or blamed, not for specified acts, but for their whole characters. Space limitations have precluded the consideration of such judgments here; but their treatment forms an important part of a more detailed examination of moral perspectives.

23. Note that, even though the grace of God may be regarded as being "freely" given, in so far as it is held to constitute a causal determinant of human action, it is treated as essentially similar to what have here been called "ultimate causes." Of considerable interest for further study would be a comparison of the perspective of ultimate moral equality—here described in purely naturalistic terms—with such religious concepts as "equality in the sight of God."

24. Indeed, the distinction between moral worth and moral credit makes it possible to give a simpler account of the judgments made by each standard than the account which proponents of the single standard view would have to give if their position were adequately worked out.

PART 5 RESPONSIBILITY

This section carries the discussion of Part Four fully into the realm of social philosophy. Most parties to the discussion agree that a person can be held morally responsible for his past action *only* if he was able to do other than he did. Put more tersely: Avoidability is a necessary condition of responsibility. We saw in Part Four that there are two senses of "avoidable." In the *categorical sense,* to say that an act is avoidable is to say that there were no antecedent conditions (causes) sufficient for its occurrence. In the *hypothetical sense,* to say that an act is avoidable is to say that *if* the actor had chosen (or, perhaps, intended) to do otherwise, he would have done otherwise (nothing would have stopped him). Avoidability in the hypothetical sense is perfectly compatible with determinism; avoidability in the categorical sense, by definition, is not. Now the question arises: In which of the senses of "avoidable"—the categorical sense, the hypothetical sense, or both—is it true that a person can be held responsible for his action only if it was avoidable?

But avoidability, however it is interpreted, is hardly the *only* condition for responsibility, and indeed there may even be reason for denying that it is a necessary condition after all. That avoidability (absence of compulsion) is not the sole factor relevant to our ascriptions of responsibility is readily seen from a quick perusal of various handbooks of criminal law, where such defenses as justification, provocation, insanity, infancy, intoxication, automatism, mistake, consent, and superior orders are also mentioned. And even if "avoidability" is given a very comprehensive sense wide enough to encompass all these diverse defenses, we shall have to distinguish among the various types and causes of "unavoidability," in particular between those that involve lack of capacity and those that involve lack of opportunity. It is probably unwise, however, to give the terms "avoidability" and "unavoidability" such wide senses in the first place, if only because we are likely then to confuse avoidability with *voluntariness,* the term traditionally used to rule out the excuses that can defeat or weaken imputations of responsibility. Indeed, some philosophers have argued plausibly enough that an act can be fully voluntary even though unavoidable (in a properly narrow sense), so that avoidability is not necessary for responsibility after all. The classic example is from Locke:

AND PUNISHMENT

Suppose a man be carried whilst fast asleep into a room where [there] is a person he longs to see and speak with, and [that he is] there locked fast in, beyond his power to get out. He awakes and is glad to find himself in so desirable company . . . He willingly stays in; that is [he] prefers his stay to going away. I ask: is not this stay voluntary? I think nobody will doubt it, and yet being locked fast in, it is evident [that] he is not at liberty *not* to stay; he has not freedom to be gone.[1]

Locke's example seems to show that one's behavior can be fully voluntary and hence properly subject to praise or blame, reward or punishment, even though one was not free in the circumstances to do otherwise. The earliest and historically most influential analysis of the concept of voluntariness is that of Aristotle in the selection that follows. Aristotle's analysis is in an essential way negative; an act is voluntary, he says, to the extent that it is *not* done because of compulsion or "in ignorance." It may be true that the man in Locke's room is there "under compulsion," but his conduct is nevertheless voluntary since he does not remain there simply *because* of the compulsion, but rather for reasons of his own.

Perhaps responsibility, in the relevant sense, is best understood as a kind of *liability* to responsive actions of various kinds by other people. Thus, to be responsible for a past action is to be properly subject (that is, liable) to credit, praise, or reward if the act was in some special way a good one; or to blame, censure, or punishment if it was an evil one. Most of the essays included here are concerned with responsibility as liability to criminal punishment. Essentially, they inquire: Under what conditions is criminal punishment reasonable and justified? This in turn takes us to the larger questions: What is punishment all about? What is its function, its aims, its justifying rationales?

A vast amount has been written on the aims and justification of criminal punishment (probably because, as a political institution devoted to the infliction of pain on human beings, it has never sat easily on the conscience of civilized man), and insofar as blame

---

[1]John Locke, *An Essay Concerning Human Understanding,* ed. A. C. Fraser (Oxford: Clarendon Press, 1894); Vol. I, p. 317.

can be construed as a "kind of verbally mediated punishment,"[2] the various traditional theories of the nature and justification of punishment find their counterparts in discussions of blame. Theories of punishment can be classified very roughly as follows:

1. *Utilitarian theories.* These theories hold that punishment is at best a necessary evil, justifiable if and only if the good of its consequences (its "social utility") outweighs its own immediate and intrinsic evil. Punishment is pain or deprivation inflicted on a person (presumably a wrongdoer) for the sake of such future goods as correction or reform of the offender, protection of society against other offenses by the same offender, and (especially) deterrence of other would-be offenders by backing up the threat of retribution.

2. *The retributive theory.* In the words of one of its critics, the retributive theory holds that "the primary justification of punishment is always to be found in the fact that an offense has been committed which deserves punishment, not in any future advantage to be gained by its infliction."[3] Two versions of the theory should be distinguished: a *moralistic version,* which maintains that the proper function of punishment is to inflict on the offender the pain "called for" or deserved by the moral gravity of his offense; and a *legalistic version,* which holds that the justification of punishment is always to be found in the fact that a rule has been broken, for the violation of which a certain penalty is specified—whether or not the offender incurs any moral guilt. This theory is not to be confused with the theory (discussed below) that vindictive satisfaction in the mind of the beholder is the ultimate justification of punishment, for its proponents have been among the leading enemies of vengeance. (Some confusion about this matter is no doubt caused by the inconstant terminology used by philosophers.)

3. *Vengeance theories.* Vengeance theories make much of the unhappy fact that, when harmful wrongs are committed, there is among men a widespread and natural lust for vengeance. Such theories are of three different kinds. The *escape-valve version,* associated with the names of James Fitzjames Stephen and Oliver Wendell Holmes, Jr., holds that legal punishment is an orderly outlet for aggressive feelings, which would otherwise demand satisfaction in socially disruptive ways. This, of course, is a variant of the utilitarian theory. The *hedonistic version* finds the justification of punishment in the pleasure it gives people (particularly the victim of the crime and his loved ones) to see the criminal suffer for his crime. Few philosophers have held this odious version of the utilitarian theory, though perhaps Lotze, Bentham, and Gabriel DeTarde come close to it. Finally, the *emotional version* of the theory, very popular among the uneducated, holds that the justification of punishment is to be found in the emotions of hate and anger it expresses, these emotions being those allegedly felt by all normal or right-thinking people.

Erewhon, the imaginary land of Samuel Butler's novel, is "nowhere" misspelled backward; and, since it is a slightly distorted mirror image of Butler's own Victorian England, or our own time, with almost everything "put backward," it is aptly named. The prevailing Erewhonian treatment of moral delinquency is very much the same as our own treatment of physical illness: Delinquents are "treated" and often "cured" by "straighteners." But the Erewhonian treatment of the physically ill is the same as our treatment of the morally delinquent: The sick are severely reprobated and punished. The aim of the wily satirist is to get his readers to see that the Erewhonians are neither more

[2]C. L. Stevenson, *Ethics and Language* (New Haven: Yale University Press, 1944), p. 307.

[3]A. C. Ewing, *The Morality of Punishment* (London: Kegan Paul, 1929), p. 13.

nor less rational than we are, all told; that *any* society that makes a fundamental distinction between disease and crime is cruelly inconsistent. The reformers, or "malcontents," in Erewhon also have their mirrored counterparts among our own moral philosophers. Substitute "crime" for the words "illness" and "consumption" in the following passage, and it becomes an accurate statement of the views of many utilitarian philosophers about punishment:

> The malcontents . . . assert that illness is the inevitable result of certain antecedent causes, which, in the great majority of cases, were beyond the control of the individual, and that therefore a man is only guilty for being in a consumption in the same way as rotten fruit is guilty for having gone rotten.

We may, of course, be driven to cutting out rotten spots or throwing away rotten fruit, just as we must, in difficult cases, incarcerate, flog, or even hang, rotten men, but in neither case is self-righteous moralizing appropriate.

Note how naturally a utilitarian account of punishment fits a deterministic world view. Indeed, determinism, in the quoted passage, is cited as a reason for holding a utilitarian theory. The Erewhonians themselves seem to be determinists, and this drives them to find some justifying myth to support their harsh standards of responsibility for illness. Their myth of the unborn invites comparison both with the Christian doctrine of original sin and Oriental doctrines of pre-existence. The reasoning of the Erewhonians, put in terms of morality rather than illness, seems to be as follows: It would be unfair to hold a person responsible for his evil ways if the causes of his character can be traced back ultimately to his parents, his earliest influences, his genes, etc. Indeed, if determinism is true, one's parents cannot help having the characters *they* have and so on back in time. Therefore, if responsibilty is to be reasonable, a person somehow must have created or chosen his own character. But to do this, he must have existed before he was born. Hence, the myth of the unborn. Aristotle, in the selection that opens this section, has a much more plausible account of the way in which one can be said to have chosen his own character, and also a famous argument to show that most of us are in fact responsible for the characters we have.

That responsibility for one's own character is undeniable—indeed inescapable—is the great motivating idea behind the twentieth-century philosophy called "existentialism," so in respect to this thesis Aristotle has found a belated and somewhat unlikely ally in Jean-Paul Sartre. The quite non-Aristotelian statement that "existence precedes essence" is simply Sartre's expression of a form of indeterminism. Nothing is "written" in advance about the outcome of human choice; to believe the opposite is simply to arm oneself with bad excuses in bad faith. The world, including our own characters, is what we freely choose to make it, and there are no eternal models, not even valid moral ideas to bind us until we freely commit ourselves to them. Sartre writes to vindicate a radical human freedom, but there is nothing naively optimistic or sentimental in his conclusion. On the contrary! Human freedom, as he conceives it, is a sobering, even dreadful thing, that not only permits but necessitates ultimate accountability and generates the whole inventory of "existential emotions." Sartre will not let us forget, however, that it also makes possible the higher "existential virtues" of courage and authenticity.

Four articles discuss the theory of criminal punishment in this section. J. D. Mabbott defends a retributive theory of the legalistic kind. M. R. Glover's critical reply to Mabbott was published in the same journal several issues later. Jonathan Glover (no relation to

M. R. Glover) presents a modified utilitarian theory of punishment which leads him to consider how, if at all, punishment is to be distinguished from "manipulation." John Rawls's very influential discussion, using some arguments foreshadowed in Mabbott's article, attempts to work out a compromise between legalistic retributivism and utilitarianism.

The final part of this section contains two essays on the nature of mental illness and the way in which it can function as an excuse for otherwise blameworthy or criminal behavior. The psychiatrist Thomas Szasz argues forcefully that the very idea of mental illness is a myth which should now be abandoned. The editor, in a quite independent article, assumes that mental illness is real enough, but offers an account that is quite different from the prevailing one of how mental illness can be an excuse.

ARISTOTLE

Conditions of Responsibility for Action*

Aristotle (B.C. 384–322) founded the Lyceum at Athens.

BOOK TWO

This book is the first of a series (II–V) dealing with the moral virtues. But first we have to ask what moral virtue or goodness is. It is a confirmed disposition to act rightly, the disposition being itself formed by a continuous series of right actions.

CHAPTER ONE

Virtue, then, is of two kinds, intellectual and moral. Of these the intellectual is in the main indebted to teaching for its production and growth, and this calls for time and experience. Moral goodness, on the other hand, is the child of habit, from which it has got its very name, ethics being derived from *ethos,* 'habit,' . . . This is an indication that none of the moral virtues is implanted in us by Nature, since nothing that Nature creates can be taught by habit to change the direction of its development. For instance a stone, the natural tendency of which is to fall down, could never, however often you threw it up in the air, be trained to go in that direction. No more can you train fire to burn downwards. Nothing in fact, if the law of its being is to behave in one way, can be habituated to behave in another. The moral virtues, then, are produced in us neither *by* Nature nor *against* Nature. Nature, indeed, prepares in us the ground for their reception, but their complete formation is the product of habit.

Consider again these powers or faculties with which Nature endows us. We acquire the ability to use them before we do use them. The senses provide us with a good illustration of this truth. We have not acquired the sense of sight from repeated acts of seeing, or the sense of hearing from repeated acts of hearing. It is the other way round. We had these senses before we used them, we did not acquire them as a result of using them. But the moral virtues we do acquire by first exercising them. The same is true of the arts and crafts in general. The craftsman has to learn how to make things, but he learns in the process of making them. So men become builders by building, harp players by playing the harp. By a similar process we become just by performing just actions, temperate by performing temperate actions, brave by performing brave actions. Look at what happens in political societies—it confirms our view. We find legislators seeking to make good men of their fellows by making good behaviour habitual with them. That is the aim of every law-giver, and when he is unable to carry it out effectively, he is a failure; nay, success or failure in this is what makes the difference between a good constitution and a bad.

Again, the creation and the destruction of any virtue are effected by identical causes and identical means; and this may be said, too, of every art. It is as a result of playing the harp that harpers become good or bad in their art. The same is true of builders and all other craftsmen. Men will become good builders as a result of building well, and bad builders

*Aristotle, *The Nicomachean Ethics,* trans. (with notes in italics) J. A. K. Thomson (Harmondsworth: Penguin Books, 1955), Book Two, chapters 1–5; Book three, Chapters 1, 5. Reprinted by permission of George Allen & Unwin Ltd.

as a result of building badly. Otherwise what would be the use of having anyone to teach a trade? Craftsmen would all be born either good or bad. Now this holds also of the virtues. It is in the course of our dealings with our fellow-men that we become just or unjust. It is our behaviour in a crisis and our habitual reactions to danger that make us brave or cowardly, as it may be. So with our desires and passions. Some men are made temperate and gentle, others profligate and passionate, the former by conducting themselves in one way, the latter by conducting themselves in another, in situations in which their feelings are involved. We may sum it all up in the generalization, 'Like activities produce like dispositions.' This makes it our duty to see that our activities have the right character, since the differences of quality in them are repeated in the dispositions that follow in their train. So it is a matter of real importance whether our early education confirms us in one set of habits or another. It would be nearer the truth to say that it makes a very great difference indeed, in fact all the difference in the world.

If, then, everything depends upon the way in which we act, clearly it is incumbent on us to inquire what this way is, never forgetting that we must not look for the precision attainable in the exact sciences.

CHAPTER TWO

Since the branch of philosophy on which we are at present engaged differs from the others in not being a subject of merely intellectual interest—I mean we are not concerned to know what goodness essentially is, but how we are to become good men, for this alone gives the study its practical value—we must apply our minds to the solution of the problems of conduct. For, as I remarked, it is our actions that determine our dispositions.

Now that when we act we should do so according to the right principle, is common ground and I propose to take it as a basis of discussion.[1] But we must begin with the admission that any theory of conduct must be content with an outline without much precision in details. We noted this when I said at the beginning of our discussion of this part of our subject that the measure of exactness of statement in any field of study must be determined by the nature of the matter studied. Now matters of conduct and considerations of what is to our advantage have no fixity

about them any more than matters affecting our health. And if this be true of moral philosophy as a whole, it is still more true that the discussion of particular problems in ethics admits of no exactitude. For they do not fall under any science or professional tradition, but those who are following some line of conduct are forced in every collocation of circumstances to think out for themselves what is suited to these circumstances, just as doctors and navigators have to do in their different *métiers*. We can do no more than give our arguments, inexact as they necessarily are, such support as is available.

After this reminder Aristotle proceeds to lay down a proposition or generalization which is cardinal in his system of ethics. Excess of deficiency in his actions impairs the moral quality of the agent.

Let us begin with the following observation. It is in the nature of moral qualities that they can be destroyed by deficiency on the one hand and excess on the other. We can see this in the instances of bodily health and strength.[2] Physical strength is destroyed by too much and also by too little exercise. Similarly health is ruined by eating and drinking either too much or too little, while it is produced, increased, and preserved by taking the right quantity of drink and victuals. Well, it is the same with temperance, courage, and the other virtues. The man who shuns and fears everything and can stand up to nothing becomes a coward. The man who is afraid of nothing at all, but marches up to every danger, becomes foolhardy. In the same way the man who indulges in every pleasure without refraining from a single one becomes incontinent. If, on the other hand, a man behaves like the Boor in comedy and turns his back on every pleasure, he will find his sensibilities becoming blunted. So also temperance and courage are destroyed both by excess and deficiency, and they are kept alive by observance of the mean.

Our virtues are employed in the same kinds of action as established them.

Let us go back to our statement that the virtues are produced and fostered as a result, and by the agency, of actions of the same quality as effect their destruction. It is also true that after the virtues have been formed they find expression in actions of that kind. We may see this in a concrete instance—bodily strength. It results from taking plenty of nourishment and going in for hard training, and it is the strong man who is best fitted to cope with such conditions. So with the virtues. It is by refraining from pleasures that we become temperate, and it is when we have become temperate that we are most able to abstain from pleasures. Or take courage. It is by habituating ourselves to make light of alarming situations and to confront them that we become brave, and it is when we have become brave that we shall be most able to face an alarming situation.

There is one way of discovering whether we are in full possession of a virtue or not. We possess it if we feel pleasure in its exercise; indeed, it is just with pleasures and pains that virtue is concerned.

CHAPTER THREE

We may use the pleasure (or pain) that accompanies the exercise of our dispositions as an index of how far they have established themselves. A man is temperate who abstaining from bodily pleasures finds this abstinence pleasant; if he finds it irksome, he is intemperate. Again, it is the man who encounters danger gladly, or at least without painful sensations, who is brave; the man who has these sensations is a coward. In a word, moral virtue has to do with pains and pleasures. There are a number of reasons for believing this. (1) Pleasure has a way of making us do what is disgraceful; pain deters us from doing what is right and fine. Hence the importance—I quote Plato—of having been brought up to find pleasure and pain in the right things. True education is just such a training. (2) The virtues operate with actions and emotions, each of which is accompanied by pleasure or pain. This is only another way of saying that virtue has to do with pleasures and pains. (3) Pain is used as an instrument of punishment. For in her remedies Nature works by opposites, and pain can be remedial. (4) When any disposition finds its complete expression it is, as we noted, in dealing with just those things by which it is its nature to be made better or worse, and which constitute the sphere of its operations. Now when men become bad it is under the influence of pleasures and pains when they seek the wrong ones among them, or seek them at the wrong time, or in the wrong manner, or in any of the wrong forms which such offences may take; and in seeking the wrong pleasures and pains they shun the right. This has led some thinkers to identify the moral virtues with conditions of the soul in which passion is eliminated or reduced to a minimum. But

this is to make too absolute a statement—it needs to be qualified by adding that such a condition must be attained 'in the right manner and at the right time' together with the other modifying circumstances.

So far, then, we have got this result. Moral goodness is a quality disposing us to act in the best way when we are dealing with pleasures and pains, while vice is one which leads us to act in the worst way when we deal with them.

The point may be brought out more clearly by some other considerations. (5) There are three kinds of things that determine our choice in all our actions—the morally fine, the expedient, the pleasant; and three that we shun—the base, the harmful, the painful. Now in his dealings with all of these it is the good man who is most likely to go right, and the bad man who tends to go wrong, and that most notably in the matter of pleasure. The sensation of pleasure is felt by us in common with all animals, accompanying everything we choose, for even the fine and the expedient have a pleasurable effect upon us. (6) The capacity for experiencing pleasure has grown in us from infancy as part of our general development, and human life, being dyed in grain with it, receives therefrom a colour hard to scrape off. (7) Pleasure and pain are also the standards by which with greater or less strictness we regulate our considered actions. Since to feel pleasure and pain rightly or wrongly is an important factor in human behaviour, it follows that we are primarily concerned with these sensations. (8) Heraclitus says it is hard to fight against anger, but it is harder still to fight against pleasure. Yet to grapple with the harder has always been the business, as of art, so of goodness, success in a task being proportionate to its difficulty. This gives us another reason for believing that morality and statesmanship must concentrate on pleasures and pains, seeing it is the man who deals rightly with them who will be good, and the man who deals with them wrongly who will be bad.

Here, then, are our conclusions. (*a*) Viture is concerned with pains and pleasures. (*b*) The actions which produce virtue are identical in character with those which increase it. (*c*) These actions differently performed destroy it. (*d*) The actions which produced it are identical with those in which it finds expression.

Aristotle now meets an obvious objection: How can a man perform (say) just actions unless he is already just?

CHAPTER FOUR

A difficulty, however, may be raised as to what we mean when we say that we must perform just actions if we are to become just, and temperate actions if we are to be temperate. It may be argued that, if I do what is just and temperate, I am just and temperate already, exactly as, if I spell words or play music correctly, I must already be literate or musical. This I take to be a false analogy, even in the arts. It is possible to spell a word right by accident or because somebody tips you the answer. But you will be a scholar only if your spelling is done as a scholar does it, that is thanks to the scholarship in your own mind. Nor will the suggested analogy with the arts bear scrutiny. A work of art is good or bad in itself—let it possess a certain quality, and that is all we ask of it. But virtuous actions are not done in a virtuous—a just or temperate—way merely because *they* have the appropriate quality. The *doer* must be in a certain frame of mind when he does them. Three conditions are involved. (1) The agent must act in full consciousness of what he is doing. (2) He must 'will' his action, and will it for its own sake. (3) The act must proceed from a fixed and unchangeable disposition. Now these requirements, if we except mere knowledge, are not counted among the necessary qualifications of an artist. For the acquisition of virtue, on the other hand, knowledge is of little or no value, but the other requirements are of immense, of sovereign, importance, since it is the repeated performance of just and temperate actions that produces virtue. Actions, to be sure, are *called* just and temperate when they are such as a just or temperate man would do. But the doer is just or temperate not because he does such things but when he does them in the way of just and temperate persons. It is therefore quite fair to say that a man becomes just by the performance of just, and temperate by the performance of temperate, action; nor is there the smallest likelihood of a man's becoming good by any other course of conduct. It is not, however, a popular line to take, most men preferring theory to practice under the impression that arguing about morals proves them to be philosophers, and that in this way they will turn out to be fine characters. Herein they resemble invalids, who listen carefully to all the doctor says but do not carry out a single one of his orders. The bodies of such people will never respond to treatment—nor will the souls of such 'philosophers.'

It is now time to produce a formal definition of virtue. In the Aristotelian system this means stating its genus and differentia—that is to say, the class of things to which it belongs and the point or points which distinguish it from other members of the class.

CHAPTER FIVE

We now come to the formal definition of virtue. Note first, however, that the human soul is conditioned in three ways. It may have (1) feelings, (2) capacities, (3) dispositions; so virtue must be one of these three. By 'feelings' I mean desire, anger, fear, daring, envy, gratification, friendliness, hatred, longing, jealousy, pity and in general all states of mind that are attended by pleasure or pain. By 'capacities' I mean those faculties in virtue of which we may be described as capable of the feelings in question—anger, for instance, or pain, or pity. By 'dispositions' I mean states of mind in virtue of which we are well or ill disposed in respect of the feelings concerned. We have, for instance, a bad disposition where angry feelings are concerned if we are disposed to become excessively or insufficiently angry, and a good disposition in this respect if we consistently feel the due amount of anger, which comes between these extremes. So with the other feelings.

Now, neither the virtues nor the vices are feelings. We are not spoken of as good or bad in respect of our feelings but of our virtues and vices. Neither are we praised or blamed for the way we feel. A man is not being praised for being frightened or angry, nor is he blamed just for being angry; it is for being angry in a particular way. But we *are* praised and blamed for our virtues and vices. Again, feeling angry or frightened is something we can't help, but our virtues are in a manner expressions of our will; at any rate there is an element of will in their formation. Finally, we are said to be 'moved' when our feelings are affected, but when it is a question of moral goodness or badness we are not said to be 'moved' but to be 'disposed' in a particular way. A similar line of reasoning will prove that the virtues and vices are not capacities either. We are not spoken of as good or bad, nor are we praised or blamed, merely because we are *capable* of feeling. Again, what capacities we have, we have by nature; but it is not nature that makes us good or bad. . . . So, if the virtues are neither feelings nor capacities, it remains that they must be dispositions. . . .

We have now to state the 'differentia' of virtue. Virtue

is a disposition; but how are we to distinguish it from other dispositions? We may say that it is such a disposition as enables the good man to perform his function well. And he performs it well when he avoids the extremes and chooses the mean in actions and feelings. . . .

BOOK THREE

Aristotle now approaches the question of moral responsibility, so important in modern ethics. It never occurred to him to doubt the freedom of the will, but he is as much alive as any modern thinker to the fact—and the importance of the fact—that our acts are not all voluntary. In the following chapter he distinguishes between the degrees of their voluntariness.

CHAPTER ONE

We have found that moral excellence or virtue has to do with feelings and actions. These may be voluntary or involuntary. It is only to the former that we assign praise or blame, though when the involuntary are concerned we may find ourselves ready to condone and on occasion to pity. It is clearly, then, incumbent on the student of moral philosophy to determine the limits of the voluntary and involuntary. Legislators also find such a definition useful when they are seeking to prescribe appropriate rewards and punishments.

Actions are commonly regarded as involuntary when they are performed (*a*) under compulsion, (*b*) as the result of ignorance. An act, it is thought, is done under compulsion when it originates in some external cause of such a nature that the agent or person subject to the compulsion contributes nothing to it. Such a situation is created, for example, when a sea captain is carried out of his course by a contrary wind or by men who have got him in their power. But the case is not always so clear. One might have to consider an action performed for some fine end or through fear of something worse to follow. For example, a tyrant who had a man's parents or children in his power might order him to do something dishonourable on condition that, if the man did it, their lives would be spared; otherwise not. In such cases it might be hard to say whether the actions are voluntary or not. A similar difficulty is created by the jettison of cargo in a storm. When the situation has no complications you never get a man voluntarily throwing away his property. But if it is to save the life of himself and his mates, any sensible person will do it. Such actions partake of both qualities, though they look more like voluntary than involuntary

acts. For at the time they are performed they are the result of a deliberate choice between alternatives, and when an action is performed the end or object of that action is held to be the end it had at the moment of its performance. It follows that the terms 'voluntary' and 'involuntary' should be used with reference to the time when the acts were being performed. Now in the imaginary cases we have stated the acts are voluntary. For the movement of the limbs instrumental to the action originates in the agent himself, and when this is so it is in a man's own power to act or not to act. Such actions therefore are voluntary. But they are so only in the special circumstances; otherwise of course they would be involuntary. For nobody would choose to do anything of the sort purely for its own sake. Occasionally indeed the performance of such actions is held to do a man credit. This happens when he submits to some disgrace or pain as the only way of achieving some great or splendid result. But if his case is just the opposite he is blamed, for it shows a degraded nature to submit to humiliations with only a paltry object in view, or at any rate not a high one. But there are also cases which are thought to merit, I will not say praise, but condonation. An example is provided when a man does something wrong because he is afraid of torture too severe for flesh and blood to endure. Though surely there are some things which a man cannot be compelled to do—which he will rather die than do, however painful the mode of death. Such a deed is matricide; the reasons which 'compelled' Alcmaeon in Euripides' play to kill his mother carry their absurdity on the face of them. Yet it is not always easy to make up our minds what is our best course in choosing one of two alternatives—such and such an action instead of such and such another—or in facing one penalty instead of another. Still harder is it to stick to our decision when made. For, generally speaking, the consequences we expect in such imbroglios are painful, and what we are forced to do far from honourable. Then we get praised or blamed according as we succumb to the compulsion or resist it.

What class of actions, then, ought we to distinguish as 'compulsory'? It is arguable that the bare description will apply to any case where the cause of the action is found in things external to the agent when he contributes nothing to the result. But it may happen that actions, though, abstractly considered, involuntary, are deliberately chosen at a given time and in given circumstances in preference to a given alternative. In that case, their origin being in the agent, these actions must be pronounced voluntary in the particular circumstances and because they are preferred to their alternatives. In themselves they are involuntary, yet they have more of the voluntary about them, since conduct is a sequence of particular acts, and the particular things done in the circumstances we have supposed are voluntary. But when it comes to saying which of two alternative lines of action should be preferred—then difficulties arise. For the differences in particular cases are many.

If it should be argued that pleasurable and honourable things exercise constraint upon us from without, and therefore actions performed under their influence are compulsory, it may be replied that this would make every action compulsory. For we all have some pleasurable or honourable motive in everything we do. Secondly, people acting under compulsion and against their will find it painful, whereas those whose actions are inspired by the pleasurable and the honourable find that these actions are accompanied by pleasure. In the third place it is absurd to accuse external influences instead of ourselves when we fall an easy prey to such inducements and to lay the blame for all dishonourable deeds on the seductions of pleasure, while claiming for ourselves credit for any fine thing we have done. It appears, then, that an action is compulsory only when it is caused by something external to itself which is not influenced by anything contributed by the person under compulsion.

Then there are acts done through ignorance. Any act of this nature is other than voluntary, but it is involuntary only when it causes the doer subsequent pain and regret. For a man who has been led into some action by ignorance and yet has no regrets, while he cannot be said to have been a voluntary agent—he did not know what he was doing—nevertheless cannot be said to have acted involuntarily, since he feels no compunction. We therefore draw a distinction. (a) When a man who has done something as the result of ignorance is sorry for it, we take it that he has acted involuntarily. (b) When such a man is not sorry, the case is different and we shall have to call him a 'non-voluntary' agent. For it is better that he should have a distinctive name in order to mark the distinction. Note, further, that there is

evidently a difference between acting *in consequence* of ignorance and acting *in* ignorance. When a man is drunk or in a passion his actions are not supposed to be the result of ignorance but of one or other of these conditions. But, as he does not realize what he is doing, he is acting *in* ignorance. To be sure every bad man is ignorant of what he ought to do and refrain from doing, and it is just this ignorance that makes people unjust and otherwise wicked. But when we use the word 'involuntary' we do not apply it in a case where the agent does not know what is for his own good. For involuntary acts are not the consequence of ignorance when the ignorance is shown in our choice of ends; what does result from such ignorance is a completely vicious condition. No, what I mean is not general ignorance—which is what gives ground for censure—but particular ignorance, ignorance that is to say of the particular circumstances or the particular persons concerned. In such cases there may be room for pity and pardon, because a man who acts in ignorance of such details is an involuntary agent. It will therefore no doubt be well to define the nature and determine the number of these particular circumstances. They are (1) the agent, (2) the act; (3) that which is the object or within the range of the act. Sometimes we must add (4) the instrument (e.g. a tool), (5) the effect or result (e.g. when a man's life is saved), (6) the manner (e.g. gently or roughly). Now nobody in his right mind could be ignorant of *all* these circumstances. Obviously he cannot be ignorant of (1) the agent—how can he fail to know himself? But a man may fail to know (2) what he is doing, as when people say that a remark 'escaped' them or that they did not know they were betraying secrets. (A good instance is that of Aeschylus' supposed revelation of the Mysteries.) Or like the man who was accused of killing another with a catapult, you might say you only wanted to show him how the thing worked. Then (3) you might mistake, say, your son for an enemy, like Merope in the play, or (4) take a naked spear instead of one with the button on, or a lump of rock in mistake for a pumice stone, or (5) you might be the death of a man with a medicine which you hoped would save his life, or (6) hit your antagonist a blow when you only meant to grip his hand, as in 'open' wrestling. Seeing then that there is the possibility of ignorance in any of these special circumstances, one who has acted in ignorance of any one of them is considered to have acted involuntarily, especially if it was the most important of them that he did not know, which by general agreement are (2) the act and (3) the effect of the act.

An involuntary act being one performed under compulsion or as the result of ignorance, a voluntary act would seem to be one of which the origin or efficient cause lies in the agent, he knowing the particular circumstances in which he is acting. I believe it to be an error to say that acts occasioned by anger or desire are involuntary. For in the first place if we maintain this we shall have to give up the view that any of the lower animals, or even children, are capable of voluntary action. In the second place, when we act from desire or anger are none of our actions voluntary? Or are our fine actions voluntary, our ignoble actions, involuntary? It is an absurd distinction, since the agent is one and the same person. It is surely paradoxical to describe as 'involuntary' acts inspired by sentiments which we quite properly desire to have. There are some things at which we *ought* to feel angry, and others which we *ought* to desire—health, for instance, and the acquisition of knowledge. Thirdly, people assume that what is involuntary must be painful and what falls in with our own wishes must be pleasant. Fourthly, what difference is there in point of voluntariness between wrong actions which are calculated and wrong actions which are done on impulse? Both are to be avoided; and the further reflection suggests itself, that the irrational emotions are no less typically human than our considered judgement. Whence it follows that actions inspired by anger or desire are equally typical of the human being who performs them. Therefore to classify these actions as 'involuntary' is surely a very strange proceeding. . . .

The question is now raised whether it is at all times in our power to be good and to do the right. The answer is yes. And it is also in our power at all times to be vicious.

CHAPTER FIVE

Since then it is the end that is the object of our wishing, and the means to the end that is the object of our deliberating and choosing, the actions which deal with means must be done by choice and must be voluntary. Now when the virtues are exercised it is upon means. So virtue also is attainable by our own exertions. And so is vice. For what it lies in our power to do, it lies in our power not to do; when we can say 'no,' we can say 'yes.' If, then, it is in our power to perform an action when it is right, it will

be equally in our power to refrain from performing it when it is wrong; and if it lies with us to refrain from doing a thing when that is right, it will also lie with us to do it when that is wrong. But if it is in our power to do the right or the wrong thing, and equally in our power to refrain from doing so; and if doing right or wrong is, as we saw, the same as being good or bad ourselves, we must conclude that it depends upon ourselves whether we are to be virtuous or vicious. The words

> To sin and suffer—that offends us still:
> But who is ever blest against his will?

must be regarded as a half-truth. It is true that no one is blest against his will, but untrue that wickedness is involuntary. Otherwise we shall have to deny the truth of what we have just been saying and maintain that a man is not the originator of his own actions, of which he might be described as the begetter. But if he demonstrably is so, and we cannot trace our actions to any other springs than those which are found within ourselves, then actions which have such an origin are themselves within our control and are voluntary. In support of this conclusion it seems possible to call in evidence the practice of both private individuals and of legislators. For they inflict pains and penalties for misbehaviour, except in cases where the offender is not held responsible, because he has acted from ignorance or under duress. On the other hand they bestow honours on those who have done some fine action. Their motive in the first case is to stop evil practices, in the second to encourage the well-doer. Now nobody encourages us to do things which it is not in our power to do and which are not voluntary. It does not help at all to be made to believe that there is no such thing as getting hot, or feeling pain or anger, and so on. We shall feel them all the same. We even find that the circumstance that an offence was committed out of ignorance is made a reason for punishment when the offender is held responsible for his ignorance, as is shown, for instance, by the sentence in a case where the accused had been drunk. It may then be doubled on the ground that the offence originated with the offender, since it was open to him to refrain from getting drunk and his drunkenness was responsible for his not knowing what he was doing when he committed the offence. We punish people, too, for breaking the law through ignorance of some point in it which it was their business to know and which they could have known without much trouble. And punishment follows also when the ignorance is thought to have been due to carelessness, it being held that the guilty party need not have shown this ignorance. He should have noticed what he was doing—it was his duty to notice. You may say that very likely he could not help it, he is just that sort of man. But there is an answer to that. Such people have only themselves to blame for having acquired a character like that by their loose living, just as they have only themselves to blame for being unjust, if they make a practice of unjust behavior, or intemperate, if they spend their time in drinking or other forms of dissipation. It is their persistent activities in certain directions that make them what they are. This is well illustrated by the behaviour of men who are training for some competition or performance: they devote their whole time to the appropriate exercises. The man, then, must be a perfect fool who is unaware that people's characters take their bias from the steady direction of their activities. If a man, well aware of what he is doing, behaves in such a way that he is bound to become unjust, we can only say that he is voluntarily unjust.

Again, while we cannot fairly argue that when a man behaves unjustly he does not wish to be unjust, or that when he plunges into dissipation he has no wish to be dissipated, it is by no means true that he can stop being unjust or dissolute merely by wishing it. You might as well expect a sick man to get better by wishing it. Yet the illness may be voluntary in the sense that it has been caused by loose living and neglecting the doctor's orders. There was a time when he need not have been ill; but once he let himself go, the opportunity was lost. When once you have thrown a stone, it is gone for good and all. Still it lay with yourself to let it lie instead of picking it up and throwing it; the origin of the act was in you. Similarly it was open to the dishonest and dissolute fellow to avoid becoming such a character; so that his original action was voluntary. But once he is hardened in vice the possibility of reforming disappears. Nor is it only vices of character that are voluntary. It is not rare to find bodily defects which are so too. Doubtless nobody blames a man for being born ugly, but we do blame those who lose their looks from want of exercise and neglect of hygiene.

We may have the same feeling when a man's physique is weakened or impaired. Thus blindness is not an object of censure but of compassion when it is the result of a congenital defect or an illness or a blow. But if it is the result of alcoholic poisoning or general debauchery, then no one has any sympathy with the blind man. It comes to this. Physical defects which could have been avoided are blamed, but not those which a man cannot help and for which he is therefore not responsible. But, this granted, we must be held responsible for moral failings which are generally reprobated.

But someone may say, 'We all aim at what appears to us to be good, but over this appearance we have no control. How the end appears is determined by the character of the individual. Now one of two things. Either the individual is in a manner responsible for his moral character or he is not. If he is, he will also be in a manner responsible for the way in which the end—that is the good—appears to him. If he is not, then none of us will be responsible for his own misdeeds. The wrongdoer will be acting wrongly because he is ignorant of the true end and thinks that by such wrongdoing he will attain the highest good. That he should aim at the end in this fashion is not a matter of his own choosing. We must be born with an eye for a moral issue which will enable us to form a correct judgement and choose what is truly good. A man who has this natural gift is one of Nature's favourites, and such an endowment is one of the greatest and noblest in the world. It is something that cannot be acquired or learned; and if a man possess it just as it was when it was bestowed upon him at birth, he will have all the native gifts and graces in their genuine and fullest form.' But if this be a sound argument, how will it be possible to maintain that virtue is more voluntary than vice? To the good and the bad man alike the end presents and establishes itself in the same way, whatever they may be, whether an instinctive process or not; and whatever they do, they do it somehow with reference to the end as they see it. One is driven then to hold one of two positions. Either (a) the view one takes of the end—whatever that view may be—is not imposed on us by Nature but is partly due to oneself. Or (b) the end is given by Nature but virtue is voluntary, because the virtuous man does voluntarily whatever he has left himself to do in order to attain his end. In either case vice will be just as voluntary as virtue. For the free agency of the bad man is just as important for his conduct as the free agency of the good man for his, even if we agree that it does not appear in the bad man's choice of an end. So if we say that the virtues are voluntary, then our vices are voluntary too. The cases are identical. . . .

Our dispositions, however, have a different kind of voluntariness from that of our actions. We are masters of an action of ours from start to finish, and it is present to our minds at every stage, so that we know what we are doing. But with dispositions it is otherwise. Their beginning is something we can control, but as they develop step by step the stages of their development elude our observation—it is

like the progress of a disease. They are, however, voluntary in the sense that it was originally in our power to exercise them for good or for evil.

NOTES

1. There will be an opportunity later of considering what is meant by this formula, in particular what is meant by 'the right principle' and how, in its ethical aspect, it is related to the moral virtues.

2. If we are to illustrate the material, it must be by concrete images.

S A M U E L   B U T L E R

Erewhon*

Samuel Butler (1835–1902), English novelist and author of The Way of All Flesh.

CURRENT OPINIONS

This is what I gathered. That in that country if a man falls into ill health, or catches any disorder, or fails bodily in any way before he is seventy years old, he is tried before a jury of his countrymen, and if convicted is held up to public scorn and sentenced more or less severely as the case may be. There are subdivisions of illness into crimes and misdemeanours as with offences amongst ourselves—a man being punished very heavily for serious illness, while failure of eyes or hearing in one over sixty-five, who has had good health hitherto, is dealt with by fine only, or imprisonment in default of payment. But if a man forges a cheque, or sets his house on fire, or robs with violence from the person, or does any other such things as are criminal in our own country, he is either taken to a hospital and most carefully tended at the public expense, or if he is in good circumstances, he lets it be known to all his friends that he is suffering from a severe fit of immorality, just as

*From Chapters 10, 12, 18, 19. *Erewhon* was first published in 1872.

we do when we are ill, and they come and visit him with great solicitude, and inquire with interest how it all came about, what symptoms first showed themselves, and so forth—questions which he will answer with perfect unreserve; for bad conduct, though considered no less deplorable than illness with ourselves, and as unquestionably indicating something seriously wrong with the individual who misbehaves, is nevertheless held to be the result of either prenatal or post-natal misfortune.

The strange part of the story, however, is that though they ascribe moral defects to the effect of misfortune either in character or surroundings, they will not listen to the plea of misfortune in cases that in England meet with sympathy and commiseration only. Ill luck of any kind, or even ill treatment at the hands of others, is considered an offence against society, inasmuch as it makes people uncomfortable to hear of it. Loss of fortune, therefore, or loss of some dear friend on whom another was much dependent, is punished hardly less severely than physical delinquency. . . .

MALCONTENTS

I confess that I felt rather unhappy when I got home, and thought more closely over the trial that I had just witnessed. [The trial referred to here is that of a man convicted of consumption. See the quotation of John Hospers' article in this volume, p. 360.] For the time I was carried away by the opinion of those among whom I was. They had no misgivings about what they were doing. There did not seem to be a person in the whole court who had the smallest doubt but that all was exactly as it should be. This universal unsuspecting confidence was imparted by sympathy to myself, in spite of all my training in opinions so widely different. So it is with most of us: that which we observe to be taken as a matter of course by those round us, we take as a matter of course ourselves. And after all, it is our duty to do this, save upon grave occasion.

But when I was alone, and began to think the trial over, it certainly did strike me as betraying a strange and untenable position. Had the judge said that he acknowledged the probable truth, namely, that the prisoner was born of unhealthy parents, or had been starved in infancy, or had met with some accidents which had developed consumption; and had he then gone on to say that though he knew all this, and bitterly regretted that the protection of society obliged him to inflict additional pain on one who had suffered so much already, yet that there was no help for it, I could have understood the position, however mistaken I might have thought it. The judge was fully persuaded that the infliction of pain upon the weak and sickly was the only means of preventing weakness and sickliness from spreading, and that ten times the suffering now inflicted upon the accused was eventually warded off from others by the present apparent severity. I could therefore perfectly understand his inflicting whatever pain he might consider necessary in order to prevent so bad an example from spreading further and lowering the Erewhonian standard; but it seemed almost childish to tell the prisoner that he could have been in good health, if he had been more fortunate in his constitution, and been exposed to less hardships when he was a boy.

I write with great diffidence, but it seems to me that there is no unfairness in punishing people for their misfortunes, or rewarding them for their sheer good luck; it is the normal condition of human life that this should be done, and no rightminded person will complain of being subjected to the common treatment. There is no alternative open to us. It is idle to say that men are not responsible for their misfortunes. What is responsibility? Surely to be responsible means to be liable to have to give an answer should it be demanded, and all things which live are responsible for their lives and actions should society see fit to question them through the mouth of its authorized agent.

What is the offence of a lamb that we should rear it, and tend it, and lull it into security, for the express purpose of killing it? Its offence is the misfortune of being something which society wants to eat, and which cannot defend itself. This is ample. Who shall limit the right of society except society itself? And what consideration for the individual is tolerable unless society be the gainer thereby? Wherefore should a man be so richly rewarded for having been the son of a millionaire, were it not clearly provable that the common welfare is thus better furthered? We cannot seriously detract from a man's merit in having been the son of a rich father without imperilling our own tenure of things which we do not wish to jeopardize; if this were otherwise we should not let him keep his money for a single hour; we would have it ourselves at once. For property *is* robbery, but then, we are all robbers or would-be robbers together, and have found it essential to organize our thieving, as we have found it necessary to organize our lust and our revenge. Property, marriage, the law; as the bed to the river, so rule and convention to the instinct; and woe to him who tampers with the banks while the flood is flowing.

But to return. Even in England a man on board a ship with yellow fever is held responsible for his mischance, no matter what his being kept in quarantine may cost him. He may catch the fever and die; we cannot help it; he must take his chance as other people do; but surely it would be desperate unkindness to add contumely to our self-protection, unless, indeed, we believe that contumely is one of our best means of self-protection. Again, take the case of maniacs. We say that they are irresponsible for their actions, but we take good care, or ought to take good care, that they shall answer to us for their insanity, and we imprison them in what we call an asylum (that modern sanctuary!) if we do not like their answers. This is a strange kind of irresponsibility. What we ought to say is that we can afford to be satisfied with a less satisfactory answer from a lunatic than from one who is not mad, because lunacy is less infectious than crime.

We kill a serpent if we go in danger by it, simply

for being such and such a serpent in such and such a place; but we never say that the serpent has only itself to blame for not having been a harmless creature. Its crime is that of being a thing which it is: but this is a capital offence, and we are right in killing it out of the way, unless we think it more danger to do so than to let it escape; nevertheless we pity the creature, even though we kill it.

But in the case of him whose trial I have described above, it was impossible that any one in the court should not have known that it was but by an accident of birth and circumstances that he was not himself also in a consumption; and yet none thought that it disgraced them to hear the judge give vent to the most cruel truisms about him. The judge himself was a kind and thoughtful person. He was a man of magnificent and benign presence. He was evidently of an iron constitution, and his face wore an expression of the maturest wisdom and experience; yet for all this, old and learned as he was, he could not see things which one would have thought would have been apparent even to a child. He could not emancipate himself from, nay, it did not even occur to him to feel, the bondage of the ideas in which he had been born and bred.

So was it also with the jury and bystanders; and— most wonderful of all—so was it even with the prisoner. Throughout he seemed fully impressed with the notion that he was being dealt with justly: he saw nothing wanton in his being told by the judge that he was to be punished, not so much as a necessary protection to society (although this was not entirely lost sight of), as because he had not been better born and bred than he was. But this led me to hope that he suffered less than he would have done if he had seen the matter in the same light that I did. And, after all, justice is relative.

I may here mention that only a few years before my arrival in the country, the treatment of all convicted invalids had been much more barbarous than now, for no physical remedy was provided, and prisoners were put to the severest labour in all sorts of weather, so that most of them soon succumbed to the extreme hardships which they suffered; this was supposed to be beneficial in some ways, inasmuch as it put the country to less expense for the maintenance of its criminal class; but the growth of luxury had induced a relaxation of the old severity, and a sensitive age would no longer tolerate what appeared to be an excess of rigour, even towards the most guilty; moreover, it was found that juries were

less willing to convict, and justice was often cheated because there was no alternative between virtually condemning a man to death and letting him go free; it was also held that the country paid in recommitals for its over-severity; for those who had been imprisoned even for trifling ailments were often permanently disabled by their imprisonment; and when a man had been once convicted, it was probable that he would seldom afterwards be off the hands of the country.

These evils had long been apparent and recognized; yet people were too indolent, and too indifferent to suffering not their own, to bestir themselves about putting an end to them, until at last a benevolent reformer devoted his whole life to effecting the necessary changes. He divided all illness into three classes—those affecting the head, the trunk, and the lower limbs—and obtained an enactment that all diseases of the head, whether interal or external, should be treated with laudanum, those of the body with castor oil, and those of the lower limbs with an embrocation of strong sulphuric acid and water.

It may be said that the classification was not sufficiently careful, and that the remedies were ill chosen; but it is a hard thing to initiate any reform, and it was necessary to familiarize the public mind with the principle, by inserting the thin end of the wedge first: it is not, therefore, to be wondered at that among so practical a people there should still be some room for improvement. The mass of the nation are well pleased with existing arrangements, and believe that their treatment of criminals leaves little or nothing to be desired; but there is an energetic minority who hold what are considered to be extreme opinions, and who are not at all disposed to rest contented until the principle lately admitted has been carried further.

I was at some pains to discover the opinions of these men, and their reasons for entertaining them. They are held in great odium by the generality of the public, and are considered as subverters of all morality whatever. The malcontents, on the other hand, assert that illness is the inevitable result of certain antecedent causes, which, in the great majority of cases, were beyond the control of the individual, and that therefore a man is only guilty for being in a consumption in the same way as rotten fruit is guilty for having gone rotten. True, the fruit must be thrown on one side as unfit for man's use, and the man in a consumption must be put in prison for the protection of his fellow-citizens; but these radicals would not punish him further than by loss of liberty and a strict surveillance. So long as he was prevented from injuring society, they would allow him to make himself useful by supplying whatever of society's wants he could supply. If he succeeded in thus earning money, they would have made him as comfortable in prison as possible, and would in no way interfere with his liberty more than was necessary to prevent him from escaping, or from becoming more severely indisposed within the prison walls; but they would deduct from his earnings the expenses of his board, lodging, surveillance, and half those of his conviction. If he was too ill to do anything for his support in prison, they would allow him nothing but bread and water, and very little of that.

They say that society is foolish in refusing to allow itself to be benefited by a man merely because he has done it harm hitherto, and that objection to the labour of the diseased classes is only protection in another form. It is an attempt to raise the natural price of a commodity by saying that such and such persons, who are able and willing to produce it, shall not do so, whereby every one has to pay more for it.

Besides, so long as a man has not been actually killed he is our fellow-creature, though perhaps a very unpleasant one. It is in a great degree the doing of others that he is what he is, or in other words, the society which now condemns him is partly answerable concerning him. They say that there is no fear of any increase of disease under these circumstances; for the loss of liberty, the surveillance, the considerable and compulsory deduction from the prisoner's earnings, the very sparing use of stimulants (of which they would allow but little to any, and none to those who did not earn them), the enforced celibacy, and above all, the loss of reputation among friends, are in their opinion as ample safeguards to society against a general neglect of health as those now resorted to. A man, therefore (so they say), should carry his profession or trade into prison with him if possible; if not, he must earn his living by the nearest thing to it that he can; but if he be a gentleman born and bred to no profession, he must pick oakum, or write art criticisms for a newspaper.

These people say further, that the greater part of the illness which exists in their country is brought about by the insane manner in which it is treated.

They believe that illness is in many cases just as curable as the moral diseases which they see daily cured round them, but that a great reform is impossible till men learn to take a juster view of what physical obliquity proceeds from. Men will hide their illnesses as long as they are scouted on its becoming known that they are ill; it is the scouting, not the physic, which produces the concealment; and if a man felt that the news of his being in ill-health would be received by his neighbours as a deplorable fact, but one as much the result of necessary antecedent causes as though he had broken into a jeweller's shop and stolen a valuable diamond necklace—as a fact which might just as easily have happened to themselves, only that they had the luck to be better born or reared; and if they also felt that they would not be made more uncomfortable in the prison than the protection of society against infection and the proper treatment of their own disease actually demanded, men would give themselves up to the police as readily on perceiving that they had taken smallpox, as they go now to the straightener when they feel that they are on the point of forging a will, or running away with somebody else's wife.

But the main argument on which they rely is that of economy: for they know that they will sooner gain their end by appealing to men's pockets, in which they have generally something of their own, than to their heads, which contain for the most part little but borrowed or stolen property; and also, they believe it to be the readiest test and the one which has most to show for itself. If a course of conduct can be shown to cost a country less, and this by no dishonourable saving and with no indirectly increased expenditure in other ways, they hold that it requires a good deal to upset the arguments in favour of its being adopted, and whether rightly or wrongly I cannot pretend to say, they think that the more medicinal and humane treatment of the diseased of which they are the advocates would in the long run be much cheaper to the country: but I did not gather that these reformers were opposed to meeting some of the more violent forms of illness with the cat-of-nine-tails, or with death; for they saw no effectual way of checking them; they would therefore both flog and hang, but they would do so pitifully.

I have perhaps dwelt too long upon opinions which can have no possible bearing upon our own, but I have not said the tenth part of what these would-be reformers urged upon me. I feel, however, that I have

BIRTH FORMULAE

I heard what follows not from Arowhena, but from Mr. Nosibor and some of the gentlemen who occasionally dined at the house: they told me that the Erewhonians believe in pre-existence; and not only this (of which I will write more fully in the next chapter), but they believe that it is of their own free act and deed in a previous state that they come to be born into this world at all. They hold that the unborn are perpetually plaguing and tormenting the married of both sexes, fluttering about them incessantly, and giving them no peace either of mind or body until they have consented to take them under their protection. If this were not so (this at least is what they urge), it would be a monstrous freedom for one man to take with another, to say that he should undergo the chances and changes of this mortal life without any option in the matter. No man would have any right to get married at all, inasmuch as he can never tell what frightful misery his doing so may entail forcibly upon a being who cannot be unhappy as long as he does not exist. They feel this so strongly that they are resolved to shift the blame on to other shoulders; and have fashioned a long mythology as to the world in which the unborn people live, and what they do, and arts and machinations to which they have recourse in order to get themselves into our own world. But of this more anon: what I would relate here is their manner of dealing with those who do come.

It is a distinguishing peculiarity of the Erewhonians that when they profess themselves to be quite certain about any matter, and avow it as a base on which they are to build a system of practise, they seldom quite believe in it. If they smell a rat about the precincts of a cherished institution, they will always stop their noses to it *if* they can.

This is what most of them did in this matter of the unborn, for I cannot (and never could) think that they seriously believed in their mythology concerning pre-existence: they did and they did not; they did not know themselves what they believed; all they did know was that it was a disease not to believe as they did. The only thing of which they were quite sure was that it was the pestering of the unborn which caused them to be brought into this world, and that they would not have been here if they would have only let peaceable people alone.

It would be hard to disprove this position, and they might have a good case if they would only leave it as it stands. But this they will not do; they must have assurance doubly sure; they must have the written word of the child itself as soon as it is born, giving the parents indemnity from all responsibility on the score of its birth, and asserting its own pre-existence. They have therefore devised something which they call a birth formula—a document which varies in words according to the caution of parents, but is much the same practically in all cases; for it has been the business of the Erewhonian lawyers during many ages to exercise their skill in perfecting it and providing for every contingency.

These formulae are printed on common paper at a moderate cost for the poor; but the rich have them written on parchment and handsomely bound, so that the getting up of a person's birth formula is a test of his social position. They commence by setting forth, That whereas A. B. was a member of the kingdom of the unborn, where he was well provided for in every way, and had no cause of discontent, etc., etc., he did of his own wanton depravity and restlessness conceive a desire to enter into this present world; that thereon having taken the necessary steps as set forth in laws of the unborn kingdom, he did with malice aforethought set himself to plague and pester two unfortunate people who had never wronged him, and who were quite contented and happy until he conceived this base design against their peace; for which wrong he now humbly entreats their pardon.

He acknowledges that he is responsible for all physical blemishes and deficiencies which may render him answerable to the laws of his country; that his parents have nothing whatever to do with any of these things; and that they have a right to kill him at once if they be so minded, though he entreats them to show their marvellous goodness and clemency by sparing his life. If they will do this, he promises to be their most obedient and abject creature during his earlier years, and indeed all his life, unless they should see fit in their abundant generosity to remit some portion of his service hereafter. And so the formula continues, going sometimes into very minute details, according to the fancies of family lawyers, who will not make it any shorter than they can help.

The deed being thus prepared, on the third or fourth day after the birth of the child, or as they call it, the "final importunity," the friends gather together, and there is a feast held, where they are all very melancholy—as a general rule, I believe, quite truly so—and make presents to the father and mother of the child in order to console them for the injury which has just been done them by the unborn.

By and by the child himself is brought down by his nurse, and the company begin to rail upon him, upbraiding him for his impertinence, and asking him what amends he proposes to make for the wrong that he has committed, and how he can look for care and nourishment from those who have perhaps already been injured by the unborn on some ten or twelve occasions; for they say of people with large families, that they have suffered terrible injuries from the unborn; till at last, when this has been carried far enough, some one suggests the formula, which is brought out and solemnly read to the child by the family straightener. This gentleman is always invited on these occasions, for the very fact of intrusion into a peaceful family shows a depravity on the part of the child which requires his professional services.

On being teased by the reading and tweaked by the nurse, the child will commonly begin to cry, which is reckoned a good sign, as showing a consciousness of guilt. He is thereon asked, Does he assent to the formula? on which, as he still continues crying and can obviously make no answer, some one of the friends comes forward and undertakes to sign the document on his behalf, feeling sure (so he says) that the child would do it if he only knew how, and that he will release the present signer from his engagement on arriving at maturity. The friend then inscribes the signature of the child at the foot of the parchment, which is held to bind the child as much as though he had signed it himself.

Even this, however, does not fully content them, for they feel a little uneasy until they have got the child's own signature after all. So when he is about fourteen, these good people partly bribe him by promises of greater liberty and good things, and partly intimidate him through their great power of making themselves actively unpleasant to him, so that though there is a show of freedom made, there is really none; they also use the offices of the teachers in the Colleges of Unreason, till at last, in one way or another, they take very good care that he shall sign the paper by which he professes to have been a free agent in coming into the world, and to take all the responsibility of having done so on to his own shoulders. And yet, though this document is obviously the most important which any one can sign in his whole life, they will have him do so at an age when neither they nor the law will for many a year allow any one else to bind him to the smallest obligation, no matter how righteously he may owe it, because they hold him too young to know what he is about, and do not consider it fair that he should commit himself to anything that may prejudice him in after years.

I own that all this seemed rather hard, and not a piece with the many admirable institutions existing among them. I once ventured to say a part of what I thought about it to one of the Professors of Unreason. I did it very tenderly, but his justification of the system was quite out of my comprehension. I remember asking him whether he did not think it would do harm to a lad's principles, by weakening his sense of the sanctity of his word and of truth generally, that he should be led into entering upon a solemn declaration as to the truth of things about which all that he can certainly know is that he knows nothing— whether, in fact, the teachers who so led him, or who taught anything as a certainty of which they were themselves uncertain, were not earning their living by impairing the truth-sense of their pupils (a delicate organisation mostly), and by vitiating one of their most sacred instincts.

The Professor, who was a delightful person, seemed greatly surprised at the view which I took, but it had no influence with him whatsoever. No one, he answered, expected that the boy either would or could know all that he said he knew; but the world was full of compromises; and there was hardly any affirmation which would bear being interpreted literally. Human language was too gross a vehicle of thought—thought being incapable of absolute translation. He added, that as there can be no translation from one language into another which shall not scant the meaning somewhat, or enlarge upon it, so there is no language which can render thought without a jarring and a harshness somewhere—and so forth; all of which seemed to come to this in the end, that it was the custom of the country, and that the Erewhonians were a conservative people; that the boy would have to begin compromising sooner or later, and this was part of his education in the art. It was perhaps to be regretted that compromise should be necessary as it was; still it was necessary, and the sooner the boy got to understand it the better for himself. But they never tell this to the boy.

From the book of their mythology about the unborn I made the extracts which will form the following chapter.

THE WORLD OF THE UNBORN

. . . Having waded through many chapters . . . I came at last to the unborn themselves, and found that they were held to be souls pure and simply, having no actual bodies, but living in a sort of gaseous yet more or less anthropomorphic existence, like that of a ghost; they have thus neither flesh nor blood nor warmth. Nevertheless they are supposed to have local habitations and cities wherein they dwell, though these are as unsubstantial as their inhabitants; they are even thought to eat and drink some thin ambrosial sustenance, and generally to be capable of doing whatever mankind can do, only after a visionary ghostly fashion as in a dream. On the other hand, as long as they remain where they are they never die—the only form of death in the unborn world being the leaving it for our own. They are believed to be extremely numerous, far more so than mankind. They arrive from unknown planets, full grown, in large batches at a time; but they can only leave the unborn world by taking the steps necessary for their arrival here—which is, in fact, by suicide.

They ought to be an exceedingly happy people, for they have no extremes of good or ill fortune; never marrying, but living in a state much like that fabled by the poets as the primitive condition of mankind. In spite of this, however, they are incessantly complaining; they know that we in this world have bodies, and indeed they know everything else about us, for they move among us whithersoever they will, and can read our thoughts, as well as survey our actions at pleasure. One would think that this should be enough for them; and most of them are indeed alive to the desperate risk which they will run by indulging themselves in that body with ''sensible warm motion'' which they so much desire; nevertheless, there are some to whom the *ennui* of a disembodied existence is so intolerable that they will venture anything for a change; so they resolve to quit. The conditions which they must accept are so uncertain, that none but the most foolish of the unborn will consent to them; and it is from these, and these only, that our own ranks are recruited.

When they have finally made up their minds to

leave, they must go before the magistrate of the nearest town, and sign an affidavit of their desire to quit their then existence. On their having done this, the magistrate reads them the conditions which they must accept, and which are so long that I can only extract some of the principal points, which are mainly the following:

First, they must take a potion which will destroy their memory and sense of identity; they must go into the world helpless, and without a will of their own; they must draw lots for their dispositions before they go, and take them, such as they are, for better or worse—neither are they to be allowed any choice in the matter of the body which they so much desire; they are simply allotted by chance, and without appeal, to two people whom it is their business to find and pester until they adopt them. Who these are to be, whether rich or poor, kind or unkind, healthy or diseased, there is no knowing; they have, in fact, to entrust themselves for many years to the care of those for whose good constitution and good sense they have no sort of guarantee.

It is curious to read the lectures which the wiser heads give to those who are meditating a change. They talk with them as we talk with a spendthrift, and with about as much success.

''To be born,'' they say, ''is a felony—it is a capital crime, for which sentence may be executed at any moment after the commission of the offence. You may perhaps happen to live for some seventy or eighty years, but what is that compared with the eternity you now enjoy? And even though the sentence were commuted, and you were allowed to live on for ever, you would in time become so terribly weary of life that execution would be the greatest mercy to you.

''Consider the infinite risk; to be born of wicked parents and trained in vice! To be born of silly parents, and trained to unrealities! Of parents who regard you as a sort of chattel or property, belonging more to them than to yourself! Again, you may draw utterly unsympathetic parents, who will never be able to understand you, and who will do their best to thwart you (as a hen when she has hatched a duckling), and then call you ungrateful because you do not love them; or, again, you may draw parents who look upon you as a thing to be cowed while it is still young, lest it should give them trouble hereafter by having wishes and feelings of its own.

"In later life, when you have been finally allowed to pass muster as a full member of the world, you will yourself become liable to the pesterings of the unborn—and a very happy life you may be led in consequence! For we solicit so strongly that a few only—nor these the best—can refuse us; and yet not to refuse is much the same as going into partnership with half a dozen different people about whom one can know absolutely nothing beforehand—not even whether one is going into partnership with men or women, nor with how many of either. Delude not yourself with thinking that you will be wiser than your parents. You may be an age in advance of those whom you have pestered, but unless you are one of the great ones you will still be an age behind those who will in their turn pester you.

"Imagine what it must be to have an unborn quartered upon you, who is of an entirely different temperament and disposition to your own; nay, half a dozen such, who will not love you though you have stinted yourself in a thousand ways to provide for their comfort and well-being—who will forget all your self-sacrifice, and of whom you may never be sure that they are not bearing a grudge against you for errors of judgment into which you may have fallen, though you had hoped that such had been long since atoned for. Ingratitude such as this is not uncommon, yet fancy what it must be to bear! It is hard upon the duckling to have been hatched by a hen, but is it not also hard upon the hen to have hatched the duckling?

"Consider it again, we pray you, not for our sake but for your own. Your initial character you must draw by lot; but whatever it is, it can only come to a tolerably successful development after long training; remember that over that training you will have no control. It is possible, and even probable, that whatever you may get in after life which is of real pleasure and service to you, will have to be won in spite of, rather than by the help of, those whom you are now about to pester, and that you will only win your freedom after years of a painful struggle in which it will be hard to say whether you have suffered most injury, or inflicted it.

"Remember also, that if you go into the world you will have free will; that you will be obliged to have it; that there is no escaping it; that you will be fettered to it during your whole life, and must on every occasion do that which on the whole seems best to you at any given time, no matter whether you are right or wrong in choosing it. Your mind will be a balance for considerations, and your action will go with the heavier scale. How it shall fall will depend upon the kind of scales which you may have drawn at birth, the bias which they will have obtained by use, and the weight of the immediate considerations. If the scales were good to start with, and if they have not been outrageously tampered with in childhood, and if the combinations into which you enter are average ones, you may come off well; but there are too many 'ifs' in this, and with the failure of any one of them your misery is assured. Reflect on this, and remember that should the ill come upon you, you will have yourself to thank, for it is your own choice to be born, and there is no compulsion in the matter. . . ."

JEAN-PAUL SARTRE

Existentialism Is a Humanism*

Jean-Paul Sartre (1905 – 1980) was a French novelist, dramatist, essayist, and philosopher. In 1964, he declined the Nobel Prize for literature.

I should like on this occasion to defend existentialism against some charges which have been brought against it.

First, it has been charged with inviting people to remain in a kind of desperate quietism because, since no solutions are possible, we should have to consider action in this world as quite impossible. We should then end up in a philosophy of contemplation; and since contemplation is a luxury, we come in the end to a bourgeois philosophy. The Communists in particular have made these charges.

On the other hand, we have been charged with dwelling on human degradation, with pointing up everywhere the sordid, shady, and slimy, and neglecting the gracious and beautiful, the bright side of human nature; for example, according to Mlle. Mercier, a Catholic critic, with forgetting the smile of the child. Both sides charge us with having ignored human solidarity, with considering man as an isolated being. The Communists say that the main reason for this is that we take pure subjectivity, the *Cartesian I think,* as our starting point; in other words, the moment in which man becomes fully aware of what it means to him to be an isolated being; as a result, we are unable to return to a state of solidarity with the men who are not ourselves, a state which we can never reach in the *cogito.*

From the Christian standpoint, we are charged with denying the reality and seriousness of human undertakings, since, if we reject God's commandments and the eternal verities, there no longer remains anything but pure caprice, with everyone permitted to do as he pleases and incapable, from his own point of view, of condemning the points of view and acts of others.

I shall try today to answer these different charges. Many people are going to be surprised at what is said here about humanism. We shall try to see in what sense it is to be understood. In any case, what can be said from the very beginning is that by Existentialism we mean a doctrine which makes human life possible and, in addition, declares that every truth and every action implies a human setting and a human subjectivity.

As is generally known, the basic charge against us is that we put the emphasis on the dark side of human life. Someone recently told me of a lady who, when she let slip a vulgar word in a moment of irritation, excused herself by saying, "I guess I'm becoming an Existentialist." Consequently, Existentialism is regarded as something ugly; that is why we are said to be naturalists; and if we are, it is rather surprising that in this day and age we cause so much more alarm and scandal than does naturalism, properly so called. The kind of person who can take in his stride such a novel as Zola's *The Earth* is disgusted as soon as he starts reading an Existentialist novel; the kind of person who is resigned to the wisdom of the ages—which is pretty sad—finds us even sadder. Yet, what can be more disillusioning than saying "true charity begins at home" or "a scoundrel will always return evil for good?"

We know the commonplace remarks made when this subject comes up, remarks which always add up to the same thing: we shouldn't struggle against the powers that be; we shouldn't resist authority; we shouldn't try to rise above our station; any station which doesn't conform to authority is romantic; any

*Reprinted with permission of Philosophical Library from *Existentialism* by Jean-Paul Sartre (New York: Philosophical Library, Inc., London, Associated Book Publishers Ltd., 1947).

effort not based on past experience is doomed to failure; experience shows that man's bent is always toward trouble, that there must be a strong hand to hold him in check, if not, there will be anarchy. There are still people who go on mumbling these melancholy old saws, the people who say, "It's only human!" whenever a more or less repugnant act is pointed out to them, the people who glut themselves on *chansons réalistes;* [satirical songs about contemporary persons or events]; these are the people who accuse Existentialism of being too gloomy, and to such an extent that I wonder whether they are complaining about it, not for its pessimism, but much rather its optimism. Can it be that what really scares them in the doctrine I shall try to present here is that it leaves to man a possibility of choice? To answer this question, we must reexamine it on a strictly philosophical plane. What is meant by the term *Existentialism?*

Most people who use the word would be rather embarrassed if they had to explain it, since, now that the word is all the rage, even the work of a musician or painter is being called "existentialist." A gossip columnist in *Clartés* signs himself *The Existentialist,* so that by this time the word has been so stretched and has taken on so broad a meaning, that it no longer means anything at all. It seems that for want of an advance-guard doctrine analogous to surrealism, the kind of people who are eager for scandal and flurry turn to this philosophy, which in other respects does not at all serve their purposes in this sphere.

Actually, it is the least scandalous, the most austere of doctrines. It is intended strictly for specialists and philosophers. Yet it can be defined easily. What complicates matters is that there are two kinds of Existentialist; first, those who are Christian, among whom I would include Jaspers and Gabriel Marcel, both Catholic; and on the other hand the atheistic Existentialists, among whom I class Heidegger, and then the French Existentialists and myself. What they have in common is that they think that existence precedes essence, or, if you prefer, that subjectivity must be the starting point.

Just what does that mean? Let us consider some object that is manufactured, for example, a book or a paper cutter; here is an object which has been made by an artisan whose inspiration came from a concept. He referred to the concept of what a paper cutter is and likewise to a known method of production, which is part of the concept, something which is, by and large, a routine. Thus, the paper cutter is at once an object produced in a certain way and, on the other hand, one having a specific use; and one cannot postulate a man who produces a paper cutter but does not know what it is used for. Therefore, let us say that, for the paper cutter, essence—that is, the ensemble of both the production routines and the properties which enable it to be both produced and defined—precedes existence. Thus, the presence of the paper cutter or book in front of me is determined. Therefore, we have here a technical view of the world whereby it can be said that production precedes existence.

When we conceive God as the Creator, he is generally thought of as a superior sort of artisan. Whatever doctrine we may be considering, whether one like that of Descartes or that of Leibnitz, we always grant that will more or less follows understanding or, at the very least, accompanies it, and that when God creates He knows exactly what He is creating. Thus, the concept of man in the mind of God is comparable to the concept of paper cutter in the mind of the manufacturer, and, following certain techniques and a conception, God produces man, just as the artisan, following a definition and a technique, makes a paper cutter. Thus, the individual man is the realization of a certain concept in the divine intelligence.

In the eighteenth century, the atheism of the *philosophes* discarded the idea of God, but not so much for the notion that essence precedes existence. To a certain extent, this idea is found everywhere; we find it in Diderot, in Voltaire, and even in Kant. Man has a human nature; this human nature, which is the concept of the human, is founded in all men, which means that each man is a particular example of a universal concept, man. In Kant, the result of this universality is that the wild man, the natural man, as well as the bourgeois, are circumscribed by the same definition and have the same basic qualities. Thus, here too the essence of man precedes the historical existence that we find in nature.

Atheistic Existentialism, which I represent, is more coherent. It states that if God does not exist, there is at least one being in whom existence precedes essence, a being who exists before he can be defined by any concept, and that this being is man, or, as Heidegger says, human reality. What is meant here by saying that existence precedes essence? It means that, first of all, man exists, turns up, appears on the scene, and only afterwards, defines himself. If man, as the Existentialist conceives him, is indefinable, it is because at first he is nothing. Only afterward will he be something, and he himself will have made what he will be. Thus, there is no human nature, since there is no God to conceive it. Not only is man what he conceives himself to be, but he is also only what he wills himself to be after this thrust toward existence.

Man is nothing else but what he makes of himself. Such is the first principle of Existentialism. It is also what is called "subjectivity," the name we are labeled with when charges are brought against us. But what do we mean by this, if not that man has a greater dignity than a stone or table? For we mean that man first exists, that is, that man first of all is the being who hurls himself toward a future and who is conscious of imagining himself as being in the future. Man is at the start a plan which is aware of itself, rather than a patch of moss, a piece of garbage, or a cauliflower; nothing exists prior to this plan; there is nothing in heaven; man will be what he will have planned to be. Not what he will want to be. Because by the word "will" we generally mean a conscious decision, which is subsequent to what we have already made of ourselves. I may want to belong to a political party, write a book, get married; but all this is only a manifestation of an earlier, more spontaneous choice that is called "will." But if existence really does precede essence, man is responsible for what he is. Thus, Existentialism's first move is to make every man aware of what he is and to make the full responsibility of his existence rest on him. And when we say that a man is responsible for himself, we do not only mean that he is responsible for his own individuality, but that he is responsible for all men.

The word "subjectivism" has two meanings, and our opponents play on the two. Subjectivism means, on the one hand, that an individual chooses and makes himself; and, on the other, that it is impossible for man to transcend human subjectivity. The second of these is the essential meaning of Existentialism. When we say that man chooses his own self, we mean that every one of us does likewise; but we also mean by that that in making this choice he also chooses all men. In fact, in creating the man that we want to be, there is not a single one of our acts which does not at the same time create an image of man as we think he ought to be. To choose to be this or that is to affirm at the same time the value of what we

choose, because we can never choose evil. We always choose the good, and nothing can be good for us without being good for all.

If, on the other hand, existence precedes essence, and if we grant that we exist and fashion our image at one and the same time, the image is valid for everybody and for our whole age. Thus, our responsibility is much greater than we might have supposed, because it involves all mankind. If I am a workingman and choose to join a Christian trade union rather than be a Communist, and if by being a member I want to show that the best thing for man is resignation, that the kingdom of man is not of this world, I am not only involving my own case—I want to be resigned for everyone. As a result, my action has involved all humanity. To take a more individual matter, if I want to marry, to have children, even if this marriage depends solely on my own circumstances or passion or wish, I am involving all humanity in monogamy and not merely myself. Therefore, I am responsible for myself and for everyone else. I am creating a certain image of man of my own choosing. In choosing myself, I choose man.

This helps us understand what the actual content is of such rather grandiloquent words as anguish, forlornness, despair. As you will see, it's all quite simple.

First, what is meant by "anguish"? The Existentialists say at once that man is anguish. What that means is this: the man who involves himself and who realizes that he is not only the person he chooses to be, but also a lawmaker who is, at the same time, choosing all mankind as well as himself, cannot escape the feeling of his total and deep responsibility. Of course, there are many people who are not anxious; but we claim that they are hiding their anxiety, that they are fleeing from it. Certainly, many people believe that when they do something, they themselves are the only ones involved, and when someone says to them, "What if everyone acted that way?" they shrug their shoulders and answer, "Everyone doesn't act that way." But really, one should always ask himself, "What would happen if everybody looked at things that way?" There is no escaping this disturbing thought except by a kind of double-dealing. A man who lies and makes excuses for himself by saying "not everybody does that," is someone with an uneasy conscience, because the act of lying implies that a universal value is conferred upon the lie.

Anguish is evident even when it conceals itself. This is the anguish that Kierkegaard called the "anguish of Abraham." You know the story: an angel has ordered Abraham to sacrifice his son; if it really were an angel who has come and said, "You are Abraham, you shall sacrifice your son," everything would be all right. But everyone might first wonder, "Is it really an angel, and am I really Abraham? What proof do I have?"

There was a madwoman who had hallucinations; someone used to speak to her on the telephone and give her orders. Her doctor asked her, "Who is it who talks to you?" She answered, "He says it's God." What proof did she really have that it was God? If an angel comes to me, what proof is there that it's an angel; and if I hear voices, what proof is there that they come from heaven and not from hell, or from the subconscious, or a pathological condition? What proves that they are addressed to me? What proof is there that I have been appointed to impose my choice and my conception of man on humanity? I'll never find any proof or sign to convince me of that. If a voice addresses me, it is always for me to decide that this is the angel's voice; if I consider that such an act is a good one, it is I who will choose to say that it is good rather than bad.

Now, I'm not being singled out as an Abraham, and yet at every moment I'm obliged to perform exemplary acts. For every man, everything happens as if all mankind had its eyes fixed on him and were guiding itself by what he does. And every man ought to say to himself, "Am I really the kind of man who has the right to act in such a way that humanity might guide itself by my actions?" And if he does not say that to himself, he is masking his anguish.

There is no question here of the kind of anguish which would lead to quietism, to inaction. It is a matter of a simple sort of anguish that anybody who has had responsibilities is familiar with. For example, when a military officer takes the responsibility for an attack and sends a certain number of men to death, he chooses to do so, and in the main he alone makes the choice. Doubtless, orders come from above, but they are too broad; he interprets them, and on this interpretation depend the lives of ten or fourteen or twenty men. In making a decision he cannot help having a certain anguish. All leaders know this anguish. That doesn't keep them from acting; on the contrary, it is the very condition of their action. For

it implies that they envisage a number of possibilities, and when they choose one, they realize that it has value only because it is chosen. We shall see that this kind of anguish, which is the kind that Existentialism describes, is explained, in addition, by a direct responsibility to the other men whom it involves. It is not a curtain separating us from action, but is part of the action itself.

When we speak of "forlornness," a term Heidegger was fond of, we mean only that God does not exist and that we have to face all the consequences of this. The Existentialist is strongly opposed to a certain kind of secular ethics which would like to abolish God with the least possible expense. About 1880, some French teachers tried to set up a secular ethics which went something like this: God is a useless and costly hypothesis; we are discarding it; but, meanwhile, in order for there to be an ethics, a society, a civilization, it is essential that certain values be taken seriously and that they be considered as having an *a priori* existence. It must be obligatory, *a priori*, to be honest, not to lie, not to beat your wife, to have children, etc., etc. So we're going to try a little device which will make it possible to show that values exist all the time, inscribed in a heaven of ideas, though otherwise God does not exist. In other words—and this, I believe, is the tendency of everything called "reformism" in France—nothing will be changed if God does not exist. We shall find ourselves with the same norms of honesty, progress, and humanism, and we shall have made of God an outdated hypothesis which will peacefully die off by itself.

The Existentialist, on the contrary, thinks it very distressing that God does not exist, because all possibility of finding values in a heaven of ideas disappears along with Him; there can no longer be an *a priori* Good, since there is no infinite and perfect consciousness to think it. Nowhere is it written that the Good exists, that we must be honest, that we must not lie; because the fact is we are on a plane where there are only men. Dostoyevsky said, "If God didn't exist, everything would be possible." That is the very starting point of Existentialism. Indeed, everything is permissible if God does not exist, and as a result man is forlorn, because neither within him nor without does he find anything to cling to. He can't start making excuses for himself.

If existence really does precede essence, there is no explaining things away by reference to a fixed and given human nature. In other words, there is no determinism, man is free, man is freedom. On the other hand, if God does not exist, we find no values or commands to turn to which legitimize our conduct. So, in the bright realm of values, we have no excuse behind us, nor justification before us. We are alone, with no excuses.

That is the idea I shall try to convey when I say that man is condemned to be free. Condemned, because he did not create himself, yet, in other respects is free; because, once thrown into the world, he is responsible for everything he does. The Existentialist does not believe in the power of passion. He will never agree that a sweeping passion is a ravaging torrent which fatally leads a man to certain acts and is therefore an excuse. He thinks that man is responsible for his passion.

The Existentialist does not think that man is going to help himself by finding in the world some omen by which to orient himself. Because he thinks that man will interpret the omen to suit himself. Therefore, he thinks that man, with no support and no aid, is condemned every moment to invent man. Ponge, in a very fine article, has said, "Man is the future of man." That's exactly it. But if it is taken to mean that this future is recorded in heaven, that God sees it, then it is false, because it would really no longer be a future to be forged, a virgin future before him, then this remark is sound. But then we are forlorn.

To give you an example which will enable you to understand forlornness better, I shall cite the case of one of my students who came to see me under the following circumstances: his father was on bad terms with his mother, and, moreover, was inclined to be a collaborationist; his older brother had been killed in the German offensive of 1940, and the young man, with somewhat immature but generous feelings, wanted to avenge him. His mother lived alone with him, very much upset by the half-treason of her husband and the death of her older son; the boy was her only consolation.

The boy was faced with the choice of leaving for England and joining the Free French Forces—that is, leaving his mother behind—or remaining with his mother and helping her to carry on. He was fully aware that the woman lived only for him and that his going off—and perhaps his death—would plunge her into despair. He was also aware that every act that he did for his mother's sake was a sure thing, in the sense that it was helping her to carry on, whereas every effort he made toward going off and fighting

was an uncertain move which might run aground and prove completely useless; for example, on his way to England he might, while passing through Spain, be detained indefinitely in a Spanish camp; he might reach England or Algiers and be stuck in an office at a desk job. As a result, he was faced with two very different kinds of action: one, concrete, immediate, but concerning only one individual; the other concerned an incomparably vaster group, a national collectivity, but for that very reason was dubious, and might be interrupted en route. And, at the same time, he was wavering between two kinds of ethics. On the one hand, an ethics of sympathy, of personal devotion; on the other, a broader ethics, but one whose efficacy was more dubious. He had to choose between the two.

Who could help him choose? Christian doctrine? No. Christian doctrine says, "Be charitable, love your neighbor, take the more rugged path, etc., etc." But which is the more rugged path? Whom should he love as a brother? The fighting man or his mother? Which does the greater good, the vague act of fighting in a group, or the concrete one of helping a particular human being to go on living? Who can decide *a priori?* Nobody. No book of ethics can tell him. The Kantian ethics says, "Never treat any person as a means, but as an end." Very well, if I stay with my mother, I'll treat her as an end and not as a means; but by virtue of this very fact, I'm running the risk of treating the people around me who are fighting, as means; and, conversely, if I go to join those who are fighting, I'll be treating them as an end, and, by doing that, I run the risk of treating my mother as a means.

If values are vague, and if they are always too broad for the concrete and specific case that we are considering, the only thing left for us is to trust our instincts. That's what this young man tried to do; and when I saw him, he said, "In the end, feeling is what counts. I ought to choose whichever pushes me in one direction. If I feel that I love my mother enough to sacrifice everything else for her—my desire for vengeance, for action, for adventure—then I'll stay with her. If, on the contrary, I feel that my love for my mother isn't enough, I'll leave."

But how is the value of a feeling determined? What gives his feeling for his mother value? Precisely the fact that he remained with her. I may say that I like so-and-so well enough to sacrifice a certain amount of money for him, but I may say so only if I've done it. I may say, "I love my mother well enough to remain with her" if I have remained with her. The only way to determine the value of this affection is, precisely, to perform an act which confirms and defines it. But, since I require this affection to justify my act, I find myself caught in a vicious circle.

On the other hand, Gide has well said that a mock feeling and a true feeling are almost indistinguishable; to decide that I love my mother and will remain with her, or to remain with her by putting on an act, amount somewhat to the same thing. In other words, the feeling is formed by the acts one performs; so, I cannot refer to it in order to act upon it. Which means that I can neither seek within myself the true condition which will impel me to act, nor apply to a system of ethics for concepts which will permit me to act. You will say, "At least, he did go to a teacher for advice." But if you seek advice from a priest, for example, you have chosen this priest; you already knew, more or less, just about what advice he was going to give you. In other words, choosing your adviser is involving yourself. The proof of this is that if you are a Christian, you will say, "Consult a priest." But some priests are collaborating, some are just marking time, some are resisting. Which to choose? If the young man chooses a priest who is resisting or collaborating, he has already decided on the kind of advice he's going to get. Therefore, in coming to see me he knew the answer I was going to give him, and I had only one answer to give: "You're free, choose, that is, invent." No general ethics can show you what is to be done; there are no omens in the world. The Catholics will reply, "But there are." Granted—but, in any case, I myself choose the meaning they have.

When I was a prisoner, I knew a rather remarkable young man who was a Jesuit. He had entered the Jesuit order in the following way: he had had a number of very bad breaks; in childhood, his father died, leaving him in poverty, and he was a scholarship student at a religious institution where he was constantly made to feel that he was being kept out of charity; then, he failed to get any of the honors and distinctions that children like; later on, at about eighteen, he bungled a love affair; finally, at twenty-two, he failed in military training, a childish enough matter, but it was the last straw.

This young fellow might well have felt that he had botched everything. It was a sign of something, but of what? He might have taken refuge in bitterness or despair. But he very wisely looked upon all this as a sign that he was not made for secular triumphs, and that only the triumphs of religion, holiness, and faith were open to him. He saw the hand of God in all this, and so he entered the order. Who can help seeing that he alone decided what the sign meant?

Some other interpretation might have been drawn from this series of setbacks; for example, that he might have done better to turn carpenter or revolutionist. Therefore, he is fully responsible for the interpretation. Forlornness implies that we ourselves choose our being. Forlornness and anguish go together.

As for "despair," the term has a very simple meaning. It means that we shall confine ourselves to reckoning only with what depends upon our will, or on the ensemble of probabilities which make our action possible. When we want something, we always have to reckon with probabilities. I may be counting on the arrival of a friend. The friend is coming by rail or streetcar; this supposes that the train will arrive on schedule, or that the streetcar will not jump the track. I am left in the realm of possibility; but possibilities are to be reckoned with only to the point where my action comports with the ensemble of these possibilities, and no further. The moment the possibilities I am considering are not rigorously involved by my action, I ought to disengage myself from them, because no God, no scheme, can adapt the world and its possibilities to my will. When Descartes said, "Conquer yourself rather than the world," he meant essentially the same thing.

The Marxists to whom I have spoken reply, "You can rely on the support of others in your action, which obviously has certain limits, because you're not going to live forever. That means: rely on both what others are doing elsewhere to help you, in China, in Russia, and what they will do later on, after your death, to carry on the action and lead it to its fulfillment, which will be the revolution. You even *have* to rely upon that, otherwise you're immortal." I reply at once that I will always rely on fellow fighters insofar as these comrades are involved with me in a common struggle, in the unity of a party or a group in which I can more or less make my weight felt; that is, one whose ranks I am in as a fighter and whose movements I am aware of at every moment. In such a situation, relying on the unity and will of the party is exactly like counting on the fact that the train will arrive on time or that the car won't jump the track. But, given that man is free and that there is no human nature for me to depend on, I cannot count on men whom I do not know by relying on human goodness or man's concern for the good of society. I don't know what will become of the Russian revolution; I may make an example of it to the extent that at the present time it is apparent that the proletariat plays a part in Russia that it plays in no other nation. But I can't swear that this will inevitably lead to a triumph of the proletariat. I've got to limit myself to what I see.

Given that men are free and that tomorrow they will freely decide what man will be, I cannot be sure that, after my death, fellow fighters will carry on my work to bring it to its maximum perfection. Tomorrow, after my death, some men may decide to set up fascism, and the others may be cowardly and muddled enough to let them do it. Fascism will then be the human reality, so much the worse for us.

Actually, things will be as man will have decided they are to be. Does that mean that I should abandon myself to quietism? No. First, I should involve myself; then, act on the old saw, "Nothing ventured, nothing gained." Nor does it mean that I shouldn't belong to a party, but rather that I shall have no illusions and shall do what I can. For example, suppose I ask myself, "Will socialization, as such, ever come about?" I know nothing about it. All I know is that I'm going to do everything in my power to bring it about. Beyond that, I can't count on anything. Quietism is the attitude of people who say, "Let others do what I can't do." The doctrine I am presenting is the very opposite of quietism, since it declares, "There is no reality except in action." Moreover, it goes further, since it adds, "Man is nothing else than his plan; he exists only to the extent that he fulfills himself; he is therefore nothing else than the ensemble of his acts, nothing else than his life." . . .

I've been reproached for asking whether Existentialism is humanistic. It's been said, "But you said in *Nausea* that the humanists were all wrong. You made fun of a certain kind of humanist. Why come back to it now?" Actually, the word "humanism" has two very different meanings. By "humanism" one can mean a theory which takes man as an end and as a higher value. Humanism in this sense can be found in Cocteau's tale *Around the World in Eighty Hours,* when a character, because he is flying over some mountains in an airplane, declares, "Man

is simply amazing." That means that I, who did not build the airplanes, shall personally benefit from these particular inventions, and that I, as man, shall personally consider myself responsible for, and honored by, acts of a few particular men. This would imply that we ascribe a value to man on the basis of the highest deeds of certain men. This humanism is absurd, because only the dog or the horse would be able to make such an overall judgment about man, which they are careful not to do, at least to my knowledge.

But it cannot be granted that a man may make a judgment about man. Existentialism spares him from any such judgment. The Existentialist will never consider man as an end because he is always in the making. Nor should we believe that there is a mankind to which we might set up a cult in the manner of Auguste Comte. The cult of mankind ends in the self-enclosed humanism of Comte, and let it be said, of fascism. This kind of humanism we can do without.

But there is another meaning of humanism. Fundamentally it is this: man is constantly outside of himself; in projecting himself, in losing himself outside of himself, he makes for man's existing; and, on the other hand, it is by pursuing transcendent goals that he is able to exist; man, being this state of passing beyond, and seizing upon things only as they bear upon this passing beyond, is at the heart, at the center of this passing beyond. There is no universe other than a human universe, the universe of human subjectivity. This connection between transcendency, as a constituent element of man—not in the sense that God is transcendent, but in the sense of passing beyond—and subjectivity, in the sense that man is not closed in on himself but is always present in a human universe, is what we call "Existentialist humanism." Humanism, because we remind man that there is no lawmaker other than himself, and that in his forlornness he will decide by himself; because we point out that man will fulfill himself as man, not in turning toward himself, but in seeking outside of himself a goal which is just this liberation, just this particular fulfillment.

From these few reflections it is evident that nothing is more unjust than the objections that have been raised against us. Existentialism is nothing else than an attempt to draw all the consequences of a coherent atheistic position. It isn't trying to plunge man into despair at all. But if one calls every attitude of unbelief despair, like the Christians, then the word is not being used in its original sense. Existentialism isn't so atheistic that it wears itself out showing that God doesn't exist. Rather, it declares that even if God did exist, that would change nothing. There

you've got our point of view. Not that we believe that God exists, but we think that the problem of His existence is not the issue. In this sense Existentialism is optimistic, a doctrine of action, and it is plain dishonesty for Christians to make no distinction between their own despair and ours and then to call us despairing.

Theories of Punishment

J. D. MABBOTT

Punishment*

J. D. Mabbott (1898–   ) taught philosophy for many years at St. John's College, Oxford.

I propose in this paper to defend a retributive theory of punishment and to reject absolutely all utilitarian considerations from its justification. I feel sure that this enterprise must arouse deep suspicion and hostility both among philosophers (who must have felt that the retributive view is the only moral theory except perhaps psychological hedonism which has been definitely detroyed by criticism) and among practical men (who have welcomed its steady decline in our penal practice).

The question I am asking is this. Under what circumstances is the punishment of some particular person justified and why? The theories of reform and deterrence which are usually considered to be the only alternatives to retribution involve well-known difficulties. These are considered fully and fairly in Dr. Ewing's book *The Morality of Punishment,* and I need not spend long over them. The central difficulty is that both would on occasion justify the punishment of an innocent man, the deter-

rent theory if he were believed to have been guilty by those likely to commit the crime in future, and the reformatory theory if he were a bad man though not a criminal. To this may be added the point against the deterrent theory that it is the threat of punishment and not punishment itself which deters, and that when deterrence seems to depend on actual punishment, to implement the threat, it really depends on publication and may be achieved if men believe that punishment has occurred even if in fact it has not. As Bentham saw, for a Utilitarian apparent justice is everything, real justice is irrelevant.

Dr. Ewing and other moralists would be inclined to compromise with retribution in the face of the above difficulties. They would admit that one fact and one fact only can justify the punishment of this man, and that is a *past* fact, that he has committed a crime. To this extent reform and deterrence theories, which look only to the consequences, are wrong. But they would add that retribution can determine only *that* a man should be punished. It cannot determine how or how much, and here reform and deterrence may come in. Even Bradley, the fiercest retributionist of modern times, says "Having once the right to punish we may modify the punishment according to the useful and the pleasant, but these

*J. D. Mabbott, "Punishment," *Mind,* XLVIII (1939), 152–167. Reprinted by permission of the author and the editor of *Mind.*

are external to the matter; they cannot give us a right to punish and nothing can do that but criminal desert." Dr. Ewing would maintain that the whole estimate of the amount and nature of a punishment may be effected by considerations of reform and deterrence. It seems to me that this is a surrender which the upholders of retribution dare not make. As I said above, it is publicity and not punishment which deters, and the publicity though often spoken of as "part of a man's punishment" is no more part of it than his arrest or his detention prior to trial, though both these may be also unpleasant and bring him into disrepute. A judge sentences a man to three years' imprisonment, not to three years *plus* three columns in the press. Similarly with reform. The visit of the prison chaplain is not part of a man's punishment nor is the visit of Miss Fields or Mickey Mouse.

The truth is that while punishing a man and punishing him justly, it is possible to deter others, and also to attempt to reform him, and if these additional goods are achieved the total state of affairs is better than it would be with the just punishment alone. But reform and deterrence are not modifications of the punishment, still less reasons for it. A parallel may be found in the case of tact and truth. If you have to tell a friend an unpleasant truth you may do all you can to put him at his ease and spare his feelings as much as possible, while still making sure that he understands your meaning. In such a case no one would say that your offer of a cigarette beforehand or your apology afterwards are modifications of the truth still less reasons for telling it. You do not tell the truth in order to spare his feelings, but having to tell the truth you also spare his feelings. So Bradley was right when he said that reform and deterrence were "external to the matter," but therefore wrong when he said that they may "modify the punishment." Reporters are admitted to our trials so that punishments may become public and help to deter others. But the punishment would be no less just were reporters excluded and deterrence not achieved. Prison authorities may make it possible that a convict may become physically or morally better. They cannot ensure either result; and the punishment would still be just if the criminal took no advantage of their arrangements and their efforts failed. Some moralists see this and exclude these "extra" arrangements for deterrence and reform. They say that it must be the punishment *itself* which reforms and deters. But it is just my point that the punishment *itself* seldom

reforms the criminal and never deters others. It is only "extra" arrangements which have any chance of achieving either result. As this is the central point of my paper, at the cost of laboured repetition I would ask the upholders of reform and deterrence two questions. Suppose it could be shown that a particular criminal had not been improved by a punishment and also that no other would-be criminal had been deterred by it, would that prove that the punishment was unjust? Suppose it were discovered that a particular criminal had lived a much better life after his release and that many would-be criminals believing him to have been guilty were influenced by his fate, but yet that the "criminal" was punished for something he had never done, would these excellent results prove the punishment just?

It will be observed that I have throughout treated punishment as a purely legal matter. A "criminal" means a man who has broken a law, not a bad man; an "innocent" man is a man who has not broken the law in connection with which he is being punished, though he may be a bad man and have broken other laws. Here I dissent from most upholders of the retributive theory—from Hegel, from Bradley, and from Dr. Ross. They maintain that the essential connection is one between punishment and moral or social wrong-doing.

My fundamental difficulty with their theory is the question of *status*. It takes two to make a punishment, and for a moral or social wrong I can find no punisher. We may be tempted to say when we hear of some brutal action "that ought to be punished"; but I cannot see how there can be duties which are nobody's duties. If I see a man ill-treating a horse in a country where cruelty to animals is not a legal offence, and I say to him "I shall now punish you," he will reply, rightly, "What has it to do with you? Who made you a judge and ruler over me?" I may have a duty to try to stop him and one way of stopping him may be to hit him, but another way may be to buy the horse. Neither the blow nor the price is a punishment. For a moral offence, God alone has the *status* necessary to punish the offender; and the theologians are becoming more and more doubtful whether even God has a duty to punish wrong-doing.

Dr. Ross would hold that not all wrong-doing is punishable, but only invasion of the rights of others; and in such a case it might be thought that the injured party had a right to punish. His right, however, is rather a right to reparation, and should not be confused with punishment proper.

This connection, on which I insist, between punishment and crime, not between punishment and moral or social wrong, alone accounts for some of our beliefs about punishment, and also meets many objections to the retributive theory as stated in its ordinary form. The first point on which it helps us is with regard to retrospective legislation. Our objection to this practice is unaccountable on reform and deterrence theories. For a man who commits a wrong before the date on which a law against it is passed, is as much in need of reform as a man who commits it afterwards; nor is deterrence likely to suffer because of additional punishments for the same offence. But the orthodox retributive theory is equally at a loss here, for if punishment is given for moral wrongdoing or for invasion of the rights of others, that immorality of invasion existed as certainly before the passing of the law as after it.

My theory also explains, where it seems to me all others do not, the case of punishment imposed by an authority who believes the law in question is a bad law. I was myself for some time disciplinary officer at a college whose rules included a rule compelling attendance at chapel. Many of those who broke this rule broke it on principle. I punished them. I certainly did not want to reform them; I respected their characters and their views. I certainly did not want to drive others into chapel through fear of penalties. Nor did I think there had been a wrong done which merited retribution. I wished I could have believed that I would have done the same thing myself. My position was clear. They had broken a rule; they knew it and I knew it. Nothing more was necessary to make punishment proper.

I know that the usual answer to this is that the judge enforces a bad law because otherwise law in general would suffer and good laws would be broken. The effect of punishing good men for breaking bad laws is that fewer bad men break good laws.

[*Excursus on Indirect Utilitarianism.* The above argument is a particular instance of a general utilitarian solution of all similar problems. When I am in funds and consider whether I should pay my debts or give the same amount to charity, I must choose the former because repayment not only benefits my creditor (for the benefit to him might be less than the good done through charity) but also upholds the general credit system. I tell the truth when a lie might do more good to the parties directly concerned, because I thus increase general trust and confidence. I keep a promise when it might do more immediate good to break it, because indirectly I bring it about that promises will be more readily made in future and this will outweigh the immediate loss involved. Dr. Ross has pointed out that the effect on the credit system of my refusal to pay a debt is greatly exaggerated. But I have a more serious objection of principle. It is that in all these cases the indirect effects do not result from my wrong action—my lie or defalcation or bad faith—but from the publication of these actions. If in any instance the breaking of the rule were to remain unknown then I could consider only the direct or immediate consequences. Thus in my "compulsory chapel" case I could have considered which of my culprits were law-abiding men generally and unlikely to break any other college rule. Then I could have sent for each of these separately and said "I shall let you off if you will tell no one I have done so." By these means the general keeping of rules would not have suffered. Would this course have been correct? It must be remembered that the proceedings need not deceive everybody. So long as they deceive would-be law-breakers the good is achieved.

As this point is of crucial importance and as it has an interest beyond the immediate issue, and gives a clue to what I regard as the true general nature of law and punishment, I may be excused for expanding and illustrating it by an example or two from other fields. Dr. Ross says that two men dying on a desert island would have duties to keep promises to each other even though their breaking them would not affect the future general confidence in promises at all. Here is certainly the same point. But as I find that desert-island morality always rouses suspicion among ordinary men I should like to quote two instances from my own experience which also illustrate the problem.

(i) A man alone with his father at his death promises him a private and quiet funeral. He finds later that both directly and indirectly the keeping of this promise will cause pain and misunderstanding. He can see no particular positive good that the quiet funeral will achieve. No one yet knows that he has made the promise nor need anyone ever know. Should he therefore act as though it had never been made?

(ii) A college has a fund given to it for the encouragement of a subject which is now expiring. Other expanding subjects are in great need of endowment. Should the authorities divert the money? Those who oppose the diversion have previously stood on the past, the promise. But one day one of them discovers the "real reason" for this slavery to a dead donor. He says "We must consider not only the value of this money for these purposes, since on all direct consequences it should be diverted at once. We must remember the effect of this diversion on the general system of benefactions. We know that benefactors like to endow special objects, and this act of ours would discourage such benefactors in future and leave learning worse off." Here again is the indirect utilitarian reason for choosing the alternative which direct utilitarianism would reject. But the immediate answer to this from the most ingenious member of the opposition was crushing and final. He said, "Divert the money but keep it dark." This is obviously correct. It is not the act of diversion which would diminish the stream of benefactions but the news of it reaching the ears of benefactors. Provided that no possible benefactor got to hear of it no indirect loss would result. But the justification of our action would depend entirely on the success of the measures for "keeping it dark." I remember how I felt and how others felt that whatever answer was right this result was certainly wrong. But it follows that indirect utilitarianism is wrong in all such cases. For its argument can always be met by "Keep it dark."]

The view, then, that a judge upholds a bad law in order that law in general should not suffer is indefensible. He upholds it simply because he has no right to dispense from punishment.

The connection of punishment with law-breaking and not with wrong-doing also escapes moral objections to the retributive theory as held by Kant and Hegel or by Bradley and Ross. It is asked how we can measure moral wrong or balance it with pain, and how pain can wipe out moral wrong. Retributivists have been pushed into holding that pain *ipso facto* represses the worse self and frees the better, when this is contrary to the vast majority of observed cases. But if punishment is not intended to measure or balance or negate moral wrong then all this is beside the mark. There is the further difficulty of reconciling punishment with repentance and with forgiveness. Repentance is the reaction morally appropriate to moral wrong and punishment added to remorse is an unnecessary evil. But if punishment is associated with law-breaking and not with the moral evil the punisher is not entitled to consider

whether the criminal is penitent any more than he may consider whether the law is good. So, too, with forgiveness. Forgiveness is not appropriate to law-breaking. (It is noteworthy that when, in divorce cases, the law has to recognize forgiveness it calls it "condonation," which is symptomatic of the difference of attitude.) Nor is forgiveness appropriate to moral evil. It is appropriate to personal injury. No one has any right to forgive me except the person I have injured. No judge or jury can do so. But the person I have injured has no right to punish me. Therefore there is no clash between punishment and forgiveness since these two duties do not fall on the same person nor in connection with the same characteristic of my act. (It is the weakness of vendetta that it tends to confuse this clear line, though even there it is only by personifying the family that the injured party and the avenger are identified. Similarly we must guard against the plausible fallacy of personifying society and regarding the criminal as "injuring society," for then once more the old dilemma about forgiveness would be insoluble.) A clergyman friend of mine catching a burglar red-handed was puzzled about his duty. In the end he ensured the man's punishment by information and evidence, and at the same time showed his own forgiveness by visiting the man in prison and employing him when he came out. I believe any "good Christian" would accept this as representing his duty. But obviously if the punishment is thought of as imposed *by* the victim or *for* the injury or immorality then the contradiction with forgiveness is hopeless.

So far as the question of the actual punishment of any individual is concerned this paper could stop here. No punishment is morally retributive or reformative or deterrent. Any criminal punished for any one of these reasons is certainly unjustly punished. The only justification for punishing any man is that he has broken a law.

In a book which has already left its mark on prison administration I have found a criminal himself confirming these views. *Walls Have Mouths,* by W. F. R. Macartney, is prefaced, and provided with appendices to each chapter, by Compton Mackenzie. It is interesting to notice how the novelist maintains that the proper object of penal servitude should be reformation,[1] whereas the prisoner himself accepts the view I have set out above. Macartney says "To punish a man is to treat him as an equal. To be punished *for an offence against rules* is a sane man's right."[2] It is striking also that he never uses "injustice" to describe the brutality or provocation which he experienced. He makes it clear that there were only two types of prisoner who were *unjustly* imprisoned, those who were insane and not responsible for the acts for which they were punished[3] and those who were innocent and had broken no law.[4] It is irrelevant, as he rightly observes, that some of these innocent men were, like Steinie Morrison, dangerous and violent characters, who on utilitarian grounds might well have been restrained. That made their punishment no whit less unjust.[5] To these general types may be added two specific instances of injustice. First, the sentences on the Dartmoor mutineers. "The Penal Servitude Act . . . lays down specific punishments for mutiny and incitement to mutiny, which include flogging. . . . Yet on the occasion of the only big mutiny in an English prison, men are not dealt with by the Act specially passed to meet mutiny in prison, but are taken out of gaol and tried under an Act expressly passed to curb and curtail the Chartists—a revolutionary movement."[6] Here again the injustice does not lie in the actual effect the sentences are likely to have on the prisoners (though Macartney has some searching suggestions about that also) but in condemning men for breaking a law they did not break and not for breaking the law they did break. The second specific instance is that of Coulton, who served his twenty years and then was brought back to prison to do another eight years and to die. This is due to the "unjust order that no lifer shall be released unless he has either relations or a job to whom he can go: and it is actually suggested that this is really for the lifer's own good. Just fancy, you admit that the man in doing years upon years in prison had expiated his crime: but, instead of releasing him, you keep him a further time—perhaps another three years—because you say he has nowhere to go. Better a ditch and hedge than prison! True, there are abnormal cases who want to stay in prison, but Lawrence wanted to be a private soldier, and men go into monasteries. Because occasionally a man wants to stay in prison, must every lifer who has lost his family during his sentence (I was doing only ten years and I lost all my family) be kept indefinitely in gaol after he has paid his debt?"[7] Why is it unjust? Because he has paid his debt. When that is over it is for the man himself to decide what is for his own good. Once again the reform and utilitarian arguments are summarily swept aside. Injustice lies not in bad treatment or treatment which is not in the man's own interest, but in restriction which, according to the law, he has not merited.

It is true that Macartney writes, in one place, a paragraph of general reflection on punishment in which he confuses, as does Compton Mackenzie, retribution with revenge and in which he seems to hold that the retributive theory has some peculiar connection with private property. "Indeed it is difficult to see how, in society as it is today constituted, a humane prison system could function. All property is sacred, although the proceeds of property may well be reprehensible, therefore any offence against property is sacrilege and must be punished. Till a system eventuates which is based not on exploitation of man by man and class by class, prisons must be dreadful places, but at least there might be an effort to ameliorate the more savage side of the retaliation, and this could be done very easily."[8] The alternative system of which no doubt he is thinking is the Russian system described in his quotations from *A Physician's Tour in Soviet Russia*, by Sir James Purves-Stewart, the system of "correctional colonies" providing curative "treatment" for the different types of criminal.[9] There are two confusions here, to one of which we shall return later. First, Macartney confuses the retributive system with the punishment of one particular type of crime, offences against property, when he must have known that the majority of offenders against property do not find themselves in Dartmoor or even in Wandsworth. After all his own offence was not one against property—it was traffic with a foreign Power—and it was one for which in the classless society of Russia the punishment is death. It is surely clear that a retributive system may be adopted for any class of crime. Secondly, Macartney confuses injustice within a penal system with the wrongfulness of a penal system. When he pleads for "humane prisons" as if the essence of the prison should be humanity, or when Compton Mackenzie says the object of penal servitude should be reform, both of them are giving up punishment altogether, not altering it. A Russian "correctional colony," if its real object is curative treatment, is no more a "prison" than is an isolation hospital or a lunatic asylum. To this distinction between abolishing injustice in punishment and abolishing punishment altogether we must now turn.

It will be objected that my original question "Why ought X to be punished?" is an illegitimate isolation of the issue. I have treated the whole set of circumstances as determined. X is a citizen of a state. About his citizenship, whether willing or unwilling, I have asked no questions. About the government, whether it is good or bad, I do not enquire. X has broken a law. Concerning the law, whether it is well-devised or not, I have not asked. Yet all these questions are surely relevant before it can be decided whether a particular punishment is just. It is the essence of my position that none of these questions is relevant. Punishment is a corollary of law-breaking by a member of the society whose law is broken. This is a static and an abstract view but I see no escape from it. Considerations of utility come in on two quite different issues. Should there be laws, and what laws should there be? As a legislator I may ask what general types of action would benefit the community, and, among these, which can be "standardized" without loss, or should be standardized to achieve their full value. This, however, is not the primary question since particular laws may be altered or repealed. The choice which is the essential *prius* of punishment is the choice that there should be laws. The choice is not Hobson's. Other methods may be considered. A government might attempt to standardize certain modes of action by means of advice. It might proclaim its view and say "Citizens are requested" to follow this or that procedure. Or again it might decide to deal with each case as it arose in the manner most effective for the common welfare. Anarchists have wavered between these two alternatives and a third—that of doing nothing to enforce a standard of behaviour but merely giving arbitrational decisions between conflicting parties, decisions binding only by consent.

I think it can be seen without detailed examination of particular laws that the method of lawmaking has its own advantages. Its orders are explicit and general. It makes behaviour reliable and predictable. Its threat of punishment may be so effective as to make punishment unnecessary. It promises to the good citizen a certain security in his life. When I have talked to business men about some inequity in the law of liability they have usually said "Better a bad law than no law, for then we know where we are."

Someone may say I am drawing an impossible line. I deny that punishment is utilitarian; yet now I say that punishment is a corollary of law and we decide whether to have laws and which laws to have on utilitarian grounds. And surely it is only this corollary which distinguishes law from good advice or exhortation. This is a misunderstanding. Punishment is a corollary not of law but of law-breaking. Legislators do not choose to punish. They hope no punishment will be needed. Their laws would succeed even if no punishment occurred. The criminal makes the essential choice: he "brings it on himself." Other men obey the law because they see its order is reasonable, because of inertia, because of fear. In this whole area, and it may be the major part of the state, law achieves its ends without punishment. Clearly, then, punishment is not a corollary of law.

We may return for a moment to the question of amount and nature of punishment. It may be thought that this also is automatic. The law will include its own penalties and the judge will have no option. This, however, is again an initial choice of principle. If the laws do include their own penalties then the judge has no option. But the legislature might adopt a system which left complete or partial freedom to the judge, as we do except in the case of murder. Once again, what are the merits (regardless of particular laws, still more of particular cases) of fixed penalties and variable penalties? At first sight it would seem that all the advantages are with the variable penalties; for men who have broken the same law differ widely in degree of wickedness and responsibility. When, however, we remember that punishment is not an attempt to balance moral guilt this advantage is diminished. But there are still degrees of responsibility; I do not mean degrees of freedom of will but, for instance, degrees of complicity in a crime. The danger of allowing complete freedom to the judicature in fixing penalties is not merely that it lays too heavy a tax on human nature but that it would lead to the judge expressing in his penalty the degree of his own moral aversion to the crime. Or he might tend on deterrent grounds to punish more heavily a crime which was spreading and for which temptation and opportunity were frequent. Or again on deterrent grounds he might "make examples" by punishing ten times as heavily those criminals who are detected in cases in which nine out of ten evade detection. Yet we should revolt from all such punishments if they involved punishing theft more heavily than blackmail or negligence more heavily than premeditated assault. The death penalty for sheep-stealing might have been defended on such deterrent grounds. But we should dislike equating sheep-stealing with murder. Fixed penalties enable us to draw these distinctions between crimes. It is not that we can say how much imprisonment is right for a sheep-stealer. But we can grade crimes in a rough scale and penalties in a rough scale, and keep our heaviest penalties for what are socially the most serious wrongs regardless of whether these penalties will reform the criminal or whether they are exactly what deterrence would require. The compromise of laying down maximum penalties and allowing judges freedom below these limits allows for the arguments on both sides.

To return to the main issue, the position I am defending is that it is essential to a legal system that the infliction of a particular punishment should *not* be determined by the good *that particular punishment* will do either to the criminal or to "society." In exactly the same way it is essential to a credit system that the repayment of a particular debt should not be determined by the good that particular payment will do. One may consider the merits of a legal system or of a credit system, but the acceptance of either involves the surrender of utilitarian considerations in particular cases as they arise. This is in effect admitted by Ewing in one place where he says "It is the penal system as a whole which deters and not the punishment of any individual offender."[10]

To show that the choice between a legal system and its alternatives is one we do and must make, I may quote an early work of Lenin in which he was defending the Marxist tenet that the state is bound to "wither away" with the establishment of a classless society. He considers the possible objection that some wrongs by man against man are not economic and therefore that the abolition of classes would not *ipso facto* eliminate crime. But he sticks to the thesis that these surviving crimes should not be dealt with by law and judicature. "We are not Utopians and do not in the least deny the possibility and inevitability of excesses by *individual persons,* and equally the need to suppress such excesses. But for this no special machine, no special instrument of repression is needed. This will be done by the armed nation itself as simply and as readily as any crowd of civilized people even in modern society parts a pair of combatants or does not allow a woman to be outraged."[11] This alternative to law and punishment has obvious demerits. Any injury not committed in the presence of the crowd, any wrong which required skill to detect or pertinacity to bring home would go untouched. The lynching mob, which is Lenin's instrument of justice, is liable to error and easily deflected from its purpose or driven to extremes. It must be a mob, for there is to be no "machine." I do not say that no alternative machine to ours could be devised but it does seem certain that the absence of all "machines" would be intolerable. An alternative machine might be based on the view that "society" is responsible for all criminality, and this curative and protective system developed. This is the system of Butler's "Erewhon" and something like it seems to be growing up in Russia except for cases of "sedition."

We choose, then, or we acquiesce in and adopt the choice of others of, a legal system as one of our instruments for the establishment of the conditions of a good life. This choice is logically prior to and independent of the actual punishment of any particular persons or the passing of any particular laws. The legislators choose particular laws within the framework of this predetermined system. Once again a small society may illustrate the reality of these choices and the distinction between them. A Headmaster launching a new school must explicitly make both decisions. First, shall we have any rules at all? Second, what rules shall we have? The first decision is a genuine one and one of great importance. Would it not be better to have an "honour" system, by which public opinion in each house or form dealt with any offence? (This is the Lenin method.) Or would complete freedom be better? Or should he issue appeals and advice? Or should he personally deal with each malefactor individually, as the case arises, in the way most likely to improve his conduct? I can well imagine an idealistic Headmaster attempting to run a school with one of these methods or with a combination of several of them and therefore without punishment. I can even imagine that with a small school of, say, twenty pupils all open to direct personal psychological pressure from authority and from each other, these methods involving no "rules" would work. The pupils would of course grow up without two very useful habits, the habit of having some regular habits and the habit of obeying rules. But I suspect that most Headmasters, especially those of large schools, would either decide at once, or quickly be driven, to realize that some rules were necessary. This decision would be "utilitarian" in the sense that it would be determined by consideration of consequences. The question "what rules?" would then arise and again the issue is utilitarian. What action must be regularized for the school to work efficiently? The hours of arrival and departure, for instance, in a day school. But the one choice which is now no longer open to the Headmaster is whether he shall punish those who break the rules. For if he were to try to avoid this he would in fact simply be returning to the discarded method of appeals and good advice. Yet the Headmaster does not decide to punish. The pupils make the decision there. He decides actually to have rules and to threaten, but only hypothetically, to punish. The one essential condition which makes actual punishment just is a condition he *cannot* fulfil—namely that a rule should be broken.

I shall add a final word of consolation to the practical reformer. Nothing that I have said is meant to counter any movement for "penal reform" but only to insist that none of these reforms have anything to do with punishment. The only type of reformer who can claim to be reforming the system of punishment is a follower of Lenin or Samuel Butler who is genuinely attacking the *system* and who believes there should be no laws and no punishments. But our great British reformers have been concerned not with punishment but with its accessories. When a man is sentenced to imprisonment he is not sentenced also to partial starvation, to physical brutality, to pneumonia from damp cells and so on. And any movement which makes his food sufficient to sustain health, which counters the permanent tendency to brutality on the part of its warders, which gives him a dry or even a light and well-aired cell, is pure gain and does not touch the theory of punishment. Reformatory influences and prisoners' aid arrangements are also entirely unaffected by what I have said. I believe myself that it would be best if all such arrangements were made optional for the prisoner, so as to leave him in these cases a freedom of choice which would make it clear that they are not part of his punishment. If it is said that every such reform lessens a man's punishment, I think that is simply muddled thinking which, if it were clear, would be mere brutality. For instance, a prisoners' aid society is said to lighten his punishment, because otherwise he would suffer not merely imprisonment but also unemployment on release. But he was sentenced to imprisonment, not imprisonment *plus* unemployment. If I promise to help a friend and through special circumstances I find that keeping my promise will involve upsetting my day's work, I do not say that I really promised to help him and to ruin my day's work. And if another friend carries on my work for me I do not regard him as carrying out part of my promise, nor as stopping me from carrying it out myself. He merely removes an indirect and regrettable consequence of my keeping my promise. So with punishment. The Prisoners' Aid Society does not alter a man's punishment nor diminish it, but merely removes an indirect and regrettable consequence of it. And anyone who thinks that a criminal cannot make this distinction and will regard all the inconvenience to him that comes to him as punishment, need only talk to a prisoner or two to find out how sharply they resent these wanton additions to a punishment which by itself they will accept as just. Macartney's chapter on "Food" in the book quoted above is a good illustration of this point, as are also his comments on Clayton's administration. "To keep a man in prison for many years at considerable expense and then to free him charged to the eyes with uncontrollable venom and hatred generated by the treatment he has received in gaol, does not appear to be sensible." Clayton "endeavoured to send a man out of prison in a reasonable state of mind. 'Well, I've done my time. They were not too bad to me. Prison is prison and not a bed of roses. Still they didn't rub it in. . . .' "[12] This "reasonable state of mind" is one in which a prisoner on release feels he has been punished but not *additionally* insulted or ill-treated. I feel convinced that penal reformers would meet with even more support if they were clear that they were *not* attempting to alter the system of punishment but to give its victims "fair play." We have no more right to starve a convict than to starve an animal. We have no more right to keep a convict in a Dartmoor cell "down which the water trickles night and day"[13] than we have to keep a child in such a place. If our reformers really want to alter the system of punishment, let them come out clearly with their alternative and preach, for instance, that no human being is responsible for any wrong-doing, that all the blame is on society, that curative or protective measures should be adopted, forcibly if necessary, as they are with infection or insanity. Short of this let them admit that the essence of prison is deprivation of liberty for the breaking of law, and that deprivation of food or of health or of books is unjust. And if our sentimentalists cry "coddling of prisoners," let us ask them also to come out clearly into the open and incorporate whatever starvation and disease and brutality they think necessary *into the sentences they propose.*[14] If it is said that some prisoners will prefer such reformed prisons, with adequate food and aired cells, to the outer world, we may retort that their numbers are probably not greater than those of the masochists who like to be flogged. Yet we do not hear the same ''coddling'' critics suggest abolition of the lash on the grounds that some criminals may like it. Even if the abolition from our prisons of all maltreatment other than that imposed by law results in a few down-and-outs breaking a window (as O. Henry's hero did) to get a night's lodging, the country will lose less than she does by her present method of sending out her discharged convicts ''charged with venom and hatred'' because of the additional and unconvenanted ''rubbing it in'' which they have received.

I hope I have established both the theoretical importance and the practical value of distinguishing between penal reform as we know and approve it—that reform which alters the accompaniments of punishment without touching its essence—and those attacks on punishment itself which are made not only by reformers who regard criminals as irresponsible and in need of treatment, but also by every judge who announces that he is punishing a man to deter others or to protect society, and by every juryman who is moved to his decision by the moral baseness of the accused rather than by his legal guilt.

NOTES

1. p. 97.
2. p. 165. My italics.
3. pp. 165–166.
4. p. 298.
5. p. 301.
6. p. 255.
7. p. 400.
8. pp. 166, 167.
9. p. 229.
10. A. C. Ewing, *The Morality of Punishment* (London: Routledge and Kegan Paul, Ltd., 1929), p. 66.
11. *The State and Revolution* (Eng. trans.), p. 93. Original italics.
12. p. 152.
13. *Op. cit.,* p. 258.
14. ''One of the minor curiosities of jail life was that they quickly provided you with a hundred worries which left you no time or energy for worrying about your sentence, long or short. . . . Rather as if you were thrown into a fire with spikes in it, and the spikes hurt you so badly that you forget about the fire. But then your punishment would *be* the spikes not the fire. Why did they pretend it was only a fire, when they knew very well about the spikes?'' (From *Lifer* by Jim Phelan, p. 40).

M. R. GLOVER

Mr. Mabbott on Punishment*

M. R. Glover (1898–   ) was a lecturer and director of Social Service Training at the University of Keele.

I find it hard to see that Mr. Mabbott in his article on punishment (*Mind,* No. 190, April 1939) has really adduced any ethical arguments that establish the retributive theory; and the considerations he brings forward are mainly logical and legal.

*M. R. Glover, ''Mr. Mabbott on Punishment,'' *Mind,* XLVIII (1939), 488–501. Reprinted by permission of the editor of *Mind.*

The logical point seems to be that the very definition of law involves punishment for its infringement, so that once you have law instead of advice or request, punishment is logically entailed; in fact, the question whether punishment should be enforced does not arise, because it has been settled already; Mr. Mabbott illustrated this from his own experience of administering a college rule of compulsory chapel. This view implies that it cannot be right to be illogical. This, of course, is the basis of Kant's moral theory; and Hobbes seems to have had the same conviction very strongly; he maintained that voluntary law-breaking was "somewhat like to that which in the disputation of scholars is called absurdity" (III, 119, Laird's reference). It does not seem clear to me that it can never be right to be illogical. I realise that the force of this opinion must be lessened by the fact that I belong to the weaker and notoriously illogical sex; but the opinion is not confined to my sex. I am told that my great-great-uncle, serving on a jury to try a boy for sheep-stealing, refused to give the verdict "guilty" and delayed the jury for an indefinite time until out of fatigue they agreed with him, although he and they and everybody else were convinced that the boy had stolen the sheep. Because the penalty was death. It is illogical to serve on a jury instead of suffering whatever the penalty may be for refusing to serve, and then not fulfil the juryman's oath to give a true verdict. But if this deliberate illogicality is the best way to get an iniquitous law altered it might be right. It is true that if everybody everywhere held themselves at liberty to be illogical, in the sense of breaking their oaths and promises, society would break down; but no sensible person would universalise the rule "break your promises"; the rule "keep your promises" might be used as rules are used in medical practice, as principles of extremely general application, which it is your duty occasionally and at your peril to break.

Secondly, Mr. Mabbott argues that punishment has nothing to do with moral wrong-doing but only with law-breaking. But if law-breaking and wrong-doing were quite distinct, I cannot see why it would be necessary to find any moral justification whatever for punishment for law-breaking, any more than for prescribing a penalty for foot-faulting at tennis.[1]

But is this momentous separation of law and morals really intended? It would, as it seems to me, imply that the whole of political activity, which is the field of law, was exempt from moral considerations. Mr. Mabbott's point, I imagine, is that laws in general have a moral basis, inasmuch as no society can live without rules, but that it is not necessary that all particular regulations should have a justification of their own in moral feeling; indeed that every real society maintains and accepts some rules whose function is to keep alive the sense of corporate order, but which taken in themselves have no moral significance. This seems to be true, but it is notorious that there is a limit to people's capacity to respect meaningless or silly regulations.[2]

If we are not prepared to divorce law and politics, those who make laws have to ask themselves both the general question, whether it is right for a man or for society to impose suffering on another human being in the interests of order, and also whether particular laws are justified. Mr. Mabbott wants to remove the real responsibility for imposing suffering from the legislator on the ground that "Punishment is the corollary not of law but of law-breaking. Legislators do not choose to punish. They hope punishment will not be needed. Their laws would succeed even if no punishment took place. The criminal makes the essential choice, he brings it on himself" (page 161). When a headmaster has decided to have rules prescribing punishments for certain offences, "the headmaster does not decide to punish. He decides actually to have certain rules and to threaten, but only hypothetically, to punish. The one essential condition which makes actual punishment just, is a condition he cannot fulfil, namely that a rule should be broken." It does not appear to me that the makers of laws and rules can be exonerated from the moral responsibility for the punishment; it seems to me as though I were to say, "I shall turn out a dangerous bull into a field, and if people trespass in order to pick fritillaries and get hurt, it is their look-out, I do not make them trespass." A railway company that decides to build a level crossing may claim that people will get hurt there only if they drive faster than they ought to drive, or cross without looking; nevertheless, the railway company always feels that it ought to take responsibility and try to save people from actualising by their own action, the only condition that can make an accident possible, by building gates. The farmer who owns the bull, the railway company and the legislator are all in the position of doing something that entails suffering for other people under certain conditions: they cannot escape the moral obligation of considering whether it is right for them to take a decision that contains this possibility.

The early Christian Fathers were very doubtful whether the coercion of one man by another with the threat of violence in the name of government was right; they thought it was a condition of affairs by no means ideal but necessitated by the Fall. Mr. Mabbott seems to me to settle this ancient question too easily by reference to the opinions of headmasters and criminals. The moral judgment of a criminal that he or another deserved to suffer is not one that I would accept without criticism; a criminal is at least as likely as anybody else to have a defective moral sensibility. Headmasters, like other men, are under a constant temptation to save time, and choose the most convenient way of achieving their estimable purposes. But the most convenient is not necessarily the most moral either for them or states; it might be right to take a lot more trouble in order to train boys by another method. This is beginning to be recognised in the case of the training of small infants. Certain methods which teach babies not to expect that their mothers will come if they cry, are very convenient for mothers; they can leave the baby alone and get on with their jobs; the baby either gets into a habit of constant hopeless crying (to the distraction of the neighbours) or gives it up as useless; some psychologists nowadays assert that these methods may do the child harm. Most mothers would agree that if this is really the case they must abandon this convenient system, and adopt one that will give them more trouble.

It is obviously possible to produce a utilitarian justification of punishment, on the ground that we do not at present know any other way of securing the order which is the necessary basis of the common good life. But this would not justify punishment if we did know another way; and the Russian experiment in curative treatment may bring a better way to light.

In Mr. Mabbott's view, however, the utilitarian argument does not stand alone, because punishment is right in itself apart from its results, as retribution. His chief ground seems to be: (1) That we all recognise that it is wrong for an innocent man to suffer, as though it followed from this that it is right for the guilty to do so; (2) That if the utility of deterrence were all that were at stake, a system of well-chosen lies would do as well as actual punishment, and since we should not approve of such lying, we are compelled really to punish. I contest both these arguments.

(1) The conviction that it is not right for the innocent to suffer does not entail the logical corollary that the guilty should; it might be right that neither should. But I would suggest that it is not really established that it is invariably more morally wrong for the innocent to suffer than for the alternative state of affairs to ensue. When I was in the North-West Frontier Province of India a few years ago, I formed the impression that the vendetta continued to flourish there partly because the Government were handicapped in their adminstration by their difficulty in securing any evidence upon which to convict known murderers; anyone who gave such evidence destined himself to be the next victim of the vendetta; so a large proportion of accused murderers got off. The opinion was therefore widely held among the people that the Government would not punish for murder, and the responsibility, which they felt very heavily, lay with the private family. It appears to me thinkable that in such a case the right thing to do would be so to alter the law of province that a man could be made to suffer the death penalty on grounds nearer to those of Oriental law; e.g., upon the conviction of the judge, not necessarily grounded on evidence given in public, that a man is guilty. The chance of an innocent man suffering might be a lesser evil than the inability of the Government to give security to anybody and to protect the lives of the people. (I believe this would be felt by the people of the province to be a great improvement on the present system which they do not at all admire or understand.)

(2) An obvious answer to the unsatisfactoriness of alleging that punishment has taken place when it has not, is that such lies cannot be efficient for very long. The unwillingness to break promise with the dead seems to me not to be a parallel because it involves another feeling altogether. I believe we value candour and good faith between persons for its own sake; and we feel that as long as we are keeping faith with the dead a certain relation with them, which is of value to us, persists and they are not wholly separated from us. Anyway the fact that lies about punishment may be wrong does not show that punishment itself is right.

The question whether there is a rightness in retribution itself, apart from its consequences, seems to me still uncertain; I think it is a matter on which our moral sensibility has no certain deliverance to make. I find myself that there are people on whom I would choose to inflict suffering if I could, in retribution for what they have done, and their suffering would seem to me fitting and proper. But I imagine most people find that when it actually lies with them to inflict pain, on someone they know and in some degree care for, in retribution (for instance to give pain by saying something, that is not expected to make them any better, in retribution for wrong they have done in causing such pain to others), we do not wish, at least in cold blood, to take this course.

It would do no good, we say. Whether either of these sentiments constitutes moral insight I do not know. But it may be remarked that those whom we agree to regard as "the best and wisest and the most just" have not shown any sign of desire that there should be retribution upon those who have done them desperate wrong.

NOTES

1. Nevertheless I should myself maintain that any human activity may become a matter of moral significance, even sport; and that there might be moral considerations involved in the rules of a game, *e.g.* over the question of body-line bowling.

2. *e.g.*, 'Solicitor' in his book *English Justice* asserts that the law of England is greatly brought into contempt in the poorer parts of London, because the laws that prescribe where you may bet, and where you may not, appear to rest on no moral considerations whatever. And it is commonly held that Prohibition in the U.S.A. caused a formidable outbreak of lawlessness, because very respectable people refused to obey a law that seemed to them to interfere with liberty without moral grounds.

JONATHAN GLOVER

Punishment in the Spirit of Utilitarianism*

Jonathan Glover (1941–   ) teaches philosophy at New College, Oxford.

1. AN APPROACH TO PUNISHMENT

The fourth question to be discussed ('whom should we punish?') is the one most closely related to the topic of responsibility. It is possible, before examining this last question, to outline an approach to punishment in the context of which to discuss questions of legal responsibility.

Traditional utilitarianism sought to resolve all moral questions into matters of whether or not certain acts or institutions were more likely than any possible others to bring about the goals of maximizing happiness and minimizing suffering. Criticisms of this doctrine are often practical ones. There are difficulties in measuring happiness, in comparing different kinds of happiness, in comparing the happiness of different people, and in predicting the consequences of one's actions. These practical difficulties are real, but they are perhaps not always as daunting as is sometimes thought. That happiness cannot be measured precisely does not seem a very formidable objection to the view that it would be increased if we produced and distributed enough food for everyone to have enough to eat. But there are other familiar criticisms of utilitarianism, of a more fundamental kind. These are moral criticisms, made from the standpoint of other values, such as justice, freedom, or the sanctity of life, that are held to have an importance that is independent of their contribution to human happiness.

The moral objections to utilitarianism may make one reluctant to say that the maximizing of happiness should be the only goal of social policy. But it is possible to outline a moral approach to punishment, retaining something of the spirit of utilitarianism, that is sufficiently different to meet many of these objections. The new doctrine would accept that to the appraisal within this moral approach of institutions or actions it is crucial whether or not, and to what extent, they benefit or harm people. (Though here, in order to allow room for moral objections to cruelty to animals, 'people' should perhaps be modified to 'conscious beings'.) But 'benefit' and 'harm' need to be interpreted more widely than the traditional utilitarian terms 'happiness' and 'suffering', or than the even narrower 'pleasure' and 'pain'. In a previous chapter[1] it was suggested that a harmful condition is one that reduces a person's pleasure or want satisfaction (whether or not he is aware of this) or one that increases his physical or mental suffering. And

*From Jonathan Glover, *Responsibility* (New Jersey: Humanities Press; London: Routledge & Kegan Paul, Ltd., 1970), pp. 150–160. Reprinted by permission of the author and the publishers.

one can talk of a condition being harmful because it reduces someone's want satisfaction by comparison with what it might be, and not merely by comparison with what it was. The concept of harm in general is to be understood along these lines. Similarly, whether some act, policy or institution benefits someone depends on whether or not it increases his pleasure or want satisfaction, or else on whether or not it reduces his physical or mental suffering. On this view, pleasure is not the only benefit, nor pain the only harm. One can see that it could be argued that people benefit from having a large area of freedom, from having their individuality respected, or from an atmosphere of social equality. All of these, while arguably of intrinsic value in themselves, could be defended as means to the maximization of want satisfaction or pleasure, or to the avoidance of suffering. Similarly, distributive justice could, up to a point, be defended in these terms. When someone is given an unfairly small share of a benefit being distributed, he may be harmed by the frustration of expectations or by the growth of resentment, over and above the harm which could be calculated merely by measuring the amount of the benefit lost.

I should not wish to defend the view that actions or policies should be judged solely in terms of human benefit or harm as outlined here. I do not wish to forgo the possibility of assigning to justice, freedom or other ends a value independent of their tendency to increase the balance of want satisfaction and pleasure over frustration and physical or mental suffering. But much of the attraction of traditional utilitarianism can be preserved by stipulating that an action or policy should be ruled out where it causes harm to anyone and yet no one benefits from it. This restriction does not rule out the pursuit of other ends, even where they do not increase the ratio of benefit over harm: all that is required is that as a result either someone benefits or else no one is harmed. It also leaves it open to us to introduce further restrictions limiting the kinds of benefit that are to count as acceptable justifications for causing harm: the pleasure a sadist gets from the suffering of another is one kind of benefit we may choose to exclude.

This restriction, that no one should be harmed where no one benefits, may seem completely trivial. It is certainly compatible with a variety of moral attitudes and beliefs. But it is not a wholly empty

restriction. If, in pursuit of some ideal of social justice, we take from the rich and give to the poor, our restriction is not flouted, for the poor benefit. But if, unable to sell the millionaire's Rolls-Royce, we confiscate it and throw it into the sea, on the grounds that equality of deprivation is better than unfair luxury, we are flouting the restriction. We may not harm even the millionaire unless someone benefits from this. (I should wish to exclude the pleasure of others at hearing of the millionaire's loss from the category of justifying benefits, as I should wish to exclude a sadist's pleasure in the physical suffering of others.)

And, more relevant to the theory of punishment, there is the difficulty the restriction raises for the more aggressive forms of retributive justice. To demand that the guilty should suffer on purely retributive grounds would be to support a policy that created harm without compensating benefits.[2] Other people's pleasure at hearing of someone getting his deserts, a possible candidate for the role of a compensating benefit, could also be excluded from the category of acceptable justifications. But, in order to prevent an indefinitely long list of arbitrary exclusions of various kinds of benefit, it is necessary to reformulate the principle which should now be stated as follows: *An action or policy is always morally unjustifiable where it causes harm to anyone, and yet no one benefits from it in an acceptable way. A benefit is only unacceptable where it consists in pleasure of any kind at the misfortunes or suffering of others.* This principle rules out any attempt to justify punishing someone merely on the grounds that he deserves it. But it does not rule out the negative principle that people should not be given any punishment that they do not deserve. Nor does the principle say that *any* harm is justifiable provided that someone benefits from it.

What kinds of penal principles would be compatible with this restriction? There is no place for retribution as a general aim justifying the institution of punishment. The reduction of the crime rate is clearly a possible justifying aim, as is the avoidance of unofficial retaliation. But I should advocate subjecting these aims to two familiar utilitarian restrictions. One is that *we are only justified in punishing where there are good grounds for supposing that we are doing less harm than we are preventing.* This can only be the case where, as well as other conditions being satisfied, there is evidence that the abolition of punishment for a particular offence would significantly increase either the frequency of the 'crime' or else the probability of unofficial retaliation. And so it seems that serious acceptance of this approach to punishment would involve a willingness to experiment far more boldly than we do now. One relevant experiment would be to refrain from punishing a crime for a trial period to see how much difference to the crime rate this made. If total suspension of punishment for a crime was found to increase its frequency, there would then be room for a further experimental period in which punishment was administered, but in smaller doses. Only by means of such investigations can we be sure that we are not inflicting pointless suffering.

There is the further utilitarian restriction that *punishment is only justified where there are good grounds for thinking that, as a method of achieving the aims in question, punishment causes less harm than any other equally effective method.* Serious acceptance of this restriction would involve being ready to experiment with other methods, such as taking more seriously the possibilities of educating people to see the undesirability of various crimes. For this we could make use both of schools[3] and of the mass media. We could also change those features of the social environment that seem to stimulate crime.[4]

The view that punishment is a necessary feature of any practically possible human society seems needlessly dogmatic. There is no adequate evidence that human nature is so static that we cannot devise a society in which prohibitions backed by sanctions would be redundant. But it must be admitted, preferably grudgingly, that we do not now live in such a society. We are sufficiently willing to harm each other in pursuit of our own ends for restraining sanctions to be necessary. It is in this context that the aims of a penal system must be considered. In a system guided by the principles mentioned, the question of punishment only arises in restricted classes of cases. These are those where the most effective method of making someone give up crime is unpleasant, or at least unwanted by the offender, or where the offender is too dangerous to let loose, or where the punishment is aimed at deterring others. (For practical purposes in many communities one other type of case can be left on one side: that in which punishment might be administered to prevent unofficial retaliation.) And it is possible that increasing knowledge derived from experiments in doing without punishment, or in finding substitutes

for it, will reduce the number of cases where punishment is permissible.

2. MANIPULATION

A frequently voiced objection to penal policies with non-retributive aims is that they appear to involve manipulation of people. In the type of policy mentioned here, the danger of manipulation comes in at two points. There may seem a hint of Brave New World in the proposal to experiment in teaching children the undesirability of various crimes. And there is perhaps a sinister sound to the proposal that punishment should often be replaced by alternative methods of treatment.

The importance people attach to being treated as responsible agents underlies some of the apparently more paradoxical objections to utilitarianism, as when critics talk of a criminal's need or right to be punished. This is one of the anti-utilitarian themes in Dostoyevsky's portrait of Raskolnikov, where we are persuaded that he feels an overwhelming need to expiate his crime by undergoing punishment. One may come to think this merely part of Dostoyevsky's private world, described with such power that one momentarily took it to be how the real world is. Philosophers have pointed out that there is something paradoxical in a desire for punishment of which most criminals are unaware, or a right to it which most of them would willingly forgo. But this dismissal is too brisk. While no doubt few people desire punishment, many are distressed if not treated as responsible agents. A refusal to punish someone can constitute a denial of his status as a responsible agent. A team of Massachusetts psychiatrists wrote about a convicted murderer: 'We find Mr. Cooper an interesting challenge in addition to being genuinely interested in him as a human being. Our impression is that he is quite treatable and might someday be a useful member of society.'[5] To see someone as 'treatable' or as 'an interesting challenge' may be well-intentioned, but it is not to see him as one's equal as a responsible agent. It is intelligible that people who are not mentally ill should sometimes prefer punishment to this sort of patronizing humanitarianism.[6]

But when some methods of preventing crime other than by punishment are described as 'manipulation', it is unclear exactly what this charge comes to. Criticisms of advertising, propaganda, bribery, blackmail, 'behaviour therapy' as a treatment for neuroses and of Brave New World, often take the form of accusations that people are being manipulated. But, if rational discussion of these matters is to be sustained, it is necessary not to allow the emotional overtones of the word 'manipulation' to blind us to its diversity of application.

One type of manipulation can easily be described. This involves influencing someone's behaviour in such a way that he has no means of knowing what is causing him to act in the way he does. To make a man do something by means of subliminal advertising, post-hypnotic suggestion or certain types of drug is normally to manipulate him in this way. While it is true that someone with great experience of post-hypnotic suggestion or subliminal advertising may be able to guess that one of these is responsible for an apparently random impulse he feels, the great majority of people is unused to these techniques and, without being told, has no means of detecting their influence.

A milder form of manipulation includes all other kinds of non-rational persuasion. Much propaganda and normal advertising falls under this category, as does 'behaviour therapy': the application of conditioning techniques in an attempt to alter a pattern of behaviour. The type of persuasion in question is non-rational in that no attempt is made to argue that what is advertised is helpful to people: instead, associations are created in people's minds that in no way reflect real causal or logical relationships. When posters advertising cigarettes depict love scenes, or election notices bear photographs of a happy family enjoying a picnic, the means of persuasion are similar in principle to behaviour therapy. When the behaviour therapist attempts to stop someone smoking by making him sick every time he has a cigarette, the treatment is on the basis of a purely non-rational association: there is no suggestion that in daily life cigarettes are likely to cause sickness. This is also true of the very different association that the cigarette advertiser wishes to create. In real life smoking no more brings about sexual gratification than politicians bring about picnics. The advertiser is not like someone who makes a false claim in a discussion: the type of advertising under consideration is manipulation because no claim is specifically made. The advertiser hopes the association will be made, but not consciously subjected to examination.

Sometimes accusations of manipulation refer not to the method of persuasion but to its aim. To persuade someone to act in a certain way by means of blackmail is a kind of manipulation, but it is not included in either of the categories mentioned above. A man influenced by blackmail is normally aware of this influence, and the persuasion is in one sense perfectly rational. The association he makes between refusal to obey the blackmailer and subsequent physical assault or public disgrace may correspond exactly to the facts of the situation: the blackmailer may carry out his threats. The key feature of this form of manipulation is not that the actions advocated are not rational means to the ends of the agent, but rather that the agent is provided with new ends in order to further the aims of the manipulator. The blackmailer furthers his own aims by providing his victim with a new end: that of avoiding the threatened unpleasantness.

This kind of manipulation is not only to be found in cases of blackmail or bribery. There are many other ways in which someone can further his own aims by providing other people with new objectives. This is perhaps the main feature that distinguishes indoctrination from education. An educator is not debarred from putting forward his own views, or those of his party or church, but his long term aim will be to further the child's own interests by providing him with the critical equipment to judge those views for himself. An indoctrinator, on the other hand, puts first his own aim of propagating a particular set of views, and tries to instil into the child the pattern of values and aims he considers desirable, giving at best a lower priority to the development of powers of critical thought. It may be objected that indoctrination is often carried out by people who believe that it is in the best interests of the person they are indoctrinating. If one considers one knows the truth about religion, morals or politics, one may think that the end of communicating this truth can justifiably be given first priority, and hence that the development of critical thought is of lesser importance. But even where the aims of the indoctrinator are altruistic, they are still his own aims, and not (at least before the indoctrination) either the present aims of his victim, or a way of realizing those present aims. It is true that educators are concerned with stimulating people to adopt new aims, as well as with imparting means of realizing present ones. But in accordance with the priorities that distinguish him from the indoctrinator, the educator prefers a rationally argued rejection of the proffered new aims to an uncritical acceptance of them. He is primarily concerned to help people discover what they want to do, while even a benevolent indoctrinator will put other aims of his own first. High-minded indoctrination is still a kind of manipulation.

It is a distaste for this third kind of manipulation that underlies much criticism of advertising. Some advertising that is neither subliminal nor based on non-rational associations is still open to the charge of manipulating people by creating in them for commercial gain desires that they would not otherwise have. The suggestion is that advertisements do not merely provide us with information about the different products we can buy, but often also deliberately create artificial or 'synthesized' wants for products that do not satisfy any of our natural desires.[7] This view as it stands is open to the objection that there is no clear way of distinguishing between wants that are natural and wants that are artificial, and to the further objection that, if there is such a distinction, there seems no reason to suppose that the creation of artificial wants is of itself undesirable. It has been pointed out that the desires for sanitation and for museums are in their different ways created rather than natural wants.[8]

But the opposition to this kind of advertising need not rest on any dubious distinction between natural and artificial desires. The central feature that makes this advertising a kind of manipulation is that it creates desires that were not previously present (but not therefore any less 'natural') for the commercial gain of the advertiser. It is in aim that advertising is distinguished from the education that creates new desires for sanitation or for museums, or a new desire to see *King Lear*. If the main aim of the advertisement was to benefit the public by providing them with a new desire to try a new form of biscuit, this would not be manipulation. But it is, because the purpose of creating the new desire is to further the aims of someone else. The educator is distinguished both from the indoctrinator and the advertiser in that his main aim is to show people what can be gained from, say, *King Lear,* so that they are in a position to make an informed choice as to whether this is the kind of play they like. He does not have as his main aim the creation of large audiences whenever *King Lear* is performed.

From the description of only these three varieties of manipulation, one can see that it is unplausible to suggest that all manipulation of people is to be

avoided at all costs. It is hard to see what reasonable objection there could be to voluntary submission to the non-rational persuasive techniques of behaviour therapy in order to cure one's neurosis. Objections are more plausible where the conditioning is not voluntarily undertaken. One may object either on the grounds of disapproving of what people are being persuaded of or to do, or else on the basis of a belief in the desirability of persuasion being carried out openly and rationally. Objections to the form of manipulation that involves giving new desires or ends to someone else in order to further one's own aims are likely to be based on some principle similar to Kant's: 'all rational beings come under the law that each of them must treat itself and all others never merely as means, but in every case at the same time as ends in themselves'.

In the approach to punishment proposed here, it would be possible to build restrictions to operate against all those kinds of manipulation that harm people. If one thinks, as one surely can, that it would be harmful to children (or adults) if they were made to hold moral beliefs by means of drugs, hypnosis or subliminal advertising, it is possible to argue against experimenting with these techniques. One might also, on similar grounds, restrict the use of other, less hidden, non-rational techniques of persuasion, such as behaviour therapy. (Though one may sometimes feel that some non-rational means of persuasion are harmless, or alternatively that the objections to some forms of crime are stronger than the objections to non-rational persuasion.)

The third type of manipulation mentioned involves giving someone new aims in order to further the aims of someone else, as in blackmail and in some types of indoctrination. This is the kind of manipulation that may involve breaking the rather obscure Kantian rule that we should never treat people 'merely as means'. It is sometimes suggested that the replacement of punishment by other forms of treatment is a policy open to criticism on these grounds. If this objection is well founded, it is necessary to weigh up the benefits to be gained by the policy, and to decide whether or not the use of these means would be too high a price to pay.

But, when the proposed policy is compared to that followed at present, the objection that it would involve this form of manipulation seems artificial. For our present policy is at least as much open to the same criticisms. At the moment, we send a man to prison, not in order to benefit him, but in order to provide him and others with new aims, which will benefit the public by reducing the number of crimes. And, if the compulsory treatment proposed is hedged about with restrictions on the types of non-rational persuasion permitted, it can hardly be said that we are treating the offender *merely* as a means. And, if the objection is that we should never treat people even partly as a means, this seems to say that under no circumstances should we ever to any degree sacrifice one person's interests to those of a greater number of people. But this moral principle, which would involve opposing the detention of a dangerous murderer against his will, is unlikely to commend itself to many.

NOTES

1. Chapter 6, section 6.

2. A person may benefit from being treated as a responsible agent. But it is hard to believe that treating someone as a responsible agent must sometimes involve inflicting retributive suffering on him.

3. The contrast between the role of schools as it often is and as it might be is brought out in Miss Leila Berg's book on Risinghill.

4. Cf. Terence Morris, *The Criminal Area,* 1958. As means of reducing the amount of crime, education and changing the social environment are not the only alternatives to the use after the offence of punishment or treatment. 'Criminals' are not one homogeneous class. But there is evidence that many of the most anti-social among them have not been loved enough as children: often they have been 'unwanted' children. It seems that one method of reducing crime (and much other misery) would be by social expenditure on much more active and efficient education about contraceptives, and upon their free provision. Utilitarians also rightly point out that some acts are prohibited by law, but should not be. Here we could reduce the crime rate by repealing the laws.

5. Quoted in Szasz, *Law, Liberty and Psychiatry,* 1963, Ch. 12.

6. Mr. Derek Parfit has pointed out to me that in a world without blame the objection on the grounds of not being treated as an equal would collapse.

7. Cf. Galbraith, *The Affluent Society,* 1958, Ch. 11.

8. Both these objections are made by Professor Richard Wollheim, *Socialism and Culture,* 1961.

JOHN RAWLS

Punishment*

John Rawls (1921–   ) teaches philosophy at Harvard. He is the author of the widely read work in social philosophy, A Theory of Justice.

In this paper I want to show the importance of the distinction between justifying a practice[1] and justifying a particular action falling under it, and I want to explain the logical basis of this distinction and how it is possible to miss its significance. While the distinction has frequently been made,[2] and is now becoming commonplace, there remains the task of explaining the tendency either to overlook it altogether, or to fail to appreciate its importance.

To show the importance of the distinction I am

*From John Rawls, "Two Concepts of Rules," Part I, *Philosophical Review,* LXIV (1955), 3–13. Reprinted by permission of the author and the *Philosophical Review.*

going to defend utilitarianism against those objections which have traditionally been made against it in connection with punishment and the obligation to keep promises. I hope to show that if one uses the distinction in question then one can state utilitarianism in a way which makes it a much better explication of our considered moral judgments than these traditional objections would seem to admit.[3] Thus the importance of the distinction is shown by the way it strengthens the utilitarian view regardless of whether that view is completely defensible or not. . . .

The subject of punishment, in the sense of attaching legal penalties to the violation of legal rules, has always been a troubling moral question.[4] The trouble about it has not been that people disagree as to whether or not punishment is justifiable. Most people have held that, freed from certain abuses, it is an acceptable institution. Only a few have rejected punishment entirely, which is rather surprising when one considers all that can be said against it. The difficulty is with the justification of punishment: various arguments for it have been given by moral philosophers, but so far none of them has won any sort of general acceptance; no justification is without those who detest it. I hope to show that the use of the aforementioned distinction enables one to state the utilitarian view in a way which allows for the sound points of its critics.

For our purposes we may say that there are two justifications of punishment. What we may call the retributive view is that punishment is justified on the grounds that wrongdoing merits punishment. It is morally fitting that a person who does wrong should suffer in proportion to his wrongdoing. That a criminal should be punished follows from his guilt, and the severity of the appropriate punishment depends on the depravity of his act. The state of affairs where a wrongdoer suffers punishment is morally better than the state of affairs where he does not; and it is better irrespective of any of the consequences of punishing him.

What we may call the utilitarian view holds that on the principle that bygones are bygones and that only future consequences are material to present decisions, punishment is justifiable only by reference to the probable consequences of maintaining it as one of the devices of the social order. Wrongs committed in the past are, as such, not relevant considerations for deciding what to do. If punishment can be shown to promote effectively the interest of society it is justifiable, otherwise it is not.

I have stated these two competing views very roughly to make one feel the conflict between them: one feels the force of *both* arguments and one wonders how they can be reconciled. From my introductory remarks it is obvious that the resolution which I am going to propose is that in this case one must distinguish between justifying a practice as a system of rules to be applied and enforced, and justifying a particular action which falls under these rules; utilitarian arguments are appropriate with regard to questions about practices, while retributive arguments fit the application of particular rules to particular cases.

We might try to get clear about this distinction by imagining how a father might answer the question of his son. Suppose the son asks, "Why was *J* put in jail yesterday?" The father answers, "Because

he robbed the bank at *B*. He was duly tried and found guilty. That's why he was put in jail yesterday." But suppose the son had asked a different question, namely, "Why do people put other people in jail?" Then the father might answer, "To protect good people from bad people" or "To stop people from doing things that would make it uneasy for all of us; for otherwise we wouldn't be able to go to bed at night and sleep in peace." There are two very different questions here. One question emphasizes the proper name: it asks why *J* was punished rather than someone else, or it asks what he was punished for. The other question asks why we have the institution of punishment; why do people punish one another rather than, say, always forgiving one another?

Thus the father says in effect that a particular man is punished, rather than some other man, because he is guilty, and he is guilty because he broke the law (past tense). In his case the law looks back, the judge looks back, the jury looks back, and a penalty is visited upon him for something he did. That a man is to be punished, and what his punishment is to be, is settled by its being shown that he broke the law and that the law assigns that penalty for the violation of it.

On the other hand we have the institution of punishment itself, and recommend and accept various changes in it, because it is thought by the (ideal) legislator and by those to whom the law applies that, as a part of a system of law impartially applied from case to case arising under it, it will have the consequence, in the long run, of furthering the interests of society.

One can say, then, that the judge and the legislator stand in different positions and look in different directions: one to the past, the other to the future. The justification of what the judge does, *qua* judge, sounds like the retributive view; the justification of what the (ideal) legislator does, *qua* legislator, sounds like the utilitarian view. Thus both views have a point (this is as it should be since intelligent and sensitive persons have been on both sides of the argument); and one's initial confusion disappears once one sees that these views apply to persons holding different offices with different duties; and situated differently with respect to the system of rules that make up the criminal law.[5]

One might say, however, that the utilitarian view is more fundamental since it applies to a more fundamental office, for the judge carries out the legislator's will so far as he can determine it. Once the legislator decides to have laws and to assign penalties for their violation (as things are there must be both the law and the penalty) an institution is set up which involves a retributive conception of particular cases. It is part of the concept of the criminal law as a system of rules that the application and enforcement of these rules in particular cases should be justifiable by arguments of a retributive character. The decision whether or not to use law rather than some other mechanism of social control, and the decision as to what laws to have and what penalties to assign, may be settled by utilitarian arguments; but if one decides to have laws then one has decided on something whose working in particular cases is retributive in form.[6]

The answer, then, to the confusion engendered by the two views of punishment is quite simple: one distinguishes two offices, that of the judge and that of the legislator, and one distinguishes their different stations with respect to the system of rules which make up the law; and then one notes that the different sorts of considerations which would usually be offered as reasons for what is done under the cover of these offices can be paired off with the competing justifications of punishment. One reconciles the two views by the time-honored device of making them apply to different situations.

But can it really be this simple? Well, this answer allows for the apparent intent of each side. Does a person who advocates the retributive view necessarily advocate, as an *institution,* legal machinery whose essential purpose is to set up and preserve a correspondence between moral turpitude and suffering? Surely not.[7] What retributionists have rightly insisted upon is that no man can be punished unless he is guilty, that is, unless he has broken the law. Their fundamental criticism of the utilitarian account is that, as they interpret it, it sanctions an innocent person's being punished (if one may call it that) for the benefit of society.

On the other hand, utilitarians agree that punishment is to be inflicted only for the violation of law. They regard this much as understood from the concept of punishment itself.[8] The point of the utilitarian account concerns the institution as a system of rules: utilitarianism seeks to limit its use by declaring it justifiable only if it can be shown to foster effectively the good of society. Historically it is a protest against the indiscriminate and ineffective use of the criminal law.[9] It seeks to dissuade us from assigning to penal institutions the improper, if not sacrilegious, task of matching suffering with moral turpitude. Like others, utilitarians want penal institutions designed so that, as far as humanly possible, only those who break the law run afoul of it. They hold that no official should have discretionary power to inflict penalties whenever he thinks it for the benefit of society; for on utilitarian grounds an institution granting such power could not be justified.[10]

The suggested way of reconciling the retributive and the utilitarian justifications of punishment seems to account for what both sides have wanted to say. There are, however, two further questions which arise, and I shall devote the remainder of this section to them.

First, will not a difference of opinion as to the proper criterion of just law make the proposed reconciliation unacceptable to retributionists? Will they not question whether, if the utilitarian principle is used as the criterion, it follows that those who have broken the law are guilty in a way which satisfies their demand that those punished deserve to be punished? To answer this difficulty, suppose that the rules of the criminal law are justified on utilitarian grounds (it is only for laws that meet his criterion that the utilitarian can be held responsible). Then it follows that the actions which the criminal law specifies as offenses are such that, if they were tolerated, terror and alarm would spread in society. Consequently, retributionists can only deny that those who are punished deserve to be punished if they deny that such actions are wrong. This they will not want to do.

The second question is whether utilitarianism doesn't justify too much. One pictures it as an engine of justification which, if consistently adopted, could be used to justify cruel and arbitrary institutions. Retributionists may be supposed to concede that utilitarians *intend* to reform the law and to make it more humane; that utilitarians do not *wish* to justify any such thing as punishment of the innocent; and that utilitarians may appeal to the fact that punishment presupposes guilt in the sense that by punishment one understands an institution attaching penalties to the infraction of legal rules, and therefore that it is logically absurd to suppose that utilitarians in justifying *punishment* might also have justified punishment (if we may call it that) of the innocent. The real question, however, is whether the utilitarian, in justifying punishment, hasn't used arguments which commit him to accepting the infliction of suffering on innocent persons if it is for the good of society (whether or not one calls this punishment). More generally, isn't the utilitarian committed in principle to accepting many practices which he, as a morally sensitive person, wouldn't want to accept? Retributionists are inclined to hold that there is no way to stop the utilitarian principle from justifying too much except by adding to it a principle which distributes certain rights to individuals. Then the amended criterion is not the greatest benefit of society *simpliciter,* but the greatest benefit of society subject to the constraint that no one's rights may be violated. Now while I think that the classical utilitarians proposed a criterion of this more complicated sort, I do not want to argue that point here.[11] What I want to show is that there is *another* way of preventing the utilitarian principle from justifying too much, or at least of making it much less likely to do so: namely, by stating utilitarianism in a way which accounts for the distinction between the justification of an institution and the justification of a particular action falling under it.

I begin by defining the institution of punishment as follows: a person is said to suffer punishment whenever he is legally deprived of some of the normal rights of a citizen on the ground that he has violated a rule of law, the violating having been established by trial according to the due process of law, provided that the deprivation is carried out by the recognized legal authorities of the state, that the rule of law clearly specifies both the offense and the attached penalty, that the courts construe statutes strictly, and that the statute was on the books prior to the time of the offense.[12] This definition specifies what I shall understand by punishment. The question is whether utilitarian arguments may be found to justify institutions widely different from this and such as one would find cruel and arbitrary.

This question is best answered, I think, by taking up a particular accusation. Consider the following from Carritt:

. . . the utilitarian must hold that we are justified in inflicting pain always and only to prevent worse pain or bring about greater happiness. This, then, is all we need to consider in so-called punishment, which must be purely preventive. But if some kind of very cruel crime becomes common, and none of the criminals can be caught, it might be highly expedient, as an example, to hang an innocent man, if a charge against him could be so framed that he were universally thought guilty; indeed this would only fail to be an ideal instance of utilitarian 'punishment' because the victim himself would not have been so likely as a real felon to commit such a crime in the future; in all other respects it would be perfectly deterrent and therefore felicific.[13]

Carritt is trying to show that there are occasions when a utilitarian argument would justify taking an action which would be generally condemned; and thus that utilitarianism justifies too much. But the failure of Carritt's argument lies in the fact that he makes no distinction between the justification of the general system of rules which constitutes penal institutions and the justification of particular applications of these rules to particular cases by the various officials whose job it is to administer them. This becomes perfectly clear when one asks who the "we" are of whom Carritt speaks. Who is this who has a sort of absolute authority on particular occasions to decide that an innocent man shall be "punished" if everyone can be convinced that he is guilty? Is this person the legislator, or the judge, or the body of private citizens, or what? It is utterly crucial to know who is to decide such matters, and by what authority, for all of this must be written into the rules of the institution. Until one knows these things one doesn't know what the institution is whose justification is being challenged; and as the utilitarian principle applies to the institution one doesn't know whether it is justifiable on utilitarian grounds or not.

Once this is understood it is clear what the countermove to Carritt's argument is. One must describe more carefully what the *institution* is which his example suggests, and then ask oneself whether or not it is likely that having this institution would be for the benefit of society in the long run. One must not content oneself with the vague thought that, when it's a question of *this* case, it would be a good thing if *somebody* did something even if an innocent person were to suffer.

Try to imagine, then, an institution (which we may call "telishment") which is such that the officials set up by it have authority to arrange a trial for the condemnation of an innocent man whenever they are of the opinion that doing so would be in the best interests of society. The discretion of officials is limited, however, by the rule that they may not condemn an innocent man to undergo such an ordeal unless there is, at the time, a wave of offenses similar to that with which they charge him and telish him for. We may imagine that the officials having the discretionary authority are the judges of the higher courts in consultation with the chief of police, the minister of justice, and a committee of the legislature.

Once one realizes that one is involved in setting up an *institution,* one sees that the hazards are very great. For example, what check is there on the officials? How is one to tell whether or not their actions are authorized? How is one to limit the risks involved in allowing such systematic deception? How is one to avoid giving anything short of complete discretion to the authorities to telish anyone they like? In addition to these considerations, it is obvious that people will come to have a very different attitude towards their penal system when telishment is adjoined to it. They will be uncertain as to whether a convicted man has been punished or telished. They will wonder whether or not they should feel sorry for him. They will wonder whether the same fate won't at any time fall on them. If one pictures how such an institution would actually work, and the enormous risks involved in it, it seems clear that it would serve no useful purpose. A utilitarian justification for this institution is most unlikely.

It happens in general that as one drops off the defining features of punishment one ends up with an institution whose utilitarian justification is highly doubtful. One reason for this is that punishment works like a kind of price system: by altering the prices one has to pay for the performance of actions it supplies a motive for avoiding some actions and doing others. The defining features are essential if punishment is to work in this way; so that an institution which lacks these features, e.g., an institution which is set up to "punish" the innocent, is likely to have about as much point as a price system (if one may call it that) where the prices of things change at random from day to day and one learns the price of something after one has agreed to buy it.[14]

If one is careful to apply the utilitarian principle to the institution which is to authorize particular actions, then there is *less* danger of its justifying too much. Carritt's example gains plausibility by its indefiniteness and by its concentration on the particular case. His argument will only hold if it can be shown that there are utilitarian arguments which

justify an institution whose publicly ascertainable offices and powers are such as to permit officials to exercise that kind of discretion in particular cases. But the requirement of having to build the arbitrary features of the particular decision into the institutional practice makes the justification much less likely to go through.

NOTES

1. I use the word "practice" throughout as a sort of technical term meaning any form of activity specified by a system of rules which defines offices, roles, moves, penalties, defenses, and so on, and which gives the activity its structure. As examples one may think of games and rituals, trials and parliaments.

2. The distinction is central to Hume's discussion of justice in *A Treatise of Human Nature,* bk. III, pt. II, esp. secs. 2–4. It is clearly stated by John Austin in the second lecture of *Lectures on Jurisprudence* (4th ed.; London, 1873), I, 116ff. (1st ed., 1832). Also it may be argued that J. S. Mill took it for granted in *Utilitarianism;* on this point cf. J. O. Urmson, "The Interpretation of the Moral Philosophy of J. S. Mill," *Philosophical Quarterly,* vol. III (1953). In addition to the arguments given by Urmson there are several clear statements of the distinction in *A System of Logic* (8th ed.; London, 1872), bk. VI, ch. xii pars. 2, 3, 7. The distinction is fundamental to J. D. Mabbott's important paper, "Punishment," *Mind,* n.s., vol. XLVIII (April, 1939). More recently the distinction has been stated with particular emphasis by S. E. Toulmin in *The Place of Reason in Ethics* (Cambridge, 1950), see esp. ch. xi, where it plays a major part in his account of moral reasoning. Toulmin doesn't explain the basis of the distinction, nor how one might overlook its importance, as I try to in this paper, and in my review of his book (*Philosophical Review,* vol. LX [October, 1951]), as some of my criticisms show, I failed to understand the force of it. See also H. D. Aiken, "The Levels of Moral Discourse," *Ethics,* vol. LXII (1952), A. M. Quinton, "Punishment," *Analysis,* vol. XIV (June, 1954), and P. H. Nowell-Smith, *Ethics* (London, 1954), pp. 236–239, 271–273.

3. On the concept of explication see the author's paper, *Philosophical Review,* vol. LX (April, 1951).

4. While this paper was being revised, Quinton's appeared; footnote 2 supra. There are several aspects in which my remarks are similar to his. Yet as I consider some further questions and rely on somewhat different arguments, I have retained the discussion of punishment and promises together as two test cases for utilitarianism.

5. Note the fact that different sorts of arguments are suited to different offices. One way of taking the differences between ethical theories is to regard them as accounts of the reasons expected in different offices.

6. In this connection see Mabbott, *op. cit.,* pp. 163–164.

7. On this point see Sir David Ross, *The Right and the Good* (Oxford, 1930), pp. 57–60.

8. See Hobbes's definition of punishment in *Leviathan,* ch. xxviii; and Bentham's definition in *The Principle of Morals and Legislation,* ch. xii, par. 36, ch. xv, par. 28, and in *The Rationale of Punishment,* (London, 1830), bk. I, ch. i. They could agree with Bradley that: "Punishment is punishment only when it is deserved. We pay the penalty, because we owe it, and for no other reason, and if punishment is inflicted for any other reason whatever than because it is merited by wrong, it is a gross im-

morality, a crying injustice, an abominable crime, and not what it pretends to be.'' *Ethical Studies* (2nd ed.; Oxford, 1927), pp. 26–27. Certainly by definition it isn't what it pretends to be. The innocent can only be punished by mistake; deliberate ''punishment'' of the innocent necessarily involves fraud.

9. Cf. Leon Radzinowicz, *A History of English Criminal Law: The Movement for Reform 1750–1833* (London, 1948), esp. ch. xi on Bentham.

10. Bentham discusses how corresponding to a punitory provision of a criminal law there is another provision which stands to it as an antagonist and which needs a name as much as the punitory. He calls it, as one might expect, the *anaetiosostic,* and of it he says: ''The punishment of guilt is the object of the former one: the preservation of innocence that of the latter.'' In the same connection he asserts that it is never thought fit to give the judge the option of deciding whether a thief (that is, a person whom he believes to be a thief, for the judge's belief is what the question must always turn upon) should hang or not, and so the law writes the provision: ''The judge shall not cause a thief to be hanged unless he have been duly convicted and sentenced in course of law'' (*The Limits of Jurisprudence Defined,* ed. C. W. Everett [New York, 1945], pp. 238–239).

11. By the classical utilitarians I understand Hobbes, Hume, Bentham, J. S. Mill, and Sidgwick.

12. All these features of punishment are mentioned by Hobbes; cf. *Leviathan,* ch. xxviii.

13. *Ethical and Political Thinking* (Oxford, 1947), p. 65.

14. The analogy with the price system suggests an answer to the question how utilitarian considerations insure that punishment is proportional to the offense. It is interesting to note that Sir David Ross, after making the distinction between justifying a penal law and justifying a particular application of it, and after stating that utilitarian considerations have a large place in determining the former, still holds back from accepting the utilitarian justification of punishment on the grounds that justice requires that punishment be proportional to the offense, and that utilitarianism is unable to account for this. Cf. *The Right and the Good,* pp. 61–62. I do not claim that utilitarianism can account for this requirement as Sir David might wish, but it happens, nevertheless, that if utilitarian considerations are followed penalties will be proportional to offenses in this sense: the order of offenses according to seriousness can be paired off with the order of penalties according to severity. Also the absolute level of penalties will be as low as possible. This follows from the assumption that people are rational (i.e., that they are able to take into account the ''prices'' the state puts on actions), the utilitarian rule that a penal system should provide a motive for preferring the less serious offense, and the principle that punishment as such is an evil. All this was carefully worked out by Bentham in *The Principles of Morals and Legislation,* chs. xiii–xv.

THOMAS SZASZ

What Is Mental Illness?*

Thomas Szasz (1920–   ) is a Hungarian-born psychoanalyst who has written numerous widely read books criticizing psychiatric practices.

A myth is, of course, not a fairy story. It is the presentation of facts belonging in one category in the idioms belonging to another. To explode a myth is accordingly not to deny the facts but to re-allocate them.

—Gilbert Ryle

At the core of virtually all contemporary psychiatric theories and practices lies the concept of mental illness. This is especially so in forensic psychiatry— that is, in those areas of life where psychiatrists seek to influence the legal process. For example, although anthropologists, political scientists, psychologists, social workers, and sociologists all address themselves to problems of human conduct, only psychiatrists are considered experts on mental illness. We shall begin, therefore, with a critical examination of this concept.[1]

Let us launch our inquiry by asking, somewhat rhetorically, whether there is such a thing as mental illness. My reply is that there is not. Of course, mental illness is not a thing or physical object. It can exist only in the same sort of way as do other theoretical concepts. Yet, to those who believe in them, familiar theories are likely to appear, sooner or later, as "objective truths" or "facts." During certain historical periods, explanatory conceptions such as deities, witches, and instincts appeared not only as theories but as *self-evident* causes of a vast number of events. Today mental illness is widely regarded in a somewhat similar fashion, that is, as the cause of innumerable diverse happenings.

As an antidote to the complacent use of the notion of mental illness—as self-evident phenomenon, theory, or cause—let us ask: What is meant by the assertion that a person is mentally ill? In this chapter I shall describe briefly the main uses of the concept of mental illness. I shall argue that this notion has outlived whatever usefulness it may have had and that it now functions as a myth.

MENTAL ILLNESS AS A SIGN OF BRAIN DISEASE

The notion of mental illness derives its main support from such phenomena as syphilis of the brain or delirious conditions—intoxications, for instance— in which persons may manifest certain disorders of thinking and behavior. Correctly speaking, however, these are diseases of the brain, not of the mind. According to one school of thought, *all* so-called mental illness is of this type. The assumption is made that some neurological defect, perhaps a very subtle one, will ultimately be found to explain all the disorders of thinking and behavior. Many contemporary psychiatrists, physicians, and other scientists hold this view, which implies that people's troubles cannot be caused by conflicting personal needs, opinions,

*From Thomas Szasz, *Law, Liberty and Psychiatry* (New York: The Macmillan Co.; London: Routledge & Kegan Paul, Ltd., 1963), pp. 12–17. Reprinted by permission of the author and the publisher. © Copyright 1963 by Thomas Szasz, M.D.

social aspirations, values, and so forth. These difficulties—which I think we may simply call *problems in living*—are thus attributed to physicochemical processes which in due time will be discovered (and no doubt corrected!) by medical research.

Mental illnesses are thus regarded as basically no different from other diseases. The only difference, in this view, between mental and bodily disease is that the former, affecting the brain, manifests itself by means of mental symptoms; whereas the latter, affecting other organ systems—for example, the skin, liver, and so on—manifests itself by means of symptoms referable to those parts of the body.

In my opinion, this view is based on two fundamental errors. In the first place, a disease of the brain, analogous to a disease of the skin or bone, is a neurological defect, not a problem in living. For example, a *defect* in a person's visual field may be explained by correlating it with certain definite lesions in the nervous system. On the other hand, a person's *belief*—whether it be in Christianity, in Communism, or in the idea that his internal organs are rotting and that his body is already dead—cannot be explained by a defect or disease of the nervous system. Explanations of this sort of occurrence—assuming that one is interested in the belief itself and does not regard it simply as a symptom or expression of something else that is more interesting—must be sought along different lines.

The second error is epistemological. It consists of interpreting communications about ourselves and the world around us as symptoms of neurological functioning. This is an error not in observation or reasoning, but rather in the organization and expression of knowledge. In the present case, the error lies in making a dualism between mental and physical symptoms, a dualism which is a habit of speech and not the result of known observations. Let us see if this is so.

In medical practice, when we speak of physical disturbances we mean either signs (for example, fever) or symptoms (for example, pain). We speak of mental symptoms, on the other hand, when we refer to a patient's communications about himself, others, and the world about him. He might state that he is Napoleon or that he is being persecuted by the Communists. These would be considered mental symptoms *only* if the observer believed that the patient was *not* Napoleon or that he was *not* being persecuted by the Communists. This makes it apparent that the statement "X is a mental symptom" involves

rendering a judgment. The judgment entails, moreover, a covert comparison or matching of the patient's ideas, concepts, or beliefs with those of the observer and the society in which they live. The notion of mental symptom is therefore inextricably tied to the *social,* and particularly the *ethical,* context in which it is made, just as the notion of bodily symptom is tied to an *anatomical* and *genetic* context.

To sum up: For those who regard mental symptoms as signs of brain disease, the concept of mental illness is unnecessary and misleading. If they mean that people so labeled suffer from diseases of the brain, it would seem better, for the sake of clarity, to say that and not something else.

MENTAL ILLNESS AS A NAME FOR PROBLEMS IN LIVING

The term "mental illness" is also widely used to describe something very different from a disease of the brain. Many people today take it for granted that living is an arduous process. Its hardship for modern man, moreover, derives not so much from a struggle for biological survival as from the stresses and strains inherent in the social intercourse of complex human personalities. In this context, the notion of mental illness is used to identify or describe some feature of an individual's so-called personality. Mental illness—as a deformity of the personality, so to speak—is regarded as the cause of interpersonal or social disharmony. It is implicit in this view that social intercourse between people is regarded as something inherently harmonious, its disturbance being due solely to the presence of mental illness in many people. Clearly, this is faulty reasoning, for it makes the abstraction "mental illness" into a *cause,* even though this abstraction was originally created to serve as a shorthand expression for certain types of human behavior. It now becomes necessary to ask: What kinds of behavior are regarded as indicative of mental illness, and by whom?

The concept of illness, whether bodily or mental, implies deviation from a clearly defined norm. In the case of physical illness, the norm is the structural and functional integrity of the human body. Although the desirability of physical health, as such, is an ethical value, what health is can be stated in anatomical and physiological terms. What is the norm deviation from which is regarded as mental illness? This question cannot be easily answered. But whatever this norm may be, we can be certain of only one thing: namely, that it must be stated in terms of psychosocial, ethical, and legal concepts. For example, notions such as "excessive repression" or "acting out an unconscious impulse" illustrate the use of psychological concepts for judging so-called mental health and illness. The idea that chronic hostility, vengefulness, or divorce are indicative of mental illness is an illustration of the use of ethical norms (that is, the desirability of love, kindness, and a stable marriage relationship). Finally, the widespread psychiatric opinion that only a mentally ill person would commit homicide illustrates the use of a legal concept as a norm of mental health. The norm from which deviation is measured, when one speaks of a mental illness, is a *psychosocial and ethical* one. Yet, the remedy is sought in terms of *medical* measures which—it is hoped and assumed— are free from wide differences of ethical value. The definition of the disorder and the terms in which its remedy is sought are therefore at odds with one another. The practical significance of this covert conflict between the alleged nature of the defect and the remedy can hardly be exaggerated.

Having identified the norms used for measuring deviations in cases of mental illness, we shall now turn to the question: Who defines the norms and hence the deviation? Two basic answers may be offered. First, it may be the person himself—that is, the patient—who decides that he deviates from a norm. For example, an artist may believe that he suffers from a work inhibition. He may implement this conclusion by seeking help *for* himself from a psychotherapist. Second, it may be someone other than the patient who decides that the latter is deviant—for example, relatives, physicians, legal authorities, society generally. A psychiatrist may then be hired by persons other than the patient to do something *to* the patient in order to correct the deviation.

These considerations underscore the importance of asking the question, "Whose agent is the psychiatrist?" and of giving a candid answer to it. The psychiatrist (or nonmedical psychotherapist) may be the agent of the patient, the relatives, the school, the military services, a business organization, a court of law, and so forth. In speaking of the psychiatrist as the agent of these persons or organizations, it is not implied that his values concerning norms, or his ideas and aims concerning the proper nature

of remedial action, must coincide with those of his employer. For example, a patient in individual psychotherapy may believe that his salvation lies in a new marriage; his psychotherapist need not share this hypothesis. As the patient's agent, however, he must not resort to social or legal force to prevent the patient from putting his beliefs into action. If his *contract* is with the patient, the psychiatrist (psychotherapist) may disagree with him or stop his treatment, but he cannot engage others to obstruct the patient's aspirations. Similarly, if a psychiatrist is retained by a court to determine the sanity of an offender, he need not fully share the legal authorities' values and intentions in regard to the criminal, nor the means deemed appropriate for dealing with him. The psychiatrist cannot testify, however, that the accused is not insane, but that the legislators are— for passing the law which decrees the offender's actions illegal. Such an opinion could be voiced, of course, but not in a courtroom, and not by a psychiatrist who is there to assist the court in performing its daily work.

Clearly, psychiatry is much more intimately related to problems of ethics than is medicine. I used the word "psychiatry" here to refer to the contemporary discipline concerned with problems in living, and not with diseases of the brain, which belong to neurology. Difficulties in human relations can be analyzed, interpreted, and given meaning only within specific social and ethical contexts. Accordingly, the psychiatrist's socio-ethical orientations will influence his ideas on what is wrong with the patient, on what deserves comment or interpretation, in what directions change might be desirable, and so forth. Even in medicine proper, these factors play a role, as illustrated by the divergent orientations which physicians, depending on their religious affiliations, have toward such things as birth control and therapeutic abortion. Can anyone really believe that a psychotherapist's ideas on religion, politics, and related issues play no role in his practical work? If, on the other hand, they do matter, what are we to infer from it? Does it not seem reasonable that perhaps we ought to have different psychiatric therapies—each recognized for the ethical positions which it embodies—for, say, Catholics and Jews, religious persons and atheists, democrats and Communists, white supremacists and Negroes, and so on? Indeed, if we look at the way psychiatry is actually practiced today, especially in the United States, we find that people seek psychiatric help in accordance with their social status and ethical beliefs. This should occasion no greater surprise than being told that practicing Catholics rarely frequent birth-control clinics.

To recapitulate: In contemporary social usage, the finding of mental illness is made by establishing a deviance in behavior from certain psychosocial, ethical, or legal norms. The judgment may be made, as in medicine, by the patient, the physician (psychiatrist), or others. Remedial action, finally, tends to be sought in a therapeutic—or covertly medical—framework. This creates a situation in which it is claimed that psychosocial, ethical, and/or legal deviations can be corrected by medical action. But is this rational?

CHOICE, RESPONSIBILITY, AND PSYCHIATRY

While I argue that mental illnesses do not exist, obviously I do not wish to imply that the social and psychological occurrences *so labeled* do not exist. Like the personal and social troubles people had in the Middle Ages, they are real enough. What concerns us is the labels we give them, and, having labeled them, what we do about them. The demonologic conception of problems in living gave rise to therapy along theological lines. Today, a belief in mental illness implies—nay, requires—therapy along medical or psychotherapeutic lines.

I do not here propose to offer a new conception of "psychiatric illness" or a new form of "therapy." My aim is more modest and yet also more ambitious. It is to suggest that the phenomena now called mental illnesses be looked at afresh and more simply, that they be removed from the category of illnesses, and that they be regarded as the expressions of man's struggle with the problem of *how* he should live. By problems in living I refer to that explosive chain reaction which began with man's fall from divine grace by partaking of the fruit of the tree of knowledge. Man's awareness of himself and of the world about him seems to be a steadily expanding one, bringing in its wake an ever larger *burden of understanding* (an expression borrowed from Susanne Langer). This burden is to be expected, and must not be misinterpreted. Our only rational means for easing it is more understanding, and appropriate action based on it. The main alternative is to behave as if the burden were not what we perceive it to be, and to take refuge in an essentially theological view of man, whether this parades in scientific guise or not. But today is not a propitious time in human history for obscuring the issue of man's responsibility for his actions, by hiding it behind the skirt of an all-explaining conception of mental illness.

CONCLUSIONS

I have tried to show that the notion of mental illness has outlived whatever usefulness it may have had and that it now functions as a convenient myth. As such, it is a true heir to religious myths in general, and to the belief in witchcraft in particular.

When I assert that mental illness is a myth, I am not saying that personal unhappiness and socially deviant behavior do not exist; but I am saying that we categorize them as diseases at our own peril.

The expression "mental illness" is a metaphor which we have come to mistake for a fact. We call people physically ill when their body-functioning violates certain anatomical and physiological norms; similarly, we call people mentally ill when their personal conduct violates certain ethical, political, and social norms. This explains why many historical figures, from Jesus to Castro, and from Job to Hitler, have been diagnosed as suffering from this or that psychiatric malady.

Another way of highlighting the distinction between physical and mental sickness is to emphasize that physical illness is usually something that *happens* to us, whereas mental illness is something we *do* (or feel or think). Brown expressed the same idea when he wrote that "Neurosis is not a disease in the medically accepted sense; . . . it is not something a person *has* but rather something that he *is*."[2]

It may be objected that whether or not we choose to call certain events in the universe "mental illness" is chiefly a semantic issue. Yes and no. The point is that when a scientific judgment becomes the basis for social action, the consequences are far-reaching. For example, when equal protection of the laws is withdrawn because a person has been labeled "mentally ill," we are confronted with an act of discrimination. Surely, from the victim's point of view, it makes little difference whether his right to vote is denied because of his race, or whether his right to stand trial is denied because of his mental illness. In the past, discrimination has been based chiefly on nationality, race, religion, and economic status; today, there is a mounting tendency to base it on psychiatric considerations. Since these practices rest on allegedly scientific grounds, and are implemented by professional persons, the ethical issues they pose are especially delicate.

Finally, the myth of mental illness encourages us to believe in its logical corollary: that social intercourse would be harmonious, satisfying, and the secure basis of a "good life" were it not for the disrupting influences of mental illness or "psychopathology." However, universal human happiness, in this form at least, is but another example of a wishful fantasy. I believe that human happiness is possible—not just for a select few, but on a scale hitherto unimaginable. But this can be achieved only if many men, not just a few, are willing and able to confront frankly, and tackle courageously, their ethical, personal, and social conflicts.

NOTES

1. In my book *The Myth of Mental Illness* (1961), I traced in detail the origin and evolution of the concept of mental illness. My present aim is to present certain less technical considerations which lead to the same conclusions as I have reached there.

2. J. A. C. Brown, *Freud and the Post-Freudians* (Baltimore: Penguin Books, 1961), p. 81.

JOEL FEINBERG

What Is So Special about Mental Illness?*

Joel Feinberg (1926–   ) teaches philosophy at the University of Arizona.

In a recent article, Professor Alan Dershowitz has very effectively put psychiatry in its proper place.[1] As far as the law and public policy are concerned, a psychiatrist is an expert on the diagnosis and treatment of mental illness. His testimony becomes relevant to questions of responsibility only when mental illness itself is relevant to such questions, and that is only when it deprives a person of the capacity to conform his conduct to the requirements of law. Mental illness should not itself be an independent ground of exculpation, but only a sign that one of the traditional standard grounds—compulsion, ignorance of fact, or excusable ignorance of law—may apply. Mental illness, then, while often relevant to questions of responsibility, is no more significant—and significant in no different way—than other sources of compulsion and misapprehension.

While this is certainly a plausible view at first sight, and an orthodox jurisprudential doctrine, I have strong doubts, nevertheless, of its adequacy as an account of the whole relevance of mental illness to moral responsibility. Indeed, I shall suggest in what follows, that mental illness has an independent significance for questions of responsibility not fully accounted for by reference to its power to deprive one of the capacity to be law-abiding.

I

At the outset we must distinguish two questions about the relation of mental illness to criminal punishment. (There are two parallel questions about the bearing of mental illness on civil commitment.)

1. How are mentally sick persons to be distinguished from normal persons?
2. When should we accept mental illness as an excuse?

The first appears to be a medical question that requires the expertise of the psychiatrist to answer; the second appears to be an essentially controversial question of public policy that cannot be answered by referring to the special expertise of any particular group.

Some psychiatrists may wish to deny this rigid separation between the two questions. They might

*From Joel Feinberg, *Doing and Deserving* (Copyright © 1970 by Princeton University Press; Princeton Paperback, 1974); pp. 272–292. Reprinted by permission of Princeton University Press.

hold it self-evident that sick people are not to be treated as responsible people; hence the criteria of illness are themselves criteria of nonresponsibility. But, obviously, this won't do. First of all, the fact of illness itself, even greatly incapacitating illness, does not automatically lead us to withhold ascription of responsibility, or else we would treat *physical* illness as an automatic excuse. But in fact we would not change our judgments of Bonnie and Clyde one jot if we discovered that they both had had 103-degree fevers during one of their bank robberies, or of Al Capone if we learned that he had ordered one of his gangland assassinations while suffering from an advanced case of chicken pox. Secondly, there are various crimes that can be committed by persons suffering from mental illnesses that can have no relevant bearing on their motivation. We may take exhibitionism to be an excuse for indecent exposure, or pedophilia for child molestation, but neither would be a plausible defense to the charge of income-tax evasion or price-fixing conspiracy. These examples show, I think, that the mere fact of mental illness, no more than the mere fact of physical illness, automatically excuses. We need some further criterion, then, for distinguishing cases of mental illness that do excuse from those that do not, and this further question is not an exclusively psychiatric one. What we want to know is this: what is it about mental illness that makes it an excuse when it is an excuse?

So much, I think, is clear. But now there are two types of moves open to us. The first is preferred by most legal writers, and it is the one about which I intend to raise some doubts. According to this view, there is nothing very special about mental disease as such. Mental illness is only one of numerous possible causes of *incapacity,* and it is incapacity—or, more precisely, the incapability to conform to law—that is incompatible with responsibility. Ultimately, there is only one kind of consideration that should lead us to exempt a person from responsibility for his wrongful deeds, and that is that he *couldn't help it.* Sometimes a mental illness compels a man to do wrong, or at least makes it unreasonably difficult for him to abstain, and in those cases we say that, because he was ill, he couldn't help what he did and, therefore, is not to be held responsible for his deviant conduct. But in other cases, as we have seen, mental illness no more compels a given wrongful act than the chicken pox does, or may be totally irrelevant to the explanation of the wrongdoing, in that the wrongdoer would have done his wrong

even if he had been perfectly healthy. What counts, then, for questions of responsibility is whether the accused could have helped himself, not whether he was mentally well or ill.

Aristotle put much the same point in somewhat different but equally familiar language. A man is responsible, said Aristotle, for all and only those of his actions that were voluntary; to whatever extent we think a given action less than voluntary, to that extent we are inclined to exempt the actor from responsibility for it. There are, according to Aristotle, two primary ways in which an action can fail to be voluntary: it can be the result of *compulsion,* or it can be done in *ignorance.* On his view a person charged with wrongdoing can have basically only *two* types of excuse: Either he couldn't help it or he didn't mean it. Thus if a hurricane wind blows you twenty yards across a street, you cannot be said to have crossed the street voluntarily, since you were compelled to do it and given no choice at all in the matter. And if you put arsenic in your wife's coffee honestly but mistakenly believing it to be sugar, you cannot be said to have poisoned her voluntarily, since you acted in genuine ignorance of what you were doing.

Now if we take just a few slight liberties with Aristotle, we can interpret most of the traditionally recognized legal excuses in terms of his categories. Acting under duress or necessity, or in self-defense, or defense of others, or defense of property, and so on, can all be treated as cases of acting under compulsion, whereas ignorance or mistake of fact, ignorance or mistake of law, and perhaps even what used to be called "moral idiocy" or ignorance of the "difference between right and wrong" can all be treated as cases of acting in responsibility-cancelling ignorance. On the view I am considering (a view which has always enjoyed favor among lawyers, and to which Professor Dershowitz, I feel sure, is friendly), the mental illness of an actor is not still a third way in which his actions might fail to be voluntary; rather, it is a factor which may or may not compel him to act in certain ways, or which may or may not delude, or mislead, or misinform him in ways that would lead him to act in ignorance. Indeed, on this view, mental illness ought not even to be an independent category of exculpation on a level with, say, self-defense or mistake of fact. Self-defense and relevant blameless mistakes of fact always excuse, whereas mental illness excuses only when it compels or deludes. We now know of the existence of inner compulsions unsuspected by Aristotle: obsessive ideas, hysterical reactions, neurotic compulsion, phobias, and addictions. Other mental illnesses characteristically produce delusions and hallucinations. But not all neurotic and psychotic disorders by any means produce compulsive or delusionary symptoms, and even those that do are not always sufficient to explain the criminal conduct of the person suffering from them.

The nineteenth-century judges who formulated the famous McNaghten Rules were presumably quite sympathetic with the view I have been describing, that there really is nothing very special about mental illness. These rules are not at all concerned with neurotically compulsive behavior—a category which simply was not before their minds at the time. Rather, they were concerned with those dramatic and conspicuous disorders that involve what we call today "paranoid delusions" and "psychotic hallucinations." The interesting thing about the rules is that they treat these aberrations precisely the same as any other innocent "mistakes of fact"; in effect the main point of this part of the McNaghten Rules is to acknowledge that mistakes of fact resulting from "disease of the mind" really are genuine and innocent and, therefore, have the same exculpatory force as more commonplace errors and false beliefs. The rules state that, "when a man acts under an insane delusion, then he is excused only when it is the case that *if* the facts were as he supposed them his act would be innocent. . . ." Thus if a man suffers the insane delusion that a passerby on the street is an enemy agent about to launch a mortal attack on him and kills him in what he thinks is "self-defense," he is excused, since if the facts were as he falsely supposed them to be, his act would have been innocent. But if (in James Vorenberg's example) he shoots his wife because, in his insane delusion, he thinks her hair has turned gray, he will be convicted, since even if her hair had turned gray, that would not have been an allowable defense. Note that the mental disease that leads to the insane delusion in these instances is given no special significance except insofar as it mediates the application of another kind of defense that can be used by mentally healthy as well as mentally ill defendants.

The McNaghten Rules do, however, make one important concession to the peculiarity of mental illness. Mentally normal persons, for the most part, are not permitted to plead *ignorance of the law* as a defense, especially for crimes that are "malum *in se.*" No normal person, for example, can plead in the state of Arizona that "he didn't know that murder is prohibited in Arizona." *That* kind of ignorance could hardly ever occur in a normal person, and even if it did, it would be negligent rather than innocent ignorance. (One should at least take the trouble to find out whether a state prohibits murder before killing someone in that state!) If a person, however, is so grossly ignorant of what is permitted that he would murder even (as the saying goes) with "a policeman at his elbow," then if his ignorance is attributable to a diseased mind and therefore innocent, he is excused. One can conceive (just barely) of such a case. Imagine a man standing on a street corner chatting with a policeman. A third person saunters up, calmly shoots and kills the man, turns to the astonished policeman and says "Good morning, officer," and starts to walk away. When the policeman apprehends him, then *he* is the astonished one. "Why, what have I done wrong?" he asks in genuine puzzlement.

In accepting this kind of ignorance when it stems from disease as an excuse, the McNaghten Rules do not really make *much* of a concession to the uniqueness of mental illness. Ignorance of law does not excuse in the normal case because the law imposes a duty on all normal persons to find out what is prohibited at their own peril. When a statute has been duly promulgated, every normal person is presumed to know about it. If any given normal person fails to be informed, his ignorance is the consequence of his own negligence, and he is to blame for it. But when the ignorance is the consequence of illness, it is involuntary or faultless ignorance and may therefore be accepted as an excuse. Again, it is not the mental illness as such which excuses, but rather the ignorance which is its indirect byproduct. The ultimate rationale of the exculpation is that the actor "didn't mean it," or given the compulsive force of his malady, that he "couldn't help" having the ignorance in which he acted. We hardly need the separate insanity defense at all if we accept the propositions that mentally ill people may be subject to internal compulsions, that mental illness can cause innocent ignorance, and that both compulsion and innocent ignorance are themselves excuses.

Suppose a mentally ill defendant is acquitted on the ground that his illness has rendered his unlawful conduct involuntary in one of these traditional ways. He may still be a menace to himself or others, even though he is perfectly innocent of any crime. Hence the state reserves to itself or to others the right to initiate civil commitment proceedings. Now whether it follows acquittal or is quite independent of any prior criminal proceedings, civil commitment can have one or both of two different purposes, and for each of these purposes the mere fact of mental illness is not a sufficient condition. The two purposes are (1) forcible detention of a dangerous person to prevent him from committing a crime and (2) compulsory therapeutic confinement of a mentally ill person "for his own good." For the purpose of preventive detention, mental illness is neither a necessary nor a sufficient condition: not necessary because mentally normal persons too can be very dangerous in certain circumstances,[2] and not sufficient because some mentally ill people, unhappy or withdrawn as they may be, are still quite harmless. Hence psychiatric testimony that a person is mentally ill is hardly sufficient to justify detaining him without a further showing of dangerousness. What is needed are very high standards of due process at detention hearings analogous to those governing criminal trials and, as Professor Dershowitz points out, clear and precise legal definitions of "harmfulness" and "danger."

The other possible purpose of civil commitment—compulsory therapy—does of course require mental illness as a necessary condition, and here psychiatric testimony is crucial. But if civil liberty has any appeal to us and if state paternalism is repugnant, we can hardly regard the simple fact of mental illness as sufficient warrant for imposing therapeutic confinement on a person against his will. To force a person to submit to our benevolence is a fearsome and ugly kind of tyranny. The traditional doctrine of *Parens Patriae* to which Professor Dershowitz refers, however, authorizes such coercion only in very special and, I think, unobjectionable circumstances. Some mental illnesses so affect the cognitive processes that a victim is unable to make inferences or decisions—a severe disablement indeed. According to the *Parens Patriae* doctrine, the state has the duty to exercise its "sovereign power of guardianship" over these intellectually defective and disordered persons who are unable to realize their needs on their own. But even on occasions where this doctrine applies, the state presumes to "decide for a man as . . . he would decide for himself if he were of sound mind."[3] By no means all mentally ill persons, however, suffer from defects of reason. Many or most of them suffer from emotional or volitional disorders that leave their cognitive faculties quite unimpaired. To impose compulsory therapy on such persons would be as objectionably paternalistic as imposing involuntary cures for warts or headaches or tooth decay.

To summarize the view I have been considering: a mere finding of mental illness is not itself a sufficient ground for exempting a person from responsibility for a given action; nor is it a sufficient ground for finding him not to be a responsible or competent person generally, with the loss of civil rights such a finding necessarily entails. At most, in criminal proceedings mental illness may be evidence that one of the traditional grounds for moral exculpation—compulsion or ignorance—applies to the case at hand, and in civil commitment hearings it may be evidence of dangerousness or of cognitive impairment. But it has no independent moral or legal significance in itself either as an excuse or as a ground for commitment.

II

I fully accept this account of the relation of mental illness to civil commitment. Preventive detention of a person who has committed no crime is a desperate move that should be made only when a person's continued liberty would constitute a clear and present danger of substantial harm to others. We should require proof of a very great danger indeed before resorting to such measures if only because people are inclined generally to overestimate threats to safety and to underestimate the social value of individual liberty. Mere evidence of mental illness by itself does not provide such proof. Nor does it by itself provide proof of that mental derangement or incompetence to grant or withhold consent that is required if compulsory therapeutic confinement is to be justified. But, for all of that, I strongly doubt that the above account does full justice to the moral significance of mental illness as it bears on blame and punishment. I shall devote the remainder of my remarks to a statement of my misgivings.

Let me turn immediately to the kind of case that troubles me. I have in mind cases of criminal conduct which appear to be both voluntary (by the usual Aristotelian tests) and sick. Let me give some examples and then contrast them with normal voluntary criminal acts.

First consider a nonviolent child molester. He is

sexually attracted to five- and six-year-old boys and girls. His rational faculties are perfectly normal. He knows that sexual contacts with children are forbidden by the criminal law, and he takes no unnecessary risks of detection. For the most part, he manages to do without sex altogether. When he does molest a child he characteristically feels guilt, if not remorse, afterward. He has no understanding of his own motivation and often regrets that his tastes are so odd.

Next in our rogues' gallery is a repetitive exhibitionist. He has been arrested numerous times for exposing his genitalia in public. He does this not to solicit or threaten, but simply to derive satisfaction from the act itself: exposure for exposure's sake. For some reason he cannot understand, he finds such exposure immensely gratifying. Still, he knows that it is offensive to others, that it is in a way publicly humiliating, that it is prohibited by law, and that the chances of being caught and punished are always very great. These things trouble him much and often, but not always, lead him to restrain himself when the impulse to self-exposure arises.

My third example is drawn from a landmark case in the criminal law, one of the first in which kleptomania was accepted as an excuse: *State* v. *McCullough,* 114 Iowa 532 (1901). The defendant, a high school student, was charged with stealing a school book worth seventy-five cents. It was discovered that stolen property in his possession included "14 silverine watches, 2 old brass watches, 2 old clocks, 24 razors, 21 pairs of cuff buttons, 15 watch chains, 6 pistols, 7 combs, 34 jack knives, 9 bicycle wrenches, 4 padlocks, 7 pair of clippers, 3 bicycle saddles, 1 box of old keys, 4 pairs of scissors, 5 pocket mirrors, 6 mouth organs, rulers, bolts, calipers, oil cans, washers, punches, pulleys, spoons, penholders, ramrods, violin strings, etc." ["etc."!]. One can barely imagine the great price in anxiety this boy must have paid for his vast accumulation of worthless junk.

Finally, consider a well-off man who shoplifts only one kind of item, women's brassieres. He could easily afford to pay for these items and, indeed, often does when there is no other way of getting them, or when he is in danger of being caught. He does not enjoy stealing them and suffers great anxiety in worrying about being found out. Yet his storerooms are overflowing with brassieres. He burgles homes

only to steal them; he assaults women only to rip off their brassieres and flee. And if you ask him for an explanation of his bizarre conduct, he will confess himself as puzzled by it as any observer.

Now, for contrast, consider some typical voluntary normal crimes. A respectable middle-aged bank teller, after weighing the risks carefully, embezzles bank funds and runs off to Mexico with his expensive lady friend. A homeowner in desperate need of cash sets his own house on fire to defraud an insurance company. A teenager steals a parked car and drives to a nearby city for a thrill. An angry man consumed with jealousy, or indignation, or vengefulness, or spite, commits criminal battery on a person he hates. A revolutionary throws a bomb at the king's carriage during an insurrection. These criminals act from a great variety of unmysterious motives—avarice, gain, lust, hate, ideological zeal; they are all rationally capable of calculating risks; they all act voluntarily.

How do the "sick" criminals in my earlier list differ from these normal ones? We might be tempted to answer that the pedophiliac, the exhibitionist, the kleptomaniac, and the fetishist are all "compulsives" and that their criminal conduct is therefore not entirely voluntary after all; but I believe it is important to understand that this answer is unsatisfactory. There is no a priori reason why the desires, impulses, and motives that lead a person to do bizarre things need necessarily be more powerful or compulsive than the desires that lead normal men to do perfectly ordinary things. It is by no means self-evident, for example, that the sex drives of a pedophiliac, an exhibitionist, or a homosexual must always be stronger than the sexual desires normal men and women may feel for one another.

There is much obscurity in the notion of the "strength of a desire," but I think several points are clear and relevant to our purposes. The first is that, strictly speaking, no impulse is "irresistible." For every case of giving in to a desire, I would argue, it will be true that, if the person had tried harder, he would have resisted it successfully. The psychological situation is never—or hardly ever—like that of the man who hangs from a windowsill by his fingernails until the sheer physical force of gravity rips his nails off and sends him plummeting to the ground, or like that of the man who dives from a sinking ship in the middle of the ocean and swims until he is exhausted and then drowns. Human endurance puts a severe limit on how long one can stay afloat in an ocean; but there is no comparable limit to our ability to resist temptation. Nevertheless, it does make sense to say that some desires are stronger than others and that some have an intensity and power that are felt as overwhelming. Some desires, in fact, may be so difficult to resist for a given person in a given state at a given time that it would be unreasonable to expect him to resist. A dieting man with a strong sweet tooth may find it difficult to resist eating an ice cream sundae for dessert; but a man who has not eaten for a week will have a much harder time still resisting the desire to eat a loaf of bread, which just happens to belong to his neighbor. Any person in a weakened condition, whether the cause be hunger or depression, fatigue or gripping emotion, will be less able to resist any given antisocial impulse than a person in a normal condition. But, again, there is no reason to suppose that bizarre appetites and odd tastes are always connected with a "weakened condition," so that they are necessarily more difficult to resist than ordinary desires. And thus there is no reason to suppose that so-called sick desires must always be compulsive or unreasonably difficult to resist.

It might seem to follow that there is *no* morally significant difference between normal and mentally ill offenders, that the one class is just as responsible as the other, provided only that their criminal actions are voluntary in the usual sense. But if this is the proper conclusion, then I am at a loss to see what difference there can be between mental illness and plain wickedness. As an ordinary citizen, before I begin to get confused by philosophy, I sometimes permit myself to feel anger and outrage at normal criminals, whereas I cannot help feeling some pity (mixed, perhaps, with repugnance) toward those whose conduct appears bizarre and unnatural. But unless I can find some morally telling difference between the two classes of criminals, then these natural attitudes must be radically reshaped, so that the fetish thief, for example, be thought as wicked as the professional burglar.

There do seem to be some striking differences between the two classes, however, and perhaps some of these can rescue my prephilosophical attitudes. Most of them have to do not with the criminal's intentions, but with his underlying motivation—the basis of the appeal in his immediate goals or objectives. The first such difference is that the sick criminal's motives appear quite *unintelligible* to us. We sometimes express our puzzlement by saying that his crimes have no apparent motive at all. We cannot

see any better than the criminal himself "what he gets out of it," and it overburdens our imaginative faculties to put ourselves in his shoes. We understand the avaricious, irascible, or jealous man's motives all too well, and we resent him for them. But where crimes resist explanation in terms of ordinary motives, we hardly know what to resent. Here the old maxim "to understand all is to forgive all" seems to be turned on its ear. It is closer to the truth to say of mentally ill wrongdoers that to forgive is to despair of understanding.

Yet mere unintelligibility of motive is not likely to advance our search for the moral significance of mental illness very far, especially if we take the criterion of unintelligibility in turn to be the frustration of our "imaginative capacities" to put ourselves in the criminal's shoes and understand what he gets out of his crimes. This test of imaginability is far too elastic and variable. On the one hand, it seems too loose, since it permits the classification as unintelligible (or even sick) of *any* particular passion or taste, provided only that it is sufficiently different from those of the person making the judgment. Some nonsmokers cannot understand what smokers get out of their noxious habit, and males can hardly understand what it is like to enjoy bearing children. On the other hand, once we begin tightening up the test of imaginability, there is likely to be no stopping place short of the point at which *all* motives become intelligible to anyone with a moderately good imagination and sense of analogy. The important thing is not that the sick criminal's motives may seem unintelligible, but rather that they are unintelligible in a certain respect or for a certain reason.

We get closer to the heart of the matter, I think, if we say that the mentally ill criminal's motives are unintelligible because they are irrational—not just unreasonable, but *irrational*. All voluntary wrongdoing, of course, is unreasonable. It is always unreasonable conduct to promote one's own good at another's expense, to be cruel, deceitful, or unfair. But in a proper sense of "rational," made familiar by economists and lawyers, wrongdoing, though unreasonable, can be perfectly rational. A wrongdoer might well calculate his own interests, and gains and risks thereto, and decide to advance them at another's expense, without making a single intellectual mistake. A rational motive, in the present sense, is simply a *self-interested* motive, or perhaps an intelligently self-interested one. The motives of mentally ill criminals are not usually very self-interested. The Supreme Court of Iowa, in overturning the conviction of young McCullough, held that the question for the jury should have been: did the accused steal because of a mental disease driving him by "an insane and irresistible impulse" to steal, or did he commit said acts "through excessive greed or avarice?" The Court's alternatives are not exhaustive. Very likely McCullough's impulses were neither irresistible nor "greedy and avaricious." Greed and avarice are forms of selfishness, excessive desires for material goods and riches for oneself. As motives they are preeminently self-interested and "rational." McCullough's sick desires, however, were not for his own good, material or otherwise. He stole objects that could do him no good at all and assumed irrational risks in the process. The desire to steal and hoard these useless trinkets was a genuine enough desire, and it was *his* desire; but it does not follow that it was a desire to promote his own good.

This point too, however, can be overstated. It may well be true that none of the mentally ill crimes we are considering is done from a self-interested motive, but this feature hardly distinguishes them (yet) from a wide variety of voluntary crimes of great blameworthiness committed by perfectly normal criminals. By no means all voluntary crimes by normal criminals are done from the motive of gain. Some are done to advance or retard a cause, to help a loved one, or to hurt an enemy, often at great cost to the criminal's self-interest. What distinguishes the sick crimes we have been considering is not that they are unselfinterested, but rather that they are *not interested at all.* They do not further *any* of the actor's interests, self *or* other-regarding, benevolent or malevolent. The fetishist's shoplifting is not rational and self-serving; he attains no economic objective by it. But neither does it hurt anyone he hates nor help anyone he loves; it neither gains him good will and prestige, nor satisfies his conscience, nor fulfills his ideals. It is, in short, not interested behavior.

But even this distinction does not quite get to the very core of the matter. The fetishist's behavior not only fails to be interested; it fails even to appear interested to him. To be sure, it is designed to fulfill the desire which is its immediate motive; but fulfillment of desire is not necessarily the same thing as abiding satisfaction. He may be gratified or relieved for an instant, but this kind of fulfillment of desire leaves only the taste of ashes in one's mouth. The important point is that his behavior tends to be *contrary to interest,* as *senseless* almost as the repetitive beating of one's head against an unyielding stone wall. Bishop Butler was one of the first to point out how profoundly misleading it is to call such behavior "self-indulgent" simply because it appears voluntary, fulfills the actor's own desire, and leads to an instant's satisfaction before a torrent of guilt and anxiety. One might as well call the thirsty marooned sailor "self-indulgent" when he drinks deeply of the sea water that will surely dry him out further, as he well knows.

I believe there is a tendency in human nature, quite opposite to the one I have already mentioned, to consider the senselessness of a crime a kind of moral aggravation. That a cruel crime seemed pointless or senseless, a source of no gain to anyone, makes the harm it caused seem in the most absolute sense *unnecessary,* and that rubs salt in our psychic wounds. The harm was *all for nothing,* we lament, as if an intelligible motive would make our wounds any less injurious or the wounder less blameable. What happens, I think, is that the senselessness of a crime, particularly when it seems contrary to the criminal's interest, is profoundly frustrating. We are naturally disposed to be angry at the selfishly cruel, the ruthlessly self-aggrandizing man; but that anger is frustrated when we learn that the criminal, for no reason *he* could understand, was hurting *himself* as well as his victim. That is simply not the way properly self-respecting wicked persons are supposed to behave! But then we become angry at him precisely because we cannot be angry in the usual ways. We blame him now for our own frustration—not only for the harm he has caused, but for his not getting anything out of it. Indignation will always out.

Still, in a calmer reflective moment, punishment of the pitiably odd is likely to seem a kind of "pouring it on." Indeed, we might well say of such people what the more forgiving Epictetus said of all wrongdoers, that they are sufficiently punished simply to be the sorts of persons they are. Their crimes are obviously profitless to themselves and serve no apparent other-regarding interest, either malevolent or benevolent. Thus if the point of punishment is to take the profit out of crime, it is superfluous to impose it upon them.

Not only are the motives of some mentally ill but non-compulsive wrongdoers *senseless,* they are senseless in the special way that permits us to speak of them as *incoherent*. Their motives do not fit together and make a coherent whole because one kind of desire, conspicuous as a sore thumb, keeps getting in the way. These desires serve ill the rest of their important interests, including their overriding interest in personal integration and internal harmony. They "gum up the works," as we would say of machinery, and throw the person out of "proper working order." The reason they do is that, insofar as these desires are fulfilled, barriers are put in the paths of the others. They are inconsistent with the others in that it is impossible for all to be jointly satisfied, even though it is possible that the others could, in principle, be satisfied together. Moreover, the "senseless" desires, because they do not cohere, are likely to seem alien, not fully expressive of their owner's essential character.[4] When a person acts to satisfy them, it is as if he were acting on somebody else's desires. And, indeed, the alien desires may have a distinct kind of unifying character of their own, as if a new person were grafted on to the old one.

The final and perhaps most important feature common to the examples of voluntary crimes by mentally ill persons is the actor's *lack of insight into his own motives*. The normal person, in rehearsing the possibilities open to him, finds some prospects appealing and others repugnant, and he usually (but not always) knows what it is about a given prospect that makes it appealing or repugnant. If robbing a bank appeals to him, the reason may be that the excitement, the romance, or (far more likely) the money attracts him; and if having more money appeals to him, he usually knows *why* it does too. Normal persons, to be sure, can be mistaken. A criminal may think it is the adventure that is attracting him, instead of the money, or vice versa. It is easy enough to be confused about these things. Often enough we can test our understanding of our own motives by experimental methods. I may think that prospect *X,* which has characteristics *a, b,* and *c,* appeals to me solely because of *a*; but then, to my surprise, prospect *Y,* which has characteristics *a* and *b,* but not *c, repels* me. Hence I conclude that it was not simply the *a*-ness of *X* after all that attracted me. Moreover, even a person who is a model of mental health will be often ignorant or mistaken about the *ultimate* basis of appeal in the things that appeal to him.

The mentally ill person, however, will be radically and fundamentally benighted about the source of the appeal in his immediate objectives, and the truth will be hid from his view by an internal iron curtain. He may think that he is constructed in such a way that little children arouse him sexually, and that is the end of the matter, hardly suspecting that it is the playful, exploratory, irresponsible, and non-threatening character of his recollected childhood experiences that moves him; or he may think that "exposure for exposure's sake" is what appeals to him in the idea of public undress, whereas really what appeals to him is the public "affirmation of masculinity, a cry of 'Look, here is proof that I am a man.' "[5] The true basis of appeal in the criminal's motivation may be, or become, obvious to an outsider, but his illness keeps him blind to it, often, I think, because this blindness is a necessary condition of the appeal itself. At any rate, his lack of self-awareness is no merely contingent thing, like the ignorance that can be charged to absentmindedness, unperceptiveness, objective ambiguities, or the garden varieties of self-deception. The ignorance is the necessary consequence, perhaps even a constituent, of the mental illness, which, taken as a collection of interconnected symptoms, is an alien condition involuntarily suffered.

III

We come back to our original question, then, in a new guise: why should the incoherent and self-concealed character of the mentally ill man's motives be a ground for special consideration when he has voluntarily committed a crime? Perhaps we should enlarge our conception of *compulsion* so that senseless, misunderstood motives automatically count as compulsive. If Jones's chronic desire to do something harmful is as powerful as, but no more powerful than, normal people's desires to do socially acceptable things, then we might think of Jones's desire as a kind of unfair burden. It is no harder for him to restrain on individual occasions, but he must be restraining it *always*; one slip and he is undone. He is really quite unlucky to have this greater burden and danger. The ordinary person is excused when he is made to do what he does not want to do; but the mentally ill man, the argument might go, is excused because of the compulsive weight of his profitless *wants* themselves.

There may be some justice in this argument, but there is little logic. When we begin to tamper this profoundly with the concept of compulsion, it is likely to come completely apart. If men can be said to be compelled by their own quite resistible desires, then what is there left to contrast compulsion with?

A more plausible move is to enlarge our conception of what it is to act "in ignorance"—the other category in the Aristotelian formula. The kleptomaniac and the fetishist have no conception of what it is that impels them to their bizarre actions. As we have seen, their conduct may well seem as puzzling to themselves as to any observer. So there is a sense in which they do not know, or realize, what it is they are really doing, and perhaps we should make this ignorance a ground for exculpation; but if we do, we shall be in danger of providing a defense for almost all criminals, normal and ill alike. The bank robber, who is deceived into thinking that it is the adventure that appeals to him when it really is the money, has this excuse available to him, as well as the bully who thinks he inflicts beatings in self-defense when it really is the sight of blood that appeals to him. Lack of insight by itself, then, can hardly be a workable extension of the ignorance defense in courts of law.

It is plain, I think, why the penal law requires rather strict interpretations of compulsion and ignorance. One of its major aims is to deter wrongdoers by providing them with a motive, namely, fear of punishment, which they would not otherwise have for refraining from crime. In close cases involving competent calculators, this new motive might be sufficient to tip the motivational scales toward self-restraint. Mentally ill but rationally competent offenders of the sort I have been discussing, provided only that they *can* restrain themselves, are eminently suited for responsibility because the fear of punishment might make some difference in their behavior. But if they truly cannot help what they do, then the fear of punishment is totally useless and might as well not be induced in them in the first place.

Thus, from the point of view of what punishment can achieve for others, it is a perfectly appropriate mode of treatment for rationally competent, noncompulsive, mentally ill persons. But from the point of view of what can be achieved for the offender himself, I still think it is altogether inappropriate. Some of the aims of an enlightened criminal law, after all, do concern the offender himself. Sometimes punishment is supposed to "reform" him by intimidation. This no doubt works once in a while for normally prudent and self-interested offenders. For others, greater claims still are made for punishment, which is expected to achieve not merely effective intimidation but also moral regeneration of the offender. But if we treat the mentally ill criminal in precisely the same way as we treat the normal one, we can only bring him to the point of hopeless despair. The prisoner, still devoid of insight into his own motives, will naturally come to wonder how his so-called illness differs from plain wickedness. His bizarre desires will be taken as simply "given," as evil impulses with no point and no reward, simply "there," an integral and irreducible part of himself; and there is no one more pitiably incorrigible than the man convinced of his own intrinsic wickedness and simply resigned to it.

I agree with Professor Dershowitz that it is outrageous to impose compulsory therapeutic treatment on an unwilling, mentally competent subject. I submit, however, that punishment imposed on the mentally ill, even though it might produce a small social gain in deterrence, is an equally odious measure. I admit that, insofar as the sick offender has voluntarily committed a crime he could have avoided, the state has a perfect right to deprive him of his liberty for a limited period; but, instead of using that time to have him break up rocks with the convicted embezzlers and burglars, we should be making every sympathetic effort to enable him to understand himself, in the hope that self-revelation will permit him to become a responsible citizen.[6] There is no easy way to avoid the problems that come from the institutional mixture of compulsion and therapy.[7] I am afraid I must leave them for my legal and psychiatric friends. My aim in this paper has been the very limited one of showing that mental illness, even without compulsion and general cognitive impairment, is a good deal more pertinent to our moral concerns than the mumps or chicken pox.

NOTES

1. Alan M. Dershowitz, "The Psychiatrist's Power in Civil Commitment: A Knife that Cuts Both Ways." An abridged version of this talk was published in *Psychology Today*, 2/9 (Feb. 1969). 43–47.

2. Consider Professor Dershowitz's example of Dallas Williams, "who at age thirty-nine had spent half his life in jail for seven convictions of assault with a deadly weapon and one conviction of manslaughter. Just before his scheduled release from jail, the government petitioned for his civil commitment. Two psychiatrists testified that although 'at the present time [he] shows no evidence of active mental illness . . . he is potentially dangerous to others and if released is likely to repeat his patterns of criminal behavior, and might commit homicide.' The judge,

in denying the government's petition and ordering Williams' release, observed that: 'the courts have no legal basis for ordering confinement on mere apprehension of future unlawful acts. They must wait until another crime is committed or the person is found insane.' Within months of his release, Williams lived up to the prediction of the psychiatrists and shot two men to death in an unprovoked attack." *Ibid.,* 44.

3. Note on "Civil Restraint, Mental Illness, and the Right to Treatment," *Yale Law Review,* 77/1 (1967), 87.

4. Hence the point of the ancient metaphor of "possession."

5. Paul H. Gebhard et al., *Report on Sex Offenders* (New York: Harper & Row, and Paul B. Hoeber, 1965), 399.

6. I.e., he is clutchable, but not necessarily punishable.

7. But see my "Crime, Clutchability, and Individuated Treatment," in *Doing and Deserving,* 252–271, for some suggestions.

PART 6 SELF-LOVE AND

Whaen people have moral problems and must decide what to do, how can they truly know what is right? When individuals disagree in their moral judgments about other persons, or about their actions or policies, how can they determine by rational means whose judgment is correct? There are so many difficulties in arguing moral questions, and moral disagreements—even among philosophers—are so intractable, that many people have concluded that the role of reason in ethical argument is severely limited, perhaps restricted to finding support for the purely factual premises. Such a view is a form of "skepticism" about ethics. Others maintain that there are no truths in ethics, or that there are no "moral absolutes," or that the "truth" of moral judgments is always relative to a given system of beliefs that itself cannot be proven correct. Phillip Montague and Walter T. Stace, in the opening articles of this section on moral philosophy, discuss the motivations for such views and the reasons given to support them. Unlike most of the other selections in Part Six, these articles are essays *about* ethics rather than essays *in* ethics; but if the conclusions of Montague and Stace are rejected, there may be little point in trying to settle the ethical issues debated in the other articles.

Another form of skeptical challenge to morality comes from a famous theory of human motivation. The theory that human beings are so constituted by nature that they are incapable of desiring or pursuing anything but their own well-being as an end in itself is called *psychological egoism*. If "true morality" requires selfless devotion to others even at the cost of one's own interests, and if all persons are inherently selfish, as this theory claims, there may be no way to motivate persons to behave morally. Genuinely disinterested acts of benevolence, on this view, do not exist, although persons sometimes appear to be acting unselfishly when they take the interests of other people to be the means for promoting their own good. This theory of motivation should be distinguished from the doctrine called *ethical egoism,* which, as its name indicates, is not a theory about how human beings in fact act but rather a moral doctrine stating how they ought to act. According to his doctrine, one ought to pursue one's own well-being, and only one's own well-being,

THE CLAIMS OF MORALITY

as an end in itself. A *psychological* egoist, insofar as he or she bothered with ethics at all, might be expected to be an *ethical* egoist; for if there is only one thing that we *can* pursue, there cannot be some other thing that we *ought* to pursue. Most psychological egoists, however, have sought some way to reconcile necessarily selfish motivation with the unselfish and even self-sacrificing conduct required by morality. Many argue, for example, that generally the best means to promote one's own happiness is to work for the public good or the happiness of others.

The essay by the editor on psychological egoism is probably the only article in this book that was not written for publication. It was distributed to students only for classroom use at Brown University, Princeton University, and U.C.L.A. during the period from 1958 to 1966. The essay contains very elementary distinctions and standard arguments reorganized and written into elementary terms. It might very well be used, because of its pedagogical intent, as the student's introduction to this section, or even perhaps to the whole volume. Most students, after much resistance, seemed to be persuaded by its arguments; but some of the best students (especially those who were psychology or biology majors) remained unconvinced to the end. Some of these unbelieving students would admit that the a priori arguments for psychological egoism are fallacious, but insisted that the biological sciences and particularly evolutionary theory may yet provide empirical evidence for the theory. How could disinterested service to others have any evolutionary advantage, they wondered, in the Darwinian world of constant struggle and "survival of the fittest"?

To this question the eminent biologist Stephen Jay Gould gives what at first may seem a surprising answer: An individual animal's sacrifice *can,* under certain circumstances, lead to "the perpetuation of his own genes" in the species. Gould's essay explains how "kin altruism" can actually have an evolutionary advantage; he does this by drawing on some basic concepts of the new discipline called "sociobiology." The philosopher Howard Kahane is also impressed by the theories of the sociobiologists. In his article here, Kahane argues that the disposition to reciprocate favors and cooperate (however grudgingly) with others can have a definite survival value in the human species. Such a disposition can provide the motivational groundwork for a conception of morality as neither egoistic nor sacrificially altruistic but rather as "rules of fair reciprocity among cooperating competitors."

Just how much weight should one's own interests have in determining what one *ought* to do in situations where the interests of others are bound to be affected by one's action? This question can be interpreted in such a way that it asks us not to weigh the rational claims of morality against those of self-interest, but rather to decide just how much of our self-interest is represented by, or included in, the claims of morality. The articles in the subsection entitled "Utilitarianism, Altruism, and Ethical Egoism" express some leading views about the nature and ground of true morality. The five philosophers—none of them *immoralists*—who wrote these selections differ among themselves over what degree of self-sacrifice, if any, and what degree of self-promotion, if any, a rational morality requires.

The theory that morality requires us to look after our own interest exclusively (or primarily) and respect the interests of others not at all (or only secondarily) may be called *ethical egoism*. But we must be very careful in our definitions, since a large number of possible "egoistic" theories do not *exactly* fit this definition. Perhaps the least misleading thing to say is that a moral theory is egoistic to the extent that it emphasizes the propriety of pursuing one's own interest. This would allow differences in degree of egoism among theories. Similarly, the theory that morality requires us totally to forget our own interests and selflessly devote ourselves to the interests of others can be called *ethical altruism*. Any particular moral theory is altruistic to the extent that it emphasizes the propriety of self-abnegation and devotion to others.

The ethical theory of John Stuart Mill (1806–1873), usually called *utilitarianism* (as Mill himself named it) but sometimes denominated *universalistic* (as opposed to egoistic) *hedonism,* is neither purely altruistic nor purely egoistic. In deciding (better *calculating*) what one ought to do, according to this theory, "everybody is to count as one and nobody as more than one." That is to say, I should consider the alternative actions open to me and their likely consequences for the interests of all those who will be directly affected by them, including of course *my own*. Then, insofar as my act will promote the happiness of the people (including *me*) it affects, just so far does it tend to be the right act for me to perform; and insofar as it promotes unhappiness (including *my* unhappiness), it tends to be wrong. Ideally, I ought to tally up the scores of the alternative acts open to me, counting my own interests as no more and no less important than anyone else's, and select that act which causes the greatest net balance all around of pleasure over pain.

Utilitarianism thus rules out partiality for self, or for family, social class, or country, and requires us to consider every human being whose happiness can be affected by our conduct to be exactly on a par. It thus has a certain initial attractiveness; but it is not without its difficulties. Should I really give all my savings to relieve the hunger of distant peoples instead of using the money to send my children to college, provided only that I thereby do more good "all around"? Do not—*ought* not—my children have a greater claim on me than does any distant stranger? And don't I owe more to those persons to whom I stand in special relation—creditors, those to whom I have made promises, neighbors, friends, teammates—than to individuals who stand in no special relation to me? And what relation can be more intimate and "special" than one's relation to oneself?

J. O. Urmson, of Oxford, would apply the test of social utility, in some cases, not to individual acts but to rules, practices, and alternative systems of morality. A system of morality, after all, is a kind of human artifact, rational only insofar as it serves to promote human welfare. If our moral rules require too much of us in the way of saintliness, heroism, and self-sacrifice, they will produce no more useful results than our human nature is prepared to yield; moreover, they will bring the "moral law" itself into disrepute, and produce widespread morbid guilt and suffering. Psychological egoists have argued in the past that human nature is such that no one is capable of deliberately and voluntarily sacrificing oneself or devoting oneself selflessly to a social cause. They have sometimes gone on to infer from this that no reasonable moral rule, therefore, can *require* the heroism that no one is capable of achieving. Urmson, on the contrary, holds that saintliness and heroism are possible, although, he concedes, they are so difficult that perhaps not many people are able to measure up to such lofty standards. For this and other reasons, a rational utilitarian moral system will recognize (as traditional Christianity does) a distinction between basic rules imposing duties and obligations, and ideals of perfection that guide aspiration but are not morally mandatory.

An ethical egoist would reject Urmson's compromise. Not only is it false, according to ethical egoism, that we *must* sacrifice our interests for the sake of others (that is, that self-sacrifice is *required* of us), it is even false that we *ought* to make such sacrifices (that is, that self-sacrifice is even an *ideal of perfection*). Some egoists[1] would concede the reasonableness of a person's assuming a great risk, or paying a great price, in order (say) to save the life of a *loved one,* but would argue that insofar as the loss of the loved one would make the person's own life miserable, the act in question clearly would *not* be self-sacrificing. These egoists, however, would still maintain that it would be unreasonable for a person to make any sacrifice at all for the sake of a complete stranger. The main point of this softened kind of ethical egoism is not to deny the reasonableness of loving and benevolent acts, but rather to give "love" and "benevolence" themselves an egoistic psychological analysis. (The editor argues in his essay "Psychological Egoism" that such analyses are generally flawed.)

Peter Singer's article, "Famine, Affluence, and Morality," draws out with relentless rigor the full consequences of the utilitarian formula that "each is to count as one and no one as more than one." Singer argues that the formula implies that we have duties to relieve the suffering of others right up to the point where doing more would cause greater misery to ourselves than it would relieve in others. Singer's conclusion is by far the most "altruistic" in this section, unless we attribute it as well to Mill (at least by implication). In the course of his argument Singer gives rebuttal to Urmson's contention that utilitarian considerations support a sharp distinction between acts of duty and acts of charity.

Ethical egoism, the view at the opposite extreme from Singer's, receives a very thorough critique in the article, "Ethical Egoism," by Paul Taylor. He considers various standard objections to the theory—including the argument that there is an inconsistency in the doctrine that *everyone* should put oneself first—and the standard egoistic rejoinders. The objections, Taylor concludes, are clearly more cogent than the rejoinders.

The final article in the subsection on utilitarianism, altruism, and ethical egoism is from a larger essay by W. D. Falk that points up the moral dangers of giving too *little* weight to one's own interests compared to others' interests. It would be a mistake to characterize

1. See, for example, Ayn Rand, "The Ethics of Emergencies," in *The Virtue of Selfishness* (New York: Signet Books, 1961).

Falk's view as "ethical egoism" of any kind; yet his eloquent essay argues that purely self-regarding directives must be included in the list of valid precepts by which the person of moral wisdom leads his or her life.

The final subsection is devoted to what Paul Taylor calls "the ultimate question" about morality: not "What does morality require of me?" but "Why should I do what morality requires if I can better serve my own interests otherwise?"—a question that arises naturally, if not frequently, in everyone's experience. Suppose you find a wallet containing $5,000 in cash. Surely the morally right thing to do (at least according to the prevailing moral code) would be to return the wallet with the money to its owner. But would this truly be the most reasonable course of action? Think of what you have to gain: an expression of gratitude, some small satisfaction at having done your duty (mixed with nagging doubts that you are a fool), and *maybe* a small reward. Now compare these benefits with what you have to lose—namely, the $5,000 itself. It would seem that the losses involved in doing your "duty" (if that's what it is) far outweigh the gains. (Perhaps the example might be still more convincing if the money belonged not to a private person but to a great corporation or the federal government.) Looking at the matter in this way, wouldn't you be a fool to return the money? Isn't it *unreasonable,* indeed profoundly contrary to reason, voluntarily to choose a loss in preference to a gain for oneself? And yet this is what morality seems continually to require of us: that we put the interests of other people ahead of our own. How, then, can it be reasonable to be moral?

One line of reply to this challenge immediately suggests itself. Not to return the property of others is tantamount to stealing it. If other people were ever to find out that you are, in effect, a thief, their opinion of you would drop drastically and your reputation might never fully recover. Moreover, if the authorities were to make this discovery about you, the consequences might be still worse. Even if no one ever found you out, you would have to live in continued anxiety and fear; and even if you got over that, you might become just a bit bolder in the face of subsequent temptations, until your very success finally would betray you, and you would be found out. The idea that it can ever *pay* to do what is morally wrong, in short, is always a miscalculation.

Glaucon and Adeimantus, two characters in Plato's *Republic,* are not satisfied with this kind of answer. That there are advantages in having the reputation of being moral and upright (or "just" as they put it) is perfectly evident; what they wish to learn from Socrates is whether there are corresponding advantages in really being, as opposed to merely seeming, morally upright. If it is reasonable to be honest only *because* dishonesty doesn't pay, then, it would seem, it is reasonable to be honest only *when* dishonesty doesn't pay; the ideally wise man would then be he who is able to have the "best of both worlds" by seeming, but not really being, moral.

Socrates' answer to the challenge of Glaucon and Adeimantus is developed in considerable detail throughout the remaining pages of the *Republic*. The essential core of that answer is included here, but without its *full* supporting argument, which includes, as ultimate premises, Plato's theory of knowledge and his theory of the nature of reality. In the end Socrates persuades Glaucon and Adeimantus to see that the elements of the unjust man's soul are necessarily discordant just as the elements of a sick man's body are out of harmony; so the question whether injustice can ever pay is as "ridiculous" as the question whether it can be more conducive to happiness to be sick than to be healthy.

Plato's *Republic* is prototypical of much of the classical literature of moral philosophy in that it consists largely of arguments designed to show that there is a necessary and invariant connection between duty and self-interest. Many of the great moralists have found unthinkable the notion that a person ever truly profits in the long run from being immoral. Whatever else morality may be, these writers argue, it must be something reasonable. And surely, they go on, it cannot be reasonable for a person deliberately to act contrary to his or her own interest. Hence, it follows that the dictates of morality (assumed to be reasonable) never require sacrifice of self-interest, appearances to the contrary. Many of the great systems of moral theory, then, are designed to account for this conclusion.

Some critics of this tradition have suggested that the main reason why it has seemed unreasonable for a person to act contrary to his or her own interest is the assumption that normal people are *incapable* of so acting, and that traditional moral philosophers, Socrates included, have tacitly assumed the truth of psychological egoism. But if people can be motivated to do their duties for duty's sake, quite apart from calculations of self-interest, as Immanuel Kant (1724–1804) argued, then the question "Why be moral?" does not arise in its usual form.

The concluding essay by Paul Taylor argues that a person's commitment to the supremacy of morality over self-interest (or the opposite) is "beyond reason, neither rational nor irrational," and yet is of the very most fundamental significance, amounting in effect to the decision to "be a certain sort of person." In the end the ultimate question (as the existentialists might have put it) is whether one can "authentically"—that is in a manner true to oneself—choose to have one sort of character rather than the other.

Ethical Skepticism

PHILLIP   MONTAGUE

Are There Objective and Absolute Moral Standards?*

Phillip Montague (1938–   ) teaches philosophy at Western Washington University.

1. MORAL ABSOLUTES AS EXCEPTIONLESS MORAL PRINCIPLES

Let us begin our discussion by considering the following question: What are some kinds of actions that are morally wrong? If you were asked this question the answers that would probably spring immediately to mind are such things as stealing, murder, lying, and failing to keep commitments, with some of you perhaps thinking of abortion, war, or law-breaking. On further reflection, however, you might be tempted to respond with a question of your own: In being asked what sorts of things are wrong, am I being asked what sorts of things are *always* wrong, no matter what the circumstances are?

You are likely to ask this last question because you no doubt realize that at least a large number of the kinds of actions you are inclined to regard as wrong can apparently have instances which are *not* wrong. Might not a situation arise in which, say, failing to keep a commitment is the *right* thing to do? Consider, for example, the following hypothetical case:

Jim Brown's employer has agreed to allow him two days off from work for a fishing trip if Brown can find a reliable replacement to fill in for him while he is gone. Brown asks his friend Joe Green if he will take the job, and Green

agrees to do so. Brown then leaves on his fishing trip confident that his friend Green will keep the commitment he made.

On his first day of work at Brown's job, however, Green receives a phone call from his wife who tells him that she has become very ill and is having difficulty caring for their two small children. Green knows that his wife is no alarmist, and would contact him only in an emergency, but he also realizes that, even if he explains the situation to Brown's employer, Brown's job will be in jeopardy if there is no one to do his work while he is on vacation. The question, then, is this: If Green does leave the job in order to care for his wife and children—thus failing in his commitment to Brown—will he be doing the wrong thing?

Most people would concede that examples of this sort at least cast considerable doubt on the idea that failing to keep commitments is without exception wrong. And of course similar examples can be constructed for other sorts of actions which we might be inclined, initially in any case, to classify as wrong (or as right or as our duty, etc.). The fact that many of these cases are genuinely puzzling, and that many of our own moral decisions are difficult and even agonizing, does indicate, however, that even when we are tempted to conclude that, say, failing to keep some particular commitment is *right,* we nevertheless hold fast to the idea that there is *something* wrong with the action. Unpacking and resolving the issues involved in such cases is one of the deepest and most perplexing problems in moral philosophy; it is also a problem which for the most part we must ignore in our discussion.

We have noted that a certain problem arises when

we try to list kinds of actions that are wrong (and we would of course have encountered the same difficulty if we tried to list kinds of actions that are right, or that we ought to perform, etc.). The problem concerns whether there are any sorts of actions which are, without exception, wrong (right, etc.), and is sometimes phrased in terms of talk about "moral absolutes." That is, those who believe that there are sorts of actions which are, without exception wrong (right, etc.) are sometimes said to believe in moral absolutes; those who deny that there are kinds of actions that are unexceptionably wrong (right, etc.) are said to deny that there are moral absolutes. We shall see later that this interpretation of what it is to believe or not to believe in "absolutes" is not the only possible one, and our discussion of moral absolutes will eventually focus on a rather different philosophical position.

Those who believe in the existence of moral absolutes (which for now we are taking to mean that there are kinds of actions which are without exception right, wrong, etc.) most commonly refer to the killing or torturing of innocent human beings as examples of actions that are always wrong, and to "good Samaritanism" as a kind of action that is always right. But even though it is extremely plausible to believe that, say, the killing of innocents is always wrong, there are cases which suggest that even this sort of action may be morally justified on occasion. The following example describes such a case:

Mike Smith is suffering severe and continually increasing pain from cancer. In an attempt to ease his suffering, Mike's physician has been giving him heavy doses of morphine, with the amount of morphine required to ease Mike's pain constantly increasing. Indeed, it is now apparent that the dosage of morphine necessary to control Mike's suffering is so large that being given the required amount would certainly kill him. In full awareness of this state of affairs—as well as of the fact that Mike's illness is terminal—his physician gives Mike the lethal injection of morphine.

There are several ways in which someone who believes that the killing of innocents is always wrong without exception might attempt to deal with the case just described. Such an individual might steadfastly stick by his principle and insist that Mike's physician committed a moral wrong in killing him. Or, our hypothetical absolutist might claim that, while Mike's doctor caused Mike's death, he didn't really *kill* Mike—and then go on to maintain that causing death differs in a morally significant way from kill-

ing. A third possible approach to the problem might involve claiming that the correct way to describe the action performed by Mike's physician is "easing Mike's suffering" and not "killing Mike" (or even "causing Mike's death").

Whatever an absolutist might say about a case like Mike Smith's, however, it is clear that such cases raise questions about the idea that even a principle like "It is wrong to kill the innocent" holds in all cases and without exception. And there are many who argue very convincingly that a careful and sensitive appraisal of actual situations reveals that any moral principle that is at all useful in guiding moral decisions will have exceptions.

The idea that there are no kinds of actions that are either right or wrong without exception (which, for the time being, we are interpreting as a denial that there are moral absolutes) is often confused with a rather different position regarding the nature of morality. This latter position states that moral matters are entirely matters of individual (or perhaps group) opinion or attitude. Someone who holds this view would claim that whether an action is right, wrong, etc., is determined by the beliefs, opinions, attitudes, or emotions of arbitrary individuals or groups. It is easy to see why this position might be interpreted as amounting to nothing more than the rejection of moral absolutes, since if, say, the wrongness of an action is determined by individual attitudes, then the obvious variations in attitude from individual to individual would evidently prevent any sort of action from always being wrong. But if we look more closely at the two positions in question we will see that they differ from each other in important ways.

Our understanding of the differences between the two positions in question will be facilitated by examining the following two questions:

1. Are there any sorts of actions which are, without exception, wrong (right, etc.)?

2. Is the wrongness (rightness, etc.) of an action determined by the beliefs, attitudes, opinions, or feelings of arbitrary individuals or groups?

It is tempting to say that someone who answers "no" to the first question must answer "yes" to the second, which would be to conclude that one who denies that there are moral absolutes must agree that morality is an individual matter. But this sort of conclusion would be mistaken; a person could answer "no" to both questions (1) and (2). Someone might say, for example, that although nothing is without exception right or wrong, what determines rightness or wrongness in a particular case are the *objective* circumstances surrounding that case—circumstances which have nothing to do with individual (or group) opinions or attitudes. Notice that, in the example we used above in connection with the question whether a particular act of commitment breaking could be right, the evident mitigating factors were in no way concerned with the attitudes, etc., of arbitrary individuals, but pertained rather to objective features of the situation.

Now that we have separated issues connected with question (2) above from those concerning question (1), let us focus on the former. This will involve departing for now from our consideration of questions regarding moral absolutes, but we will return to these questions later; and when we return we will be better able to deal with them as a result of the discussion we will engage in next.

2. MORAL SUBJECTIVISM

Let us refer to a person who gives an affirmative answer to question (2) (from the preceding section) as a "moral subjectivist." We can then call someone who answers this question negatively a "moral objectivist." The terms "subjectivist" and "objectivist" (as well as "objective" and "subjective") have different meanings in ordinary usage, so it is important in the discussion which follows that we not lose sight of the fact that these expressions are being used in a special way here. It is not uncommon, for example, to hear someone's view of a situation characterized as subjective (or as objective), with the emphasis in such descriptions being placed on the extent to which the person allows his own attitudes, feelings, etc., to influence his judgments concerning the situation. But in such cases there need not be (and usually is not) any suggestion that the individual's attitudes, etc., are *determining* the situation to be a certain way. And it is this last condition which is crucial to applications of "subjective" in the way we are using this term here.

Although subjectivism might be adopted outside the moral realm (and outside the more general sphere of norms and values), it is much more common to find the position put forward within these areas. And it is easy to see why this should be the case. For suppose two chemists were to disagree regarding

what to expect from a particular experiment. It would be reasonable to suppose that their dispute, which is, of course, not a moral one, could be resolved—that we could discover which of them (if either) is correct—by performing the experiment. There is apparently in this case an objective criterion, namely how the experiment actually turns out, for assessing each of the chemist's views. But moral disagreements are apparently different. In particular it is difficult to see what the analogue would be in a moral disagreement to actually carrying out the experiment in our example of the disagreement between the two chemists. What objective criterion would we use to determine which of two individuals disagreeing over a moral matter is correct?

Suppose, for example, John and Marsha are two young people who decide to live together without marrying. When they announce their decision to Marsha's mother Mrs. Jones, she becomes very upset and urges them to reconsider because, she claims, they would be doing something morally wrong. John and Marsha disagree. They accuse Mrs. Jones of narrow-minded adherence to an outdated morality and maintain that what they are doing is not morally wrong. Without attempting here to resolve the dispute between Mrs. Jones and John and Marsha, let us note how difficult it is to produce an acceptable objective criterion to settle the matter. Of course we might come up with *something* in the way of a criterion—perhaps divine law or parental authority—but the question whether such a criterion is *acceptable* would raise its head, and we would again appear forced to appeal to individual opinions or attitudes.

The moral subjectivist simply denies the existence of objective criteria for resolving moral issues. He would insist that the rightness or wrongness of John and Marsha's contemplated action depends upon the viewpoint of any individual who happens to hold a view regarding the issue, and the search for objective criteria is therefore bound to be a vain one. If the subjectivist is *correct* in his approach to morality, then there is no way of choosing between the position of Mrs. Jones on the one hand, and that of John and Marsha on the other: their positions are evidently equally acceptable.

3. THE PROBLEM OF CONTRADICTIONS

With the understanding of moral subjectivism we now have, we can consider whether the position is acceptable as a general approach to morality.

The first thing that must occur to anyone studying moral subjectivism seriously is that the view allows the possibility that an action can be both right and not right, or wrong and not wrong, etc. This possibility exists because, as we have seen, the subjectivist claims that the moral character of an action is determined by individual subjective states; and these states can vary from person to person, even when directed toward the same action on the same occasion. Hence one and the same action can evidently be determined to have—simultaneously—radically different moral characters. This kind of result must give us pause, even if it turns out in the end not to be a problem.

To sharpen the point at issue here, let us focus on the version of subjectivism which says this:

(1) If someone thinks that an action is right (wrong, etc.) then it *is* right (wrong, etc.); if someone thinks that an action isn't right (wrong, etc.) then it *isn't* right (wrong, etc.).

Statement (1) obviously expresses the subjectivist's way of thinking because it implies that the rightness (wrongness, etc.) of an action is determined by individual opinion. We will now suppose that statement (1) is true and examine its implications as applied to the example employed above involving John, Marsha, and Mrs. Jones.

Let us abbreviate John and Marsha's contemplated act of living together by the letter A; their living together can then be expressed by talking about their performance of A. As we have already indicated, Mrs. Jones thinks that performing A is wrong, while John and Marsha think it isn't wrong. Now let us examine the two statements.

(2) Mrs. Jones thinks that performing A is wrong.
(3) John and Marsha think that performing A isn't wrong.

In light of Statement (1), it is clear that from (1) and (2) follows

(4) Performing A is wrong.

and from (1) and (3) it follows that

(5) Performing A isn't wrong.

It is precisely this sort of result which we noted earlier is allowed for by subjectivism. Now what about (4) and (5)? In particular, can they both be true?

In attempting to answer this last question, we must be careful to distinguish it from these similar sounding but very different questions: "*Which* of the two statements (4) and (5) is true?" and "How do we *know* which of the two statements is true?" Remember, we are asking whether (4) and (5) can be true together, and this question can be answered without determining which of the two is true much less whether we *know* which is true. Having separated the question we are interested in from these others, it should now be clear that, at least on the face of the matter, (4) and (5) contradict each other and hence cannot both be true. And if subjectivism—at least as expressed in (1) and (2)—does generate such contradictory conclusions, then the position is certainly untenable. What we must now determine is whether moral subjectivism can avoid the kind of problem we have just described.

4. AN APPROACH TO THE PROBLEM OF CONTRADICTIONS

One way a subjectivist might try to avoid the problem of contradictions is this: he might admit that, *as they stand,* (4) and (5) do contradict each other, and hence cannot be true together; but then he could go on to claim that no self-respecting subjectivist would conclude that some action could be *simply* right or *simply* wrong. In connection with statements (4) and (5), our hypothetical subjectivist might continue, we must say that performing A is wrong *to Mrs. Jones;* and performing A isn't wrong *to John and Marsha.* It is statements like these last two, with their references to *individuals,* we might be informed, which are the proper conclusions of subjectivism; and such statements clearly do not contradict each other.

If we accept the line of reasoning just presented, then for statements (4) and (5) we should substitute these statements:

(6) Performing A is wrong to Mrs. Jones.
(7) Performing A isn't wrong to John and Marsha.

And the subjectivist who offers (6) and (7) as alternatives to (4) and (5) is evidently correct at least in asserting that (6) and (7) are not contradictory. Moreover, in containing references to individuals, (6) and (7) appear to be much closer than (4) and (5) to the spirit of moral subjectivism, which emphasizes the role of individual subjective states as determiners of morality. But if we take a closer look at (6) and (7), particularly in light of their alleged status as conclusions of subjectivism, we will see that simply substituting them for (4) and (5) gives rise to problems.

Recall that we derived (4) logically from (1) (a version of subjectivism) and (2), while we derived (5) from (1) and (3). Statements (4) and (5) are thus obvious and straightforward consequences of subjectivism as expressed in (1). But (6) and (7) are not in this way consequences of subjectivism. The phrases "to Mrs. Jones" and "to John and Marsha" were added to (4) and (5) as a means of avoiding contradictions, and not because the additions are justified by anything we have said so far about subjectivism—in particular not by anything contained in (1). Thus the claim made above by our hypothetical subjectivist that statements like (6) and (7) are the only proper consequences of subjectivism is certainly a questionable one, given what we have said up to this point.

The defender of subjectivism does, however, have an out: he can claim that (1) is simply a misstatement of subjectivism. He can say that, just as (6) and (7) have references to individuals, so must (1); and if we are to have a correct statement of moral subjectivism we must substitute for (1) the following:

> (1') If someone thinks that an action is right (wrong, etc.), then it is right (wrong, etc.) *to that individual;* if someone thinks that an action isn't right (wrong, etc.), then it isn't right (wrong) *to that individual.*

Having added these references to individuals to (1) to obtain (1'), we can now see that (6) is a logical consequence of (1') and (2), and (7) is a logical consequence of (1') and (3). We have now apparently arrived at *noncontradictory* consequences of subjectivism, and in doing so have formulated, in (1'), what looks like a more satisfactory statement of this position than is contained in (1).

But the situation is not quite as happy for the moral subjectivist as it might appear. Consider in particular the phrases "to Mrs. Jones," "to John and Marsha" and "to that individual" as they are used in (6), (7), and (1') respectively. What precisely do these phrases mean? We can use such expressions in nonmoral contexts—in saying, for example, that, *to certain primitive people,* the earth is flat; or that, *to children,* Santa Claus is real. But such statements translate

very naturally into talk about beliefs or opinions in this way: certain primitive people think, or believe that the earth is flat; children think or believe that Santa Claus is real. It is no less natural to interpret (6) and (7) in a similar fashion:

> (6') Mrs. Jones thinks that performing A is wrong.
> (7') John and Marsha think that performing A isn't wrong.

And (1') turns out to look like this:

> (1'') If someone thinks that an action is right (wrong, etc.), then that individual thinks it is right (wrong, etc.); if someone thinks that an action isn't right (wrong, etc.), then that individual thinks it isn't right (wrong, etc.)

Now there are several things to be noted at this point. First, while (1'') may be true, it is terribly uninteresting; secondly, (6') and (7') simply duplicate (2) and (3) which we assumed at the outset of our discussion; and thirdly, all references to what *is* right (wrong, etc.) have disappeared from our discussion, being replaced by references to what individuals *think* is right (wrong, etc.). Freedom from contradiction has thus been purchased at a very high price: rather than an interesting (albeit problematic) theory about right and wrong, we now have some trivial remarks about what individuals think is right or wrong.

But perhaps the subjectivist who urges us to substitute (6) and (7) for (4) and (5) as a means of avoiding contradictions has something in mind which does not lead to the unsatisfactory results we have just noted. Perhaps there is a way to construe the references to Mrs. Jones and to John and Marsha in (6) and (7) which does not force us to interpret these statements as concerned with what Mrs. Jones and John and Marsha *think* is right as expressed in (6') and (7'). Whether such alternatives exist for the subjectivist is a question we shall examine in the next section.

5. SUBJECTIVE RELATIVISM

Recall that we considered above the idea that

> (4) Performing A is wrong

and

> (5) Performing A isn't wrong

are importantly different from obviously contradictory pairs of statements like and

(9) This isn't rectangular

in that (8) and (9) are complete statements as they stand, while (4) and (5) are not. It was suggested that converting (4) and (5) into complete statements requires the addition to each of phrases like "to Mrs. Jones" and "to John and Marsha."

What the subjectivist can now say is this: we are deceived by the (superficial) grammatical forms of (4) and (5) (which *look* exactly like (8) and (9)) into thinking that (4) says of A that it has the property or characteristic of being right, and that (5) says of A that it lacks this property or characteristic; and this assumption leads to the conclusion that (4) and (5) cannot be true together, since one and the same thing cannot simultaneously possess and not possess a given property. But, our subjectivist continues, we must recognize that (4) and (5) are not concerned with the ascription of *properties*. These statements should be compared not with "This is rectangular" and "This isn't rectangular" but with something like "He is the father" and "He isn't the father," where the latter deal not with *properties* but with *relations*.

If we look at the statements "He is the father" and "He isn't the father" we can see their grammatical similarity to "This is rectangular" and "This isn't rectangular." At the same time we can notice that, while the latter pair of statements cannot be true together, the former can—if we interpret them as shorthand for, say, "He is the father of Jimmie" and "He isn't the father of Johnnie." The point is that "is the father" is implicitly relational even if it does not appear to be. And, in comparing "is right" to "is the father," while contrasting the former to "is rectangular," the subjectivist is claiming that "is right" is implicitly relational also. If the subjectivist is correct in this claim, then (4) and (5) are in a real sense incomplete; the need to complete them—as well as the way to do so—is suggested by the idea that

(6) Performing A is wrong to Mrs. Jones

and

(7) Performing A isn't wrong to John and Marsha

be substituted for (4) and (5) as expressions of what the subjectivist sees as the proper form of moral judgments. Of course a great deal needs to be said by the subjectivist regarding the nature of the rela-

tions that rightness, wrongness, etc., are supposed to be, but before turning to that issue let us investigate further exactly how this relational form of subjectivism differs from the version we examined initially.

One way we might become clearer regarding how these two forms of subjectivism differ is in terms of the following lists of expressions:

is red	is the father
is rectangular	is taller
is six feet tall	is before
is an apple	is next to
etc.	etc.

You can no doubt add expressions to each of these lists because you recognize the principles according to which they are constructed: the lefthand column contains expressions which refer to properties, the righthand column expressions referring to relations. Our initial assumption about the expressions "is right," "is wrong," etc., would have located them in the lefthand column. This assumption is the natural one to make, particularly in view of the superficial grammar of these expressions, and is reflected in our adoption of (1) in the preceding chapter as an expression of moral subjectivism. In claiming, however, that "is right," "is wrong," etc., are relational expressions, the subjectivist is rejecting the assumption that these expressions belong in the lefthand column, and insisting that they should be placed in the righthand column.

We have now described two versions of subjectivism, one of which views moral expressions as referring to properties, the other viewing these expressions as referring to relations, and it will be convenient to give these two versions labels. One label is suggested by the terms "relation" and "relational" which are central to one form of subjectivism we have considered, and we will refer to this form of subjectivism as "subjective relativism." The other version of subjectivism, that according to which rightness, wrongness, etc., are properties (and not relations), we will refer to as "subjective absolutism." What we have said so far then, suggests that subjective absolutism has serious difficulties (leading either to contradictions or to triviality), and hence that if moral subjectivism is to be acceptable at all, it must be interpreted in its relativistic (relational) form. Whether even in this latter form moral subjectivism is a tenable theory of morality remains to be seen.

We are clearly using "relativism" and "absolutism" in a special way here, though our use is by no means entirely eccentric or out of line with normal philosophical usage. Although some philosophers interpret relativism, at least in its *philosophical* form (and we will examine a *nonphilosophical* form later) as the view that different individuals or groups have fundamentally different moral standards which are equally acceptable, such an interpretation must be based on our way of viewing relativism (i.e., as a claim about the relational nature of moral concepts) if it is to avoid contradictions. For example, suppose it is claimed by someone that some group of people regard human sacrifice as right while others regard it as not being right, that this is a fundamental moral disagreement, and that the views of the disagreeing groups are equally acceptable. Does this mean that "Human sacrifice is right" and "Human sacrifice isn't right" are *both* true? How could this be unless we interpret rightness as relational? And if we cannot avoid contradictions without this last assumption, then relativism (again, as a philosophical position) must be interpreted as at least implying a view about the nature of moral concepts, viz., that they are relational.

The term "absolutism" appears in philosophical discussions much less commonly than does "relativism," and it is difficult to say how our use of the former expression squares with ordinary philosophical usage. We can note, however, that there is an important difference between our use of "absolutism" and nontechnical talk about "moral absolutes," some of which occurred at the very beginning of our discussion. When most people speak of moral absolutes they apparently have in mind things that are right, wrong, etc., regardless of particular circumstances. For example, someone who claims that our duty not to lie is a moral absolute would normally be interpreted as saying that each and every act of lying, irrespective of the situation in which it is performed, is a failure to do one's duty. Another way to describe this view is by saying that it holds that moral rules or principles have no exceptions.

The difference between this last position and absolutism as we are interpreting the latter here is this: an absolutist (someone who holds that rightness, wrongness, etc., are properties) can allow for exceptions to moral rules in that he could say, for example, that one particular act of lying has the *property* of being right, while another act of lying has the *property* of being wrong. He could say this even if he is an *objective* absolutist, by maintaining that what determines whether an action has the property of being right are *objective* features of the situation in which the action is performed. In connection with our example of John and Marsha's plans to live together, an objective absolutist could deny that each and every act of living together out of wedlock is either right or wrong; he could maintain that John and Marsha's living together would not be wrong because they are mature individuals with a healthy relationship, a knowledge of contraceptive devices, etc. (note the *objective* character of these considerations); and at the same time he could assert that it would be wrong for Al and Salome to live together, citing their immaturity, their basic dislike for each other, etc. (which again are objective considerations).

We will discuss no further the question whether there are moral absolutes in the sense of exceptionless moral principles. For our purposes, then, the use of "absolute" or "absolutism" will be confined to discussing the idea that rightness, wrongness, etc., are properties, and will be contrasted to our use of "relative" and "relativism" which refer to the view that moral concepts are relational.

6. EVALUATING SUBJECTIVE RELATIVISM

We have succeeded in our discussion up to this point in distilling from a confused mixture of views (which often pass as a single unified position), a form of moral subjectivism which is fairly well defined, and which is also free from potential contradictions. This form of subjectivism, which we are calling subjective relativism, is a position at which any moral subjectivist wishing to avoid both confusion and contradictions in his theory of morality must arrive. It is moral subjectivism in its most acceptable form, and what we will now do is examine subjective relativism to see just how acceptable it is as a theory of morality.

As with any theory, philosophical or otherwise, an obvious way to assess the acceptability of subjective relativism is by examining its implications. This approach at least provides a method of falsification in the sense that if the implications of the theory are unacceptable, then the theory must be rejected. Of course the fact that a theory's implications are not unacceptable does not guarantee the truth of the theory, though it may give us a reason not to reject it out of hand.

Consider how this process works in the case of a scientific theory. Suppose, for example, that a theory of combustion is proposed which states that when an object burns, a certain substance departs from the object, and that this substance is not recoverable after combustion occurs. This theory implies, then, that the products of combustion will weigh less—or at least not more than—the object weighed before it burned. But now assume that we weigh an object, burn it, collect the products of combustion and weigh them, only to discover that the products of combustion weigh *more* than the original object. How could we continue to accept the original theory, the implications of which are inconsistent with the results of our experiment? Clearly we would be required to abandon the theory, at least in its stated form, and explain combustion in a way which squares with the results of our experiment.

The process of evaluating philosophical theories is analogous, but with an important difference: observation cannot be relied upon to assess the implications of a philosophical theory in the way that it can be for a scientific theory. This fact in no way implies, however, that the truth or falsity of a philosophical theory is merely a matter of opinion, that it is at bottom a subjective matter. For even though we cannot rely in any simple way on *observation* to test philosophical theories, we still want to know whether these theories correspond to *reality,* that is, to *objective* reality. How we make such determinations is not easy to explain, but some indication of how the procedure works can be gained by actually examining a proposed theory. And we shall do this for subjective relativism as a proposed theory of morality.

We have stated that, according to subjective relativism, moral concepts such as that of being right and of being wrong are relations. We have also noted that the words we ordinarily use to express these concepts—words like "right" and "wrong"— are not obviously relational. It is up to the subjective relativist to show, then, that these expressions are *implicitly* relational—that they can be paraphrased so as to reveal their relational character. And in so doing, the subjective relativist must preserve the subjective nature of his theory according to which whether an action is right, wrong, etc., is determined by individual (or group) subjective states. Let us consider an example of subjective relativism to see how the theory might work.

If someone were to claim that an action's being right consists simply in its being approved of by someone, he would be putting forward a form of subjective relativism. The theory is subjective in that whether an action is right or wrong depends upon whether some (arbitrary) individual approves of it; it is relativistic because approval is a relational concept holding between individuals and what it is they approve of. Note that on this view the rightness of an action amounts to *nothing more than* its being approved of by someone, i.e., its standing in the approval relation to someone. Since one and the same action could stand in the approval relation to (i.e., be approved of by) one individual, and not stand in this relation to (i.e. not be approved of by) another individual, the action could be right and not right. But this is to say nothing about any property or characteristic of the action, as would be the case on an absolutist approach to morality.

Someone who adopts this form of subjective relativism would presumably regard statements (4) and (5) above as incomplete in an important sense, with (6) and (7) as not in the same way incomplete, but nevertheless as requiring translations along these lines:

(10) Performing A is not approved by Mrs. Jones.
(11) Performing A is approved of by John and Marsha.

It is important to realize that, on the view we are considering, (10) and (11) entirely capture the meanings of (4) and (5). What is being maintained is that an action's being right consists simply in its being approved of by someone; A's being right consists simply in its being approved of by John and Marsha, or by anyone else who happens to approve of A's being performed. In connection with this last phrase it should be noted that, in accordance with the basic tenets of subjectivism, the attitudes of those intimately involved in the performance of an action have no privileged position regarding whether the action is right.

We have been examining in our remarks about approval and disapproval what has been described as an example of subjective relativism, with the implication that the theory could be exemplified in alternative ways. But if we search for examples different from the one we chose, i.e., if we attempt to express subjective relativism in terms of something other than approval and disapproval, we will discover how difficult it is to produce a version of the theory which differs very much from the latter. We will likely conclude that all forms of subjective relativism will identify moral concepts like rightness and wrongness with positive or negative attitudes, one example of which is approval. This conclusion suggests that subjective relativism as a whole can be investigated in terms of the example of this theory cited above, provided that nothing we say pertains to the nature of approval and disapproval as such, as distinct from other positive and negative attitudes. In the discussion which follows we shall operate on this assumption as we examine the implications of subjective relativism for various aspects of morality.

Consider first what such a theory implies regarding the nature of moral decision making. If subjective relativism is true, then deciding whether a certain course of action is the right one to pursue would, *at its best,* consist simply in discovering whether someone approves of that course of action. *Why* it is approved of by some individual (assuming that it is) is irrelevant to whether the action is right; all that matters is *that* it is approved of. Now, do we really want to say that this kind of procedure, i.e., simply finding out whether someone approves of an action, represents moral decision making at its best? Or would we rather require that one who is trying to decide whether some action is right examine the action to see what its consequences would be, whether it would be the honest thing to do, etc., to the end of determining whether or not the totality of relevant data at hand confirms that the action is right? Clearly, this latter procedure, which involves determining an action's morally relevant features and weighing the positive against the negative features, is the way moral decision making is carried out by the mature, morally sensitive and rational individual. And if this is true, then there is something seriously wrong with subjective relativism, because subjective relativism gives us no reason to suppose that anyone with a real grip on the nature of morality would go through the often difficult and sometimes agonizing procedure we have put forward here as representing moral decision making at its best. According to subjective relativism, the individual who really knows what morality is all about bases his decision regarding whether some action is right on the answer to one question: Does anyone approve of performing the action? But moral decision making surely involves more than this. We can make this same point by supposing that some individual facing a moral decision discovers that someone (perhaps he himself) approves of the action, while someone else disapproves of it, which implies that the action is both right and not right. How does he decide what to do? All morally relevant considerations have been accounted for (since on subjective relativism these considerations consist entirely in individual approvings and disapprovings); and thus deciding what to do could be a matter of coin-flipping, or anything else that, in a particular case, might motivate a decision. But is this really what morality is all about?

When we attempt to apply subjective relativism to particular cases, we can see that its implications are again open to serious question. Suppose, for example, we were wondering whether the director of a World War II concentration camp did the right thing in ordering the execution of several thousand Jewish prisoners. (That we are unlikely to have any genuine doubts regarding this issue should not distract us from the point we are trying to make by using it as an example.) If subjective relativism is true, and if the camp director (or anyone else—Hitler, for example) approved of the action, then it was right. Of course, if someone did not approve of the action it was not right, but this would not change it from being right to not being right; it would be right and not right simultaneously. And in concluding that the action is both right and not right (i.e., that it is approved of by someone and not approved of by someone else), we have exhausted the moral content of the discussion. It is not open to one party in a moral dispute to say, for example, "It is irrelevant that you approve of the action; it is wrong," because according to the subjective relativist, the fact that someone approves of an action is *crucially* relevant to whether the action is right. Note too that two individuals arguing over the rightness of the action in question either must be arguing simply about whether *someone* approves of the action (since this is, according to the subjectivist, all that rightness amounts to)—which is surely a peculiar view of the nature of such disputes; or their argument consists in nothing more than a statement by one party that he approves of the action—which is not really a dispute at all. And again we have a picture of an aspect of morality which bears little resemblance to the reality of acceptable moral practice.

There is one more area which is worth examining

in connection with our evaluation of subjective relativism. This is the area of moral education. What we must ask ourselves is this: If subjective relativism is true, how does one go about morally educating one's children? Remember that the subjective relativist identifies rightness and wrongness with attitudes of approval and disapproval; and hence if subjective relativism is true, and if moral education is aimed at providing an understanding of the true nature of morality, then someone interested in giving a child a good moral education must attempt to convey to him this necessary connection between rightness and wrongness on the one hand, and approval and disapproval on the other. Not only is it extremely difficult to see how one would carry out such a procedure, but it is also quite clear that in actual practice moral education works rather differently. Children are urged not to perform certain actions *because these actions involve injuring others,* or *because these actions involve cheating,* etc. And these kinds of reasons are obviously independent of individual attitudes of approval and disapproval, and hence objective. What we are saying then is that subjective relativism implies a mistaken—and perhaps even an impossible—view of the nature of moral education; and this constitutes a serious flaw in the theory.

While the foreoing considerations may not constitute a *refutation* of subjective relativism and of subjectivism in general, they do raise questions which the subjective relativist must take seriously and may have difficulty answering. How these questions might be answered is not easy to see, and, as a matter of fact, few if any moral subjectivists even attempt to deal with them.

Because so many serious difficulties surround subjective relativism, one might wonder why anyone would hold this position. At least a partial answer to this question may lie in the fact that subjective relativism is seldom if ever held in its pure form as *the* moral outlook of a given individual. Rather, it is usually found as part of a confused mixture of moral views held by some individual, some of which are in conflict, and no one of which has even been examined very carefully by that individual to determine its adequacy or its relation to his other views. Someone who puts forward a version of subjectivism on one occasion may very well adhere to the objectivist point of view on another, and never realize that he has adopted incompatible positions on the two occasions. It is unlikely that anyone will be inclined toward subjectivism in a situation where he has strong feelings regarding the morality of some action, particularly if he believes that he himself has been wronged; but the subjectivist point of view may nevertheless be expressed by an individual regarding some action the moral character of which he is indifferent to. Given that the difficulties with subjectivism become really clear only when this position is well understood, it is not surprising that the view is not repudiated by those who do not understand it, and who as a result have given no real consideration to its implications. On its face subjectivism seems attractive to many, perhaps because it *appears* to allow for tolerance of the moral views of others in a way that objectivism does not; and objectivism is viewed by many who have not examined it too closely as surrounded by insurmountable difficulties. So as a result we find people espousing subjectivism at least on occasion, and this notwithstanding the serious difficulties we have noted as attaching to the position.

The foregoing remarks may to some degree explain why subjectivism is not rejected by those who hold it, but they do not show why these individuals find the view attractive. There is no doubt a host of reasons which would account for the appeal of subjectivism and we cannot examine all of them here. But there is one reason which stands out partly because it crops up so frequently, and partly because it possesses a fair amount of initial plausibility. This we will examine in the discussion which follows.

7. CULTURAL RELATIVISM

An argument very commonly offered in support of subjective relativism in its "group" version rests on assertions regarding differences among the moral beliefs of different cultures. The argument goes something like this: What is right in one culture may not be right in another culture; hence there is no universal right and wrong as would be the case if objectivism were true; therefore right and wrong are subjective and relative to individual cultures. This conclusion could be put more precisely employing the definition given above for subjective relativism in this way: rightness, wrongness, etc., are relations which hold between actions and cultural groups in virtue of the attitudes of the individuals in those groups. The only difference, then, between this version of subjective relativism and the one we focused on earlier is that in the one case the rightness and wrongness relations hold between actions and cultural groups, while in the other they hold between actions and individuals.

The first premise of the above argument states that what is right in one culture may not be right in another. This view is sometimes referred to as "cultural relativism," and as normally put forward it is meant to be some sort of sociological and anthropological thesis. It is not intended, then, to be a philosophical claim—a claim about the nature of morality as is subjective relativism—but rather a claim that is at least quasi-scientific. And this fact, together with some of the results of our earlier analysis of subjectivism, suggests an alternative, more illuminating way to formulate cultural relativism.

Talk about what is right or wrong *in a culture* is very much like talk (which we examined earlier) about what is right or wrong *to an individual*. That is, to say that something is right in a culture is apparently to say that it is believed to be right by the individuals in that culture. Thus, cultural relativism can be interpreted as saying that what the individuals in one culture believe is right may be believed not to be right by the individuals in another culture. And this is a thesis that sociologists and anthropologists might investigate according to the means appropriate to their disciplines. It is not, of course, a philosophical position.

Now let us consider the second step of our argument, namely, that there is no universal right and wrong as would be the case if objectivism were true. Note that this step is meant to follow from the first, which is a statement of cultural relativism. It is quite clear, however, that if a denial of "universal right and wrong" follows from cultural relativism, then the notion that there is no universal right and wrong must mean that there is nothing universally *believed* to be right and nothing universally *believed* to be wrong. And this last statement is completely compatible with objectivism. That is, one who believes that there are objective moral truths need not maintain that these truths are universally *accepted*.

We can now see that the main conclusion of the argument, which states that subjective relativism is true, simply fails to follow from the preceding steps in the argument. That is, even if there is disagreement among cultures regarding what is right, this does not show that the rightness and wrongness of actions is determined by the attitudes, feelings, etc., of individuals in those cultures. Unless we assume at the outset that subjective relativism is true (which cannot be done if we are trying to prove the truth of this position), we would have to recognize the possibility that the members of a cultural group could be *mistaken* in what they regard as right or wrong.

A cultural relativist might of course deny that references to what is right in a culture translate into references to what members of the culture believe is right. He might claim, along the lines of our earlier discussion, that "right in a culture" is meant to express the idea that rightness is a relation which holds between an action and a culture. But to take this line would be to make a philosophical claim about the nature of moral concepts, and would run counter to the idea that cultural relativism is a (quasi) scientific thesis open to empirical investigation.

We have been concerned so far with the question whether subjective relativism follows from cultural relativism (which it does not), and have not considered whether cultural relativism is true. This lack of attention to cultural relativism itself is quite appropriate since we are concerned here with moral *philosophy,* but there is a matter related to questions regarding the truth of cultural relativism which falls within the scope of our inquiry and which is worth looking at, even if very briefly.

The idea that widespread differences exist among the moral views of different cultures has, in the recent past, been propounded often and emphatically by many writers in the social sciences. Lately, however, an increasing number of social scientists have been taking a different view and have begun emphasizing similarities in the moral views of members of different cultures. In part this change in attitude can be attributed to a recognition that what might appear to be a difference in *moral* views can more accurately be characterized as a difference in non-moral views together with an underlying commonality in moral outlook.

For example, the story is told of a culture in which a son is regarded as obligated to kill his father when the latter reaches age sixty. Given just this much information about the culture and the practice in question it is tempting to conclude that the members of that culture differ radically from members of our culture in their moral beliefs and attitudes. We, after all, believe it is immoral to take a human life, and regard patricide as especially wrong. But suppose that in the culture we are considering, those who belong to it believe (a) that at the moment of death one enters heaven; (b) one's physical and mental condition in the afterlife is exactly what it is at the moment of death; and (c) men are at the peak of their physical and mental powers when they are sixty. Then what appeared at first to be peculiarities in moral outlook on the part of the cultural group in question regarding the sanctity of life and respect for parents, turn out to be located rather in a nonmoral outlook of the group. A man in that culture who kills his father is doing so out of concern for the latter's well-being—to prevent him, for example, from spending eternity blind or senile. It is not at all clear that, if we shared the relevant non-moral beliefs of this other culture, we would not believe with them that sons should kill their fathers at the appropriate time.

We must take care not to conclude from the foregoing remarks that genuine moral disagreements among cultures are nonexistent. Someone who claims that it is right to kill one's father when he is sixty surely disagrees—and disagrees *morally*—with someone who maintains that doing so is wrong. But moral disagreements can take place at different levels, and in our remarks about the possibility of *nonmoral* disagreements, we are questioning the idea that widespread moral disagreements among cultures exist at a *fundamental* level. It is quite possible, that is, for cultures to share a common fundamental moral outlook, but nevertheless to differ in their conclusions about particular cases in virtue of differences in their nonmoral views. And of course disagreements of this sort can arise *within* particular cultures, as is witnessed by differing opinions that exist within our own regarding the morality of abortion, homosexuality, and premarital intercourse. That is, two individuals might agree for example that homicide is wrong, and yet disagree over whether abortion is wrong, because one believes abortion is homicide and the other does not.

It is worth noting in connection with the notion that members of other cultures can be mistaken in their moral beliefs, that such an idea does not require us to believe that individuals whom we regard as holding mistaken moral views are wicked, or that they are blameworthy or morally culpable for performing actions prescribed by those views. One might say, for example, of a group of primitive people who believe that slavery is right that they are mistaken

in their belief, without insisting that they are blameworthy for practicing slavery. This distinction between concepts such as right and wrong on the one hand, and blameworthiness, culpability and wickedness on the other is an important one and a difficult one to be clear about. Unfortunately we cannot take time here to discuss it further.

We can conclude, then, that cultural relativism does not warrant adopting the subjective point of view toward morality. As we noted above, there may be other ways one might attempt to argue for subjectivism; but such arguments are extremely difficult to uncover, and it is hard to imagine that any exist which are powerful enough to overcome the difficulties with subjective relativism that we described in our earlier discussion.

8. SUMMARY

We have been engaged throughout the preceding paragraphs in a rather exhaustive study of the subjectivist approach to morality. Our study began with an attempt to produce a clear-cut version of subjectivism, proceeded to an evaluation of the version we did arrive at, and concluded with an examination of one argument commonly offered in support of subjectivism. We found it necessary to devote considerable attention to the first stage of our investigation because subjectivism often shows up as a mixture of views which conflict with each other; and until these views are sorted out it is really impossible to determine whether subjectivism is a viable theory of morality. We finally decided that a form of subjective relativism, which identifies rightness and wrongness with approval and disapproval (viewing the latter as relations holding between individuals and actions), is probably the most acceptable form of subjectivism and we evaluated this position by examining its implications. In a variety of areas of morality these implications turned out to be at best problematic and at worst totally unacceptable. We then wondered why, given its difficulties, anyone would be attracted to subjectivism, and this led to our examination of a possible reason for the position's popularity. Upon close scrutiny this reason turned out to involve several confusions and provided no real support for subjectivism.

WALTER T. STACE

Ethical Relativism*

Any ethical position which denies that there is a single moral standard which is equally applicable to all men at all times may fairly be called a species of ethical relativity. There is not, the relativist asserts, merely one moral law, one code, one standard. There are many moral laws, codes, standards. What morality ordains in one place or age may be quite different from what morality ordains in another place or age. The moral code of Chinamen is quite different from that of Europeans, that of African savages quite different from both. Any morality, therefore, is relative to the age, the place, and the circumstances in which it is found. It is in no sense absolute.

This does not mean merely—as one might at first sight be inclined to suppose—that the very same kind of action which is *thought* right in one country and period may be *thought* wrong in another. This would be a mere platitude, the truth of which everyone would have to admit. Even the absolutist would admit this—would even wish to emphasize it—since he is well aware that different people have different sets of moral ideas, and his whole point is that some of these sets of ideas are false. What the relativist means to assert is, not this platitude, but that the very same kind of action which *is* right in one country and period may *be* wrong in another. And this, far from being a platitude, is a very startling assertion.

It is very important to grasp thoroughly the difference between the two ideas. For there is reason to think that many minds tend to find ethical relativity attractive because they fail to keep them clearly apart. It is so very obvious that moral ideas differ from country to country and from age to age. And it is so very easy, if you are mentally lazy, to suppose that to say

this means the same as to say that no universal moral standard exists,—or in other words that it implies ethical relativity. We fail to see that the word "standard" is used in two different senses. It is perfectly true that, in one sense, there are many variable moral standards. We speak of judging a man by the standard of his time. And this implies that different times have different standards. And this, of course, is quite true. But when the word ' standard" is used in this sense it means simply the set of moral ideas current during the period in question. It means what people *think* right, whether as a matter of fact it *is* right or not. On the other hand when the absolutist asserts that there exists a single universal moral "standard," he is not using the word in this sense at all. He means by "standard" what *is* right as distinct from what people merely think right. His point is that although what people think right varies in different countries and periods, yet what actually is right is everywhere and always the same. And it follows that when the ethical relativist disputes the position of the absolutist and denies that any universal moral standard exists he too means by "standard" what actually is right. But it is exceedingly easy, if we are not careful, to slip loosely from using the word in the first sense to using it in the second sense; and to suppose that the variability of moral beliefs is the same thing as the variability of what really is moral. And unless we keep the two senses of the word "standard" distinct, we are likely to think the creed of ethical relativity much more plausible than it actually is.

The genuine relativist, then, does not merely mean that Chinamen may think right what Frenchmen think wrong. He means that what *is* wrong for the Frenchman may *be* right for the Chinaman. And if one enquires how, in those circumstances, one is to know what actually is right in China or in France, the answer comes quite glibly. What is right in China is the

*Reprinted with permission of Macmillan Publishing Co., Inc. from *The Concept of Morals* by W. T. Stace. Copyright 1937 by Macmillan Publishing Company, Inc., renewed 1965 by Walter T. Stace.

same as what people think right in China; and what is right in France is the same as what people think right in France. So that, if you want to know what is moral in any particular country or age all you have to do is to ascertain what are the moral ideas current in that age or country. Those ideas are, *for that age or country,* right. Thus what is morally right is identified with what is thought to be morally right, and the distinction which we made above between these two is simply denied. To put the same thing in another way, it is denied that there can be or ought to be any distinction between the two senses of the word "standard." There is only one kind of standard of right and wrong, namely, the moral ideas current in any particular age or country.

Moral right *means* what people think morally right. It has no other meaning. What Frenchmen think right is, therefore, right *for Frenchmen.* And evidently one must conclude—though I am not aware that relativists are anxious to draw one's attention to such unsavory but yet absolutely necessary conclusions from their creed—that cannibalism is right for people who believe in it, that human sacrifice is right for those races which practice it, and that burning widows alive was right for Hindus until the British stepped in and compelled the Hindus to behave immorally by allowing their widows to remain alive.

When it is said that, according to the ethical relativist, what is thought right in any social group is right for that group, one must be careful not to misinterpret this. The relativist does not, of course, mean that there actually is an objective moral standard in France and a different objective standard in England, and that French and British opinions respectively give us correct information about these different standards. His point is rather that there are no objectively true moral standards at all. There is no single universal objective standard. Nor are there a variety of local objective standards. All standards are subjective. People's subjective feelings about morality are the only standards which exist.

To sum up. The ethical relativist consistently denies, it would seem, whatever the ethical absolutist asserts. For the absolutist there is a single universal moral standard. For the relativist there is no such standard. There are only local, ephemeral, and variable standards. For the absolutist there are two senses of the word "standard." Standards in the sense of sets of current moral ideas are relative and changeable. But the standard in the sense of what is actually morally right is absolute and unchanging. For the relativist no such distinction can be made. There is only

one meaning of the word "standard," namely, that which refers to local and variable sets of moral ideas. Or if it is insisted that the word must be allowed two meanings, then the relativist will say that there is at any rate no actual example of a standard in the absolute sense, and that the word as thus used is an empty name to which nothing in reality corresponds; so that the distinction between the two meanings becomes empty and useless. Finally—though this is merely saying the same thing in another way—the absolutist makes a distinction between what actually is right and what is thought right. The relativist rejects this distinction and identifies what is moral with what is thought by certain human beings or groups of human beings. . . .

I shall now proceed to consider, first, the main arguments which can be urged in favor of ethical relativity; and secondly, the arguments which can be urged against it. . . . The first is that which relies upon the actual varieties of moral "standards" found in the world. It was easy enough to believe in a single absolute morality in older times when there was no anthropology, when all humanity was divided clearly into two groups, Christian peoples and the "heathen." Christian peoples knew and possessed the one true morality. The rest were savages whose moral ideas could be ignored. But all this is changed. Greater knowledge has brought greater tolerance. We can no longer exalt our own morality as alone true, while dismissing all other moralities as false or inferior. The investigations of anthropologists have shown that there exist side by side in the world a bewildering variety of moral codes. On this topic endless volumes have been written, masses of evidence piled up. Anthropologists have ransacked the Melanesian Islands, the jungles of New Guinea, the steppes of Siberia, the deserts of Australia, the forests of central Africa, and have brought back with them countless examples of weird, extravagant, and fantastic "moral" customs with which to confound us. We learn that all kinds of horrible practices are, in this, that, or the other place, regarded as essential to virtue. We find that there is nothing, or next to nothing, which has always and everywhere been regarded as morally good by all men. Where then is our universal morality? Can we, in face of all this evidence, deny that it is nothing but an empty dream?

This argument, taken by itself, is a very weak one. It relies upon a single set of facts—the variable moral customs of the world. But this variability of moral ideas is admitted by both parties to the dispute, and is capable of ready explanation upon the hypothesis of either party. The relativist says that the facts are to be explained by the non-existence of any absolute moral standard. The absolutist says that they are to be explained by human ignorance of what the absolute moral standard is. And he can truly point out that men have differed widely in their opinions about all manner of topics including the subject-matters of the physical sciences—just as much as they differ about morals. And if the various different opinions which men have held about the shape of the earth do not prove that it has no one real shape, neither do the various opinions which they have held about morality prove that there is no one true morality.

Thus the facts can be explained equally plausibly on either hypothesis. There is nothing in the facts themselves which compels us to prefer the relativistic hypothesis to that of the absolutist. And therefore the argument fails to prove the relativist conclusion. If that conclusion is to be established, it must be by means of other considerations.

This is the essential point. But I will add some supplementary remarks. The work of the anthropologists, upon which ethical relativists seem to rely so heavily, has as a matter of fact added absolutely nothing *in principle* to what has always been known about the variability of moral ideas. Educated people have known all along that the Greeks tolerated sodomy, which in modern times has been regarded in some countries as an abominable crime; that the Hindus thought it a sacred duty to burn their widows; that trickery, now thought despicable, was once believed to be a virtue; that terrible torture was thought by our own ancestors only a few centuries ago to be a justifiable weapon of justice; that it was only yesterday that western peoples came to believe that slavery is immoral. Even the ancients knew very well that moral customs and ideas vary—witness the writings of Herodotus. Thus the principle of the variability of moral ideas was well understood long before modern anthropology was ever heard of. Anthropology has added nothing to the knowledge of this principle except a mass of new and extreme examples of it drawn from very remote sources. But to multiply examples of a principle already well known and universally admitted adds nothing to the argument which is built upon that principle. The discoveries of the anthropologists have no doubt been of the highest importance in their own sphere. But in my considered opinion they have thrown no new light upon the special problems of the moral philosopher.

Although the multiplication of examples has no logical bearing on the argument, it does have an immense *psychological* effect upon people's minds. These masses of anthropological learning are impressive. They are propounded in the sacred name of "science." If they are quoted in support of ethical relativity—as they often are—people *think* that they must prove something important. They bewilder and over-awe the simple-minded, batter down their resistance, make them ready to receive humbly the doctrine of ethical relativity from those who have acquired a reputation by their immense learning and their claims to be "scientific." Perhaps this is why so much ado is made by ethical relativists regarding the anthropological evidence. But we must refuse to be impressed. We must discount all this mass of evidence about the extraordinary moral customs of remote peoples. Once we have admitted—as everyone who is instructed must have admitted these last two thousand years without any anthropology at all—the principle that moral ideas vary, all this new evidence adds nothing to the argument. And the argument itself proves nothing for the reasons already given. . . .

The second argument in favor of ethical relativity is also a very strong one. And it does not suffer from the disadvantage that it is dependent upon the acceptance of any particular philosophy such as radical empiricism. It makes its appeal to considerations of a quite general character. It consists in alleging that no one has ever been able to discover upon what foundation an absolute morality could rest, or from what source a universally binding moral code could derive its authority.

If, for example, it is an absolute and unalterable moral rule that all men ought to be unselfish, from whence does this *command* issue? For a command it certainly is, phrase it how you please. There is no difference in meaning between the sentence "You ought to be unselfish" and the sentence "Be unselfish." Now a command implies a commander. An obligation implies some authority which obliges. Who is this commander, what this authority? Thus the vastly difficult question is raised of *the basis of moral obligation.* Now the argument of the relativist would be that it is impossible to find any basis for a universally binding moral law; but that it is quite easy to discover a basis for morality if moral codes are admitted to be variable, ephemeral, and relative to time, place, and circumstance.

In this book I am assuming that it is no longer possible to solve this difficulty by saying naïvely that the universal moral law is based upon the uniform commands of God to all men. There will be many, no doubt, who will dispute this. But I am not writing for them. I am writing for those who feel the necessity of finding for morality a basis independent of particular religious dogmas. And I shall therefore make no attempt to argue the matter.

The problem which the absolutist has to face, then, is this. The religious basis of the one absolute morality having disappeared, can there be found for it any other, any secular, basis? If not, then it would seem that we cannot any longer believe in absolutism. We shall have to fall back upon belief in a variety of perhaps mutually inconsistent moral codes operating over restricted areas and limited periods. No one of these will be better, or more true, than any other. Each will be good and true for those living in those areas and periods. We shall have to fall back, in a word, on ethical relativity.

For there is no great difficulty in discovering the foundations of morality, or rather of moralities, if we adopt the relativistic hypothesis. Even if we cannot be quite certain *precisely* what these foundations are— and relativists themselves are not entirely agreed about them—we can at least see in a general way the *sort* of foundations they must have. We can see that the question on this basis is not in principle impossible of answer—although the details may be obscure; while, if we adopt the absolutist hypothesis—so the argument runs—no kind of answer is conceivable at all. . . .

This argument is undoubtedly very strong. It *is* absolutely essential to solve the problem of the basis of moral obligation if we are to believe in any kind of moral standards other than those provided by mere custom or by irrational emotions. It is idle to talk about a universal morality unless we can point to the source of its authority—or at least to do so is to indulge in a faith which is without rational ground. To cherish a blind faith in morality may be, for the average man whose business is primarily to live aright and not to theorize, sufficient. Perhaps it is his wisest course. But it will not do for the philosopher. His function, or at least one of his functions, is precisely to discover the rational grounds of our everyday beliefs—if they have any. Philosophically and intellectually, then, we cannot accept belief in a universally binding morality unless we can discover upon what foundation its obligatory character rests.

But in spite of the strength of the argument thus posed in favor of ethical relativity, it is not impregna-ble. For it leaves open one loop-hole. It is always possible that some theory, not yet examined, may provide a basis for a universal moral obligation. The argument rests upon the negative proposition that *there is no theory which can provide a basis for a universal morality.* But it is notoriously difficult to prove a negative. How can you prove that there are no green swans? All you can show is that none have been found so far. And then it is always possible that one will be found tomorrow. . . .

It is time that we turned our attention from the case in favor of ethical relativity to the case against it. Now the case against it consists, to a very large extent, in urging that, if taken seriously and pressed to its logical conclusion, ethical relativity can only end in destroying the conception of morality altogether, in undermining its practical efficacy, in rendering meaningless many almost universally accepted truths about human affairs, in robbing human beings of any incentive to strive for a better world, in taking the life-blood out of every ideal and every aspiration which has ever ennobled the life of man. . . .

First of all, then, ethical relativity, in asserting that the moral standards of particular social groups are the only standards which exist, renders meaningless all propositions which attempt to compare these standards with one another in respect to their moral worth. And this is a very serious matter indeed. We are accustomed to think that the moral ideas of one nation or social group may be "higher" or "lower" than those of another. We believe, for example, that Christian ethical ideals are nobler than those of the savage races of central Africa. Probably most of us would think that the Chinese moral standards are higher than those of the inhabitants of New Guinea. In short we habitually compare one civilization with another and judge the sets of ethical ideas to be found in them to be some better, some worse. The fact that such judgments are very difficult to make with any justice, and that they are frequently made on very superficial and preju-diced grounds, has no bearing on the question now at issue. The question is whether such judgments have any *meaning.* We habitually assume that they have.

But on the basis of ethical relativity they can have none whatever. For the relativist must hold that there is no *common* standard which can be applied to the various civilizations judged. Any such comparison of moral standards implies the existence of some superior standard which is applicable to both. And the existence of any such standard is precisely what the relativist denies. According to him the Christian standard is applicable only to Christians, the Chinese standard only to Chinese, the New Guinea standard only to the inhabitants of New Guinea.

What is true of comparisons between the moral standards of different races will also be true of comparisons between those of different ages. It is not unusual to ask such questions as whether the standard of our own day is superior to that which existed among our ancestors five hundred years ago. And when we remember that our ancestors employed slaves, practiced barbaric physical tortures, and burnt people alive, we may be inclined to think that it is. At any rate we assume that the question is one which has meaning and is capable of rational discussion. But if the ethical relativist is right, whatever we assert on this subject must be totally meaningless. For here again there is no common standard which could form the basis of any such judgments.

This in its turn implies that the whole notion of moral *progress* is a sheer delusion. Progress means an advance from lower to higher, from worse to better. But on the basis of ethical relativity it has no meaning to say that the standards of this age are better (or worse) than those of a previous age. For there is no common standard by which both can be measured. Thus it is nonsense to say that the morality of the New Testament is higher than that of the Old. And Jesus Christ, if he imagined that he was introducing into the world a higher ethical standard than existed before his time, was merely deluded. . . .

I come now to a second point. Up to the present I have allowed it to be taken tacitly for granted that, though judgments comparing different races and ages in respect of the worth of their moral codes are impossible for the ethical relativist, yet judgments of comparison between individuals living within the same social group would be quite possible. For individuals living within the same social group would be subject to the same moral code, that of their group, and this would therefore constitute, as between these individuals, a common standard by which they could both be measured. We have not here, as we had in the other case, the difficulty of the absence of any common standard of comparison. It should therefore be possible for the ethical relativist to say quite meaningfully that President Lincoln was a better man than some criminal or moral imbecile of his own time and coun-

try, or that Jesus was a better man than Judas Iscariot.

But is even this minimum of moral judgment really possible on relativist grounds? It seems to me that it is not. For when once the whole of humanity is abandoned as the area covered by a single moral standard, what smaller areas are to be adopted as the *loci* of different standards? Where are we to draw the lines of demarcation? We can split up humanity, perhaps,—though the procedure will be very arbitrary—into races, races into nations, nations into tribes, tribes into families, families into individuals. Where are we going to draw the *moral* boundaries? Does the *locus* of a particular moral standard reside in a race, a nation, a tribe, a family, or an individual? Perhaps the blessed phrase "social group" will be dragged in to save the situation. Each such group, we shall be told, has its own moral code which is, for it, right. But what *is* a "group"? Can anyone define it or give its boundaries? This is the seat of that ambiguity in the theory of ethical relativity to which reference was made on an earlier page.

The difficulty is not, as might be thought, merely an academic difficulty of logical definition. If that were all, I should not press the point. But the ambiguity has practical consequences which are disastrous for morality. No one is likely to say that moral codes are confined within the arbitrary limits of the geographical divisions of countries. Nor are the notions of race, nation, or political state likely to help us. To bring out the essentially practical character of the difficulty let us put it in the form of concrete questions. Does the American nation constitute a "group" having a single moral standard? Or does the standard of what I ought to do change continuously as I cross the continent in a railway train? Do different States of the Union have different moral codes? Perhaps every town and village has its own peculiar standard. This may at first sight seem reasonable enough. "In Rome do as Rome does" may seem as good a rule in morals as it is in etiquette. But can we stop there? Within the village are numerous cliques each having its own set of ideas. Why should not each of these claim to be bound only by its own special and peculiar moral standards? And if it comes to that, why should not the gangsters of Chicago claim to constitute a group having its own morality, so that its murders and debaucheries must be viewed as "right" by the only standard which can legitimately be applied to it? And if it be answered that the nation will not tolerate this, that may be so. But this is to put the foundation of right simply in the superior force of the majority. In that case whoever is stronger will be right, however monstrous his ideas and actions. And if we cannot deny to any set of people the right to have its own morality, is it not clear that, in the end, we cannot even deny this right to the individual? Every individual man and woman can put up, on this view, an irrefutable claim to be judged by no standard except his or her own.

If these arguments are valid, the ethical relativist cannot really maintain that there is anywhere to be found a moral standard binding upon anybody against his will. And he cannot maintain that, even within the social group, there is a common standard as between individuals. And if that is so, then even judgments to the effect that one man is morally better than another become meaningless. All moral valuation thus vanishes. There is nothing to prevent each man from being a rule unto himself. The result will be moral chaos and the collapse of all effective standards. . . .

But even if we assume that the difficulty about defining moral groups has been surmounted, a further difficulty presents itself. Suppose that we have now definitely decided what are the exact boundaries of the social group within which a moral standard is to be operative. And we will assume—as is invariably done by relativists themselves—that this group is to be some actually existing social community such as a tribe or nation. How are we to know, even then, what actually *is* the moral standard within that group? How is anyone to know? How is even a member of the group to know? For there are certain to be within the group—at least this will be true among advanced peoples—wide differences of opinion as to what is right, what wrong. Whose opinion, then, is to be taken as representing *the* moral standard of the group? Either we must take the opinion of the majority within the group, or the opinion of some minority. If we rely upon the ideas of the majority, the results will be disastrous. Wherever there is found among a people a small band of select spirits, or perhaps one man, working for the establishment of higher and nobler ideals than those commonly accepted by the group, we shall be compelled to hold that, for that people at that time, the majority are right, and that the reformers are wrong and are preaching what is immoral. We shall have to maintain, for example, that Jesus was preaching immoral doctrines to the Jews. Moral goodness will have to be equated always with the mediocre and sometimes with the definitely base and ignoble. If on the other hand we said that the moral standard of the group is to be identified with the moral opinions of some minority, then what minority is this to be? We cannot answer that it is to be the minority composed of the best and most enlightened individuals of the group. This would involve us in a palpably vicious circle. For by what standard are these individuals to be judged the best and the most enlightened? There is no principle by which we could select the right minority. And therefore we should have to consider every minority as good as every other. And this means that we should have no logical right whatever to resist the claim of the gangsters of Chicago— if such a claim were made—that their practices represent the highest standards of American morality. It means in the end that every individual is to be bound by no standard save his own.

The ethical relativists are great empiricists. *What* is the actually moral standard of any group can only be discovered, they tell us, by an examination on the ground of the moral opinions and customs of that group. But will they tell us how they propose to decide, when they get to the ground, which of the many moral opinions they are sure to find there is *the* right one in that group? To some extent they will be able to do this for the Melanesian Islanders—from whom apparently all lessons in the nature of morality are in future to be taken. But it is certain that they cannot do it for advanced peoples whose members have learned to think for themselves and to entertain among themselves a wide variety of opinions. They cannot do it unless they accept the calamitous view that the ethical opinion of the majority is always right. We are left therefore once more with the conclusion that, even within a particular social group, anybody's moral opinion is as good as anybody else's, and that every man is entitled to be judged by his own standards.

Finally, not only is ethical relativity disastrous in its consequences for moral theory. It cannot be doubted that it must tend to be equally disastrous in its impact upon practical conduct. If men come really to believe that one moral standard is as good as another, they will conclude that their own moral standard has nothing special to recommend it. They might as well then slip down to some lower and easier standard. It is true that, for a time, it may be possible to hold one view in theory and to act practically upon another. But ideas, even philosophical ideas, are not so ineffectual that they can remain forever idle in the upper chambers of the intellect. In the end they seep down to the level of practice. They get themselves acted on.

JOEL FEINBERG

Psychological Egoism*

A. THE THEORY

1. "Psychological egosim" is the name given to a theory widely held by ordinary people, and at one time almost universally accepted by political economists, philosophers, and psychologists, according to which all human actions when properly understood can be seen to be motivated by selfish desires. More precisely, psychological egoism is the doctrine that the only thing anyone is capable of desiring or pursuing ultimately (as an end in itself) is his *own* self-interest. No psychological egoist denies that people sometimes do desire things other than their own welfare—the happiness of other people, for example; but all psychological egoists insist that people are capable of desiring the happiness of others only when they take it to be a *means* to their own happiness. In short, purely altruistic and benevolent actions and desires do not exist; but people sometimes appear to be acting unselfishly and disinterestedly when they take the interests of others to be means to the promotion of their own self-interest.

2. This theory is called *psychological* egoism to indicate that it is not a theory about what *ought* to be the case, but rather about what, as a matter of fact, *is* the case. That is, the theory claims to be a description of psychological facts, not a prescription of ethical ideals. It asserts, however, not merely that all men do as a contingent matter of fact "put their own interests first," but also that they are capable of nothing else, human nature being what it is. Universal selfishness is not just an accident or a coinci-

*From materials composed for philosophy students at Brown University, 1958.

dence on this view; rather, it is an unavoidable consequence of psychological laws.

The theory is to be distinguished from another doctrine, so-called "ethical egoism," according to which all people *ought* to pursue their own well-being. This doctrine, being a prescription of what *ought* to be the case, makes no claim to be a psychological theory of human motives; hence the word "ethical" appears in its name to distinguish it from *psychological* egoism.

3. There are a number of types of motives and desires which might reasonably be called "egoistic" or "selfish," and corresponding to each of them is a possible version of psychological egoism. Perhaps the most common version of the theory is that apparently held by Jeremy Bentham.[1] According to this version, all persons have only one ultimate motive in all their voluntary behavior and that motive is a selfish one; more specifically, it is one particular kind of selfish motive—namely, a desire for one's own *pleasure*. According to this version of the theory, "the only kind of ultimate desire is the desire to get or to prolong pleasant experiences, and to avoid or to cut short unpleasant experiences for oneself."[2] This form of psychological egoism is often given the cumbersome name—*psychological egoistic hedonism*.

B. PRIMA FACIE REASONS IN SUPPORT OF THE THEORY

4. Psychological egoism has seemed plausible to many people for a variety of reasons, of which the following are typical:

a. "Every action of mine is prompted by motives or desires or impulses which are *my* motives and not somebody else's. This fact might be expressed by saying that whenever I act I am always pursuing my own ends or trying to satisfy my own desires. And from this we might pass on to—'I am always pursuing something for myself or seeking my own satisfaction.' Here is what seems like a proper description of a man acting selfishly, and if the description applies to all actions of all men, then it follows that all men in all their actions are selfish."[3]

b. It is a truism that when a person gets what he wants he characteristically feels pleasure. This has suggested to many people that what we really want in every case is our own pleasure, and that we pursue other things only as a means.

c. *Self-Deception.* Often we deceive ourselves into thinking that we desire something fine or noble when what we really want is to be thought well of by others or to be able to congratulate ourselves, or to be able to enjoy the pleasures of a good conscience. It is a well-known fact that people tend to conceal their true motives from themselves by camouflaging them with words like "virtue," "duty," etc. Since we are so often misled concerning both our own real motives and the real motives of others, is it not reasonable to suspect that we might *always* be deceived when we think motives disinterested and altruistic? Indeed, it is a simple matter to explain away all allegedly unselfish motives: "Once the conviction that selfishness is universal finds root in a person's mind, it is very likely to burgeon out in a thousand corroborating generalizations. It will be discovered that a friendly smile is really only an attempt to win an approving nod from a more or less gullible recording angel; that a charitable deed is, for its performer, only an opportunity to congratulate himself on the good fortune or the cleverness that enables him to be charitable; that a public benefaction is just plain good business advertising. It will emerge that gods are worshipped only because they indulge men's selfish fears, or tastes, or hopes; that the 'golden rule' is no more than an eminently sound success formula; that social and political codes are created and subscribed to only because they serve to restrain other men's egoism as much as one's own, morality being only a special sort of 'racket' or intrigue using weapons of persuasion in place of bombs and machine guns. Under this interpretation of human nature, the categories of commercialism replace those of disinterested service and the spirit of the horse trader broods over the face of the earth."[4]

d. *Moral education.* Morality, good manners, decency, and other virtues must be teachable. Psychological egoists often notice that moral education and the inculcation of manners usually utilize what Bentham calls the "sanctions of pleasure and pain."[5] Children are made to acquire the civilizing virtues only by the method of enticing rewards and painful punishments. Much the same is true of the history of the race. People in general have been inclined to behave well only when it is made plain to them that there is "something in it for them." Is it not then highly probable that just such a mechanism of human motivation as Bentham describes must be presupposed by our methods of moral education?

C. CRITIQUE OF PSYCHOLOGICAL EGOISM: CONFUSIONS IN THE ARGUMENTS

5. *Non-Empirical Character of the Arguments.* If the arguments of the psychological egoist consisted for the most part of carefully acquired empirical evidence (well-documented reports of controlled experiments, surveys, interviews, laboratory data, and so on), then the critical philosopher would have no business carping at them. After all, since psychological egoism purports to be a scientific theory of human motives, it is the concern of the experimental psychologist, not the philosopher, to accept or reject it. But as a matter of fact, empirical evidence of the required sort is seldom presented in support of psychological egoism. Psychologists, on the whole, shy away from generalizations about human motives which are so sweeping and so vaguely formulated that they are virtually incapable of scientific testing. It is usually the "armchair scientist" who holds the theory of universal selfishness, and his usual arguments are either based simply on his "impressions" or else are largely of a non-empirical sort. The latter are often shot full of a very subtle kind of logical

confusion, and this makes their criticism a matter of special interest to the analytic philosopher.

6. The psychological egoist's first argument (4a, above) is a good example of logical confusion. It begins with a truism—namely, that all of my motives and desires are *my* motives and desires and not someone else's. (Who would deny this?) But from this simple tautology nothing whatever concerning the nature of my motives or the objective of my desires can possibly follow. The fallacy of this argument consists in its violation of the general logical rule that analytic statements (tautologies) cannot entail synthetic (factual) ones.[6] That every voluntary act is prompted by the agent's own motives is a tautology; hence, it cannot be equivalent to "A person is always seeking something for himself" or "All of a person's motives are selfish," which are synthetic. What the egoist must prove is not merely:

(i) Every voluntary action is prompted by a motive of the agent's own.

but rather:

(ii) Every voluntary action is prompted by a motive of a quite particular kind, viz. a selfish one.

Statement (i) is obviously true, but it cannot all by itself give any logical support to statement (ii).

The source of the confusion in this argument is readily apparent. It is not the genesis of an action or the *origin* or its motives which makes it a "selfish" one, but rather the "purpose" of the act or the *objective* of its motives; *not where the motive comes from* (in voluntary actions it always comes from the agent) but *what it aims at* determines whether or not it is selfish. There is surely a valid distinction between voluntary behavior, in which the agent's action is motivated by purposes of his own, and *selfish* behavior in which the agent's motives are of one exclusive sort. The egoist's argument assimilates all voluntary action into the class of selfish action, by requiring, in effect, that an unselfish action be one which is not really motivated at all. In the words of Lucius Garvin, "to say that an act proceeds from our own . . . desire is only to say that the act is our own. To demand that we should act on motives that are not our own is to ask us to make ourselves living contradictions in terms."[7]

7. But if argument 4a fails to prove its point, argument 4b does no better. From the fact that all our successful actions (those in which we get what we were after) are accompanied or followed by pleasure it does not follow, as the egoist claims, that the *objective* of every action is to get pleasure for oneself. To begin with, the premise of the argument is not, strictly speaking, even true. Fulfillment of desire (simply getting what one was after) is no guarantee of satisfaction (pleasant feelings of gratification in the mind of the agent). Sometimes when we get what we want we *also* get, as a kind of extra dividend, a warm, glowing feeling of contentment; but often, far too often, we get no dividend at all, or, even worse, the bitter taste of ashes. Indeed, it has been said that the characteristic psychological problem of our time is the *dissatisfaction* that attends the fulfillment of our very most powerful desires.

Even if we grant, however, for the sake of argument, that getting what one wants *usually* yields satisfaction, the egoist's conclusion does not follow. We can concede that we normally get pleasure (in the sense of satisfaction) when our desires are satisfied, *no matter what our desires are for;* but it does not follow from this roughly accurate generalization that the only thing we ever desire is our own satisfaction. Pleasure may well be the usual accompaniment of all actions in which the agent gets what he wants; but to infer from this that what the agent always wants is his own pleasure is like arguing, in William James's example,[8] that because an ocean liner constantly consumes coal on its trans-Atlantic passage that therefore the *purpose* of its voyage is to consume coal. The immediate inference from even constant accompaniment to purpose (or motive) is always a *non sequitur*.

Perhaps there is a sense of "satisfaction" (desire fulfillment) such that it is certainly and universally true that we get satisfaction whenever we get what we want. But satisfaction in this sense is simply the "coming into existence of that which is desired." Hence, to say that desire fulfillment always yields "satisfaction" in this sense is to say no more than that we always get what we want when we get what we want, which is to utter a tautology like "a rose is a rose." It can no more entail a synthetic truth in psychology (like the egoistic thesis) than "a rose is a rose" can entail significant information in botany.

8. *Disinterested Benevolence.* The fallacy in argument 4b then consists, as Garvin puts it, "in the supposition that the apparently unselfish desire to benefit others is transformed into a selfish one by

the fact that we derive pleasure from carrying it out."[9] Not only is this argument fallacious; it also provides us with a suggestion of a counter-argument to show that its conclusion (psychological egoistic hedonism) is false. Not only is the presence of pleasure (satisfaction) as a by-product of an action no proof that the action was selfish; in some special cases it provides rather conclusive proof that the action was *unselfish*. For in those special cases the fact that we get pleasure from a particular action *presupposes that we desired something else*—something other than our own pleasure—as an end in itself and not merely as a means to our own pleasant state of mind.

This way of turning the egoistic hedonist's argument back on him can be illustrated by taking a typical egoist argument, one attributed (perhaps apocryphally) to Abraham Lincoln, and then examining it closely:

Mr. Lincoln once remarked to a fellow-passenger on an old-time mud-coach that all men were prompted by selfishness in doing good. His fellow-passenger was antagonizing this position when they were passing over a corduroy bridge that spanned a slough. As they crossed this bridge they espied an old razor-backed sow on the bank making a terrible noise because her pigs had got into the slough and were in danger of drowning. As the old coach began to climb the hill, Mr. Lincoln called out, "Driver, can't you stop just a moment?" Then Mr. Lincoln jumped out, ran back and lifted the little pigs out of the mud and water and placed them on the bank. When he returned, his companion remarked: "Now Abe, where does selfishness come in on this little episode?" "Why, bless your soul Ed, that was the very essence of selfishness. I should have had no peace of mind all day had I gone on and left that suffering old sow worrying over those pigs. I did it to get peace of mind, don't you see?"[10]

If Lincoln had cared not a whit for the welfare of the little pigs and their "suffering" mother, but only for his own "peace of mind," it would be difficult to explain how he could have derived pleasure from helping them. The very fact that he did feel satisfaction as a result of helping the pigs presupposes that he had a preexisting desire for something other than his own happiness. Then when *that* desire was satisfied, Lincoln of course derived pleasure. The *object* of Lincoln's desire was not pleasure; rather pleasure was the *consequence* of his preexisting desire for something else. If Lincoln had been wholly indifferent to the plight of the little pigs as he claimed, how could he possibly have derived any pleasure from

helping them? He could not have achieved peace of mind from rescuing the pigs, had he not a prior concern—on which his peace of mind depended—for the welfare of the pigs for its own sake.

In general, the psychological hedonist analyzes apparent benevolence into a desire for "benevolent pleasure." No doubt the benevolent person does get pleasure from his benevolence, but in most cases, this is only because he has previously desired the good of some person, or animal, or mankind at large. Where there is no such desire, benevolent conduct is not generally found to give pleasure to the agent.

9. *Malevolence*. Difficult cases for the psychological egoist include not only instances of disinterested benevolence, but also cases of "disinterested malevolence." Indeed, malice and hatred are generally no more "selfish" than benevolence. Both are motives likely to cause an agent to sacrifice his own interests—in the case of benevolence, in order to help someone else, in the case of malevolence in order to harm someone else. The selfish person is concerned ultimately only with his own pleasure, happiness, or power; the benevolent person is often equally concerned with the happiness of others; to the malevolent person, the *injury* of another is often an end in itself—an end to be pursued sometimes with no thought for his own interests. There is reason to think that people have as often sacrificed themselves to injure or kill others as to help or to save others, and with as much "heroism" in the one case as in the other. The unselfish nature of malevolence was first noticed by the Anglican Bishop and moral philosopher Joseph Butler (1692–1752), who regretted that people are no more selfish than they are.[11]

10. *Lack of Evidence for Universal Self-Deception*. The more cynical sort of psychological egoist who is impressed by the widespread phenomenon of self-deception (see 4c above) cannot be so quickly disposed of, for he has committed no *logical* mistakes. We can only argue that the acknowledged frequency of self-deception is insufficient evidence for his universal generalization. His argument is not fallacious, but inconclusive.

No one but the agent himself can ever be certain what conscious motives really prompted his action, and where motives are disreputable, even the agent may not admit to himself the true nature of his desires. Thus, for every apparent case of altruistic behavior, the psychological egoist can argue, with some plausibility, that the true motivation *might* be selfish, appearance to the contrary. Philanthropic acts are really motivated by the desire to receive gratitude; acts of self-sacrifice, when truly understood, are seen to be motivated by the desire to feel self-esteem; and so on. We must concede to the egoist that all apparent altruism might be deceptive in this way; but such a sweeping generalization requires considerable empirical evidence, and such evidence is not presently available.

11. *The "Paradox of Hedonism" and Its Consequences for Education.* The psychological egoistic Hedonist (e.g., Jeremy Bentham) has the simplest possible theory of human motivation. According to this variety of egoistic theory, all human motives without exception can be reduced to one—namely, the desire for one's own pleasure. But this theory, despite its attractive simplicity, or perhaps because of it, involves one immediately in a paradox. Astute observers of human affairs from the time of the ancient Greeks have often noticed that pleasure, happiness, and satisfaction are states of mind which stand in a very peculiar relation to desire. An exclusive desire for happiness is the surest way to prevent happiness from coming into being. Happiness has a way of "sneaking up" on persons when they are preoccupied with other things; but when persons deliberately and single-mindedly set off in pursuit of happiness, it vanishes utterly from sight and cannot be captured. This is the famous "paradox of hedonism": the single-minded pursuit of happiness is necessarily self-defeating, for *the way to get happiness is to forget it;* then perhaps it will come to you. If you aim exclusively at pleasure itself, with no concern for the things that bring pleasure, then pleasure will never come. To derive satisfaction, one must ordinarily first desire something other than satisfaction, and then find the means to get what one desires.

To feel the full force of the paradox of hedonism the reader should conduct an experiment in his imagination. Imagine a person (let's call him "Jones") who is, first of all, devoid of intellectual curiosity. He has no desire to acquire any kind of knowledge for its own sake, and thus is utterly indifferent to questions of science, mathematics, and philosophy. Imagine further that the beauties of nature leave Jones cold: he is unimpressed by the autumn foliage, the snow-capped mountains, and the rolling oceans.

Long walks in the country on spring mornings and skiing forays in the winter are to him equally a bore. Moreover, let us suppose that Jones can find no appeal in art. Novels are dull, poetry a pain, paintings nonsense and music just noise. Suppose further that Jones has neither the participant's nor the spectator's passion for baseball, football, tennis, or any other sport. Swimming to him is a cruel aquatic form of calisthenics, the sun only a cause of sunburn. Dancing is coeducational idiocy, conversation a waste of time, the other sex an unappealing mystery. Politics is a fraud, religion mere superstition; and the misery of millions of underprivileged human beings is nothing to be concerned with or excited about. Suppose finally that Jones has no talent for any kind of handicraft, industry, or commerce, and that he does not regret that fact.

What then is Jones interested in? He must desire something. To be sure, he does. Jones has an overwhelming passion for, a complete preoccupation with, his own happiness. The one exclusive desire of his life is *to be happy.* It takes little imagination at this point to see that Jones's one desire is bound to be frustrated. People who—like Jones—most hotly pursue their own happiness are the least likely to find it. Happy people are those who successfully pursue such things as aesthetic or religious experience, self-expression, service to others, victory in competitions, knowledge, power, and so on. If none of these things in themselves and for their own sakes mean anything to a person, if they are valued at all then only as a means to one's own pleasant states of mind—then that pleasure can never come. The way to achieve happiness is to pursue something else.

Almost all people at one time or another in their lives feel pleasure. Some people (though perhaps not many) really do live lives which are on the whole happy. But if pleasure and happiness presuppose desires for something other than pleasure and happiness, then the existence of pleasure and happiness in the experience of some people proves that those people have strong desires for something other than their own happiness—egoistic hedonism to the contrary.

The implications of the "paradox of hedonism" for educational theory should be obvious. The parents least likely to raise a happy child are those who, even with the best intentions, train their child to seek happiness directly. How often have we heard parents say:

I don't care if my child does not become an intellectual, or a sports star, or a great artist. I just want her to be a plain average sort of person. Happiness does not require great ambitions and great frustrations; it's not worth it to suffer and become neurotic for the sake of science, art, or do-goodism. I just want my child to be happy.

This can be a dangerous mistake, for it is the child (and the adult for that matter) without "outer-directed" interests who is the most likely to be unhappy. The pure egoist would be the most wretched of persons.

The educator might well beware of "life adjustment" as the conscious goal of the educational process for similar reasons. "Life adjustment" can be achieved only as a by-product of other pursuits. A whole curriculum of "life adjustment courses" unsupplemented by courses designed to incite an interest in things other than life adjustment would be tragically self-defeating.

As for moral education, it is probably true that punishment and reward are indispensable means of inculcation. But if the child comes to believe that the *sole* reasons for being moral are that he will escape the pain of punishment thereby and/or that he will gain the pleasure of a good reputation, then what is to prevent him from doing the immoral thing whenever he is sure that he will not be found out? While punishment and reward then are important tools for the moral educator, they obviously have their limitations. Beware of the man who does the moral thing only out of fear of pain or love of pleasure. He is not likely to be wholly trustworthy. Moral education is truly successful when it produces persons who are willing to do the right thing *simply because it is right,* and not merely because it is popular or safe.

12. *Pleasure as Sensation.* One final argument against psychological hedonism should suffice to put that form of the egoistic psychology to rest once and for all. The egoistic hedonist claims that all desires can be reduced to the single desire for one's own *pleasure.* Now the word "pleasure" is ambiguous. On the one hand, it can stand for a certain indefinable, but very familiar and specific kind of sensation, or more accurately, a property of sensations; and it is generally, if not exclusively, associated with the senses. For example, certain taste sensations such as sweetness, thermal sensations of the sort derived from a hot bath or the feel of the August sun while one lies on a sandy beach, erotic sensations, olfactory sensations (say) of the fragrance of flowers or perfume, and tactual and kinesthetic

sensations from a good massage, are all pleasant in this sense. Let us call this sense of "pleasure," which is the converse of "physical pain," pleasure $_1$.

On the other hand, the word "pleasure" is often used simply as a synonym for "satisfaction" (in the sense of gratification, not mere desire fulfillment.) In this sense, the existence of pleasure presupposes the prior existence of desire. Knowledge, religious experience, aesthetic expression, and other so-called "spiritual activities" often give pleasure in this sense. In fact, as we have seen, we tend to get pleasure in this sense whenever we get what we desire, no matter what we desire. The masochist even derives pleasure (in the sense of "satisfaction") from his own physically painful sensations. Let us call the sense of "pleasure" which means "satisfaction"—pleasure $_2$.

Now we can evaluate the psychological hedonist's claim that the sole human motive is a desire for one's own pleasure, bearing in mind (as he often does not) the ambiguity of the word "pleasure." First, let us take the hedonist to be saying that it is the desire for pleasure $_1$ (pleasant sensation) which is the sole ultimate desire of all people and the sole desire capable of providing a motive for action. Now I have little doubt that all (or most) people desire their own pleasure, *sometimes.* But even this familiar kind of desire occurs, I think, rather rarely. When I am very hungry, I often desire to eat, or, more specifically, to eat this piece of steak and these potatoes. Much less often do I desire to eat certain morsels simply for the sake of the pleasant gustatory sensations they might cause. I have, on the other hand, been motivated in the latter way when I have gone to especially exotic (and expensive) French or Chinese restaurants; but normally, pleasant gastronomic sensations are simply a happy consequence or by-product of my eating, not the antecedently desired objective of my eating. There are, of course, others who take gustatory sensations far more seriously: the *gourmet* who eats only to savor the textures and flavors of fine foods, and the wine fancier who "collects" the exquisitely subtle and very pleasant tastes of rare old wines. Such people are truly absorbed in their taste sensations when they eat and drink, and there may even be some (rich) persons whose desire for such sensations is the sole motive for eating and drinking. It should take little argument, however, to convince the reader that such persons are extremely rare.

Similarly, I usually derive pleasure from taking a hot bath, and on occasion (though not very often) I even decide to bathe simply for the sake of such sensations. Even if this is equally true of everyone, however, it hardly provides grounds for inferring that *no one ever* bathes from *any* other motive. It should be empirically obvious that we sometimes bathe simply in order to get clean, or to please others, or simply from habit.

The view then that we are never after anything in our actions but our own pleasure—that all people are complete "gourmets" of one sort or another—is not only morally cynical; it is also contrary to common sense and everyday experience. In fact, the view that pleasant sensations play such an enormous role in human affairs is so patently false, on the available evidence, that we must conclude that the psychological hedonist has the other sense of "pleasure"—satisfaction—in mind when he states his thesis. If, on the other hand, he really does try to reduce the apparent multitude of human motives to the one desire for pleasant sensations, then the abundance of historical counter-examples justifies our rejection out of hand of his thesis. It surely seems incredible that the Christian martyrs were ardently pursuing their own pleasure when they marched off to face the lions, or that what the Russian soldiers at Stalingrad "really" wanted when they doused themselves with gasoline, ignited themselves, and then threw the flaming torches of their own bodies on German tanks, was simply the experience of pleasant physical sensations.

13. *Pleasure as Satisfaction.* Let us consider now the other interpretation of the hedonist's thesis, that according to which it is one's own pleasure$_2$ (satisfaction) and not merely pleasure$_1$ (pleasant sensation) which is the sole ultimate objective of all voluntary behavior. In one respect, the "satisfaction thesis" is even less plausible than the "physical sensation thesis"; for the latter at least is a genuine empirical hypothesis, testable in experience, though contrary to the facts which experience discloses. The former, however, is so confused that it cannot even be completely stated without paradox. It is, so to speak, defeated in its own formulation. Any attempted explication of the theory that all men at all times desire only their own satisfaction leads to an *infinite regress* in the following way:

"All men desire only satisfaction."
"Satisfaction of what?"
"Satisfaction of their desires."
"Their desires for what?"
"Their desires for satisfaction."
"Satisfaction of what?"
"Their desires."
"For what?"
"For satisfaction"—etc., *ad infinitum*.

In short, psychological hedonism interpreted in this way attributes to all people as their sole motive a wholly vacuous and infinitely self-defeating desire. The source of this absurdity is in the notion that satisfaction can, so to speak, feed on itself, and perform the miracle of perpetual self-regeneration in the absence of desires for anything other than itself.

To summarize the argument of sections 11 and 12: The word "pleasure" is ambiguous. Pleasure$_1$ means a certain indefinable characteristic of physical sensation. Pleasure$_2$ refers to the feeling of satisfaction that often comes when one gets what one desires whatever be the nature of that which one desires. Now, if the hedonist means pleasure$_1$ when he says that one's own pleasure is the ultimate objective of all of one's behavior, then his view is not supported by the facts. On the other hand, if he means pleasure$_2$, then his theory cannot even be clearly formulated, since it leads to the following infinite regress: "I desire only satisfaction of my desire for satisfaction of my desire for satisfaction . . . etc., *ad infinitum*." I conclude then that psychological hedonism (the most common form of psychological egoism), however interpreted, is untenable.

D. CRITIQUE OF PSYCHOLOGICAL EGOISM: UNCLEAR LOGICAL STATUS OF THE THEORY

14. There remain, however, other possible forms of the egoistic psychology. The egoist might admit that not all human motives can be reduced to the one ultimate desire for one's own pleasure, or happiness, and yet still maintain that our ultimate motives, whether they be desire for happiness (J. S. Mill), self-fulfillment (Aristotle), power (Hobbes), or whatever, are always *self-regarding* motives. He might still maintain that, given our common human nature, wholly disinterested action impelled by exclusively other-regarding motives is psychologically impossible, and that therefore there is a profoundly important sense in which it is true that, whether they be hedonists or not, *all people are selfish.*

Now it seems to me that this highly paradoxical claim cannot be finally evaluated until it is properly understood, and that it cannot be properly understood until one knows what the psychological egoist is willing to accept as evidence either for or against it. In short, there are two things that must be decided: (a) whether the theory is true or false and (b) whether its truth or falsity (its truth value) depends entirely on the *meanings* of the words in which it is expressed or whether it is made true or false by certain *facts,* in this case the facts of psychology.

15. *Analytic Statements.* Statements whose truth is determined solely by the meanings of the words in which they are expressed, and thus can be held immune from empirical evidence, are often called analytic statements or tautologies. The following are examples of tautologies:

(1) All bachelors are unmarried.
(2) All effects have causes.
(3) Either Providence is the capital of Rhode Island or it is not.

The truth of (1) is derived solely from the meaning of the word "bachelor," which is defined (in part) as "unmarried man." To find out whether (1) is true or false we need not conduct interviews, compile statistics, or perform experiments. All empirical evidence is superfluous and irrelevant; for if we know the meanings of "bachelor" and "unmarried," then we know not only that (1) is true, but that it is *necessarily* true—i.e., that it cannot possibly be false, that no future experiences or observations could possibly upset it, that to deny it would be to assert a logical contradiction. But notice that what a tautology gains in certainty ("necessary truth") it loses in descriptive content. Statement (1) imparts no information whatever about any matter of fact; it simply records our determination to use certain words in a certain way. As we say, "It is true by definition."

Similarly, (2) is (necessarily) true solely in virtue of the meanings of the words "cause" and "effect" and thus requires no further observations to confirm it. And of course, no possible observations could falsify it, since it asserts no matter of fact. And finally, statement (3) is (necessarily) true solely in virtue of the meaning of the English expression "either . . . or". Such terms as "either . . . or," "If . . . then," "and," and "not" are called by logicians "logical constants." The *definitions* of logical constants are made explicit in the so-called "laws of thought"—the law of contradiction, the

law of the excluded middle, and the law of identity. These "laws" are not laws in the same sense as are (say) the laws of physics. Rather, they are merely consequences of the *definitions* of logical constants, and as such, though they are necessarily true, they impart no information about the world. "Either Providence is the capital of Rhode Island or it is not" tells us nothing about geography; and "Either it is now raining or else it is not" tells us nothing about the weather. You don't have to look at a map or look out the window to know that they are true. Rather, they are known to be true *a priori* (independently of experience); and, like all (or many)[12] *a priori* statements, they are *vacuous,* i.e., devoid of informative content.

The denial of an analytic statement is called a contradiction. The following are typical examples of contradictions: "Some bachelors are married," "Some causes have no effects," "Providence both is and is not the capital of Rhode Island." As in the case of tautologies, the truth value of contradictions (their falsehood) is logically necessary, not contingent on any facts of experience, and uninformative. Their falsity is derived from the meanings (definitions) of the words in which they are expressed.

16. *Synthetic Statements.* On the other hand, statements whose truth or falsity is derived not from the meanings of words but rather from the facts of experience (observations) are called *synthetic*.[13] Prior to experience, there can be no good reason to think either that they are true or that they are false. That is to say, their truth value is *contingent;* and they can be confirmed or disconfirmed only by *empirical* evidence,[14] i.e., controlled observations of the world. Unlike analytic statements, they do impart information about matters of fact. Obviously, "It is raining in Newport now," if true, is more informative than "Either it is raining in Newport now or it is not," even though the former *could* be false, while the latter is necessarily true. I take the following to be examples of synthetic (contingent) statements:

(1') All bachelors are neurotic.
(2') All events have causes.
(3') Providence is the capital of Rhode Island.
(3'') Newport is the capital of Rhode Island.

Statement (3') is true; (3'') is false; and (1') is a matter for a psychologist (not for a philosopher) to decide; and the psychologist himself can only decide *empirically*, i.e., by making many observations. The status of (2') is very difficult and its truth value is a matter of great controversy. That is because its truth or falsity depends on *all* the facts ("all events"); and, needless to say, not all of the evidence is in.

17. *Empirical Hypotheses.* Perhaps the most interesting subclass of synthetic statements are those generalizations of experience of the sort characteristically made by scientists; e.g., "All released objects heavier than air fall," "All swans are white," "All men have Oedipus complexes." I shall call such statements "empirical hypotheses" to indicate that their function is to sum up past experience and enable us successfully to predict or anticipate future experience.[15] They are never logically certain, since it is always at least conceivable that future experience will disconfirm them. For example, zoologists once believed that all swans are white, until black swans were discovered in Australia. The most important characteristic of empirical hypotheses for our present purposes is their relation to evidence. A person can be said to understand an empirical hypothesis only if he knows how to recognize evidence against it. *If a person asserts or believes a general statement in such a way that he cannot conceive of any possible experience which he would count as evidence against it, then he cannot be said to be asserting or believing an empirical hypothesis.* We can refer to this important characteristic of empirical hypotheses as *falsifiability in principle*.

Some statements only appear to be empirical hypotheses but are in fact disguised tautologies reflecting the speaker's determination to use words in certain (often eccentric) ways. For example, a zoologist might refuse to allow the existence of "Australian swans" to count as evidence against the generalization that all swans are white, on the grounds that the black Australian swans are not "really" swans at all. This would indicate that he is holding *whiteness* to be part of the definition of "swan," and that therefore, the statement "All swans are white" is, for him, "true by definition"— and thus just as immune from counterevidence as the statement "All spinsters are unmarried." Similarly, most of us would refuse to allow any possible experience to count as evidence against "2 + 2 = 4" or "Either unicorns exist or they do not," indicating

that the propositions of arithmetic and logic are not empirical hypotheses.

18. *Ordinary Language and Equivocation.* Philosophers, even more than ordinary people, are prone to make startling and paradoxical claims that take the form of universal generalizations and hence resemble empirical hypotheses. For example, "All things are mental (there are no physical objects)," "All things are good (there is no evil)," "All voluntary behavior is selfish," etc. Let us confine out attention for the moment to the latter which is a rough statement of psychological egoism. At first sight, the statement "All voluntary behavior is selfish" seems obviously false. One might reply to the psychological egoist in some such manner as this:

I *know* some behavior, at least, is unselfish, because I saw my Aunt Emma yesterday give her last cent to a beggar. Now she will have to go a whole week with nothing to eat. Surely, *that* was not selfish of her.

Nevertheless, the psychological egoist is likely not to be convinced, and insist that, in this case, if we knew enough about Aunt Emma, we would learn that her primary motive in helping the beggar was to promote her own happiness or assuage her own conscience, or increase her own self-esteem, etc. We might then present the egoist with even more difficult cases for his theory—saints, martyrs, military heroes, patriots, and others who have sacrificed themselves for a cause. If psychological egoists nevertheless refuse to accept any of these as examples of unselfish behavior, then we have a right to be puzzled about what they are saying. Until we know what they would count as *unselfish* behavior, we can't very well know what they mean when they say that all voluntary behavior is *selfish*. And at this point we may suspect that they are holding their theory in a "privileged position"—that of immunity to evidence, that they would allow no *conceivable* behavior to count as evidence against it. What they say then, if true, must be true in virtue of the way he defines—or redefines— the word "selfish." And in that case, it cannot be an empirical hypothesis.

If what the psychological egoist says is "true by redefinition," then I can "agree" with him and say "It is true that in *your* sense of the word 'selfish' my Aunt Emma's behavior was selfish; but in the ordinary sense of 'selfish,' which implies blameworthiness, she surely was not selfish." There is no point of course in arguing about a mere word. The important thing is not what particular words a man uses, but rather whether what he wishes to say in those words is true. Departures from ordinary language can often be justified by their utility for certain purposes; but they are dangerous when they invite equivocation. The psychological egoist may be saying something which is true when he says that Emma is selfish in *his* sense, but if he doesn't realize that his sense of "selfish" differs from the ordinary one, he may be tempted to infer that Emma is selfish in the ordinary sense which implies blameworthiness; and this of course would be unfair and illegitimate. It is indeed an extraordinary extension of the meaning of the word "self-indulgent" (as C. G. Chesterton remarks somewhere) which allows a philosopher to say that a man is self-indulgent when he wants to be burned at the stake.

19. *The Fallacy of the Suppressed Correlative.* Certain words in the English language operate in pairs—e.g., "selfish-unselfish," "good-bad," "large-small," "mental-physical." To assert that a thing has one of the above characteristics is to *contrast* it with the opposite in the pair. To know the meaning of one term in the pair, we must know the meaning of the correlative term with which it is contrasted. If we could not conceive of what it would be like for a thing to be bad, for example, then we could not possibly understand what is being said of a thing when it is called "good." Similarly, unless we had a notion of what it would be like for action to be *unselfish*, we could hardly understand the sentence "So-and-so acted selfishly"; for we would have nothing to contrast "selfishly" with. The so-called "fallacy of the suppressed correlative"[16] is committed by a person who consciously or unconsciously redefines one of the terms in a contrasting pair in such a way that its new meaning incorporates the sense of its correlative.

Webster's Collegiate Dictionary defines "selfish" (in part) as "regarding one's own comfort, advantage, etc. in disregard of, or at the expense of that of others." In this ordinary and proper sense of "selfish," Aunt Emma's action in giving her last cent to the beggar certainly was *not* selfish. Emma *disregarded* her *own* comfort (it is not "comfortable" to go a week without eating) and advantage (there is no "advantage" in malnutrition) *for the sake of* (not "at the expense of") another. Similarly, the martyr marching off to the stake is foregoing (not indulging) his "comfort" and indeed his very life for the sake of (not at the expense of) a cause. If

Emma and the martyr then are "selfish," they must be so in a strange new sense of the word.

A careful examination of the egoist's arguments (see especially 4b above) reveals what new sense he gives to the word "selfish." He redefines the word so that it means (roughly) "motivated," or perhaps "intentional." "After all," says the egoist, "Aunt Emma had some *purpose* in giving the beggar all her money, and this purpose (desire, intention, motive, aim) was *her* purpose and no one else's. She was out to further some aim of her own, wasn't she? Therefore, she was pursuing her own ends (acting from her own motives); she was after something *for herself* in so acting, and that's what I mean by calling her action selfish. Moreover, all intentional action—action done 'on purpose,' deliberately from the agent's own motives—is selfish in the same sense." We can see now, from this reply, that since the egoist apparently means by "selfish" simply "motivated," when he says that all motivated action is selfish *he is not asserting a synthetic empirical hypothesis about human motives; rather, his statement is a tautology roughly equivalent to "all motivated actions are motivated."* And if that is the case, then what he says is true enough; but, like all tautologies, it is empty, uninteresting, and trivial.

Moreover, in redefining "selfish" in this way, the psychological egoist has committed the fallacy of the suppressed correlative. For what can we now contrast "selfish voluntary action" with? Not only are there no *actual* cases of unselfish voluntary actions on the new definition; there are not even any *theoretically possible* or *conceivable* cases of unselfish voluntary actions. And if we cannot even conceive of what an unselfish voluntary action would be like, how can we give any sense to the expression "selfish voluntary action"? The egoist, so to speak, has so blown up the sense of "selfish" that, like inflated currency, it will no longer buy anything.

20. *Psychological Egoism as a Linguistic Proposal.* There is still one way out for the egoist. He might admit that his theory is not really a psychological hypothesis about human nature designed to account for the facts and enable us to predict or anticipate future events. He may even willingly concede that his theory is really a disguised redefinition of a word. Still, he might argue, he has made no claim to be giving an accurate description of actual linguistic usage. Rather, he is making a proposal

to *revise* our usage in the interest of economy and convenience, just as the biologists once proposed that we change the ordinary meaning of "insect" in such a way that spiders are no longer called insects, and the ordinary meaning of "fish" so that whales and seals are no longer called fish.

What are we to say to this suggestion? First of all, stipulative definitions (proposals to revise usage) are never true or false. They are simply useful or not useful. Would it be useful to redefine "selfish" in the way the egoist recommends? It is difficult to see what would be gained thereby. The egoist has noticed some respects in which actions normally called "selfish" and actions normally called "unselfish" are alike, namely they are both motivated and they both can give satisfaction—either in prospect or in retrospect—to the agent. Because of these likenesses, the egoist feels justified in attaching the label "selfish" to *all* actions. Thus one word—"selfish"—must for him do the work of two words ("selfish" and "unselfish" in their old meanings); and, as a result, a very real distinction, that between actions for the sake of others and actions at the expense of others, can no longer be expressed in the language. Because the egoist has noticed some respects in which two types of actions are alike, he wishes to make it impossible to describe the respects in which they differ. It is difficult to see any utility in this state of affairs.

But suppose we adopt the egoist's "proposal" nevertheless. Now we would have to say that all actions are selfish; but, in addition, we would want to say that there are two different kinds of selfish actions, those which regard the interests of others and those which disregard the interests of others, and, furthermore, that only the latter are blameworthy. After a time our ear would adjust to the new uses of the word "selfish," and we would find nothing at all strange in such statements as "Some selfish actions are morally praiseworthy." After a while, we might even invent two new words, perhaps "selfitic" and "unselfitic," to distinguish the two important classes of "selfish" actions. Then we would be right back where we started, with new linguistic tools ("selfish" for "motivated," "selfitic" for "selfish," and "unselfitic" for "unselfish") to do the same old necessary jobs. That is, until some new egoistic philosopher arose to announce with an air of discovery that "All selfish behavior is really selfitic—there are no truly unselfitic selfish actions." Then, God help us!

NOTES

1. See his *Introduction to the Principles of Morals and Legislation* (1789), Chap. I, first paragraph: "Nature has placed mankind under the governance of two sovereign masters, *pain* and *pleasure*. It is for them alone to point out what we ought to do, as well as to determine what we shall do. . . . They govern us in all we do, in all we say, in all we think: every effort we can make to throw off our subjection will serve but to demonstrate and confirm it."

2. C. D. Broad, *Ethics and the History of Philosophy* (New York: The Humanities Press, 1952), Essay 10—"Egoism as a Theory of Human Motives," p. 218. This essay is highly recommended.

3. Austin Duncan-Jones, *Butler's Moral Philosophy* (London; Penguin Books, 1952), p. 96. Duncan-Jones goes on to reject this argument. See p. 512f.

4. Lucius Garvin, *A Modern Introduction to Ethics* (Boston: Houghton Mifflin, 1953), p. 37. Quoted here by permission of the author and publisher.

5. *Op. cit.,* Chap. III.

6. See Part D, 15 and 16, below.

7. *Op. cit.,* p. 39.

8. *The Principles of Psychology,* (New York: Henry Holt, 1890), Vol. II, p. 558.

9. *Op. cit.,* p. 39.

10. Quoted from the *Springfield* (Illinois) *Monitor,* by F. C. Sharp in his *Ethics* (New York: Appleton-Century, 1928), p. 75.

11. See his *Fifteen Sermons on Human Nature Preached at the Rolls Chapel* (1726), especially the first and eleventh.

12. Whether or not there are some *a priori* statements that are not merely analytic, and hence *not* vacuous, is still a highly controversial question among philosophers.

13. Some philosophers (those called "rationalists") believe that there are some synthetic statements whose truth can be known *a priori* (see footnote 12). If they are right, then the statement above is not entirely accurate.

14. Again, subject to the qualification in footnotes 12 and 13.

15. The three examples given above all have the generic character there indicated, but they also differ from one another in various other ways, some of which are quite important. For our present purposes however, we can ignore the ways in which they differ from one another and concentrate on their common character as generalizations of experience ("inductive generalizations"). As such they are sharply contrasted with such a generalization as "All puppies are young dogs," which is analytic.

16. The phrase was coined by J. Lowenberg. See his article "What is Empirical?" in the *Journal of Philosophy,* May 1940.

STEPHEN JAY GOULD

So Cleverly Kind an Animal*

Stephen Jay Gould (1941–   ) is Professor of Geology at Harvard University and also teaches in the Departments of Biology and History of Science. He writes a regular column for Natural History *magazine.*

In *Civilization and Its Discontents,* Sigmund Freud examined the agonizing dilemma of human social life. We are by nature selfish and aggressive, yet any successful civilization demands that we suppress our biological inclinations and act altruistically for common good and harmony. Freud argued further that as civilizations become increasingly complex and "modern," we must renounce more and more of our innate selves. This we do imperfectly, with guilt, pain, and hardship; the price of civilization is individual suffering.

It is impossible to overlook the extent to which civilization is built up upon a renunciation of instinct, how much it presupposes precisely the nonsatisfaction . . . of powerful instincts. This "cultural frustration" dominates the large field of social relationships between human beings.

Freud's argument is a particularly forceful variation on a ubiquitous theme in speculations about "human nature." What we criticize in ourselves, we attribute to our animal past. These are the shackles of our apish ancestry—brutality, aggression, selfishness; in short, general nastiness. What we prize and strive for (with pitifully limited success), we consider as a unique overlay, conceived by our rationality and imposed upon an unwilling body. Our hopes for a better future lie in reason and kindness—the mental

*From Stephen Jay Gould, *Ever Since Darwin* (New York: W. W. Norton, 1977), pp. 260–271. Reprinted by permission from *Natural History,* November 1976. Copyright American Museum of Natural History, 1976.

transcendence of our biological limitations. "Build thee more stately mansions, O my soul."

Little more than ancient prejudice supports this common belief. It certainly gains no justification from science—so profound is our ignorance about the biology of human behavior. It arises from such sources as the theology of the human soul and the "dualism" of philosophers who sought separate realms for mind and body. It has roots in an attitude that I attack in several of these essays: our desire to view the history of life as progressive and to place ourselves on top of the heap (with all the prerogatives of domination). We seek a criterion for our uniqueness, settle (naturally) upon our minds, and define the noble results of human consciousness as something intrinsically apart from biology. But why? Why should our nastiness be the baggage of an apish past and our kindness uniquely human? Why should we not seek continuity with other animals for our "noble" traits as well?

One nagging scientific argument does seem to support this ancient prejudice. The essential ingredient of human kindness is altruism—sacrifice of our personal comfort, even our lives in extreme cases, for the benefit of others. Yet, if we accept the Darwinian mechanism of evolution, how can altruism be part of biology? Natural selection dictates that organisms act in their own self-interest. They know nothing of such abstract concepts as "the good of the species." They "struggle" continuously to increase the representation of their genes at the expense of their fellows. And that, for all its baldness, is all there is to it; we have discovered no higher principle in nature. Individual advantage, Darwin argues, is the only criterion of success in nature. The harmony of life goes no deeper. The balance of nature arises from interaction between competing teams, each trying to win the prize for itself alone, not from the cooperative sharing of limited resources.

How, then, could anything but selfishness ever evolve as a biological trait of behavior? If altruism is the cement of stable societies, then human society must be fundamentally outside nature. There is one way around this dilemma. Can an apparently altruistic act be "selfish" in this Darwinian sense? Can an individual's sacrifice ever lead to the perpetuation of his own genes? The answer to this seemingly contradictory proposition is "yes." We owe the resolution of this paradox to the theory of "kin selection" developed in the early 1960s by W. D. Hamilton, a British theoretical biologist. It has been stressed as the cornerstone for a biological theory of society in E. O. Wilson's *Sociobiology*. (I criticized the deterministic aspects of Wilson's speculations on human behavior in [another] essay. I also praised his general theory of altruism, and continue this theme now.)

The legacy of brilliant men includes undeveloped foresight. English biologist J. B. S. Haldane probably anticipated every good idea that evolutionary theorists will invent during this century. Haldane, arguing about altruism one evening in a pub, reportedly made some quick calculations on the back of an envelope, and announced: "I will lay down my life for two brothers or eight cousins." What did Haldane mean by such a cryptic comment? Human chromosomes come in pairs: We receive one set from our mother's egg; the other from our father's sperm. Thus, we possess a paternal and a maternal copy of each gene (this is not true among males for genes located on sex chromosomes, since the maternal X chromosome is so much longer—i.e. has so many more genes—than the paternal Y chromosome; most genes on the X chromosome have no corresponding copy on the short Y). Take any human gene. What is the probability that a brother will share the same gene? Suppose that it is on a maternal chromosome (the argument works the same way for paternal chromosomes). Each egg cell contains one chromosome of each pair—that is, one half the mother's genes. The egg cell that made your brother either had the same chromosome you received or the other member of the pair. The chance that you share your brother's gene is an even fifty-fifty. Your brother shares half your genes and is, in the Darwinian calculus, the same as half of you.

Suppose, then, that you are walking down the road with three brothers. A monster approaches with clearly murderous intent. Your brothers do not see it. You have only two alternatives: Approach it and give a rousing Bronx cheer, thereby warning your brothers, who hide and escape, and insuring your own demise; or hide and watch the monster feast on your three brothers. What, as an accomplished player of the Darwinian game, should you do? The answer must be, step right up and cheer—for you have only yourself to lose, while your three brothers represent one and a half of you. Better that they should live to propagate 150 percent of your genes. Your apparently altruistic act is genetically "selfish," for it maximizes the contribution of your genes to the next generation.

According to the theory of kin selection, animals evolve behaviors that endanger or sacrifice themselves only if such altruistic acts increase their own genetic potential by benefiting kin. Altruism and the society of kin must go hand in hand; the benefits of kin selection may even propel the evolution of social interaction. While my absurd example of four brothers and a monster is simplistic, the situation becomes much more complex with twelfth cousins, four times removed. Hamilton's theory does not only belabor the obvious.

Hamilton's theory has had stunning success in explaining some persistent biological puzzles in the evolution of social behavior in the Hymenoptera—ants, bees, and wasps. Why has true sociality evolved independently at least eleven times in the Hymenoptera and only once among other insects (the termites)? Why are sterile worker castes always female in the Hymenoptera, but both male and female in termites? The answers seem to lie in the workings of kin selection within the unusual genetic system of the Hymenoptera.

Most sexually reproducing animals are diploid; their cells contain two sets of chromosomes—one derived from their mother, the other from their father. Termites, like most insects, are diploid. The social Hymenoptera, on the other hand, are haplodiploid. Females develop from fertilized eggs as normal diploid individuals with maternal and paternal sets of chromosomes. But males develop from unfertilized eggs and possess only the maternal set of chromosomes; they are, in technical parlance, haploid (half the normal number of chromosomes).

In diploid organisms, genetic relationships of sibs and parents are symmetrical: parents share half their genes with their children, and each sib (on average) shares half its genes with any other sib, male or female. But in haplodiploid species, genetic relationships are asymmetrical, permitting kin selection to work in an unusual and potent way. Consider the relationship of a queen ant to her sons and daughters, and the relationship of these daughters to their sisters and brothers:

1. The queen is related by 1/2 to both her sons and daughters; each of her offspring carries 1/2 her chromosomes and, therefore, 1/2 her genes.

2. Sisters are related to their brothers, not by 1/2 as in diploid organisms, but only by 1/4. Take any of a sister's genes. Chances are 1/2 that it is a paternal gene. If so, she cannot share it with her brother (who has no paternal genes). If it is a maternal gene, then chances are 1/2 that her brother has it as well. Her total relationship with her brother is the average of zero (for paternal genes) and 1/2 (for maternal genes), or 1/4.

3. Sisters are related to their sisters by 3/4. Again, take any gene. If it is paternal, then her sister must share it (since fathers have only one set of chromosomes to pass to all daughters). If it is maternal, then her sister has a fifty-fifty chance of sharing it, as before. Sisters are related by the average of 1 (for paternal genes) and 1/2 (for maternal genes), or 3/4.

These asymmetries seem to provide a simple and elegant explanation for that most altruistic of animal behaviors—the "willingness" of sterile female workers to forego their own reproduction in order to help their mothers raise more sisters. As long as a worker can invest preferentially in her sisters, she will perpetuate more of her genes by helping her mother raise fertile sisters (3/4 relationship) than by raising fertile daughters herself (1/2 relationship). But a male has no inclination toward sterility and labor. He would much rather raise daughters, who share all his genes, than help sisters, who share only 1/2 of them. (I do not mean to attribute conscious will to creatures with such rudimentary brains. I use such phrases as "he would rather" only as a convenient shortcut for "in the course of evolution, males who did not behave this way have been placed at a selective disadvantage and gradually eliminated.")

My colleagues R. L. Trivers and H. Hare have recently reported the following important discovery in *Science* (January 23, 1976): they argue that queens and workers should prefer different sex ratios for fertile offspring. The queen favors a 1:1 ratio of males to females since she is equally related (by 1/2) to her sons and daughters. But the workers raise the off-

spring and can impose their preferences upon the queen by selective nurturing of her eggs. Workers would rather raise fertile sisters (relationship 3/4) than brothers (relationship 1/4). But they must raise some brothers, lest their sisters fail to find mates. So they compromise by favoring sisters to the extent of their stronger relationship to them. Since they are three times more related to sisters than brothers, they should invest three times more energy in raising sisters. Workers invest energy by feeding; the extent of feeding is reflected in the adult weight of fertile offspring. Trivers and Hare therefore measured the ratio of female/male weight for all fertile offspring taken together in nests of 21 different ant species. The average weight ratio—or investment ratio—is remarkably close to 3:1. This is impressive enough, but the clincher in the argument comes from studies of slave-making ants. Here, the workers are captured members of other species. They have no genetic relationship to the daughters of their imposed queen and should not favor them over the queen's sons. Sure enough, in these situations, the female/male weight ratio is 1:1—even though it is again 3:1 when workers of the enslaved species are not captured but work, instead, for their own queen.

Kin selection, operating on the peculiar genetics of haplodiploidy, seems to explain the key features of social behavior in ants, bees, and wasps. But what can it do for us? How can it help us understand the contradictory amalgam of impulses toward selfishness and altruism that form our own personalities? I am willing to admit—and this is only my intuition, since we have no facts to constrain us—that it probably resolves Freud's dilemma of the first paragraph. Our selfish and aggressive urges may have evolved by the Darwinian route of individual advantage, but our altruistic tendencies need not represent a unique overlay imposed by the demands of civilization. These tendencies may have arisen by the same Darwinian route via kin selection. Basic human kindness may be as "animal" as human nastiness.

But here I stop—short of any deterministic speculation that attributes *specific* behaviors to the possession of specific altruist or opportunist genes. Our genetic makeup permits a wide range of behaviors—from Ebenezer Scrooge before to Ebenezer Scrooge after. I do not believe that the miser hoards through opportunist genes or that the philanthropist gives because nature endowed him with more than the normal complement of altruist genes. Upbringing, culture, class, status, and all the intangibles that we call "free will," determine how we restrict our behaviors from the wide spectrum—extreme altruism to extreme selfishness—that our genes permit.

As an example of deterministic speculations based on altruism and kin selection, E. O. Wilson has proposed a genetic explanation of homosexuality (*New York Times Magazine,* October 12, 1975). Since exclusive homosexuals do not bear children, how could a homosexuality gene ever be selected in a Darwinian world? Suppose that our ancestors organized socially as small, competing groups of very close kin. Some groups contained only heterosexual members. Others included homosexuals who functioned as "helpers" in hunting or child rearing: they bore no children but they helped kin to raise their close genetic relatives. If groups with homosexual helpers prevailed in competition over exclusively heterosexual groups, then homosexuality genes would have been maintained by kin selection. There is nothing illogical in this proposal, but it has no facts going for it either. We have identified no homosexuality gene, and we know nothing relevant to this hypothesis about the social organization of our ancestors.

Wilson's intent is admirable; he attempts to affirm the intrinsic dignity of a common and much maligned sexual behavior by arguing that it is natural for some people—and adaptive to boot (at least under an ancestral form of social organization). But the strategy is a dangerous one, for it backfires if the genetic speculation is wrong. If you defend a behavior by arguing that people are programmed directly for it, then how do you continue to defend it if your speculation is wrong, for the behavior then becomes unnatural and worthy of condemnation. Better to stick resolutely to a philosophical position on human liberty: what free adults do with each other in their own private lives is their business alone. It need not be vindicated—and must not be condemned—by genetic speculation.

Although I worry long and hard about the deterministic uses of kin selection, I applaud the insight it offers for my favored theme of biological potentiality. For it extends the realm of genetic potential even further by including the capacity for kindness, once viewed as intrinsically unique to human culture. Sigmund Freud argued that the history of our greatest scientific insights has reflected, ironically, a continuous retreat of our species from center stage in the cosmos. Before Copernicus and Newton, we thought we lived at the hub of the universe. Before Darwin, we thought that a benevolent God had created us. Before Freud, we imagined ourselves as rational creatures (surely one of the least modest statements in intellectual history). If kin selection marks another stage in this retreat, it will serve us well by nudging our thinking away from domination and toward a perception of respect and unity with other animals.

HOWARD KAHANE

Making the World Safe for Reciprocity*

Howard Kahane (1928–   ) teaches philosophy at the University of Maryland Baltimore County.

Our societies are based on the mammalian plan: the individual strives for personal reproductive success foremost and that of his immediate kin secondarily; further grudging cooperation represents a compromise struck in order to enjoy the benefits of group membership.

> E. O. Wilson *(On Human Nature)*

Among human beings, immediate impulses—for food, sex, and so on—often are overruled by prospects of greater satisfaction later. We delay immediate gratification of certain motivating interests in order to maximize satisfaction of those and other interests over the long run. Doing so is simply a matter of prudence.

Are there any other instances when it is rational to constrain our immediate impulses or desires? Or is the rational person simply one who tries to maximize his or her own motivating interests in the long run? How we answer such questions depends, as it always does in philosophy, on what kinds of reasons or evidence we are willing to accept as relevant.

The question whether *morality* constitutes a constraint on the prudent management of motivating interests is a good example, because morality does seem to require us at least sometimes to put the interests of other people ahead of our own. But does it really? And if so, how and under what conditions?

I. REASON AND MORALITY

In the history of philosophy, all sorts of reasons have been provided to justify particular moral theories. Immanuel Kant, for instance, looked to reason alone, divorced from any tugs of desire or self-

interest, to provide all that is relevant or needed to develop a correct moral theory. Others have looked to some feature of the "external" world—the world outside of ourselves. G. E. Moore, for instance, argued that there is such a thing as "non-natural" objective goodness, and that we can somehow apprehend it in our experiences of the external world, even though not quite as we apprehend "natural" qualities such as colors and sounds.

But there is another sort of appeal we can make, aside from an appeal to reason alone or to some feature of the external world; namely an appeal to our own deepest desires and goals, our own most important motivating interests. Morality, on this view, stems from and serves some of our most important interests. Egoists, for instance, have often supported their view by arguing that in the last analysis we are basically selfish creatures, however much prudentially motivated altruistic behavior may mask that fact.

This appeal to our own interests is especially attractive to those who think of moral decision making as a kind of rational decision making. From our viewpoint, it is clear that *morally right decisions must be rationally right decisions*. Otherwise, only fools would care to make them. True morality, assuming there is such a thing, cannot run counter to our interests—the desire to be moral has to *be* one of our motivating interests. But which one? What precisely is the desire to be moral?

To answer this question, we need to know at least roughly what our most fundamental motivators are, so that we can determine which are closest to those commonly thought of as moral. This will also enable us to evaluate standard moral theories such as egoism and utilitarianism that have been proposed by moral theorists, since the right moral theory must be the one that best furthers our motivating interests.

*Copyright © Howard Kahane, 1981. This essay was commissioned by the editor expressly for the fifth edition of this anthology.

The point of this paper is to argue that current scientific theories about the "nature of human nature"—in particular some theories proposed by sociobiologists[1]—support neither egoism nor utilitarianism, but a version of what is called "contract ethics," specifically the view that the correct rules of morality are just the rules of *fair reciprocity* among cooperating competitors. On this view, what we are obligated to do is (roughly) to keep fair agreements or contracts, implicit as well as explicit, because in doing so we best satisfy basic human motivating interests. Let me explain further.

II. NATURAL SELECTION AND HUMAN NATURE

Although many of us have been taught otherwise, in fact the *gene* is the basic unit of survival in natural selection—not the species, as commonly thought, nor, obviously, individual animals or plants. Individual animals and plants can, in fact, be profitably thought of as "gene survival machines."[2]

On the whole, of course, what is good for a given organism's genes is good for that individual's own survival and successful procreation. However, genes do not program us directly to do what is best for our (and their) survival, but rather indirectly by giving us *motivating interests* (appetites, feelings, etc.[3]), which move us to actions that on the whole were good for gene survival during the vast sweep of evolutionary time. (It remains to be seen, of course, whether our genes will move us now and in the future to actions that result in human survival, given the way human beings have been swiftly changing their environment in the past few hundred years.)

Once we think of ourselves and other living things as gene survival machines, the question arises as to how *altruistic behavior* (behavior likely to benefit some other individual at the expense of the doer) could have evolved in a world of tooth and claw. What genetic survival value does altruism have? The sociobiologist's answer to this question distinguishes between two importantly different sorts of altruism: kin altruism and reciprocal altruism. A *kin altruistic* act is simply an altruistic act likely to benefit close genetic relatives of the doer. Genes of survival machines programmed to engage in certain kinds of kin altruistic behavior clearly have a survival advantage over genes of competing survival machines not so programmed, even though these altruistic acts may reduce the survival chances of the actors themselves.

For instance, a bird programmed to feed its young will reproduce more successfully than birds not so programmed, thus increasing the survival chances of its genes in spite of reducing its own survival chances.

Kin altruism obviously is an important part of the human repertoire; in virtually every human society the young are given special care by their own kin, and sacrifices for close kin are much more common than for unrelated members of a group. (Of course, all sorts of people, philosophers in particular, accept the idea that birds and other "lower" animals are programmed to do things like feed their young, but vehemently reject the idea that homo sapiens could be so programmed. See the postscript to this article for a defense of the view that we are indeed just like all other living things in this respect.)

The evolutionary function of the other sort of altruism, *reciprocal altruism*[4] or *R-altruism*—which, I shall argue, provides the key to a good understanding of the basic function of morality and the moral sentiments—is a little harder to explain. In particular, it is difficult to understand *delayed* reciprocal altruism, in which one party reciprocates after receiving the benefit of the others' altruism. Why should it be advantageous to reciprocate, especially when the benefits of the others' altruism have already been obtained? The answer is that (roughly) reciprocating is advantageous when the benefit to each party is greater than the effort expended in reciprocating, *and* when this benefit on the whole cannot be obtained as easily—at least not for long—without expending the effort involved in reciprocating. Consider the altruistic behavior of grooming observed among many bird and mammal species (commonly seen among primates in zoos). Since grooming is vital to health and thus to survival, the benefits of being groomed are clearly greater for each party than the effort they expend in reciprocating, and this benefit cannot be obtained as easily in any other way.

We should expect then that among higher social animals, including homo sapiens, interests and feelings tending to promote these two kinds of altruism will be favored by natural selection. This would explain the origin and function of emotions such as love, empathy, embarrassment, shame, and guilt. But altruistic sentiments and motives cannot increase to the point where they drive out all competing selfish ones; genetic competition among individual members of a species prevents this. During the long period of time (one or two million years?) during which upright primates evolved into today's homo sapiens, essentially two sorts of genetic competition favored selfish behavior. First, competition among groups (in-group competing against out-group) favored aggressive, hostile sentiments that are valuable in warfare. Second, competition within each group (for mates and a share of the material necessities of life) favored sentiments such as greed, envy, and lust.

Completely altruistic human beings thus had no chance to evolve. Even if they had, they would have lost out in competition to more selfishly programmed individuals within their own group. Total altruism is not an "evolutionarily stable strategy."[5] A population composed primarily of "saints," who act altruistically even towards those who don't return the favor, would be easy pickings for "sinners," programmed never to reciprocate. Thus sinners, guided by fewer feelings of empathy, love, and guilt, would tend to increase in a population at the expense of saints until lack of cooperation pushed the whole group to extinction. So neither "saint" nor "sinner" is an evolutionarily stable strategy for human beings.

Once organisms evolve sufficient intelligence to recognize individual members of their group, another basic strategy becomes possible, namely "grudging reciprocity." An intelligent individual can be programmed to learn who is trustworthy and who isn't, and to reciprocate only with those who are. The strategy of grudging reciprocity clearly has an advantage over that of saint or sinner, and also over any random combination of the two, because it allows for the advantages of cooperative ventures while generally avoiding the disadvantages encountered by saints or sinners. If the point of R-altruistic acts is to receive the benefits of reciprocity, then those organisms programmed to be altruistic only toward those non-kin who in fact reciprocate obviously have a much better chance for genetic survival than saints or sinners. In fact, the basic strategy of grudger comes modestly close to being an evolutionarily stable strategy. Our best theory at this stage, therefore, is that human beings will tend basically to be grudgers (with all sorts of complexities and individual variations). And that is a conclusion many of us find supported by our experiences with our fellow human beings.

III. REJECTION OF NON-CONTRACT MORAL THEORIES

The competitive behavior programs just discussed are extremely crude, to say the least. While it is almost certain that the vast majority of human beings have a large stock of grudging sentiments (some people obviously are provisioned more heavily than

others), there are other strategies and many subtleties as yet uninvestigated by sociobiologists. The genetic programming of real flesh-and-blood human beings will almost certainly turn out to be many times more complex than that of mere grudger, even though grudging is its focus.

Even so, it should already be clear that none of the standard non-contract moral theories come close to dovetailing with the sociobiological account of human nature, and are unlikely to do so with the more subtle accounts we can expect soon. So before arguing for the evolutionary function of two key concepts of contract theories of morality, namely fairness and retribution, let's see why three standard non-contract theories must be rejected by anyone who approaches morality via rational decision-making and an investigation of human nature, the approach taken in this paper.

(1) Utilitarianism has been the dominant moral theory in American philosophy in recent years. One plausible way to put the theory of classical utilitarianism is this: ". . . Society is rightly ordered, and therefore just, when its major institutions are arranged so as to achieve the greatest net balance of satisfaction summed up over all the individuals belonging to it."[6]

What sort of human interest could such a theory answer to? It would have to be an interest in the *end* that utilitarianism promotes, which is to maximize human satisfaction, however distributed. That human beings could have such an interest finds no support in sociobiological theory or any other scientific theory of human nature. It is incredible to think that anyone would have a motive for sacrificing a significant amount of personal pleasure, or the pleasure of a friend or relative, in order to modestly increase the satisfaction of several total strangers or perhaps even serious rivals (except, of course, where contractual fairness requires it, as described later).

Utilitarianism fails to take account of our special interest in benefiting some human beings (ourselves, close kin, close friends, fair reciprocators) and harming others (in-group cheaters, members of hostile out-groups), because it fails properly to take account of the competitive as well as the cooperative aspects of human nature and human interactions. Utilitarianism thus cannot be in accord with anyone's rational interest. Utilitarianism would be the right theory for a person who had an extremely strong interest in sheer human satisfaction, without concern for who gets it—an interest strong enough to frequently overcome all opposing selfish interests. Most of us do wish happiness for other people, even total strangers (not including gross cheaters), because we have feelings such as empathy. We *wish* this happiness and occasionally care enough to make modest sacrifices to benefit strangers; but no one is called immoral for failing to do so, for that would mean branding almost everybody immoral.

(2) Similarly, moral theories that require us to act out of love for all human beings (for instance, the situation ethics of Joseph Fletcher) have very little in common with the view of human nature given by sociobiologists or any other social scientists. As Dawkins says, "Much as we might wish to believe otherwise, universal love and the welfare of the species as a whole are concepts which simply do not make evolutionary sense."[7]

(3) Ethical egoism also clearly is not consistent with any scientific view of human nature. However, the situation is complicated by the fact that different theories can be construed as egoistic. There is the theory that we should always act so as to satisfy our strictly selfish immediate desires and motives, and never do altruistic acts. This clearly is not a rational theory because it fails to take account of selfish or prudential reasons for withholding immediate satisfaction and even acting altruistically. It would rule out, for example, giving a business acquaintance an expensive present in expectation of receiving a great deal more in return later. Clearly, an egoism permitting or even requiring such prudential altruism is more sensible than one that does not.

But this more sensible version is not sensible enough, because almost all of us have a great many altruistic sentiments that are slighted by this version of egoism. For example, we desire to benefit our own children by providing funds for their education without expecting any benefits for ourselves (not to be confused with a selfish desire to see them educated so that they can better care for us when we get old).

An aspiring egoist therefore must appeal to an even broader conception of human motivations, taking into account our altruistic motives, by saying that the right moral principle is just to do whatever we feel like doing except when overruled by prudence, which requires the sacrifice of relatively trivial impulses to increase satisfaction of more important ones over the long run.

This brings us to the crux of the matter, because among our motivating interests are desires for things like *fairness, justice,* and *retribution.* Should we count these as altruistic or selfish? If we take them to be altruistic, or at least not selfish, then again egoism is not a rational theory for those of us—just about all of us—who are motivated strongly to be fair, seek retribution, etc.

But if we take them to be selfish, then our "egoistic" system amounts to just the theory that morality concerns the satisfaction of our whole package of interests. When we add our moral desires for fairness and so on to our stock of selfish and altruistic desires, we end up with just about the sum total of our motivating interests. This means that we have implicitly changed the idea of selfishness so that a person becomes automatically selfish simply by acting to satisfy his or her own motivating interests—selfish, altruistic, or whatever. In other words, we end up with a theory that may well be correct (I think it is) but isn't really egoistic.

The discussion of these complexities should make it clear that there are two constraints on a strictly self-regarding theory and thus two reasons why a strictly self-regarding egoism fails to match our basic motivating interests. The first is the constraint of directly altruistic feelings, motivating us to benefit others even though no personal benefit is sought (although successful altruism may yeild personal benefit). The second is the constraint of strictly moral sentiments, such as the desire for fairness and retribution, motivating us to such actions as keeping agreements even though we may have no altruistic feelings toward the other parties in the agreement.

A theory that permits or requires satisfaction of altruistic desires as well as selfish ones, but forbids satisfaction of strictly moral desires, does share in the spirit of egoism, whether the theory is egoistic or not. Specifically, it is egoistic in its view that it is rational to ignore any *moral* tugs on behavior, rational to forget about duty, fairness, and retribution when deciding what to do. One force moving people to accept egoism is the feeling that morality itself, as opposed to any merely altruistic desires or motives, is a sham and delusion, one reason why some forms of egoism can be characterized as simply the denial that there is any such thing as binding moral obligation.

Well, *is* morality a sham and delusion? Or, translated into the terms of rational decision theory, is it ever rational to act out of a sense of duty or fairness, even when doing so satisfies no other desire to benefit either ourselves or anyone else? *That* is the key moral question for those of us who view the whole issue from the point of view of rational decision-making. And the answer depends on whether we have strong desires for our interests in things such as duty and fairness. While interests vary considerably from person to person, most of us do have a rather strong interest in these things. This can easily be proved by watching our own deliberative processes in action, and attending to the regret, shame, and guilt we feel when we fail to take fairness or justice into account. But our ideas on these matters tend to be confused. (One reason why it is hard to sort out our thoughts is that philosophers, theologians, and all sorts of authority figures bombard us with contradictory and often self-serving ideas on the subject.)

A good moral theory should help us cut through the confusion and characterize morality so that we recognize the tug of its chief features, and notice their conformity with stongly held desires and interests that the theory itself helps put into sharp focus. This, it seems to me, is what a good contractual theory of moral obligation can do for us.

IV. FAIRNESS, RETRIBUTION, AND CONTRACT ETHICS

The idea that human beings are necessarily cooperating competitors who are at best grudging reciprocators suggests that the chief survival function of moral sentiments—such as our desires to be fair, to do our duty, and to punish wrongdoers—is just to balance our strong selfish urges,[8] assuring sufficient reciprocity to obtain the benefits of cooperative ventures. This in turn suggests and is consistent with a contract theory of moral obligation, since contracts are just agreements to cooperate between competing parties. But the sociobiological theories appealed to are themselves much too simple to provide more than an approximation of the basics of human nature, and as yet are only modestly supported by evidence. Nevertheless, these theories do have predictive and explanatory power: We can test them by seeing whether at least some kinds of human behavior and motivation encountered in everyday life are consistent with (and thus perhaps explained by) the theory that human beings are essentially grudgers and that morality is the oil needed to grease the cooperative machinery required to make grudging a viable evolutionary strategy.

In fact, the more we look, the more we find that human behavior and motives do more or less conform to this view of the human predicament. Let us consider two kinds of everyday motivating interests, namely our interests in *fairness* and in *retribution,* which are key to any plausible theory of contract ethics.

(1) A serious threat to grudging as an evolutionary stable strategy is the profit in cheating on a reciprocal arrangement *if* one is smart enough not to get caught. In fact, there must have been (and must still be) a push towards genes programming those motivating interests and abilities that do lead to increases in the frequency and subtlety of cheating.[9] Implicit, however, in any reasonably subtle form of cheating, and in any good defense against the cheating of others, is the notion of a *fair* agreement or arrangement. Getting the edge in a reciprocal arrangement requires knowledge of what a fair arrangement would be like, because the cheater wants to get more than a fair share of the returns or to expend less than a fair share of the effort whenever possible. Reciprocators thus need the ability to determine at least in a rough way, first, when a reciprocal arrangement is likely to return more than it takes, and second, (since benefit often is relative[10]) how each participant stands to benefit compared to the relative amount of the work that person is likely to do. Roughly speaking, a fair arrangement is one in which the return to each party in the long run is likely to be commensurate with that party's share of the total work—so that those who do more get more.[11]

It is important to notice that the idea of fairness presupposes some sort of *competition*—otherwise there would be nothing to be fair about. For example, the question of fair wages to be paid to assembly line workers arises from competition between employer and employee over company profits, the fruits of their common labor. When cooperation is required to reach a goal, a fair arrangement is the one which divides the fruits of that combined labor according to each reciprocator's share in the effort, so that the mere arrangement itself, as opposed to the relative amount of productivity of each party, yields no competitive advantage to any party.[12]

Our sense of fairness thus seems to promote the needed cooperation between human competitors in essentially three ways: (1) It enables us to tell which arrangements are fair; (2) it increases the chances that we ourselves will be fair and carry out our part of fair reciprocal arrangements, even when we dislike the other parties; and (3) it helps us to spot the cheating of others, even when that cheating is quite subtle. Without a sense of fairness—which means not just an understanding of which arrangements are fair but also a feeling of outrage when treated unfairly and (to a lesser extent) a feeling of guilt when we fail others —cooperation between non-kin members of a group would be much more limited. For example, the universal human practice of sharing food, even with non-kin, one of the important practices developed by early members of the genus homo, could not have evolved very far, because there would have been no mechanism assuring genetic advantage in such a practice to any party.

(2) The other vital feature of any serious cooperative venture among human competitors is that of retribution. But to understand the importance of retribution for a contract theory, we must understand the difference between it and two related concepts, namely revenge and restitution. While these terms are quite ambiguous, the senses intended here are these. *Revenge* is the striking back at those who harm us, *because* they have harmed us, whether or not they were justified in doing so. (Revenge clearly is not an idea of any great value for moral theory.) *Restitution* is the harming of wrongdoers, or the benefiting of those harmed by the wrongdoing, so as to "restore the balance" of fair competition destroyed by the original wrongdoing.

Requiring a runner who jumps the gun in a race to come back to the starting line constitutes restitution in this sense, because that restores fair competition between the runners. Restitution restores fairness to a competition but does not inflict a penalty on those who were unfair. It is justified in general when there is no truly guilty party (in the sense that no one had a guilty intent) or when guilt cannot be assessed. (In running competitions, repeated gun-jumping is taken as evidence of intent, and brings retribution in the form of ejection from the competition—a harm greater than any possible gain from intentionally starting too soon.)

Retribution is the infliction of a harm greater than that caused by a breach of agreement, not to restore the balance but rather to punish the offender. This means making the offender's chances in competition

with others less than they were before the agreement was violated.

While the details of the evolution of our strong sense of retribution have not been worked out, its general evolutionary function seems clear, namely to assure that the cost of cheating is high. It functions to deter moral lawbreakers, just as legal sanctions or penalties function to deter legal lawbreakers. If there were no sense of outrage at cheaters, then those moral lawbreakers would have a field day, just as the elimination of penalties for legal lawbreaking would make crime a much better paying proposition.[13]

In any event, let us now look at the difference between a self-interested enlightened theory of fair reciprocity and a genuinely egoistic theory. The desire to cheat on one's selfish long-run interests is tempered by motives of prudence (for example, the prudence that keeps an overweight person on a diet). The desire to cheat on one's kin-altruistic interests is blocked by feelings of affection and empathy. But the desire to cheat on one's R-altruistic interests (in fairness) often is not impeded by any altruistic feelings. Consider for instance the case of a person who no longer cares for, even hates, his or her spouse, or the case of a businessman who never did care for his partner. These are the key cases for morality, the cases where duty and inclination clash, where a person must resist the temptation to cheat. The theory of fair reciprocity requires us to keep fair reciprocal arrangements even when cheating would be more profitable and is not tempered by feelings of affection or friendship. Egoism, however, if it is to be a genuine alternative to other theories, must be construed so that it allows or perhaps even requires cheating in such cases.

This brings us to the point that being moral, in the sense of keeping fair bargains, is not in everyone's rational interest, precisely because some individuals lack the usual regard for fairness and its attendant feelings of guilt when one is unfair. When cheating can be gotten away with, those who do not care to be fair to others have no *reason* to keep agreements with anyone but close friends or kin. These people are rationally justified in moving in the direction of egoism. But the rest of us, for whom, to put it mildly, cheating takes the luster off of accomplishment, require a different sort of moral theory, of the type, it seems to me, described here.

Finally, it should be clear that certain *social* contract theories are a special case of the general contract theory described in the previous paragraphs. We can construe social rules and conventions as multiple agreements between the various members of a society, and think of a just society as one in which the social arrangements necessary to gain the benefits of cooperation do not favor the chances of any particular members of society in their competition with other members.

POSTSCRIPT ON GENETICALLY DETERMINED BEHAVIOR

The sociobiological theories, on which the preceding discussion was based, rest themselves on the idea that human behavior, like all animal behavior, is genetically determined. Libertarians, who reject every sort of determinism on philosophical grounds, obviously cannot accept such an idea. But many determinists reject it also, in particular those who believe human beings are unlike other animals in that human behavior is determined chiefly by culture, that is, by environmental factors. But their rejection of genetic explanations of human behavior, it seems to me, confuses the issue at hand with another issue, illustrated by the often acrimonious debate over the causes of American racial differences in I.Q. test scores. (Some argue that these differences are environmental and can be eliminated by changing environment, others that they are genetic and thus cannot be so eliminated.) To see more clearly what is at issue in that controversy, let's consider a case that has not aroused such intense passions: the question whether height, which like intelligence differs from person to person, is genetically determined or due to environmental factors.

There are three possible positions we can take about height differences: (1) A person's height is determined completely by genetic factors; (2) height is determined completely by environmental factors; or (3) genes lay down a range of variability within which cultural factors determine exact height. Experience shows that with respect to height, the third position is correct, but that (except in extreme cases such as those resulting in adult cripples) the range of variability possible in a single person is very small compared to the range of height variability that occurs from person to person resulting from genetic differences. In other words, we can indeed influence height by manipulation of the environment, but only to a small extent compared to the variability determined by genes. That is why, informally, differences in height are usually said to be genetic: Beyond a relatively small range, *they cannot be manipulated by changing the environment*. We cannot make pygmies into six-footers by feeding them Danish pastry nor Danes into pygmies by a reverse food switch.

However, behavior traits such as, for example, the response to motion pictures of couples engaging in sexual intercourse, are so easily influenced by changes in environment that they are informally said to be environmental or cultural in origin. All this means is that such traits can be manipulated over a reasonably wide range by changing the environment.

While sociobiological theory has as yet nothing to say about the cause of racial I.Q. test score differences, experimental results seem to indicate that such differences are largely cultural. But this does not mean that intelligent human behavior is not genetically programmed. It just means that the range of variability laid down by the genes is greater for the trait of intelligence than for a trait such as height; large differences in environment do seem to lead to modestly large differences in I.Q. test scores.

Listen to two psychologists on the issue of heredity versus environment:

Let us get two facts straight. First, of course the environment has a strong effect on a person's development. We do not need sophisticated studies to prove that a child raised in a neglectful or abusive family will generally not turn out as well as a child raised in a warm, supportive one. . . . Changes in environment cause changes in behavior, a process called malleability. Improvements in the former improve the latter. Second, it also is true that human beings are not infinitely adjustable. Malleability does not mean that given the same environment all individuals will end up alike. Common sense and a sheaf of studies indicate that people bring idiosyncratic responses to the same situations. Even in a perfect world, some people will be unhappier than others. The reason for these individual differences has much to do with genetic makeup.

Too many people believe the myth that if a characteristic is genetic, it cannot be changed. This is nonsense. Human behavior is much more complicated than a particular physical trait, such as blue eyes. Although genes may dictate color of hair or eyes, they do not specify that Sally will have an I.Q. of 139 rather than 125 or 150. Genes do not fix behavior; rather they establish a range of possible reactions to the range of possible experiences that the environment provides.

How people behave or what their measured I.Q.'s turn out to be depends on the quality of their environments and on the genetic endowments they have at birth. Some elements of the environment, such as having nurturing parents, are better for everyone, but some individuals respond better to one environment and others respond better to another. What occurs is an interaction between genes and environment, . . .[14]

Listen also to Richard Dawkins on the concept of genetically controlled behavior:

If I speak . . . of a hypothetical gene "for saving a companion from drowning," and you find such a concept incredible, . . . recall that we are not talking about the gene as the sole antecedent cause of all the complex muscular contractions, sensory integrations, and even conscious decisions, which are involved in saving somebody from drowning. We are saying nothing about the question whether learning, experience, or environmental influences enter into the development of behavior. All you have to concede is that it is possible for a single gene, other things being equal and lots of other factors being present, to make a body more likely to save somebody from drowning than its allele [an alternative gene at the same spot on a chromosome] would.[15]

Anyone who denies the possibility claimed by Dawkins will have to deny that things such as musical and athletic abilities are determined in part by heredity. Does anyone seriously believe that we can shape randomly chosen individuals into musical geniuses or great athletes merely by giving them just the right environment? (No one denies that improvements in environment can improve a person's skill in these areas.) Way back in the 1930s, when environmentalists were rejecting his theories out of hand, Abraham Meyerson once remarked in exasperation, "Environmentalists seem to believe that if cats gave birth to kittens in a stove, the offspring would be biscuits." That's a bit caustic, of course, but it does seem that the concept of genetically determined behavior is an idea whose time has come.

NOTES

1. Sociobiologists are trying to determine what human beings are like by applying the basic ideas of the theories of natural selection, genetics, and biology, given that we are a certain kind of social animal and have evolved over a period of about two billion years.

2. The phrase comes from Richard Dawkins' excellent book, *The Selfish Gene* (New York and Oxford: Oxford University Press, 1976). See also the September, 1978, issue of *Scientific American*, devoted entirely to the theory of evolution. It is important to understand that the theory of natural selection does *not* ever explain behavior as arising "for the good of the species," any more than for the good of primates, mammals, chordates, or animals in general.

3. For an interesting theory of the emotions, linking into a

chain the idea of a *stimulus* triggering a cognition, leading to a *feeling*, resulting in *behavior* serving some evolutionary *function* (for example, perceiving a threat by an enemy, construing it as danger, feeling fear, and running away to protect life and limb), see Robert Plutchik, *Emotion: A Psychoevolutionary Synthesis* (New York: Harper & Row, 1980), or his article "A Language for the Emotions," in *Psychology Today*, February 1980.

4. The term seems to have been coined by R. L. Trivers, who worked out the first comprehensive theory of reciprocal altruism.

5. The idea of an evolutionarily stable strategy was developed by W. D. Hamilton, R. H. MacArthur, and John Maynard Smith. See Dawkins' *The Selfish Gene* for more on this crucial idea.

6. John Rawls, *A Theory of Justice* (Cambridge, Mass.: Harvard University Press, 1971, p. 22). Rawls goes on to present some serious objections to utilitarianism.

7. *The Selfish Gene*, pp. 2–3.

8. And also some of our altruistic ones; for instance, the urge of the person who engages in backstabbing at work in order to provide better for family and friends.

9. Some theorists believe that the advantages of an increased ability to cheat subtly and to detect subtle cheating constituted the major reason for the amazingly rapid increase in intelligence that occurred in the last million years or so of human evolution (in particular, the increased mathematical skill in counting and in comparing the sizes of two bunches of things). One reason for this belief is that the most important force shaping human evolution during that time was (as it still is) competition among human beings for the necessities of life—not competition with other animals for resources nor defense against wild predators, although defense against bacteria and viruses surely played an important role.

10. It does someone little good, for example, to gain an improvement in housing if competitors for mates gain an even greater improvement.

11. The profitability of subtle cheating helps explain why puzzling features of human nature such as self-deception have evolved—puzzling since straight thinking seems to be so valuable. One advantage of deceiving ourselves (not being consciously aware of unconscious motivating forces or not attending to conscious motives) is that we are better able to deceive others when self-deceived—remember that others are programmed to detect the difference between honest and dishonest talking. (There are, of course, several other functions of self-deception—for instance, to allow us to ignore general rules of conduct, such as the one to be fair with others, when following the rules would result in too great a loss.)

12. Similar remarks apply to "winner-take-all" competitions. Thus, the rules of sporting events are fair when they do not favor the winning chances of any competitor, as they would, say, if red-haired runners in a hundred-meter dash were required to start five meters back. Horse races in which horses are assigned different weights to carry may be fair to wagerers, but not to the horses if they really are trying to win.

13. But the fact that punishment has deterrence value does not constitute a *justification* for the practice of punishment. According to a rational decision theory, punishment is justified because it satisfies strong motivating interests—in inflicting harm on wrongdoers (often resulting in our own satisfaction, but that too cannot be the primary motive for punishing, even though some who punish are gratified to experience satisfaction).

14. Sandra Scarr and Richard A. Weinberg, "Attitudes, Interests, and I.Q.," *Human Nature*, April 1978. (Scarr and Weinberg also present solid evidence supporting the theory that statistical differences in I.Q. between whites and blacks in the United States are chiefly cultural in origin.)

15. *The Selfish Gene*, p. 66.

JOHN STUART MILL

Utilitarianism*

John Stuart Mill (1806–1873) was one of the leading British moral philosophers of the nineteenth century. He also wrote important works on logic, economics, education, and feminism, and served for a time as a Member of Parliament.

1. GENERAL REMARKS

There are a few circumstances, among those which make up the present condition of human knowledge, more unlike what might have been expected, or more significant of the backward state in which speculation on the most important subjects still lingers, than the little progress which has been made in the decision of the controversy respecting the criterion of right and wrong. From the dawn of philosophy, the question concerning the *summum bonum* or, what is the same thing, concerning the foundation of morality, has been accounted the main problem in speculative thought, has occupied the most gifted intellects and divided them into sects and schools, carrying on a vigorous warfare against one another. And, after more than two thousand years, the same discussions continue, philosophers are still ranged under the same contending banners, and neither thinkers nor mankind at large seem nearer to being unanimous on the subject than when the youth Socrates listened to the old Protagoras, and asserted (if Plato's dialogue be grounded on a real conversation) the theory of utilitarianism against the popular morality of the so-called Sophist.

*From J. S. Mill, *Utilitarianism,* Chaps. 1–4. First published in 1863.

It is true that similar confusion and uncertainty, and in some cases similar discordance, exist respecting the first principles of all the sciences, not excepting that which is deemed the most certain of them—mathematics—without much impairing, generally indeed without impairing at all, the trustworthiness of the conclusions of those sciences. An apparent anomaly, the explanation of which is that the detailed doctrines of a science are not usually deduced from, nor depend for their evidence upon, what are called its first principles. Were it not so, there would be no science more precarious, or whose conclusions were more insufficiently made out, than algebra, which derives none of its certainty from what are commonly taught to learners as its elements, since these, as laid down by some of its most eminent teachers, are as full of fictions as English law, and of mysteries as theology. The truths which are ultimately accepted as the first principles of a science are really the last results of metaphysical analysis practiced on the elementary notions with which the science is conversant, and their relation to the science is not that of foundations to an edifice, but of roots to a tree, which may perform their office equally well though they be never dug down to and exposed to light. But though, in science the particular truths precede the general theory, the contrary might be expected to be the case with a practical art, such as morals or legislation. All action is for the sake of some end; and rules of action, it seems natural to suppose, must take their whole character and color from the end to which they are subservient. When we engage in a pursuit, a clear and precise conception of what we are pursuing would seem to be the first thing we need, instead of the last we are to look forward to. A test of right and wrong must be the means, one would think, of ascertaining what is right or wrong, and not a consequence of having already ascertained it.

The difficulty is not avoided by having recourse to the popular theory of a natural faculty, a sense or instinct, informing us of right and wrong. For, besides that the existence of such a moral instinct is itself one of the matters in dispute, those believers in it who have any pretensions to philosophy have been obliged to abandon the idea that it discerns what is right or wrong in the particular case in hand, as our other senses discern the sight or sound actually present. Our moral faculty, according to all those of its interpreters who are entitled to the name of thinkers, supplies us only with the general principles of moral judgments; it is a branch of our reason, not of our sensitive faculty, and must be looked to for the abstract doctrines of morality, not for perception of it in the concrete. The intuitive, no less than what may be termed the inductive, school of ethics, insists on the necessity of general laws. They both agree that the morality of an individual action is not a question of direct perception, but of the application of a law to an individual case. They recognize also, to a great extent, the same moral laws, but differ as to their evidence, and the source from which they derive their authority. According to the one opinion, the principles of morals are evident *a priori,* requiring nothing to command assent, except that the meaning of the terms be understood. According to the other doctrine, right and wrong, as well as truth and falsehood, are questions of observation and experience. But both hold equally that morality must be deduced from principles, and the intuitive school affirm, as strongly as the inductive, that there is a science of morals. Yet they seldom attempt to make out a list of the *a priori* principles which are to serve as the premises of the science; still more rarely do they make any effort to reduce those various principles to one first principle, or common ground of obligation. They either assume the ordinary precepts of morals as of *a priori* authority, or they lay down as the common groundwork of those maxims some generality much less obviously authoritative than the maxims themselves, and which has never succeeded in gaining popular acceptance. Yet, to support their pretensions, there ought either to be some one fundamental principle or law at the root of all morality, or, if there be several, there should be a determinate order of precedence among them, and the one principle, or the rule for deciding between the various principles when they conflict, ought to be self-evident.

To inquire how far the bad effects of this deficiency have been mitigated in practice, or to what extent the moral beliefs of mankind have been vitiated or made uncertain by the absence of any distinct recognition of an ultimate standard, would imply a complete survey and criticism of past and present ethical doctrine. It would, however, be easy to show that whatever steadiness or consistency these moral beliefs have attained has been mainly due to the tacit influence of a standard not recognized. Although the nonexistence of an acknowledged first principle has made ethics not so much a guide as a consecration of men's actual sentiments, still, as men's sentiments, both of favor and of aversion, are greatly influenced by what they suppose to be the effects of things upon their happiness, the principle of utility, or, as Bentham latterly called it, the greatest-happiness principle, has had a large share in forming the moral doctrines even of those who most scornfully reject its authority. Nor is there any school of thought which refuses to admit that the influence of actions on happiness is a most material and even predominant consideration in many of the details of morals, however unwilling to acknowledge it as the fundamental principle of morality and the source of moral obligation. I might go much further, and say that, to all those *a priori* moralists who deem it necessary to argue at all, utilitarian arguments are indispensable. It is not my present purpose to criticize these thinkers, but I cannot help referring, for illustration, to a systematic treatise by one of the most illustrious of them—the *Metaphysics of Ethics,* by Kant. This remarkable man, whose system of thought will long remain one of the landmarks in the history of philosophical speculation, does, in the treatise in question, lay down a universal first principle as the origin and ground of moral obligation. It is this: "So act, that the rule on which thou actest would admit of being adopted as a law by all rational beings." But when he begins to deduce from this precept any of the actual duties of morality, he fails, almost grotesquely, to show that there would be any contradiction, any logical (not to say physical) impossibility, in the adoption by all rational beings of the most outrageously immoral rules of conduct. All he shows is that the *consequences* of their universal adoption would be such as no one would choose to incur.

On the present occasion, I shall, without further discussion of the other theories, attempt to contribute something towards the understanding and appreciation of the Utilitarian or Happiness theory and towards such proof as it is susceptible of. It is evident that this cannot be proof in the ordinary and popular meaning of the term. Questions of ultimate ends are not amenable to direct proof. Whatever can be proved to be good, must be so by being shown to be a means to something admitted to be good without proof. The medical art is proved to be good by its conducing to health, but how is it possible to prove that health is good? The art of music is good, for the reason, among others, that it produces pleasure, but what proof is it possible to give that pleasure is good? If, then, it is asserted that there is a comprehensive formula, including all things which are in themselves good, and that whatever else is good is not so as an end, but as a mean, the formula may be accepted or rejected, but is not a subject of what is commonly understood by proof. We are not, however, to infer that its acceptance or rejection must depend on blind impulse or arbitrary choice. There is a larger meaning of the word "proof," in which this question is as amenable to it as any other of the disputed questions of philosophy. The subject is within the cognizance of the rational faculty, and neither does that faculty deal with it solely in the way of intuition. Considerations may be presented capable of determining the intellect either to give or withhold its assent to the doctrine, and this is equivalent to proof.

We shall examine presently of what nature are these considerations, in what manner they apply to the case, and what rational grounds, therefore, can be given for accepting or rejecting the utilitarian formula. But it is a preliminary condition of rational acceptance or rejection that the formula should be correctly understood. I believe that the very imperfect notion ordinarily formed of its meaning is the chief obstacle which impedes its reception, and that, could it be cleared even from only the grosser misconceptions, the question would be greatly simplified, and a large proportion of its difficulties removed. Before, therefore, I attempt to enter into the philosophical grounds which can be given for assenting to the utilitarian standard, I shall offer some illustrations of the doctrine itself, with the view of showing more clearly what it is, distinguishing it from what it is not, and disposing of such of the practical objections to it as either originate in, or are closely connected with, mistaken interpretations of its meaning. Having thus pre-pared the ground, I shall afterwards endeavor to throw such light as I can upon the question, considered as one of philosophical theory.

2. WHAT UTILITARIANISM IS

A passing remark is all that needs be given to the ignorant blunder of supposing that those who stand up for utility, as the test of right and wrong, use the term in that restricted and merely colloquial sense in which utility is opposed to pleasure. An apology is due to the philosophical opponents of utilitarianism for even the momentary appearance of confounding them with any one capable of so absurd a misconception, which is the more extraordinary, inasmuch as the contrary accusation, of referring every thing to pleasure, and that, too, in its grossest form, is another of the common charges against utilitarianism, and, as has been pointedly remarked by an able writer, the same sort of persons, and often the very same persons, denounce the theory "as impracticably dry when the word 'utility' precedes the word 'pleasure,' and as too practicably voluptuous when the word 'pleasure' precedes the word 'utility.' " Those who know any thing about the matter are aware that every writer from Epicurus to Bentham who maintained the theory of utility meant by it, not something to be contradistinguished from pleasure, but pleasure itself, together with exemption from pain, and, instead of opposing the useful to the agreeable or the ornamental, have always declared that the useful means these, among other things. Yet the common herd, including the herd of writers, not only in newspapers and periodicals, but in books of weight and pretension, are perpetually falling into this shallow mistake. Having caught up the word "utilitarian," while knowing nothing whatever about it but its sound, they habitually express by it the rejection or the neglect of pleasure in some of its forms, of beauty, of ornament, or of amusement. Nor is the term thus ignorantly misapplied solely in disparagement, but occasionally in compliment, as though it implied superiority to frivolity and the mere pleasures of the moment. And this perverted use is the only one in which the word is popularly known, and the one from which the new generation are acquiring their sole notion of its meaning. Those who introduced the word, but who had for many years discontinued it as a distinctive appellation, may well feel themselves called upon to resume it, if by doing so they can hope to contribute any thing towards rescuing it from this utter degradation.[1]

The creed which accepts as the foundation of morals Utility, or the Greatest-happiness Principle, holds that actions are right in proportion as they tend to promote happiness, wrong as they tend to produce the reverse of happiness. By happiness is intended pleasure and the absence of pain, by unhappiness, pain and the privation of pleasure. To give a clear view of the moral standard set up by the theory, much more requires to be said, in particular, what things it includes in the ideas of pain and pleasure, and to what extent this is left an open question. But these supplementary explanations do not affect the theory of life on which this theory of morality is grounded—namely, that pleasure and freedom from pain are the only things desirable as ends, and that all desirable things (which are as numerous in the utilitarian as in any other scheme) are desirable either for the pleasure inherent in themselves, or as means to the promotion of pleasure and the prevention of pain.

Now, such a theory of life excites in many minds, and among them in some of the most estimable in feeling and purpose, inveterate dislike. To suppose that life has (as they express it) no higher end than pleasure—no better and nobler object of desire and pursuit—they designate as utterly mean and groveling, as a doctrine worthy only of swine, to whom the followers of Epicurus were, at a very early period, contemptuously likened; and modern holders of the doctrine are occasionally made the subject of equally polite comparisons by its German, French, and English assailants.

When thus attacked, the Epicureans have always answered, that it is not they, but their accusers, who represent human nature in a degrading light, since the accusation supposes human beings to be capable of no pleasures except those of which swine are capable. If this supposition were true, the charge could not be gainsaid but would then be no longer an imputation; for, if the sources of pleasure were precisely the same to human beings and to swine, the rule of life which is good enough for the one would be good enough for the other. The comparison of the Epicurean life to that of beasts is felt as degrading, precisely because a beast's pleasures do not satisfy a human being's conceptions of happiness. Human beings have faculties more elevated than the animal appetites, and, when once made conscious of them, do not regard any thing

as happiness which does not include their gratification. I do not, indeed, consider the Epicureans to have been by any means faultless in drawing out their scheme of consequences from the utilitarian principle. To do this in any sufficient manner, many Stoic as well as Christian elements require to be included. But there is no known Epicurean theory of life which does not assign to the pleasures of the intellect, of the feelings and imagination, and of the moral sentiments, a much higher value as pleasures than to those of mere sensation. It must be admitted, however, that utilitarian writers in general have placed the superiority of mental over bodily pleasures chiefly in the greater permanency, safety, uncostliness, etc., of the former—that is, in their circumstantial advantages rather than in their intrinsic nature. And, on all these points, utilitarians have fully proved their case, but they might have taken the other, and, as it may be called, higher ground, with entire consistency. It is quite compatible with the principle of utility to recognize the fact that some *kinds* of pleasure are more desirable and more valuable than others. It would be absurd that while, in estimating all other things, quality is considered as well as quantity, the estimation of pleasures should be supposed to depend on quantity alone.

If I am asked what I mean by difference of quality in pleasures, or what makes one pleasure more valuable than another, merely as a pleasure, except its being greater in amount, there is but one possible answer. Of two pleasures, if there be one to which all or almost all who have experience of both give a decided preference, irrespective of any feeling of moral obligation to prefer it, that is the more desirable pleasure. If one of the two is, by those who are competently acquainted with both, placed so far above the other that they prefer it, even though knowing it to be attended with a greater amount of discontent, and would not resign it for any quantity of the other pleasure which their nature is capable of, we are justified in ascribing to the preferred enjoyment a superiority in quality so far outweighing quantity, as to render it, in comparison, of small account.

Now, it is an unquestionable fact, that those who are equally acquainted with and equally capable of appreciating and enjoying both do give a most marked preference to the manner of existence which employs their higher faculties. Few human creatures would consent to be changed into any of the lower animals for a promise of the fullest allowance of a beast's pleasures; no intelligent human being would consent to

be a fool, no instructed person would be an ig-
noramus, no person of feeling and conscience would
be selfish and base, even though they should be persuaded that the fool, the dunce, or the rascal is better
satisfied with his lot than they are with theirs. They
would not resign what they possess more than he for
the most complete satisfaction of all the desires which
they have in common with him. If they ever fancy
they would, it is only in cases of unhappiness so extreme that, to escape from it, they would exchange
their lot for almost any other, however undesirable in
their own eyes. A being of higher faculties requires
more to make him happy, is capable probably of more
acute suffering, and certainly accessible to it at more
points, than one of an inferior type, but, in spite of
these liabilities, he can never really wish to sink into
what he feels to be a lower grade of existence. We
may give what explanation we please of this unwillingness: we may attribute it to pride, a name which is
given indiscriminately to some of the most and to
some of the least estimable feelings of which mankind
are capable; we may refer it to the love of liberty and
personal independence—an appeal to which was with
the Stoics one of the most effective means for the inculcation of it; to the love of power, or to the love of
excitement, both of which do really enter into and
contribute to it; but its most appropriate appellation is
a sense of dignity, which all human beings possess in
one form or other, and in some, though by no means
in exact, proportion to their higher faculties, and
which is so essential a part of the happiness of those in
whom it is strong, that nothing which conflicts with it
could be, otherwise than momentarily, an object of
desire to them. Whoever supposes that this preference
takes place at a sacrifice of happiness, that the
superior being, in any thing like equal circumstances,
is not happier than the inferior—confounds the two
very different ideas of happiness and content. It is indisputable that the being whose capacities of enjoyment are low has the greatest chance of having them
fully satisfied, and a highly endowed being will always feel that any happiness which he can look for, as
the world is constituted, is imperfect. But he can learn
to bear its imperfections, if they are at all bearable,
and they will not make him envy the being who is
indeed unconscious of the imperfections, but only because he feels not at all the good which those imperfections qualify. It is better to be a human being dissatisfied than a pig satisfied, better to be Socrates
dissatisfied than a fool satisfied. And if the fool or
the pig are of a different opinion, it is because they

only know their own side of the question. The other
party to the comparison knows both sides.

It may be objected that many who are capable of
the higher pleasures occasionally, under the influence
of temptation, postpone them to the lower. But this is
quite compatible with a full appreciation of the intrinsic superiority of the higher. Men often, from infirmity of character, make their election for the nearer
good, though they know it to be the less valuable, and
this no less when the choice is between two bodily
pleasures than when it is between bodily and mental.
They pursue sensual indulgences to the injury of
health, though perfectly aware that health is the
greater good. It may be further objected, that many
who begin with youthful enthusiasm for everything
noble, as they advance in years sink into indolence
and selfishness. But I do not believe that those who
undergo this very common change voluntarily choose
the lower description of pleasures in preference to the
higher. I believe that, before they devote themselves
exclusively to the one, they have already become incapable of the other. Capacity for the nobler feelings
is in most natures a very tender plant, easily killed,
not only by hostile influences but by mere want of
sustenance, and, in the majority of young persons, it
speedily dies away if the occupations to which their
position in life has devoted them, and the society into
which it has thrown them, are not favorable to keeping that higher capacity in exercise. Men lose their
high aspirations as they lose their intellectual tastes,
because they have not time or opportunity for indulging them, and they addict themselves to inferior pleasures, not because they deliberately prefer them, but
because they are either the only ones to which they
have access or the only ones which they are any
longer capable of enjoying. It may be questioned
whether any one who has remained equally susceptible to both classes of pleasures ever knowingly and
calmly preferred the lower, though many in all ages
have broken down in an ineffectual attempt to combine both.

From this verdict of the only competent judges, I
apprehend there can be no appeal. On a question
which is the best worth having of two pleasures, or
which of two modes of existence is the most grateful
to the feelings, apart from its moral attributes and
from its consequences, the judgment of those who are
qualified by knowledge of both, or, if they differ, that
of the majority among them, must be admitted as fi-

nal. And there needs be the less hesitation to accept this judgment respecting the quality of pleasures, since there is no other tribunal to be referred to even on the question of quantity. What means are there of determining which is the acutest of two pains, or the intensest of two pleasurable sensations, except the general suffrage of those who are familiar with both? Neither pains nor pleasures are homogeneous, and pain is always heterogeneous with pleasure. What is there to decide whether a particular pleasure is worth purchasing at the cost of a particular pain, except the feelings and judgment of the experienced? When, therefore, those feelings and judgment declare the pleasures derived from the higher faculties to be preferable *in kind,* apart from the question of intensity, to those of which the animal nature disjoined from the higher faculties is susceptible, they are entitled on this subject to the same regard.

I have dwelt on this point, as being a necessary part of a perfectly just conception of Utility or Happiness, considered as the directive rule of human conduct. But it is by no means an indispensable condition to the acceptance of the utilitarian standard, for that standard is not the agent's own greatest happiness, but the greatest amount of happiness altogether; and if it may possibly be doubted whether a noble character is always the happier for its nobleness, there can be no doubt that it makes other people happier, and that the world in general is immensely a gainer by it. Utilitarianism, therefore, could only attain its end by the general cultivation of nobleness of character, even if each individual were only benefited by the nobleness of others, and his own, so far as happiness is concerned, were a sheer deduction from the benefit. But the bare enunciation of such an absurdity as this last renders refutation superfluous.

According to the Greatest-happiness Principle, as above explained, the ultimate end with reference to and for the sake of which all other things are desirable (whether we are considering our own good or that of other people) is an existence exempt as far as possible from pain, and as rich as possible in enjoyments, both in point of quantity and quality; the test of quality, and the rule for measuring it against quantity, being the preference felt by those who in their opportunities of experience, to which must be added their habits of self-consciousness and self-observation, are best furnished with the means of comparison. This being, ac-

cording to the utilitarian opinion, the end of human action is necessarily also the standard of morality; which may accordingly be defined, the rules and precepts for human conduct by the observance of which an existence such as has been described might be, to the greatest extent possible, secured to all mankind, and not to them only but, so far as the nature of things admits, to the whole sentient creation.

Against this doctrine, however, arises another class of objectors who say that happiness, in any form, cannot be the rational purpose of human life and action, because, in the first place, it is unattainable; and they contemptuously ask, What right hast thou to be happy? a question which Mr. Carlyle clinches by the addition, What right, a short time ago, hadst thou even *to be?* Next they say that men can do *without* happiness, that all noble human beings have felt this, and could not have become noble but by learning the lesson of *Entsagen* or renunciation, which lesson, thoroughly learned and submitted to, they affirm to be the beginning and necessary condition of all virtue.

The first of these objections would go to the root of the matter, were it well founded; for, if no happiness is to be had at all by human beings, the attainment of it cannot be the end of morality, or of any rational conduct. Though, even in that case, something might still be said for the utilitarian theory, since utility includes not solely the pursuit of happiness, but the prevention or mitigation of unhappiness; and, if the former aim be chimerical, there will be all the greater scope and more imperative need for the latter, so long at least as mankind think fit to live, and do not take refuge in the simultaneous act of suicide recommended under certain conditions by Novalis. When, however, it is thus positively asserted to be impossible that human life should be happy, the assertion, if not something like a verbal quibble, is at least an exaggeration. If by happiness be meant a continuity of highly pleasurable excitement, it is evident enough that this is impossible. A state of exalted pleasure lasts only moments, or in some cases, and with some intermissions, hours or days, and is the occasional brilliant flash of enjoyment, not its permanent and steady flame. Of this the philosophers who have taught that happiness is the end of life were as fully aware as those who taunt them. The happiness which they meant was not a life of rapture, but moments of such, in an existence made up of few and transitory pains, many and various pleasures, with a decided predominance of the active over the passive, and having, as the foundation of the whole, not to expect more from life than it is capable of bestowing. A life thus composed, to those who have been fortunate enough to obtain it, has always appeared worthy of the name of "happiness." And such an existence is even now the lot of many, during some considerable portion of their lives. The present wretched education and wretched social arrangements are the only real hindrance to its being attainable by almost all.

The objectors, perhaps, may doubt whether human beings, if taught to consider happiness as the end of life, would be satisfied with such a moderate share of it. But great numbers of mankind have been satisfied with much less. The main constituents of a satisfied life appear to be two, either of which by itself is often found sufficient for the purpose—tranquillity and excitement. With much tranquillity, many find that they can be content with very little pleasure; with much excitement, many can reconcile themselves to a considerable quantity of pain. There is assuredly no inherent impossibility in enabling even the mass of mankind to unite both, since the two are so far from being incompatible, that they are in natural alliance, the prolongation of either being a preparation for, and exciting a wish for, the other. It is only those in whom indolence amounts to a vice that do not desire excitement after an interval of repose; it is only those in whom the need of excitement is a disease, that feel the tranquillity which follows excitement dull and insipid, instead of pleasurable in direct proportion to the excitement which preceded it. When people who are tolerably fortunate in their outward lot do not find in life sufficient enjoyment to make it valuable to them, the cause generally is caring for nobody but themselves. To those who have neither public nor private affections, the excitements of life are much curtailed and, in any case, dwindle in value as the time approaches when all selfish interests must be terminated by death; while those who leave after them objects of personal affection, and especially those who have also cultivated a fellow feeling with the collective interests of mankind, retain as lively an interest in life on the eve of death as in the vigor of youth and health. Next to selfishness, the principal cause which makes life unsatisfactory is want of mental cultivation. A cultivated mind—I do not mean that of a philosopher, but any mind to which the fountains of knowledge have been opened, and which has been taught, in any tolerable degree, to exercise its faculties—finds sources of inexhaustible interest in all that surrounds it, in the objects of nature, the achievements of art, the imaginations of poetry, the incidents of history, the ways of mankind past and present, and their prospects in the future. It is possible, indeed, to become indifferent to all this, and that, too, without having exhausted a thousandth part of it, but only when one has had from the beginning no moral or human interest in these things, and has sought in them only the gratification of curiosity.

Now, there is absolutely no reason in the nature of things why an amount of mental culture sufficient to give an intelligent interest in these objects of contemplation should not be the inheritance of every one born in a civilized country. As little is there an inherent necessity that any human being should be a selfish egotist, devoid of every feeling or care but those which center in his own miserable individuality. Something far superior to this is sufficiently common even now to give ample earnest of what the human species may be made. Genuine private affections and a sincere interest in the public good are possible, though in unequal degrees, to every rightly brought up human being. In a world in which there is so much to interest, so much to enjoy, and so much also to correct and improve, every one who has this moderate amount of moral and intellectual requisites is capable of an existence which may be called enviable; and unless such a person, through bad laws or subjection to the will of others, is denied the liberty to use the sources of happiness within his reach, he will not fail to find this enviable existence, if he escape the positive evils of life, the great sources of physical and mental suffering—such as indigence, disease, and the unkindness, worthlessness, or premature loss, of objects of affection. The main stress of the problem lies, therefore, in the contest with these calamities, from which it is a rare good fortune entirely to escape, which, as things now are, cannot be obviated, and often cannot be in any material degree mitigated. Yet no one whose opinion deserves a moment's consideration can doubt that most of the great positive evils of the world are in themselves removable, and will, if human affairs continue to improve, be in the end reduced within narrow limits. Poverty, in any sense implying suffering, may be completely extinguished by the wisdom of society, combined with the good sense and providence of individuals. Even that most intractable of enemies, disease, may be indefinitely reduced in dimensions by good physical and moral education, and proper control of noxious influence, while the progress of science holds out a promise for the future of still more direct conquests over this detestable foe. And every advance in that direction relieves us from some, not only of the chances which cut short our own lives but, what concerns us still more, which deprive us of those in whom our happiness is wrapped up. As for vicissitudes of fortune and other disappointments connected with worldly circumstances, these are principally the effect either of gross imprudence, of ill-regulated desires, or of bad or imperfect social institutions. All the grand sources, in short, of human suffering are in a great degree, many of them almost entirely, conquerable by human care and effort; and though their removal is grievously slow, though a long succession of generations will perish in the breach before the conquest is completed, and this world becomes all that, if will and knowledge were not wanting, it might easily be made—yet every mind sufficiently intelligent and generous to bear a part, however small and unconspicuous, in the endeavor will draw a noble enjoyment from the contest itself, which he would not, for any bribe in the form of selfish indulgence, consent to be without.

And this leads to the true estimation of what is said by the objectors concerning the possibility and the obligation of learning to do without happiness. Unquestionably, it is possible to do without happiness; it is done involuntarily by nineteen-twentieths of mankind, even in those parts of our present world which are least deep in barbarism, and it often has to be done voluntarily by the hero or the martyr, for the sake of something which he prizes more than his individual happiness. But this something—what is it, unless the happiness of others, or some of the requisites of happiness? It is noble to be capable of resigning entirely one's own portion of happiness, or chances of it; but, after all, this self-sacrifice must be for some end; it is not its own end, and if we are told that its end is not happiness but virtue, which is better than happiness, I ask, Would the sacrifice be made if the hero or martyr did not believe that it would earn for others immunity from similar sacrifices? Would it be made if he thought that his renunciation of happiness for himself would produce no fruit for any of his fellow-creatures but to make their lot like his, and place them also in the condition of persons who have renounced happiness? All honor to those who can abnegate for themselves the personal enjoyment of life, when by such renunciation they contribute worthily to increase the amount of happiness in the world, but he who does it,

or professes to do it, for any other purpose is no more deserving of admiration than the ascetic mounted on his pillar. He may be an inspiriting proof of what men *can* do, but assuredly not an example of what they *should*.

Though it is only in a very imperfect state of the world's arrangements that any one can best serve the happiness of others by the absolute sacrifice of his own, yet, so long as the world is in that imperfect state, I fully acknowledge that the readiness to make such a sacrifice is the highest virtue which can be found in man. I will add that in this condition of the world, paradoxical as the assertion may be, the conscious ability to do without happiness gives the best prospect of realizing such happiness as is attainable. For nothing except that consciousness can raise a person above the chances of life, by making him feel that, let fate and fortune do their worst, they have not power to subdue him; which, once felt, frees him from excess of anxiety concerning the evils of life, and enables him, like many a Stoic in the worst times of the Roman Empire, to cultivate in tranquillity the sources of satisfaction accessible to him, without concerning himself about the uncertainty of their duration, any more than about their inevitable end.

Meanwhile, let utilitarians never cease to claim the morality of self-devotion as a possession which belongs by as good a right to them as either to the Stoic or to the Transcendentalist. The utilitarian morality does recognize in human beings the power of sacrificing their own greatest good for the good of others. It only refuses to admit that the sacrifice is itself a good. A sacrifice which does not increase, or tend to increase, the sum total of happiness, it considers as wasted. The only self-renunciation which it applauds is devotion to the happiness, or to some of the means of happiness, of others, either of mankind collectively, or of individuals within the limits imposed by the collective interests of mankind.

I must again repeat what the assailants of utilitarianism seldom have the justice to acknowledge, that the happiness which forms the utilitarian standard of what is right in conduct is not the agent's own happiness but that of all concerned. As between his own happiness and that of others, utilitarianism requires him to be as strictly impartial as a disinterested and benevolent spectator. In the golden rule of Jesus of Nazareth, we read the complete spirit of the ethics of utility. To do as you would be done by, and to love your neighbor as yourself, constitute the ideal perfection of utilitarian morality. As the means of making the nearest approach to this ideal, utility would enjoin, first, that laws and social arrangements should place the happiness or (as, speaking practically, it may be called) the interest of every individual as nearly as possible in harmony with the interest of the whole; and secondly, that education and opinion, which have so vast a power over human character, should so use that power as to establish in the mind of every individual an indissoluble association between his own happiness and the good of the whole—especially between his own happiness, and the practice of such modes of conduct, negative and positive, as regard for the universal happiness prescribes—so that not only he may be unable to conceive the possibility of happiness to himself consistently with conduct opposed to the general good, but also that a direct impulse to promote the general good may be in every individual one of the habitual motives of action, and the sentiments connected therewith may fill a large and prominent place in every human being's sentient existence. If the impugners of the utilitarian morality represented it to their own minds in this its true character, I know not what recommendation possessed by any other morality they could possibly affirm to be wanting to it, what more beautiful or more exalted developments of human nature any other ethical system can be supposed to foster, or what springs of action, not accessible to the utilitarian, such systems rely on for giving effect to their mandates.

The objectors to utilitarianism cannot always be charged with representing it in a discreditable light. On the contrary, those among them who entertain any thing like a just idea of its disinterested character sometimes find fault with its standard as being too high for humanity. They say it is exacting too much to require that people shall always act from the inducement of promoting the general interests of society. But this is to mistake the very meaning of a standard of morals, and confound the rule of action with the motive of it. It is the business of ethics to tell us what are our duties or by what test we may know them, but no system of ethics requires that the sole motive of all we do shall be a feeling of duty; on the contrary, ninety-nine hundredths of all our actions are done from other motives, and rightly so done, if the rule of duty does not condemn them. It is the more unjust to utilitarianism that this particular misapprehension should be made a ground of objection to it, inasmuch as utilitarian moralists have gone beyond almost all others in affirming that the motive has nothing to do with the morality of the action though much with the worth of

the agent. He who saves a fellow creature from drowning does what is morally right, whether his motive be duty or the hope of being paid for his trouble; he who betrays the friend that trusts him is guilty of a crime, even if his object be to serve another friend to whom he is under greater obligations.[2] But to speak only of actions done from the motive of duty, and in direct obedience to principle: it is a misapprehension of the utilitarian mode of thought to conceive it as implying that people should fix their minds upon so wide a generality as the world or society at large. The great majority of good actions are intended, not for the benefit of the world but for that of individuals, of which the good of the world is made up; and the thoughts of the most virtuous man need not on these occasions travel beyond the particular persons concerned, except so far as is necessary to assure himself that, in benefiting them, he is not violating the rights—that is, the legitimate and authorized expectations—of any one else. The multiplication of happiness is, according to the utilitarian ethics, the object of virtue; the occasions on which any person (except one in a thousand) has it in his power to do this on an extended scale—in other words, to be a public benefactor—are but exceptional, and on these occasions alone is he called on to consider public utility; in every other case, private utility, the interest or happiness of some few persons, is all he has to attend to. Those alone, the influence of whose actions extends to society in general, need concern themselves habitually about so large an object. In the case of abstinences indeed—of things which people forbear to do from moral considerations, though the consequences in the particular case might be beneficial—it would be unworthy of an intelligent agent not to be consciously aware that the action is of a class which, if practised generally, would be generally injurious, and that this is the ground of the obligation to abstain from it. The amount of regard for the public interest implied in this recognition is no greater than is demanded by every system of morals, for they all enjoin to abstain from whatever is manifestly pernicious to society.

The same considerations dispose of another reproach against the doctrine of utility, founded on a still grosser misconception of the purpose of a standard of morality, and of the very meaning of the words "right" and "wrong." It is often affirmed that utilitarianism renders men cold and unsympathizing, that it chills their moral feelings towards individuals, that it makes them regard only the dry and hard consideration of the consequences of actions, not taking into their moral estimate the qualities from which those actions emanate. If the assertion means that they do not allow their judgment respecting the rightness or wrongness of an action to be influenced by their opinion of the qualities of the person who does it, this is a complaint, not against utilitarianism but against having any standard of morality at all; for certainly no known ethical standard decides an action to be good or bad because it is done by a good or bad man, still less because done by an amiable, a brave, or a benevolent man, or the contrary. These considerations are relevant, not to the estimation of actions, but of persons, and there is nothing in the utilitarian theory inconsistent with the fact that there are other things which interest us in persons besides the rightness and wrongness of their actions. The Stoics indeed, with the paradoxical misuse of language which was part of their system and by which they strove to raise themselves above all concern about any thing but virtue, were fond of saying that he who has that has everything, that he, and one he, is rich, is beautiful, is a king. But no claim of this description is made for the virtuous man by the utilitarian doctrine. Utilitarians are quite aware that there are other desirable possessions and qualities besides virtue, and are perfectly willing to allow to all of them their full worth. They are also aware that a right action does not necessarily indicate a virtuous character, and that actions which are blamable often proceed from qualities entitled to praise. When this is apparent in any particular case, it modifies their estimation, not certainly of the act but of the agent. I grant that they are notwithstanding of opinion that, in the long run, the best proof of a good character is good actions, and resolutely refuse to consider any mental disposition as good, of which the predominant tendency is to produce bad conduct. This makes them unpopular with many people; but it is an unpopularity which they must share with every one who regards the distinction between right and wrong in a serious light, and the reproach is not one which a conscientious utilitarian need be anxious to repel.

If no more be meant by the objection than that many utilitarians look on the morality of actions, as measured by the utilitarian standards, with too exclusive a regard, and do not lay sufficient stress upon the other beauties of character which go towards making

a human being lovable or admirable, this may be admitted. Utilitarians who have cultivated their moral feelings but not their sympathies nor their artistic perceptions, do fall into this mistake, and so do all other moralists under the same conditions. What can be said in excuse for other moralists is equally available for them, namely that, if there is to be any error, it is better that it should be on that side. As a matter of fact, we may affirm that among utilitarians, as among adherents of other systems, there is every imaginable degree of rigidity and of laxity in the application of their standard; some are even puritanically rigorous, while others are as indulgent as can possibly be desired by sinner or by sentimentalist. But on the whole, a doctrine which brings prominently forward the interest that mankind have in the repression and prevention of conduct which violates the moral law, is likely to be inferior to no other in turning the sanctions of opinion against such violations. It is true, the question, What does violate the moral law? is one on which those who recognize different standards of morality are likely now and then to differ. But difference of opinion on moral questions was not first introduced into the world by utilitariansim, while that doctrine does supply, if not always an easy, at all events a tangible and intelligible mode of deciding such differences.

It may not be superfluous to notice a few more of the common misapprehensions of utilitarian ethics, even those which are so obvious and gross that it might appear impossible for any person of candor and intelligence to fall into them, since persons even of considerable mental endowments often give themselves so little trouble to understand the bearings of any opinion against which they entertain a prejudice, and men are in general so little conscious of this voluntary ignorance as a defect, that the vulgarest misunderstandings of ethical doctrines are continually met with in the deliberate writings of persons of the greatest pretensions both to high principle and to philosophy. We not uncommonly hear the doctrine of utility inveighed against as a *godless* doctrine. If it be necessary to say any thing at all against so mere an assumption, we may say that the question depends upon what idea we have formed of the moral character of the Deity. If it be a true belief that God desires, above all things, the happiness of his creatures, and that this was his purpose in their creation, utility is not only not a godless doctrine but more profoundly religious than any other. If it be meant that utilitariansim does not recognize the revealed will of God as the supreme law of morals, I answer that an utilitarian, who believes in the perfect goodness and wisdom of God, necessarily believes that whatever God has thought fit to reveal on the subject of morals must fulfil the requirements of utility in a supreme degree. But others besides utilitarians have been of opinion that the Christian revelation was intended, and is fitted, to inform the hearts and minds of mankind with a spirit which should enable them to find for themselves what is right and incline them to do it when found, rather than to tell them, except in a very general way, what it is, and that we need a doctrine of ethics, carefully followed out, to *interpret* to us the will of God. Whether this opinion is correct or not, it is superfluous here to discuss, since whatever aid religion, either natural or revealed, can afford to ethical investigation, is as open to the utilitarian moralist as to any other. He can use it as the testimony of God to the usefulness or hurtfulness of any given course of action, by as good a right as others can use it for the indication of a transcendental law, having no connection with usefulness or with happiness.

Again: Utility is often summarily stigmatized as an immoral doctrine by giving it the name of Expediency and, taking advantage of the popular use of that term, to contrast it with Principle. But the Expedient, in the sense in which it is opposed to the Right, generally means that which is expedient for the particular interest of the agent himself, as when a minister sacrifices the interests of his country to keep himself in place. When it means any thing better than this, it means that which is expedient for some immediate object, some temporary purpose, but which violates a rule whose observance is expedient in a much higher degree. The Expedient, in this sense, instead of being the same thing with the useful, is a branch of the hurtful. Thus it would often be expedient, for the purpose of getting over some momentary embarrassment or attaining some object immediately useful to ourselves or others, to tell a lie. But inasmuch as the cultivation in ourselves of a sensitive feeling on the subject of veracity is one of the most useful, and the enfeeblement of that feeling one of those most hurtful, things to which our conduct can be instrumental, and inasmuch as any, even unintentional, deviation from truth does that much towards weakening the trustworthiness of human assertion, which is not only the principal support of all present social well-being, but the insufficiency of which does more than any one thing that can be named to keep back civilization, virtue, every thing on which human happiness on the largest scale

depends—we feel that the violation, for a present advantage, of a rule of such transcendent expediency is not expedient, and that he who, for the sake of a convenience to himself or to some other individual, does what depends on him to deprive mankind of the good, and inflict upon them the evil, involved in the greater or less reliance which they can place in each other's word, acts the part of one of their worst enemies. Yet that even this rule, sacred as it is, admits of possible exceptions is acknowledged by all moralists, the chief of which is, when the withholding of some fact (as of information from a malefactor, or of bad news from a person dangerously ill) would save an individual (especially an individual other than one's self) from great and unmerited evil and when the withholding can only be effected by denial. But in order that the exception may not extend itself beyond the need and may have the least possible effect in weakening reliance on veracity, it ought to be recognized and, if possible, its limits defined, and, if the principle of utility is good for any thing, it must be good for weighing these conflicting utilities against one another, and marking out the region within which one or the other preponderates.

Again: defenders of utility often find themselves called upon to reply to such objections as this—that there is not time, previous to action, for calculating and weighing the effects of any line of conduct on the general happiness. This is exactly as if any one were to say that it is impossible to guide our conduct by Christianity, because there is not time, on every occasion on which any thing has to be done, to read through the Old and New Testaments. The answer to the objection is that there has been ample time, namely, the whole past duration of the human species. During all that time, mankind have been learning by experience the tendencies of actions, on which experience all the prudence as well as all the morality of life are dependent. People talk as if the commencement of this course of experience had hitherto been put off and as if, at the moment when some man feels tempted to meddle with the property or life of another, he had to begin considering for the first time whether murder and theft are injurious to human happiness. Even then, I do not think that he would find the question very puzzling, but at all events the matter is now done to his hand. It is truly a whimsical supposition that, if mankind were agreed in considering utility to be the test of morality, they would remain without any agreement as to what *is* useful, and would take no measures for having their notions on the subject taught to the young and enforced by law and opinion. There is no difficulty in proving any ethical standard whatever to work ill, if we suppose universal idiocy to be conjoined with it; but on any hypothesis short of that, mankind must by this time have acquired positive beliefs as to the effects of some actions on their happiness, and the beliefs which have thus come down are the rules of morality for the multitude, and for the philosopher, until he has succeeded in finding better. That philosophers might easily do this, even now, on many subjects, that the received code of ethics is by no means of divine right, and that mankind have still much to learn as to the effects of actions on the general happiness—I admit or, rather, earnestly maintain. The corollaries from the principle of utility, like the precepts of every practical art, admit of indefinite improvement and, in a progressive state of the human mind, their improvement is perpetually going on. But to consider the rules of morality as improvable is one thing; to pass over the intermediate generalizations entirely, and endeavor to test each individual action directly by the first principle, is another. It is a strange notion, that the acknowledgment of a first principle is inconsistent with the admission of secondary ones. To inform a traveler respecting the place of his ultimate destination is not to forbid the use of landmarks and direction posts on the way. The proposition that happiness is the end and aim of morality does not mean that no road ought to be laid down to that goal, or that persons going thither should not be advised to take one direction rather than another. Men really ought to leave off talking a kind of nonsense on this subject which they would neither talk nor listen to on other matters of practical concernment. Nobody argues that the art of navigation is not founded on astronomy, because sailors cannot wait to calculate the ''Nautical Almanac.'' Being rational creatures, they go to sea with it ready calculated, and all rational creatures go out upon the sea of life with their minds made up on the common questions of right and wrong, as well as on many of the far more difficult questions of wise and foolish. And this, as long as foresight is a human quality, it is to be presumed they will continue to do. Whatever we adopt as the fundamental principle of morality, we require subordinate principles to apply it by; the impos-

sibility of doing without them, being common to all systems, can afford no argument against any one in particular; but gravely to argue as if no such secondary principles could be had, and as if mankind had remained till now and always must remain without drawing any general conclusions from the experience of human life, is as high a pitch, I think, as absurdity has ever reached in philosophical controversy.

The remainder of the stock arguments against utilitarianism mostly consist in laying to its charge the common infirmities of human nature, and the general difficulties which embarrass conscientious persons in shaping their course through life. We are told that an utilitarian will be apt to make his own particular case an exception to moral rules and, when under temptation, will see an utility in the breach of a rule greater than he will see in its observance. But is utility the only creed which is able to furnish us with excuses for evil-doing, and means of cheating our own conscience? They are afforded in abundance by all doctrines which recognize as a fact in morals the existence of conflicting considerations, which all doctrines do that have been believed by sane persons. It is not the fault of any creed, but of the complicated nature of human affairs, that rules of conduct cannot be so framed as to require no exceptions, and that hardly any kind of action can safely be laid down as either always obligatory or always condemnable. There is no ethical creed which does not temper the rigidity of its laws by giving a certain latitude, under the moral responsibility of the agent, for accommodation to peculiarities of circumstances and, under every creed, at the opening thus made, self-deception and dishonest casuistry get in. There exists no moral system under which there do not arise unequivocal cases of conflicting obligation. These are the real difficulties, the knotty points both in the theory of ethics and in the conscientious guidance of personal conduct. They are overcome practically with greater or with less success according to the intellect and virtue of the individual, but it can hardly be pretended that any one will be the less qualified for dealing with them, from possessing an ultimate standard to which conflicting rights and duties can be referred. If utility is the ultimate source of moral obligations, utility may be invoked to decide between them when their demands are incompatible. Though the application of the standard may be difficult, it is better than none at all; while in other systems, the moral laws all claiming independent authority, there is no common umpire entitled to interfere between them, their claims to precedence one over another rest on little better than sophistry, and unless determined, as they generally are, by the unacknowledged influence of considerations of utility, afford a free scope for the action of personal desires and partialities. We must remember that only in these cases of conflict between secondary principles is it requisite that first principles should be appealed to. There is no case of moral obligation in which some secondary principle is not involved and, if only one, there can seldom be any real doubt which one it is, in the mind of any person by whom the principle itself is recognized.

3. OF THE ULTIMATE SANCTION OF THE PRINCIPLE OF UTILITY

The question is often asked, and properly so, in regard to any supposed moral standard, What is its sanction? what are the motives to obey it? or, more specifically, what is the source of its obligation? whence does it derive its binding force? It is a necessary part of moral philosophy to provide the answer to this question, which, though frequently assuming the shape of an objection to the utilitarian morality, as if it had some special applicability to that above others, really arises in regard to all standards. It arises, in fact, whenever a person is called on to *adopt* a standard or refer morality to any basis on which he has not been accustomed to rest it. For the customary morality, that which education and opinion have consecrated, is the only one which presents itself to the mind with the feeling of being *in itself* obligatory; and, when a person is asked to believe that this morality *derives* its obligation from some general principle round which custom has not thrown the same halo, the assertion is to him a paradox: the supposed corollaries seem to have a more binding force than the original theorem; the superstructure seems to stand better without than with what is represented as its foundation. He says to himself, ''I feel that I am bound not to rob or murder, betray or deceive, but why am I bound to promote the general happiness? If my own happiness lies in something else, why may I not give that the preference?''

If the view adopted by the utilitarian philosophy of the nature of the moral sense be correct, this difficulty will always present itself, until the influences which form moral character have taken the same hold of the principle which they have taken of some of the consequences, until, by the improvement of education, the feeling of unity with our fellow creatures shall be

(what it cannot be denied that Christ intended it to be) as deeply rooted in our character and, to our own consciousness, as completely a part of our nature, as the horror of crime is in an ordinarily well brought up young person. In the mean time, however, the difficulty has no peculiar application to the doctrine of utility, but is inherent in every attempt to analyze morality, and reduce it to principles, which, unless the principle is already in men's minds invested with as much sacredness as any of its applications, always seems to divest them of a part of their sanctity.

The principle of utility either has, or there is no reason why it might not have, all the sanctions which belong to any other system of morals. Those sanctions are either external or internal. Of the external sanctions it is not necessary to speak at any length. They are the hope of favor and the fear of displeasure from our fellow creatures, or from the Ruler of the universe, along with whatever we may have of sympathy or affection for them or of love and awe of him, inclining us to do his will independently of selfish consequences. There is evidently no reason why all these motives for observance should not attach themselves to the utilitarian morality as completely and as powerfully as to any other. Indeed, those of them which refer to our fellow creatures are sure to do so, in proportion to the amount of general intelligence; for, whether there be any other ground of moral obligation than the general happiness or not, men do desire happiness and, however imperfect may be their own practice, they desire and commend all conduct in others towards themselves by which they think their happiness is promoted. With regard to the religious motive, if men believe, as most profess to do, in the goodness of God, those who think that conduciveness to the general happiness is the essence, or even only the criterion of good, must necessarily believe that it is also that which God approves. The whole force, therefore, of external reward and punishment, whether physical or moral, and whether proceeding from God or from our fellow men, together with all that the capacities of human nature admit of disinterested devotion to either, become available to enforce the utilitarian morality, in proportion as that morality is recognized, and the more powerfully, the more the appliances of education and general cultivation are bent to the purpose.

So far as to external sanctions. The internal sanction of duty, whatever our standard of duty may be, is one and the same—a feeling in our own mind, a pain, more or less intense, attendant on violation of duty, which, in properly cultivated moral natures, rises in the more serious cases into shrinking from it as an impossibility. This feeling, when disinterested, and connecting itself with the pure idea of duty and not with some particular form of it, or with any of the merely accessory circumstances, is the essence of Conscience; though in that complex phenomenon, as it actually exists, the simple fact is, in general, all incrusted over with collateral associations, derived from sympathy, from love, and still more from fear, from all the forms of religious feeling, from the recollections of childhood, and of all our past life, from self-esteem, desire of the esteem of others, and occasionally even self-abasement. This extreme complication is, I apprehend, the origin of the sort of mystical character which, by a tendency of the human mind of which there are many other examples, is apt to be attributed to the idea of moral obligation, and which leads people to believe that the idea cannot possibly attach itself to any other objects than those which, by a supposed mysterious law, are found in our present experience to excite it. Its binding force, however, consists in the existence of a mass of feeling which must be broken through in order to do what violates our standard of right, and which, if we do nevertheless violate that standard, will probably have to be encountered afterwards in the form of remorse. Whatever theory we have of the nature or origin of conscience, this is what essentially constitutes it.

The ultimate sanction, therefore, of all morality (external motives apart) being a subjective feeling in our own minds, I see nothing embarrassing, to those whose standard is utility, in the question, What is the sanction of that particular standard? We may answer, The same as of all other moral standards—the conscientious feelings of mankind. Undoubtedly this sanction has no binding efficacy on those who do not possess the feelings it appeals to, but neither will these persons be more obedient to any other moral principle than to the utilitarian one. On them, morality of any kind has no hold but through the external sanctions. Meanwhile the feelings exist—a fact in human nature, the reality of which, and the great power with which they are capable of acting on those in whom they have been duly cultivated, are proved by experience. No reason has ever been shown why

they may not be cultivated to as great intensity in connection with the utilitarian as with any other rule of morals.

There is, I am aware, a disposition to believe that a person who sees in moral obligation a transcendental fact, an objective reality belonging to the province of "things in themselves," is likely to be more obedient to it than one who believes it to be entirely subjective, having its seat in human consciousness only. But, whatever a person's opinion may be on this point of ontology, the force he is really urged by is his own subjective feeling and is exactly measured by its strength. No one's belief that Duty is an objective reality is stronger than the belief that God is so, yet the belief in God, apart from the expectation of actual reward and punishment, only operates on conduct through, and in proportion to, the subjective religious feeling. The sanction, so far as it is disinterested, is always in the mind itself; and the notion, therefore, of the transcendental moralists must be that this sanction will not exist *in* the mind, unless it is believed to have its root out of the mind, and that if a person is able to say to himself, "This which is restraining me, and which is called my conscience, is only a feeling in my own mind," he may possibly draw the conclusion that, when the feeling ceases, the obligation ceases, and that, if he find the feeling inconvenient, he may disregard it and endeavor to get rid of it. But is this danger confined to the utilitarian morality? Does the belief that moral obligation has its seat outside the mind make the feeling of it too strong to be got rid of? The fact is so far otherwise that all moralists admit and lament the ease with which, in the generality of mind, conscience can be silenced or stifled. The question, Need I obey my conscience? is quite as often put to themselves by persons who never heard of the principle of utility as by its adherents. Those whose conscientious feelings are so weak as to allow of their asking this question, if they answer it affirmatively, will not do so because they believe in the transcendental theory but because of the external sanctions.

It is not necessary, for the present purpose, to decide whether the feeling of duty is innate or implanted. Assuming it to be innate, it is an open question to what objects it naturally attaches itself, for the philosophic supporters of that theory are now agreed that the intuitive perception is of principles of morality and not of the details. If there by any thing innate in the matter, I see no reason why the feeling which is innate should not be that of regard to the pleasures and pains of others. If there is any principle of morals which is intuitively obligatory, I should say it must be that. If so, the intuitive ethics would coincide with the utilitarian, and there would be no further quarrel between them. Even as it is, the intuitive moralists, though they believe that there are other intuitive moral obligations, do already believe this to be one, for they unanimously hold that a large *portion* of morality turns upon the consideration due to the interests of our fellow creatures. Therefore, if the belief in the transcendental origin of moral obligation gives any additional efficacy to the internal sanction, it appears to me that the utilitarian principle has already the benefit of it.

On the other hand, if, as is my own belief, the moral feelings are not innate but acquired, they are not for that reason the less natural. It is natural to man to speak, to reason, to build cities, to cultivate the ground, though these are acquired faculties. The moral feelings are not indeed a part of our nature, in the sense of being in any perceptible degree present in all of us, but this, unhappily, is a fact admitted by those who believe the most strenuously in their transcendental origin. Like the other acquired capacities above referred to, the moral faculty, if not a part of our nature, is a natural outgrowth from it, capable like them, in a certain small degree, of springing up spontaneously, and susceptible of being brought by cultivation to a high degree of development. Unhappily, it is also susceptible, by a sufficient use of the external sanctions and of the force of early impressions, of being cultivated in almost any direction, so that there is hardly any thing so absurd or so mischievous that it may not, by means of these influences, be made to act on the human mind with all the authority of conscience. To doubt that the same potency might be given by the same means to the principle of utility, even if it had no foundation in human nature, would be flying in the face of all experience.

But moral associations which are wholly of artificial creation, when intellectual culture goes on, yield by degrees to the dissolving force of analysis; and if the feeling of duty, when associated with utility, would appear equally arbitrary, if there were no leading department of our nature, no powerful class of sentiments, with which that association would harmonize, which would make us feel it congenial, and incline us not only to foster it in others (for which we have abundant interested motives), but also to cherish it in ourselves, if there were not, in short, a natural basis of sentiment for utilitarian morality—it might well happen that this association also, even after it

had been implanted by education, might be analyzed away.

But there *is* this basis of powerful natural sentiment, and this it is, which, when once the general happiness is recognized as the ethical standard, will constitute the strength of the utilitarian morality. This firm foundation is that of the social feelings of mankind: the desire to be in unity with our fellow creatures, which is already a powerful principle in human nature, and happily one of those which tend to become stronger, even without express inculcation from the influences of advancing civilization. The social state is at once so natural, so necessary, and so habitual to man, that except in some unusual circumstances, or by an effort of voluntary abstraction, he never conceives himself otherwise than as a member of a body, and this association is riveted more and more as mankind are further removed from the state of savage independence. Any condition, therefore, which is essential to a state of society, becomes more and more an inseparable part of every person's conception of the state of things which he is born into, and which is the destiny of a human being. Now, society between human beings, except in the relation of master and slave, is manifestly impossible on any other footing than that the interests of all are to be consulted. Society between equals can only exist on the understanding that the interests of all are to be regarded equally. And since, in all states of civilization, every person except an absolute monarch has equals, every one is obliged to live on these terms with somebody, and in every age, some advance is made towards a state in which it will be impossible to live permanently on other terms with anybody. In this way, people grow up unable to conceive as possible to them a state of total disregard of other people's interests. They are under a necessity of conceiving themselves as at least abstaining from all the grosser injuries, and (if only for their own protection) living in a state of constant protest against them. They are also familiar with the fact of cooperating with others, and proposing to themselves a collective, not an individual, interest as the aim (at least for the time being) of their actions. So long as they are cooperating, their ends are identified with those of others; there is at least a temporary feeling that the interests of others are their own interests. Not only does all strengthening of social ties, and all healthy growth of society, give to each individual a stronger personal interest in practically consulting the welfare of others; it also leads him to identify his *feelings* more and more with their good, or at least with an ever greater degree of practical consideration for it. He comes, as though instinctively, to be conscious of himself as a being who *of course* pays regard to others. The good of others becomes to him a thing naturally and necessarily to be attended to, like any of the physical conditions of our existence. Now, whatever amount of this feeling a person has, he is urged by the strongest motives, both of interest and of sympathy, to demonstrate it and, to the utmost of his power, encourage it in others, and, even if he has none of it himself, he is as greatly interested as any one else that others should have it. Consequently, the smallest germs of the feeling are laid hold of and nourished by the contagion of sympathy and the influences of education, and a complete web of corroborative association is woven round it by the powerful agency of the external sanctions. This mode of conceiving ourselves and human life, as civilization goes on, is felt to be more and more natural. Every step in political improvement renders it more so, by removing the sources of opposition of interest and leveling those inequalities of legal privilege between individuals or classes, owing to which there are large portions of mankind whose happiness it is still practicable to disregard. In an improving state of the human mind, the influences are constantly on the increase which tend to generate in each individual a feeling of unity with all the rest, which, if perfect, would make him never think of or desire any beneficial condition for himself, in the benefits of which they are not included. If we now suppose this feeling of unity to be taught as a religion, and the whole force of education, of institutions, and of opinion directed, as it once was in the case of religion, to make every person grow up from infancy surrounded on all sides both by the profession and the practice of it, I think that no one who can realize this conception will feel any misgiving about the sufficiency of the ultimate sanction for the Happiness morality. To any ethical student who finds the realization difficult, I recommend, as a means of facilitating it, the second of M. Comte's two principal works, the *Traité de Politique Positive*. I entertain the strongest objections to the system of politics and morals set forth in that treatise; but I think it has superabundantly shown the possibility of giving to the service of humanity, even without the aid of belief in a Providence, both the psychological power and the social efficacy of a religion, making it take hold of human life, and color all thought, feeling, and action, in a manner of which the greatest ascendancy ever exercised by any religion may be but a type and foretaste, and of which the danger is, not that it should be insufficient, but that it should be so excessive as to interfere unduly with human freedom and individuality.

Neither is it necessary to the feeling which constitutes the binding force of the utilitarian morality on those who recognize it, to wait for those social influences which would make its obligation felt by mankind at large. In the comparatively early state of human advancement in which we now live, a person cannot indeed feel that entireness of sympathy with all others which would make any real discordance in the general direction of their conduct in life impossible, but already a person in whom the social feeling is at all developed cannot bring himself to think of the rest of his fellow creatures as struggling rivals with him for the means of happiness, whom he must desire to see defeated in their object in order that he may succeed in his. The deeply rooted conception which every individual even now has of himself as a social being tends to make him feel it one of his natural wants that there should be harmony between his feelings and aims and those of his fellow creatures. If differences of opinion and of mental culture make it impossible for him to share many of their actual feelings—perhaps make him denounce and defy those feelings—he still needs to be conscious that his real aim and theirs do not conflict, that he is not opposing himself to what they really wish for—namely, their own good—but is, on the contrary, promoting it. This feeling in most individuals is much inferior in strength to their selfish feelings, and is often wanting altogether. But to those who have it, it possesses all the characters of a natural feeling. It does not present itself to their minds as a superstition of education, or a law despotically imposed by the power of society, but as an attribute which it would not be well for them to be without. This conviction is the ultimate sanction of the greatest-happiness morality. This it is which makes any mind of well-developed feelings work with, and not against, the outward motives to care for others, afforded by what I have called the external sanctions, and when those sanctions are wanting, or act in an opposite direction, constitutes in itself a powerful internal binding force, in proportion to the sensitiveness and thoughtfulness of the character; since few but those whose mind is a moral blank could bear to lay out their course of life on the plan of paying no regard to others, except so far as their own private interest compels.

4. OF WHAT SORT OF PROOF THE PRINCIPLE OF UTILITY IS SUSCEPTIBLE

It has already been remarked that questions of ultimate ends do not admit of proof, in the ordinary acceptation of the term. To be incapable of proof by reasoning is common to all first principles, to the first premises of our knowledge, as well as to those of our conduct. But the former, being matters of fact, may be the subject of a direct appeal to the faculties which judge of fact, namely, our senses, and our internal consciousness. Can an appeal be made to the same faculties on questions of practical ends? Or by what other faculty is cognizance taken of them?

Questions about ends are, in other words, questions what things are desirable. The utilitarian doctrine is that happiness is desirable, and the only thing desirable, as an end, all other things being only desirable as means to that end. What ought to be required of this doctrine—what conditions is it requisite that the doctrine should fulfill—to make good its claim to be believed?

The only proof capable of being given that an object is visible is that people actually see it, the only proof that a sound is audible is that people hear it, and so of the other sources of our experience. In like manner, I apprehend, the sole evidence it is possible to produce that any thing is desirable is that people do actually desire it. If the end which the utilitarian doctrine proposes to itself were not, in theory and in practice, acknowledged to be an end, nothing could ever convince any person that it was so. No reason can be given why the general happiness is desirable, except that each person, so far as he believes it to be attainable, desires his own happiness. This, however, being a fact, we have not only all the proof which the case admits of, but all which it is possible to require, that happiness is a good, that each person's happiness is a good to that person, and the general happiness, therefore, a good to the aggregate of all persons.[3] Happiness has made out its title as *one* of the ends of conduct, and consequently one of the criteria of morality.

But it has not, by this alone, proved itself to be the sole criterion. To do that, it would seem, by the same rule, necessary to show, not only that people desire happiness, but that they never desire any thing else. Now, it is palpable that they do desire things, which, in common language, are decidedly distinguished

from happiness. They desire, for example, virtue and the absence of vice, no less really than pleasure and the absence of pain. The desire of virtue is not as universal, but it is as authentic a fact, as the desire of happiness, and hence the opponents of the utilitarian standard deem that they have a right to infer that there are other ends of human action besides happiness, and that happiness is not the standard of approbation and disapprobation.

But does the utilitarian doctrine deny that people desire virtue, or maintain that virtue is not a thing to be desired? The very reverse. It maintains not only that virtue is to be desired, but that it is to be desired disinterestedly, for itself. Whatever may be the opinion of utilitarian moralists as to the original conditions by which virtue is made virtue, however they may believe (as they do) that actions and dispositions are only virtuous because they promote another end than virtue—yet, this being granted, and it having been decided, from considerations of this description, what *is* virtuous, they not only place virtue at the very head of the things which are good as means to the ultimate end, but they also recognize, as a psychological fact, the possibility of its being to the individual a good in itself, without looking to any end beyond it, and hold that the mind is not in a right state, not in a state conformable to utility, not in the state most conducive to the general happiness, unless it does love virtue in this manner—as a thing desirable in itself, even although, in the individual instance, it should not produce those other desirable consequences which it tends to produce, and on account of which it is held to be virtue. This option is not, in the smallest degree, a departure from the Happiness principle. The ingredients of happiness are very various, and each of them is desirable in itself and not merely when considered as swelling an aggregate. The principle of utility does not mean that any given pleasure—as music, for instance—or any given exemption from pain—as, for example, health—are to be looked upon as means to a collective something termed happiness, and to be desired on that account. They are desired and desirable in and for themselves; besides being means, they are a part of the end. Virtue, according to the utilitarian doctrine, is not naturally and originally part of the end, but it is capable of becoming so and, in those who love it disinterestedly, it has become so, and is desired and cherished, not as a means to happiness, but as a part of their happiness

To illustrate this further: we may remember that virtue is not the only thing, originally a means, and which, if it were not a means to anything else, would be and remain indifferent, but which, by association with what it is a means to, comes to be desired for itself, and that, too, with the utmost intensity. What, for example, shall we say of the love of money? There is nothing originally more desirable about money than about any heap of glittering pebbles. Its worth is solely that of the things which it will buy, the desires for other things than itself, which it is a means of gratifying. Yet the love of money is not only one of the strongest moving forces of human life, but money is, in many cases, desired in and for itself; the desire to possess it is often stronger than the desire to use it, and goes on increasing when all the desires which point to ends beyond it, to be compassed by it, are falling off. It may, then, be said truly, that money is desired, not for the sake of an end but as part of the end. From being a means to happiness, it has come to be itself a principal ingredient of the individual's conception of happiness. The same may be said of the majority of the great objects of human life—power, for example, or fame, except that to each of these there is a certain amount of immediate pleasure annexed, which has at least the semblance of being naturally inherent in them, a thing which cannot be said of money. Still, however, the strongest natural attraction, both of power and of fame, is the immense aid they give to the attainment of our other wishes, and it is the strong association thus generated between them and all our objects of desire which gives to the direct desire of them the intensity it often assumes, so as in some characters to surpass in strength all other desires. In these cases, the means have become a part of the end, and a more important part of it than any of the things which they are means to. What was once desired as an instrument for the attainment of happiness has come to be desired for its own sake. In being desired for its own sake, it is, however, desired as *part* of happiness. The person is made, or thinks he would be made, happy by its mere possession, and is made unhappy by failure to obtain it. The desire of it is not a different thing from the desire of happiness, any more than the love of music or the desire of health. They are included in happiness. They are some of the elements of which the desire of happiness is made up. Happiness is not an abstract idea but a concrete whole, and these are some of its parts. And

the utilitarian standard sanctions and approves their being so. Life would be a poor thing, very ill provided with sources of happiness, if there were not this provision of nature, by which things originally indifferent, but conducive to, or otherwise associated with, the satisfaction of our primitive desires, become in themselves sources of pleasure more valuable than the primitive pleasures, both in permanency, in the space of human existence that they are capable of covering, and even in intensity.

Virtue, according to the utilitarian conception, is a good of this description. There was no original desire of it, or motive to it, save its conduciveness to pleasure, and especially to protection from pain. But through the association thus formed, it may be felt a good in itself, and desired as such with as great intensity as any other good, and with this difference between it and the love of money, of power, or of fame—that all of these may, and often do, render the individual noxious to the other members of the society to which he belongs, whereas there is nothing which makes him so much a blessing to them as the cultivation of the disinterested love of virtue. And consequently the utilitarian standard, while it tolerates and approves those other acquired desires, up to the point beyond which they would be more injurious to the general happiness than promotive of it, enjoins and requires the cultivation of the love of virtue up to the greatest strength possible, as being above all things important to the general happiness.

It results from the preceding considerations that there is in reality nothing desired except happiness. Whatever is desired otherwise than as a means to some end beyond itself, and ultimately to happiness, is desired as itself a part of happiness, and is not desired for itself until it has become so. Those who desire virtue for its own sake desire it either because the consciousness of it is a pleasure, or because the consciousness of being without it is a pain, or for both reasons united; as in truth the pleasure and pain seldom exist separately, but almost always together, the same person feeling pleasure in the degree of virtue attained, and pain in not having attained more. If one of these gave him no pleasure, and the other no pain, he would not love or desire virtue, or would desire it only for the other benefits which it might produce to himself or to persons whom he cared for.

We have now, then, an answer to the question of what sort of proof the principle of utility is suceptible. If the opinion which I have now stated is psychologically true, if human nature is so constituted as to desire nothing which is not either a part of happiness or a means of happiness—we can have no other proof, and we require no other, that these are the only things desirable. If so, happiness is the sole end of human action, and the promotion of it the test by which to judge of all human conduct, from whence it necessarily follows that it must be the criterion of morality, since a part is included in the whole.

And, now, to decide whether this is really so, whether mankind do desire nothing for itself but that which is a pleasure to them, or of which the absence is a pain—we have evidently arrived at a question of fact and experience, dependent, like all similar questions, upon evidence. It can only be determined by practised self-consciousness and self-observation, assisted by observation of others. I believe that these sources of evidence, impartially consulted, will declare that desiring a thing and finding it pleasant, aversion to it and thinking of it as painful, are phenomena entirely inseparable, or rather two parts of the same phenomenon—in strictness of language, two different modes of naming the same psychological fact; that to think of an object as desirable (unless for the sake of its consequences), and to think of it as pleasant, are one and the same thing; and that to desire any thing, except in proportion as the idea of it is pleasant, is a physical and metaphysical impossibility.

So obvious does this appear to me that I expect it will hardly be disputed, and the objection made will be, not that desire can possibly be directed to any thing ultimately except pleasure and exemption from pain, but that the will is a different thing from desire; that a person of confirmed virtue, or any other person whose purposes are fixed, carries out his purposes without any thought of the pleasure he has in contemplating them, or expects to derive from their fulfilment, and persists in acting on them, even though these pleasures are much diminished by changes in his character, or decay of his passive sensibilities, or are outweighed by the pains which the pursuit of the purposes may bring upon him. All this I fully admit, and have stated it elsewhere as positively and emphatically as any one. Will, the active phenomenon, is a different thing from desire, the state of passive sensibility and, though originally an offshoot from it, may in time take root and detach itself from the parent stock; so much so, that in the case of an habitual purpose, instead of willing the thing because we desire it, we often desire it only because we will it. This, however, is but an instance of that familiar fact, the power of habit, and is nowise confined to the case of virtu-

ous actions. Many indifferent things, which men originally did from a motive of some sort, they continue to do from habit. Sometimes this is done unconsciously, the consciousness coming only after the action; at other times with conscious volition, but volition which has become habitual, and is put in operation by the force of habit, in opposition, perhaps, to the deliberate preference, as often happens with those who have contracted habits of vicious or hurtful indulgence. Third and last comes the case in which the habitual act of will in the individual instance is not in contradiction to the general intention prevailing at other times, but in fulfilment of it, as in the case of the person of confirmed virtue, and of all who pursue deliberately and consistently any determinate end. The distinction between will and desire, thus understood, is an authentic and highly important psychological fact, but the fact consists solely in this—that will, like all other parts of our constitution, is amenable to habit, and that we may will from habit what we no longer desire for itself, or desire only because we will it. It is not the less true that will, in the beginning, is entirely produced by desire, including in that term the repelling influence of pain, as well as the attractive one of pleasure. Let us take into consideration no longer the person who has a confirmed will to do right, but him in whom that virtuous will is still feeble, conquerable by temptation, and not to be fully relied on; by what means can it be strengthened? How can the will to be virtuous, where it does not exist in sufficient force, be implanted or awakened? Only by making the person *desire* virtue, by making him think of it in a pleasurable light, or of its absence in a painful one. It is by associating the doing right with pleasure, or the doing wrong with pain, or by eliciting and impressing and bringing home to the person's experience the pleasure naturally involved in the one or the pain in the other, that it is possible to call forth that will to be virtuous which, when confirmed, acts without any thought of either pleasure or pain. Will is the child of desire, and passes out of the domination of its parent only to come under that of habit. That which is the result of habit affords no presumption of being intrinsically good, and there would be no reason for wishing that the purpose of virtue should become independent of pleasure and pain, were it not that the influence of the pleasurable and painful associations which prompt to virtue is not sufficiently to be depended on for unerring constancy of action until it has acquired the support of habit. Both in feeling and in conduct, habit is the only thing which imparts certainty, and it is because of the importance to others of being able to rely absolutely on one's feelings and conduct, and to one's self of being able to rely on one's own, that the will to do right ought to be cultivated into this habitual independence. In other words, this state of the will is a means to good, not intrinsically a good, and does not contradict the doctrine that nothing is a good to human beings but in so far as it is either itself pleasurable or a means of attaining pleasure or averting pain.

But if this doctrine be true, the principle of utility is proved. Whether it is so or not, must now be left to the consideration of the thoughtful reader.

NOTES

1. The author of this essay has reason for believing himself to be the first person who brought the word "utilitarian" into use. He did not invent it, but adopted it from a passing expression in Mr. Galt's *Annals of the Parish*. After using it as a designation for several years, he and others abandoned it from a growing dislike to any thing resembling a badge or watchword of sectarian distinction. But as a name for one single opinion, not a set of opinions—to denote the recognition of utility as a standard, not any particular way of applying it—the term supplies a want in the language, and offers, in many cases, a convenient mode of avoiding tiresome circumlocution.

2. The following footnote was added by Mill in the second edition:

An opponent, whose intellectual and moral fairness it is a pleasure to acknowledge (the Rev. J. Llewellyn Davies), has objected to this passage, saying, "Surely the rightness or wrongness of saving a man from drowning does depend very much upon the motive with which it is done. Suppose that a tyrant, when his enemy jumped into the sea to escape from him, saved him from drowning simply in order that he might inflict upon him more exquisite tortures, would it tend to clearness to speak of that rescue as 'a morally right action'? Or suppose again, according to one of the stock illustrations of ethical inquiries, that a man betrayed a trust received from a friend, because the discharge of it would fatally injure that friend himself or someone belonging to him, would Utilitarianism compel one to call the betrayal 'a crime' as much as if it had been done from the meanest motive?"

I submit that he who saves another from drowning in order to kill him by torture afterwards does not differ only in motive from him who does the same thing from duty or benevolence; the act itself is different. The rescue of the man is, in the case supposed, only the necessary first step of an act far more atrocious than leaving him to drown would have been. Had Mr. Davies said, "The rightness or wrongness of saving a man from drowning does depend very much"—not upon the motive, but—"upon the *intention*," no utilitarian would have differed from him. Mr. Davies, by an oversight too common not to be quite venial, has in this case confounded the very different ideas of Motive and Intention. There is no point which utilitarian thinkers (and Bentham preeminently) have taken more pains to illustrate than this. The morality of the action depends entirely upon the intention—that is, upon what the agent *wills to do*. But the motive, that is, the feeling which makes him will so to do, if it makes no difference in the act, makes none in the morality; though it makes a great difference in our moral estimation of the agent, especially if it indicates a good or bad habitual *disposition*—a bent of character from which useful, or from which hurtful actions are likely to arise.

3. In a letter written in 1868 to an unidentified correspondent, and published in the second volume of *Letters* (ed. Elliot), Mill said: "As to the sentence you quote from my *Utilitarianism:* when I said that the general happiness is a good to the aggregate of all persons I did not mean that every human being's happiness is a good to every other human being, though I think in a good state of society and education it would be so. I merely meant in this particular sentence to argue that since A's happiness is a good, B's a good, C's a good, etc., the sum of all these goods must be a good."

J. O. URMSON

Saints and Heroes*

James O. Urmson (1915–   ) taught philosophy for many years at Corpus Christi College, Oxford. He now teaches at Stanford University.

Moral philosophers tend to discriminate, explicitly or implicitly, three types of action from the point of view of moral worth. First, they recognize actions that are a duty, or obligatory, or that we ought to perform, treating these terms as approximately synonymous; second, they recognize actions that are right in so far as they are permissible from a moral standpoint and not ruled out by moral considerations, but that are not morally required of us, like the lead of this or that card at bridge; third, they recognize actions that are wrong, that we ought not to do. Some moral philosophers, indeed, could hardly discriminate even these three types of action consistently with the rest of their philosophy. Moore, for example, could hardly recognize a class of morally indifferent actions, permissible but not enjoined, since it is to be presumed that good or ill of some sort will result from the most trivial of our actions. But most moral philosophers recognize these three types of action and attempt to provide a moral theory that will make intelligible such a three-fold classification.

To my mind this threefold classification, or any classification that is merely a variation on or elaboration of it, is totally inadequate to the facts of morality; any moral theory that leaves room only for such a classification will in consequence also be inadequate. My main task in this paper will be to show the inadequacy of such a classification by drawing attention to two of the types of action that most conspicuously

lie outside such a classification; I shall go on to hazard some views on what sort of theory will most easily cope with the facts to which I draw attention, but the facts are here the primary interest.

We sometimes call a person a saint, or an action saintly, using the word "saintly" in a purely moral sense with no religious implications; also we sometimes call a person a hero or an action heroic. It is too clear to need argument that the words "saint" and "hero" are at least normally used in such a way as to be favorably evaluative; it would be impossible to claim that this evaluation is always moral, for clearly we sometimes call a person a saint when evaluating him religiously rather than morally and may call a person the hero of a game or athletic contest in which no moral qualities were displayed, but I shall take it that no formal argument is necessary to show that at least sometimes we use both words for moral evaluation.

If "hero" and "saint" can be words of moral evaluation, we may proceed to the attempt to make explicit the criteria that we implicitly employ for their use in moral contexts. It appears that we so use them in more than one type of situation, and that there is a close parallel between the ways in which the two terms "hero" and "saint" are used; we shall here notice three types of situation in which they are used which seem to be sufficiently different to merit distinction. As the first two types of situation to be noticed are ones that can be readily subsumed under the threefold classification mentioned above, it will be sufficient here to note them and pass on to the third type of situation, which, since it cannot be subsumed under that classification, is for the purposes of this paper the most interesting.

A person may be called a saint (1) if he does his duty regularly in contexts in which inclination, desire, or self-interest would lead most people not

*J. O. Urmson, "Saints and Heroes," in *Essays in Moral Philosophy*, ed. A. I. Melden (Seattle: University of Washington Press, 1958), pp. 198–216. Reprinted by permission of the author and the publisher.

to do it, and does so as a result of exercising abnormal self-control; parallel to this a person may be called a hero (1) if he does his duty in contexts in which terror, fear, or a drive to self-preservation would lead most men not to do it, and does so by exercising abnormal self-control. Similarly for actions: an action may be called saintly (1) if it is a case of duty done by virtue of self-control in a context in which most men would be led astray by inclination or self-interest, and an action may be called heroic (1) if it is a case of duty done by virtue of self-control in a context in which most men would be led astray by fear or a drive for self-preservation. The only difference between the saintly and the heroic in this sort of situation is that the one involves resistance to desire and self-interest; the other, resistance to fear and self-preservation. This is quite a clear difference, though there may be marginal cases, or cases in which motives were mixed, in which it would be equally appropriate to call an action indifferently saintly or heroic. It is easy to give examples of both the heroic and the saintly as distinguished above: the unmarried daughter does the saintly deed of staying at home to tend her ailing and widowed father; the terrified doctor heroically stays by his patients in a plague-ridden city.

A person may be called a saint (2) if he does his duty in contexts in which inclination or self-interest would lead most men not to do it, not, as in the previous paragraph, by abnormal self-control, but without effort; parallel to this a person may be called a hero (2) if he does his duty in contexts in which fear would lead most men not to do it, and does so without effort. The corresponding accounts of a saintly (2) or heroic (2) action can easily be derived. Here we have the conspicuously virtuous deed, in the Aristotelian sense, as opposed to the conspicuously self-controlled, encratic deed of the previous paragraph. People thus purged of temptation or disciplined against fear may be rare, but Aristotle thought there could be such; there is a tendency today to think of such people as merely lucky or unimaginative, but Aristotle thought more highly of them than of people who need to exercise self-control.

It is clear that, in the two types of situation so far considered, we are dealing with actions that fall under the concept of duty. Roughly, we are calling a person saintly or heroic because he does his duty in such difficult contexts that most men would fail

in them. Since for the purposes of this paper I am merely conceding that we do use the terms "saintly" and "heroic" in these ways, it is unnecessary here to spend time arguing that we do so use them or in illustrating such uses. So used, the threefold classification of actions whose adequacy I wish to deny can clearly embrace them. I shall therefore pass immediately to a third use of the terms "heroic" and "saintly," which I am not merely willing to concede but obliged to establish.

I contend, then, that we may also call a person a saint (3) if he does actions that are far beyond the limits of his duty, whether by control of contrary inclination and interest or without effort; parallel to this we may call a person a hero (3) if he does actions that are far beyond the bounds of his duty, whether by control of natural fear or without effort. Such actions are saintly (3) or heroic (3). Here, as it seems to me, we have the hero or saint, heroic or saintly deed, par excellence; until now we have been considering but minor saints and heroes. We have considered the, certainly, heroic action of the doctor who does his duty by sticking to his patients in a plague-stricken city; we have now to consider the case of the doctor, who, no differently situated from countless other doctors in other places, volunteers to join the depleted medical forces in that city. Previously we were considering the soldier who heroically does his duty in the face of such dangers as would cause most to shirk—the sort of man who is rightly awarded the Military Medal in the British Army; we have now to consider the case of the soldier who does more than his superior officers would ever ask him to do—the man to whom, often posthumously, the Victoria Cross is awarded. Similarly, we have to turn from saintly self-discipline in the way of duty to the dedicated, self-effacing life in the service of others which is not even contemplated by the majority of upright, kind, and honest men, let alone expected of them.

Let us be clear that we are not now considering cases of natural affection, such as the sacrifice made by a mother for her child; such cases may be said with some justice not to fall under the concept of morality but to be admirable in some different way. Such cases as are here under consideration may be taken to be as little bound up with such emotions as affection as any moral action may be. We may consider an example of what is meant by "heroism" (3) in more detail to bring this out.

We may imagine a squad of soldiers to be practicing the throwing of live hand grenades; a grenade slips from the hand of one of them and rolls on the ground near the squad; one of them sacrifices his life by throwing himself on the grenade and protecting his comrades with his own body. It is quite unreasonable to suppose that such a man must be impelled by the sort of emotion that he might be impelled by if his best friend were in the squad; he might only just have joined the squad; it is clearly an action having moral status. But if the soldier had not thrown himself on the grenade would he have failed in his duty? Though clearly he is superior in some way to his comrades, can we possibly say that they failed in their duty by not trying to be the one who sacrificed himself? If he had not done so, could anyone have said to him, "You ought to have thrown yourself on that grenade"? Could a superior have decently ordered him to do it? The answer to all these questions is plainly negative. We clearly have here a case of a moral action, a heroic action, which cannot be subsumed under the classification whose inadequacy we are exposing.

But someone may not be happy with this conclusion, and for more respectable reasons than a desire to save the traditional doctrine. He may reason as follows: in so far as the soldier had time to feel or think at all, he presumably felt that he ought to do that deed; he considered it the proper thing to do; he, if no one else, might have reproached himself for failing to do his duty if he had shirked the deed. So, it may be argued, if an act presents itself to us in the way this act may be supposed to have presented itself to this soldier, then it is our duty to do it; we have no option. This objection to my thesis clearly has some substance, but it involves a misconception of what is at issue. I have no desire to present the act of heroism as one that is naturally regarded as optional by the hero, as something he might or might not do; I concede that he might regard himself as being obliged to act as he does. But if he were to survive the action only a modesty so excessive as to appear false could make him say, "I only did my duty," for we know, and he knows, that he has done more than duty requires. Further, though he might say to himself that so to act was a duty, he could not say so even beforehand to anyone else, and no one else could ever say it. Subjectively, we may say, at the time of action, the deed presented itself as a duty, but it was not a duty.

Another illustration, this time of saintliness, may help. It is recorded by Bonaventura that after Francis of Assisi had finished preaching to the birds on a celebrated occasion his companions gathered around him to praise and admire. But Francis himself was not a bit pleased; he was full of self-reproach that he had hitherto failed in what he now considered to be his duty to preach to the feathered world. There is indeed no degree of saintliness that a suitable person may not come to consider it to be his duty to achieve. Yet there is a world of difference between this failure to have preached hitherto to the birds and a case of straightforward breach of duty, however venial. First, Francis could without absurdity reproach himself for his failure to do his duty, but it would be quite ridiculous for anyone else to do so, as one could have done if he had failed to keep his vows, for example. Second, it is not recorded that Francis ever reproached anyone else for failure to preach to the birds as a breach of duty. He could claim this action for himself as a duty and could perhaps have exhorted others to preach to the birds; but there could be no question of reproaches for not so acting.

To sum up on this point, then, it seems clear that there is no action, however quixotic, heroic, or saintly, which the agent may not regard himself as obliged to perform, as much as he may feel himself obliged to tell the truth and to keep his promises. Such actions do not present themselves as optional to the agent when he is deliberating; but, since he alone can call such an action of his a duty, and then only from the deliberative viewpoint, only for himself and not for others, and not even for himself as a piece of objective reporting, and since nobody else can call on him to perform such an act as they can call on him to tell the truth and to keep his promises, there is here a most important difference from the rock-bottom duties which are duties for all and from every point of view, and to which anyone may draw attention. Thus we need not deny the points made by our imaginary objector in order to substantiate the point that some acts of heroism and saintliness cannot be adequately subsumed under the concept of duty.

Let us then take it as established that we have to deal in ethics not with a simple trichotomy of duties, permissible actions, and wrong actions, or any substantially similar conceptual scheme, but with something more complicated. We have to add at least the complication of actions that are certainly of moral worth but that fall outside the notion of a duty and seem to go beyond it, actions worthy of being called heroic or saintly. It should indeed be noted that heroic or saintly actions are not the sole, but merely conspicuous, cases of actions that exceed the basic demands of duty; there can be cases of disinterested kindness and generosity, for example, that are clearly more than basic duty requires and yet hardly ask for the high titles, "saintly" and "heroic." Indeed, every case of "going the second mile" is a case in point, for it cannot be one's duty to go the second mile in the same basic sense as it is to go the first—otherwise it could be argued first that it is one's duty to go two miles and therefore that the spirit of the rule of the second mile requires that one go altogether four miles, and by repetition one could establish the need to go every time on an infinite journey. It is possible to go just beyond one's duty by being a little more generous, forbearing, helpful, or forgiving than fair dealing demands, or to go a very long way beyond the basic code of duties with the saint or the hero. When I here draw attention to the heroic and saintly deed, I do so merely in order to have conspicuous cases of a whole realm of actions that lie outside the trichotomy I have criticized and therefore, as I believe, outside the purview of most ethical theories.

Before considering the implications for ethics of the facts we have up to now been concerned to note, it might be of value to draw attention to a less exalted parallel to these facts. If we belong to a club there will be rules of the club, written or unwritten, calling upon us to fulfill certain basic requirements that are a condition of membership, and that may be said to be the duties of membership. It may perhaps be such a basic requirement that we pay a subscription. It will probably be indifferent whether we pay this subscription by check or in cash—both procedures will be "right"—and almost certainly it will be quite indifferent what sort of hat we wear at the meetings. Here, then, we have conformity to rule which is the analogue of doing one's duty, breach of rule which is the analogue of wrongdoing, and a host of indifferent actions, in accordance with the traditional trichotomy. But among the rule-abiding members of such a club what differences there can be! It is very likely that there will be one, or perhaps two or three, to whose devotion and loyal service the success of the club is due far more than to the activities of all the other members together; these are the saints and the heroes of the clubs, who do more for them by far than any member could possibly be asked

to do, whose many services could not possibly be demanded in the rules. Behind them come a motley selection, varying from the keen to the lukewarm, whose contributions vary in value and descend sometimes to almost nothing beyond what the rules demand. The moral contribution of people to society can vary in value in the same way.

So much, then, for the simple facts to which I have wished to draw attention. They are simple facts and, unless I have misrepresented them, they are facts of which we are all, in a way, perfectly well aware. It would be absurd to suggest that moral philosophers have hitherto been unaware of the existence of saints and heroes and have never even alluded to them in their works. But it does seem that these facts have been neglected in their general, systematic accounts of morality. It is indeed easy to see that on some of the best-known theories there is no room for such facts. If for Moore, and for most utilitarians, any action is a duty that will produce the greatest possible good in the circumstances, for them the most heroic self-sacrifice or saintly self-forgetfulness will be duties on all fours with truth-telling and promise-keeping. For Kant, beyond the counsels of prudence and the rules of skill, there is only the categorical imperative of duty, and every duty is equally and utterly binding on all men; it is true that he recognizes the limiting case of the holy will, but the holy will is not a will that goes beyond duty but a will that is beyond morality through being incapable of acting except in accordance with the imperative. The nearest to an equivalent to a holy will in the cases we have been noting is the saintly will in the second sense we distinguished—the will that effortlessly does its duty when most would fail—but this is not a true parallel and in any case does not fall within the class of moral actions that go beyond duty to which our attention is primarily given. It is also true that Kant recognized virtues and talents as having conditional value, but not moral value, whereas the acts of heroism and saintliness we have considered have full moral worth, and their value is as unconditional as anyone could wish. Without committing ourselves to a scholarly examination of Kant's ethical works, it is surely evident that Kant could not consistently do justice to the facts before us. Intuitionism seems to me so obscurantist that I should not wish to prophesy what an intuitionist might feel himself entitled to say; but those intuitionists with whose works I am acquainted found their theories on an intuition of the fitting, the prima facie duty or the claim; the act that has this character to the highest degree at any time is a duty. While they recognize greater and lesser, stronger and weaker, claims, this is only in order to be able to deal with the problem of the conflict of duties; they assign no place to the act that, while not a duty, is of high moral importance.

Simple utilitarianism, Kantianism, and intuitionism, then, have no obvious theoretical niche for the saint and the hero. It is possible, no doubt, to revise these theories to accommodate the facts, but until so modified successfully they must surely be treated as unacceptable, and the modifications required might well detract from their plausibility. The intuitionists, for example, might lay claim to the intuition of a nonnatural characteristic of saintliness, of heroism, of decency, of sportingness, and so on, but this would give to their theory still more the appearance of utilizing the advantages of theft over honest toil.

Thus as moral theorists we need to discover some theory that will allow for both absolute duties, which, in Mill's phrase, can be exacted from a man like a debt, to omit which is to do wrong and to deserve censure, and which may be embodied in formal rules or principles, and also for a range of actions which are of moral value and which an agent may feel called upon to perform, but which cannot be demanded and whose omission cannot be called wrongdoing. Traditional moral theories, I have suggested, fail to do this. It would be well beyond the scope of this paper, and probably beyond my capacity, to produce here and now a full moral theory designed to accommodate all these facts, including the facts of saintliness and heroism. But I do think that of all traditional theories utilitarianism can be most easily modified to accommodate the facts, and would like before ending this paper to bring forward some considerations tending to support this point of view.

Moore went to great pains to determine exactly the nature of the intrinsically good, and Mill to discover the *summum bonum,* Moore's aim being to explain thereby directly the rightness and wrongness of particular actions and Mill's to justify a set of moral principles in the light of which the rightness or wrongness of particular actions can be decided. But, though there can be very tricky problems of duty, they do not naturally present themselves as problems whose solution depends upon an exact determination of an ultimate end; while the moral principles that come most readily to mind—truth-telling; promise-keeping; abstinence from murder, theft, and violence; and the like—make a nice dis-

crimination of the supreme good seem irrelevant. We do not need to debate whether it is Moore's string of intrinsic goods or Mill's happiness that is achieved by conformity to such principles; it is enough to see that without them social life would be impossible and any life would indeed be solitary, poor, nasty, brutish, and short. Even self-interest (which some have seen as the sole foundation of morality) is sufficient ground to render it wise to preach, if not to practice, such principles. Such considerations as these, which are not novel, have led some utilitarians to treat avoidance of the *summum malum* rather than the achievement of the *summum bonum* as the foundation of morality. Yet to others this has seemed, with some justification, to assign to morality too ignoble a place.

But the facts we have been considering earlier in this paper are surely relevant at this point. It is absurd to ask just what ideal is being served by abstinence from murder; but on the other hand nobody could see in acts of heroism such as we have been considering a mere avoidance of antisocial behavior. Here we have something more gracious, actions that need to be inspired by a positive ideal. If duty can, as Mill said, be exacted from persons as a debt, it is because duty is a minimum requirement for living together; the positive contribution of actions that go beyond duty could not be so exacted.

It may, however, be objected that this is a glorification of the higher flights of morality at the expense of duty, toward which an unduly cynical attitude is being taken. In so far as the suggestion is that we are forgetting how hard the way of duty may be and that doing one's duty can at times deserve to be called heroic and saintly, the answer is that we have mentioned this and acknowledge it; it is not forgotten but irrelevant to the point at issue, which is the place of duty in a moral classification of actions, not the problem of the worth of moral agents. But I may be taken to be acquiescing in a low and circumscribed view of duty which I may be advised to enlarge. We should, it may be said, hitch our wagons to the stars and not be content to say: you must do this and that as duties, and it would be very nice if you were to do these other things but we do not expect them of you. Is it perhaps only an imperfect conception of duty which finds it not to comprise the whole of morality? I want to examine this difficulty quite frankly, and to explain why I think that we properly recognize morality that goes beyond duty; for it seems to me incontestable that properly or improperly we do so.

No intelligent person will claim infallibility for his moral views. But allowing for this one must claim that one's moral code is ideal so far as one can see; for to say, "I recognize moral code A but see clearly that moral code B is superior to it," is but a way of saying that one recognizes moral code B but is only prepared to live up to moral code A. In some sense, then, everybody must be prepared to justify his moral code as ideal; but some philosophers have misunderstood this sense. Many philosophers have thought it necessary, if they were to defend their moral code as ideal, to try to show that it had a superhuman, a priori validity. Kant, for example, tried to show that the moral principles he accepted were such as any rational being, whether man or angel, must inevitably accept; the reputedly empiricist Locke thought that it must be possible to work out a deductive justification of moral laws. In making such claims such philosophers have unintentionally done morality a disservice; for their failure to show that the moral code was ideal in the sense of being a rationally justifiable system independent of time, place, circumstance, and human nature has led many to conclude that there can be no justification of a moral code, that moral codes are a matter of taste or convention.

But morality, I take it, is something that should serve human needs, not something that incidentally sweeps man up with itself, and to show that a morality was ideal would be to show that it best served man—man as he is and as he can be expected to become, not man as he would be if he were perfectly rational or an incorporeal angel. Just as it would be fatuous to build our machines so that they would give the best results according to an abstract conception of mechanical principles, and is much more desirable to design them to withstand to some extent our ham-fistedness, ignorance, and carelessness, so our morality must be one that will work. In the only sense of "ideal" that is of importance in action, it is part of the ideal that a moral code should actually help to contribute to human well-being, and a moral code that would work only for angels (for whom it would in any case be unnecessary) would be a far from ideal moral code for human beings. There is, indeed, a place for ideals that are practically unworkable in human affairs, as there is a place for the blueprint of a machine that will never go into production; but

it is not the place of such ideals to serve as a basic code of duties.

If, then, we are aiming at a moral code that will best serve human needs, a code that is ideal in the sense that a world in which such a code is acknowledged will be a better place than a world in which some other sort of moral code is acknowledged, it seems that there are ample grounds why our code should distinguish between basic rules, summarily set forth in simple rules and binding on all, and the higher flights of morality of which saintliness and heroism are outstanding examples. These grounds I shall enumerate at once.

1. It is important to give a special status of urgency, and to exert exceptional pressure, in those matters in which compliance with the demands of morality by all is indispensable. An army without men of heroic valor would be impoverished, but without general attention to the duties laid down in military law it would become a mere rabble. Similarly, while life in a world without its saints and heroes would be impoverished, it would only be poor and not necessarily brutish or short as when basic duties are neglected.

2. If we are to exact basic duties like debts, and censure failure, such duties must be, in ordinary circumstances, within the capacity of the ordinary man. It would be silly for us to say to ourselves, our children, and our fellow men, "This and that you and everyone else must do," if the acts in question are such that manifestly but few could bring themselves to do them, though we may ourselves resolve to try to be of that few. To take a parallel from positive law, the prohibition laws asked too much of the American people and were consequently broken systematically; and as people got used to breaking the law a general lowering of respect for the law naturally followed; it no longer seemed that a law was something that everybody could be expected to obey. Similarly in Britain the gambling laws, some of which are utterly unpractical, have fallen into contempt as a body. So, if we were to represent the heroic act of sacrificing one's life for one's comrades as a basic duty, the effect would be to lower the degree of urgency and stringency that the notion of duty does in fact possess. The basic moral code must not be in part too far beyond the capacity of the ordinary men or ordinary occasions, or a general breakdown of compliance with the moral code would be an inevitable consequence; duty would seem to be something high and unattainable, and not for "the

likes of us.'' Admirers of the Sermon on the Mount do not in practice, and could not, treat failure to turn the other cheek and to give one's cloak also as being on all fours with breaches of the Ten Commandments, however earnestly they themselves try to live a Christian life.

3. A moral code, if it is to be a code, must be formulable, and if it is to be a code to be observed it must be formulable in rules of manageable complexity. The ordinary man has to apply and interpret this code without recourse to a Supreme Court or House of Lords. But one can have such rules only in cases in which a type of action that is reasonably easy to recognize is almost invariably desirable or undesirable, as killing is almost invariably undesirble and promise-keeping almost invariably desirable. Where no definite rule of manageable complexity can be justified, we cannot work on that moral plane on which types of action can be enjoined or condemned as duty or crime. It has no doubt often been the case that a person who has gone off to distant parts to nurse lepers has thereby done a deed of great moral worth. But such an action is not merely too far beyond average human capacity to be regarded as a duty, as was insisted in (2) above; it would be quite ridiculous for everyone, however circumstanced, to be expected to go off and nurse lepers. But it would be absurd to try to formulate complicated rules to determine in just what circumstances such an action is a duty. This same point can readily be applied to such less spectacular matters as excusing legitimate debts or nursing sick neighbors.

4. It is part of the notion of a duty that we have a right to demand compliance from others even when we are interested parties. I may demand that you keep your promises to me, tell me the truth, and do me no violence, and I may reproach you if you transgress. But however admirable the tending of strangers in sickness may be it is not a basic duty, and we are not entitled to reproach those to whom we are strangers if they do not tend us in sickness; nor can I tell you, if you fail to give me a cigarette when I have run out, that you have failed in your duty to me, however much you may subsequently reproach yourself for your meanness if you do so fail. A line must be drawn between what we can expect and demand from others and what we can merely hope for and receive with gratitude when we get it; duty falls on one side of this line, and other acts with moral value on the other, and rightly so.

5. In the case of basic moral duties we act to some extent under constraint. We have no choice but to apply pressure on each other to conform in these fundamental matters; here moral principles are like public laws rather than like private ideas. But free choice of the better course of action is always preferable to action under pressure, even when the pressure is but moral. When possible, therefore, it is better that pressure should not be applied and that there should be encouragement and commendation for performance rather than outright demands and censure in the event of nonperformance. There are no doubt degrees in this matter. Some pressure may reasonably be brought to persuade a person to go some way beyond basic duty in the direction of kindliness and forbearance, to be not merely a just man but also not too hard a man. But, while there is nothing whatever objectionable in the idea of someone's being pressed to carry out such a basic duty as promise-keeping, there is something horrifying in the thought of pressure being brought on him to perform an act of heroism. Though the man might feel himself morally called upon to do the deed, it would be a moral outrage to apply pressure on him to do such a deed as sacrificing his life for others.

These five points make it clear why I do not think that the distinction of basic duty from other acts of moral worth, which I claim to detect in ordinary moral thought, is a sign of the inferiority of our everyday moral thinking to that of the general run of moral theorists. It in no way involves anyone in acquiescing in a second best. No doubt from the agent's point of view it is imperative that he should endeavor to live up to the highest ideals of behavior that he can think of, and if an action falls within the ideal it is for him irrelevant whether or not it is a duty or some more supererogatory act. But it simply does not follow that the distinction is in every way unimportant, for it is important that we should not demand ideal conduct from others in the way in which we must demand basic morality from them, or blame them equally for failures in all fields. It is not cynicism to make the minimum positive demands upon one's fellow men; but to characterize an act as a duty is so to demand it.

Thus we may regard the imperatives of duty as prohibiting behavior that is intolerable if men are to live together in society and demanding the minimum of cooperation toward the same end; that is why we have to treat compliance as compulsory and dereliction as liable to public censure. We do not need to ask with Bentham whether pushpin is as good as poetry, with Mill whether it is better to be Socrates dissatisfied or a fool satisfied, or with Moore whether a beautiful world with no one to see it would have intrinsic worth; what is and what is not tolerable in society depends on no such nice discrimination. Utilitarians, when attempting to justify the main rules of duty in terms of a *summum bonum,* have surely invoked many different types of utilitarian justification, ranging from the avoidance of the intolerable to the fulfillment of the last detail of a most rarefied ideal.

Thus I wish to suggest that utilitarianism can best accommodate the facts to which I have drawn attention; but I have not wished to support any particular view about the supreme good or the importance of pleasure. By utilitarianism I mean only a theory that moral justification of actions must be in terms of results. We can be content to say that duty is mainly concerned with the avoidance of intolerable results,

while other forms of moral behavior have more positive aims.

To summarize, I have suggested that the trichotomy of duties, indifferent actions, and wrongdoing is inadequate. There are many kinds of action that involve going beyond duty proper, saintly and heroic actions being conspicuous examples of such kinds of action. It has been my main concern to note this point and to ask moral philosophers to theorize in a way that does not tacitly deny it, as most traditional theories have. But I have also been so rash as to suggest that we may look upon our duties as basic requirements to be universally demanded as providing the only tolerable basis of social life. The higher flights of morality can then be regarded as more positive contributions that go beyond what is universally to be exacted; but while not exacted publicly they are clearly equally pressing *in foro interno* on those who are not content merely to avoid the intolerable. Whether this should be called a version of utilitarianism, as I suggest, is a matter of small moment.

PETER SINGER

Famine, Affluence, and Morality*

Peter Singer (1946–   ), author of the best-selling Animal Liberation, *teaches moral philosophy at LaTrobe University in Australia.*

As I write this, in November 1971, people are dying in East Bengal from lack of food, shelter, and medical care. The suffering and death that are occurring there now are not inevitable, not unavoidable in any fatalistic sense of the term. Constant poverty, a cyclone, and a civil war have turned at least nine million people into destitute refugees; nevertheless,

*Peter Singer, "Famine, Affluence, and Morality," *Philosophy & Public Affairs,* Vol 1, No. 3 (Spring, 1972), pp. 229–43. © 1972 by Princeton University Press. Reprinted by permission of the author and the publisher.

it is not beyond the capacity of the richer nations to give enough assistance to reduce any further suffering to very small proportions. The decisions and actions of human beings can prevent this kind of suffering. Unfortunately, human beings have not made the necessary decisions. At the individual level, people have, with very few exceptions, not responded to the situation in any significant way. Generally speaking, people have not given large sums to relief funds; they have not written to their parliamentary representatives demanding increased government assistance; they have not demonstrated in the streets, held symbolic fasts, or done anything else directed toward providing the refugees with the means to satisfy their essential needs. At the government level, no government has given the sort of massive aid that would enable the refugees to survive for more than a few days. Britain, for instance, has given rather more than most countries. It has, to date, given £14,750,000. For comparative purposes, Britain's share of the nonrecoverable development costs of the Anglo-French Concorde project is already in excess of £275,000,000, and on present estimates will reach £440,000,000. The implication is that the British government values a supersonic transport more than thirty times as highly as it values the lives of the nine million refugees. Australia is another country which, on a per capita basis, is well up in the "aid to Bengal" table. Australia's aid, however, amounts to less than one-twelfth of the cost of Sydney's new opera house. The total amount given, from all sources, now stands at about £65,000,000. The estimated cost of keeping the refugees alive for one year is £464,000,000. Most of the refugees have now been in the camps for more than six months. The World Bank has said that India needs a minimum of £300,000,000 in assistance from other countries before the end of the year. It seems obvious that assistance on this scale will not be forthcoming. India will be forced to choose between letting the refugees starve or diverting funds from her own development program, which will mean that more of her own people will starve in the future.[1]

These are the essential facts about the present situation in Bengal. So far as it concerns us here, there is nothing unique about this situation except its magnitude. The Bengal emergency is just the latest and most acute of a series of major emergencies in various parts of the world, arising both from natural and from man-made causes. There are also many parts of the world in which people die from malnutrition and lack of food independent of any special emergency. I take Bengal as my example only because it is the present concern, and because the size of the problem has ensured that it has been given adequate publicity. Neither individuals nor governments can claim to be unaware of what is happening there.

What are the moral implications of a situation like this? In what follows, I shall argue that the way people in relatively affluent countries react to a situation like that in Bengal cannot be justified; indeed, the whole way we look at moral issues—our moral conceptual scheme—needs to be altered, and with it, the way of life that has come to be taken for granted in our society.

In arguing for this conclusion I will not, of course, claim to be morally neutral. I shall, however, try to argue for the moral position that I take, so that anyone who accepts certain assumptions, to be made explicit, will, I hope, accept my conclusion.

I begin with the assumption that suffering and death from lack of food, shelter, and medical care are bad. I think most people will agree about this, although one may reach the same view by different routes. I shall not argue for this view. People can hold all sorts of eccentric positions, and perhaps from some of them it would not follow that death by starvation is in itself bad. It is difficult, perhaps impossible, to refute such positions, and so for brevity I will henceforth take this assumption as accepted. Those who disagree need read no further.

My next point is this: if it is in our power to prevent something bad from happening, without thereby sacrificing anything of comparable moral importance, we ought, morally, to do it. By "without sacrificing anything of comparable moral importance" I mean without causing anything else comparably bad to happen, or doing something that is wrong in itself, or failing to promote some moral good, comparable in significance to the bad thing that we can prevent. This principle seems almost as uncontroversial as the last one. It requires us only to prevent what is bad, and not to promote what is good, and it requires this of us only when we can do it without sacrificing anything that is, from the moral point of view, comparably important. I could even, as far as the application of my argument to the Bengal emergency is concerned, qualify the point so as to make it: if it is in our power to prevent something very bad from happening, without thereby sacrificing anything morally significant, we ought, morally, to do it. An application of this principle would be as follows: if I am walking past a shallow pond and see a child drowning in it, I ought to wade in and pull the child out. This will mean getting my clothes muddy, but this is insignificant, while the death of the child would presumably be a very bad thing.

The uncontroversial appearance of the principle just stated is deceptive. If it were acted upon, even in its qualified form, our lives, our society, and our world would be fundamentally changed. For the principle takes, firstly, no account of proximity or distance. It makes no moral difference whether the person I can help is a neighbor's child ten yards from me or a Bengali whose name I shall never know, ten thousand miles away. Secondly, the principle makes no distinction between cases in which I am the only person who could possibly do anything and cases in which I am just one among millions in the same position.

I do not think I need to say much in defense of the refusal to take proximity and distance into account. The fact that a person is physically near to us, so that we have personal contact with him, may make it more likely that we *shall* assist him, but this does not show that we *ought* to help him rather than another who happens to be further away. If we accept any principle of impartiality, universalizability, equality, or whatever, we cannot discriminate against someone merely because he is far away from us (or we are far away from him). Admittedly, it is possible that we are in a better position to judge what needs to be done to help a person near to us than one far away, and perhaps also to provide the assistance we judge to be necessary. If this were the case, it would be a reason for helping those near to us first. This may once have been a justification for being more concerned with the poor in one's own town than with the famine victims in India. Unfortunately for those who like to keep their moral responsibilities limited, instant communication and swift transportation have changed the situation. From the moral point of view, the development of the world into a "global village" has made an important, though still unrecognized, difference to our moral situation. Expert observers and supervisors, sent out by famine relief organizations or permanently stationed in famine-prone areas, can direct our aid to a refugee in Bengal almost as effectively as we could get it to someone in our own block. There would seem, therefore, to be no possible justification for discriminating on geographical grounds.

There may be a greater need to defend the second implication of my principle—that the fact that there are millions of other people in the same position, in respect to the Bengali refugees, as I am, does not make the situation significantly different from a situation in which I am the only person who can prevent something very bad from occurring. Again, of course, I admit that there is a psychological difference between the cases; one feels less guilty about doing nothing if one can point to others, similarly placed, who have also done nothing. Yet this can make no real difference to our moral obligations.[2] Should I consider that I am less obliged to pull the drowning child out of the pond if on looking around I see other people, no further away than I am, who have also noticed the child but are doing nothing? One has only to ask this question to see the absurdity of the view that numbers lessen obligation. It is a view that is an ideal excuse for inactivity; unfortunately most of the major evils—poverty, overpopulation, pollution—are problems in which everyone is almost equally involved.

The view that numbers do make a difference can be made plausible if stated in this way: if everyone in circumstances like mine gave £5 to the Bengal Relief Fund, there would be enough to provide food, shelter, and medical care for the refugees; there is no reason why I should give more than anyone else in the same circumstances as I am; therefore I have no obligation to give more than £5. Each premise in this argument is true, and the argument looks sound. It may convince us, unless we notice that it is based on a hypothetical premise, although the conclusion is not stated hypothetically. The argument would be sound if the conclusion were: if everyone in circumstances like mine were to give £5, I would have no obligation to give more than £5. If the conclusion were so stated, however, it would be obvious that the argument has no bearing on a situation in which it is not the case that everyone else gives £5. This, of course, is the actual situation. It is more or less certain that not everyone in circumstances like mine will give £5. So there will not be enough to provide the needed food, shelter, and medical care. Therefore by giving more than £5 I will prevent more suffering than I would if I gave just £5.

It might be thought that this argument has an absurd consequence. Since the situation appears to be that very few people are likely to give substantial amounts, it follows that I and everyone else in similar circumstances ought to give as much as possible, that is, at least up to the point at which by giving more one would begin to cause serious suffering for oneself and one's dependents—perhaps even beyond this point to the point of marginal utility, at which by giving more one would cause oneself and one's dependents as much suffering as one would prevent in Bengal. If everyone does this, however, there will be more than can be used for the benefit of the refugees, and some of the sacrifice will have been unnecessary. Thus, if everyone does what he ought to do, the result will not be as good as it would be if everyone did a little less than he ought to do, or if only some do all that they ought to do.

The paradox here arises only if we assume that the actions in question—sending money to the relief funds—are performed more or less simultaneously, and are also unexpected. For if it is to be expected that everyone is going to contribute something, then clearly each is not obliged to give as much as he would have been obliged to had others not been giving too. And if everyone is not acting more or less simultaneously, then those giving later will know how much more is needed, and will have no obligation to give more than is necessary to reach this amount. To say this is not to deny the principle that people in the same circumstances have the same obligations, but to point out that the fact that others have given, or may be expected to give, is a relevant circumstance: those giving after it has become known that many others are giving and those giving before are not in the same circumstances. So the seemingly absurd consequence of the principle I have put forward can occur only if people are in error about the actual circumstances—that is, if they think they are giving when others are not, but in fact they are giving when others are. The result of everyone doing what he really ought to do cannot be worse than the result of everyone doing less than he ought to do, although the result of everyone doing what he reasonably believes he ought to do could be.

If my argument so far has been sound, neither our distance from a preventable evil nor the number of other people who, in respect to that evil, are in the same situation as we are, lessens our obligation to mitigate or prevent that evil. I shall therefore take as established the principle I asserted earlier. As I have already said, I need to assert it only in its qualified form: if it is in our power to prevent something very bad from happening, without thereby sacrificing anything else morally significant, we ought, morally, to do it.

The outcome of this argument is that our traditional moral categories are upset. The traditional distinction between duty and charity cannot be drawn, or at least, not in the place we normally draw it. Giving money to the Bengal Relief Fund is regarded as an act of charity in our society. The bodies which collect money are known as "charities." These organizations see themselves in this way—if you send them a check, you will be thanked for your "generosity." Because giving money is regarded as an act of charity, it is not thought that there is anything wrong with not giving. The charitable man may be praised, but the man who is not charitable is not condemned. People do not feel in any way ashamed or guilty about spending money on new clothes or a new car instead of giving it to famine relief. (Indeed, the alternative does not occur to them.) This way of looking at the matter cannot be justified. When we buy new clothes not to keep ourselves warm but to look "well-dressed" we are not providing for any important need. We would not be sacrificing anything significant if we were to continue to wear our old clothes, and give the money to famine relief. By doing so, we would be preventing another person from starving. It follows from what I have said earlier that we ought to give money away, rather than spend it on clothes which we do not need to keep us warm. To do so is not charitable, or generous. Nor is it the kind of act which philosophers and theologians have called "supererogatory"—an act which it would be good to do, but not wrong not to do. On the contrary, we ought to give the money away, and it is wrong not to do so.

I am not maintaining that there are no acts which are charitable, or that there are no acts which it would be good to do but not wrong not to do. It may be possible to redraw the distinction between duty and charity in some other place. All I am arguing here is that the present way of drawing the distinction, which makes it an act of charity for a man living at the level of affluence which most people in the "developed nations" enjoy to give money to save someone else from starvation, cannot be supported. It is beyond the scope of my argument to consider whether the distinction should be redrawn or abolished altogether. There would be many other possible ways of drawing the distinction—for instance, one might decide that it is good to make other people as happy as possible, but not wrong not to do so.

Despite the limited nature of the revision in our moral conceptual scheme which I am proposing, the revision would, given the extent of both affluence and famine in the world today, have radical implications. These implications may lead to further objections, distinct from those I have already considered. I shall discuss two of these.

One objection to the position I have taken might be simply that it is too drastic a revision of our moral scheme. People do not ordinarily judge in the way

I have suggested they should. Most people reserve their moral condemnation for those who violate some moral norm, such as the norm against taking another person's property. They do not condemn those who indulge in luxury instead of giving to famine relief. But given that I did not set out to present a morally neutral description of the way people make moral judgments, the way people do in fact judge has nothing to do with the validity of my conclusion. My conclusion follows from the principle which I advanced earlier, and unless that principle is rejected, or the arguments shown to be unsound, I think the conclusion must stand, however strange it appears.

It might, nevertheless, be interesting to consider why our society, and most other societies, do judge differently from the way I have suggested they should. In a well-known article, J. O. Urmson suggests that the imperatives of duty, which tell us what we must do, as distinct from what it would be good to do but not wrong not to do, function so as to prohibit behavior that is intolerable if men are to live together in society.[3] This may explain the origin and continued existence of the present division between acts of duty and acts of charity. Moral attitudes are shaped by the needs of society, and no doubt society needs people who will observe the rules that make social existence tolerable. From the point of view of a particular society, it is essential to prevent violations of norms against killing, stealing, and so on. It is quite inessential, however, to help people outside one's own society.

If this is an explanation of our common distinction between duty and supererogation, however, it is not a justification of it. The moral point of view requires us to look beyond the interests of our own society. Previously, as I have already mentioned, this may hardly have been feasible, but it is quite feasible now. From the moral point of view, the prevention of the starvation of millions of people outside our society must be considered at least as pressing as the upholding of property norms within our society.

It has been argued by some writers, among them Sidgwick and Urmson, that we need to have a basic moral code which is not too far beyond the capacities of the ordinary man, for otherwise there will be a general breakdown of compliance with the moral code. Crudely stated, this argument suggests that if we tell people that they ought to refrain from murder and give everything they do not really need to famine relief, they will do neither, whereas if we tell them that they ought to refrain from murder and that it is good to give to famine relief but not wrong not to do so, they will at least refrain from murder. The issue here is: Where should we draw the line between conduct that is required and conduct that is good although not required, so as to get the best possible result? This would seem to be an empirical question, although a very difficult one. One objection to the Sidgwick-Urmson line of argument is that it takes insufficient account of the effect that moral standards can have on the decisions we make. Given a society in which a wealthy man who gives five percent of his income to famine relief is regarded as most generous, it is not surprising that a proposal that we all ought to give away half our incomes will be thought to be absurdly unrealistic. In a society which held that no man should have more than enough while others have less than they need, such a proposal might seem narrow-minded. What it is possible for a man to do and what he is likely to do are both, I think, very greatly influenced by what people around him are doing and expecting him to do. In any case, the possibility that by spreading the idea that we ought to be doing very much more than we are to relieve famine we shall bring about a general breakdown of moral behavior seems remote. If the stakes are an end to widespread starvation, it is worth the risk. Finally, it should be emphasized that these considerations are relevant only to the issue of what we should require from others, and not to what we ourselves ought to do.

The second objection to my attack on the present distinction between duty and charity is one which has from time to time been made against utilitarianism. It follows from some forms of utilitarian theory that we all ought, morally, to be working full time to increase the balance of happiness over misery. The position I have taken here would not lead to this conclusion in all circumstances, for if there were no bad occurrences that we could prevent without sacrificing something of comparable moral importance, my argument would have no application. Given the present conditions in many parts of the world, however, it does follow from my argument that we ought, morally, to be working full time to relieve great suffering of the sort that occurs as a result of famine or other disasters. Of course, mitigating circumstances can be adduced—for instance, that if we wear ourselves out through overwork, we shall be less effective than we would otherwise have been. Nevertheless, when all considerations of this sort have been taken into account, the conclusion remains: we ought to be preventing as much suffering as we can without sacrificing something else of comparable moral importance. This conclusion is one which we may be reluctant to face. I cannot see, though, why it should be regarded as a criticism of the position for which I have argued, rather than a criticism of our ordinary standards of behavior. Since most people are self-interested to some degree, very few of us are likely to do everything that we ought to do. It would, however, hardly be honest to take this as evidence that it is not the case that we ought to do it.

It may still be thought that my conclusions are so wildly out of line with what everyone else thinks and has always thought that there must be something wrong with the argument somewhere. In order to show that my conclusions, while certainly contrary to contemporary Western moral standards, would not have seemed so extraordinary at other times and in other places, I would like to quote a passage from a writer not normally thought of as a way-out radical, Thomas Aquinas.

Now, according to the natural order instituted by divine providence, material goods are provided for the satisfaction of human needs. Therefore the division and appropriation of property, which proceeds from human law, must not hinder the satisfaction of man's necessity from such goods. Equally, whatever a man has in super-abundance is owed, of natural right, to the poor for their sustenance. So Ambrosius says, and it is also to be found in the *Decretum Gratiani:* "The bread which you withhold belongs to the hungry; the clothing you shut away, to the naked; and the money you bury in the earth is the redemption and freedom of the penniless."[4]

I now want to consider a number of points, more practical than philosophical, which are relevant to the application of the moral conclusion we have reached. These points challenge not the idea that we ought to be doing all we can to prevent starvation, but the idea that giving away a great deal of money is the best means to this end.

It is sometimes said that overseas aid should be a government responsibility, and that therefore one ought not to give to privately run charities. Giving privately, it is said, allows the government and the noncontributing members of society to escape their responsibilities.

This argument seems to assume that the more people there are who give to privately organized famine relief funds, the less likely it is that the government will take over full responsibility for such aid. This assumption is unsupported, and does not strike me as at all plausible. The opposite view— that if no one gives voluntarily, a government will assume that its citizens are uninterested in famine relief and would not wish to be forced into giving aid—seems more plausible. In any case, unless there were a definite probability that by refusing to give one would be helping to bring about massive government assistance, people who do refuse to make voluntary contributions are refusing to prevent a certain amount of suffering without being able to point to any tangible beneficial consequence of their refusal. So the onus of showing how their refusal will bring about government action is on those who refuse to give.

I do not, of course, want to dispute the contention that governments of affluent nations should be giving many times the amount of genuine, no-strings-attached aid that they are giving now. I agree, too, that giving privately is not enough, and that we ought to be campaigning actively for entirely new standards for both public and private contributions to famine relief. Indeed, I would sympathize with someone who thought that campaigning was more important than giving oneself, although I doubt whether preaching what one does not practice would be very effective. Unfortunately, for many people the idea that "it's the government's responsibility" is a reason for not giving which does not appear to entail any political action either.

Another, more serious reason for not giving to famine relief funds is that until there is effective population control, relieving famine merely postpones starvation. If we save the Bengal refugees now, others, perhaps the children of these refugees, will face starvation in a few years' time. In support of this, one may cite the now well-known facts about the population explosion and the relatively limited scope for expanded production.

This point, like the previous one, is an argument against relieving suffering that is happening now, because of a belief about what might happen in the future; it is unlike the previous point in that very good evidence can be adduced in support of this belief abut the future. I will not go into the evidence here. I accept that the earth cannot support indefinitely a population rising at the present rate. This certainly poses a problem for anyone who thinks it important to prevent famine. Again, however, one could accept the argument without drawing the conclusion that it absolves one from any obligation to do anything to prevent famine. The conclusion that should be drawn is that the best means of preventing famine, in the long run, is population control. It would then follow from the position reached earlier that one ought to be doing all one can to promote population control (unless one held that all forms of population control were wrong in themselves, or would have significantly bad consequences). Since there are organizations working specifically for population control, one would then support them rather than more orthodox methods of preventing famine.

A third point raised by the conclusion reached earlier relates to the question of just how much we all ought to be giving away. One possibility, which has already been mentioned, is that we ought to give until we reach the level of marginal utility—that is, the level at which, by giving more, I would cause as much suffering to myself or my dependents as I would relieve by my gift. This would mean, of course, that one would reduce oneself to very nearly the material circumstances of a Bengali refugee. It will be recalled that earlier I put forward both a strong and a moderate version of the principle of preventing bad occurrences. The strong version, which required us to prevent bad things from happening unless in doing so we would be sacrificing something of comparable moral significance, does seem to require reducing ourselves to the level of marginal utility. I should also say that the strong version seems to me to be the correct one. I proposed the more moderate version—that we should prevent bad occurrences unless, to do so, we had to sacrifice something morally significant—only in order to show that even on this surely undeniable principle a great change in our way of life is required. On the more moderate principle, it may not follow that we ought to reduce ourselves to the level of marginal utility, for one might hold that to reduce oneself and one's family to this level is to cause something significantly bad to happen. Whether this is so I shall not discuss, since, as I have said, I can see no good reason for holding the moderate version of the principle rather

than the strong version. Even if we accepted the principle only in its moderate form, however, it should be clear that we would have to give away enough to ensure that the consumer society, dependent as it is on people spending on trivia rather than giving to famine relief, would slow down and perhaps disappear entirely. There are several reasons why this would be desirable in itself. The value and necessity of economic growth are now being questioned not only by conservationists, but by economists as well.[5] There is no doubt, too, that the consumer society has had a distorting effect on the goals and purposes of its members. Yet looking at the matter purely from the point of view of overseas aid, there must be a limit to the extent to which we should deliberately slow down our economy; for it might be the case that if we gave away, say, forty percent of our Gross National Product, we would slow down the economy so much that in absolute terms we would be giving less than if we gave twenty-five percent of the much larger GNP that we would have if we limited our contribution to this smaller percentage.

I mention this only as an indication of the sort of factor that one would have to take into account in working out an ideal. Since Western societies generally consider one percent of the GNP an acceptable level for overseas aid, the matter is entirely academic. Nor does it affect the question of how much an individual should give in a society in which very few are giving substantial amounts.

It is sometimes said, though less often now than it used to be, that philosophers have no special role to play in public affairs, since most public issues depend primarily on an assessment of facts. On questions of fact, it is said, philosophers as such have no special expertise, and so it has been possible to engage in philosophy without committing oneself to any position on major public issues. No doubt there are some issues of social policy and foreign policy about which it can truly be said that a really expert assessment of the facts is required before taking sides or acting, but the issue of famine is surely not one of these. The facts about the existence of suffering are beyond dispute. Nor, I think, is it disputed that we can do something about it, either through orthodox methods of famine relief or through population control or both. This is therefore an issue on which philosophers are competent to take a position. The issue is one which faces everyone who has more money than he needs to support himself and his dependents, or who is in a position to take some sort of political action. These categories must include practically every teacher and student of philosophy in the universities of the Western world. If philosophy is to deal with matters that are relevant to both teachers and students, this is an issue that philosophers should discuss.

Discussion, though, is not enough. What is the point of relating philosophy to public (and personal) affairs if we do not take our conclusions seriously? In this instance, taking our conclusion seriously means acting upon it. The philosopher will not find it any easier than anyone else to alter his attitudes and way of life to the extent that, if I am right, is involved in doing everything that we ought to be doing. At the very least, though, one can make a start. The philosopher who does so will have to sacrifice some of the benefits of the consumer society, but he can find compensation in the satisfaction of a way of life in which theory and practice, if not yet in harmony, are at least coming together.

NOTES

1. There was also a third possibility: that India would go to war to enable the refugees to return to their lands. Since I wrote this paper, India has taken this way out. The situation is no longer that described above, but this does not affect my argument, as the next paragraph indicates.

2. In view of the special sense philosophers often give to the term, I should say that I use "obligation" simply as the abstract noun derived from "ought," so that "I have an obligation to" means no more, and no less, than "I ought to." This usage is in accordance with the definition of "ought" given by the *Shorter Oxford English Dictionary:* "the general verb to express duty or obligation." I do not think any issue of substance hangs on the way the term is used; sentences in which I use "obligation" could all be rewritten, although somewhat clumsily, as sentences in which a clause containing "ought" replaces the term "obligation."

3. J. O. Urmson, "Saints and Heroes," in *Essays in Moral Philosophy,* ed. Abraham I. Melden (Seattle and London, 1958), p. 214 (included in this anthology. pp. 541–548). For a related but significantly different view see also Henry Sidgwick, *The Methods of Ethics,* 7th edn. (London, 1907), pp. 220–221, 492–493.

4. *Summa Theologica,* II-II, Question 66, Article 7, in *Aquinas, Selected Political Writings,* ed. A. P. d'Entreves, trans. J. G. Dawson (Oxford, 1948), p. 171.

5. See, for instance, John Kenneth Galbraith, *The New Industrial State* (Boston, 1967); and E. J. Mishan, *The Costs of Economic Growth* (London, 1967).

P A U L   W .   T A Y L O R

Ethical Egoism*

Paul W. Taylor (1923–   ) teaches philosophy at Brooklyn College and the Graduate Center of the City University of New York.

The distinction between psychological egoism and ethical egoism [is] made as follows. Psychological egoism is intended to be a factual, explanatory account of human motivation, stating a universal empirical truth about man's nature. Ethical egoism, on the other hand, is intended as a normative theory which

*From Paul W. Taylor, *Principles of Ethics, An Introduction* (Belmont, Calif.: Wadsworth Publishing Co., 1975), Chap. 3. Reprinted by permission of the publisher and the author.

sets up an ultimate standard or principle for determining right and wrong conduct. Psychological egoism means to tell us why people act the way they do, while ethical egoism attempts to tell us how people ought to act. The question now is, What reasons are there for accepting, or rejecting, the principle of ethical egoism as a guide to conduct?

One proposed argument for accepting the principle has already been examined. This states (1) that psychological egoism is true, and (2) that ethical egoism provides the only normative principle which it is psychologically possible for people to comply with. Since the purpose of accepting a normative principle is to guide people's conduct, once psychological egoism is accepted, ethical egoism must be accepted, too. For if psychological egoism is true, each person's actions can only be motivated by what he believes will promote his self-interest. What actually *will* promote his self-interest must then become the sole basis for judging conduct. No other principle could function as a norm for human conduct because every individual, being egoistically motivated, would be unable to use a nonegoistic principle in deciding how to act.

Some reasons for questioning the truth of psychological egoism have been brought out in the preceding section of this chapter, and its final acceptance or rejection is left open. Whatever one's views on psychological egoism might be, however, the normative principle of ethical egoism must still be considered on its own merits. For some ethical egoists do not believe that their theory presupposes the acceptance of psychological egoism. Furthermore, they do not appeal to psychological egoism in support of their theory since they think psychological egoism actually gives a false account of human motivation. These ethical egoists hold that a person *can* be altruistically motivated to perform actions which he himself correctly believes to be contrary to his own self-interest. Nevertheless, these ethical egoists continue, no action is *right* unless it does further the individual's well-being. So let us now inquire into the grounds for accepting—or rejecting—ethical egoism independently of any stand we might take regarding the truth or falsity of psychological egoism.

When the ethical egoist is asked why everyone ought to act so as to promote his own self-interest, there are two sorts of reply he might make. First, he can simply assert that this is an ultimate principle of normative ethics. Or secondly, he might argue that this principle, if consistently followed by everyone, would have better results than some other guiding norm. Putting aside the first reply for the moment, let us look at the second.

The claim that everyone's following one principle would have *better* results than everyone's following another principle presupposes a standard of goodness or value by which some results are judged superior to others. If this standard were anything but the fulfillment of everyone's self-interest to the greatest possible extent, it would seem that the position is not (universal) ethical egoism. Yet the fulfillment of everyone's self-interest in this argument constitutes an *end* to which the practice of each person following the rule "Do what will most promote my own interests" is taken as a *means*. Now suppose there were another, more effective means for bringing about this same end. For example, suppose that everyone's following the rule "Do what will most promote the interests of all people affected by my action" would actually tend to result in the fulfillment of everyone's self-interest to a greater extent than would result from everyone's complying with "Do what will most promote my own interests." In that case, the egoist would have to admit that it is our duty to follow the first rule. But that rule . . . is a principle of utilitarianism, not of egoism. To justify his own theory, the egoist would have to show that the universal following of the rule of self-interest will in fact more effectively promote everyone's self-interest than will the universal practice of utilitarianism. Whether this can indeed be shown is left to the reader's judgment, after consideration of utilitarianism. . . .

However, most ethical egoists have supported their theory in the first way mentioned above. They have held each person's promotion of his own self-interest to be the supreme norm or ultimate principle of ethics, not merely a means to some further end. . . .

What objections might be raised against the theory of universal ethical egoism, and what replies might be given to those objections? The most frequent criticism of universal ethical egoism is that it must be false because it contains an *internal inconsistency*. The argument goes as follows. The universal ethical egoist says that each person should promote his own self-interest. There will be many situations, however, in which a conflict of interest occurs between the egoist and others. In such situations, if others pursue their ends the egoist himself will be hindered or prevented from pursuing his own, and vice versa. Yet according to his theory, an action ought to be done whenever it furthers the interests of the agent, *whoever that agent may be*. It follows that in all cases of conflict of interest between the egoist himself and others, the principle of universal ethical egoism entails contradictory ought-statements. For it entails that another person ought to do a certain action (because it would promote his interests) and at the same time it entails that he ought not to, since his doing it would interfere with the egoist's pursuit of his own interests. Similarly, if the egoist's action would benefit him, then according to his theory he ought to do it. However, in a situation where his action conflicts with another's self-interest, that other would *correctly* judge that the action ought not to be done. Thus the two contradictory judgments: "The egoist ought to do the act" and "The egoist ought not to do the act" would both be true of the same action. It follows, therefore, that universal ethical egoism is internally inconsistent.

The egoist's reply to this argument is that, according to his theory, he need not *assert* that others ought to pursue their interests when doing so conflicts with the promotion of his own. He can simply keep quiet about the matter. Indeed, if he is to further his interests in the most effective way possible he should publicly urge others to be altruistic, since by following his counsel they will not interfere with him but, on the contrary, will help him attain his goals. If, then, he is true to the egoist principle that he ought to do everything that will most effectively further his own ends, he will not advocate publicly that everyone be an ethical egoist. Instead, he will declare that all persons should be altruists—at least with regard to the way they treat him!

It has seemed to the critics of egoism, however, that this reply does not get rid of the inconsistency. They point out that it follows from the theory of universal egoism that *each and every person* ought to think in the way described above. Thus everyone ought to urge others to be altruistic as a means to promoting his self-interest. And since each person's pursuit of self-interest requires that he not become altruistic himself, the theory implies that no one should be an altruist. Hence, every individual ought to do something (namely, promote his own self-interest by getting others to be altruistic) and at the same time ought to prevent another from doing what that other ought to do (namely, getting others to be altruistic without becoming altruistic himself).

The logical consequence of universal ethical egoism thus appears to be that everyone should do a certain sort of thing while actually it is impossible that everyone do it successfully. If one person succeeds in doing it (that is, succeeds in getting another to be altruistic while remaining egoistic himself), someone else must fail to do it (if he happens to be the person whom the other has successfully made altruistic). Ethical egoism need not be *advocated* universally for this internal inconsistency to arise. It is an inconsistency that arises from everyone's *practicing* ethical egoism by *not* advocating that everyone become an ethical egoist.

It should be noted that these considerations apply to what we [can call] "universal ethical egoism." The other two forms of ethical egoism, which [are] desig-nated by the terms "individual" and "personal," can escape the foregoing difficulties, since neither claims that every person should promote his own self-interest. The "individual" ethical egoist holds that *he* should promote his self-interest and that all others should also promote his, the ethical egoist's, self-interest. There is nothing internally inconsistent with everyone's putting this principle into practice. The "personal" ethical egoist, on the other hand, asserts that *he* should promote his own self-interest and simply has nothing to say, one way or the other, concerning what anyone else ought to do. Here also, no contradiction is involved in what the personal ethical egoist claims ought to be done.

Can we accept, then, either of these forms of ethical egoism as a justifiable normative system? That there remain certain problems which each of them has to face becomes clear from the following reflections.

Consider, first, the position of the individual ethical egoist. He says that his interests ought to be furthered not only by his own actions but also by those of everyone else. One implication of his view is that his wishes, desires, and needs have a right to be fulfilled even at the cost of frustrating the wants of others. His ultimate principle, in other words, entails an inequality of rights among persons. We can then formulate a challenge which will reasonably be addressed to the egoist by all others: "Why should your self-interest count more than anyone else's? On what grounds do your wants and needs make a higher claim to fulfillment than those of anyone else? Unless you can show that you merit special consideration, there is no reason why others owe you a duty (namely, to further your interests) which you do not owe to them. And your theory itself offers no basis for your claim to special consideration, since anyone else can propose the same ultimate principle on his own behalf and thus endow his interests with a higher claim to fulfillment than yours. Your theory provides no *reasons* why you should be given unique treatment." It is difficult to see how the egoist could reply to this challenge. As long as others knew that it was contrary to their interests to accept his principle, they would need to be shown why they should accept it before they could have a reason to do the actions it required of them. But the only way the individual egoist could justify others' accepting his principle would be by pointing out some *characteristic* of himself that made him deserving of special consideration. If he were to do this, however, the possession of the given characteristic would be the supreme principle of his system, not the principle of egoism itself. He would then have to admit that if anyone else were found to have the attribute in question, that person's interest would have a claim to fulfillment equal to his own. And this would be giving up individual ethical egoism.

Let us look, next, at the position of personal ethical egoism. The personal egoist escapes the foregoing criticism since he does not claim that others ought to promote his self-interest. He simply says that he ought to do those actions that will most benefit him, and makes no ought-statements about anyone else's actions (not even the statement that they ought not to interfere with or frustrate him in the pursuit of his interests). It is important to realize that the principle of personal ethical egoism does not provide any basis for judging the rightness or wrongness of the conduct of any individual other than the egoist himself. Once we see clearly that personal ethical egoism has this implication, we see how it is possible to raise the following objection to it. (It is an objection, be it noted, which cannot be raised against the theories of universal or individual ethical egoism.)

How can personal ethical egoism be considered a normative ethical system at all? Since it tells only one person in the world what *he* ought and ought not to do but remains completely silent about the actions of everyone else, it turns out to be nothing more than a private policy of action adopted by one person with regard to himself alone. It is a policy by which he can guide his own conduct, but it cannot serve to guide anyone else's. Consequently it does not qualify as a moral principle. Even if everyone were to accept the principle, it would leave all but one person completely in the dark about what they morally ought or ought not to do. It may indeed be *consistent* for someone to adopt the principle for himself and use it as a policy governing his own actions. But such a personal policy cannot provide others with moral reasons for or against doing anything they please.

This argument assumes that an ethical system must give an account of *moral* reasons for action and that a *moral* reason for action cannot be merely a personal policy adopted by one individual as a guide to his own conduct alone. If a statement about the properties or consequences of an action constitutes a moral reason for (or against) the action, then it must be a reason for *anyone's* performing (or refraining from) that kind of conduct, whenever *anyone* is in a situation in which doing and refraining from an action of the given kind are alternatives open to him. . . .

W. D. F A L K

Morality, Self, and Others*

W. David Falk (1906–) was born in Germany and taught philosophy in England, Scotland, Australia, and the United States. For many years he was at the University of North Carolina.

1

In: And how can you say that I never had a moral education? As a child, I was taught that one ought not to maltreat other children, ought to share one's sweets with them, ought to keep tidy and clean; as an adolescent, that one ought to keep one's word, to work, to save, to leave off drink, not to waste the best of years of one's life, to let reason govern one's emotions and actions. Nor did I simply learn that one is *called upon* to act in these ways by paternal authority and social custom on pain of censure. I learned to appreciate that one *ought* to do these things *on their merits,* and that what one ought to do on its merits does not depend on the request or enjoinders of anyone. The facts in the case themselves make one liable, as a reflective person, to act in these ways

*Reprinted from *Morality and the Language of Conduct,* ed. Hector-Neri Castañeda and George Nakhnikian, pp. 25–47, by permission of The Wayne State University Press, the author and the editors. Copyright © 1963, The Wayne State University Press. Parts 4, 5, and 6 are here omitted.

of one's own accord: they provide one with choice-supporting reasons sufficient to determine one if one knows them and takes diligent account of them.

Out: I know you were taught all this. But why did your teacher say that you ought to act in these ways?

In: Why? For very cogent reasons. My tutor was a student of the Ancients. The moral man, "the man of practical wisdom," he kept quoting Aristotle, "is the man who knows how to deliberate well about what is good and useful for himself." And surely, he would say, you can see for yourself: if you don't act sociably, who will act sociably towards you? Uncleanliness breeds disease. Without work, how are you to live? Without savings, what about your future? Drink leaves one a wreck. Indulging one's sorrows makes them worse. The wasted years, one day you will regret them when it is too late. People who cannot govern themselves are helpless before fortune, without the aid and comfort of inner strength.

Out: And so you think that you had a moral education? Let me tell you, you never even made a start. For what were you taught? That there are things that you ought to do or to avoid on your own account. But one does not learn about morality that way. What one *morally* ought to do is what one ought to do on account of others, or for the sake of some good state of things in general. Now had you been taught to appreciate that you ought to keep clean so as to be pleasing to others, and that you ought to do what moral custom requires for the sake of the general good, then, and then only, would you have learned the rudiments of moral duty.

In: Very well, my upbringing was too narrow. One would hardly be a human being if the good of others, or of society at large, could not weigh with one as a cogent reason for doing what will promote it. So one has not fully learned about living like a rational and moral being unless one has learned to appreciate that one ought to do things out of regard for others, and not only out of regard for oneself.

Out: No, you have still not got my point. I am saying that only insofar as you ought to do things— no matter whether for yourself or for others—for the sake of others, is the reason a moral reason and the ought a moral ought. Reasons of self-regard are not moral reasons at all, and you can forget about them in the reckoning of your *moral* obligations.

In: But this seems artificial. A moral education surely should teach one all about the principles of orderly living and the reasons which tell in their favor. And if there are also perfectly good personal reasons which tell in their favor, why suppress them?

To be sure, in talking to people in ordinary life, we do no such thing. If they say "Why ought I to act sociably?" we say "For the general good as well as your own." If they say "Why ought I to be provident?" we say "For your own good as well as that of others." In short, we offer mixed reasons, and none of these reasons can be spared. One ought not to lie because this is a good social rule, and equally because the habit of evasiveness is destructive of oneself as a person. And one ought not to take a drink or indulge one's sorrows, or waste the best years of one's life primarily out of proper regard for oneself, much as there may be other-regarding reasons as well. If morality were all social service, and one had no moral responsibilities towards oneself or towards others, the moral inconveniences of life would be far less than they are. So I don't see the point of saying "But one has no *moral* commitment to do anything except insofar as one ought to do it on account of others." To say this seems like encouraging people not to bother about doing things insofar as they ought to do them only for personal reasons, as after all this is not a moral ought.

Out: But one does not speak of a moral duty to do things for one's own sake. If one ought to save in order to provide for one's own future, one regards this as a precept not of morals but of prudence. It would be different if one ought to save in order to provide for one's dependents. Moral commitments are those which one has as a moral being, and what makes one a moral being is that one has commitments towards others and does not evade them.

In: Not everyone will agree that as a moral being one has only commitments towards others or that only such commitments are properly "moral." The Greeks, for example, took a wider view. For Plato the equivalent of a moral being was the just or right-living person, and of a moral commitment the right and just course—the one which the right-living person would be led to take. And this right-living person was one who would keep himself in good shape as a sane and self-possessed being, and who would do whatever good and sufficient reasons directed him to do. This is why for Plato and the Greeks temperance and prudence were no less among the just man's commitments than paying his debts and not willfully harming others, and why the one was not treated any less as a moral commitment than the other. The Greeks placed the essence of man as a moral being in his capacity to direct himself on rational grounds; and his commitments as a moral being were therefore all those which he seriously incurred as a properly self-directing being.

Out: Citing the Greeks only shows how distant their concept of morality is from ours. We will not call every rational commitment "moral" or equate the moral with the rational man.

In: This is broadly so, although not entirely. Our concept of morality vacillates between the Greek and the Christian tradition. We associate "moral" with "social" commitment, and the "morally good man" with the "selfless man." But we also speak of man as a "moral agent," of his "moral freedom" and "moral powers"; and here we refer to his whole capacity of self-direction by good and sufficient reasons. One may speak without strain of a personal and social ethic, and refer to the negligent disregard of oneself as a vice, and a sign of moral defect. We call the improvident man "morally weak," and we call the man who can resist drink in company on account of his health or who sticks to his vocation in adversity a man of "moral strength and character." There is certainly little difference in the qualities needed to live up to a social or a personal ought. It takes self-denial to provide for one's future, moral courage to stick to one's vocation. One may show one's mettle as a moral agent here no less than in selfless care for others. There are contemporary moralists who call "moral" any "authentic" commitment of a self-governing person, whether its grounds are social or personal. What justifies them is the broader use of the term which is also part of our language and tradition.

Out: And how eccentric this use is. Our very concept of a moral being is inseparable from the notion of submission of self to a good other than one's own. It is not conceivable that a man should have moral duties on a desert island, devoid of man or beast. Would one say that he still had a moral duty to do what was good for him? You may as well go on and say that if a shipwrecked fellow arrived to share his vegetables, it might be his moral duty to let him starve rather than starve himself.

In: The good of others need not always have the overriding claim on one, if this is what you mean. One could say to a good-hearted and weak-willed person, "For your own sake, you ought to stop neglecting your future, even if this hurts others." This

would not be a typically "moral" ought, but one may be giving sound moral advice.

Out: And so, if beneficence had the better of this person, you should call him morally irresponsible and blameworthy. On your showing, he has evaded a moral commitment, and for such evasions one is held morally responsible and liable to censure. But surely, even if I granted your case, one would not call him blameworthy and a morally bad man; as indeed in any case where a person fails to do what his own good requires we do not call him morally bad, but only imprudent, unwise, rash. It is quite a different offense to be slack about brushing one's teeth, than to be negligent about providing dentures for others. And this is so precisely because the second is a moral offense and the first is not and because one is blameworthy for the one and not for the other.

In: I agree that there is a difference. One is only called morally bad and is held answerable to *others* for neglecting what one ought to do out of regard for them. And this is understandable enough. After all, insofar as one fails to do only what one's own good requires, the failing is no one's concern but one's own. But then I should not say that such self-neglect was in no sense morally irresponsible and blameworthy. If it does not call for blame by others, it still calls for self-reproach. A rational person is responsible to himself for not being evasive about anything that he is convinced that he really ought to do. And the lack of moral strength and courage in personal matters, although commonly viewed as an amicable vice, is an amicable vice only in the estimation of others since it is not directly a threat to them.

However, we are not making headway. You find it repugnant to call a commitment "moral" unless its grounds are social and unless its nonobservance makes one liable not only to social censure but also to self-reproach; and so be it. Perhaps our disagreement is only verbal, and despite some misgivings, I am ready to settle for your usage. Let us only speak of a moral ought where one ought to do things on account of others. But let us not be misled. For it still does not follow that if one ought to do things on one's own account, this ought may not still be otherwise functioning *like* a moral ought.

Out: How could it be like a moral ought if it is not a moral ought?

In: Because when one thinks of a moral ought, one thinks not only that its grounds are social but also that it has a special force and cogency. A moral ought commits one in all seriousness and in every way, without leaving any reasonable option to act otherwise. Your view comes to saying that if an ought is to be moral it must satisfy two conditions: it must seriously bind one in every way, and it must do so for other-regarding reasons. On your showing, a personal ought cannot be moral, as it cannot satisfy one of these conditions simply by having personal grounds. But it may still satisfy the other condition, and be as cogently binding and action-guiding in its force and function as a moral ought. This is why I can only accept your usage with one proviso: that one may also say that there are other than strictly moral commitments which a right-living person may have to reckon with no less than his strictly moral ones.

Out: Surely you don't expect me to fall for this. When I say ''Don't count the purely personal ought as moral'' I am not saying ''Count it as well, but call it by another name.'' My point is precisely that it does not function like a moral ought at all. Personal reasons do not commit one to do anything with the same cogency as social reasons. In fact, in calling them reasons of prudence or expediency, we deprecate them. We regard them as inferior, and often disreputable, guides to action. So I won't let you reduce my position to triviality. That only the social commitments are essentially moral must be taken as implying that only they have the characteristic moral force.

In: I thought that this was at the back of our discussion all along. It usually is so with people who are so insistent on your usage, although part of the trouble is that one can never be sure. First one is told that a moral ought is one that commits one on other-regarding grounds and that a personal ought is not a moral ought *for this reason.* But then comes the further suggestion that it is not only different from a moral ought in this way, but is also otherwise inferior. It gives directives, but directives of a somehow shady kind. One way or other, the idea is that a commitment that has personal grounds is either not properly a commitment at all, or, if one in any way, then one that belongs in some limbo of disrepute. But your argument so far has done nothing to prove this point. From your language rule, it only follows that the personal ought must be unlike a moral ought in one essential respect, but not, except by way of confusion, that it must be therefore also unlike a moral ought in other respects too. You might as well say ''Surely a lay-analyst is not a doctor,'' as one is not a doctor without a medical degree, and take this to

be proof that a lay-analyst cannot otherwise cure like a doctor either. ''No lay-analyst is a doctor'' is strictly and trivially true in one way, and may be misleading and tendentiously false in another. And the same with ''No personal ought is a *moral* ought.'' Your language rule makes this strictly and trivially true; but it does not go to show that a personal ought cannot otherwise be *like* a moral ought by being seriously committing or by taking precedence in a conscientious calculus of action-guiding considerations. My point is that, even if this were so, your appeal to usage cannot settle this matter. Logical grammar can decree that only social reasons are properly called ''moral.'' But it cannot decide what reasons can, or cannot, be seriously committing for human beings.

Out: But what I am saying seems substantially true. What one ought to do on account of others is the prototype of the categorically binding ought. Personal reasons have not got the binding cogency of other-regarding reasons, and one deprecates them as inferior and disreputable.

In: And there is some truth in this. Personal and social reasons are not on the same footing in the economy of action-guiding considerations. Personal reasons are very commonly less thoroughly committing, they are often inferior reasons, and not rarely discreditable. But why this is so is a different matter and has not yet been touched on in any way. What is more, personal reasons need not always be in this inferior position. They are often not intrinsically discreditable, and become inferior guides to action only where there are other reasons in the case deserving of prior considerations. Take someone concerned for his health, or future, or self-respect. Surely these are respectable aspirations and there may be things which he ought to do on account of them without violating other claims. His health requires that he be temperate, his self-respect that he live without evasion. Would it not then be positively remiss of him not to act in these ways? If he did not, one would say that he had failed to do what a man in his position really ought to have done, and precisely for the reason which he had. And, if one can say this, what remains of the blemish?

This is why it remains perplexing to me why commitments on personal grounds should be excluded from the orbit of moral teaching, and why modern moralists, unlike the Ancients, should disdain to mention them as an integral part of the moral life. For they may also be cogent and sometimes over-ridingly cogent commitments to action. And if they are not the whole of morals, why not count them as part of them? For it also seems natural to say that to teach someone all about morality is to teach him about all the valid directives for action; about all those things which he might not otherwise do readily but which, for good and compelling reasons in the nature in the case, he ought to do and would have to break himself into doing whether for the sake of others or his own.

There is, I agree, one tendency to say that the moral man acts in accordance with precepts of self-lessness. But there is also another tendency to say that he is the man to organize his life in accordance with all valid precepts. Our disagreement has exhib-ited the kind of shuttle-service between rival con-siderations better known as the dialectic of a problem. It may be that this shuttle-service is maintained by a cleft in the very concept of morality. This concept may have grown from conflicting or only partially overlapping observations, which are not fully recon-ciled in ordinary thinking.

Out: If this is so, I would have to be shown, for common sense still seems to me right in its dispar-agement of personal reasons.

In: Very well, then we shall have to consider why personal reasons should function as a less cogent guide to action than social ones. I shall admit that in more ways than one the personal ought presents a special case, but not that it presents a case for dis-paragement except in special contexts. After this, the question of whether the personal ought is properly called moral or not will appear less important, partly because it will have become plainer why there is a question. Nor shall I try to offer a ruling on this point. With a background of discourse as intricate and full of nuance as in this case, discretion is the better part of valor, and clarification is a safer bet than decision.

2

Whenever one remarks that clearly there are things which one ought to avoid or do if only for one's own sake, someone is sure to say, "No doubt; but any such ought is only a precept of prudence or expedi-ency." It is a textbook cliché against Hobbes that

his account of morality comes to just this. And this is said as if it were an obvious truth and enough to discredit all such precepts in one go. This assumes a great deal and settles nothing.

What it assumes is this: that everything that one ever does for one's own sake, one does as a matter of prudence *or* expediency; that there is no difference between these two; that morality always differs from prudence as a scent differs from a bad smell; and that everyone knows how so and why.

None of this will do.

In the first place, not everything done for oneself is done for reasons of prudence. That one ought to insure one's house, save for one's old age, not put all one's money into one venture, are precepts of prudence. But it is not a precept of prudence, though it may be a good precept, that someone ought to undergo a dangerous operation as a long shot to restoring his health rather than linger under a dis-ability forever after.

The point is that prudence is only one way of looking after oneself. To act prudently is to play safe, for near-certain gains at small risks. But some good things one cannot get in this way. To get them at all one has to gamble, taking the risk of not getting them even so, or of coming to harm in the process. If one values them enough, one will do better by oneself to throw prudence to the winds, to play for high stakes, knowing full well the risk and the price of failure. Explorers, artists, scientists, mountain-eers are types who may serve themselves better by this course. So will most people at some juncture. Thus, if someone values security, then that he ought to save in order to be secure is a precept of prudence. But that someone ought to stick to his vocation when his heart is in it enough to make it worth risking security or health or life itself is not a precept of *prudence,* but of *courage.*

One says sometimes, "I ought to save, as I *want* to be prudent," but sometimes "as I *ought* to be prudent." One may also decide that in one's own best interests one ought to be prudent rather than daring, or daring rather than prudent, as the case may be. Now, that one ought to do something as it would be prudent is a dictate of prudence. But that one really ought to be prudent, in one's own best inter-ests, would not be a dictate of prudence again. One then ought to play safe in order to serve oneself *best* and not in order to serve oneself *safely.*

A dictate of prudence where one wants to be pru-dent but ought to be courageous in one's own best interests is a dictate of timidity. A dictate of courage, where one feels reckless but ought to be prudent, is a dictate of foolhardiness. Both will then plainly be morally imperfect precepts. But there is nothing obviously imperfect about a dictate of prudence where one ought to be prudent, or a dictate of courage where one ought to be daring. Such precepts seem near-moral enough to allow one to call the habit of acting on them a virtue. The Ancients considered both prudence and courage as moral virtues. Oddly enough, in our time, one is more ready to view courage on one's own behalf as a moral virtue than prudence. It needs the reminder that precepts of self-protection may be precepts of courage as well as of prudence for one to see that any precept of self-protection may have a moral flavor. I think that the dim view which we take of prudence corresponds to a belief that to be daring is harder than to be level-headed, a belief most likely justified within our own insurance-minded culture. But such belief would have seemed strange to Bishop Butler and the fashionable eighteenth-century gentlemen to whom he addressed himself. Prudence in Butler's time, as throughout the ancient world, was not yet the cheap commodity which it is with us; and the price of virtue varies with the market.

There are other precepts of self-protection which are not "just a matter of prudence" either. That one ought not to take to drugs or drink, indulge oneself in one's sorrows, waste one's talents, commit suicide just in the despair of the moment, are precepts made of sterner stuff. One wants to say, "Surely, it is more than just a matter of prudence that one ought to avoid these things." And rightly so. The effect on oneself of taking to drugs or drink, or of any of the others, is not conjectural, but quite certain. To avoid them is therefore more than a matter of *taking no risks*. Sometimes, when one looks down a precipice, one feels drawn to jump. If one refrains, it will hardly be said of one, "How prudent he is, he takes no chances." The avoidance of excesses of all kinds in one's own best interests is in this class. The habit of avoiding them the Greeks called temperance, a virtue distinct from prudence.

Another error is to equate the prudent with the expedient, and, again, the expedient with everything that is for one's own good. To save may be prudent; but whether it is expedient or convenient to start now is another matter. With a lot of money to spare at the moment it will be expedient; otherwise it will not. But it may be prudent all the same. Again, one marries in the hope of finding happiness; but marriage in this hope is not a marriage of convenience. The point is that reasons of expediency are reasons of a special sort: reasons for doing something on the ground that it is incidentally at hand to serve one's purpose, or because it serves a purpose quite incidental to the purpose for which one would normally be doing this thing. One marries for reasons of expediency when one marries for money, but not when in hope of finding happiness. Hobbes said that "men never act except with a view to some good to themselves." This would be quite different from saying that "they never act except with a view to what is expedient."

There is also this difference between the prudent and the expedient: one can speak of "rules of prudence," but less well of "rules of expediency." The expedient is what happens to serve. It is not therefore easily bottled in rules.

The word "prudence" is used too freely in still one more context. When one wishes to justify the social virtues to people, a traditional and inviting move is to refer them, among other things at least, to their own good. "You ought to hold the peace, be honest, share with others." "Why?" "Because an order in which such practices were universal is of vital concern to you; and your one hope of helping to make such an order is in doing your share." The classical formulation of this standard move is Hooker's, quoted with approval by Locke: "If I cannot but wish to receive good . . . how should I look to have any part of my desire herein satisfied, unless I myself be careful to satisfy the like desire: my desire therefore to be loved of my equals in nature, as much as possible may be, imposes upon me a *natural duty* of bearing to themward fully the like affection."

Now, it is said again, "So defended, the social duties come to no more than precepts of prudence"; and this goes with the veiled suggestion that it is morally improper to use this defense. But, even if so defended, the social duties are not necessarily reduced purely to precepts of prudence. For they may be recommended in this way either as mere *rules* or as *principles* of self-protection; and as principles they would be misdescribed as mere precepts of prudence. The distinction is this: When one says, "People ought to practice the social values, if only for their own benefit," one may be saying, "They ought to practice them for this reason as a *rule*, i.e., normally, as much as each time this is likely to be for their own good." Or one may be saying, "They ought to practice them for this reason not merely as a rule but as a *matter of principle*, i.e., every time, whether at that time this is likely to be for their good or not." And one might defend the adoption of this principle by saying, "Because your best, even if slim, hope of contributing to a society fit for you to live in lies in adding to the number of principled people who will do their share each time, without special regard for their good at that time."

Now this seems to me a precept of courage rather than one of prudence. The game of attempting by one's actions to make society a place fit for one to live in is a gamble worth the risk only because of the known price of not attempting it. This gamble is a root condition of social living. One is sure to give hostages to fortune, but again, what other hope has one got? Hence, if a man practiced the social virtues, thinking that he ought to as a matter of principle, and on these grounds, one will praise him for his *wisdom*, his firm grasp of vital issues, his steadfastness, his courage. But one will not necessarily congratulate him on his prudence. For many times the prudent course might have been otherwise. It may be wise to persist in being honest with cheats, or forbearing with the aggressive, or helpful to those slow to require helpfulness; but it might have been more prudent to persist for no longer than there was requital, or not even to start before requital was assured.

Now would it be a moral precept or not that, if only out of proper care for oneself, one ought to act on principles of wisdom and courage? That one ought to risk life in order to gain it? And, assuming a society of men acting fixedly on these principles but no others, would it or would it not contain men of moral virtue? One might as well ask, "Is a ski an article of footwear?" There is no more of a straight answer here than there. One may say, "Not quite"; and the point of saying this needs going into. But it would be more misleading to say, "Not at all." For it is part of the meaning of "moral precept" that it prescribes what a man would do in his wisdom—if he were to consider things widely, looking past the immediate concerns of self and giving essentials due weight before incidentals. As it is also part of what is meant by one's moral capacities that one can live by such considerations, it becomes fruitless after a time to press the point whether such precepts are properly called moral.

There are then varieties of the personal ought, differing in the considerations on which they are based and the qualities needed to follow them; and they all seem at least akin to a "moral" ought in their action-guiding force and function. But I grant that one does not want to speak of more than a kinship, and the point of this needs considering. One's hesitancy derives from various sources which have to be traced one by one.

Some of the hesitancy comes from contexts where one can say disparagingly, "He did this *only* for reasons of prudence, *only* for reasons of expediency, *only* for himself." This plainly applies sometimes, but it does not apply always. One would hardly say of someone without dependents, "He thought that he ought to save, but *only* for reasons of prudence"; or of someone, "He thought that he ought to have the carpenter in along with the plumber, but *only* for reasons of expediency or convenience"; or "He thought that he ought to become a doctor, but *only* because the career would suit him." "Only" has no point here. Why else should a man without dependents save, except to be prudent? Why else should anyone have the carpenter in along with the plumber, except for convenience? What better reason is there normally for choosing a career than that it will suit one? On the other hand, there is point in saying, "He held the peace only because it was prudent," "He saved only because it was convenient," "He practices the social virtues only for self-protection." It is plain why "only" applies here and is disparaging. One says "only" because something is done for the wrong or for not quite the right reason—done for *one* reason where there is *another* and nearer reason for doing it anyway. Personal reasons are often in this position, and then they are disparaged as inferior. One saves "only" because it is expedient, if one ought to have saved anyway for reasons of prudence. One holds the peace "only" because it was prudent when one ought to have done so anyway as a matter of principle and even if it had not been prudent. And one practices the social virtues "only" for self-protection when one does not *also* practice them for the general good.

The last case is different from the others. Plainly, one ought to practice the social virtues as principles of general good. But on none but perhaps pure Christian principles would it hold, or necessarily hold, that one ought to practice them on this ground unconditionally, however great the provocation to oneself. The case for the social virtues is weakened when the social environment becomes hostile and intractable by peaceable means; it is correspondingly strengthened where they can also be justified as wise principles of self-protection. That someone practices forbearance "only" as a wise principle of self-protection is not therefore to say that he practices it for a reason which is neither here nor there; but rather for a reason which falls short of all the reason there is. This was, in effect, the view of the Old Natural Law moralists—Hooker, Grotius, Puffendorf: the social virtues derive joint support from our natural concern for our own good and for that of society. Hobbes streamlined this account by denying the second, which provoked subsequent moralists to deny the first. Both Hobbes's sophistical toughness and the well-bred innocence of the academic moralists since are distorted visions which are less convincing than the unsqueamish common sense of the philosophers and divines of earlier times.

3

So far we have met no reason for deprecating every personal ought. Men often have cause to be temperate, courageous, wise for their own good. This is often the only, or the nearest, reason why they should. It is then pointless to go on complaining, "But they still only act so for their own sakes." "Only" is a dangerous word.

Even so one feels that somehow a commitment that has only personal grounds is morally inferior. "One ought to risk one's life in order to gain it" seems near-moral enough. But compare it with "One ought to risk one's life in order to save others." This still seems different. And this is so not only because the one has a personal reason and the other has not, but also because where the reason is social rather than personal, the ought itself feels different—more binding, more relentless, and more properly called "moral" for this reason. The real inferiority of the personal ought seems here to lie in a lack of formal stringency.

There are such differences of stringency between "I ought to save, as I *want* to provide for my future" and "I ought to save, as I *ought* to provide for my children." The first prescribes saving as a means to an end which one *is* seeking; the second as a means to an end which in turn one *ought* to seek. The first therefore commits one formally less than the second. It leaves one at liberty to escape the commitment

by renouncing the ultimate end, which the second does not. One may, as Kant did, call the first ought hypothetical and non-moral, and the second categorical and moral on account of this difference. The distinction is made to rest on a formal difference of the binding force and not at all on any material difference in the justifying grounds. The formally "moral" commitment is to an ultimate end or rule of life and to what one ought to do on account of it in any particular case.

Now the personal ought comes more typically as non-moral and the social ought as moral in form. One says, "You don't *want* to make your misery worse, so you ought not to dwell on it"; "You *want* to secure your future, so you ought to be prudent and save." One might also say "You *want* to provide for your children, so you ought to save"; and then formally this too would be a non-moral ought although its grounds are other-regarding. But this is the less typical case. One is often more grudging about the needs of others than one's own. So there is here less occasion for saying, "You ought to do this on account of an end which you *are* seeking"; and more for saying, "You ought to do it on account of an end which in turn you *ought* to seek."

This typical difference between the personal and the social ought raises two questions: one, whether it is an inherent feature of the personal ought to be never more than non-moral in form; the other, whether, even if this were so, it would be any the worse as a possibly serious commitment. Both of these positions have been taken. One's own good one always seeks. It is not therefore among the ends which one ever ought to seek in the absence of a sufficient inclination. But with the good of others, or the avoidance of harm to them, it is different. Here are ends which one does not always seek, but ought to seek all the same: ends which one may still have reason for seeking on their own account; which one would be led to seek on a diligently comprehending and imaginative review of them (of what doing good, or harm, inherently amount to). Only the social ought, therefore, may bind one to the choice of the final end as well as of the means, while the personal ought binds one only to the means on account of an end which one wants already. The personal ought is therefore only non-moral in form, and "only" once again signifies a defect. But all this is misleading. One does not always seek one's own good as much as one has reasonable ground for seeking it, and about this I shall say more later. But even supposing that one did, then all precepts of self-regard would prescribe what one ought to do consistently with an already desired end. But they would not therefore be negligible or improper all the time.

It is true that what one ought to do consistently with a desired end need not be what one really ought to do at all. The end, or the means toward it, may prove undesirable on further scrutiny either by reason of what it is in itself or of the special circumstances of the case. I ought to save as I wish for security, and there is nothing inherently wrong with the end or the means, and so far so good. But I also ought to support my mother, and I cannot do both. Then maybe I ought not to do *all told* what otherwise I ought to have done. But in this case, the precept of prudence would have been less than "only" non-moral. It would have been invalid all told, and counter-moral altogether. But surely not every case is like this.

For often there is nothing wrong with the things which one cares for on one's own behalf, and one really does care for them. Even if one had the abstract option to give them up, one has no serious wish to do so. One often does care for one's life or health or career or the regard of others and one often *may* without violating other claims. And one always *may* care, if one does, for one's peace of mind or self-respect. And so what one ought to do as far as these ends go one really ought to do. As one wants to live, one really ought to look after one's health. As one wants to be liked by others, one really ought to keep a civil tongue. As one wants to live after one's own fashion, one really ought to stick to one's vocation in adversity. As one wants to be able to respect oneself or, in Hume's phrase, "bear one's own survey," one really ought to conduct oneself as one thinks that one has good reasons for doing. All these precepts tell one what one ought to do consistently with a personal end which one actually has at heart; and where they hold after scrutiny, they hold no less validly and conclusively than any fully "moral" precept. The conscientious man would have to take notice of them no less than of the others. They deserve to be called "semi-moral" at least.

I keep allowing that a distinction remains. "I ought to work hard, as I *want* to succeed" is still a different kind of commitment from "I ought to work hard as I *ought* to provide for others." The difference is partly in the end, personal in the one case, impersonal in the other. But this quite apart, there is another reason for the difference. The second ought has a quality of sternness which is lacking from the first, and which is a product of its *form,* not of its *content.* For the second is an ought twice over. It says that one ought to take steps for an end which one ought to pursue ultimately. The first is an ought only once; it says that one ought to take steps for an end with regard to which one is at liberty as far as it goes. So the second ought subjects one to a regimen which is complete. It commits one *through and through,* whereas the semi-moral ought does not. And this through-and-throughness gives to the moral ought its notorious stern flavor. It makes it more imposing and often more onerous. One is having one's socks pulled up all over. And additional qualities are required of one for appreciating it and acting on it: not only forethought and consistency, but also the ability to appreciate an end as committing by reason of its own nature, which, among other things, requires sympathetic understanding and imagination. No wonder that a moral ought inspires those confronted with it with awe. The semi-moral ought cannot compete with this, though when it comes to the precepts of wisdom and courage on one's own behalf they come near enough.

However, having given the formally moral ought its due, I want to add that respect for it should be no reason for slighting the other. For in the first place, and as a reassurance to those who regard lack of onerousness as a defect, though the semi-moral ought is not so bad, it may be bad enough. How hard it is to pull up one's socks does not necessarily depend on their number; two commodious socks may respond more readily than one shrunken one. One semi-moral and one moral case may serve as examples. If one really *wants* to do a thing and do it well, one ought to take trouble. And if one really *ought* to do good to the sick, one ought to telephone and inquire how they are getting on. The first requires a lot: putting oneself into harness, forgoing all sorts of things which one would rather do, particularly at that moment, coping with aches and pains and anxieties, playing the endless game of snakes and ladders with achievement, and yet going on, nursing one's purpose. The second, though in form a commitment through and through, requires nothing but getting up and dialing a number. It may need a great deal not to put things off, not to dwell on one's miseries, not to spend improvidently, all simply because one really ought not to in one's own best interest. The ought that lays down the law on these things may be little imposing in form. But such is the bulk of the stuff which compounds the "moral" inconveniences of ordinary life. And one also measures oneself and others by the show that is made on this front.

But then it is not the lack of onerousness as much as that of formal stringency that is felt to discredit the semi-moral ought. It still is not binding like the moral ought, simply as it is not committing through and through. Moreover, its very subservience to an end which is only desired seems something amiss, as if a man should rather act always for the sake of ends which he ultimately ought to seek, and not just of ends which he happens to be seeking even if nothing is wrong with them.

This sense of guilt about the non-obligatory rests partly on excessive zeal for original sin. What the natural man in one desires never can be quite as it should. It is always "Tell me what you want to do, and I shall tell you what you ought to do instead." But there is also a failure to see that not every semi-moral commitment is renounceable at will. Not every situation need confront one with a commitment through and through, and it is improper to demand that it should or to deplore that it does not.

When one ought to do a thing on account of some desired end, then one need not always be at liberty to escape the commitment by renouncing the end. It depends on whether one is free to give up the end itself, and this is not always so. One says of some ends, "If you want to seek it you may, and if you don't want to you need not." There is here no reason against seeking the end, nor reason enough to tell one to seek it in the absence of a desire for it. And one is free to escape a commitment on account of such an end simply by giving up the end. But in the case of other ends one will say, "If you want to seek it you may, but if you do not want to you still ought to all the same." Again there is no reason against seeking the end if one wants to, but here there would be still reason for seeking it even if one did not want to. A commitment on account of such an end one may not escape at will as one is not here free to give up the end. It is arguable whether commitments on personal grounds are not often in this position. One ought to be temperate as one wants to preserve one's health. And although this is a semi-moral ought as

far as it goes one need not be free to get out of it at will. For even if one ceased to care about the end, one might still here have reasonable ground for caring, and ought to care all the same.

An ought of this kind commits one on account of an end which one seeks as well as ought to seek. And this makes it like an ought through and through, but still not quite. There can be ends which one seeks and ought to seek. But insofar as one *is* seeking such an end, it is strained to say that one also *ought* to seek it at the same time. One would rather say that if one were not seeking it already, then one ought to be seeking it all the same. This is why, if someone is perfectly willing about an end, a commitment on account of this end would still not for him have the form of a commitment through and through; and this although it is potentially such a commitment and would turn into one as soon as he ceased to be readily inclined towards the end.

The point is that ought applies only where there is a case for pulling one's socks up. The same action may be viewed in otherwise the same circumstances either as one which one ought to do, or as one which one wants to and may do, according to the psychological starting point. One normally wants to have one's breakfast, and one would find it improper to have it put before one with the remark, "You ought to eat this morning." "Why ought I? Don't I eat every morning anyway?" But if one were convalescent, the remark would be in place. Nor would one say to a notoriously indulgent parent, "You ought not to be harsh with your children" (though one might wonder whether he *may* be so indulgent). The remark applies to a parent bad at controlling his temper. If I resolved to become an early riser and succeeded, I might report in retrospect, "For the first month it was a duty, but afterwards it ceased to be a duty and became a habit, if not a pleasure."

None of this should be surprising. Ought is an action-guiding concept. It expresses the notion that one is liable to direction by reasons in the case which would motivate one if one gave them due consideration. And one cannot be *liable* to direction by reasons except in a matter of doing what one is not fully motivated to do already. This is why it cannot be an obligation for one to do what one wants to do anyway, much as it might become an obligation for one to do it if one ceased to want to. This is also why, when one really wants to do something, the natural question to ask is not, "And *ought* I to do this thing?" but rather, "And *may* I do it?" or "Would there be anything wrong with it?" or "Ought I perhaps *not* to do it?" One looks for possible reasons against, not for possible reasons for. And what point would there be in doing anything more? When one really wants to do something, one already has, *for* doing it, all the reason one needs. And this is also why one only says "You ought to" to others when one takes it that there is a case for changing their present frame of mind. But to wonder whether one ought to (as distinct from wondering whether one may, or perhaps ought not to) where one already wants to would be like wondering whether to sit down when seated; and to say "You ought to" to someone quite ready to, would be like advising a sitting man to take a seat.

There is no ought for those blessed with wants which are not wrong.

One may object: "But surely one can say that everyone ought to do good, and if there were benevolent people this would not make this false." And this is correct, but no refutation. What raises a problem are general statements like "People ought to do good," "One ought to be tolerant." But one may make a general statement without having to specify all the conditions when it shall or shall not hold. One says in general, "Butter will melt in the sun"; and if someone interjected, "But *not* when one has just melted it on the kitchen stove," this would be no rebuttal. "*This* butter will melt in the sun," when I am bringing it dripping from the kitchen, would be different. This particular butter is not *liable* to melt, even though it remains true that butter is. The same with "People ought to do good." This is a general statement, and one need not state the obvious: that it will not apply to someone whose heart needs no melting as it is soft already. Nor does one use "one ought to" directively to people, except for general purposes of propaganda. "I ought to" and "you ought to" are in a logically different class.

One makes general ought-statements about standard ends and practices towards which people commonly have no sufficient inclination. These ought-statements apply particularly to doing things for others, and less so to doing things for oneself. And this alone could explain why one normally does not say that people ought to care for their own good. For the question of whether they *ought* to does not here normally arise. They can be trusted with a modicum of well adjustment towards this end—they seek it, and, within limits, they may seek it. Hence, what one ought to do on account of one's own good is commonly a commitment on account of a desired end, much as it might also turn into a commitment through and through with a loss of immediate interest in the end. Nor could one reasonably hope that such commitments were more imposing in form than they are. On the contrary, one may say that the less imposing the ought, the better designed for living the man.

Why Be Moral?

PLATO

The Immoralists' Challenge*

Plato (B.C. 427?–347) lived and taught in Athens. Most of his surviving works have the form of fictitious dialogues between Socrates (who had been his teacher) and other Athenian intellectuals.

With these words I was thinking that I had made an end of the discussion; but the end, in truth, proved to be only a beginning. For Glaucon, who is always the most pugnacious of men, was dissatisfied at Thrasymachus' retirement; he wanted to have the battle out. So he said to me: Socrates, do you wish really to persuade us, or only to seem to have persuaded us, that to be just is always better than to be unjust?

I should wish really to persuade you, I replied, if I could.

Then you certainly have not succeeded. Let me ask you now:—How would you arrange goods—are there not some which we welcome for their own sakes, and independently of their consequences, as, for example, harmless pleasures and enjoyments, which delight us at the time, although nothing follows from them?

I agree in thinking that there is such a class, I replied.

Is there not also a second class of goods, such as knowledge, sight, health, which are desirable not only in themselves, but also for their results?

Certainly, I said.

And would you not recognize a third class, such as gymnastic, and the care of the sick, and the physi-

cian's art; also the various ways of money-making—these do us good but we regard them as disagreeable; and no one would choose them for their own sakes, but only for the sake of some reward or result which flows from them?

There is, I said, this third class also. But why do you ask?

Because I want to know in which of the three classes you would place justice?

In the highest class, I replied, among those goods which he who would be happy desires both for their own sake and for the sake of their results.

Then the many are of another mind; they think that justice is to be reckoned in the troublesome class, among goods which are to be pursued for the sake of rewards and of reputation, but in themselves are disagreeable and rather to be avoided.

I know, I said, that this is their manner of thinking, and that this was the thesis which Thrasymachus was maintaining just now, when he censured justice and praised injustice. But I am too stupid to be convinced by him.

I wish, he said, that you would hear me as well as him, and then I shall see whether you and I agree. For Thrasymachus seems to me, like a snake, to have been charmed by your voice sooner than he ought to have been; but to my mind the nature of justice and injustice have not yet been made clear. Setting aside their rewards and results, I want to know what they are in themselves, and how they inwardly work in the soul. If you please, then, I will revive the argument of Thrasymachus. And first I will speak of the nature and origin of justice accord-

*From Plato, *The Republic*, ii. 357A–367E, trans. B. Jowett.

ing to the common view of them. Secondly, I will show that all men who practice justice do so against their will, of necessity, but not as a good. And thirdly, I will argue that there is reason in this view, for the life of the unjust is after all better far than the life of the just—if what they say is true, Socrates, since I myself am not of their opinion. But still I acknowledge that I am perplexed when I hear the voices of Thrasymachus and myriads of others dinning in my ears; and, on the other hand, I have never yet heard the superiority of justice to injustice maintained by any one in a satisfactory way. I want to hear justice praised in respect of itself; then I shall be satisfied, and you are the person from whom I think that I am most likely to hear this; and therefore I will praise the unjust life to the utmost of my power, and my manner of speaking will indicate the manner in which I desire to hear you too praising justice and censuring injustice. Will you say whether you approve of my proposal?

Indeed I do; nor can I imagine any theme about which a man of sense would oftener wish to converse.

I am delighted, he replied, to hear you say so, and shall begin by speaking, as I proposed, of the nature and origin of justice.

They say that to do injustice is, by nature, good; to suffer injustice, evil; but that the evil is greater than the good. And so when men have both done and suffered injustice and have had experience of both, not being able to avoid the one and obtain the other, they think that they had better agree among themselves to have neither; hence there arise laws and mutual covenants; and that which is ordained by law is termed by them lawful and just. This they affirm to be the origin and nature of justice;—it is a mean or compromise, between the best of all, which is to do injustice and not be punished, and the worst of all, which is to suffer injustice without the power of retaliation; and justice, being at a middle point between the two, is tolerated not as a good, but as the lesser evil, and honoured by reason of the inability of men to do injustice. For no man who is worthy to be called a man would ever submit to such an agreement if he were able to resist; he would be mad if he did. Such is the received account, Socrates, of the nature and origin of justice.

Now that those who practice justice do so involuntarily and because they have not the power to be unjust will best appear if we imagine something of

this kind: having given both to the just and the unjust power to do what they will, let us watch and see whither desire will lead them; then we shall discover in the very act the just and unjust man to be proceeding along the same road, following their interest, which all natures deem to be their good, and are only diverted into the path of justice by the force of law. The liberty which we are supposing may be most completely given to them in the form of such a power as is said to have been possessed by Gyges the ancestor of Croesus the Lydian. According to the tradition, Gyges was a shepherd in the service of the king of Lydia; there was a great storm, and an earthquake made an opening in the earth at the place where he was feeding his flock. Amazed at the sight, he descended into the opening, where, among other marvels, he beheld a hollow brazen horse, having doors, at which he stooping and looking in saw a dead body of stature, as appeared to him, more than human, and having nothing on but a gold ring; this he took from the finger of the dead and reascended. Now the shepherds met together, according to custom, that they might send their monthly report about the flocks to the king; into their assembly he came having the ring on his finger, and as he was sitting among them he chanced to turn the collet of the ring inside his hand, when instantly he became invisible to the rest of the company and they began to speak of him as if he were no longer present. He was astonished at this, and again touching the ring he turned the collet outwards and reappeared; he made several trials of the ring, and always with the same result—when he turned the collet inwards he became invisible, when outwards he reappeared. Whereupon he contrived to be chosen one of the messengers who were sent to the court; where as soon as he arrived he seduced the queen, and with her help conspired against the king and slew him, and took the kingdom. Suppose now that there were two such magic rings, and the just put on one of them and the unjust the other; no man can be imagined to be of such an iron nature that he would stand fast in justice. No man would keep his hands off what was not his own when he could safely take what he liked out of the market, or go into houses and lie with any one at his pleasure, or kill or release from prison whom he would, and in all respects be like a God among men. Then the actions of the just would be as the actions of the unjust; they would both come at last to the same point. And this we may truly affirm to be a great proof that a man is just, not willingly or because he thinks that justice is any good to him individually, but of necessity, for wherever any one thinks that he can safely be unjust, there he is unjust. For all men believe in their hearts that injustice is far more profitable to the individual than justice, and he who argues as I have been supposing, will say that they are right. If you could imagine any one obtaining this power of becoming invisible, and never doing any wrong or touching what was another's, he would be thought by the lookers-on to be a most wretched idiot, although they would praise him to one another's faces, and keep up appearances with one another from a fear that they too might suffer injustice. Enough of this.

Now, if we are to form a real judgment of the life of the just and unjust, we must isolate them; there is no other way; and how is the isolation to be effected? I answer: Let the unjust man be entirely unjust, and the just man entirely just; nothing is to be taken away from either of them, and both are to be perfectly furnished for the work of their respective lives. First, let the unjust be like other distinguished masters of craft; like the skillful pilot or physician, who knows intuitively his own powers and keeps within their limits, and who, if he fails at any point, is able to recover himself. So let the unjust make his unjust attempts in the right way, and lie hidden if he means to be great in his injustice (he who is found out is nobody): for the highest reach of injustice is: to be deemed just when you are not. Therefore I say that in the perfectly unjust man we must assume the most perfect injustice; there is to be no deduction, but we must allow him, while doing the most unjust acts, to have acquired the greatest reputation for justice. If he have taken a false step he must be able to recover himself; he must be one who can speak with effect, if any of his deeds come to light, and who can force his way where force is required by his courage and strength, and command of money and friends. And at his side let us place the just man in his nobleness and simplicity, wishing, as Aeschylus says, to be and not to seem good. There must be no seeming, for if he seem to be just he will be honoured and rewarded, and then we shall not know whether he is just for the sake of justice or for the sake of honours and rewards; therefore, let him be clothed in justice only, and have no other covering; and h must be imagined in a state of life the opposite of the former. Let him be the best of men, and let him be thought the worst; then he will have been put to the proof; and we shall see whether he will be affected by the fear of infamy and its consequences. And let him continue thus to the hour of death; being just and seeming to be unjust. When both have reached the uttermost extreme, the one of justice and the other of injustice, let judgment be given which of them is the happier of the two.

Heavens! my dear Glaucon, I said, how energetically you polish them up for the decision, first one and then the other, as if they were two statues.

I do my best, he said. And now that we know what they are like there is no difficulty in tracing out the sort of life which awaits either of them. This I will proceed to describe; but as you may think the description a little too coarse, I ask you to suppose, Socrates, that the words which follow are not mine.—Let me put them into the mouths of the eulogists of injustice: They will tell you that the just man who is thought unjust will be scourged, racked, bound—will have his eyes burnt out; and, at last, after suffering every kind of evil, he will be impaled: Then he will understand that he ought to seem only, and not to be, just; the words of Aeschylus may be more truly spoken of the unjust than of the just. For the unjust is pursuing a reality; he does not live with a view to appearances—he wants to be really unjust and not to seem only:—

> His mind has a soil deep and fertile,
> Out of which spring his prudent counsels.[1]

In the first place, he is thought just, and therefore bears rule in the city; he can marry whom he will, and give in marriage to whom he will; also he can trade and deal where he likes, and always to his own advantage, because he has no misgivings about injustice; and at every contest, whether in public or private, he gets the better of his antagonists, and gains at their expense, and is rich, and out of his gains he can benefit his friends, and harm his enemies; moreover, he can offer sacrifices, and dedicate gifts to the gods abundantly and magnificently, and can honour the gods or any man whom he wants to honour in a far better style than the just, and therefore he is likely to be dearer than they are to the gods. And thus, Socrates, gods and men are said to unite in making the life of the unjust better than the life of the just.

I was going to say something in answer to Glaucon, when Adeimantus, his brother, interposed: Socrates, he said, you do not suppose that there is nothing more to be urged?

Why, what else is there? I answered.

The strongest point of all has not been even mentioned, he replied.

Well, then, according to the proverb, 'Let brother help brother'—if he fails in any part do you assist him; although I must confess that Glaucon has already said quite enough to lay me in the dust, and take from me the power of helping justice.

Nonsense, he replied. But let me add something more: There is another side to Glaucon's argument about the praise and censure of justice and injustice, which is equally required in order to bring out what I believe to be his meaning. Parents and tutors are always telling their sons and their wards that they are to be just; but why? not for the sake of justice, but for the sake of character and reputation; in the hope of obtaining for him who is reputed just some of those offices, marriages, and the like which Glaucon has enumerated among the advantages accruing to the unjust from the reputation of justice. More, however, is made of appearances by this class of persons than by the others; for they throw in the good opinion of the gods, and will tell you of a shower of benefits which the heavens, as they say, rain upon the pious; and this accords with the testimony of the noble Hesiod and Homer, the first of whom says, that the gods make the oaks of the just—

To bear acorns at their summit, and bees in the middle;
And the sheep are bowed down with the weight of their
    fleeces.[2]

and many other blessings of a like kind are provided for them. And Homer has a very similar strain; for he speaks of one whose fame is—

As the fame of some blameless king who, like a god,
Maintains justice; to whom the black earth brings forth
Wheat and barley, whose trees are bowed with fruit,
And his sheep never fail to bear, and the sea gives him
    fish.[3]

Still grander are the gifts of heaven which Musaeus and his son[4] vouchsafe to the just; they take them down into the world below, where they have the saints lying on couches at a feast, everlastingly drunk, crowned with garlands; their idea seems to be that an immortality of drunkenness is the highest meed of virtue. Some extend their rewards yet further; the posterity, as they say, of the faithful and just shall survive to the third and fourth generation. This is the style in which they praise justice. But about the wicked there is another strain; they bury them in a slough in Hades, and make them carry water in a sieve; also while they are yet living they bring them to infamy, and inflict upon them the punishments which Glaucon described as the portion of the just who are reputed to be unjust; nothing else does their invention supply. Such is their manner of praising the one and censuring the other.

Once more, Socrates, I will ask you to consider another way of speaking about justice and injustice, which is not confined to the poets, but is found in prose writers. The universal voice of mankind is always declaring that justice and virtue are honourable, but grievous and toilsome; and that the pleasures of vice and injustice are easy of attainment, and are only censured by law and opinion. They say also that honesty is for the most part less profitable than dishonesty; and they are quite ready to call wicked men happy, and to honour them both in public and private when they are rich or in any other way influential, while they despise and overlook those who may be weak and poor, even though acknowledging them to be better than the others. But most extraordinary of all is their mode of speaking about virtue and the gods: they say that the gods apportion calamity and misery to many good men, and good and happiness to the wicked. And mendicant prophets go to rich men's doors and persuade them that they have a power committed to them by the gods of making an atonement for a man's own or his ancestor's sins by sacrifices or charms, with rejoicings and feasts; and they promise to harm an enemy, whether just or unjust, at a small cost; with magic arts and incantations binding heaven, as they say, to execute their will. And the poets are the authorities to whom they appeal, now smoothing the path of vice with words of Hesiod:—

Vice may be had in abundance without trouble; the way
is smooth and her dwelling-place is near. But before virtue
the gods have set toil,[5]

and a tedious and uphill road: then citing Homer as a witness that the gods may be influenced by men; for he also says:—

The gods, too, may be turned from their purpose; and men pray to them and avert their wrath by sacrifices and soothing entreaties, and by libations and the odour of fat, when they have sinned and transgressed.[6]

And they produce a host of books written by Musaeus and Orpheus, who were children of the Moon and the Muses—that is what they say—according to which they perform their ritual, and persuade not only individuals, but whole cities, that expiations and atonements for sin may be made by sacrifices and amusements which fill a vacant hour, and are equally at the service of the living and the dead; the latter sort they call mysteries, and they redeem us from the pains of hell, but if we neglect them no one knows what awaits us.

He proceeded: And now when the young hear all this said about virtue and vice, and the way in which gods and men regard them, how are their minds likely to be affected, my dear Socrates,—those of them, I mean, who are quickwitted, and, like bees on the wing, light on every flower, and from all that they hear are prone to draw conclusions as to what manner of persons they should be and in what way they should walk if they would make the best of life? Probably the youth will say to himself in the words of Pindar—

Can I by justice or by crooked ways of deceit ascend a loftier tower which may be a fortress to me all my days?

For what men say is that, if I am really just and am not also thought just, profit there is none, but the pain and loss on the other hand are unmistakable. But if, though unjust, I acquire the reputation of justice, a heavenly life is promised to me. Since then, as philosophers prove, appearance tyrannizes over truth and is lord of happiness, to appearance I must devote myself. I will describe around me a picture and shadow of virtue to be the vestibule and exterior of my house; behind I will trail the subtle and crafty fox, as Archilochus, greatest of sages, recommends. But I hear some one exclaiming that the concealment of wickedness is often difficult; to which I answer, Nothing great is easy. Nevertheless, the argument indicates this, if we would be happy, to be the path along which we should proceed. With a view to concealment we will establish secret brotherhoods and political clubs. And there are professors of rhetoric who teach the art of persuading courts and assemblies; and so, partly by persuasion and partly by force, I shall make unlawful gains and not be punished. Still I hear a voice saying that

the gods cannot be deceived, neither can they be compelled. But what if there are no gods? or, suppose them to have no care of human things—why in either case should we mind about concealment? And even if there are gods, and they do care about us, yet we know of them only from tradition and the genealogies of the poets; and these are the very persons who say that they may be influenced and turned by 'sacrifices and soothing entreaties and by offerings.' Let us be consistent then, and believe both or neither. If the poets speak truly, why then we had better be unjust, and offer of the fruits of injustice; for if we are just, although we may escape the vengeance of heaven, we shall lose the gains of injustice; but, if we are unjust, we shall keep the gains, and by our sinning and praying, and praying and sinning, the gods will be propitiated, and we shall not be punished. 'But there is a world below in which either we or our posterity will suffer for our unjust deeds.' Yes, my friend, will be the reflection, but there are mysteries and atoning deities, and these have great power. That is what mighty cities declare; and the children of the gods, who were their poets and prophets, bear a like testimony.

On what principle, then, shall we any longer choose justice rather than the worst injustice? When, if we only unite the latter with a deceitful regard to appearances, we shall fare to our mind both with gods and men, in life and after death, as the most numerous and the highest authorities tell us. Knowing all this, Socrates, how can a man who has any superiority of mind or person or rank or wealth, be willing to honour justice; or indeed to refrain from laughing when he hears justice praised? And even if there should be some one who is able to disprove the truth of my words, and who is satisfied that justice is best, still he is not angry with the unjust, but is very ready to forgive them, because he also knows that men are not just of their own free will; unless, peradventure, there be some whom the divinity within him may have inspired with a hatred of injustice, or who has attained knowledge of the truth—but no other man. He only blames injustice who, owing to cowardice or age or some weakness, has not the power of being unjust. And this is proved by the fact that when he obtains the power, he immediately becomes unjust as far as he can be.

The cause of all this, Socrates, was indicated by us at the beginning of the argument, when my brother and I told you how astonished we were to find that of all the professing panegyrists of justice—beginning with the ancient heroes of whom any memorial has been preserved to us, and ending with the men of our own time—no one has ever blamed injustice or praised justice except with a view to the glories, honours, and benefits which flow from them. No one has ever adequately described either in verse or prose the true essential nature of either of them abiding in the soul, and invisible to any human or divine eye; or shown that of all the things of a man's soul which he has within him, justice is the greatest good, and injustice the greatest evil. Had this been the universal strain, had you sought to persuade us of this from our youth upwards, we should not have been on the watch to keep one another from doing wrong, but every one would have been his own watchman, because afraid, if he did wrong, of harbouring in himself the greatest of evils. I dare say that Thrasymachus and others would seriously hold the language which I have been merely repeating, and words even stronger than these about justice and injustice, grossly, as I conceive, perverting their true nature. But I speak in this vehement manner, as I must frankly confess to you, because I want to hear from you the opposite side; and I would ask you to show not only the superiority which justice has over injustice, but what effect they have on the possessor of them which makes the one to be a good and the other an evil to him. And please, as Glaucon requested of you, to exclude reputations; for unless you take away from each of them his true reputation and add on the false, we shall say that you do not praise justice, but the appearance of it; we shall think that you are only exhorting us to keep injustice dark, and that you really agree with Thrasymachus in thinking that justice is another's good and the interest of the stronger, and that injustice is a man's own profit and interest, though injurious to the weaker. Now as you have admitted that justice is one of that highest class of goods which are desired indeed for their results, but in a far greater degree for their own sakes—like sight or hearing or knowledge or health, or any other real and natural and not merely conventional good—I would ask you in your praise of justice to regard one point only: I mean the essential good and evil which justice and injustice work in the possessors of them. Let others praise justice and censure injustice, magnifying the rewards and honours of the one and abusing the other; that is a manner of arguing which, coming from them, I am ready to tolerate, but from you who have spent your whole life in the consideration of this question, unless I hear the contrary from your own lips, I expect something better. And therefore, I say, not only prove to us that justice is better than injustice, but show what they either of them do to the possessor of them, which makes the one to be a good and the other an evil, whether seen or unseen by gods and men.

NOTES

1. *Seven against Thebes,* 574.
2. Hesiod, *Works and Days,* 230.
3. Homer, *Od.* xix. 109.
4. Eumolpus.
5. Hesiod, *Works and Days,* 287.
6. Homer, *Iliad,* ix. 493.

PLATO

Socrates' Answer (in part)*

BOOK II

I had always admired the genius of Glaucon and Adeimantus, but on hearing these words I was quite delighted, and said: Sons of an illustrious father,[1] that was not a bad beginning of the elegiac verses which the admirer of Glaucon made in honour of you after you had distinguished yourselves at the battle of Megara:—

'Sons of Ariston,' he sang, 'divine offspring of an illustrious hero.'

The epithet is very appropriate, for there is something truly divine in being able to argue as you have done for the superiority of injustice, and remaining unconvinced by your own arguments. And I do believe that you are not convinced—this I infer from your general character, for had I judged only from your speeches I should have mistrusted you. But now, the greater my confidence in you, the greater is my difficulty in knowing what to say. For on the one hand I cannot offer any help, because I feel that I am unequal to the task; and my inability is brought home to me by the fact that you were not satisfied with the answer which I made to Thrasymachus, proving, as I thought, the superiority which justice has over injustice. And yet I cannot refuse to help, while breath and speech remain to me; I am afraid that there would be an impiety in being present when justice is evil spoken of and not lifting up a hand in her defence. And therefore I had best give such help as I can.

Glaucon and the rest entreated me by all means not to let the question drop, but, in the first place, to inquire thoroughly into the nature of justice and injustice, and secondly, to discover the truth about their relative advantages. I told them, what I really thought, that the inquiry would be of a serious nature, and would require very good eyes. Seeing then, I said, that we are no great wits, I think that we had better adopt a method which I may illustrate thus; suppose that a short-sighted person had been asked to read small letters from a distance; and someone observed that the same inscription was written elsewhere on a larger scale—if they were the same, and he could read the larger letters first and then proceed to the lesser, this would have been thought a rare piece of good fortune.

Very true, said Adeimantus; but how does the illustration apply to our inquiry about justice?

I will tell you, I replied; justice is, as you know, sometimes spoken of as the virtue of an individual, and sometimes as the virtue of a State.[2]

True, he replied.

And is not a State larger than an individual?

It is.

Then in the larger, justice is likely to be more abundant and more easily discernible. I propose therefore that we inquire into the nature of justice and injustice, first as they appear in the State, and secondly in the individual, proceeding from the greater to the lesser and comparing them.

That, he said, is an excellent proposal.

And if we imagine the State in process of creation, we shall see the justice and injustice of the State in process of creation also.

I dare say.

When the State is completed there may be a hope that the object of our search will be more easily discovered.

Yes, far more easily.

But ought we to attempt to construct one? I said; for to do so, as I am inclined to think, will be a very serious task. Reflect therefore.

I have reflected, said Adeimantus, and am anxious that you should proceed.

A State, I said, arises, as I conceive, out of the

*From Plato, *The Republic*, ii. 367E–376E, iii. 412B–iv. 445B, trans. B. Jowett.

needs of mankind, no one is self-sufficing, but all of us have many wants. Can any other origin of a State be imagined?

There can be no other.

Then, as we have many wants, and many persons are needed to supply them, one takes a helper for one purpose and another for another; and when these partners and helpers are gathered together in one habitation the body of inhabitants is termed a State.

True, he said.

And it is in the belief that it is for his own good, that one man gives to another or receives from him in exchange.

Very true.

Then, I said, let us construct a State in theory from the beginning; and yet the true creator, it seems, will be necessity.

Of course, he replied.

Now the first and greatest of necessities is food, which is the condition of life and existence.

Certainly.

The second is a dwelling, and the third clothing and the like.

True.

And now let us see what must be the size³ of a city able to supply such a demand: We may suppose that one man is a husbandman, another a builder, someone else a weaver—shall we add to them a shoemaker, or perhaps some other purveyor to our bodily wants?

By all means.

The simplest possible State must include four or five men.

Clearly.

And how will they proceed? Will each bring the result of his labours into a common stock?—the individual husbandman, for example, producing for four, and labouring four times as long and as much as he need in the provision of food with which he supplies others as well as himself; or will he have nothing to do with others and not be at the trouble of producing for them, but provide for himself alone a fourth of the food in a fourth of the time, and in the remaining three fourths of his time be employed in making a house or a coat or a pair of shoes, not bothering to form a partnership with others, but supplying himself all his own wants?

Adeimantus thought that he should aim at producing food only and not at producing everything.

Probably, I replied, that would be the better way; and when I hear you say this, I am myself reminded that we are not all alike; there are diversities of natures among us which are adapted to different occupations.

Very true.

And will you have a work better done when every workman tries his hand at many occupations, or when each has only one?

When he has only one.

Further, there can be no doubt that a work is spoilt when not done at the right time?

No doubt.

For business is not disposed to wait until the doer of the business is at leisure; but the doer must follow up his opportunity, and make the business his first object.

He must.

And if so, we must infer that all things are produced more plentifully and easily and of a better quality when one man does one thing which is natural to him and does it at the right time, leaving other crafts alone.

Undoubtedly.

Then more than four citizens will be required to furnish all that has been mentioned; for the husbandman will not make his own plough or mattock, or other implements of agriculture, if they are to be good for anything. Neither will the builder make his tools—and he too needs many; and in like manner the weaver and shoemaker.

True.

Then carpenters, and smiths, and many other artisans, will be sharers in our little State, which is already beginning to grow?

True.

Yet even if we add neatherds, shepherds, and other herdsmen, in order that our husbandmen may have oxen to plough with, and builders as well as husbandmen may have draught cattle, and curriers and weavers fleeces and hides,—still our State will not be very large.

That is true; yet neither will it be a very small State which contains all these.

Then, again, there is the situation of the city—to find a place where nothing need be imported is well-nigh impossible.

Impossible.

Then there must be another class of citizens who will bring the required supply from another city?

There must.

But if the trader goes empty-handed, having nothing which they require who would supply his need, he will come back empty handed.

That is probable.

And therefore what they produce at home must be not only enough for themselves, but such both in quantity and quality as to accommodate those from whom their wants are supplied.

Very true.

Then more husbandmen and more artisans will be required?

They will.

Not to mention those who serve as importers and exporters of goods, who are called, I believe, merchants?

Yes.

Then we shall want merchants?

We shall.

And if merchandise is to be carried over the sea, we shall also require men who have been bred to various nautical occupations.

Yes, a large class.

Then, again, within the city, how will they exchange their productions? To secure such an exchange was, as you will remember, one of our principal objects when we formed them into a society and constituted a State.

Clearly they will buy and sell.

Then they will need a market-place, and a money-token for purposes of exchange.

Certainly.

Suppose now that a husbandman, or an artisan, brings some productions to market, and comes at a time when there is no one to exchange with him— is he to sit idle in the market-place, taking a holiday from his work?

Not at all; he will find people there who, seeing the want, undertake the office of salesmen. In well-ordered states they are commonly those who are weakest in bodily strength, and therefore of little use for any other purpose; their duty is to be in the market, and to give money in exchange for goods to those who desire to sell and to take money from those who desire to buy.

This want, then, creates a class of retail-traders in our State. Is not 'retailer' the term which is applied to those who sit in the market-place engaged in buying and selling, while those who wander from one city to another are called merchants?

Yes, he said.

And there is another class of servants, who are intellectually hardly on the level of association; still they have plenty of bodily strength for labour, which accordingly they sell, and are called, if I do not mistake, hirelings, hire being the name which is given to the price of their labour.

True.

Then hirelings will help to make up our population?

Yes.

And now, Adeimantus, is our State matured and perfected?

I think so.

Where, then, is justice within it, and where is injustice, and at what stage did they make their entrance?

Probably in the dealings of these citizens with one another. I cannot suggest where else they may be found.

I dare say that you are right in your suggestion, I said; we had better think the matter out, and not shrink from the inquiry.

Let us then consider, first of all, what will be their way of life; now that we have thus established them. Will they not work at the production of corn, and wine, and clothes, and shoes? And when they are housed, in summer they will commonly work stripped and barefoot, but in winter substantially clothed and shod. They will feed on barley-meal and flour of wheat, baking the one and kneading the other, making noble cakes and loaves; these they will serve up on a mat of reeds or on clean leaves, themselves reclining the while upon beds strewn with yew or myrtle. And they and their children will feast, drinking of the wine which they have made, wearing garlands on their heads, and hymning the praises of the gods, in happy converse with one another. And they will take care that their families do not exceed their means; having an eye to poverty or war.

But, said Glaucon, interposing, you have not given them a relish to their meal.

True, I replied, I had forgotten; of course they must have a relish—salt, and olives, and cheese, and they will boil roots and herbs such as country people prepare; for a dessert we shall give them figs, and peas, and beans; and they will roast myrtleberries and acorns at the fire, sipping their wine in moderation. And with such a diet they may be expected to live in peace and health to a good old age, and bequeath a similar life to their children after them.

Yes, Socrates, he said, and if you were providing

for a city of pigs, how else would you feed the beasts?

But what would you have, Glaucon? I replied.

Why, he said, you should give them the ordinary conveniences of life. People who are to be comfortable are accustomed to lie on sofas, and dine off tables, and they should have sauces and sweets in the modern style.

Yes, I said, now I understand: the question which you would have me consider is, not only how a State, but how a luxurious State is created; and possibly there is no harm in this, for by extending our inquiry to such a State we shall be more likely to see how political justice and injustice originate. In my opinion the true and healthy constitution of the State is the one which I have described. But if you wish also to see a State at fever-heat, I have no objection. For I suspect that many will not be satisfied with the simpler way of life. They will be for adding sofas, and tables, and other furniture; also dainties, and perfumes, and incense, and courtezans, and cakes, all these not of one sort only, but in every variety; we must go beyond the necessaries of which I was at first speaking, such as houses, and clothes, and shoes: the arts of the painter and the embroiderer will have to be set in motion, and gold and ivory and all sorts of materials must be procured.

True, he said.

Then we must enlarge our borders; for the original healthy State is no longer sufficient. Now will the city have to fill and swell with a multitude of callings which are not required by any natural want; such as the tribe of hunters, and again imitators, of whom one large class have to do with forms and colours; another will be the votaries of music—poets and their attendant train of rhapsodists, players, dancers, contractors; also makers of divers kinds of articles, including those which serve for the adornment of women. And we shall want more servants. Will not tutors be also in request, and nurses wet and dry, tirewomen and barbers, as well as confectioners and cooks? Then we shall also now need swineherds, who were not needed and therefore had no place in our former State. They must not be forgotten: also a vast number of cattle will be required, if meat is to be eaten.

Certainly.

And living in this way we shall have much greater need of physicians than before?

Much greater.

And the country which was once enough to support the original inhabitants will now have become too small?

Quite true.

Then a slice of our neighbours' land will be wanted by us for pasture and tillage, and they will want a slice of ours, if, like ourselves, they exceed the limit of necessity, and give themselves up to the unlimited accumulation of wealth?

That, Socrates, will be inevitable.

And so we shall go to war, Glaucon. Shall we not?

Most certainly, he replied.

Then, without determining as yet whether war does good or harm, thus much we may affirm, that now we have discovered war to be derived from causes which are also the causes of almost all the evils in States, private as well as public.

Undoubtedly.

And our State must once more enlarge; and this time the enlargement will be nothing short of a whole army, which will have to go out and fight with the invaders for all that we have, as well as for the things and persons whom we were describing above.

Why? he said; are they not capable of defending themselves?

No, I said; not if we were right in the principle which was acknowledged by all of us when we were framing the State: the principle, as you will remember, was that one man cannot practise many arts with success.

Very true, he said.

But is not armed combat in war an art?

Certainly.

And an art requiring as much attention as shoe-making?

Quite true.

And the shoemaker was not allowed by us to be a husbandman, or a weaver, or a builder—in order that we might have our shoes well made; but to him and to every other worker was assigned one work for which he was by nature fitted, and at that he was to continue working all his life long and at no other; he was not to let opportunities slip, and then he would become a good workman. Now can anything be more important than that the work of a soldier should be well done? Or is war an art so easily acquired that a man may be a warrior who is also a husbandman, or shoemaker, or other artisan; although no one in the world would be a good dice- or chess-player who merely took up the game as a recreation, and had not from his earliest years devoted himself to this and nothing else? No equipment will make a man a skilled workman, or athlete, nor be of any use to him who has not learned how to handle it, and has never bestowed sufficient attention upon it. How then will he who takes up a shield or other implement of war become a good fighter all in a day, whether with heavy-armed or any other kind of troops?

Yes, he said, the tools which would teach men their own use would be beyond price.

And just as the duties of the guardian surpass all others in importance, I said, so does his business require the most skill and practice, as well as undivided attention.

No doubt, he replied.

Will he not also require natural aptitude for his calling?

Certainly.

Then it will be our duty to select, if we can, natures which are fitted for the task of guarding the city?

It will.

It is no light task, then, that we have undertaken, I said; but we must be brave and do our best.

We must.

Do you agree that the noble youth is very like a well-bred dog in respect of guarding and watching?

What do you mean?

I mean that both of them ought to be quick to see, and swift to overtake the enemy when they see him; and strong too if, when they have caught him, they have to fight with him.

All these qualities, he replied, will certainly be required by them.

Well, and your guardian must be brave if he is to fight well?

Certainly.

And is he likely to be brave who has no spirit, whether horse or dog or any other animal? Have you never observed how invincible and unconquerable is spirit and how the presence of it makes the soul of any creature to be absolutely fearless and indomitable?

I have.

Then now we have a clear notion of the bodily qualities which are required in the guardian.

True.

And also of the mental ones; his soul is to be full of spirit?

True again.

But how can these spirited natures fail to be savage with one another, and with everybody else?

A difficulty by no means easy to overcome, he replied.

Whereas, I said, they ought to be dangerous to their enemies, and gentle to their friends; if not, they will destroy themselves without waiting for their enemies to destroy them.

True, he said.

What is to be done then? I said; how shall we find a gentle nature which has also a high spirit, for the one is the contradiction of the other?

True.

He will not be a good guardian who is wanting in either of these two qualities; and yet the combination of them appears to be impossible; and hence we must infer that to be a good guardian is impossible.

I am afraid that what you say is true, he replied.

Here feeling perplexed I began to think over what had preceded.—My friend, I said, no wonder that we are in a perplexity; for we have lost sight of the image which we had before us.

What do you mean? he said.

It has escaped our notice that there do exist natures gifted with those opposite qualities.

Where?

Many animals, I replied, furnish examples of them, but most of all the dog, to which we compared the guardian: you know the disposition of a well-bred dog, perfectly gentle to its familiars and acquaintances, and the reverse to strangers.

Yes, I know.

Then there is nothing impossible or out of the order of nature in our finding a guardian who has a similar combination of qualities?

Certainly not.

Would not he who is fitted to be a guardian, besides the spirited nature, need to have the qualities of a philosopher?

I do not apprehend your meaning.

The trait of which I am speaking, I replied, may also be seen in the dog, and is remarkable in the animal.

What trait?

Why, a dog, whenever he sees a stranger, is angry; when an acquaintance, he welcomes him, although the one has never done him any harm, nor the other any good. Did this never strike you as curious?

The point never struck me before; but I quite recognize the truth of your remark.

And surely this instinct of the dog is very charming;—your dog is a true philosopher.

Why?

Why, because he distinguishes the face of a friend and of an enemy only by the criterion of knowing and not knowing. And must not an animal be a lover of learning who determines what is or is not friendly to him by the test of knowledge and ignorance?

Most assuredly.

And is not the love of learning the love of wisdom, which is philosophy?

They are the same, he replied.

And may we not say confidently of man also, that he who is likely to be gentle to his friends and acquaintances, must by nature be a lover of wisdom and knowledge?

That we may safely affirm.

Then he who is to be a really good and noble guardian of the State will require to unite in himself philosophy and spirit and swiftness and strength?

Undoubtedly.

Then we have found the desired natures; and now that we have found them, how are they to be reared and educated? Is not this an inquiry which may be expected to throw light on the greater inquiry which is our final end—How do justice and injustice grow up in States? for we do not want either to omit what is to the point or to draw out the argument to an inconvenient length.

Adeimantus thought that the inquiry would be of great service to us.

Then, I said, my dear friend, the task must not be given up, even if somewhat long.

Certainly not.

Come then, and let us pass a leisure hour in story-telling, and our story shall be the education of our heroes. . . .

[Socrates' account of the primary education of the Guardians (376E–412B) is omitted here. In it he discusses censorship of literature, the molding influence of dramatic recitation, music and meter, and physical training. The argument resumes below with his account of how rulers are to be selected.—Ed.]

BOOK III

Such, then, are our principles of nurture and education: Where would be the use of going into further details about the dances of our citizens, or about their hunting and coursing, their gymnastic and equestrian contests? For these all follow the general principle, and having found that, we shall have no difficulty in discovering them.

I dare say that there will be no difficulty.

Very good, I said; then what is the next question? Must we not ask who are to be rulers and who subjects?

Certainly.

There can be no doubt that the elder must rule the younger.

Clearly.

And that the best of these must rule.

That is also clear.

Now, are the best husbandmen those who are most devoted to husbandry?

Yes.

And as we are to have the best of guardians for our city, must they not be those who have most the character of guardians?

Yes.

And to this end they ought to be wise and efficient, and to have a special care of the State?

True.

And a man will be most likely to care about that which he loves?

To be sure.

And he will be most likely to love that which he regards as having the same interests with himself, and that of which the good or evil fortune is supposed by him at any time most to affect his own?

Very true, he replied.

Then there must be a selection. Let us note among the guardians those who in their whole life show the greatest eagerness to do what they suppose to be for the good of their country, and the greatest repugnance to do what is against her interests.

Those are the right men.

And they will have to be watched at every age, in order that we may see whether they preserve their resolution, and never yield either to force or to enchantment, so as to forget or cast off their sense of duty to the State.

How cast off? he said.

I will explain to you, I replied. A resolution may go out of a man's mind either with his will or against his will; with his will when he gets rid of a falsehood and learns better, against his will whenever he is deprived of a truth.

I understand, he said, the willing loss of a resolution; the meaning of the unwilling I have yet to learn.

Why, I said, do you not see that men are unwillingly deprived of good, and willingly of evil? Is not to have lost the truth an evil, and to possess the truth a good? and you would agree that to conceive things as they are is to possess the truth?

Yes, he replied; I agree with you in thinking that mankind are deprived of truth against their will.

And is not this involuntary deprivation caused either by theft, or force, or enchantment?

Still, he replied, I do not understand you.

I must have been talking darkly like the tragedians. As for theft, I only mean that some men are changed by persuasion and that others forget; argument steals away the beliefs of one class, and time of the other. Now you understand me?

Yes.

Those again who are forced, are those whom the violence of some pain or grief compels to change their opinion.

I understand, he said, and you are quite right.

And you would also acknowledge that the enchanted are those who change their minds either under the softer influence of pleasure, or the sterner shock of fear?

Yes, he said; everything that deceives may be said to enchant.

Therefore, as I was just now saying, we must inquire who are the best guardians of their own conviction that they should always do what they judge most advantageous to the State. We must watch them from their youth upwards, and make them perform actions in which they are most likely to forget or to be deceived, and he who remembers and is not deceived is to be selected, and he who fails in the trial is to be rejected. That will be the way?

Yes.

And there should also be toils and pains and conflicts prescribed for them, in which they will be made to give further proof of the same qualities.

Very right, he replied.

And then, I said, we must try them with enchantments—that is the third sort of test—and see what will be their behaviour: like those who take colts amid noise and tumult to see if they are of a timid nature, so must we take our youth amid terrors of some kind, and thence pass them into pleasures, and prove them more thoroughly than gold is proved in the furnace, that we may discover whether they are armed against all enchantments, and of a noble bearing always, good guardians of themselves and of the music which they have learned, and retaining under all circumstances a rhythmical and harmonious

nature, such as will be most serviceable to themselves and to the State. And he who at every age, as boy and youth and in mature life, has come out of the trial victorious and pure, shall be appointed a ruler and guardian of the State; he shall be honoured in life and death, and shall receive sepulture and other memorials of honour, the greatest that we have to give. But him who fails, we must reject. I am inclined to think that this is the sort of way in which our rulers and guardians should be chosen and appointed. I speak generally, and not with any pretension to exactness.

And, speaking generally, I agree with you, he said.

And perhaps the word 'guardian' in the fullest sense ought to be applied to this higher class only who both preserve us against foreign enemies and maintain peace among our citizens at home, that the one may not have the will, or the others the power, to harm us. The young men whom we before called guardians may be more properly designated auxiliaries and supporters of the principles of the rulers.

I agree with you, he said.

How then may we devise one of those needful falsehoods of which we lately spoke—just one royal lie which may deceive the rulers, if that be possible, and at any rate the rest of the city?

What sort of lie? he said.

Nothing new, I replied; only an old Phoenician[4] tale of what has often occurred before now in other places (as the poets say, and have made the world believe), though not in our time, and I do not know whether such an event could ever happen again, or could now even be made to seem probable.

How your words seem to hesitate on your lips!

You will not wonder, I replied, at my hesitation when you have heard.

Speak, he said, and fear not.

Well then, I will speak, although I really know not how to look you in the face, or in what words to utter the audacious fiction, which I propose to communicate gradually, first to the rulers, then to the soldiers, and lastly to the people. They are to be told that the education and training which they seemed to receive from us in youth was but a dream; in reality during all that time they were being formed and fed in the womb of the earth, where they themselves and their arms and appurtenances were manufactured;

when they were completed, the earth, their mother, sent them up; and so, their country being their mother and also their nurse, they are bound to advise for her good, and to defend her against attacks; and the other citizens they are to regard as children of the earth and their own brothers.

You had good reason, he said, to be ashamed of the lie which you were going to tell.

No doubt, I replied, but listen to the continuation of the tale. Citizens, we shall say to them in our tale, you are brothers, yet God has framed you differently. Some of you have the power of command, and in the composition of these he has mingled gold, wherefore also they have the greatest honour; others he has made of silver, to be auxiliaries; others again who are to be husbandmen and craftsmen he has composed of brass and iron; and the species will generally be preserved in the children. But as all are of the same original stock, a golden parent will sometimes have a silver son, a silver parent a golden son, and so forth. And God proclaims as a first principle to the rulers, and above all else, that there is nothing which they should so anxiously guard, or of which they are to be such good guardians, as of the mixture of elements in the soul. First, if one of their own offspring has an admixture of brass or iron, they shall in no wise have pity on it, but give it the rank which is its due and send it down to the husbandmen or artisans. On the other hand, if there are sons of artisans who have an admixture of gold or silver in them, they will be raised to honour, and become guardians or auxiliaries. For an oracle says that when a man of brass or iron guards the State, it will be destroyed. Such is the tale; is there any possibility of making our citizens believe in it?

Not in the first generation, he replied; but their sons may be made to believe in the tale, and their sons' sons, and posterity after them.

I see the difficulty, I replied; yet the fostering of such a belief will make them care more for the city and for one another. Enough, however, of the fiction, which may now fly abroad upon the wings of rumour, while we arm our earth-born heroes, and lead them forth under the command of their rulers. Let them look round and select a spot whence they can best suppress insurrection, if any prove refractory within, and also defend themselves against enemies, who like wolves may come down on the fold from without; there let them encamp, and when they have

encamped, let them sacrifice to the proper gods and prepare their lodging.

Just so, he said.

And this must be such as will shield them against the cold of winter and the heat of summer.

I suppose that you mean houses, he replied.

Yes, I said; but they must be the houses of soldiers, and not of shopkeepers.

What is the difference? he said.

That I will endeavour to explain, I replied. To keep watchdogs, who, from want of discipline or hunger or some evil habit or other, would turn upon the sheep and worry them, and behave not like dogs but wolves, would be a foul and monstrous thing in a shepherd?

Truly monstrous, he said.

And therefore every care must be taken that our auxiliaries, being stronger than our citizens, may not behave in this fashion and become like savage tyrants instead of friends and allies?

Yes, great care should be taken.

And if they have really received a good education, will not that furnish the best safeguard?

But they have received it, he replied.

I cannot be so confident, my dear Glaucon, I said; but I believe the truth is as I said, that a sound education, whatever that may be, will have the greatest tendency to civilize and humanize them in their relations to one another, and to those who are under their protection.

Very true, he replied.

And not only their education, but their habitations, and all that belongs to them, should be such as will neither impair their virtue as guardians, nor tempt them to prey upon the other citizens. Any man of sense must acknowledge that.

He must.

Then now let us consider what will be their way of life, if they are to realize our idea of them. In the first place, none of them should have any property of his own beyond what is absolutely necessary; neither should they have a private house or store closed against anyone who has a mind to enter; their provisions should be only such as are required by trained warriors, who are men of temperance and courage; they should agree to receive from the citizens a fixed rate of pay, enough to meet the expenses of the year and no more; and they will go to mess and live together like soldiers in a camp. Gold and silver we will tell them that they have from God; the diviner metal is within them, and they have therefore no need of the dross which is current among men, and ought not to pollute the divine by any such earthly admixture; for that commoner metal has been the sources of many unholy deeds, but their own is undefiled. And they alone of all the citizens may not touch or handle silver or gold, or be under the same roof with them, or wear them, or drink from them. And this will be their salvation, and they will be the saviours of the State. But should they ever acquire homes or lands or moneys of their own, they will become householders and husbandmen instead of guardians, enemies and tyrants instead of allies of the other citizens; hating and being hated, plotting and being plotted against, they will pass their whole life in much greater terror of internal than of external enemies, and the hour of ruin, both to themselves and to the rest of the State, will be at hand. For all which reasons may we not say that thus shall our State be ordered, and that these shall be the regulations appointed by us for our guardians concerning their lodging and all other matters?

Yes, said Glaucon.

BOOK IV

Here Adeimantus interposed a question: How would you answer, Socrates, said he, if a person were to say that you are not making these men very happy, and that they are themselves to blame; the city in fact belongs to them, but they reap no advantage from it; whereas other men acquire lands, and build large and handsome houses, and have everything handsome about them, offering sacrifices to the gods on their own account, and practising hospitality; moreover, they have the gold and silver which you have just mentioned, and all that is usual among the favourites of fortune; but our poor citizens are no better than mercenaries who are quartered in the city and are always mounting guard?

Yes, I said; and you may add that they are only fed, and not paid in addition to their food like other men; and therefore they cannot, if they would, take a private journey abroad; they have no money to spend on a mistress or any other luxurious fancy, which, as the world goes, is thought to be happiness; and many other accusations of the same nature might be added.

But, said he, let us suppose all this to be included in the charge.

You mean to ask, I said, what will be our answer?

Yes.

If we proceed along the old path, my belief, I said, is that we shall find the answer. And our answer will be that, even as they are, our guardians may very likely be the happiest of men; but that our aim in founding the State was not the disproportionate happiness of any one class, but the greatest happiness of the whole; we thought that in a State which is ordered with a view to the good of the whole we should be most likely to find justice, and in the worst-ordered State injustice: and, having found them, we might then decide upon the answer to our first question. At present, I take it, we are fashioning the happy State, not piecemeal, or with a view of making a few happy citizens, but as a whole; and by-and-by we will proceed to view the opposite kind of State. Suppose that we were painting a statue, and someone came up to us and said, Why do you not put the most beautiful colours on the most beautiful parts of the body—the eyes ought to be purple, but you have made them black—to him we might fairly answer, 'Sir, you would not surely have us beautify the eyes to such a degree that they are no longer eyes; consider rather whether, by giving this and the other features their due proportion, we make the whole beautiful.' And so I say to you, do not compel us to assign to the guardians a sort of happiness which will make them no guardians at all; for we too can clothe our husbandmen in royal apparel, and set crowns of gold on their heads, and bid them till the ground as much as they like, and no more. Our potters also might be allowed to repose on couches, and feast by the fireside, passing round the winecup, while their wheel is conveniently at hand, so that they may make a few pots when they feel inclined; in this way we might make every class happy—and then, as you imagine, the whole State would be happy. But do not put this idea into our heads; for, if we listen to you, the husbandman will be no longer a husbandman, the potter will cease to be a potter, and no one will have the character of any distinct class in the State. Now this is not of much consequence where the corruption of society, and pretension to be what you are not, is confined to cobblers; but when the guardians of the laws and of the government are only seeming and not real guardians, then see how they turn the State upside down; and on the other hand they alone have the power of giving order and happiness to the State. We mean our guardians to be true saviours and not the destroyers of the State, whereas our opponent is thinking of peasants at a festival, who are enjoying a life of revelry, not of citizens who are doing their duty to the State. But, if so, we mean different things, and he is speaking of something which is not a State. And therefore we must consider whether in appointing our guardians we look to their greatest happiness individually, or whether our aim is not to ensure that happiness appears in the State as a whole. What these guardians or auxiliaries must be compelled or induced to do (and the same may be said of every other trade), is to become as expert as possible in their professional work. And thus the whole State will grow up in a noble order, and the several classes will receive the proportion of happiness which nature assigns to them.

I think that you are quite right.

I wonder whether you will agree with another remark which occurs to me.

What may that be?

There seem to be two causes of the deterioration of the arts.

What are they?

Wealth, I said, and poverty.

How do they act?

The process is as follows: When a potter becomes rich, will he, think you, any longer take the same pains with his art?

Certainly not.

He will grow more indolent and careless?

Very true.

And the result will be that he becomes a worse potter?

Yes; he greatly deteriorates.

But, on the other hand, if he has no money and cannot provide himself with tools or other requirements of his craft, his own work will not be equally good, and he will not teach his sons or apprentices to work equally well.

Certainly not.

Then, under the influence either of poverty or of wealth, workmen and their work are equally liable to degenerate?

That is evident.

Here then is a discovery of new evils, I said, against which the guardians will have to watch, or they will creep into the city unobserved.

What evils?

Wealth, I said, and poverty; the one is the parent of luxury and indolence, and the other of meanness

and viciousness, and both of a revolutionary spirit.

That is very true, he replied; but still I should like to know, Socrates, how our city will be able to go to war, especially against an enemy who is rich and powerful, if deprived of the sinews of war.

Evidently it would be difficult, I replied, to wage war with one such enemy; but it will be easier where there are two of them.

How so? he asked.

In the first place, I said, if we have to fight, our side will be trained warriors fighting against an army of rich men.

That is true, he said.

And do you not suppose, Adeimantus, that a single boxer who was perfect in his art would easily be a match for two stout and well-to-do gentlemen who were not boxers?

Hardly, if they came upon him at once.

What, not, I said, if he were able to run away and then turn and strike at the first who came up? And supposing he were to do this several times under the heat of a scorching sun, might he not, being an expert, overturn more than one stout personage?

Certainly, he said, there would be nothing wonderful in that.

And yet rich men probably have more instruction in the science and practise of boxing than they have in military science.

Likely enough.

Then we may assume that our athletes will be able to fight with two or three times their own number?

I will accept that, for I think you right.

And suppose that, before engaging, our citizens send an embassy to one of the two cities, telling them what is the truth: 'Silver and gold we neither have nor are permitted to have, but you may; do you therefore come and help us in war, and take the spoils of the other city.' Who, on hearing these words, would choose to fight against lean wiry dogs, rather than, with the dogs on their side, against fat and tender sheep.

That is not likely; and yet there might be a danger to the poor State if the wealth of many States were to be gathered into one.

But how simple of you to think that the term State is applicable at all to any but our own!

Why so?

You ought to speak of other States in the plural number; not one of them is a city, but many cities, as they say in the game. Each will contain not less than two divisions, one the city of the poor, the other of the rich, which are at war with one another; and within each there are many smaller divisions. You would be altogether beside the mark if you treated these as a single State; but if you deal with them as many, and give the wealth or power or persons of the one to the others, you will always have a great many friends and not many enemies. And your State, while the wise order which has now been prescribed continues to prevail in her, will be the greatest of States, I do not mean to say in reputation or appearance, but in deed and truth, though she number not more than a thousand defenders. A single State of that size you will hardly find, either among Hellenes or barbarians, though many that appear to be as great and many times greater.

That is most true, he said.

Hence, I said, it can be seen what will be the best limit for our rulers to fix when they are considering the size of the State and the amount of territory which they are to include, and beyond which they will not go.

What limit would you propose?

I would allow the State to increase so far as is consistent with unity; that, I think, is the proper limit.

Very good, he said.

Here then, I said, is another order which will have to be conveyed to our guardians: Let them guard against our city becoming small, or great only in appearance. It must attain an adequate size, but it must remain one.

And perhaps, said he, you do not think this is a very severe order?

And here is another, said I, which is lighter still,—I mean the duty, of which some mention was made before, of degrading the offspring of the guardians when inferior, and of elevating into the rank of guardians the offspring of the lower classes, when naturally superior. The intention was that, in the case of the citizens generally, each individual should be put to the use for which nature intended him, one to one work, and then every man would do his own business, and become one and not many; and so the whole city would be one and not many.

Yes, he said; that is not so difficult.

The regulations which we are prescribing, my good Adeimantus, are not, as might be supposed, a number of great principles, but trifles all, if care be taken, as the saying is, of the one great thing,—a thing, however, which I would rather call, not great, but sufficient for our purpose.

What may that be? he asked.

Education, I said, and nurture: if our citizens are well educated, and grow into sensible men, they will easily see their way through all these, as well as other matters which I omit; such, for example, as marriage, the possession of women and the procreation of children, which will all follow the general principle that friends have all things in common, as the proverb says.

That will be the best way of settling them.

Also, I said, the State, if once started well, moves with accumulating force like a wheel. For where good nurture and education are maintained, they implant good constitutions, and these good constitutions taking root in a good education improve more and more, and this improvement affects the breed in man as in other animals.

Very possibly, he said.

Then to sum up: This is the principle to which our rulers should cling throughout, taking care that neglect does not creep in—that music and gymnastic be preserved in their original form, and no innovation made. They must do their utmost to maintain them intact. And when anyone says that

'Mankind most regard the newest song which the singers have',[5]

they will be afraid that he may be praising, not new songs, but a new kind of song; and this ought not to be praised, or conceived to be the meaning of the poet; for any musical innovation is to be shunned, as likely to bring danger to the whole State. So Damon tells me, and I can quite believe him;—he says that when modes of music change, the fundamental laws of the State always change with them.

Yes, said Adeimantus; and you may add my suffrage to Damon's and your own.

Then, I said, our guardians must lay the foundations of their fortress in music?

Yes, he said; the lawlessness of which you speak too easily steals in.

Yes, I replied, in the form of amusement, and as though it were harmless.

Why, yes, he said, and harmless it would be; were it not that little by little this spirit of licence, finding a home, imperceptibly penetrates into manners and customs; whence issuing with greater force it invades contracts between man and man, and from contracts goes on to laws and constitutions, in utter recklessness, ending at last, Socrates, by an overthrow of all rights, private as well as public.

Is that true? I said.

That is my belief, he replied.

Then, as I was saying, our boys should be trained from the first in a stricter system, for if childish amusement becomes lawless, it will produce lawless children, who can never grow up into well-conducted and virtuous citizens.

Very true, he said.

And when boys who have made a good beginning in play, have later gained the habit of good order through music, then this habit accompanies them in all their actions and is a principle of growth to them, and is able to correct anything in the State which had been allowed to lapse. It is the reverse of the picture I have just drawn.

Very true, he said.

Thus educated, they will discover for themselves any lesser rules which their predecessors have altogether neglected.

What do you mean?

I mean such things as these:—when the young are to be silent before their elders; how they are to show respect to them by standing and making them sit; what honour is due to parents; what garments or shoes are to be worn; the mode of dressing the hair; deportment and manners in general. You would agree with me?

Yes.

But there is, I think, small wisdom in legislating about such matters,—precise written enactments cannot create these observances, and are not likely to make them lasting.

Impossible.

It would seem, Adeimantus, that the direction in which education starts a man will determine his future life. Does not like always attract like?

To be sure.

Until some one grand result is reached which may be good, and may be the reverse of good?

That is not to be denied.

And for this reason, I said, I, for my part, should not attempt to extend legislation to such details.

Naturally enough, he replied.

Well, and about the business of the agora, and the ordinary dealings between man and man, or again about agreements with artisans; about insult and injury, or the commencement of actions, and

the appointment of juries, what would you say? there may also arise questions about any impositions and exactions of market and harbour dues which may be required, and in general about the regulations of markets, police, harbours, and the like. But, oh heavens! shall we condescend to legislate on any of these particulars?

No, he said, it is unseemly to impose laws about them on good men; what regulations are necessary they will find out soon enough for themselves.

Yes, I said, my friend, if God will only preserve to them the laws which we have given them.

And without divine help, said Adeimantus, they will go on for ever making and mending their laws and their lives in the hope of attaining perfection.

You would compare them, I said, to those invalids who, having no self-restraint, will not leave off their habits of intemperance?

Exactly.

Yes, I said; and what a delightful life they lead! they are always doctoring their disorders, with no result except to increase and complicate them, and always fancying that they will be cured by any nostrum which anybody advises them to try.

Such cases are very common, he said, with invalids of this sort.

Yes, I replied; and the charming thing is that they deem him their worst enemy who tells them the truth, which is simply that, unless they give up gorging and drinking and wenching and idling, neither drug nor cautery nor amputation nor spell nor amulet nor any other remedy will avail.

Charming? he replied. I see nothing charming in going into a passion with a man who tells you what is right.

These gentlemen, I said, do not seem to be in your good graces.

Assuredly not.

Nor would you approve if a whole State behaves in this way, and that brings me back to my point. For when, in certain ill-ordered States, the citizens are forbidden under pain of death to alter the constitution; and yet he who most sweetly courts those who live under this régime and indulges them and fawns upon them and is skilful in anticipating and gratifying their humours is honoured as a great and good statesman—do not these States resemble the persons whom I was describing?

Yes, he said; the fault is the same; and I am very far from approving it.

But what of these ready and eager ministers of

political corruption? I said. Do you not admire their coolness and dexterity?

Yes, he said, I do; but not of all of them, for there are some whom the applause of the multitude has deluded into the belief that they are really statesmen.

What do you mean? I said; you should have more feeling for them. When a man cannot measure, and a great many others who cannot measure declare that he is four cubits high, can he help believing what they say?

Nay, he said, certainly not in that case.

Well, then, do not be angry with them; for are they not as good as a play, trying their hand at paltry reforms such as I was describing; they are always fancying that by legislation they will make an end of frauds in contracts, and the other rascalities which I was mentioning, not knowing that they are in reality cutting off the heads of a hydra?

Yes, he said; that is just what they are doing.

I conceive, I said, that the true legislator will not trouble himself with this class of enactments whether concerning laws or the constitution either in an ill-ordered or in a well-ordered State; for in the former they are quite useless, and in the latter they will either be of a kind which anyone can devise, or will naturally flow out of our previous regulations.

What, then, he said, is still remaining to us of the work of legislation?

Nothing to us, I replied; but to Apollo, the god of Delphi, there remains the ordering of the greatest and noblest and chiefest things of all.

Which are they? he said.

The institution of temples and sacrifices, and the entire service of gods, demigods, and heroes; also the ordering of the repositories of the dead, and the rites which have to be observed by him who would propitiate the inhabitants of the world below. These are matters of which we are ignorant ourselves, and as founders of a city we should be unwise in trusting them to any interpreter but the ancestral one. For it is Apollo who, sitting at the navel of the earth, is the ancestral interpreter of such observances to all mankind.

You are right, and we will do as you propose.

So now the foundation of your city, son of Ariston, is finished. What comes next? Provide yourself with a bright light and search, and get your bother and Polemarchus and the rest of our friends to help, and let us see where in it we can discover justice and where injustice, and in what they differ from one another, and which of them the man who would be happy should have for his portion, whether seen or unseen by gods and men.

Nonsense, said Glaucon: did you not promise to search yourself, saying that for you not to help justice in her need would be an impiety?

Your reminder is true, and I will be as good as my word; but you must join.

We will, he replied.

Well, then, I hope to make the discovery in this way: I mean to begin with the assumption that our State, if rightly ordered, is perfect.

That is most certain.

And being perfect, is therefore wise and valiant and temperate and just.

That is likewise clear.

And whichever of these qualities we first find in the State, the one which is not yet found will be the residue?

Very good.

If in some other instance there were four things, in one of which we were most interested, the one sought for might come to light first, and there would be no further trouble; or if we came to know the other three first, we should thereby attain the object of our search, for it must clearly be the part remaining.

Very true, he said.

And is not a similar method to be pursued about the virtues, which are also four in number?

Clearly.

First among the virtues found in the State, wisdom comes into view, and in this I detect a certain peculiarity.

What is that?

The State which we have been describing has, I think, true wisdom. You would agree that it is good in counsel?

Yes.

And this good counsel is clearly a kind of knowledge, for not by ignorance, but by knowledge, do men counsel well?

Clearly.

And the kinds of knowledge in a State are many and diverse?

Of course.

There is the knowledge of the carpenter; but is that the sort of knowledge which gives a city the title of wise and good in counsel?

Certainly not; that would only give a city the reputation of skill in carpentering.

Then a city is not to be called wise because possessing a knowledge which counsels for the best about wooden implements?

Certainly not.

Nor by reason of a knowledge which advises about brazen pots, he said, nor as possessing any other similar knowledge?

Not by reason of any of them, he said.

Nor yet by reason of a knowledge which cultivates the earth; that would give the city the name of agricultural?

Yes.

Well, I said, and is there any knowledge in our recently founded State among any of the citizens which advises not about any particular thing in the State, but about the whole, and considers how it can best conduct itself in relation with itself and with other States?

There certainly is.

And what is this knowledge, and among whom is it found? I asked.

It is the knowledge of guarding, he replied, and is found in those rulers whom we were just now describing as perfect guardians.[6]

And what is the name which the city derives from the possession of this sort of knowledge?

The name of good in counsel and truly wise.

And will there be in our city more of these true guardians or more smiths?

The smiths, he replied, will be far more numerous.

Will not the guardians probably be the smallest of all the classes who receive a name from the profession of some kind of knowledge?

Much the smallest.

And so by reason of the smallest part or class, and of the knowledge which resides in this presiding and ruling part of itself, the whole State, being thus constituted according to nature, will be wise; and this, which can claim a share in the only knowledge worthy to be called wisdom, has been ordained by nature to be of all classes the least.

Most true.

Thus, then, I said, the nature and place in the State of one of the four virtues has somehow or other been discovered.

And, in my humble opinion, very satisfactorily discovered, he replied.

Again, I said, there is no difficulty in seeing the nature of courage, and in what part that quality resides which gives the name of courageous to the State.

How do you mean?

Why, I said, everyone who calls any State courageous or cowardly, will be thinking of the part which fights and goes out to war on the State's behalf.

No one, he replied, would ever think of any other.

The rest of the citizens may be courageous or may be cowardly, but their courage or cowardice will not, as I conceive, have the effect of making the city either the one or the other.

No.

The city will be courageous also by one part of herself, in which resides the power to preserve under all circumstances that opinion about the nature and description of things to be feared in which our legislator educated them; and this is what you term courage.

I should like to hear what you are saying once more, for I do not think that I perfectly understand you.

I mean that courage is a kind of preservation.

Preservation of what kind?

Of the opinion respecting things to be feared, what they are and of what nature, which the law implants through education; and I mean by the words 'under all circumstances' to intimate that in pleasure or in pain, or under the influence of desire or fear, a man preserves and does not lose this opinion. Shall I give you an illustration?

If you please.

You know, I said, that dyers, when they want to dye wool for making the true sea-purple, begin by choosing the white from among all the colours available; this they prepare and dress with much care and pains, in order that the white ground may take the purple hue in full perfection. The dyeing then proceeds; and whatever is dyed in this manner becomes a fast colour, and no washing either with lyes or without them can take away the bloom. But, when the ground has not been duly prepared, you will have noticed how poor is the look either of purple or of any other colour.

Yes, he said; I know that they have a washed-out and ridiculous appearance.

Then now, I said, you will understand that our object in selecting our soldiers, and educating them in music and gymnastic, was very similar; we were contriving influences which would prepare them to take the dye of the laws in perfection, and the colour of their opinion about dangers and of every other opinion was to be indelibly fixed by their nurture and training, not to be washed away by such potent lyes as pleasure—mightier agent far in washing the soul than any soda or lye—or by sorrow, fear, and desire, the mightiest of all other solvents. And this sort of universal saving power of true opinion in conformity with law about real and false dangers I call and maintain to be courage, unless you disagree.

But I agree, he replied; for I suppose that you mean to exclude mere right belief about dangers when it has grown up without instruction, such as that of a wild beast or of a slave—this, in your opinion, is something not quite in accordance with law, which in any case should have another name than courage.

Most certainly.

Then I concede courage to be such as you describe.

Excellent, said I, and if you add the words 'of a citizen', you will not be far wrong;—hereafter, if you agree, we will carry the examination of courage further, but at present we are seeking not for courage but justice; and for the purpose of our inquiry we have said enough.

You are right, he replied.

Two virtues remain to be discovered in the State—first, temperance, and then justice which is the end of our search.

Very true.

Now, can we find justice without troubling ourselves about temperance?

I do not know how that can be accomplished, he said, nor do I desire that justice should be brought to light and temperance lost sight of; and therefore I wish that you would do me the favour of considering temperance first.

Certainly, I replied, I should not be justified in refusing your request.

Then consider, he said.

Yes, I replied; I will; and as far as I can at present see, temperance has more of the nature of harmony and symphony than have the preceding virtues.

How so? he asked.

Temperance, I replied, is the ordering or controlling of certain pleasures and desires; this is curiously enough implied in the saying of 'a man being his own master'; and other traces of the same notion may be found in language, may they not?

No doubt, he said.

There is something ridiculous in the expression 'master of himself'; for the master must also be the servant and the servant the master, since in all these modes of speaking the same person is denoted.

Certainly.

The meaning of this expression is, I believe, that there is within the man's own soul a better and also a worse principle; and when the better has the worse under control, then he is said to be master of himself; and this is a term of praise: but when, owing to evil education or association, the better principle, which is also the smaller, is overwhelmed by the greater mass of the worse—in this case he is blamed and is called the slave of self and dissolute.

Yes, there is reason in that.

And now, I said, look at our newly created State, and there you will find one of these two conditions realized; for the State, as you will acknowledge, may be justly called master of itself, if the words 'temperance' and 'self-mastery' truly express the rule of the better part over the worse.

On looking, he said, I see that what you say is true.

Let me further note that the manifold and complex pleasures and desires and pains are generally found in children and women and servants, and in the freemen so called who are of the lowest and more numerous class.

Certainly, he said.

Whereas the simple and moderate desires, which follow reason and are under the guidance of mind and true opinion, are to be found only in a few, and those the best born and best educated.

Very true.

These too, as you may perceive, have a place in your State; and the meaner desires of the many are held down by the desires and wisdom of the more virtuous few.

That I perceive, he said.

Then if there be any city which may be described as master of its own pleasures and desires, and master of itself, ours may claim such a designation?

Certainly, he replied.

It may also for all these reasons be called temperate?

Yes.

And if there be any State in which rulers and subjects will be agreed as to the question who are to rule, that again will be our State? Do you think so?

I do, emphatically.

And the citizens being thus agreed among themselves, in which class will temperance be found—in the rulers or in the subjects?

In both, as I should imagine, he replied.

Do you observe that we were not badly inspired

in our guess that temperance bore some resemblance to harmony?

Why so?

Why, because temperance is unlike courage and wisdom, each of which resides in a part only, the one making the State wise and the other valiant; not so temperance, which extends to the whole, and runs through all the notes of the scale, and produces a unison of the weaker and the stronger and the middle class, whether you suppose them to be stronger or weaker in wisdom or power or numbers or wealth, or anything else you please. Most truly then may we deem this unity of mind to be temperance, an agreement of the naturally superior and inferior as to the right to rule of either both in states and individuals.

I entirely agree with you.

And so, I said, we may consider three out of the four virtues to have been discovered in our State. What remainder is there of qualities which make a state virtuous? For this, it is evident, must be justice.

The inference is obvious.

The time then has arrived, Glaucon, when, like huntsmen, we should surround the cover, and look sharp that justice does not steal away, and pass out of sight and escape us; for beyond a doubt she is somewhere in this country: watch therefore and strive to catch a sight of her, and if you see her first, let me know.

Would that I could! but you will do right to regard me rather as a follower who has just eyes enough to see what you show him.

Offer up a prayer with me and follow.

I will, but you must show me the way.

Here is no path, I said, and the wood is dark and perplexing; still we must push on.

Let us push on.

Here I saw something: Halloo! I said, I begin to perceive a track, and I believe that the quarry will not escape.

Good news, he said.

Truly, I said, we are stupid fellows.

Why so?

Why, my dear friend, far back from the beginning of our inquiry, justice has been lying at our feet, and we never saw her; nothing could be more ridiculous. Like people who go about looking for what they have in their hands, we looked not at what we were seeking, but at what was far off in the distance; and that, I suppose, was how we missed her.

What do you mean?

I mean to say that for a long time past we have been talking or hearing of justice, and yet have failed to recognize that we were in some sense actually describing it.

I grow impatient at the length of your exordium.

Well then, tell me, I said, whether I am right or not: You remember the original principle which we laid down at the foundation of the State; we decided, and more than once insisted, that one man should practise one occupation only, that to which his nature was best adapted;—now justice, in my view, either is this principle or is some form of it.

Yes, we did.

Further, we affirmed that justice was doing one's own business, and not being a busybody; we said so again and again, and many others have said the same to us.

Yes, we said so.

Then to attend to one's own business, in some form or another, may be assumed to be justice. Do you know my evidence for this?

No, but I should like to be told.

Because I think that this is the virtuous quality which remains in the State when the other virtues of temperance and courage and wisdom are abstracted; and that this not only made it possible for them to appear, but is also their preservative as long as they remain, and we were saying that if the three were discovered by us, justice would be the fourth or remaining one.

That follows of necessity.

If we are asked to determine which of these four qualities by its presence will contribute most to the excellence of our State, whether the agreement of rulers and subjects, or the preservation in the soldiers of the opinion which the law ordains about the true nature of dangers, or wisdom and watchfulness in the rulers, or this other which is found in children and women, slave and freeman, artisan, ruler, subject (I mean the quality of every one doing his own work, and not being a busybody), the decision is not so easy.

Certainly, he replied, there would be a difficulty in saying which.

Then the attention of each individual to his own work appears to be a quality rivalling wisdom, temperance, and courage, with reference to the excellence of the State.

Yes, he said.

And the only virtue which, from that point of view, is of equal importance with them, is justice?

Exactly.

Let us look at the question also in this way: Are not the rulers in a State those to whom you would entrust the office of determining suits at law?

Certainly.

In the decision of such suits will any principle be prior to this, that a man may neither take what is another's nor be deprived of what is his own?

No.

Because it is a just principle?

Yes.

Then on this view also justice will be admitted to be the having and doing what is a man's own, and belongs to him?

Very true.

Think, now, and say whether you agree with me or not. Suppose a carpenter sets out to do the business of a cobbler, or a cobbler that of a carpenter; and suppose them to exchange their implements or social position, or the same person to try to undertake the work of both, or whatever be the change; do you think that any great harm would result to the State?

Not much.

But when the cobbler or any other man whom nature designed to be a trader, having his heart lifted up by wealth or strength or the number of his followers or any like advantage, attempts to force his way into the class of warriors, or a warrior into that of legislators and guardians, to which he ought not to aspire, and when these exchange their implements and their social position with those above them; or when one man would be trader, legislator, and warrior all in one, then I think you will agree with me in saying that this interchange and this meddling of one with another is the ruin of the State.

Most true.

Seeing then, I said, that there are three distinct classes, any meddling of one with another, or the change of one into another, is the greatest harm to the State, and may be most justly termed evil-doing?

Precisely.

And the greatest degree of evil-doing to one's own city would be termed by you injustice?

Certainly.

This then is injustice; and on the other hand when the three main classes, traders, auxiliaries, and guardians, each do their own business, that is justice, and will make the city just.

I agree with you.

We will not, I said, be over-positive as yet; but if, on trial, this conception of justice be verified in the individual as well as in the State, there will be no longer any room for doubt; if it be not verified, we must have a fresh inquiry. First let us complete the old investigation, which we began, as you remember, under the impression that, if we could previously examine justice on the larger scale, there would be less difficulty in discerning her in the individual. That larger example appeared to be the State, and accordingly we constructed as good a one as we could, knowing well that in the good State justice would be found. Let the discovery which we made be now applied to the individual—if they agree, we shall be satisfied; or, if there be a difference in the individual, we will come back to the State and have another trial of the theory. The friction of the two when rubbed together may possibly strike the light of justice, from which we can kindle a steady flame in our souls.

That will be in regular course; let us do as you say.

I proceeded to ask: When two things, a greater and less, are called by the same name, are they like or unlike in so far as they are called the same?

Like, he replied.

The just man then, if we regard the idea of justice only, will be like the just State?

He will.

And a State was thought by us to be just when the three classes in the State severally did their own business; and also thought to be temperate and valiant and wise by reason of certain other affections and qualities of these same classes?

True, he said.

And so of the individual: we may assume that he has the same three principles in his own soul which are found in the State; and he may be rightly described in the same terms, because he is affected in the same manner?

Certainly, he said.

Once more then, O my friend, we have alighted upon an easy question—whether the soul has these three principles or not?

An easy question? Nay, rather, Socrates, the proverb holds that hard is the good.

Very true, I said; and I must impress upon you, Glaucon, that in my opinion our present methods of argument are not at all adequate to the accurate solution of this question; the true method is another and a longer one. Still we may arrive at a solution not below the level of the previous inquiry.

May we not be satisfied with that? he said;—under the circumstances, I am quite content.

I too, I replied, shall be extremely well satisfied.

Then faint not in pursuing the speculation, he said.

Must we not perforce acknowledge, I said, that in each of us there are the same principles and habits which there are in the State; for it is from the individual that the State derives them. Take the quality of passion or spirit;—it would be ridiculous to imagine that this quality, when found in States, is not derived from the individuals who are supposed to possess it, e.g. the Thracians, Scythians, and in general the northern nations; and the same may be said of the love of knowledge, which may be claimed as the special characteristic of our part of the world, or of the love of money, which may, with equal truth, be attributed to the Phoenicians and Egyptians.

Exactly so, he said.

This is a fact, and there is no difficulty in perceiving it.

None whatever.

But the question is not quite so easy when we proceed to ask whether these principles are three or one; whether, that is to say, we learn with one part of our nature, are angry with another, and with a third part desire the satisfaction of our natural appetites; or whether the whole soul comes into play in each sort of action—to determine that is the difficulty.

Yes, he said; there lies the difficulty.

Then let us now try and determine whether they are the same or different.

How?

Clearly the same thing cannot act or be acted upon in the same part or in relation to the same thing at the same time, in contrary ways; and therefore whenever this contradiction occurs in things apparently the same, we know that they are really not the same, but different.

Good.

For example, I said, can the same thing be at rest and in motion at the same time in the same part?

Impossible.

Now, I said, let us have still more precise understanding, lest we should hereafter fall out by the way. Imagine the case of a man who is standing and also moving his hands and his head, and suppose a person to say that one and the same person is in motion and at rest at the same moment—to such a mode of speech we should object, and should rather say that one part of him is in motion while another is at rest.

Very true.

And suppose the objector to refine still further, and to draw the nice distinction that not only parts of tops, but whole tops, when they spin round with their pegs fixed on the spot, are at rest and in motion at the same time (and he may say the same of anything which revolves in the same spot), his objection would not be admitted by us, because in such cases things are not at rest and in motion in the same parts of themselves; we should rather say that they have both an axis and a circumference; and that the axis stands still, for there is no deviation from the perpendicular; and that the circumference goes round. But if, while revolving, the axis inclines either to the right or left, forwards or backwards, then in no point of view can they be at rest.

That is the correct mode of describing them, he replied.

Then none of these objections will confuse us, or incline us to believe that the same thing at the same time, in the same part or in relation to the same thing, can be contrary or act or be acted upon in contrary ways.

Certainly not, according to my way of thinking.

Yet, I said, that we may not be compelled to examine all such objections, and prove at length that they are untrue, let us assume their absurdity, and go forward on the understanding that hereafter, if this assumption turn out to be untrue, all the consequences which follow from it shall be withdrawn.

Yes, he said, that will be the best way.

Well, I said, would you not allow that assent and dissent, desire and aversion, attraction and repulsion, are all of them opposites, whether they are regarded as active or passive (for that makes no difference in the fact of their opposition)?

Yes, he said, they are opposites.

Well, I said, and hunger and thirst, and the desires in general, and again willing and wishing,—all these you would refer to the classes already mentioned. You would say—would you not?—that the soul of him who desires is either seeking after the object of desire; or is drawing towards herself the thing which she wishes to possess: or again,—for she may merely consent that something should be offered to her—intimates her wish to have it by a nod of assent, as if she had been asked a question?

Very true.

And what would you say of unwillingness and dislike and the absence of desire; should not these be referred to the opposite class of repulsion and rejection?

Certainly.

Admitting this to be true of desire generally, let us suppose a particular class of desires, and out of these we will select hunger and thirst, as they are termed, which are the most obvious of them?

Let us take that class, he said.

The object of one is food, and of the other drink?

Yes.

And here comes the point: is not thirst the desire which the soul has of drink, and of drink only, not of drink qualified by anything else; for example, warm or cold, or much or little, or, in a word, drink of any particular sort? But if there is heat additional to the thirst, it will bring with it the desire of cold drink; or, if cold, then that of warm drink. And again, if the thirst is qualified by abundance or by smallness, it will become a desire for much or little drink, as the case may be: but thirst pure and simple will desire drink pure and simple, which is the natural satisfaction of thirst, as food is of hunger?

Yes, he said; the simple desire is, as you say, in every case of the simple object, and the qualified desire of the qualified object.

But here a confusion may arise; and I should wish to guard against an opponent starting up and saying that no man desires drink only, but good drink, or food only, but good food; for good is the universal object of desire, and if thirst be a desire, it will necessarily be thirst after good drink (or whatever its object is); and the same is true of every other desire.

Yes, he replied, the opponent might seem to be talking sense.

Nevertheless I should still maintain that of relatives some have a quality attached to either term of the relation; others are simple and have their correlatives simple.

I do not know what you mean.

Well, you know of course that the greater is relative to the less?

Certainly.

And the much greater to the much less?

Yes.

And the sometime greater to the sometime less, and the greater that is to be to the less that is to be?

Certainly, he said.

And so of more and less, and of other correlative terms, such as the double and the half, or again, the heavier and the lighter, the swifter and the slower; and of hot and cold, and of any other relatives;—is not this true of all of them?

Yes.

And does not the same principle hold in the sciences? The object of science is knowledge (assuming that to be the true definition), but the object of a particular science is a particular kind of knowledge; I mean, for example, that the science of house-building is a kind of knowledge which is defined and distinguished from other kinds and is therefore termed architecture.

Certainly.

Because it has a particular quality which no other has?

Yes.

And it has this particular quality because it has an object of a particular kind; and this is true of the other arts and sciences?

Yes.

Now, then, if I have made myself clear, you will understand my original meaning in what I said about relatives. My meaning was, that if one term of a relation is taken alone, the other is taken alone; if one term is qualified, the other is also qualified. I do not mean to say that relative terms must possess all the same qualities as their correlates; that the science of health is healthy, or that of disease necessarily diseased, or that the sciences of good and evil are therefore good and evil; but only that, when the term science is no longer used absolutely, but has a qualified object which in this case is the nature of health and disease, it becomes defined, and is hence called not merely science, but the science of medicine.

I quite understand, and I think as you do.

Would you not say that thirst is one of these essentially relative terms, having clearly a relation——

Yes, thirst is relative to drink.

And a certain kind of thirst is relative to a certain kind of drink; but thirst taken alone is neither of much nor little, nor of good nor bad, nor of any particular kind of drink, but of drink only?

Certainly.

Then the soul of the thirsty one, in so far as he is thirsty, desires only drink; for this she yearns, and for this she strives?

That is plain.

And if you suppose something which pulls a thirsty soul away from drink, that must be different from the thirsty principle which draws him like a beast to drink; for, as we were saying, the same thing cannot at the same time with the same part of itself act in contrary ways about the same.

Impossible.

No more than you can say that the hands of the archer push and pull the bow at the same time, but what you say is that one hand pushes and the other pulls.

Exactly so, he replied.

Now are there times when men are thirsty, and yet unwilling to drink?

Yes, he said, it constantly happens.

And in such a case what is one to say? Would you not say that there was something in the soul bidding a man to drink, and something else forbidding him, which is other and stronger than the principle which bids him?

I should say so.

And the prohibition in such cases is derived from reasoning, whereas the motives which lead and attract proceed from passions and diseases?

Clearly.

Then we may fairly assume that they are two, and that they differ from one another; the one with which a man reasons, we may call the rational principle of the soul, the other, with which he loves and hungers and thirsts and feels the flutterings of any other desire, may be termed the irrational or appetitive, the ally of sundry pleasures and satisfactions?

Yes, he said, we may fairly assume them to be different.

So much, then, for the definition of two of the principles existing in the soul. And what now of passion, or spirit? Is it a third, or akin to one of the preceding?

I should be inclined to say—akin to desire.

Well, I said, there is a story which I remember to have heard, and in which I put faith. The story is, that Leontius, the son of Aglaion, coming up one day from the Piraeus, under the north wall on the outside, observed some dead bodies lying on the ground at the place of execution. He felt a desire to see them, and also a dread and abhorrence of them; for a time he struggled and covered his eyes, but at length the desire got the better of him; and forcing them open, he ran up to the dead bodies, saying, Look, ye wretches, take your fill of the fair sight.

I have heard the story myself, he said.

The moral of the tale is that anger at times goes to war with desire, as though they were two distinct things.

Yes; that is the meaning, he said.

And are there not many other cases in which we observe that when a man's desires violently prevail over his reason, he reviles himself, and is angry at the violence within him, and that in this struggle, which is like the struggle of factions in a State, his spirit is on the side of his reason;—but for the passionate or spirited element to take part with the desires when reason decides that she should not be opposed, is a sort of thing which I believe that you never observed occurring in yourself, nor, as I should imagine, in anyone else?

Certainly not.

Suppose that a man thinks he has done a wrong to another, the nobler he is the less able is he to feel indignant at any suffering, such as hunger, or cold, or any other pain which the injured person may inflict upon him—these he deems to be just, and, as I say, his spirit refuses to be excited by them.

True, he said.

But when a man thinks that he is the sufferer of the wrong, then the spirit within him boils and chafes, and is on the side of what it believes to be justice; and though it suffers hunger or cold or other pain, it is only the more determined to persevere and conquer. Such a noble spirit will not be quelled until it has achieved its object or been slain, or until it has been recalled by the reason within, like a dog by the shepherd?

The illustration is perfect, he replied; and in our State, as we were saying, the auxiliaries were to be dogs, and to hear the voice of the rulers, who are their shepherds.

Yes, I said, you understand me admirably; there is, however, a further point which I wish you to consider.

What point?

You remember that passion or spirit appeared at first sight to be a kind of desire, but now we should say quite the contrary; for in the conflict of the soul spirit is arrayed on the side of the rational principle.

Most assuredly.

But a further question arises: Is passion different from reason also, or only a kind of reason; in which latter case, instead of three principles in the soul, there will only be two, the rational and the concupiscent? or rather, as the State was composed of three classes, traders, auxiliaries, counsellors, so may there not be in the individual soul a third element which is passion or spirit, and when not corrupted by bad education is the natural auxiliary of reason?

Yes, he said, there must be a third.

Yes, I replied, if passion, which has already been shown to be different from desire, turn out also to be different from reason.

But that is easily proved:—We may observe even in young children that they are full of spirit almost as soon as they are born, whereas some of them never seem to attain to the use of reason, and most of them late enough.

Excellent, I said, and you may see passion equally in brute animals, which is a further proof of the truth of what you are saying. And we may once more appeal to the words of Homer, which have been already quoted by us.

He smote his breast, and thus rebuked his heart;[7]

for in this verse Homer has clearly supposed the power which reasons about the better and worse to be different from the unreasoning anger which is rebuked by it.

Very true, he said.

And so, after much tossing, we have reached land, and are fairly agreed that the same principles which exist in the State exist also in the individual, and that they are three in number.

Exactly.

Must we not then infer that the individual is wise in the same way and in virtue of the same quality which makes the State wise?

Certainly.

Also that the State is brave in the same way and by the same quality as an individual is brave, and that there is the same correspondence in regard to the other virtues?

Assuredly.

Therefore the individual will be acknowledged by us to be just in the same way in which the State has been found just?

That follows of course.

We cannot but remember that the justice of the State consisted in each of the three classes doing the work of its own class?

I do not think we have forgotten, he said.

We must now record in our memory that the individual in whom the several components of his nature do their own work will be just, and will do his own work?

Yes, he said, we must record that important fact.

First, it is proper for the rational principle, which is wise, and has the care of the whole soul, to rule, and for the spirit to be the subject and ally?

Certainly.

And, as we were saying, the blending of music and gymnastic will bring them into accord, nerving and sustaining the reason with noble words and lessons, and moderating and soothing and civilizing the wildness of passion by harmony and rhythm?

Quite true, he said.

And these two, thus nurtured and educated, and having learned truly to know their own functions, will rule over the concupiscent, which in each of us is the largest part of the soul and by nature most insatiable of gain; over this they will keep guard, lest, waxing great and strong with the fullness of bodily pleasures, as they are termed, the concupiscent soul, no longer confined to her own sphere, should attempt to enslave and rule those who are not her natural-born subjects, and overturn the whole life of man?

Very true, he said.

Both together will they not be the best defenders of the whole soul and the whole body against attacks from without; the one counselling, and the other going out to fight as the leader directs, and courageously executing his commands and counsels?

True.

Likewise it is by reference to spirit that an individual man is deemed courageous, because his spirit retains in pleasure and pain the commands of reason about what he ought or ought not to fear?

Right, he replied.

And we call him wise on account of that little part which rules, and which proclaims these commands; the part in which is situated the knowledge of what is for the interest of each of the three parts and of the whole?

Assuredly.

And would you not say that he is temperate who has these same elements in friendly harmony, in whom the one ruling principle of reason, and the two subject ones of spirit and desire, are equally agreed that reason ought to rule, and do not rebel?

Certainly, he said, that is a precise account of temperance whether in the State or individual.

And, finally, I said, a man will be just in that way and by that quality which we have often mentioned.

That is very certain.

And is justice dimmer in the individual, and is her form different, or is she the same which we found her to be in the State?

There is no difference in my opinion, he said.

Because, if any doubt is still lingering in our minds, a few commonplace instances will satisfy us of the truth of what I am saying.

What sort of instances do you mean?

If the case is put to us, must we not admit that the just State, or the man of similar nature who has been trained in the principles of such a State, will be less likely than the unjust to make away with a deposit of gold or silver? Would any one deny this?

No one, he replied.

Will such a man ever be involved in sacrilege or theft, or treachery either to his friends or to his country?

Never.

Neither will he ever, for any reason, break faith where there have been oaths or agreements?

Impossible.

No one will be less likely to commit adultery, neglect his father and mother, or fail in his religious duties?

No one.

And the reason for all this is that each part of him is doing its own business, whether in ruling or being ruled?

Exactly so.

Are you satisfied then that the quality which makes such men and such states is justice, or do you hope to discover some other?

Not I, indeed.

Then our dream has been realized, and the suspicion which we expressed that, at the beginning of our work of construction, some divine power must have conducted us to a primary form of justice, has now been verified?

Yes, certainly.

And the division of labour which required the carpenter and the shoemaker and the rest of them to devote himself to the work for which he is naturally fitted, and to do nothing else, was a shadow of justice, and for that reason it was of use?

Clearly.

And in reality justice was such as we were describing, being concerned however, not with a man's external affairs, but with an inner relationship in which he himself is more truly concerned; for the just man does not permit the several elements within him to interfere with one another, or any of them to do the work of others,—he sets in order his own

inner life, and is his own master and his own law, and at peace with himself; and when he has bound together the three principles within him, which may be compared to the higher, lower, and middle notes of the scale, and any that are intermediate between them—when he has bound all these together, and is no longer many, but has become one entirely temperate and perfectly adjusted nature, then he proceeds to act, if he has to act, whether in a matter of property, or in the treatment of the body, or in some affair of politics or private business; always thinking and calling that which preserves and co-operates with this harmonious condition, just and good action, and the knowledge which presides over it, wisdom, and that which at any time impairs this condition, he will call unjust action, and the opinion which presides over it ignorance.

You have said the exact truth, Socrates.

Very good; and if we were to affirm that we had discovered the just man and the just State, and the nature of justice in each of them, we should not be far from the truth?

Most certainly not.

May we say so, then?

Let us say so.

And now, I said, injustice has to be considered.

Clearly.

Must not injustice be a strife which arises among the same three principles—a meddlesomeness, and interference, and rising up of a part of the soul against the whole, an assertion of unlawful authority, which is made by a rebellious subject against a true prince, of whom he is the natural vassal,—what is all this confusion and delusion but injustice and intemperance and cowardice and ignorance, and, in short, every form of vice?

Exactly so.

And if the nature of justice and injustice is known, then the meaning of acting unjustly and being unjust, or again of acting justly, is now also perfectly clear?

How so? he said.

Why, I said, they are like disease and health; being in the soul just what disease and health are in the body.

How so? he said.

Why, I said, that which is healthy causes health, and that which is unhealthy causes disease.

Yes.

And just actions cause justice, and unjust actions cause injustice?

That is certain.

And the creation of health is the institution of a natural order and government of one by another in the parts of the body; and the creation of disease is the production of a state of things at variance with this natural order?

True.

And is not the creation of justice the institution of a natural order and government of one by another in the parts of the soul, and the creation of injustice the production of a state of things at variance with the natural order?

Exactly so, he said.

Then virtue is the health and beauty and well-being of the soul, and vice the disease and weakness and deformity of the same?

True.

And how are virtue and vice acquired—is it not by good and evil practices?

Assuredly.

The time has come, then, to answer the final question of the comparative advantage of justice and injustice: Which is the more profitable, to be just and act justly and honourably, whether one's character is or is not known, or to be unjust and act unjustly, if one is unpunished, that is to say unreformed?

In my judgement, Socrates, the question has now become ridiculous. We know that, when the *bodily* constitution is gone, life is no longer endurable, though pampered with all kinds of meats and drinks, and having all wealth and all power; and shall we be told that when the natural health of our vital principle* is undermined and corrupted, life is still worth having to a man, if only he be allowed to do whatever he likes, except to take steps to acquire justice and virtue and escape from injustice and vice; assuming them both to be such as we have described?

Yes, I said, the question is, as you say, ridiculous.

*["the very principle whereby we live" in the translation of F. M. Cornford—Ed.]

NOTES

1. [They were Plato's elder brothers. He avoids pronouncing his father's name, like the Pythagoreans who would only refer to their founders as ἐκεῖνος, 'that man'.]

2. [Or 'city': and so throughout the following passage.]

3. [Reading, in 369 d 6, πόση πόλις for the πως η πόλις of the MSS. (R. W. Chapman in *C.R.* 1 (1936), p. 167.)]

4. Cf. *Laws* 663·e.

5. *Odyssey* i. 352.

6. [Cf. iii. 414 a.]

7. *Od.* xx. 17, quoted *supra*, iii. 390d.

I M M A N U E L   K A N T

Fragments of a Moral Catechism*

Immanuel Kant (1724–1804), the greatest of the German philosophers, spent his entire career at the University of Königsberg in East Prussia.

The teacher seeks in his pupil's reason what he wants to teach him; and if perhaps the student does not know the answer to the question, then (directing his student's reason) he suggests it to him.

*From Immanuel Kant, *The Metaphysical Principles of Virtue*, translated by James Ellington (Indianapolis and New York: Bobbs-Merrill, 1964), pp. 148–53. Originally published in German in 1797. Reprinted by permission of the translator.

1. Teacher: What is your greatest, yes, your whole desire in life?

Student: (remains silent).

Teacher: That everything should always go according to your wish and will.

2. What does one call such a condition?

Student: (remains silent).

Teacher: It is called happiness (constant well-being, a pleasant life, complete satisfaction with one's condition).

3. If you had all happiness (all that is possible in the world) in your possession, would you keep it all for yourself or share it with your fellow men?

Student: I would share it and make other people happy and contented also.

4. Teacher: That shows quite well that you have a good heart. But let us see if you have good understanding. Would you give the sluggard soft pillows to while away his life in sweet idleness? Or the drunkard wine and other intoxicating spirits? Or the deceiver a charming appearance and captivating manners so as to dupe others? Or the violent person audacity and a hard fist so as to be able to overpower others? There are all so many means which each of these people wishes in order to be happy in his fashion.

Student: No, not that.

5. Teacher: So, you see, if you had all happiness at your disposal and the best will besides, you still would not, without reflection, bestow that happiness upon everyone who sought it, but would first inquire to what extent each person was worthy of happiness. But as for yourself, you would probably have no hesitation about first providing yourself with everything you reckon in your happiness?

Student: Yes.

Teacher: But does it not also occur to you to ask whether you yourself might be worthy of happiness?

Student: By all means.

Teacher: That something in you which strains after happiness is inclination. But that which restricts your inclination, on condition that you first be worthy of happiness, is your reason, and your being able by means of your reason to restrain and subdue your inclination is the freedom of your will.

6. The rule and direction for knowing how you go about sharing in happiness, without also becoming unworthy of it, lies entirely in your reason. This amounts to saying that you don't have to learn this rule of conduct by experience or from other people's instruction; your own reason teaches and even tells you what you have to do. For instance, if a situation presents itself in which you can get yourself or a friend a great advantage by an artfully thought out lie (and without hurting anybody else either), what does your reason say to that?

Student: I should not lie, though the advantage to me and my friend be as great as ever you please. Lying is mean and makes a man unworthy to be happy. Here is an unconditional constraint by a command (or prohibition) of reason, which I must obey. In the face of this, all my inclinations must be silent.

Teacher: What does one call this necessity, laid upon man directly by his reason, to act in accordance with its law?

Student: It is called duty.

Teacher: Accordingly, the observance of man's duty is the universal and sole condition of his worthiness to be happy; and these two are one and the same.

7. But if, besides, we are conscious of such a good and efficacious will, by which we think ourselves worthy (at least not unworthy) to be happy, can we make this the foundation of any secure hope of sharing in happiness?

Student: No, not upon that alone. For it is not always within our power to provide ourselves with it. Moreover, the course of nature does not adjust itself to our merit; the fortunes of life (our welfare generally) depend upon circumstances which are far from being all within the power of man. Our happiness, therefore, remains always only a wish, which can never even become a hope unless some other power is added.

8. Teacher: Has reason its own grounds for assuming that there really is such a power that distributes happiness according to the merit and guilt of men, governs the whole of nature, and rules the world with supreme wisdom, i.e., for believing in God?

Student: Yes. For we see in those works of nature which we can judge of such extensive and profound wisdom that we cannot explain it to ourselves otherwise than as the inexpressibly great art of a Creator. From this Creator we also have cause to promise ourselves a no less wise regulation of the moral order, the supreme ornament of the world: a regulation, namely, that if we do not make ourselves unworthy of happiness by violating our duty, then we can hope to become partakers of it.

In this catechism, which ought to go through all the articles of virtue and vice, the greatest attention must be paid to the consideration that a command of duty is not founded upon the advantages or disadvantages of observing it, either for the man it ought to obligate or even for other people, but, rather, is founded quite purely upon moral principle. Any mention of advantages or disadvantages is only incidental, as a supplement that is dispensable in itself, but serves as a vehicle for the taste of those who are frail by nature. The ignominy of vice, not the harmfulness of it (for the agent himself), must above all be strikingly represented. For if the dignity of virtue in action is not exalted above everything else, the very concept of duty disappears and dissolves into mere pragmatic prescriptions. Then the nobility of man in his own consciousness disappears, and he is for sale, to be bought at any price which tempting inclinations may offer him.

When these things have been wisely and accurately evolved from man's own reason according to the variety of the circumstances of age, sex, and rank which are encountered, then there is still something which must make the decision, which inwardly moves the soul and sets man in a position in which he cannot but regard himself with the greatest admiration for the original predisposition residing within him, the impression of which never fades away. When, at the conclusion of the student's instruction, his duties in their order are once more summarily enumerated (recapitulated) for him, when in each one of these duties he is made mindful of the fact that no evil, hardship, nor any of life's suffering, nor even threat of death —any or all of which might be inflicted upon him for remaining true to his duties—can rob him of his consciousness of being superior to such evils and being master of them, then the following question lies very close to him: What is that in you which may dare to do battle against all the forces of nature within you and round about you, and to conquer them when they come into conflict with your moral principles? When this question, whose solution completely transcends the power of speculative reason, but which nonetheless presents itself of its own accord, is taken to heart, then even the incomprehensibility of this self-knowledge must give the soul an exaltation which only animates it into more strongly holding its duty sacred the more it is assailed.

In this catechistic moral instruction it would be of the greatest advantage to moral education to present some casuistical questions with every analysis of a duty, and to let the assembled students test their understanding by having each one of them declare how he thinks the captious problem proposed to him might be solved. This is so not only because such a procedure is a cultivation of the reason especially suited to the ability of a beginner (inasmuch as these questions, which concern what duty is, can be resolved far more easily than questions of speculation), and is, accordingly, the most appropriate kind of procedure for generally sharpening the understanding of the young; but this is especially so because it lies in the nature of man to love what he by his own work has brought to the condition of a science (whose outcome he now knows), and so the student by such exercises is drawn imperceptibly to serve the interest of morality.

But it is of the greatest importance in education not to intermix (amalgamate) the moral catechism with the religious catechism, still less to let it follow upon the latter, but always to bring the moral catechism to a state of the clearest insight and indeed with the greatest diligence and minuteness of detail. For otherwise nothing will come of religion later on but the hypocrisy of acknowledging one's duties from fear, and of feigning an interest in them which is not of the heart.

PAUL W. TAYLOR

The Ultimate Question*

THE DEMAND FOR A JUSTIFICATION OF MORALITY

There is one problem of ethics that perhaps deserves, more than any other, to be called the Ultimate Question. It is the question of the rationality of the moral life itself. It may be expressed thus: Is the commitment to live by moral principles a commitment grounded on reason or is it, in the final analysis, an arbitrary decision?

The Ultimate Question is not itself a moral question. That is to say it does not ask what we morally ought to do or even how we can discover our moral duty. It is, instead, a question about the justification of morality as a whole. Why, it asks, should we be concerned with morality at all? If living by moral principles can at times be so difficult, if our moral integrity may, in some circumstances, require the sacrifice of our happiness or even of our life, why not simply reject the whole moral "game" and live amorally? In short, why be moral?

It is important to see exactly why this is not a moral question or a question about what actions are morally right. When a person asks why he should be moral, he assumes he already knows what "being moral" means. He could not understand his own question when he asked, "Why should I do what is morally right, especially when it conflicts with my self-interest?" unless he understood the meaning of doing what is morally right. Moreover, if his question concerns a *particular* case of conflict between moral duty and self-interest, then it is assumed that the questioner accepts the fact that, in the specific circumstances referred to, a certain action *is* his duty. He recognizes it as an action which, from the moral point of view, he

ought to perform. But he also recognizes it as conduct which, from the standpoint of his self-interest, would be irrational. He then asks, Why, after all, should I do it? In effect he is asking, Why should moral duty *outweigh* or *override* self-interest when there is a conflict between them? . . .

The demand for an ultimate justification of morality was first stated in its classic form in Plato's *Republic*. Glaucon and Adeimantus, two of the figures participating in the dialogue, challenge Socrates, the protagonist, to justify the living of a morally upright life. Their challenge is presented in the form of the . . . story, which is known as The Myth of Gyges. . . . [See the articles by Plato in this volume, pp. 569 and 575.]

Here is a classic statement of the case against morality. Socrates' attempt to reply to it, which forms the main argument of Plato's *Republic,* consists in trying to show that moral virtue is its own reward and that only the just (morally upright) man is truly happy. Thus, in effect, Socrates claims that in the long run there is no real conflict between duty and self-interest. Philosophers have been disputing about this ever since.

In order to see exactly what is at stake in trying to answer the question, Why be moral? we must recognize how it differs from a question about the nature of moral reasoning. For the question, Why be moral? arises the moment when someone realizes that, if he commits himself to the principles of moral reasoning, he may find himself in circumstances where his reasoning leads to the conclusion that he ought to do an act which entails some inconvenience, unpleasantness, or frustration for himself. It might even lead to the conclusion that in the given situation confronting him he must give up his life. He then wants to know why he should follow the rules of moral reasoning.

*From Paul W. Taylor, *Principles of Ethics, An Introduction* (Belmont, Calif.: Wadsworth Publishing Co., 1975), Chap. 9. Reprinted by permission of the publisher and the author.

It should be noted that this problem does not arise for the ethical egoist, who *identifies* moral reasoning with prudential reasoning. As we saw, . . . ethical egoism is the view that each person ought to do whatever will most further his self-interest in the long run. If this is taken as an ultimate moral principle then the question, Why be moral? becomes the question, Why seek the furtherance of my self-interest in the long run? Such a question would only be asked by someone who did not want to give up his pleasures or who was satisfied with pursuing short-range goals in life, and who realized at the same time that his long-range interests might not be furthered by his continuing to live in the way he had been living. The answer to his question, of course, would be that, if he is not willing to put up with inconveniences and discomforts and if he is not able to discipline himself to sacrifice his short-range goals when his pursuit of them prevents him from achieving lasting satisfactions in life, then he will not in fact be happy. But for the ethical egoist, no sacrifice of his self-interest *as a whole* would ever be justified and no such sacrifice would ever be morally required of him.

Since the Ultimate Question arises only when it is logically possible for there to be a conflict between the demands of morality and the pursuit of self-interest, we shall be concerned from this point on with nonegoist moral principles only. We are not assuming that morality is superior to self-interest, but only that it is possible for them to be in conflict. Under this assumption, then, the next point to realize is that the Ultimate Question lies outside the framework of the logic of moral reasoning itself. For the logic of moral reasoning tells us what a good reason in ethics is. It defines the method of reasoning a person should use *if* he were to commit himself to trying to find out what he morally ought to do. In asking, Why be moral? on the other hand, one is challenging the reasonableness of being committed to trying to find out what one morally ought to do. It is a challenge to the whole enterprise of moral reasoning and moral conduct. The challenge can be put this way: Suppose there is a valid method of moral reasoning and suppose, by following it, I do find out what I morally ought to do. Why should I bother to act in accordance with this knowledge? Why shouldn't I follow my self-interest instead? In other words, granted that there is a logic of moral reasoning, why should I choose to let this logic outweigh the logic of self-interest or prudence when there is a conflict between them? In making this challenge the person is not questioning the validity of moral reasoning. Rather, he is asking why such reasoning should guide his conduct when he could just as well choose to have his conduct guided by another set of rules of reasoning, namely, the furtherance of his own self-interest. Thus, he is demanding a justification for morality (the commitment to use moral reasoning as a guide to conduct) *as a whole*. . . .

IS THE ULTIMATE QUESTION AN ABSURDITY?

One view that has been taken by philosophers regarding the Ultimate Question is that it cannot be answered because it is absurd. It has been seen that a person who asks why he should do what is morally right already presupposes that he knows, or at least believes, that certain acts *are* right. In asking his question, therefore, he is not asking what he morally ought to do. He already has an answer to this. What, then, does he want to know? It seems that he wants to know why he should do what he knows to be right. It is as if he is saying, "I know what my moral duty is—now tell me why I ought to act in accordance with this knowledge." This, however, is absurd. For if the person knows that something is his duty, then he already knows why he ought to do it, namely, *just because it is his duty*.

When it is understood in this way, the Ultimate Question cannot be answered. But the reason it cannot is that no real question is being asked. For suppose we try to answer it by showing the person why he ought to do a certain action. We are then giving him moral reasons for doing that particular action. This, however, will not be accepted by him as an answer to the question he is asking. *His* question is, Why should I do what is right?, not, Why is this action the right thing to do? So if we show him that it is the right thing to do, he will not be satisfied. He will still ask for reasons for being *committed to doing* what he *acknowledges* to be something he ethically ought to do. Therefore it is no answer to give him moral reasons for doing the action in question. One cannot cite moral reasons for being moral (that is, for being committed to do what one believes to be right). Someone who wants to justify being moral is asking why he ought to use moral reasons as actual guides in his practical life. To give him such reasons is to assume that he will accept them as reasons for action. But this is the very thing he is questioning.

Once we become aware of this, however, we can see that there is a deep confusion behind the question

"Why be moral?" when it is interpreted as a demand for reasons for doing what one acknowledges to be morally right. A moral reason is, by its very nature, a *"reason for acting."* It is not merely a "reason for believing," that is, a reason for accepting or acknowledging the truth of a proposition such as, Act X is morally right. To show why act X is morally right is to give moral reasons why a person should actually perform it. At the same time, it justifies accepting the statement "Act X is morally right" as true. It has been pointed out that the person who asks, Why be moral? is asking (under the present interpretation), Why should I *do* what I *believe* to be morally right? It can now be seen that he is confused in asking this. For he is assuming a separation between moral belief and moral action that isn't possible. To *believe* that an action is morally right is to have a reason for *doing* it, namely, that it is morally right. It is this confusion that explains why his question cannot be answered by giving him moral reasons for being moral. The point is that, once a person accepts moral reasons for *believing* that some action ought to be done, he has all the basis he needs for *doing* it, to wit, those very reasons for believing it ought to be done.

Given this interpretation of the Ultimate Question, it can be dismissed as resting on a mistake. It is not worth trying to answer, since a clear-thinking person would never ask it.

THE MEANING OF THE ULTIMATE QUESTION

Does the foregoing argument successfully dispose of the Ultimate Question? Some philosophers are convinced that it does not. They claim that there is a genuine question behind the apparent oddity of asking why one ought to do something while acknowledging that a moral person would have good reason to do it. The true significance of the question, they say, has to do with a choice or decision to be made between two sorts of reasons: moral reasons and reasons of self-interest. To hold that a person who asks why he ought to do what is morally right already knows why (namely, because it *is* morally right), is to miss the real point of the Ultimate Question. It is true that one cannot give moral arguments for being moral, just as one cannot give prudential arguments for being prudent. Nevertheless there may be moral reasons *for,* and prudential reasons *against,* a certain action, and there may be moral reasons *against* and prudential reasons *for* another action. In situations of that sort,

one must act either morally or in one's self-interest; one cannot do both. How is one to decide?

It is here that the question, Why be moral? does not seem at all absurd. This was why Socrates took seriously the challenge to morality expressed in the Myth of Gyges. He realized that, in normal circumstances of life, we do not ask for a justification of morality because society sees to it that it is generally in a person's self-interest to be moral. It pays to avoid social disapproval and to maintain a good reputation. But the philosopher cannot be satisfied with this, since it is possible to imagine a case where a person has the power (as described in the Myth of Gyges) to act immorally and escape social sanctions. Why, then, should he not act immorally? Unless there is a *reason* for his not doing so, morality reduces to the self-interested avoidance of social disapproval. Conformity to the actual moral code of one's own society would then be one's highest duty. This entails, of course, normative ethical relativism. The norms of each society would determine what is right and wrong in it, and no society's code as a whole could be shown to be unjust or evil. But to take the Ultimate Question seriously is to seek a reason for being moral even when it doesn't pay, and even when being moral involves a clash with what is socially approved.

So let us now interpret the Ultimate Question as asking, When moral reasons and reasons of self-interest are in conflict, why should one follow the first rather than the second (assuming that one had the power to do either)?

One possible response to the question so understood might be to try to strengthen in the questioner the desire to be moral, so that he will in fact act morally even when it is contrary to his self-interest. The Ultimate Question is then being taken as a demand for *motivating* reasons (reasons that will actually move a person to act) rather than as a demand for *justifying* reasons (reasons that show why an act ought to be done). Now it may sometimes be true that a person who asks, Why be moral? in real life does want to be motivated to such conduct. We then answer him, not by presenting him with a sound philosophical argument, but by trying to persuade or influence him so that he will feel inspired to do what is right. We try to reinforce his moral motives and strengthen his sense of duty. If he is a child we give him a moral upbringing. We not only try to instill in him a desire to abide by moral rules (of honesty, fairness, nonmaleficence, et cetera), we also try to develop his capacity and inclination to reason morally for himself. If we are successful in this, he will not feel the need to ask the question, Why be moral? in later life. He will have been motivated to be moral and thus not find it psychologically necessary to ask to be motivated.

The philosopher, however, is not interested in engaging in this kind of response. For him the Ultimate Question is a demand for a justification for being moral, not a request to be motivated to be moral. The difference is not always easy to grasp. (Indeed, there is a whole theory in psychology—the behaviorism of Professor B. F. Skinner—which overlooks the difference!) A person's motivation, we have seen, has to do with his desires, his actual tendencies to aim at certain ends or goals. Here the relevant questions are, Does this individual have a desire to be moral, and if so, how strong is that desire? In particular, is it strong enough to overcome the motive to pursue his self-interest in cases of conflict between what he believes to be morally right and what he believes will serve his own interests? Justification, on the other hand, has to do with reasons, not with desires. To justify being moral is to vindicate the belief that moral reasons outweigh or override reasons of self-interest when they conflict. It is to show why moral reasons take priority over, and hence are superior to, prudential reasons. Now the idea of one sort of reasons taking priority over, or being superior to, another sort is not to be confused with the idea of one sort of reasons having greater motivational strength than another sort. A person's believing that moral reasons are better or weightier grounds for an action than prudential ones does not imply that he will always be more strongly motivated to do what is moral than what is prudent. If there is such a discrepancy in a person between justifying reasons and their motivational effectiveness, the person is said to have "weakness of will," and he may even recognize this in himself as a flaw in his character. It is then possible for him to consider an action *unjustified* (because it is morally wrong though prudentially expedient) and still actually do it. In that case his desires and actions are simply not consistent with his moral beliefs.

To justify anyone's being moral, as distinct from motivating some particular individual to be moral, is to give a sound argument in support of the claim that moral reasons take priority over reasons of self-interest whenever they conflict. If we were able to discover, or construct, such an argument, it would follow that everyone ought to be motivated by moral reasons for acting rather than by prudential reasons for acting in cases of conflict. Whether any given individual will in fact be so motivated depends on the strength of his desires, not on the soundness of an argument. Even if a person's desire to be moral were indeed strengthened by his reading or hearing such an argument, thus motivating him to be moral, this is irrelevant to the question of whether the argument actually showed the moral reasons to be superior to those of self-interest. Similarly, the argument might not convince someone intellectually, nor persuade him to act morally, nor reinforce his moral motivation. But the failure of the argument to bring about such results in any given individual is strictly irrelevant to the philosophical acceptability of the argument's content.

Suppose, then, that the Ultimate Question is understood to mean, Why do moral reasons outweigh prudential reasons in cases of conflict, rather than the other way around? Now it will not do to reply, Because morality *by definition* is that set of principles which outweigh all other principles that might conflict with them. This is not an acceptable answer because a person might decide to make reasons of self-interest *his* highest overriding principles. Then, by the given definition, self-interest would become morality in his case, and there could be no conflict between moral reasons and prudential reasons. In short, he would be an ethical egoist, and we saw earlier that the Ultimate Question presupposes that ethical egoism is false. (If ethical egoism were true, the whole issue would cease to be a meaningful problem.)

It has now become clear where the crux of the matter lies. The Ultimate Question places before us a challenge that concerns our *ultimate normative commitments*. It asks: Are there any reasons that would justify our commitment to moral principles as being the supreme overriding norms of our practical life (where "moral principles" are not by definition supreme and where it is logically possible for them to be in conflict with prudential principles)? We shall take this as our final formulation of the Ultimate Question. What answers might be proposed for it when it is understood this way?

TWO PROPOSED ANSWERS TO THE ULTIMATE QUESTION

(1) The first answer is that there are reasons that justify *everyone's* commitment to the priority of moral principles over self-interest. For suppose *everyone* took the opposite position and made a com-

mitment such that, whenever self-interest and morality conflict, considerations of self-interest are to override moral considerations. The consequence would be the total collapse of any social order. Each person would be out for himself and would know that every other person was out for himself. Thus, each could have no confidence that others would refrain from harming him. Everyone would live in continual fear of everyone else, since all would realize that no constraints upon self-interest would be operative (even when such constraints were required by moral principles of fairness and respect for life). A world where the priority rule, "Self-interest is to take precedence over morality," was generally accepted would be a world where no one could attain his goals. Each would lack the basic security of being able to count on others not to interfere with his pursuit of his own ends.

The conclusion is evident. The whole point of any individual's committing himself to the supremacy of self-interest over morality is to promote his own welfare. But if this commitment were made by everyone, each would be unable to promote his self-interest to as great a degree as he would when everyone made the opposite commitment. This is the paradox of universal selfishness. No one would be as well off as he would be under universal conformity to moral rules. The very purpose of universal selfishness, in other words, is undermined by its practice. The priority of self-interest over morality is therefore a self-defeating commitment. It frustrates its own purpose and is consequently irrational. Commitment to the priority of morality over self-interest, on the contrary, is self-fulfilling. Its purpose is to create a social order where everyone benefits from mutual trust. This trust is only possible under the condition that everyone makes a firm commitment to the supremacy of such moral principles as justice and nonmaleficence. For only under that condition can each person count on others not to harm him or interfere with his pursuit of his own goals.

Is this an acceptable answer to the Ultimate Question? Does it provide a sound argument to justify being moral? It seems not, for it is open to the following objection. The answer that has been proposed overlooks an important distinction, which can be brought out by comparing these two questions: (a) Why should I be moral? (b) Why should people in general be moral? The argument given above is an adequate answer to (b), but not to (a). And it is (a) that is the Ultimate Question. The person who asks, Why be moral? is asking why he, *as an individual,* should commit himself to the priority of moral principles over his self-interest. If such a person were given the argument stated above, he would reply, Yes, I agree that if *everyone* were to commit himself to the supremacy of self-interest, it would lead to the frustration of my own as well as everyone else's self-interest. So I agree that it would be irrational for everyone to do this. However, this does not show that it would be irrational for *me* to make such a commitment. For in the world as it is (where others are at least sometimes committed to being moral), by making the commitment to self-interest over morality I would thereby gain a major advantage for myself. This would be especially true if I kept my commitment a secret from others. My self-interest would be promoted by such a commitment on my part, and hence it would not be self-defeating, but quite the contrary. So how can it be shown to be irrational?

When the person who asks the Ultimate Question takes this stand, it is true that the answer to (b) will not provide him with an answer to *his* question, which is (a). But a new aspect of the situation has now come to light; we see that such a person is assuming that his case is an exception to a general rule. The argument against everyone's making a commitment to self-interest, he claims, does not hold for him. Why not? Because his commitment to self-interest can be self-fulfilling only when others do not make a similar commitment. We can then ask him, Why should your case be considered an exception? What is so special about you that makes your commitment justifiable when those of, others in circumstances similar to yours, are not? Indeed, by your own argument you can be justified in making your commitment only on the condition that others do *not* make the same commitment. Now unless you can show that you deserve to be treated as a special case, you have provided no justification for considering yourself an exception.

There is, however, a reply that can be made to this objection—a reply available to the person who asks question (a). He can say, Since I am asking for reasons that support an *ultimate* normative commitment, I am seeking to justify commitment to *any* principle as a supreme one, including the principle that I am not to make my case an exception to a general rule. After all, I can always point to some property that I have and that no one else has as the basis for claiming that my own case is to be treated differently from theirs.

That is, I can commit myself to the *principle* (as a supreme one) that having the attribute in question is a relevant difference between one person and another, as far as the promotion of self-interest is concerned. The Ultimate Question can now simply be restated to include this principle, thus: Why ought a person— *any* person—having that property not be considered an exception to the general rule that moral reasons override reasons of self-interest?

To see how such a position is perfectly consistent, consider the property of having six toes on each foot with a wart on each toe. Suppose someone endowed by nature with that property states that he adopts, as an ultimate normative commitment, the principle that *anyone* with such feet is to be permitted to further his interests whenever they conflict with the interest of others. It is not possible, then, to claim that he is making an unjustifiable exception in his own favor (knowing that he alone has the property in question). For he is quite willing to universalize that principle, letting *everyone* commit himself to it and letting it be applied to *all* cases where the property in question is exemplified. Thus he is not claiming that his own case is to be treated differently from others' *merely because it is his own*. Instead, he is committing himself to the principle (as a supreme one) that having the property in question is a relevant difference between persons.

Given this commitment, the Ultimate Question can be rephrased as follows. Instead of asking "Why should I be moral?" the individual now can ask, "Why should I not adopt the principle that anyone having six toes on each foot with a wart on each toe is an exception to the general rule that moral reasons override reasons of self-interest?" This question cannot be answered by asserting that there is no relevant difference between the questioner's case and that of others, for this would simply mean that the one who asserts this does not subscribe to the principle adopted by the questioner. To make such a statement is not to show why the questioner is mistaken, illogical, or unjustified in adopting his principle. It is merely to indicate that one has not made the same ultimate normative commitment that the questioner has. So an adequate answer has not yet been given to question (a): Why should I (as an individual) be moral?

(2) A second way to respond to the Ultimate Question can be seen as emerging from the foregoing considerations. When the Ultimate Question is interpreted as question (a),—Why should I be moral?—what is being asked for are reasons that would justify an individual's making an ultimate choice of the priority of morality over self-interest. But an *ultimate* choice, by its very nature, cannot be based on reasons, since any arguments given to justify it will themselves presuppose a principle that has already been chosen, from which it follows that the choice being justified is not an ultimate one. Let us set out this argument fully and explicitly.

To give "reasons for choosing" is to show that a person is justified in choosing one thing rather than another when he can do one or the other but not both. Giving such reasons is possible only within the framework of some principle according to which the reasons given do indeed warrant the choice based on them. (That doing X will satisfy a desire is a reason for choosing to do X only because one accepts the *principle*, What satisfies a desire is a good thing to do.) Thus giving reasons for choosing already presupposes commitment to a principle. Now suppose one were to give reasons for choosing one principle rather than another—that is, justification for a commitment to follow one as a guide to conduct rather than another. Then to give reasons for choosing *that* principle would presuppose commitment to some higher principle. And if reasons for choosing this higher principle were offered, commitment to still another at a higher level would be presupposed. And so on, for any higher principle. Therefore, with regard to any choice, if reasons for choosing are given to justify it, it cannot be an *ultimate* choice—the choice of a *highest* principle. Now the Ultimate Question is precisely the demand for reasons for making an ultimate choice. Such a demand is incoherent, as can be seen from the fact that it asks for what is impossible. No reasons can be given for an ultimate choice, for an ultimate choice rules out the possibility of reasons for choosing.

We are now in a position to understand how the challenge expressed in the Ultimate Question is to be met. We simply say to the person who poses the question, "We cannot give you reasons that will show what choice you must make. You must decide for yourself. You cannot avoid this final responsibility. The choice of how you are to live, of the supreme normative axioms of your conduct, is a choice that no one can make but yourself. Even your own reason cannot do this job for you. As we have seen, your acceptance of any reasons for choosing will presuppose some principle that has already been chosen by you. Thus it is a matter, not of your reason, but of your will. You must *decide* what shall be your ultimate commitment, and this requires an exercise of your capacity to make an autonomous, self-directed choice about the kind of life you are to live. In this sort of situation to ask for reasons is actually an unconscious attempt to evade the burden of an ultimate choice. Such an attempt is futile, however, for it is an attempt to deny what cannot be denied: that each individual must finally answer for himself the question of what principles he is to live by.''

This line of thought has led some philosophers to the following conclusion. To make an ultimate commitment is nothing less than *to define oneself*. It is to decide to be a certain kind of person. There is no way to escape this choice, the reason being that we *are* at every moment what we choose to *make* ourselves, and we can always choose to create a different self and so define our nature in a new way. Most of our decisions and choices, it is true, are not consciously directed to alternatives of this ultimate kind. But that is because we make most decisions and choices within the framework of a way of life. Our way of life is our mode or ''style'' of carrying on human existence. It is the expression of our own conception of what it means to be human, and it includes our commitment to the very principles that determine what we accept as reasons for acting and reasons for choosing. Hence, though we make decisions and choices in daily life that are not themselves ultimate, we do so only in terms of the conceptual system embodied in the ultimate principles of our way of life.

Since our way of life is our way of defining ourselves, it is not imposed on us from the outside. Nor is it merely a reflection of the kind of person we already are. For our being a certain kind of person is due to our having chosen to live in a certain way, not the other way around. (This is a logical point about the concepts of a way of life and of personhood, not a psychological account of the origins of our ''personality.'' To exist as a person by choosing to define oneself in a certain way is logically prior to having a ''personality'' as that is empirically explained and described by the science of psychology.) At every moment, whether we realize it or not, we are choosing our way of life, since at each instant there is some way of life that may be correctly ascribed to us. The fact that we do not change our mode of living from one moment to the next does not show that no choice is being made. For if we do not change, we are choosing to continue to be what we have been. And so we are still creating ourselves, making ourselves in a certain image of man, defining our own nature by living as we do. Thus, whether our way of life is one in which morality outweighs self-interest (in cases of conflict between them) or one in which self-interest overrides morality, it is *our* way of life because we have *made* it so. It is we who determine which shall be supreme, ethics or ego. As an ultimate choice, it is a matter of how we decide to live and to define ourselves. And whether our past decisions continue to mold our way of life in the present is something only we have the power to determine. The decision to change or not to change is forever inescapable. We cannot free ourselves from the responsibility to define our selfhood at every moment. At the same time, at every moment we have the ''existential'' freedom to define our selfhood as we will.

THE COMMITMENT TO BE MORAL

Do these considerations necessarily imply that a person's commitment to the supremacy of moral principles over self-interest is an *arbitrary* decision, like the tossing of a coin? As an ultimate choice it can be called extrarational, beyond reason, neither rational nor irrational. But one can say the same of the contrary choice, by which a person commits himself to the priority of self-interest over morality. Is this all there is to be said?

Something further can indeed be said, but this something further is not the giving of a reason that would justify the choice of one alternative rather than the other. It is, instead, a matter of bringing clearly before one's mind a full recognition of the *nature* of the choice, an ultimate one. Now if it is true that in some sense ultimate choices cannot be avoided—that everyone must make them, and at every moment of life—then making such choices is simply a necessary aspect of one's autonomy as an individual. Thus suppose someone said, ''I refuse to make an ultimate choice between morality and self-interest.'' He would actually be making an ultimate choice, namely, not to commit himself in advance but to wait until he finds himself in a situation of conflict between morality and self-interest and then commit himself on the spur of the moment. His supreme commitment is to whatever principles he chooses to follow as an immediate reaction to particular situations confronting him with the necessity to choose. This is the way he is defining *his* nature. And his decision to refuse to commit himself in advance is itself an exercise of his autonomy as an individual! It seems, then, that there can be no genuine counter-instance to the generalizations that ultimate choices must be made at every moment by each person, and that such choices realize or express the autonomy of each individual.

Now this is of great significance. For if every person, as a person, must bear the responsibility of making his own ultimate choices at every moment of his life, anything that took away or diminished the possibility of someone's exercise of this autonomy would be a violation of the very foundation of rational action and choice in that person's life. In not allowing the person to define himself, it would deny him existence as a person. What is more, to interfere with or destroy someone's capacity for making ultimate choices would be to negate that person's responsibility to answer the Ultimate Question for himself. So if the Ultimate Question is not an absurdity and if one individual can never answer it for another but each must find his own answer, then, as far as solving the Ultimate Question is concerned, each person must be unhindered in the exercise of his autonomy as a maker of ultimate choices.

The necessary conditions for each person's asking and answering the Ultimate Question are now seen to impose a restriction upon human conduct: that no one shall deprive another of his capacity to make ultimate choices, nor interfere with his exercise of that capacity. To put it another way, each person must respect every other person's autonomy. If, in any particular set of circumstances, one person's acting from self-interest would transgress this primary rule of respect for everyone's autonomy, then his action must not be permitted. To allow him to do it would be to deny the principle which lies at the very foundation of all rational action and choice. For the freedom to make ultimate choices is necessarily presupposed by anyone's having *any* reasons for acting and reasons for choosing, whether they be moral or prudential reasons.

It seems plausible to hold that respect for the autonomy of persons is itself a moral principle. If this is so, then the choice between *this* principle and the pursuit of self-interest, even when it is an ultimate choice, is not arbitrary. Although one cannot give reasons for choosing this moral principle, one can examine fully the true nature of the choice and recognize that commitment to the principle in question is a precondition for all ultimate choices made by anyone,

and hence a precondition for anyone's being able to carry on practical reasoning.

Let us then suppose, as our final consideration, that a person who has followed the foregoing argument still wants to know why he should be moral to the extent of respecting the autonomy of others. He admits that he can meaningfully ask this question only because others are respecting *his* autonomy and that, if he were not to respect *their* autonomy, they would be unable to find an answer, or even seek an answer, to the Ultimate Question. But he says, "Why should I care whether they seek an answer, or find one?"

There are no reasons that can be given which provide an answer to his question. He must decide for himself what he is to care about in his life. The only thing that can be done is to point out to him that this is a decision of a fundamental kind. It is the decision to be a certain sort of person. Can he face himself openly and unevasively and still decide not to respect the autonomy of others, having clearly before his mind the full meaning of such a choice? If he can, then he has determined what conception of being human shall be exemplified in his life and this is all one can say about his decision. No argument can be given to show that his decision is irrational or that it is based on false assumptions.

This, after all, is in keeping with the idea emphasized above: that each person must take upon himself the responsibility for his ultimate normative commitment. In subscribing to the basic principles of his way of life, a person chooses to define himself in a certain way. If he decides to be the kind of person who deprives another of the capacity for an autonomous choice of a way of life, he cannot be said to be inconsistent. One can only ask, Can he make such a decision *authentically,* that is, sincerely acknowledging it as his own and at the same time making the decision, as it were, with his whole being? If he can, he knows what sort of conception of man he chooses to exemplify. And if he is willing to choose to be that sort of person—one who denies the personhood of another in the very act of defining his own personhood—nothing more can be said.

Commitment to moral principles, then, is finally a matter of one's will, not of one's reason. Reason can make clear to us the nature of the commitment and can lead us to a full awareness of the alternatives among which we must choose. But reason alone cannot tell us what choice to make. We must not expect, therefore, that someone might provide us with an argument showing which alternative *ought* to be chosen. There is simply no way to evade the responsibility—a responsibility that rests upon each of us alone—for defining our own selves. It is up to us to answer, each in his own way, that haunting question, Who am I? We give our answer to it by deciding whether our lives shall exemplify, to whatever extent is in our power, the principles of morality, or some other principles. Even to say, "Let each one decide for himself," is to express a doctrine that imposes a restraint upon action. And it is possible for a person to commit himself to some other principle contrary to this one, without being inconsistent. As long as he understands and acknowledges the nature of his choice and does not try to evade the fact that it is *his* choice, such a person cannot be shown to have chosen against the dictates of reason.

It is simply that he decides to be a certain kind of human being. Whether we also decide to be that kind of human being ourselves is a question only we can answer. For no one can escape the necessity to determine for himself what the answer, in his own life, shall be.

Suggestions for Further Reading

PART 1. REASON AND RELIGIOUS BELIEF

Virtually all the important writings on the ontological argument from St. Anselm to the present have recently been brought together in one volume, *The Ontological Argument,* edited by Alvin Plantinga, with an introduction by Richard Taylor (New York: Doubleday Anchor Books, 1965). The leading contemporary proponent of the argument is Alvin Plantinga; see his *God, Freedom, and Evil* (Grand Rapids, Mich.: Eerdman's, 1978). For a discussion of the philosophical issues involving possibility, actuality, and existence that arise in Rowe's article, see Michael J. Loux, *The Possible and the Actual: Readings in the Metaphysics of Modality* (Ithaca, N.Y.: Cornell University Press, 1979).

Anthony Kenny's *Five Ways: St. Thomas Aquinas's Proofs of God's Existence* (London: Routledge & Kegan Paul, 1969) is an excellent and thorough commentary by a skilled English analytic philosopher. A very useful collection of critical essays on the first cause argument and other arguments similar in form to it can be found in *The Cosmological Arguments,* edited by Donald Burrill (New York: Doubleday Anchor Books, 1967). For serious students, William L. Rowe's *The Cosmological Argument* (Princeton, N.J.: Princeton University Press, 1975) is strongly recommended.

John Stuart Mill's "Theism" in his *Three Essays on Religion* (1875) contains a historically important discussion of the argument from design. A recent defense of the argument can be found in Richard Taylor's *Metaphysics* (Englewood Cliffs, N.J.: Prentice-Hall, 1974), Chap. 10.

David Hume's writings on religion have been gathered together in a useful volume with an excellent introductory essay by Richard Wollheim, *David Hume on Religion* (New York: Meridian Books, 1964). The definitive edition of Hume's *Dialogues* can be found in *The Natural History of Religion and Dialogues Concerning Natural Religion,* edited by A. Wayne Colver and John V. Price (London: Oxford University Press, 1977). A very useful paperback edition with commentary is that of Nelson Pike (Indianapolis: Bobbs-Merrill, 1971). An interesting recent exchange on the argument from design is that between Wesley C. Salmon, "Religion and Science: A New Look at Hume's Dialogues" and Nancy Cartwright, "Comments on Wesley Salmon's 'Science and Religion,' " *Philosophical Studies,* Vol. 33 (1978).

For more on the problem of evil, see *God and Evil,* edited by Nelson Pike (Englewood Cliffs, N.J.: Prentice-Hall, 1964) and the helpful bibliography contained therein. A theistic rejoinder to the inductive argument from evil for the nonexistence of God is given by Alvin Plantinga in "The Probabilistic Argument from Evil," *Philosophical Studies,* Vol. 35 (1979).

For contemporary discussions on the meaning of religious statements, verification, falsifiability, and related problems, see the following excellent collections: *New Essays in Philosophical Theology,* edited by Antony Flew and Alasdair MacIntyre (New York: Macmillan, 1955); *Faith and the Philosophers,* edited by John Hick (New York: St. Martin's Press, 1964); and *The Logic of God,* edited by M. Diamond and T. V. Litzenburg (Indianapolis: Bobbs-Merrill, 1975). See also Alasdair MacIntyre, "The Logical Status of Religious Belief" in *Metaphysical Beliefs* (London: S.C.M. Press, 1957); and Frederick Ferre, *Language, Logic, and God* (London: Eyre & Spottiswood, 1962). John Wisdom's "Gods" in *Philosophy and Psychoanalysis* (Oxford: Blackwell, 1957) is a very important article.

For sympathetic discussions of religious mysticism, see W. R. Inge, *Mysticism in Religion* (Chicago: University of Chicago Press, 1948) and W. T. Stace, *Mysticism and Philosophy* (Philadelphia: Lippincott, 1960). For an unsympathetic discussion based on psychological analysis, see J. H. Leuba, *The Psychology of Religious Mysticism* (New York:

Harcourt, Brace & World, 1925). See also Sigmund Freud's analysis of apparent mystic experiences in his *Civilization and Its Discontents* (New York: W. W. Norton, 1962), pp. 11–16. For a helpful discussion of the religious significance of "mind-expanding drugs," see Huston Smith's article, "Do Drugs Have Religious Import?", *Journal of Philosophy,* Vol. 61 (1964). An important recent book on this subject is R. C. Zaehner's *Zen, Drugs, and Mysticism* (New York: Pantheon Books, 1972).

For views opposed to William James's on the reasonableness of beliefs based on no adequate evidence, see W. K. Clifford's "The Ethics of Belief" in his *Lectures and Essays,* Vol. II (London: Macmillan, 1879). The classic statement of "agnosticism" (that in the absence of evidence belief should be suspended) is T. H. Huxley's in his *Essays Upon Controversial Questions* (1889).

There is an important fideist tradition in modern Protestant theology which is often called "Christian Existentialism." Its clearest statements can be found in Søren Kierkegaard's *Concluding Unscientific Postscript,* as selected by E. L. Miller in his valuable collection, *Philosophical and Religious Issues* (Belmont, Calif.: Wadsworth Publishing Co., 1972), and in *Dynamics of Faith* by Paul Tillich (New York: Harper & Row, 1957).

Many of the topics in Part One are discussed in the following important books: John Hick, *Faith and Knowledge* (Ithaca, N.Y.: Cornell University Press, 1957); Alvin Plantinga, *God and Other Minds* (Ithaca, N.Y.: Cornell University Press, 1968); James F. Ross, *Philosophical Theology* (Indianapolis: Bobbs-Merrill, 1969); Wallace I. Matson, *The Existence of God* (Ithaca, N.Y.: Cornell University Press, 1965), and two books by Antony Flew—*God and Philosophy* (London: Hutchinson and Co., 1966), and *The Presumption of Atheism & Other Essays* (London: Elek/Pemberton, 1976). The books by Hick, Plantinga, and Ross are sympathetic to religious belief; those by Matson and Flew are written from nontheistic points of view. Two good elementary texts are: John Hick, *Philosophy of Religion* (Englewood Cliffs, N.J.: Prentice-Hall, 1963) and John King-Farlow, *Reason and Religion* (London: Darton, Longman & Todd, 1969). Terence Penelhum's *Religion and Rationality* (New York: Random House, 1971) is an important contribution to its subject, and readily accessible to the beginner. *Understanding Religious Convictions*

by J. W. McClendon and J. M. Smith (Notre Dame, Indiana: University of Notre Dame Press, 1975) is an important and original work. A very clear and comprehensive text is William Rowe's *Philosophy of Religion: An Introduction* (Belmont, Calif.: Wadsworth Publishing Co., 1978). Perhaps the best of the many anthologies in the philosophy of religion is Baruch Brody, *Readings in the Philosophy of Religion: An Analytic Approach* (Englewood Cliffs, N.J.: Prentice-Hall, 1974).

PART 2. HUMAN KNOWLEDGE: ITS GROUNDS AND LIMITS

The most useful of all beginning texts in the theory of knowledge is Adam Morton's *A Guide Through the Theory of Knowledge* (Belmont, Calif.: Wadsworth Publishing Co., 1977). For another good general introduction along historical lines (from Descartes to the present) see Bruce Aune's *Rationalism, Empiricism, and Pragmatism: An Introduction* (New York: Random House, 1970). The following general introductions are also recommended: A. J. Ayer, *The Problem of Knowledge* (Baltimore: Penguin Books, 1956); R. M. Chisholm, *Theory of Knowledge* (Englewood Cliffs, N.J.: Prentice-Hall, 1966); and Bertrand Russell, *The Problems of Philosophy* (London: Oxford University Press, 1912). *Meaning and Knowledge,* edited by Ernest Nagel and Richard B. Brandt (New York: Harcourt, Brace & World, 1965) is an excellent collection of primary materials from classical and contemporary sources divided by problems.

The following more recent anthologies are also highly recommended: *Knowing,* edited by Michael D. Roth and Leon Galis (New York: Random House, 1970); *Empirical Knowledge: Readings from Contemporary Sources,* edited by Roderick M. Chisholm and Robert J. Swartz (Englewood Cliffs, N.J.: Prentice-Hall, 1973); *Essays on Knowledge and Justification,* edited by George S. Pappas and Marshall Swain (Ithaca, N.Y.: Cornell University Press, 1978); and *Justification and Knowledge: New Studies in Epistemology,* edited by George S. Pappas (Dortrecht, Holland: D. Reidel, 1980).

For general accounts of the period from Descartes through Mill in histories of philosophy, see Frederick Copleston, S.J., *A History of Philosophy* (Westminster, Md.: Westminster Press, 1960), Vols. IV, V, VI; and Frank Thilly and Ledger Wood, *A History of Philosophy,* 3rd ed. (New York: Holt, 1957).

Norman Kemp Smith has written valuable commentaries on Descartes and Hume: *The Philosophy of*

David Hume (London: Macmillan, 1964); *New Studies in the Philosophy of Descartes* (London: Macmillan, 1963). A recent prize-winning study of Hume is *Hume,* by Barry Stroud (The Arguments of the Philosophers Series; London and Boston: Routledge & Kegan Paul, 1977). The following are also valuable studies of individual philosophers: D. J. O'Connor, *John Locke* (Baltimore: Penguin Books, 1955); Harry G. Frankfurt, *Demons, Dreamers, and Madmen* (on Descartes's first two meditations—Indianapolis: Bobbs-Merrill, 1970); G. J. Warnock, *Berkeley* (Baltimore: Penguin Books, 1953); D. F. Pears, ed., *David Hume, A Symposium* (London: Macmillan, 1963); and *Descartes: Critical and Interpretive Essays,* edited by Michael Hooker (Baltimore: Johns Hopkins University Press, 1978).

John Locke's theory of perception is found in *An Essay Concerning Human Understanding,* especially Book II, Chaps. 8, 9, and Book IV, Chap. 11. For an illuminating discussion of the kind of argument used in Berkeley's first dialogue, see A. J. Ayer, *The Foundations of Empirical Knowledge* (London: Macmillan, 1940) Chap. 1. Ayer is criticized in turn by J. L. Austin in *Sense and Sensibilia* (New York: Oxford University Press, 1964).

Other important books on perceptual knowledge include: D. M. Armstrong, *Perception and the Physical World* (London: Routledge & Kegan Paul, 1961); Roderick M. Chisholm, *Perceiving* (Ithaca, N.Y.: Cornell University Press, 1957); H. H. Price, *Perception* (London: Methuen, 1933); Wilfrid Sellars, *Science, Perception, and Reality* (London: Routledge & Kegan Paul, 1963), Chap. 3; and Fred I. Dretske, *Seeing and Knowing* (Chicago: University of Chicago Press, 1969). A very clear and thorough treatment of the philosophy of perception for beginners can be found in James Cornman and Keith Lehrer, *Philosophical Problems and Arguments: An Introduction* (New York: Macmillan, 1968). George Berkeley's other works on perception have been collected in his *Philosophical Writings,* edited by David M. Armstrong (London: Macmillan, 1974).

Recent efforts to deal with Hume's skeptical doubts about induction include: Max Black, "The Justification of Induction" in *Language and Philosophy* (Ithaca, N.Y.: Cornell University Press, 1949); Hans Reichenbach, *Experience and Prediction* (Chicago: University of Chicago Press, 1938); Bertrand Russell, *Human Knowledge* (New York: Simon & Schuster, 1948), Part 5; and Wesley C. Salmon, *The Foundations of Scientific Inference* (Pittsburgh: University of Pittsburgh Press, 1976). For a readable survey of various attempts to dissolve or evade Hume's problem or to justify induction, see Wesley C. Salmon, "Unfinished Business: The Problem of Induction," *Philosophical Studies,* Vol. 33 (1978); Salmon finds all of these attempts inadequate. A useful anthology is *The Justification of Induction,* edited by Richard Swinburne (Oxford: Oxford University Press, 1974).

Important new contributions to the theory of knowledge can be found in the following works: George Pitcher, *A Theory of Perception* (Princeton, N.J.: Princeton University Press, 1971); Keith Lehrer, *Knowledge* (Oxford: Clarendon Press, 1974); and Peter Unger, *Ignorance* (Oxford: Oxford University Press, 1975). Unger argues ingeniously in favor of skepticism. *The Web of Belief,* 2nd ed., by W. V. Quine and J. S. Ullian (New York: Random House, 1978) will be very helpful to beginning students.

PART 3. MIND AND ITS PLACE IN NATURE

The philosophy of mind has been greatly enriched in the last few decades largely because of the stimulation of Ludwig Wittgenstein. The beginning student will experience difficulties with Wittgenstein's *Philosophical Investigations* (Oxford: Basil Blackwell, 1958) but he will find useful guides in George Pitcher's *The Philosophy of Wittgenstein* (Englewood Cliffs, N.J.: Prentice-Hall, 1964) and *The Private-Language Problem* by John Turk Saunders and Donald F. Henze (New York: Random House, 1967). Another great influence on recent work is Gilbert Ryle's *The Concept of Mind* (New York: Barnes & Noble, 1949). Ryle's position was attacked by Jerry Fodor in *Psychological Explanation: An Introduction to the Philosophy of Psychology* (New York: Random House, 1968), and *The Language of Thought* (Cambridge Mass.: Harvard University Press, 1979).

Important articles on the mind-body problem and related topics have been widely anthologized. See, for example, the following paperback collections: Donald Gustafson, ed., *Essays in Philosophical Psychology* (Garden City, N.Y.: Doubleday Anchor, 1964); Stuart Hampshire, ed., *Philosophy of Mind* (New York: Harper & Row, 1966); and Antony Flew, ed., *Body, Mind, and Death* (New York: Macmillan, 1964). A very large and useful collection of articles on the mind-body problem from Descartes to an article written in 1961 is G. N. A. Vesey's *Body and Mind* (London: George Allen & Unwin, 1964). Clear and helpful elementary books on the subject are Jerome Shaffer's *Philosophy of Mind* (Englewood Cliffs, N.J.: Prentice-Hall, 1967) and Alan R. White's *The Philosophy of Mind* (New York: Random House, 1967).

Descartes' views on the relation between mind and body are also found in his *On the Passions of the Soul* (1630). For an account of the views of Descartes' chief contemporary materialistic critic (Pierre Gassendi), see *The Philosophy of Gassendi* by G. S. Brett (New York, 1908).

Important and subtle books emphasizing the unity of mind and body are P. F. Strawson, *Individuals* (London: Methuen, 1959), Part I; and G. N. A. Vesey, *The Embodied Mind* (London: George Allen & Unwin, 1965).

Two anthologies between them contain virtually all of the influential defenses and criticisms of the theory of brain-mind identity. These are: John O'Connor, ed., *Modern Materialism: Readings on Mind-Body Identity* (New York: Harcourt, Brace, and World, 1969); and *The Mind/Brain Identity Theory,* edited by Clive V. Borst (New York: Macmillan, 1970). The most readable book-length defense and elaboration of the theory is David M. Armstrong's *A Materialist Theory of the Mind* (London: Routledge & Kegan Paul; New York: Humanities Press, 1968). Also strongly recommended is Armstrong's latest work, *The Nature of Mind* (Queensland, Australia: Queensland University Press, 1980).

Some recent work has distinguished between the claim that each particular mental event ("token") is identical with each particular brain event and the view that there are interesting correlations between "types" of mental events and types of brain events. See Donald Davidson's "Mental Events," in *Experience and Theory,* edited by Lawrence Foster and Joe W. Swanson (Amherst, Mass.: University of Massachusetts Press, 1970); and Jerry Fodor's *The Language of Thought* (Cambridge, Mass.: Harvard University Press, 1979). Much recent discussion has centered on Saul Kripke's attack on the identity theory in "Identity and Necessity," in *Identity and Individuation,* edited by Milton Munitz (New York: New York University Press, 1971); and "Naming and Necessity" in *Semantics of Natural Language,* edited by Donald Davidson and Gilbert Harman. (These articles, however, may be rather difficult for beginners.)

An early statement of the other leading form of materialism (epiphenomenalism) is found in Shadworth Hodgson, *The Metaphysics of Experience* (London: Longmans, Green, 1898), Vol. II. Epiphenomenalism finds expression in the form of a beautiful parable in George Santayana's "Normal Madness," in *Dialogues in Limbo* (New York: Scribners, 1926). The latest important work to suggest a theory like epiphenomenalism is Keith Campbell's *Body and Mind* (New York: Doubleday Anchor Books, 1971). James Cornman's theory is spelled out in more detail in two of his books: *Materialism and Sensations* (New Haven: Yale University Press, 1971), and *Perception, Common Sense, and Science* (New Haven: Yale University Press, 1975).

Among noted twentieth-century philosophers who have argued for the possibility of the mind's survival of the death of its body, two stand out for the clarity of their writing: C. J. Ducasse and H. H. Price. See Ducasse's *A Critical Examination of the Belief in a Life after Death* (Springfield, Ill.: Charles C. Thomas, 1961), and also his *Nature, Mind, and Death* (La Salle, Ill.: Open Court, 1951), Chaps. 20 and 21. See Price's *Personal Identity and Survival* (London: Society for Psychical Research, 1958). For the case against survival see Corliss Lamont , *The Illusion of Immortality* (New York: G. P. Putnam's, 1935), and C. Cohen, *The Other Side of Death* (London: The Pioneer Press, 1922). *Man's Concern with Death* containing original articles by Arnold Toynbee, A. K. Mant, Ninian Smart, John Hinton, Simon Yudkin, Eric Rhode, Rosaline Heywood, and H. H. Price (London: Hodder & Stoughton, 1968) is an excellent collection. Terence Penelhum's *Survival and Disembodied Existence* (New York: Humanities Press, 1970) is a very clear discussion of the conceptual problems raised by the doctrine of survival.

The leading classical and contemporary works on the problem of personal identity are listed in the footnote at the end of John Perry's article on p. 325.

The prevailing current materialist theory in the philosophy of mind is functionalism, which holds that mental states are functional states, distinguishable by the functional role they play within a system. For an early exposition of this view see Hilary Putnam's "Minds and Machines," in *Dimensions of Mind,* edited by Sidney Hook (New York: New York University Press, 1960). A very readable introductory article acquainting the reader with recent issues in the field is D. C. Dennett's "Current Issues in the Philosophy of Mind," *American Philosophical Quar-*

terly, Vol. 15 (1978). See also Gilbert Harman's *Thought* (Princeton, N.J.: Princeton University Press, 1973). Functionalism has provided a philosophical basis for much recent work in cognitive psychology, psycholinguistics, and artificial intelligence modeling. For a good introduction to this literature see D. C. Dennett's *Brainstorms: Philosophical Essays on Mind and Psychology* (Montgomery, Vermont: Bradford Books, 1978). A collection of essays on these topics is *Perception and Cognition: Issues in the Foundations of Psychology,* Minnesota Studies in the Philosophy of Science, Vol. IX, edited by C. Wade Savage (Minneapolis: University of Minnesota Press, 1978).

PART 4. DETERMINISM AND FREE WILL

One common method of arguing for determinism is to claim that events cannot be made fully intelligible unless they are, at least in principle, subject to causal explanation. A very lucid and elementary theory of the general nature of explanation is that of John Hospers in his article "What is Explanation?" in *Essays in Conceptual Analysis,* edited by Antony Flew (London: Macmillan; New York: St. Martin's Press, 1956). Hospers' account of explanation is of the sort that finds its classic statement in "Studies in the Logic of Explanation," by Carl G. Hempel and Paul Oppenheim, *Philosophy of Science,* Vol. 15 (1948). Also see Hempel's elementary text, *The Philosophy of Natural Science* (Englewood Cliffs, N.J.: Prentice-Hall, 1966) and Ernest Nagel's *The Structure of Science* (New York: Harcourt, Brace, & World, 1961), Chaps. 2, 3. For critical discussions of the Hempel-Oppenheim theory, especially as it applies to historical explanation, see *Philosophy and History,* edited by Sidney Hook (New York: New York University Press, 1963), especially Part III. Other useful articles are: "Why Questions," by Sylvain Bromberger, in *Mind and Cosmos,* edited by R. Colodny (Pittsburgh, 1965); and "Explanation in Everyday Life, in Science, and in History," by John Passmore, *History and Theory,* Vol. II (1962). See also Wesley C. Salmon's " 'Why Ask, Why?' An Inquiry Concerning Scientific Explanation," *Proceedings of the American Philosophical Association,* Vol. 51 (1978).

Indeterminist writers often support their case against determinism by arguing that human actions (unlike other events) can be rendered intelligible by explanations in terms other than "causes" or "laws of nature." In his book, *The Concept of Motivation* (London: Routledge & Kegan Paul; New York: Humanities Press, 1958), R. S. Peters argues that human behavior is subject to "his reason" explanations that stand in contrast to the causal explanations scientists seek when investigating nonhuman behavior. The nature of psychological explanation is thus of critical importance for the resolution of the problem of determinism and free will. Almost all of the important recent work on the explanation of human actions is contained in one or the other of two remarkably thorough recent anthologies: *Readings in the Theory of Action,* edited by Norman S. Care and Charles Landesman (Bloomington, Ind.: Indiana University Press, 1968), and *The Nature of Human Action,* edited by Myles Brand (Glenview, Ill.: Scott, Foresman and Co., 1970). The leading presentation, perhaps, of the position opposed to that of R. S. Peters is included in both these volumes. It is Donald Davidson's "Actions, Reasons, and Causes." See also Alvin I. Goldman's *A Theory of Human Action* (Princeton, N.J.: Princeton University Press, 1970) for a development of themes suggested in Goldman's article in this volume. For a discussion of these issues at an introductory level see Lawrence H. Davis, *Theory of Action* (Englewood Cliffs, N.J.: Prentice-Hall, 1979).

At least five very valuable symposia on the problem of determinism and free will have appeared in recent years: *Free Will and Determinism,* edited by Bernard Berofsky (New York: Harper & Row, 1966); *Determinism and Freedom in the Age of Modern Science,* edited by Sidney Hook (New York: New York University Press, 1958); *Freedom and Determinism,* edited by Keith Lehrer (New York: Random House, 1966); *Free Will,* edited by Sidney Morgenbesser and James Walsh (Englewood Cliffs, N.J., Prentice-Hall, 1962)—all of which are inexpensive paperbacks; and *Freedom and the Will,* edited by D. F. Pears (London: Macmillan; New York: St. Martin's Press, 1963). Most of the essays in the Pears volume originated as talks in the Third Programme of the British Broadcasting Corporation.

The reconciling determinist position is defended in Thomas Hobbes's *Leviathan* (1651), Chap. 21; in David Hume's *Treatise of Human Nature,* Book II, Part III; and in John Stuart Mill's *System of Logic* (1843), Book VI, Chap. 2. More recent influential arguments for the theory are found in Chapter 7 of Moritz Schlick's *Problems of Ethics* (Englewood Cliffs, N.J.: Prentice-Hall, 1939); in A. J. Ayer, "Freedom and Necessity" in his *Philosophical Es-*

says (London: Macmillan; New York: St. Martin's Press, 1954); in R. B. Hobart's "Free Will as Involving Determinism and Inconceivable Without It," *Mind,* 1934; and in Charles L. Stevenson, *Facts and Values* (New Haven and London: Yale University Press, 1963), Chap. 7.

Determinist theories of a relatively nonreconciling ("hard") kind are found in Baruch Spinoza, *Ethics,* Part III; in *System of Nature* by Baron D'Holbach (1770); in Arthur Schopenhauer, *Essay on the Freedom of the Will* (New York: Liberal Arts Press, 1960; first published in 1841); and in essays by Paul Edwards and John Hospers in the Sidney Hook anthology, *Determinism and Freedom in the Age of Modern Science* (New York: New York University Press, 1958). See also the speeches of the great criminal lawyer Clarence Darrow, in *Attorney for the Damned,* edited by Arthur Weinberg (New York: Simon & Schuster, 1957), especially Part One.

Indeterminist theories are defended in C. A. Campbell, *Skepticism and Construction* (London: Allen & Unwin, 1931); William James, "The Dilemma of Determinism," first published in 1884 and now widely anthologized; Charles S. Peirce, "The Doctrine of Necessity Examined," reprinted in *The Philosophy of Peirce,* edited by J. Buchler (New York: Harcourt, Brace, 1950); Thomas Reid, *Essays on the Powers of the Human Mind* (1812), Vol. III; and Jean-Paul Sartre, *Being and Nothingness* (New York: Philosophical Library, 1956). Two recent articles by indeterminists who argue for the incompatibility of freedom and determinism are: Peter van Inwagen, "The Incompatibility of Free Will and Determinism," *Philosophical Studies,* Vol. 27 (1975); and G. E. M. Anscombe, "Soft Determinism," in *Contemporary Aspects of Philosophy,* edited by Gilbert Ryle (Stocksfield, England: Oriel Press, 1976). Perhaps the most important of the recent defenses of libertarianism are the various articles of Roderick Chisholm. See especially his Lindley Lecture "Human Freedom and the Self" (Department of Philosophy, University of Kansas, 1964), and his *Person and Object: A Metaphysical Study* (London: George Allen & Unwin, Ltd., 1976), Chap. 2.

For the debate over deliberation and foreknowledge see the books and articles cited in the footnotes of Goldman's original article, especially the works by Cranston, Canfield, Cox, and R. Taylor. An important article defending the position opposed to that of Goldman is Carl Ginet's "Can the Will Be Caused?" *Philosophical Review,* Vol. 71 (1962). A kind of precursor of the Ginet article is "Decision, Intention, and Certainty," by H. L. A. Hart and Stuart Hampshire, *Mind,* Vol. 67 (1958).

For discussions of blame and blameworthiness, consult the footnote references in Elizabeth Beardsley's article included in this volume. See also Chap. 18 of Richard Brandt's *Ethical Theory* (Englewood Cliffs, N.J.: Prentice-Hall, 1958), and the following articles: R. B. Brandt, "Blameworthiness and Obligation," in A. I. Melden, ed., *Essays in Moral Philosophy* (Seattle: University of Washington Press, 1958); E. L. Beardsley, "A Plea for Deserts," *American Philosophical Quarterly,* Vol. 6 (1969), and "Moral Disapproval and Moral Indignation," *Philosophy and Phenomenological Research,* Vol. 31 (1970); L. Kenner, "On Blaming," *Mind,* Vol. 76 (1967); J. E. R. Squires, "Blame," *The Philosophical Quarterly,* Vol. 18 (1968); and Elizabeth Beardsley's latest contribution, "Blaming," *Philosophia,* Vol. 8 (1979). See also "Action and Responsibility" in *Doing and Deserving* by Joel Feinberg (Princeton, N.J.: Princeton University Press, 1970).

PART 5. RESPONSIBILITY AND PUNISHMENT

For a large and unusually complete collection of readings on criminal punishment and other problems concerning responsibility in law and morals, see Herbert Morris, ed., *Freedom and Responsibility* (Stanford, Calif.: Stanford University Press, 1961). Excellent general discussions of the topics of this and the preceding section are also found in Richard B. Brandt, *Ethical Theory* (Englewood Cliffs, N.J.: Prentice-Hall, 1959), Chap. 18–20 and in John Hospers, *Human Conduct* (New York: Harcourt, Brace & World, 1961), Chap. 9 and 10.

For a general account of Aristotle's ethics, see W. D. Ross, *Aristotle* (New York: Meridian Books, 1959), Chap. 7; and W. F. R. Hardie, *Aristotle's Ethical Theory* (Oxford: Clarendon Press, 1968). An excellent analysis of Aristotle's theory of personal responsibility against the background of centuries of Greek thought on the subject is found in Arthur W. H. Adkins, *Merit and Responsibility* (Oxford: Clarendon Press, 1960), Chap. 15.

Views similar to those of Butler's Erewhonian "malcontents" are expressed in Plato's *Protagoras* (324–325), *Gorgias* (479–480 and 525–526), and *Republic* (380); in Robert Owen, *Letters to the*

Human Race (London, 1850); and in Leo Tolstoy, *What I Believe* (Oxford Centenary Edition, 1933), Vol. II. See also Tolstoy's novel *Resurrection*. For more recent versions of the view that all crime is sickness, see Benjamin Karpman, "Criminality, Insanity, and the Law," *Journal of Criminal Law and Criminology* (1939), and *The Criminal Mind,* by Philip Q. Roche, M.D. (New York: Grove Press, 1958). For the contrary view, that only some criminals are mentally ill, see Paul Schilder, *Psychoanalysis, Man, and Society* (New York: Norton, 1951). For analyses of the concepts of mental health and illness, see Joseph Margolis, *Psychotherapy and Morality* (New York: Random House, 1966), Chaps 1–3; Georg von Wright, *The Varieties of Goodness* (London: Routledge & Kegan Paul, 1963), Chap. III; and Jonathan Glover, *Responsibility* (New York: Humanities Press, 1970).

The following are good collections of articles in and about existentialism: *Existentialist Philosophy,* edited by James A Gould and Willis H. Truitt (Belmont, Calif.: Wadsworth Publishing Co., 1973); and *Existentialism,* edited by Robert C. Solomon (New York: Random House, 1974). Perhaps the best treatment in English of the existentialist theory of freedom and choice is Frederick A. Olafson, *Principles and Persons: An Ethical Interpretation of Existentialism* (Baltimore: Johns Hopkins University Press, 1967), Chap. 7.

Classical sources of the utilitarian theory of punishment are: Jeremy Bentham, *An Introduction to the Principles of Morals and Legislation* (Oxford: Basil Blackwell, 1948) and *The Rationale of Punishment* (1830). An excellent little commentary is David Lyons's *Jeremy Bentham* (London: Macmillan, 1972). See also the Marquis de Beccaria, *An Essay on Crimes and Punishments* (Indianapolis: Bobbs-Merrill, 1963; first published in 1764); Hastings Rashdall, *Theory of Good and Evil* (Oxford: Clarendon Press, 1924), Vol. I, Chap. 9; and H. Wechsler and J. Michael, "A Rationale of the Law of Homicide," *Columbia Law Review,* 1937.

The most influential statements of the retributive theory are found in the writings of Immanuel Kant (1724–1804) and Georg W. F. Hegel (1770–1831). Kant's chief work on the subject is his *Philosophy of Law* (1797), which the beginning student will find difficult. A very clear commentary is found in *The Rationale of Legal Punishment* by Edmund L. Pincoffs (New York: Humanities Press, Inc., 1966), Chap. 1. Other statements and defenses of the Kantian

version of the retributive theory can be found in Josef Kohler's *Philosophy of Law* (Boston: Boston Book Co., 1914), and Rudolf Stammler, *The Theory of Justice* (New York: Macmillan, 1925). The main source of Hegel's theory of punishment is *Hegel's Philosophy of Right,* translated by T. M. Knox (Oxford: Oxford University Press, 1953), especially sections 90–104. An excellent critique of retributivism is found in Chapter I of A. C. Ewing's *The Morality of Punishment* (London: Kegan Paul, 1929). Refined versions of retributivism are expressed in "The Retributivist Hits Back," by K. G. Armstrong, *Mind,* Vol. 70 (1961); H. J. McCloskey, "A Non-Utilitarian Approach to Punishment," *Inquiry* (1965); Herbert Morris, "Persons and Punishment," *The Monist* (October, 1968); and Herbert Fingarette, "Punishment and Suffering," *Proceedings of the American Philosophical Association* (1977).

For discussions sympathetic to the view that vengeance is a legitimate function of criminal punishment, see James Fitzjames Stephen, *History of the Criminal Law* (1883), Vol. I, p. 478 and Vol. II, pp. 81–82 *et passim;* G. de Tarde, *Penal Philosophy* (Boston: Little, Brown, 1912); and Oliver Wendell Holmes, Jr., *The Common Law* (Boston: Little, Brown, 1881).

A developed theory of the sort suggested by the Mabbott and Rawls selections is to be found in S. I. Benn and R. S. Peters, *Social Principles and the Democratic State* (London: Allen & Unwin, 1959), Chap. 8.

The following are more recent books on the philosophy of punishment and the criminal law: H. B. Acton, *The Philosophy of Punishment* (Oxford: Blackwell's, 1969); Gertrude Ezorsky, ed., *Philosophical Perspectives on Punishment* (Albany, N.Y.: State University of New York Press, 1971); Joel Feinberg, *Doing and Deserving* (Princeton, N.J.: Princeton University Press, 1970); H. L. A. Hart, *Punishment and Responsibility* (New York and Oxford: Oxford University Press, 1968); John Kleinig, *Punishment and Desert* (The Hague: Martinus Nijhoff, 1973); Aryeh Neier, *Crime and Punishment: A Radical Solution* (New York: Stein and Day, 1976); Edmund L. Pincoffs, *The Rationale of Legal Punishment* (New York: Humanities Press, 1966); Ernest Vann Den Haag, *Punishing Criminals* (New York: Basic Books, 1975); Andrew von Hirsch, *Doing Justice* (New York: Hill and Wang, 1976); James Q. Wilson, *Thinking About Crime* (New York: Random House, 1977; J. B. Cederblom and W. L. Blizek, eds., *Justice and Punishment* (Cambridge, Mass.: Ballinger, 1977); Herbert Morris, *On Guilt and Innocence: Essays in Legal Philosophy and Moral Psychology* (Berkeley: University of California Press. 1976); Jeffrie G. Murphy, *Retribution, Justice, and Therapy: Essays in the Philosophy of Law* (Dortrecht, Holland: D. Reidel Publishing Co., 1979); and Hugo Bedau, *Retribution and the Theory of Punishment* (Totowa, N.J.: Rowman and Littlefield, 1981).

Jeffrie G. Murphy's anthology, *Punishment and Rehabilitation* (Belmont, Calif.: Wadsworth Publishing Co., 1973), is a well-selected collection of essays on mental illness as an excuse and related matters. Three important books on the subject are: Herbert Fingarette, *The Meaning of Criminal Insanity* (Berkeley, Los Angeles, and London: University of California Press, 1972); Abraham S. Goldstein, *The Insanity Defense* (New Haven: Yale University Press, 1967); and Antony Flew, *Crime or Disease?* (New York: Harper & Row, 1973).

PART 6. SELF-LOVE AND THE CLAIMS OF MORALITY

J. L. Mackie has recently published an original and very clear book defending a subjectivist theory of ethics; see his *Ethics* (Harmondsworth and New York: Penguin Books, 1977). The latest important defense of ethical relativism is Gilbert Harman's *The Nature of Morality: An Introduction to Ethics* (New York: Oxford University Press, 1977). For other discussions of ethical relativism, see R. B. Brandt, "Ethical Relativism," in *The Encyclopedia of Philosophy,* edited by Paul Edwards (New York: Macmillan, 1967); Robert Coburn, "Relativism and the Basis of Morality," *Philosophical Review,* Vol. 85 (1976); and Charles L. Stevenson, *Facts and Values* (New Haven, Conn.: Yale University Press, 1963), Chap. 5. *Ethical Relativism,* edited by John Ladd (Belmont, Calif.: Wadsworth Publishing Co., 1973), is a very useful anthology. G. E. Moore's *Ethics* (London: Home University Library, 1912) contains a historically important attempt to refute ethical skepticism. For other essays on ethical reasoning, see Joel Feinberg and Henry West (editors), *Moral Philosophy: Classic Texts and Contemporary Problems* (Belmont, Calif.: Wadsworth Publishing Co., 1977), Chap. 5, and Paul

W. Taylor, *Problems of Moral Philosophy,* 3rd ed. (Belmont, Calif.: Wadsworth Publishing Co., 1978), Chap. 2.

Classic sources of psychological egoism include Thomas Hobbes, *On Liberty and Necessity* and *Leviathan,* 1654; Claude Helvetius, *De l'Esprit,* 1759; and Jeremy Bentham, *Introduction to the Principles of Morals and Legislation,* 1780. A typical eighteenth-century statement and use of the theory is in Bernard De Mandeville's *The Fable of the Bees, or Private Vices, Public Benefits* (London, 1723). Mandeville believed that human beings are incorrigibly greedy, conceited, and vainglorious; yet these very vices, he argued, can be motives for the noblest conduct. "The moral virtues," he concluded, "are the political offspring which flattery begot on pride."

Philosophical works arguing against psychological egoism are legion. Among the best of them are: C. D. Broad, "Egoism as a Theory of Human Motives," in *Ethics and the History of Philosophy* (New York: Humanities Press, 1952); Joseph Butler, *Fifteen Sermons Upon Human Nature* (London, 1729), especially Sermon Eleven—"Upon the Love of Our Neighbor"; Austin Duncan-Jones, *Butler's Moral Philosophy* (Harmondsworth: Penguin Books, 1952), Chap. 4; William James, *The Principles of Psychology* (New York: Henry Holt, 1890), Vol. II, Chap. XXVI; Hastings Rashdall, *The Theory of Good and Evil* (London: Oxford University Press, 1924), Vol. I, Chap. 2; Frank C. Sharp, *Ethics* (New York: Appleton-Century, 1928), Book III; and Henry Sidgwick, *Methods of Ethics,* Book I, Chap. 4.

The primary source of the theory of sociobiology is E. O. Wilson, *On Human Nature* (Cambridge, Mass.: Harvard University Press, 1975). For other sources and philosophical responses, see the exceptionally useful collection, *The Sociobiology Debate, Readings on Ethical and Scientific Issues,* edited by Arthur L. Caplan (New York: Harper & Row, 1978).

Important discussions of ethical egoism are contained in Richard C. Brandt, *Ethical Theory* (Englewood Cliffs, N.J.: Prentice-Hall, 1959), Chap. 14; W. D. Glasglow, "The Contradiction in Ethical Egoism," *Philosophical Studies,* Vol. 19 (1968); Brian Medlin, "Ultimate Principles and Ethical Egoism," *Australasian Journal of Philosophy,* Vol. 35 (1957); Laurence Thomas, "Ethical Egoism and Psychological Dispositions," *American Philosophical Quarterly,* Vol. 17 (1980); Moritz Schlick, *Problems of Ethics* (Englewood Cliffs, N.J.: Prentice-Hall, 1939), Chap. 3; and Henry Sidgwick, *The*

Methods of Ethics, 7th ed. (New York and London: Macmillan, 1907), Book II.

The classic source of the utilitarian moral philosophy is Jeremy Bentham, *An Introduction to the Principles of Morals and Legislation* (London: The Athlone Press, 1970; first published in 1789). The most useful edition of Mill's *Utilitarianism* is that edited by Samuel Gorovitz (Indianapolis: Bobbs-Merrill, 1971). In addition to Mill's text, this edition contains twenty-eight critical and interpretive essays by recent philosophers. Other classical sources include Henry Sidgwick, *Methods of Ethics* (London: Macmillan, 1963; first published in 1874), and G. E. Moore, *Ethics* (London: Oxford University Press, 1912). Influential recent books are: David Lyons, *Forms and Limits of Utilitarianism* (Oxford: Clarendon Press, 1965); and J. J. C. Smart (for) and Bernard Williams (against), *Utilitarianism: For and Against* (Cambridge, Eng.: Cambridge University Press, 1973). An excellent paperback collection of important recent papers on utilitarianism is Michael D. Bayles, ed., *Contemporary Utilitarianism* (Garden City, N.Y.: Doubleday Anchor, 1968). A bibliography of articles on duty and supererogation, including some articles criticizing Urmson's "Saints and Heroes" can be found in Joel Feinberg, ed., *Moral Concepts* (Oxford: Oxford University Press, 1969).

For various answers to, and discussions of, the question "Why Should I Be Moral?" see the following: H. A. Prichard, *Duty and Interest* (Oxford: Clarendon Press, 1928); Frank C. Sharp, *Ethics* (New York: Appleton-Century, 1928); Kurt Baier, *The Moral Point of View* (Ithaca, N.Y.: Cornell University Press, 1958), Chaps. 11, 12; John Hospers, *Human Conduct* (New York: Harcourt, Brace & World, 1961), Chap. 4; and David P. Gauthier, "Morality and Advantage," *Philosophical Review,* Vol. 76 (1967).

For commentaries on Plato's *Republic,* see A. E. Taylor, *Plato, the Man and His Work* (New York: Humanities Press, 1927), Chap. XI; R. C. Cross and A. D. Woozley, *Plato's Republic, A Philosophical Commentary* (London: Macmillan, 1964); Terrence Irwin, *Plato's Moral Theory* (Oxford: Clarendon Press, 1977), Chaps. 7, 8; and Nicholas P. White, *A Companion to Plato's Republic* (Indianapolis: Hackett Publishing Co., 1979).

Two recent books on morality and self-interest deserve mention: Thomas G. Nagel, *The Possibility of Altruism* (Oxford: Clarendon Press, 1970), and Robert G. Olson, *The Morality of Self-Interest* (New York: Harcourt, Brace & World, 1965). Nagel's book is of first importance but it will be difficult for the beginner. *Morality and Rational Self-Interest,* edited by D. P. Gautier (Englewood Cliffs, N.J.: Prentice-Hall, 1970), and *Egoism and Altruism,* edited by Ronald D. Milo (Belmont, Calif.: Wadsworth Publishing Co., 1973) are useful anthologies. For a general introduction for the beginner to the main problems of philosophical ethics, consult Paul Taylor's *Principles of Ethics* (Belmont, Calif.: Wadsworth Publishing Co., 1975).